Relationship

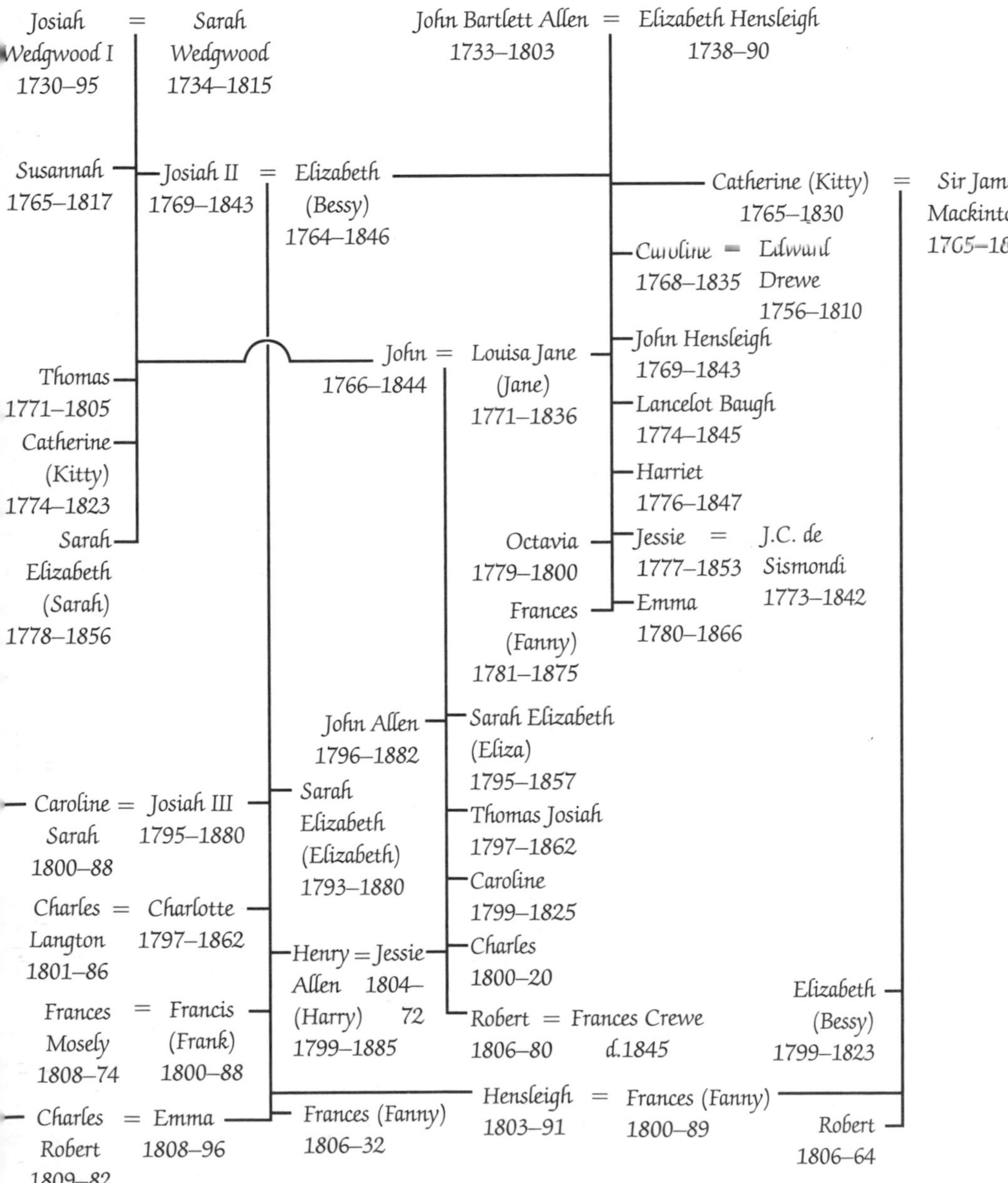

THE CORRESPONDENCE OF
CHARLES DARWIN

Editors

FREDERICK BURKHARDT DUNCAN M. PORTER

SHEILA ANN DEAN SAMANTHA EVANS

SHELLEY INNES

ANDREW SCLATER ALISON PEARN

PAUL WHITE

Research Associates

ANNE SCHLABACH BURKHARDT

ANNA-K. MAYER

This edition of the Correspondence of Charles Darwin is sponsored by the American Council of Learned Societies. Its preparation is made possible by the co-operation of Cambridge University Library and the American Philosophical Society.

Support for editing has been received from the Alfred P. Sloan Foundation, the Andrew W. Mellon Foundation, the National Endowment for the Humanities, the National Science Foundation, the Pew Charitable Trusts, the British Academy, the British Ecological Society, the Isaac Newton Trust, the Natural Environment Research Council, the Royal Society of London, the Stifterverband für die Deutsche Wissenschaft, and the Wellcome Trust. The National Endowment for the Humanities grants (Nos. RE-23166-75-513, RE-27067-77-1359, RE-00082-80-1628, RE-20166-82, RE-20480-85, RE-20764-89, RE-20913-91, RE-21097-93, RZ-20393-99, and RZ-20849-02) were from its Program for Editions; the National Science Foundation funding of the work was under grants Nos. SOC-75-15840, SES-7912492, SES-8517189, SBR-9020874, and SES-0135528. Any opinions, findings, conclusions, or recommendations expressed in this publication are those of the editors and do not necessarily reflect the views of the grantors.

Charles Darwin on his horse, Tommy
By permission of the Syndics of Cambridge University Library

THE CORRESPONDENCE OF
CHARLES DARWIN

VOLUME 14 1866

CAMBRIDGE
UNIVERSITY PRESS

PUBLISHED BY THE PRESS SYNDICATE OF THE UNIVERSITY OF CAMBRIDGE
The Pitt Building, Trumpington Street, Cambridge, United Kingdom

CAMBRIDGE UNIVERSITY PRESS
The Edinburgh Building, Cambridge CB2 2RU, UK
40 West 20th Street, New York, NY 10011-4211, USA
477 Williamstown Road, Port Melbourne, VIC 3207, Australia
Ruiz de Alarcón 13, 28014 Madrid, Spain
Dock House, The Waterfront, Cape Town 8001, South Africa

http://www.cambridge.org

First published 2004

Citation:
Burkhardt, Frederick *et al.*, eds. 2004. *The correspondence of Charles Darwin.*
Vol. 14. Cambridge: Cambridge University Press.

Printed in the United Kingdom at the University Press, Cambridge

Typeface Monotype Baskerville 10/12 pt. *System* EmTex

A catalogue record for this book is available from the British Library

ISBN 0 521 84459 2 hardback

CONTENTS

List of illustrations	vi
List of letters	vii
Introduction	xiii
Acknowledgments	xxvi
List of provenances	xxix
Note on editorial policy	xxxi
Darwin/Wedgwood genealogy	xxxviii
Abbreviations and symbols	xl
THE CORRESPONDENCE, 1866	1
Appendixes	
I. Translations	455
II. Chronology	481
III. Diploma	483
IV. Presentation list for the fourth edition of *Origin*	484
Manuscript alterations and comments	487
Biographical register and index to correspondents	493
Bibliography	551
Notes on manuscript sources	599
Index	603

ILLUSTRATIONS

Charles Darwin on his horse, Tommy — frontispicce

Blumenau, Brazil — facing p. 56

Tynron School — 57

Charles Darwin, 1866 — 88

Elizabeth Darwin — 89

Herbert Spencer — 184

John Traherne Moggridge — 184

Fritz Müller — 185

George Bentham — 185

Mary Everest Boole — 216

Ernst Haeckel — 217

Julius Victor Carus — 217

CALENDAR LIST OF LETTERS

The following list is in the order of the entries in the *Calendar of the correspondence of Charles Darwin*. The first part includes all those letters that are listed in the *Calendar* for the year 1866, and those that have been redated into 1866. Alongside the *Calendar* numbers are the corrected dates of each letter. A date or comment printed in italic type indicates that the letter has been omitted from this volume.

Letters acquired after the publication of the first edition of the *Calendar*, in 1985, have been given numbers corresponding to the chronological ordering of the original *Calendar* listing with the addition of an alphabetical marker. Many of these letters are summarised in a 'Supplement' to a new edition of the *Calendar* (Cambridge University Press, 1994). The marker 'f' denotes letters acquired after the second edition of the *Calendar* went to press in 1994.

3144. 8 May [1866]
4728. [1 Oct 1866]
4731. *Rejected for publication.*
4932. 6 Nov [1866]
4950. 10 Dec [1866]
4960. [April? 1866]
4961. [1866]
4962. [23 June 1866]
4963. [1866?]
4964. [after 13 May 1866]
4965. [before 20 Feb 1866?]
4966. [1866?]
4967. *Cancel: same as 4085, vol. 11.*
4968. [6 and 7? Jan 1866]
4968a. 3 Jan [1866]
4969. *4 Jan [1867]*
4970. 6 Jan [1866]
4971. *8 Jan [1868?]*
4972. 11 Jan 1866
4973. 11 Jan 1866
4974. 11 Jan 1866
4975. 13 [Dec] 1866
4976. 15 [Jan 1866]
4977. 16 Jan [1866]
4978. 16 Jan 1866
4979. [after 24 Jan 1866]
4980. 20 Jan [1866]
4981. 21 [Jan 1866]
4982. 22 Jan 1866
4983. 22 Jan [1866]
4984. 23 Jan 1866
4985. 28 Jan 1866
4986. 28 Jan 1866
4987. 29 Jan 1866
4988. *31 Jan [1863 or 1866?]. To be published in next supplement.*
4989. [6 Feb 1866]
4990. 1 Feb 1866
4991. *Enclosure to 5160.*
4992. 1 Feb [1866]
4993. 1 Feb [1866]
4994. 2 Feb 1866
4995. 3 Feb [1866]
4995f. 3 Feb 1866
4996. 4 Feb 1866
4997. 4 Feb 1866
4998. 5 Feb 1866
4999. 7 Feb [1866]
5000. 9 Feb 1866
5001. [before 10 Feb 1866]
5002. 10 Feb [1866]
5003. 10 Feb [1866]
5003f. [6–10 Feb 1866]
5004. 11 Feb [1866]
5004a. 13 Feb 1866
5005. 14 Feb 1866
5006. [23 April 1866]
5007. 15 Feb [1866]
5008. 15 Feb 1866
5008a. 15 Feb [1866]
5008b. 16 Feb [1866]
5009. 17 Feb [1866]

5010. 19 Feb [1866]
5011. 20 Feb 1866
5011f. 20 Feb 1866
5012. 21 Feb [1866]
5013. 21 Feb 1866
5014. 21 Feb [1866]
5015. 22 Feb [1866]
5016. 22 Feb [1866]
5017. [26 or 27 Feb 1866]
5017a. *See footnotes to 5417 (this volume).*
5018. 25 Feb 1866
5019. *28 Feb [1862]*
5020. [28 Feb 1866]
5021. 28 Feb 1866
5022. Mar 1866
5023. Mar 1866
5024. 1 Mar 1866
5025. [3 Mar 1866]
5026. 4 Mar 1866
5027. 5 Mar 1866
5027a. 6 Mar 1866
5028. 8 Mar [1866]
5029. 8 Mar 1866
5030. *10 Mar [1863 or 1866?]. To be published in next supplement.*
5031. 10 Mar 1866
5032. *12 [Mar 1860]*
5033. 12 Mar 1866
5034. 13 Mar 1866
5035. 16 Mar 1866
5036. 17 Mar [1866]
5037. [18–30 Mar 1866]
5038. 23 Mar 1866
5039. 28 Mar 1866
5040. 28 Mar [1866]
5041. 28 Mar 1866
5042. 31 Mar [1866]
5043. 31 Mar 1866
5044. [after 19 Apr 1866]
5045. 2 Apr 1866
5046. 4 Apr [1866]
5047. [6 Apr 1866]
5048. 7 Apr 1866
5049. 8 Apr 1866
5050. [9 and] 15 Apr [1866]
5051. [9 Apr 1866]
5052. 9 Apr 1866
5053. 10 Apr [1866]
5053a. 10 Apr 1866
5054. [5 Apr 1866]
5055. 12 Apr 1866
5056. 13 Apr 1866
5057. 16 Apr [1866]
5058. 16 Apr [1866]
5059. 16 Apr 1866
5059f. [before 19 Apr 1866]
5060. 19 Apr 1866
5061. [19] Apr [1866]
5062. 20 Apr 1866
5062a. 20 Apr [1866]
5063. 21 Apr 1866
5064. [22 Apr 1866]
5064a. [23 Apr 1866?]
5065. 24 Apr 1866
5066. *20 Apr [1876]*
5067. 26 Apr 1866
5068. 26 Apr 1866
5069. [26 Apr 1866]
5070. 27 Apr [1866]
5071. [28 Apr 1866]
5072. [29 Apr 1866]
5073. [16 Apr 1866]
5074. [14–21 Apr 1866]
5075. [*c.* 10 May 1866]
5076. [after 28 Apr 1866]
5077. [19 Mar 1866]
5078. [21 Mar 1866]
5079. 5 May [1866]
5080. 5 May [1866]
5080a. *6 May [1864]. To be published in next supplement.*
5081. 7 May 1866
5082. 7 May 1866
5083. 10 May [1866?]
5084. 10 May [1866]
5085. 10 May 1866
5086. 10 May 1866
5087. 11 May 1866
5088. [12 May 1866]
5089. 13 May 1866
5090. *Enclosure to 3550, vol. 10.*
5090f. 14 May 1866
5091. 16 May [1866]
5092. 16 May [1866]
5093. [17 May 1866]
5094. 17 May 1866
5095. 18 May 1866
5096. 21 May [1866]
5097. 23 May 1866
5098. *23 May [1874 or 1875?]*
5099. 25 May [1866]
5100. 25 May 1866

5101. 25 May [1866]
5102. 20 May 1866
5103. 28 May [1866]
5104. 29 May 1866
5105. 30 May [1866]
5106. 31 May [1866]
5107. [31 May 1866]
5108. [7 May – 11 June 1866]
5109. [18 June 1866]
5110. [2 June 1866]
5111. 3 June 1866
5112. [4 June 1866]
5113. 5 June [1866]
5114. 6 June 1866
5115. 8 June [1866]
5116. 9 June 1866
5117. 11 June [1866]
5118. 12 June [1866]
5119. 12 June [1866]
5120. [13 or 14 June 1866]
5121. 14 June [1866]
5122. *15 June [1862?]. Published in supplement to vol. 13.*
5123. 15 June [1866]
5123a. 15 [June 1866]
5124. 18 June 1866
5125. 19 [June 1866]
5126. 19 June 1866
5127. *[1 May 1864]. To be published in next supplement.*
5128. 20 June [1866]
5129. 21 June [1866]
5130. 21 June [1866]
5131. 22 June [1866]
5132. [24 June 1866]
5133. 27 June 1866
5134. 29 June [1866]
5135. 30 June [1866]
5136. 30 [June 1866]
5137. [July–Sept 1866]
5138. 1 July [1866]
5139. 2 July 1866
5140. 2 July 1866
5141. 3 July 1866
5142. [2–4 July 1866]
5143. 4 July 1866
5144. 4 July [1866]
5145. 5 July [1866]
5146. 5 July 1866
5147. 5 and 6 July [1866]
5148. [6 Feb 1866]
5149. 6 July 1866
5150. 7 Feb 1866
5151. 7 July 1866
5152. 9 July [1866]
5153. 10 Feb 1866
5154. 12 July 1866
5155. 15 July [1866]
5156. 16 July 1866
5157. 17 July 1866
5158. 17 July 1866
5159. 17 July 1866
5160. 18 July 1866
5161. 18 July [1866]
5162. 21 [July 1866]
5163. 22 July [1866?]
5163f. 22 July [1866]
5164. 23 July [1866]
5165. [24 July 1866]
5166. 24 July 1866
5167. 30 July [1866]
5168. 31 July 1866
5169. 1 Aug [1866]
5170. 2 Aug [1866]
5171. 2 Aug 1866
5172. 2 Aug [1866]
5173. 2 Aug 1866
5174. 3 and 4 Aug [1866]
5175. 3 Aug [1866]
5176. 4 Aug [1866]
5177. 4 Aug [1866]
5178. 4 Aug 1866
5179. 4 Aug 1866
5180. [after 4 Aug 1866]
5181. 5 Aug [1866]
5182. [6 Aug 1866]
5183. 7 Aug 1866
5184. 7 Aug 1866
5185. 8 Aug [1866]
5186. 9 Aug 1866
5187. 10 Aug [1866]
5188. [before 11 Aug 1866]
5189. [before 11 Aug 1866]
5190. 12 Aug [1866]
5191. [17 Aug 1866]
5192. 18 Aug 1866
5193. 18 Aug [1866]
5194. 20 Aug [1866]
5195. 20 Aug [1866]
5196. 23 Aug [1866]
5197. 24 Aug [1866]
5198. 27 Aug 1866
5199. [28 Aug] 1866
5200. 30 Aug [1866]

5201. 31 Aug 1866
5202. [Sept 1866]
5203. [before 25 Sept 1866]
5204. [28 July? 1866]
5205. *1 Sept [1867]*
5206. [4 Sept 1866]
5207. 8 Sept 1866
5208. 8[–9] Sept [1866]
5209. 9 Sept 1866
5210. 10 Sept [1866]
5211. 12 Sept 1866
5212. 14 Sept [1866]
5213. 17 Sept [1866]
5214. 19 Sept 1866
5215. 20 Sept 1866
5216. 25 Sept [1866]
5217. 25 Sept [1866]
5218. 25 Sept 1866
5219. 26 Sept [1866]
5220. 27 Sept [1866]
5221. 27 Sept 1866
5222. 28 Sept 1866
5223. 29 Sept 1866
5224. [20 Oct 1866]
5225. 1 Oct 1866
5226. 1 and 3 Oct 1866
5227. 2 Oct [1866]
5227f. 2 Oct 1866
5228. [4 Oct 1866]
5229. 4 Oct [1866]
5230. 4 Oct [1866]
5231. 4 Oct [1866]
5232. 5 Oct 1866
5233. 7 Oct [1866]
5234. 8 Oct 1866
5235. 8 Oct 1866
5236. 9 Oct [1866]
5237. 10 Oct 1866
5238. 11 Oct [1866]
5239. 12 Oct [1866]
5240. 12 Oct [1866]
5240a. [2 Oct 1866]
5241. 13 Oct [1866]
5242. 14 Oct 1866
5243. 15 Oct 1866
5244. 16 Oct [1866]
5245. 16 Oct [1866]
5246. 18 Oct [1866]
5247. 19 Oct 1866
5248. 19 Oct 1866
5249. [19? Oct 1866]
5250. 19 Oct [1866]
5251. *21 Oct [1864]*
5252. [21 Oct 1866]
5253. 23 Oct [1866]
5254. 23 Oct 1866
5255. 25 Oct [1866]
5256. 26 Oct 1866
5257. [21 Oct 1866]
5258. 28 Oct 1866
5259. 30 Oct 1866
5260. 31 Oct [1866]
5261. [before 10 Dec 1866]
5262. 1 Nov [1866]
5263. 1 Nov [1866]
5264. [2 Nov 1866]
5265. 2 Nov 1866
5266. 3 Nov 1866
5267. 3 Nov [1866]
5268. 6 Nov [1866]
5269. 7 Nov 1866
5270. 7 Nov 1866
5271. 8 Nov [1866]
5272. 9 Nov [1866]
5273. 10 Nov 1866
5274. 10 Nov 1866
5275. 11 Nov 1866
5276. 12 Nov 1866
5277. 13 Nov [1866]
5278. 15 Nov 1866
5279. 15 Nov 1866
5280. 19 Nov 1866
5281. 20 Nov [1866]
5282. 21 Nov 1866
5283. [22 Nov 1866]
5284. [23 Nov 1866]
5284a. 24 Nov [1866]
5285. 27 Nov 1866
5286. 27 Nov [1866]
5287. 30 Nov 1866
5287a. [after 30 Nov 1866]
5288. [Dec 1866?]
5289. 1 Dec [1866]
5290. 1 Dec [1866]
5291. 1 Dec 1866
5292. 1 Dec 1866
5292a. 1 Dec 1866
5293. 4 Dec [1866]
5294. 4 Dec 1866
5295. 5 Dec [1866]
5296. *5 Dec [1865]*
5297. 7 Dec [1866]

5297f. 7 Dec 1866
5298. 8 Dec 1866
5299. 10 Dec [1866]
5300. 10 Dec [1866]
5301. 12 Dec [1866]
5302. [12 Dec 1866]
5303. 13 Dec 1866
5304. 13 Dec 1866
5305. 14 Dec 1866
5306. 14 Dec [1866]
5307. 14 Dec 1866
5308. *Cancel. Not by Darwin.*
5309. 15 Dec [1866]
5309f. 16 Dec [1866?]
5310. 17 Dec [1866]
5311. 18 [Dec 1866]
5312. 18 Dec [1866]
5313. 19 Dec 1866
5314. *19 Dec [1858]. Published in supplement to vol. 13.*
5314f. 21 and 22 Dec [1866]
5315. 22 Dec [1866]
5316. 22 Dec 1866
5317. 22 Dec [1866]
5318. 24 Dec [1866]
5319. [28 Nov 1866]
5320. 24 Dec [1866]
5321. 24 Dec [1866]
5322. 24 Dec [1866]
5323. 24 [Dec 1866]
5324. 25 Dec 1866
5325. 25 Dec 1866
5326. 28 [Dec 1866]
5327. 28 Dec [1866]
5328. [29 Dec 1866]
5329. 31 Dec 1866
5330. 31 Dec [1866]
5331. [late Dec 1866 and] 1 Jan 1867
5417. 24 Feb [1866]
5427. 2 Mar [1866]
5481f. [before 21 Feb 1866]
5524. 3 May [1866]
10344. [after 9 June 1866]
13780. [4 Nov 1866?]
13793. [after 12 Oct 1866]
13850. [after 28 Apr 1866?]
13851. [after 4 Apr 1866]
13863. [1 Oct 1866]
13868. 13 Apr [1866]

INTRODUCTION

The year 1866 began well for Charles Darwin, as his health, after several years of illness, was now considerably improved. His increased vigour was apparent in a busy year that included two trips to London, to the great delight of his friends, the entertaining of a number of scientific admirers at Down, among them Robert Caspary, John Traherne Moggridge, and Ernst Haeckel, and also a meeting with Herbert Spencer, who was visiting Darwin's neighbour, Sir John Lubbock. In February, Darwin received a request from his publisher, John Murray, for a new edition of *On the origin of species* (*Origin*). Darwin set to energetically, and the fourth, and much revised, edition was with the printers in July. Much to Darwin's annoyance, however, publication was delayed by Murray, who judged that it would sell better if released later in the year. The correspondence includes some pithy remarks on publishers, decried on one occasion by Joseph Dalton Hooker as 'Penny-wise Pound foolish, Penurious, Pragmatical Prigs' (letter from J. D. Hooker, [29 December 1866]). But the crowning achievement of the year was the completion of the major part of what was to become *The variation of animals and plants under domestication* (*Variation*). Although it was not published until 1868, all but the concluding chapter of the work was submitted by Darwin to his publisher in December. Much of Darwin's correspondence in 1866 was focussed on issues surrounding the completion of this lengthy work, including further discussion of 'pangenesis', his hypothesis of hereditary transmission.

Debate about Darwin's theory of transmutation continued in various quarters, with important commentaries appearing in France, Germany, and Italy. In the United States, Louis Agassiz renewed his defence of special creation on the basis of alleged evidence of a global ice age, while Asa Gray pressed Darwin's American publisher for a revised edition of *Origin*. Closer to home, Darwin's theory featured in the presidential address by William Robert Grove at the annual meeting of the British Association for the Advancement of Science. Fuller consideration of Darwin's work was given by Hooker in an evening speech on insular floras at the same meeting. Prior to the event, the details of Hooker's proposed talk formed the basis of a lengthy and lively exchange of letters between the two friends. The year's successes and frustrations were punctuated by family bereavement. Two of Darwin's sisters died, Emily Catherine Langton in January, and Susan Darwin in October. In his correspondence, Darwin responded philosophically to these deaths, regarding both as a merciful release from painful illness.

Among Darwin's first letters in the new year was a report on his condition to his doctor, Henry Bence Jones: 'I am able now to walk daily on an average $3\frac{1}{2}$ miles

& often one mile at a stretch. . . . I feel altogether much more vigorous & active. I read more, & what is delightful, I am able to write easy work for about 1½ hours every day' (letter to H. B. Jones, 3 January [1866]). Darwin had first consulted Jones in July 1865 and attributed his improved health by the end of that year to the diet and exercise he had prescribed. 'I have not yet much taste for common meat,' he continued, 'but eat a little game or fowl twice a day & eggs, omelet or maccaroni or cheese at the other meals & these I think suit me best.' He sought Jones's approval to increase his intake of coffee to two cups a day, since coffee, with the '10 drops of Muriatic acid twice a day (with Cayenne & ginger)', appeared to have had a beneficial effect on his troublesome stomach, although he still usually suffered daily bouts of flatulence. Jones replied in encouraging terms, enclosing a revised diet, which unfortunately does not survive, and recommending the addition of an occasional baked potato. He also advised a holiday, and the acquisition of a 'rough pony' so that his patient could be 'shaken once daily to make the chemistry go on better' (letter from H. B. Jones, 10 February [1866]). Darwin began riding the cob, Tommy, on 4 June 1866, and in a letter to his cousin William Darwin Fox on 24 August [1866], he wrote, 'I attribute my improvement partly to Bence Jones' diet & partly, wonderful to relate, to my riding every day which I enjoy much.' The new exercise regime led to Darwin's being teased by his neighbour, John Lubbock, about the prospect of riding to hounds: 'I . . . fully expect to see you out with our beagles before the season is over' (letter from John Lubbock, 4 August 1866). More predictably, however, Darwin immediately converted his renewed vigour into scientific work, remarking to Fox, 'I don't believe in your theory of moderate mental work doing me any harm—any how I can't be idle' (letter to W. D. Fox, 24 August [1866]).

Since the publication of *Origin* in November 1859, Darwin had continued gathering and organising information on variation in domesticated plants and animals in order to write the first of a projected three volumes detailing the evidence on which his theory of the transmutation of species by natural selection was based. The work relied heavily on Darwin's extensive correspondence over several decades with plant and animal breeders, such as the pigeon and poultry expert William Bernhard Tegetmeier. In January, Darwin wrote to Tegetmeier that he was getting on with his 'everlasting volume', and began a series of detailed queries and instructions, extending over the course of the year, on some of the book's illustrations, the production of which Tegetmeier had agreed to supervise (letter to W. B. Tegetmeier, 16 January [1866]). Darwin found the evidence of variation in domesticated pigeons the most useful and complete for his purposes, and he took great care to ensure that the visual presentation of this evidence supported his argument for the common descent of all domestic varieties from *Columbia livia*, the rock pigeon.

In addition to the material on pigeons, the first volume of *Variation* included discussions of other domesticated animals, and of cultivated plants. The second volume contained chapters on inheritance, reversion, crossing, sterility, hybridism, and the causes and laws of variation. Finally, in an admittedly speculative chapter headed 'Provisional hypothesis of pangenesis', Darwin proposed that the various phenomena of development and hereditary transmission could be explained by the operation of 'gemmules', minute particles thrown off by the body's individual cells, and capable of generating new cells when needed. Gemmules circulated in the body's fluids, and could cohere by mutual attraction in, for example, the reproductive organs, or the tissues of a bud. Darwin had submitted a preliminary sketch of pangenesis to Thomas Henry Huxley in 1865 (see *Correspondence* vol. 13), and continued to refine his hypothesis in 1866. He wrote to Hooker on 16 May [1866], 'I . . . am at work on a Chap. on Reversion which to me is a most interesting subject & brimful of my dear little mysterious gemmules.' Darwin collected information on anomalous cases of reproduction, such as graft hybrids, soliciting assistance from the American botanist Asa Gray, the nurseryman Thomas Rivers, and the German botanist Robert Caspary. Darwin was particularly interested in recent work by Caspary on a graft hybrid then known as *Cytisus adami*, in which the scion apparently produced buds with blended characters; Darwin had tried to propagate the species some years before without success.

Darwin had originally intended his work on variation to form just two chapters of the 'big book' on species of which *Origin* was an abstract; but when he completed all but the final chapter of the manuscript in December, he was worried that it was too big. 'You must congratulate me', he wrote to Hooker, 'when you hear that I have sent M.S. (such an awful, confounded pile, two volumes I much fear) of "Domestic Animals & Cult. Plants" to Printers' (letter to J. D. Hooker, 24 December [1866]). When finally published in 1868, it filled two lengthy volumes, even with much of the text set in small type. The compilation and writing of *Variation* had been a major task, occupying much of Darwin's working time since the publication of *Origin*. Although he was still debating whether to grasp the nettle and insert a chapter on human origins, his relief at its completion is palpable.

There had been, however, one last interruption. On 21 February Darwin received notification from John Murray that stocks of the third edition of *Origin* were exhausted. Darwin replied the next day, 'I am much pleased but even more grieved . . .; for after ten months intermission I am now able to work nearly two hours daily at my next book; but this will be now stopped by the Origin. Natural Hist. progresses so quickly that I must make a good many corrections.' It had been five years since the third edition was issued. The intervening period had seen the publication of a wide range of researches that Darwin regarded as supportive of his theory of transmutation. These included his own work on botanical dimorphism and trimorphism, published between 1861 and 1864, which raised questions about hybrid sterility as a criterion for species. The implications of Darwin's botanical research and that of other plant hybridisers had been a subject of debate between Darwin and Huxley, who had asserted the importance of producing new 'physiological species' by means of artificial selection as a necessary condition for proof of Darwin's theory. Shortly after the new edition was published, Darwin wrote to Huxley, 'do read the Chapt. on Hybridism . . ., for I am very anxious to make you think less seriously on that difficulty.— I have improved the Chapt. a good deal I think, & have come to more definite views' (letter to T. H. Huxley, 22 December [1866]).

The fourth edition of *Origin* also incorporated the work of some of Darwin's closest scientific friends and correspondents. Hooker's research on alpine floras, Henry Walter Bates's article on mimetic butterflies, Lubbock's observations of diving Hymenoptera and insect metamorphosis, Benjamin Dann Walsh's theory of phytophagic varieties and species of insects, Fritz Müller's research on crustacean embryology, and Alfred Russel Wallace's conclusions on varieties and species of Malayan Lepidoptera were all inserted into Darwin's 'long argument' for descent with modification. Darwin also added material obtained through correspondence in 1866, including observations by the American naturalist Jeffries Wyman on the irregular shape of bee cells, long regarded as works of geometric perfection and therefore of divine design. Finally, the new edition of *Origin* allowed Darwin to respond to his former friend, and now bitter antagonist, Richard Owen, whose harsh criticism of *Origin* Darwin had regarded as unjust. Darwin expanded his historical preface to include a lengthy account of Owen's alleged claim to have discovered the principle of natural selection in 1850: 'This belief in Professor Owen that he then gave to the world the theory of natural selection will surprise all those who are acquainted with the several passages in his works, reviews, and lectures, published since the "Origin," in which he strenuously opposes the theory' (*Origin* 4th ed., p. xviii).

Much of Darwin's correspondence in February and early March was also concerned with an extended discussion of glacial theory, prompted in part by the Harvard naturalist Louis Agassiz's recent claims. Agassiz undertook an ambitious expedition to Brazil in 1865 and 1866, partly with a view to finding support for his hypothesis that the entire earth had been frozen during the Ice Age, destroying all life; this was a direct challenge to Darwin's theory of descent. Agassiz claimed to have found evidence of glaciation in the Amazon basin. Darwin was sceptical of Agassiz's findings, however, and allusions to Agassiz's 'absurd views' and his burning desire to disprove Darwin's theories are reiterated in correspondence throughout the year, as in his remark to Lyell, 'I quite follow you in thinking Agassiz glacier-mad' (letter to Charles Lyell, 8[–9] September [1866]).

Darwin had first heard of Agassiz's views through a letter to Lyell's wife, Mary Elizabeth Lyell, from Elizabeth Cabot Cary Agassiz, who had accompanied her husband to South America. Lyell circulated this and other letters (several of which have survived and appear in this volume), drawing Darwin, Hooker, and the botanist Charles James Fox Bunbury into the discussion of glacial theory. Lyell's own interest in the subject was keen, as he was preparing a greatly expanded discussion of climatic change, including a new chapter on astronomical influences, for the tenth edition of his *Principles of geology*. The discussion partly turned on the weighing of different causes of glaciation, and the relative value attached to different forms of evidence in geology, geography, botany, palaeontology, and physics. Although Darwin never advanced a theory of the glacial epoch, his views on geographical distribution depended upon a 'mundane cold period', and he was sceptical of some speculations of physicists against a general cooling of the globe. 'I am bigotted to the last inch, & will not yield', he wrote to Hooker, who attached greater weight to physical and astronomical arguments, such as that of the Scottish autodidact James Croll, who traced the glacial epoch to a period of extreme eccentricity of the earth's orbit. Darwin favoured evidence from observed distributions, such as the presence of the same temperate species on distant mountains, and remarked to Hooker on his strong preference for specific facts over general theories: 'I will maintain to the death that y^r^ case of Fernando Po & Abyssinia is worth ten times more than the belief of a dozen physicists' (letter to J. D. Hooker, [28 February 1866]). Darwin also ventured to inform Lyell that he did not support Lyell's theory of the cause of glaciation, which involved the massing of land at the poles. 'I must confess that I cannot believe in change of land & water being more than a subsidiary agent', Darwin wrote on 8 March [1866], prefacing his remark with, 'I hope you will own that I have generally been a good & docile pupil to you'.

In April Darwin went with his wife, Emma, and daughter Henrietta, to London, staying for two weeks with his brother, Erasmus Alvey Darwin. Owing to improved health, Darwin was able to make a number of social calls, sit for the photographer Ernest Edwards, and visit the gardens of the Zoological Society at Regent's Park. He also astonished the metropolitan scientific community by attending a reception at the Royal Society of London. Some of his friends did not recognise him owing to the beard he had grown over the past few years. Emma described the Royal Society event in a letter to George: 'Your father . . . entered at the same time with Dr B. J. who received him with triumph. All his friends gave him the most cordial reception as soon as they knew who he was, for he had to name himself to all who had not seen him lately. The P. of Wales was there & Gen. Sabine presented your father who made 2 of the best bows he cd muster. The P. muttered some little civility but he cd not hear what, & that was all' (Stephen Keynes, private collection). Darwin's friends were indeed delighted at his return to scientific society; Hooker remarked, 'I am longing to know how you go on, after the startling apparition of your face at R.S. Soirèe—which I dreamed of 2 nights running. Tyndall came up to me in raptures at seeing you—& told me to worship Bence Jones in future—' (letter from J. D. Hooker, 13 May 1866). Darwin himself was jubilant: 'I have been so well most days since being in London, like what I was 7 or 8 years ago— one day I paid 3 calls! & then went for $\frac{3}{4}$ to Zoolog. Garden!!!!!!!!!' (letter to J. D. Hooker, [28 April 1866]).

Darwin's increasing renown both within Britain and abroad is evident from his portrayal in various popular publications, and from the visits he received from admirers and followers. A photograph of Darwin by Edwards was published with a biographical sketch in a volume edited by Lovell Reeve and Edward Walford,

Portraits of men of eminence in literature, science and art. Another of Edwards's photographs served as the basis for a handsome engraving that accompanied a lengthy review article in the *Quarterly Journal of Science*. Though not uncritical, the review described Darwin as 'one of the noblest, most exalted, and most brilliant intellects of our age' (Anon 1866, p. 176). At Down, Darwin received a number of visitors whom he had known previously only through correspondence. George Henslow, the son of his Cambridge mentor, John Stevens Henslow, stayed for two days in April and discussed mechanisms for insect pollination in the legume genera *Medicago*, *Indigofera*, and *Cytisus*. Darwin contributed an observational note to Henslow's paper on the subject, read several weeks later at the Linnean Society of London (Henslow 1866a). In June, Darwin was visited by the orchid specialist John Traherne Moggridge, whose work on the self-pollinating bee ophrys (*Ophrys apifera*) and related orchids was of particular interest. The visit had been precipitated by a meeting between Moggridge and Henrietta during her travels in France. 'I have just had the eventful interview with Mogg', she wrote in May, 'He didn't scold me at all about fusca & lutea & we talked orchids very amicably—but the little man wants to see you— I told him that he might come & pay a morning call but that most likely you wdn't see him & he said he shd be delighted to come on those terms so you are in for it' (letter from H. E. Darwin, [*c*. 10 May 1866]). Henrietta's letter demonstrates her own interest in Darwin's botanical work ('I happened to have an orchid in my hand for him to name & oddly enough it was the other orchis that fertilises itself. . . . It is rather horrible to have another self fertiliser, isn't it?'), as well as the role that she and Emma continued to play in safeguarding Darwin's health and securing his privacy. Similarly, Hooker was called upon to act as intermediary between Darwin and the German botanist Robert Caspary, who wished to visit Down in May: 'ask him by all means to come & sleep here, if he has spare time, but at same time tell him the truth how little exertion I can stand. I sh^{d} like very much to see him, though I dread all exertion' (letter to J. D. Hooker, [12 May 1866]). Darwin's interest in Caspary's research on graft hybrids and self-pollinating waterlilies prevailed over considerations of health in this case.

Nor could Darwin refuse a request from his most zealous admirer and advocate, Ernst Haeckel. The German zoologist had written to Darwin on 11 January 1866, 'Every time I succeed in making a new discovery in the intellectual field of the contemplation of nature that you have newly opened up for us, I want to hurry to Down, Bromley, Kent, in order to talk to you about it.' Haeckel was in England in August en route to Madeira. His visit to Down House is described in a letter from Henrietta to George: 'when first he entered he was so agitated he forgot all the little English he knew & he & Papa shook hands repeatedly. Papa reiteratedly remarking that he was very glad to see him & Haeckel receiving it in dead silence. . . . He told us that there are over 200 medallions of Papa made by a man from W^{ms} photo in circulation amongst the students in Jena' (DAR 245: 269). Haeckel continued to promote Darwinism in Germany. His vast work, *Generelle Morphologie*, published in 1866, was dedicated to Darwin (as well as to Carl Gegenbaur, Johann Wolfgang von

Goethe, and Jean-Baptiste de Lamarck), and credited Darwin with having effected a reformation in descent theory and a new era in science. Darwin received the book with gracious thanks: 'You confer on my book, the "Origin of Species", the most magnificent eulogium which it has ever received' (letter to Ernst Haeckel, 18 August [1866]). Darwin clearly admired parts of the book, but he expressed to Huxley and others certain reservations and worries that its formidable length and difficult language would make its translation into English problematic: 'I have been able to read a page or two here & there, & have been interested & instructed by parts. But my *vague* impression is that too much space is given to methodical details, & I can find hardly any facts or detailed new views. The number of new words, to a man like myself weak in his Greek, is something dreadful' (letter to T. H. Huxley, 22 December [1866]).

Further interest in Darwin's theory in Germany is indicated by correspondence with several publishers who sought permission to translate Darwin's works, including a new edition of *Origin*. A son of the publisher Friedrich Emil Suchsland wrote to Darwin in March asking permission for a new translation of *Origin*, and claiming that Darwin's theory had been widely misunderstood as a result of shortcomings in the previous translation. Two German editions of *Origin*, translated by Heinrich Georg Bronn, had been published in 1860 and 1863 by the firm E. Schweizerbart'sche Verlagsbuchhandlung; these included numerous notes and a critical epilogue that was partly inspired by Bronn's adherence to *Naturphilosophie*, the German idealist tradition of science. Some recent German commentaries on Darwin's theory, such as that of Carl Wilhelm von Nägeli, were also influenced by the authors' commitments to this tradition, with its assumptions about progressive, teleological development (see for example, letter to C. W. Nägeli, 12 June [1866]). Also in March, however, Christian Friedrich Schweizerbart wrote to Darwin offering to publish a revised edition himself. Negotiations were complicated by debates about a suitable translator, Bronn having died in 1862. Finally, Julius Victor Carus, a naturalist who was sympathetic to Darwin and had previously translated Huxley's *Man's place in nature*, was settled upon. Carus immediately began work on the new translation (Bronn and Carus trans. 1867), incorporating the revisions Darwin had made to the fourth English edition, and corresponding with Darwin about various details.

Less success was achieved across the Atlantic, despite much effort expended by Asa Gray in trying to secure a new American edition of *Origin*. Gray had negotiated the original contract between Darwin and the New York publisher D. Appleton and Co. in 1860. Unfortunately, Appleton had produced the 1860 edition using stereotypes, solid plates in which the type was permanently fixed. Substantial alterations, such as Darwin had made to the fourth English edition, would consequently require the recasting of the entire volume, a process that Appleton was unwilling to undertake. The firm apparently offered to incorporate some changes, but their proposal was unsatisfactory to Darwin. Gray then approached another American firm, Ticknor & Fields, but they declined Gray's offer, and a revised American edition was not published until 1870.

Despite the demands of completing *Variation* and preparing a fourth edition of *Origin*, Darwin still found time in the spring and summer to continue botanical researches on dimorphism and dichogamy. As he had done since 1862, Darwin relied on assistance from his eldest son, William, who made observations of the common broom (*Cytisus scoparius*) and the white broom (*C. multiflorus*) in his botanical notebook (DAR 186: 43). His drawings of *C. scoparius*, sent to Darwin with his letter of 8 May [1866], allowed detailed comparisons of pollen-grains of long-styled and short-styled forms, and illustrated the floral mechanism peculiar to *Cytisus* that facilitated cross-pollination by insects. Darwin and William also exchanged over a dozen letters in May and June on the subject of *Rhamnus catharticus* (now *R. cathartica*). Darwin had become interested in *Rhamnus* (buckthorn) in 1861, when Asa Gray informed him that a North American species presented 'an initial state of dimorphism' (*Correspondence* vol. 9, letter from Asa Gray, 11 October 1861). Darwin wished to establish whether dioecious plants had hermaphrodite ancestors, by observing gradation in the development of separate sexes. William gathered numerous specimens of *R. catharticus*, the only species of *Rhamnus* native to Britain, and made detailed observations and drawings. He initially reported that the species was 'merely ordinaryly diœcious' (letter from W. E. Darwin, [7 May – 11 June 1866]). On examining more specimens later in the season, he detected two floral forms of each sex and speculated: 'I cannot help thinking the Rhamnus is a case of dimorphic becoming diœcious' (letter from W. E. Darwin, 20 June [1866]). Darwin was excited by William's find, and urged him to continue his observations with a view to publishing the results: 'If your case turns out true . . . it will be a most interesting discovery & I vow you shall write a paper & publish it; but it must be well worked out first.' Darwin also counselled his son on the necessary disappointments that accompanied scientific inquiry: 'Do not be discouraged if the whole case blows up— I am well accustomed to such explosions' (letter to W. E. Darwin, 22 June [1866]). He urged further observations the following summer, including experiments to assess the relative fertility of the pollen from the different male forms. Darwin evidently continued his observations, planting cuttings sent by William; however, no further correspondence or notes on the subject have been found. When Darwin eventually published the results in *Forms of flowers*, pp. 293–5, he credited observations of the different flower forms to William, but remarked that the plant showed no evidence of having once been heterostyled.

A more wide-ranging set of discussions engaged Darwin and Hooker for much of the summer, prompted by Hooker's decision to give a public lecture at the August meeting of the British Association for the Advancement of Science in Nottingham. Hooker had accepted an invitation from the president of the association, William Robert Grove, to speak 'on the Darwinian theory', and wrote to Darwin on 16 January 1866, 'I am utterly disgusted with my bravado. . . . the difficulty of the subject & impossibility of my doing it justice had charms for me. The Lord have mercy on your bantling in my hand'. The actual subject of Hooker's address was insular floras, a topic of long-standing interest to both men, and a source of ongoing debate for its bearing both on Darwin's theory of transmutation, and on competing theories of the geographical distribution of plants. Darwin had consistently argued against migration by means of continental extension, as proposed by Edward Forbes and others. He favoured instead migration by occasional transport, including the dispersal of seeds by wind, sea currents, floating ice, and birds. Hooker had never accepted Darwin's arguments on this score as conclusive, and raised a host of botanical objections. The preparation of his insular floras lecture offered a new occasion for airing these differences, and for a reassessment of the problem in light of recent evidence. The exchange was often heated, and there were moments when Darwin expressed concern about Hooker's arguments against his distribution theory: 'When you exorcise at Nottingham occasional means of transport, be honest, & admit how little is known on the subject' (letter to J. D. Hooker, 3 and 4 August [1866]). And on the next day: 'It makes me rather miserable to see how differently we look at every thing' (letter to J. D. Hooker, 5 August [1866]). Yet both men seemed to relish this fresh opportunity for intense debate. As Darwin remarked to Lyell earlier in the year: 'a squabble with or about Hooker always does me a world of good, & we have been at it many a long year' (letter to Charles Lyell, 15 February [1866]). Hooker tried to set Darwin's mind at ease: 'You must not let me worry you. I am an obstinate pig—but you must not be miserable at my looking at the same thing in a different light from you' (letter from J. D. Hooker, 7 August 1866). The two exchanged letters with great rapidity in the weeks leading up to the meeting, their correspondence breaking off only when Hooker visited Down on 18 August, bringing his 'blessed mss' (letter from J. D. Hooker, [17 August 1866]). Hooker reported in a letter dated [28 August] 1866: 'The whole thing went off . . . in very good style— . . . I never was so glad to get a thing out of hand & mind.' In the end, Hooker argued that both theories, continental extension and occasional transport, faced 'insuperable obstacles', though he granted that the latter offered a 'rational solution of many of the most puzzling phenomena' that oceanic islands presented. Hooker also asserted that the facts regarding oceanic floras strongly supported 'Mr. Darwin's derivative theory of species', and concluded with a humorous reference to the famous Oxford meeting of the British Association in 1860, where the bishop of Oxford, Samuel Wilberforce, had held forth against *Origin* (J. D. Hooker 1866a, pp. 50, 75–6).

Darwin's work also featured significantly in another speech at the Nottingham meeting. William Robert Grove had approached Hooker in May for information on recent research supportive of Darwin's theory for his presidential address. Hooker produced a list of corroborative works, including his own essays on Arctic and Australian floras, Darwin's *Orchids* and papers on botanical dimorphism, Bates's and Wallace's work on mimetic butterflies, and Wallace's work on human races. Darwin replied with a modified list, adding Fritz Müller's *Für Darwin*, and a recent fossil discovery in pre-Silurian strata; he thought his own work on orchids and *Primula* of 'too indirect a bearing to be worth noticing' (letter to J. D. Hooker, 31 May [1866]). Most of these works and discoveries were mentioned in Grove's address; however, Darwin's theory was described only in terms of its general contrast with creationist accounts of species. Darwin was displeased that the address did not discuss what was specific to his theory. In a letter that has not been found, he voiced his criticisms to Grove, who replied that he had wanted the address to be accessible to non-specialists, and that the 'adaptation view' was in fact consistent both with the origin of species by natural selection, and with special creation (letter from W. R. Grove, 31 August 1866). Hooker later explained that Grove had shown 'little appreciation' of the difficulties of Darwin's theory and had intended Hooker to be 'champion of the cause': 'I was to "back him up" & "to carry Darwinism through the ranks of the enemy" after he had sounded the charge' (letter from J. D. Hooker, [4 September 1866]).

Darwin discussed the details of transmutation theory during the year with Alfred Russel Wallace. They corresponded in February on non-blending characteristics with reference to Darwin's crosses between different varieties of sweetpea and Wallace's work on different female forms of a Malayan species of butterfly. In July, Wallace sent a lengthy commentary on the term 'natural selection'. Darwin's metaphorical use of the expression had been a subject of long discussion in previous years with Lyell, Gray, and Hooker. Wallace's remarks were prompted by several recent reviews in which *Origin* had been criticised for inconsistencies with respect to the role of design in nature. A similar criticism had been made by the editor of the *Quarterly Journal of Science*, James Samuelson, in his letter of 8 April 1866. Wallace argued that the extended analogy that Darwin had drawn between natural selection and artificial or human selection had encouraged readers to attribute intelligent choice to nature. Wallace also pointed out passages in which Darwin had written of nature as 'favouring' or 'seeking' the good of a species, and warned against personifying nature too much. In place of 'natural selection', Wallace suggested that Darwin substitute 'survival of the fittest', an expression first used by Herbert Spencer in an 1864 instalment of *Principles of biology*. (Letter from A. R. Wallace, 2 July 1866.) Darwin agreed that Spencer's term had merit, but argued that it could not be directly substituted as, unlike the term 'natural selection', it could not be used as a substantive governing a verb. Although it was too late to alter the fourth edition of *Origin*, Darwin did insert Spencer's expression at numerous places in the fifth edition, as well as in *Variation*. Darwin continued to read the instalments of *Principles of biology*, praising 'its prodigality of original thought', while noting that 'each suggestion, to be of real value to science, w^{d} require years of work' (letter to J. D. Hooker, 30 June [1866]). He met Spencer during a visit to the Lubbocks in October, and remarked on his use of 'awesomely long words' (letter to J. D. Hooker, 2 October [1866]). He later expressed amusement at Hooker's description of Spencer as a 'thinking pump': 'I read aloud your simile of H. Spencer to a thinking pump, & it was unanimously voted first-rate, & not a bit the worse for being unintelligible' (letter from J. D. Hooker, 14 December 1866, letter to J. D. Hooker, 24 December [1866]).

Fritz Müller, the German naturalist living in Brazil, became a regular correspondent of Darwin's in 1866. Having sent Müller copies of his earlier botanical publications at the end of 1865, Darwin wrote in January 1866, sending his *Journal of researches* and offering Müller a copy of the second German edition of *Origin*. Müller was happy to receive all Darwin's works and read them carefully. A modest request from Darwin on 23 May 1866, 'will you be so kind as to observe whether Oxalis with you exhibits different forms', inspired Müller to make thorough and detailed observations of dimorphism and trimorphism not only in *Oxalis*, but in several other genera, which he sent to Darwin along with diagrams, drawings, specimens, and seeds. With the rich Brazilian orchid flora at his disposal, Müller was able to send Darwin a wealth of new information on orchid pollination. Some of Müller's observations were added to *Variation*, the fifth edition of *Origin*, and Darwin's later botanical works. Müller seemed almost to anticipate what would be useful to Darwin, causing the latter to remark, 'It is quite curious how by coincidence you have been observing the same subjects that have lately interested me' (letter to Fritz Müller, 25 September [1866]). Not surprisingly, Müller was on Darwin's list to receive a pre-publication copy of the fourth edition of *Origin*, and within a few weeks of reading it, he was able to send evidence confirming Darwin's hypothesis that the lancelet, then classified as a primitive fish, would have an invertebrate as its closest competitor in the struggle for existence (letter from Fritz Müller, 1 December 1866). By the close of the year, Darwin had already planted several of the bulbs and seeds sent by Müller, and began a letter, 'I have so much to thank you for that I hardly know how to begin' (letter to Fritz Müller, [before 10 December 1866]).

On occasion, issues of national or international concern were registered in Darwin's correspondence, and even touched upon the publication of his work. In the summer months, much of the attention of the British press was directed toward war on the continent, as Prussia's efforts to expand its power and dominions led to armed conflict with other German states and Austria in June and July. Writing on 10 May from Württemberg, one of the states bordering Prussia, Darwin's German publisher, Christian Friedrich Schweizerbart, warned that should war break out, 'business would be totally paralysed'. Similarly, John Murray gave as a reason for his decision to delay the publication of *Origin* until November the distraction of the British public with 'gaieties travelling & War Bulletins' (letter from John Murray, 18 July 1866). Slavery, a subject of extensive correspondence between Darwin and Asa Gray for many years, was legally abolished in the United States with the ratification of the Thirteenth Amendment to the Constitution in December 1865. Despite concerns about the ongoing difficulties of reconstruction in the southern states, Darwin rejoiced over this latest development: 'I declare I can hardly yet realise the grand, magnificent fact that Slavery is at end in your country' (letter to Asa Gray, 16 April [1866]). Similar sentiments may have been behind Darwin's decision to support the Jamaica Committee, which had formed in December 1865 to lobby for the criminal prosecution of the colonial governor Edward John Eyre. In his efforts to suppress an uprising of the ex-slave population in Jamaica, Eyre had executed a leading revolutionary without trial. An opposing committee for Eyre's defence was formed in August 1866, and both sides in the controversy sought to enlist the support of prominent individuals. Darwin was asked by Herbert Spencer to sign a list of those in favour of prosecution on 2 November 1866. Spencer enclosed a letter by Huxley to the *Pall Mall Gazette*, responding to the imputation that his views on 'the development of species' had inclined him to regard 'the negro' as well as 'the ape' as a brother. 'I am glad to hear from Spencer', Huxley wrote on 11 November, 'that you are on the right (that is *my*) side in the Jamaica business— But it is wonderful how people who commonly act together are divided about it—'. The issue did in fact divide Darwin and Hooker, who remarked on 3 November that the application of high political principles was absurd when colonial officials were chosen from among 'heaven born politicians; Geograph. Soc: Lions, & nine days wonders'. Darwin confessed, 'You will shriek at me when you hear that I have just subscribed to the Jamaica committee. For the more I hear about it the more atrocious the case appears—' (letter to J. D. Hooker, 20 November [1866]).

The year was marked by several deaths within Darwin's family and circle of friends, provoking sombre thoughts. Darwin's younger sister Emily Catherine Langton died in February, and his elder sister Susan Darwin died in October. On learning of Catherine's poor state of health, Hooker, who had lost his father the previous year, wrote on 23 January 1866: 'I have been so haunted by death & his dart ... that I can hardly bear to look at my children asleep in bed'. Darwin's two sisters had lived together in the family house in Shrewsbury after their father's death in 1848 until Catherine married in 1863. Catherine had written shortly before her death that she was 'grieved indeed at poor Susan's loneliness' (letter from E. C. Langton to Emma and Charles Darwin, [6 and 7? January 1866]), and Darwin later remarked to Lyell, 'We are uneasy about Susan, but she has hitherto borne it better than we c^{d} have hoped' (letter to Charles Lyell, 7 February [1866]). Susan had been a particular favourite among the family at Down and her company was frequently enjoyed during her visits to Darwin's brother, Erasmus, in London. When her death seemed near, Darwin wrote to Hooker: 'we must soon hear of the end of a most sweet & loving character' (letter to J. D. Hooker, 2 October [1866]). In the following month, the family house and estate were put up for sale, bringing an end to the family's Shrewsbury era. The disposal of Susan's property prompted thoughts of the provision Darwin hoped to make for his children at his death, and brought an urgent request that his eldest son William make a will of his own. Another particularly sad loss came in April, when the young daughter of Hooker's colleague at Kew, Daniel Oliver, died suddenly. 'How grieved I am to hear about poor Oliver's loss', Darwin wrote to Hooker, 'There is nothing in this world like the bitterness of such a loss,—unless indeed the wife herself' (letter to J. D. Hooker, [9 April 1866]).

It was against this background that Darwin made a rare statement of his religious views, replying to the educator Mary Everest Boole, who asked whether he thought the theory of natural selection compatible with belief in God as a 'personal and Infinitely good Being' (letter from M. E. Boole, 13 December 1866). Darwin answered, 'it has always appeared to me more satisfactory to look at the immense amount of pain & suffering in this world, as the inevitable result of the natural sequence of events . . . rather than from the direct intervention of God' (letter to M. E. Boole, 14 December 1866). But amidst such loss and sober reflection, the year ended on a bright note, with the renewal of old friendships, and enthusiasm over family successes and scientific work. One of the officers on the *Beagle* voyage, Bartholomew James Sulivan, wrote on 25 December of the achievements of his sons, newly promoted in the navy, and of the Admiralty's plans to return to the site in Patagonia where he had discovered the fossilised bones of several extinct mammals years before. Darwin replied on the last day of the year, reporting the success of his son George, who had recently won a scholarship to Trinity College, Cambridge. He asked Sulivan about the possibility of obtaining information on the expression of emotions among 'Fuegians', and added what was by no means an afterthought, 'I have just sent off to the printers a great bundle of M.S for a book on "domestic animals".'

ACKNOWLEDGMENTS

The editors are grateful to the late George Pember Darwin and to William Huxley Darwin for permission to publish the Darwin letters and manuscripts. They also thank the Syndics of Cambridge University Library and other owners of manuscript letters who have generously made them available.

The work for this edition has been supported by grants from the National Endowment for the Humanities (NEH), the National Science Foundation (NSF), and the Wellcome Trust. The Alfred P. Sloan Foundation, the Pew Charitable Trusts, and the Andrew W. Mellon Foundation provided grants to match NEH funding, and the Mellon Foundation awarded grants to Cambridge University that made it possible to put the entire Darwin correspondence into machine-readable form. Research and editorial work have also been supported by grants from the Royal Society of London, the British Academy, the British Ecological Society, the Isaac Newton Trust, the Jephcott Charitable Trust, the Natural Environment Research Council, and the Wilkinson Charitable Foundation. The Stifterverband für die Deutsche Wissenschaft provided funds to edit Darwin's correspondence with German naturalists.

Cambridge University Library and the American Philosophical Society (APS) have generously made working space and many services available to the editors.

Since the project began in 1975, the editors have been fortunate in benefiting from the interest, experience, and practical help of many people, and hope that they have adequately expressed their thanks to them individually as the work proceeded.

Without the expert help of John L. Dawson of the Literary and Linguistic Computing Centre of Cambridge University, the initial computerisation of the correspondence would not have been possible. Iain Burke, Peter Dunn, Ray Horne, Patricia Killiard, Adrian Miller, Chris Sendall, Tomasz Waldoch, and Ellis Weinberger have helped maintain and extend our access to the Library's electronic resources, and provided essential technical support. Simon Buck provided invaluable assistance in setting up automatic typesetting procedures, and we are grateful to Robin Fairbairns for expert help in their maintenance and development. Gratitude is expressed to the late C. A. Tripp for providing the editors with an invaluable tool for searching texts.

English Heritage has responded most generously to requests for information and for material from the collections at Down House, Downe. We are particularly grateful to Tori Reeve, curator of Down House, Nick Biddle, formerly grounds curator of Down House, and the staff of the English Heritage Picture Library. Richard Darwin Keynes kindly made available Darwin family material in his possession. Ursula Mommens has also provided letters and other materials that belonged to her grandfather, Francis Darwin.

Libraries all over the world have given indispensable help by making available photocopies of Darwin correspondence and other manuscripts in their collections. The institutions and individuals that furnished copies of letters for this volume can be found in the List of provenances. The editors are extremely indebted to them all. We are also grateful to the many people who have transmitted information regarding the whereabouts of particular letters.

Virginia Murray of John Murray (publishers) Ltd has graciously provided the editors with copies of the Darwin correspondence in the Murray archive and with related information. Leonard G. Wilson kindly provided the editors with photocopies of manuscript material in the possession of the family of Sir Charles Lyell. George Beccaloni, Milton Forsyth, the late Quentin Keynes, Chris Kohler, Joseph Sakmyster, and John Wilson have generously provided photocopies of or information about newly found letters.

The editors make daily use of the incomparable facilities of Cambridge University Library and have benefited greatly from its services and from the help and expertise of its staff, particularly the staff of the Manuscripts Department. We are especially grateful to the former University Librarian, Frederick W. Ratcliffe, to his successor, Peter K. Fox, and to the Keeper of Manuscripts and Archives, Patrick Zutshi, for their generous support. Other members of the library's staff who have frequently responded to the editors' requests are: Marjolein Allen, Wendy Aylett, Gerry Bye, Kathleen Cann, Colin Clarkson, Barry Eaden, Les Goodey, David J. Hall, John Hall, Tony Harper, Isabel Holowaty, Brian Jenkins, Morag Law, Elisabeth Leedham-Green, David Lowe, Peter Meadows, Anne Murray, William Noblett, Adam Perkins, Jayne Ringrose, Mark Scudder, Clive Simmonds, Nicholas Smith, Anne Taylor, Nicola Thwaite, Godfrey Waller, and Cynthia Webster. The fetchers in the Rare Books reading room have also patiently dealt with the editors' often complex requirements, as have the staff of the Map Room.

At the American Philosophical Society Library, a splendid collection of Darwiniana and works in the history of science has been available to the editors since the inception of the project. Whitfield J. Bell Jr, secretary of the society until 1983, serves on the United States Advisory Committee for the project and has done his utmost to further its work. The editors have also benefited from the co-operation of the late Edward Carter II, Robert S. Cox, Roy C. Goodman, Carl F. Miller, Elizabeth Carroll-Horrocks, and Bertram Dodelin, all of the APS Library.

Thanks are due to the faculty and staff of the Department of Science and Technology Studies, Cornell University, for accomodating one of the Project's editors, to staff at Cornell University Libraries, including David Corson at the Kroch library, for help with research enquiries, and to Frank Strickland of the College of Arts and Sciences, Cornell University, for invaluable computing support.

The editors would like to acknowledge the assistance of Rodney Dennis, Jennie Rathbun, and Susan Halpert of the Houghton Library, Constance Carter of the Science Division of the Library of Congress, and Judith Warnement and Jean Cargill of the Gray Herbarium of Harvard University, who have all been exceptionally helpful in providing material from the collections in their charge.

In Britain, the editors have often received assistance from Mary Sampson, archivist of the Royal Society; Rex E. R. Banks, Vicki Veness, and the late John Thackray of the Natural History Museum Library; Gina Douglas, librarian of the Linnean Society of London; and Sylvia FitzGerald, John Flanagan, and Kate Pickard of the Library of the Royal Botanic Gardens, Kew. We would also like to thank Malcolm P. Marjoram of the British Library (Manuscripts); Richard G. Williams, Mrs Felton, and Anne Barrett (college archivist) of Imperial College of Science, Technology and Medicine; Christine Fyfe, archivist of Keele University; George R. Else, of the Department of Entomology, Natural History Museum, London; and Douglas Ferguson and Candace Guite of Christ's College, Cambridge. Invaluable assistance has been received from local studies librarians and county archivists, too numerous to name individually, although Elizabeth Silverthorne of Bromley Central Library and Donald Gibson of the Centre for Kentish Studies deserve special mention for their repeated assistance.

Among the others who have advised and assisted the editors in their work are David Allen, Nick Gill, Ruth Goldstone, Deirdre Haxton, Julius Held, Sandra Herbert, Randal Keynes, Desmond King-Hele, Gren Lucas, Jim Moore, Muriel Palmer, Henri Quinn, Jim Secord, and Garry J. Tee. The editors are also pleased to acknowledge the invaluable support of the members of the British and United States Advisory Committees.

For help with particular research enquiries in volume 14, the editors would like to thank, besides those already mentioned, Christine Brandon-Jones, David Brown, Hugh Brown of the International Registry of Sunken Ships, Robin K. Campbell, Robert Dressler, Jennifer Fox, Kristi Mercer of the Illinois State Geological Survey, John Smith of Trinity College, Cambridge, and James Williams of the Dumfriesshire & Galloway Natural History & Antiquarian Society.

Thanks are also due to all former staff of the Darwin Correspondence Project: Sarah Benton, Heidi Bradshaw, Janet Browne, P. Thomas Carroll, Mario Di Gregorio, Kate Fletcher, Hedy Franks, Joy Harvey, Arne Hessenbruch, Thomas Junker, David Kohn, Jyothi Krishnan-Unni, Sarah Lavelle, Anna K. Mayer, William Montgomery, Perry O'Donovan, Stephen V. Pocock, Marsha L. Richmond, the late Peter Saunders, Anne Secord, the late Sydney Smith, Nora Carroll Stevenson, Jonathan R. Topham, Tylor Veak, and Sarah Wilmot.

The editors also gratefully acknowledge the valuable assistance of Rosemary Clarkson, Philip Hardie, Tracey A. B. Slotta, and Béatrice Willis, and extend thanks to Jean Macqueen for providing the index to the volume.

In addition, we would like to acknowledge the contribution of colleagues who left the staff during the preparation of this volume. Charlotte Bowman has retired after serving brilliantly as assistant editor for over twenty years, and during 2003 we lost the valuable services of Rhonda Edwards and Kathleen Lane, whom we wish well in all they undertake in the future.

LIST OF PROVENANCES

The following list gives the locations of the original versions of the letters printed in this volume. The editors are grateful to all the institutions and individuals listed for allowing access to the letters in their care. Access to material in DAR 261 and DAR 263, formerly at Down House, Downe, Kent, England, is courtesy of English Heritage.

American Philosophical Society, Philadelphia, Pennsylvania, USA
Archiv der Berlin-Brandenburgischen Akademie der Wissenschaften, Berlin, Germany
Archives de la famille de Candolle, Geneva, Switzerland
Archives, The New York Botanical Garden, Bronx, New York, USA
Beinecke Rare Book and Manuscript Library, Yale University, New Haven, Connecticut, USA
Henry Bristow (dealer)
British Library, London, England
Bodleian Library, Oxford, England
Boston Public Library, Boston, Massachusetts, USA
Christie's (dealers), London, England
Cleveland Health Sciences Library, Cleveland, Ohio, USA
Roy Davids (dealer)
Field Museum of Natural History, Chicago, Illinois, USA
Fitzwilliam Museum, Cambridge, England
Gardeners' Chronicle and Agricultural Gazette (publication)
Gray Herbarium of Harvard University, Cambridge, Massachusetts, USA
Gunther 1975 (publication)
Ernst-Haeckel-Haus, Friedrich-Schiller-Universität Jena, Germany
Eilo Hildebrand (private collection)
Imperial College of Science, Technology, and Medicine, London, England
Keele University Library, Keele, Staffordshire, England
Linnean Society of London, Piccadilly, London, England
K. M. Lyell ed. 1881 (publication)
ML (publication)
Möller ed. 1915–21 (publication)
Morristown National Historical Park, New Jersey, USA
Museo Civico di Storia Naturale, Milan, Italy
Muséum National d'Histoire Naturelle (Département Systématique & Evolution; Cryptogamie), Paris, France

John Murray Archive, London, England
National Library of Australia, Canberra, Australia
The Natural History Museum, Cromwell Road, London, England
North Star Rare Books & Manuscripts (dealer)
A. Pritchard comp. 1897 (publication)
Remember When Auctions (dealer)
Rendells (dealer)
Royal Botanic Gardens, Kew, Richmond, Surrey, England
Royal Horticultural Society, London, England
Royal Institution of Great Britain, London, England
Senckenbergische Naturforschende Gesellschaft, Frankfurt am Main, Germany
Herb Sewell (private collection)
Michael Silverman (dealer)
Smithsonian Institution Libraries, Washington DC, USA
Sotheby's London (dealer), London, England
Sotheby's New York (dealer), New York, USA
Staatsbibliothek zu Berlin, Germany
E. Sulivan (private collection)
Alexander Turnbull Library (National Library of New Zealand), Wellington, New Zealand
University Library, Basel, Switzerland
R. Wallace ed. 1899 (publication)
Jeffries Wyman Jr (private collection)
Wedgwood Museum Trust, Barlaston, Stoke-on-Trent, England
Wellcome Library for the History and Understanding of Medicine, London, England
John Wilson (dealer)

A NOTE ON EDITORIAL POLICY

The first and chief objective of this edition is to provide complete and authoritative texts of Darwin's correspondence. For every letter to or from Darwin, the text that is available to the editors is always given in full. The editors have occasionally included letters that are not to or from Darwin if they are relevant to the published correspondence. Volumes of the *Correspondence* are published in chronological order. Occasional supplements will be published containing letters that have come to light or have been redated since the relevant volumes of the *Correspondence* appeared. Letters that can only be given a wide date range, in some instances spanning several decades, are printed in the supplement following the volume containing letters at the end of their date range. The first such supplement was in volume 7 and included letters from 1828 to 1857. The second supplement was in volume 13, and included letters from 1822 to 1864.

Dating of letters and identification of correspondents

In so far as it is possible, the letters have been dated, arranged in chronological order, and the recipients or senders identified. Darwin seldom wrote the full date on his letters and, unless the addressee was well known to him, usually wrote only 'Dear Sir' or 'Dear Madam'. After the adoption of adhesive postage stamps in the 1840s, the separate covers that came into use with them were usually not preserved, and thus the dates and the names of many recipients of Darwin's letters have had to be derived from other evidence. The notes made by Francis Darwin on letters sent to him for his editions of his father's correspondence have been helpful, as have matching letters in the correspondence, but many dates and recipients have had to be deduced from the subject-matter or references in the letters themselves.

Transcription policy

Whenever possible, transcriptions have been made from manuscripts. If the manuscript was inaccessible but a photocopy or other facsimile version was available, that version has been used as the source. In many cases, the editors have had recourse to Francis Darwin's large collection of copies of letters, compiled in the 1880s. Other copies, published letters, or drafts have been transcribed when they provided texts that were otherwise unavailable.

The method of transcription employed in this edition is adapted from that described by Fredson Bowers in 'Transcription of manuscripts: the record of variants',

Studies in Bibliography 29 (1976): 212–64. This system is based on accepted principles of modern textual editing and has been widely adopted in literary editions.

The case for using the principles and techniques of this form of textual editing for historical and non-literary documents, both in manuscript and print, has been forcefully argued by G. Thomas Tanselle in 'The editing of historical documents', *Studies in Bibliography* 31 (1978): 1–56. The editors of the *Correspondence* followed Dr Tanselle in his conclusion that a 'scholarly edition of letters or journals should not contain a text which has editorially been corrected, made consistent, or otherwise smoothed out' (p. 48), but they have not wholly subscribed to the statement made earlier in the article that: 'In the case of notebooks, diaries, letters and the like, whatever state they are in constitutes their finished form, and the question of whether the writer "intended" something else is irrelevant' (p. 47). The editors have preserved the spelling, punctuation, and grammar of the original, but they have found it impossible to set aside entirely the question of authorial intent. One obvious reason is that in reading Darwin's writing, there must necessarily be reliance upon both context and intent. Even when Darwin's general intent is clear, there are cases in which alternative readings are, or may be, possible, and therefore the transcription decided upon must to some extent be conjectural. Where the editors are uncertain of their transcription, the doubtful text has been enclosed in italic square brackets.

A major editorial decision was to adopt the so-called 'clear-text' method of transcription, which so far as possible keeps the text free of brackets recording deletions, insertions, and other alterations in the places at which they occur. Darwin's changes are, however, recorded in the back matter of the volume, under 'Manuscript alterations and comments', in notes keyed to the printed text by paragraph and line number. All lines above the first paragraph of the letter (that is, date, address, or salutation) are referred to as paragraph '0'. Separate paragraph numbers are used for subscriptions and postscripts. This practice enables the reader who wishes to do so to reconstruct the manuscript versions of Darwin's autograph letters, while furnishing printed versions that are uninterrupted by editorial interpolations. The Manuscript alterations and comments record all alterations made by Darwin in his letters and any editorial amendments made in transcription, and also where part of a letter has been written by an amanuensis; they do not record alterations made by amanuenses. No attempt has been made to record systematically all alterations to the text of copies of Darwin letters included in the correspondence, but ambiguous passages in copies are noted. The editors believe it would be impracticable to attempt to go further without reliable information about the texts of the original versions of the letters concerned. Letters to Darwin have been transcribed without recording any of the writers' alterations unless they reflect significant changes in substance or impede the sense; in such cases footnotes bring them to the reader's attention.

Misspellings have been preserved, even when it is clear that they were unintentional: for instance, 'lawer' for 'lawyer'. Such errors often indicate excitement or haste and may exhibit, over a series of letters, a habit of carelessness in writing to a particular correspondent or about a particular subject.

Capital letters have also been transcribed as they occur except in certain cases, such as 'm', 'k', and 'c', which are frequently written somewhat larger than others as initial letters of words. In these cases an attempt has been made to follow the normal practice of the writers.

In some instances that are not misspellings in a strict sense, editorial corrections have been made. In his early manuscripts and letters Darwin consistently wrote 'bl' so that it looks like 'lb' as in 'albe' for 'able', 'talbe' for 'table'. Because the form of the letters is so consistent in different words, the editors consider that this is most unlikely to be a misspelling but must be explained simply as a peculiarity of Darwin's handwriting. Consequently, the affected words have been transcribed as normally spelled and no record of any alteration is given in the textual apparatus. Elsewhere, though, there are misformed letters that the editors have recorded because they do, or could, affect the meaning of the word in which they appear. The main example is the occasional inadvertent crossing of 'l'. When the editors are satisfied that the intended letter was 'l' and not 't', as, for example, in 'stippers' or 'istand', then 'l' has been transcribed, but the actual form of the word in the manuscript has been given in the Manuscript alterations and comments.

If the only source for a letter is a copy, the editors have frequently retained corrections made to the text when it is clear that they were based upon comparison with the original. Francis Darwin's corrections of misreadings by copyists have usually been followed; corrections to the text that appear to be editorial alterations have not been retained.

Editorial interpolations in the text are in square brackets. Italic square brackets enclose conjectured readings and descriptions of illegible passages. To avoid confusion, in the few instances in which Darwin himself used square brackets, they have been altered by the editors to parentheses with the change recorded in the Manuscript alterations and comments. In letters to Darwin, square brackets have been changed to parentheses silently.

Material that is irrecoverable because the manuscript has been torn or damaged is indicated by angle brackets; any text supplied within them is obviously the responsibility of the editors. Occasionally, the editors are able to supply missing sections of text by using ultraviolet light (where text has been lost owing to damp) or by reference to transcripts or photocopies of manuscript material made before the damage occurred.

Words and passages that have been underlined for emphasis are printed in italics in accordance with conventional practice. Where the author of a letter has indicated greater emphasis by underlining a word or passage two or more times, the text is printed in bold type.

Paragraphs are often not clearly indicated in the letters. Darwin and others sometimes marked a change of subject by leaving a somewhat larger space than usual between sentences; sometimes Darwin employed a longer dash. In these cases, and when the subject is clearly changed in very long stretches of text, a new paragraph has been started by the editors without comment. The beginnings of letters, valedictions, and postscripts are also treated as new paragraphs regardless of whether they appear as new paragraphs in the manuscript. Special manuscript devices delimiting sections or paragraphs, for example, blank spaces left between sections of text and lines drawn across the page, are treated as normal paragraph indicators and are not specially marked or recorded unless their omission leaves the text unclear.

Occasionally punctuation marking the end of a clause or sentence is not present in the manuscript, but the author has made his or her intention clear by allowing, for example, extra space or a line break to function as punctuation. In such cases, the editors have inserted an extra space following the sentence or clause to set it off from the following text.

Additions to a letter that run over into the margins, or are continued at its head or foot, are transcribed at the point in the text at which the editors believe they were intended to be read. The placement of such an addition is only recorded in a footnote if it seems to the editors to have some significance or if the position at which it should be transcribed is unclear. Enclosures are transcribed following the letter.

The hand-drawn illustrations and diagrams that occur in some letters are reproduced as faithfully as possible and are usually positioned as they were in the original text. In some cases, however, it has been necessary to reduce the size of a diagram or enhance an outline for clarity; any such alterations are recorded in footnotes. The location of diagrams within a letter is sometimes changed for typesetting reasons. Tables have been reproduced as close to the original format as possible, given typesetting constraints.

Some Darwin letters and a few letters to Darwin are known only from entries in the catalogues of book and manuscript dealers or mentions in other published sources. Whatever information these sources provide about the content of such letters has been reproduced without substantial change. Any errors detected are included in footnotes.

Format of published letters

The format in which the transcriptions are printed in the *Correspondence* is as follows:

1. *Order of letters*. The letters are arranged in chronological sequence. A letter that can be dated only approximately is placed at the earliest date on which the editors believe it could have been written. The basis of a date supplied by the editors is given in a footnote unless it is derived from a postmark, watermark, or endorsement that is recorded in the physical description of the letter (see section 4, below). Letters with the same date, or with a range of dates commencing with that date, are printed in the alphabetical order of their senders or recipients unless their contents dictate a clear alternative order. Letters dated only to a year or a range of years precede letters that are dated to a particular month or range of months, and these, in turn, precede those that are dated to a particular day or range of dates commencing with a particular day.

2. *Headline*. This gives the name of the sender or recipient of the letter and its date. The date is given in a standard form, but those elements not taken directly from the letter text are supplied in square brackets. The name of the sender or recipient is enclosed in square brackets only where the editors regard the attribution as doubtful.

3. *The letter text*. The transcribed text follows as closely as possible the layout of the source, although no attempt is made to produce a type-facsimile of the manuscript: word-spacing and line-division in the running text are not adhered to. Similarly, the typography of printed sources is not replicated. Dates and addresses given by authors are transcribed as they appear, except that if both the date and the address are at the head of the letter they are always printed on separate lines with the address first, regardless of the manuscript order. If no address is given on a letter by Darwin, the editors have supplied one, when able to do so, in square brackets at the head of the letter. Similarly, if Darwin was writing from an address different from the one given on the letter, his actual location is given in square brackets. Addresses on printed stationery are transcribed in italics. Addresses, dates, and valedictions have been run into single lines to save space, but the positions of line-breaks in the original are marked by vertical bars.

4. *Physical description*. All letters are complete and in the hand of the sender unless otherwise indicated. If a letter was written by an amanuensis, or exists only as a draft or a copy, or is incomplete, or is in some other way unusual, then the editors provide the information needed to complete the description. Postmarks, endorsements, and watermarks are recorded only when they are evidence for the date or address of the letter.

5. *Source*. The final line provides the provenance of the text. Some sources are given in abbreviated form (for example, DAR 140: 18) but are listed in full in the List of provenances unless the source is a published work. Letters in private collections are also indicated. References to published works are given in author–date or short-title form, with full titles and publication details supplied in the Bibliography at the end of the volume.

6. *Darwin's annotations*. Darwin frequently made notes in the margins of the letters he received, scored significant passages, and crossed through details that were of no further interest to him. These annotations are transcribed or described following the letter text. They are keyed to the letter text by paragraph and line numbers. Most notes are short, but occasionally they run from a paragraph to several pages, and sometimes they are written on separate sheets appended to the letter. Extended notes relating to a letter are transcribed whenever practicable following the annotations as 'CD notes'.

Quotations from Darwin manuscripts in footnotes and elsewhere, and the text of his annotations and notes on letters, are transcribed in 'descriptive' style. In this method the alterations in the text are recorded in brackets at the places where they occur. For example:

'See Daubeny ['vol. 1' *del*] for *descriptions of volcanoes in [*interl*] S.A.' *ink*

means that Darwin originally wrote in ink 'See Daubeny vol. 1 for S.A.' and then deleted 'vol. 1' and inserted 'descriptions of volcanoes in' after 'for'. The asterisk before 'descriptions' marks the beginning of the interlined phrase, which ends at the bracket. The asterisk is used when the alteration applies to more than the immediately preceding word. The final text can be read simply by skipping the material in brackets. Descriptive style is also used in the Manuscript alterations and comments.

Editorial matter

Each volume is self-contained, having its own index, bibliography, and biographical register. A chronology of Darwin's activities covering the period of each volume and translations of foreign-language letters are supplied, and additional appendixes give supplementary material where appropriate to assist the understanding of the correspondence. A cumulative index is planned once the edition is complete. References are supplied for all persons, publications, and subjects mentioned, even though some repetition of material in earlier volumes is involved.

If the name of a person mentioned in a letter is incomplete or incorrectly spelled, the full, correct form is given in a footnote. Brief biographies of persons mentioned in the letters, and dates of each correspondent's letters to and from Darwin in the current volume, are given in the Biographical register and index to correspondents. Where a personal name serves as a company name, it is listed according to the family name but retains its original order: for example, 'E. Schweizerbart'sche Verlagsbuchhandlung' is listed under 'S', not 'E'.

Short titles are used for references to Darwin's books and articles and to collections of his letters (e.g., *Descent*, 'Parallel roads of Glen Roy', *LL*). They are also used for some standard reference works and for works with no identifiable author (e.g., *Alum. Cantab.*, *Wellesley index*, *DNB*). For all other works, author–date references are used. References to the Bible are to the authorised King James version unless otherwise stated. Words not in *Chambers dictionary* are usually defined in the footnotes with a source supplied. The full titles and publication details of all the books referred to are given in the Bibliography. References to archival material, for instance that in the Darwin Archive at Cambridge University Library, are not necessarily exhaustive.

Darwin and his correspondents writing in English consistently used the term 'fertilisation' for the processes that are now distinguished as fertilisation (the fusion of female and male gametes) and pollination (the transfer of pollen from anther to stigma); the first usage known to the editors of a distinct term for pollination in English was in 1873 (letter from A. W. Bennett, 12 July 1873 (*Calendar* no. 8976)). 'Fertilisation' in Darwin's letters and publications often, but not always, can be regarded as referring to what is now termed pollination. In the footnotes, the editors, where possible, have used the modern terms where these can assist in explaining the details of experimental work. When Darwin or his correspondents are quoted directly, their original usage is never altered.

The editors use the abbreviation 'CD' for Charles Darwin throughout the footnotes. A list of all abbreviations used by the editors in this volume is given on p. xl.

The Wedgwood and

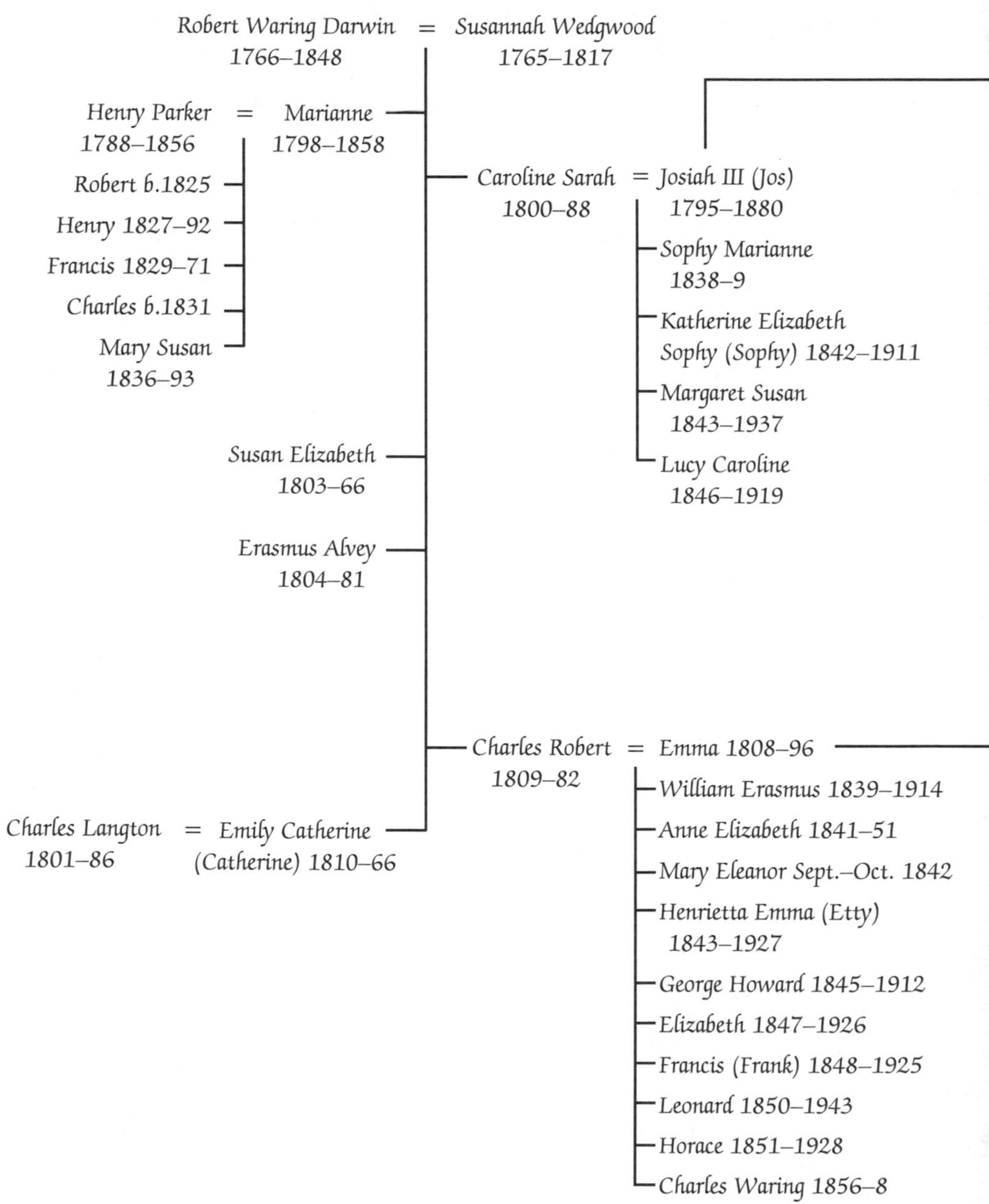

arwin Families up to 1866

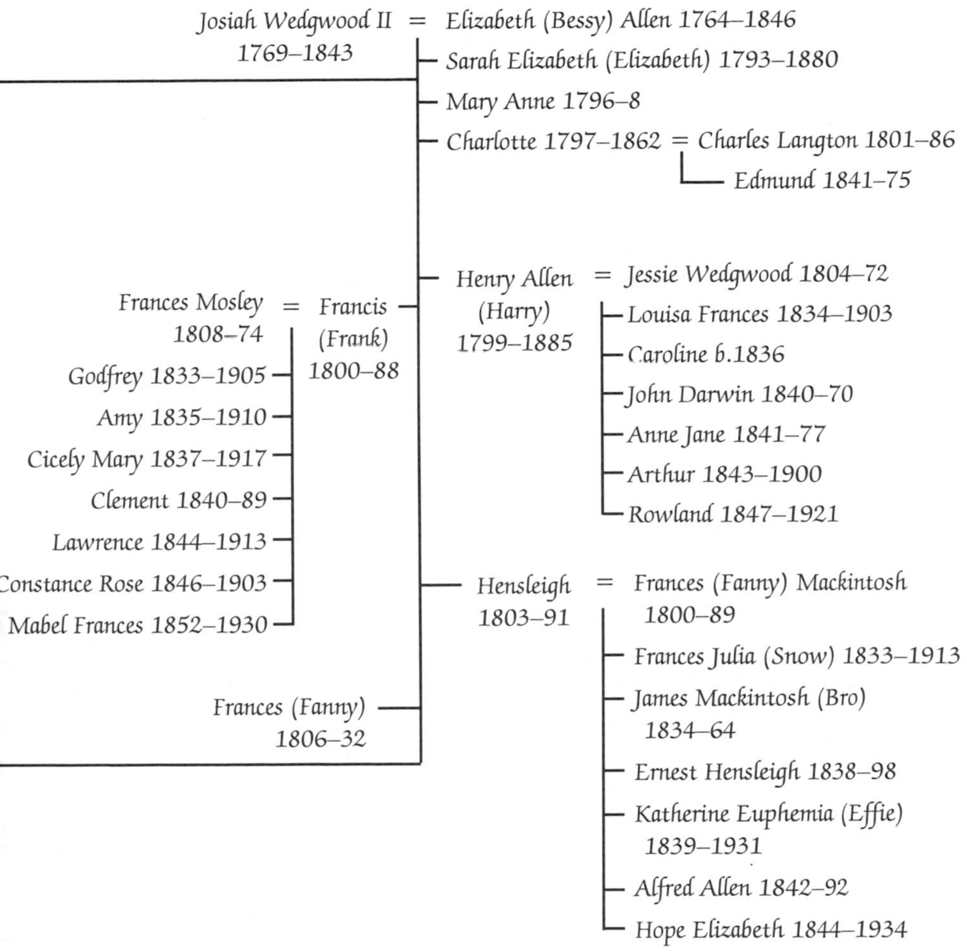

ABBREVIATIONS

AL	autograph letter
ALS	autograph letter signed
DS	document signed
LS	letter in hand of amanuensis, signed by sender
LS(A)	letter in hand of amanuensis with additions by sender
Mem	memorandum
(S)	signed with sender's name by amanuensis
CD	Charles Darwin
CUL	Cambridge University Library
DAR	Darwin Archive, Cambridge University Library
del	deleted
illeg	illegible
interl	interlined
underl	underlined

TRANSCRIPTION CONVENTIONS

[some text]	'some text' is an editorial insertion
*/*some text*/*	'some text' is the conjectured reading of an ambiguous word or passage
[some text]	'some text' is a description of a word or passage that cannot be transcribed, e.g., '*3 words illeg*'
⟨ ⟩	word(s) destroyed
⟨some text⟩	'some text' is a suggested reading for a destroyed word or passage
⟨*some text*⟩	'some text' is a description of a destroyed word or passage, e.g., '*3 lines excised*'

THE CORRESPONDENCE OF CHARLES DARWIN 1866

To George Howard Darwin [1866]

Dear George

Can you or any of your friends answer me this.[1] In a family of 10 5 of the children squinted & 5 did not & they came alternately—.[2] But you must understand it is indifferent whether a squinter or a non squinter comes first. What I want to know is what are the chances against their coming alternately.[3]

Yours affec | Ch. Darwin | Ch. Darwin | Ch. Darwin[4]

P.S This case of the squinting & other such cases are real.

Endorsement: '66
L(S)
DAR 210.1: 1

[1] George Darwin was studying mathematics at Cambridge University (*Alum. Cantab.*).

[2] A case of squinting in five of ten siblings was reported in Streatfield 1857–9, and was referred to in Sedgwick 1861, which CD cited (in relation to a different subject) in *Variation* 2: 328 n. However, Streatfield stated that squinting affected only the boys among ten siblings, not that alternate children squinted. CD briefly discussed squinting in *Variation* 2: 9, in the chapter on inheritance, but relied exclusively on evidence provided by William Bowman.

[3] At the top of the letter, George calculated a 1:126 chance of squinters and non-squinters being born alternately in a family of ten, by dividing twice the square of the factorial of five by the factorial of ten. At the end of his working, he multiplied 126 by two; the reason for this is unclear. George's reply to CD has not been found.

[4] The letter is in the hand of CD's daughter Elizabeth. The signatures are copied from CD's own.

To a local landowner[1] [1866?][2]

Dear Sir.

As you are now so little on your Farm, you may not be aware that the necks of your horses are badly galled, as I have been informed by two persons.[3] I hope you will immediately attend to this, for though I sh^{d} be very sorry to give trouble or annoyance to yourself from whom I have always received much civility, I must for the sake of humanity attend to this.[4] A conviction for working Horses with galled necks is easily obtainable, on sufficient evidence being produced & I was most unwillingly compelled, after vainly remonstrating with Mr Ainslie by letter on the subject, to get the Officer of the Royal Humane Soc. to come down here & attend to the case, & Mr Ainslie was fined by the Magistrates at the Bromley Session.—[5] I sincerely hope that you will at once make enquiries & give strict orders to your Bailiff not to work any horse with a wounded neck[6]—

& | I remain | Dear Sir | Y^rs^ faithfully | Ch. Darwin

Draft
DAR 96: 27r

[1] The recipient has not been identified; he was apparently a farmer or landowner in Down or its neighbourhood.
[2] The year is conjectured from the endorsement ''66' in Francis Darwin's hand.
[3] CD's informants have not been identified.
[4] For CD's interest in animals, and their humane treatment, see Atkins 1974, pp. 78–84, and n. 5, below. CD's original wording of this sentence referred to his obligation 'as a magistrate' to become involved in this matter (see 'Manuscript alterations and comments').
[5] In 1852, CD had arranged for an officer of the Society for the Prevention of Cruelty to Animals to inspect horses owned by Robert Ainslie of Tromer Lodge, Down (letter from Emma Darwin to William Erasmus Darwin, [23 April 1852] (DAR 219.1: 4)). CD refers, apparently in error, to the Royal Humane Society, which was established in 1774 to promote better techniques and resources for saving people from drowning (P. J. Bishop 1974). CD was himself a magistrate from 1857 (Milner 1994, pp. 90–4). For information on the Darwins' involvement with the Royal Society for the Prevention of Cruelty to Animals and the campaign for humane vermin traps, see *Correspondence* vol. 11, Appendix IX. For the society's emphasis on 'humane' objectives between 1837 and 1870, see Fairholm and Pain 1924, pp. 162–4.
[6] The bailiff has not been identified.

From Charles John Robinson [1866?][1]

Harewood | Ross. Herefordshire

My dear Mr Darwin,

I cannot resist the pleasure of telling you how gratified I have been to hear of your restoration to health.

Your name was mentioned the other night at dinner at the Deanery[2] & my neighbour M^r^. Herbert—(our County Court Judge)—in answer to my enquiries, gave me the very welcome news.[3]

I pay him a visit next week in order to meet your old friend Charles Whitley.[4]

In the few years that have passed since I last had the pleasure of seeing you I have had to endure many sorrows. The loss of my wife in her first confinement &—almost simultaneously—the death of my father & mother—have left me very solitary.[5]

If I am not wholly forgotten, allow me to offer my kind regards to M^rs^. & Miss Darwin as well as to yourself—[6] for whom I trust there are many years of health & fame in store.

Yours very sincerely, | Charles J Robinson

I have a small living (Norton Canon) in this county, where I am building a Vicarage house—restoring Church & School[7] & otherwise following the ordinary imprudent course w^{h}. my brethren adopt.

DAR 176: 188

[1] The year is conjectured from the references to CD's improving health and to the dinner at Hereford Deanery. CD's health had been improving since the end of 1865, an improvement he attributed to treatment by Henry Bence Jones (*Correspondence* vol. 13, letter to T. H. Huxley, 4 October [1865] and n. 3). Robinson's informant about CD's health, John Maurice Herbert, had learned the news of the good effects of Jones's treatment 'some few months' before writing to CD in May 1867 (*Correspondence* vol. 15, letter from J. M. Herbert, 3 May 1867). The dinner at the Deanery is likely to have taken place some time before the death of Herbert's friend, the dean of Hereford, Richard Dawes, in March 1867 (see *DNB* and *Correspondence* vol. 15, letter from J. M. Herbert, 3 May 1867).

[2] Robinson refers to the Deanery at Hereford.

[3] Herbert, a Cambridge friend of CD's (*Correspondence* vol. 1), was a County Court judge on the South Wales circuit from 1847 to 1882 (*Modern English biography*). See also n. 1, above.

[4] Charles Thomas Whitley had been at Shrewsbury School and Cambridge with CD; he was Herbert's cousin (*LL* 1: 166, *Modern English biography*).

[5] Robinson's first wife has not been further identified. He later married Emma Harriet Agnes Crocker; they had four daughters by 1881. Robinson's parents were Eleanor Rocke and Charles Frederick Robinson of Ashcott, near Glastonbury. (*Biograph and Review* 6 (1881): 144–6.)

[6] Robinson refers to Emma Darwin and Henrietta Emma Darwin; he had met them and CD at Ilkley, Yorkshire, in October 1859 (letter from Emma Darwin to William Erasmus Darwin, [24 or 31 October 1859] (DAR 210.6: 50)).

[7] Robinson was vicar of Norton Canon, Herefordshire, between 1865 and 1877; on his building and restoration works see *Biograph and Review* 6 (1881): 144–6.

To Henry Bence Jones 3 January [1866][1]

Down. | Bromley. | Kent. S.E.
Jan 3.

My dear Dr Bence Jones

I have a good report to make.[2] I am able now to walk daily on an average $3\frac{1}{2}$ miles & often one mile at a stretch.[3]

My weight now with slight fluctuations keeps steady at the lowest point to which it has sunk.[4] I feel altogether much more vigorous & active. I read more, & what is delightful, I am able to write easy work for about $1\frac{1}{2}$ hours every day.[5] The only drawback is that on most days 3 hours after luncheon or dinner, I have a sharpish headache on one side, & with bad flatulence lasting to the next meal.[6] I forgot to say that taking the whole day, the flatulence is somewhat diminished especially on my better days. One day when my head & stomach were extra bad, in despair I took a cup of coffee without sugar, & it acted really like a charm & has continued to do so; for I now take a cup of coffee each day with luncheon or dinner, & I believe I have never once had headache and flatulence after the meal with coffee.[7] I have transposed luncheon & dinner & made other changes, but as far as I can discover it is the coffee which is effectual. Under these circumstances may I try coffee with both luncheon & dinner. I have not yet much taste for common meat, but eat a little game or fowl twice a day & eggs, omelet or maccaroni or cheese at the other meals & these I think suit me best. I have not taken to *[2 words illeg]* much starch for I have such horror about acid.[8]

There is an odd change in my stomach, for the last 20 years coffee & cheese have disagreed with me, now they suit me eminently well.[9] I took 10^{g} oxyde of Iron for a fortnight but did not miss it when I left it off 10 days ago: I will do as you like about retaking it.[10] I have taken 10 drops of Muriatic acid twice a day (with Cayenne & ginger) for above 3 weeks & it suits me *excellently*.[11] May I continue it longer? I hope you will be pleased with my report. I shall be grateful for any further advice

yours very faithfully with | cordial thanks | Ch. Darwin

LS(A)
DAR 249: 86

[1] The year is established by the relationship between this letter and the letter from H. B. Jones, 10 February [1866].

[2] CD became a patient of Jones's during the summer of 1865; on Jones's recommendation, CD had begun a strict diet (see *Correspondence* vol. 13, letter to Asa Gray, 15 August [1865] and n. 12). CD reported some improvement in his condition in September 1865 (see, for example, *Correspondence* vol. 13, letter to J. D. Hooker, 27 [or 28 September 1865]). For further discussion of CD's health, see Bowlby 1990, Browne 1998, Colp 1998, and Browne 2002, pp. 262–9. See also *Correspondence* vol. 13, Appendix IV, for an account of CD's health in the preceding months.

[3] In his notes on his health, submitted to John Chapman in May 1865, CD mentioned that he could not walk more than half a mile (see *Correspondence* vol. 13, Appendix IV). Emma Darwin's diary listed regular walks on the sandwalk (see Atkins 1974, pp. 25–6) between July and early October and walks of between 3 and $5\frac{2}{3}$ miles between 5 and 17 October 1865 (DAR 242).

[4] In the letter to J. D. Hooker, 27 [or 28 September 1865], CD recorded the beneficial effect of his loss of 15 lbs since starting Jones's diet (see *Correspondence* vol. 13). Emma Darwin's diary (DAR 242) shows CD's weight to have been in the range of 11 st. 2 lbs (156 lbs) to 11 st. 4 lbs (158 lbs) during August 1865. Thereafter, her weekly records show CD's progressive loss of weight to 10 st. 4 lbs (144 lbs) by early December 1865. His weight remained stable until late January 1866, rising later in the year to around $10\frac{1}{2}$ st. (147 lbs). CD was about six feet in height (*LL* 1: 109).

[5] In his notes on his health dated May 1865, CD wrote that reading caused his ears to sing and interfered with his vision (see *Correspondence* vol. 13, Appendix IV). CD also mentioned the problem in letters (see, for example, *Correspondence* vol. 13, letter to J. D. Hooker 27 [or 28 September 1865]). In his letter to J. D. Hooker, 22 December [1865] (*Correspondence* vol. 13), CD said he was able to write for an hour on most days. CD wrote in his 'Journal' that he resumed his work on *Variation* on 25 December 1865 (see *Correspondence* vol. 13, Appendix II).

[6] In his May 1865 notes on his health, CD had stated that he seldom suffered from headaches, but noted his chronic flatulence (see *Correspondence* vol. 13, Appendix IV). CD subsequently underwent Chapman's ice treatment for flatulence and other problems (see *Correspondence* vol. 13, letter to John Chapman, 7 June 1865).

[7] The entry in Emma Darwin's diary (DAR 242) for 8 December 1865 reads 'left off sugar'. No other references to the beneficial effects of coffee on CD's health have been found.

[8] In 1864, CD's illness had caused him to vomit 'acid & morbid secretion' (see *Correspondence* vol. 12, letter to J. D. Hooker, [20–]22 February [1864]); these symptoms were treated with antacids by William Jenner (see *Correspondence* vol. 12, letter to J. D. Hooker, 13 April [1864] and n. 6). CD's

continuing problem with acidity was recorded in the notes on his health of May 1865 (*Correspondence* vol. 13, Appendix IV and n. 5).

9 CD seems to have drunk coffee without problems as a young man (see, for example, *Correspondence* vol. 7, letter to W. D. Fox, 13 November [1858]).

10 CD began taking iron in 1864, Emma Darwin's diary (DAR 242) recording 'began iron' on 12 April, and 'began phosph. iron' on 21 August and 21 September. CD took phosphate of iron on Jenner's advice (see *Correspondence* vol. 12, letters from William Jenner, 15 October 1864 and 9 November 1864). It is not known when, or for what reason, CD started to take oxide of iron; contemporary preparations of oxide of iron and their medicinal properties are described in Royle and Headland 1865, pp. 139–43.

11 Muriatic acid was the contemporary term for hydrochloric acid (Royle and Headland 1865, p. 49). A recipe for a remedy consisting of 'Oxley's essence of Ginger' and tincture of cayenne in brandy is given by CD in the letter to G. H. Darwin, 22 January 1873 (*Calendar* no. 8747). Cayenne is derived from species of *Capsicum* and was used for the treatment of gout and flatulence (Beasley 1865, p. 161). Ginger was valued for its beneficial effects on the stomach (Beasley 1865, p. 537).

From Emily Catherine Langton to Emma and Charles Darwin [6 and 7? January 1866][1]

Dearest Emma & Charles

I am so rapidly weaker I can lose no time in sending you all & Elizabeth my dearest farewell.[2] It is grievous to think I shall never see any of your dear faces. On New Year's day I knew this, and what a different world it seems to me.

What I want to say is that poor Susan feels my loss so cruelly—[3] I left off this last night as I was too exhausted to go on—

I am grieved indeed at poor Susan's loneliness, but there seems no help.

My dearest husband will feel my loss too; *what a nurse he is*, if he was not deaf—[4]

Every body's love & goodness to me are past speech—

May God bless you all & may we meet hereafter.

E.C.L—

Sunday.

The Wedgwood Museum Trust (Temporary deposit at Keele University): W/M202

1 The date is conjectured from the reference to New Year's day; in 1866, the following Saturday and Sunday were 6 and 7 January. It is also possible that the letter was written on a later weekend in January. Emily Catherine Langton (Catherine) died in early February 1866 (see letter from J. D. Hooker, 4 February 1866 and n. 1).

2 Sarah Elizabeth Wedgwood, known as Elizabeth, was Emma Darwin's sister and Catherine's cousin (Freeman 1978). Catherine had been in poor health since at least the time of her marriage to Charles Langton in 1863 (see *Correspondence* vol. 11, letter to J. D. Hooker, 25 [August 1863], and Wedgwood and Wedgwood 1980, p. 272). She had discussed her poor health and inability to pay social visits in a letter to Henrietta Emma Darwin of [November 1865] (DAR 219.8: 3).

3 Susan Elizabeth Darwin, CD and Catherine's sister, lived at the Mount (their childhood home) in Shrewsbury. She and Catherine had lived together there after their father's death in 1848 until Catherine moved to another house in Shrewsbury following her marriage to Charles Langton in 1863 (Freeman 1978).

[4] Catherine refers to Charles Langton.

To Philip Lutley Sclater 6 January [1866][1]

Down. | *Bromley.* | *Kent. S.E.*
Jan 6

Dear Sclater

I know that you are one of the busiest of men, but I want to beg a little bit of information & I trust to your kindness for I do not know to whom else to apply. Mr Swinhoe writes to me of a domestic race of duck in China as perhaps descended from Anas pœcilorhyncha.[2] Now do you consider this form as deserving to be called a distinct species from A. Boschas & may I quote your opinion??[3]

How does it differ? I suppose it has the curled tail feathers & wing-marks. Is it a native of China? I sh^{d} be very grateful for a few lines giving me information on these heads.[4]

Pray forgive me troubling you & believe me
yours very sincerely | Charles Darwin

P.S. After nine months inaction from illness, I have just begun to do a little work—[5]

LS(A)
American Philosophical Society (311)

[1] The year is established by the content of the postscript (see n. 5, below).

[2] CD probably refers to the missing portion of the letter from Robert Swinhoe, [before 1 October 1865?] (*Correspondence* vol. 13); the surviving portion includes a discussion of ducks, but not of *Anas poecilorhyncha*, the spot-billed duck of Asia. Robert Swinhoe, the British consul in Formosa (now Taiwan), had earlier informed CD of a supposed 'thorough race' of duck that had developed from hybrids of the muscovy duck (*Carina moschata*; then also *A. moschata*) and the Chinese domestic duck (see *Correspondence* vol. 10, letter from Robert Swinhoe, 12 November 1862).

[3] No reply from Sclater has been found; in his discussion of breeds of domestic ducks and their descent from the mallard, *Anas boschas* (now *A. platyrhynchos*), in *Variation* 1: 276–87, CD did not cite information from Sclater or Swinhoe.

[4] *Anas poecilorhyncha* is distributed throughout Asia. Its lack of curled tail-feathers distinguishes it from *A. boschas*, although both species have conspicuous wing patches (*Birds of the world* 1: 605, 607). CD mentioned *A. boschas*, but not *A. poecilorhyncha*, in *Variation.*

[5] CD recorded being ill from 22 April until December 1865 (see *Correspondence* vol. 13, Appendix II).

From Ernst Haeckel[1] 11 January 1866

Jena (Saxe-Weimar)
11. Januar 1866

Hochverehrter theurer Herr!

Indem ich Ihnen zunächst ein recht glückliches neues Jahr wünsche und vor Allem, dass Ihre theure Gesundheit wieder ganz gekräftigt werden möge, zeige ich Ihnen den Empfang Ihrer beiden freundlichen Briefe (vom 6. Dec. and 5. Jan.)[2]

an, welche mir, wie alle Erinnerungen an Sie, stets von dem grössten Werthe sind und bleiben werden.[3]

Dass Sie meine letzten Arbeiten richtig empfangen haben, ist mir lieb.[4] Mein Buchhändler (*Engelmann in Leipzig*) hatte ⟨sie⟩ schon im vorigen September an *Willia⟨ms &⟩ Norgate* abgesandt.[5] Der *Prot⟨ogenes⟩ primordialis* (in dem Blatt: "⟨Sarcodekörper⟩ der Rhizopoden") ist Ihnen ⟨hoffentlich⟩ von besonderem Interesse.[6] Ich g⟨laube, dass⟩ solche Organismen (ganz hom⟨ogene⟩ Eiweiss-Klumpen oder Protoplasma ⟨ ⟩ im Anfange des organischen Lebens ⟨auf der⟩ Erde spontan entstanden sind, und ⟨dass⟩ sich aus ihnen durch "natural Sele⟨ction"⟩ zunächst verschiedenartige *Zellen* und daraus weiter durch Differenzirung die wenigen grossen *Hauptklassen* des Thier- und Pflanzen-Reichs gebildet haben, unter welche wir alle verschiedenen Organismen unterordnen können.[7] Ich nehme solcher Hauptklassen (Typen, Branches, Embranchemens) ungefähr 10 oder 12 im Ganzen an und werde diese Annahme in meinem jetzt erscheinenden allgemeinen Buche dadurch zu beweisen suchen, dass ich einen ganzen *Stammbaum* (eine genealogische Tabelle) für jede derselben aufstelle.[8] Der Druck dieses Buches schreitet jetzt rüstig vorwärts; indess wird es wohl immer noch einige Monate dauern, bis es erscheinen wird.[9] Ein sehr wichtiges Capitel (*die allgemeinen Principien ⟨u⟩nd Gesetze der embryonalen* und der ihr *⟨par⟩allelen palaeontologischen Entwickelung*) ⟨will⟩ ich noch ganz umarbeiten. Dieses und ⟨einige an⟩dere Capitel habe ich schon ⟨mehrere⟩ male umgearbeitet.[10] Aber es ⟨ist se⟩hr schwierig, auf einem solchen ⟨neuen⟩ und uncultivirten Felde vorwärts ⟨zu k⟩ommen. Es ist wie ein dichter ⟨noch u⟩nbetretener Urwald, in welchem ⟨da⟩s Unkraut der Vorurtheile und die ⟨Dorn⟩en der Dogmen jeden Schritt aufhalten.

Wie viel ich mich bei dieser schweren Arbeit, die meine ganzen Kräfte in Anspruch nimmt, und mich dadurch zugleich am besten von meinem unglücklichen Schicksal ablenkt,[11] mich mit *Ihnen*, theuer Herr, beschäftige, können Sie denken, und jedesmal, wenn mir eine neue Entdeckung auf dem intellectuellen Gebiete der philosophischen Naturbetrachtung welches Sie uns neu eröffnet haben, gelungen ist, möchte ich nach Down. Bromley. Kent. springen, um mich mit Ihnen darüber zu unterhalten. Ich bin gewiss, dass Sie sich darüber freuen würden und weiss im Voraus, dass Ihnen mein Buch viele Freude machen wird. Denn es hat noch Niemand die *gesammte Morphologie* auf den von Darwin entdeckten Principien umgearbeitet und mit *Intensität* und *Consequenz* die Descendenz Theorie auf *alle Zweige* derselben anzuwenden versucht. Es ist mir aber sehr schwer, Ihnen jetzt *Einzelnes* daraus mitzutheilen, da das Ganze eine fortlaufende *Kette philosophischer Untersuchungen* bildet.

Als lehrreichsten Beweis, zu welchen Thorheiten das Dogma von der Species-Constanz, und die teleologisch–dogmatische Behandlung der Morphologie führt, setze ich in meinem Buche den Ansichten von *Darwin* stets diejenigen von *Agassiz* gegenüber, welcher in der That das Maximum von Verkehrtheit und von unnatürlicher Behandlung der Natur geleistet hat.[12] Da aber seine Ansichten immer noch viele Anhänger finden, sieht man, wie weit wir noch im Allgemeinen zurück sind.[13]

Meine öffentlichen Vorlesungen "über Darwins Theorie" sind, wie ich Ihnen wohl schon geschrieben habe, in diesem Winter die besuchtesten von allen Vorlesungen, die hier gehalten werden,[14] und ich hoffe, dass ich dadurch viele fruchtbare Samenkörner ausstreue, welche zu kräftigen Stützen der Descendenz-Theorie heranwachsen werden.

Ich habe nun noch eine grosse Bitte, mein theurer Herr, die ich Ihnen schon lange vortragen wollte. Einer meiner lebhaftesten Wünsche ist, ein grösseres Portrait von Ihnen zu besitzen. Zwar habe ich über meinem Schreibtische die grössere Photographie (ohne vollen Bart) hängen, welche der zweiten Ausgabe Ihres Werkes vorgebunden war;[15] und darunter habe ich die *vortreffliche* kleinere Photographie, welche Sie mir vor 2 Jahren zu schicken die Güte hatten.[16] Allein die erstere ist gewiss schlecht, und die zweite zu *klein*, um mich zu befriedigen. Ich habe schon in allen Buchhandlungen in Berlin und anderen grösseren Orten gefragt, ob keine grössere Lithographie oder Photographie von Ihnen existirt, habe aber keine bekommen können. Vielleicht giebt es eine solche in England, und Sie würden mir eine ausserordentliche Freude machen, wollten Sie mir eine solche schicken. Ich bekomme sehr oft Besuch von vielen Schülern und Freunden, welche Ihr Bild sehen wollen, und ich bin dann immer betrübt, dass Ihre kleine Photographie (mit vollem Bart) nicht viermal oder sechsmal vergrössert werden kann. Um die kleine Photographie (in Visiten-Karten-Format) bin ich schon oft gebeten worden. Wenn Sie mir von dieser etwa $\frac{1}{2}$ oder 1 Dutzend schicken könnten, so würde ich Ihnen dafür ebenso viele Photographien von deutschen Verehrern Darwins und Anhängern seiner Lehre zurück-schicken. Entschuldigen Sie meine, vielleicht kindische Bitte; aber sie liegt mir zu sehr am Herzen.[17]

Beifolgend lege ich eine Photographie von mir vom vorigen Oktober bei, damit Sie sehen, wie alt ich in 2 Jahren geworden bin.[18]

Indem ich Ihnen, theurer Herr, von ganzem Herzen die baldigste Kräftigung Ihrer Gesundheit wünsche, damit Sie uns und der Wissenschaft noch lange erhalten bleiben mögen, bleibe ich | von ganzem Herzen | Ihr treulichst ergebener | Ernst Haeckel.

DAR 166: 41

[1] For a translation of this letter, see Appendix I.

[2] For the letter to Haeckel of 6 December [1865], see *Correspondence* vol. 13; the letter to Haeckel of 5 January 1866 has not been found.

[3] CD and Haeckel had been corresponding since 1863 or earlier. Their earliest extant correspondence refers to earlier letters (see *Correspondence* vol. 11, letter to Ernst Haeckel, 30 December [1863] – 3 January [1864]).

[4] In his letter of 11 November 1865, Haeckel listed three publications that were to be sent to CD (see *Correspondence* vol. 13). These were Haeckel 1865a, 1865b and 1865c, all papers on marine invertebrates of the class Coelenterata. A lightly annotated copy of Haeckel 1865a, inscribed by the author, is in the Darwin Pamphlet Collection–CUL. CD's copy of Haeckel 1865b was listed in CD's library catalogue (DAR 240), but was not listed in later catalogues. It has not been found in the Darwin Library–CUL or at Down. In his letter to Haeckel of 6 December [1865], CD acknowledged receipt of two

other papers of Haeckel's (Haeckel 1864 and 1865d). For a discussion of the role of Coelenterata in nineteenth-century debates over zoological classification and theories of descent, see Winsor 1976.

5 Wilhelm Engelmann was a publisher of scientific books (*NDB*; see also *Correspondence* vol. 13, letter from Ernst Haeckel, 11 November 1865). Williams & Norgate, booksellers and publishers of Covent Garden, London, and of Edinburgh, specialised in foreign and scientific literature (*Modern English biography* s.v. Williams, Edmund Sidney).

6 The reference is to Haeckel 1865a, a paper on rhizopods in which his newly discovered primitive species, *Protogenes primordialis*, was described and illustrated. Haeckel had previously drawn CD's attention to this 'organism', emphasising its significance for his transmutation theory (see *Correspondence* vol. 13, letter from Ernst Haeckel, 11 November 1865 and nn. 11 and 12); a protoplasmic aggregate, without differentiation, organisation, or nucleus, it was able to surround and assimilate foreign bodies, and to reproduce by simple division (Haeckel 1865a, pp. 360–3). It is not recognised in modern taxonomic literature.

7 In his book *Generelle Morphologie der Organismen*, published later in 1866, Haeckel classified *Protogenes primordialis* in a new phylum, the Monera, comprising the most basic forms of life; he argued that the Rhizopoda might have evolved from a *Protogenes* species (Haeckel 1866, 2: XXII–XXIII). The taxonomic hierarchy proposed by Haeckel reflected CD's transmutation theory, being based on descent from primitive life forms (Haeckel 1866, 2: XVII–XXII; see also n. 8, below). For discussions of Haeckel's theories of protoplasm and the development of living organisms from inorganic matter, see Rehbock 1975 and Rupke 1976. On the Victorian debates over spontaneous generation, see Strick 2000.

8 The reference is to Haeckel 1866. Haeckel had previously written to CD about his work on this book (see *Correspondence* vol. 12, letter from Ernst Haeckel, 26 October 1864 and n. 8, and *Correspondence* vol. 13, letter from Ernst Haeckel, 11 November 1865 and n. 4). Inside the back cover of the second volume are eight genealogical trees, drawn by Haeckel, displaying the possible relationships among all living organisms. The first tree summarises all subsequent trees and has a central section representing the kingdom of 'Protista' (including unicellular organisms, fungi and sponges) flanked by the animal and plant kingdoms. Haeckel showed eleven main classes (subkingdoms): six within the plant and five within the animal kingdom (for a definition of Haeckel's taxonomic categories, see Haeckel 1866, 2: 374–91). Haeckel's evolutionary trees established a standard iconography for phylogeny (see, for example, S. J. Gould 1990, pp. 263–7). Their epistemological significance is considered in Bouquet 1995, pp. 47–51. CD earlier used a tree-like diagram to illustrate the divergence of offspring from parental types (*Origin*, facing p. 117; see also Winsor 1976, pp. 172–4). For Haeckel's theoretical discussion of his phylogenetic categories, see Haeckel 1866, 2: XVII–XX, XXXI–XXXII, XLVIII–L, and 406–17.

9 Haeckel 1866 was published on or after 14 September 1866, the date appearing at the foot of the foreword.

10 Haeckel probably refers to chapter 21, 'Begriff und Aufgabe der Phylogenie' (Concept and function of phylogeny; Haeckel 1866, 2: 303–22), in which he developed arguments in support of the principle that ontogeny recapitulates phylogeny: 'During its own rapid development . . . an individual repeats the most important changes in form evolved by its ancestors during their long and slow palaeontological development' (Haeckel 1866, 2: 300; translated in S. J. Gould 1977, p. 76). For an extensive modern examination of Haeckel's attempted theoretical connection of long-term evolutionary change with short-term growth and development, and a comparison with CD's views, see S. J. Gould 1977.

11 After Haeckel's wife, Anna Sethe, died on 16 February 1864, Haeckel wrote to CD: 'a stroke of fate has destroyed all prospects of happiness in my life, and . . . I shall pursue the one goal in my life, namely to disseminate, to support and to perfect your theory of descent' (English translation; see *Correspondence* vol. 12, letter from Ernst Haeckel, 9 [July 1864]; see also *Correspondence* vol. 13, letter from Ernst Haeckel, 11 November 1865 and n. 13).

12 There are approximately ten references to Louis Agassiz in Haeckel 1866; most make no direct comparison with CD. For more on Agassiz's and Haeckel's interpretations of taxonomic hierarchies, and their differing implications for evolutionary theory, see Bryant 1995, pp. 197–202 and 207 *et seq.*

13 For Agassiz's views on the constancy of species, and his arguments against CD and Haeckel during the 1860s, see Morris 1997. On support for Agassiz's anti-Darwinian rhetoric in the early 1860s, see Lurie 1960, pp. 309–11.

14 According to Haeckel, over 150 people from a wide range of disciplines regularly attended his public lectures on CD's theory in the academic year 1864 to 1865 (see *Correspondence* vol. 13, letter from Ernst Haeckel, 11 November 1865). Records of the university of Jena indicate that 120 people attended the lectures on Darwinian theory given by Haeckel in the main lecture theatre during the winter of 1865 to 1866 (Uschmann 1959, pp. 43–6, 196–8).

15 This photograph, procured from London by the German publisher, E. Schweizerbart'sche Verlagsbuchhandlung, was used as the frontispiece to the second German edition of *Origin* (see *Correspondence* vol. 10, letter from E. Schweizerbart'sche Verlagsbuchhandlung, 7 June 1862 and n. 5); it was taken by Maull & Polyblank, *circa* 1857. The photograph is reproduced as the frontispiece to *Correspondence* vol. 8.

16 Haeckel refers to the first photograph of CD with a beard, taken in 1864 by his son William Erasmus Darwin. The photograph is reproduced as the frontispiece to *Correspondence* vol. 12. See *ibid.*, letter to Ernst Haeckel, 19 July [1864] and n. 7.

17 CD exchanged photographs with many of his correspondents during the 1860s (see *Correspondence* vols. 9–13, and Browne 1998, pp. 253–80).

18 The photograph has not been found. However, there is a portrait of Haeckel dated 1865 at the Ernst Haeckel Haus in Jena. An earlier portrait, presumably taken during 1863, was sent to CD in summer 1864, and included Haeckel's late wife, Anna Sethe (see *Correspondence* vol. 12, letter from Ernst Haeckel, 10 August 1864; see also *ibid.*, plate facing p. 280).

To Fritz Müller 11 January 1866

Down. | Bromley. | Kent. S.E.
Jan 11 1866

My dear Sir

I received your interesting letter of Nov 5. some little time ago,[1] & despatched immediately a copy of my Journal of researches.[2] I fear that you will think me troublesome in my offers; but have you the 2nd German Edition of the Origin? which is a translation with additions of the 3rd English Ed.[3] & is I think considerably improved compared with the 1st Ed.[4] I have some spare copies which are of no use to me & it wd be a pleasure to me to send you one, if it wd be of any use to you. You wd never require to re-read the book, but you might wish to refer to some passage. I am particularly obliged for your photograph, for one likes to have a picture in one's mind of any one about whom one is interested.[5] I have received & read with interest your paper on the Spunge with horny Spicula.[6] Owing to ill-health & being busy when formerly well, I have for some years neglected periodical scientific literature & have lately been reading up & have thus read translations of several of your papers;[7] amongst which I have been particularly glad to read & see the drawings of the Metamorphoses of Peneus. This seems to me the most interesting discovery in embryology which has been made for years.[8]

I am much obliged to you for telling me a little of your plans for the future; what a strange but to my taste, interesting life you will lead when you retire to your estate on the Itajahi![9] You refer in your letter to the facts which Agassiz is collecting, against our views, on the Amazons.[10] Though he has done so much for science, he seems to me so wild & paradoxical in all his views that I cannot regard his opinions as of any value—[11]

Believe me my dear Sir | yours very sincerely | Ch. Darwin

P.S. I did not at all know that your island had lately risen.[12] Near Rio I c[d] find no such evidence;[13] you ought to collect & send the paper to some Geolog. Journal—[14]

LS
British Library (Loan 10: 5)

[1] See letter from Fritz Müller, 5 November 1865 (*Correspondence* vol. 13).

[2] No request by Müller for a copy of *Journal of researches* has been found. For CD's offer to send the book to Müller, see *Correspondence* vol. 13, letter to Fritz Müller, 20 September [1865]; for Müller's receipt of the book, see this volume, letter from Fritz Müller, 13 February 1866 and n. 2.

[3] Christian Friedrich Schweizerbart of Stuttgart published the German editions of *Origin* during CD's lifetime. The second German edition appeared in 1863; the first and second German editions were translated by Heinrich Georg Bronn, who died in 1862. John Murray published the third English edition of *Origin* in 1861.

[4] For CD's additions and corrections to the second German edition, see *Correspondence* vol. 10, Appendix VIII. On the additional material incorporated in the third English edition, including the 'Historical sketch of the recent progress of opinion on the origin of species', see *Origin* 3d ed., pp. xi–ii, and Peckham ed. 1959, p. 20. The first and second German editions (Bronn trans. 1860 and 1863) included a final chapter containing Bronn's own comments, which CD addressed in the third English edition of *Origin* (see *Correspondence* vol. 8, letter to H. G. Bronn, 5 October [1860]).

[5] CD had asked for a photograph of Müller in his letter of 10 August [1865] (*Correspondence* vol. 13), and Müller promised to send one when he had had one made (*ibid.*, letter from Müller, 10 October 1865). It is likely that the photograph was enclosed with the letter from Fritz Müller, 5 November 1865 (*Correspondence* vol. 13). Although the photograph has not been found in the Darwin Archive, it was probably a copy of the photographic 'carte' or 'carte de visite' reproduced in Möller 1915–21, 3: 84 with the caption 'ca. 1866' (see plate opposite p. 185). Earlier in 1865, CD had sent a photograph of himself to Müller (see *Correspondence* vol. 13, letter from Fritz Müller, 10 October 1865).

[6] CD refers to F. Müller 1865a. In his letter of 10 October 1865 (*Correspondence* vol. 13), Müller mentioned that Max Johann Sigismund Schultze of Berlin would be sending an offprint of the paper to CD. In the same letter, Müller discussed the content of F. Müller 1865a, including his application of CD's theory to his study of Brazilian sponges. For CD's response to Müller's conclusions about spicules, see *Correspondence* vol. 13, letter to Fritz Müller, 9 December [1865]. An offprint of F. Müller 1865a, with a note in CD's hand on the front cover, is in the Darwin Pamphlet Collection–CUL.

[7] In the summer of 1865, CD had been reading back issues from the previous ten years of *Annals and Magazine of Natural History* (see *Correspondence* vol. 13, letter to A. R. Wallace, 22 September [1865] and n. 4, and letters to J. D. Hooker, 27 [or 28 September 1865] and n. 12, and 22 and 28 [October 1865]). Between 1857 and 1865, the journal published twelve translations of papers by Müller, all on crustaceans.

[8] The reference is to F. Müller 1864a, a paper in the *Annals and Magazine of Natural History* describing and illustrating metamorphosis in a species of the prawn *Peneus*. In the paper, Müller illustrated the free-swimming nauplius larva of *Peneus* for the first time (F. Müller 1864a, plate IV and p. 115); in *Für Darwin*, he interpreted it as the earliest developmental stage of the higher crustaceans (Malacostraca) and argued that it had been suppressed by natural selection in other species of prawn (F. Müller 1864c, pp. 38–41, 82–4, and Dallas trans. 1869, pp. 57–62, 123–26). CD revised the fourth edition of *Origin* during the spring of 1866 (see 'Journal', Appendix II), adding references to Müller's work on *Peneus* (*Origin* 4th ed., pp. 523–4, 530–1). CD made further reference to *Peneus*, citing F. Müller 1864c, in describing his provisional hypothesis of pangenesis in *Variation* 2: 368.

[9] Müller was working as a mathematics teacher at Destêrro (now Florianópolis), on Santa Catarina island, Brazil; he had written to CD that, in 1870 or 1871, he intended to return to his 'small homestead' beside the Itajahy river (now called Itajaí Açu), where he had lived from 1854 to 1856 (see *Correspondence* vol. 13, letter from Fritz Müller, 5 November 1865 and n. 13). The river is in the north-east of Santa Catarina state in Brazil (*Columbia gazetteer of the world*); Müller's homestead was later incorporated within the town of Blumenau. See plate opposite p. 56. For more on Müller's life in Brazil, see West 2003.

[10] Müller had informed CD of Louis Agassiz's expedition to Brazil, and his intended challenge to CD's transmutation theory using evidence gained from the geographical distribution of fish in the Amazon River basin (see *Correspondence* vol. 13, letter from Fritz Müller, 5 November 1865 and n. 14). The expedition, which left New York on 1 April 1865 and returned on 6 August 1866, was financed by Nathaniel Thayer and received substantial support from steamship companies and the Brazilian government (see Lurie 1960, pp. 345–9). The Amazon expedition was conceived as part of Agassiz's wider programme to disprove Darwinian theory empirically by collecting fish from every river system in the world (Lurie 1960, pp. 336–7; Winsor 1991, pp. 66–76). Agassiz never published a formal description of the expedition's specimens, or an analysis of their variation and distribution (see Winsor 1991, pp. 66–76). His informal comments on the fish of South America are given in J. L. R. Agassiz and Agassiz 1868, pp. 216–27, 237–41, and 377–84.

[11] In his most recent book, Agassiz had stated his opposition to 'the transmutation theory': in his view it was 'opposed to the processes of Nature, ... [and] contradicted by the facts of Embryology and Paleontology'; he added that the experiments upon domesticated animals and cultivated plants, on which its adherents based their views, were 'entirely foreign' to the 'processes of Nature' (J. L. R. Agassiz 1863, pp. iii–v; there is a lightly annotated copy in the Darwin Library–Down (see *Marginalia* 1: 13)). For CD's recent comments on Agassiz and his work, see *Correspondence* vol. 12, letter to B. D. Walsh, 4 December [1864], and *Correspondence* vol. 13, letter to Fritz Müller, 20 September [1865] and n. 12. On Agassiz's controversial professional style and deteriorating reputation through the 1860s, see Winsor 1991, pp. 27–42 and 44–65.

[12] In his letter to CD of 5 November 1865, Müller referred to the landscape and vegetation of Santa Catarina island (see *Correspondence* vol. 13). The source of CD's information on the island having risen has not been found. However, in a letter to M. J. S. Schultze dated 11 March 1865 (Möller 1915–21, 2: 62), Müller described finding old tubes of *Vermetus* on rocks above the shoreline of the island. The Vermetidae are a family of marine molluscs that inhabit worm-like shell tubes usually attached to rocks (George and George 1979, p. 89). Müller argued that the island had risen by at least four feet because the old tubes were that much higher than their present habitat.

[13] During the *Beagle* voyage, CD made a series of observations of the uplift of land along the eastern coast of South America (see *South America*, pp. 1–26), and wrote: 'Between Rio de Janeiro and Cape Frio, I crossed sandy tracts abounding with sea-shells, at the distance of a league from the coast; but whether these tracts have been formed by upheaval, or through the mere accumulation of drift sand, I am not prepared to assert' (*ibid.*, p. 3, n. 6). CD's extensive interpretations of uplift on both the eastern and western seaboards of South America are in *South America*, pp. 1–57.

[14] No publication by Müller about either *Vermetus* or the rising of Santa Catarina island has been found.

From Jeffries Wyman 11 January 1866

Cambridge [Massachusetts]
Jan. 11th. 1866

Dear Sir

Having lately given some attention to the study of the cells of the bee I have been struck with the fact that the deviations from the form alledged to have been measured by Maraldi & which was calculated by Koenig, are much greater than is mentioned in any of the descriptions I have seen.[1] The conclusion to which I have been led, is, that whatever the *typical* form of the cell be, it is rarely, if ever, realised.[2] As you have given your own careful attention to this subject, I feel that I run the risk of writing what may be already better known to you than to myself.[3] Then it occurs to me that cumulative evidence is worth something. At all events I will state what I have to say briefly.

1st After repeated measurments of hundreds of worker cells I find, as Reaumer did in the drone cells, that the diameters are very frequently variable, so that nine cells measured in the direction of one diameter will sometimes fill a space, which it will require ten to fill if measured in the direction of another.[4] 2d. The terminal rhombs are the most variable parts of the cell. I have shown this very satisfactorily by means of plaster casts, & even by the coccoons from old brood cells which give a very good model of the base— Sometimes the rhombs are all of different sizes, & at others one is nearly eliminated, the other two making nearly the whole of the partition between two adjoining cells. 3d. The introduction of the fourth side to the base does not always, or even generally depend upon the transition from worker to drone cells, as stated by Huber,[5] but either upon an incorrect allinement of the cells on opposite sides of the comb, or upon an increase of the size of the cells on one side not corresponding with that on the other. 4th the most remarkable deviation which I have noticed is a sort of rotation as it were of the cells, so that those of the two sides, differed in position about 30°.

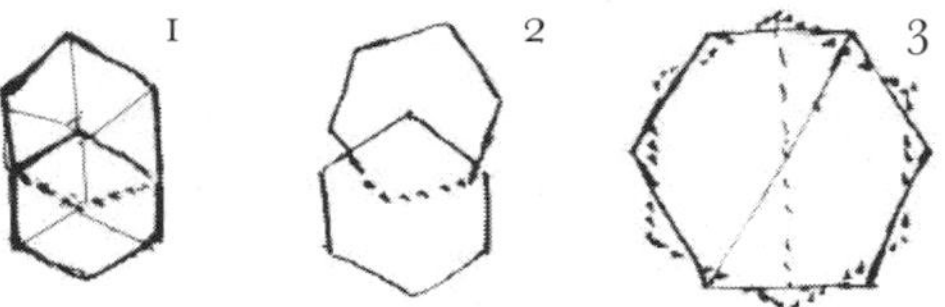

Fig 1 being the normal position, 2 & 3 are the abnormal ones— in 2 the angle of one cell corresponds with the centre of the other, but instead of pointing to one of the angles of the other cell it points to one of the sides. In 3 the cells were fitted together by their whole bases, &, projected on to the same plane, are concentric. In both of these cases the rhombic faces became impracticable, & the bees compromised on a *flat* bottom to the cell— I found this arrangement in a large part of a worker brood-comb, & in the whole of a piece of drone comb. 5th. Lastly there is no regular mode of transition from worker to drone cells, but this may be effected in several ways, viz by means of irregular polygonal cells, by a gradual change of size, so that no line of separation is noticeable between the two kinds; & by the close approximation of worker & drone cells making an abrupt change; but as the worker cells are one fifth smaller than the drone cells, & therefore fail to fill up the space, a new row is intercalated for this purpose.

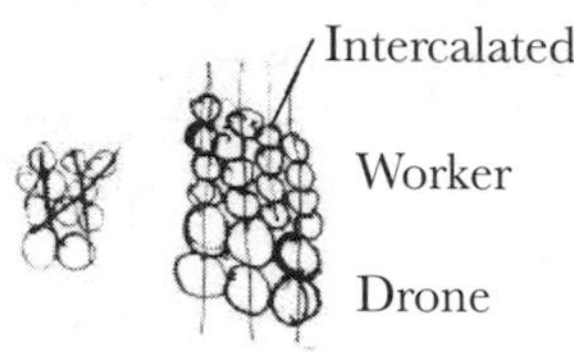

These intercalated rows however do come at regular intervals, & the emergency is often met by thickened walls.

I have studied the cells with reference to the hexagonal shape, & it seems to me that the view taken by Mr Waterhouse & yourself is the most tenable one.[6] Fearing that you may not have seen the work, I take the liberty of calling your attention to the so called "fossil tadpole nests", in Prof Hitchcocks report on the Ichnology of Massachusetts. Have you not there exactly the phenomenon in question? A lot of tadpoles get together each wiggling about on a centre, as is is necessary in a crowd, each excavates a place in the mud, but their respective cavities soon come in collision & a flat wall between them results, & in many cases a hexagonal cell almost as true as that of the bee—[7]

One thing seems entirely clear, that the hexagonal cell results from the cooperation of several bees & is never made by a single bee, & if he have no antagonist in the construction of a wall it is curvilinear.[8] In some of my wasps nests from S America it appears that even in working with paste board, the outer walls of the new cells are always curved *at first*, but when other cells are made outside of them they are flattened so as to conform to those that have preceded them.

Before I close allow me to mention the observations of Mr Putnam on the cells of our humble bees—which he has shown are at first a mass of pollen & honey, on which an egg is placed, & into which the larva eats as soon as hatched.[9] The cavity thus formed is the beginning of the cell.— This is increased by additions of pollen, which is gradually consumed; eventually wax is applied to the exterior in a very thin layer.[10] I requested Mr Putnam to send you a copy of his paper, which perhaps you will have received before this reaches you.

I fear I have trespassed upon your time, but hope you will excuse me on the score of good intention

With great respect | Truly yours | J. Wyman

Charles Darwin, Esq. | Downe Bromley Kent.

DAR 181: 191

CD ANNOTATIONS

1.4 The conclusion . . . realised. 1.6] *scored pencil*

3.3 attention . . . Massachusetts. 3.5] *scored pencil*
4.1 One . . . single bee, 4.2] *double scored pencil*
5.1 Before . . . bees— 5.2] *double scored pencil*
On cover: 'Size [*above del* 'Thickness'] of Cells & irregularities—good—Wyman' *ink*

[1] Giacomo Filippo Maraldi's geometrical measurements of hive-bee (honey-bee) cells (Maraldi 1712, pp. 304–9) and Johann Samuel Koenig's calculations (Koenig 1739) were cited in Réaumur 1734–42, 5: 382, 388–9. The base of each cell, a hexagonal prism, is composed of three parallelograms (rhombs), for which Koenig calculated the internal angles required to achieve the most efficient relationship between volume and the amount of wax required to build the cell. As Koenig's theoretical figures corresponded closely with Maraldi's empirical measurements (Réaumur 1734–42, 5: 388–90), the notion arose that the dimensions of hive-bee cells were more or less standard.

[2] Wyman's conclusion is cited in *Origin* 4th ed., pp. 271–2: 'I hear from Prof. Wyman, who has made numerous careful measurements, that the accuracy of the workmanship of the bee has been greatly exaggerated; so much so, that, as he adds, whatever the typical form of the cell may be, it is rarely, if ever, realised.'

[3] Differences in the shapes of the cells made by various kinds of bees presented a potential problem for natural selection (see, for example, *Correspondence* vol. 7, and *Correspondence* vol. 11; see also *Origin*, p. 224). The issue continued to interest CD after the publication of *Origin* (see, for example, *Correspondence* vol. 8, letter to W. H. Miller 1 December [1860], and *Correspondence* vol. 12, letter to A. R. Wallace, 1 January 1864 and n. 2). CD's notes on bees' cells are in DAR 48B. For a detailed examination of CD's effort to demonstrate that the complex geometry of the cell could be achieved through the gradual evolution of complex instinct, see Prete 1990.

[4] Brood combs include cells of different sizes. The smallest and most abundant cells of hive-bee combs are occupied by the larvae of workers, while the larvae of drones occupy larger cells (Stanek 1969, p. 177, and Seeley 1995, pp. 177–8). In his measurements of hive-bee cells, René Antoine Ferchault de Réaumur recorded greater variability among the diameters of drone cells than among those of worker cells (Réaumur 1734–42, 5: 397–400).

[5] François Huber contended that the transition from worker cells to drone cells required that the pyramidal base of each cell be made up of four rhombs rather than three, as found typically in the worker cell (see F. Huber 1814, 2: 222–4). In his annotated copy of F. Huber 1814 in the Darwin Library–CUL, CD scored parts of this passage (see *Marginalia* 1: 412). Further detail on structural aspects of the transition from worker to drone cells is given in the appendix to F. Huber 1814, written by his son, Jean Pierre Huber (*ibid.*, 2: 231–51).

[6] In contrast to François Huber, who held that the bee cell was the product of the bee's ability to construct geometrical forms, George Robert Waterhouse considered that the hexagonal cell of the hive-bee, and the rhombs of its base, originated in the form of a simple cylinder with a curved base. In his theoretical model, a number of pliable wax cylinders when packed tightly together under even pressure became hexagonal ([Waterhouse] 1835, pp. 153–5). In *Origin*, p. 225, CD wrote: 'I was led to investigate this subject by Mr. Waterhouse, who has shown that the form of the cell stands in close relation to the presence of adjoining cells; and the following view may, perhaps, be considered only as a modification of his theory.' CD went on to propose an underlying instinct by which bees build cell walls according to a scheme of intersecting circles, adding that the hive-bee's hexagonal cells resulted from the natural selection of successive slight modifications in instinct that conferred increasing economy in the use of wax (*Origin*, p. 235). See also *Correspondence* vol. 7, letter from G. R. Waterhouse, 13 February 1858, and letter to W. B. Tegetmeier, 17 [October 1858] and nn. 3 and 4.

[7] Edward Hitchcock established the science of ichnology (*Proceedings of the American Philosophical Society* 9 (1864): 445). Hitchcock observed both mud and fossils containing cavities that were hexagonal in form like bee cells; he concluded that in both cases the cavities had been formed by tadpoles (Hitchcock 1858, pp. 121–3 and plates 21 and 50). See also *Correspondence* vol. 13, letter from Edward Cresy, 10 September 1865 and n. 11.

[8] In preparing the fourth edition of *Origin* during the spring of 1866 (see 'Journal', Appendix II), CD deleted a sentence in which he had cautiously entertained the possibility that hive-bees construct each cell as 'an isolated hexagon' (see *Origin*, p. 233, and Peckham ed. 1959, p. 410).

[9] The reference is to Frederic Ward Putnam and Putnam 1863a, an annotated copy of which is in the Darwin Pamphlet Collection–CUL.

[10] CD's annotations on Putnam's paper included the scoring of passages on the formation by adult humble-bees (*Bombus*) of a thin wax wall around the pupa, and Putnam's rejection of the view that eggs were laid in pre-formed cells (Putnam 1863a, pp. 101–4).

To Joseph Dalton Hooker 15 [January 1866]

Down. | *Bromley.* | *Kent. S.E.*
15th

My dear H.

I remember when I lent you Wichura on Hybrids,[1] (since returned) talking with you on Verlot's memoir on variation of plants in French.—

I have lost it & am in despair— Did I lend it you? Let me have one line in answer; but do *not* hunt for it, if you remember nothing. I must *immediately* order fresh copy & what is only bad job read the whole again—[2] Post going

Yours affect | C. Darwin

Endorsement: 'Jany 66.'
DAR 115: 280

[1] CD reminded Hooker of his loan of Wichura 1865, a paper on hybrid willows, three times in 1865 (see *Correspondence* vol. 13, letters to J. D. Hooker, [17 June 1865], [29 July 1865], and 22 and 28 [October 1865]). Hooker is likely to have borrowed the work during his visit to Down between 4 and 6 March 1865 (Emma Darwin's diary (DAR 242)). There is an annotated copy of Wichura 1865 in the Darwin Library–CUL (see *Marginalia* 1: 871–3).

[2] CD probably needed Bernard Verlot's *Sur la production et la fixation des variétés dans les plantes d'ornement* (Verlot 1865) for his work on the fourth edition of *Origin* and *Variation.* In a number of chapters of *Variation*, CD included examples of variability in plants from Verlot 1865. A passage on the production of fertile and sterile forms in varieties of garden stock (Verlot 1865, p. 84) was cited in *Origin* 4th ed., p. 284, where CD described similar alternation between reproductive and sterile forms of ants. CD previously expressed his high opinion of Verlot 1865 in the letter to Hooker of [29 July 1865] (*Correspondence* vol. 13). There is an annotated copy of Verlot 1865 in the Darwin Library–CUL (see *Marginalia* 1: 817–19).

From J. D. Hooker 16 January 1866

Kew
Jany 16/66

Dear Darwin

I have mislaid your note,[1] from which you may guess what a mess of correspondence I am in. Letters come in like hail here, & I may whistle for any assistance I will get before April 1. (the financial year)—[2]

Certainly I have not & never saw the French book you ask about.[3] I do hope it will turn up. Rereading a book in any such a case is a disgusting bore: & in your case is simply purgatorial. Can you read to yourself now?[4]

I have been wondering how you go on, & hoping to get down to see you—but Smith is now away for a fortnight,[5] & when he returns I expect to have to run down to Staffordshire with my Cousin R. Palgrave who is designing a pretty monument to my father, chiefly of slabs of Wedgwood ware—for Kew G.[6] I have not settled to go yet. If I could manage to return to Town in time on Saturday 27th I might run down that night to Down.[7] I will let you know in good time.

In tossing over old Geological mss the other day I found a prophecy of your's. You bet 5 to 1, that in 20 years, it would be generally admitted, that Coal was formed by submarine plants,—this was I suppose in 1846— What odds will you take now in 1866?—[8]

Would you believe it, I have in cold blood, accepted an invitation to deliver an evening address on the Darwinian theory at Nottingham.[9] I am utterly disgusted with my bravado. The fact is that Grove asked me, & I feel that I ought to make amends for hateing him so heartily as I did once.—[10] Also as I must do something at Nottingham I am one of those who would rather be hung for a sheep than a lamb—a very long way— Also the difficulty of the subject & impossibility of my doing it justice had charms for me. The Lord have mercy on your bantling in my hand— this strictly private at present.

Do you read Pall-Mall Gazette?[11] it is so good.—

Ever Yrs affec | J D Hooker

DAR 102: 53–4

CD ANNOTATION

6.1 Do you ... so good.—] *scored pencil*

[1] Letter to J. D. Hooker, 15 [January 1866].

[2] Hooker succeeded his father as director of the Royal Botanic Gardens, Kew, on 1 November 1865 (R. Desmond 1999, p. 221). He had previously commented on the volume of work associated with his post (see *Correspondence* vol. 13, letter from J. D. Hooker, [3 November 1865] and n. 3).

[3] The reference is to Verlot 1865 (see letter to J. D. Hooker, 15 [January 1866] and n. 2).

[4] In 1865, CD had complained that reading made his head 'sing violently' (see *Correspondence* vol. 13, letter to J. D. Hooker, 27 [or 28 September 1865], and Appendix IV and n. 3). His wife and daughters often read to him, but usually not on scientific matters (see *Autobiography*, pp. 138–9, *Correspondence* vol. 12, letter to Asa Gray, 29 October [1864], and *Correspondence* vol. 13, letter to J. D. Hooker, 27 [or 28 September 1865]).

[5] John Smith (1821–88) was the curator of the Royal Botanic Gardens, Kew (R. Desmond 1995, p. 430).

[6] William Jackson Hooker died in August 1865 (see *Correspondence* vol. 13, letter to J. D. Hooker, 16 August [1865] and n. 1). Reginald Francis Douce Palgrave was an amateur sculptor and W. J. Hooker's nephew (*DNB*, L. Huxley ed. 1918, 1: 18–19). Palgrave designed the stone surround to the memorial in St Anne's Church, Kew, the centrepiece of which is a 'white on jasper' Wedgwood medallion of W. J. Hooker, sculpted by Thomas Woolner (Allan 1967, p. 216, and plate facing p. 241). The carved fern fronds designed by Palgrave commemorate W. J. Hooker's fame as a pteridologist. The Wedgwood works were at Etruria, Staffordshire.

[7] According to Emma Darwin's diary (DAR 242), Hooker next visited Down from 24 to 26 March.

[8] In his letter to J. D. Hooker, [1 May 1847] (*Correspondence* vol. 4), CD wrote: 'I am delighted to hear that . . . Binney considers coal a sort of submarine peat. I w^d. bet 5 to 1 that in 20 years this will be generally admitted.' Edward William Binney was the author of *On the origin of coal* (Binney 1846), a lightly annotated copy of which is in the Darwin Pamphlet collection–CUL. The origin of coal had long been a subject of difference between CD and Hooker (see *Correspondence* vols. 3 and 4; see also *Autobiography*, p. 105, and Affolter 1980, pp. 4–5). Worthen 1866, pp. 68–9, states:

> It is now generally admitted and believed that coal is the carbonized residuum of vegetable matter that grew upon a low, swampy surface, during the coal measure epoch; and being subsequently submerged and covered by deposits of sand and clay, the vegetable accumulation underwent the necessary chemical change and was transformed into coal, while above the coal, sandstones, shales and limestones were slowly accumulating. Subsequently these marine formations were raised above the ocean's level, and another growth of vegetable matter accumulated to form another bed of coal; and this process must have been repeated as often as successive seams of coal and the intervening marine deposits were found.

For a contemporary summary of successive theories of the origin of coal, see Smyth 1867, chapter 3, especially pp. 41–4.

[9] On the evening of 27 August 1866, Hooker delivered a lecture to an audience of about 2000 at the meeting of the British Association for the Advancement of Science at Nottingham. The text was published under the title 'Insular floras' in *Gardeners' Chronicle* (1867): 6–7, 27, 50–1, 75–76 (see also *Journal of Botany* 5 (1867): 23–31, and L. Huxley ed. 1918, 2: 98–105, 498). The address did not appear in the *Report of the thirty-sixth meeting of the British Association for the Advancement of Science.*

[10] William Robert Grove was president of the British Association for the Advancement of Science in 1866. For Hooker's and CD's attitudes to Grove, see *Correspondence* vol. 8, letter to J. D. Hooker, 8 February [1860].

[11] The *Pall Mall Gazette* was an evening newspaper; it first appeared on 7 February 1865 (*Reader*, 11 February 1865, p. 167). It featured articles on political and social questions by well-known writers (Ellegård 1990, p. 379, North 1997, pp. 3716–17).

To William Bernhard Tegetmeier 16 January [1866]

Down. | Bromley. | Kent. S.E.
Jan 16th

My dear Sir

At last after 10 months' illness I am better & able daily to do one or two hours' work, & so am going on with my everlasting volume.[1] Therefore I want to know what progress has been made with the wood-blocks or rather drawings of the pigeons.—[2] If not finished, I sh^d. wish no time to be lost.— Could you aid me in getting a common Dovecot pigeon not chequered (with wing-bars, & tail-bar) drawn, in order to show standard of comparison for the other breeds.[3]

Lastly, will you be so kind as to return me the Pigeon Book by Belgian man, as I want to consult it before long.[4] Do you think you could get Mr Zurhorst to try his experiment again this Spring on the eggs from Cochin crossed by Spanish & let me see eggs.?—[5]

I hope that you & your family are all well—

Pray believe me | My dear Sir | Yours sincerely | Ch. Darwin

P.S. If there is a difficulty about getting a dead non-chequered Dovecot half-wild

Pigeon for drawing, I could cut out a fairly good drawing out of Dixons Dovecot Book,[6] but then the pigeon in comparison with others would not be in true proportion or scale.—

Endorsement: '1866'
Archives of The New York Botanical Garden (Charles Finney Cox Collection) (Tegetmeier 93)

[1] For CD's illness in 1865, see the letter to H. B. Jones, 3 January [1866] and nn. 2–8, and *Correspondence* vol. 13, Appendixes II and IV. CD also refers to his work on *Variation*, which had occupied him intermittently since January 1860 (see *Correspondence* vol. 13, letter to John Murray, 4 April [1865] and n. 3). In 1866, CD worked on *Variation* continuously except between 1 March and 10 May (see 'Journal', Appendix II).

[2] CD and Tegetmeier corresponded in 1865 about the engagement of Luke Wells to make drawings of pigeons for *Variation* (see, for example, *Correspondence* vol. 13, letter to W. B. Tegetmeier, 6 April [1865] and nn. 3 and 4). Tegetmeier made arrangements for this with the publisher (see *Correspondence* vol. 13, letter from W. B. Tegetmeier to John Murray and R. F. Cooke, 17 April 1865, and letter from R. F. Cooke to W. B. Tegetmeier, 18 April 1865).

[3] CD used an illustration of a dead specimen of *Columba livia* in *Variation* 1: 135, and presented the species as the 'standard of comparison' in his detailed comparisons of different breeds (*Variation* 1: 134 *et seq.*); see also n. 6, below. A dovecot pigeon, with wing and tail bars and without chequering, would closely resemble *C. livia*, the rock pigeon, which CD held to be the progenitor of all breeds of pigeon (*Variation* 1: 131–224; see also *Origin*, p. 23). On the relationship of dovecot pigeons to *C. livia*, see *Variation* 1: 185–7.

[4] The reference is to Chapuis 1865. CD had sent Tegetmeier his copy in June 1865 (see *Correspondence* vol. 13, letter from W. B. Tegetmeier, 20 June 1865 and n. 3). There is a lightly annotated copy in the Darwin Library–CUL (see *Marginalia* 1: 165).

[5] No reference to an earlier experiment by Frederick William Zurhorst has been found. For the inconclusive results of CD's suggested experiment on the eggs resulting from a cross between Cochin and Spanish fowl, see the letter from W. B. Tegetmeier, 10 December [1866]. For CD's discussion of variability in the size and colour of eggs among different breeds of fowl, see *Variation* 1: 248–9.

[6] CD refers to Dixon 1851, an annotated copy of which is in the Darwin Library–CUL (see *Marginalia* 1: 199–201); the illustration of the 'dovehouse pigeon' was not cut out of this copy. CD had previously sought permission from the publisher to use an illustration of the dovecot pigeon from Dixon 1851 (*Correspondence* vol. 13, letter to John Murray, 31 March [1865] and n. 17). For details of the varieties of pigeon illustrated in *Variation*, see *Correspondence* vol. 13, letter to W. B. Tegetmeier, 6 April [1865] and n. 4. See also n. 3 above.

To Ernst Haeckel 20 January [1866]

Down. | *Bromley.* | *Kent. S.E.*
Jan 20

My dear Sir

I thank you for your kind note of Jan. 11.[1] You think much too highly of my work, but I confess it gratifies me not a little to read your frequently repeated expressions about my Origin of Species. No other photographs have been taken of me besides that published by Bronn & that by my son of which I enclose half a dozen copies.[2] Do not trouble yourself to make up an equal number but I sh[d] value greatly photographs of some of the leading naturalists in whom your country so abounds. I have only yourself Fritz Muller, Rütemeyer, & the Philolog. Schleicher.[3]

I am heartily glad that your book is making such good progress:[4] I shall try & read it through, but it will take me an immense time, for I am a wretched German scholar & never improve. I wish I c^d^ get it translated & will keep it in mind, but fear it will be impossible as there is but little sale for purely scientific works in England.[5]

I have read your account of the protogenes primordialis with much interest: nothing can be so wonderful as the vitality & movements of these fluid bodies.[6] I have not yet read your larger paper on Medusæ.[7] My health is better & I am now able to work one or two hours a day on the Variation of Domestic Animals & Plants; but I make slow progress.[8]

Pray believe me with every good wish yours sincerely | Ch. Darwin

The photographs are in a separate envelope as the postage is less—[9]

Endorsement: '/1866.'
LS
Ernst-Haeckel-Haus (Bestand A-Abt. 1-52/8)

[1] See letter from Ernst Haeckel, 11 January 1866.

[2] See letter from Ernst Haeckel, 11 January 1866 and n. 15. CD refers to Heinrich Georg Bronn and the frontispiece to Bronn trans. 1863. The photographs sent by CD to Haeckel with this letter were probably copies of the portrait taken in spring 1864 by his son, William Erasmus Darwin (see *Correspondence* vol. 12, frontispiece, and letter from W. E. Darwin, [19 May 1864] and n. 8). William also photographed CD in 1861 (*Correspondence* vol. 9, frontispiece, and letter to Asa Gray, 11 April [1861] and n. 19).

[3] Haeckel had offered to send CD photographs of German scientists who admired him (see letter from Ernst Haeckel, 11 January 1866). Haeckel sent his own photograph to CD in summer 1864 (see *Correspondence* vol. 12, letter from Ernst Haeckel, 10 August 1864 and nn. 2 and 3), and also enclosed a photograph taken in October 1865 with his letter of 11 January 1866. Fritz Müller sent a photograph of himself in 1865 (see letter to Fritz Müller, 11 January 1866 and n. 5). There is no reference in CD's extant correspondence with Ludwig Rütimeyer to a photograph of Rütimeyer. August Schleicher enclosed his photograph with his letter to CD of 9 February 1865 (see *Correspondence* vol. 13). He was a philologist.

[4] The reference is to Haeckel 1866 (see letter from Ernst Haeckel, 11 January 1866 and nn. 7–9).

[5] Haeckel 1866, a two-volume work of over 1000 pages, was published on or after 14 September 1866, the date appearing at the end of the foreword; it has never been translated into English.

[6] See letter from Ernst Haeckel, 11 January 1866 and nn. 6 and 7. *Protogenes primordialis* was not mentioned by name in *Variation*. However, the question of whether cell-like bodies without walls and nuclei might be classified as cells was raised by CD, with a reference to Haeckel's recent classification of cells (*Variation* 2: 370 and n. 25). For Haeckel's classification, see Haeckel 1866, 1: 269–88.

[7] The monograph (Haeckel 1865b), on the Geryonidae (now called Geryoniidae), was one of three papers by Haeckel sent to CD on Haeckel's behalf by Wilhelm Engelmann (see letter from Ernst Haeckel, 11 January 1866 and n. 4). For CD's interest in Haeckel's work on the medusae, see *Correspondence* vol. 13, letter to J. D. Hooker, 4 May [1865] and n. 10.

[8] For CD's health in the preceding months, see the letter to H. B. Jones, 3 January [1866] and nn. 2–8. For CD's work on *Variation* in 1866, see the letter to W. B. Tegetmeier, 16 January [1866] and n. 1.

[9] See n. 3, above. A letter to Germany weighing half an ounce cost 6*d*.; printed papers, probably including photographs, were charged at a lesser rate if not accompanied by a letter (*Post Office London directory* 1866).

To J. D. Hooker 21 [January 1866]

Down.
Sunday 21

My dear Hooker

I am ashamed of myself. I have found Verlot,[1] which had been swept up with some other pamphlet on a quite different subject.— I cannot say that I am sorry I wrote, as it got a note from you.—[2] How I wish that you were not so overworked with correspondence & all sorts of things.

I write now chiefly to say that though scarcely anything or rather nothing would give me so much pleasure as seeing you here for a day, yet I may have to put you off next Sunday (if you are able to come);[3] for my poor sister M^rs. Langton is dying at Shrewsbury, or rather in a hopeless state, & whether or not she may linger for some time I do not think the Doctors know.[4] I am sure I wish all was over with her. In case of her death I sh^d. not like to have anyone, even you, in the House.— I will write, if I hear she gets nearer her end.— Poor thing she suffers much.—

I continue much the same & am able to write for 1½ or even 2 hours & read a little to myself; but my stomach keeps very bad.—[5] What a horrid wretch you are to remind me of my coal-plant prophecy. The coal-formation will ever be an enigma to be.—[6]

I rejoice over the Nottingham Lecture.[7] I am sure you will do it excellently— you know the subject so well & by all accounts did the Bishop so well at Oxford.—[8] Will it be printed; if not you really *must* let me read M.S. By Jove I do not envy you the job; for I cannot conceive anything more difficult than making such a lecture; I do not mean on your subject, but on any blessed subject whatever.—

Yours affect | C. Darwin

We take in Pall Mall Gazette & agree it is admirable.—[9]

Endorsement: 'Jany 1866.'
DAR 115: 281

[1] CD had asked Hooker whether he had lent him Verlot 1865 (see letter to J. D. Hooker, 15 [January 1866]).

[2] Letter from J. D. Hooker, 16 January 1866.

[3] Hooker had suggested that he might travel from London to visit CD at Down House on the evening of Saturday 27 January (see letter from J. D. Hooker, 16 January 1866).

[4] See letter from E. C. Langton to Emma and Charles Darwin, [6 and 7? January 1866] and nn. 1 and 2.

[5] For CD's state of health, see also the letter to H. B. Jones, 3 January [1866]; in his letters to P. L. Sclater, 6 January [1866], and Ernst Haeckel, 20 January [1866], CD reported having recovered sufficiently to work for limited periods each day.

[6] See letter from J. D. Hooker, 16 January 1866 and n. 8. In the late 1840s, CD had argued with Hooker about the origin of coal (see *Correspondence* vol. 4, letter to J. D. Hooker, [5 October 1847] and n. 6). The origin of coal tested CD's knowledge of biology to such an extent that he likened his interest in the debates to watching a good game without knowing the rules (*Correspondence* vol. 4, letter to J. D. Hooker, [2 June 1847]). Divergent opinions on the subject also led him to write: 'I

suppose the coal was rained down [from Heaven] to puzzle mortals' (*Correspondence* vol. 4, letter to J. D. Hooker, [5 October 1847]).

7 CD refers to Hooker's proposed lecture on CD's theory of transmutation for the August 1866 meeting of the British Association for the Advancement of Science at Nottingham (see letter from J. D. Hooker, 16 January 1866 and n. 9).

8 Samuel Wilberforce, bishop of Oxford, spoke against *Origin* at the British Association for the Advancement of Science meeting in Oxford in 1860. For Hooker's response to Wilberforce's lecture, see *Correspondence* vol. 8, Appendix VI.

9 See letter from J. D. Hooker, 16 January 1866 and n. 11.

From W. B. Tegetmeier 22 January [1866][1]

Muswell Hill
Jany 22./65

My dear Sir

I was very glad to see your writing again.[2] I had heard from Mr Wallace that you were better but would not trouble you with letters.[3]

I have already engraved

Barb—
Short faced tumbler
African owl
Fantail
and. Carrier.[4]

There remain to be done the Pouter and Blue Rock.[5] of the latter I shall a pure wild bred specimen from Sutherlandshire on Tuesday[6] That compleates the pigeons— of the fowls the Spanish cock head is engraved: Polish in Engravers hands— Hamburgh (rose comb) is being drawn—[7]

I returned Chappuis, (with thanks) by post on Friday.[8] The author has sent me a copy—

The experiment respecting the eggs shall be tried as soon as possible both by myself and Mr Zurhorst—[9]

—Now I want to ask an especial favour which will cost you I hope but little trouble and do me much service

—The Unfortunate "poultry book which was never completed, has at last got into the hands of a solvent publisher[10]

It is commenced *de novo* And as all the original matter of Johnson & Wingfield is expunged the book will go by my name only.—.[11] All the matter to which you have referred will be retained and I therefore beg to ask you as a great favour to refer to the *Poultry book by W B Tegetmeier*—[12] I do this the more readily as a very small number only 500 of the incomplete edition was printed and I should doubt whether a single copy except that in the British Museum could be obtained for reference Whereas if I live there is no doubt of this present edition being finished and as 4000 of the first part are sold it will be a well known authority—

Trusting you will excuse my troubling you on this subject | Believe me | My dear Sir | Yours very truly | W B Tegetmeier

C Darwin Esq

DAR 178: 71

CD ANNOTATION
4.1 The experiment . . . Zurhorst— 4.2] *double scored pencil*

1 The year is established by the publication date of the first part of Tegetmeier 1867 (see n. 11, below). Tegetmeier mistakenly dated the letter '65' instead of '66.'

2 Letter to W. B. Tegetmeier, 16 January [1866].

3 The reference is to Alfred Russel Wallace. For CD's recently improved health, see the letter to H. B. Jones, 3 January [1866] and nn. 2–8.

4 Tegetmeier supervised the procurement of illustrations of pigeons and poultry, and their engraving, for *Variation* (see letter to W. B. Tegetmeier, 16 January [1866] and n. 2). Tegetmeier refers to illustrations that appear in the first volume of *Variation* with the captions 'English Barb' (p. 145), 'Short-faced English Tumbler' (p. 152), 'African Owl' (p. 149), 'English Fantail' (p. 147), and 'English Carrier' (p. 140).

5 The two engravings entitled 'The Rock-pigeon, or Columba livia' and 'English Pouter' appear in *Variation* 1: 135 and 137, respectively. The rock pigeon is a slaty-blue colour (*Variation* 1: 183, 195).

6 No record survives of the bird from Sutherlandshire (a former Scottish county, subsumed after 1974 into Highland Region); the dead rock pigeon illustrated in *Variation* was apparently obtained instead from the Orkney Islands or the Isle of Lewis (see letter from W. B. Tegetmeier, 4 July 1866).

7 CD asked Tegetmeier to arrange for Luke Wells to draw these breeds (see *Correspondence* vol. 13, letter to W. B. Tegetmeier, [7 April 1865]). The engravers were Butterworth and Heath (*ibid.*, letter from W. B. Tegetmeier to John Murray and R. F. Cooke, 17 April 1865). The illustrations appeared in *Variation* 1: 226, 228–29.

8 The reference is to Chapuis 1865 (see letter to W. B. Tegetmeier, 16 January [1866] and n. 4).

9 Tegetmeier refers to CD's request that Tegetmeier ask Frederick William Zurhorst to repeat an experiment on eggs from a cross between Cochin and Spanish fowl (see letter to W. B. Tegetmeier, 16 January [1866] and n. 5). Neither a discussion, nor the results, of Zurhorst's original cross have been found.

10 The first edition of the *The poultry book* was by William Wriothesley Wingfield and George William Johnson (Wingfield and Johnson 1853). In 1856 and 1857, a revised edition, edited by Tegetmeier, was published in parts by William S. Orr and Co. (*Correspondence* vol. 6, letter to W. B. Tegetmeier, 18 May [1857] and nn. 4–6); however, the publishers went out of business before the edition was completed. The eleven unbound parts of the incomplete edition (Wingfield and Johnson 1856–7) are in the Darwin Library–CUL and are annotated by CD (see *Marginalia* 1: 798–800). See also n. 11 below.

11 Wingfield and Johnson 1856–7 was superseded by Tegetmeier 1867, published by George Routledge & Sons. The work retained most of the original plates and Tegetmeier's text from Wingfield and Johnson 1856–7; it included four additional parts and new figures and plates. Twelve parts of Tegetmeier 1867 were issued in 1866 and three in 1867. The unbound copies, heavily annotated by CD, are in the Darwin Library–CUL (see *Marginalia* 1: 800–3).

12 Tegetmeier had previously asked CD to cite him personally rather than refer to Wingfield and Johnson 1856–7 (see *Correspondence* vol. 13, letter from W. B. Tegetmeier, [29 March – 7 April 1865]). CD replied that he was still obliged to refer occasionally to Wingfield and Johnson 1856–7 for details of work by others than Tegetmeier (*ibid.*, letter to W. B. Tegetmeier, 2 June [1865]). However, CD was able to change the references, as Tegetmeier 1867 is cited frequently in the chapter on fowls in *Variation* (1: 225–75), not Wingfield and Johnson 1856–7.

To Alfred Russel Wallace 22 January 1866

Down. | *Bromley.* | *Kent. S.E.*
Jan 22. 1866

My dear Wallace

I thank you for your paper on Pigeons, which interested me, as every thing that you write does.[1] Who w^{d} ever have dreamed that monkeys influenced the distribution of pigeons & parrots![2]

But I have had a still higher satisfaction; for I finished yesterday your paper in Linn. Trans.[3] It is admirably done. I cannot conceive that the most firm believer in Species c^{d} read it without being staggered. Such papers will make many more converts among naturalists than long-winded books such as I shall write if I have strength.

I have been particularly struck with your remarks on Dimorphism; but I cannot quite understand one point (p. 22) & sh^{d} be grateful for an explanation for I want fully to understand you.

How can one female form be selected & the intermediate forms die out, without also the other extreme form also dying out from not having the advantages of the first selected form; for as I understand, both female forms occur on the same Island.[4] I quite agree with your distinction between dimorphic forms & varieties; but I doubt whether your criterion of dimorphic forms not producing intermediate offspring will suffice; for I know of a good many varieties which must be so called, that will not blend or intermix, but produce offspring quite like either parent.[5]

I have been particularly struck with your remarks on Geog. Distrib. in Celebes. It is impossible that any thing c^{d} be better put, & w^{d} give a cold shudder to the immutable naturalists.[6]

And now I am going to ask a question which you will not like. How does y^{r} Journal get on?[7] It will be a shame if you do not popularize your researches. my health is so far improved that I am able to work one or 2 hours a day—

Believe me dear Wallace | yours very sincerely | Ch. Darwin

LS
British Library (Add 46434, f. 61)

[1] The reference is to A. R. Wallace 1865. A lightly annotated copy is in the Darwin Archive–CUL (DAR 133: 11).

[2] CD marked the passage in which Wallace noted that the largest populations of pigeons, and of parrots, occurred in a part of the Malay archipelago from which monkeys and squirrels were absent (A. R. Wallace 1865, p. 366; see also *ML* 1: 265). Wallace suggested that the birds consumed fruits that formed part of the diets of these mammals; he also noted the monkeys' habits of destroying eggs and young birds (A. R. Wallace 1865, p. 366).

[3] The reference is to A. R. Wallace 1864b, a paper on variation and geographical distribution as illustrated by butterflies of the family Papilionidae in the Malayan region. CD was aware of its theme through the summary printed in the *Reader* in 1864; however, the paper was not published in full until 1865. CD's unbound, annotated, copy is in the Darwin Archive–CUL. For CD's earlier favourable impressions of its content, see *Correspondence* vol. 12, letter to A. R. Wallace, 28 [May 1864] and n. 4. CD referred to the content of A. R. Wallace 1864b in considering taxonomic distinctions between variable forms, local forms, geographical races or subspecies, and true species in *Origin* 4th ed.,

pp. 53–4; CD also referred to Wallace's work on polymorphic butterflies in the chapter on pangenesis in *Variation* 2: 399–400. See also *Descent*, chapter 11.

4 The passage to which CD refers concerns Wallace's interpretation of the origins of dimorphism and polymorphism in *Papilio* (A. R. Wallace 1864b, p. 22). In observing wing patterns in *P. memnon*, Wallace had noted three different forms of female, two of which occurred in Java. One form (plate 1, fig. 4, in A. R. Wallace 1864b) was a mimic of *P. coon*. Wallace argued that such polymorphic variants resulted from natural selection and conferred various advantages on females in particular, since, being slower than males, they were more vulnerable to predation. Wallace wrote that natural selection thus explained the development of the differently camouflaged wing colours and patterns in female forms, as well as the phenomenon of mimicry. In his own copy of A. R. Wallace 1864b, CD wrote on page 22: 'just like neuters'. See also A. R. Wallace 1905, 1: 401–3.

5 Wallace urged that it was important to distinguish between varieties, which he defined as producing intermediate offspring when crossed, and dimorphic forms, the progeny of which he claimed would resemble one parent (A. R. Wallace 1864b, p. 10). However, CD had earlier written of varieties producing offspring that were not intermediate but resembled one parent (*Origin*, pp. 273–5). CD described this phenomenon in greater detail in *Variation* 2: 92–4.

6 Compared with other islands of the archipelago, Celebes had many more species of Papilionidae that were unique to it. Celebes also had 3 unique species of mammals, 5 unique species of birds and 190 unique hymenopterous species. Furthermore, Wallace observed that members of the Papilionidae on Celebes exhibited certain common characteristics that distinguished them from their counterparts on other islands. Wallace used this information to argue for the mutability of species and against the notion that all species had been created exactly as and where they were found (A. R. Wallace 1864b, pp. 30–2).

7 Four months earlier, CD had enquired about progress on Wallace's 'journal' (*Correspondence* vol. 13, letter to A. R. Wallace, 22 September [1865] and n. 3). After his return from Malaya in 1862, Wallace spent five years organising his collections and writing articles. It was not until 1867 that he began in earnest to write *The Malay Archipelego*, his most popular book; it was published in 1869 (A. R. Wallace 1905, 1: 385–408). There is an annotated copy inscribed by the author in the Darwin Library–CUL (see *Marginalia* 1: 840–2), and the first volume bears a printed dedication testifying to Wallace's personal friendship for CD and to his 'deep admiration for his genius and works'.

From J. D. Hooker 23 January 1866

Kew
Jany 23d/66.

Dear Darwin

I am truly grieved to hear of Mrs Langton's state—[1] I have been so haunted by death & his dart—this 6 or 8 years, that I can hardly bear to look at my children asleep in bed—[2] I used to think a child asleep not only the loveliest thing in creation, but the most gratifying in every respect:— leaving nothing to be desired except that it would not grow older— all is changed now.—

May you soon my very dear friend be relieved of your aching sympathy for one so dear to you.

I go to the North on Saturday & shall be at the Etruria works on Monday. & back to Kew same night[3]

Your ever affectionate | Jos D Hooker

Frances is very sorry indeed,[4] she liked Mrs Langton so much

DAR 102: 55–6

[1] Emily Catherine Langton, CD's younger sister, was dying (see letter to J. D. Hooker, 21 [January 1866]).
[2] Hooker's father-in-law, John Stevens Henslow, died in May 1861 (see *Correspondence* vol. 9), his daughter Maria Elizabeth in September 1863 (see *Correspondence* vol. 11, letter from J. D. Hooker, 1 October 1863 and n. 1), and his father, William Jackson Hooker, in August 1865 (see *Correspondence* vol. 13). Extracts from Hooker's letters expressing his reactions to these losses are collected in L. Huxley ed. 1918, 2: 60–5. See also *Correspondence* vol. 13, letter from J. D. Hooker, [26 September 1865].
[3] Hooker and his cousin, Reginald Francis Douce Palgrave, travelled to the Wedgwood pottery works in Etruria, Staffordshire, in connection with a Wedgwood medallion to form the centrepiece of a memorial to William Jackson Hooker (see letter from J. D. Hooker, 16 January 1866 and n. 6).
[4] Hooker refers to his wife, Frances Harriet Hooker.

From W. B. Tegetmeier [after 24 January 1866][1]

Muswell Hill | N

My dear Sir

I write a hasty line to acknowledge the receipt of yours with enclosure—

The expenses and trouble which I have incurred have been so slight that your remittance far overpays them.[2]

I have heard from Mr Zurhorst and shall meet him next week. we will both repeat experiments and consequently their will be but little chance of error I shall arrange with him as to our exact modes of trial—[3]

If you would like I can send you a set of engravings as far as they are done.[4]

Believe me | Very truly Yours | W B Tegetmeier

C. Darwin Esq.

Mr Blyth is writing some articles on Indian Cattle, (Gaours and Gayals) in the Field.[5] I can cut them out and send you if you like, I am sure you will be sorry to hear they are from a place of enforced temporary quietness a private asylum in fact—[6]

DAR 178: 70

[1] The date is established by the relationship between this letter and the date of CD's payment to Tegetmeier (see n. 2, below).
[2] CD's letter has not been found. On 24 January 1866, CD recorded a payment of £3 3*s*. to Tegetmeier for woodcuts (CD's Classed account books (Down House MS)); CD had previously invited Tegetmeier to commission and supervise the engravings of pigeons and fowl for *Variation*, for a fee of two guineas (*Correspondence* vol. 13, letter to W. B. Tegetmeier, 14 March [1865] and nn. 11 and 12).
[3] CD had wanted Frederick William Zurhorst to repeat an earlier experiment (see letter to W. B. Tegetmeier, 16 January [1866] and n. 5).
[4] See letter from W. B. Tegetmeier, 22 January [1866], for a list of engravings of pigeons and fowl that had been made for *Variation*.
[5] Edward Blyth published two short articles on Indian cattle in the *Field*, dealing chiefly with gaurs, *Bos gaurus*, and gayals, *B. gaurus frontalis* (Blyth 1866a and Blyth 1866b; see also Grzimek ed. 1972, pp. 360–4). CD cited Blyth as an authority on feral cattle and briefly referred to the gayal in *Variation* 1: 79–80, 82.

[6] Edward Blyth formerly wrote frequently to CD from India on biological topics (see *Correspondence* vols. 5–7); he left India for England in 1862 (*Correspondence* vol. 10, letter from Edward Blyth, 23 November 1862 and n. 4). Blyth was apparently incapacitated during 1865 and 1866, and may have been confined to a private asylum; by 1869, his sister complained of his 'excessive drinking' (letter from Clara Sarah Blyth to Alfred Newton, 28 June 1869, Alfred Newton papers–CUL; see also letters from Clara Sarah Blyth to Alfred Newton, 1 December 1865 and 31 March 1866, Alfred Newton papers–CUL). Blyth's mental problems and alcoholism are further considered in Brandon-Jones 1995, pp. 92–3, and Brandon-Jones 1997, pp. 172–3 and n. 150.

From Ernst Haeckel[1] 28 January 1866

Jena (Saxe-Weimar)
28. Jan. 66.

Theurer hochverehrter Herr!

Herzlichsten Dank für die gütige Übersendung Ihrer werthvollen Porträts, durch welche Sie meinen Freunden eine grosse Freude gemacht haben.[2] Mit Ausnahme von Schleiden, welcher nicht mehr hier ist,[3] habe ich den andern fünf Naturforschern Ihr Bild geschickt, und sie haben mir dagegen das Ihrige für Sie gegeben.[4]

Sie erhalten also beifolgend die Portraits von den bedeutendsten und eifrigsten Naturforschern, welche in Deutschland Ihre Lehre verbreiten. Es sind dies aber fast die einzigen bedeutenden Naturforscher, welche bei uns *offen* für Ihre Lehre kämpfen, weil die meisten Anderen, welche von ihrer Wahrheit überzeugt sind, zu feige und furchtsam sind, um dies offen auszudrücken. Sie geben zwar privatim die Wahrheit zu, haben aber Angst, dieselbe öffentlich auszusprechen, und fürchten ihre Consequenzen.[5]

Alle sechs Naturforscher, deren Bilder Sie erhalten, haben schon offen und frei, wie ich, für die Wahrheit der Darwin-Theorie gesprochen und geschrieben. A. Braun und Virchow, auch Leydig, sind meine Lehrer.[6] Der jüngste, Dohrn, welcher jetzt mein Assistent ist, hat noch wenig geschrieben; ich hoffe aber viel von ihm, weil er fast eben so aufrichtig Ihrer Lehre ergeben ist, wie ich selbst, und darin eine totale Reform der ganzen morphologischen und physiologischen Wissenschaft findet, wie ich ihn gelehrt habe.[7] Glauben Sie nicht, dass ich Ihr Verdienst überschätze. Man *kann* dies *nicht* überschätzen, wenn man den traurigen Zustand der Zoologie und Botanik bedenkt, in welchen sie durch das Species-Dogma gerathen ist, und zu dessen totaler Reform Sie *zuerst* den Anstoss gegeben haben.— Ich würde Ihnen gern Englisch schreiben; ich kann es aber nicht schreiben, bloss lesen.— Es freut mich ausserordentlich zu hören, dass es Ihnen besser geht. Möge Ihre Besserung immer so fort schreiten!

Das ist der aufrichtigste Wunsch Ihres von ganzem Herzen ergebenen Ernst Haeckel

DAR 166: 42

[1] For a translation of this letter, see Appendix I.

[2] See letter to Ernst Haeckel, 20 January [1866]. Haeckel requested photographs of CD in his letter of 11 January 1866.

[3] Matthias Jacob Schleiden had resigned from his professorship of botany at Jena in 1862; from 1864, he lived elsewhere as a private scholar (*ADB*, *DBE*).

[4] CD had sent six photographs of himself for Haeckel to forward to German scientists (see letter to Ernst Haeckel, 20 January [1866]). The photographs CD received were evidently of Alexander Carl Heinrich Braun, Rudolf Carl Virchow, Franz von Leydig, and Anton Dohrn, probably together with that of Schleiden, and one other, possibly Carl Gegenbaur, whom Haeckel had mentioned in letters to CD (see nn. 6 and 7, below, and *Correspondence* vol. 12).

[5] On the reception of CD's theory in Germany, see *Correspondence* vol. 11, letter from Friedrich Rolle, 26 January 1863 and nn. 6–14, and *Correspondence* vol. 12, letters from Ernst Haeckel, 9 [July 1864], 10 August 1864, and 26 October 1864. See also Corsi and Weindling 1985, Montgomery 1988, Junker 1989, Engels ed. 1995, and Nyhart 1995.

[6] In the early 1850s, Haeckel attended Braun's lectures at the University of Berlin, and between 1852 and 1856, Virchow's and von Leydig's lectures at the University of Würzburg (*DSB*, Krauße 1987, pp. 18–28, and *DBE*). Haeckel had previously informed CD of Braun's and Virchow's support for his work in his letters of 9 [July 1864] and 26 October 1864 (*Correspondence* vol. 12).

[7] Dohrn was a student of Haeckel's at Jena. By January 1866, he had published more than a dozen scientific papers, including his 1865 article 'Die Darwin'sche Theorie und das Experiment' (Dohrn 1865; see also Kühn 1950, pp. 18, 186–7). For an account of Dohrn's relationship with Haeckel, see Heuss 1991, pp. 35–47.

From Friedrich Rolle[1] 28 January 1866

Homburg vor der Hoehe bei Frankfurt am Main
den 28 Januar 1866.

Geehrtester Herr!

Nachdem Ihnen im vorigen Sommer Heft I von meinem Buche "Der Mensch" zugekommen ist, wie ich aus Ihrer gütigen Anmeldung ersah, wird Ihnen Heft 2–5 seither durch meinen Buchhaendler auch zugekommen sein.[2]

Ich hoffe dass meine Arbeit Ihren Beifall findet; sie ist nach den Grundzügen Ihrer Theorie entworfen; über Einzelheiten kann man allerdings verschiedner Ansicht sein; die Grundzüge des Ganzen stehen aber bereits so bestimmt gezeichnet, dass der wesentliche Geist der Anschauung schon ziemlich fest gegeben erscheint.

Wo Zweifel vorliegen, habe ich mich bemüht, vorsichtig zu urtheilen.

So namentlich in Bezug auf Einheit oder Mehrheit des Ursprungs—und ob die Einheit des Menschengeschlechts diesseits oder jenseits der menschlichen Stufe liegt.[3]

Allerdings entscheiden darüber in letzter Spruchfaellung nur Funde.

Aber rationelle Vermuthungen sind auch schon erlaubt—und beleuchten den Weg den man voraussichtlich gehen wird und die Schwierigkeiten welche man noch zu überwinden [haben] wird.

Es scheint mir dass die Wurzeln des menschlichen Stamms

in den Negern von Afrika

in den büschelig-kraushaarigen Menschen von Südafrika und jenen von Neuguinea, Tasmanien usw.

endlich drittens einem nicht naeher bekannten kurzkoepfigen Volke (Brachycephali) von Südasien liegen moegen.

Wo und wie diese drei Wurzeln ausgegangen sind, ist mir noch dunkel.

Aber alle schlichthaarigen Culturvoelker scheinen mir vervollkommete Culturvoelker zu sein, bei welchen Langkoepfe, Mittelkoepfe und Kurzkoepfe vielfach gemischt sind.[4]

Dies würde also aehnlich wie bei den Hausthier-Rassen sein.

In der Nomenclatur hat Bronn "natural selection" mit "natürliche Auswahl" ins deutsche übersetzt. Ich übersetzte mit "natürliche Auslese" dieser Ausdruck kommt dem Begriffe des Passiven schon naeher.[5] Neuerlich habe ich begonnen mit "Entfallung" oder "Aussterbe-Etat" zu übersetzen. "Entfallen" ist "to fall out of" (dilabi, elabi)[6]

z. B. Der Ur und der Wisent sind auf den Aussterbe-Etat gelangt und entfallen.[7]

⟨*6 lines excised*⟩

Vertreter kaempfen mit dem Widerstand der aelteren Schule und werden offenbar beim Besetzen der Aemter zurückgesetzt.

D^{r}. Jaeger in Wien hat Unglück, der Wiener zoologische Garten ist in Concurs und Jaeger hat wenig A⟨ussi⟩cht in Wien seine Stellung zu halten.[8]

D^{r}. Weinland hat sein⟨e⟩ Ste⟨llung⟩ in Frankfurt verlasse⟨n.⟩[9] ⟨Er gab in⟩ Würtemberg eine Zeitschrift "Der Thiergarten" heraus, sie sollte ein Organ für Zucht der Hausthiere und Vertretung der Transmutations-Theorie werden. Leider hat sie nur einen Jahrgang 1864 erlebt und eingehen müssen.[10]

Aber Prof. Rütimeyer in Basel ist sehr thaetig, aus der Palaeontologie der Säugethiere die Abstammung und Transmutation der Säugethiere zu entwickeln.[11]

Er sandte mir ⟨*6 lines excised*⟩

Eine Gegenschrift schrieb Professor Goeppert (Ueber die Darwin'sche Transmutations-Theorie in Beziehung auf die fossilen Pflanzen) im Neuen Jahrbuch für Mineralogie. Jahrgang 1865. Stuttgart. (pag. 296–306.)[12]

Mit d⟨en⟩ besten Wünschen fur Ihr Wohlsein und ⟨Ihre⟩ fernere erfolgreiche T⟨haetig⟩ke⟨it⟩ g⟨eeh⟩rtester Herr | ⟨Ihr er⟩gebenster Diener | D^{r}. Friedr. Rolle

DAR 176: 202

1 For a translation of this letter, see Appendix I.

2 In May 1865, CD had thanked Rolle for the first part of Rolle's *Der Mensch* (Rolle 1866), a study of the development of human society in the light of *Origin* and recent discoveries in geology (*Correspondence* vol. 13, letter to Friedrich Rolle, 6 May [1865]). It was published by Friedrich Emil Suchsland of Frankfurt-am-Main in five parts; the first part on 1 May 1865 (*Börsenblatt für den Deutschen Buchhandel und die mit ihm verwandten Geschäftszweige* 32 (1865): 954), the second and third parts on 17 November 1865 (*ibid.* 32 (1865): 2634), and the fourth and fifth parts on 15 January 1866 (*ibid.* 33 (1866): 103). CD's lightly annotated copy of Rolle 1866 is in the Darwin Pamphlet Collection–CUL. CD cited Rolle 1866 in *Descent* 1: 4 and 246 n.

3 In his complex discussion, Rolle contrasted his scientific treatment of the origin of human beings with theological explanations, allowing that humans might have derived from one or several pairs of parents. He also considered evidence for the genus *Homo* comprising one or more species, and whether human races had arisen relatively recently, as geographical varieties of a single species, or as distinct and immutable species of more distant origin (Rolle 1866, pp. 253–7). For more on Rolle's work, and CD's use of it, see Martin and Uschmann 1969, pp. 28–36, 68–9.

4 Rolle discussed the primeval races from which he considered humans to have originated in Rolle

1866, pp. 257–64. Rolle believed that certain physical traits, including the straightness of the hair and the shape of the skull, defined a superior type: 'Diese höhere Form der Menschheit trägt mehr oder minder den Charakter einer Aristokratie der Cultur . . .' ('This higher form of mankind bears more or less the character of an aristocracy of civilisation . . .') (Rolle 1866, pp. 260–1). For more on craniometry in relation to racial difference in the period, see S. J. Gould 1997, pp. 62–141, especially pp. 130–2; see also Bowler 1987, pp. 55–6, and Stocking 1987.

5 In his translation of *Origin* (Bronn trans. 1860), Heinrich Georg Bronn used 'natürliche Züchtung', 'natürliche Zuchtwahl', and 'natürliche Auswahl' to translate CD's 'natural selection'. See also Browne 2002, pp. 141–2. Rolle used both 'natürliche Auslese' and 'natürliche Auswahl' (Rolle 1866, pp. 72, 105), although only the former appeared in the section and chapter titles of Rolle's books (Rolle 1863, p. 155; Rolle 1866, p. 104). While the different translations implied differing degrees of choice, CD wished to dispel notions that natural selection implied conscious choice (*Origin* 3d ed., pp. 84–5).

6 Rolle used various terms to describe the process of extinction. For his use of the words 'Entfallung' and 'Aussterbe-Etat', see Rolle 1866, pp. 142–4. The former denotes 'falling out' or disappearance, and the latter a state of extinction. 'Dilabi': to fall apart; 'elabi': to fall away (Latin; see Lewis and Short 1969).

7 Aurochs and wisent are mentioned several times in Rolle 1866 (pp. 317, 324–5, 328). The aurochs, *Bos primigenius*, became extinct in western Europe in 1627 (Grzimek ed. 1972, p. 369), whereas wisent (or European bison), *Bison bonasus bonasus*, were in danger of extinction in the nineteenth century (*ibid.*, pp. 394–5).

8 The zoologist Gustav Jäger was CD's most active supporter in Vienna, where Rolle had worked before leaving in March 1862 to settle in Homburg (*Correspondence* vol. 11, letter from Friedrich Rolle, 26 January 1863 and n. 4). Jäger was an organiser and director of the zoological garden in Vienna; in March 1866, Jäger was replaced as director. The zoological garden had financial problems from its outset in 1863 and closed in September 1866 (Weinreich 1993, 48–64).

9 David Friedrich Weinland was a supporter of CD (*Correspondence* vol. 11, letter from Friedrich Rolle, 26 January 1863 and n. 12). In December 1863, Weinland moved from Frankfurt to his parents' estate in Württemberg, having resigned as secretary of the zoological society in Frankfurt and editor of *Der Zoologischer Garten*, the foremost journal for zoological gardens in Germany (Weinland 1863).

10 Weinland founded *Der Thiergarten* in 1864. Only one volume appeared, comprising twelve parts.

11 Ludwig Rütimeyer had recently published a history of the genus *Bos* based on palaeontological work (Rütimeyer 1865). For Rütimeyer's earlier correspondence with CD on the origins of domestic cattle, and references to Rütimeyer in CD's publications, see *Correspondence* vol. 13, letter from Ludwig Rütimeyer, 3 January 1865 and nn. 3 and 4.

12 Rolle refers to Göppert 1865a, in which the author rejected the principle of genealogical connections among extinct and living species of plants (Göppert 1865a, p. 297). The *Neues Jahrbuch für Mineralogie* (1865): 301–6 contained a different paper in which Heinrich Robert Göppert considered transmutation in relation to geology (Göppert 1865b). In 1864 and 1865, Göppert had published a series of papers criticising CD's theory of common descent from the perspective of botanical palaeontology (see, for example, Göppert 1864, of which there is a lightly annotated copy in the Darwin Pamphlet Collection–CUL). For Göppert's views on transmutation, see Junker 1989, pp. 95–98.

From Frederic Ward Putnam 29 January 1866

Essex Institute, | Salem, Mass.
Jan 29 *1866*

Charles Darwin Esq.
Dear Sir:

Professor J. Wyman, of Cambridge, has requested me to send you a copy of a short paper which I read at a meeting of the Essex Institute Oct. 1863, on the habits of some of our species of Humble Bees (Bombus), thinking that you might be interested in my observations on the formation of the cells in the nest of Bombus.[1] I, therefore, take the liberty of mailing a copy of the paper to you. You will notice on reading the paper that I state that *the larvæ make the cells & not the old bees*.[2] I have examined so many nests of the several species of Bombus during the last 3 years that I feel confident I have made no mistake in regard to this point.

You will, I think, be interested in D^r. Packards account of the "Humble Bees & their Parasites" sent under the same cover with my "Notes &c"[3]

I shall soon publish an account of a singular specimen of an Eel which was found in a well. This eel, which is our common species Anguilla bostoniensis, is of most singular shape. Having the head much shortened & broader than is normal, & with the eyes & pectoral fins very much developed.[4] The enclosed rough sketch will give you an idea of the shape of the head.[5] The rest of the specimen is normal. The well in which the eel was found is situated nearly a mile from either salt or fresh water.[6] How the eel got into the well & what caused it to be so singularly formed I will not undertake to say.

I am, sir, | very respectfully, | your ob't. sv't, | F. W. Putnam, | Supt. E.I.

DAR 174: 81

1 Putnam refers to Jeffries Wyman, to Putnam 1863a, and to the genus *Bombus*. See letter from Jeffries Wyman, 11 January 1866. An annotated copy of Putnam 1863a is in the Darwin Pamphlet Collection–CUL.

2 Putnam 1863a, p. 102, describes how *Bombus* larvae determined the position of cells by making cavities in the surrounding pollen mass. The larvae then initiated the cells by spinning cocoons around themselves. However, thereafter adults built the walls of the cells by covering the cocoons with wax. In CD's copy of the paper, the passage describing this process is scored in pencil.

3 The reference is to Alpheus Spring Packard Jr and Packard 1864, a lightly annotated copy of which is in the Darwin Pamphlet Collection–CUL, in a paper cover that also contains Putnam 1863a and another paper by Putnam on leaf-cutting bees (Putnam 1863b).

4 Putnam exhibited the malformed eel (*Anguilla bostoniensis*, now *A. rostrata*) at the meeting of the Boston Society of Natural History on 7 February 1866. The eel had been recovered from a well that had dried out during the previous season. At the meeting, Wyman attributed the deformities of the eel to the retention of the proportions of the embryonic head, citing similar observations in calves and birds and in a breed of cattle in Buenos Aires with short, broad heads and large eyes. (*Proceedings of the Boston Society of Natural History* (1866) 10: 295–6.) For information on the survival of eels out of water and on their movement through subterranean waters, see Tesch 1977, pp. 213–4, 234–5.

5 The enclosure has not been found.

6 The well was in Lynn (*Proceedings of the Boston Society of Natural History* (1866) 10: 295), a small city in Essex county, eastern Massachusetts (*Columbia gazetteer of the world*).

From Frederic William Farrar 1 February [1866][1]

Harrow. N.W.
Feb. 1.

Dear Sir,

I am about to make a request, which I must preface by asking you to pardon it, if it should seem presumptious.

I have been told by a gentleman of influence & position in the Royal Society—that my two works on Language, together with my contributions to Ethnology, constitute a sufficient justification to my offering myself as a candidate for admission into the Royal Society.[2] The first book—The Origin of Language—was the earliest work devoted to that subject since the beginning of this century, & every succeeding writer has noticed it with approval—including both Prof Pott of Berlin, & Mons. Ernest Renan.[3] The latter book you have done me the honour to read & approve.[4]

It is indeed very *late* to offer myself as the election takes place early in March, but if I am not taking too great a liberty in asking if you would be one of those who would, from general knowledge, sign my certificate, I cannot help thinking that your name alone would go far to secure my election.[5]

Once more offering my apologies if, in writing thus, I trespass too far on your indulgence, I remain, dear Sir, | Very faithfully your's, | Frederic W Farrar.

DAR 164: 36

1 The year is established by the relationship between this letter and the letter to F. W. Farrar, 3 February [1866].

2 The two works on language were *An essay on the origin of language* (Farrar 1860) and *Chapters on language* (Farrar 1865). For Farrar's contributions to ethnology, see, for example, Farrar 1857, 1864a, 1864b, 1864c, and 1864d. Farrar also wrote anonymously for the *Anthropological Review*; see *Correspondence* vol. 13, letter from F. W. Farrar, 6 November 1865 and n. 8.

3 Farrar refers to Farrar 1860, August Friedrich Pott, and Joseph-Ernest Renan. Farrar 1860 referred repeatedly to Renan's work; Pott was also cited.

4 CD praised Farrar 1865 in his letter to Farrar of 2 November [1865] (*Correspondence* vol. 13). CD's lightly annotated presentation copy of Farrar 1865 is in the Darwin Library–Down (see *Marginalia* 1: 226). CD later cited Farrar 1865 in *Descent* 1: 56 n.

5 For information on certificates and other details of election to fellowship of the Royal Society of London, see M. B. Hall 1984, especially p. 142. See also Lyons 1944, pp. 152–3, 272–8. Farrar was elected to fellowship of the Royal Society on 7 June 1866; CD, who was one of twenty signatories to Farrar's certificate, specified that his support was based upon a general, rather than a personal, knowledge of Farrar's work (Royal Society of London, certificates of election and candidature).

To Ernst Haeckel 1 February 1866

Down Bromley Kent
Feb 1. 1866

My dear Sir

I write merely to say that I received safely this morning the photographs.[1]

I thank you cordially for all the trouble you have taken. I value them much & all the more as I did not know that some of these distinguished men had ever taken any part in the discussion on the modification of species.[2]

Believe me my dear Sir | yours truly obliged | Ch. Darwin

LS
Ernst-Haeckel-Haus (Bestand A-Abt. 1-52/9)

1 See letter from Ernst Haeckel, 28 January 1866 and n. 4.

[2] See letter from Ernst Haeckel, 28 January 1866 and n. 5.

To Friedrich Rolle 1 February [1866][1]

Down Bromley Kent
Feb 1

My dear Sir

I have received safely all five numbers of your work "Der Mensch" & your obliging note of Jan. 28.[2] I have not as yet had time to do more than turn over the pages of the four latter numbers; nor shall I be able for some little time, as my health is weak, but when I do read them I have no doubt I shall find interesting matter, & I thank you sincerely for sending them to me.

Your letter contained several points new to me. I was not aware that Rütimeier for whom I feel much respect, had ever expressed himself on the subject of the modification of species.[3] I am sorry to hear what you tell me about D[r] Weinland & Jager[4] I am not at all surprized at what you say about disagreeing with me on some points, for no two men c[d] think independently on so complex a subject without differing to a certain extent[5]

With my best thanks for your kindness pray believe me my dear Sir | yours very faithfully | Ch. Darwin

LS
Senckenbergische Naturforschende Gesellschaft, Frankfurt am Main

[1] The year is established by the relationship between this letter and the letter from Friedrich Rolle, 28 January 1866.
[2] CD refers to Rolle 1866 and the letter from Friedrich Rolle, 28 January 1866.
[3] CD refers to Ludwig Rütimeyer; see letter from Friedrich Rolle, 28 January 1866 and n. 11.
[4] CD refers to David Friedrich Weinland and Gustav Jäger; see letter from Friedrich Rolle, 28 January 1866 and nn. 8–10.
[5] See letter from Friedrich Rolle, 28 January 1866 and nn. 3 and 4.

To Jeffries Wyman 2 February 1866

Down. | Bromley. | Kent. S.E.
Feb 2 1866

Dear Sir

I am very much obliged to you for your interesting letter of Jan 11th.[1] I was aware that the cells of Bees varied a little in dimensions, but did not in the least know to what a degree the variability extended.[2] Your statements make the proposition of some, I think, French savant that the size of the cell sh[d] be the standard of all measurements, quite ludicrous.[3] This variability of size agrees well with the view which we both I think take of all instincts.[4] Your case of the 2 cells separated by a flat bottom appears to me particularly interesting.[5]

As so much has been written of late about Bees cells, I cannot but think that your facts w[d] be well worth publishing in a separate paper: should you intend doing so, I sh[d] be grateful for a copy.[6] I had not heard of the fossil tadpole-nests,[7] nor of M[r] Puttnam's paper on the cells of humble bees; I wish he had sent me a copy of it.[8]

With respect to your remark that the hexagonal cell always results from the co-operation of several bees, you must remember the comb began by the solitary female wasp.[9] M[r] F. Smith of the Brit. Museum has lately adduced in Proc. of Ent. Soc. of London several cases of hexagonal combs made by single insects, & others with hexagonal cells at the extreme circumference;[10] But in the specimens which I have seen, the hexagons were not very perfect at the circumference. I am glad that you have been attending a little to this subject; I formerly found it very interesting but I have not looked over my notes for several years.[11]

I may add that Prof. Miller carefully measured for me the thickness of the cell-walls & found great variability in their thickness.[12] With my best thanks for your kindness in writing

I remain dear Sir yours very faithfully | Ch. Darwin

LS(A)
Jeffries Wyman Jr (private collection)

1 See letter from Jeffries Wyman, 11 January 1866.

2 See letter from Jeffries Wyman, 11 January 1866 and n. 2. In successive editions of *Origin*, CD modified his account of the cell-making instinct of the hive-bee to incorporate evidence of variability in the structure of cells (see Peckham ed. 1959, pp. 52, 54, 402–12). For more on CD's deliberation over the problem of the hive-bee's cell-building instinct, see Prete 1990.

3 René Antoine Ferchault de Réaumur suggested that the cell of the hive-bee might formerly have been adopted in preference to the pendulum-based standards as a standard unit of measurement (Réaumur 1734–42, 5: 398–9). On pendulums and their limitations as standards of measurement, see McGreevy 1995, 1: 140–2. Although Réaumur had acknowledged that individual cells varied slightly in their dimensions, he observed negligible variation in the mean size of a large sample of cells (*ibid.*, pp. 379–98).

4 For CD's view that the shape of the cell of the bee had developed as a result of successive modifications of instinct, see the letter from Jeffries Wyman, 11 January 1866, n. 6.

5 CD refers to the flattened bases of the abnormal cells illustrated by figures 2 and 3 in the letter from Wyman of 11 January 1866. CD had argued in *Origin*, pp. 224–7, that the regular shape of the individual cell of the hive-bee, with its pyramidal base, is due to the way that the cells are aggregated to form the comb.

6 In his letter of 11 January 1866, Wyman had not informed CD of his paper 'Notes on the cells of the bee' (Wyman 1866), which he read on 9 January 1866 at a meeting of the American Academy of Arts and Sciences, and in which he referred to CD. There is an annotated, inscribed, copy in the Darwin Pamphlet Collection–CUL.

7 See letter from Jeffries Wyman, 11 January 1866 and n. 7.

8 At Wyman's suggestion, Frederic Ward Putnam had sent CD a copy of Putnam 1863a, which CD would not yet have received (see letter from Jeffries Wyman, 11 January 1866 and nn. 9 and 10, and letter from F. W. Putnam, 29 January 1866). There is an annotated copy in the Darwin Pamphlet Collection–CUL.

9 CD wrote of the queen wasp's ability to make hexagonal cells in *Origin*, p. 233. CD had obtained information about wasps' nests from Erasmus Alvey Darwin, Frederick Smith, and George Robert

Waterhouse in 1858 (*Correspondence* vol. 7); see also *Correspondence* vol. 8, letter from J. S. Henslow, 7 April 1860.

10 The comb of the wasp is built by the queen alone (F. Smith 1864, p. 139). Smith described only one species of wasp, *Apoica pallida*, as building hexagonal combs (*ibid.*, p. 137–8). However, he named three further species as capable of building isolated hexagonal cells (*ibid.*, p. 140), and gave several examples of hexagonal cells occurring at the edge of the comb (*ibid.*, pp. 135–6).

11 Notes made by CD about bee cells, many dating from between 1858 and 1860, are in the Darwin Archive–CUL (DAR 48: B1–78). See letter from Jeffries Wyman, 11 January 1866 and n. 3.

12 In 1860, CD obtained information from William Hallowes Miller on the thickness of the cell walls of the hive-bee (see *Correspondence* vol. 8). Miller's information on bee cells is cited in *Origin* 3d ed., p. 252.

From Charles James Fox Bunbury to Charles Lyell 3 February 1866[1]

Barton,
February 3rd, '66.

My dear Lyell

I thank you much for sending me Madame Agassiz's letter to Mary, which I have read with much curiosity and interest.[2] The variety of new fish and other novelties which Agassiz has discovered are not half so astonishing to me as the rapid growth of that country.[3] How completely Brazil seems to be revolutionized by the one single agency of *steam*. Madame Agassiz speaks of the voyage from Para to the Barra de Rio Negro taking *five* days;[4] when the botanist Spruce explored that country, no longer ago than 1850, the voyage from Para to Santorin, which is little more than half way to the Barra, often required a *month*.[5] Still, I should have more confidence in observations made by men who have been a long time stationary in chosen spots, like Bates and Wallace and Spruce, than in those made at steam pace.[6]

Agassiz's observation on "glacial phenomena," in Brazil are certainly very astonishing indeed; so astonishing that I have very great difficulty in believing them.[7] They shake my faith in the glacial system altogether;—or perhaps they ought rather to shake the faith in Agassiz. They seem to threaten a *reductio ad absurdum* of the whole theory. If Brazil was ever covered with glaciers, I can see no reason why the whole earth should not have been so. Probably the whole terrestrial globe was once "one entire and perfect *icicle*."[8] Seriously,—to answer your questions;—there is nothing in the least *northern*, nothing that is not characteristically Brazillian, in the flora of the Organ mountains.[9] I did not myself ascend any of the peaks, but Gardner did, and made very rich collections, of which he has given an account in Sir W. Hooker's Journal, and more compendiously in his volume of Travels.[10] The vegetation consists of very curious dwarfish forms of those families and genera which are characteristic of *tropical* America, and especially of Brazil; together with representatives of some other groups which are widely diffused, but by no means *northern*. So also the vegetation of the table lands has many peculiar forms, but is composed mainly of under-shrubby and herbaceous species, of the same families and genera which in the forests appear as trees and tall climbers.[11]

Certainly, IF Brazil was ever covered with glaciers it seems to me certain that *the whole* of the tropical flora must have come into existence *since*. I also think it clear, on the same IF, that the absence of "glacial action" from Southern Europe must be due to some other cause than climate.[12]

Again, to answer your last question.— Brazil (I speak not merely of the small part which I saw, but of what I have read of, and I have read a good many books of travels in that country), seems to be very deficient in lakes, with the exception of lagoons ("broads" they would be called in Norfolk), on the coast; of these there are plenty, but they are evidently formed in the same way as the Norfolk broads, by the natural damming up of the outfall of the abundant waters. Where I travelled, in the higher lands of the interior, the running streams were absolutely innumerable, but scarcely so much as a permanent pond to be seen.[13]

Many thanks to dear Mary for her kind message.[14] With much love to her, believe me ever

Your affectionate friend | Charles J. F. Bunbury

I think Joseph Hooker will be as sceptical as myself about the *glaciation* of Brazil.[15]

F. J. Bunbury ed. 1891–3, *Later life* 1: 134–6.

[1] This letter was apparently sent by Lyell to CD (see the postscript to the letter to Charles Lyell, 7 February [1866]).

[2] Bunbury refers to Elizabeth Cabot Cary Agassiz and Mary Elizabeth Lyell. The letter has not been found, but an extract was apparently also sent to CD (see letter to Charles Lyell, 7 February [1866] and n. 2).

[3] Bunbury refers to Brazil, where Louis Agassiz was leading a scientific expedition; Agassiz planned to challenge CD's transmutation theory with the results of a survey of the fish of the Amazon river (see letter to Fritz Müller, 11 January 1866 and n. 10). At Pará (see n. 4, below), during a single week in 1865, Agassiz had identified sixty-three species of fish, a greater number than had previously been recorded in the Amazon basin as a whole (J. L. R. Agassiz and Agassiz 1868, p. 150). By the end of the expedition, Agassiz had identified about 1800 new species of fish (Marcou 1896, 2: 155).

[4] On the impact of railways, industrial engines, and steam navigation on Brazil in the latter part of the nineteenth century, see, for example, Dean 1995, pp. 204–10. Pará is a city in Brazil, near the mouth of the Amazon river; the Barra de Rio Negro is apparently the place where the Rio Negro joins the Amazon river near Manaus (*Columbia gazetteer of the world*, s.v. Rio Negro). The journey from Pará to Manaus could be made by steamer in five days in 1866, though Agassiz planned to allow longer for the journey, so that he could carry out scientific work (J. L. R. Agassiz and Agassiz 1868, p. 145; see also n. 6, below).

[5] Bunbury refers to Santarém, on the banks of the Tapajós river at its influx into the Amazon (*Columbia gazetteer of the world*); Richard Spruce made the 474-mile journey from Pará to Santarém between 10 October and 19 November 1849 (Spruce 1908, 1: 54–76).

[6] Henry Walter Bates and Alfred Russel Wallace undertook a joint expedition to the Amazon between 1848 and 1850 (A. R. Wallace 1853, Bates 1863). Spruce published numerous papers about his botanical expedition to the Amazon in the *Journal of Botany* between 1850 and 1855. Agassiz's expedition left Pará on 20 August 1865 and arrived at Manaus on 4 September (J. L. R. Agassiz and Agassiz 1868, pp. 143, 152–85).

[7] Evidently the letter from E. C. C. Agassiz to M. E. Lyell (see n. 2, above) had contained information on Louis Agassiz's observations of glacial action in Brazil. Before arriving in Brazil, Agassiz had lectured on the possibility that the Amazon basin had been formed by glacial action (J. L. R. Agassiz and

Agassiz 1868, p. 15). The evidence he subsequently reported of former glacial action in the Amazon basin is presented in J. L. R. Agassiz and Coutinho 1868. The accumulation of such evidence in the closing months of 1865 is reported in J. L. R. Agassiz and Agassiz 1868, pp. 69–70, 86–97, 99–101, 250. For more on Agassiz's controversial claims of former glaciation in Brazil, see Brice and Figueirôa 2001.

8 In the late 1830s, Agassiz had pioneered the concept of a former ice age that had affected part of the globe (see, for example, Lurie 1960, pp. 94–106). In 1840, Lyell and others came to accept Agassiz's glacial theory (see, for example, Lurie 1960, p. 100), although Lyell subsequently rejected Agassiz's views (Boylan 1998). Through his observations in the Amazon basin in 1865 and 1866, Agassiz sought to demonstrate that the entire earth had been frozen during the ice age (J. L. R. Agassiz and Agassiz 1868, pp. 399, 425; see also Brice and Figueirôa 2001, pp. 162–70). This represented a challenge to CD's transmutation theory by denying the possibility that plants and animals living after the ice age were the descendants of ones living before it (see, for example, Lurie 1960, pp. 353–4). It also challenged CD's theory of the geographical distribution of species, as presented in chapters 11 and 12 of *Origin*, in which CD argued that the tropics and the wider equatorial area had been a retreat for temperate species during the ice age (*Origin*, pp. 376–9). For an account of the development of glacial theory during the early to mid Victorian period, see Rudwick 1969 and Imbrie and Imbrie 1979, pp. 19–46.

9 The Serra dos Orgãos, or Organ Mountains, are a coastal range in central Rio de Janeiro state (*Columbia gazetteer of the world*). Lyell's evident interest in the 'northern' origin of species there apparently relates to CD's theory of geographical distribution and the retreat of temperate species to the equatorial region during the ice age (see n. 8, above). In 1841, Bunbury had communicated information on the flora of Brazil to the Linnean Society (*Proceedings of the Linnean Society of London* 1 (1849): 108–10).

10 Between 1842 and 1848, George Gardner contributed a number of papers on the flora of Brazil to the *London Journal of Botany*; these included Gardner 1843 and 1845, a detailed description of plants on the Organ mountains. The *London Journal of Botany* was edited by William Jackson Hooker between 1842 and 1848 (Allan 1967, p. 143). In Gardner's *Travels* (Gardner 1846a), the accounts of the flora of the Organ mountains are on pp. 40–6, 63–70, 527–31. A further account appeared in Gardner 1846b.

11 Species common to the pasture lands (described by Bunbury as tableland) at the foot of the Organ mountains and those of the adjacent virgin forests are enumerated in Gardner 1846b, p. 275–9. Bunbury visited the area in 1833 (F. J. Bunbury ed. 1891–3, *Early life*, p. 90).

12 Bunbury apparently considered that, if Agassiz's claims that there had been glaciers in Brazil were correct, it would follow that southern Europe had also been glaciated, even though the physical evidence was lacking. Various natural agents that could have destroyed such evidence in Europe had been considered by Lyell in letters written to Leonard Horner from Switzerland and Italy in 1857 (K. M. Lyell ed. 1881, 2: 249–72). Lyell later noted that evidence gathered in Europe and North America suggested that former glaciation had extended ten or more degrees further south in North America than in Europe (C. Lyell 1867–8, 1: 298).

13 See also F. J. Bunbury ed. 1891–3, *Early life*, pp. 84–100, 113–42.

14 Mary Elizabeth Lyell was the sister of Bunbury's wife, Frances Joanna Bunbury.

15 Bunbury refers to Joseph Dalton Hooker. See letter to Charles Lyell, 15 February [1866].

To F. W. Farrar 3 February [1866][1]

Down. | *Bromley.* | *Kent. S.E.*
Feb 3.

My dear Sir

I shall have real pleasure in signing your certificate if you can send it to me here, for I have not strength to go to London.[2] For the same reason I can be of little use in speaking to other members of the Royal Soc—which otherwise I sh[d] have had much pleasure in doing.

Do not be disappointed if you are not elected this year, for the number of applicants in all branches of science is great; & very many excellent men are not elected the first year.[3]

With my best wishes for your success | I remain my dear Sir | yours sincerely | Ch. Darwin

LS
National Library of Australia (MS 5907)

[1] The year is established by the relationship between this letter and the letter from F. W. Farrar, 5 February 1866.

[2] Farrar had asked CD to sign his certificate as a candidate for fellowship of the Royal Society of London (see letter from F. W. Farrar, 1 February [1866]).

[3] Farrar was one of fifteen new fellows, excluding foreign fellows, elected on 7 June 1866 (*Proceedings of the Royal Society of London* 15 (1866–7): 189).

From J. D. Hooker 4 February 1866

Kew
Feby 4 /66.

Dear Darwin

I hear nothing of your sister having hardly time to look at the papers.[1]

I now write in the vainest chance of you being able to help me to a medicine that may check vomiting— we have a most dear friend—at death's door from not being able to keep any food on the stomach. This is a daughter of my Indian friend Campbell, a young lady of some 20–22 who was for 8 years under my charge when her parents were in India.[2] She has been out of health for 4 or 5 years; lost her voice & otherwise suffered in chest & stomach— Some 6 months ago she had an eruption in fauces & mouth & now her stomach seems so affected that no food whatever lies on it; & she is we fear dying from exhaustion. Ice did good for a time, under Chapman,[3] & of course all the usual remedies have been tried— You may know of some unusual ones; if so—please write to

D[r]. Campbell
104 Lansdowne Road
Notting Hill
W

if not do not trouble.

I have no news except that D. of Somerset will send 2 large ships one to survey Corea, & the other Straits of Magellan, & asks me to look out for 2 naturalists, who shall be "high class men"—[4] This looks promising— I wish I could go! Do you know of any one?

Ever yr affec | J D Hooker

DAR 102: 57–8

CD ANNOTATIONS
1.1 I hear] *cross in margin, pencil*
3.2 Straits of Magellan] *cross in margin, pencil*
Top of letter: 'Report' *pencil*

1 CD wrote of the serious illness of his sister, Emily Catherine Langton, in his letter to Hooker of 21 [January 1866]. Notice of her death was printed in *The Times*, 6 February 1866, p. 1. The date of death is registered in Shrewsbury as 1 February 1866, although it was given as 2 February in *The Times*, and the *Darwin pedigree*, p. 11.

2 Archibald Campbell was superintendent of Darjeeling for the East India Company from 1840 until 1862 (Buchanan 1908, pp. 441–2). Campbell accompanied Hooker on his second Himalayan journey and was imprisoned with him by the Sikkim rajah in 1849 (J. D. Hooker 1854, 2: 202–38). Hooker apparently refers to Campbell's eldest daughter, Helen Maria, born at Darjeeling in 1842 (D. Campbell comp. 1925, p. 36).

3 The physician John Chapman advocated the application of ice to the spine especially for the treatment of seasickness and cholera (*DNB*). In 1865 Chapman had treated CD, whose symptoms included vomiting (see *Correspondence* vol. 13, letters to John Chapman, 16 May [1865] and 7 June 1865, and Appendix IV).

4 Edward Adolphus Seymour Seymour, twelfth duke of Somerset, was first lord of the Admiralty (*DNB*). It is likely that the proposed expedition to Korea was that on which Cuthbert Collingwood served as naturalist (see letter from Cuthbert Collingwood, 15 February 1866). That expedition covered many areas of the China Sea during 1866 and 1867, but did not ultimately reach Korea (see Collingwood 1868 and Day 1967, p. 84). On Hooker's recommendation, Robert Oliver Cunningham was appointed naturalist to the expedition in HMS *Nassau* to the Straits of Magellan, under the command of Richard Charles Mayne (Day 1967, p. 84). An account of the natural history of the voyage is given in Cunningham 1871. The printed dedications to Hooker in Collingwood 1868 and Cunningham 1871 express thanks for his assistance in facilitating the authors' voyages.

From A. R. Wallace 4 February 1866

9, St Mark's Crescent, | Regent's Park, N.W.
Feb. 4th. *1866*

My dear Darwin

I am very glad to hear you are a little better, & hope we shall soon have the pleasure of seeing your volume on "Variation under domestication".[1]

I do not see the difficulty you seem to feel about 2 or more female forms of one species.[2] The *most common* or *typical* female form must have certain characters or qualities which are sufficiently advantageous to it, to enable it to maintain its existence;—in general such as vary much from it, die out. But occasionally a variation may occur which has special advantageous characters of its own, (such as mimicking a protected species) & then this variation will maintain itself by selection.[3] In no less than 3 of my *polymorphic* species of Papilio, one of the female forms mimics the *Polydorus* group, which like the *Æneas* group in America seem to have some special protection. In two or three other cases one of the female forms is confined to a restricted locality to the conditions of which it is probably specially adapted. In other cases one of the female forms resembles *the male*, and perhaps receives a protection from the abundance of the males, in the crowd of which it is passed over.[4]

I think these considerations render the production of two or three forms of female very conceivable. The physiological difficulty is to me greater, of how each of two forms of female, produces offspring like the other female as well as like itself, but no intermediates.

If you "*know varieties that will not blend or intermix, but produce offspring quite like either parent*",—is not that the very physiological test of a species which is wanting for the *complete proof* of the "origin of species:"?[5]

I have by no means given up the idea of writing my travels, but I think I shall be able to do it better for the delay, as I can introduce chapters giving popular sketches of the subjects treated of in my various papers.[6]

I hope, if things go as I wish this summer, to begin work at it next winter.[7] But I feel myself incorrigibly lazy, & have no such system of collecting & arranging facts or of making the most of my materials, as you, & many of our hard working naturalists possess in perfection.

With best wishes | Believe me Dear Darwin | Yours most sincerely | Alfred R. Wallace

C. Darwin Esq.

DAR 106: B31–2

[1] In his letter to Wallace of 22 January 1866, CD noted that his health had improved to the extent that he was able to work one or two hours per day. *Variation* was published in 1868.

[2] After reading Wallace's report of three different forms of female in *Papilio memnon* (A. R. Wallace 1864b, p. 22), CD had expressed difficulty in understanding how two different forms of female could persist on one island (see letter to A. R. Wallace, 22 January 1866 and n. 4). Wallace later wrote a fuller explanation of how the different forms of female had arisen within the species (*ML* 1: 265–6, n. 3).

[3] By protected species, Wallace means species possessing 'some hidden means of protection' (A. R. Wallace 1864b, p. 21).

[4] See A. R. Wallace 1864b, pp. 24–7.

[5] The quotation is from the letter to A. R. Wallace, 22 January 1866, in which CD considered Wallace's criterion for distinguishing between varieties and dimorphic forms. For CD's example of the red cowslip as a new 'physiological' species, exhibiting a high degree of sterility when crossed with the common cowslip, and for Thomas Henry Huxley's origination of the term 'physiological species' as part of his appeal for proof of the theory of natural selection, see *Correspondence* vol. 12, letter to Asa Gray, 13 September [1864] and n. 13. See also T. H. Huxley 1863a, pp. 107–8.

[6] Wallace had travelled throughout the Malay Archipelago from 1854 until 1862, and had started 'a small book' about his travels by January 1864 (*Correspondence* vol. 12, letter from A. R. Wallace, 2 January 1864 and nn. 7 and 10). CD enquired about the book's progress in his letters to Wallace of 22 September [1865] (*Correspondence* vol. 13) and 22 January 1866. The two-volume narrative, *The Malay Archipelago*, was published in 1869 (A. R. Wallace 1869); in the preface, p. viii, Wallace explained, 'I could, indeed, at once have printed my notes and journals, leaving all reference to questions of natural history for a future work; but I felt that this would be as unsatisfactory to myself, as it would be disappointing to my friends, and uninstructive to the public.' Between 1862 and 1869, Wallace published over thirty papers based on his collections (A. R. Wallace 1869, 1: viii–xiv). For a bibliography of Wallace's work, see C. H. Smith ed. 1991, pp. 372–437.

[7] Wallace spent much of 1867 and 1868 writing A. R. Wallace 1869 (A. R. Wallace 1905, 1: 405–6). See also letter to A. R. Wallace, 22 January 1866 and n. 7.

From F. W. Farrar 5 February 1866

Harrow. | N.W.
Feb. 5. 1866.

My dear Sir,

Accept my grateful thanks for your kind & prompt reply to my bold request.[1] The certificate shall be sent to you, probably in a few days.[2] Among many others, Mr. Crawfurd, Prof. J. Clerk Maxwell, Prof. T. Hewitt Key, Gen[l] Sir A Scott Waugh (of the Indian Trigonometrical Survey), & Mr Evans will be supporters of my claim;[3] & as the names of gentlemen eminent in many *different* branches of science will be on my certificate, I have authority sufficient at least to justify my candidature if not to ensure my success.[4] One of my qualifications will be a steady endeavour to promote by every means in my power the study of science (& especially of botany) at our Public Schools. The little "Flora of Harrow" which I forward to you by post, & which is entirely the work of Harrow boys under my guidance & encouragement, will I hope be some proof of this fact.[5] Pray do not take the trouble to acknowledge its arrival.

If I should succeed I shall attribute my success far more to the influence of your great name than to any other circumstance.

Believe me, my dear Sir, | Sincerely and gratefully your's | Frederic W Farrar.

DAR 164: 37

[1] See letter to F. W. Farrar, 3 February [1866].

[2] CD had agreed to sign Farrar's certificate of candidature for election to fellowship of the Royal Society of London; see letter from F. W. Farrar, 1 February [1866], and letter to F. W. Farrar, 3 February [1866].

[3] John Crawfurd, James Clerk Maxwell, Thomas Hewitt Key, Andrew Scott Waugh, and John Evans were among the twenty fellows who signed Farrar's certificate (Royal Society of London, Certificates of election and candidature).

[4] Farrar was elected a fellow of the Royal Society on 7 June 1866 (*Proceedings of the Royal Society of London* 15 (1866–7): 189).

[5] Farrar was a master at Harrow, a boys' public school in Harrow-on-the-Hill, Middlesex (*DNB*). Farrar's preface to *The flora of Harrow* (Melvill 1864) refers to the schoolboys' botanical work.

To Frederick Ransome [6 February 1866][1]

[Down]

My dr Sir

I have been ill for a long time & have therefore not commun with you— Last Spring (in hope of forming a new Co[y]) you asked for delay in paying me the £100, which you promised as a final settlement of the loan of £250. I hope you are now prepared to pay it & finally settle the affair—[2] I trust the Companies is more prosperous than when you last wrote & I beg leave to remain

Adraft
DAR 96: 13

[1] The date is established by the relationship between this letter and the letter from Frederick Ransome, 7 February 1866.

[2] CD had purchased shares in Ransome's Patent Siliceous Stone Company in 1852, and had subsequently made several loans to Ransome; in March 1864, CD received a promissory note from Ransome for £100 (CD's Investment book (Down House MS)). In 1865, Ransome started another company, the Patent Concrete Stone Company, and asked CD to extend his loan another year. See *Correspondence* vol. 13, letters from Frederick Ransome, 6 March 1865 and 9 March 1865.

From James Shaw [6–10 February 1866][1]

To Dr Darwin | with Mr Shaw's Compl^s^

The Appreciation of Beauty by Animals.

At a meeting of the Natural History & Antiquarian Society held in Dumfries on Tuesday 6th. Feb. 1866 Mr Shaw of Tynron read a paper on the above topic. Sir W^m^. Jardine Bart of Applegirth in the Chair.[2]

Mr Shaw remarked the subject of beauty in animal and vegetable had, in an Essay by the Duke of Argyll, been called a theological one, not a natural-history one, and that his Grace had thrown it by way of a stumbling block in front of Dr Darwin's theory.[3] The writer had reason to believe that Dr Darwin was not likely to fall over this stumbling block but that he saw his way to at least a partial solution of the problem.

Mr Shaw then attempted to prove that in man from the most civilized to the most barbarous, from the infant to the man of grey hairs, tribute was paid to external loveliness, and that passion was so remarkable in the savage that a great modern thinker had suggested that ornament not comfort was at the origin of clothes.[4] At considerable length he adduced striking instances of taste, love of cleanliness, pleasure in personal decoration, courtesy towards their own image in mirror or picture, pride and ostentation, in some of the most lively and loving birds.

He then showed that in certain cases some birds, as the Australian Bower Bird, the Magpie, the Cornish chough, the Raven, the Daw &c went beyond themselves and out of their own species in their appreciation of beauty and their attempts to conserve it—their tastes being, as was to be expected, more similar to those of savages and apes & children in the objects of their selection than to those of civilized men.[5]

Having quoted Mr Montagu's observations concerning the manner in which singing birds attract towards them the females at the mating season by means of song, he repelled that naturalist's conclusion that the ear alone guided the female to its choice, since Nature at the pairing season was at as much pains to please the eye as to delight the ear.[6] He then asked if it was merely a coincidence or was it that beauty was attractive to the beautiful that humming-birds & butterflies were so often found hovering over flowers the rivals of themselves in gorgeousness.

Mr. Darwin thought these flowers might be decoys, by which their seed-sower was drawn to its task.[7]

Allusion was made to the intoxicating effect of light on insects, so like its effects on human babies and to the fact that it was among insects that the fire-flies are found. The fire-flies were attracted into the dwellings in St. Domingo by torches for the purpose of killing mosquitoes, and what more likely than that their own torches should be elements of sexual attraction & an animal having a little more gayety, a little more light, in its organization than its companions of the same species would thus draw more readily towards it a partner and by its beauty secure further perpetuity and extension of the charm. More than one observer has connected this living light with the attractions of sex.

The writer then remarked on the wonderful similarity of the construction of the eye and on the fact that although beauty in animal & vegetable was wide-spread—so in the kingdoms of animated nature was the seeing faculty, and doubtless other eyes, as well as human had preferences in the things that they saw.[8]

A conversation ensued.

Dr. Dickson[9] thought that this paper went to undermine Dr. Darwin's theory, as it exalted feebleness into a favoured condition by allowing beauty to be an element in the preservation of races or of individuals.

Dr. Grierson[10] thought that beauty and health went together—the beauty of a peach-cheek depended on the health of its possessor.

Mr. Shaw thought that Dr. Dickson misconceived Dr. Darwin's views if he was under the impression that they accounted only for the existence of the strongest. Take the illustration of the wolves, where adaptation, not strength was the favouring circumstance.[11]

The Chairman, Sir Wm. Jardine, said that more facts ought to be collected before forming such high conclusions.

In reply to a question Mr. Shaw said that it seemed to him that nature had placed its spangles and glowing colours just where they were most readily seen. Birds and some other beasts had got their crowns and their coronets, their breast-knots & shoulder-knots their trains and painted eyes and ornamented cheeks and ears like Kings and Queens. In cases where the animal ornaments were not patent at once powerful muscles were provided for erection and display.[12]

Memorandum
DAR 84.1: 14–17

CD ANNOTATION

1.1 The Appreciation of Beauty by Animals] *enclosed in square brackets, pencil*; '(Sexual Selection' *added below, pencil, square bracket in original MS*

[1] The date range is established by the date on which Shaw read his paper (see n. 2, below) and by CD's reply to Shaw of 11 February [1866].

[2] The text, which is handwritten, is that of a newspaper report of the paper Shaw read to the Dumfriesshire and Galloway Natural History and Antiquarian Society on 6 February 1866 (see R. Wallace ed. 1899, p. lvi); the newspaper in which it was published has not been identified. A fuller account of Shaw's paper later appeared in the *Transactions and Journal of the Proceedings of the Dumfriesshire and Galloway Natural History and Antiquarian Society* for the session 1864–5 (Shaw 1866a).

[3] Shaw's paper referred to 'The reign of law', by George Douglas Campbell, eighth duke of Argyll (G. D. Campbell 1865, pp. 229–31). Campbell accepted that the development of natural processes could be accounted for by CD's transmutation theory but maintained that their origination was under divine control; he also challenged CD's belief in the functional origin of beauty as expressed in, for example, *Orchids*, pp. 351–2 (G. D. Campbell 1862, pp. 394–5). For further discussion on the natural or divine origins of beauty, see *Correspondence* vol. 13, letter to Charles Lyell, 22 January [1865], and letter from James Shaw, 20 November 1865 and n. 7. For a commentary on the tensions between religion and science in CD's philosophy of nature, see Sloan 2001; for a Christian perspective on beauty as a product of the evolutionary process, see, for example, Haught 2000, pp. 126–37.

[4] Shaw refers to Thomas Carlyle and to *Sartor resartus* ([Carlyle] 1838). See also R. Wallace ed. 1899, p. lviii, and *Correspondence* vol. 13, letter from James Shaw, 20 November 1865.

[5] In the full published version (Shaw 1866a, see n. 2 above), Shaw suggested that an interest in shiny objects was common to Africans, children, and many other human groups.

[6] The writer refers to a passage on birdsong in Montagu 1831, pp. 475–80; George Montagu wrote that male songbirds did not in general search for females but attracted them by song (*ibid.*, p. 475). Montagu was later cited on this point by CD (*Descent* 2: 52 and n.). Montagu also wrote, 'we cannot suppose birds discriminate the colours . . . because some distinct species are so exactly alike that a mixture might take place' (Montagu 1831, p. 475).

[7] In Shaw 1866a, the flower of the bee orchis (or ophrys) is cited as CD's example of a decoy. However, the bee ophrys, *Ophrys apifera*, is frequently self-pollinated and rarely attracts insects (*Orchids*, pp. 63–72). Shaw was apparently mistaken in citing this example, although CD gave examples of various mechanisms by which many other species of orchid lured pollinators to their flowers (*Orchids*, pp. 346–60 and *passim*).

[8] CD discussed the development of the eye by natural selection in *Origin*, pp. 186–90.

[9] John Dickson was a co-founder and secretary of the Dumfriesshire and Galloway Natural History and Antiquarian Society (Gladstone 1913, pp. 9–10, 34).

[10] Thomas Boyle Grierson was a co-founder and vice-president of the Dumfriesshire and Galloway Natural History and Antiquarian Society (Gladstone 1913, p. 10).

[11] Shaw's reference was to *Origin*, pp. 90–1, where CD used the example of wolves to argue that different environments would lead to the selection of different adaptations and ultimately to the emergence of distinct varieties.

[12] Shaw's point about beauty in animals being prominently positioned, such as on the head, is developed further in Shaw 1866b. See also *Descent* 2: 71 and n.

To A. R. Wallace [6 February 1866][1]

Down Bromley SE
Tuesday

My dear Wallace

After I had despatched my last note, the simple explanation which you give had occurred to me, & seems satisfactory.[2]

I do not think you understand what I mean by the non-blending of certain varieties.[3] It does not refer to fertility; an instance will explain; I crossed the Painted

Lady & Purple sweet-peas, which are very differently coloured vars, & got, even out of the same pod, both varieties perfect but none intermediate.[4] Something of this kind I sh^{d}. think must occur at first with your butterflies & the 3 forms of Lythrum;[5] tho' these cases are in appearance so wonderful, I do not know that they are really more so than every female in the world producing *distinct* male & female offspring.

I am heartily glad that you mean to go on preparing your journal.[6]

Believe me yours | very sincerely | Ch. Darwin

LS(A)
British Library (Add 46434, f. 64)

[1] The date is established by the relationship between this letter and the letter from A. R. Wallace, 4 February 1866. In 1866, the first Tuesday after 4 February was 6 February.

[2] The reference is to the letter to A. R. Wallace, 22 January 1866, in which CD asked about the coexistence of different female forms in a Malayan species of butterfly (see letter to A. R. Wallace, 22 January 1866 and nn. 4–6). In his reply, Wallace emphasised that polymorphic forms of butterfly were consistent with natural selection, particularly when the survival of certain forms was secured by mimicry of protected species (see letter from A. R. Wallace, 4 February 1866).

[3] In his letter to Wallace of 22 January 1866, CD had mentioned that he knew of a good many varieties that would not blend or intermix; Wallace in his reply had asked whether such varieties were not new species (see letter from A. R. Wallace, 4 February 1866 and n. 5). For more on CD's examination of the relationship between hybrid sterility and the origination of new species, see *Origin*, chapter 8, and *Correspondence* vol. 10, Appendix VI.

[4] CD's results from crossing these two sweetpea varieties are described in *Variation* 2: 93–4 and *Cross and self fertilisation*, pp. 154–9. In those accounts, CD added that the early flowers resembling one or other parent were followed later in the season by others that were intermediate in colour between the parents. See also *Correspondence* vol. 8, letters to M. T. Masters, 7 April [1860] and 13 April [1860], and letter from William Masters, [after 7 April 1860]. For an interpretation of CD's experiment with sweetpeas and comparison with the work of Gregor Mendel, see Dawkins 2003. On CD's continuing interest in the cross-pollination of leguminous flowers, see *Correspondence* vol. 6, letters to *Gardeners' Chronicle*, [before 6 December 1856] and 18 October [1857], *Correspondence* vol. 7, letter to *Gardeners' Chronicle*, [before 13 November 1858] and this volume, letter to *Gardeners' Chronicle*, [before 11 August 1866].

[5] CD refers to A. R. Wallace 1864b and to 'Three forms of *Lythrum salicaria*'. In the exposition of his provisional hypothesis of pangenesis, CD wrote, 'With those animals and plants which habitually produce several forms, as with certain butterflies described by Mr. Wallace, in which three female forms and the male exist, or as with the trimorphic species of Lythrum and Oxalis, gemmules capable of reproducing several widely-different forms must be latent in each individual' (*Variation* 2: 399–400). Wallace's work on dimorphic butterflies had been likened to CD's on dimorphism in *Linum* and *Primula*, owing to the lack of intermediate offspring (*Reader*, 16 April 1864, pp. 491–3).

[6] See letter from A. R. Wallace, 4 February 1866 and n. 7.

To Charles Lyell 7 February [1866][1]

Down
Feb 7.

My dear Lyell

I am very much obliged for your note & the extract which have interested me extremely.[2] I cannot disbelieve for a moment Agassiz on Glacial action after all his experience, as you say, & after that capital book with plates which he early published;[3] as for his inferences & reasoning on the valley of the Amazon that is quite another question; nor can he have seen all the regions to which Mrs A. alludes.[4]

Her letter is not very clear to me & I do not understand what she means by "to a height of more than 3000 ft".[5] There are no erratic boulders (to which I particularly attended) in the low country round Rio. It is possible or even probable that this area may have subsided; for I c^d^ detect no evidence of elevation or any tertiary formations or volcanic action.[6]

The Organ M^ts^. are from 6000 to 7000 ft in height & I am only a little surprized at their bearing the marks of glacial action.[7] For some temperate genera of plants viz Vaccineum, Andromeda, Gaultheria, Hypericum, Drosera, Habenaria, inhabit these M^ts^. & I look at this almost as good evidence of a cold period as Glacial action.[8] That there are not more temperate plants can be accounted for by the isolated position of these Mountains.

There are no erratic boulders on the Pacific coast North of Chiloe & but few glaciers in the Cordillera; but it by no means follows I think that there may not have been formerly gigantic glaciers on the Eastern & *more humid* side.[9]

In the 3rd Ed. of the Origin p 403, you will find a brief allusion, on authority of Mr D. Forbes, on the former much lower extension of glaciers in the equatorial Cordillera.[10] Pray also look at p 407 at what I say on the nature of Tropical vegetation (which I could now much improve) during the glacial period.[11] I feel a strong conviction that soon every one will believe that the whole world was cooler during the glacial period.[12]

Remember Hooker's wonderful case recently discovered of the identity of so many temperate plants on the summit of Fernando Po & on the M^ts^. of Abyssynia:[13] I look at as certain that these plants crossed the whole of Africa from E. to W. during this same period. I wish I had published a long chapter written in full & almost ready for the press on this subject which I wrote ten years ago.[14] It was impossible in the Origin to give a fair abstract.[15]

My health is considerably improved, so that I am able to work nearly 2 hours a day & so make some little progress with my everlasting book on domestic varieties.[16]

You will have heard of my sister Catherine's easy death last Friday morning.[17] She suffered much, & we all look at her death as a blessing for there was much fear of prolonged & greater suffering. We are uneasy about Susan, but she has hitherto borne it better than we c^d^ have hoped.[18]

Emma joins me in love to Lady Lyell[19] & believe me dear Lyell | yours affectionately | Charles Darwin

Remember glacial action of Lebanon, when you speak of no glacial action in S. & on Himalaya & in S.E. Australia.—[20]

P.S. I have been very glad to see Sir C. Bunbury's letter.[21] If the genera which I name from Gardner are not considered by him, as usually temperate forms, I am of course silenced;[22] but Hooker looked over the M.S chapter some ten years ago & did not score out my remarks on them,[23] & he is generally ready enough to pitch into my ignorance, & snub me as I often deserve.— My wonder was how any, even so few, temperate forms reached the mountains of Brazil; & I supposed they travelled by the rather high land & ranges (name forgotten) which stretch from the Cordillera towards Brazil— Cordillera genera of Plants have, also, somehow reached the Silla of Caraccas.[24]

When I think of the vegetation of N. Zealand & W. coast of S. America, where glaciers now descend to, or very near, to the sea, I feel it rash to conclude that **all** Tropical forms w^{d} be destroyed by a considerably cooler period under the Equator.—[25]

LS(A)
American Philosophical Society (312)

1 The year is established by the reference to the death of Emily Catherine Langton (Catherine; see n. 17, below).

2 The letter from Lyell has not been found; the extract was probably part of a letter from Elizabeth Cabot Cary Agassiz to Mary Elizabeth Lyell, describing the progress of Louis Agassiz's expedition to Brazil (see n. 4, below, and letter from C. J. F. Bunbury to Charles Lyell, 3 February 1866 and n. 2).

3 CD refers to J. L. R. Agassiz 1840b; Louis Agassiz was among the first to formulate a theory of ancient glaciation (see, for example, Imbrie and Imbrie 1979, pp. 30–1): CD read J. L. R. Agassiz 1840b and expressed his admiration of it in his letter to Louis Agassiz, 1 March [1841] (*Correspondence* vol. 2).

4 Agassiz's view that glacial action had created the valley of the Amazon was apparently conveyed in the letter from E. C. C. Agassiz to M. E. Lyell (see n. 2, above). For more on Agassiz's interest in former glacial action in South America and its implications, see the letter from C. J. F. Bunbury to Charles Lyell, 3 February 1866 and nn. 7 and 8. For a narrative of Agassiz's Brazilian expedition, and its scientific findings, see J. L. R. Agassiz and Agassiz 1868. In the tenth edition of *Principles of geology* (C. Lyell 1867–8, 1: 468–9), Lyell said that Agassiz had failed to discover proofs of former glaciation in the Amazon basin.

5 Elizabeth Agassiz apparently referred to the altitude of certain features around Rio de Janeiro in her letter (see n. 2, above), but see also n. 7, below. See also the letter from C. J. F. Bunbury to Charles Lyell, 20 February 1866 and n. 9.

6 CD had explored the area around Rio de Janeiro, Brazil, in 1832 while on the *Beagle* voyage (*Journal of researches*, pp. 21–43). CD wrote that erratic boulders were not found on the intertropical plains of South America, including the valley of the Amazon (*ibid.*, pp. 288–9). However, Agassiz claimed to have found drift and erratic boulders on the sides of the valley at Tijuca, near Rio (Hartt 1870, pp. 27–30; see also J. L. R. Agassiz and Agassiz 1868, pp. 399–401). Agassiz also noted that, while elevation was consistent with the physical geography of certain parts of the Brazilian coast, the Amazon basin appeared to have subsided and showed no evidence of deposits of marine origin (J. L. R. Agassiz 1866b, pp. 450–3).

7 The Serra dos Orgãos, or Organ Mountains, are a coastal range in central Rio de Janeiro state; the highest peaks just exceed 7000 ft (*Columbia gazetteer of the world*), although Agassiz estimated their height at between 2000 and 3000 ft (J. L. R. Agassiz and Agassiz 1868, pp. 46, 69). Agassiz's description of the Organ Mountains, including reference to 'glacial phenomena', is given in J. L. R. Agassiz and Agassiz 1868, pp. 492–3, and Hartt 1870, pp. 15–18. CD referred to these mountains in the fourth and later editions of *Origin* (for example, *Origin* 4th ed., pp. 444–5); only in the fourth edition did he mention Agassiz's reported discovery of marks of glacial action.

8 CD believed that temperate plants retreated to mountains in the tropics at the end of a former ice age, as warmer temperatures returned (see also letter from C. J. F. Bunbury to Charles Lyell,

3 February 1866 and nn. 8 and 9). George Gardner had recorded the presence of *Andromeda*, *Drosera*, *Gaultheria*, *Habenaria*, *Hypericum*, and *Vaccinium* in the Organ Mountains (Gardner 1846b, pp. 281–4).

9 CD gave an account of the glaciers of South America in *Journal of researches*, pp. 279–90, and speculated on the relationship between former climate and the range of certain tender plant species in that continent (*ibid.*, pp. 268–71, 291).

10 In *Origin* 3d ed., pp. 403–4, CD wrote:

> Mr. D. Forbes . . . informs me that he found in the Cordillera, from lat. 13° to 30° S., at about the height of 12,000 feet, strongly-furrowed rocks, resembling those with which he was familiar in Norway, and likewise great masses of detritus, including grooved pebbles.

See also *Correspondence* vol. 13, Supplement, letter to David Forbes, 11 December [1860] and n. 8, and *Correspondence* vol. 8, letter from David Forbes, [November? 1860] (now redated to [after 11 December 1860]).

11 In *Origin* 3d ed., p. 407, CD wrote:

> As the cold came slowly on, all the tropical plants and other productions will have retreated from both sides towards the equator. . . . The tropical plants probably suffered much extinction; how much no one can say; perhaps formerly the tropics supported as many species as we see at the present day crowded together at the Cape of Good Hope, and in parts of temperate Australia. . . . But the great fact to bear in mind is, that all tropical productions will have suffered to a certain extent.

12 CD's belief that the non-glaciated parts of the earth experienced a cooler climate during the glacial period is expressed in *Origin*, pp. 369–80 (see also, for example, *Correspondence* vol. 6, letter to Charles Lyell, 8 July [1856], and *Correspondence* vol. 11, letter to J. D. Hooker, 26 [March 1863]). Lyell, however, believed that the earth was formerly hotter (Fleming 1998, p. 163) and resisted arguments in favour of a glacial period (Boylan 1998). Later, CD modified his views on geographical distribution to allow for former periods of warmer climate during glaciation in alternate hemispheres (*Origin* 5th ed., pp. 451–9). For more on contemporary publications that influenced CD's position on former climate change, see the letter to J. D. Hooker, [28 February 1866] and n. 7.

13 CD refers to J. D. Hooker 1861; CD's annotated copy is in his collection of unbound journals in the Darwin Library–CUL. Abyssinia is now Ethiopia; Fernando Po, an island off the coast of West Africa in the Gulf of Guinea, is now known as Bioko (*Columbia gazetteer of the world*). Joseph Dalton Hooker concluded that a close relationship existed between the temperate flora of Fernando Po, growing above 5000 feet on Clarence Peak, and that of Abyssinia, situated 1800 miles away on the other side of the continent.

14 CD refers to the chapter 'Geographical distribution' in his 'big book' on species (*Natural selection*, pp. 534–66). In that chapter, CD had also proposed that plants migrated during a recent ice age from Abyssinia to Cape Province (now part of the Republic of South Africa), that is from north-east to south-west Africa (*ibid.*, pp. 551–2). See also n. 13, above.

15 Chapters 11 and 12 of *Origin*, pp. 346–410, were devoted to geographical distribution. In chapter 11, CD considered dispersal during the glacial period and mentioned the occurrence on mountains in Abyssinia of species otherwise found in Europe or the Cape of Good Hope (now part of the Republic of South Africa) (*Origin*, p. 375).

16 CD refers to *Variation*. On CD's health and his resumption of work on *Variation*, see the letter to H. B. Jones, 3 January [1866] and n. 5.

17 The date of death of CD's younger sister, Catherine, was registered as Thursday 1 February 1866 (see also letter from J. D. Hooker, 4 February 1866 and n. 1).

18 Susan Elizabeth Darwin, CD's sister, had suffered distress and loneliness during Catherine's final illness (see letter from E. C. Langton to Emma and Charles Darwin, [6 and 7? January 1866]).

19 Mary Elizabeth Lyell.

20 For Hooker's report of former glacial action on the mountains of Lebanon, see *Correspondence* vol. 8, letter to T. H. Huxley, 1 November [1860] and n. 4; see also J. D. Hooker 1862, pp. 12 and 17. CD's

lightly annotated copy of J. D. Hooker 1862 is in his unbound journals in the Darwin Library–CUL. CD added Hooker's information on Lebanese glaciation to *Origin* 4th ed., p. 442 (see also Peckham ed. 1959, pp. 591–2). CD referred to former glaciation in the Himalayas and south-east Australia in *Origin*, p. 373 (see also *Correspondence* vol. 7, letter from J. D. Hooker, 25 January 1859 and n. 9). The evidence for glaciation in Australia was provided by William Branwhite Clarke, though it was not attributed to him by name (see *Correspondence* vol. 9, letter from W. B. Clarke, [August 1861] and nn. 4 and 5); an attribution of the information to Clarke was added in the fourth and later editions of *Origin* (*Origin* 4th ed., p. 443).

21 The reference is apparently to the letter from C. J. F. Bunbury to Charles Lyell, 3 February 1866.

22 In his letter to Lyell (see n. 21, above), Charles James Fox Bunbury maintained that the flora of the Organ mountains was Brazilian rather than northern in character. CD refers here to the temperate genera listed in the third paragraph of the present letter. See also n. 8, above. These genera were cited by CD in *Natural selection*, p. 551 (see also *Origin*, p. 374).

23 Hooker had commented on the manuscript of *Natural selection*, without criticising CD's use, on page 551, of Gardner's information to argue that 'Those few temperate forms which were able to penetrate the lowlands of Tropical America during the Glacial epoch, would be most of all modified, & when the climate again became hot, could only survive on high land' (see *Correspondence* vol. 6, letter from J. D. Hooker, 9 November 1856 and n. 2). CD argued similarly in *Origin*, pp. 378–9.

24 For CD, the Cordillera included all the mountain ranges that run parallel to the west coast of South America (see *Journal of researches*, p. 237). Silla de Caracas is a mountain in the coastal range near Caracas, Venezuela, close to the Caribbean Sea (*Columbia gazetteer of the world*). Citing information from the German naturalist Alexander von Humboldt, CD wrote of plant species that are found both on the Silla de Caracas and in the lower latitudes of the Cordillera in *Natural selection*, p. 551; see also *Origin*, pp. 374–5. This information came from Humboldt and Bonpland 1822, pp. 491–9, CD's annotated copy of which is in the Darwin Library–CUL (see *Marginalia* 1: 417).

25 Examples of South American glaciers descending to the sea in the proximity of tropical vegetation are given in *Journal of researches*, pp. 282–7. For Julius von Haast's evidence of subtropical vegetation growing beside a glacier near the New Zealand coast, see J. F. J. von Haast 1864; see also *Correspondence* vol. 12, letter from J. D. Hooker, 15 June 1864 and n. 10. CD marked Haast's observation of this phenomenon in his unbound copy of J. F. J. von Haast 1864, p. 475, which is in the Darwin Library–CUL.

From Frederick Ransome 7 February 1866

Rushmere Lodge | Norwood Lane
Feby 7th/66

My dear Sir

I am duly in recᵗ. of your favour of yesterdays date—[1] I had intended running over to Down to see you personally on the subject of your communication—but the death of another near relative prevented my doing so—

I am most unwilling to trespass longer upon your kind indulgence but under present circumstances I am compelled to ask you to allow the payment of the principal sum to be postponed a short time longer and allow me to pay you Interest thereon—

You will see by the enclosed circular,[2] the very satisfactory way in which my Invention is gaining ground with the public and we have just taken the premises alluded to and are about immediately to commence the erection of important works—for which upwards of *£16.000* have already been subscribed but in order to secure this desireable result I have been compelled to accept shares and debentures to a large amount—and it would be extremely detrimental to the Interests of our Company were I at the present moment to attempt to dispose of them in the open market—[3]

I think you will agree with me that the names of M^r. Bessemer[4] and so many of his personal friends—are a guarantee for the high estimate formed of the value of our property but pending the development up to a point at which I can receive dividend upon the large Stake I hold—my Income is so limited—that it is difficult for me to spare even £100 without disposing of some of my Shares—which at the present time would be extremely undesireable—

Will you kindly consent to hold the Acc^e. a little longer allowing me to pay Int^t thereon until I can more conveniently redeem it? and upon hearing from you to this effect I will immediately send you Cheque for Interest to present time.

Believe me my dear Sir | very faithfully yours | Fred^k. Ransome

C. Darwin Esq

DAR 99: 26–7

1 Letter to Frederick Ransome, [6 February 1866].
2 The circular has not been found.
3 Ransome had invented an artificial sandstone in 1848 (*Modern English biography*). He was patentee and general manager of the Patent Concrete Stone Company (*Post Office London directory* 1866). The company did not go into full production until 1867 (*Engineering*, 28 June 1867, pp. 671–2).
4 Henry Bessemer had invested in Ransome's company, which was located next to Bessemer's new steel works in East Greenwich, London (*Engineering*, 28 June 1867, pp. 671–2).

From Lionel Smith Beale 9 February 1866

61 Grosvenor Sq
Feby 9th 1866

My dear Sir

I send you the numbers you wish to see— Please keep them as long as you like & then let me have them back—[1]

I fear the notion will hardly be intelligible without what has preceded I enclose a list of the journals in which other papers were printed but the whole will be republished[2]—though I fear not for some time as I have much work of another kind to get through—[3]

If you should be in London with an evening to spare I should be glad to tell you my conclusions & the facts on which they rest in few words or if you are disengaged some Sunday afternoon I would come down to you with pleasure if you will allow me—[4]

It is useless asking you to *read* what I have written as there is very much & distributed in many difft journals

Yours Faithfully | Lionel S Beale

DAR 160: 101

[1] The reference is apparently to numbers of an unidentified periodical containing articles by Beale, who wrote on medicine and microscopy (see *Royal Society catalogue of scientific papers*). During 1865, Beale had published a number of articles on cell biology, based on his examination of their microscopic constituents. Of these, 'An inquiry into the nature of the phenomena which constitute "inflammation": two lectures delivered at the Royal College of Physicians' was serialised in the *Medical Times and Gazette* (1865), pt 1: 593–4, 619–21, 645–6, pt 2: 135–6, 191–3, 273–4, 329–31. CD ordered a copy of the second lecture (see this volume, letter to Williams & Norgate, 10 February [1866]); CD referred to it in *Variation* 2: 378.

[2] The list has not been found (but see *Royal Society catalogue of scientific papers*). In *Variation* 2: 370, CD cited Beale's notion of 'germinal matter' and 'formed material' from his *On the structure and growth of tissues and of life* (Beale 1865, pp. 21–63). CD's annotated copy of Beale 1865 is in the Darwin Library–CUL (see *Marginalia* 1: 37–8). The endpaper bears CD's annotation 'Used for pangenesis and of no other use'. See also *Variation* 2: 382. In the *Medical Times and Gazette* (1865) pt 2: 331, the intention to print further papers on inflammation was announced although none of the titles of Beale's subsequent papers in the journal specified that subject.

[3] In 1866, Beale was working on Todd *et al.* 1866, a new edition of a work by Robert Bentley Todd and William Bowman. The first volume of the work appeared in or after June 1866; *Archives of Medicine*, an annual publication of which Beale was founder and editor, did not appear in 1866. For Beale's other activities, see *DSB*.

[4] No record of a meeting between CD and Beale has been found in the Darwin Archive–CUL.

To *Gardeners' Chronicle* [before 10 February 1866][1]

Will any of your botanical readers have the kindness to inform me, whether in those monœcious or diœcious plants, in which the flowers are widely different, it has ever been observed that half the flower, or only a segment of it, has been of one sex and the other half or segment of the opposite sex;[2] in the same manner as so frequently occurs with insects?[3]

Charles Darwin

Gardeners' Chronicle and Agricultural Gazette, 10 February 1866, p. 127

[1] The letter was published in the *Gardeners' Chronicle* on 10 February 1866 under the heading 'Partial change of sex in unisexual flowers'. See also *Collected papers* 2: 130–1. Apparently, the editors' note was the only reply to this letter (see n. 2, below).

[2] CD refers to plants with unisexual male and female flowers that are borne separately, on the same (monoecious) plant or on distinct (dioecious) plants. Under the printed letter, the editors noted their observation of willow flowers with one stamen and a stalked carpel, and cited instances of anthers developing from an ovary in members of the Euphorbiaceae. The sole reference to the variable development of the male and female parts of unisexual flowers in *Variation* is the mention of John Scott's observations in maize (*Variation* 1: 321; see also *Correspondence* vol. 12, letter from John Scott, 12 [February 1864] and n. 8, and Scott 1863). For examples of CD's early interest in transitional states between hermaphroditism and unisexuality in plants and animals, see *Notebooks*, Notebook C, 167; Notebook D, 157–9. CD later devoted a chapter to the subject in *Forms of flowers* (pp. 278–309).

[3] Gynandromorphy, that is, the occurrence of male and female characters in the same individual, is illustrated by a beetle and some moths in Westwood 1831, of which there is a copy in the Darwin

Library–CUL. Westwood 1831 contains references to further papers on gynandromorphy in insects from the first volume of the *Zoological Journal* and the fifteenth volume of the *Transactions of the Linnean Society of London*, both of which CD had read earlier (see 'CD's reading notebooks', *Correspondence* vol. 4, Appendix IV). CD alluded to half-male and half-female insects in earlier discussions of the possibility that flowers are fundamentally bilateral (see *Correspondence* vol. 4, letter to J. D. Hooker, [2 June 1847] and n. 4). In *Variation* 2: 400, he considered insects in which exactly one half or one quarter of the body resembled the male, and the other half or three quarters the female, as examples of the latency of characters.

From H. B. Jones 10 February [1866]

Royal Institution of Great Britain

My dear Mr Darwin

I wish I had got over your flatulence; but it is not easy & your progress must be slow.[1] However you have done famously so far; and a good change in May abroad or at home ought to do you great good.[2] I wish you could get a rough pony & be shaken once daily to make the chemistry go on better[3] I think the mineral acid sh^d^ be continued & take a dose of the Potass-ammonia when the flatulence is worst[4]

If you are on a good diet & change it for a worse one in a fortnight I do not see the wisdom of the change[5] I send you a model diet with the Exception of a potatoe which is intended to tempt you.[6]

It should be baked in the oven & made so that it crumbles with the pressure of a fork

I am very glad to hear that you were able to work a little

Y^rs^ most truly | H Bence Jones

Feb 10

Endorsement: '(Feb. 10th 1866.) | Diet Table'
DAR 168: 77

1 In his letter to Jones of 3 January [1866], CD had complained of continuing flatulence while noting the beneficial effect of coffee on the condition. As the present letter lacks direct replies to CD's observation about oxide of iron and question about taking coffee in his letter of 3 January [1866], it is likely that Jones's reply to that letter, and a further letter from CD, are missing.

2 CD went to stay with his brother, Erasmus Alvey Darwin, from 21 April until 2 May 1866; on 29 May, CD went to Leith Hill Place, Surrey, returning to Down on 2 June (CD's 'Journal', Appendix II). Leith Hill Place was the home of Emma Darwin's brother, Josiah Wedgwood III (Freeman 1978).

3 CD began riding the cob, Tommy, on 4 June 1866 (Freeman 1978, p. 276; Emma Darwin's diary (DAR 242)).

4 In the letter to H. B. Jones, 3 January [1866], CD reported that taking muriatic acid with cayenne pepper and ginger suited him '*excellently*'. Mineral acid is a generic term for inorganic acids, including hydrochloric (formerly muriatic) acid (*OED*). On the use of acids in the treatment of stomach disorders, see Ringer 1869, pp. 80–2. 'Potass-ammonia' probably refers to a chalk-potash and ammonia remedy for acidity (see *Correspondence* vol. 12, letter from William Jenner, [after 24 November] 1864 and n. 3).

5 In the letter to H. B. Jones, 3 January [1866], CD wrote of various alterations to his diet.

6 The enclosure has not been found.

From Frederick Ransome 10 February 1866

Rushmere Lodge
Feby 10/66

My dear Sir

I beg to thank you most sincerely for the kind expressions contained in your's of the 8th Inst. and for the consideration you have manifested for my convenience—[1]

I now enclose cheque £5 in payment of Interest for the past year receipt of which kindly acknowledge & oblige[2]

My dear Sir | Yours very faithfy | Fredk. Ransome

Chas. Darwin Esqre—

DAR 99: 21

[1] CD's letter of 8 February 1866 has not been found. See, however, letter to Frederick Ransome, [6 February 1866] and n. 2, and letter from Frederick Ransome, 7 February 1866.

[2] The last entry relating to Ransome's company in CD's Investment book (Down House MS) is dated 2 March 1866, and records a payment of £5 for one year's interest on a loan.

To Williams & Norgate[1] 10 February [1866][2]

Down. | Bromley. | Kent. S.E.
Feb. 10th

Dear Sir

Please get for me & send to "care of G. Snow Nag's Head,"[3] Owens Anatomy of Vertebrates.—[4]

I will take in for present year the Annals & Mag. of Nat. Hist,[5] & it may be sent by post monthly or bimonthly or with the Poultry Book.—[6]

Please & try & procure for me & send **soon by Post**, the 3 following numbers of the "Medical Times & Gazette", viz

for August 19th. 1865
—Sept. 9th. do
Sept 23rd. do[7]

Dear Sir | Yours faithfully | C. Darwin

It is a great misfor. that the Nat. Hist. Revw. has ceased.—[8]

Fitzwilliam Museum, Cambridge

[1] The recipient is identified by the references to works published or sold by Williams & Norgate (see nn. 4–6 and 8, below).

[2] The year is established by the date publication of the *Natural History Review* ceased; see n. 8, below.

[3] The carrier service between Down and London, operated weekly by George Snow, returned from the Nag's Head public house in Borough High Street, London (*Post Office London directory* 1866, and Freeman 1978, p. 261).

[4] The first of the three volumes of *On the anatomy of vertebrates* (Owen 1866–8) was published on 14 December 1865, bearing the date 1866 on the title page; the second volume was scheduled to appear

on 1 March 1866 (*Reader* 6 (1865): 655). The third volume did not appear until 1868. There are annotated copies of all three volumes in the Darwin Library–CUL (*Marginalia* 1: 645–8). The work was published by Longmans, Green, and Co., with whom Williams & Norgate had a collaborative relationship (see, for example, *Correspondence* vol. 13, letter to J. D. Hooker, [29 July 1865], n. 19; Freeman 1977, pp. 116–17).

5 CD's annotated set of the *Annals and Magazine of Natural History* is in the Darwin Library–CUL and runs from 1838 to 1855 inclusive, and from 1865 to 1873 inclusive. CD may have stopped subscribing between 1856 and 1864 (see also *Correspondence* vol. 8, letter to John Lubbock, [18 November 1860]). From 1866, the journal was published by Longmans, Green, Reader, and Dyer, successor to Longmans, Green, and Co (see n. 4, above; *Post Office London directory* 1865 and 1866). The covers of several unbound parts in CD's set bear Williams & Norgate's trade label.

6 *The poultry book* (Tegetmeier 1867) was published monthly from January 1866. There is an annotated copy of the unbound set of the fifteen published parts in the Darwin Library–CUL (see *Marginalia* 1: 500–3); the covers of several of the parts bear Williams & Norgate's trade label.

7 These numbers contained the second of a pair of lectures on inflammation by Lionel Smith Beale (see letter from L. S. Beale, 9 February 1866 and n. 1).

8 Williams & Norgate were the publishers of the quarterly *Natural History Review*; CD subscribed to the new series of the journal from its appearance in 1861. The final part of its fifth and last volume appeared in October 1865 (see also *Correspondence* vol. 13, letter from J. D. Hooker, 13 July 1865 and n. 28).

To James Shaw 11 February [1866][1]

Down, Bromley,
11th Feb.

Dear Sir,—

I am much obliged to you for your kindness in sending me an abstract of your paper on beauty.[2] In my opinion you take quite a correct view of the subject. It is clear that Dr. Dickson has either never seen my book, or overlooked the discussion on sexual selection.[3] If you have any precise facts on birds' 'courtesy towards their own image in mirror or picture' I should very much like to hear them.[4] Butterflies offer an excellent instance of beauty being displayed in conspicuous parts; for those kinds which habitually display the underside of the wing have this side gaudily coloured, and this is not so in the reverse case.[5] I daresay you will know that the males of many foreign butterflies are much more brilliantly coloured than the females, as in the case of birds.[6] I can adduce good evidence from two large classes of facts (too large to specify), that flowers have become beautiful to make them conspicuous to insects.[7]

With my best thanks for your kindness and clear exposition of my views, I remain, etc., | Ch. Darwin.

Copy
R. Wallace ed. 1899, pp. lvi–lvii

1 The year is established by the relationship between this letter and the letter from James Shaw, 14 February 1866.

[2] See memorandum from James Shaw, [6–10 February 1866] and n. 2.

[3] For John Dickson's interpretation of Shaw's paper as a challenge to CD's transmutation theory, and for Shaw's response, see the memorandum from James Shaw, [6–10 February 1866]. CD discussed sexual selection in *Origin*, pp. 87–90.

[4] See memorandum from James Shaw, [6–10 February 1866].

[5] CD later discussed this point in more detail in *Descent* 1: 396–7, citing A. R. Wallace 1864b.

[6] Henry Walter Bates emphasised that the colours of butterflies were generally more beautiful in males than in females, and noted that 'handsome' butterflies were more numerous in tropical than in temperate zones (Bates 1863, 1: 20 1). There is an annotated copy of Bates 1863 in the Darwin Library–CUL, in which CD scored and underlined text containing this information (see *Marginalia* 1: 35–6). CD also received letters from Bates with information about colour in relation to sexual selection in butterflies (*Correspondence* vol. 9, letters from H. W. Bates, 28 March 1861 and [1 December] 1861). Later, CD wrote that colour differences between male and female butterflies were due to sexual selection acting on males, whereas females retained 'primordial or very ancient' colouring (*Descent* 1: 419). For more on beauty in birds, and the differing views of CD and George Douglas Campbell, eighth duke of Argyll, on the subject, see *Correspondence* vol. 13, letter to Charles Lyell, 22 January [1865] and nn. 5–7.

[7] See *Origin* 4th ed., p. 239; see also memorandum from James Shaw, [6–10 February 1866] and n. 7.

From Fritz Müller[1] 13 February 1866

Desterro,
13. Februar 1866.

Verehrter Herr!

Ich empfing Ihre freundlichen Briefe vom 17. October und vom 9. Dezember und auch Ihr "Journal of Researches", wofür ich Ihnen noch meinen aufrichtigen Dank sagen darf.[2] Ich lese das Buch jetzt mit ausserordentlichem Interesse.

Sie bemerken (S. 30), dass bei all den verschiedenen Arten von leuchtenden Thieren, welche Sie beobachtet haben, das Licht von deutlich grüner Farbe gewesen ist.[3] Ich habe dieselbe Beobachtung gemacht bei Seethieren (Renilla, Noctiluca, Beroë u. s. w.), aber bei den Insecten giebt es einige Ausnahmen. Die verschiedenen Arten von leuchtenden Elateren, welche ich gesehen habe, besitzen ausser den beiden Lichtern am Thorax noch einen leuchtenden Fleck an der Bauchseite des ersten Hinterleibsegments; wenn das Insect in Ruhe ist oder umherkriecht, so ist dieser Fleck nicht sichtbar; er wird aber sichtbar, sobald der Hinterleib in die Höhe gebogen wird oder wenn der Elater fliegt. Das Licht dieses Flecks ist sogar heller als das der beiden anderen und von gelber Farbe, sehr verschieden von dem grünlichen Licht der Thorax-Flecken.

. . . . . Eine kleine Art von Elater hat zwei leuchtende Punkte mehr, welche wie diejenige der Glühwürmer an dem hinteren Theil des Abdomen gelegen sind. Ungefähr vor 12 Jahren fand ich in dem Urwalde am Itajahy-Fluss[4] eine sehr merkwürdige leuchtende Käferlarve, welche leuchtende Flecke an allen ihren Leibesringeln hatte; einige von diesen Flecken (wenn ich mich recht entsinne, diejenigen des Vorderendes) waren von leuchtendem Roth, einige waren gelb, und der grösste Theil grün. Die Larve konnte alle oder auch einige von ihren leuchtenden Flecken verdunkeln; wenn sie gereizt wurde, so strahlten alle ein prächtiges Licht aus.[5] Die Larve scheint sehr selten zu sein; mein Bruder, der am Itajahy seit 1852 lebt,[6] hat sie nur ein einziges Mal gefunden.

Es ist mir sehr schmeichelhaft, dass Sie meine Bemerkungen über Kletterpflanzen für werth gehalten haben, der Linnaean Soc. vorgelegt zu werden.[7]

. . . . . Im letzten Monat habe ich drei Wochen zu einer Reise nach dem Itajahy-Fluss verwendet, wo ich mich wiederum an der Pracht unserer Urwälder erfreute. Ich sah mich nach Kletterpflanzen um; aber ich habe nur einen einzigen Fall von einer Pflanze bemerkt, welche einen dicken Stamm erkletterte (ungefähr 5 Fuss im Umfang); nach dem Bau des Holzes und dem bitteren Geschmack glaube ich, dass es eine Menispermee war; sie hatte ungefähr 3 Zoll Durchmesser und kletterte in einer lockeren Spirale von links nach rechts. Die meisten Kletterpflanzen, welche dicke Bäume erstiegen, waren Wurzelklimmer (Farne, Aroideen, Begonia u. s. w.); ich fand auch einige Rankenklimmer (Haplolophium, Bignonia, Cissus u. s. w.).—[8] Am oberen Itajahy sah ich zahlreiche schwarze Schnüre (von einigen Linien bis zu beinah ein Zoll Durchmesser[)], spiralig um die Stämme einiger mächtigen Bäume gewunden, und ich glaubte zuerst, es wären Kletterpflanzen, welche die Bäume erstiegen; später aber fand ich, dass es Luftwurzeln waren von einem Philodendron, welches auf den Zweigen jener Bäume lebte und von dort die Wurzeln nach der Erde sandte. Es giebt einige andere Arten von Philodendron, deren Luftwurzeln immer frei von den Zweigen herunterhängen und senkrecht zur Erde wachsen, wobei sie oftmals eine Länge von mehr als 50 m erreichen.[9]

. . . . . Was Orchideen anbetrifft, so habe ich die gute Gelegenheit, Arten aus all den verschiedenen Gruppen zu beobachten und so viele von den wundervollen Anpassungen zu sehen, welche in Ihrem Orchideen-Buch beschrieben sind, und mich so von der Richtigkeit Ihrer Beobachtungen zu überzeugen. . . . .[10]

Incomplete
Möller ed. 1915–21, 2: 79–80

[1] For a translation of this letter, see Appendix I. According to Alfred Möller, all Fritz Müller's letters to CD were written in English (see Möller ed. 1915–21, 2: 72 n.); most of them have not been found. Many of the letters were later sent by Francis Darwin to Möller, who translated them into German for his *Fritz Müller: Werke, Briefe und Leben* (Möller ed. 1915–21). Möller also found final drafts of some Müller letters among the Fritz Müller papers and included these in their original English form (*ibid.*, 2: 72 n.). Where the original English versions are missing, the published version, usually appearing in German translation, has been used.

[2] See *Correspondence* vol. 13, letters to Fritz Müller, 17 October [1865] and 9 December [1865]; for CD's offer to send a copy of the *Journal of researches*, see *Correspondence* vol. 13, letter to Fritz Müller, 20 September [1865] and n. 14. CD probably sent the second edition, which had been reprinted in 1860 (Freeman 1977, p. 40).

[3] In *Journal of researches* 2d ed., pp. 29–30, CD had written:

> It is remarkable that in all the different kinds of glowworms, shining elaters, and various marine animals (such as the crustacea, medusæ, nereidæ, a coralline of the genus Clytia, and Pyrosoma), which I have observed, the light has been of a well-marked green colour.

[4] The river to which Müller refers is the Itajaí Açu in Santa Catarina province, Brazil.

Blumenau colony, Santa Catarina province, Brazil, 1867: from a drawing by Fritz Müller
Möller ed. 1915–21, 3: 91

Tynron School, where James Shaw was schoolmaster
R. Wallace ed. 1899, facing p. xxiii

[5] As evidence against the role of luminosity in the behaviour of mating insects, CD cited Müller's observation that a beetle larva was the most luminous insect that he had seen in Brazil (*Descent* 1: 345).

[6] Fritz Müller and his brother August emigrated together from Germany to Brazil in 1852. For an account of their settlement on the Itajaí Açu river, and Fritz Müller's return visits from Desterro, where he taught mathematics from 1856, see Möller ed. 1915–21, 3: 45 *et seq.*; see also West 2003, pp. 65–96.

[7] CD had edited comments relating to 'Climbing plants', made by Müller in three letters to CD, and communicated them to the Linnean Society (see *Correspondence* vol. 13, letter from Fritz Müller, [12 and 31 August, and 10 October 1865] and n. 1); the paper was read on 7 December 1865, and published as F. Müller 1865b.

[8] CD added to F. Müller 1865b a short account of the climbing of a trunk roughly five feet in circumference by a probable member of the Menispermaceae (see also *Correspondence* vol. 13, letter from Fritz Müller, [12 and 31 August, and 10 October 1865] and n. 19). The structures of the wood of the climbing plants listed in this letter are described and illustrated in F. Müller 1866b, of which there is an annotated copy in the Darwin Pamphlet Collection–CUL.

[9] CD added Müller's description of the aerial roots to *Climbing plants* 2d ed., p. 188 n., and added:

> These roots therefore seem to be true twiners, though they use their powers to descend, instead of to ascend like twining plants. The aërial roots of some other species of Philodendron hang vertically downwards, sometimes for a length of more than fifty feet.

[10] Müller refers to *Orchids*; CD added new information provided by Müller to the second edition. See, for example, letters from Fritz Müller, 2 August 1866, n. 5, and 1 December 1866, n.4.

From James Shaw 14 February 1866

Tynron, Dumfriesshire,
14 Feby 1866

Dear Sir,

I rec^{d} your kind and encouraging letter.[1] I had but very lately remarked the fact to which you refer about butterflies wings and am thankful to you for the hint concerning the male foreign butterflies being prettier than the females, as I did not know that.[2]

With regard to birds admiring themselves and showing courtesy to their image in mirror or picture my chief authority was second-hand. It is quoted from Bennett (I suspect he who was Vice-President of the Zoological Society) in the article "Birds of Paradise" Knight's English Encyclopaedia. It was a male nine years caged. The picture was full-length drawn by a Chinese artist. Bennett says he was the eye-witness.[3]

A gentleman, whose name I could get yet, came up to me after I had read my paper[4] and said—"I believe you. I have a pet Canary which flew out of my cage. I searched all the room for it and espied it on the top of a small statuette pluming its feathers before the mirror. Previously I had shown it its likeness there".

I had a kitten which used to divert itself before the mirror and even (as I thought) peeped behind it like a child, often altering its position with its paw.

I am in a situation here where I have considerable leisure time, and now that, with your encouragement, I have got thoroughly alive to this most interesting question, I will endeavour, through time, to pick up any more precise facts of the sort through my own experience or that of my scholars when I may trouble you with a selection of them.[5]

I am | Dear Sir, | Yours most respectfully, | James Shaw.

DAR 177: 150

[1] See letter to James Shaw, 11 February [1866].

[2] See letter to James Shaw, 11 February [1866] and n. 6. Shaw remarked on differences in beauty between female and male butterflies in Shaw 1866b.

[3] Edward Turner Bennett, vice-secretary of the Zoological Society of London until 1831, then secretary (*DNB*), was not the source. *The English cyclopædia*, edited by Charles Knight, gave George Bennett's *Wanderings* (Bennett 1834) as the source of a description of a male *Paradisea apoda* that reacted with comparable courtesy to a portrait of itself, painted by an unnamed Chinese artist, and to its own reflection in a mirror (*English cyclopædia* 1: 474–80); the original account, published in Bennett 1834, 2: 41–8, did not refer to self-admiration. CD later questioned whether jealousy of a supposed rival or other causes led birds to observe themselves in mirrors (*Descent* 2: 111).

[4] Shaw 1866a; see memorandum from James Shaw, [6–10 February 1866].

[5] Shaw was master of the rural parish school of Tynron, Dumfriesshire, from 1862; this post enabled him to devote much time to natural history and literature (R. Wallace ed. 1899, pp. xxiii–xxxi). After CD's death, Shaw referred to CD's interest in beauty and sexual selection in an essay entitled 'Dandies – animal and human' (published in R. Wallace ed. 1899, pp. 250–62).

From Cuthbert Collingwood 15 February 1866

14 Gloucester Plac⟨e⟩ Greenwich S.⟨E.⟩
Feb 15/66

Dear Sir

I am shortly going out to the East in the capacity of *Naturalist* (unpaid) to the "Rifleman" surveying vessel, with my friend Capt J. W. Reed— We shall proceed overland to Hong Kong & first do some business among the reefs in the China sea,[1] & I hope also to have opportunity of collecting among the islands of the East Indian Archipelago—[2]

I naturally recur to the "Journal of Researches" by yourself, & also to the problems held out for solution in the "Origin of species", & I should be sorry to go without having first communicated with you—

I very much regret to hear from D^r^. Hooker[3] that your health is so very poor at present, & I can hardly hope for a personal interview with you, but should you wish to make any communication, or suggestion, I shall receive it with the greatest respect & pleasure, & shall indeed be very glad of any hint which your experience may enable you to give me—

My time is now limited—& although I could not move in the matter sooner, I find myself now within little more than a week of starting on my journey—

I shall have to run down to Liverpool for a few days to wind up my affairs there,[4] & then I shall be able to devote the rest of my time to preparations for my voyage—

I am dear Sir | very truly yours | C. Collingwood

Chas Darwin Esq

DAR 161: 212

CD ANNOTATION[5]

Head of letter: 'Means of Distribution.— Domestic animals— greatly neglected Gestures of Savages—' *added pencil*

[1] On the Admiralty's requirement for a naturalist to join a survey in the China Sea in 1866, see the letter from J. D. Hooker, 4 February 1866 and n. 4. For Collingwood's overland journey to Hong Kong, see Collingwood 1868, pp. 1–22. John William Reed was master in command of the surveying vessel HMS *Rifleman* in the China Sea (*Navy list* 1864–6); apparently Collingwood and Reed did not travel together (Collingwood 1868). In April 1866, Collingwood joined HMS *Serpent* at Hong Kong, under the command of Charles J. Bullock (Collingwood 1868, p. 22).

[2] Collingwood wrote at least seventeen scientific papers based on his maritime and terrestrial observations in the China Sea and published between 1867 and 1869 (see *Royal Society catalogue of scientific papers*). He gave a general account of his journey in Collingwood 1868; there is a lightly annotated presentation copy in the Darwin Library–CUL (see *Marginalia* 1: 169).

[3] Joseph Dalton Hooker.

[4] Collingwood was lecturer in botany at the Royal Infirmary Medical School, Liverpool (*DNB*).

[5] CD's annotations relate to his letter to Collingwood of 16 February [1866].

To Charles Lyell 15 February [1866][1]

Down
Thursday | Feb 15th

My dear Lyell

Many thanks for Hooker's letter.[2] It is a real pleasure to me to read his letters, they are alway written with such spirit. I quite agree that Agassiz could never mistake weathered-blocks & glacial action;[3] though the mistake has, I know, been made in 2 or 3 quarters of the world. I have often fought with Hooker about the Physicists putting their veto on the world having been cooler; it seems to me as irrational, as if, when Geologists first brought forward some evidence of elevation & subsidence, a former Hooker had declared that this cd not possibly be admitted until Geologists cd explain what made the earth rise & fall.[4] It seems that I erred greatly about some of the plants on the Organ Mts.,[5] but I am very glad to hear about Fuchsia &c. I cannot make out what Hooker does believe, he seems to admit the former cooler climate, & almost in the same breath, to spurn the idea. To retort Hooker's words "It is inexplicable to me" how he can compare the transport of seeds from the Andes to the Organs Mts. with that from a continent to an island: not to mention the much greater distance, there are no currents of water from one to the other, & what on earth shd make a bird fly that distance without resting many times.[6] I do not at all suppose that nearly all tropical forms were exterminated during the cool period, but in somewhat depopulated areas, into which there cd be no migration, probably many closely allied species will have been formed since this period. Hooker's paper in Nat. Hist. Rev. is *well worth* studying; but I cannot remember that he gives good grounds for his conviction that certain orders of plants c^{d} not withstand a rather cooler climate, even if it came on most gradually.[7] We have only just learnt under how cool a temperature several tropical Orchids can flourish.[8] I clearly saw Hookers difficulty about the preservation of tropical forms during the cool period, & tried my best to retain one spot after another as a hot-house for their preservation; but it w^{d} not hold good, & it was a mere piece of truckling on my part when I suggested that longitudinal belts of the world were cooled one after the other.[9] I shall very much like to see Agassiz' letter whenever you receive one.[10]

I have written a long letter; but a squabble with or about Hooker always does me a world of good, & we have been at it many a long year. I cannot quite understand whether he attacks me as a Wriggler or a Hammerer but I am very sure that a deal of wriggling has to be done.[11]

With many thanks | yours affectionately | Charles Darwin

LS(A)
American Philosophical Society (313)

[1] The year is established by the relationship between this letter and the letter from J. D. Hooker, 21 February 1866; Lyell apparently sent this letter or a copy of it to Joseph Dalton Hooker.

[2] The letter from Lyell, and its enclosure, evidently a letter from Hooker to Lyell, have not been found.

[3] On Louis Agassiz's view that the valley of the Amazon in Brazil was of glacial origin, see the letter from C. F. J. Bunbury to Charles Lyell, 3 February 1866 and nn. 7 and 8, and the letter to Charles Lyell, 7 February [1866]. Agassiz himself wrote of the difficulties of distinguishing between weathered rocks and glacial drift around Tijuca in Brazil (J. L. R. Agassiz and Agassiz 1868, pp. 86–8), and differed from other geologists in Brazil in his interpretation of glacial phenomena in that country (Brice and Figueirôa 2001, pp. 166–72).

[4] For an example of earlier correspondence between CD and Hooker on changes in global temperature, see *Correspondence* vol. 12, letter to J. D. Hooker, [20–]22 February [1864] and nn. 10 and 11. See also letter to Charles Lyell, 7 February [1866] and n. 12. The physicist William Thomson (later Lord Kelvin) had recently calculated the age of the earth on the basis that it had been cooling progressively during geological time (W. Thomson 1865). CD and Hooker had exchanged letters on elevation and subsidence, for example in November 1862; Hooker had protested, 'I set out on Biological grounds & hold myself as independent of theories of subsidence as you do of the opinions of Physicists on heat of Globe!!' (*Correspondence* vol. 10, letter from J. D. Hooker, 2 November 1862).

[5] CD had written in *Origin*, p. 374: 'On the highest mountains of Brazil, some few European genera were found by Gardner, which do not exist in the wide intervening hot countries.' In *Origin* 4th ed., pp. 444–5, this was changed to: 'On the Organ mountains of Brazil, some few European temperate, some antarctic, and some Andean genera were found by Gardner, which did not exist in the low intervening hot countries.' CD referred to George Gardner and Gardner 1846b (see also letter to Charles Lyell, 7 February [1866] and nn. 22 and 23).

[6] CD and Hooker had long failed to agree on the mechanisms of the geographical distribution of plants (see, for example, *Correspondence* vol. 5, letter to J. D. Hooker, 7 April [1855], and *Correspondence* vol. 11, letters from J. D. Hooker, [7 May 1863] and n. 11, and [24 May 1863] and nn. 7 and 8).

[7] CD apparently refers to the anonymous review article 'New colonial floras' in the *Natural History Review* n.s. (1865) 5: 46–63. The article contained a section on the vulnerability of plants to intertropical glaciation, with comments on CD's views about the survival of tropical species. CD previously thought that the review's author was Daniel Oliver (see *Correspondence* vol. 13, letter to J. D. Hooker, 19 January

[1865] and n. 7); however, Hooker is named as the possible author in *ML* 1: 479 n. There is an unbound annotated copy of the paper in the Darwin Library–CUL.

8 During 1864, the *Gardeners' Chronicle* had published discussions about the temperature of greenhouses for tropical orchids. CD subscribed to the magazine; his copies are in the Cory Library, Cambridge University Botanic Garden. The discussion was generated in part by James Bateman's 'Lecture on cool orchids' (*ibid.*, 21 May 1864, pp. 483–5) and the publication of his pamphlet on the subject (Bateman 1864).

9 Hooker had questioned how tropical species could survive a former cold period, and expressed anxiety over the lack of suitable 'greenhouse' temperatures during such a period (see *Correspondence* vol. 6, letter from J. D. Hooker, 9 November 1856). In *Origin*, p. 374, CD proposed 'broad longitudinal belts, having been simultaneously colder from pole to pole' to explain the 'distribution of identical and allied species' across and between continents, although this passage was altered in the fifth and later editions of *Origin* (Peckham ed. 1959, p. 595). For earlier letters from CD to Hooker concerning the possible migration of temperate species across the equator during a former glacial period, see, for example, *Correspondence* vol. 13, letter to J. D. Hooker, 19 January [1865] and n. 8, and *Correspondence* vol. 13, Supplement, letter to J. D. Hooker, [14 November 1858]. For a brief history of CD and Hooker's differences concerning the geographical distribution of plants, see R. Desmond 1999, pp. 254–60.

10 No such letter has been found.

11 The ability to 'wriggle' out of theoretical difficulties had long been a joke between CD and Hooker (see *Correspondence* vol. 13, letter to J. D. Hooker, 19 January [1865] and n. 9). The word 'hammerer' may be used here to mean a geologist (see *OED*), or may refer to Hooker's criticism of CD's 'sledge-hammer hypothesis' (see also letter from J. D. Hooker, 21 February 1866).

From John Traherne Moggridge 15 February [1866][1]

Maison Fontana | Mentone
Feb. 15

Dear Sir

As we are sending a parcel by *Grand Vitesse* to my brother at Leicester, I take the opportunity of enclosing a box of Ophryses for you.[2]

I have great doubts as to their fate, for the French railways do not really understand either speed or precision.

Thank you very much for your letter of Jan. 26, in accordance with which I am marking plants both under cultivation & wild.[3]

I am now so far restored to health that I do not think it likely that I shall return next year to Mentone; I shall therefore endeavour to get some one of my friends to carry out the scheme in 1867.[4]

I have, as you suggest, selected & marked some plants which correspond to the early forms figured in my Plates;[5] but I find variation so very prevalent, that I generally prefer making careful sketches of each of the marked plants.—

I have, however, obtained one bit of evidence which would tend to shew that there is a considerable degree of stability in the early forms (such as A plate 43);[6] for the other day I again gathered the flowers from a certain well marked & separate group of plants, which I have by chance observed as each of the last three previous Springs have come round, & they have uniformly presented the green sepals & petals of **Oph.** *aranifera*. Thus no marked change has taken place throughout four successive years.—[7]

I feel quite sure also that there is a great tendency among seedlings to retain a resemblance to the parent plant; as I always notice that when a few isolated plants are closely grouped together they almost invariably have most of their peculiarities in common.[8]

I am keeping a register of the difference of character which may frequently be found in flowers on the same spike: for I often find that though the lowest flowers may have a complex marking, those above present either the simple Π marked or an approach to it, & *vice versâ*.—[9]

thus:—

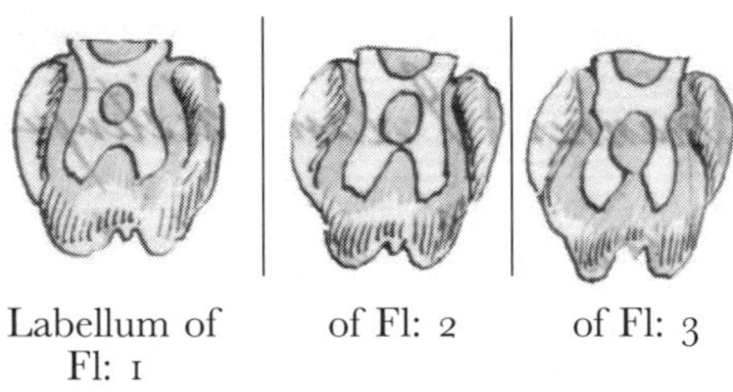

Labellum of Fl: 1   of Fl: 2   of Fl: 3

or thus:—

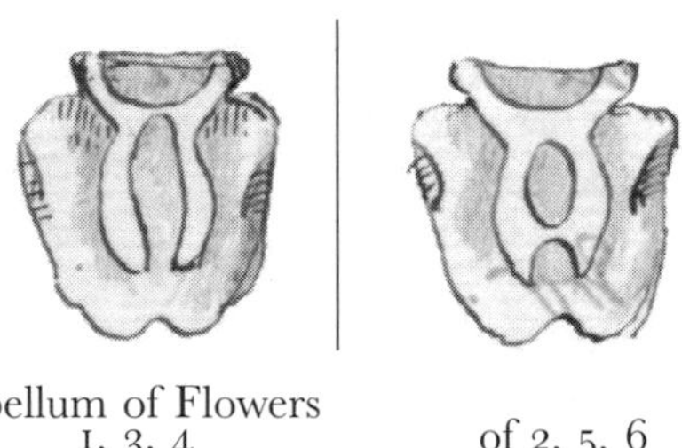

Labellum of Flowers 1, 3, 4   of 2, 5, 6

With respect to the Insects concerned in the fertilization of the Ophryses I have as yet no information to give, except indeed that one day lately I captured a small black ant gnawing the bracts of one of these plants.[10] I am thinking of making an attempt to capture these mysterious visitors by smearing the labellum of a few plants with some viscid (& unattractive) matter

I find it a very accurate method for marking my Ophrys plants to fasten round each a little zinc label, such as they use in the Hotels here for the numbers on keys thus

—In this manner I can distinguish a very large series of individuals.

Believe me dear Sir | y^{rs} very truly | J. Traherne Moggridge

Ch. Darwin Es^{qr}

DAR Pamphlet collection G368 (bound in part of Moggridge 1865–8)

CD ANNOTATIONS
0.3 Dear Sir . . . careful sketches of each 5.3] *crossed ink*
4.1 I am now . . . Mentone; 4.2] *2 crosses in margin, pencil*
9.1 With respect to . . . the labellum of a few 9.4] *crossed ink*
Top of first page: 'Box | Health | Facts' *pencil*

1 The year is established by Moggridge's reference to 1867 as 'next year'.

2 Moggridge refers to his father, Matthew Moggridge, who accompanied him to Mentone (*Proceedings of the Linnean Society of London* 1882–3, pp. 42–3) and to his brother Matthew Weston Moggridge, curate of St John's Church, Leicester (*Crockford's clerical directory* 1868). French railways offered two classes of goods service: *grande vitesse*, or express, and *petite vitesse* (Monkswell 1911, p. 85). Moggridge had sent a previous consignment of *Ophrys* specimens in December 1865 (*Correspondence* vol. 13, letter from J. T. Moggridge, 27 December [1865] and n. 2; see also Moggridge 1865–8, text accompanying plate XLV).

3 The letter of 26 January has not been found. CD had earlier written to Moggridge asking him to mark spider orchids at Mentone (probably *Ophrys arachnites*, the late spider ophrys) and subsequently to send them for cultivation at Down; CD's object was to determine whether the plants 'kept constant' when planted in England (*Correspondence* vol. 13, letter to J. T. Moggridge, 13 October [1865] and n. 5). It is likely, however, that this scheme was extended in a missing letter to include related forms of *Ophrys* described in Moggridge 1865–8. Moggridge could have marked plants of *O. aranifera* (the spider ophrys) and a closely related form in flower at Mentone in February, but not other forms (including *O. arachnites*) which flower later (see Moggridge 1865–8, text accompanying plates XLIV–XLV).

4 Moggridge evidently returned to Mentone during the winter of 1866 to 1867 and wrote from Mentone to CD on 6 March [1867] (*Correspondence* vol. 15). That letter prompted CD's note dated 9 March 1867: 'Mr M now informs me that with natural plants no marked change from last year.—' The note is on CD's annotated copy of part of Moggridge 1865–8 (*Contributions to the flora of Mentone*); the copy is in the Darwin Pamphlet Collection–CUL and is bound together with the present letter. Specimens collected at Mentone in spring 1867 are also recorded in Moggridge 1869 ('Ueber Ophrys insectifera L. (part)').

5 CD had received copies of plates XLIII–XLV, and their accompanying text, from Moggridge 1865–8 (*Correspondence* vol. 13, letter to J. T. Moggridge, 13 October [1865] and n. 2). The plates illustrated variation in the flowers of thirteen forms of *Ophrys insectifera* L., under which taxon Moggridge included *O. aranifera*, *O. arachnites* (the late spider ophrys), *O. scolopax*, and *O. apifera* (the bee ophrys), and were arranged in order of flowering date. For the earliest, that is those that flowered in February at Mentone, see n. 3, above. Moggridge refers to forms rather than species because his object was to identify forms that were intermediate between the named species (see Moggridge 1865–8, text accompanying plate XLIII).

6 Moggridge refers to *Ophrys aranifera*; in his copy of Moggridge 1865–8, CD annotated flower A, plate XLIII: 'O. aranifera Hudson'.

7 In the text accompanying plate XLIV, Moggridge described his observations at Mentone, over four seasons, of a series of intermediate forms between the earliest flowering form, *Ophrys aranifera*, and the latest, *O. apifera.* By late February, he observed the first variant, a form having brown petals and pale sepals, rather than the green petals and darker sepals characteristic of *O. aranifera* (Moggridge 1865–8). In *Orchids* 2d ed., p. 59, CD wrote: 'Mr. Moggridge further shows that in Italy *O. aranifera* flowers first, and *O. apifera* last, the intermediate forms at intermediate periods.'

8 A fuller account of parental influences on the inheritance of characters in *Ophrys* is given in Moggridge 1869, pp. 6–7.

9 Similar variation in the markings of flowers on the same spike of a form that was intermediate between *Ophrys aranifera* and *O. arachnites* is illustrated in Moggridge 1865–8, plate XLIV; a further example was considered in Moggridge 1869, p. 6.

[10] CD had noted that in Britain *Ophrys* species were seldom visited by pollinating insects (*Orchids*, pp. 62, 66, 68). CD also referred to the pollination of the bee ophrys, *O. apifera*, as his 'greatest puzzle' (*Correspondence* vol. 11, letter to P. H. Gosse, 2 June [1863] and n. 12). See also *Correspondence* vol. 8, letter to *Gardeners' Chronicle*, [4–5 June 1860] (*Collected papers* 2: 34).

To Cuthbert Collingwood 16 February [1866]

Down | Bromley Kent
Feb 16

Dear Sir

I am sorry that the state of my health & your short time will prevent us meeting.[1] You have my cordial good wishes for your health & success in every way. As I do not know the Malay Arch. or coast of China I have no special suggestions, nor indeed any general ones of any novelty; but I may mention a few points which I shd myself especially attend to if I were going myself on the expedition. Enquire after & search any caverns in the Malay Arch. for fossil bones & all recent deposits for the same.[2] If you have the means nothing w^d^ give more valuable results than *deep* sea dredging in the Tropics.[3] If you ascend any moderately lofty M^ts^. & are acquainted with glacial action, it w^d^ be well to observe on this subject.[4] If you fish in open ocean for minute surface animals, look out for seeds, & attend to all occasional means of distribution.[5] Domestic animals have generally been neglected by travelling naturalistss. Their history, peculiarities, & care taken in breeding them ought to be attended to.[6] I may add one little point which I have been surprised has been so rarely noticed, viz. are the gestures & expression of countenance under various emotions with real savages the same as with us?[7]

With my repeated good wishes, | I remain dear Sir | yours very faithfully | Ch. Darwin

LS
Postmark: FE 17 66
DAR 185: 96

[1] Collingwood had asked CD for suggestions on his forthcoming work as naturalist aboard a ship on the China Sea (see letter from Cuthbert Collingwood, 15 February 1866).

[2] Recent discoveries of fossils and human bones in caves had thrown new light on environmental conditions and species distribution during the Quaternary period (see, for example, *Correspondence* vol. 12, letter from J. D. Hooker, 29 March 1864 and n. 18). Collingwood reported exploring various caves during his expedition, but not the recovery of bones or fossils (Collingwood 1868, pp. 86, 123, 233).

[3] CD was probably interested in deep-sea dredging in connection with the imperfection of the geological record. CD had contended that many organisms would not become fossilised at the bottom of the sea in the Malay Archipelago, where he believed conditions to have been similar to those of a former European archipelago (*Origin*, pp. 299–300). Later in 1866, Collingwood dredged to a depth of approximately sixty fathoms in the China Sea, recovering sponges, branching corals, members of the genera *Comatula* and *Gorgonia*, zoophytes, tunicates, shells, nymphons (sea spiders), crabs, a new species of nudibranch, and various foraminiferous organisms (Collingwood 1868, pp. 125–7).

[4] Glacial action was on CD's mind in early 1866, partly as a result of Louis Agassiz's reported finding of evidence of former glaciation in Brazil (see, for example, letter to Charles Lyell, 15 February [1866]). CD substantially altered the section on glacial action in *Origin* 4th ed., pp. 442–56, on which he worked between March and May 1866 (see CD's 'Journal' (Appendix II) and Peckham ed. 1959, pp. 591–610). Collingwood 1868 did not include information on glaciation.

[5] CD had addressed long-standing questions concerning the dispersal of seeds by water or ice in recent correspondence (see, for example, the letter to Charles Lyell, 15 February [1866] and n. 6). Collingwood 1868 did not include information on this subject.

[6] CD included information on domestic animals in the first chapter of *Origin*; the subject was of central importance to his research for *Variation*, on which he continued to work in 1866 (see CD's 'Journal' (Appendix II)); however, Collingwood 1868 did not include information on the subject.

[7] This is one of the earliest extant letters requesting information for *Expression*. See also *Expression*, pp. 15–17. Collingwood later sent CD a copy of the published account of his expedition (Collingwood 1868), in which social aspects of the life of indigenous peoples were described, but not human expression. For earlier correspondence on human expression, see, for example, *Correspondence* vol. 8, letter from Thomas Bridges, [October 1860 or after], and *Correspondence* vol. 10, letter to J. D. Hooker, 24 December [1862] and n. 8. For the scope of CD's earlier interest in human expression, see, for example, *Notebooks*, and his observations of his infant son, William (*Correspondence* vol. 2).

From Erasmus Alvey Darwin 17 February [1866][1]

Feb 17.

Dear Charles

A thought has just come into my head which might save Susan[2] from a little worry, tho' I dont the least know that there is any necessity for it.

Susan will have to pay to Catherine's Estate half the value of the Shrewsbury furniture,[3] & if she has not got the money which is probable enough, my idea was that she should give a note of hand & the interest might run on till her death so that she would have no farther trouble.[4] I of course would advance the money with pleasure, only perhaps it would be simpler if you accepted Susan's note as part of the proceeds of Catherine's Estate. Let me know what you think of the plan before I make any suggestion to Susan.

yours affec. | E D

DAR 105: B53–4

[1] The year is established by the references to the estate of Emily Catherine Langton (Catherine), who died in February 1866 (see letter from J. D. Hooker, 4 February 1866 and n. 1).

[2] Susan Elizabeth Darwin, CD and Erasmus's sister.

[3] In his will of 27 September 1845 (Department of Manuscripts and Records, National Library of Wales), Robert Waring Darwin requested that his executors, Erasmus Alvey Darwin and CD, give his unmarried daughters the option of purchasing the furniture at the Mount, the family home in Shrewsbury, Shropshire, if they chose to continue living there. Susan and Catherine, who were unmarried when Robert died in 1848, presumably purchased the furniture. They lived together at the Mount until Catherine married Charles Langton in 1863 (see *Correspondence* vol. 11).

[4] Susan Elizabeth Darwin died 3 October 1866 (*Darwin pedigree*).

From E. A. Darwin 19 February [1866][1]

Feb 19

Dear Charles

Thanks for your note & I will when the time comes act upon it.[2] My notion was that no money would pass but that you would accept the note as part of your (childrens) share of C's estate.[3] Langton[4] however suggests that (with Legatees consent) there need be no distribution till after Susans[5] death. I was glad to hear from Caroline that her day dream is to pay me a visit which shows she must have some feeling of strength.[6]

I have taken a little hint with regard to my own will— I have left the contents of my house with one or two exceptions to you, in order that merely by request to you I can leave any little things & so save my Exōr bother for which I hope he will be grateful, & I have put in George[7] instead of Susan as a second name.

I took the opportunity of William being here to coach him a little about where he would find all necessary directions.[8]

I hear from Susan that George has had some great success—[9] I wish you would pluck up heart to come & pay me another little visit. The Jos's are coming to Elizabeths house when she goes to Tenby.[10]

Yours affec. | E D

DAR 105: B40–1

1 The year is established by the relationship between this letter and the letter from E. A. Darwin, 17 February [1866].

2 The letter from CD has not been found.

3 See letter from E. A. Darwin, 17 February [1866]. Emily Catherine Langton (Catherine) died in February 1866 (see letter from J. D. Hooker, 4 February 1866 and n. 1).

4 Charles Langton was the widower of Emily Catherine Langton.

5 Susan Elizabeth Darwin was the younger of CD and Erasmus's two surviving sisters.

6 Caroline Sarah Wedgwood, CD and Erasmus's elder surviving sister, had attended Catherine when she was dying (undated letter from H. E. Darwin to G. H. Darwin (DAR 245: 273)).

7 George Howard Darwin was CD's second son. On Erasmus's death in 1881, George and William Erasmus Darwin appear to have acted as executors (see letter from G. H. Darwin, 28 August 1881 (*Calendar* no. 13301)).

8 William Erasmus Darwin was CD's eldest son.

9 George became an undergraduate scholar of the foundation of Trinity College, Cambridge, in 1866 (*Cambridge University calendar* 1867, p. 400, F. Darwin 1916).

10 The references are to the family of Josiah Wedgwood III, who lived at Leith Hill Place, Surrey, and to Sarah Elizabeth Wedgwood (Elizabeth), who lived at Hartfield, East Sussex. Elizabeth's aunts, Emma and Frances Allen, lived near Tenby at Cresselly, South Wales (*Darwin pedigree*, Freeman 1978).

From E. A. Darwin [before 20 February 1866?][1]

Dear Charles

Perhaps this is in Georges way if his Pedigree does not go so high as this man professes.[2]

Lyell[3] was here yesterday & was calculating in an envious kind of way how much work you could do, & he came to the conclusion that counting every thing you could do more than any of the philosophers.

E D

DAR 105: B52

[1] The date is conjectured from the relationship between this letter and the letter from H. E. Darwin to G. H. Darwin, [20 February 1866] (DAR 245: 275). The letter of [20 February 1866] enclosed a letter originally sent to E. A. Darwin and conveyed an offer of one guinea from CD to enable George Howard Darwin to visit 'the man in London & try & discover whether it was *male* line'. The date of DAR 245: 275 is established from references to various family visits, which are also recorded in Emma Darwin's diary (DAR 242).

[2] The enclosure has not been found. The reference is to CD's second son, George, who was interested in family history. A number of family pedigrees and related notes are among his papers, for example in DAR 210.14 and the Francis Galton archive, University College, London (Freeman 1984, p. vii).

[3] Charles Lyell.

From C. J. F. Bunbury to Charles Lyell 20 February 1866

Barton
February 20th, 1866.

My Dear Lyell,

Very many thanks for sending me Hooker's and Darwin's letters, which I have read with great interest.[1] I agree in almost everything that Hooker says, as far as I can make him out, but his letter is *very* hard to read. I differ from Darwin as to the plants which he quotes, as instances of the occurrence of temperate forms on the Organ Mountains; he seems to consider as a "temperate" genus every genus which is found *at all* in temperate climates, and here I think him mistaken.[2] I think I mentioned in my former letter, that, besides the strictly tropical forms on those peaks, there are species of genera which are very widely spread, and not specially either tropical or the reverse.[3] Such a genus is Hypericum, one of those which Darwin enumerates; it is found in almost all parts of the world, *except* very cold countries. Clematis (which he does not mention) is another instance of the same kind. Drosera and Habernaria (as Hooker points out) have certainly their maximum within the tropics.[4] If there are Vacciniums on the Organ mountains, they are of the sub-genus (Gaylussacia of Humboldt), which belongs specially to South America, and of which there is a species even on the coast of Brazil, in the island of St. Catherine.[5]

If the Brazilian mountains were once a branch of the Andes (which I infer is Darwin's notion) I should have expected a greater number of the peculiar characteristic forms of the Upper Andes to be found on the mountains of Minus, &c., such as those "Rhododendrons of the Andes" (Befarius), of which Humboldt talks so much.[6] There are some such: Gaultherias, Gaylussacias, Escallonias, &c., but not so many as one would expect. The strongest case, perhaps, in favour of Darwin's view and against mine, is the genus Drimys (the Winter Bark). Whether the

American forms of Drimys be all varieties of one species, or a group of closely allied species, they certainly afford a most striking instance of a group of very near relations ranging along the Andes, from Cape Horn all through South America into Mexico, and re-appearing conspicuously on the table land of Brazil.[7] I do not know whether they are found anywhere *between* Minas and the Andes. It is certainly quite allowable for Darwin to say, that they must have migrated to the Brazilian uplands when these were more closely connected with the Andes than they now are. Fuchsia comes nearly into the same category with Drimys, except that there is a greater variety of forms, and some of them more decidedly distinct. I doubt whether either Fuchsia or Drimys is found very high up on the Andes.[8]

I acknowledge that, in my former letter, I did not sufficiently consider the possibility of the Organ mountains and those of Minas having been formerly much higher than now, and of their upper regions having been "*glaciated*" while in that position. But after all, as Hooker says, the information in Madame Agassiz's letter is almost too vague to afford any safe ground for fighting upon. I think the meaning *must* be, that the "glacial" marks were observed *down to* (not *up* to) 3000 feet. This is a most material point.[9]

I do not agree with Darwin, that the nature of the vegetation of New Zealand, gives us reason to believe that tropical families of plants could bear a cold climate. However luxuriant the vegetation of New Zealand, it does not, I think, include any really tropical types.[10] I am not sure, however, about Chiloe and Valdivia.[11]

I am very glad to hear that Darwin's health is better.[12]

Believe me ever your very affectionate Friend | Charles J. F. Bunbury

You may perhaps perceive that a certain degree of change has come over me while I have been writing this letter. I feel that I was perhaps too absolute in my first incredulity as to the possibility of glaciers on the Brazilian mountains: though I still think it quite incredible *if they had only their present elevation*; and I have recollected (as I noticed above) some instances of Brazilian plants which might with some plausibility be supposed to have migrated from the Andes.[13]

F. J. Bunbury ed. 1891–3, *Later life* 1: 144–7

1 The reference is to the letter from CD to Charles Lyell, 7 February [1866], possibly also to the letter to Charles Lyell, 15 February [1866] and, probably, to the letter from Joseph Dalton Hooker to Lyell that was mentioned in CD's letter to Charles Lyell, 15 February [1866]. The letter from Hooker has not been found.

2 For the 'temperate' genera mentioned by CD as occurring on the Serra dos Orgãos, Rio de Janeiro state, Brazil, see the letter to Charles Lyell, 7 February [1866] and nn. 7 and 8. See also letter to Charles Lyell, 15 February [1866] and n. 5.

3 For Bunbury's earlier remarks on the plant species of the Serra dos Orgãos occurring elsewhere in Brazil, see the letter from C. J. F. Bunbury to Charles Lyell, 3 February 1866.

4 CD had described *Hypericum*, *Drosera*, and *Habenaria* as 'temperate' genera (see letter to Charles Lyell, 7 February [1866] and n. 8).

5 See letter to Charles Lyell, 7 February [1866] and n. 8. *Gaylussacia* is closely allied to *Vaccinium* (Lindley 1853, pp. 757–8). A single species was described in Humboldt *et al.* 1815–25, 3: 215–6. CD made a note of Bunbury's objection that *Vaccinium* plants on the Organ mountains in Brazil were not temperate

species, but members of the tropical subgenus *Gaylussacia* (DAR 50: E47). See also letter to Charles Lyell, 22 February [1866], n. 2.

6 The reference is apparently to the mountains of Minas Gerais, a state in eastern Brazil, to the north of Rio de Janeiro and to the east of the Andes (*Columbia gazetteer of the world*). Five species of *Befaria* from the Andes are described with additional observations in Humboldt and Bonpland 1808–13, 2: 118–26. The genus is now named *Bejaria* (Luteyn 2002, p. 18).

7 Detailed information on the wide distribution, through South America and Mexico, of *Drimys winteri*, Winter's bark, had earlier been communicated to CD (see *Correspondence* vol. 2, letter from J. D. Hooker, [12 December 1843 – 11 January 1844]). CD had observed *D. winteri* growing south of latitude 55°, that is, south of the Beagle Channel in Tierra del Fuego (*Journal of researches*, p. 272).

8 Descriptions of Andean and other South American species of *Fuchsia*, with information on their distribution and subspecific variation, are given in Munz 1943. CD included a report of *Fuchsia* thriving near the snowline in Tierra del Fuego in his *Journal of researches*, pp. 271–2.

9 CD had questioned the same passage in the letter from Elizabeth Cabot Cary Agassiz, and recognised its bearing on the evidence for the former elevation or subsidence of the Amazon basin (see letter to Charles Lyell, 7 February [1866] and n. 5).

10 CD had argued that types of vegetation observed close to glaciers near the New Zealand coast suggested that, under similar conditions, tropical plants could have survived a former period of global cooling (see the letter to Charles Lyell, 7 February [1866] and n. 25).

11 Chiloé and Valdivia are on the coast of southern Chile at latitude 42° and 40°, respectively; see letter to Charles Lyell, 7 February [1866] and n. 25. CD had written of the luxuriant vegetation of Chiloé, noting that peaches could be grown 'with care' there, while at the more northerly Valdivia they fruited abundantly (*Journal of researches*, pp. 268 and 271).

12 See the letter to Charles Lyell, 7 February [1866] and n. 16.

13 In his journal entry for 20 February 1866, written after receiving from Lyell letters by Hooker and CD, Bunbury recorded his initial disagreement with some of CD's botanical inferences, and with CD's support for Agassiz's claim that glaciation might have affected the Serra dos Orgãos. However, Bunbury acknowledged that CD also suggested that the South American mountains had formerly been higher (see letter to Charles Lyell, 7 February [1866]). In support of CD's argument that former glaciation might be indicated by the distribution of temperate species in the mountains of eastern and western South America (see letter to Charles Lyell, 7 February [1866]), Bunbury's journal entry acknowledged that temperate species of *Gaultheria*, *Gaylussacia*, *Fuchsia*, and *Drimys*, in particular, might have spread from the Andes to the Brazilian mountains. See F. J. Bunbury ed. 1891–3, *Later life* 1: 143–4.

From Cuthbert Collingwood 20 February 1866

14 Gloucester Place | Greenwich SE
Feb 20/66

Dear Sir

I thank you sincerely for your kind letter,[1] & I shall not fail to attend to the points mentioned in it. I hardly hoped to see you, but I could not leave without having had some communication with you, & am most desirous of obtaining suggestions by which I may turn my cruise to good account—[2]

I leave by the Marseilles mail next Monday

I am dear Sir | very truly yours | Cuthbert Collingwood

Charles Darwin Esq

DAR 161: 213

[1] See letter to Cuthbert Collingwood, 16 February [1866].

[2] Collingwood was about to leave to take up a post as naturalist aboard a ship on the China Sea; he gave an account of his journey in Collingwood 1868. See also letter from Cuthbert Collingwood, 15 February 1866 and n. 1.

From Kent Church Penitentiary Society[1] [before 21 February 1866][2]

⟨*about a third of a page missing*⟩ for Discharged Female ⟨*4 or 5 words*⟩ maintained by the donations ⟨*2 or 3 words*⟩ ⟨ ⟩d by annual subscriptions. These funds ⟨*1 or 2 words*⟩ ⟨ ⟩uate, a laundry was commenced three years ago, ⟨ ⟩s from which have since that time more than ⟨cov⟩ered one half of the total expenditure.—[3]

Since the first formation of "The Home" seventy one cases have been received from the Prisons of East and West Kent, of whom fifty-three have been satisfactorily dealt with.—[4]

Notwithstanding this success, it has been found that a small establishment is proportionately very expensive, and that the Home, while benefiting the class of female domestic servants only, did not enlist that general sympathy and support which could alone ensure its permanence.

It was therefore unanimously resolved at the last Annual General Meeting of the Subscribers, that the present Home should be closed, and that the Association should be ⟨*about a third of a page missing*⟩ the reception of s⟨ ⟩ ⟨*5 or 6 words*⟩ may deem fit objects for its inter⟨ ⟩ ⟨*2 or 3 words*⟩

It has been calculated that ⟨*3 or 4 words*⟩ are annually discharged from the Gaols of ⟨*2 or 3 words*⟩ of whom a considerable percentage might be res⟨ ⟩ ⟨*1 or 2 words*⟩ means of admission to such Refuges, Homes, or penitentiaries, or by assisting them to emigrate:—

Owing to a deficiency caused by the fitting up of the laūndry at the late Home, and by the expense of transferring its inmates to another Refuge, the Society is now burdened with a debt. We beg respectfully to ask you to co-operate with us by a donation in paying this off at once, so that the Society's means of usefulness may not be crippled during the present year.—

We wish also earnestly to solicit an annual subscription toward this most important work, not only on the ground of philanthropy, but also on that of sound social economy.[5]

Incomplete
DAR 142: 92

[1] Kent Church Penitentiary Society was founded in 1860, in association with the Church Penitentiary Association for the Reclamation of Fallen Women, founded by William Ewart Gladstone in 1848 (Nokes 1895, pp. 15, 26; R. Jenkins 1995, p. 76).

[2] The date is established by the reference to the removal of the home, and by entries in CD's Classed account books (Down House MS). St Mary's Home, or the Kent Penitentiary, moved from Tenterden, Kent, to Stone, Kent, in the first half of 1866 (Nokes 1895, p. 27). CD made a payment of £1 10*s.*

to 'Book hawk & Kent penitents' on 21 February 1866, and thereafter usually recorded an annual donation of £1 or more to what he variously described as 'Church. Eng. Pen. Soc.', 'Kent Female Pen.', and 'Kent Penitent'.

3 Other means of earning money having failed, a laundry was set up at the penitentiary in Tenterden, and in 1866 earned £40 (Nokes 1895, pp. 19–20).

4 According to Nokes 1895, p. 34, the girls and women were generally sent by clergymen or district visitors, or brought by their friends, or received through refuges. They were trained to domestic service.

5 See n. 2, above.

To Robert Caspary 21 February [1866][1]

Dear Sir

I hope you will excuse the liberty which I take in begging a favour of you. You read a paper at the Amsterdam Hort: Congress on cases like that of Cytisus Adami. Would you have the kindness to tell me where this has been, or will be, published? and if you have a spare copy I should be grateful for it.[2] If you do not intend to publish it I beg you not to take the trouble to answer this note as I shall understand your silence.

I am very much interested in this subject which I hope you will receive as some excuse for my troubling you.[3]

With very sincere respect I beg leave to remain | Dear Sir | yours faithfully | Ch. Darwin

Down Bromley, Kent | Feb. 21st.

LS(A)

Beinecke Rare Book and Manuscript Library, Yale University, General Collection Manuscript Miscellany, Group 1559, Item F-2

1 The year is established by the relationship between this letter and the letter from Robert Caspary, 25 February 1866.

2 Caspary delivered the paper on *Cytisus adami* (now +*Laburnocytisus adamii*) and other hybrids that he believed were produced by grafting at the International Congress of Botany and Horticulture held at Amsterdam from 7 to 12 April 1865 (Caspary 1865a). CD had read a notice of the paper in the *Gardeners' Chronicle*, 29 April 1865, p. 386 (see *Correspondence* vol. 13, letter to J. D. Hooker, [1 May 1865], and letter from M. T. Masters, 12 July 1865). The paper appeared in *Bulletin du Congrès International de Botanique et d'Horticulture réuni à Amsterdam* (1865): 65–80; CD's offprint of the paper, bound with an annotated handwritten English translation, is in the Darwin Pamphlet Collection–CUL.

3 CD had long been interested in *Cytisus adami* (now +*Laburnocytisus adamii*), a hybrid produced by grafting a scion of *Cytisus purpureus* (a dwarf purple broom) onto a stock of *Laburnum anagyroides* (the common yellow laburnum). See *Correspondence* vols. 4–6, 10, and 11. Unlike most grafts, which preserve the floral character of the scion, +*L. adamii* has branches of purplish-yellow flowers, which regularly revert to those of both parent species (Bean 1970–88, 2: 510–11). CD had tried to propagate the hybrid by seed, and to produce the hybrid by crossing, but without success (see *Correspondence* vol. 6, letter to J. D. Hooker, 8 September [1856], and *Correspondence* vol. 10, letter to Daniel Oliver, 24 July [1862]). CD discussed the plant in *Variation* 1: 387–97, 405–11, and 2: 37, 364–5, noting the 'extraordinary fact' that two distinct species could 'unite by their cellular tissue, and subsequently produce a plant bearing

leaves and sterile flowers intermediate in character between the scion and stock, and producing buds liable to reversion; in short, resembling in every important respect a hybrid formed in the ordinary way by seminal reproduction' (*Variation* 1: 390). He argued that the plant was a graft-hybrid, and not a product of sexual union, citing Caspary 1865a and other information obtained from Caspary's letters (*Variation* 1: 388–9). Because it displayed both fusion and reversion of characters, +*L. adamii* served to illustrate the similarity of asexual and sexual modes of reproduction, an important aspect of CD's theory of pangenesis (see *Variation* 1: 411, 2: 364–5, and Olby 1985, pp. 76–80).

From J. D. Hooker 21 February 1866

Kew
Feby 21/66.

Dear old Darwin

I have been atrociously busy & am so still—but have all along been itching to have a shot at you. I hear you are disgustingly well & entitled to no sort of consideration— How I should chuckle when well, if I were an habitual invalid, & feel I was cheating my life & old time out of what they would have witheld if they could. Your restored health has brought peace to me— long may it last. The Busks come here today for the night & the Lyells meet them at dinner— I hope Lady L. will take sufficiently to Mrs. Busk who is no end of times better than some of the Lyells friends.[1] All the same I cannot add that she is a special favorite of mine.

As to this Agassian affair,[2] I wish I could explain to you my crude notions as to glacial period & your position towards it & *the Universe at large*—[3]

I suppose I hold this doctrine, that there was a glacial period, but that it was not one of universal cold; because I think that the existing distributer of glaciers is sufficiently demonstrative of the proposition, that by comparatively slight re-dispositions of sea & land & perhaps axis of globe, you may account for all the leading Palæontological phenomena upon which the glacial period is established, & more than all the purely geological & existing Botanical phenomena by which it is supported. Remember this, that the extent of the glacial action is deduced from 3 phenomena, 1. glacial blocks boulders &c. a purely geological argument, that does not carry the action very far south;—2 Palæontology—which carries the action further & wider:—3 existing distribution of existing plants & animals, which carries its action across every latitude & according to you *simultaneously in every longitude.*[4]

Now the value of these phenomena differs greatly.— the Geological is irrefragable— the Palæontological is open to the objection, that the glacial organisms may have been suited to warmer distribution then than now—or that under a less struggle for existence they had a wide climatic distribution. The third phenomenon is unsupported by the 1st & 2d. & is open to the further objections that the tropical alpine dispersion of glacial plants may be accounted for by the action of birds winds &c, that the phenomena of tropical vegetation, whether as to its extent, variety, or distribution, is against it,[5] & that the Physicists deny its possibility on grounds as good as those of existing plants.

You attach little importance to the Physicists objection;[6]—I attach great;— because in the main, physical phenomena regulate the production & distribution of organisms; & because the your theory in contrast to it is a crude one not in harmony with the fact, that the relations of Life to conditions are intricate, & the results can only be accounted for after exploring a Labyrinth of conflicting facts. This is why I call yours a sledge-hammer hypothesis. I know no phenomena so subtle or so difficult to attach their true value to, as this of the distribution of Arctic & temperate types over tropical mts.[7] To account for it at all, requires a far greater amount of Geographical change than you are disposed to admit.—eg in the case of Panama, which must have been occupied by mountains at least 4 or 5000 feet higher than at present; whilst the dispersion of temperate forms from Japan to Tasmania & from Algeria to the Cape without intermediate mts requires what every botanist will consider an extinction of thousands of tropical *genera* & even orders. You are surely illogical when you found on the distribution of a very few temperate genera & species, a glacial extension that does violence to a host of tropical species genera & orders.[8] You are illogical when you deny to the physicist the right to maintain as an argument in favor of this absence of a colder period, the phenomena of tropical distribution, & claim that of temperate in your own justification.—

The question resolves itself into this—putting aside the physicists has there been time enough since the glacial epoch, to have repeopled the tropics with its forms, & to have distributed them as they are now distributed.— if yes, then why has so little change been produced in the same time in temperate latitudes. But here you may ask, is the tropical differentiation greater than the temperate & is tropical distribution of types more general than temperate. I think it is, but to answer that one must see how many orders genera are common in each Zone to the several continents. & balance results.

Your argument drawn from the fact, that a geologist had a right to insist on elevation before the *means* of elevation were shown,[9] is not applicable in this case. I do not deny your universal cold period because you cannot show how the cold was brought about, but because the Physicists profess to prove that the earth must have been *hotter* if anything at your Epoch—[10] It is not as if it were an open question whether the earth were then hotter or colder or equal in temperature. if it were so I would go along with you a great way.

With regard to tropical orchids requiring cool treatment,[11] that is no argument, they are cool climate species & were killed before by the heat— no tropical orchid is cultivable in a cool house even when it is never exposed to frost.

I want to get to Down soon but have little prospect, just now. except for a Sunday soon[12]

Ever Yr affec | J D Hooker

DAR 102: 59, 62–4

CD ANNOTATIONS

2.1 As to] *opening square bracket ink*

End of letter: '(Not very important general arguments)' *pencil*

[1] Hooker refers to George and Ellen Busk, and Charles and Mary Elizabeth Lyell. Both families lived in Harley Street (*Post Office London directory*), but Mary Lyell did not invite the Busks to social gatherings (see *Correspondence* vol. 13, letter from J. D. Hooker, [2 June 1865] and n. 16).

[2] Hooker refers to reported claims that Louis Agassiz had found evidence of former glacial action in the Amazon basin in Brazil. See letter from C. J. F. Bunbury to Charles Lyell, 3 February 1866, and the letters to Charles Lyell, 7 February [1866] and 15 February [1866]. See also letter from C. J. F. Bunbury to Charles Lyell, 20 February 1866.

[3] Hooker's comments were apparently prompted by reading CD's letter to Charles Lyell, 15 February [1866]; that letter was in turn prompted by CD's reading a letter from Hooker to Lyell (see letter to Charles Lyell, 15 February [1866] and n. 2). For the controversies surrounding Agassiz's work on global cooling, glaciation, and the implications of possible glaciation in the Amazon basin, see the letter from C. J. F. Bunbury to Charles Lyell, 3 February 1866 and n. 8.

[4] Hooker drew a sketch map of Europe and America, showing his estimate of the southern limit of the glacial sea, in a memorandum enclosed with his letter to CD of 9 November 1856 (*Correspondence* vol. 6). For a modern view of the geographical extent of the last ice age, see Imbrie and Imbrie 1979, pp. 12–13. On estimating the extent of glaciation by geological and biological methods in the nineteenth century, see, for example, Rudwick 1969. For a contemporary theory of the influence of the relative positions of land and sea on terrestrial temperature, see C. Lyell 1853, 1: 105–10; and for the theories about the variation in the tilt of the earth's axis, see Imbrie and Imbrie 1979, pp. 69–75. During his Brazilian expedition, Agassiz claimed to have gathered evidence of glaciation from erratic blocks and palaeontology (see, for example, Hartt 1870, pp. 28–31, 467–72). CD explained the present distribution of species in part by their migration north and south along broad longitudinal belts that had formerly been colder from pole to pole (see the letter to Charles Lyell, 15 February [1866], n. 9).

[5] In an earlier paper on the temperate flora of Cameroon and Nigeria, Hooker had juxtaposed CD's theory of temperate species moving overland to the tropics at the onset of the glacial period (and their colonisation of northern latitudes or high tropical altitudes on the return of warm conditions) with the explanation of transport of seeds by birds and winds (J. D. Hooker 1863, pp. 180–1). CD's lightly annotated copy of J. D. Hooker 1863 is among the unbound journals in the Darwin Library–CUL. On the existence of temperate plants on tropical mountains, see also n. 7, below. On the survival of tropical vegetation around the formerly cold equator, see n. 8, below.

[6] CD's view of the distribution of plants (see n. 4, above), which relied on a cold period, was not compatible with the opinion of contemporary physicists that the temperature had then been warmer than CD had believed (see letter to Charles Lyell, 15 February [1866] and n. 4). For a perspective on contemporary understanding of the physics of climate change, see Fleming 1998.

[7] Hooker had earlier expressed concern about the difficulty of explaining the presence of European genera among the plants on tropical mountains (see *Correspondence* vol. 11, letters from J. D. Hooker, [7 May 1863] and n. 11, and [24 May 1863] and n. 8).

[8] For earlier discussions of the problem of the survival of tropical plants during a mundane glacial period, see *Correspondence* vol. 11, letter to J. D. Hooker, 17 March [1863] and nn. 15–18, and letter from J. D. Hooker, [24 March 1863]. See also the section on 'Dispersal during the glacial period' in *Origin*, pp. 365–82.

[9] See the letter to Charles Lyell, 15 February [1866].

[10] The prevailing theories of climate change, based on contemporary physics, are reviewed in Croll 1864; they were not compatible with CD's views of geographical distribution (see also n. 6, above). More recently, James Croll had proposed a succession of ice ages affecting each hemisphere alternately (see, for example, Croll 1865a, pp. 270–1); in the hemisphere that was not glaciated, Croll argued that winter temperatures, in particular, would have been higher than at the present day (Croll 1865a, pp. 271, 436).

[11] See letter to Charles Lyell, 15 February [1866].

[12] Hooker's next recorded visit to Down was from Saturday 24 March to Monday 26 March 1866 (Emma Darwin's diary (DAR 242)).

From John Murray 21 February [1866][1]

50^A. Albemarle S^t. | W.
Feby 21

My Dear Sir

I have the pleasure to inform you that the Third Edition of your Origin of Species, printed 1861 is now exhausted.[2] Will it be agreable to you that I send to press a new Edition, & if so have you any changes to make?—

The demand for the work after 3 Editions is necessarily slow & limited— I w^d therefore propose to print no more than 1250 copies I propose as before to give you $\frac{2}{3}$^d of the profits of the Edition, but I hope that instead of paying you on the publication of the work in consideration of the altered circumstances, you will kindly wait until the sale shall have in part at least, repaid the outlay of paper, printing &c[3]

When you do me the favor to answer this, I w^d fain hear about your health, wch I sincerely hope has improved since you last did me the favor to write.[4]

I remain My Dear Sir | Your faithful servant | John Murray

Charles Darwin Esqr

DAR 171: 333

1 The year is established by the relationship between this letter and the letter to John Murray, 22 February [1866].

2 The print run of the third edition of *Origin* was 2000 copies (Peckham ed. 1959, p. 776). It was published in April 1861 (see *Correspondence* vol. 9).

3 The print run of the fourth edition of *Origin* was 1500 copies. The production cost of the book exceeded the sum paid to the author, which was slightly less than two-thirds of the profit. See Peckham ed. 1959, p. 776.

4 In his most recent known letter to Murray, CD had written, 'I am now better but know not in the least whether I shall keep well enough to work', having reported his recent loss of five or six weeks owing to illness (*Correspondence* vol. 13, letter to John Murray, 2 June [1865]).

To Charles Lyell 22 February [1866][1]

Down.
Feb. 22

My dear Lyell

I have been particularly glad to see my errors pointed out by Bunbury,[2] who adds nearly as much as he takes away.[3] I believe now I have notes about Drimys & Fuchsia &c in my Portfolio on this subject, but knowing nothing of Botany, they had escaped me.—[4] I have also vague remembrance, but cannot hunt up my notes, that some of fossil mammals of caves of Brazil are Andean, as Vicunas, Bears & Goat-like animal &c.—[5]

I am all the gladder to have seen all these letters,[6] as I have heard, almost to my sorrow, this morning that Murray wants new Edit. of Origin, & I must alter a few words about Organ Mountains.[7] I suppose I might add "that I have been informed that Agassiz has detected Glacial markings on these mountains".—[8]

It goes to my heart that all my present work will be stopped for a month or two or three.—

Yours affectionately | C. Darwin

American Philosophical Society (314)

[1] The year is established by the relationship between this letter and the letter from C. J. F. Bunbury to Charles Lyell, 20 February 1866 (see n. 2, below).

[2] CD refers to Charles James Fox Bunbury and the letter from Bunbury to Lyell of 20 February 1866 (see this volume).

[3] CD had noted Bunbury's admission (letter from C. J. F. Bunbury to Charles Lyell, 20 February 1866) that *Gaultheria*, *Gaylussacia*, and *Escallonia* were common to the flora of the Andes and the Organ Mountains. CD's note ends: 'Drimys (he admits) or Winter's Bark is in favour of me & Fuchsia— Drimys ranges along Andes to Mexico & reappears conspicuously on Table-land of Brazil' (DAR 50: E47). For Bunbury's comments on CD's views as expressed in the letter to Charles Lyell, 7 February [1866], see the letter from C. J. F. Bunbury to Charles Lyell, 20 February 1866, n. 13.

[4] CD's notes on the geographical distribution of plants were in his portfolio number 20. CD kept a number of such portfolios, amassed over a long period of time and since dispersed. The likely contents of some portfolios were reconstructed when some of CD's papers were catalogued in 1932 (see DAR 220: 13). However, CD's earlier notes on the distribution of *Fuchsia* and *Drimys* in South America have not been found in the Darwin Archive–CUL.

[5] CD may refer to notes made in 1839 and 1840 (see *Notebooks*, Torn Apart Notebook, Frag 6^{r}, 79 (pp. 464–5)). These two notes concerned fossil mammals in the caves of South America and referred to Edward Blyth's belief 'in the existence of Molina's Pudu— or goat' (see also Blyth 1841, pp. 255–6, in which the relationship between the Pudu and the fossil *Antilope Mariquensis* is considered).

[6] The letters were those from Bunbury, Joseph Dalton Hooker, and Elizabeth Cabot Cary Agassiz (see n. 2, above, letter to Charles Lyell, 7 February [1866] and n. 2, and letter to Charles Lyell, 15 February [1866] and n. 2).

[7] See letter from John Murray, 21 February [1866]. For the changes to the fourth edition of *Origin*, see the letter to Charles Lyell, 15 February [1866] and n. 5. See also letter from C. J. F. Bunbury to Charles Lyell, 20 February 1866.

[8] For CD's temporary alteration to the text of *Origin* on this point, see the letter to Charles Lyell, 7 February [1866] and n. 7.

To John Murray 22 February [1866][1]

Down Bromley | Kent.
Feb 22—

My dear Sir

I am much pleased but even more grieved about the Origin;[2] for after ten months intermission I am now able to work nearly two hours daily at my next book;[3] but this will be now stopped by the Origin. Natural Hist. progresses so quickly that I must make a good many corrections.[4] It will save me a good deal of labour if you will make a special request to Messrs Clowes[5] that the sheets are corrected with extra care, & only those sheets sent to me which contain corrections of more than a word or two. The former editions were corrected with *admirable* care. I will begin to work in a few days & as soon as a few sheets are ready shall I send them off to Mess[rs] Clowes?

I must cut up my present single copy, so must request you to send (to "care of G. Snow Nag's Head Borough")[6] a new bound copy as I must have one by me.

With respect to payment, will it suit you when half the copies are sold?[7]

I hope you will let me have a few presentation copies as before.[8]

I fear my Orchis book has been a poor affair. What state is it in?[9]

I enclose a cheque for your account.[10]

I was going to have written to you about woodcuts.[11] Now Alas there is less hurry, but yet I may as well settle the affair. Ten blocks of pigeons & poultry are almost completed;[12] but I require 32 or 33 of heads of animals—but chiefly of bones & skulls: there will often be 3 or 4 little bones in the same cut.[13] Now I do not know that M[r] G. B. Sowerby has had any experience in drawing bones, but sh[d] rather prefer him as he is patient with me & I am familiar with his ways.[14] What do you wish & advise? If M[r] Sowerby is employed, how is he, or indeed any one, to be restricted about price? Whoever draws for me will have to come down here to receive instructions & take away the specimens.[15]

How long a time ought I to grant for these 32 woodcuts?

I am sorry to give you so much trouble with so many questions, & shall be grateful for answers & will give no more trouble.

I am very much interested in my present book on Domestic Animals &c; but cannot form the most remote idea whether the public will care for it. If it had not been for the Origin I think I sh[d] certainly have gone to press with it early this autumn.[16]

I am much obliged for your kind enquiries about my health, & remain my dear Sir | yours very sincerely | Charles Darwin

P.S. I find my copy of Origin is so bescribbled,[17] that I must correct on clean sheets— if you have unbound copy, so much the better.— *Please send by* **Post**.—

LS(A)
John Murray Archive

[1] The year is established by the references to the fourth edition of *Origin* and to CD's work on *Variation.*

[2] CD refers to Murray's plans to print a fourth edition of *Origin*; see letter from John Murray, 21 February [1866].

[3] CD refers to *Variation*, on which he had been engaged intermittently since January 1860 (see *Correspondence* vols. 8–13, CD's 'Journal' (Appendix II)).

[4] CD revised the fourth more extensively than earlier editions of *Origin* (Peckham ed. 1959, p. 21). He worked on the revisions between 1 March and 10 May 1866 (see CD's 'Journal' (Appendix II)).

[5] William Clowes & Sons.

[6] George Snow operated a carrier service between London and Down, calling at the Nag's Head inn, Borough High Street, London (*Post Office directory of the six home counties* 1866, Freeman 1978).

[7] Murray had paid CD on publication of the earlier editions, but had suggested deferring payment for the fourth edition until he had recouped some of the publication costs. See letter from John Murray, 21 February [1866].

[8] Murray had allowed CD twelve copies of the first edition of *Origin*, eighteen of the second edition, and six of the third edition (Peckham ed. 1959, pp. 775–6).

[9] CD had previously expressed concern about the sales of *Orchids* (see *Correspondence* vol. 11, letter to John Murray, 22 January [1863] and n. 3). For more on the publishing history of *Orchids*, see Freeman 1977, pp. 112–15.

[10] CD's Classed account books (Down House MS) contain an entry of £1.10.0 for 'Presentation copies', dated 21 February 1866.

[11] CD and Murray exchanged several letters regarding woodcuts for illustrations in *Variation* in 1865; see *Correspondence* vol. 13, letters to John Murray, 31 March [1865], 4 April [1865], and 2 June [1865], and letter from John Murray, 1 April 1865.

[12] The ten woodcuts of pigeons and poultry for *Variation* were being made from drawings by Luke Wells, under the supervision of William Bernhard Tegetmeier (see letter from W. B. Tegetmeier, 22 January [1866] and nn. 4–7).

[13] In the published volumes of *Variation*, there were forty woodcuts of animals, including twenty-five illustrating skulls and bones.

[14] George Brettingham Sowerby Jr drew the figures for *Fossil Cirripedia* (1854), *Living Cirripedia* (1851, 1854), and *Orchids* (1862). CD had already asked Murray about Sowerby's contributing drawings of bones and skulls to *Variation* (see *Correspondence* vol. 13, letter to John Murray, 31 March [1865] and n. 4).

[15] No record of a visit to Down by Sowerby in 1866 has been found; for his earlier visits, see *Correspondence* vol. 13, letter to John Murray, 31 March [1865] and n. 4.

[16] CD refers to *Variation* and the fourth edition of *Origin*; see nn. 3 and 4, above.

[17] CD's own annotated copies of *Origin* are in the Rare Books Room–CUL; they include all those published before 1866, that is the first, second, and third English editions, and the first American edition.

From John Murray 24 February [1866][1]

50, Albemarle St. | *W.*
Feby 24

My Dear Sir

I have despatched by Book post today a copy of the "Origin" in sheets for correction[2] The printer will guarantee a correct reprint of all that you send to press unaltered & will send you proofs of sheets in wch you make corrections—[3]

I shall be happy to pay you two thirds of the profits of the Edition as soon as one half of the copies are sold—as you suggest[4]

I can see no objection to your employing Mr Sowerby to draw the bones & heads for your book on Domesticated animals.[5] I w^d^ stipulate that after he has seen all that you require, he sh^d^ send me in writing his estimate of the cost of drawing the 32 or 33 subjects—& a statement of the time within wch he will undertake to draw them—[6]

I have no doubt this work will be as interesting to the Public as it has been to you

I remain | My Dear Sir | Yours very faithfully | John Murray

I have still near 600 copies of the Book on Orchids on hand—but the deficiency on it has been reduced to £30.—[7]

Charles Darwin Esqr

DAR 171: 346

[1] The year is established by the relationship between this letter and the letter to John Murray, 22 February [1866].
[2] In order to make revisions and corrections for the fourth edition, CD had requested a clean copy of *Origin* (see letter to John Murray, 22 February [1866]).
[3] See letter to John Murray, 22 February [1866].
[4] See letter to John Murray, 22 February [1866]. Murray made a copy of this sentence that survives in the Murray Archives (see *Calendar* no. 5017a).
[5] Murray refers to George Brettingham Sowerby Jr and *Variation*. See letter to John Murray, 22 February [1866] and nn. 13 and 14.
[6] CD had raised the question of fixing a price with Sowerby in his letter to Murray of 22 February [1866]. Sowerby had nearly completed his illustrations for *Variation* in October 1866 (see letter to G. B. Sowerby Jr, 19 October [1866]).
[7] There is a statement of Murray's account for *Orchids* in DAR 171.3: 524–5, annotated by CD: 'Feb— 27— 1866. Still about 600 copies on Hand & 30£ deficient.—'

From Robert Caspary 25 February 1866

Koenigsberg in Pr.
25th. Febr. 1866

My dear Sir

Many thanks for your letter.[1] I stand indeed to you under very great obligations for your kindly sending me all your publications and I should have long ago written to you to thank you, had I not been afraid of giving you more trouble by my letters, than my thanks would be worth.[2] That your papers were most useful to me and others here, you will see from the account, which I gave of some in connexion with some other publications, which your observations and hypotheses elicited.[3] The account, which I add, is accompanied with a few lines on those peculiar appearances, of which I am now convinced that they are caused by a sort of hybridism in consequence of grafting. The account is published in: Schriften der physikalisch-œkonomischen Gesellschaft zu Koenigsberg Jahrgang VI Sitzungsberichts, p. 4.[4]

The account of what I said on the same subject at the Amsterdam-congress—is printed about 4 or 5 months ago but has not yet been published.[5] At the time I corrected the letterpress, which Professor Rauwenhoff[6] at Rotterdam sent me, being the editor of the transactions of that congress. I write at once to Professor Rauwenhoff to tell him, that he might send you directly a copy; I have none. The transactions of that Congress will be published in 8o.[7]

I collected material or rather was allways at the look-out for material for more than 10 years on the hybridization and muling by grafting. The case of Cytisus Adami I had an opportunity of examining in a most perfect development at Bonn—[8] As regards the Bizarrin[9] I saw no case, nor any person living, who ever had observed one, except Professor Passerini at Parma,[10] who is about of procuring me one or two trees, which exhibit Bizarrin, but I am afraid our climate will be too severe for it, as it is for Cytisus Adami.

If I had 3 or 4 weeks to spare I should prepare a full paper on the matter, not being able at present to add any thing. But I shall not have time to do so before 2— or 3 months have elapsed, as I am very hard at work to finish some papers on Nymphaeaceae, which I promised to Professor Miquel and V. Martius.[11] Having finished those papers I took the resolution of writing down at full length my observations on Cytisus Adami and similar subjects. The account on them which I gave at the Amsterdam Congress is a very brief one.[12]

At the close of the paper, I add, I mentioned the seeds of Euryale, ripened by flowers, which remained under water and did not open.[13] Now I got last year many of that description *and some allready germinated*.

I take the liberty of adding my photography and asking for yours—[14] You could do me no greater favor, than if you would send it me.

Yours most respectfully and faithfully | R. Caspary

DAR 161: 118

1 Letter to Robert Caspary, 21 February [1866].

2 Caspary's name is on CD's presentation list for *Origin* (see *Correspondence* vol. 8, Appendix III). No record that CD sent Caspary any of his other publications has been found.

3 Caspary 1865b discussed recent botanical work relevant to CD's hypothesis, presented in *Origin*, pp. 96–101, that occasional or habitual intercrossing occurred between hermaphrodite individuals. Caspary reviewed CD's arguments in *Orchids*, 'Dimorphic condition in *Primula*', 'Two forms in species of *Linum*', and 'Three forms of *Lythrum salicaria*', and described various cleistogamic (small, unopening) flowers that presented a challenge to CD's hypothesis. CD's annotated copy of Caspary 1865b is in the Darwin Pamphlet Collection–CUL. For CD's interest in cleistogamic flowers, see *Correspondence* vols. 10–12.

4 Caspary refers to Caspary 1865c, a short paper in which he claimed to have observed 'an unquestionable instance of the origination of a hybrid by grafting': a white moss-rose that had been grafted onto a stock of *Rosa centifolia* developed shoots and flowers of both forms, as well as flowers and stalks that were compounded of both forms. Caspary suggested that the peculiar features of this hybrid were analogous to those of *Cytisus adami* (now +*Laburnocytisus adamii*), and the 'bizzarria orange', and thus lent support to the view that these were also graft hybrids. CD's annotated copy of Caspary 1865c is in the Darwin Pamphlet Collection–CUL, bound with a handwritten English translation of part of the paper. On *Cytisus adami* and CD's interest in graft hybrids, see the letter to Robert Caspary, 21 February [1866] and n. 3; see also n. 9, below.

5 Caspary refers to Caspary 1865a. See letter to Robert Caspary, 21 February [1866] and n. 2.

6 Nicolas Willem Pieter Rauwenhoff.

7 8°: i.e., octavo.

8 Caspary was director of the herbarium at the University of Bonn from 1856 to 1858 (*ADB*).

9 In Caspary 1865a, pp. 66–9, the bizzarria orange is described as the earliest recorded case of a graft hybrid: produced in Italy in 1644, by grafting a scion of the bitter orange (*Citrus bigarradia*, now *C. aurantium*) onto a stock of the citron (*C. medica*), the plant developed leaves, flowers, and fruit of both parent forms, as well as compound fruit. In *Variation* 1: 391, CD described the bizzarria orange as a 'strictly parallel case to that of *Cytisus adami*'. See also n. 4, above.

10 Giovanni Passerini.

11 Caspary contributed articles on the family Nymphaeaceae to the *Annales Musei Botanici Lugduno-Batavi*, edited by Friedrich Anton Wilhelm Miquel (Caspary 1866b), and to Karl Friedrich Philipp von Martius's *Flora Brasiliensis* (Caspary [1878]).

12 Caspary refers to Caspary 1865a.

13 In Caspary 1865b, p. 20, the self-fertility of the waterlily, *Euryale ferox*, and the apparent ability of its unopened flowers to set seed under water, are described. CD's copy of Caspary 1865b is bound with

a page of notes on *E. ferox* and other species with cleistogamic flowers; the notes were used in *Cross and self fertilisation*, p. 365.

[14] Caspary's photograph has not been found in the Darwin Archive–CUL.

From J. D. Hooker [26 or 27 February 1866][1]

Dear Darwin

You may care to see the last paragraph of enclosed from John Scott— I hope he has repaid you your money loan.[2]

I had a long talk with Lyell[3] on Sunday— he wants to see my last to you—[4] I fear I made some allusion to Busks that may not be showable[5]—not that there was anything in the letter otherwise worth his seeing. His head is full of Summer apogees, & winter perigees & precession of the Equinoxes & God knows what all. By way of making matters worse, I gave him a dose of radiant-heat, humidity & absorption of Caloric, which will muddle the effect of his astronomical causes of heat & cold on the Globe.[6]

Poor Harvey is very ill indeed of hæmorrhage from the lungs & I fear we shall lose him.[7]

I am still very busy in the Garden & hardly ever stir from Kew.[8]

Ever Yr affte | J D Hooker

[Enclosure]

Royal Botanic Gardens | Calcutta
22^d January 1866

Sir,

Dr. Anderson who, I regret to say, has been suffering much of late from attacks of inflammation in the liver with fever, desired me previous to his leaving for Moulmein—where he has been advised to go for a few weeks—to advise you of the despatch of a dry box of plants containing the enclosed enumeration.[9]

Coelogyne Hookeriana we had sent us only a few weeks ago from Sikkim, and have only retained a few pseudo-bulbs for trial here, as I think there are small hopes of us succeeding in keeping them through our hot season.[10] Even **now** they are impatient to the heat,—a good omen to the cool culturist at home—showing an inaptitude to climate, by a premature disposition to flower and the withering and dropping of these without opening.

I have sent you a few of the Bengal terrestrial orchids[11]—all my *present stock* in *[pots]*—having only lately commenced collecting these with a view to the establishment of an indigenous and exotic herbaceous garden, which Dr. Anderson has long wished to have... In one of the small tins enclosed are seeds of two species of Calami—[12] those in the upper portion are C. Jenkinsianus Griff. collected this season by Dr. Anderson in the Terai—[13] in the lower portion you have seeds from an unnamed species in our gardens. It seems to approach very closely to, if not identical with C. Lewisianus Griff.—a truly magnificent species though perhaps requiring a little more room than you can well spare. I have already succeeded in raising plants from the same produce as seeds sent you, and am much interested with them under the impression that they are in all probability **hybrids**—the seeds being produced in a plant with which a *male plant* of another noble and distinct species, C. angustifolius Griff., is entangled and both of which flowered at the same time,—and likewise at some distance from any others.

I have sent you three young plants of *Nipa*, along with the ungerminated seed. I wished to have sent you more in the latter state, but as I had only your list of desiderata on the day of packing, there was little time to search for them, and my collectors said that they could find no others ungerminated. I with some hesitation enclosed you three of the youngest in slightly *moistened charcoal*, trusting that they are sufficiently secured to prevent communicating damp to the other contents. It will be well therefore to get the box secured as early as possible after the arrival of the mail in case of injury by frost.

I would now only express my sincere thanks for the very excellent appointment which through your recommendation has been made me,[14] and should further feel obliged by your remembering me at your convenience, to my esteemed benefactor, Mr. Darwin, whom—from the press of incumbent duties, and a consequent want of time to pursue those experimental enquiries in which he takes such a lively interest, I have not lately had the pleasure of communicating with.[15]

I remain | Sir | Yours respectfully | J Scott

J. D. Hooker Esq. M.D.

DAR 102: 65–6; Royal Botanic Gardens, Kew, DC vol. 156 doc. 1048

[1] The date range is established by the relationship between this letter, the letter from J. D. Hooker, 21 February 1866, the letter to J. D. Hooker, [28 February 1866], and the letter from Charles Lyell, 1 March 1866. This letter indicates that Charles Lyell had asked to see Hooker's letter to CD of 21 February 1866 on Sunday 25 February; he had received it by Thursday 1 March (see letter from Charles Lyell, 1 March 1866). CD wrote to Hooker on the Wednesday of that week confirming that he had sent Hooker's letter of 21 February on to Lyell (see letter to J. D. Hooker, [28 February 1866]). This letter must therefore have been written on Monday 26 or Tuesday 27 February.

[2] Hooker had expressed concern about John Scott's repayment of money given to him by CD (*Correspondence* vol. 13, letter from J. D. Hooker, [23] December 1865 and n. 12). CD had advanced funds to Scott in 1864 so that Scott could travel to India to seek employment (see *Correspondence* vol. 12, letter to John Scott, 21 May [1864], and letters from John Scott, 10 June [1864] (second letter) and 2 August 1864). CD gave Scott £25 on 10 June 1864 and £10 on 31 July 1864 (CD's Classed account books (Down House MS)). CD entered the amounts under 'Gifts [and] Annual Subscriptions.' In August 1864, CD gave Scott a further £80 (CD's Account books–cash account (Down House MS)).

[3] Charles Lyell.

[4] Letter from J. D. Hooker, 21 February 1866.

[5] Hooker refers to George and Ellen Busk; see letter from J. D. Hooker, 21 February 1866.

[6] CD and Hooker had been arguing about the causes and extent of the glacial period (see letter from J. D. Hooker, 21 February 1866; see also letter from Charles Lyell, 1 March 1866). Lyell too was interested in the subject, and incorporated new information upon it into the tenth edition of his *Principles of geology* (C. Lyell 1867–8, vol. 1, chapter 10 *et seq.*). For background on contemporary geological, astronomical, and physical theories of changes in climate, and Lyell's position with regard to them, see Fleming 1998.

[7] William Henry Harvey died of pulmonary consumption on 15 May 1866 (*DNB*).

[8] Following the death of his father, William Jackson Hooker, in 1865, J. D. Hooker had been appointed director of the Royal Botanic Gardens, Kew (see *Correspondence* vol. 13, letter from J. D. Hooker, [3 November 1865] and n. 3).

[9] Thomas Anderson was superintendent of the Calcutta botanic gardens; he appointed Scott as curator in 1865 (*Correspondence* vol. 13, letter from J. D. Hooker, [23] December 1865 and n. 11). Moulmein (now Mawlamyine) was the chief town of British Burma (*Columbia gazetteer of the world*).

[10] Sikkim is a mountainous state in the Himalayas, in north-eastern India, bordering Nepal and Tibet (*Columbia gazetteer of the world*).

[11] What Scott refers to as Bengal is an area that now includes Bangladesh and the Indian state of western Bengal (*Columbia gazetteer of the world*).

[12] Scott refers to the genus of climbing palms, *Calamus* (*OED*).

[13] The Terai is a region of marshy land in southern Nepal and northern India, lying between the lower foothills of the Himalayas and the plains (*Columbia gazetteer of the world*).

[14] On Hooker's recommendations of Scott for a post in India, see *Correspondence* vol. 13.

[15] For CD's financial assistance to Scott, see n. 2, above. For Scott's assistance to CD on botanical experiments, see *Correspondence* vols. 10–13.

From John Edward Gray 28 February 1866

BM
28 Feb 66

My Dear Darwin

It was very pleasant to see your handwriting & to receive the *Larva* of the Batrachian from California[1]

I hope that you are better than when I last heard of you I have been complaining had two attacks of Rheumatic Iritis which shut me up in a Dark Room for 6 or 8 weeks & I find I am growing an Old Man.[2]

The specimen sent agrees in some respects with *Protonopsis horrida* the Mud devil, hellbender or alligators of the Lakes[3] but if it is it is in a state that I have not seen it before

It is also like the *Axolotl* in some respects but yet larger & different from any of them I have seen bythby I hear in Paris they have breed the *Axolotl* & they have specimens with & without external gills[4]

I will examine the Beast & see if I can make it out as soon as I am done with the Bats[5]

The Bats like the *Paradoxuri*[6] regularly worry me there are specimens so alike externally that the best men have regarded them all the same species but when you examine the Bones they prove to belong to several genera & when you have decided that such ansuch specimens are different genera you are not then able to discover any external character to seperate them from each other

On the other hand the specimens of several genera seem to regularly appear Black Brown & red coats not in different seasons & localities because specimens caught at the same time & place present these Variations in colour

With kindest Regards | Ever yours sincly | J E Gray

DAR 165: 209

[1] The letter to Gray has not been found; CD evidently also sent the specimen of a 'very curious fish' from California that CD had been sent by Thomas Gold Appleton. The supposed fish had legs that Appleton believed assisted it to migrate to water when the mountain lakes in which it lived dried up; Appleton considered it to be a 'most remarkable corroboration' of adaptation in the 'Struggle for life' (see *Correspondence* vol. 13, letter from T. G. Appleton, 5 December [1865]).

[2] Gray had suffered poor health in 1865 (see *Correspondence* vol. 13, letter to J. E. Gray, 27 January [1865] and n. 3).

[3] The reference is to *Cryptobranchus alleganiensis*, a large salamander that lives in mountain rivers of the north-eastern United States (S. C. Bishop 1994, Grzimek ed. 1974, pp. 316–17). It was formerly named *Protonopsis horrida* (Boulenger 1882).

[4] The axolotl (*Ambystoma mexicanum*) is a large neotenic salamander, originating in lakes near Mexico City (Grzimek ed. 1974, p. 319). Specimens were sent in 1863 from Mexico to Paris, where Auguste-Henri-André Duméril observed their breeding at the Muséum d'Histoire Naturelle; he noted that some individuals underwent metamorphosis, while others retained their larval anatomy, including their external gills, during otherwise normal development (Duméril 1866, pp. 277–8). For more information on the impact of the axolotl on nineteenth-century zoology, see H. M. Smith 1989.

[5] Gray published several taxonomic revisions of bat genera in the *Proceedings of the Zoological Society of London* in 1866, and in the *Annals and Magazine of Natural History* in 1865 and 1866. He subsequently compiled a catalogue of the fruit-eating bats in the British Museum (J. E. Gray ed. 1870).

[6] Gray apparently refers to palm civets, members of the tribe Paradoxurina of the family Viverridae of carnivorous mammals; variability in the form of skulls and teeth in the African and Asian genera *Nandinia*, *Paradoxurus*, *Paguma*, and *Arctogale* had made classification within the tribe complex (J. E. Gray ed. 1869, pp. 43, 59–77).

To J. D. Hooker [28 February 1866][1]

Down
Wednesday

My dear Hooker

I have forwarded your letter to Lyell at his request: I did not do so at first on account of the nice little sentence about M[rs] Busk "*being no end of times better than Lyell's friends*"[2] I cut off this part, & told him it was about a private affair, & sent the remainder.[3] I dare say there is a great deal of truth in your remarks on the glacial affair but we are in a muddle & shall never agree.[4] I am bigotted to the last inch, & will not yield. I cannot think how you can attach so much weight to the physicists, seeing how Hopkins Hennessey, Haughton & Thompson have enormously disagreed about the rate of cooling of the crust;[5] remembering Herschel's speculations about cold space,[6] & bearing in mind all the recent speculations on change of axis;[7] I will maintain to the death that y[r] case of Fernando Po & Abyssinia is worth ten times more than the belief of a dozen physicists.[8]

Your remarks on my regarding temperate plants & disregarding the tropical plants made me at first uncomfortable, but I soon recovered.[9] You say that all Botanists would agree that many tropical plants could not withstand a somewhat cooler climate. But I have come not to care at all for *general* beliefs without the special facts. I have suffered too often from this; thus I found in every book the *general* statement that a host of flowers were fertilised in the bud,[10]—that seeds could not withstand salt-water &c &c.—[11] I would far more trust such graphic accounts, as that by you of the mixed vegetation on the Himalayas[12] & other such accounts. And with respect to Tropical plants withstanding the slowly coming on cool period I trust to such facts as yours (& others) about seeds of same species from mountains & plains having acquired a slightly different climatal constitution.[13] I know all that I have said will excite in you savage contempt towards me. Do not answer this rigmarole, but attack me to your heart's content & to that of mine, whenever you can come here, & may it be soon.—[14]

Hearty thanks, my dear kind friend for all that you say about my improved health; but it is hardly so good as you suppose. Twenty-four hours never pass without 5 or 6 paroxysms of great discomfort of stomach & singing head

Here is a horrid bore (though at same time it pleases me a little) my work on Domestication is stopped for a month or two by a new Edit. of Origin being wanted.[15]

Your's ever affectionately | Ch. Darwin

DAR 94: 31–2

[1] The date is established by the relationship between this letter, the letter from J. D. Hooker, [26 or 27 February 1866], and the letter from Charles Lyell, 1 March 1866. See also letter from J. D. Hooker, [26 or 27 February 1866], n. 1. In 1866, 28 February was a Wednesday.

[2] CD had been informed by Hooker that Charles Lyell wished to read Hooker's letter of 21 February 1866 (see letter from J. D. Hooker, [26 or 27 February 1866]). CD refers to Ellen Busk.

[3] No accompanying letter from CD to Lyell has been found. The letter from J. D. Hooker, 21 February 1866, is in the Darwin Archive–CUL (DAR 102: 59, 62–4); a copy of the first page, omitting the opening paragraph in which Hooker referred to Ellen and George Busk and Mary Elizabeth and Charles Lyell, is at DAR 102: 61.

[4] See letter from J. D. Hooker, 21 February 1866.

[5] CD refers to William Hopkins, Henry Hennessy, Samuel Haughton, and William Thomson (later Lord Kelvin), all of whom contributed to research on the rate of cooling of the earth's crust. See Hennessy 1864 for a discussion of the differing positions of Hopkins, Hennessy, and Thomson. In 1865, Haughton estimated the earth to be at least 1280 million years old by calculating the rate of cooling of the crust (Haughton 1865, pp. 99–102). See also letters to Charles Lyell, 7 February [1866] and n. 12, and 15 February [1866] and n. 4.

[6] In 1830, in a paper read before the Geological Society of London, John Frederick William Herschel had considered uncertainties about the temperature of space in relation to the changes in the earth's climate that were implied by evidence from palaeontology (Herschel 1830, pp. 297–9).

[7] CD probably refers to discussions arising from James Croll's astronomical explanations of climate change (Croll 1864; see also Imbrie and Imbrie 1979, pp. 81–96). In letters to the *Reader* (for example, Croll 1865a and 1865b), Croll had developed his views, prompting further discussion in the review's 'Scientific correspondence' columns between September and December 1865. Hooker had drawn CD's attention to Croll's work on shifts in the earth's centre of gravity caused by the weight of ice during the glacial period in the letter from F. H. Hooker, 6 September [1865] (*Correspondence* vol. 13). The subject was expanded further in Croll 1866a and 1866b, the latter appearing with a short introductory note by Lyell. All but one issue of the *Reader* in January and February 1866 contained comments by correspondents who made implicit or explicit references to Croll's work. In 1860, CD had commented on Sir Henry James's 'wild speculations' about climate change in relation to change of the earth's axis (*Correspondence* vol. 8, letter to Charles Lyell, 8 October [1860] and n. 7). CD cited Croll on climate change in *Origin* 5th ed., pp. 451–2.

[8] In a paper read before the Linnean Society in 1861 (J. D. Hooker 1861), Hooker had emphasised the affinity between the vegetation of Clarence Peak, Fernando Po, off the coast of West Africa, and that of Abyssinia, 1800 miles distant on the other side of Africa. On the inferences that CD drew from this affinity in relation to a possible former cold period, see *Correspondence* vol. 10, letter from J. D. Hooker, 28 June 1862, n. 9.

[9] See letter from J. D. Hooker, 21 February 1866.

[10] In 'Two forms in species of *Linum*', pp. 80–1 (*Collected papers* 2: 103), CD had written: 'In botanical works many flowers are said to be fertilized in the bud. This rests solely, as far as I can discover, on the anthers opening in the bud. . . . I have reason to believe that some flowers are frequently fertilized without expanding; but my observations lead me to disbelieve that this is ever the invariable course with all the flowers of any species whatever.'

[11] CD had conducted a series of experiments in the 1850s, the results of which were published in his 1857 paper 'On the action of sea-water on the germination of seeds' (*Journal of the Proceedings of the Linnean Society (Botany)* 1: 130–40; *Collected papers* 1: 264–73).

[12] J. D. Hooker 1852.

[13] See, for example, J. D. Hooker 1853–5, p. xi.

[14] Hooker next visited Down from 24 to 26 March 1866 (Emma Darwin's diary (DAR 242)).

[15] CD refers to *Variation*. John Murray had proposed that CD produce a fourth edition of *Origin* (see letter from John Murray, 21 February [1866]).

From Maxwell Tylden Masters March 1866

International Horticultural Exhibition, | *& Botanical Congress,* | *Office, 1, William Street,* Lowndes Square, | *Knightsbridge, S.W.*

March *1866*

Sir/

I am desired by the Committee of the Botanical Congress[1] to ask you to allow your name to be added to the list of its members which already comprises those of

Prof A. de Candolle President
Prof Babington
J. J. Bennett Esq
Rev[d]. M J Berkeley
Prof Bentley
D[r]. J. E. Gray
D[r]. Welwitsch
John Miers Esq
W. Carruthers Esq[2]
and others—

A Programme will shortly be sent to you[3]

in the meantime I beg the favor of an early reply and am Sir | Your obedient Servant | Maxwell. T. Masters | MD | Hon. Sec. Congress—

P.S. | Private— not official!

My dear Sir/

Owing to D[r]. Seemann's somewhat sudden departure and the establishment of a congress committee only during the last few days I am ignorant if any communication has been sent you—[4] Pray excuse me for troubling you twice over if I have done so

DAR 171: 74

[1] Masters was secretary of the International Horticultural Exhibition and Botanical Congress, held in South Kensington, London, from 22 to 31 May 1866. CD became one of the twenty-four vice-presidents of the committee of the botanical congress. Earlier international botanical and horticultural congresses had been held in Brussels (1864) and Amsterdam (1865). (*International Horticultural Exhibition* 1866, pp. 6–9, 16.)

[2] The references are to Alphonse de Candolle, Charles Cardale Babington, John Joseph Bennett, Miles Joseph Berkeley, Robert Bentley, John Edward Gray, Friedrich Welwitsch, John Miers, and William Carruthers.

[3] The congress programme has not been found in the Darwin Archive–CUL; however, the papers were published, with a detailed report of the exhibition and congress, in *International Horticultural Exhibition* 1866.

[4] Masters refers to Berthold Carl Seemann, who was absent from Britain between March and August 1866 on an expedition to Nicaragua (*Journal of Botany* 10 (1872): 5). No letter from Seemann to CD about the congress has been found.

From Frederick Smith March 1866

British Museum
March 1866

⟨*one page obscured*⟩ or four places—and I have distinct recollection of my own daughter being stung twice or thrice by a wasp that was shut up in the crevaces of her bonnet. In fact I dont recollect any instance of a wasp leaving its sting in the wound.—[1]

If you have contrary experience you know much more of the matter than I do.—

Neither Bombus or Apathus leave their sting in the wound to my knowledge.[2] Pompilus and all the Crabronidae sting repeatedly without damage to the ⟨w⟩eapon of defence[3] and ⟨*3 or 4 words missing*⟩ use their ⟨*3 or 4 words missing*⟩ on being ⟨cau⟩ght— The most severe and excrutiating pain—although not of long duration—is that produced by the sting of Mutilla, these insects have the sting nearly the length of the abdomen and are most dangerous insects to handle— thus in the extensive Genera Philanthus & Cerceris—both furnished with formidable stings, it is a matter of impossibility to persuade them to use them—[4] I have many times experimented in various ways but never succeeded in inducing them to sting— Philanthus you will recollect—preys upon the *[*Spica*]* *[one line illegible]* which they paralyze by stin⟨ging.⟩ Cerceris more frequently selects different *[*Curculios*]*—some species ⟨ ⟩licti &c. but none of them will use their sting when caught in the hand—

I may sum up by saying that as far as my observations have l⟨ed⟩ me— I know of no insects that leave their stings in the wound except the species of Honey Bees and I once saw an instance of an Ichneumon—Ophius leaving its ovipositor in a wound[5] ⟨prod⟩uced by piercing a Ladys ⟨ ⟩ and with great subsequent pain & inflammation ⟨ ⟩ ⟨ ⟩ Ever yours | sincerely | F Smith

Ch Darwin Esq

Damaged
DAR 177: 197

CD ANNOTATIONS

Glued to first page: '⟨ ⟩ wasps leave ⟨ ⟩ stings in wound— Knows only of Hive bees *doing so [*interl*]— Certain genera have very long stings but will never use them as organ of defence when captured.! *(Marked passage) [*added pencil margin*] Proof that *using* a weapon is a distinct ⟨ ⟩t;— it does ⟨ ⟩ [*one word illeg*] having it—' *added pencil*
1.1 or four . . . I do.— 2.2] *crossed pencil*
3.1 Neither . . . hand— 3.12] *enclosed in square brackets, pencil*
4.1 I may . . . F. Smith 4.5] *crossed pencil*

1 In *Journal of researches* 2d ed., pp. 35–6, CD described repeated stinging of a spider by a *Pepsis* wasp. Later, in *Origin*, p. 202, CD wrote, 'Can we consider the sting of the wasp or of the bee as perfect, which, when used against many attacking animals, cannot be withdrawn . . . and so inevitably causes the death of the insect . . . ?' However, in the fourth and later editions, only the bee was mentioned, in this sentence, as dying after stinging (Peckham ed. 1959, p. 374). For earlier correspondence about the effects of stinging on the survival of bees and wasps, see *Correspondence* vol. 9, letter from John Innes, [before 6 April 1861], and letter from J. D. Glennie Jr, 6 April 1861. For more on the stinging behaviour of solitary wasps and an interpretation of its evolution, see Steiner 1986, pp. 65–7.

2 *Bombus*, the humble-bee, and *Apathus* (now *Psithyrus*), the cuckoo bumble-bee, are closely related, the latter laying its eggs in the nests of the former (*ML* 1: 262, n. 1).

3 *Pompilus* and Crabronidae are a genus and a family of predatory wasps, respectively.

4 *Mutilla*, *Philanthus*, and *Cerceris* are genera of predatory wasps. On the sequence of stimuli required to induce stinging in *Philanthus*, see Tinbergen 1969, pp. 47–8.

5 *Ophius* is a genus of parasitic ichneumon wasps.

From Charles Lyell 1 March 1866

53 Harley Street
March 1st./66.

My dear Darwin

Please sign the memorial & return it by return of post as no time is to be lost.[1] I have had Hooker's letter copied.[2] I feel sure that the whole globe must at times have been superficially cooler— Still I think that during extreme excentricity the sun would make great efforts to compensate in perihelion for the chill of a long winter in aphelion in one hemisphere & a cool summer in the other—[3]

I think you will turn out to be right in regard to meridianal lines of mountain chains by which the migrations across the equator took place while the was contemporaneous tropical heat of certain low lands, where plants requiring heat &

Charles Darwin in 1866
Photograph by Ernest Edwards
By permission of the Syndics of Cambridge University Library

Elizabeth Darwin
Photograph taken by Leonard Darwin, *c.* 1865?
By permission of the Syndics of Cambridge University Library

moisture were saved from extinction, by the heat of the earth's surface, which was stored up in perihelion being prevented from radiating off freely into space by a blanket of aqueous vapour caused by the melting of ice & snow.[4] But though I am inclined to profit by Croll's maximum excentricity for the glacial period, I consider it quite subordinate to geographical causes or the relative position of land & sea & the abnormal excess of land in polar regions.[5] It is a vast subject & if one applies to the astronomer there is no end to the number of uncertain data which it has never been worth their while to calculate for their own purposes. The worst of all the uncertainties is that which relates to the temperature of space[6]

believe me | ever most truly yrs | Cha Lyell

DAR 91: 89–90

[1] The memorial has not been identified, but may be that submitted by CD and others to W. E. Gladstone, 14 May 1866 (see this volume).

[2] Lyell refers to the letter from J. D. Hooker, 21 February 1866. CD had forwarded part of the letter to Lyell, having been told by Joseph Dalton Hooker that Lyell wished to see it (see letter from J. D. Hooker, [26 or 27 February 1866], and letter to J. D. Hooker, [28 February 1866] and n. 3).

[3] For CD's belief that the entire earth was cooler during the glacial period, see the letter to Charles Lyell, 7 February [1866] and n. 12. Hooker had disagreed with CD on this and related topics in his letter to CD of 21 February 1866. The effects on global climate of aphelion and perihelion, eccentricity of the earth's orbit, and other astronomical phenomena are discussed in chapter 13 of C. Lyell 1867–8.

[4] Lyell refers to CD's argument in *Origin*, pp. 377–8, that temperate plants may have crossed through the tropical regions near the equator during a glacial period by means of mountain ranges, which would have remained cooler, while tropical plants were preserved in the greater heat of the low-lying areas. This would account for the existence of similar species in both the northern and southern temperate zones. For some years, Hooker challenged CD on the problem of the survival of tropical plants in 'so very cool a greenhouse' as would be required to allow temperate plants to cross the equator, suggesting that the distribution of plants and animals could be better explained by land-bridges and continental extension (see *Correspondence* vol. 11, letter to J. D. Hooker, 5 March [1863] and n. 17). In the fourth edition of *Origin*, CD admitted that the survival of tropical species was a difficulty for his theory (*Origin* 4th ed., pp. 450–1), but this text was not retained in later editions (see Peckham ed. 1959, pp. 599–603). CD later explained the survival of tropical plants according to James Croll's theory of ice ages that alternated between hemispheres, and during which the temperature of the non-glaciated hemisphere rose (*Origin* 5th ed., pp. 450–61; see also n. 5, below). Lyell, however, had invoked alternate meridional belts of cooler and warmer temperature to explain the survival of species during the glacial period (C. Lyell 1863, pp. 366–7).

[5] Croll had recently published a paper relating the occurrence of ice ages to the eccentricity of the earth's orbit and to the longitude of the perihelion (Croll 1866a). For more on changes in global temperature, including the significance of Croll's work to CD's theory of the migration of plants during the glacial period, see the letter to Charles Lyell, 7 February [1866] and n. 12, and the letter from J. D. Hooker, 21 February 1866 and n. 10; see also the letter to J. D. Hooker, [28 February 1866] and n. 7. Lyell explained former changes in climate in relation to geographical and astronomical causes in C. Lyell 1867–8, chapters 12 and 13, respectively. For a summary of Lyell's position on former climate changes, see Ospovat 1977 and Fleming 1998.

[6] CD wrote of uncertainties about the temperature of space, in the light of recent contributions by physicists and astronomers to the understanding of glaciation, in the letter to J. D. Hooker, [28 February 1866].

To Thomas Gold Appleton 2 March [1866][1]

Down Bromley Kent
Mar 2.

My dear Mr Appleton

I am very much obliged to you for your kind note & wish to aid my heretical transmutation doctrines.[2] I hope you will be so good as to give my sincere thanks to Mr C. C. Fuller for all the trouble which he has taken.[3]

The creature I am sorry to say is not a fish; but the larva of some Batrachian or Frog-like animal.

I have sent the specimen to the British Museum where they are glad to have it for they have nothing exactly the same, but tell me that it is closely allied to the Axoltl of Mexico & to the Mud devil of the lakes of N. America.[4]

We often remember the very pleasant visit you paid us many years ago, & sincerely wish it c^d be repeated.[5]

My wife joins in very kind remembrances to you & I remain | my dear Mr Appleton | yours very sincerely | Charles Darwin

LS
Boston Public Library Rare Books and Print Departments–Courtesy of the Trustees

1 The year is established by the relationship between this letter and the letter from J. E. Gray, 28 February 1866.

2 See *Correspondence* vol. 13, letter from T. G. Appleton, 5 December [1865].

3 Colonel Charles C. Fuller gave Appleton a specimen of a 'very curious fish' with legs, which Appleton forwarded to CD (see *Correspondence* vol. 13, letter from T. G. Appleton, 5 December [1865]). Fuller has not been further identified.

4 For the report on the specimen by John Edward Gray of the British Museum, see the letter from J. E. Gray, 28 February 1866.

5 Appleton had visited Down House in October 1849 (Emma Darwin's diary (DAR 242)). Emma Darwin's cousin, Robert James Mackintosh, had married Appleton's sister (Wedgwood and Wedgwood 1980, pp. 248–9).

To Charles Lyell [3 March 1866][1]

Down
Saturday

My dear Lyell

I returned the memorial this morning & hope it may be successful.—[2]

I wish I had earlier known how interested you were on mundane cool period, for *perhaps* I could have given you additional facts.[3] I worked in some new facts in last German Edit. of Origin & they will appear in the new Eng. Edit, but this will be too late for you.[4] There is one rather important consideration, as it seems to me, viz that it can be proved that individuals of the same plant, growing N. & S, or growing on mountains & plains, certainly become acclimatised & transmit different constitutional powers of withstanding cold to their seedlings; & this would come into play with the slowly advancing glacial period.—[5]

You must have given up already so much time to subject that I do not suppose my M.S., which I wrote some ten years ago, would be worth your reading: it is at your service & is well copied out but long, viz 47 Pages folio.— —[6] Do not answer on this account.—

It is curious how, I find, facts turning up in support of same view: but the other day I read a paper on the representative closely allied Petrels of N. & S. oceans.—[7]

Very many thanks for your note.—[8]

Ever yours | C. Darwin

American Philosophical Society (315)

[1] The date is established by the relationship between this letter and the letter from Charles Lyell, 1 March 1866. In 1866, 3 March was the first Saturday after 1 March.

[2] See letter from Charles Lyell, 1 March 1866 and n. 1.

[3] Lyell altered the text of the tenth edition of *Principles of geology* (C. Lyell 1867–8) to include detailed discussion of former climate changes, and in particular the effect of glaciation on climate. For a comparison with the ninth edition, and a summary of the changes and extensive additions incorporated into chapters 10 to 13 of the tenth edition, see C. Lyell 1867–8, p. iv.

[4] CD refers to Bronn trans. 1863, and to the fourth edition of *Origin*, published in November 1866 (*Publishers' Circular* 1866). CD's additions about glaciation in Bronn trans. 1863 are listed in *Correspondence* vol. 10, Appendix VIII, pp. 718–20; the majority of these were incorporated by CD in his revision of chapter 11, 'Geographical distribution', in the fourth edition of *Origin*. Lyell finished work on the tenth edition of *Principles of geology* in November 1866 (C. Lyell 1867–8, 1: vi). Lyell referred to the fourth edition of *Origin* in C. Lyell 1867–8, 1: 264, but not in connection with the mundane cold period.

[5] In *Origin* 4th ed., p. 448, CD wrote: 'Nor must it be overlooked that, as the cold will have come on very slowly, it is almost certain that many of the inhabitants of the tropics will have become in some degree acclimatised; in the same manner as the same species of plant when living on lowlands and highlands certainly transmit to their seedlings different constitutional powers of resisting cold.' Lyell included a similar passage on acclimatisation in the chapter on natural selection in the tenth edition of *Principles of geology* (C. Lyell 1867–8, 2: 319–40).

[6] CD's manuscript and notes for chapter 11 of his 'big book' on species, 'Geographical distribution', were written in 1856. The manuscript CD refers to is in the Darwin Archive–CUL, DAR 14: D1–47 (see *Natural selection*, pp. 534–66).

[7] CD apparently refers to his theory of migration during the glacial period, on which Lyell had commented in his letter of 1 March 1866, and to Hutton 1865 ('Notes on some of the birds inhabiting the southern ocean'). Frederick Wollaston Hutton noted a close resemblance between species of petrel inhabiting the northern hemisphere and distinct species inhabiting the southern hemisphere; Hutton termed these similar species 'analogues' and suggested that they had originated when southern species migrated northwards during the glacial period and subsequently became isolated. There is an annotated presentation copy of Hutton 1865 in the Darwin Pamphlet Collection–CUL.

[8] Letter from Charles Lyell, 1 March 1866.

To Robert Caspary 4 March 1866

Down. | *Bromley.* | *Kent. S.E.*
Mar. 4. 1866

My dear Sir

I am extremely obliged to you for your kind letter & photograph, which I am very glad to possess.[1] I enclose one of myself the only one I have, taken by one of my sons.[2] I am also very grateful for the two papers & for that received yesterday of the Amsterdam Congress. These papers will be of the *highest* possible interest to me; but I have as yet read only that on the rose, for I am a very poor German scholar, & I suffer much from weak health.[3]

One ought not to wish on any side in Science, but I cannot help wishing to believe in the graft & stock producing buds with blended characters. Perhaps this very wish makes me too cautious, for I am not fully persuaded by your rose case; I hope your longer paper will have a more convincing effect.[4] In a work which I hope to publish this autumn "on Domesticated animals & cultivated plants", I have a chapter devoted to the same subject as your paper.[5] I shall be particularly glad to read your criticisms on my view that no plant is perpetually self-fertilized. I still retain faith in this view & believe that the exceptional cases will some day be explained.[6]

With cordial thanks & sincere respect I remain | my dear Sir yours very faithfully | Charles Darwin

LS
DAR 92: A38–9

[1] Caspary enclosed his photograph with his letter of 25 February 1866. The photograph has not been found in the Darwin Archive–CUL.

[2] CD probably refers to a copy of the photograph taken by his son William Erasmus Darwin in April or May 1864; see *Correspondence* vol. 12, frontispiece, and letter from W. E. Darwin, [19 May 1864] and n. 8. CD continued to send this photograph to correspondents during 1865 (*Correspondence* vol. 13).

[3] The paper 'of the Amsterdam Congress' was Caspary 1865a; see letter to Robert Caspary, 21 February [1866] and n. 2. The paper 'on the rose' was Caspary 1865c; see letter from Robert Caspary, 25 February 1866 and n. 4. The third paper was Caspary 1865b; see letter from Robert Caspary, 25 February 1866 and n. 3.

[4] Caspary 1865c described a hybrid rose that displayed both blended characters and those of the parental forms (see letter from Robert Caspary, 25 February 1866 and n. 4). CD wrote on the front of his copy of Caspary 1865c: 'I cannot yet tell whether to put amongst sports or effects of grafting'. For CD's interest in the blending of characteristics of scion and stock, see also the letter to Robert Caspary, 21 February [1866], n. 3. Caspary 1865a contained a more extensive discussion of graft hybrids than Caspary 1865c.

[5] CD referred to Caspary 1865a and 1865c in his chapter 'On bud variation, and on certain anomalous modes of reproduction and variation', in *Variation* (see *Variation* 1: 380, 388–9). *Variation* was published in 1868.

[6] See letter from Robert Caspary, 25 February 1866 and n. 3. CD reiterated his views on the advantages of crossing in *Variation* 2: 174–6.

From Charles Lyell 5 March 1866

March 5th, 1866

. . . In the beginning of Hooker's letter to you he speaks hypothetically of a change in the earth's axis as having possibly co-operated with redistribution of land and sea in causing the cold of the Glacial period.[1] Now, when we consider how extremely modern, zoologically and botanically, the Glacial period is proved to be, I am shocked at any one introducing, with what I may call so much levity, so organic a change as a deviation in the axis of the planet . . .[2]

Incomplete
ML 2: 158

[1] Lyell refers to Joseph Dalton Hooker. See letter from J. D. Hooker, 21 February 1866. CD had forwarded part of that letter to Lyell at Hooker's request (see letter from J. D. Hooker, [26 or 27 February 1866], and letter to J. D. Hooker, [28 February 1866] and n. 2).

[2] James Croll had newly calculated that the glacial epoch ended 80,000 years before 1800, having begun 240,000 years earlier; he estimated that the coldest period occurred between 200,000 and 210,000 years before 1800 (Croll 1866a). In his letter of 21 February 1866, Hooker expressed the view that the evidence on which belief in the glacial period was founded could have been produced by various earlier global circumstances, including a slight shift in the earth's axis. Hooker may have misinterpreted Croll 1865a as implying a change in the axis of the earth (see *Correspondence* vol. 13, letter from F. H. Hooker, 6 September [1865] and n. 6); however, Croll 1865a concerned the effect of icecaps on the centre of gravity, rather than the axis, of the earth (see also Fleming 1998, p. 166). Lyell did not believe that the earth's centre of gravity had altered much either (see *Reader*, 13 January 1866, p. 44).

From Fritz Müller[1] 6 March 1866

Desterro, Brazil,
6. März 1866.

Verehrter Herr!

Da ich einen Brief vor ein paar Wochen abgeschickt habe, so schreibe ich Ihnen heute nur, um Ihnen zu sagen, dass ich Ihren freundlichen Brief vom 11. Januar richtig empfing, und um Ihnen für das neue werthvolle Geschenk zu danken, das Sie mir anzubieten die Güte haben.[2] Da alles, was von Ihnen kommt, mir immer sehr angenehm sein wird, und da alles, was sich auf Ihre Theorie bezieht, meiner grössten Theilnahme immer sicher ist, so werde ich auch mit grosser Befriedigung und herzlichem Dank die zweite Auflage der deutschen Uebersetzung der "Origin" in Empfang nehmen.

Die letzten zwei Sommer (von 1863 auf 64 sowohl als von 64 auf 65) waren hier ungewöhnlich trocken und diese Trockenheit scheint, obwohl sie nicht stark genug war, dem Ackerbau viel Schaden zu thun, dennoch manche Veränderungen in der relativen Häufigkeit vieler unserer Thiere und Pflanzen hervorgebracht zu haben;[3] verschiedene Arten sind augenscheinlich aus Oertlichkeiten verschwunden, wo sie früher in Menge vorkamen.— So waren die Ränder einiger Gräben nahe bei der "Villa do Itajahy"[4] früher bedeckt von einer sehr zierlichen Aeschynomene, von der ich, als ich letzthin dort vorbeikam, nicht ein einziges Exemplar fand; die Stelle dieser Art war besetzt von einer anderen noch schöneren Leguminose, nemlich Daubentonia.[5] Diese letztere sah ich nie vor der grossen Ueberschwemmung vor dem Jahre 1855; seitdem ist sie an den Ufern des Itajahy sehr häufig geworden.—[6] In einem kleinen Graben nahe der Küste lebten früher Myriaden eines zarten Closterium;[7] dieser Graben trocknete vollständig aus und blieb so, bis der gegenwärtige regnerische Sommer ihn wieder mit Wasser füllte; nun sind die Conferve, die Cypris, die Cyclops u.s.w. wieder erschienen,[8] aber vergeblich sah ich mich um nach dem Closterium, von dem Max Schultze einige Zeichnungen für sein Archiv zu haben wünschte.—[9] Vor ein paar Tagen wollte ich einem Freunde die Bewegung in den Wurzelhaaren einer Hydrocharidee (Limnobium) zeigen;[10] ich ging deswegen nach einem Graben, den ich in früheren Jahren jeden Tag überschreiten musste und der damals ausschliesslich von dieser Pflanze bedeckt war; jetzt konnte ich kaum ein paar Exemplare sammeln, da die Pflanze vollständig durch eine ausserordentlich häufige Heteranthera ersetzt war.—[11] Unsere einzige Orchidee aus der Ophrys-Gruppe (Bonatea) scheint auch der Dürre auf unserer Insel unterlegen zu sein, sie kommt nur noch auf dem Festlande vor.—[12] Orchestia Darwinii war in Folge der Dürre ausserordentlich selten geworden; jetzt ist der grössere Theil des Gebietes, welches sie früher mit Ausschluss jeder andern Art von Amphipoden einnahm, in Beschlag genommen von Orch. Tucuranna, und obwohl sie auf dem kleinen Gebiet, welches sie noch inne hat, sehr zahlreich vorkommt, so gelang es mir doch nicht, ein einziges Exemplar einer der beiden Formen von Männchen zu finden, welche früher beide offenbar gleich häufig waren.—[13] Ohne Zweifel wird es noch eine grosse Anzahl anderer Pflanzen und Thiere geben, welche durch jene Dürre beeinflusst sind; auf alle, die ich erwähnte, zu achten, wurde ich durch verschiedene anderweite Beweggründe veranlasst und stellte so zufällig die Veränderung fest.

Auch zu Zeiten, wo kein aussergewöhnlicher Wechsel in den physikalischen Bedingungen das Ergebniss des "Kampfes ums Dasein" beeinflusst, sind die relativen Zahlen der verschiedenen thierischen und pflanzlichen Bewohner eines Landes oder Meeres keineswegs unveränderlich, sondern, wie ich meine, erheblich wechselnde Grössen, und dies wahrscheinlich noch vielmehr dort, wo Urvegetation das ganze Land bedeckt, als wo menschliche Kultur den wilden Thieren und Pflanzen kaum ein Mindestmass von Fläche übrig gelassen hat, auf dem sie um ihr Dasein kämpfen. Ich entsinne mich, dass auf dem schmalen Küstenstreifen dicht bei meinem Hause vielfacher Wechsel in der Fauna innerhalb der letzten 10 Jahre stattgefunden hat;[14] unglücklicherweise sah ich in früheren Jahren solche Veränderungen nicht voraus, auch glaubte ich nicht, dass sie von irgend welcher wissenschaftlicher Wichtigkeit wären; ich bin daher jetzt nicht im Stande, genauen Bericht von ihnen zu geben. Einer der Fälle, die mich am meisten in Erstaunen setzten, ist der folgende: Ein kleiner Felsen nahe bei der Küste, nur ein paar Fuss breit, war während der ersten Jahre meines hiesigen Aufenthaltes mit grossen Büschen eines braunen Bryozoon bedeckt; vor ungefähr 6 oder 7 Jahren sah ich zum ersten Male an einem benachbarten Felsen einige Exemplare eines anderen sehr zierlichen weissen Bryozoon, welches einige Jahre hindurch recht selten blieb; ungefähr 4 oder 5 Jahre danach wurde dieses aber plötzlich sehr häufig und bedeckte alle Felsen in der Nachbarschaft; auf unserm kleinen Felsen war jeder Ast des braunen Bryozoon mit Büschchen des weissen besetzt, und alle Exemplare des ersteren starben ab. Aber die Herrschaft der weissen Art war von kurzer Dauer; ungefähr ein halbes Jahr nach ihrer grössten Verbreitung begannen sie abzusterben und immer seltener zu werden; gegenwärtig kenne ich keinen Felsen mehr, von dem man sie beschaffen könnte. Was mir nun aber das Merkwürdigste erschien, ist, dass die braune Bryozoe, nachdem der weisse Eindringling verschwunden war, ihre Herrschaft auf dem

Felsen nicht wieder aufgenommen hat, obwohl sie ihn doch früher viele Jahre fast ausschliesslich bedeckt hatte; aber da ist jetzt eine vollständig neue Fauna, in der unter den befestigten Arten eine Clavellina[15] vorherrscht.

Incomplete
Möller ed. 1915–21, 2: 80–2

[1] For a translation of this letter, see Appendix I. For an account of the reconstruction of Fritz Müller's letters to CD, see the letter from Fritz Müller, 13 February 1866, n. 1.

[2] Müller refers to his letter to CD of 13 February 1866; in his letter to Fritz Müller of 11 January 1866, CD offered to send him a copy of the second German edition of *Origin* (Bronn trans. 1863).

[3] For an account of deforestation, agricultural intensification, and climatic instability in coastal south-eastern Brazil during the nineteenth century, see Dean 1995, pp. 191–6 *et seq.*

[4] Müller refers to the town of Itajahy (now Itajaí) at the mouth of the Itajaí Açu river on the Brazilian mainland.

[5] *Aeschynomeme* and *Daubentonia* (now *Sesbania*) are both large genera of leguminous plants (Mabberley 1997).

[6] Müller refers to the Itajaí Açu river. Müller's homestead was beside the river about twenty-five miles inland from the the town of Itajahy, and was later incorporated within the town of Blumenau. In November 1855, flooding had caused the river to rise nearly ten metres above its normal level (Möller 1915–21, 3: 63–4).

[7] *Closterium* is a genus of freshwater green algae.

[8] Müller refers to filamentous freshwater algae; to *Cypris*, a genus of ostracods or minute freshwater crustaceans; and to *Cyclops*, a genus of copepods that are also minute freshwater crustaceans. Müller referred to *Cypris*, *Cyclops*, and other copepods in several parts of *Für Darwin* (F. Müller 1864c; translated as Dallas trans. 1869).

[9] Max Johann Sigismund Schultze founded *Archiv für mikroskopische Anatomie* in 1865; the journal did not publish illustrations of *Closterium* during its first ten years, the period of Schultze's editorship (Möller 1915–21, 2: IV *et seq.*). Schultze corresponded with Müller and in 1857 gave him a microscope to assist his biological work (*ibid.*, 1: 75).

[10] *Limnobium* is a genus of the family Hydrocharitaceae; protoplasmic streaming, that is, the movement of the contents of the protoplasm within individual cells, may be observed in the root hairs of the floating herb *L. spongia* (Mabberley 1997).

[11] *Heteranthera* is a genus of aquatic plants in the family Pontederiaceae.

[12] The flora of Santa Catarina state, where Müller lived, includes one species of the orchid genus *Bonatea*, *B. pratensis*, now *Habenaria pratensis*.

[13] Müller refers to the small crustaceans *Orchestia darwinii* and *O. tucurauna* (see F. Müller 1864c, p. 54, and Dallas trans. 1869, pp. 79–80).

[14] Müller refers to the coast of the island of Santa Catarina, Brazil. As well as his homestead beside the Itajaí Açu river in the mainland part of Santa Catarina state, Müller had a house at Destêrro on the island of Santa Catarina (*DSB*).

[15] Müller refers to *Clavelina*, a genus of sea squirts in the class Ascidiacea.

From George Henslow 8 March 1866

10 South Crescent | Bedford Sq W.C.
March 8/66

My dear Sir,

I must apologise for letting your kind letter of Dec 6th. lie unreplied, but I found I was unable to leave London in January, even to *attempt* to see you.[1] I sincerely hope you are better, as I have been given to understand you are, under Dr B. Jones' treatment.[2]

Very many thanks for the paper on Kidney Beans,[3] & the offer of a duplicate No. of your "tendril papers", which I feel disposed to accept, even now, if you will allow me; as I have marked & scored my copy all over that it is hardly fit to bind up with the rest of the journals.[4]

The Editor of the Popular Science Review has asked me to write another article for the July No. on *Naudin's* researches on *hybrids*: &c. & I thought I should like to study the subject first, & compare *other* writers & observers with his: can you oblige me with any references to such; or any papers on hybridization &c. if you could I should feel much obliged.[5]

I feel much tempted to run down, & take the liberty of calling upon you *in Easter week* if agreeable to yourself; as I shall have a holiday then: but perhaps you will kindly let me know if you are *then*, well enough to see me.

Yours very Sincerely | Geo Henslow

DAR 166: 153

[1] CD's letter to Henslow has not been found. In his letter to CD of 2 December 1865 (*Correspondence* vol. 13), Henslow had suggested that he visit CD in January 1866.

[2] CD became a patient of Henry Bence Jones in 1865; see *Correspondence* vol. 13, letter to J. D. Hooker, 27 [or 28 September 1865] and n. 14. On CD's continuing treatment by Jones during the early part of 1866, see the letter to H. B. Jones, 3 January [1866], and the letter from H. B. Jones, 10 February [1866].

[3] In his letter of 2 December 1865 (*Correspondence* vol. 13), Henslow asked CD whether he might keep a copy of CD's paper 'On the agency of bees in the fertilisation of papilionaceous flowers, and on the crossing of kidney beans' (*Correspondence* vol. 7, letter to *Gardeners' Chronicle*, [before 13 November 1858]; *Collected papers* 2: 19–25). For more on Henslow's interest in this topic, see *Correspondence* vol. 13, letter from George Henslow, 1 November 1865 and n. 9.

[4] 'Climbing plants' had been published as a double issue of the *Journal of the Linnean Society* (*Botany*) in June 1865; for more on the paper, its offprints, and separate commercial publication, see *Correspondence* vol. 13, letter to Asa Gray, 19 April [1865] and n. 16. Henslow's summary of 'Climbing plants' appeared in the January 1866 issue of *Popular Science Review* (Henslow 1866c).

[5] Henslow refers to Charles Victor Naudin; his review of Naudin 1858, 1863, and 1864 included references to the work of CD, Karl Friedrich von Gärtner, William Herbert, John Scott, and Max Ernst Wichura (Henslow 1866b).

To Charles Lyell 8 March [1866][1]

Down | ☞ **Bromley** Kent
Mar 8

My dear Lyell

Many thanks for your interesting letter.[2] From the serene elevation of my old age I look down with amazement at your youth, vigour & indomitable energy.[3]

With respect to Hooker & the axis of the earth, I suspect he is too much over worked to consider now any subject properly.[4] His mind is so acute & critical that I always expect to hear a torrent of objections to any thing proposed; but he is so candid that he often comes round in a year or two. I have never thought on the causes of the glacial period, for I feel that the subject is beyond me;[5] but, though I hope you will own that I have generally been a good & docile pupil to you, yet I must confess that I cannot believe in change of land & water being more than a subsidiary agent:[6] I have come to this conclusion from reflecting on the geograph. distribution of the inhabitants of the sea on the opposite sides of all our continents, & of the inhabitants of the continents themselves.[7]

But now to business— I send by this post the M.S.: if any will be of use to you, I think it will be the pages tied together by green ribbon, which have appeared in the second German & French editions & will come in this summer in the English edition.[8] Please return these pages in *about a week's time*; the rest you may keep as long as you like. This rest is the old M.S. which I abstracted for the Origin[9] & I doubt whether you will find it of any use; but if you read it possibly one or two facts may be new to you. I have thought it best also to send some pencil notes & a letter from Hooker after he had read this 10 y^r old M.S.[10]

Yours most sincerely | C. Darwin

LS(A)
American Philosophical Society (316)

1 The year is established by the relationship between this letter and the letter from Charles Lyell, 5 March 1866.

2 See letter from Charles Lyell, 5 March 1866.

3 CD was in fact twelve years younger than Lyell.

4 CD refers to Joseph Dalton Hooker, and to the letter from J. D. Hooker, 21 February 1866, which CD had forwarded to Lyell at Hooker's request (see letter from J. D. Hooker, [26 or 27 February 1866], and letter to J. D. Hooker, [28 February 1866]). Hooker referred to the demands of his work and lack of time in all his letters to CD in February 1866 (see letters from J. D. Hooker, 4 February 1866, 21 February 1866, and [26 or 27 February 1866]).

5 Although every edition of *Origin* has lengthy discussions of how the glacial period affected the distribution of plants and animals, consideration of the causes of glaciation appeared only in the fifth and sixth editions (*Origin* 5th ed., pp. 451–2, and *Origin* 6th ed., p. 336; see also letter from Charles Lyell, 10 March 1866, n. 8).

6 According to Lyell, former extremes of climate were induced by changes in the position of land and sea on the surface of the globe (see C. Lyell 1853, pp. 110–11, and subsequent editions of his *Principles of geology*). On CD's earlier disagreement with Lyell's view, see *Correspondence* vol. 12, letter to J. D. Hooker, 23 September [1864] and n. 10. CD had formerly refrained from expressing his disagreement directly to Lyell (see *Correspondence* vol. 10, letter to A. C. Ramsay, 5 September [1862]).

7 In *Origin* 4th ed., p. 427, CD enumerated 'several facts in distribution' as evidence against the view that there had been large changes in the position and extent of continents. CD's facts included the great difference in the marine faunas on the opposite sides of continents, and the similarity between contemporary organisms in some areas and their counterparts of the Tertiary era. For more on CD's views about geographical distribution and the former extent of continents, see, for example, *Correspondence* vol. 13, letter to J. D. Hooker, 22 and 28 [October 1865] and nn. 11 and 12.

8 CD refers to the chapter on geographical distribution in the manuscript of his 'big book' on species (*Natural selection*, pp. 534–66; see letter to Charles Lyell, [3 March 1866] and n. 6). CD also refers to manuscript pages of additions to the second German edition of *Origin* (Bronn trans. 1863), and the second French edition (Royer trans. 1866). The fourth edition of *Origin* was published in November 1866 (*Publishers' Circular* 1866). For details of the additions and corrections to the second German edition of *Origin*, see *Correspondence* vol. 10, Appendix VIII.

[9] CD refers to the manuscript of chapter 11 of his 'big book' on species; see n. 8, above. The chapter was reworked as chapter 11, and page 399 in chapter 12, of *Origin.*

[10] Hooker's pencil notes on the manuscript of chapter 11 of CD's 'big book' on species are in the Darwin Archive–CUL (DAR 100: 109–10). CD also refers to the letter from J. D. Hooker, 9 November 1856 (*Correspondence* vol. 6). Hooker's notes on the chapter are reproduced as a memorandum with that letter in *Correspondence* vol. 6, and in *Natural selection*, pp. 575–7. A copy of the manuscript of the chapter, with annotations by Hooker, is in the Darwin Archive–CUL (DAR 14: D1–47).

From Charles Lyell 10 March 1866

53 Harley Street:
March 10, 1866.

My dear Darwin,—

Your precious MS. has arrived safe.[1] I will return it registered in a few days. I am much obliged to you for the privilege of reading it; and in regard to the notes prepared for the new edition,[2] I am amused to find how many of the topics are the same as those treated of in the letters of yourself, Hooker, and Bunbury, in commenting on the observations by Agassiz of marks of glaciation in the Organ Mountains.[3] By the way, you allude to Hooker's discovery of moraines in the Sikhim Mountains, which I believe are only about 7° farther from the equator than the Organ Mountains.[4] It is very interesting to read Hooker's letter dated 1856, and to see the impression which the MS. made on him, causing him to feel, as he says, 'shaky as to species' so long before the 'Origin' was published.[5] We certainly ran no small risk of that work never seeing the light, until Wallace and others would have anticipated it in some measure.[6] But it was only by the whole body of doctrine being brought together, systematised, and launched at once upon the public, that so great an effect could have been wrought in the public mind.

I have been doing my best to do justice to the astronomical causes of former changes of climate, as I think you will see in my new edition, but I am more than ever convinced that the geographical changes are, as I always maintained, the principal and not the subsidiary ones.[7] If you snub them, it will be peculiarly ungrateful in you, if you want to have so much general refrigeration at a former period.[8] In my winter of the great year, I gave you in 1830 cold enough to annihilate every living being.[9] The ice now prevailing at both poles is owing to an abnormal excess of land, as I shall show by calculation.[10] Variations in eccentricity have no doubt intensified the cold when certain geographical combinations favoured them, but only in exceptional cases, such as ought to have occurred very rarely, as paleontology proves to have been the case.[11]

Ever most truly yours, | Charles Lyell.

K. M. Lyell ed. 1881, 2: 408–9

[1] CD had sent Lyell the manuscript for chapter 11 of his 'big book' on species (*Natural selection*, pp. 534–66), and notes for additions to editions of *Origin* (see letter to Charles Lyell, 8 March [1866] and nn. 8 and 9; see also letter to Charles Lyell, [3 March 1866] and n. 6).

[2] Lyell refers to notes for additions to the fourth edition of *Origin* (see n. 1, above).

[3] Lyell refers to the letters from C. J. F. Bunbury to Charles Lyell, 3 February 1866 and 20 February 1866, the letters to Charles Lyell, 7 February [1866], 15 February [1866], and 22 February [1866], and the letter from J. D. Hooker, 21 February 1866. Lyell had sought comment from CD, Joseph Dalton Hooker, and Charles James Fox Bunbury on Louis Agassiz's claim that he had found evidence of former glacial action in the Organ Mountains of Brazil (see letter to Charles Lyell, 7 February [1866]).

[4] In the manuscript that he sent Lyell (see n. 1, above), CD wrote, citing J. D. Hooker 1854: 'Looking south we find in the Himalaya abundant evidence of the former much lower descent of the Glaciers, which have left behind them enormous Moraines' (DAR 14: D16 v.; see also *Natural selection*, p. 545 and n. 5). Hooker had described moraines and other evidence of former glaciation in valleys in Sikkim and elsewhere in the Himalayas in J. D. Hooker 1854, 1: 248, 380. The mountains of Sikkim are near latitude 28° N, and the Organ Mountains of Brazil are near latitude 23° S (*Times atlas*).

[5] CD sent Lyell Hooker's letter of 9 November 1856 (*Correspondence* vol. 6) with the manuscript of chapter 11 of his 'big book' on species (see n. 1, above).

[6] The publication of *Origin* was precipitated by a letter from Alfred Russel Wallace to CD containing Wallace's manuscript 'On the tendency of varieties to depart indefinitely from the original type'. See *Correspondence* vol. 7, letter to Charles Lyell, 18 [June 1858] and n. 3, and Appendixes III and IV.

[7] CD had expressed the view that geographical changes were subsidiary causes of former climate change (see letter to Charles Lyell, 8 March [1866] and nn. 6 and 7). In C. Lyell 1867–8, Lyell considered the geographical causes of former changes in climate in chapter 12; the corresponding astronomical causes are considered in chapter 13.

[8] Lyell refers to CD's manuscript (see n. 1, above), in which CD's theory of geographical distribution was based upon the premise that glaciation had at some stage affected the whole earth or 'a few great meridional belts' (DAR 14: D20, D34; see also *Natural selection*, pp. 548, 557). In *Origin*, the causes of the glacial period were first considered in the fifth edition, in which CD referred to James Croll's astronomical theory of glaciation (*Origin* 5th ed., pp. 451–2); in the sixth and final edition, CD referred briefly to Lyell's theory that glaciation was caused by changes in the relative positions of land and water and related it to Croll's theory (*Origin* 6th ed., p. 336; see also Peckham ed. 1959, pp. 593–4).

[9] Lyell thought that the earth's climate varied according to great cycles of change; in the first edition of *Principles of geology*, published between 1830 and 1833, a complete cycle was termed the 'great year', during the winter of which 'not only land as extensive as our existing continents, but immense tracts of sea in the frigid and temperate zones, would ... present a solid surface covered with snow' (C. Lyell 1830–3, 1: 116–23; quotation from pp. 119–20). For commentaries on Lyell's concept of the 'great year', see Secord 1997, pp. xviii–xix, and Leeder 1998, p. 108.

[10] In the tenth edition of *Principles of geology*, Lyell argued that the current proportion of land to sea in polar regions was greater than it once had been, and that consequently the temperature of the earth as a whole was cooler (C. Lyell 1867–8, 1: 247–8).

[11] Croll had recently estimated the dates of recurrent glacial periods as a function of periods of maximum eccentricity in the earth's orbit (Croll 1866a). Lyell challenged these estimated periods of glaciation on the grounds that palaeontological evidence indicated that some coincided with long periods of equable temperatures (C. Lyell 1867–8, 1: 299–300).

From George Henslow 12 March 1866

10 South Crescent | Bedford Sq | W.C.
Mch 12/66

My dear Sir,

I beg to thank you very much for your kind offer of a bed, which I shall be very thankful to accept, that I may not be compelled to run away so soon: & I am, indeed, rejoiced to hear you are so much better. I must thank you also for your valuable suggestions & references as to papers on Hybridism.—[1]

I am busy just now with a course of lectures (4) at Royal Institution, I enclose a Syllabus.—[2]

If Easter Monday would be convenient to you; (April 2) I shall be very happy to come & see you on that day.—[3]

Yours very truly | G Henslow.

Very many thanks for the copy of the tendril paper.—[4]

DAR 166: 154

[1] CD's letter to Henslow has not been found. Henslow had asked CD for references to works on hybridism for a paper he was writing on Charles Victor Naudin's research on hybridity, and had suggested that he might visit CD at Easter; see letter from George Henslow, 8 March 1866 and n. 5.

[2] The syllabus has not been found and was not enclosed (see letter from George Henslow, 17 March [1866]). Henslow gave four lectures on structural and systematic botany 'considered with reference to education & self-instruction' at the Royal Institution of Great Britain on Saturdays between 3 and 24 March 1866 (Greenaway ed. 1976, 12: 123, 126).

[3] Henslow was a dinner guest at Down on 2 April 1866 (Emma Darwin's diary (DAR 242)).

[4] 'Climbing plants'. See letter from George Henslow, 8 March 1866 and n. 4.

From Benjamin Dann Walsh 13 March 1866

Rock Island. Illinois. U.S.
March 13. 1866

Chas. Darwin Esq.
My dear Sir,

I send you herewith a copy of a recent Paper for yourself, & another for M^r. Wallace, which I must beg you to forward to him. I do not know & cannot find out his address, or I would not put you to this trouble.[1] He was kind enough to send me a copy of his Memoir on the *Malayan Papilionidæ*, which I am highly delighted with.[2]

Since my Paper was printed, I have had forwarded to me an extract from Jurine's "Nouvelle Methode &c" (Tome 1. Introd. p. 19), in which he notices the "bullæ" I have written about as occurring in certain Aculeate Hymenoptera, e.g. *Andrena* & *Nomada* among the Bees, though he says Hymenoptera "des deux premièrs ordres n'ont pas de bulles aux ailes, ou s'ils en ont, ce n'est qu'un petit nombre, et elles y sont très-irregulièrement placées."[3] Whereas, after examining hundreds of Eureopean species, belonging to scores of different genera of *Ichneumonidæ*, besides the N.A. genera already examined, I find that the "bullæ" in any given genus are just as constant & regular as any other generic character, & that the species on the two sides of the Atlantic follow precisely the same laws in this respect.[4]

Jurine says he was at first inclined to suppose that the 'bullæ" were apertures through which the air contained in the veins (which he considered as air-tubes) penetrated the membrane of the wing; but that, on reflecting that a very great number of Hymenoptera had no "bullæ" at all, he came to the conclusion that they were caused by the foldings of the wing (les plis de l'aile.)[5] But in the first place the wings of Hymenoptera are not folded, in the sense in which the wings of Coleoptera may be said to be folded, & in the second place it is impossible to fold up the wing of an *Ichneumon*, so as to make a fold wherever there is a "bullæ", without making additional folds in certain veins which never have any bullæ.

As I find these singular "bullæ" are far more general in Hymenoptera than I had supposed, & wherever they appear are homologous, I partly incline now to believe that they must be connected in some unknown manner with the circulatory system.[6] At all events in certain genera, e.g. *Metopius* & *Xylonomus*, very fine fibres seem to issue cross-wise from them into the membrane of the wing. But even if we make this assumption, I do not see that this explains the colorational phenomena, i.e. that in a black wing the bullæ & the adjacent membrane should be uniformly white or whitish. It is a very puzzling subject certainly. Singularly enough, Jurine has entirely overlooked what I have called the spots F & G, which are just as plain & constant in the Bee as in the Ichneumon.[7]

Yours very truly | Benj. D. Walsh

P.S. Do you know anything of a Quaker gentleman, "Mr. Wilson Armistead, Virginia House, Leeds?" He sent me a circular & a letter, stating that he was about to publish an illustrated Book on the Galls of the whole world & soliciting assistance.[8] I answered him by Mail last autumn, & afterwards on Oct. 13. 1865 sent him through the Smithsonian Institution a large Box containing specimens of Galls. Since then I have not heard a word from him, which does not strike me as particularly polite. But perhaps he is sick or dead. He stated that he was recommended by Prof. Westwood to apply to me.[9]

Field Museum of Natural History, Chicago

CD ANNOTATION

Left of signature: 'Wallace | 9 St Marks Crescent | Regents Park | N. W'[10]

1 Walsh refers to the second part of his essay 'On phytophagic varieties and phytophagic species' (Walsh 1864–5). CD's annotated copy is in the Darwin Pamphlet Collection–CUL. Alfred Russel Wallace leased a house at 9 St Mark's Crescent, London, in April 1865 (Raby 2001, p. 182; see also CD's annotation).

2 Walsh refers to Wallace 1864b.

3 The reference is to *Nouvelle méthode de classer les hyménoptères et les diptères*, by Louis Jurine (Jurine 1807, p. 20). The quotation may be translated as follows: Hymenoptera 'of the two first orders do not have bullae on their wings, or if they do have them, they are but few in number, and are positioned very irregularly'. Walsh had observed that 'blister-like spots' or 'bullae' appeared in identical number and pattern on the wings of different species of parasitic wasps in the family Ichneumonidae (Walsh 1864–5, pp. 209–15). Jurine did not class the Ichneumonidae among the two first orders of Hymenoptera, however (see Jurine 1807, p. (1)).

4 Walsh's further observations on bullae in the Ichneumonidae are reported in Walsh 1866b, pp. 241–8.

5 See Jurine 1807, p. 20, and Walsh 1866b, p. 245.

6 In Walsh 1866b, pp. 246–8, Walsh remarked that the bullae were located along wing-veins, which were blood-conducting tubes, but that their connection with the circulatory system was uncertain.

[7] Walsh identified five bullae (A to E), and two additional minute spots (F and G) on the wings of species of *Ichneumon* (Walsh 1864–5, pp. 209–15, and Walsh 1866b, pp. 241–2).
[8] Armistead published several papers on gall insects, but his book on the subject was unfinished at the time of his death in 1868 (*Royal Society catalogue of scientific papers*, *Entomologist* 4 (1868): 49).
[9] Walsh refers to John Obadiah Westwood.
[10] See n. 1, above.

From Rudolf Suchsland 16 March 1866

Swansea.
16th March 1866.

Sir,

Excuse the liberty I take in addressing you, without having the honour of your personal acquaintance. My object in writing to you is to ask your permission in the name of my father, Mr. F. E. Suchsland, publishing bookseller & head of the firm: Joh. Chr. Hermann'sche Verlagsbuchhandlung at Francfort on the Maine,[1] to publish a German translation of your works, especially of the renowned book: "On the origin of species by means of natural selection, or the preservation of the favoured races in the struggle for life".

It is true that one German translation by Professor Bronn of Heidelberg already exists; but as it is not generally considered a successful reproduction, I think, annother and more liberal translation has not only become a necessity for Germany considering the great importance and propagation of your theory there, but is also in your own interest.[2]

My father has already published two books by Dr. Rolle, which he took the liberty of sending to you viz: "Charles Darwin's Lehre von der Entstehung der Arten im Pflanzen- & Thierreich in ihrer Anwendung auf die Schöpfungsgeschichte dargestellt & erläutert von Dr. Fr. Rolle." & "Der Mensch, seine Abstammung & Gesittung im Lichte der Darwinschen Lehre von der Artentstehung & auf Grundlage der neueren geologischen Entdeckungen dargestellt von Dr. Fr. Rolle."[3]

These two books have contributed greatly to the propagation of your theory in Germany.[4] The first of them has been translated into the Russian language, while the second has been prohibited by the Russian Government.[5]

My father would, of course, try to secure the services of an eminent man of science for the purpose of translating your works & would also interest Dr. Rolle in the undertaking.[6] But before doing so, he wishes to be sure of your consent & to know your conditions.

I deem it necessary to remark, that, at present, my father could not guarantee an immediate fixed payment seeing that the cost of translating and publishing would amount to no inconsiderable sum.

I shall feel much obliged by an early answer & remain | yours | most respectfully | R. Suchsland | 25. Belle Vue street | Swansea.

Charles Darwin Esq. | Down | South Kent.

DAR 177: 271

[1] Friedrich Emil Suchsland was owner and head of Johann Christian Hermann'sche Verlagsbuchhandlung in Frankfurt (*Börsenblatt für den deutschen Buchhandel* 3 (1836): 830 and 36 (1869): 434).

[2] Two editions of Heinrich Georg Bronn's translation of *Origin* had been published (Bronn trans. 1860 and Bronn trans. 1863); they included an afterword in which Bronn commented on CD's transmutation theory (see also Montgomery 1988, p. 91). In his letter to the *Athenæum* of 18 April [1863], CD mentioned Bronn as an opponent of his transmutation theory (*Correspondence* vol. 11). For a contemporary account of German opinion of CD's theory, see the letter from Ernst Haeckel, 28 January 1866 and n. 5.

[3] In 1862, CD had been sent a copy of Friedrich Rolle's *Ch. Darwin's Lehre* (Rolle 1863; see *Correspondence* vol. 10, letter to Friedrich Rolle, 17 October [1862]); CD commented on the work in his letter to Friedrich Rolle, 30 January [1863] (*Correspondence* vol. 11). CD's annotated copies of the four parts of Rolle 1863 are in the Darwin Pamphlet Collection–CUL. CD received the five parts of Rolle's *Der Mensch* (Rolle 1866) in 1865 and 1866 (see letter from Friedrich Rolle, 28 January 1866 and n. 2). CD's lightly annotated copy of Rolle 1866 is in the Darwin Pamphlet Collection–CUL.

[4] Following the publication of Rolle 1863, Rolle gave an account of the response to CD's transmutation theory in Germany and informed CD of his efforts to propagate CD's theory in his letter to CD of 26 January 1863 (*Correspondence* vol. 11).

[5] *Ch. Darwin's Lehre* (Rolle 1863) was published in two Russian translations (Vladimirskii trans. 1864 and Usov trans. 1865). No Russian edition of *Der Mensch* (Rolle 1866) has been found; for an account of Russian censorship in the nineteenth century, see Choldin 1985. For more on the controversies associated with the reception of CD's transmutation theory in Russia, see Rogers 1988.

[6] For details of works by Rolle published by Johann Christian Hermann'sche Verlagsbuchhandlung, see Martin and Uschmann 1969, pp. 132–6. On the relationship between Rolle and Friedrich Emil Suchsland, see Martin and Uschmann 1969, pp. 30–1.

From George Henslow 17 March [1866][1]

10 South Crescent | Bedford Sq W.C.
Sat 17th Mch.

My dear Sir,

I wrote so hurridly that I forgot to thank you for your kind remarks about my paper on tendrils.[2] It has given me very great satisfaction & pleasure to hear that my résumé met with so decided an approval from you.—

I forgot also to enclose a copy of my Syllabus.[3]

I will ascertain if there will be any alteration in the trains for *April* & then write & ask if it will be convt. for you to see me on monday 2d..[4]

In mean time, believe me to be | My dear Sir | Yours very faithfully | Geo Henslow

C. Darwin Esq

DAR 166: 155

[1] The year is established by the relationship between this letter and the letter from George Henslow, 12 March 1866.

[2] Henslow refers to his letter of 12 March 1866 and his summary of 'Climbing plants' (Henslow 1866c), upon which CD apparently commented in a letter that has not been found.

[3] See letter from George Henslow, 12 March 1866 and n. 2.
[4] See letter from George Henslow, 12 March 1866 and n. 3.

From George Henslow [18–30 March 1866][1]

10 South Crescent | Bedford Sq | W.C.

My dear Sir,

I beg to thank you for your kind letter;[2] I should much like to have been able to accede to your proposal but my duties here forbid my availing myself of them: for I not only have a botanical class every *Sat^{y}.* evening, but am engaged every *Sunday* at St Stephens West^{r}. so that I could not possible go to Down on a Saturday:[3] so that if still agreeable to you I will come on April 2.[4]

Yours very truly | Geo. Henslow

DAR 166: 156

[1] The date range is established from the relationship between this letter and the letter from George Henslow, 17 March [1866], and from the assumption that CD had invited Henslow for a Saturday before 2 April. In 1866, the last Saturday before 2 April was 31 March.
[2] CD's letter to Henslow has not been found.
[3] Henslow probably refers to the botanical lectures that he gave at the Royal Institution on Saturdays in March 1866 (see letter from George Henslow, 12 March 1866 and n. 2); he was also headmaster of the Grammar School, Store Street, London (R. Desmond 1994), and may have given botanical classes there. Henslow probably also refers to St Stephen's Church, Rochester Row, Westminster.
[4] See letter from George Henslow, 12 March 1866 and n. 3.

From J. D. Hooker [19 March 1866][1]

Kew
Monday.

My dear Darwin

May I come to you on Saturday?[2] My wife & I are going to hear Acis & Galatea at the C.P., with a Lady friend, who lives hard by, & with whom *she* returns to sleep.[3] If you could meet me at Sydenham, with a trap of any kind, at about $5\frac{1}{2}$ PM I would go on to you. At some Hotel or the Sydenham station would perhaps be better than the palace itself, to meet the trap

Ever Yr affec | J D Hooker

DAR 102: 68

[1] The date is established by the date of Hooker's visit to Down, and by the date of the performance of *Acis and Galatea* (see nn. 2 and 3, below). In 1866, 19 March was the first Monday before 24 March.
[2] Hooker visited Down from Saturday 24 March to Monday 26 March 1866 (Emma Darwin's diary (DAR 242)).
[3] Hooker's wife was Frances Harriet Hooker. George Frideric Handel's *Acis and Galatea* was performed on 24 March 1866 at the Crystal Palace in Sydenham (*Athenæum*, 17 March 1866, p. 349). The friend has not been identified.

From J. D. Hooker to Emma Darwin [21 March 1866][1]

Kew
Wednesday

Dear Mrs Darwin

Thanks for your kind note.[2] Mrs Hooker is going to spend Sunday, with a Lady friend near Sydenham, she would have been delighted to come, but I think she had better wait for better weather. And now that your husband is "restored to his friends" I hope I may ask to bring her before long.[3]

I am counting the days till Saturday[4]

Ever most sincerely Yrs | Jos D Hooker

DAR 102: 67

[1] The date is established by the relationship between this letter and the letter from J. D. Hooker, [19 March 1866]. In 1866, the Wednesday after 19 March was 21 March.
[2] Emma Darwin's letter has not been found.
[3] Frances Harriet Hooker and J. D. Hooker visited Down in June 1866 (Emma Darwin's diary (DAR 242)).
[4] Hooker arrived at Down on Saturday 24 March 1866 (Emma Darwin's diary (DAR 242)).

From E. Schweizerbart'sche Verlagsbuchhandlung[1] 23 March 1866

Stuttgart
den 23 März 1866.

Verehrtester Herr!

Seit ich zum letztenmale das Vergnügen hatte, mich brieflich mit Ihnen über die 2te Auflage der deutschen Bearbeitung von "on the origin etc und die Uebersetzung der Orchideen zu unterhalten, sind nun schon $3\frac{1}{2}$ Jahre verflossen.[2]

Ihr berühmtes Werk hat auch in Deutschland viele Freunde gefunden, aber an Gegnern hat es ebensowenig gefehlt, wie diess bei einem in die früheren Anschauungen so tief einschneidenden Buche nicht anders seyn konnte.[3] Wie der unvergeßliche Bronn in seinem Prospecte sagte: "dass kein Naturforscher der sich nicht mit den in diesem Buche niedergelegten Thatsachen und neuen Gesichtspunkten vertraut gemacht auf der Höhe der Wissenschaft stehe etc"[4] So überzeuge ich mich, daß der Absatz der deutschen Ausgabe—wenn auch klein gegenüber dem in England—doch nachhaltig ist und namentlich jüngere Naturforscher für das Buch sehr eingenommen sind, von welchen es auch immer neu in Anregung gebracht wird.[5] Ich erlaube mir nun, verehrter Herr, Sie in Kenntniß zu setzen, dass ich wieder an eine neue Auflage denken muss und daß—falls Sie für diese neue deutsche Auflage Zusätze zu geben für angemeßen finden sollten, es mir sehr angenehm wäre, solche recht bald zu erhalten um den Druck der Auflage beginnen lassen zu können.[6]

Die Revision des Drucks so wie die Übersetzung der etwaigen Zusätze oder Aenderungen werde ich dem Herrn Professor Geinitz—in Dresden übertragen, der an des Herrn Bronn's Stelle in die Redaction des Jahrbuchs f. Min. u Palaeontologie eingetreten ist.[7]

Ihren gütigen Nachrichten hierauf sehe ich entgegen und bin mit größter Hochachtung und Verehrung Ihr | ergebenster | E. Schweizerbart.[8]

DAR 177: 71

[1] For a translation of this letter, see Appendix I. The letter was written by Christian Friedrich Schweizerbart, head of the Stuttgart publishing firm E. Schweizerbart'sche Verlagsbuchhandlung (see n. 8, below).

[2] See *Correspondence* vol. 10, letter from E. Schweizerbart'sche Verlagsbuchhandlung, 16 October 1862. The firm had published two German editions of *Origin* (Bronn trans. 1860 and 1863), and a German edition of *Orchids* (Bronn trans. 1862).

[3] On the reception of *Origin* in Germany, see the letter from Ernst Haeckel, 28 January 1866 and n. 5.

[4] Heinrich Georg Bronn's prospectus for the first German edition of *Origin* was published in *Neues Jahrbuch für Mineralogie, Geologie und Palaeontologie* (Bronn 1860a); Bronn was co-editor of the journal.

[5] A thousand copies of the second German edition of *Origin* (Bronn trans. 1863) were printed. See *Correspondence* vol. 10, letter from E. Schweizerbart'sche Verlagsbuchhandlung, 7 June 1862.

[6] See also letter from Rudolf Suchsland, 16 March 1866. Suchsland had criticised Bronn's translation of *Origin*, and had asked permission on behalf of his father, Friedrich Emil Suchsland, to publish a new translation.

[7] After Bronn's death in 1862, Hans Bruno Geinitz replaced him as editor of the *Neues Jahrbuch für Mineralogie, Geologie und Palaeontologie* (*Jubiläums-Katalog*, p. xvii). In the event, Geinitz was unable to undertake the revision, and the third German edition of *Origin* (Bronn and Carus trans. 1867) was overseen by Julius Victor Carus (see letter from E. Schweizerbart'sche Verlagsbuchhandlung, 10 May 1866).

[8] In his business communications, C. F. Schweizerbart continued to use the signature of his uncle, Wilhelm Emanuel Schweizerbart, from whom he had purchased the publishing firm in 1841 (*Jubiläums-Katalog*, pp. x–xi).

From Albert Müller 28 March 1866

2, Camden Villas, | Jasmin Grove, Penge | SE.
28th. March 1866.

Dear Sir.

I hope you will kindly excuse the liberty, I take in calling your attention to the latest work of my countryman Prof. O. Heer, "Die Urwelt der Schweiz". Zürich 1865.—[1] On pg 599 & seq., in a footnote, the author refers to your valuable observation, that f. sanguinea keeps less slaves in this country than in Switzerland;[2] but he adds. 'es sind diess aber unbedeutende Unterschiede, die nach den Jahreszeiten und auch nach den verschiedenen Stöcken wechseln". etc.—[3]

If it does not give you too much trouble, I should feel much obliged by your informing me at your convenience, to what circumstances you attribute the fact that these slaves are captured in greater numbers in Switzerland than in England.—

It seems to me that British ants, being through climate etc. in a harder struggle for life & food, ought rather be found to keep more slaves to attend to their wants, than their Swiss brethren, which have a richer fauna & flora to fall back upon & therefore less labour to perform.—

Apologizing for my intruding upon you, I am, | Dear Sir, | your's obediently | Albert Müller

Charles Darwin Esqre.

DAR 171: 280

1 Müller refers to Oswald Heer and Heer 1865.

2 In *Origin*, pp. 219–24, CD discussed the slave-making behaviour of the ant species *Formica sanguinea*. He remarked that in England the slave-ants stayed almost entirely within the nest, whereas in Switzerland they performed various activities outside the nest such as searching for aphids. These differences, CD suggested, were probably due to the slaves being captured in greater numbers in Switzerland than in England (*ibid.*, p. 221).

3 CD's remarks on *Formica sanguinea* are discussed in a note in Heer 1865, pp. 599–601. The passage quoted by Müller is on page 600 and may be translated: 'But these are insignificant differences, which vary with the seasons and also with different colonies.'

To Albert Müller 28 March [1866][1]

Down Bromley Kent
March 28th

Dear Sir

I shd. have been very glad to have given you the desired information, had it been in my power; but I can assign no reason for fewer slaves being captured in England than in Switzerland.[2] That this is the case, can hardly be doubted after Mr Smith's & my own examination of so many nests.—[3] I forget whether I stated in the *earlier* edition of the Origin that I had found one nest with the slaves going out in search of food.—[4]

I remain Dear Sir | Yours faithfully | Ch. Darwin

University Library, Basel, Allgemeine Autographensammlung, D

1 The year is established by the relationship between this letter and the letter from Albert Müller, 28 March 1866.

2 See letter from Albert Müller, 28 March 1866 and nn. 2 and 3.

3 CD's discussion of slave-making by *Formica sanguinea* and other ant species in *Origin*, pp. 219–24, was based primarily on observations made by him and the entomologist Frederick Smith in Britain (see *Correspondence* vols. 7 and 8). CD's observations of slave-making ants, made between 1858 and 1860, are in DAR 205.11: 88–107. CD's information on *F. sanguinea* in Switzerland was based on Huber 1810.

4 In *Origin*, p. 221, CD stated: 'I observed a few slaves mingled with their masters leaving the nest, and marching along the same road to a tall Scotch-fir-tree ... which they ascended together, probably in search of aphides or cocci.' This passage was unaltered in subsequent editions.

From Robert Swinhoe 28 March 1866

Amoy.
28 March, 1866.

Charles Darwin, Esq.r
My dear Sir,

On returning to my post at Takow after a 10 day's revel in the heart of the Formosan Mountains, I found orders awaiting me to repair to Amoy to relieve my brother-in-law M.r Pedder who goes home by this mail.[1] My sister, M.rs Pedder, has kindly offered to take home a small parcel for me.[2] It occurred to me on her making this offer that I was under promise to procure for you some Chinese Honey-comb, or rather comb of the Chinese Honey-Bee.[3] Enclosed in this box are several pieces of the article you desire, which my man procured after a long hunt through the town, this not being the season for gathering the honey— I hope you will be pleased with the present, and that you may find it to answer your purpose—[4]

If you have anything further that I can assist you in, do not fail to let me know of it. Now that I am in China *proper* again & once more within the line of regular communication I can the more easily procure any article you desire and find opportunities for forwarding such to you—

Your's sincerely, | Robert Swinhoe.

DAR 177: 329

[1] Swinhoe was in the British diplomatic service in Takow, Formosa (now Taiwan), and Amoy, China (P. B. Hall 1987). William Henry Pedder was British consul in Amoy (*Foreign Office list*).

[2] Mrs Pedder has not been further identified.

[3] The earlier correspondence between Swinhoe and CD about the comb of the Chinese honey-bee (*Apis indica*) has not been found. Swinhoe may have previously sent CD a specimen of the honey-bee from Amoy (see *Correspondence* vol. 12, letter to Frederick Smith, [*c.* 17 February 1864?] and n. 8).

[4] In 1863, Thomas White Woodbury had suggested to CD that it would be interesting to compare the size of the cells of *Apis indica* with those in the combs of European species of honey-bee (see *Correspondence* vol. 11, letter from T. W. Woodbury, 17 March 1863).

To Richard Kippist 31 March [1866]

Down Bromley | Kent
March 31

My dear Sir

Will you have kindness to grant me a favour. I have been for some time elected Honorary member of a *few* foreign Societies, & as I see everyone gives their titles in list of members I sh.d like to do so;[1] but I have mislaid most of the diplomas, & do not know how they sh.d be called.[2] Will you have the kindness to enter them in proper fashion, & then pass on the list to the *Royal Soc.* for its list of members[3]

I am honorary member of the Royal Soc. of Berlin,[4] ="Regia Scientarum academica Suecica" (which I suppose is same as Stockholm of which I am member)[5]

=Regia Scient. Soc. Upsalensis=[6] =Nat. Cæs. Cur.=[7] =Neuchatel,[8] (but probably this is not usually specified)— Philadelphia=[9] & Edinburgh.=[10]

By accident I have got two copies of little Book by Rütimeyer, so send one for Library of Linn. Soc.—[11]

My dear Sir | Yours sincerely | Ch. Darwin

Endorsement: '1866'
Linnean Society of London, Misc. loose letters, case 1: C. Darwin (4)

1 CD refers to the *List of the Linnean Society of London.*
2 CD mentioned that he had lost several of his diplomas in his letter to J. D. Hooker, 22 December [1865] (*Correspondence* vol. 13); in his reply of [23] December 1865, Joseph Dalton Hooker told CD that Kippist was responsible for maintaining the list of the Linnean Society's members that included their titles and diplomas. CD's extant diplomas are in DAR 229.
3 CD refers to the *List of the Royal Society.*
4 CD was elected a corresponding member of the Königliche-Preussische Akademie der Wissenschaften (Royal Prussian Academy of Sciences), Berlin, in 1863. See *Correspondence* vol. 11, Appendix III.
5 CD was elected a foreign member of the Regia Scientiarum Academia Svecica (Royal Swedish Academy of Sciences) in Stockholm in 1865. See *Correspondence* vol. 13, Appendix III.
6 CD was elected a fellow of the Regia Scientiarum Societas Upsaliensis (Royal Society of Sciences of Upsala) in 1860 (*LL* 3: 376; DAR 229: 2).
7 CD was elected a member of the Academia Caesarea Leopoldino-Carolina Naturae Curiosorum of Dresden in 1857. See *Correspondence* vol. 6.
8 CD was elected a corresponding member of the Société des Sciences Naturelles de Neuchâtel in 1863. See *Correspondence* vol. 11.
9 CD was elected a corresponding member of the Academy of Natural Sciences of Philadelphia in 1860. See *Correspondence* vol. 8.
10 CD was elected an honorary member of the Royal Society of Edinburgh in 1865 (see *Correspondence* vol. 13, Appendix III). CD held a number of other honorary memberships; these are listed in *LL* 3: 373–6, and in Freeman 1977, pp. 107–10.
11 The reference is probably to Rütimeyer 1863. CD's annotated copy is in the Darwin Library–CUL (see *Marginalia* 1: 718).

From Albert Müller 31 March 1866

2. Camden Villas, | Jasmin Grove | Penge SE.
31st. March 1866.

Dear Sir.

Whilst thanking you for your kind note of the 28th.,[1] I cannot help observing, that if our time would only devote a tithe of the energy it gives to the description of new species, to observations on the habits of living creatures, we should soon have "more light" on that most puzzling question, whether the theory of the descent from one ancestor can really bear the weight not so much of reasoning, but of facts.— I only hope, we may get more extensive evidence in your intended work, which has my best wishes.—[2]

Your's obediently | Albert Müller

Charles Darwin Esqre.

DAR 171: 281

[1] See letter to Albert Müller, 28 March [1866].
[2] Müller refers to *Variation*.

From Harriet Lubbock [April? 1866][1]

My dear M[r] Darwin

So many Thanks for y[r] kind Note.[2] I am only just returned from Leicestersh or wou[d] have written sooner. John & Ellen are away from home[3] but I am sure will quite agree with you so I send you 3£ 1 for each of us.[4] I hope dear M[rs] Darwin is pretty well I heard she had been ill wh I was very sorry for.[5] pray give her my very kind love—

I assure you all Lubbocks feel proud to get a Note from you & prize them so I can only thank you heartily for yours & hope you will believe me | Your much obliged | Harriet Lubbock

DAR 170: 18

[1] The year is established by the reference to the £3 donation (see n. 4, below). The month is conjectured from the reference to Emma Darwin's illness (see n. 5, below), and from the date of the Lubbocks' return from Europe (see n. 3, below).
[2] CD's note has not been found.
[3] John and Ellen Frances Lubbock were in Europe in the spring of 1866 (Hutchinson 1914, 1: 85–6). The letter from J. D. Hooker, [after 28 April 1866], suggests that John Lubbock had returned by the end of April. Harriet Lubbock was John Lubbock's mother.
[4] CD was treasurer of the Down Coal and Clothing Club, a local charity that supplied parishioners with coal and clothes in exchange for regular savings. The only year in which contributions of £1 each from John Lubbock, Ellen Lubbock, and Harriet Lubbock are recorded in the Coal and Clothing Club account book (Down House MS) is 1866. On CD's charitable work, see J. R. Moore 1985, p. 466, and Browne 2002, pp. 452–4.
[5] Emma Darwin's diary (DAR 242) records that she fell ill with influenza on 9 April 1866. CD's letter to Asa Gray, 16 April [1866], reports that she was still unwell; however, she had evidently recovered by 17 April as she recorded in her diary that she 'drove out' on that day.

From Rudolf Suchsland 2 April 1866

25. Belle Vue street | Swansea
2nd April 1866.

Ch. Darwin Esq. | Down | Bromley.
Sir,

I have to-day received an answer from my father, who is much obliged for your two letters.[1] He wrote to Mr. Schweizerbart at once after receiving the first one, but did not get an answer; it is plain, therefore, that Mr. Schweizerbart's proposal to you was only made in consequence of my father's letter, a translation of which I take the liberty to enclose.[2]

Neither my father nor I can pretend to judge, whether Prof. Geinitz is the right man to correct & revise the new edition; but I do not think it is doing him any wrong to say, that he has never before made himself thoroughly acquainted with your theory & under those circumstances it is a great question, whether the new edition will be an improvement on the preceding ones.[3]

A translation made by a good naturalist under Dr. Rolle's superintendance would, no doubt, propagate your ideas more correctly in Germany & would prevent your being misunderstood by German scientific men, which is now only too often the case.[4] In corroboration of this allow me to quote an article by Jurgen Bona Meyer, who is considered an eminent philosopher, in the last number of the "Preussische Jahrbücher" about "Darwin's theory" from Bronn's translation.[5] He certainly would have judged more favourably, if a more correct translation had been accessible to him.

Considering all this, it would perhaps be the best if more than one translation were published with your consent. A work of such vast importance should not be treated like every day publications. But, of course, as to that, you are the best judge. In case your final decision has already been taken, my father would be much obliged for your permission to publish the additions to the 8th English edition of "the Origin etc".[6]

He also desires me to ask you, whether you have published anything besides the following works:

Fertilizing of Foreign Orchids by Insects.
Geological Observations[7]
Natural History & Geography of H.M.S. Beagle[8]
Origin of Species
Researches into Natural History & Geology.
Observations on Volcanic Islands[9]
Voyage of a Naturalist round the World[10]
Zoology of the Voyage of H.M.S. Beagle.[11]

An answer at your early convenience will much oblige yours, dear Sir, most respectfully | R. Suchsland.

[Enclosure]

Translation

Frankfort ^{a}/M.
22nd March 1866.

Mr. Chr. Fr. Schweizerbart[12]
Stuttgart.

Dear Sir,

I have been asked to publish a new translation of Ch. Darwin's Origin of Species, the gentlemen, who will undertake the translation being of opinion, that Bronn's translation is very incorrect as to language & meaning & that, considering the importance of Darwin's theory, a new & thouroughly successful translation has become a necessity for Germany.[13]

I can, of course, not accept this proposal, without having satisfied your claims & therefore take the liberty to inquire, whether you are inclined to dispose of the remaining copies of the second edition for a moderate sum. If so, be good enough to let me know the number of copies remaining unsold.

An answer pr return of post will much oblige yours etc.

(signed) F. E. Suchsland | Firm: Hermannsche Verlagsbuchhandlung.

DAR 177: 272

1 CD's letters to Rudolf Suchsland's father, Friedrich Emil Suchsland, have not been found.

2 See enclosure. For Suchsland's earlier request for permission to publish a new German translation of *Origin*, see the letter from Rudolf Suchsland, 16 March 1866. Christian Friedrich Schweizerbart was director of the firm that had published two German editions of *Origin* (Bronn trans. 1860 and 1863); for the firm's proposal for a third edition, see the letter from E. Schweizerbart'sche Verlagsbuchhandlung, 23 March 1866.

3 The first and second German editions had been translated by Heinrich Georg Bronn, who died in 1862. Schweizerbart had suggested that the translation of the third edition be overseen by Hans Bruno Geinitz (see letter from E. Schweizerbart'sche Verlagsbuchhandlung, 23 March 1866).

4 The reference is to Friedrich Rolle. See letter from Rudolf Suchsland, 16 March 1866. See also letter from Friedrich Rolle, 28 January 1866 and n. 5.

5 Suchsland refers to a long review of the second German edition of *Origin* (Bronn trans. 1863) by Jürgen Bona Meyer in the *Preussische Jahrbücher* for March and April 1866 (Meyer 1866). No enclosure containing a quotation from Meyer has been found; however, a copy of the review is in the Darwin Pamphlet Collection–CUL. Meyer's criticisms were similar to those of Carl Wilhelm von Nägeli, and he was supportive of Nägeli's theory of species (see Meyer 1866, pp. 432–3, and letter to C. W. von Nägeli, 12 June [1866] and nn. 7, 8, and 10).

6 Suchsland wrote '8' in error. CD was preparing the fourth edition of *Origin*, which was published in November 1866 (*Publishers' Circular*).

7 The references are to *Orchids*, and *South America*.

8 This is a reference to *Journal of researches*.

9 The references are to *Origin*, *Journal of researches* 2d ed., and *Volcanic islands*.

10 The spine of *Journal of researches* (1860) reads *Naturalist's voyage round the world*. See Freeman 1977, p. 32.

11 *Zoology*.

12 Christian Friedrich Schweizerbart (see n. 2, above).

13 See nn. 3 and 4 above.

To J. D. Hooker 4 April [1866][1]

Down—
April 4th.

My dear Hooker

We have had G. Henslow here for two days & are very much pleased with him: there is something very engaging about him.—[2]

Many thanks about the Bonatea & the Water-lilies & about the Cucumber case.[3] Ask Mr Smith whether by any odd chance he has ever seen a bud with blended character arising from junction of stock & graft.—[4]

I will not forget about orchids; but it is not likely we shall have any to send you.— It was really **very** good in you to write about Pangenesis; for all such remarks lead one to see what points to bring out clearly.—[5] I think you do not understand my notions on Pangenesis

Firstly.— I do not suppose that each cell can reproduce the whole species. The essence of my notion is that each cell, by throwing off an atom or gemmule (which grows or increases under proper conditions) reproduces the parent-cell & nothing more; but I believe that the gemmules of all the cells congregate at certain points & form ovules & buds & pollen-grains.[6] I daresay they may congregate within a preexisting cell, passing through its walls like contents of pollen-tubes into embryonic sack; & it was partly on this account that I wished to learn about first appearance of buds.—[7] When you speak of "a single detached cell of Begonia becoming a perfect plant"; I presume you do *not* mean that each cell, when separated by the knife, will grow; but that a fragment of a leaf will produce buds at apparently every & any point;[8] if you mean more, I sh$^{d.}$ be specially grateful for information.—

Secondly.— I do *not* suppose that gemmules are preserved in each species of all its preexisting states up to the "irrepressible monad"; but am forced to admit that wonderfully many are thus preserved & are capable of development, judging from reversion; but reversion does not go to such astounding lengths as you put it.[9]

Thirdly. I do not suppose that a cell contains gemmules of any future state; but only that when a cell is modified by the action of the surrounding cells or of the external conditions, that the so modified cell throws off similarly modified atoms of its contents or gemmules which reproduce the modified cell.—[10]

I have made a memorandum to ask you, (for I am very curious on subject,) when we meet, what R. Brown & Griffith predicted:[11] I conjecture such cases would come under what I call "correlation" in the Origin.—[12] I am not surprised that you think Pangenesis is only a statement of the concrete; so now it almost appears to me; yet I declare it has been nothing less than revelation to me as clearing away mist & connecting various classes of facts. The key-stone of the view is that the reproductive organs do not form the reproductive male & female elements,—only collect them (i.e. the gemmules of each separate cell) by some mysterious power in due proportions & fit them for mutual action & separate existence.—

If any remarks or sneers on this subject occur to you, for the love of Heaven, make a memorandum that I may sometime hear them.—

Ever yours affect. | C. Darwin

DAR 115: 282, 282b

[1] The year is established by the reference to George Henslow's visit (see n. 2, below), and by the discussion of CD's hypothesis of pangenesis.

[2] Emma Darwin's diary (DAR 242) records that Henslow arrived at Down on 2 April 1866.

[3] No letter from Hooker containing information on these plants has been found. In *Variation* 1: 403, CD states that Hooker had informed him of an observation made by John Smith (1798–1888), the retired curator of the Royal Botanic Gardens, Kew, that the development of the ovary in the South African orchid *Bonatea speciosa* 'could be effected by mechanical irritation of the stigma'. CD had previously studied dried specimens of *B. speciosa* (*Orchids*, p. 304 n.). For CD's interest in the plant, see *Orchids*, pp. 302–5, and *Correspondence* vol. 13, letter from Roland Trimen, 13 December 1865, n. 1. CD was interested in waterlilies as possible exceptions to his view that it was necessary for individuals to cross

at least occasionally (see letter from Robert Caspary, 25 February 1866 and n. 13). On the cucumber case, see the letter to J. D. Hooker, [5 April 1866] and n. 2.

4 CD refers either to John Smith (1798–1888), or to John Smith (1821–88), curator of the Royal Botanic Gardens, Kew. CD was interested in the effect of stock on scion tissue for its bearing on his theory of pangenesis. See letter to Robert Caspary, 21 February [1866] and n. 3.

5 The letter from Hooker on pangenesis has not been found. CD's theory of the transmission and development of hereditary characters was published in the chapter headed 'Provisional hypothesis of pangenesis' in *Variation* 2: 357–404. He had discussed his hypothesis with Thomas Henry Huxley at the end of May 1865, enclosing a thirty-page draft of the chapter (see *Correspondence* vol. 13, letters to T. H. Huxley, 27 May [1865] and 30 May [1865]). For more on CD's ideas on heredity and generation, which developed over a thirty-year period, see Kohn 1980, Hodge 1985, and Olby 1985. On CD's hypothesis of pangenesis, see Geison 1969 and Endersby 2003.

6 In *Variation* 2: 358, CD states that his hypothesis of pangenesis involves the supposition that 'every separate atom or unit, reproduces itself'. On the mutual affinity and aggregation of gemmules in buds and sexual elements, see *ibid.*, pp. 374, 380–1.

7 See *Variation* 2: 387–8.

8 In *Variation* 2: 379, CD remarked that with certain kinds of plants even a minute fragment of a leaf would reproduce the whole plant. CD referred specifically to 'a leaf of a Begonia' in *Variation* 2d ed., 2: 374.

9 CD described the dormancy of gemmules, and reversion, in *Variation* 2: 374, 398–402, adding, 'but there is no reason to suppose that all dormant gemmules would be transmitted and propagated for ever' (p. 402).

10 On variability resulting from modifications of gemmules, see *Variation* 2: 394–7.

11 CD refers to Robert Brown and probably to William Griffith; however, the predictions alluded to have not been identified. CD had read some of Brown's works (see *Correspondence* vol. 4, Appendix IV, and *Marginalia* 1: 94). CD had also read William Griffith's *Journals of travels* in 1859 on Hooker's recommendation; it contains numerous botanical observations and speculations (Griffith 1847–8; see *Correspondence* vol. 4, Appendix IV).

12 CD discussed 'correlation of growth' in *Origin*, pp. 143–50: he wrote, 'the whole organisation is so tied together during its growth and development, that when slight variations in any one part occur, and are accumulated through natural selection, other parts become modified' (p. 143). CD gave numerous examples of correlated variability in *Variation*, and discussed correlation in detail in chapter 25 (2: 319–38).

From John Walton [after 4 April 1866][1]

I remember hearing the late professor Dicks of Edinburgh[2] say in a lecture at the Veternary college there that he once knew an instance of a fully developed tooth being found in the testicul of a horse that I thought a very singular place for a tooth to grow in perhaps the very last member of the body where one would have expected it.[3]

I have often remarked the great fleetness of hares in countries where greyhound coursing is much followed. I have lived in places where few or no greyhounds were kept and the hares though not more numerous were so slow that they were not unfrequently caught by the sheep dogs in a [*fore*] course while when tried with greyhounds they made no sport but in countries where many greyhounds are kept where the landlord of each village public house has his coursing dog & where dogs are constantly being excercised and tried they do not catch one hare out of three they are sliped at so fleet do they get by being bred by natural selection from the strongest & fleetest sires & dams.[4]

I have now Sir jotted down the few things that come into my mind while I read your book if they are of the least use to you as confirmatory evidence I shall be glad to think it a little return for the pleasure received by me from your writings

I am Sir | Your Obedient Servant | John Walton *[j^r]*

Incomplete
DAR 47: 210

CD ANNOTATIONS
1.1 I remember ... it. 1.5] *crossed pencil*
2.1 I have] *after opening square bracket, pencil*; 'Selection'[5] *pencil*
3.1 I have now ... writings 3.3] *crossed pencil*

[1] The date is established by the reference to William Dick (see n. 2, below). The correspondent has not been further identified.

[2] William Dick, professor at the Veterinary College, Edinburgh, died on 4 April 1866 (*Modern English biography*).

[3] In *Variation*, CD briefly discussed cases in which teeth or hair appeared in unusual parts of the body, and in ovarian tumours; he argued that his theory of pangenesis could explain such abnormalities (see *Variation* 2: 369–70, 391–3).

[4] CD remarked on the modifications of rabbits owing to use and disuse of parts of their bodies in *Variation* 1: 124–30, and discussed the specific effects of use and disuse in domestic and wild animals, including the importance of exercise in strengthening muscles, in *Variation* 2: 295–9. In *Origin*, pp. 90–1, CD had described how, in animals who prey on other animals in the wild, natural selection might preserve the swiftest, giving the example of wolves; he also compared wolves with greyhounds.

[5] CD's annotation may refer to the section of chapter 4 of *Origin*, 'Illustrations of the action of natural selection', pp. 90–6, or to his chapters on selection in *Variation* 2: 192–249. Walton's example was not added to *Variation* or to later editions of *Origin*.

To J. D. Hooker [5 April 1866][1]

Down
Thursday

My dear Hooker.—

Please ask Mr Smith (who I sh^d. think w^d be trustworthy) 1st. where the Sion House Cucumber is crossed by foreign a var. whether the fruit is *always*, *generally* or *only rarely* affected? 2^d Is there any other change besides flavour, & what is flavour that a change in it can be detected?— 3^d Has Mr S. *himself* crossed the Sion H. with foreign pollen?—[2]

I w^d. not trouble you, but this case sounds of real value to me.—

Yours affect | C. D.

We hope to go to 6 Queen Anne St next Wednesday, if both are well enough, but this depends on the doctrine of chances.—[3]

DAR 115: 286

[1] The date is established by the relationship between this letter and the letter to J. D. Hooker, [9 April 1866]. In 1866, 5 April was the Thursday before 9 April.

[2] CD had thanked Hooker for the 'cucumber case' in his letter of 4 April [1866]. John Smith (1821–88), curator of the Royal Botanic Gardens, Kew, had previously been gardener to the duke of Northumberland at Syon House, Middlesex (R. Desmond 1994). CD was interested in the possible effects of the male element on the female element in crossing. In *Variation* 1: 397–403, he gave numerous examples of plants in which the internal or external characteristics of the fruit were modified as a result of pollination by another plant. CD noted that such modifications had been observed in cucumbers in England but did not provide corroborative evidence (*ibid.*, p. 399). See also *Correspondence* vol. 6, letter from J. D. Hooker, [2 December 1857].

[3] Six Queen Anne Street was the London address of CD's brother, Erasmus Alvey Darwin. CD and Emma Darwin both fell ill with influenza in the following week, and did not go to London until 21 April (Emma Darwin's diary (DAR 242)).

From J. D. Hooker [6 April 1866][1]

Kew
Friday.

Dear Darwin

You will find a brief notice of *Begonia Phyllomaniaca* in Hook. Lond. Journ. Bot. IV. 206[2] but not worth referring to & a longer one in Martius huge "Flora Brasiliensis"—[3] I *gather from it* that the plant produces *ramenta*, that sometimes consist of a mere utricle, & that these may become new plants, but the description is far from clear.

I will go into the matter of this & other cases of the kind as soon as I can. Very many thanks for the explicit account of Pangenesis—which I completely misunderstood.[4] I think I now follow your idea, but it takes a deal of thought, it is so very speculative— it is 1000 times more difficult to grasp than Atomic theory or Latent heat.[5]

We are in great sorrow—on account of poor Oliver having lost his little girl, only two days after he got into my late house here:[6] a sweet little thing of 3 or 4, was taken ill just as my child was, before they left Acton.[7] Their Doctor (a Homæopathist) made no objection to their bringing the child across to Kew, where it died yesterday. I can hardly bear to think of it: poor Oliver finds comfort in the fact that it was taken ill before he left Acton, as his wife had a great prejudice against Kew & he truly says that it would have been fatal to his comfort ever after in the house, if the seizure had taken place in it. He has one other child, younger.[8]

I do hope the poor fellow will leave Kew at once with his wife— the interment takes place tomorrow at a Friends' cemetry at Isleworth.[9]

The Doctor had pronounced the child quite out of danger a few hours before it died—but I felt sure that the apparent improvement was a fatal symptom. It was a very lovely child, but delicate looking though it never ailed any-thing.

Ever my dear old Darwin | Yrs affec | Jos D Hooker

DAR 102: 69–70

[1] The date is established by the relationship between this letter and the letter to J. D. Hooker, 4 April [1866]. In 1866, the first Friday after 4 April was 6 April.

[2] See letter to J. D. Hooker, 4 April [1866]. The description of *Begonia phyllomaniaca* appeared in the *London Journal of Botany* 4 (1852): 206–7. The journal was edited by William Jackson Hooker. The plant is described as producing from the stem, branches, and petioles innumerable leaflets, which, when detached and placed in moist soil, produce perfect plants.

[3] Hooker refers to Karl Friedrich Philipp von Martius's *Flora Brasiliensis* (Martius ed. 1840–1906, vol. 4 part 1 (1852–63): 386–7).

[4] See letter to J. D. Hooker, 4 April [1866].

[5] On the development of the atomic theory of matter in the nineteenth century, see Brock and Knight 1967, and Rocke 1984. On the concept of latent heat in relation to other theories of heat in the nineteenth century, see Brush 1983, pp. 46–54.

[6] Daniel Oliver's daughter has not been identified. On becoming director of the Royal Botanic Gardens, Kew, in November 1865, Hooker had moved from 55 Kew Green to 49 Kew Green (R. Desmond 1995, p. 416). Oliver had been given increased responsibilities at Kew, following Hooker's appointment as director (see *Correspondence* vol. 13, letter from J. D. Hooker, [3 November 1865]).

[7] Maria Elizabeth Hooker had died in 1863 at the age of 6 (see *Correspondence* vol. 11, letter from J. D. Hooker, [28 September 1863]). Acton is about two miles north of Kew.

[8] Oliver and his wife, Hannah, had a son, Francis Wall Oliver.

[9] Isleworth, a large village on the Thames, about one mile from Kew, had a Society of Friends' Meeting House (*Post Office directory of the six home counties* 1866).

From George Henslow 7 April 1866

10 South Crescent | Bedford Sq | W.C.
April 7th /66

My dear Sir

I send by this post a few copies of the "*Science Gossip*", which I happen to have as duplicates, so that you can obtain a knowledge of their General character.[1] Also one or two N^os. of the Leisure Hour in which I have written short papers, that may perhaps interest you, as being connected with my *fathers* doings. Please to accept them. (One has not my name attached viz: "*Phosphate Nodules*".)—[2]

I have already exhibited the Coryanthes—you so kindly gave me—to the delight & astonishment of several: it certainly is a most wonderful contrivance.[3]

With regard to the remark I made about the relative N^os. expressive of the fertility of Primrose.— I was referring to the Tab. II p. 89. *P. veris*

		By calculation good pods		Weight of seed in grains
Long: styled Homo^c.	as	100	to	**42***
long styled Hetero^c.	"	100	:	62
Short styled: Homo^c.	"	100	:	30
Short styled Hetero^c.	"	100	:	**44***[4]

Comparing these (*) it seems, they run very close![5] does *that proportion* mean that the seed from every *100 good pods* weighed, *on average* (by calculation of course) 42 grains?

Again thanking you for a very pleasant visit last Monday,[6]

Believe me | My dear Sir, | Yours very faithfully | Geo Henslow

C. Darwin Esq.

DAR 166: 157

[1] *Hardwicke's Science-Gossip: an Illustrated Medium of Interchange and Gossip for Students and Lovers of Nature* was established in 1865. Published monthly, it was advertised as 'a medium of exchange and Chit-chat . . . for lighter and more varied information', complementing the publisher's other journal, *Popular Science Review* (back page of issue 2).

[2] Henslow's article 'Phosphate nodules' described the introduction of phosphates as a manure for root crops by Henslow's father, John Stevens Henslow; it was published in *Leisure Hour*, 11 July 1863, pp. 436–8 ([Henslow] 1863). Henslow also refers to his signed article 'The wild flowers of Shakespear', which appeared in *Leisure Hour*, 9 April 1864, pp. 229–31 (Henslow 1864).

[3] CD probably gave Henslow a plant of the orchid genus *Coryanthes* when Henslow visited Down from 2 to 3 or 4 April 1866 (letter to J. D. Hooker, 4 April [1866]). CD had described *Coryanthes* in *Orchids*, pp. 277–8, remarking that drops of the secreted nectar were collected in the hollowed end of the labellum 'just like a bucket suspended some way beneath a dripping spring of water'. The section on *Coryanthes* is considerably expanded in the second edition (*Orchids* 2d ed., pp. 173–6). See also *Origin* 4th ed., p. 230, 'Fertilization of orchids', p. 151 (*Collected papers* 2: 153–4), and *Correspondence* vol. 12.

[4] The table is an extract from table II in 'Dimorphic condition in *Primula*', p. 89 (*Collected papers* 2: 56); the four lines show, successively, the results of pollination of long-styled flowers of *Primula veris* by own pollen and pollen from short-styled flowers, and of pollination of short-styled flowers by own pollen and pollen from long-styled flowers.

[5] In 'Dimorphic condition in *Primula*', p. 88 (*Collected papers* 2: 56), CD calculated that homomorphic unions yielded a weight of 35 grains of seed per 100 'good capsules', while heteromorphic unions yielded 54 grains. Henslow here shows that the difference is narrowed considerably if the second and third rows of results are omitted.

[6] See n. 3, above.

From James Samuelson 8 April 1866

6 Montpellier Terrace | New Brighton Cheshire
Apl 8/66

Dear Sir.

I am glad you consider the notice of your works an unprejudiced one.[1] It seems, strangely enough, to find favor with the rigid orthodox as well as with those who are disposed to consider the subject without reference to theology. & I hope it will give a stimulus to the perusal of your works.

I cannot, for my own part, conceive how any one who considers the past and present of organic life, without theological bias, can find it reasonable to suppose that animals have sprung into existence as it was formerly believed, and a gradual development appears to me the only **sensible** mode of explaining the matter.

On the other hand, unless you are greatly misunderstood, by me as well as others, I am at a loss to comprehend how you can have arrived at the metaphysical result stated or implied, at p 492 of the 'Origin'. (3^{d} Ed^{n}.) "not by means superior to, though analogous with" &c.[2]

Assuming your theory to be correct; that the metaphysical causes—in other words that the creative or divine power which makes or has made new species is *not* superior to, though analogous with, human reason; what is the use of continuing *your* efforts to make a new species? It is only on the assumption that "Nature" acts in a manner superior to though analogous with human reason, that the question of artificial selection can have the slightest weight in determining the natural method of creating species;—I am not going to read you a sermon! *You have had enough of those I should think*! but judging from some of the explanatory remarks you have introduced into your last edition, referred to by your reviewer at p. 153 (J of S.) I should say that you have, from conviction, not coercion, somewhat changed your views as regards the nature of the metaphysical influences at work; or at least that you have felt yourself to be misunderstood, in the amount of power attributable to "Natural Selection".[3]

I think you are still misunderstood, in a way which is calculated to impede the progress of your views.

As to 'Natural selection' modifying the Egg—seed &c, "by preserving favorable variations",[4] I confess myself totally unable to perceive how you can, in a large majority of cases, ascertain anything whatever as to the influences which are at work in or upon the ovum, germ, or spermatozoon. In the lower & lowest forms of life, these are at present often *less* than microscopic, & when our powers increase, I do not think we shall be much wiser in that respect. I say this with every deference to your large experience and observation; though as you may perhaps be aware, I have devoted many years to this particular branch of Science. You will probably have seen that I sent a paper last Autumn to the Royal Society in which I have sought to show *by experiment* that the developmental theory must, in the case of the infusoria, take the place of that of spontaneous generation; but although in the paper (of which an abstract only appeared in the proceedings) I have expressed my conviction that one and the same form of zoospore, monad, or whatever you choose to call it, may become developed into what are now believed to be distinct species of Infusoria, (& I sent an illustration of what I believe to be such a phenomenon) yet I cannot go so far back as the "ovum, germ, or seed" in forming a judgment upon the causes of variation.[5]

You will consider me very un-Editorial, I know, for entering upon this discussion, but I received your note, & reply to it, not in my official capacity, but as a *young* fellow-observer—if you will not be scandalised by the comparison.

Believe me, Dear Sir, | With every regard, Yrs truly | James Samuelson

C Darwin Esq

DAR 177: 27

[1] An anonymous article, 'Darwin and his teachings', appeared in the April 1866 issue of the *Quarterly Journal of Science* (Anon. 1866). A lightly annotated presentation copy is in the Darwin Pamphlet Collection–CUL. The article reviewed the third edition of *Origin*, and referred to *Journal of researches*, *Orchids*, and 'Climbing plants'. CD's letter to Samuelson has not been found.

[2] Samuelson refers to a sentence in the second paragraph of the last chapter of *Origin*, p. 459 (*Origin* 3d ed., p. 492):

> Nothing at first can appear more difficult to believe than that the more complex organs and instincts should have been perfected, not by means superior to, though analogous with, human reason, but by the accumulation of innumerable slight variations, each good for the individual possessor.

[3] The review compared the first and third editions of *Origin*, noting places in which CD had substituted 'natural selection' for 'nature', and had inserted new material in an attempt to clarify the meaning of natural selection (Anon. 1866, pp. 152–4). The reviewer claimed that natural selection was 'of itself not sufficient to explain the phenomena, past and present, of nature' (*ibid.*, p. 152).

[4] In *Origin*, p. 127, CD wrote: 'Natural selection, on the principle of qualities being inherited at corresponding ages, can modify the egg, seed, or young, as easily as the adult.' Previously in the same chapter, he had discussed the transmission of characters 'by natural selection preserving the same favourable variations' (p. 104). CD attempted to explain hereditary transmission in his provisional hypothesis of pangenesis (see *Variation*, ch. 27).

[5] Samuelson's paper 'On the development of certain infusoria' was read at the 8 November 1865 meeting of the Royal Society. An abstract was published in the *Proceedings of the Royal Society of London* 14 (1865): 546–7. The paper described the successive appearance, in organic infusions, of what seemed to be distinct species of Protozoa rising in the developmental scale: monads, amoeba, and ciliated infusoria. Samuelson claimed, however, that the monadic forms were in fact the larval stage of infusoria (species of *Cercomonas*). He also reported further experiments, designed to refute the theory of spontaneous generation, showing that organic forms appeared in pure distilled water only if it had been exposed to the atmosphere for some time.

From J. E. Gray 9 April 1866

British Museum
9 April 1866

My Dear Darwin

I fear it is only as Compliment but I should be glad for many reasons if it was not

Will you come and dine with us on the 16 of **May** at 7. to meet Professor De. Candolle, who has promised to dine with me on that day[1]

With kindest Regard to Mrs Darwin[2] & yourself

Ever Yours Sincerely | J. E Gray

Charles Darwin Esq | &c &c

DAR 165: 210

[1] CD did not travel to London on 16 May to dine with Gray and Alphonse de Candolle; see letter to J. D. Hooker, 16 May [1866], and letter from Alphonse de Candolle, 3 June 1866.

[2] Emma Darwin.

To J. D. Hooker [9 April 1866][1]

Down
Monday

My dear Hooker

I write one line to thank you for your note & to say how grieved I am to hear about poor Oliver's loss.—[2] There is nothing in this world like the bitterness of such a loss,—unless indeed the wife herself. If you have any good opportunity say a kind word from me to poor Oliver.—

I have been bad in bed with influenza sore throat & rheumatism.—[3]

How curious your note on the odd Begonia coinciding with article in Gard: Chronicle on ditto.—[4] I read some word wrong in your former note about **flavour** of crossed Sion H. Cucumber, & was surprised: I have ordered seed to cross.[5]

I am astonished that Pangenesis seems perplexing to you; that it is abominably wildly, horridly speculative, (worthy *even* of Herbert Spencer) I fully plead guilty to.[6]

Ever yours | C. D.

DAR 115: 284

[1] The date is established by the relationship between this letter and the letter from J. D. Hooker, [6 April 1866]. In 1866, the Monday after 6 April was 9 April.

[2] Hooker informed CD of the death of Daniel Oliver's daughter in his letter of [6 April 1866].

[3] Emma Darwin's diary (DAR 242) records that CD fell ill with a cold on 6 April 1866, and that he contracted influenza on 8 April.

[4] See letter from J. D. Hooker, [6 April 1866] and n. 2. An editorial in the *Gardeners' Chronicle*, 7 April 1866, pp. 313–14, considered *Begonia phyllomaniaca* as an example of sports arising by 'prolification of the leaf'.

[5] See letter to J. D. Hooker, [5 April 1866] and n. 2. Hooker's note on the cucumber has not been found. CD crossed the 'Sion House cucumber' with another variety, and compared offspring of the crossed and self-pollinated plants in height, number, and seed production; his notes, dated 30 October to 30 December [1866], are in DAR 78: 190–1.

[6] See letter from J. D. Hooker, [6 April 1866]. Hooker and CD had previously criticised the speculative nature of Spencer's work (see, for example, *Correspondence* vol. 12, letter from J. D. Hooker, 24 January 1864, and letter to J. D. Hooker, 3 November [1864]).

To Fritz Müller [9 and] 15 April [1866][1]

Down. | Bromley. | Kent. S.E.
April 15th.

My dear Sir,

I am very much obliged by your letter of February the 13th abounding with so many highly interesting facts.[2] Your account of the Rubiaceous plant is one of the most extraordinary that I have ever read, and I am glad you are going to publish it.[3] I have long wished some one to observe the fertilization of Scævola, and you must permit me to tell you what I have observed: First for the allied genus of Leschenaultia: utterly disbelieving that it fertilizes itself, I introduced a camel-hair brush into the flower in the same way as a bee would enter, and I found that the flowers were thus fertilized, which never otherwise happens;[4] I then searched for the stigma, and found it *outside* the indusium with the pollen tubes penetrating it: and I convinced Dr Hooker that botanists were quite wrong in supposing that the stigma lay inside the indusium.[5] In *Scævola microcarpa* the structure is very different, for the immature stigma lies at the base within the indusium; and as the stigma grows it pushes the pollen out of the indusium and it then clings to the hairs which fringe the lips of the indusium; and when an insect enters the flower, the pollen (as I have seen) is swept from these long hairs onto the insect's back. The stigma continues to grow, but is not apparently ready for impregnation until it is developed into two long protruding horns, at which period all the pollen has been pushed out of the indusium. But my observations are here at fault, for I did not observe the penetration of the pollen tubes. the case is almost paralell with that of lobelia.[6] Now I hope you will get two plants of Scævola, and protect one from insects, leaving the other uncovered, and observe the result both in the number of capsules produced, and in the average number of seed in each. It would be well to fertilize half a dozen flowers under the net, to prove that the cover is not injurious to fertility.[7]

With respect to your case of Aristolochia, I think further observation would convince you that it is not fertilized *only* by larvæ, for in a nearly parallel case of an Arum and an Aristolochia, I found that insects flew from flower to flower.[8] I would suggest to you to observe any cases of flowers which catch insects by their probosces, as occurs with some of the Apocyneæ, I have never been able to conceive for what purpose (if any) this is effected;[9] at the same time, if I tempt you to neglect your Zoological work for these miscellaneous observations I shall be guilty of a great crime

To return for a moment to the indusium; how curious it is that the pollen should be thus collected in a special receptacle, afterwards to be swept out by insects' agency!

I am surprised at what you tell me about the fewness of the flowers of your native Orchids which produce seed-capsules.[10] What a contrast with our temperate European species with the exception of some sp. of Ophrys!— I now know of 3 or 4 cases of self-fertilising orchids; but all these are provided with means for an occasional cross.—[11] I am sorry to say Dr. Crüger is dead from a fever.—[12]

I received yesterday your paper in Bot. Zeitung on the wood of Climbing Plants:[13] I have read as yet only your very interesting & curious remarks on the subject as bearing on the change of species;[14] you have pleased me by the very high compliment which you pay to my paper.—[15]

I have been at work since March 1st on a new English Edition of my Origin, of which when published I will send you a copy.[16] I have much regretted the time it has cost me, as it has stopped my other work. On the other hand it will be useful for a new 3d German Edition which is now wanted.[17] I have corrected it largely & added some discussions, but not nearly so much as I wished to do, for being able to work only two hours daily, I found I shd. never get it finished.— I have taken some facts & views from your work "Fur Darwin"; but not *one quarter* of what I sh$^{d.}$ have liked to have quoted.[18]

With the more cordial respect & thanks, Believe me my dear Sir Yours most sincerely | Ch. Darwin

LS(A)
British Library (Loan 10: 6)

[1] The year is established by the reference to the letter from Fritz Müller, 13 February 1866. The original date of '9th' was crossed out and '15th.' written below.

[2] See letter from Fritz Müller, 13 February 1866.

[3] The discussion of the rubiaceous plant was evidently in a missing portion of Müller's letter of 13 February 1866. Müller described the plant in the 27 April 1866 issue of *Botanische Zeitung* (F. Müller 1866a). Uncertain whether the plant was a species of *Posoqueria*, Müller named it *Martha (posoqueria?) fragrans.* The species is now known as *Posoqueria densiflora.* In *Forms of flowers*, p. 131 n., and *Cross and self fertilisation*, pp. 5, 391, CD mentioned 'Posoqueria fragrans', as described by Müller, among plants in which special movements of certain floral organs ensure cross-pollination.

[4] In his letter of 5 November 1865 (*Correspondence* vol. 13), Müller had mentioned a *Scaevola* growing on the east coast of the island of Santa Catarina, Brazil. CD began experiments with another member of the Goodeniaceae, *Leschenaultia*, in April 1860 (see *Correspondence* vol. 8). His initial results were reported in the letter to the *Journal of Horticulture*, [17 May 1861] (*Correspondence* vol. 9). CD's notes on pollination in *Leschenaultia* are in in his Experimental notebook (DAR 157a), and DAR 265.

[5] CD discussed *Leschenaultia* in 1860 with Joseph Dalton Hooker, who disagreed with CD's view that the stigma was outside the indusium (see *Correspondence* vol. 8, letter to J. D. Hooker, 18 April [1860], and letter from J. D. Hooker, [28 April 1860]). In 1862, CD made further observations that confirmed his view; these were corroborated by Hooker (see *Correspondence* vol. 10, letter from J. D. Hooker, [16 May 1862]). CD later published an account of his observations in a letter to the *Gardeners' Chronicle*, [before 9 September 1871] (*Calendar* no. 7926; *Collected papers* 2: 162–5).

[6] CD described pollination in *Scaevola microcarpa*, noting its analogy with *Lobelia*, in a letter to J. D. Hooker, 7 June [1860] (*Correspondence* vol. 8). His notes on *Scaevola* are in his Experimental notebook (DAR 157a). CD discussed the cross-pollination mechanism of *Lobelia* in *Origin*, pp. 98–9, and *Cross and self fertilisation*, p. 176. See also *Correspondence* vol. 6, letter to Asa Gray, 5 September [1857]. CD's notes on *Lobelia* are in DAR 49: 85, 88, 88v. It appears in a list of plants, 'apparently adapted to prevent self fertilization', in DAR 117: 71. For more on the pollination mechanisms of *Scaevola*, *Leschenaultia*, *Lobelia*, and related genera, see *ML* 2: 257–9.

[7] Müller was unable to perform the experiments with *Scaevola* because all his specimens died (*Correspondence* vol. 15, letter from Fritz Müller, 4 March 1867).

[8] The information on *Aristolochia* is probably in a missing portion of Müller's letter of 13 February 1866. CD compared *Arum maculatum*, the filaments of which are constructed so as to trap insects, with *Aristolochia* in *Cross and self fertilisation*, pp. 417–18; he reported experiments made in 1842 that indicated that insects were able to escape from *Arum maculatum* and carry pollen to another plant.

[9] The sub-family *Apocyneae* (family *Apocynaceae*) includes the American fly-trap (*Apocynum androsaemifolium*); it is cross-pollinated by insects, which can become caught by their probosces or legs. CD was familiar with this species (see *Correspondence* vol. 8, letter to Daniel Oliver, [21 November 1860] and n. 5, and letter from Daniel Oliver, 23 November 1860). The original text has been corrected in CD's hand from 'Asclepiadae' to 'Apocyneae'; on contemporary disagreements about the inclusion of particular species within these families, see Lindley 1853, p. 625.

[10] The information on orchids was probably in a missing portion of Müller's letter of 13 February 1866.

[11] In *Orchids*, pp. 358–9, CD had remarked on the rarity of self-pollination among orchids, and stated that only the bee ophrys (*Ophrys apifera*) had 'special and perfectly efficient contrivances' for self-pollination. CD later described a number of other species in which self-pollination regularly occurred, noting

that in each case structures were present that enabled the plants to be cross-pollinated by insects (see 'Fertilization of orchids', p. 158 (*Collected papers* 2: 155), and *Orchids* 2d ed., pp. 291–2).

12 Hermann Crüger had died in February 1864 (R. Desmond 1994).

13 CD refers to F. Müller 1866b and to the journal *Botanische Zeitung*. Müller had enclosed his manuscript of the article in his letter of 10 October 1865 (*Correspondence* vol. 13), requesting that CD forward it to Max Johann Sigismund Schultze for publication. CD's annotated copy, with a separate sheet of notes in his own hand, is in the Darwin Pamphlet Collection–CUL.

14 Müller stated that all the woody climbing plants he observed had clefts or fissures in their trunks; he described a *Bignonia* that had such clefts only in the portion of the plant that climbed, and remarked that such a feature could not have arisen through special creation, but was best explained by CD's theory (F. Müller 1866b, p. 68). In his notes on Müller's paper, CD wrote, 'he shows that great majority of Climbers have cleft wood—& that this might easily, being useful (how?) have been acquired through natural selection— On other hand certain great peculiarities do not appear in different Fam, as might have been expected if structure of each had been due to independent creation' (square brackets in original).

15 In F. Müller 1866b, p. 68, Müller thanked CD for sending him a copy of 'Climbing plants', noting that the work had inspired him to make further observations.

16 Müller's name appears on CD's presentation list for the fourth edition of *Origin* (see Appendix IV).

17 See letter from E. Schweizerbart'sche Verlagsbuchhandlung, 23 March 1866.

18 CD refers to F. Müller 1864c. CD had added references to F. Müller 1864c to the fourth edition of *Origin*. No new references to Müller 1864c were added to the third German edition (Bronn and Carus trans. 1867).

From E. A. Darwin 10 April [1866][1]

10 April—

Dear Charles

A man has sent to offer me "two most beautiful autographic Proof impressions of the portrait of C D Esq by Maguire" 7/6

What are they?[2]

I was sorry to hear of your heap of maladies & I suppose I shant see you till I dont know when[3]

E D

Georgina[4] wished me to ask you to bring with you the Quarterly Journal of Science with the Review upon yourself—[5]

DAR 105: B42–3

1 The year is established by the reference to the review of CD's works in the *Quarterly Journal of Science* (see n. 5, below).

2 CD's portrait had been drawn by Thomas Herbert Maguire in 1849 as part of a series commissioned for Ipswich Museum; a limited number of prints were issued for public sale (see *Correspondence* vol. 4). It is reproduced in *Calendar*, p. viii.

3 See letter to J. D. Hooker, [9 April 1866] and n. 2. CD had planned to visit Erasmus in London (see letter to J. D. Hooker, [5 April 1866] and n. 3).

4 Georgina Tollet, a friend of the Darwin and Wedgwood families, lived near Erasmus at 14 Queen Anne Street, London (Freeman 1978).

5 The article 'Darwin and his teachings' appeared in the April 1866 issue of the *Quarterly Journal of Science* (Anon. 1866). See letter from James Samuelson, 8 April 1866.

From William Reeves 10 April 1866

Royal Irish Academy, | *19 Dawson Street,* | *Dublin*
April 10. *1866*

Sir

I am directed to inform you that, at the Stated General Meeting of the Royal Irish Academy, held on the 16th. March last, you were elected an Honorary Member of the same, in the department of Science.

A formal Diploma of the appointment will presently be forwarded to you.[1]

I have the honour to remain | Sir | your obedient humble Servant | William Reeves, D. D. | Secretary

Charles Darwin Esqre.

DAR 230: 16

[1] The diploma has not been found in the Darwin Archive–CUL. For a list of CD's honorary memberships, see Freeman 1978, pp. 107–10.

From Friedrich Rolle 12 April 1866[1]

Homburg vor der Hoehe | bei Frankfurt am Main
den 12 April 1866.

Geehrtester Herr!

Da ich gestern von meinem Verleger erfuhr, dass er mit mit Ihnen betreffs Uebersetzung von Schriften in Verbindung getreten ist und dass Prof. *Geinitz* in *Dresden* die neue Auflage Ihres Werks "On the Origin" besorgen wird,[2] erlaube ich mir die Gelegenheit zu benützen, erstlich meine Freude auszusprechen, daß Ihnen die Zusendung meines Werks "Der Mensch" zugekommen ist und Ihr Interesse erregte,[3] zweitens ein Blatt mit Auszügen aus *Leonhardt's* und *Geinitz* "Jahrbuch" Ihnen mitzutheilen, aus dem Sie entnehmen werden, dass die Redaction *Gegner* von Ihrer Lehre ist und vorzugsweise dem *Compromisse* des *Widerstand's* angehoert.[4] *Für* Ihre Theorie finde ich nichts darin, aber die Critiken des Jahrbuchs sind ungünstig und haemisch!

Nur ein Original-Artikel des Jahrbuchs behandelt Ihre Theorie und auch ist dieser von einem *Gegner* verfasst.

Goeppert. Ueber die Darwinsche Transmutations-Theorie mit Beziehung auf die fossilen Arten.

·/· Neues Jahrbuch für Min. 1865. pag. 296.·/·[5]

Da meine vorigen Notizen über Literatur Ihrer Theorie Ihr Interesse fanden, beehre ich mich, noch damit fortzufahren[6]

G. Schwartz von Mohrenstern. Ueber die Familie der Rissoiden. II Rissoa. (Denkschriften der Kaiserlichen Akademie der Wissenschaften 1864. XIX. 4°) Wien 58 pag. 4 Taf.[7] (Ist auch als Separat-Abdruck erschienen)

Diese treffliche Arbeit gibt eine Monographie und den genealogischen Stammbaum der Gattung Rissoa. Sie gibt eine genealogische Tafel, aus der man die geologische Reihenfolge und unter Zugrundelegung der *Darwin'schen* Theorie die wahrscheinliche Abstammung der fossilen und lebenden Rissoen erkennt.[8] (Bei der Abfassung von Text und Tafel wurde ich von dem Verfasser zu Rath gezogen und half ihm dazu, seine eignen Ansichten mit den Ihrigen in Uebereinstimmung zu bringen und zu befestigen.

Von D^r^. *Gustav Jaeger* erschien in Wien ein Werk "Zoologische Briefe", welches die logischen Elemente der Transmutationslehre eroertert. Er bringt mehrere sehr originelle Tabellen zur Versinnlichung von Genealogie der Species in directer Projection und nach Eintritt von Abzweigungen, Erloeschungen und Auswanderungen Ein Theil dieser Arbeit war schon geschrieben, ehe Ihre Origin of Species in Deutschland bekannt war![9]

Von Prof. *Virchow* in *Berlin*, dem berühmten Physiologen und Landtagsabgeordneten erschien das erste Heft einer Reihe von Vortraegen; derselbe hat mir mündlich mitgetheilt, dass er vom Standpunkt der Embryologie aus *für* Ihre Theorie auftreten werde. Jenes Werk enthaelt eine Abhandlung über Archaeologie von demselben in populaerer Fassung.[10]

In der Hoffnung, dass meine Notizen Sie interessiren | empfiehlt sich hochachtungsvoll | Ihr ergebenster | D^r^. Rolle

DAR 176: 203

CD ANNOTATIONS
6.1 Ueber . . . Wien 6.2] *double-scored pencil*
8.1 Von . . . Genealogie 8.3] *double-scored pencil*
9.1 Von . . . Fassung. 9.5] *scored pencil*

[1] For a translation of this letter, see Appendix I. The letter was sent as an enclosure to the letter from Rudolf Suchsland, 16 April 1866.

[2] Rolle refers to the publisher Friedrich Emil Suchsland. See letters from Rudolf Suchsland, 16 March 1866 and 2 April 1866. Two German editions of *Origin* had been published by E. Schweizerbart'sche Verlagsbuchhandlung; Hans Bruno Geinitz had been asked to undertake the revisions necessary for a third German edition (see letter from E. Schweizerbart'sche Verlagsbuchhandlung, 23 March 1866).

[3] The reference is to Rolle 1866. See letter to Friedrich Rolle, 1 February [1866].

[4] The list of excerpts has not been found. Rolle refers to the *Neues Jahrbuch für Mineralogie, Geologie und Palaeontologie*, edited by Gustav von Leonhard and Geinitz.

[5] The reference is to Göppert 1865a. See letter from Friedrich Rolle, 28 January 1866 and n. 12.

[6] In his letter of 28 January 1866, Rolle had discussed recent work by Ludwig Rütimeyer and David Friedrich Weinland.

[7] The reference is to Schwartz von Mohrenstern 1864; however, Rolle apparently confused this paper with an earlier article on Rissoidae, a mollusc family, that appeared in volume 19 of *Denkschriften der kaiserlichen Akademie der Wissenschaften. Mathematisch-naturwissenschaftliche Classe* (*Wien*) (Schwartz von Mohrenstern 1861).

[8] The genealogical tree is on plate 4 of Schwartz von Mohrenstern 1864.

[9] Rolle refers to Jäger 1864. The genealogical trees appear in plates 1 to 5. In the preface, Gustav Jäger suggests that parts of the work were written prior to the publication of *Origin* (Jäger 1864, p. vi). The first German edition of *Origin* was published in 1860 (Bronn trans. 1860).

[10] The reference is to *Ueber Hünengräber und Pfahlbauten* (Megalithic graves and lake-dwellings) by Rudolf Carl Virchow (Virchow 1866).

From J. E. Gray 13 April 1866

BM
13 April 1866

My Dear Darwin

I have sent you a Botanical work which I fear is not much in your way, except as proving what good workers there were formerly, and it also contains some curious instances of the introduction of some garden plants[1]

Like "Leach mollusca it is publish in memoriam of person kind to me when I was a lad working to support my self[2] & some dependent on me who, I am glad to say have all done well[3]

Did you see the account in the Annals [extracted] from the Boston Journal of a Whale (*Beluga*) that was harnessed onto a carriage but the more [curious] part of the paper is that this *Beluga* was not so tame as the *Tursio*[4]

I hear there is a Porpoise at Hastings that has been kept in a pond a month [Couch] gave the account of one that live in a Pond (of Salt Water?) for much longer[5]

My Catalogue of Whales is out but our printers only gave me one copy[6]

With kindest Regards to M[rs] Darwin[7] & yourself | Ever yours sincerely | J E Gray

DAR 165: 211

1 The reference is to *The genera of plants* by Richard Anthony Salisbury (Salisbury 1866). The work was based on a manuscript, unfinished at the time of Salisbury's death in 1829, that Gray had obtained in 1864 (see Gunther 1975, pp. 42, 157).

2 Gray refers to *Molluscorum Britanniæ synopsis* by William Elford Leach (Leach 1852). Gray had arranged for the book's publication, having obtained printed proofs and manuscript pages of the work, which had been interrupted when the author fell ill in 1820. In his preface, Gray expressed his debt to the author for having afforded him the opportunity to study zoology (Leach 1852, p. vii). Similarly, Gray noted the kindness he had received from Salisbury in his preface to Salisbury 1866, p. iv. On Gray's early career and his relations with Salisbury and Leach, see Gunther 1975, pp. 19–30.

3 Gray was the second of five children. He partly supported his parents and younger siblings from an early age. His younger brother, George Robert, became assistant keeper at the British Museum. The youngest of his sisters, Charlotte Frances, married Samuel Birch, who became keeper of oriental antiquities at the British Museum. See Gunther 1975, pp. 19, 21–23, 28.

4 The note 'Domesticated whales' appeared in *Annals and Magazine of Natural History*, April 1866, p. 312. It described a 'White Whale' that 'was sufficiently well trained during the time he was in confinement to allow himself to be harnessed to a car, in which he drew a young lady around the tank'. The notice was extracted from the article 'Description of a "White Fish", or "White Whale," (*Beluga borealis* Lesson.)' in the *Boston Journal of Natural History* (1863): 603–12 (Wyman 1863). *Tursio* is now known as *Tursiops*, the genus of bottle-nosed dolphins.

5 Gray may refer to the ichthyologist Jonathan Couch. A frequent contributor to natural history journals, he collected extensive materials for a book on the British Cetacea (the order includes porpoises), which was never completed (Couch 1871, p. 17). The account of the porpoise has not been found.

6 Gray refers to *Catalogue of seals and whales in the British Museum* (J. E. Gray 1866).

7 Emma Darwin.

To [H. B. Jones?] 13 April [1866][1]

Down, Bromley, Kent
April 13

[CD's plans have changed and he will be in London the following week and therefore able to call on his correspondent.][2]

Incomplete[3]
Sotheby's, London (17 December 1973)

[1] The correspondent is conjectured to be Jones on the basis of his visit to CD in London on 23 April 1866 (see letter to H. B. Jones, [23 April 1866?]). The date of 13 April is given in the sale catalogue. The year is established by the dates of CD's visit to London in 1866 (see n. 2, below). No records have been found of an April visit to London that was delayed in any other year.

[2] CD visited London from 21 April to 1 May 1866 (Emma Darwin's diary (DAR 242). He had planned to go to London on 11 April, but had to postpone his visit because of poor health (see letter to J. D. Hooker, [5 April 1866], and letter from E. A. Darwin, 10 April [1866]).

[3] The original letter is complete and is described in the sale catalogue as being one page long.

To Henrietta Emma Darwin [14–21 April 1866][1]

My dear Etty.

I doubt whether the Ophrys which you sent had been self-fertilised;[2] it is more probable that the pollen-mass had by some accident been knocked on to the stigma.— In the Bee both pollen-masses fall quite symmetrically & spontaneously on the stigma.—[3] I am so sorry about all the illness of your companions.[4]

Try & find out from Battersby whether he has himself observed changes in same plant from O. aranifera into O. scolopax & O. apifera.—[5] Tell him I sh[d]. be most grateful for information, but I suspect, that what he says is borrowed from Moggridge.—[6] If your Ophrys is not O. lutea, you will have to eat humble-pye to Mogg.—[7]

Mamma is better to day; but we have had a poor House— Everything now looks brighter; & I for one am nearly on the sound list[8]

My dearest Etty— yours affect | C. Darwin

Mamma tells me to add that your Mentone Letter has arrived & is satisfactory. It begins to appear a terribly long time since you left us.[9]

My dear Etty | Yours affect. C. D

Endorsement: S. France | May | 1866
DAR 185: 59

[1] The year is established by the endorsement. The date range is established by the reference to Emma Darwin's and CD's poor health (see n. 8, below), and by the absence of any mention of CD's visit to London from 21 April to 2 May, which suggests that the letter was written prior to this visit.

[2] It is likely that Henrietta sent a specimen either of *Ophrys lutea* or of *O. fusca* (see n. 7, below); no letter from Henrietta mentioning the specimen has been found. Henrietta apparently believed that she had

found another example of self-fertilisation in *Ophrys*; however, CD had noted that the condition was rare among orchids generally, and that *O. apifera* was the only species of *Ophrys* to be self-fertile (see *Orchids*, pp. 358–9).

3 In his letter to J. T. Moggridge, 13 October [1865] (*Correspondence* vol. 13), CD wrote, 'no single point in natural history interests and perplexes me so much as the self-fertilisation of the Bee orchis'. CD described the pollination mechanism of the bee ophrys (*Ophrys apifera*) in *Orchids*, pp. 63–72, noting that, despite its adaptations facilitating self-pollination, it retained features associated with insect pollination.

4 Henrietta was in France with Elinor Mary Bonham-Carter and Elinor's aunt, Julia Smith (letter from H. E. Darwin to G. H. Darwin, [March 1866] (DAR 245: 276)). Henrietta's letters indicate that both of her travelling companions were unwell for much of April (Emma Darwin to H. E. Darwin, [6 April 1866] (DAR 219.9: 40), and H. E. Darwin to George Darwin, 2 May 1866 (DAR 245: 270)).

5 Charles Henry Battersby was an Irish physician who practised medicine part of the year in Cannes, France, and collected plants in that region (R. Desmond 1994); in *Orchids* 2d ed., p. 106 n., he is acknowledged for supplying CD with specimens.

6 In *Contributions to the flora of Mentone* (Moggridge 1865–8, pls. XIX, XLIII–XLV), John Traherne Moggridge had classified *Ophrys apifera*, *O. aranifera*, *O. arachnites*, and *O. scolopax* as varieties of a single species, *O. insectifera*. See letter from J. T. Moggridge, 15 February [1866] and nn. 5 and 7.

7 Moggridge described *Ophrys lutea* in *Contributions to the flora of Mentone* (Moggridge 1865–8, pl. XLVI), expressing some uncertainty about its classification as a distinct species, and noting its close relationship with *O. fusca*. Henrietta met Moggridge in Cannes around 10 May. See also letter from H. E. Darwin, [*c.* 10 May 1866].

8 Emma Darwin and CD both had influenza during the second and third weeks of April; Emma Darwin's diary (DAR 242) records that CD had a cold from 6 April, and influenza from 8 April, recovering by 14 April; while Emma had influenza from 9 April. In his letter to Asa Gray, 16 April [1866], CD wrote that Emma was still unwell.

9 The letter has not been found. Henrietta visited Mentone twice during her stay in France (letter from Emma Darwin to H. E. Darwin, [6 April 1866] (DAR 219.9: 40), and letter from H. E. Darwin to G. H. Darwin, 2 May 1866 (DAR 245: 270)). According to Emma Darwin's diary (DAR 242), Henrietta went abroad on 15 March.

To Asa Gray 16 April [1866][1]

Down. | *Bromley.* | *Kent. S.E.*
April. 16th

My dear Gray

I have been a scandalously ungrateful, & idle dog for not having thanked you very long ago for the second article on climbing plants, which pleased me *greatly*.[2] But, as I have before said, now that I work a little, I seldom feel inclined to write to anyone,[3] but this evening the spirit has moved me to do so, though I have little to say, & my dear amanuensis is poorly with influenza, which has likewise knocked me up for a week.—[4]

Hooker paid us a visit of a day about a fortnight ago & I was delighted to see him looking well & in good spirits:[5] he hopes before long not to be so terribly overworked & is going soon to write a paper on the St. Helena Flora from Burchell's collections.[6] I have lately had a letter from Fritz Müller in S. Brazil, full of curious observations.[7] One case, which he is going to publish in Germany, is of a Rubiaceous plant with very long tubular corolla & with stigma in the middle: when an insect or any object touches the filament of the stamens, these suddenly & violently bend & eject the pollen, which had been previously shed & collected into a ball between the anthers, against the intruding object. But the curious point is that this same movement closes the tube of the corolla, so that the insect cannot then fertilise the flower; but in about 8 hours the tube opens & then an insect dusted with the ejected pollen from a *distinct* flower can do the work of fertilisation.[8]

I was well at work on my new Book, when in beginning of March, Murray required new Edit. of Origin, & I have been correcting & adding matter of some importance ever since.[9] It almost broke my heart to give up so much time, but I have been comforted by finding that it will likewise serve for a new German Edition, which is wanted.[10]

All this has makes me regret *extremely* that the American edition was stereotyped; for the book is now considerably improved from what it was in the 2d. edition, which is the one reprinted in America.— I suppose nothing can be done: the corrections are far too numerous & minute for alteration in stereotypes.[11] I presume the sale has stopped; & even if it had not quite stopped, it would, I fear, be useless to ask Publishers, either the same or any others, to bring out an amended edition.— I will send you a copy whenever it is published, for the chance of your liking to have one.—[12]

I will just ask on bare chance, whether you have any *new* facts on the *direct* influence of pollen on the fruit borne by the mother-plant; for this subject has come to interest me greatly:[13] also whether you know of any cases of bud with *blended* character produced at junction of stock & graft: I have been reading a paper by Caspary on this subject.[14]

I hope all the Fenian row in your country, will not be the cause of more trouble & hatred between our two countries.[15] It seems blowing over at present; as I hope are your troubles about your President & the South.—[16] I declare I can hardly yet realise the grand, magnificent fact that Slavery is at end in your country.[17] Farewell my good & kind friend—

Yours most sincerely | C. Darwin

I work daily now between 2 & 3 hours! & walk 3 or 4 miles daily!! yet never escape much discomfort.—

Gray Herbarium of Harvard University (96)

[1] The year is established by the relationship between this letter and the letter from Asa Gray, 7 May 1866.

[2] The second part of Gray's review of 'Climbing plants' (A. Gray 1865–6) appeared in the January 1866 issue of the *American Journal of Science and Arts*. CD had praised the first part of the review (see *Correspondence* vol. 13, letter to Asa Gray, 19 October [1865]). CD's lightly annotated copy of Gray 1865–6 is in the Darwin Pamphlet Collection–CUL.

[3] In his letter to Gray of 28 May [1864] (*Correspondence* vol. 12), CD remarked that the pleasure of doing work on *Lythrum*, following many months of 'inaction', had 'disinclined [him] for the exertion of writing letters'. CD's health had been poor for much of 1864 and 1865; he began to report some

improvement in September 1865 (see *Correspondence* vol. 12, and *Correspondence* vol. 13, letter to J. D. Hooker, 27 [or 28 September 1865]).

4 According to Emma Darwin's diary (DAR 242), she came down with influenza on 9 April. CD had contracted influenza the previous day, having gone to bed with a cold on 6 April. By 14 April, CD had recovered.

5 Joseph Dalton Hooker had visited Down from 24 to 26 March 1866 (Emma Darwin's diary (DAR 242)).

6 William John Burchell had collected plants while serving as botanist to the East India Company on St Helena from 1805 to 1810 (R. Desmond 1994). Hooker did not publish a paper on Burchell's St Helena collections; however, he mentioned the collections in his paper on insular floras (J. D. Hooker 1866a, p. 27). See also *Correspondence* vol. 13, letter from J. D. Hooker, [19 April 1865] and n. 14.

7 See letter from Fritz Müller, 13 February 1866.

8 See letter to Fritz Müller, [9 and] 15 April [1866] and n. 3.

9 In his letter to Charles Lyell, 22 February [1866], CD had complained of having to stop work on *Variation* in order to undertake revisions for the fourth edition of *Origin* as requested by his publisher, John Murray. See also letter from John Murray, 21 February [1866], and letter to John Murray, 22 February [1866].

10 On the publication of a third German edition of *Origin*, see the letter from E. Schweizerbart'sche Verlagsbuchhandlung, 23 March 1866.

11 Gray had arranged for the publication of *Origin* in the United States by the New York firm D. Appleton and Co. in 1860. The firm had used the process of stereotyping, in which the type of each page of text was set into a solid plate. See *Correspondence* vol. 8, letter from Asa Gray, 23 January 1860 and n. 2. After the first three print-runs had nearly sold out, Appleton agreed to produce a revised edition (*Origin* US ed.), incorporating a historical sketch in the form of a preface, additional material added to the end of chapter 4 on natural selection, and a seven-page supplement containing other additions and alterations. On the differences between the American edition and the second English edition, see *Correspondence* vol. 8, Appendix VI.

12 The American edition of *Origin* was reprinted a further six times by D. Appleton and Co. between 1861 and 1870, when a new edition was issued (Freeman 1977). Gray's name appears on CD's presentation list for the fourth edition of *Origin* (see Appendix IV).

13 In *Variation* 1: 397–403, CD discussed cases in which the pollen of one plant, when applied to another species or variety, affected the shape, colour, or flavour of its fruit. Such modifications, CD argued, were not due to the effect of the pollen on the 'germ'. CD returned to the subject in his chapter on pangenesis; on the direct action of the male element on the female, he wrote, 'We are thus brought half-way towards a graft-hybrid, in which the cellular tissue of one form, instead of its pollen, is believed to hybridise the tissues of a distinct form' (*ibid.*, 2: 365). See letter to J. D. Hooker, [5 April 1866] and n. 2.

14 The reference is to Caspary 1865a. On CD's interest in graft-hybrids, see the letter to Robert Caspary, 21 February [1866] and n. 3, and the letter from Robert Caspary, 25 February 1866 and nn. 4 and 9.

15 From 1864, Canadian and British government officials had expressed concern about the possible invasion of Canada by Fenian forces (Winks 1960, pp. 323–6; B. Jenkins 1974–80, 2: 391–2). Fenian troops, composed largely of Union Army veterans, made several raids across the US border into Canadian territory in 1866 (Senior 1991). The Fenian Brotherhood was established in 1859 as the North American branch of the Irish Republican Brotherhood. The Fenians sought political independence for Ireland. The movement had substantial support within Irish American communities in the United States, although the actual membership of the brotherhood was small. On the history of the Fenians, see Rafferty 1999.

16 The president of the United States, Andrew Johnson, had clashed with Congress over the policy of reconstruction in the southern states following the American Civil War. Johnson had vetoed congressional bills concerning the readmission of former Confederate states into the Union, on the

grounds that they contravened powers of the individual states as guaranteed by the Constitution. For a discussion of Johnson's policy and congressional debates on reconstruction, see McKitrick 1988, pp. 258–9, 274–325.

17 Slavery was outlawed in the United States by the Thirteenth Amendment to the United States Constitution. The amendment had been passed by the House of Representatives in January 1865; by December it had received the required vote from two-thirds of the state legislatures to be made into law. See *EB* and McKitrick 1988, p. 169. For CD's opposition to slavery and his extensive correspondence with Gray on slavery and the American Civil War, see *Journal of researches* 2d ed., pp. 499–500, *Correspondence* vols. 1, 9–13, Colp 1978, and Browne 1995, pp. 196–9, 213–14, 244–6.

To George Henslow 16 April [1866][1]

Down Bromley Kent
April 16

My dear Mr. Henslow

I received yesterday the Botanische Zeitung Nor 10 for March 9 1866 with paper by Dr. Hildebrand of Bonn, who describes carefully what you showed me in Indigofera![2] & it seems that the irritability had been described by De Candolle & Treviranus,—who, however, mistook the proportion—[3] Hildebrand also describes analogous movement in Medicago & to certain extent in Cytisus.—[4]

I am sorry for this. Dr H. also sends me long paper with good engravings on Salvia[5]—but not yet read— All these are in German— In Haste

Yours very sincerely | Ch. Darwin

Linnean Society of London, C451: Opuscula

1 The year is established by the reference to the receipt of *Botanische Zeitung* for 9 March 1866.

2 Friedrich Hildebrand's paper described mechanisms for insect pollination in *Indigofera*, *Medicago*, and other genera (Hildebrand 1866a). A lightly annotated copy is in the Darwin Pamphlet Collection–CUL. Henslow was preparing a paper in which he argued that the flowers of *Indigofera* were adapted to assist the pollination of one flower by another (Henslow 1866a). The published paper contained a discussion of Hildebrand 1866a, and a brief note by CD on similar mechanisms in *Cytisus scoparius*. Henslow commented that, although Hildebrand had described the same structure as 'adapted for fertilization by insects', he did not infer that it was 'especially purposed for the *intercrossing of distinct flowers*' (Henslow 1866a, p. 356). Henslow discussed *Indigofera* with CD during his visit to Down from 2 to 3 or 4 April 1866 (letter to Friedrich Hildebrand, 20 April [1866] and n. 3).

3 Hildebrand noted that Augustin Pyramus de Candolle and Ludolph Christian Treviranus had previously described the mechanism by which the stigma and stamens were released from the keel of the flowers of *Indigofera*, but had not noted that the mechanism permitted cross-pollination by insects (Hildebrand 1866a, pp. 74–5). Henslow also criticised Candolle and Treviranus in Henslow 1866a, pp. 356–7. CD may refer to the proportion of flowers pollinated without insect aid to those pollinated by insects.

4 See Hildebrand 1866a, pp. 74–5. Henslow had written a paper on pollination mechanisms in *Medicago sativa* (Henslow 1865). See *Correspondence* vol. 13, letters from George Henslow, 1 November 1865 and 6 November 1865.

5 The reference is to Hildebrand 1866b. CD's heavily annotated copy is in the Darwin Pamphlet Collection–CUL. Henslow had described the movement of the anthers and stigma that facilitated insect pollination in *Salvia* in his letter to CD of 1 November 1865 (*Correspondence* vol. 13). On CD's interest in *Salvia*, see *ibid.*, letter from George Henslow, 6 November 1865, n. 3.

To J. D. Hooker [16 April 1866][1]

Down
Monday

My dear H.

Will you tell me for new Edit. of Origin how many plants are proper to New Zealand (excluding of course naturalised plants). I do not care for any great accuracy but do not like to reprint old & false number.—[2]

We have been just extremely pleased by George being second in Mathematicks at Trinity (which considering size of College is great honour) & getting an 80£ Scholarship, for next five years.—[3]

Yours affect— | C. Darwin

DAR 115: 283

[1] The date is established by the reference to George Howard Darwin's examination (see n. 3, below), and by the relationship between this letter and the letter to J. D. Hooker, [22 April 1866]. In 1866, the Monday before 22 April was 16 April. An endorsement, 'April 9/66', in Hooker's hand is presumably in error.

[2] In *Origin*, CD noted the relatively small number of indigenous species of flowering plants on oceanic islands as compared with those on equal continental areas, giving the number for New Zealand as 750 (*Origin*, p. 389); in the fourth edition, this number was changed to 960 (*Origin* 4th ed., p. 463).

[3] George Howard Darwin achieved first class in the examination held at Trinity College for 'junior sophs' (second year undergraduates) in 1866 (*Cambridge University calendar* 1867, p. 397). In a letter to Henrietta Emma Darwin, [30 March 1866] (DAR 251: 2239), George wrote that the examination began on 4 April, and that the results would be available on 13 April.

From Rudolf Suchsland 16 April 1866

25. Belle Vue Street. | Swansea.
16th April 1866.

Dear Sir,

Yesterday I received a letter from my father, who desires me to thank you for your very interesting communications & to inform you, that under the existing circumstances, he has given up the idea of publishing a new translation of the "Origin of Species".[1]

Nevertheless he wishes to call your attention to the fact, that Prof. Geinitz of Dresden has until now only written against your theory.[2] You will find this corroborated by a letter from Dr. Rolle addressed to you, which I take the liberty to enclose.[3] Dr. Rolle was therefore greatly astonished to hear that Prof. Geinitz was going to superintend the publication of the new edition.

My father begs further to communicate to you the following literary notices, which may perhaps interest you.

Prof. Dr. Oscar Schmidt & Prof. Franz Unger (the celebrated Botanist) have published: "The age of mankind & the Paradise" two lectures, in which Darwin's theory is highly commended. Prof Schmidt acknowledges openly, that having formerly been an adversary of this theory, he has now become a most decided follower of the same.[4]

Prof. Ernst Hallier of Jena has published: "Darwin's theory & the Specification," a little book full of self-praise, in which the author speaks against Bronn's translation.[5] Count Mariani of Florence has written a most interesting book called: "Confessions of a Metaphysician". The first volume contains the Ontology particularly directed against Hegel; the second volume, Kosmology pays special attention to Darwin's theory.[6]

Hoping that I have not tired you, I remain, dear Sir, | yours | most respectfully | R. Suchsland.

Chas. Darwin Esq. | Down.

DAR 177: 273

[1] CD's letters have not been found. On Friedrich Emil Suchsland's interest in publishing a new German edition of *Origin*, see the letter from Rudolf Suchsland, 2 April 1866 and n. 2.

[2] Christian Friedrich Schweizerbart, the publisher of the first and second German editions of *Origin* (Bronn trans. 1860 and 1863), had suggested that Hans Bruno Geinitz would undertake the translation of a third German edition. See letter from E. Schweizerbart'sche Verlagsbuchhandlung, 23 March 1866.

[3] See letter from Friedrich Rolle, 12 April 1866.

[4] The reference is to Schmidt and Unger 1866, two lectures given at the University of Graz. There is a copy in the Darwin Pamphlet Collection–CUL. Unger's lecture, 'Steiermark zur Zeit der Braunkohlenbildung' (Styria during the time of brown coal formation), contained a brief remark that CD's theory was compatible with the creation of humans by 'organic means' (*ibid.*, pp. 44–5). Oskar Schmidt's lecture, 'Das Alter der Menscheit: nach den neueren geologischen Forschungen und Darwin's Hypothese' (The age of mankind as determined by new geological researches and Darwin's hypothesis), contained an afterword in which Schmidt discussed recent research by Fritz Müller, Carl Gegenbaur, and others that was supportive of CD's theory. Schmidt added that he had been especially convinced by Gegenbaur's work (*ibid.*, pp. 31–6).

[5] Hallier's review, 'Darwin's Lehre und die Specification', claimed that Heinrich Georg Bronn's translation of *Origin* (Bronn trans. 1863) contained many scientific errors, and gave rise to misunderstandings and 'teleological readings' not present in the original (Hallier 1865, pp. 61–2). There is a copy in the Darwin Pamphlet Collection–CUL.

[6] The reference is to *Confessioni di un Metafisico* by Terenzio Mamiani della Rovere (Mamiani della Rovere 1865), and to Georg Wilhelm Friedrich Hegel. For more on Mamiani della Rovere, see Corsi and Weindling 1985, p. 720.

To George Henslow [before 19 April 1866][1]

In the Broom, if the flowers be protected from insects, the parts (stamen and pistil) do not spring out, and scarcely any pods are produced. In a flower lately expanded, when a bee alights on the keel, the shorter stamens alone are ejected, and they dust the abdomen of the insect. When the flower is a day or two older, if a bee alights on the keel, the pistil and longer stamens spring violently out, and the hairs on the pistil deposit plenty of pollen on the bee's back, against which the stigma is rubbed. When the bee flies away, the pistil curls still more, and the stigmatic surface becomes up-turned, and stands close to the protruded anthers of the shorter stamens. We have seen that the bee gets dusted in its abdomen from the shorter stamens of the younger flowers; and this pollen will be left on the up-turned stigma of the curled pistil of the older flowers. Thus both the upper and lower surface of the bee gets dusted with pollen, which will be transferred to the stigma at two different periods.[2]

Mem, incomplete
Journal of the Linnean Society (Botany) 9 (1867): 358[3]

[1] The date is established by the relationship between this memorandum and the date, 19 April 1866, on which it was read to the Linnean Society as part of Henslow 1866a (see n. 2, below).

[2] Henslow included this note, 'kindly communicated . . . by Mr. Darwin', in his paper on pollination in *Indigofera* (Henslow 1866a; see also letter to George Henslow, 16 April [1866] and n. 2). CD was interested in dichogamy in *Cytisus scoparius*, the common broom, as well as in its mechanism for insect pollination. His notes date from May 1857, and include measurements of stamens of different lengths, and observations of the curling of the pistil, and of bee visits (DAR 76). CD's son, William Erasmus Darwin, also made extensive observations on broom (see letter from W. E. Darwin, 8 May [1866]).

[3] The original letter has not been found.

From James Shaw 19 April 1866

Tynron Parish School, Dumfriesshire.
19th April 1866.

Dear Sir,

According to promise & in answer to your wish expressed in your note of 11 Feb. I proceed to give a few facts in connection with the love of beauty by animals.[1] The facts I daresay are very humble & commonplace but shall be as correctly reported as possible.

I have a black bantam cock and hen. The cock is fully two years old and is a great pet, allowing me to lift him whenever I please with the slightest possible remonstrance and evidently well pleased at attention paid him. I have tried him several times with the mirror he being handsome & having a very pretty rose-comb. He never once pecked at his shadow there but walked mincingly & slowly before it on his toes or drew up a foot as he does when one speaks coaxingly to him. I took him one day into the parlour & placed the mirror on the carpet. There were no crumbs to be had, yet for ten minutes he seemed quite pleasantly employed surveying his likeness and walking mincingly before it and saluting it with a good many crows. The hen bantam was not altogether indifferent to the mirror, holding up its foot and looking. My Spanish cock pecked at himself in it as did the hen, latterly however he became content with a short stare without pecking.

Having carried my bantam cock one day out to the garden where I was working a little, beside a circle of snow drops, I was surprised at him tearing off the flowers with his bill. In less than a minute he picked off more than a dozen flowers. I carried him out next morning when he tore off about half a dozen.

Dr. Grierson Thornhill[2] who has a museum & is well versed in natural history has informed me that he had a monkey which was a pest in the garden owing to its disposition to tear off the flowers from their stalks. He showed it a large book of coloured drawings of animals— it clutched at the insects, and started back at the serpents.—

Mrs Hunter Milton Tynron to whom I read my paper &c[3] said that she had a pet canary which leaped about the table at meal-times but of all articles on the table nothing was so attractive to it as a polished cruet in which it saw its reflection. It was continually hopping about that article and sorting its tufts before it. She has often seen her peacock unfurling its feathers and strutting with self-complacency before the mirror of the glass door when the sun was shining on it or before the window. When she took it into the room it did the same before the mirrored wardrope, but its satisfaction out-of-doors before the window was more marked.

Mr Mitchell of the Dumfries Courier[4] has shown me his canary a male nine years old— not quite yellow, but with an olive stained plumage. It submits to the introduction of his finger on which it perched & he brought it out to me. When he opens the door of its cage one of the first things it does is to fly towards the mirror and perch itself on some article before it where it can see itself. It never pecks at its shadow but looks quietly at it or trims its feathers before it. It sometimes flies backwards & forwards before the mirror. Mr Mitchell I understand has had the canary 9 years— he says it is as well known as himself in Dumfries. Mr M. is quite convinced that the mirror is an article of luxury grateful to the canary.

Mrs Hunter Milton Tynron had a parrot very aristocratic in its tastes. It would allow genteel well dressed people to pay it attentions but not the servants or ill-dressed people.

Mr Macfarlane writer Falkirk says to me in a note.[5] When I was a boy & kept pigeons had it been legal & honourable I was firmly convinced that by the use of mirrors I could have attracted towards my dovecots half the pigeons of the parish.

The hints which you kindly gave me of the possibility of proving that "the beauty of flowers and some kinds of fruit are modified &c by bird & insect are very suggestive indeed.[6]

I felt when you first flashed the light of your discovery on me like an astronomer at sight of a new planet. On the poetical side of the suggestion there are a thousand lyrics to be sung by poets and other eloquent persons yet to come. Birds and insects to build up a world of beauty is more astonishing than how coral reefs are built up.[7]

Before the heat of public controversy sets in on these theories I find many testimonies in their favour by unprejudiced observers.

I caught the Revd Mr Wood[8] for instance, full of the conviction that the Atalanta butterfly slowly hovering & displaying its gaudy wings in the sunshine was conscious of its own splendour and describing the great part played by colour in the loves of the sticklebacks in an aquarium.

I have read a review of your 'Teachings' in the Quarterly Journal of Science.[9] It is well-intentioned but perhaps the reviewer like myself is no great naturalist, at least I thought so. I was more interested in your portrait which is there & which I had never seen before.[10]

This is a pastoral district & I daresay anecdotes about sheep & collies could be more plentifully collected than these I humbly submit.

I am Dear Sir | Yours respectfully | Ja.ˢ Shaw.

DAR 84.1: 10–13

CD ANNOTATIONS

5.4 She has . . . before the window. 5.6] *scored pencil*
6.3 When . . . before it. 6.6] *scored pencil*
6.8 Mr M . . . canary. 6.9] *scored pencil*
7.1 Mrs Hunter . . . people. 7.3] *scored pencil*
10.3 Birds . . . up. 10.5] *scored pencil*
Top of letter: '(Appreciation of Beauty)' *pencil*

1 See letter to James Shaw, 11 February [1866]. CD had asked Shaw for information about birds that displayed 'courtesy towards their own image in mirror or picture', to which Shaw had alluded in a recent paper, 'The appreciation of beauty by animals' (Shaw 1866a; see letter from James Shaw, [6–10 February 1866]).

2 The reference is to Thomas Boyle Grierson of Thornhill, Dumfriesshire. See also letter from James Shaw, [6–10 February 1866] and n. 10.

3 Mrs Hunter, of Milnton, Tynron, Dumfriesshire (*County directory of Scotland*, 1862) has not been further identified. The reference is to Shaw 1866a.

4 Donald Mitchell was a reporter for the Dumfries Courier and a member of the Dumfriesshire and Galloway Natural History and Antiquarian Society (*Dumfries Courier*, 4 October 1876; *Transactions and Journal of the Proceedings of the Dumfriesshire & Galloway Natural History and Antiquarian Society* (1862–3): 16).

5 Robert Macfarlane of Thornhill, Falkirk (*County directory of Scotland* 1868) has not been further identified.

6 See letter to James Shaw, 11 February [1866].

7 Shaw alludes to CD's work *Coral reefs*.

8 James Julius Wood was minister of the Free Church in Dumfries (*Modern English biography*).

9 Shaw refers to Anon. 1866. For further discussion of the review, see the letter from James Samuelson, 8 April 1866, and the letter from A. R. Wallace, 2 July 1866.

10 The portrait, a lithograph apparently based on a photograph taken by Ernest Edwards, appeared in *Quarterly Journal of Science*, facing p. 151. CD may have sat for Edwards during his visit to London from 8 to 20 November 1865 (*Correspondence* vol. 13).

To B. D. Walsh [19] April [1866]

Down. | Bromley. | Kent. S.E.
April 20th[1]

My dear Sir

I forwarded the paper at once to Wallace "9 St. Mark's Terrace Regents Park, London. N.W." & pray at any time use me in the same way.[2]

I have been much interested by your remarks on Halesidota[3] & especially on the 18 spots on Doryphora.—[4] What an indefatigable worker you are!

I know nothing about Mr. Wilson Armistead, except that he is going to publish on galls & consequently I sent him a good collection which I had from Ceylon:[5] he was profuse in his thanks to me,[6] so that I do not think it likely that he would be intentionally ungrateful to you.—

I see that you have been attacking Mr Scudder; & you will do the subject of the change of species wonderfully good service; for everyone in the U. States must now be aware that if he argues foolishly or misquotes, you will be down on him like a clap of thunder.[7] I have followed Sir C. Lyell's[8] advice, (who is a very wise man) & always avoided controversy; but Lyell's arguments (except as far as loss of time is concerned) do not apply to any third party, who has energy & courage & wit enough to enter the arena.—

My health is considerably improved so that I work 2–3 hours daily;[9] but all my new work has been stopped since the 1st of March, by correcting & adding to a new Edit. of the Origin.[10] But I have found that I cd. not do nearly justice to the subject. I have referred to your work, but have not used it to *one quarter* of the extent, which I shd. have liked to have done.[11] I will send you a copy when it is published in the course of the summer; for it is somewhat improved since the American Edition, which was so unfortunately stereotyped.—[12] If you can remember look in Histor: Sketch at my account of Owen's views: it is rich & shows what a muddle those who "utter sonorous commonplaces about carrying out the Plan of Creation &c" fall into.—[13]

My dear Sir | Yours most sincerely | Ch. Darwin

You will have seen an account of poor Whewell's death from a fall from a Horse.[14]

My second son is now at your old College of Trinity, & has just gained a Scholarship, being the second man of his year, which pleases me much.—[15]

Postmark: AP 19 66
Field Museum of Natural History, Chicago (Walsh 7)

1 CD evidently misdated the letter: the cover is postmarked 19 April 1866.

2 CD refers to the second part of Walsh 1864–5 and to Alfred Russel Wallace (see letter from B. D. Walsh, 13 March 1866).

3 Walsh had observed four stable colour variants in the gall insect, *Halesidota tessellaris*; the differences in colour were distinguishable at a certain stage in the development of the larvae, but not at the imago stage. On this basis, Walsh proposed a new species, *H. Harrissii*, arguing that species distinctions should not be made solely on the basis of comparisons between adult forms (Walsh 1864–5, pp. 197–200). He drew an analogy between the gall insects and the 'alternate generations' of certain Radiata, in which distinct hydroids produce similar jellyfish (*ibid.*, p. 203); this passage is scored in CD's copy (Darwin Pamphlet Collection–CUL).

4 Walsh described eighteen spots, arranged in a particular pattern, on the thorax of two species of *Doryphora*. He remarked that the presence of such identical markings was explicable if the two species had arisen from a common ancestor, whereas there was no reason for 'Nature to plagiarize from herself a merely ornamental design' when millions of other patterns were available (Walsh 1864–5, pp. 207–8); this section is scored in CD's copy.

5 See letter from B. D. Walsh, 13 March 1866 and n. 8. CD had received galls from George Henry Kendrick Thwaites, director of the Peradiniya botanic gardens in Ceylon, in 1863 (see *Correspondence* vol. 11, letter to G. H. K. Thwaites, 30 March [1863] and n. 10). The galls are described in *Variation* 2: 282.

6 No correspondence between CD and Armistead has been found.

7 In the postscript to Walsh 1864–5, Walsh criticised a recent paper by Samuel Hubbard Scudder, in which a passage from *Origin* was misquoted (Walsh 1864–5, p. 216; see also Scudder 1866, pp. 26–7).

Walsh concluded: 'A theory must be strong indeed, when, as would seem from the practice of certain Naturalists, it can only be refuted by misstating it.'

8 Charles Lyell.

9 Following long periods of illness in 1864 and 1865, CD began to report improvement in his health in September 1865 (see *Correspondence* vol. 12, and *Correspondence* vol. 13, letter to J. D. Hooker, 27 [or 28 September 1865]).

10 CD had agreed to produce a fourth edition of *Origin* in February (see letter to John Murray, 22 February [1866]).

11 CD added two references to Walsh in the fourth edition of *Origin*, citing his work on phytophagic forms (Walsh 1864–5), and his 'law of equable variability', according to which characters highly variable in one species tend to be variable in allied species (Walsh 1863, p. 213). See *Origin* 4th ed., pp. 55, 187.

12 Walsh's name appears on CD's presentation list for the fourth edition of *Origin* (see Appendix IV); the book was not published until November 1866 (see letter from John Murray, 18 July [1866]). On the use of stereotypes in the production of the American edition of *Origin* in 1860, see the letter to Asa Gray, 16 April [1866] and n. 11.

13 CD considerably revised his account of Richard Owen's work in his historical sketch to *Origin* 4th ed., pp. xvii–xviii (Peckham ed. 1959, pp. 64–6). See letter to J. D. Hooker, 31 May [1866] and n. 11. CD quotes from Walsh 1864–5, p. 215.

14 William Whewell, an acquaintance of CD's since his undergraduate days at Cambridge, had died on 6 March 1866 (*DNB*). Walsh had been a student and fellow at Trinity College, Cambridge, while Whewell was fellow and junior tutor there (*Alum. Cantab.*).

15 CD refers to George Howard Darwin. See letter to J. D. Hooker, [16 April 1866] and n. 3.

From George Henslow [after 19 April 1866][1]

10 Sth Crescent | Bedford Sq | W.C.

Dear Mr Darwin

Many thanks for your letter.[2] I have got the Botanische Zeitung from the Linn: Soc: & mean to get a friend to translate it to me. It is a bother Dr Hildebrand hitting on the very same thing! I however read my note upon the structure of *Indigoferae* at last meeting of Soc: Linn: & called attention, at the same time, to Dr Hildebrands paper.[3]

I am glad to say the Governors of St. Bartholomew's Hospital have withdrawn their restriction & have elected me their *Botanical Lecturer* at last![4] So I begin my duties in May.—

Thanks for explanation about *Primula*.[5] I see that *2d* & *3d* column of Table II brings out the difference more palpably. viz: that of the total No. of pods produced & of good Pods.

$$\text{homo}\left\{\begin{matrix}5\\6\end{matrix}\right\} : \text{Hetero}\left\{\begin{matrix}14\\11\end{matrix}\right\}\text{—}^{6}$$

Have you ever noticed a sort of *intermediate form*? viz: *stamens low down*, but stigma *only slightly* above them, with the Corolla generally larger? as in enclosed.—[7]

Yrs very truly | G Henslow

DAR 166: 160

[1] The date is established by the reference to Henslow 1866a (see n. 3, below).
[2] Letter to George Henslow, 16 April [1866].
[3] See letter to George Henslow, 16 April [1866] and n. 2. Henslow discussed Friedrich Hildebrand's article on pollination mechanisms in *Indigofera* and other plants (Hildebrand 1866a) in his paper read at the Linnean Society on 19 April 1866 (Henslow 1866a).
[4] Henslow may refer to the requirement that members of staff of St Bartholomew's Hospital serve a medical apprenticeship (see Medvei and Thornton eds. 1974, p. 265).
[5] CD's explanation has not been found; see, however, the letter from George Henslow, 7 April 1866 and n. 5. Henslow refers to CD's calculations of the weight of seeds in pods of *Primula veris* in 'Dimorphic condition in Primula'.
[6] The figures are taken from table II in 'Dimorphic condition in Primula', p. 89, and show, in the first and second columns, respectively, the number of 'good pods' produced in homomorphic and heteromorphic crosses of *Primula veris*. The upper row shows the results for long-styled flowers, and the lower row for short-styled (*Collected papers* 2: 56).
[7] In addition to the long-styled and short-styled forms of *Primula sinensis*, CD had been experimenting with 'equal-styled' specimens since 1862. CD concluded that these specimens were variations of the long-styled form, and not a third, distinct form. See *Correspondence* vol. 10 and 'Illegitimate offspring of dimorphic and trimorphic plants', pp. 414–18. His notes are in DAR 108: 29, 38v., 56–66, 85–7, 134–5. He also carried out experiments with an equal-styled variety of *P. veris* that had been described by John Scott (see *Correspondence* vol. 11, letter to John Scott, 1 and 3 August [1863] and n. 13). See also 'Illegitimate offspring of dimorphic and trimorphic plants', pp. 426–30, *Forms of flowers*, pp. 234–8, and *Variation* 2: 109 n. See also *Correspondence* vol. 12.

To Friedrich Hildebrand 20 April [1866]

Down. | Bromley. | Kent. S.E.
April 20th

Dear Sir

I am very much obliged to you for so kindly sending me your most interesting papers.[1] The cases of Lopezia & Schizanthus are quite new to me.[2] A Botanical friend, Mr. Henslow, was staying here a fortnight since, & detected & showed to me the curious movements in Indigofera, which grew in my greenhouse.—[3]

You may perhaps like to hear that in 1860 I watched Bombus lapidarius sucking the flowers of Pedicularis sylvatica, & I saw all that you describe: when the Bee forced its head into the corolla, the slit in the upper helmet-like petal opened & the anthers & stigma were rubbed on its back, so that its back was white with pollen.—[4]

Several years ago I protected Medicago lupulina from insects, & its fertility was much impaired, but not wholly prevented.[5] I know of many cases in which in the same genus one species requires insect aid & another is sufficiently or fully fertile without such aid; but in this latter case the flowers are nevertheless repeatedly crossed by adjoining plants.

I have not yet read your paper on Salvia, but I recognize the beautiful structures in your excellent drawings with which I am familiar.—[6]

I hope that you will continue your interesting researches, & with sincere respect, | remain Dear Sir | Yours truly obliged | Ch. Darwin

Postmark: AP 20 66
Morristown National Historical Park (Lloyd W. Smith MS 698)

[1] CD had received copies of Hildebrand 1866a and 1866b. See letter to George Henslow, 16 April [1866] and nn. 2 and 5.
[2] For Hildebrand's descriptions of *Lopezia coronata* and *Schizanthus pinnatus*, see Hildebrand 1866a, pp. 75–7.
[3] George Henslow had visited CD from 2 to 3 or 4 April 1866 (Emma Darwin's diary (DAR 242)). He had been preparing a paper on pollination mechanisms in *Indigofera* (see letter to George Henslow, 16 April [1866] and n. 2).
[4] *Pedicularis sylvatica*, commonly known as lousewort, is described in Hildebrand 1866a, pp. 10–11. CD reported his observations of bees visiting *P. sylvatica* in *Cross and self fertilisation*, p. 422.
[5] CD had written a note on *Medicago lupulina* that was included in a paper by Henslow on cross-pollination by insects in *Medicago sativa* (Henslow 1865). See *Correspondence* vol. 13, letter to George Henslow, [2–5 November 1865]. CD's observations were also published in *Cross and self fertilisation*, p. 368. His notes on *M. lupulina*, dated 1859, are in DAR 157a: 45.
[6] CD refers to Hildebrand 1866b. See letter to George Henslow, 16 April [1866] and n. 5.

From M. T. Masters 20 April 1866

International Horticultural Exhibition, | & Botanical Congress, | Office, 1, William Street, Lowndes Square, S.W.
April 20 *1866*

My dear Sir/

I hope you will not attribute the fact of my not having sent you Caspary's paper (read at Amsterdam) to my negligence—[1] the truth is it is not yet published but I believe it soon will be when I will forward it to you as soon as I shall have looked it through in in the interests of the Gard. Chron.[2] in the meantime it may interest you to know that Caspary intends to read an elaborate paper at our congress on the motion observed in the branches of trees as the result of cold—[3] His paper is minute in detail and accompanied with diagrams &c

The principal conclusions at w^h. he arrives are

1. That there is in frosty weather a lateral movement (to the left hand) of the branches & in direct proportion to the intensity of the cold.

2. There is also a vertical movement from above downwards

3. Sometimes a similar movement in the reverse direction i.e. upwards

4 In other cases the branches rise in mild weather & droop in frost—

Another Paper which concerns you is one of Lecoq's on the migration of plants w̄h special reference to the mountain flora of Auvergne nearly identical with those of the Alps & Pyrenees—[4] He disagrees with you as to the glacial epoch and its effect in producing the present distribution of plants He says the former greater extension of glaciers was rather due to a higher than to a lower temperature and says he has anticipated Frankland & Tyndall in this point see his book Des glaciers et des Climats"—[5] He considers that birds and the winds have effected the colonization of Alpine & Articc plants in the Auvergne mountains[6]—but while disagreeing with you on most points he shares your views as to Origin of Species and has anticipated you— see his Etudes sur la geographie botanique de l'Europe tom i. p. 140. tom iv. p 245–277.[7]

—The other papers that I have got (more than we quite know what to do with!) are mostly technical either horticultural or botanical should anything turn up that I think will be likely to interest you I will let you know before hand.[8] De C's address is chiefly on the relations of Veg^{l}. Physiol. to Horticult. & of the services w^{h}. Horticulturists (not devoted to £·s·d only) might render to Veg. Phys & Bot.[9]

If all this is caviare pray excuse me and believe me though hastily yet with great respect | yours faithfully | Maxwell. T. Masters

DAR 171: 75

[1] The reference is to Robert Caspary's paper on graft hybrids (Caspary 1865a). See letter to Robert Caspary, 21 February [1866] and n. 2. CD had received a copy of the paper (see letter to Robert Caspary, 4 March 1866).

[2] Masters had become the principal editor of *Gardeners' Chronicle* in 1865, upon the death of John Lindley (*DNB*).

[3] Caspary's paper 'On the change of the direction of the branches of woody plants' was read at the International Horticultural Exhibition and Botanical Congress on 23 May 1866. The paper was published in the congress proceedings (Caspary 1866a). An abstract was printed in *Gardeners' Chronicle*, 2 June 1866, pp. 513–14.

[4] Henri Lecoq's paper on the migration of alpine plants was delivered at the International Horticultural Exhibition and Botanical Congress and published in the congress proceedings (Lecoq 1866).

[5] Lecoq disputed CD's argument in *Origin*, pp. 365–82, that Alpine species had migrated during a cold period to lowlands formerly occupied by temperate species, and that with a return of warmer temperatures after the glacial epoch, some of these Alpine species had ascended mountains while others retreated to Arctic regions. Lecoq claimed that glaciers in Europe had been caused not by a general lowering of temperature, but by a condensation of vapour in higher altitudes during a comparatively warm period (see Lecoq 1866, pp. 162–3). Lecoq referred to his work, *Des glaciers et des climats* (Lecoq 1847), as containing the first exposition of theories on glacial formation that were later proposed by Edward Frankland and John Tyndall. In several papers published in 1864, Frankland argued that the glacial epoch was caused by increased precipitation owing to a warming of the oceans (see Frankland 1864a and 1864b, and *Correspondence* vol. 12). In support of his theory, Frankland cited Tyndall's research on the formation of glaciers by a process of freezing and melting, implying a fluctuation of temperatures rather than an absolute reduction in temperature (Frankland 1864a, pp. 168–9; see also Tyndall and Huxley 1857, Tyndall 1860, and *Correspondence* vol. 6). Tyndall's glacial research is discussed in Rowlinson 1971 and Hevley 1996.

[6] See Lecoq 1866, pp. 163–4.

[7] The reference is to Lecoq 1854–8. There is an annotated copy in the Darwin Library–CUL (see *Marginalia* 1: 488–96). Before he read Lecoq 1854–8, CD added a note to his historical sketch in the American edition of *Origin*, stating his belief that Lecoq's views on modification and descent were similar to those of Naudin (*Correspondence* vol. 8, Appendix IV, p. 575). After reading it, he replaced the note with a quotation from Lecoq 1854–8, 1: 250, which suggested that Lecoq's views agreed with those of Etienne Geoffroy Saint-Hilaire and Johann Wolfgang von Goethe. CD added the remark, 'Some other passages scattered through M. Lecoq's large work, make it a little doubtful how far he extends his views on the modification of species'. See *Origin* 4th ed., p. xx, and Peckham ed. 1959, pp. 68–9. For CD's negative assessment of the work, see *Correspondence* vol. 9, letter to J. D. Hooker, [9 December 1861].

[8] For a list of the papers presented at the congress, see *International Horticultural Exhibition* 1866.

[9] Alphonse de Candolle gave the presidential address at the opening meeting of the International Horticultural Exhibition and Botanical Congress on 23 May 1866 (Candolle 1866).

To Friedrich Rolle[1] 21 April 1866

Down, Bromley | Kent S.E.
April 21. 1866.

Dear Sir,

I write one line to thank you incesely[2] for your great kindness in taking the time to inform me of so many interesting publications. Some of which as that on Rissoa and Virchows work I must procure[3]

I suspected that Geinitz was opposed to me, but I hope that will not present[4] him taking care in correcting Bronn's translation[5]

I had nothing wathever to do with the selection as this lay entirely withe the Publisher of the German edition

We have I[6] yet heard positively that Prof. Geinitz will undertake the whole affair

With my respected and sincere Thanks

I remain, dear Sir | Your very faithfully | Ch. Darwin

Copy
Senckenbergische Naturforschende Gesellschaft, Frankfurt am Main

[1] The original letter to Rolle has not been found. The letter text is based on a transcription made by Rolle for Francis Darwin, who prepared editions of CD's letters (*LL* and *ML*). Rolle's transcription contains many obvious errors, and was not published in *LL* or *ML*.
[2] For 'incesely' read 'sincerely'.
[3] See letter from Friedrich Rolle, 12 April 1866. Rolle refers to Schwartz von Mohrenstern 1864, Rudolf Carl Virchow, and Virchow 1866.
[4] For 'present' read 'prevent'.
[5] See letter from Friedrich Rolle, 12 April 1866. CD's German publisher, Christian Friedrich Schweizerbart, had asked Hans Bruno Geinitz to prepare a third German edition of *Origin*. The first two German editions had been translated by Heinrich Georg Bronn (Bronn trans. 1860 and Bronn trans. 1863). See letter from E. Schweizerbart'sche Verlagsbuchhandlung, 23 March 1866 and n. 7.
[6] For 'have I' read 'haven't'.

To J. D. Hooker [22 April 1866]

6. Queen Anne St | W.
Sunday

My dear Hooker

Many thanks about New Zealand Flora,[1] received just as we were coming here for a week.—[2]

If M[rs] Hooker or yourself are in London, we hope much that you will call, but you must not of course think for a moment of coming on purpose; though of course we sh[d]. only be too glad to see M[rs]. Hooker or both—[3]

Ever yours | C. Darwin

Endorsement: 'April 22/66'
DAR 115: 285

[1] See letter to J. D. Hooker, [16 April 1866] and n. 2. Hooker's reply has not been found.

[2] The Darwins were in London from 21 April to 1 May 1866 (Emma Darwin's diary (DAR 242)); 6 Queen Anne Street was the residence of CD's brother, Erasmus Alvey Darwin.
[3] CD refers to Frances Harriet Hooker.

To H. B. Jones [23 April 1866?][1]

6. Queen Anne St | *W.*
Monday

My dear Dr. Bence Jones

I had hoped to have saved you trouble & called on you, but I find I hardly can with comfort to myself.[2] Will you, therefore, be so good as to call here on me, that I may consult you & report progress—[3]

Ever yours | Most truly obliged | Ch. Darwin

Wellcome Library for the History and Understanding of Medicine, Bence Jones autograph letter file

[1] The date is conjectured from the fact that it is the only date on which a payment was made to Jones on a Monday, coinciding with a visit by CD to London. CD was in London from 21 April to 1 May 1866 (Emma Darwin's diary (DAR 242)). CD's Classed account books (Down House MS) record a payment to Jones on 23 April 1866, a Monday.
[2] See letter to [H. B. Jones?], 13 April [1866].
[3] On CD's health, see the letter to H. B. Jones, 3 January [1866] and the letter from H. B. Jones, 10 February [1866].

To James Shaw [23 April 1866][1]

Down. | *Bromley.* | *Kent. S.E.* [6 Queen Anne Street, London]
Monday

Dear Sir

I am much obliged for your kind letter & all the great trouble which you have taken in sending me the various & interesting facts on birds admiring themselves.—[2] I am very glad to hear of these facts.— I have just finished revising & adding to a new Edition of the Origin, & in this I have given, without going into details (so that I shall not be able to use your facts) some remarks on the subject of beauty.[3] When the Edition is published in the course of the summer I will do myself the pleasure of sending you a copy.—[4]

With my best thanks I remain Dear Sir | Yours very faithfully | Ch. Darwin

American Philosophical Society (317)

[1] The date is established by the relationship between this letter and the letter from James Shaw, 19 April 1866, and by Shaw's statement that he received this letter in April 1866 (R. Wallace ed. 1899, p. lvii). In 1866, 23 April was the first Monday after 19 April.
[2] See letter from James Shaw, 19 April 1866.
[3] CD discussed beauty in the fourth edition of *Origin*, pp. 237–41. He briefly discussed cases in which birds looked at themselves in a mirror in *Descent* 2: 111.
[4] Shaw's name appears on CD's presentation list for the fourth edition of *Origin* (see Appendix IV).

From Charles Wentworth Dilke 24 April 1866

76, Sloane Street SW.
24 April 1866

Dear Sir

Mr. & Madame de Candolle[1] dine with my Mother in Law[2] & myself on Thursday the 17th of May at a quarter before seven. If Mrs Darwin & yourself would give us the pleasure of your company we should be pleased.[3]

Yours truly | C Wentworth Dilke

C Darwin Esq

DAR 162: 181

[1] Dilke refers to Alphonse de Candolle and his wife, Jeanne-Victoire-Laure de Candolle.

[2] Dilke's mother-in-law, Caroline A. Duncombe Chatfield, had lived at Dilke's London residence since his marriage in 1840 (Gwynn and Tuckwell 1917, 1: 8).

[3] Dilke refers to Emma Darwin. CD and Emma did not attend the dinner. See letter from Alphonse de Candolle, 3 June 1866.

From Robert Caspary 26 April 1866

Koenigsberg in Pr
26: of April 1866

My dear Sir,

I delayed answering your kind letter of the 4th of March[1] hoping to be able to express to you the most bright prospect, that I should go to the congress of botanists to be held at London and that I should be perhaps there fortunate enough as to make your personal acquaintance.[2]

Will your health be strong enough as to enable you to partake of the congress; You are as I see member of the committee.[3] How very glad I should be to meet you somewhere, particularly if I could spend a few quiet hours with you.[4] It was only a few days ago that the decision, that I should go the congress fell to the positive.

I express to you at the same time my warmest thanks for your photography; the circumstance that it is a home-made one, enheightens rather the interest, which I take in it[5]

I shall leave this place by about the 12th of May and go directly without any delay to London. I have a long list of books—and plants; which I want to study at the British Museum and at Kew or to *[get]* in some garden or other.[6] I am only sorry, that I can not spend more than 3 weeks at the utmost to the whol tour, as I can not interrupt longer my course of lectures—[7]

I sent to Dr M. Masters a paper, destined for the congress, on a rather curious subject; on the motion or changement which the direction of branches undergos by frost.[8] I examined last winter 10 species of trees as regards this change by dayly observations. Some trees bend their branches in frost down, others lift them up and still others lift them up in mild frost and head them down in severe frost. All have a movement to the side.

I the hope of seeing you soon face to face with most sincere respect yours very truly | Rob. Caspary

DAR 161: 119

[1] Letter to Robert Caspary, 4 March 1866.
[2] Caspary refers to the International Horticultural Exhibition and Botanical Congress, held in London from 22 to 31 May 1866.
[3] CD was a vice-president of the committee of the botanical congress (see letter from M. T. Masters, March 1866 and n. 1).
[4] CD did not attend the congress. Caspary visited CD at Down on 27 May 1866 (Emma Darwin's diary (DAR 242)).
[5] CD enclosed his photograph with the letter to Robert Caspary, 4 March 1866. It was probably a copy of the photograph taken by his son William Erasmus Darwin in April or May 1864 (see *Correspondence* vol. 12, frontispiece).
[6] Caspary refers to the Royal Botanic Gardens, Kew.
[7] Caspary was professor of botany and director of the botanic garden at the University of Königsberg.
[8] The reference is to Maxwell Tylden Masters and Caspary 1866a. See letter from M. T. Masters, 20 April 1866 and n. 3.

From William Robert Grove 26 April 1866

Apr 26/66

Dear Darwin

Very sorry to have missed you when you called.[1] Are you going to leave London if so I will come & see you this evening, if you are disengaged

If not I will come next Sunday say about 3 pm.

I am worked beyond endurance

Ever yours | W R Grove

DAR 165: 230

[1] CD was in London from 21 April to 1 May 1866 (Emma Darwin's diary (DAR 242)).

To W. R. Grove [26 April 1866][1]

[6 Queen Anne Street, London]

Dear Grove

I am sorry to say that I am so tired this evening that I could talk to no one, though I am sure I am very much obliged to you for offering to come.

I have a half-sort of engagement to go, if able, to Kew on Sunday afternoon.[2] Would you excuse me proposing to call on you for half an hour on Sunday morning at 10 or $10\frac{1}{2}$ or 11.—

To save you trouble, of writing I will say, if I do *not* hear to contrary that I will call about 10; but of course if you are tired or have other engagement put me off without least scruple[3]

Yours very sincerely | Ch. Darwin

Royal Institution of Great Britain (RI MS GR/1a/99)

[1] The date is established by the relationship between this letter and the letter from W. R. Grove, 26 April 1866.
[2] See letter to J. D. Hooker, [28 April 1866].
[3] CD called on Grove on 29 April 1866 (letter from Emma Darwin to H. E. Darwin, 30 April [1866] (DAR 219.9: 42)).

To Thomas Rivers 27 April [1866][1]

Down. | *Bromley.* | *Kent. S.E.* [6 Queen Anne Street, London]
April 27th

My dear Sir

From reading your last article in Journal of Hort. I am going to beg a favour; & favours you have always granted me at least twice over.— It is to make a memorandum, & send me, when partially in flower, a raceme of *Cytisus purpureus-elongatus.* & at same time, if you have it, a raceme of C. Adami.—[2] My tree of latter is dead, but I could probably get flowers by sending to Westerham;[3] yet I shd. prefer flowers from you, for then I shd. have them fresh at same time with those of C. purp-elongatus. These flowers ought to be enclosed in tin-foil or in very small tin-cannister & sent by Post.—

Why I want them is that Prof. Caspary states that in C. Adami the pollen *in appearance* is good, whilst the ovules are bad. Now this does not occur in any known *sterile* ordinary hybrid, & Caspary hence argues that C. Adami is not a common hybrid. So that I am very curious to examine pollen & ovules of C. purp-elongatus; as I likewise will of Watererer's *supposed* hybrid between C. laburnum & alpinus.—[4]

Mr Robson does not know what he is talking about & in how odious a spirit he answered you.—[5]

If you will kindly grant me the above favour, do not trouble yourself to write, but when time comes send me the flowers to dissect. My health at last is better, & I am able to do a little work.

My dear Sir | yours sincerely | Ch. Darwin

Remember When Auctions (Cat. 41)

[1] The year is established by the relationship between this letter and the letter from Thomas Rivers, 17 May 1866.
[2] Rivers's article on fruit culture in the *Journal of Horticulture* for 24 April 1866 mentioned shields of *Cytisus purpureus* and a specimen of 'Cytisus purpureus elongatus' that Rivers had in his own nursery garden (Rivers 1866b, p. 306). 'Cytisus purpureus elongatus', described by Rivers as a distinct variety, was a hybrid between *C. purpureus* and *C. elongatus*, but is not recognised in modern taxonomy. *C. adami* is now +*Laburnocytisus adamii.*
[3] The florist, nurseryman, and seedsman John Cattell had premises at Westerham, Kent (R. Desmond 1994, *Post Office directory of the six home counties* 1859–66).
[4] On CD's interest in Robert Caspary's paper on graft hybrids such as *Cytisus adami* (Caspary 1865a), see the letter to Asa Gray, 16 April [1866] and n. 14. CD described the ovules and pollen-grains

of '*Cytisus purpureo-elongatus*' in *Variation* 1: 389. He described 'Waterer's laburnum' in *Variation* 1: 390, reporting that his specimen, though usually infertile, yielded some good seeds in 1866. The species is now known as *Laburnum* x *watereri*, a hybrid of *L. alpinum* and *L. anagyroides*.

5 Rivers had criticised an article by John Robson in the *Journal of Horticulture* on the grafting of trees and shrubs (Robson 1866a), in particular Robson's claim that the budding or grafting of a purple *Cytisus* onto the common *Laburnum* produced a staining of the bark and foliage (see Rivers 1866a). Robson defended his claim in a subsequent issue of the journal (Robson 1866b), prompting a further reply from Rivers (Rivers 1866b).

To J. D. Hooker [28 April 1866]

6. Queen Anne St
Saturday

My dear Hooker

I have had a baddish day & the higher powers have settled that I am not fit for Kew & I believe they, i.e. she is, right, so I must give up my great treat.[1]

I want a Book **very** much, which is not in Royal or Linn: & I went for it to B. Mus. but my strength failed, when there.—[2] It is "Annales de la Soc. Hort. de Paris Tom. VII. 1830".[3] Can you lend it me & send by Post, to Down.

When poor Oliver can stand being bothered please ask him for reference for microscopical appearance & structure of a bud, when it can first be discerned.[4] This account must not be in German. & must be in Book, which I can borrow from Linn. Soc.—

I have been so well most days since being in London, like what I was 7 or 8 years ago— one day I paid 3 calls! & then went for $\frac{3}{4}$ to Zoolog. Garden!!!!!!!!![5]

My dear old friend | C. D.—

Victoria Lily & Euryale ferox

☞ This means a memorandum about crossing.—[6]

We return on Monday morning or perhaps Tuesday[7]

Endorsement: 'April 28/66.'
DAR 115: 287

1 CD refers to Emma Darwin; he had planned to visit the Royal Botanic Gardens, Kew, on 29 April (see letter to W. R. Grove, [26 April 1866]).

2 CD refers to the Royal Society of London, the Linnean Society, and the British Museum.

3 CD refers to the *Annales de le Société d'Horticulture de Paris*. Volume 7 contained an account of *Cytisus adami* (Prévost 1830) that is cited in *Variation* 1: 390. For CD's interest in *C. adami* (now +*Laburnocytisus adamii*), see the letter to Asa Gray, 16 April [1866] and n. 14, and the letter to Thomas Rivers, 27 April [1866].

4 Daniel Oliver's daughter had died early in April (see letter from J. D. Hooker, [6 April 1866]).

5 CD was in London from 21 April to 1 May 1866 (Emma Darwin's diary (DAR 242)). He refers to the gardens of the Zoological Society of London in Regent's Park.

6 CD wished to test Robert Caspary's claim that the giant waterlily of the Amazon, *Victoria regia* (synonym *Euryale amazonica*, now *Victoria amazonica*), and the related species, *Euryale ferox*, were perpetually self-fertilised, contrary to CD's view that occasional cross-pollination was necessary (see Caspary

1865b, pp. 19–20, and letter from Robert Caspary, 25 February 1866 and n. 13). CD discussed pollination and the setting of seed in *E. amazonica* and *E. ferox* in *Cross and self fertilisation*, pp. 358, 365.

[7] According to Emma Darwin's diary (DAR 242), the Darwins returned home on Tuesday 1 May.

From J. D. Hooker [after 28 April 1866][1]

in their case (as in our's) depend on the favor of the public. The Director of the Adelaide Garden[2] writes that no born colonist there *ever saw a parasitic orchid.*

The W. Ind. Gardens are roaring for E. Ind. Orchids & vice versa:—& we roar for all!—

Oliver will answer in a day or two about buds,[3] the books are at binders.[4]

I go to Torquay tomorrow Lubbock goes by same Train.[5]

Lyell has been writing to me about the Coal-plants of Melville Island. But as we have not the plants, it is no use speculating on them.[6] I have glanced at Lyells 1st. Ed. & do not doubt he there means *all Globe* cooler by massing land at Poles. I doubt it greatly—& suspect that he would only thereby *redistribute* amounts of heat & cold—as I gathered was his view from subsequent Editions.[7] He makes no allusion to effect of vapor, which I am sure will throw out all his calculations.[8]

Ever Yrs affec | J D Hooker

Incomplete
DAR 102: 60

CD ANNOTATION
1.1 in ... calculations. 5.6] *crossed pencil*

[1] The date is established by the relationship between this letter and the letter to J. D. Hooker, [28 April 1866].

[2] Moritz Richard Schomburgk became director of the Adelaide Botanic Garden in 1865.

[3] Hooker refers to Daniel Oliver; see letter to J. D. Hooker, [28 April 1866].

[4] See letter to J. D. Hooker, [28 April 1866] and n. 3.

[5] Hooker refers to John Lubbock.

[6] Charles Lyell was preparing the tenth edition of *Principles of geology.* He revised his discussion of Carboniferous plants collected on Melville Island in the Arctic Ocean off Canada. Lyell noted that the collection had since been lost, but that further fossil plants had been obtained from the island, indicating the spread of Miocene plants over the Arctic regions nearly as far as the north pole (C. Lyell 1867–8, 1: 225; see also *ibid.*, pp. 89–90). For more discussion of coal plants, see the letter from J. D. Hooker, 16 January 1866 and n. 8, and the letter to J. D. Hooker, 21 [January 1866] and n. 6.

[7] In the first edition of *Principles of geology*, Lyell argued that the earth's temperature was determined to a significant degree by the relative position of land and sea, adding that a concentration of land at the poles would produce a general cooling of the earth's surface (C. Lyell 1830–3, 1: 108–21). Lyell's argument remained largely unchanged in later editions (see, for example, C. Lyell 1853, 1: 104–10, and C. Lyell 1867–8, 1: 266). For further discussion of Lyell's theory, see the letters from Charles Lyell, 1 March 1866 and n. 3, and 10 March 1866, and the letter to Charles Lyell, 8 March [1866]; see also Fleming 1998.

[8] In the tenth edition of *Principles of geology*, Lyell briefly considered whether the glacial period was one of higher mean temperature, 'because an excess of snow implies an excess of evaporation, and

consequently of heat'; however, he dismissed this view as a 'fallacy' that had arisen 'from omitting the element of time from the calculation'. He argued, 'If the summer's warmth cannot get rid of all the winter's snow, even by a few feet in a century, there will, in the course of thousands of years, be as large a store of ice formed as geologists may require' (C. Lyell 1867–8, 1: 288).

From William Turner [after 28 April 1866?][1]

One evening, some summers' ago, I was sitting with a friend in his garden, when, during a pause in the conversation, our attention was attracted by a slight tap-tap, several times repeated— We quietly rose from our seats & stepped to some bushes, from amidst which the sound proceeded— On peering between the branches we saw a bird holding in its beak the shell of a common garden snail which it was tapping with some force against a flat stone lying on the ground— After a time the shell broke into several pieces & the bird then extracted the snail with its beak. The ground for some distance around the stone was covered with numerous fragments of snails' shells & the conclusion was naturally drawn that the bird had been in the habit of resorting to this particular stone for the purpose of aiding it in breaking the shells of the snails on which it fed—

Wm Turner

Incomplete
DAR 178: 197

[1] The date is conjectured from the likelihood that the information in the letter was communicated after the Royal Society of London soirée on 28 April 1866 at which CD first met Turner (see letter to William Turner, 5 June [1866]). Subsequent correspondence with Turner is confined to medical topics relevant to *Variation*, *Descent*, and *Expression*.

To William Robinson [29 April 1866][1]

6. Queen Anne St
Sunday

Dear Sir.—

I was very sorry to have missed seeing you & hope I shall be more fortunate when I may next be in London; for I return home tomorrow morning.[2]

I am much obliged for your obliging offer of assistance, which I will keep in mind.[3] I may mention (though it is improbable that you can aid me) one point.— If you have Euryale ferox & if it produces more than one flower at a time, I wish you would cross some & fertilise some others with their own pollen, in order to see, when the seeds are counted (which I would undertake), whether the cross aids at all in increasing fertility. Properly pollen ought to be taken for the cross from a distinct plant.— The Euryale is dead at Kew, where they w^d^. have made the trial on a large scale for me.—[4] Prof Caspary has advanced this plant as a case of self-fertilisation for many generations with unimpaired fertility.[5]

If you have two distinct plants of any Nymphæa, I sh[d]. much like the above trial to be made, but the flowers which are fertilised *with own pollen* ought to be protected, whilst expanded from insects.—

With my thanks for your kind offer. Dear Sir | Yours very faithfully | Ch. Darwin

Royal Horticultural Society, Lindley Library (Box 2, Package 16)

[1] The date is established by the relationship between this letter, the letter to J. D. Hooker, [28 April 1866], and the letter to William Robinson, 5 May [1866]. In 1866, the intervening Sunday was 29 April.

[2] CD was in London from 21 April to 1 May 1866 (Emma Darwin's diary (DAR 242)). In the letter to J. D. Hooker, [28 April 1866], he wrote that he would return home on Monday 30 April, or Tuesday 1 May 1866.

[3] No letter from William Robinson offering assistance has been found.

[4] On CD's interest in *Euryale ferox*, see the letter to J. D. Hooker, [28 April 1866] and n. 6.

[5] CD refers to Robert Caspary. See letter to J. D. Hooker, [28 April 1866] and n. 6.

To Robert Hunt 3 May [1866][1]

Down Bromley Kent
May 3

My dear Sir

I am much obliged for your note. I enclose a copy of a sketch of the principal events in my life which will give you all the facts & more that you require.[2]

Believe me my dear Sir | yours very faithfully | Ch. Darwin

[Enclosure]

Charles Robert Darwin born Feb 12 1809 at Shrewsbury, son of D[r] Robert Waring Darwin F.R.S. & grandson of D[r] Erasmus Darwin F.R.S author of the Botanic Garden, Zoonomia &c[3] & grandson by the mother's side of Josiah Wedgwood F.R.S the celebrated potter.[4] Educated at Shrewsbury school under D[r] Butler afterwards Bishop of Lichfield.[5]

In the winter of 1825 went to the Edinburgh University for two years, & thence to Christ's College Cambridge, where he took his B.A. degree in 1831. In the autumn of 1831 Captain Fitz Roy R.N.,[6] having offered to give up part of his own cabin to any Naturalist who would accompany H.M.S Beagle in her surveying voyage & circumnavigation, Mr Darwin volunteered his services without salary, but on condition that he should have the entire disposal of his collections. The Beagle sailed from England Dec. 27 1831 & returned Oct. 22. 1836.[7] Mr Darwin published a volume as part of Captain Fitz Roy's general work descriptive of the voyage, in 1839.[8] This volume was republished in a modified form under the title of "Journal of researches" &c in 1845 & has since been several times reprinted.[9] Between the year 1840 & 1843 Mr Darwin edited the Zoology of the Voyage of the Beagle giving an account of the habits & ranges of the various animals therein described. In aid of the publication of this & the following works the Lords of the Treasury granted

£1000.[10] In 1842 Mr Darwin published his work on "The Structure & distribution of Coral Reefs".[11] In 1845, "Geological Observations on Volcanic Islands", & in 1846, "Geological Observations on South America".[12] In 1851 & 1854 Mr Darwin published two volumes by aid of the Ray Society on Pedunculated & Sessile Cirripedes, & the Paleontographical Society published for him two volumes on the Fossil Species of the same class.[13] Towards the close of 1859 Mr Darwin published his "Origin of Species, of which four English editions have appeared, & nine foreign editions in French, German, Dutch, Italian & Russian.[14] Above one hundred reviews, pamphlets & separate books have been published on this work.[15]

In 1862 Mr D. published a book "On the various contrivances by which Orchids are fertilized."[16]

Of separate papers published by Mr D. the more important have been "On the connection of certain Volcanic Phenomena in South America"; "On the Distribution of Erratic boulders in S. America"; "on the formation of Mould by Earthworms" & on the Geology of the Falkland I's;" all published in the Trans. of the Geolog. Soc.[17]

In the journal of the Linnean Soc. three papers by him have appeared on the Dimorphous & Trimorphous states of Primula, Linum & Lythrum; & one paper "On the Movements & habits of Climbing Plants", which has also been published as a separate work.[18]

The Royal Soc. in 1853 awarded to Mr D. the Royal Medal, & in 1864, the Copley medal. In 1859 the Geolog. Soc. awarded him the Wollaston medal.[19]

Mr D. married his cousin Emma Wedgwood in the beginning of 1839 by whom he has a large family.[20]

He has lived for the last 26 years at Down near Farnborough Kent, & is a magistrate for that county.[21]

LS
The Natural History Museum, London (Gen. Lib. MSS/HUN: 49).

[1] The year is established by the publication date of the fifth volume of Reeve and Walford eds. 1863–7, *Portraits of men of eminence*. A photograph of CD and a memoir edited by Hunt appeared in this volume, which was published in 1866. The letter is bound with Hunt's proof copy of the text at the Natural History Museum, London (De Beer ed. 1959a, p. 37).

[2] See n. 1, above. Hunt also later wrote on scientific practitioners for the *DNB*. He had corresponded with CD about light in 1855 (see *Correspondence* vol. 5).

[3] E. Darwin 1789–91 and 1794–6; see also E. Darwin 1797, 1800, and 1803.

[4] CD refers to Josiah Wedgwood I. Wedgwood's daughter Susannah married Robert Waring Darwin in 1796.

[5] Samuel Butler.

[6] Robert FitzRoy.

[7] On this period of CD's life see *Correspondence* vol. 1.

[8] *Journal and remarks.*

[9] *Journal and remarks*, volume 3 of FitzRoy's *Narrative*, was issued in its own right as *Journal of researches* in the same year, 1839, and reprinted in 1840. A second edition was printed in 1845 and reprinted in 1852 and 1860. See Freeman 1977.

[10] CD began work on *Zoology* in October 1837; publication of the parts began in February 1838 and was completed in October 1843 (*Correspondence* vol. 2, Appendix II). On the publication of *Zoology* and on the Treasury grant, see Freeman 1977 and *Correspondence* vol. 2.

[11] *Coral reefs.*

[12] *Volcanic islands* was published in 1844 and *South America* in 1846.

[13] CD refers to *Living Cirripedia* (1851) and (1854), and *Fossil Cirripedia* (1851) and (1854). On the publication of these books, see *Correspondence* vol. 5.

[14] By the end of 1866 there had been four English editions of *Origin*, one Dutch (Winkler trans. 1860), two French (Royer trans. 1862 and 1866), two German (Bronn trans. 1860 and 1863), one Italian (Canestrini and Salimbeni trans. 1864), and two Russian (Rachinskii trans. 1864 and 1865). There had also been one US edition.

[15] CD maintained a list of reviews of *Origin* and his other works; the list is now in DAR 262.8: 9–18 (Down House MS). See also *Correspondence* vol. 8, Appendix VII. On the worldwide reception of Darwin's work, see Glick ed. 1988.

[16] *Orchids.*

[17] 'Volcanic phenomena and the formation of mountain chains'; 'Distribution of erratic boulders'; 'Formation of mould'; 'On the geology of the Falkland Islands'.

[18] 'Dimorphic condition in *Primula*'; 'Two forms in species of *Linum*'; 'Three forms of *Lythrum salicaria*'; 'Climbing plants' and *Climbing plants.*

[19] See *Correspondence* vol. 5, letter from J. D. Hooker, [4 November 1853]; *Correspondence* vol. 12 and Appendix IV; and *Correspondence* vol. 7, letter to John Phillips, 21 January [1859].

[20] On CD's marriage to Emma, see *Correspondence* vol. 2. The marriage took place on 29 January 1839 (*Correspondence* vol. 2, Appendix II). CD and Emma had seven surviving children.

[21] CD moved to Down in September 1842 (see *Correspondence* vol. 2). He was a county magistrate from 1857 (J. R. Moore 1985, p. 467; see also Milner 1994, pp. 90–5).

To Julius von Haast 5 May [1866][1]

Down. | Bromley. | Kent. S.E.
May 5th

My dear Dr. Haast

I have just received the list of candidate proposed by Council of Royal Soc. & I am heartily sorry that your name is not there; but you are certain to be elected another year.—[2]

I write now to say that I regret extremely, that though I wrote especially on the subject, your proposal paper was never sent for my signature & when I enquired it was too late as the paper was already suspended. But I hope to be in London this summer, health permitting, & will then attach my name;[3] but in truth such attached names do not much signify, as the Council judges by what is said by those present, & this year the Council is extraordinarily deficient in members who have attended to Natural History & Geology.—[4]

With every good wish, believe me | Yours very sincerely | Ch. Darwin

Alexander Turnbull Library

[1] The year is established by the relationship between this letter and the letter to Julius von Haast, 26 December [1865] (*Correspondence* vol. 13).

[2] In his letter of 27 September 1865 (*Correspondence* vol. 13), Haast had asked CD to support his candidacy for fellowship of the Royal Society of London. Haast had also sought support from Joseph Dalton

Hooker, who had arranged for Haast to be nominated by Andrew Crombie Ramsay; Hooker had reservations about Haast being elected in 1866, before the election of his superior in New Zealand, James Hector (see *ibid.*, letter from J. D. Hooker, [23] December 1865). CD agreed to sign Haast's certificate (see *ibid.*, letter to Julius von Haast, 26 December [1865]), remarking that Haast would probably not be elected for a year or two. Haast was elected to the Royal Society in 1867 (*Record of the Royal Society of London*).

[3] CD had asked Hooker to send him Haast's certificate to sign (*Correspondence* vol. 13, letter to J. D. Hooker, 22 December [1865]). CD is listed as one of Haast's proposers for the fellowship of the Royal Society in 1867 (Royal Society of London archives, EC/1867/06).

[4] For a list of the twenty-one members who served on the Royal Society council for 1866, see *Proceedings of the Royal Society of London* 14 (1865): 513. CD had expressed his concerns about the poor representation of natural history on the Royal Society council in a letter to J. D. Hooker, [31 December 1865] (*Correspondence* vol. 13). See also *Correspondence* vol. 11, letter from Edward Sabine to John Phillips, 12 November 1863, and *Correspondence* vol. 12, Appendix IV.

To William Robinson 5 May [1866][1]

Down. | Bromley. | Kent. S.E.
May 5th

Dear Sir

I write one line to thank you & to say that it w^d. be superfluous to castrate the flowers, which are crossed with pollen from a distinct plant, grown under as different circumstances as may be. The flowers fertilised with their actually own pollen sh^d. certainly be protected from insects.[2]

Dear Sir | yours much obliged | C. Darwin

P.S. I was glad to see your Election to Linn. Soc.—[3]

Royal Horticultural Society (Box 2, Package 19)

[1] The year is established by the date of Robinson's election to the Linnean Society (see n. 3, below).

[2] Robinson's letter has not been found; see, however, the letter to William Robinson, [29 April 1866] and nn. 4 and 6. CD had asked Robinson to make crosses of the waterlily *Euryale ferox*, and to compare the number of seeds in crossed individuals with that in self-pollinated specimens. CD asked for a similar experiment to be made with any species of *Nymphaea*, and instructed Robinson to protect the self-pollinated individuals from insects. Presumably it was not necessary to remove the anthers from the flowers because of the prepotency of the pollen from other individuals (see *Cross and self fertilisation*, p. 2).

[3] Robinson was elected a fellow of the Linnean Society on 19 April 1866 (*List of the Linnean Society of London* 1866).

From Robert Caspary 7 May 1866

Koenigsberg in Pr.
7th of May 1866

My dear Sir

I am very much obliged to you indeed for your very kind letter and for the invitation to go to see you.[1] What should I like better, than to do this? But at the same time I hear with greatest sympathy, that your health is weak and that you must avoid excitements of all kind.[2] I am afraid therefore, that, what would give me not only greatest pleasure, but would be a matter of greatest scientific and mental interest to me, namely to call upon you and make your personal acquaintance, would be a fateague to you, nay even more, would be perhaps a real injury to your health. Therefore I must at present consider it rather unfair, to decide already now upon my accepting your kind invitation. It will be time enough to do so, when I have come to London and after having met our common friend Dr. J. D. Hooker; may he decide, whether it is possible, that I may go to see you, without injury to your precious health, which God the strengthen, that you are long still kept to your family, your friends and to science.[3] The scientific congress is badely off, that you are unable to partake of it.[4]

I regret much that just 10 years ago, when I was for the last time in England, I did not follow the advice of your friend Dr. Hooker to go and see you— But having in sight at that time the finishing of a peculiar object and being very short of time, I could not follow Hooker's advice.

Now, my dear Sir, do all in your power to strengthen your health, avoid every, even little thing, which weakens it. May your health be spared to finish as much, of the scientific objects, the elaboration of which you have in hands, as possible— These wishes, I should say rather prayers I have the warmer for you, as I have the same in a similar case in my own family. My father in law Prof. Alex. Braun, whose signification in science you know as I,[5] is also in very poor health for months, although his suffering is rather an acute one from repeated colds, which he caught. But he can not recover now and continues to be very feable, having not left the bed for weeks. This state seems to me the more dangerous, as he suffers from colds each winter, and in the last winters really severely.

With sincerest regard, believe me, my dear Sir, yours very faithfully | Rob. Caspary

DAR 161: 120

1 CD's letter has not been found. CD was interested in Caspary's work on graft hybrids (see letters to Robert Caspary, 21 February [1866] and 4 March 1866).

2 On CD's recent state of health, see the letter to J. D. Hooker, [28 April 1866]. On his long-standing practice of avoiding conversations with visitors and other social occasions for reasons of health, see *Correspondence* vol. 13, Appendix IV and n. 9.

3 On the advice of Joseph Dalton Hooker, Caspary visited CD at Down on 27 May 1866 (see letter to J. D. Hooker, [12 May 1866], and letter from Robert Caspary, 25 May 1866 and n. 2).

4 Caspary had hoped to meet CD at the International Horticultural Exhibition and Botanical Congress, held in South Kensington, London, from 22 to 31 May 1866 (see letter from Robert Caspary, 26 April 1866). CD was a member of the congress committee (see letter from M. T. Masters, March 1866 and n. 1); however, he did not attend (see letter to Friedrich Hildebrand, 16 May [1866]).

5 CD had read Alexander Carl Heinrich Braun's work on rejuvenescence (Braun 1853; see *Correspondence* vol. 11, letter to J. D. Hooker, 13 January [1863]); it is cited in the discussion of graft hybrids in *Variation* 1: 388.

From William Erasmus Darwin [7 May – 11 June 1866][1]

Southton[2]
Monday

My Dear Father,

I went over yesterday to Isle of Wight to get Buckthorn, but unluckily it was not properly out.[3] I send a few flowers (male) but will send you some more when I have got each sex. As far as I can judge it is merely ordinaryly diœcious, but I have only roughly looked at a bud. The petals in female certainly are smaller, & the sterile stamens exist, as do the stigmas in male flower. the buds have an odd little husklike scale on them, which

Incomplete
DAR 109: A76

CD ANNOTATIONS
1.4 female certainly . . . stamens exist 1.5] *scored pencil*
Top of p. 2: '1866 Rhamnus catharticus' *pencil*

1 The year is established by CD's annotation. The date range is established by the flowering season of *Rhamnus cathartica* (May to June), and by the relationship between this letter and the letter from W. E. Darwin, [18 June 1866]. In 1866, the first Monday in May was 7 May.

2 William Erasmus Darwin lived in Southampton, where he was a partner in the Southampton and Hampshire Bank.

3 CD became interested in *Rhamnus* (buckthorn) in 1861, when Asa Gray informed him that a North American species, *R. lanceolatus* (now called *R. lanceolata*) was dimorphic; CD had then written to Joseph Dalton Hooker about obtaining a specimen (see *Correspondence* vol. 9, letter from Asa Gray, 11 October 1861, and second letter to J. D. Hooker, 1 November [1861]). CD had asked William to collect specimens from the Isle of Wight in 1864 (see *Correspondence* vol. 12, letter from H. E. Darwin to W. E. Darwin, [18 May 1864], and letter from W. E. Darwin, [19 May 1864]). It is the only species of *Rhamnus* native to Britain (Stace 1997, p. 463).

From Asa Gray 7 May 1866

Cambridge, Mass.
May 7, 1866.

My Dear Darwin

I am so delighted to get a letter from you, written with your own hand, and to see that you can work again a little.[1]

I am distracted with every sort of bothering occupation at this season, and am good for nothing either for scientific work or for correspondence. But I write a hurried line to say something about a new ed. of *Origin*.[2]

As to the Amer. ed. I have nothing from the Appleton's for years; the sale, I suppose, has gone on slowly, but they have made no returns.[3] Now would be a good time to bring out here a new ed., and if you would send me the sheets—or say that you will send them, I will write to the Appleton's asking them in the first instance if they will bring it out, and allow you the paltry 5 per cent on sales. And if they decline I would arrange with a Boston publisher, and have the work brought out in a handsome form, as a standard author.[4]

Please write me a line that I can initiate proceedings upon. Of course I also wish a copy of the new ed. for myself.[5]

I have no new facts about the influence of pollen on *fruit*,—nor about influence of grafts.[6]

I have got a little plant of *Bignonia capreolata* growing here. I punched a lot of holes into the shady side of a lath; the tendrils thrust their ends in,—also into crevice; but did not stay; either the movement of stem or tendril, or at length the shortening of the body of the tendril by coiling—which it does promptly—brought all away. I have stuck some cotton on to the lath at the proper height for the next pair of tendrils. The tendril near by stuck fast at once, and is beginning to develop the disks. And now the tendril of the other leaf has bent abruptly round, and seized the cotton with avidity.[7] Are there any new observations I can make.

The *Fenian scare* we have supposed here was mainly a plan of certain rogues here to fleece their poor countrymen & women here—poor servants & working-men: nothing more could come of it.[8] But I sadly fear many here have enjoyed the trouble it has given and the alarm it has excited,—especially among our neighbors in New Brunswick[9]—who rather enjoyed our woes 2 or 3 years ago.[10]

—Yes, Slavery is thoroughly done for.[11] We have a bad set to deal with at the South; and *holding Wolf by the* ears is no pleasant nor hopeful occupation,—as, the temper of the wolf does not improve under the holding. But we shall jangle out of the difficulty in time, even with such a crooked character as our President to deal with also.[12]

Take good care of your health; and bring out the book on Variation soon.[13]

Ever Yours affectionately | A. Gray

DAR 165: 150

CD ANNOTATION

6.8 Are there . . . can make.] *double scored pencil*

1 See letter to Asa Gray, 16 April [1866].

2 In his letter to Gray of 16 April [1866], CD mentioned that he had been working on a new edition of *Origin*, which had been requested by his publisher John Murray.

3 See letter to Asa Gray, 16 April [1866] and n. 11. Gray had negotiated with the publisher, D. Appleton & Co., the author's share of the profits of the US edition of *Origin* (see *Correspondence* vol. 7, letter to Asa Gray, 21 December [1859], and letter to John Murray, 22 December [1859], and *Correspondence* vol. 8). By 1 May 1860, 1750 of a print-run of 2500 copies had been sold (see *Correspondence* vol. 8, letter to Asa Gray, 22 May [1860] and enclosure 1). The edition was reprinted in 1861, 1864, and 1865 (Freeman 1977); however, no record of these print-runs or of the volumes sold between 1861 and 1865 has been found. See letter from Asa Gray, 3 July 1866.

4 Gray refers to the Boston publishing firm of Ticknor & Fields (see letter from Asa Gray, 27 August 1866). D. Appleton and Co. did not publish a new edition of *Origin* until 1870 (Freeman 1977).

5 Gray's name appears on the presentation list for the fourth edition of *Origin* (see Appendix IV).

6 See letter to Asa Gray, 16 April [1866] and nn. 13 and 14. See also letter to Thomas Rivers, 27 April [1866].

7 CD had been interested in the development of adhesive disks at the ends of tendrils in *Bignonia caproleata*; the plant was unable to climb on smooth surfaces, but CD had observed that the tendrils

penetrated the loose fibres of wool (see *Correspondence* vol. 12, letter to J. D. Hooker, 4 December [1864] and n. 13). He had discussed the adhesive properties of the plant with Gray, who believed that he had seen the plant climbing trees covered with mosses and lichens (see *ibid.*, letter to Asa Gray, 28 May [1864], and letter from Asa Gray, 11 July 1864). *Bignonia caproleata* is discussed in 'Climbing plants', pp. 56–9, 102–5, and 113. See also *Correspondence* vol. 13, letter from Fritz Müller, [12 and 31 August, and 10 October 1865].

8 On the Fenian movement in the United States, see the letter to Asa Gray, 16 April [1866] and n. 15.

9 Fenian troops made several raids into Canadian territory in 1866, including an attempt to capture Campobello Island, New Brunswick, in early April (Senior 1991).

10 Gray refers to losses incurred by the Union army in the American Civil War. A majority of the Canadian press, including most major newspapers, had been anti-Union during the war; the New Brunswick press had been predominantly anti-Union (Winks 1960, pp. 221–2).

11 See letter to Asa Gray, 16 April [1866] and n. 17.

12 On Andrew Johnson's clashes with the United States Congress over the policy of reconstruction in the southern states, see the letter to Asa Gray, 16 April [1866] and n. 16.

13 See letter to Asa Gray, 16 April [1866] and n. 9. *Variation* was published in January 1868 (Freeman 1977).

From W. E. Darwin 8 May [1866][1]

Southampton
May 8.

My Dear Father.

I have got the broom and examined it:[2] I enclose outlines of pollen grains,[3] also sketches of anthers,[4] though you probably know the differences in them.

As you will see there is not much difference in the two sets of pollen, which is odd as the the arrangements are so marked to separate the Stamens. The stamens are of two kinds, 5 on thin filaments with Versatile anthers, 5 on thick filaments with adnate anthers.[5]

4 of the stamens with thin filaments & versatile anthers tho' shortish in the bud become the long stamens of the flower when ready for opening and have the lobe of the anther nearest the stigma larger and, I think a little turned in, so as when ready, to fit into the cup beneath the stigma.

the remaining stamen on thin filament has a more versatile filament than any of the others & instead of lengthening, bends back with the 4 stamens on thick filaments.[6] The *5* stamens on thick filaments with adnate anthers always shed their pollen before the others; as the flower gets old the difference in size of filaments does not show so much.

The long stamened anthers are certainly larger & I think have more pollen than the short ones.

I have just taken up my botany as much as I have time for, and am grinding up Asa Gray's Structural botany, & find it very nice[7]

I hope you are none the worse for your London Expedition.[8] I return Etty's letter.[9]

I have got some more of your photographs ready if you should want any.[10]

Your affect son | W E Darwin

[Enclosure 1][11]

Broom

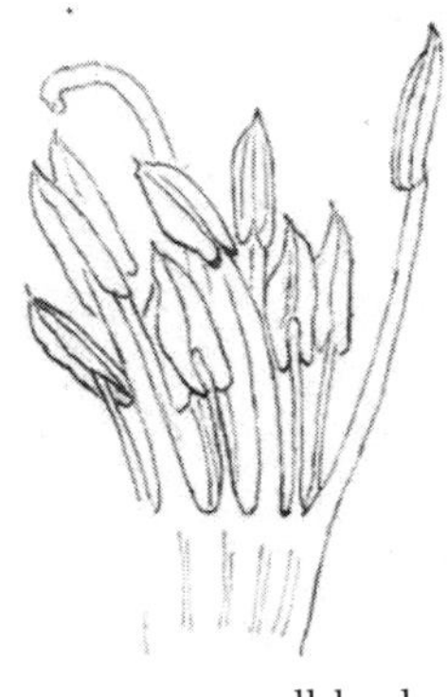

a very small bud

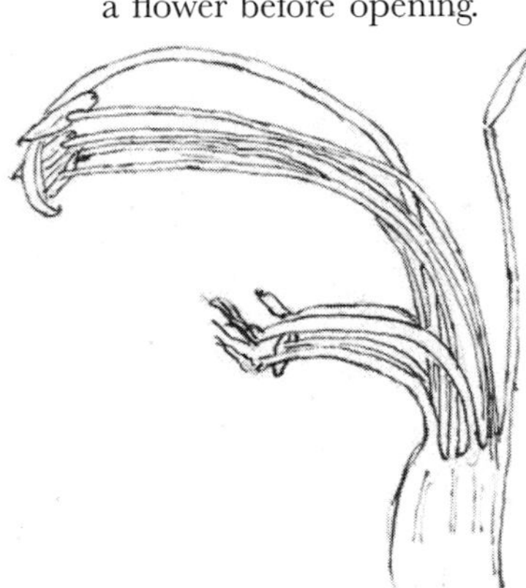

a flower before opening.

a bud before stigma bending

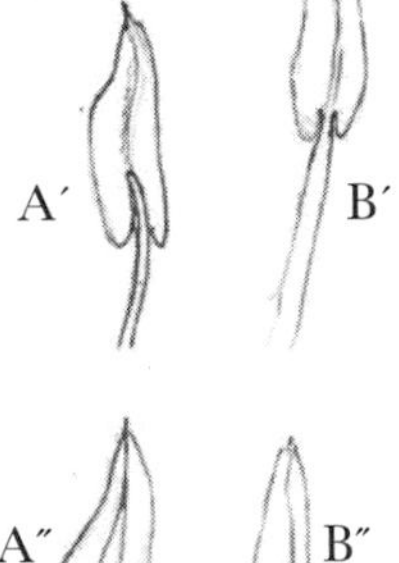

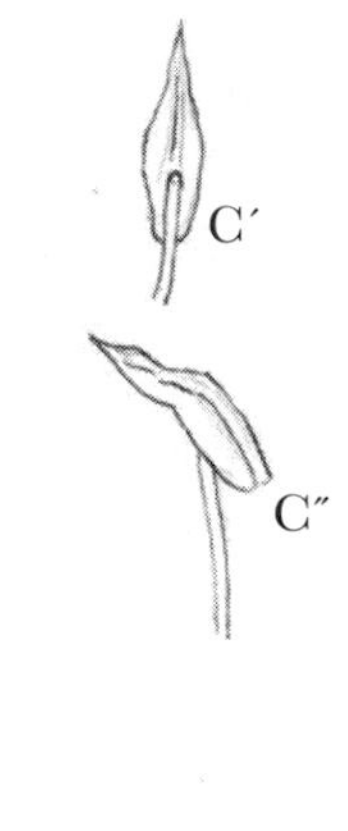

A′ A″	back & front view of versatile irregularly lobed anther of long stamens			
B′ B″	—D°—	adnate regularly	—D°—	short stamens
C′ C″	D°	of 5th versatile anther on thin filaments—		

[Enclosure 2][12]

Broom
drawn with Camera

Long stamens anthers

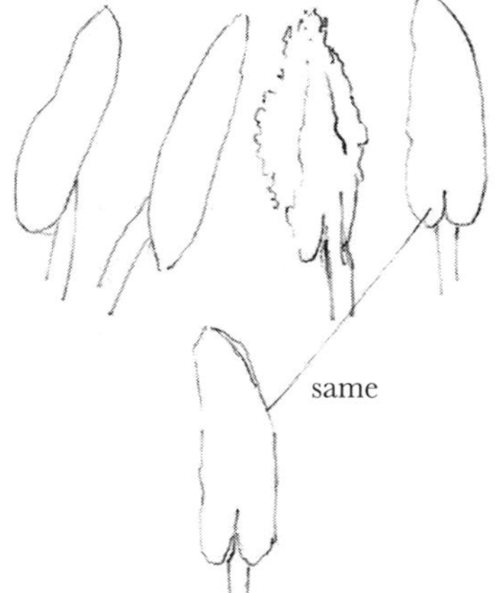

short stamens Anthers

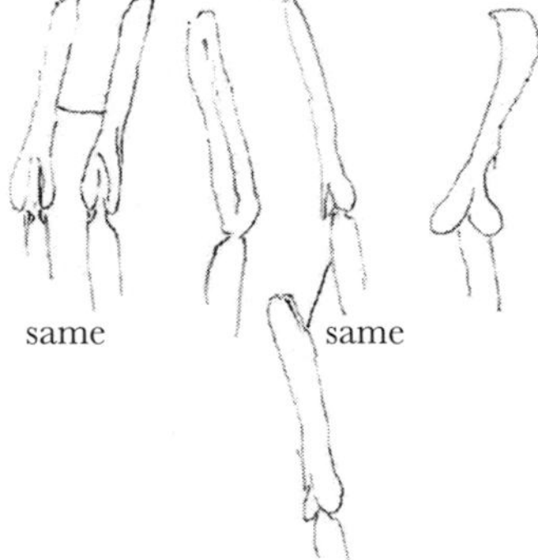

Long stamens pollen

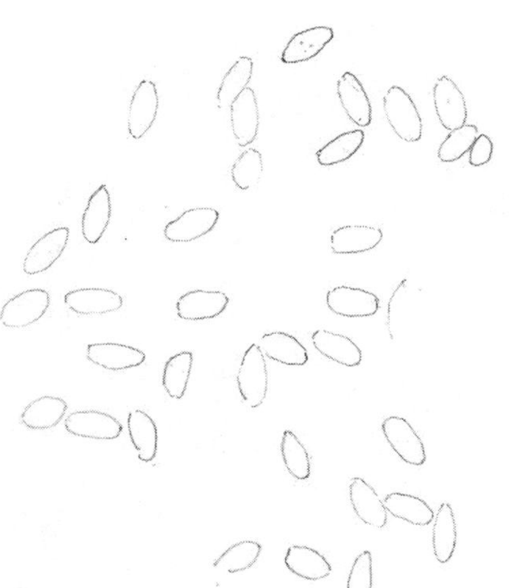

short stamens pollen

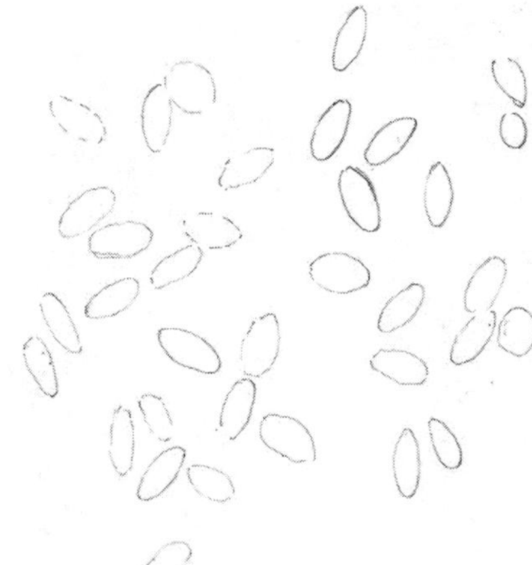

[Enclosure 3]

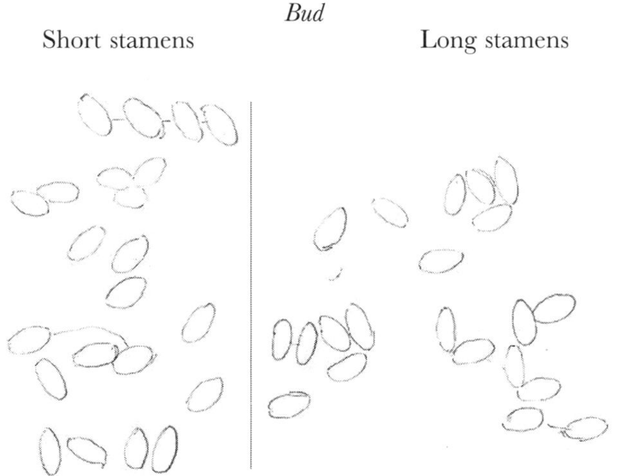

Wellish out flower

Short stamens Long stamens

[Enclosure 4]

from bud

short stamens

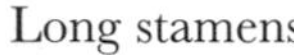

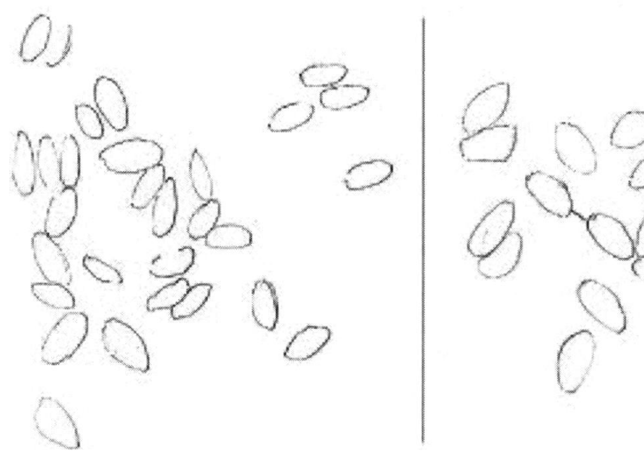

DAR 76: B52, 66–72

CD ANNOTATIONS
4.1 the remaining stamen] '5th' *interl after* 'remaining' *pencil*
4.2 bends back] 'back' *del pencil*; 'upwards' *added above* 'back' *pencil*
4.2 the 4] 'the' *del pencil*; '4' *double underl pencil*; '5' *added above, pencil, del pencil*
Enclosure 1
A′ ... stamens] '& thin filaments' *added pencil*
B′ ... stamens] 'with thick filaments' *added pencil*
Verso: 'Broom— Dichog— | Broom— Dichog' *blue crayon*

1 The year is established by the reference to CD's visit to London (see n. 8, below).

2 CD was interested in dichogamy in the common broom (*Cytisus scoparius*, then also known as *Sarothamnus scoparius*). In a note written on 29 May 1857 or later, he indicated that 'a great many' plants were '$\frac{1}{2}$ dichogamous' (DAR 76: B53): that is, their stamens shed half their pollen before the stigma of the same flower became receptive. *Cytisus scoparius* appears in a list of plants 'apparently adapted to prevent self fertilization' in William Erasmus Darwin's notebook (DAR 117: 71). Further notes on broom by William are in DAR 186: 43. William had given CD extensive assistance in his research on floral dimorphism, including drawings made with a camera lucida (see *Correspondence* vols. 10–12).

3 See enclosures 2, 3, and 4.

4 See enclosure 2.

5 CD was interested in the sizes of pollen-grains from stamens of different lengths in plants that, unlike *Cytisus scoparius*, were heterostyled; William had previously sketched and measured pollen-grains from several of those species (see, for example, *Correspondence* vol. 12, letter from W. E. Darwin, 14 April [1864], and *Forms of flowers*, pp. 248–52). CD did not mention the size of pollen-grains in his discussion of *Sarothamnus scoparius* in *Cross and self fertilisation*, pp. 163–4.

[6] See enclosure 1. In addition to dichogamy in broom, CD was also interested in the flower's particular mechanism for insect pollination (see memorandum to George Henslow, [before 19 April 1866]).

[7] William refers to A. Gray 1858. CD had encouraged his son's interest in botany after he had taken up a position as a banker in Southampton (see, for example, *Correspondence* vol. 10, letter to W. E. Darwin, 14 February [1862]).

[8] According to Emma Darwin's diary (DAR 242), CD was in London from 21 April to 1 May 1866.

[9] William may refer to the letter from H. E. Darwin, [*c.* 10 May 1866].

[10] William had taken a photograph of CD in spring 1864 (see *Correspondence* vol. 12, frontispiece, and letter from W. E. Darwin, [19 May 1864] and n. 8). CD had sent six copies of this photo to Ernst Haeckel and one to Robert Caspary (see letter to Ernst Haeckel, 20 January [1866], and letter to Robert Caspary, 4 March 1866).

[11] The sketches are reproduced at approximately 75 per cent of their original size.

[12] The remaining sketches associated with this letter are reproduced at approximately 40 per cent of their original size.

From H. E. Darwin [*c.* 10 May 1866][1]

My dear Papa

I have just had the eventful interview with Mogg[2] He didn't scold me at all about fusca & lutea[3] & we talked orchids very amicably—but the little man wants to see you— I told him that he might come & pay a morning call but that most likely you wdn't see him & he said he shd be delighted to come on those terms so you are in for it[4] I was quite civil I beg to state. Well he was exceeding civil & I happened to have an orchid in my hand for him to name & oddly enough it was the other orchis that fertilises itself—i.e. orchis secundiflora = Neotinea intacta in Seeman's Journal of Bot. for 1865—[5] He is going to send you some[6] They shall be sent to Dow[n] He seems to have been making most careful observations about the different ophrys. he showed me a great many of his drawings of the links between them all.[7] It is rather horrible to have another self fertiliser, isn't it? He will send you some of secundiflora & I am to have some to bring too.

I hope I shall know my plans by tomorrow & then I shall know my plans.

yours dear Papa | H.E.D.

DAR 162: 67

[1] The year is established by the reference to John Traherne Moggridge's visit to Down (see n. 4, below); the date is established by the relationship between this letter and the letter from J. T. Moggridge, 10 May [1866].

[2] Henrietta had met Moggridge in Cannes (see letter from J. T. Moggridge, 21 May [1866]).

[3] On *Ophrys lutea* and *O. fusca*, see the letter to H. E. Darwin, [14–21 April 1866] and n. 7.

[4] Moggridge visited CD at Down from 23 to 25 June 1866 (Emma Darwin's diary (DAR 242)). For CD's apprehension regarding visitors, see *Correspondence* vol. 13, Appendix IV and n. 9.

[5] Henrietta refers to the article '*Neotinea intacta, Rchb. fil.*, the new Irish orchid', by Heinrich Gustav Reichenbach, which appeared in the January 1865 issue of *Journal of Botany*, edited by Berthold Carl Seemann. Reichenbach observed that pollination occurs within the bud in *N. intacta* (syn. *Orchis secundiflorum*), and reported similar observations of other orchids, concluding: 'With such facts before

us, it is hard to believe that any Orchid is incapable of fertilizing itself, and requires some as yet undiscovered insect to act as sexual agent' (Reichenbach 1865, p. 2). CD had claimed that self-pollination was rare in orchids (*Orchids*, pp. 358–60).

6 See letter from J. T. Moggridge, 10 May [1866]. In *Orchids* 2d ed., p. 27, CD described pollination in specimens of *Neotinea intacta* received from Moggridge: although 'remarkable for producing seeds without the aid of insects', the flower was so structured that it could be pollinated by insects if they visited, although not as well as other orchids. CD remarked that *N. intacta* and *O. apifera* were among the few orchids that regularly self-pollinated without the aid of insects (*ibid.*, p. 291). On CD's interest in the self-pollinating bee orchid (*O. apifera*), see the letter to H. E. Darwin, [14–21 April 1866] and n. 3.

7 See letter to H. E. Darwin, [14–21 April 1866] and n. 6.

From John Gould 10 May 1866

26, Charlotte Street, | Bedford Square, W.C.
10th. May 66

My Dear Darwin

The singular Humming bird with the four central tail feathers tipped with white is the type of my genus *urosticte* and its specific name is *benjamini*. This term was given to it by a Frenchman (Bourcier)[1]

How absurd it is that so beautiful and singular a creature should be hereafter distinguished by by such a soubriquet but so it must be according to the now received laws of Scientific nomenclature with regard to specific names[2]

You will find a short remark of mine on this bird at page 110 of the octavo introduction to the Trochilidae commencing with words "I must now ask those"[3]

In the Folio work there are some about the female[4]

Believe me | My dear Darwin | Yours Very Sincerely | John Gould

Chas Darwin Esq—

DAR 84.1: 20–1

CD ANNOTATION

Top of letter: 'Case like Pigeon quote—tail feather'[5] *pencil*

1 Gould refers to a humming-bird species found in Ecuador and first described as *Trochilus benjamini* by the French ornithologist, Jules Bourcier (see Bourcier 1851). Gould placed the species within a new genus, *Urosticte*; only the males of the species had white tips on their central tail-feathers (see J. Gould 1861a, pp. 110–11, and 1861b, 3: 190). CD may have discussed the bird with Gould during his recent stay in London from 21 April to 1 May. See also nn. 3 and 4, below.

2 CD had served on a committee appointed by the British Association for the Advancement of Science in 1842 to report on zoological nomenclature (see *Correspondence* vol. 2, letter to H. E. Strickland, 17 February [1842]). The committee drew up rules for the naming of species and genera that were widely accepted as standard by zoologists in most countries until the 1890s (Stresemann 1975, pp. 264–7). One of the rules stipulated that 'the name originally given by the founder of a group or the describer of a species should be permanently retained' (Strickland *et al.* 1842, p. 109). See also *Correspondence* vol. 2, letter to H. E. Strickland, 31 May [1842], and *Correspondence* vol. 4, letters to H. E. Strickland, 29 January [1849] and [4 February 1849].

[3] Gould described the white-tipped central tail-feathers of *Urosticte benjamini* in *An introduction to the Trochilidæ, or family of humming-birds* (J. Gould 1861a, pp. 110–11). Although Gould remarked that the coloured feathers were displayed by males of the species to attract females, he concluded: 'that ornament and variety is the sole object [of such markings], I have myself little doubt' (J. Gould 1861a, p. 110). CD's annotated presentation copy of J. Gould 1861a is in the Darwin Library–CUL; Gould's description and remarks are underlined (see *Marginalia* 1: 342–4). The question of beauty in humming-birds had recently been raised by George Douglas Campbell, the Duke of Argyll, in a series of articles critical of CD's theory of descent by natural selection (G. D. Campbell 1865, pp. 230–2; see letter from James Shaw, [6–10 February 1866] and n. 3). CD discussed Gould's description of *U. benjamini*, and Campbell's criticisms, in *Descent* 2: 151–2. CD argued that the white-tipped central feathers could be explained by the theory of sexual selection.

[4] Gould refers to *A monograph of the Trochilidae, or family of humming-birds*, in which he noted that females of the species *Urosticte benjamini* had all but their two central tail-feathers tipped with white (J. Gould 1861b, 3: 190).

[5] CD may refer to a pigeon breed in which the males alone had black striations. The breed is described in Chapuis 1865, which CD had recently consulted for his work on pigeons in *Variation* (see *Correspondence* vol. 13, letter to W. B. Tegetmeier, 2 June [1865], and this volume, letter to W. B. Tegetmeier, 16 January [1866] and n. 4). CD cited the case from Chapuis 1865 in *Variation* 2: 74, and *Descent* 1: 285, 293–4, 2: 157.

From J. T. Moggridge 10 May [1866][1]

Villa Christiana | Cannes
May 10

Dear Mr. Darwin

I send you per *grand Vitesse*[2] a box of Orchids.—

I fear that the hot weather will spoil many of them—

I have quite failed to obtain any *self-fertilizing* specimens of Oph. scolopax Cav.[3]

I send Oph. apifera Huds.[4]
— scolopax Cav.
— Bertolonii Guss
Serapias Cordigera L.[5]
Orchis papilionacea L. (?)
Neotinea intacta Rchb.[6]

We propose starting for England on Monday next & I shall hope to bring a box of Orchids with me—

Believe me yrs. very sincerely | J. Traherne Moggridge.

Ch. Darwin Esqre

DAR 171: 205

[1] The year is established by the relationship between this letter and the letter from H. E. Darwin, [*c.* 10 May 1866].

[2] See letter from J. T. Moggridge, 15 February [1866] and n. 2.

[3] Moggridge had observed two forms of *Ophrys scolopax*; one found at Cannes was self-fertile, another found at Mentone was not (see *Correspondence* vol. 12, letter to J. T. Moggridge, 19 June [1864] and

n. 6, and Moggridge 1864, p. 252). CD cited Moggridge's description of the orchid in 'Fertilization of orchids', p. 145 (*Collected papers* 2: 142), and *Orchids* 2d ed., pp. 52, 292–3.

4 For CD's interest in *Ophrys apifera*, see the letter to H. E. Darwin, [14–21 April 1866] and n. 3.

5 In *Orchids* 2d ed., p. 27, CD referred to Moggridge's description of *Serapias cordigera* (Moggridge 1864, p. 258). See also *Correspondence* vol. 12, letter to J. T. Moggridge, 19 June [1864] and plate facing p. 248.

6 See letter from H. E. Darwin, [*c.* 10 May 1866] and n. 5.

From E. Schweizerbart'sche Verlagsbuchhandlung[1] 10 May 1866

Stuttgart
den 10 Mai 1866.

Verehrtester Herr

Für Ihre gütige und baldige Antwort auf meinen Brief bin ich Ihnen recht verbunden und wollen Sie es nur nicht als Unaufmerksamkeit meiner auslegen wenn ich Ihnen so spät Nachricht darauf gebe.[2] Die Sache hat sich aus mehreren Ursachen verzögert. Herr Prof. Geinitz den Herr Prof Leonhard in meinem Namen befragte ob er Zeit und Lust hätte sich sowohl der Durschsicht einer neuen Auflage Ihres Werkes als auch der Uebertragung eines anderen Werkes aus Ihrer Feder zu unterziehen, gab ihm etwas spät eine ablehnende Antwort, was mich veranlasste selbst noch an ihn zu schreiben; aber ich hatte auch keinen bessern Erfolg.[3] Herr Geinitz schrieb mir darauf anliegenden Brief und empfahl mir nochmals Herrn Prof Carus in Leipzig.[4]

Sie wissen aus den Tagesblättern in welch kritischen Zuständen wir in Deutschland uns dermalen befinden, wo der an Verrath am Vaterland gränzende Uebermuth eines einzigen Menschen uns in den BürgerKrieg zu treiben im Begriffe steht, in dem er gegen alles Recht und gegen den Willen der ganzen deutschen Nation seine ehrgeizigen Plane verfolgt und sich mit dem Ausland selbst verbündet![5] Dass unter solchen Umständen die Geschäfte total gelähmt werden ist unvermeidlich. Ich werde daher auch mich auf das Nöthigste beschränken, da man neue Bücher jetzt nur zwecklos aussenden würde.

Wie Ihnen bekannt ist, hat herr Prof. G. Leonhard schon mit Herrn Bronn das "*Jahrbuch*" gemeinschaftlich redigirt und hat auch jetzt das Geschäftliche der Redaction zu besorgen.[6] Da nun die Uebersetzung von *Bronn* ist und die Durchsicht der neuen Auflage nur mühsam ist, Herr Leonhard aber bei mir *die Geologie von Russland* Murchisons, auch die Schrift von Sedgewick & Murchison: "*die palaeozoischen Gesteine*" ins Deutsche übertragen hat, so dürfte er hinreichend Kenntnisse der Englischen Sprache haben um die 3te Aufl. nach der neuesten engl. Aufl. Ihres Origins, zu revidiren;[7] ich habe ihm daher auch den Antrag gemacht, vor dem mir entfernst wohnenden H^{r} Carus, weil ich gegen die Wittwe des Uebersetzers, *Bronn*, dann wieder Verpflichtungen habe und ich der Ansicht bin dass Herr Leonhard leichter sich mit uns verständigt, da er doch der familie Bronn längst befreundet ist.[8]

Ich möchte Sie also, verehrter Herr, ersuchen mir das betreffende Material für die 3t. deutsche Aufl. zu senden, dann haben wir Muse es jezt mit der 2t deutschen Aufl. zu vergleichen und die nöthigen Abänderungen zu machen.[9]

Was die von einigen Personen gerügten Mängel an der Arbeit des Hr Bronn betrifft, so glaube ich dass wesentliche Unrichtigkeiten nicht im Texte enthalten sind; denn Hr Bronn hat ausser den alten Sprachen auch die bedeutendsten neuen Sprachen inne und wenn irgend Jemand so war er ganz besonders durch seine eigenen Arbeiten zu der Uebertragung Ihres Buches geeignet, da er ein ganz eminentes Wissen besass.[10]

In Beziehung auf Ihr anderes Werk* das Sie so freundlich waren mir in den AushängeBogen für die Uebersetzung überlassen zu wollen, so nehme ich das Offert gerne an, aber für den Augenblick wird man damit noch zuwarten müssen, bis sich der Politische Horizont abgeklärt hat. Für dieses Werk denke ich mich dann an Herrn Carus zu wenden, möchte Sie aber bitten vorerst **mir** die davon schon gedruckten Bogen (Sheets) zu senden.[11]

Seyen Sie überzeugt dass mir selbst sehr viel daran liegt dass die Arbeit gut ausgeführt wird, denn ich lege grossen Werth darauf, dass Sie, der so freundlich uns entgegen kam, auch ganz zufrieden gestellt werden.

Dass Sie sich wieder wohl befinden haben wir mit vielem Vergnügen gelesen.

Weiteren gütigen Nachrichten sehe ich nun entgegen und bin mit grosser Hochachtung Ihr ganz ergebenster | E. Schweizerbart[12]

*Domestic animals & cultivated Plants &c

[Enclosure]

Geehrtester Herr Schweizerbart!

So geehrt ich mich auch durch das mir von *Darwin* und von Ihnen geschenkte Vertrauen bezüglich einer Revision der neuen deutschen Auflage seines berühmten Werkes und der Uebersetzung eines neuen Werkes[13] von diesem ausgezeichneten Naturforscher fühle, so ist es mir dennoch nicht möglich, diese Arbeit zu übernehmen. Gerade durch mein schon im vorigen Jahre beendetes Steinkohlenbuch sind mir manche andere wissenschaftlich höchst anziehende Arbeiten länger liegen geblieben, als ich verantworten kann, und diese werden mich neben den unausgesetzten ebenfalls viel Zeit in Anspruch nehmenden Arbeiten für unser Jahrbuch, für das unter meiner Direction stehende Königliche Museum und für meine Vorlesungen an der polytechnischen Schule mehrere Jahre vollauf beschäftigen.[14]

Wiewohl ich nicht zu den *extremen* Anhängern des Darwinianismus gehöre, so verfolge ich diesen wichtigen uns durch Darwin bezeichneten Weg doch mit grossem Interesse und höre nicht auf, bei meinen specielleren Arbeiten die Thatsachen mit aller Unparteilichkeit zu prüfen.[15]

Ich hatte mir erlaubt, Ihre Aufmerksamkeit auf Prof. Victor Carus in Leipzig an meiner Stelle zu richten und glaube noch heute, dass er gerade die geeigneteste Persönlichkeit hierzu ist, nicht allein, weil er ein grosser Verehrer der Darwin'schen

Lehre ist, sondern auch, weil er nach einem mehrjährigen Aufenthalte auf der Universität Oxford, der englischen Sprache vollkommen mächtig ist und als Professor der Physiologie namentlich auch diesen Fragen näher steht, als ich es vom geologisch–palaeontologischen Standpunkte kann.[16]

Ich verbleibe mit grösster Hochachtung
Ihr ganz ergebener | H. B. Geinitz

Dresden d. 29. Apr. 1866.
Herrn E. Schweizerbart in Stuttgart.

DAR 177: 72

[1] For a translation of this letter, see Appendix I. The letter was written by Christian Friedrich Schweizerbart, head of the Stuttgart publishing firm E. Schweizerbart'sche Verlagsbuchhandlung.

[2] The letter to E. Schweizerbart'sche Verlagsbuchhandlung has not been found; however, see the letter from E. Schweizerbart'sche Verlagsbuchhandlung, 23 March 1866.

[3] Schweizerbart refers to a third German edition of *Origin* and to *Variation*. Gustav von Leonhard was co-editor with Hans Bruno Geinitz of the *Neues Jahrbuch für Mineralogie, Geologie und Palaeontologie*, published by E. Schweizerbart'sche Verlagsbuchhandlung.

[4] Julius Victor Carus. See enclosure.

[5] Schweizerbart refers to the measures taken by Otto von Bismarck to expand Prussian influence and territory within the German lands. Many of Bismarck's efforts were directed against Austria, the other principal power in the German confederation of states. On 9 April 1866, Prussia had formed an alliance with Italy, effective for ninety days, that committed the two states to assist each other in the event of war with Austria. On Bismarck's diplomacy during the years leading up to the Austro-Prussian war, and the opposition to his policies by liberal political parties and the German press, see Sheehan 1989, Pflanze 1990, vol. 1, and Wawro 1996.

[6] Leonhard assumed editorial responsibilities for the *Neues Jahrbuch für Mineralogie, Geognosie, Geologie und Petrefaktenkunde* in 1861. He edited the journal jointly with Heinrich Georg Bronn until the latter's death in July 1862, when the name of the journal was changed to *Neues Jahrbuch für Mineralogie, Geologie und Palaeontologie*. Bronn was succeeded as co-editor by Geinitz in 1863. See *Jubiläums-Katalog*, p. xvii.

[7] The first two German editions of *Origin* had been translated by Bronn (Bronn trans. 1860 and Bronn trans. 1863), who had arranged for its publication by E. Schweizerbart'sche Verlagsbuchhandlung (see *Correspondence* vol. 8). Leonhard had translated Murchison and Sedgwick 1842 and Murchison *et al.* 1845 into German; both translations were also published by E. Schweizerbart'sche Verlagsbuchhandlung (Leonhard trans. 1844 and 1848). In the event, the third German edition was overseen by Carus (Bronn and Carus trans. 1867). The references are to Adam Sedgwick and Roderick Impey Murchison.

[8] Bronn's widow has not been further identified.

[9] The second German edition of *Origin* (Bronn trans. 1863) was based on the third English edition, but with additional changes (see *Correspondence* vol. 10, Appendix VIII). The third German edition was based on the fourth English edition.

[10] For criticisms of Bronn's translation of *Origin*, see the letters from Rudolf Suchsland, 16 March 1866 and 2 April 1866; see also letter from Rufolf Oldenbourg, 28 October 1866, letters from J. V. Carus, 7 November 1866 and 15 November 1866, and letter to J. V. Carus, 10 November 1866.

[11] CD's letter to Schweizerbart has not been found. The reference is to proofs of *Variation*. A German edition of *Variation*, translated by Carus, was published by E. Schweizerbart'sche Verlagsbuchhandlung in 1868 (Carus trans. 1868).

[12] See letter from E. Schweizerbart'sche Verlagsbuchhandlung, 23 March 1866, n. 8.

[13] Geinitz refers to a third German edition of *Origin* and to *Variation*.

[14] Geinitz refers to H. B. Geinitz ed. 1865. He was director of the Mineralogisches Museum, and professor of geology and mineralogy at the Technische Bildungsanstalt, Dresden (*ADB*).
[15] On the reception of CD's work in Germany, see the letter from Ernst Haeckel, 28 January 1866 and n. 5.
[16] Carus had been conservator of the comparative anatomy collection at Oxford from 1849 to 1851; in 1853 he was appointed professor of comparative anatomy at Leipzig University (*DSB*).

To ? 10 May [1866?][1]

Down. | *Bromley.* | *Kent. S.E.*
May 10th

My dear Sir

Many thanks for your note & kind desire for me not to answer.—[2] The case seemed worth enquiry, so I wrote to Mr Dorrell, a head man in Messrs. Clowes enormous establishment[3] & he assures me that the difference in apparent length of arms is by no means common with compositors,[4] & that when it occurs it is only apparent from one shoulder drooping. Hence compositors often walk with one arm retained in a peculiar position. He says when the apparently unequal arms are measured there is no real difference in their length.— File-makers, I may add, get into a habit of standing in so peculiar a position, that they always speak of one of their legs as the hind leg, even when not at work.—

With many thanks | Yours very sincerely | Ch. Darwin

Endorsement: **1866.**
American Philosophical Society (B/D25.292)

[1] The year is conjectured from the endorsement, which is in an unknown hand.
[2] The note has not been found.
[3] Dorrell was evidently in charge of typesetting at the firm of William Clowes and Sons, printers to CD's publisher, John Murray; he was probably a member of the family firm Edmund Robson Dorrell & Son, booksellers with premises next to Clowes on Charing Cross (S.W.), London (*Post Office London directory* 1866). CD later wrote to Dorrell about the printing and typesetting of *Descent* (letter to Mr Dorrell, 9 August 1870, *Calendar* no. 7298).
[4] CD discussed modifications to the body parts of animals in relation to their use or disuse in *Origin*, pp. 11, 134–9, *Variation* 2: 295–303, and *Descent* 1: 116–21, where he considered the effects of different occupations.

From Friedrich Hildebrand 11 May 1866

Bonn
May 11th 1866

Most honoured Sir

I must thank you for your very kind letter in which you approved my lastly published papers;[1] I expect the copies of a little treatise on the Trimorphismus of Oxalis, to send you one of them: a great many of the former species were only founded on the different length of the styles and therefore must be united.[2] It is a pity that the Oxalis are not much to be found in the gardens, I could not get of any more than one form (fresh specimens) and have only experimentized with the long-styled form of Oxalis rosea.[3]

I am sorry that I cannot follow the invitation to your botanical congress, from the Program I see that you will be there as Vice President[4]— perhaps you will have an opportunity to read the adjoining notices of the fertilisation of Corydalis cava, I hope the results of my experiments will be of some interest for you and some other botanist.—[5] I am very glad to see by your letter, written with your own hand that you are quite recovered now, with my best wishes for your further health

I remain | dear Sir | yours | F Hildebrand

DAR 166: 203

[1] Hildebrand 1866a and 1866b. See letter to Friedrich Hildebrand, 20 April [1866].

[2] Hildebrand refers to Hildebrand 1866c. CD's heavily annotated copy is in the Darwin Pamphlet Collection–CUL. Hildebrand criticised existing classifications of *Oxalis* in which style length had been used as a species characteristic, and species descriptions had been based on only a few specimens (*ibid.*, p. 353). See letter to Friedrich Hildebrand, 16 May [1866] and n. 10.

[3] Although Hildebrand only experimented with the long-styled form, he stated that had he been able to cross other forms, it was 'highly probable' that the results would have been analogous to those that CD had obtained with *Lythrum salicaria* (Hildebrand 1866c, p. 373; see also 'Three forms of *Lythrum salicaria*'). CD summarised Hildebrand's experiments with *O. rosea* in *Forms of flowers*, pp. 178–9, noting, 'The same rule holds good with Oxalis as with *Lythrum salicaria*; namely, that in any two unions, the greater the inequality in length between the pistils and stamens . . . the less fertile is the union.'

[4] CD had been asked to join the committee of the International Horticultural Exhibition and Botanical Congress, held in London from 22 to 31 May 1866 (see letter from M. T. Masters, March 1866). CD did not attend the meeting; however, he is listed as a vice-president in the *International Horticultural Exhibition* 1866, p. 16.

[5] Hildebrand's paper 'On the necessity for insect agency in the fertilisation of *Corydalis cava*' was published in the *International Horticultural Exhibition* 1866, pp. 157–8 (Hildebrand 1866d). A copy of the paper is in the Darwin Pamphlet Collection–CUL. An expanded version of the paper was also published in German (Hildebrand 1866–7b); a copy is in the Darwin Pamphlet Collection–CUL. A brief notice of the paper appeared in the 2 June 1866 issue of *Gardeners' Chronicle*, p. 516; CD underlined the passage in which Hildebrand reported that perfect fertilisation was only ensured by crossing flowers on different plants. CD's annotated copies of the *Gardeners' Chronicle* are in the Cory Library, Cambridge Botanic Garden.

To J. D. Hooker [12 May 1866]

Down.
Saturday

My dear Hooker

Caspary wrote to me a little time ago that he wanted to meet him;[1] I answered that I sh^{d}. be very glad to see him here, but that I doubted whether it was worth his while, as I could talk so little with anyone.—[2] He writes me a very nice letter & says he shall consult you.—[3] Therefore I write to beg you to ask him by all means to come & sleep here, if he has spare time, but at same time tell him the truth how little exertion I can stand. I sh^d like very much to see him, though I dread all exertion.—[4]

Yours affect | C. Darwin

London did me no harm,[5] but I have not been quite so brilliant lately, I am pleased to see that you will be D.C.L of Oxford.—[6]

Endorsement: 'May 12th/66'
DAR 115: 288

1 See letter from Robert Caspary, 26 April 1866. CD wrote 'him' rather than 'me' in error.
2 The letter to Caspary has not been found.
3 See letter from Robert Caspary, 7 May 1866.
4 CD often remarked that conversation with visitors made him exhausted or sick, and he frequently excused himself from social occasions on these grounds (see *Correspondence* vol. 13, Appendix IV and n. 9).
5 CD had visited London from 21 April to 1 May 1866 (Emma Darwin's diary (DAR 242)).
6 Hooker received the honorary degree of doctor of civil law from Oxford University on 13 June 1866 (*The Times*, 13 June 1866, p. 9).

From J. D. Hooker 13 May 1866

Kew
May 13/66.

My dear Darwin

This may interest you.[1] I can talk with A. Gray now calmly & dispassionately, which I could not do during the war, holding as I then did, that whatever the rights of the N. may have been, they had no right to resort to bloodshed to procure their ends—[2]

I am longing to know how you go on, after the startling apparition of your face at R.S. Soirèe—which I dreamed of 2 nights running.[3] Tyndall came up to me in raptures at seeing you—& told me to worship Bence Jones in future—[4]

Tylor was here & spent the day last week, I like him much & have persuaded him to draw up questions to be sent to Consuls & especially missionaries, through whose wives a lot of *most* curious information could be obtained—[5] Tying the umbilical cord has always appeared to me to be the greatest mystery of humanity— how ever did such a custom originate & spread— it is to me an unanswerable argument in favor of unity of species of man.[6]

What shocking twaddle is old Crawfurds paper on cultivated plants!.[7]

A fine Surveying ship is going to survey Magellans straits & I am doing my utmost to get a good Naturalist with Zoological acquirements especially to be sent out.[8] Capt Mayne (son of Head Beak) & who wrote a fair book on Brit Columbia, is going out—a nice fellow.[9] What a nuisance this "international" week will be[10]

Mrs Oliver has been very ill indeed—but is better I hope though still confined to bed— She has had a little daughter, prematurely—but her complaint is of the throat & mucous membranes.[11]

Lowe (Revd.) of Madeira is here— he has had a second winter in Cape de Verde with Wollaston, both in a Mr Gray's Yacht,[12] He describes the interior as most beautiful & most wild & picturesque. He has got a good many of the Cameroons plants on the high Mts. which you will be glad to know of—[13] I must get a list for you.[14]

I hope these commercial failures have not affected you or your's.[15] my balance being on the wrong side at my Bankers is a comfort!

Has Woolner begun your bust?[16] Huxley has a 7th. daughter![17]

I hear the Miss Horners are in a state of frantic excitement about Katy—[18] I have often thought what a picturesque Joan of Arc Susan would make.—[19] N.B. my ideas of J. A. are wholly derived from Etty's & Millais' pictures:[20] I do not know even in whose reign she lived, if in any;[21] and as I have no Wedgwood Medallion of her I have no means of knowing.[22] By the way my pursuit of that blue art is over, & the crockery shops know me no more. I have never time to go to London now, and hope never to have again.— I do hope to have time to get to Down with my wife this summer if Mrs Darwin will take F. in & let me go up & down— What are your plans for June or July?[23]

What news of Etty?[24]

If you could run up to Town to take one peep of this Hort show on 22d. it would repay you I am sure & I would meet you there.[25] I expect it will recall the Tropics— we are sending 8 Van loads of Palms &c

Wallace is married you see—a daughter of Mr Mitten a very acute cryptogamic Botanist of Hurst Pier point[26]

Ever Yours affec | J D Hooker

DAR 102: 71–4

[1] The enclosure, a letter from Asa Gray to J. D. Hooker (see letter to J. D. Hooker, 16 May [1866]) has not been found.

[2] Hooker and Asa Gray had disagreed sharply over the American Civil War, and by December 1861 had ceased to discuss it in their letters (see *Correspondence* vol. 9, letter from J. D. Hooker, [29 December 1861], and *Correspondence* vol. 10, letter from Asa Gray, 18 February 1862). CD sometimes shared letters from Gray that contained comments on the war with Hooker (see, for example, *Correspondence* vol. 10, letter from J. D. Hooker, [19 January 1862], and *Correspondence* vol. 11, letter from J. D. Hooker, [1 March 1863]).

[3] CD had attended a reception at the Royal Society of London on 28 April 1866 (Emma Darwin's diary (DAR 242)). The event is described in the *Athenæum*, 5 May 1866, pp. 597–8. According to Emma Darwin, many of CD's old friends did not recognise him because of the beard that he had grown: 'He was obliged to name himself to almost all of them, as his beard alters him so' (*Emma Darwin* (1915) 2: 185).

[4] Hooker refers to John Tyndall and to the physician Henry Bence Jones. CD began to consult Jones in the summer of 1865 (see letter to H. B. Jones, 3 January [1866] and n. 2; see also letter to H. B. Jones, [23 April 1866?]).

[5] CD had read Edward Burnett Tylor's book *The early history of mankind* (Tylor 1865) in 1865 and had asked Hooker whether he knew the author (see *Correspondence* vol. 13, letter to J. D. Hooker, [10 July 1865], and letter from J. D. Hooker, 13 July 1865). CD cited Tylor 1865 in *Descent* 1: 232 on the close similarity in the customs and habits of different human races.

6 For CD's views on whether humans had descended from a single ancestral stock, see *Descent* 2: 385–405, and *Correspondence* vol. 13, letter from F. W. Farrar, 6 November 1865, n. 3.

7 Hooker refers to John Crawfurd's paper 'On the migration of cultivated plants in reference to ethnology' (Crawfurd 1866). The paper asserted that the migration of cultivated plants was 'wholly the work of man' (*ibid.*, p. 317), and discussed the migration through human agency of plants used as foodstuffs. CD had read Crawfurd's ethnological works on India and China (see *Correspondence* vol. 4, Appendix IV). Crawfurd had written a critical review of *Origin* (see *Correspondence* vol. 7, letter to Charles Lyell, 2 December [1859]).

8 HMS *Nassau* surveyed the Straits of Magellan from 1866 to 1869; the naturalist on the voyage was Robert Oliver Cunningham. See letter from J. D. Hooker, 4 February 1866 and n. 4.

9 Richard Charles Mayne was the commander of HMS *Nassau*, and the author of *Four years in British Columbia and Vancouver Island* (Mayne 1862). Mayne had served on an expedition to British Columbia from 1857 to 1861 (*Modern English biography*). His father, Richard Mayne, was the commissioner of London police. 'Beak' refers to a magistrate.

10 The International Horticultural Exhibition and Botanical Congress was held in South Kensington, London, from 22 to 31 May 1866.

11 Hooker refers to Hannah Oliver, the wife of Daniel Oliver. Their daughter has not been identified.

12 Richard Thomas Lowe and Thomas Vernon Wollaston visited the Cape Verde Islands, off the west coast of Africa, in 1866 on a yacht owned by John Gray, to collect plants, insects, and molluscs (Cook 1995). Gray, a friend of Wollaston's, has not been further identified.

13 In a paper on the flora of the Cameroon Mountains, Hooker had noted that temperate plants that were common in Europe were present in the higher elevations of this equatorial region of Africa (J. D. Hooker 1863). That these same species had been found in the Cape Verde Islands, located some 1000 miles to the west of the Cameroon Mountains, provided further evidence for CD's argument, first presented in *Origin*, pp. 377–8, that temperate species had migrated into tropical regions during a Pleistocene glacial period. CD added information on the Cameroon and Cape Verde vegetation in his discussion of the topic in *Origin* 4th ed., p. 445. For more on the Cameroon flora, see *Correspondence* vols. 10 and 11.

14 No such list has been found.

15 On 11 May 1866, the closure of a large lending firm, Overend, Gurney & Co., a joint-stock company with limited liability, led to a commercial panic in London and other financial centres, with a number of banks closing doors and other firms temporarily suspending payments (*Annual Register* (1866), pp. 44–5).

16 Hooker had suggested in 1863 and 1864 that CD sit for the sculptor Thomas Woolner (see *Correspondence* vol. 11, letter from Emma Darwin to J. D. Hooker, 26 December [1863], and *Correspondence* vol. 12, letters from J. D. Hooker, 24 January 1864 and 26 August 1864). CD did not sit for Woolner until 1868 (see letter to J. D. Hooker, 26 November [1868] (*Calendar* no. 6476)).

17 Ethel Gladys Huxley was the seventh child, and fifth daughter, of Thomas Henry Huxley and his wife Henrietta (R. W. Clark 1968).

18 Ann Susan and Joanna Horner were the daughters of Leonard and Anne Susan Horner; their sister, Katharine Murray Horner, was married to Henry Lyell, Charles Lyell's younger brother (Freeman 1978).

19 Hooker refers to Ann Susan Horner.

20 Hooker refers to Henrietta Emma Darwin and John Everett Millais. Millais's painting 'Joan of Arc' was exhibited at the Royal Academy in London in 1865 (Graves 1905–6, 5: 245).

21 Joan of Arc was instrumental in placing Charles VII on the throne of France in 1429 (*EB*).

22 Hooker had been an avid collector of Wedgwood ware, and was particularly interested in medallions (see *Correspondence* vols. 11 and 12, and this volume, letter from J. D. Hooker, [22 November 1866]).

23 Hooker visited Down from 23 to 25 June 1866; his wife, Frances Harriet Hooker, visited from 23 to 29 June (Emma Darwin's diary (DAR 242)).

24 Henrietta Emma Darwin was in France (see letter from H. E. Darwin, [*c.* 10 May 1866] and n. 2).

[25] See n. 10, above. CD did not attend the congress (see letter from Robert Caspary, 7 May 1866 and n. 4).
[26] Alfred Russel Wallace had married Annie Mitten, the daughter of William Mitten, in April 1866 (see Raby 2001, p. 187).

From Daniel Oliver [after 13 May 1866][1]

Bot. Zeit. of *1865* to see if there were any memoirs wh. you ought to see. You may have seen them before this. The only likely ones were

p. 1. Hildebrand, on Dichogamy & Dimorphism
13. do of *Geranium pratense*— *Pulmonaria officinalis*.[2]
p. 50. Notice of yr. paper on *Lythrum*[3]
p. 245. Hildebrd. Experiments on Hybridizing Orchids.[4]

Happily I can at length I think report improvet. in Mrs. Oliver.[5] She has had a long & serious illness but at last she is so far recovered that we have already had her out in bath-chair twice & hope in a week or so to remove her from Kew.— Very many thanks for your kind enquiries & very kind message of sympathy wh. were very welcome during our late bitter trial[6]

Ever very sincerely | D Oliver

Incomplete
DAR 173: 31

[1] The date is established by the relationship between this letter and the letter from J. D. Hooker, 13 May 1866.
[2] The reference is to the two-part article by Friedrich Hildebrand, 'Experimente zur Dichogamie und zum Dimorphismus', that appeared in *Botanische Zeitung* (Hildebrand 1865a). CD had received a copy of the paper in February 1865; see *Correspondence* vol. 13, letter to J. D. Hooker, 15 [February 1865] and n. 2.
[3] The review 'Darwin, über die geschlechtlichen Beziehungen der 3 Formen von *Lythrum Salicaria*' appeared in the January 1865 issue of *Botanische Zeitung*, pp. 50–2 (Hildebrand 1865b), under the initials 'F. H.'. In his letter to CD of 24 July 1866, Hildebrand confirmed that he was the author.
[4] Oliver refers to Hildebrand 1865c.
[5] The reference is to Oliver's wife, Hannah.
[6] CD had asked Hooker to convey his sympathies regarding the recent death of the Olivers' daughter (see letter to J. D. Hooker, [9 April 1866].

To William Ewart Gladstone 14 May 1866

London,
May 14, 1866.

To the Rt. Hon. the Chancellor of the Exchequer.

Sir,—

It having been stated that the Scientific men of the Metropolis are, as a body, entirely opposed to the removal of the Natural History Collections from their present situation in the British Museum, we, the undersigned Fellows of the Royal, Linnean, Geological, and Zoological Societies of London, beg leave to offer to you the following expression of our opinion upon the subject.[1]

We are of opinion that it is of fundamental importance to the progress of the Natural Sciences in this country, that the administration of the National Natural History Collections should be separated from that of the Library and Art Collections, and placed under one Officer, who should be immediately responsible to one of the Queen's Ministers.[2]

We regard the exact locality of the National Museum of Natural History as a question of comparatively minor importance, provided that it be conveniently accessible and within the Metropolitan district.[3]

George Bentham, F.R.S., F.L.S., F.Z.S.
William B. Carpenter, M.D., F.R.S., F.L.S., F.G.S.
W. S. Dallas, F.L.S.
Charles Darwin, F.R.S., F.L.S., F.Z.S.
F. Ducane Godman, F.L.S., F.Z.S.
J. H. Gurney, F.Z.S.
Edward Hamilton, M.D., F.L.S., F.Z.S.
Joseph D. Hooker, M.D., F.R.S., F.L.S., F.G.S.
Thomas H. Huxley, F.R.S., V.P.Z.S., F.L.S. F.G.S.
John Kirk, F.L.S., C.M.Z.S.
Lilford,[4] F.L.S., F.Z.S.
Alfred Newton, M.A., F.L.S. F.Z.S.
W. Kitchen Parker, F.R.S., F.Z.S.
Andrew Ramsay, F.R.S., V.P.G.S.
Arthur Russell, M.P., F.R.G.S., F.Z.S.
Osbert Salvin, M.A., F.L.S., F.Z.S.
P. L. Sclater, F.R.S., F.L.S., F.Z.S.
G. Sclater-Booth, M.P., F.Z.S.
S. James A. Salter, M.B., F.R.S., F.L.S., F.Z.S.
W. H. Simpson, M.A., F.Z.S.
J. Emerson Tennent, F.R.S., F.Z.S.
Thomas Thomson, M.D., F.R.S., F.L.S.
H. B. Tristram, M.A., F.L.S.
Walden,[5] F.Z.S., F.L.S.
Alfred R. Wallace, F.R.G.S., F.Z.S.

London, *May 14th*, 1866.

Gunther 1975, p. 238 (facsimile of printed copy of memorial)

[1] No recent statement regarding the opposition of the scientific community to the removal of the natural history collections of the British Museum has been found. CD had signed two memorials in 1858 on the location and organisation of the natural history collections; the first of these proposed the

enlargement of the existing Bloomsbury site (see *Correspondence* vol. 7, Appendix VI, and n. 3, below). A version of the text of the present memorial was printed in the *Athenæum*, 23 June 1866, p. 836; it may be the memorial referred to in the letter from Charles Lyell, 1 March 1866.

2 In 1856, a new post had been created for Richard Owen as superintendent of the natural history departments of the British Museum; however, all of the museum's collections had remained under the direction of the principal librarian, Anthony Panizzi. The second memorial of 1858 (see n. 1, above) had proposed that a museum and library of scientific zoology be placed under one person who was directly responsible to a government minister, and that most of the botanical collections be consolidated with the herbarium at the Royal Botanic Gardens, Kew, which was already under the supervision of a director responsible to the minister of Works. See also *Correspondence* vol. 13, Supplement, letter to John Russell, [10 March 1847]. In June 1865, Panizzi had announced his plans to retire in the following year, and questions about the future administration of the museum were raised in Parliament in February and March 1866 (see *Hansard's Parliamentary Debates*, 3d ser. 181 (1866): 814–15, and 182 (1866): 730–1, and Fagan 1880, 2: 257–62). For more on the debates over museum administration and relocation, see Stearn 1981, pp. 34–46; on Owen's role in the debates, see Rupke 1994, pp. 31–47.

3 CD had earlier been apprehensive about the removal of the natural history collections from the British Museum in Bloomsbury to South Kensington, which he thought was less accessible to the public (see *Correspondence* vol. 7, letter to J. D. Hooker, 29 [October 1858]); on the opposition of others to the proposed removal, see Rupke 1994, pp. 37–9. In February 1866, Alfred Waterhouse was appointed to complete an existing design for a new natural history museum in South Kensington, although other locations for the museum continued to be considered until 1870. Construction of the British Museum of Natural History began in 1873 and was completed in 1880. On the construction of the museum, see Stearn 1981, pp. 43–9, and Forgan and Gooday 1994.

4 Thomas Littleton Powys, fourth Baron Lilford.

5 Arthur Hay, Viscount Walden.

To Friedrich Hildebrand 16 May [1866][1]

Down. | Bromley. | Kent. S.E.
May 16

My dear Sir

The state of my health prevents my attending the Hort. Congress;[2] but I forwarded yesterday your paper to the Secretary & if they are not overwhelmed with papers, yours will be gladly received.[3] I have made many observations on the Fumariacæ & convinced myself that they were adapted for insect-agency;[4] but I never observed anything nearly so curious as your most interesting facts.[5] I hope you will repeat your experiments on the Corydalis on a larger scale, & especially on several distinct plants;[6] for your plant might have been individually peculiar, like certain individual plants of Lobelia &c described by Gärtner,[7] & of Passiflora & orchids described by Mr Scott.[8]

I hope you will send me your paper on Oxalis.[9] Three years ago I received a large collection of Oxalis from the Cape of Good Hope, & the sender told me that some of the forms were trimorphic. Of the plants which I raised from the bulbs, none of the species presented more than one form, excepting two. And these 2 species exhibited only two forms, but from their structure & from getting plenty of seed when I fertilized the pistil with pollen from the stamens of equal height, I felt sure that they were trimorphic.[10]

Since writing to you before I have read your admirable memoir on Salvia & it has interested me almost as much as when I first investigated the structure of Orchids.[11] Your paper illustrates several points in my Origin of Species, especially the transition of organs. Knowing only 2 or 3 species in the genus, I had often marvelled how one cell of the anther c[d] have been transformed into the moveable plate or spoon; & how well you show the gradations; but I am surprized that you did not more strongly insist on this point.[12]

I shall be still more surprized if you do not ultimately come to the same belief with me, as shown by so many beautiful contrivances, that all plants require, from some unknown cause, to be occasionally fertilized by pollen from a distinct individual.[13]

With sincere respect believe me my dear Sir | yours very faithfully | Ch. Darwin.

LS
Courtesy of Eilo Hildebrand (photocopy)

1 The year is established by the relationship between this letter and the letter from Friedrich Hildebrand, 11 May 1866.

2 Hildebrand had hoped to meet CD in London at the the International Horticultural Exhibition and Botanical Congress (see letter from Friedrich Hildebrand, 11 May 1866 and n. 4).

3 See letter from Friedrich Hildebrand, 11 May 1866 and n. 5. Hildebrand's paper on *Corydalis cava* was published in the report of the congress (Hildebrand 1866d). Maxwell Tylden Masters was honorary secretary of the congress (see letter from M. T. Masters, March 1866).

4 CD began experiments on the pollination mechanisms of the Fumariaceae in 1858, following his correspondence with Asa Gray, who argued that self-fertilisation occurred in the family (see *Correspondence* vol. 6; see also *Correspondence* vols. 7 and 9–11). CD's notes on Fumariaceae species, made between 1858 and 1863, are in DAR 76: B13–21. CD published a notice on pollination in Fumariaceae in *Nature* 9 (1874): 460 (*Collected papers* 2: 182–3). His experiments indicated that some species were self-sterile, and thus required insect agency for fertilisation, while others were fertile without insect aid (*Cross and self fertilisation*, pp. 329–59, 366).

5 In his paper on *Corydalis cava* (Hildebrand 1866d), Hildebrand reported that individual flowers of the species were self-sterile, even though the stigma was in contact with pollen from the same flower; he also described various degrees of fertility when different flowers from the same plant, from different plants, or from different varieties, were crossed. CD discussed Hildebrand's experiments on *C. cava* in *Variation* 2: 132–3, remarking that the case was 'highly instructive', as it showed how widely different the action of the same pollen was, depending on whether it was placed on the stigma of the same flower, or on that of another flower on the same raceme, or on that of a distinct plant. CD added information on *C. cava* from Hildebrand to *Origin* 5th ed., p. 304. See also *Cross and self fertilisation*, pp. 331, 340–2. CD had experimented with *C. solida* and *C. lutea*, finding them to be self-sterile (see *Cross and self fertilisation*, pp. 358–9).

6 Most of Hildebrand's crossing experiments involved as many as five plants; however, one experiment, which involved pollinating flowers on the same raceme with one another, and which resulted in some limited seed production, was performed with only one specimen (see Hildebrand 1866d, p. 157).

7 Karl Friedrich von Gärtner had observed two self-sterile plants of *Lobelia fulgens*, a species generally self-fertile (see Gärtner 1849, pp. 64, 357). CD's heavily annotated copy of Gärtner 1849 is in the

Darwin Library–CUL (see *Marginalia* 1: 256–98). CD discussed Gärtner's findings in *Variation* 2: 136. See also *Correspondence* vol. 11, letter to John Scott, 6 March 1863.

8 CD discussed cases in which individual plants within a species were self-sterile in *Variation* 2: 136–8, including examples of *Passiflora* observed by John Scott and Robertson Munro. Scott had also observed that one of several self-pollinated plants of the orchid *Oncidium divaricatum* produced seed capsules, but without any good seed; the other specimens were all self-sterile (Scott 1864, p. 548). CD's annotated copy of Scott 1864 is in the Darwin Pamphlet Collection–CUL. CD reported the observation in *Variation* 2: 164. See also CD's concluding remarks on why individual plants, or species, might be self-sterile in *Variation* 2: 141–2, and *Cross and self fertilisation*, pp. 341–5.

9 Hildebrand 1866c. See letter from Friedrich Hildebrand, 11 May 1866 and nn. 2 and 3.

10 Roland Trimen had sent CD bulbs of *Oxalis* from South Africa in 1864 (see *Correspondence* vol. 12, letters to Roland Trimen, 13 May 1864 and 25 November 1864). CD experimented on the genus from 1864 to 1868; his notes are in DAR 109: B3–27, B101, B108, B110, B115, and DAR 111: A44–8, A64, A67–8, B33–5, B43. He discussed Hildebrand's findings and his own experimental work on *Oxalis* in *Forms of flowers*, pp. 169–83.

11 CD refers to Hildebrand 1866b. In his letter to CD of 21 June 1864 (*Correspondence* vol. 12), Hildebrand stated that his research on pollination mechanisms in *Salvia* and other plants had been inspired by CD's *Orchids*. For CD's interest in *Salvia*, see *Correspondence* vol. 12, letter to Friedrich Hildebrand, 25 June [1864], and this volume, letter to Friedrich Hildebrand, 20 April [1866]. CD cited Hildebrand's work on *Salvia* in *Cross and self fertilisation*, p. 93 n. CD's heavily annotated copy of Hildebrand 1866b is in the Darwin Pamphlet Collection–CUL.

12 CD discussed the development of organs by transitional gradations in *Origin*, pp. 179–94. He added a lengthy section on pollination mechanisms in *Origin* 4th ed., pp. 229–31. Hildebrand 1866b described gradations in the length of the connective (the portion of the filament connecting the two lobes of the anther) in *Salvia*; the connective allowed for varying degrees of movement. Hildebrand also described the flattened lobe or 'cell' characteristic of one pair of anthers in different species of the genus. CD's experiments with *Salvia coccinea* and *S. tenori*, and his observations of *S. grahami*, are described in *Cross and self fertilisation.*

13 CD had first publicly stated his belief that it was a 'law of nature that every organic being should occasionally be crossed with a distinct individual of the same species' in a letter to the *Gardeners' Chronicle*, [before 13 November 1858] (*Correspondence* vol. 7). He reiterated this view in *Origin*, p. 97, and *Orchids*, p. 359. However, CD continued to investigate possible cases of perpetual self-fertilisation (see *Correspondence* vols. 12 and 13, and 'Three forms of *Lythrum salicaria*', pp. 191–2 n. (*Collected papers* 2: 130–1)). See also letter to Robert Caspary, 4 March 1866 and n. 6. Hildebrand did not make any theoretical generalisation based on his results in Hildebrand 1866b. He later came to support CD's views on crossing (see Hildebrand 1867, p. 5).

To J. D. Hooker 16 May [1866][1]

Down. | Bromley. | Kent. S.E.
May 16

My dear Hooker

I have been very glad to see Asa Gray's letter;[2] but how I sh^{d} have liked to have seen yours to him; if you had been half a man you w^{d} have sent it me, though this w^{d} have been something new in correspondence.[3]

I have been wonderfully interested about the C. de Verd Alpine plants.[4] After giving your Fernando Po case, may I give, in the new Ed. of Origin, the enclosed sentence;[5] & if so, return it in enclosed envelope, without adding a word as I know how busy you must be: If I do not receive it back I shall understand that for some reason I must not give it.

I sh[d] have liked beyond any thing to have seen the Hort. Exhib. but without 2 or 3 days hardening in London it w[d] be impossible for me.[6] Do not forget about Caspary,[7] & if you can remember it, please say to Decandolle & you can say it with perfect truth, how greatly I regret not seeing him in London.[8]

My dissipation in London did me no harm, perhaps good, though I have lately had a poorish week; & I enjoyed extremely seeing my old friends at the Royal Soc. & their reception of me pleased me greatly.[9] I saw Tyler there & was much struck with his pleasant manner.[10] Can you lend me Crawford's paper on Cult. plants?[11] What you say about "twaddle" gives me a shudder for I fear it is applicable to my 2 Chaps on the same subject.[12] I have often had it at my pen or tongue's end to ask you to read these 2 Chapters; but they are fearfully dull; yet I c[d] not pass the subject over.

I am getting on with my work & have finished correcting but not revising the Origin, which I think I have considerably improved.[13] I have now begun again at my other book & am at work on a Chap. on Reversion which to me is a most interesting subject & brimful of my dear little mysterious gemmules.[14]

Hildebrand of Bonn has sent thro' me to the Congress a curious paper on the fertilization of Corydalis.[15] The horrid man has been taking the bread out of my mouth, as he has out of G. Henslow's,[16] for the Fumariacæ have been a pet subject with me & he has likewise just made out the trimorphism of Oxalis.[17]

Lastly, but by no means least, we shall be delighted to see Mrs Hooker & yourself & as many children as you have at home at the end of the first week in June or in any part of the 3 following weeks when we shall certainly be at home, & we hope you will be able to give us a week.[18]

yours affectionately | Ch Darwin

L(S)
DAR 115: 289, 289b

[1] The year is established by the relationship between this letter and the letter from J. D. Hooker, 13 May 1866.

[2] Hooker had enclosed a letter from Asa Gray. See letter from J. D. Hooker, 13 May 1866 and n. 1.

[3] For Hooker's notes on the content of his letter to Gray, see the letter from J. D. Hooker, [17 May 1866].

[4] See letter from J. D. Hooker, 13 May 1866 and n. 13.

[5] The enclosure has not been found. CD had praised Hooker's 1861 paper on the vegetation of Clarence Peak on Fernando Po, now known as Bioko Island, in his letter to Charles Lyell, 7 February [1866], and his letter to J. D. Hooker, [28 February 1866]. CD cited information from J. D. Hooker 1861 in *Origin* 4th ed., p. 445, and added the following sentences to his discussion of the migration of temperate

plants during the glacial period:

> It now also appears, as I hear from Dr. Hooker, that some of these same temperate plants have been discovered by the Rev. R. T. Lowe on the mountains of the Cape de Verde islands. This extension of the same temperate forms, almost under the equator, across the whole continent of Africa and to the mountains of the Cape de Verde archipelago, is one of the most astonishing facts ever recorded in the distribution of plants.

[6] In his letter of 13 May 1866, Hooker had suggested that he meet CD in London at the International Horticultural Exhibition and Botanical Congress.

[7] Robert Caspary wished to meet CD; Hooker was to inform Caspary that he could visit CD at Down House (see letter from Robert Caspary, 7 May 1866, and letter to J. D. Hooker, [12 May 1866]).

[8] CD had been invited to dinner at the home of John Edward Gray on 16 May; Alphonse de Candolle had also been invited (see letter from J. E. Gray, 9 April 1866). CD had also been invited to meet Candolle at the home of Charles Wentworth Dilke (see letter from C. W. Dilke, 24 April 1866).

[9] CD had stayed in London with his brother Erasmus from 21 April to 1 May; he attended a reception at the Royal Society of London on 28 April (see letter from J. D. Hooker, 13 May 1866 and n. 3).

[10] CD refers to Edward Burnett Tylor. See letter from J. D. Hooker, 13 May 1866 and n. 5.

[11] Crawfurd 1866. See letter from J. D. Hooker, 13 May 1866 and n. 7.

[12] See letter from J. D. Hooker, 13 May 1866. CD refers to chapters 9 and 10 of *Variation*, which were on cultivated plants.

[13] CD had been working on the fourth edition of *Origin* since 1 March (see 'Journal', Appendix II).

[14] CD discussed reversion, or the appearance in organisms of ancestral traits not evident in the parent forms, in chapter 13 of *Variation*. CD's hypothesis of pangenesis, presented in chapter 27, proposed that characteristics of an organism were inherited through 'gemmules' that were thrown off by the body's cells, and that aggregated either into buds or into the elements of sexual reproduction. CD attempted to explain the phenomenon of reversion by suggesting that gemmules could remain inactive for generations (*Variation* 2: 372–3, 398–402). For a further discussion of pangenesis, see the letter to J. D. Hooker, 4 April [1866]; see also *Correspondence* vol. 13, letters to T. H. Huxley, 27 May [1865] and 12 July [1865].

[15] Hildebrand 1866d. See letter to Friedrich Hildebrand, 16 May [1866] and nn. 3–5.

[16] See letter to George Henslow, 16 April [1866]. Hildebrand had published a paper on the pollination mechanisms of *Indigofera* and *Medicago sativa* (Hildebrand 1866a); the paper contained observations similar to those made independently by Henslow.

[17] CD refers to Hildebrand 1866c. See letter from Friedrich Hildebrand, 11 May 1866 and nn. 2 and 3, and letter to Friedrich Hildebrand, 16 May [1866] and n. 10.

[18] Hooker and his wife, Frances Harriet Hooker, arrived at Down on 23 June 1866. He left on 25 June, and she left on 29 June (Emma Darwin's diary (DAR 242)).

From J. D. Hooker [17 May 1866][1]

Kew
Thursday.

Dear Darwin

Harvey is gone, he died last Tuesday after much suffering at last,[2] attended by his wife & my Mother & Sister,[3] to whom he had long been as a son & brother. I shall never see his like again:—for purity of Spirit & sweetness of Temper he was equalled only by Henslow;[4] but then he had besides an exquisite sensibility of temperament & extreme delicacy of feeling that in other people are combined with irritability or vanity. A more unassuming or unselfish man never lived, & when I think how much purer & better he was than I am I smite my self reproaching conscience & feel stricken with shame & sorrow, almost with remorse. He will be buried at Torquay on Saturday, but it will be utterly impossible for me to go to the funeral His loss to Science will be very great, He was a good most painstaking & most conscientious working Botanist. & he leaves no successor fit for his Chair or Herbari⟨um s⟩tudies[5] I do not know how it is, but the demand for systematic Botany is enormously greater than for any other branch of Nat. Hist. Science of a practical sort I mean—& all Harveys works were useful & good.—[6]

I have no heart to write more now—

I saw Caspary for a moment yesterday, but forgot your message in the hurry, I will see him again tomorrow & give it[7]

Ever Yr affec | J D Hooker

P.S. | Many thanks for yours of 16th. just arrived—[8]

Crawfurds paper was such trash that I tore it up— I will get you a copy.[9]

Pray do let me have your chapters on same subject: they cannot be dull to me.[10]

My letter to A Gray was proving by law of N.S. that America will have an aristocracy—& the greater the security of life & property the firmer the aristocratic element (& be d—d to it) I am glad you did not see it— it was so far in advance of your weak elements of knowledge! that you would have been rendered miserable. Joking apart it was only what I wrote you before about effect of the interbreeding of wealth beauty & intellect[11]—acting on the fact, that when struggle is strong the lower classes will have no time for politics & let power lapse to those with above endowments.

May we go to you on 23d. June.[12]

DAR 102: 75–6

CD ANNOTATIONS

Before P.S.: 'Harvey' *added pencil*

7.1 *Pray* . . . to me.] *scored pencil*

9.1 23d.] *underl pencil*

[1] The date is established by the reference to William Henry Harvey's death (see n. 2, below), and by the relationship between this letter and the letter to J. D. Hooker, 16 May [1866]. In 1866, 17 May was the first Thursday after 15 May.

[2] Hooker had remarked that Harvey was very ill in his letter to CD of [26 or 27 February 1866]. Harvey died on 15 May 1866 (*DNB*).

[3] Hooker refers to Elizabeth Lecky Harvey, Maria Hooker, and Elizabeth Evans-Lombe.

[4] John Stevens Henslow was Hooker's father-in-law and CD's mentor at Cambridge (see Walters and Stow 2001).

[5] Harvey had been professor of botany and keeper of the herbarium at Trinity College, Dublin (*DNB*).

[6] Harvey was best known for his work on algae (for example, Harvey 1846–51), and the flora of South Africa (for example, Harvey 1859–63).

[7] Hooker refers to Robert Caspary. See letter to J. D. Hooker, 16 May [1866] and n. 7.

[8] Letter to J. D. Hooker, 16 May [1866].

[9] CD had requested a copy of John Crawfurd's paper 'On the migration of cultivated plants in reference to ethnology' (Crawfurd 1866), which Hooker had criticised as 'shocking twaddle'. See letter from J. D. Hooker, 13 May 1866 and n. 7, and letter to J. D. Hooker, 16 May [1866].

[10] Hooker refers to the chapters on cultivated plants that CD had written for *Variation* (see letter to J. D. Hooker, 16 May [1866] and n. 12).

[11] Having seen Asa Gray's reply to Hooker, CD remarked that he would like to have seen Hooker's original letter to Gray (see letter to J. D. Hooker, 16 May [1866] and n. 2). In previous correspondence, Hooker had suggested that the accumulation of wealth, intelligence, and beauty in an aristocratic class was an outcome of natural selection. See, for example, *Correspondence* vol. 10, letter from J. D. Hooker, [23 March 1862], and *Correspondence* vol. 11, letter from J. D. Hooker, [2]9 June 1863. For CD's views on hereditary aristocracy, see *Correspondence* vol. 10, letter to J. D. Hooker, 25 [and 26] January [1862], and *Descent* 2: 356.

[12] See letter to J. D. Hooker, 16 May [1866] and n. 18.

From Thomas Rivers 17 May 1866

Bonks Hill, | Sawbridgeworth.
May 17/66

My dear Sir/

I hope to be at home when the Cytissus & Laburnum show their flowers & to a certainty will send you some of each.[1]

I found to day a curious (to me) instance of the Wistaria frutescens turning back on its own shoots— they will make a light package but too long for the post so I intend to send them *per* rail tomorrow paid to London.[2]

I rejoice much to hear of y^r. restoration to health & hope to meet you on Saturday at D^r. Gray's[3]

I am My d^r Sir | Y^rs. very truly | Th^os. Rivers

I am trying to get the stain by cutting out the buds of Negundo variegata leaving the shields[4] this is the most thorough variegation I know of in deciduous trees.

DAR 176: 165

[1] See letter to Thomas Rivers, 27 April [1866]. CD had requested that Rivers send him specimens of '*Cytisus purpureus-elongatus*' and *C. adami*. On CD's interest in *Cytisus*, see the letter to Robert Caspary, 21 February [1866] and n. 2, and the letter from Robert Caspary, 25 February 1866 and nn. 4 and 9.

[2] *Wisteria frutescens* is a species native to the south-eastern United States. CD had briefly discussed the climbing habit of *Wisteria* in 'Climbing plants', pp. 21–2. He had also remarked that hanging shoots of some climbing plants twined back around themselves in order to grow upwards (*ibid.*, p. 14). For CD's interest in *Wisteria*, see also *Correspondence* vol. 12.

[3] John Edward Gray had invited CD to dine on Wednesday 16 May (see letter from J. E. Gray, 9 April 1866); however, CD evidently declined (see letter to J. D. Hooker, 16 May [1866] and n. 8). No record that CD dined at Gray's on 19 May has been found.

[4] Rivers refers to the variegated tree *Acer negundo* 'Variegatum'; the variety is described in Bean 1970–88, 1: 214. A 'shield' is 'a shield-shaped portion of a branch, containing a bud, cut for use as a graft' (*OED*). Rivers was interested in the possible effect of scion wood on the coloration of stock tissue in *Acer*; by removing the bud from the shield, he would have prevented the scion from making new growth (see Rivers 1866a, p. 237). CD had previously consulted Rivers about cases of stock being affected by grafts (see *Correspondence* vol. 10, letter to Thomas Rivers, 28 December [1862], and *Correspondence* vol. 11, letter to Thomas Rivers, 7 January [1863]). CD had also asked Asa Gray about cases of buds with blended characters produced at the junction of stock and graft (see letter to Asa Gray, 16 April [1866]).

From George Henslow 18 May 1866

10 South Crescent | Bedford Square | W.C.
May 18/66

Dear Mr. Darwin

I have at last written my article on Hybridism for the Popular Science Review,[1] & have much to thank you for so kindly lending me yr books &c. on the subject.[2] I will forward them to the address given to me within a few days.

I have wanted to ask you whether you would mind running over the proof sheet (about 8 pp.) so that you might give me a hint or two as to any passage you might think objectionable, or any statement too *positively* asserted &c, as being a subject I knew nothing about previously, I might have been led into making some wrong or hazardous statement. If however, ill health, time &c. should prevent you, pray do not hesitate a moment in saying so & obliging[3]

Yours faithfully | Geo. Henslow.

DAR 166: 159

[1] In his letter of 8 March 1866, Henslow had informed CD of his intention to write on Charles Victor Naudin's research on hybridity. The article appeared in *Popular Science Review* 5 (1866): 304–13 (Henslow 1866b).

[2] Henslow had asked CD for references to relevant works on hybridism. See letter from George Henslow, 12 March 1866 and n. 1.

[3] CD returned the proof-sheet with his letter to Henslow of 12 June [1866].

From Thomas Rivers 20 May 1866

Bonks Hill, | *Sawbridgeworth.*
May 20/66

My Dear Sir/

My son[1] was struck last year by observing in his garden the apparent instinct of a "Haricot" French bean—a variety called a dwarf F. B but which puts forth slender twining shoots— one of these was taking an upright direction when suddenly & in calm weather it turned off abruptly to the N.E, & caught hold of the young shoot of a plum tree trained to the wall in front of which the row of beans was growing the tree here made what gardeners call "foreright" shoots[2] & to one of these the bean attached itself. My son was amused & took a sketch which I enclose, it will perhaps give you an idea of what took place.[3] The row of beans was 2½ feet from the end of the plum shoots,

The Wistaria (Glycine) from which I cut the shoots sent to you are from a tree turned to a S.W. aspect so that their return voyage was due N.E.[4]

I hope to see you at the Congress on Wednesday next[5] I am deputed to follow Decandolle in a short lecture on Horticulture the subject "raising new kinds of fruit from seed"[6]

I have plenty in me but whether it will come out I can't say

I am My dr Sir | Yrs. very truly | Thos. Rivers

[Enclosure]

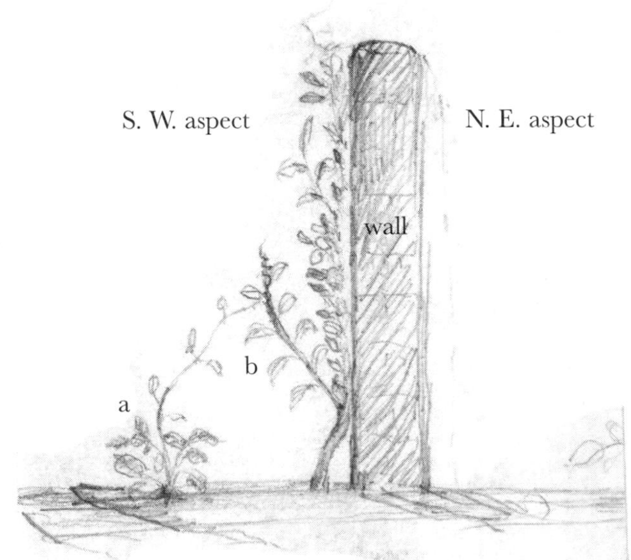

The bean, a, $2\frac{1}{2}$ feet from the shoot of the tree, b

DAR 176: 166; 176: 188.1

1 T. Francis Rivers.
2 Foreright: 'Of a branch etc.: Shooting straight out' (*OED*).
3 See enclosure. Rivers had described the climbing bean in his letter to CD of 6 July 1865 (*Correspondence* vol. 13). CD had briefly discussed varieties of *Phaseolus* in 'Climbing plants', pp. 6 and 25, including '"Fulmer's dwarf forcing-bean," on which occasionally a long twining shoot appeared' (p. 25).
4 See letter from Thomas Rivers, 17 May 1866 and n. 2. *Wisteria frutescens* was formerly also known as *Glycine frutescens.*
5 CD did not attend the International Horticultural Exhibition and Botanical Congress (see letter from Friedrich Hildebrand, 11 May 1866 and n. 4).
6 Rivers read a paper, 'On seedling peaches and nectarines', following the presidential address delivered by Alphonse de Candolle at the opening meeting of the congress on 23 May 1866 (*Gardeners' Chronicle*, 26 May 1866, p. 490).

From J. T. Moggridge 21 May [1866][1]

7a. Eastbourne Terr. | Hyde Park. | W.
May 21

Dear Mr. Darwin

I send a small box containing two plants of what I take to be **Orchis** *coriophora*, gathered at Cannes; also a spike of **Serapias** *cordigera* Linn. which happens to be tolerably well preserved.— —[2]

The marshy field where the *self-fertilising* **Oph**: *scolopax* used to grow has now begun to feel the effects of drainage & the Ophryses generally are dying out there— —

Herbert Spencer in 1866–7
Duncan 1908, facing p. 127
By permission of the Syndics of Cambridge University Library

John Traherne Moggridge
Courtesy of Hunt Institute for Botanical Documentation, Carnegie Mellon University, Pittsburgh, PA, USA

Fritz Müller in 1866
Möller ed. 1915–21, 3: 84

George Bentham
Journal of Botany 13 (1884): facing p. 353
By permission of the Syndics of Cambridge University Library

—[3] *Perhaps* these plants may have been hybrids between **Oph**. *scolopax* & *apifera*, & thus, having a more precarious tenure of life, are the first to disappear completely—[4]

Talking of hybrids, I have had a most valuable lesson lately upon hybrid Cistuses from Dr Bornet at Antibes— — He has been making observations for several years in M. Thuret's garden,[5] &, though he says that it must be yet some years before he can publish his observations, I think that some important points are already cleared up—

Firstly the old dictum about the hybrid having the foliage of the mother & the habit of the father plant, does not hold in the least.— Secondly, it appears that some characters are more sure of reappearing than others; as for ex: the hairyness of one parent seems to be always transmitted; & the scorpioid inflorescence of **Cistus** *monspeliensis* is always found in its descendants— — —[6]

D^r^. Bornet seems to be a most conscientious observer; his energy is not even daunted by the very early hours at which the flowers open, & he is to be found regularly at work between 5· & 6· a.m. upon the fertilisation!—

I had great pleasure in making Miss Darwin's acquaintance at Cannes,[7] & I much wish that it were possible that I might some day have the priviledge of seeing & speaking to her Father—[8]

believe me | y^rs^. very sincerely | J. Traherne Moggridge.

I think that we shall be at the above adress for a month at least.

DAR 171: 206

[1] The year is established by the reference to meeting Henrietta Emma Darwin at Cannes (see letter to H. E. Darwin, [14–21 April 1866], and letter from H. E. Darwin, [*c.* 10 May 1866]).

[2] On *Serapias cordigera*, see the letter from J. T. Moggridge, 10 May [1866] and n. 4.

[3] Moggridge had observed a self-fertile form of *Ophrys scolopax* in 1864 (see letter from J. T. Moggridge, 10 May [1866], n. 2).

[4] Moggridge had argued that *Ophrys scolopax* and *O. apifera*, together with *O. arachnites* and *O. aranifera*, were varieties of a single species, *O. insectifera* (see letter to H. E. Darwin, [14–21 April 1866] and n. 6).

[5] Edouard Bornet worked for many years with Gustave Adolphe Thuret, at Thuret's garden in Antibes, France (*DBF*).

[6] CD did not refer to this information on the transmission of characters in *Cistus* in any of his published works; however, in *Variation* 1: 389 and 2: 140, CD cited information from Bornet on the fertility of *Cistus* hybrids. See also letter to J. T. Moggridge, 13 November [1866].

[7] Henrietta Emma Darwin had met Moggridge during her stay in the south of France. See letter from H. E. Darwin, [*c.* 10 May 1866].

[8] Moggridge visited Down from 23 to 25 June 1866 (Emma Darwin's diary (DAR 242)).

To Fritz Müller 23 May 1866

Down Bromley Kent
May 23. 1866

My dear Sir

I thank you sincerely for your two letters of Mar. 6 & Ap. 3rd.[1] Your account of the Orchis with affinities toward Cephalanthera, Vanilla, & Glossodia is extremely curious.[2] I am much surprized at the course of the vessels; but Dr Crüger partly convinced me (as well as some observations which I have made on some other plants) that vessels often fail to give true homologies: at present I feel quite in the dark on the subject.[3] As I am not likely to take up Orchids again, I did not like to retain your really beautiful drawings as they might be of use to yourself.[4]

I am very much obliged for all the facts which you give me in your former letter on the changes in the flora & fauna in your ditches & especially on the sea coast.[5] If ever I have strength to publish my larger work these facts will come in very useful.[6] The only analogous facts which I have met with refer to frequent changes in the Fuci growing on the same part on our shores.[7]

That is a singular fact of which you tell me about the male Orchestia externally like a female.[8]

I have rec^d^ your little pamphlet about poor old Gray's absurd blunders.[9] Such men do much harm in Nat. History; but he has done wonderfully well in accumulating materials for the Brit. Museum.[10] You must have read carefully my book on the Lepadidæ to have picked out Gray's method of classifying Scalpellum[11] As you attend to plants, will you be so kind as to observe whether Oxalis with you exhibits different forms; for Dr Hildebrand of Bonn writes to me that the C of Good Hope species are trimorphic like Lythrum, as indeed I was aware as I have been experimenting on some for the last two years.[12] I suspect that aquatic & marsh-plants are apt to be dimorphic so if you see any with a pistil much longer or shorter than the stamens pray look at the flowers of 3 or 4 other plants.[13] I have almost finished correcting the new Ed. of the Origin[14] & I am pleased to hear that my labour will be so much the more advantageous as a 3rd German Ed. is immediately to be printed revised by Prof. Leonhard.[15] As you feel interested on the subject, I may mention that I have lately read two pamphlets in our favour, by good men, one by Oscar Schmidt & the other by Carl Nägeli.[16] I think Rutimeyer, for whom I feel much respect is also with us; by the way he quoted in one of his last works your account of the metamorphoses of the "Garneelen".[17]

With sincere thanks for all your kindness pray believe me | yours very truly | Ch. Darwin

P.S. I will keep safely your note on the curious Orchis & can return it to you if you sh^d^ desire it[18]

LS
British Library (Loan 10: 7)

[1] Müller's letter of 6 March 1866 is incomplete (see letter from Fritz Müller, 6 March 1866 and n. 1); the letter of 3 April 1866 has not been found.

[2] Müller's account of the orchid was contained in his letter of 3 April 1866 (see n. 1, above; see also letter from Fritz Müller, 2 August 1866). He also discussed the orchid in letters to Max Johann Sigismund Schultze, 2 June 1866, and Hermann Müller, 1 July 1866; the letters are reproduced in Möller ed. 1915–21, 2: 83–4, 86–9. Müller described the orchid as similar to *Cephalanthera* in form and foliage but with flowers closely resembling *Vanilla.* He thought the flower was noteworthy in that the two stamens of the outer whorl were not merged with the labellum as CD had described (see *Orchids*,

p. 294), but were clearly present in rudimentary form, though infertile (see Möller ed. 1915–21, 2: 84, 87). Müller did not mention *Glossodia* in the letters to Schultze and Hermann Müller.

3 Hermann Crüger had argued that the 'production and multiplication of vascular cords and their distribution' was related to 'physiologic activity' (Crüger 1864, p. 132), and cast doubt on CD's claim in *Orchids*, p. 290, that tracing the spiral vessels of orchids could help determine the homologies of the parts relative to other flowers. CD added a reference to Crüger 1864 to *Orchids* 2d ed., p. 235, while maintaining his former claim.

4 The drawings have not been found.

5 See letter from Fritz Müller, 6 March 1866.

6 The 'larger work' was presumably the 'second work' referred to in *Variation* 1: 4, in which CD planned to 'discuss the variability of organic beings in a state of nature'. This work was never written.

7 *Fucus* is a genus of seaweed with species known to occur in all three intertidal zones. CD had written about the geographical range of *F. giganteus* in *Journal of researches*, p. 304. In his 'big book' on species (*Natural selection*, p. 284), CD quoted William Henry Harvey on environmentally induced changes in *F. vesiculosus*.

8 The information on the external similarity of the male and female forms of this amphipod must have been contained either in the missing portion of Müller's letter of 6 March 1866 or in his missing letter of 3 April 1866 (see n. 1, above). Müller had earlier discussed dimorphism in males within the genus (see F. Müller 1864c, pp. 16–17).

9 Müller's paper (F. Müller 1864b) was a critique of the generic diagnosis of a type of sea-pen (Pennatulacea) in the family Renilla (now Renillidae), given by John Edward Gray. Gray had proposed that the species *Renilla edwardsii* should be put into a new genus, which he called *Herklotsia* (see J. E. Gray 1860). Müller argued that Gray's diagnosis was severely flawed, partly because of the disparity between live and preserved specimens of the organism, but also because of Gray's use of inaccurate terminology (see F. Müller 1864b, p. 353). *Herklotsia* is now considered to be an invalid genus, and is placed in synonymy with *Renilla* (see Williams 1995, p. 101). Müller's paper is not in the Darwin Pamphlet Collection–CUL.

10 Gray was keeper of the zoological collections at the British Museum. He had facilitated CD's classificatory work on barnacles by arranging access to the museum's specimens, providing CD with his own collection, and advising him on procuring other collections (see *Correspondence* vol. 4, Appendix II).

11 Müller had prefaced his paper with a quotation from *Living Cirripedia* (1851), p. 216, in which CD claimed that the 'inordinate multiplication of genera' destroyed 'the main advantages of classification'. The statement was made in the context of a critique of Gray's adoption of generic names for four species that CD included in a single genus, *Scalpellum.*

12 Friedrich Hildebrand had written a paper on trimorphism in *Oxalis* that he had promised to send to CD when it was published (Hildebrand 1866c). See letter from Friedrich Hildebrand, 11 May 1866 and nn. 2 and 3, and letter to Friedrich Hildebrand, 16 May [1866] and n. 10.

13 CD had earlier speculated whether there might be an unusual proportion of aquatic plants with separate sexes (see *Correspondence* vol. 11, letter to Daniel Oliver, 20 [January 1863]). See also *Forms of flowers*, p. 257 n.

14 CD had begun preparing the fourth edition of *Origin* on 1 March 1866 (see CD's 'Journal', Appendix II).

15 CD's German publisher had recently informed CD that he had asked Gustav von Leonhard to undertake the translation of the third German edition of *Origin* (see letter from E. Schweizerbart'sche Verlagsbuchhandlung, 10 May 1866 and nn. 6 and 7).

16 CD refers to Oskar Schmidt and Carl Wilhelm von Nägeli, and to Schmidt and Unger 1866, pp. 3–36, and Nägeli 1865, both of which are in the Darwin Pamphlet Collection–CUL. CD's copy of Nägeli 1865 is heavily annotated and there is a partial manuscript translation, beginning on page 15, of the German text, along with a page of notes by CD, in the Darwin Pamphlet Collection–CUL. For more on Schmidt and Unger 1866, see the letter from Rudolf Suchsland, 16 April 1866 and n. 4.

[17] CD refers to Ludwig Rütimeyer and to Müller's paper on prawns, F. Müller 1863 (translated into English as F. Müller 1864a; the modern German spelling is 'Garnelen'). No reference to F. Müller 1863 has been found in any of Rütimeyer's publications.

[18] Müller's note on the orchid was contained in the letter of 3 April 1866 (see nn. 1 and 2, above). It has not been found.

From Robert Caspary 25 May 1866

Kew gardens | House of Dr. J. D. Hooker
25th. of May | 1866

My dear Sir,

Having spoken to Dr. Hooker about my wish to visit you, he advises me to follow your kind invitation to go and see you.[1] Consequently I shall leave London, Charing-Cross station, on Sunday 27th of May in the morning by an early train to get out to you[2] I can not say exactly by what train, as no timetable is here. My time is so much taken up here by researches of several kinds, that I could no see Dr Hooker earlier for deciding upon my visiting you. Send me away from you, as soon as you feel in any degree tired.

In the hope of seeing you soon I remain, dear Sir, with the highest regards | your most sincerely | Rob. Caspary

DAR 161: 121

[1] CD had asked Joseph Dalton Hooker to convey his invitation to Caspary. See letter to J. D. Hooker, 16 May [1866] and n. 7.

[2] According to Emma Darwin's diary (DAR 242), Caspary visited CD at Down on 27 May 1866.

From J. T. Moggridge 25 May [1866][1]

7a. Eastbourne Terr. | Hyde Park | W.
May 25.

Dear Mr. Darwin

I thank you most heartily for your very kind offer of hospitality, & accept for June 23.—[2]

I have seen quite enough of invalid life to understand the laws of a sick house,[3] & I only hope that no ceremony may prevent the issue of the necessary instructions—

—With renewed thanks believe me | very sincerely yours | J. Traherne Moggridge.

DAR 171: 207

CD ANNOTATION

Top of letter: 'Will leave L. at 4°·30 or 5°·— | Sowerby'[4] *pencil*

[1] The year is established by the date of Moggridge's visit to Down (see n. 2 below).

[2] The letter to Moggridge has not been found. Moggridge arrived at Down on 23 June and departed on 25 June 1866 (Emma Darwin's diary (DAR 242)).

[3] Moggridge spent each winter in Mentone, in the south of France, because of ill health (*Gardeners' Chronicle* n.s. 2 (1874): 723).

[4] CD may refer to George Brettingham Sowerby Jr, who had been employed to produce illustrations for *Variation* (see letter to John Murray, 22 February [1866] and n. 14, and letter to G. B. Sowerby Jr, 19 October [1866]).

From John Murray 25 May [1866][1]

50^A., Albemarle S^t. | W.
May 25

My Dear Sir

The printing of the new Edition of your work on Species is now nearly completed —& I write to inform you that I have directed that the Edition shall be limited to 1000 copies.[2] Calculating, as far as I can upon the recent demand for the work that number may last from 3 to 5 years. I hope this will be agreeable to you.

I rejoice to hear so good an account of your improved health & am only sorry I had no opportunity of bearing witness to it myself—having missed seeing you at the R^l. Society Soirée[3] & elsewhere— I remain My Dear Sir | Yours very faithfully | John Murray

Chas Darwin Esq

DAR 171: 334

CD ANNOTATIONS[4]
2.1 I rejoice . . . improved] *scored pencil*
2.1 your improved] 'Future book' *added pencil*
Head of letter: 'Additions Lithograph Plates) Advertise a little | * Future Book [*del pencil*] | Copies— [*after del illeg*] I shall give away a good n^o.' *added pencil*

[1] The year is established by the references to the fourth edition of *Origin* and to the Royal Society of London soirée (see nn. 2 and 3, below).

[2] Murray printed 1500 copies of the fourth edition of *Origin* (Peckham ed. 1959, p. 776); it was published in November 1866 (*Publishers' Circular* 1866). See also letter from John Murray, 30 May [1866].

[3] CD attended a reception at the Royal Society on 28 April 1866 (Emma Darwin's diary (DAR 242)). See letter from J. D. Hooker, 13 May 1866 and n. 3.

[4] CD's annotations were made for his letter to John Murray, 28 May [1866].

To John Murray 28 May [1866][1]

Down. | Bromley. | Kent. S.E.
May 28

My dear Sir

You are much the best judge about the number of copies to print off.[2] I have corrected the vol. thoroughly & improved it I think a good deal; but have added, which perhaps you will be sorry to hear, about 50 pages.[3] I hope you will think it worth while to advertise the book as added to & corrected.[4] I suppose you have remembered the lithographed Diagram.[5]

I trust to your kindness to give me a few copies, for I shall have to give away a dozen or two in addition.[6]

I am much obliged for your kind expressions about my improved health; & now that the Origin is nearly finished I hope to make real progress in my next book—[7]

My dear Sir | yours sincerely | Ch. Darwin

LS
John Murray Archive

[1] The year is established by the relationship between this letter and the letter from John Murray, 25 May [1866].
[2] See letter from John Murray, 25 May [1866] and n. 2.
[3] CD had been revising *Origin* since 1 March 1866 (see CD's 'Journal', Appendix II), after Murray had informed him that a new edition was called for (see letter from John Murray, 21 February [1866]). The fourth edition of *Origin* is fifty-seven pages longer than the third edition. The front matter included a list of significant additions.
[4] CD had made the same recommendation to Murray for the third edition of *Origin* (see *Correspondence* vol. 9, letter to John Murray, 30 April [1861]). In a letter to H. W. Bates, 9 April [1863] (*Correspondence* vol. 11), CD expressed his suspicion that Murray had not advertised *Origin* much.
[5] As with previous editions, the fourth edition of *Origin* contained only one plate, a diagram illustrating divergence of character (Peckham ed. 1959, p. 211).
[6] For a presentation list for the fourth edition of *Origin*, see Appendix IV.
[7] CD refers to *Variation*, published in 1868.

From J. D. Hooker 29 May 1866

Kew
May 29/66

Dear Darwin

The enclosed may amuse you slightly.[1]

Did you see Caspary?[2]

Grove asked me to give him, in brief, the principal confirmatory evidences of your theory &c.[3] I thought of

1 Your Orchid book & Primula &c[4]

2. Wallaces speculations on Man[5]

3. Do— Malayan Butterflies[6]

4. Bates Amazon ditto & his book everywhere[7]

5. My Arctic Essay & Australian do—[8]

Can you put me up to any more?— it is for his speech at Nottingham.[9]

This International show has been a tremendous worry & I am glad that it is all over[10]

Ever Yr affec | J D Hooker

DAR 102: 77

CD ANNOTATION

End of letter: 'Fritz Muller— | Eozoon— Candense— | Archeopteryx'[11] *pencil*

[1] Hooker evidently intended to send CD a letter from Asa Gray, but failed to enclose it (see letter to J. D. Hooker, [31 May 1866], and letter to J. D. Hooker, [4 June 1866]).

[2] Robert Caspary had visited CD on 27 May 1866 (Emma Darwin's diary (DAR 242)).

[3] William Robert Grove was president of the British Association for the Advancement of Science in 1866; the information was for his presidential address, which was to be delivered on 22 August 1866 (see n. 9, below).

[4] *Orchids* and 'Dimorphic condition in *Primula*'. Hooker also alludes to CD's other papers on botanical dimorphism and trimorphism, 'Two forms in species of *Linum*' and 'Three forms of *Lythrum salicaria*'.

[5] Hooker refers to Alfred Russel Wallace's paper, 'The origin of human races and the antiquity of man deduced from the theory of "natural selection"' (A. R. Wallace 1864a).

[6] A. R. Wallace 1864b.

[7] Hooker refers to Henry Walter Bates's paper on mimetic butterflies (Bates 1861) and his book, *The naturalist on the river Amazons* (Bates 1863).

[8] Hooker had endorsed CD's theory of evolution by natural selection and applied the theory to the distribution of plants in his essays on Australian and Arctic floras (J. D. Hooker 1859 and J. D. Hooker 1860a).

[9] In his presidential address at the British Association meeting in Nottingham (W. R. Grove 1866), Grove presented evidence for the 'derivative hypothesis', or 'gradual succession', of species, as opposed to development by 'sudden leaps' or 'sudden creations'. Grove cited Bates's research on butterflies, Wallace's observations of butterflies and birds of the Malay region, and Hooker's work on Australian and Arctic plants as being supportive of gradual succession. Grove also referred to Benjamin Dann Walsh's recent paper on phytophagic insect species and varieties (Walsh 1864–5), and to John Lubbock's observations of diving hymenopterous insects. The only work by Darwin specifically mentioned in the address was *Origin* (see W. R. Grove 1866, pp. lxxi–lxxx).

[10] Hooker refers to the International Horticultural Exhibition and Botanical Congress held in South Kensington, London, from 22 to 31 May 1866. See letter from J. D. Hooker, 13 May 1866 and nn. 10 and 25.

[11] CD's annotations are notes for his letter to Hooker of 31 May [1866].

From John Murray 30 May [1866][1]

50^{A}, Albemarle S^{t}. | W.
May 30

My Dear Sir

I have received your obliging note & reflecting upon the large & very important additions wch you have made in this Edition of your work on Species, wch I had observed myself in the proof sheets I propose to print 1500, instead of 1000 copies—[2] Counting on your assent.

You shall have 18 copies of the new Ed^{n} for yourself[3]

I remain | My Dear Sir | Yours very faithfully | John Murray

Ch Darwin Esq

DAR 171: 335

[1] The year is established by the relationship between this letter and the letter to John Murray, 28 May [1866].

[2] See letter to John Murray, 28 May [1866]. Murray had originally stated that he would print 1000 copies (see letter from John Murray, 25 May [1866] and n. 2).
[3] See Appendix IV for a presentation list for the fourth edition of *Origin*.

To J. D. Hooker 31 May [1866][1]

Leith Hill Place
May 31

returning home on Saturday[2]
My dear H.

Your list of Books & Papers seems to me very good; but my Orchid paper & Primula has too indirect a bearing to be worth noticing.—[3]

The Eozoon is one of most important facts,[4] & in much lesser degree the Archeopteryx[5] "Fritz Müller Fur Darwin" is perhaps the most important contribution.—[6]

I have worked into new Edit. of Origin the more important new facts & views known to me & if Grove thought it worth while, I could send him soon clean sheets by half-dozens with pencil marks to passages.[7] I thought of this when I saw him in London,[8] but hardly liked to offer this, nor do I now like to do so, as it seems pushing myself so forward.—

The new Edit. of Origin has caused me two great vexations; I forgot Bates' paper on variation, but I remembered in time his mimetic work, & now strange to say I find I have forgotten your Arctic paper.!![9] I know how it arose. I indexed for my bigger work[10] & never expected that a new Edition of Origin, w$^{d.}$ be wanted. I cannot say how all this has vexed me. Everything which I have read during last 4 years I find is quite washy in my mind.

I am not well today so farewell. | Yours affect. | C. Darwin

I now find that Owen claims to have been the originator of Natural Selection:[11] —Asa Gray always said he w$^{d.}$ do so.—[12]

I liked Caspary *very much*.—[13]

DAR 115: 290

[1] The year is established by the relationship between this letter and the letter from J. D. Hooker, 29 May 1866.
[2] CD went to Leith Hill Place in Surrey, the home of his sister Caroline and his brother-in-law Josiah Wedgwood III, on 29 May; he returned to Down on Saturday 2 June 1866 (Emma Darwin's diary (DAR 242)).
[3] William Robert Grove had asked Hooker for recent evidence supporting CD's theory for use in preparing his presidential address for the British Association for the Advancement of Science. See letter from J. D. Hooker, 29 May 1866 and nn. 3 and 4.
[4] In 1864, John William Dawson identified samples taken from pre-Silurian strata in eastern Canada as fossilised Foraminifera, single-celled protists with shells; he named the species *Eozoon canadense*, the 'Dawn animal from Canada' (Dawson 1864). Further samples were sent to William Benjamin Carpenter, an expert on Foraminifera, who confirmed Dawson's interpretation (Carpenter 1864). CD

added information on the discovery of *Eozoon canadense* to *Origin* 4th ed., p. 371, as substantiating his claim, made in *Origin*, p. 307, that life existed before the Silurian period. The interpretation of the samples as pre-Silurian fossils remained controversial, however (see, for example, Carpenter 1866, and King and Rowney 1866); and by the end of the century, comparisons with similar, more recent, formations indicated that the samples were mineral in origin (see Schopf 2000).

5 *Archaeopteryx*, a Jurassic fossil bird with reptilian features, was discovered in Bavaria in 1861 and described by Richard Owen (Owen 1862). For CD's interest in the discovery, see *Correspondence* vol. 11, letters to Hugh Falconer, 5 [and 6] January [1863] and 20 [January 1863]. In *Origin* 4th ed., p. 367, CD noted the discovery of *Archaeopteryx* as evidence against the view that the whole class of birds had suddenly come into existence during the Eocene period.

6 F. Müller 1864c, a study of the Crustacea, was supportive of CD's theory of transmutation. For CD's enthusiasm about the book, see *Correspondence* vol. 13.

7 In his letter of 25 May [1866], John Murray had informed CD that the printing of the fourth edition of *Origin* was nearly completed. Grove's address included discussions of *Eozoon canadense* and Fritz Müller's work (W. R. Grove 1866, p. lxxiv); it did not mention *Archaeopteryx*, or CD's work on orchids or *Primula*. See also letter from J. D. Hooker, 29 May 1866, n. 9.

8 CD met Grove in London on 29 April (see letter to W. R. Grove, [26 April 1866] and n. 3).

9 CD refers to Henry Walter Bates and Bates 1860, which discussed the variability of different species of butterflies, Bates 1861, and J. D. Hooker 1860a. See letter from J. D. Hooker, 29 May 1866, nn. 7 and 8.

10 CD refers to *Variation*. CD referred to J. D. Hooker 1860a in *Variation* 2: 256.

11 A review in the *London Review of Politics, Society, Literature, Art, and Science*, 28 April 1866, pp. 482–3, of the first two volumes of Richard Owen's *On the anatomy of vertebrates* (Owen 1866–8) claimed that even though Owen repudiated Darwinian views, he made 'a significant though partial admission ... of the truth of the principles of Natural Selection'; the reviewer quoted what he found to be the relevant passage in Owen's book. In a letter to the editor of the *London Review*, 5 May 1866, p. 516, Owen confirmed the 'essential identity of the passage cited with the basis of that [Darwinian] theory, the power, viz., of species to accommodate themselves, or bow to the influences of surrounding circumstances'; he added that the cited statement in his recent book was almost identical to that expressed in his 1850 paper on the *Dinornis* (Owen 1850), and that if he was thought to have followed the view of Darwin's *Origin*, the fact that he had published this work in 1850 actually placed CD in the position of 'adoptor'. Following Owen's letter, the editor wrote: 'So far as we can gather ... [Owen] denies the Darwinian doctrine, admits the accuracy of its basis, and claims to be the first to point out the truth of the principle on which it is founded.' CD revised his discussion of Owen's work in the historical sketch in the fourth edition of *Origin*, including the following passage (p. xviii):

> Professor Owen now believes that he promulgated the theory of natural selection in a passage read before the Zoological Society in February, 1850. . . . This belief in Professor Owen that he then gave to the world the theory of natural selection will surprise all those who are acquainted with the several passages in his works, reviews, and lectures, published since the 'Origin,' in which he strenuously opposes the theory; and it will please all those who are interested on this side of the question, as it may be presumed that his opposition will now cease. It should, however, be stated that the passage above referred to in the 'Zoological Transactions,' as I find on consulting it, applies exclusively to the extermination and preservation of animals, and in no way to their gradual modification, origination, or natural selection.

CD considerably modified this passage in the fifth edition (see Peckham ed. 1959, p. 66). See also Rupke 1994, pp. 246–7.

12 In an unsigned review of *Origin*, Asa Gray had stated that Owen might have been harbouring 'some transmutation theory of his own conceiving', which might yet see the light ([A. Gray] 1860, p. 115). See also *Correspondence* vol. 11, letters from Asa Gray, 26 May 1863 and 21 July 1863. For a discussion of Owen's views on evolution, see Rupke 1994, pp. 220–58.

13 Robert Caspary had visited CD at Down on 27 May 1866 (Emma Darwin's diary (DAR 242)).

To J. D. Hooker [31 May 1866][1]

My dear H.

I forgot in my morning's note[2] to say that you began your note[3] by saying that "the enclosed may amuse you"— Nothing was enclosed— I sh^{d}. much like to be amused, for my stomach & the whole Universe is this day demoniacal in my eyes—

C. D.

DAR 115: 290a

1 The date is established by the relationship between this letter and the letter to J. D. Hooker, 31 May [1866].
2 Letter to J. D. Hooker, 31 May [1866].
3 Letter from J. D. Hooker, 29 May 1866.

From J. D. Hooker [2 June 1866][1]

Kew.
Saturday

Dear Darwin

I grieve to hear of your state again.[2]

I assure you I am more grieved that you should vex yourself about the omissions as you call them—[3] As to mine they *prove nothing* & there was no call to notice them. they can only claim to be illustrations of using your methods.[4]

Ever Yr aff | J D Hooker

DAR 102: 78

1 The date is established by the relationship between this letter and the letter to J. D. Hooker, 31 May [1866]. In 1866, the first Saturday after 31 May was 2 June.
2 CD had complained of poor health and stomach troubles (see letters to J. D. Hooker, 31 May [1866] and [31 May 1866]).
3 CD had forgotten to include references to Bates 1860 and J. D. Hooker 1860a in his revisions for the fourth edition of *Origin* (see letter to J. D. Hooker, 31 May [1866] and n. 9).
4 Hooker had supported CD's theory in J. D. Hooker 1859 and J. D. Hooker 1860a (see letter from J. D. Hooker, 29 May 1866 and n. 8).

From Alphonse de Candolle[1] 3 June 1866

Londres
3 Juin 1866

Mon cher Monsieur

je viens de passer 15 jours à Londres de la manière la plus agréable. Une chose cependant me fait de la peine, mais comme elle resulte seulement d'une erreur de ma part je suis bien aise de vous l'expliquer. La première fois que j'ai assisté à une séance du Comité relatif au Congrès botanique j'ai demandé de vos nouvelles et si nous aurions le plaisir de vous voir.[2] Un de ces messieurs m'a repondu que vous etiez malade et il a ajouté (ou j'ai mal compris ce qu'il a dit en anglais) que vous étiez absent. J'ai cru que vous etiez allé dans le midi et avec beaucoup de regrets j'ai renoncé à l'idée de vous rencontrer. Ensuite j'ai appris par Mr Caspary[3] et par Sir Charles Lyell que vous êtes à la campagne, mais c'etait trop tard pour que je puisse aller vous presenter mes compliments. Permettez moi de vous dire que c'est un véritable sujet de regrets pour moi, d'autant plus que nous allons nous diriger, madame de Candolle[4] et moi, du côté d'Oxford et du nord de la Grande Bretagne, de sorte qu'il ne me sera pas possible de reparer ma négligence.

Sir Charles Lyell et vous n'avez peutêtre pas une idée très exacte de ce que Mr Lecoq a dit sur les plantes d'Auvergne et sur l'epoque glaciaire.[5] J'avais l'impression qu'il a surtout combattu l'idée d'un abaissement de température comme cause de l'extension des glaciers et qu'il a insisté sur la possibilité de grands glaciers quand il y a beaucoup d'humidité dans l'air. Je n'ai pas le souvenir qu'il ait nié completement l'epoque glaciaire.[6] Il a insisté sur la possibilité de transports de graines a de grandes distances par les vents, oiseaux etc, ce que j'ai examiné soigneusement, et je persiste, pour mon compte, a croire—qu'on a pris souvent des possibilités pour des réalités.[7] L'observation m'a montré que dans 2 ou 3 siècles, dans les pays où l'on a le plus observé, aucune phanerogame ne s'est naturalisée autrement qu'a la suite d'une action directe ou indirecte de *l'homme*. Il faudra lire le discours improvisé de Lecoq, dans le Compte rendu pour s'en faire mieux l'idée.[8]

Mr Ruprecht a publié en allemand dans le Bulletin de l'Academie de St Petersbourg un mêmoire curieux sur la terre noire du midi de la Russie.[9] Il prouve par les debris végétaux et par l'absence de tout dépôt marin ou autre sur cette terre que c'etait une île considérable remontant à l'époque tertiaire, où les graminées ont formé une énorme accumulation de detritus. Alors nous aurions là une source de nos végétaux d'Europe, avant et pendant l'epoque glaciaire. J'ai fait traduire cet article pour la Bibliotheque universelle de Genève, a fin de pouvoir mieux le comprendre, car à premiere lecture d'un texte allemand assez mal redigé je ne puis pas apprecier bien l'opinion de l'auteur.[10] J'ai lieu de croire Mr Ruprecht un bon observateur et ce quil dit meritera votre attention ainsi que celle de Sir Charles et des autres géologues—

Agréer, mon cher Monsieur, l'assurance de mon dévouement très sincère et tous mes vœux pour une amélioration dans votre santé | Alph. de Candolle

PS. Mes respects, je vous prie, à Madame Charles Darwin.

DAR 161: 12

CD ANNOTATION
2.10 aucune] *cross after, pencil*

1 For a translation of this letter, see Appendix I.

2 Candolle had delivered the presidential address at the opening meeting of the International Horticultural Exhibition and Botanical Congress on 23 May 1866 (A. de Candolle 1866). CD was on

the congress committee, but did not attend the meeting for reasons of health (see letter from M. T. Masters, March 1866, and letter to Friedrich Hildebrand, 16 May [1866]). CD had been invited to two dinner parties at which Candolle was to be present (letter from J. E. Gray, 9 April 1866, and letter from C. W. Dilke, 24 April 1866), and had asked Joseph Dalton Hooker to convey his regrets at not seeing Candolle in London (letter to J. D. Hooker, 16 May [1866] and n. 8).

3 Robert Caspary had attended the Botanical Congress, and had visited CD at Down (letter from Robert Caspary, 7 May 1866 and n. 3).

4 Jeanne-Victoire-Laure de Candolle.

5 See letter from M. T. Masters, 20 April 1866. Maxwell Tylden Masters had informed CD of a paper on the migration of plants to be delivered by Henri Lecoq at the International Horticultural Exhibition and Botanical Congress (Lecoq 1866). CD had been corresponding at length with Charles Lyell about plant dispersal during the glacial period (see, for example, letter to Charles Lyell, 7 February [1866]).

6 See letter from M. T. Masters, 20 April 1866 and n. 5.

7 See letter from M. T. Masters, 20 April 1866 and n. 6.

8 Candolle refers to Lecoq 1866.

9 Franz Josef Ruprecht's paper, 'Neuere geo-botanische Untersuchungen über den Tschornosjom' (New geo-botanical studies of the Russian black earth), appeared in the 1866 volume of the *Bulletin de l'Académie Impériale des Sciences de St.-Pétersbourg* (Ruprecht 1865).

10 Candolle refers to Ruprecht 1866. Ruprecht published mainly in Russian; for a bibliography of his works, see *Bulletin de l'Académie Impériale des Sciences de St.-Pétersbourg* 16 (1871): Supplement.

To J. D. Hooker [4 June 1866]

My dear Hooker.—

Many thanks for Asa Gray, as I always like to read him.[1] I was very uncomfortable for two days & all the world looked dismal to me, but everything looks brighter again now.—[2] I knew that *you* would not care a bit about my omission,[3] but I was much vexed at my own stupidity & strange forgetfulness; it seemed to me on that day like softening of the Brain! & I could have improved my own work by considering all your excellent remarks.[4] Well it is too late—

Cordial thanks & farewell— Ask Oliver to do a little favour for me.[5]

C. Darwin

Endorsement: 'June 4/66'
DAR 115: 291

1 Hooker evidently enclosed a letter from Asa Gray with his letter of [2 June 1866]. There is a letter from Gray to Hooker, dated 10 May 1866, in the archives of the Royal Botanic Gardens, Kew (Asa Gray letters, ff. 411–12).

2 CD had complained of poor health and stomach troubles (see letters to J. D. Hooker, 31 May [1866] and [31 May 1866]).

3 See letter to J. D. Hooker, [2 June 1866] and n. 3.

4 Hooker had supported CD's transmutation theory in his essay on Arctic flora (J. D. Hooker 1860a).

5 The favour was probably detailed in an enclosure. The enclosure has not been found; see, however, the letter from Daniel Oliver, 9 June 1866.

To William Turner 5 June [1866][1]

Down,
June 5,

My dear Sir

I thank you sincerely for having sent me so many of your papers, several of which have interested me much;[2] and the one on cellular pathology might have been written "to order," it was so exactly what I wanted to know.[3] It was a real pleasure to me to have had the good fortune to have met you at the Royal Soc. Soirée.[4]

My dear Sir | Yours sincerely | Ch. Darwin.

Copy
DAR 148: 150

[1] The year is established by the reference to the soirée at the Royal Society of London (see n. 4, below).

[2] Signed author's offprints of Turner 1863, 1864b, and 1866b are in the Darwin Pamphlet Collection–CUL. The papers are lightly annotated. Copies of Turner 1864a, 1865, and 1866a are also in the Darwin Pamphlet Collection–CUL, and are lightly annotated.

[3] CD discussed cell theory in his chapter on pangenesis in *Variation*, and cited Turner's paper on cellular pathology (Turner 1863) as supportive of the view that all cells develop from pre-existing cells (see *Variation* 2: 370 and Turner 1863, pp. 5–6). On CD's use of cell theory in his work on generation and heredity, see Geison 1969 and Bowler 1989, pp. 59–60.

[4] CD had attended a reception at the Royal Society on 28 April 1866 (Emma Darwin's diary (DAR 242)).

From Thomas Rivers 6 June 1866

Nurseries, Sawbridgeworth, Herts, | *Great Eastern Railway.*[1]
June 6/66

My Dear Sir/

By this post I trust you will receive a tin box in which are some flowers of the Cytissus purpureus elongatus[2] You will also find two "plates" or "shields" with the buds cut out these buds are of the variety of Negundo fraxinifolia with variegated leaves I did this in spring hoping to obtain a stain as occurred in the purple Laburnum[3]

I enclose a leaf of this variety & one from the stock *below* the bud; four buds were cut out on four separate stocks but no stain has taken place either above or below the buds

I am Dear Sir | Yrs. very truly | Thos. Rivers

DAR 176: 167

[1] In this letter and later ones, the location of Rivers's nursery is followed on the letterhead by: '*Harlow Station is the most convenient for passengers*'.

[2] See letter from Thomas Rivers, 17 May 1866 and n. 1. In *Variation* 1: 390, CD reported cases in which *Cytisus* hybrids had arisen spontaneously, including a hybrid of *C. purpureus* and *C. elongatus*.

[3] The name 'Negundo fraxinifolia' was never published; however, Rivers refers to the variegated tree, *Acer negundo* 'Variegatum', and to *Cytisus purpureus*. Rivers had been trying to determine the effect of scion wood on the coloration of stock tissue in *Acer*. See letter from Thomas Rivers, 17 May 1866 and n. 4.

To Thomas Rivers 8 June [1866][1]

Down. | Bromley. | Kent. S.E.
June 8th

My dear Sir

I thank you most cordially for the Cytisus, after examining which I forwarded to Prof. Caspary at Kœnigsberg;[2] so you have killed two birds with one act of kindness. The C. adami case gets more & more perplexing. I wish your experiments with the buds of the Negundo had succeeded.—[3] If you will not think me an insufferable bore, I wish you wd. observe whether Cytisus purpureus-elongatus produces any pods & inform me:—[4]

With many thanks | My dear Sir | Yours very sincerely | Ch. Darwin

John Wilson (Catalogue 63)

[1] The year is established by the relationship between this letter and the letter from Thomas Rivers, 6 June 1866.

[2] See letter from Thomas Rivers, 6 June 1866. CD was interested in Robert Caspary's research on *Cytisus adami* (now +*Laburnocytisus adami*). See letter to Thomas Rivers, 27 April [1866] and n. 4.

[3] See letter from Thomas Rivers, 6 June 1866 and n. 3. CD cited Rivers on the transmission of colour from the bud of a purple-leaved hazel to a rootstock of the common green-leaved hazel in *Variation* 1: 395.

[4] See letter from Thomas Rivers, 6 June 1866 and n. 2. In *Variation* 1: 388–90, CD discussed the viability of ovules and pollen in *Cytisus* hybrids, and reported a case of a sterile hybrid of *Cytisus purpureus* and *C. elongatus* that had been described by Alexander Carl Heinrich Braun (see Braun 1853, p. xxiii).

From Daniel Oliver 9 June 1866

Royal Gardens Kew
June 9/1866

My dear Sir/

Your plant is, I think, *Anchusa italica*[1]

Schacht's '*Lehrbuch*'[2] I am afraid you will not find at Linn. Soc. If you think it worth while referring to I suppose we might make an exception again to our stringent rule about lending books![3]

very sincerely yrs | Dl. Oliver

DAR 173: 32

[1] *Anchusa italica* (now treated as a synonym of *A. azurea*) is a Mediterranean herbaceous perennial that was introduced to British gardens in the nineteenth century (Coats 1968, pp. 15–17). CD evidently enclosed a request for Oliver to identify the plant in his letter to J. D. Hooker, [4 June 1866].

[2] Oliver refers to the *Lehrbuch der Anatomie und Physiologie der Gewächse* (Textbook on the anatomy and physiology of perennials) by Hermann Schacht (Schacht 1856–9). In his chapter on pangenesis in *Variation* 2: 384, CD cited Schacht 1856–9, 2: 12, on 'adventitious buds', which CD said might be formed 'almost anywhere' in plants.

[3] CD occasionally requested books from the library of the Royal Botanic Gardens, Kew, when he was unable to obtain a copy from the Linnean Society (see, for example, *Correspondence* vol. 8, letter to J. D. Hooker, 26 November [1860]).

From Robert Caspary [after 9 June 1866][1]

been open for some days certainly and 4 were not yet quite open), giving altogether 1182 grains, amongst them 30 bad ones; this gives *2,5/100* bad grains; but this result is not fair, as I took in account *all bad* grains I could find, but only those few good ones—comparatively speaking—which happened to be with the bad ones on the same fields of the Microscope. Therefore the percentage of bad grains is still less than 2,5.[2] I repeat the percentage of all:

	good grains	bad grains
Cytisus purpureus	92,3	7,7
— Laburnum	93,3	6,6
— alpinus[3]	96,3	3,7
— Watereri	79,7	20,3
— purp.-elong.	15,2	84,8
— Adami	97,5	2,5
	or rather more.	or rather less.[4]

The worst of all as regards the pollen is therefore Cytis. purp.-elong. then Cyt. Watereri; better than all Cytisus Adami. I found allways as often as I examined the pollen of any good species, more or less abortive grains. Sometimes one scarcely finds one *good* grain; this remarkable fact is shown by the pollen of Cochlearia armoracia, *of which I saw never any fruit!* although I looked for it since 1851.[5]

As regards Rhamnus Cathartica I have been rather unfortunate. I have 6 bushes of it in the botanic Garden here, about a week ago in full flower, but all male— I looked them over and over again, but I found no female flower or hermaphrodite upon them—[6] Fig 1 represents a mere male flower, which has a quite abortive germen;[7] Fig 2 a flower with a germen somewhat better, although not perfect—[8] Such germens I found only partly on one bush. No body could tell me here, where I could find a female or hermaphrodite bush— The places about Koenigsberg, in which the plant was formerly plentifull, are all gone; culture has eradicated all the woods in the neighbourhood of the town. I went on the 9th. June with 20 students to the only wood, about 7 engl. miles distant from here, in which I could expect to find Rham. cathart. I explained the object to the students; we searched attentively, but could find no trace of Rhamn. cathart.

That Cytisus has as many other Leguminosae (f. i. Lupinus) short and long stamens, the anthers of which are unequal, in the same flower, you will be aware. As regards the size of the pollen I could find no difference in the two sets of anthers[9]

[Enclosure]

Rhamnus cathartica L.
♂ h.b.rgm. 7.6.1866[10]

Fig 1

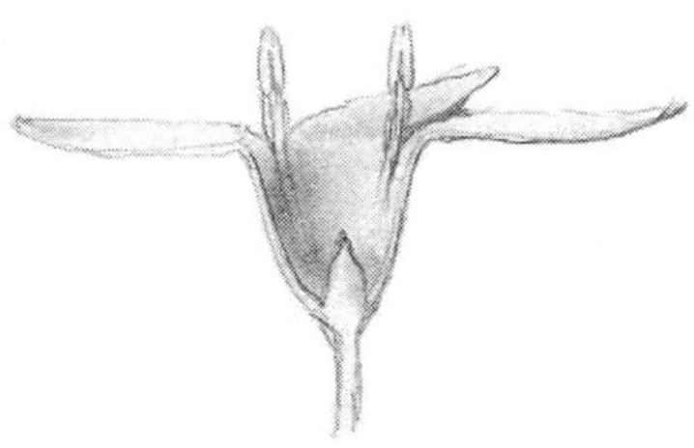

germen tertiam calicis tubis partem aequans. Pistillum omnino abortivum. Antherae defloratae! Germen abortivum, tamen styli indoles adest.[11]

Fig 2

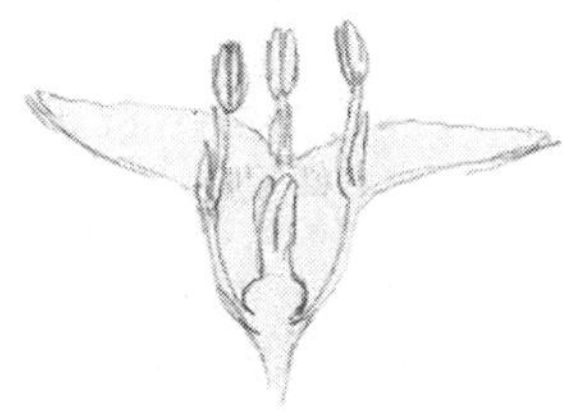

Frutex ♂ h. b. rgm.
Stigmata haud expansa: Pistillum tubum calicis fere aequans[12]

AL incomplete
DAR 109: A81; DAR 111: B45, B48b, B48c

CD ANNOTATIONS
1.1 been … 1851. 2.5] *crossed red crayon*
2.5 1851.] *Line across page after, blue crayon*
3.1 As regards] *opening square bracket red crayon*
3.4 Fig. 1 … one bush. 3.6] *double scored ink*
3.7 The places … anthers 4.3] *crossed pencil*; 'I have specimen of Rhamnus' *added pencil*[13]
Enclosure: expansa] 'To left' *pencil*[14]

[1] The date is established by the date of the enclosure, and by Caspary's remark that he searched for *Rhamnus cathartica* on 9 June.

[2] Caspary refers to the probable viability, based on external appearance, of pollen in *Cytisus adami* (now + *Laburnocytisus adami*).

[3] Now called *Laburnum alpinum*.

[4] CD reported Caspary's findings on the percentage of bad pollen in *Cytisus* species in *Variation* 1: 388. CD added that such a high proportion of good pollen in the hybrid *C. adami* was contrary to what usually occurs in hybrids, including those of the same genus, '*C. purpureo-elongatus*', and *C. alpino-laburnum* (called '*C. Watereri*' by Caspary; now *Laburnum* x *watereri*, a hybrid of *L. alpinum* and *L. anagyroides*). This fact, together with the irregular shape of the ovules in *C. adami*, was taken by Caspary as evidence that the species was a graft-hybrid. For CD's interest in graft-hybrids, see the letter to Thomas Rivers, 27 April [1866] and n. 4. Caspary had visited CD on 27 May 1866 (Emma Darwin's diary (DAR 242)); CD had forwarded flowers of '*Cytisus purpureo-elongatus*' to Caspary that he had received from Rivers (see letter to Thomas Rivers, 8 June [1866]).

[5] A species commonly known as horseradish.

[6] CD was interested in the different flower forms of *Rhamnus cathartica*. See letter from W. E. Darwin, [7 May – 11 June 1866] and n. 3.

[7] 'Germen': ovary (*OED*).

[8] See Caspary's sketches. CD and his son William eventually concluded that the species had two male and two female forms, distinguished by the length of their pistils. CD included Caspary's drawings in *Forms of flowers*, p. 294, where they are captioned 'short-styled male' and 'long-styled male'.

[9] For CD's interest in pollen-grains of different sizes in heteromorphic species, see the letter from W. E. Darwin, 8 May [1866] and n. 5.

[10] 'h.b.rgm' = possibly an abbreviation of 'hortus botanicus regium', indicating that the specimen was from the botanic gardens at Königsberg.

[11] 'Ovary one-third as long as calyx tube. Pistil entirely abortive. Anthers withered! Ovary abortive, nevertheless rudimentary style is present.'

[12] 'Shrub' (see n. 10, above). 'Stigmas not at all spread out: pistil nearly as long as calyx tube'.

[13] CD had received male flowers of *Rhamnus cathartica* from William with his letter of [7 May – 11 June 1866].

[14] CD's annotation refers to the position of the sketch in *Forms of flowers*, p. 294.

From George Henslow 11 June [1866][1]

10 Sth Crescent | Bedford Sq | W.C.
11th June.

Dear Mr Darwin

I greatly regret my carelessness in not writing again to tell you, I did *not* send the books, but have them still.[2] The reason was, that when I took my M.S.S. to Hardwicke, he said he would put it in type *immediately* & send me the proofs in a few days.[3] Then I thought, If that was the case, I had better keep the books till the Proof came, in case I might have to refer to them again: I did so, & hoping to get the proof, as he promised I did not write, but it only arrived on Saty. night last!

I am much obliged for your kindness in so readily acceding to my request to look over the sheets which I send enclosed. Please do not hesitate to make any disparaging comments you may think fit; or any suggestion you may deem desirable

I have added a little postscript for your consideration as to whether you would allow me to subjoin.[4]

I should be obliged by the return of the proof at your earliest convenience as publishers are apt to get rather importunate sometimes!

AL
DAR 166: 161

[1] The year is established by the relationship between this letter and the letter from George Henslow, 18 May 1866.
[2] CD had lent Henslow books for an article on Charles Victor Naudin's research on hybridity (Henslow 1866b). See letter from George Henslow, 18 May 1866 and n. 2.
[3] Robert Hardwicke was the publisher of *Popular Science Review*. The journal was published quarterly; Henslow's article appeared in the third issue for 1866.
[4] See letter to George Henslow, 12 June [1866] and n. 3.

To George Henslow 12 June [1866][1]

Down. | Bromley. | Kent. S.E.
June 12th

My dear Mr Henslow.

I have read over your Proofs, & have appended some criticisms.—[2] I think your paper will do good by calling attention to subject. Several sentences appear to me to require making clear.—

It would really be of no use, I shd. prefer your not stating that I had read over the proofs, as it makes me to certain extent responsible; & I am not sure that I shd agree with all.[3]

I shd be much obliged if you would inform me, whether Naudin does really say that *ovules* (*not* seed) of Hybrid Luffa & Cucumis are imperfect.—[4]

Kindly tell me when the books are sent to 6. Queen Anne St & be so good as to direct them plainly.[5] If sent there on Thursday morning I could get one of my servants who will be in London to call for them— But do not send them, if not finished with.—

In Haste | Yours very sincerely | C. Darwin

Fitzwilliam Museum, Cambridge

[1] The year is established by the relationship between this letter and the letter from George Henslow, 11 June [1866].
[2] Henslow had sent CD the proof-sheets for an article on Charles Victor Naudin's research on hybridity (Henslow 1866b) with his letter of 11 June [1866]. For an indication of the nature of CD's comments, see the letter from George Henslow, [13 or 14 June 1866].
[3] In his letter to CD of 11 June [1866], Henslow had asked whether he might add a postscript to his article, evidently acknowledging that CD had read it in proof.
[4] Henslow had reported that, according to Naudin, sterility in hybrids was a result of defective ovules (Henslow 1866b, p. 307). Henslow's article accurately summarised the discussion in Naudin 1863, pp. 181–2, as follows: 'In order to account for the sterility of hybrids, M. Naudin remarks that we must, in all probability, go to the *ovules* to look for the cause, as the pistil often presents every sign of fertility, while the ovules, either all, or some only, remain abortive, as is the case with *Luffa acutangulo* + *cylindrica* and *Cucumis Meloni* + *trigonus*' (Henslow 1866b, p. 307).

[5] See letter from George Henslow, 11 June [1866] and n. 2. Six Queen Anne Street, London, was the address of CD's brother, Erasmus Alvey Darwin.

To Carl Wilhelm von Nägeli 12 June [1866][1]

Down Bromley, | Kent S.E.
June 12

Dear Sir

I hope you will excuse the liberty which I take in writing to you. I have just read though imperfectly your "Enstehung & Begriff" & have been so greatly interested by it that I have sent it to be translated, as I am a poor German Scholar.[2] I have just finished a new edition of my origin which will be translated into German,[3] & my object in writing to you is to say that if you should see this edition you would think that I had borrowed from you without acknowledgement, two discussions on the beauty of flowers & fruit; but I assure you every word was printed off before I had opened your pamphlet.[4] Should you like to possess a copy of either the German or English New Edition I should be proud to send one.[5] I may add, with respect to the beauty of Flowers, that I have already hinted the same views as you hold in my paper on Lythrum.[6]

Many of your criticisms on my views are the best which I have met with, but I could answer some at least to my own satisfaction;[7] & I regret extremely that I had not read your pamphlet before printing my new edition— On one or two points, I think you have a little misunderstood me, though I daresay I have not been cautious in expressing myself. The remark which has struck me most is that on the position of the leaves not having been acquired thro' natural selection from not being of any special importance to the plant.[8] I well remember being formerly troubled by an analagous difficulty, namely the position of the ovules their anatropous condition &c.[9]

It was owing to forgetfulness that I did not notice this difficulty in the Origin. Although I can offer no explanation of such facts, & only hope to see that they may be explained, yet I hardly see how they support the doctrine of some law of necessary development for it is not clear to me that a plant with its leaves placed at some particular angle or with its ovules in some particular position, thus stands higher than another plant.[10] But I must apologise for troubling you with these remarks.

As I much wish to possess your photograph, I take the liberty of enclosing my own[11] & with sincere respect I remain | Dear Sir | Yours faithfully | Ch. Darwin.

Copy
DAR 147: 181

[1] The year is established by the reference to Nägeli 1865 and to publication of the fourth edition of *Origin* (see n. 3 below).

[2] CD refers to *Entstehung und Begriff der naturhistorischen Art* (The origin and concept of natural historical species; Nägeli 1865), in which Nägeli discussed the mechanisms and principles operative in the

development and transmutation of species; a heavily annotated copy is in the Darwin Pamphlet Collection–CUL. A handwritten English translation is also in the Darwin Archive–CUL; it contains CD's annotations and a list of notes. The translation was probably made by Camilla Ludwig, a former governess at Down House, who was occasionally employed to translate German works (see, for example, *Correspondence* vol. 13, letter to Fritz Müller, 10 August [1865] and n. 1). An entry in CD's Classed account books (Down House MS) for 16 May 1866 records a payment of £1 to 'Miss Ludwig' under the heading 'Science'.

[3] The fourth edition of *Origin* was published in 1866; the third German edition (Bronn and Carus trans. 1867) was based on this edition.

[4] In the fourth edition of *Origin*, CD added several pages (pp. 238–41) on the subject of beauty in relation to natural selection, including a discussion (pp. 239–40) of brightly coloured flowers and fruit as adaptations for attracting insects, birds, or other animals. The same point is reiterated in the concluding chapter, p. 557. See also Peckham ed. 1959, pp. 370–1, 737. Nägeli had described observations and experiments that indicated that plants were rendered attractive to insects by their brightly coloured flowers, leaves, or fruit, or by their scent or nectar (Nägeli 1865, pp. 21–5).

[5] Nägeli's name is not on CD's presentation list for the fourth edition of *Origin* (see Appendix IV); no presentation list for the third German edition (Bronn and Carus trans. 1867) has been found.

[6] In 'Three forms of *Lythrum salicaria*', CD described adaptations in flowers that facilitated pollination by insects, concluding that the features he described provided 'one more instance of the supreme dominating power of insects over all the minor structural details of flowers' (p. 176; *Collected papers* 2: 112).

[7] Nägeli regarded natural selection as one mechanism of species development, but argued that it was insufficient by itself to explain various features of plants. For Nägeli's criticisms of CD's theory, see Nägeli 1865, pp. 26–30. See also letter to Fritz Müller, 23 May 1866.

[8] In his annotated copy of Nägeli 1865, CD noted as a 'very good objection' the point that various morphological structures in plants, such as phyllotaxy, conferred no apparent competitive advantage and so could not have developed as a result of natural selection (Nägeli 1865, pp. 27–8). On Nägeli's 'misunderstanding' of CD's theory, see also the letter to J. V. Carus, 21 November 1866 and n. 6.

[9] In 1863, CD had asked Daniel Oliver whether the ovules of *Primula* were 'anatropal' (inverted with respect to the funicle), or 'amphitropal' (attached laterally to the funicle). See *Correspondence* vol. 11, letter to Daniel Oliver, [12 April 1863], and letter from Daniel Oliver, 14 April 1863. See also letter to J. V. Carus, 21 November 1866.

[10] Nägeli argued that 'higher' species evolved through the operation of a 'perfectibility principle' ('Vervollkommnungsprincip'; what CD refers to here as a 'law of necessary development'): a tendency within each organism to develop more complicated structures. Nägeli claimed that this principle operated in conjunction with the natural selection of useful variations (see Nägeli 1865, pp. 16–17, 28–30). CD added a discussion of Nägeli 1865 to *Origin* 5th ed., p. 151, noting that, according to Nägeli, natural selection would not act on the arrangement of leaves on the axis or on the position of the ovules (see Peckham ed. 1959, pp. 233–4).

[11] CD probably sent the photograph taken by his son William Erasmus Darwin in 1864 (see *Correspondence* vol. 12, frontispiece and letter from W. E. Darwin, [19 May 1864]).

From George Henslow [13 or 14 June 1866][1]

10 South Crescent | Bedford Sq | W.C.

My dear Mr Darwin,

Very many thanks for your kindness in looking over the proof & for your valuable criticisms.[2]

I cannot make out however, whether *you* believe in the fact of *reversion*.—[3] Of course on the whole of this subject, *I* personally have no opinion to offer at all: as I am simply endeavouring to arrive at the present position of the subject from various authors:—& as to *reversion*, came to the conclusion stated in my paper, from the various works on the subject. If however *you* think it a fact, I will modify my state^ts: accordingly (without, of course, alluding to you)

I should be much obliged, however, if you would kindly give me your positive opinion on that point: as it is a very important one, since it is **the** one Naudin especially observed.[4]

the 3 passages you marked as "obscure" oddly enough, were all quotations from *Berkeleys* Translations in Journal of Hort: Soc: Jan/66 I have endeavoured to elucidate them, as far as I can.[5]

I have felt *immense* difficulty in drawing up this paper, as I have not had a *scrap* of experience of my own—so that I greatly feared it would be defective, yet, as you kindly suggest, if it call attention to the subject that is all I can desire or wish to expect.—[6]

If you would give me y^r opinion on "*reversion*" as soon as possible I will be much obliged.

I have looked at Naudin's remarks on "*ovules*". & find it to be correct— Offered, however, as a matter to be provd. (p 181–2: in Nouvelles recherches sur l'hybridite)[7]

Y^rs truly | G Henslow

DAR 166: 158

CD ANNOTATION

7.1 Offered, . . . provd. 7.2] *double scored blue crayon*

1 The date range is established by the relationship between this letter and the letters to George Henslow, 12 June [1866] and 15 [June 1866].

2 CD had commented on the proof pages for Henslow 1866b; see letter to George Henslow, 12 June [1866].

3 In a brief discussion of reversion in *Origin*, pp. 13–15, CD questioned the widely held view that domestic varieties invariably reverted to their aboriginal stock when they ran wild, stating, more cautiously: 'our varieties certainly do occasionally revert in some of their characteristics to ancestral forms' (*ibid.*, p. 15). He also discussed the sporadic appearance in domestic pigeon breeds of features characteristic of the parent rock-pigeon as an example of reversion (*ibid.*, pp. 159–61).

4 In his paper, Henslow discussed work by Charles Victor Naudin (Naudin 1858, 1863, and 1864) that argued that all hybrids inevitably reverted to their parent forms; Henslow concluded: 'Naudin's experiments . . . have very satisfactorily shown that reversions do take place, at least amongst cultivated plants; though it would seem to occur rarely among individuals in a wild state' (Henslow 1866b, p. 313). Henslow remarked that, as Naudin had failed to protect his hybrid plants from insects, the possibility that they were pollinated by the parent forms remained open. Henslow also criticised Naudin for having worked exclusively with cultivated plants, in which characteristics were less stable than in wild forms (*ibid.*, pp. 311–13). CD had previously criticised Naudin's experiments for ignoring insect agency (see, for example, *Correspondence* vol. 10, letter to J. D. Hooker, 30 [June

1862] and n. 11, and *Correspondence* vol. 12, letter to J. D. Hooker, 22 [May 1864]), and for focusing exclusively on cultivated plants (see *Correspondence* vol. 13, letter to M. E. Wichura, 3 February [1865]).

5 Henslow quoted from Miles Joseph Berkeley's translation of Naudin 1864, which appeared in the *Journal of the Royal Horticultural Society* for January 1866, pp. 1–9 (see Henslow 1866b, pp. 310–11).

6 See letter to George Henslow, 12 June [1866].

7 See letter to George Henslow, 12 June [1866], and n. 4.

From J. T. Moggridge 14 June [1866][1]

7.a. Eastbourne Terr. | W.
June 14

Dear Mr. Darwin

I should very much like to spend the Sunday with you at Down—[2]

I shall take the earlier of the two trains you mention, or at any rate try to take it, thus having the later one to rely upon in case of losing the first.

With many thanks believe me | yrs. very sincerely | J. Traherne Moggridge.

DAR 171: 208

1 The year is established by the date of Moggridge's visit to Down (see n. 2, below).

2 The letter inviting Moggridge to Down has not been found; see, however, the letter from J. T. Moggridge, 25 May [1866]. According to Emma Darwin's diary (DAR 242), Moggridge arrived on 23 June and left on 25 June 1866.

To George Henslow 15 [June 1866][1]

Down. | Bromley. | Kent. S.E.
15th

My dear Mr Henslow.

I do most strongly believe in Reversion. There can be no shadow of doubt both in uncrossed & in crossed varieties.— I have seen many instances.[2]

The evidence of Kölreuter & Gärtner is distinct for Hybrids, & **some** of Naudin's cases leave no doubt whatever in my mind.—[3] I have been writing a chapter on subject, & the cases of Reversion in ordinary Hybrids appeared so clear that I have not thought it worth while to give instances, only references.[4] So that I have discussed only more curious cases. Think over that of Cytisus adami—[5]

I had forgotten whether Herbert gave cases.[6] But I know that he believed to largest extent in Reversion, as I remember in conversation[7] & as I think is stated in his remarks on stripes in Asses & Horses—[8] but this latter case does not concern you, as it does not refer to Hybrids.— I fully believe that Gärtner is right when he says that Reversion occurs only rarely in hybrids made from plants, *which have not been cultivated*[9] Hence wide difference in Wichura's & Naudin's results.—[10]

Your's very sincerely | Ch. Darwin

DAR Library: tipped into George Henslow's copy of *Variation*

[1] The date is established by the relationship between this letter and the letter from George Henslow, 19 June 1866.

[2] See letter from George Henslow, [13 or 14 June 1866] and n. 3; see also n. 4, below.

[3] CD discussed the works of Joseph Gottlieb Kölreuter, Karl Friedrich von Gärtner, and Charles Victor Naudin for their bearing on reversion in *Variation* 1: 392 and 2: 36–7, 48–50.

[4] CD devoted chapter 13 in *Variation* to reversion, and gave numerous examples in other chapters. CD entered in his 'Journal' (Appendix II) for 10 May 1866, 'began going over Ch. XIII of Dom. Animals'; see letter to J. D. Hooker, 16 May [1866] and n. 14.

[5] For CD's interest in the graft hybrid *Cytisus adami* (now +*Laburnocytisus adamii*), some tissues of which often revert to those of one or other parent, see the letter to Robert Caspary, 21 February [1866] and n. 3, and the letter from Robert Caspary, 25 February 1866 and nn. 4 and 9.

[6] William Herbert published many works on hybrid plants; CD had discussed Herbert 1837 and 1846 in detail in the manuscript for his 'big book' on species (see *Natural selection*). Heavily annotated copies of Herbert 1837 and 1846 are in the Darwin Library–CUL (see *Marginalia* 1: 372–6). CD cited Herbert on cases of reversion in *Variation* 1: 377, 388.

[7] CD corresponded with Herbert on reversion in 1839 (see *Correspondence* vol. 2), and visited him in 1845 and 1847 (see *Correspondence* vol. 3, letter to Charles Lyell, 8 October [1845] and n. 5, and *Correspondence* vol. 4, letter to J. D. Hooker, [2 June 1847]).

[8] The example of a dun pony with a black stripe down its back is mentioned in Herbert 1837, p. 340, as evidence that the horse may have originated from the wild ass. CD had referred to this case in his unpublished 'big book' on species (see *Natural selection*, p. 332, n. 2). In *Origin*, pp. 163–7, and *Variation* 1: 55–64 and 2: 41–3, CD discussed stripes in asses and horses as cases of partial reversion in colour to a common progenitor.

[9] CD refers to Gärtner 1849, pp. 474, 582.

[10] Naudin's claim that all hybrids inevitably undergo reversion had been based exclusively on experiments with cultivated plants. However, Max Ernst Wichura's experiments on uncultivated hybrid willows had led him to question whether hybrids ever reverted to their parent forms (Wichura 1865, p. 23). CD discussed Wichura's and Naudin's findings in *Variation* 2: 50, and explained the discrepancy in their results using Gärtner's observation of the comparative frequency of reversions in hybrids whose parent species had long been cultivated. See also *Origin* 4th ed., pp. 332–3, and letter from George Henslow, [13 or 14 June 1866], n. 4.

To Andrew Crombie Ramsay 15 June [1866][1]

Down. | Bromley. | Kent. S.E.
June 15

Dear Ramsay

I am very much obliged to you for your kind present of the Geological Survey of N. Wales.[2] I shall not be able to read it immediately but I have no doubt when I do that I shall find much of interest to me, for this has been the case with all that I have read of your writing

Looking over the pages makes me long to be able to wander over some of the mountains with which I was formerly familiar but did not understand.[3]

Believe me dear Ramsay | yours sincerely | Charles Darwin

LS
DAR 261.9: 8

[1] The year is established by the reference to Ramsay 1866 (see n. 2 below).

[2] Ramsay evidently sent CD volume 3 of the *Memoirs of the Geological Survey of Great Britain and of the Museum of Economic Geology in London*, which contained his memoir, 'The geology of North Wales' (Ramsay 1866). He had informed CD that the work was about to go to press in his letter of 18 August 1864 (*Correspondence* vol. 12).

[3] CD had done his first geological field work on a tour of North Wales led by Adam Sedgwick in 1831; he had returned in 1842 to study evidence of glaciation (see *Correspondence* vols. 1 and 2). For CD's other visits to Wales, see Freeman 1978, p. 286, and Lucas 2002a and 2002b.

From W. E. Darwin [18 June 1866][1]

Southampton
Monday.

My Dear Father,

I send you the 3 kinds of Buckthorn.[2] I went to the place yesterday, and marked some shrubs, there seemed about as many female trees, as there were of the other two put together As soon as I have examined pollen etc of the two I will let you know.

Your affect son W E Darwin

DAR 109: A70

CD ANNOTATIONS
Top of letter: '*[*Abor^{d}*]* | **abort** *[*ovules*]* | $\frac{1}{2}$ *[*fms*]*' *red crayon*[3]
Verso: 'barely $\frac{12}{7000}$ *[*altho looks*]* beautifully *[*impressive*]* | $\frac{12}{7000}$ or $\frac{12-13}{7000}$ middle sp p' *pencil*[4]

[1] The date is established by the relationship between this letter and the letter to W. E. Darwin, 19 [June 1866]. In 1866, 18 June was the Monday before 19 June.

[2] William had promised to send specimens of the different flowers produced by *Rhamnus cathartica* (buckthorn) from the Isle of Wight (see letter from W. E. Darwin, [7 May – 11 June 1866] and n. 3). William and CD initially thought that the species might have hermaphrodite, as well as male and female forms; however, they later determined that the plant had two male and two female forms (see letter to W. E. Darwin, 19 [June 1866] and n. 4, and letter from W. E. Darwin, 20 June [1866] and n. 6).

[3] CD described the partially aborted pistil in the male flowers of *Rhamnus cathartica* in a note dated 19 June 1866 in DAR 109: A41. See letter to W. E. Darwin, 19 [June 1866] and n. 4.

[4] These annotations refer to the size in inches of pollen-grains in the different flower forms of *Rhamnus cathartica*. See letter to W. E. Darwin, 22 June [1866].

From George Maw 18 June 1866

Benthall Hall, | nr. Broseley.
June 18th. 1866.

Dear Sir

Some months ago you asked me whether any examples of *bud* sports had come under my notice[1] & think therefore you will like to have the accompanying fragment of a Fern-leaved Beech bearing a branch of the ordinary form of foliage[2] It is from the garden of Mr W De Crewdson of Helme Lodge Nr Kendal[3] The tree I am informed is about twenty years old, an occasional leaf of intermediate character occurs here & there, but for the most part the branches bearing the two forms are well marked & distinct.

Believe me Dr Sir | very truly yrs | George Maw

C Darwin Esq.

DAR 171: 101

[1] The letter to Maw has not been found. CD had written to several correspondents in March and April for information on bud variations in which characteristics of parent or ancestral species appeared either in pure or blended form (see letter to Robert Caspary, 4 March 1866, letter to J. D. Hooker, 4 April [1866], and letter to Asa Gray, 16 April [1866]).

[2] Maw refers to *Fagus sylvatica* 'Asplenifolia', a graft hybrid that bears both fern-like leaves and normal leaves of the species. Adventitious buds often give rise to shoots bearing normal leaves, and intermediate forms of leaves may also occur (A. Mitchell 1996, p. 233). For CD's interest in graft hybrids, see the letter to Thomas Rivers, 27 April [1866] and n. 4.

[3] William Dilwerth Crewsden resided at Helm Lodge, Kendal, Westmorland (*Post Office directory of Northumberland*).

To W. E. Darwin 19 [June 1866][1]

Down
19th

My dear old W.

very many thanks for Rhamnus, which I have so long wished to see.—[2] As a species it seems one step less unisexual than Holly.[3] It wd be interesting to know whether the male or Hermaphrodite flowers with rather longer pistil bear any fruit— As stamens are in female far more rudimentary than the pistil is in the male,, at least in the Hermaphrodite, flowers,[4] the species probably once existed in state of Thyme, ie, some plants, hermaphrodite & some female, but none as pure males—[5]

And this is just what I wanted to know— I see no evidence of its having once been dimorphic like Primula.—[6]

You are the man to do a job thoroughily

Your affect Father | C. Darwin

Do not forget the white Broom.—[7]

Thanks about N.W. R. Shares. I shall sell. I can get £113 for each share.—[8]

DAR 185: 14

[1] The date is established by the relationship between this letter and CD's note, dated 19 June 1866, on *Rhamnus cathartica* (see n. 4, below).

[2] See letters from W. E. Darwin, [7 May – 11 June 1866] and [18 June 1866] and n. 2.

[3] CD had been interested in the English holly (*Ilex aquifolium*) as 'a good case of gradation' in the development of separate sexes: the plant's female flowers had fully formed stamens, but no pollen

(*Correspondence* vol. 9, letter to Asa Gray, 17 September [1861]). In *Forms of flowers*, pp. 297–8, CD placed *Ilex aquifolium* among plants that either showed a tendency to become dioecious or had apparently become dioecious 'within a recent period'.

4 On examining the flowers, CD considered that the third form of *Rhamnus cathartica* was a male, and not a hermaphrodite. In a note dated 19 June 1866 (DAR 109: A41) CD wrote: 'W. sent me fl. of *Rhamnus Catharticus*. . . . Female fl. with very rudimentary stamens. . . . Male fl. with rudiment of pistil— . . . Thirdly a kind of Herm: with quite [*interl*] small but larger pistil than in male fl. good sized stamens & petals as in male fl. It is apparently male with pistil not so completely aborted'. CD's further notes on *R. cathartica* and other *Rhamnus* species are in DAR 109: A42–4, 50, and DAR 111: A19, B8, 45–6, 48b.

5 Species of thyme were taken by CD to be representative of a class of plants he later called 'gynodioecious' (see *Correspondence* vols. 12 and 13, and *Forms of flowers*, pp. 298–303).

6 CD had discovered the phenomenon later called heterostyly in *Primula*, in which the existence of two flower-forms (long-styled and short-styled) assists cross-pollination (see 'Dimorphic condition in *Primula*' and *Forms of flowers*, pp. 14–50).

7 Information on the white broom (*Cytisus multiflorus*) may have been in the missing portion of the letter from W. E. Darwin, [7 May – 11 June 1866]. William's notes on *C. multiflorus* are in DAR 186: 43. On CD's interest in dichogamy in the common broom, see the letter to George Henslow, [before 19 April 1866], and the letter from W. E. Darwin, 8 May [1866] and n. 2; on his interest in hybrid brooms, see the letter to George Henslow, 15 [June 1866] and n. 5.

8 The reference to 'N.W.R.' shares may have been in the missing portion of the letter from W. E. Darwin, [7 May – 11 June 1866]. From 1846, CD's Investment book (Down House MS) lists shares of London & North West Railway under Emma Darwin's trust property. CD's Investment book (Down House MS) records £72 18*s.* 9*d.* for sale of 'N.W.R.' shares on 21 June 1866 under the heading 'Capital paid up'.

From George Henslow 19 June 1866

10 South Crescent | Bedford Sq: | W.C.
June 19/66

My dear M^r. Darwin,

Very many thanks for yr kind letter; I have altered my paper accordingly somewhat materially.—[1]

Again, thanks for the books so kindly lent.[2] I have taken them to y^r Brothers, 6. Queen Anne St—with your address upon them.[3] & moreover told the footman they were for you.—

Hoping y^r health is improving, believe me | D^r. Mr Darwin | Y^rs very truly | Geo. Henslow

DAR 166: 162

1 In his letter to Henslow of 15 [June 1866], CD had replied to Henslow's questions on reversion. Henslow also refers to Henslow 1866b, the proof-sheets of which he had sent to CD for comment (see letter from George Henslow, 11 June [1866]).

2 CD had lent Henslow books on hybridism (see letter from George Henslow, 18 May 1866 and n. 2).

3 CD requested that Henslow return his books to his brother, Erasmus Alvey Darwin, who lived at 6 Queen Anne Street, London (see letter to George Henslow, 12 June [1866]).

From W. E. Darwin 20 June [1866][1]

Southampton
June 20

My Dear Father

I enclose you some orders for dividends for your signature please forward them to Uncle Ras,[2] and ask him to sign & post them.

I cannot help thinking the Rhamnus is a case of dimorphic becoming diœcious;[3] I will tell more in a day or two but I have not time today, & George & Edmund come here tomorrow.[4] I thought it must be as you say at first, but I found that the pollen of long pistilled male was the largest, which seemed odd if that was *less* of a male flower than the short pistilled;[5] so I examined the female flowers, & I think I have found two sizes among them corresponding to the two males flowers.[6] Mem. I am prob^ly. wrong; will write in a day or two

your affection— | W. E. Darwin

DAR 109: A77

CD ANNOTATIONS
1.1 I enclose . . . post them 1.2] *crossed blue pencil*
2.3 I found . . . largest 2.4] *underl red pencil*

1 The year is established by the relationship between this letter and the letter to W. E. Darwin, 19 [June 1866].

2 The reference is to Erasmus Alvey Darwin.

3 In his letter to William of 19 [June 1866], CD stated that he thought *Rhamnus cathartica* had once existed in hermaphrodite and female forms, and that he saw no evidence that it had ever been dimorphic.

4 William refers to his brother George Howard Darwin and their cousin Edmund Langton.

5 In his research on *Primula*, CD had observed that pollen-grains from short-styled forms were consistently larger than those from long-styled forms (see 'Dimorphic condition in *Primula*', pp. 78–9; *Collected papers* 2: 45–7; see also 'Three forms of *Lythrum salicaria*', pp. 178, 190–1; *Collected papers* 2: 113, 123, 125). In *Forms of flowers*, p. 294, he noted William's 'very remarkable' observation that larger pollen-grains were produced in male flowers with longer, rather than shorter, pistils, in *Rhamnus cathartica*. CD added that heterostyled plants tended to produce larger pollen-grains in flowers with shorter pistils, but that *R. cathartica* showed no evidence of having ever been heterostyled.

6 William's notes on *Rhamnus cathartica* are in DAR 186: 43 and contain sketches of the four flower forms. In *Forms of flowers*, pp. 294–5, CD described *Rhamnus cathartica* as dioecious, with each sex having two 'sub-forms'. See also letter from W. E. Darwin, [18 June 1866] and n. 2, and letter to W. E. Darwin, 19 [June 1866] and n. 4.

From W. E. Darwin 21 June [1866][1]

Southton
June 21

My Dear Father,

I send 2 females with outlines of my sketches, the 4 females outlined are from 4 different trees.[2]

I have all particulars down about them if you care for them.
I should it say it certainly was case of dimorphic become diœcious[3]
Broomfield says "dioecious said to be polygamous".[4]

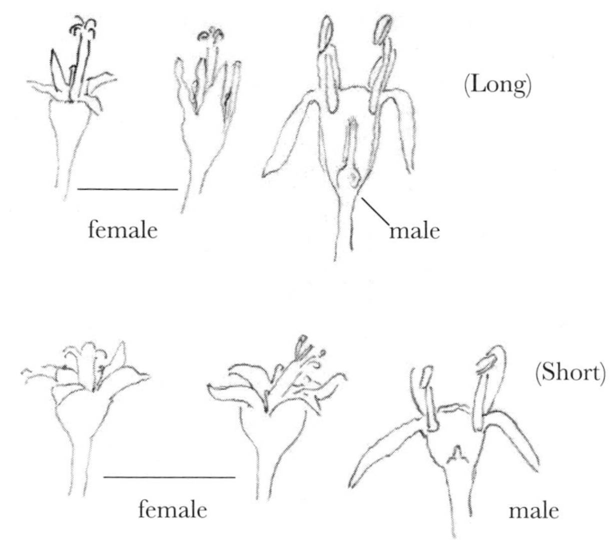

AL incomplete
DAR 109: A80

CD ANNOTATIONS
1.1 4 females] 'flowers' *added pencil*; *erased*
End of letter: 'Primordial'[5] *pencil*

[1] The year is established by the relationship between this letter and the letter from W. E. Darwin, 20 June [1866].
[2] William's original sketches of *Rhamnus cathartica*, together with extensive notes on each specimen, are in DAR 186: 43.
[3] See letter from W. E. Darwin, 20 June [1866] and nn. 3 and 6.
[4] William refers to the description of *Rhamnus cathartica* in Bromfield 1856, a flora of the Isle of Wight. The description reads: 'dioecious, or sometimes, it is said, polygamous' (Bromfield 1856, p. 107).
[5] See letter to W. E. Darwin, 22 June [1866].

To George Maw 21 June [1866]

Down. | *Bromley.* | *Kent. S.E.*
June 21st

My dear Sir

I am very much obliged to you for your great kindness in remembering my desire for information about sports, & for the curious & nicely dried specimen received yesterday. As it happens I have already seen this case, but I am not the less grateful to you for your kindness—[1]

Pray believe me | Yours very faithfully | Ch. Darwin

Postmark: London S X JL*[U]* 22 66; Broseley JU 2*[3]* 66
Royal Horticultural Society, Lindley Library

[1] Maw had sent CD a fragment of a fern-leaved beech (*Fagus sylvatica* 'Asplenifolia') bearing a branch of the normal form of foliage (see letter from George Maw, 18 June 1866 and n. 2). In *Variation* 1: 382, CD referred to other cases in which the buds of the fern-leaved beech had reverted to the normal form; or had reverted only partially, so that branches bore both normal and fern-like leaves, as well as variously shaped leaves. CD cited information from Braun 1853, p. 315, and *Gardeners' Chronicle* 1841, p. 329.

To W. E. Darwin 22 June [1866][1]

Down
June 22nd.

Dear William—

I have forwarded the business letters.[2]

If your case turns out true (wh. it probably won't) it will be a most interesting discovery & I vow you shall write a paper & publish it; but it must be well worked out first.[3] I presume the case is as follows; let us take a long & short-styled primrose and suppose the female organs to abort in both & then we shd have two males; & now take another pair & abort the male organs in both & we shd. have two females; & the case wd be like that of the Rhamnus. In all my speculations I never dreamed of such a case. Now the great thing is to be sure that the pollen grains differ in size in the two males. I have more confidence in measuring a few choice grains with the micrometer than with the camera.[4] You say that the grains are largest in what you call the pistillate males i.e. what primordially must have been the long-styled forms. Now it is a universal law in the most different orders, as in Primula Hottonia, Mitchella, Pulmonaria, Menyanthes, Sethia, Lythrum, and Oxalis that the pollen grains from the longer stamens in the short styled form are the largest; & this is unfortunately against yr. view.[5] But as the pollen is equal in the two forms of Linum there may be some way of wriggling out of this difficulty.[6]

Is there any difference in length in the stamens of the two male forms? Are you pretty sure that the two male forms do not graduate into each other; & so with the two female forms? It wd be eminently well to ascertain whether yr. pistillate male sets a few berries. I could detect no difference in length in the rudimentary stamens of the two females. If you are sure about the difference in size in the pollen of the two males, the case must be extraordinary whether or no we can understand it. If you have marked all four forms I would get you in the autumn when the leaves are shedding, to cut me off some branches & I daresay we could make them strike & then I could experimentise on them; I suppose the bushes would be two big to dig up? I could give you the results of any experiments for *your* paper but this is looking a long way ahead.[7]

Do not be discouraged if the whole case blows up— I am well accustomed to such explosions.

y^r^ affectate Father | Ch. Darwin (miserable forgery)[8] | Ch. Darwin

It w^d^ be well to look at ovules in pistillate male:—[9] Asa Gray says in letter that Rhamnus lanceolatus of U. States, has 2 forms, which differ only in pistils— The long-styled is much the most fruitful, but the short-styled does bear some fruit.— He adds that the stamens in the 2 forms were not rigorously compared.—[10]

LS(A)
DAR 185: 15

1 The year is established by the relationship between this letter and the letter from W. E. Darwin, 20 June [1866].

2 With his letter of 20 June [1866], William had sent some orders for dividends to be signed and forwarded to CD's brother, Erasmus Alvey Darwin.

3 William had observed four flower forms, two male and two female, in *Rhamnus cathartica*, and believed that the plant had once been dimorphic. See letters from W. E. Darwin, 20 June [1866] and 21 June [1866].

4 William frequently measured the sizes of pollen-grains with the aid of a camera lucida (see, for example, letter from W. E. Darwin, 8 May [1866] and n. 2).

5 See letter from W. E. Darwin, 20 June [1866] and n. 5. CD discussed each of these genera in *Forms of flowers*.

6 Although *Linum* species are heterostyled, CD had found that the pollen-grains of the two forms, unlike other heterostyled genera that he had observed, were indistinguishable under the microscope ('Two forms in species of *Linum*', p. 75; *Collected papers* 2: 98).

7 The account of *Rhamnus cathartica* was not published until 1877 in *Forms of flowers* (pp. 293–5). CD credited William with many of the observations, and added that he could 'form no satisfactory theory how the four forms . . . originated' (p. 295).

8 The letter down to, and including, the first signature is in Henrietta Emma Darwin's hand; the remainder is in CD's hand.

9 See CD's annotations to the letter from W. E. Darwin, [18 June 1866] and n. 3.

10 Asa Gray had described two hermaphrodite forms of *Rhamnus lanceolatus* in his letter of 11 October 1861 (*Correspondence* vol. 9), noting that the long-styled form was more fruitful. However, in *Forms of flowers*, pp. 295–6, CD reported on Gray's authority that the short-styled form was more fruitful.

From W. E. Darwin [23 June 1866][1]

Southampton
Saturday

My dear Father,

I will go over to Isle of W on Tuesday & mark the females. I suppose it would not do to cut slips at present.[2]

Both the males have entirely abortive ovules, and both the females incomplete stamens:[3]

Do you want a slip of all 4 kinds? I cannot understand how they got called polygamous.[4]

I am sorry to hear Mama is laid up[5]

Your affect son | W. E. Darwin

DAR 109: A75

CD ANNOTATIONS
2.1 Both ... ovules] *scored red crayon*
3.1 of all 4 kinds?] *scored red crayon*

[1] The date is established by the relationship between this letter and the letter to W. E. Darwin, 22 June [1866], and by the reference to Emma Darwin's poor health (see n. 5, below). In 1866, 23 June was a Saturday.
[2] In his letter of 22 June [1866], CD had indicated that William should mark the four flower forms of *Rhamnus cathartica* on the Isle of Wight, in order to take cuttings in autumn.
[3] See letter to W. E. Darwin, 22 June [1866] and n. 9.
[4] See letter from W. E. Darwin, 21 June [1866] and n. 4.
[5] Emma Darwin's diary (DAR 242) records a 'feverish attack' on 21 June 1866.

To W. E. Darwin [24 June 1866][1]

Down
Sunday

My dear W.

Send me **dry** in paper a few youngish flowers of two males, that I may put pollen of both close together under microscope. Attend well to gradation between the 2 males & between the 2 females— I feel great interest in your discovery, if it will but hold good.—[2]

Please send 3 or 4 twigs, about as thick as tobacco-pipes, (of *last year's shoots* bearing this year's sprouts) of all 4 forms, & we will try whether they will strike, but the chance is poor.—[3] Tie up & damp each lot of 3 or 4 separately; ; & then tie 4 bundles close together into one & perhaps roll the whole in tin-foil.— I will repay postage—but it need not be more than about a shilling—

Your affect. Father | C. Darwin

Thanks for note by George about ovules.[4] I suppose there is no difference in length of stamens in the 2 males.—[5]

I wish to Heaven pollen-grains had *not* been largest in your "pistillate males":—[6]

Hooker is here & very pleasant.[7] I have been telling him about Rhamnus & he is much surprised; but I fear, I fear.

Does Rhamnus grow in sandy, or clay soil— In sun or shade??[8]

DAR 185: 16

[1] The date is established by the relationship between this letter and the letter to W. E. Darwin, 22 June [1866], and by the reference to Joseph Dalton Hooker's visit (see n. 7, below). In 1866, 24 June was the first Sunday after 22 June.
[2] William had discovered that there were four flower forms in *Rhamnus cathartica*, two male and two female, and speculated that the plant might once have been dimorphic (see letter from W. E. Darwin, 20 June [1866]).
[3] In his letter to William of 22 June [1866], CD had suggested waiting until autumn to plant the slips.
[4] The note from George Howard Darwin has not been found. George had visited his brother William on 21 June (see letter from W. E. Darwin, 20 June [1866]).

[5] CD had asked the same question in his letter to W. E. Darwin, 22 June [1866].
[6] See letter to W. E. Darwin, 22 June [1866] and n. 5.
[7] Hooker visited CD at Down from 23 to 25 June 1866 (Emma Darwin's diary (DAR 242)).
[8] *Rhamnus cathartica* is found in peaty habitats; it grows well in dry or moist soil, in full sun or light dappled shade (*The new Royal Horticultural Society dictionary of gardening*; London: Macmillan, 1992).

From Bartholomew James Sulivan 27 June 1866

Bournemouth
June 27/66

My dear Darwin

I am indeed glad to get such a cheering letter from you—and to hear that you have such a prospect of restored health.[1] Up to three months ago I was in hopes I was getting better, for I had lost all the pains in joints &c. and my pulse and general circulation was stronger;[2] but either from my head not being able to stand this—or because the complaint was making more progress, I became very unwell with head symptoms—such as pain in the frontal region if I stoop or cough or on the least thing trying my head; & though for some time time I have been regularly under the best doctor here I get little—if any—better. I believe it is entirely caused by congestion of all the small vessels of the brain.

about three months since my eldest boy came home promoted—having got the annual surveying promotion from the surveying ship in Mediterranean:[3] he had suffered from Rheumatism—and was advised to try the hot air baths of D^r. Barter at Blarney—Co. Cork—[4]

He came back in six weeks well & strong: & the Doctor assured him that they would do my head great good— Finding him still very confident about it after sending him particulars of my case, and as I get no better here I think of going over there with my wife and eldest daughter next week.[5] I shall also escape the bother I have with the work of my house because some builders here think nothing of breaking contracts & delaying work they have pledged themselves to do, and it is with difficulty I have been able to get common exertions made to finish it though promised me by 1st of August, & not likely to be ready by 1st of October.

And now having tried your patience with personal matters, I must tell you that my boy is going out as 2nd Lieut with Mayne,[6] and that I have been looking forward to interesting Mayne & his Naturalist in a further search for "*my bones*",[7] having been giving my boy full particulars, & I meant to urge it on Richards (Hydrographer), also—who was my second Lieut. & with me cutting them out.[8] So with the aid of First Lord I have no doubt it will be easily managed[9] If I were well I should enjoy going with them and being landed at Falklands, for the summer, after a months good work at the "diggings"—[10] I look forward to going on Board Nassau at Portsmouth & pointing every thing out to Mayne. His vessel is a very long unhandy vessel for Gallegos, & I should not like to take her in there in such a tide & intricate channel, but there is a nice safe anchorage just outside; inside a good bank, & so thoroughly sheltered, & this removes all objection on that score.

Mary Everest Boole
Cobham 1951, frontispiece
By permission of the Syndics of Cambridge University Library

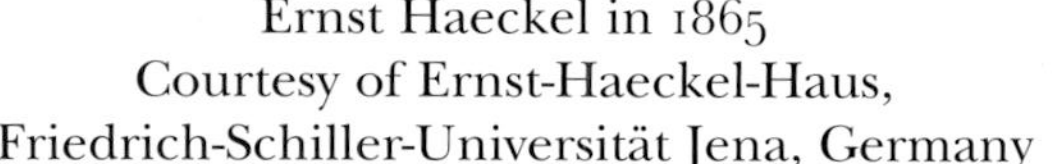

Ernst Haeckel in 1865
Courtesy of Ernst-Haeckel-Haus,
Friedrich-Schiller-Universität Jena, Germany

Julius Victor Carus
Courtesy of the Imperial College of Science,
Technology and Medicine Archives, London

They could pitch a tent on the far shore of the River opposite the bones, & in three or four days load all their boats twice over, with a good party—but to get the bones out carefully there would be work for a month—[11]

The Nassau is not going out for the survey of Straits of M. Her chief object is the better survey of the Smythe & Baker channels, & the best anchorages on them;[12] which is much wanted now that many large steamers go that way. at the same time she will make larger plans of some of the Harbours in the Straits. In one, through one channel in not being surveyed, a French screw line of battle ship was nearly lost and had to go back leaking to Rio Janeiro.

She will also complete the sounding of Possession Bay, & the best positions for anchoring outside the narrows; this was left very unfinished.[13]

I have seen published lists of the FitzRoy subscription.[14] I had one sent me but cannot now lay my hand on it— It was through that, that I knew of your handsome contribution to it.[15] I have heard twice from M^rs. FitzRoy:[16] but do not know what has been done with the testimonial fund. I suppose you saw that his Son was promoted into a death vacancy soon after going out in Commodores ship last year to Africa, so he has a good start—being a Commander about 26,—as times go.[17]

My second boy went out in a new surveying ship to N America, under Hope; and on his arrival had a Lieuts commission given him in a death vacancy, which had afterwards to *be cancelled* because his ship did not get on the station *till two hours after the death*.[18] I was not sorry as his elder brother was not then promoted.

all my party are well. my wife joins me in kind regards to Mrs Darwin & your daughters—[19] Believe me my dear Darwin | Yours most sincerely | B J Sulivan

I will take care to have written particulars prepared if I am not able myself to see Mayne & the Naturalist. Hooker[20] should ask Richards to further it & I will write also. B J S

DAR 177: 286

1 The letter from CD to Sulivan has not been found.

2 Sulivan had suffered health problems in 1864, and had resigned his position as chief naval officer in the Marine Department at the Board of Trade in 1865 because of his continued ill health (see *Correspondence* vol. 13, letter from B. J. Sulivan, 8 May [1865]).

3 James Young Falkland Sulivan had served as sub-lieutenant on HMS *Firefly*, stationed in the Mediterranean, from November 1864; he was promoted to the rank of lieutenant in January 1866 (*Navy list*). See also *Correspondence* vol. 13, letter from B. J. Sulivan, 8 May [1865].

4 The physician Richard Barter ran a hydrotherapy establishment in Blarney, County Cork, Ireland, offering hot-air baths and Turkish baths (*DNB*).

5 Sulivan refers to his wife, Sophia, and to their eldest daughter, Sophia Henrietta. Sulivan did undergo treatment by Barter (see Sulivan ed. 1896, p. 391).

6 James Young Falkland Sulivan served as lieutenant on HMS *Nassau* from 1866 to 1867 (*Navy list*); the vessel surveyed the Straits of Magellan from 1866 to 1869 (Cunningham 1871). Richard Charles Mayne was the commander of the *Nassau* during the survey expedition (see letter from J. D. Hooker, 13 May 1866 and n. 9).

7 The naturalist on HMS *Nassau* was Robert Oliver Cunningham (see letter from J. D. Hooker, 4 February 1866 and n. 4). In January 1845, while commanding HMS *Philomel*, Sulivan had discovered the fossil bones of mammals at the base of a cliff along the Río Gallegos in Patagonia (see *Correspondence*

vol. 3, letters from B. J. Sulivan, 13 January – 12 February 1845, and 4 July 1845). Six casks of bones were collected and sent to Richard Owen, who described several of the findings (*ibid.*, letter to Richard Owen, 21 [June 1846]; *Report of the 16th meeting of the British Association for the Advancement of Science held at Southampton in 1846*, Transactions of the sections, p. 66, and Owen 1853). For CD's interest in the findings, see *Correspondence* vol. 3, letter to J. D. Hooker, [4 June 1845], and letter to C. G. Ehrenberg, 29 October [1845]. For Sulivan's interest in returning to the site, see *Correspondence* vol. 4, letter to Richard Owen, 28 April [1850], and *Correspondence* vol. 10, letter from Arthur Mellersh, 30 November [1862]. Sulivan's discovery is discussed in Brinkman 2003.

8 George Henry Richards was lieutenant on HMS *Philomel* (Sulivan ed. 1896, p. 56); he became hydrographer to the Admiralty in 1863 (*Modern English biography*).

9 The first lord of the Admiralty was Edward Adolphus Seymour Seymour, twelfth duke of Somerset (*DNB*).

10 Sulivan had surveyed the Falkland Islands from 1837 to 1839, and lived there from 1848 to 1851 (*DNB*).

11 The search for the fossils took place in December 1867 and May 1868. The ship's naturalist, Cunningham, reported that the strata were rapidly disintegrating, and that few specimens of any size or value were found, except for one fossil cranium of a large quadruped, later identified by Thomas Henry Huxley as a new genus of mammal allied to *Anoplotherium* (Cunningham 1871, pp. 279–82, 469–73).

12 The Smyth Channel is north of the western end of the Strait of Magellan, between the Archipiélago de la Reina Adelaida and the Península de Muñoz Gamero. The Baker Channel is at the southern end of the Golfo de Penas. (*Times atlas.*)

13 Possession Bay is on the north side of Bahía de Lomas, at the eastern entrance to the Strait of Magellan (Mapa de Chile, 1: 3.000.000. Instituto Geográfico Militar, Santiago, 1975). HMS *Beagle* had visited Possession Bay on 24 January 1834 (*Narrative*, Appendix).

14 Robert FitzRoy commanded HMS *Beagle* during the 1831 to 1836 voyage on which Sulivan was second lieutenant and CD naturalist and companion to FitzRoy (see *Correspondence* vol. 1). FitzRoy committed suicide on 30 April 1865 (*Correspondence* vol. 13). A testimonial fund was set up for his family (see *Correspondence* vol. 13, letter from Charles Shaw, 3 October 1865).

15 CD had subscribed £100 to the FitzRoy testimonial fund (CD's Classed account books (Down House MS), 4 October 1865).

16 Maria Isabella FitzRoy.

17 Robert O'Brien FitzRoy had served as flag lieutenant of HMS *Bristol*, stationed on the west coast of Africa, from 7 October 1865, and became commander of the vessel on 1 February 1866; the commodore of the vessel was Geoffrey Thomas Phipps Hornby (*Navy list*).

18 Thomas Edward Sulivan was sub-lieutenant on HMS *Gannet* from July 1865; from December 1866, he was lieutenant on HMS *Duncan* (*Navy list*). James Hope was navy commander-in-chief in North America and the West Indies (*DNB*).

19 Sulivan refers to Emma, Henrietta Emma, and Elizabeth Darwin.

20 Joseph Dalton Hooker.

From W. E. Darwin 29 June [1866][1]

Southampton.
June 29th

My Dear Father,

I enclose what flowers I could find of the different kinds; I am afraid it is doubtful whether you will find any pollen, as the flowers are very much past. I suppose it will turn out all rubbish, & I think gradations will probably turn up.[2]

Still I think it ought to be the explanation, as it is much neater— And I do not quite see how supposing it to have been originally hermaphrodite & female explains it, as tho' one can understand hermaphrodite become male, why should the female become male?[3]

I enclose outlines of pollen, & styles cut off close to ovary.[4]

There is a great difference in the length of papillæ on the two male flower stigmas;[5] the long styled is much the roughest

I hope the twigs will grow;[6] one has taken root in my friend Dunn's garden.[7]

I am going to look at the white broom this evening.[8]

I am glad the boys are going a trip in Wales.[9]

I hope mamma is pretty brisk[10]

[Enclosure 1][11]

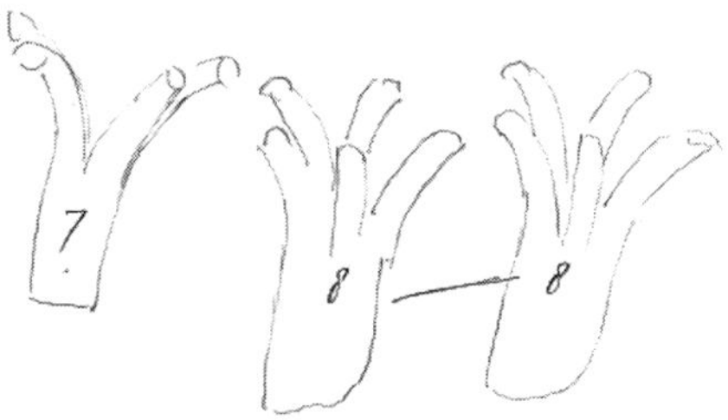

[Enclosure 2]

1 2 3 4 from one short styled female shrub | 9.10.11 from one long styled female shrub
5 6 7 8 from another Do— | 12 13 14.15 from another —Do—

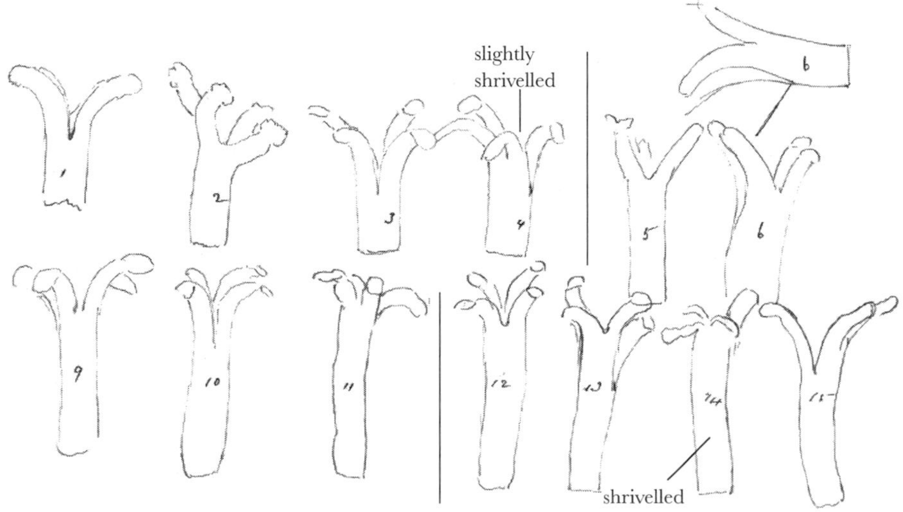

[Enclosure 3]

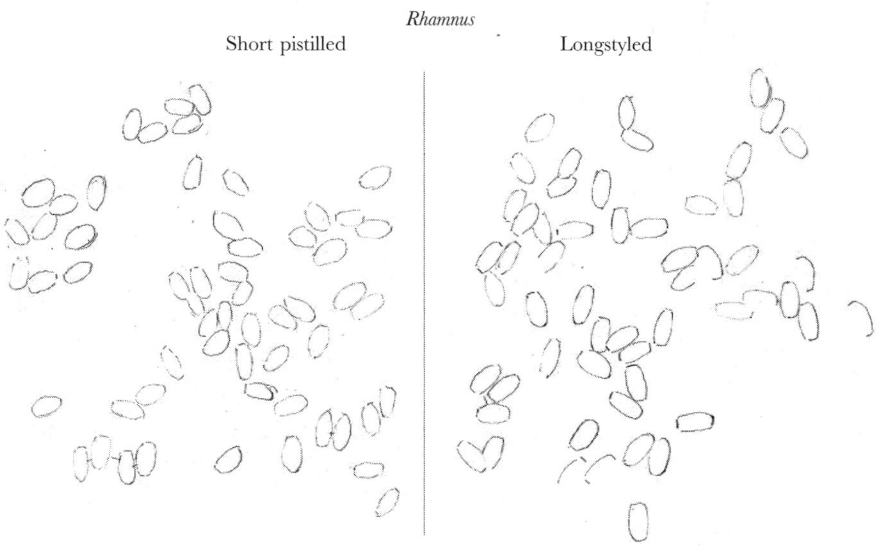

[Enclosure 4]

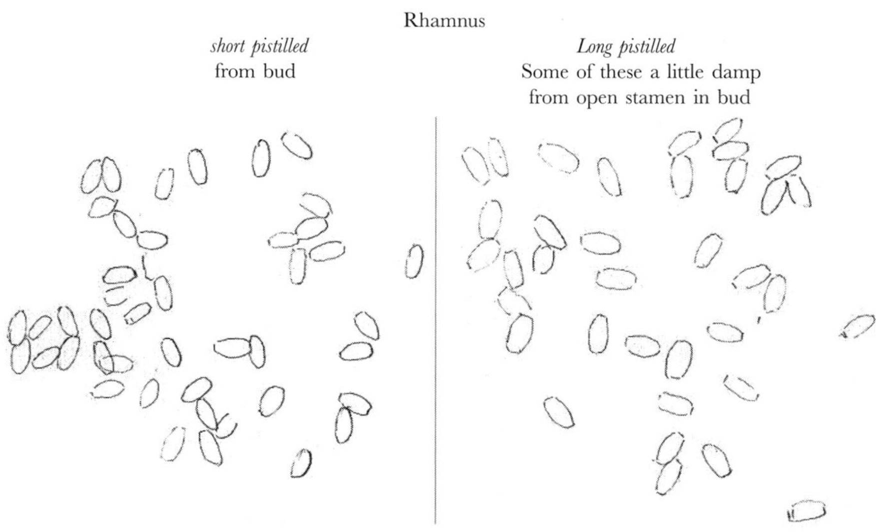

AL incomplete?
DAR 109: A78–9, A47–9

CD ANNOTATIONS
4.1 There is . . . roughest 4.2] *scored red crayon*
Enclosure 1: 'In ♀ flower do the reverting stamens differ in length—the longer'[12] *pencil*
Enclosure 2: 'short st | *[*Mean length*]* | Females with aborted anther' *pencil*
Enclosure 3: 'Very little difference' *pencil*
Enclosure 4: 'Certainly larger— first *[*instance*]* of what ought to occur if once *[1 word illeg]*' *pencil*

1 The year is established by the relationship between this letter and the letter to W. E. Darwin, [24 June 1866].
2 In the letter to W. E. Darwin, [24 June 1866], CD had requested that William send him 'a few youngish flowers' of the two male forms of *Rhamnus cathartica.* William had discovered two male and two female forms in the species, and speculated that the plant may once have been dimorphic (see letter from W. E. Darwin, 20 June [1866]). CD had advised William to look for gradations in his letters of 22 June [1866] and [24 June 1866].
3 CD had initially suggested that *Rhamnus cathartica* had once existed in hermaphrodite and female forms (see letter to W. E. Darwin, 19 [June 1866]). He later suggested that if William's belief proved true, then two hermaphrodite forms, long-styled and short-styled, had given rise to four unisexual forms (see letter to W. E. Darwin, 22 June [1866]).
4 See enclosure.
5 In *Forms of flowers*, p. 294, CD noted that on some male flowers of *Rhamnus cathartica*, the pistil was 'much more developed, with the papillae on the stigmatic surfaces moderately large'.
6 William had sent twigs of *Rhamnus cathartica* so that CD could plant them as cuttings (see letters to W. E. Darwin, [24 June 1866] and 30 [June 1866]).
7 The reference is to Robert Dunn, curate of Gatecombe, Isle of Wight (*Alum. Cantab.*).
8 See letter to W. E. Darwin, 19 [June 1866] and n. 7.
9 According to Emma Darwin's diary (DAR 242), Francis and Horace Darwin went to Wales on 7 July 1866 and returned on 16 July.
10 Emma Darwin had been unwell. See letter from W. E. Darwin, [23 June 1866] and n. 5.
11 The diagrams associated with this letter are reproduced at approximately 40 per cent of their original size.
12 In *Forms of flowers*, pp. 294–5, CD notes that the two female forms of *Rhamnus cathartica* are distinguished only by their pistils; the stamens of both forms are described as 'in an extremely rudimentary condition'.

To W. E. Darwin 30 [June 1866][1]

Down. | Bromley. | Kent. S.E.
30th

My dear William

The cuttings arrived in good time & were at once planted, & this morning your grand collection of sketches arrived: many thanks for all your great trouble—[2] Your drawings show considerable difference in the two pollens, & I now believe in your discovery, which seems to me, a very curious one.—[3]

The anthers received this morning contained pollen too shrivelled to measure.—[4] Next summer I must get you to send me some fresh flowers, & you must look a little more for gradation in form.—[5] It will not do for you to publish, I think, till we have tested power of the two pollens on the two females.— It is just possible size of grains may vary in different trees.— The whole case seems to me **eminently** well worth working out.—

I have to pay Elinor Carter £2" 16" 8 for your expences at Paris.—[6] You must let me hear sometime how balance is between your journey & Etty's napoleons—[7]

your affect Father | C. Darwin

I suppose stamens do not differ in length in the two males[8]

DAR 185: 17

[1] The date is established by the relationship between this letter and the letter from W. E. Darwin, 29 June [1866].

[2] CD had requested that William send him one-year-old shoots from which to propagate the four different forms of *Rhamnus cathartica* (see letter to W. E. Darwin, [24 June 1866]). William had sent drawings of pollen and styles of *Rhamnus cathartica* with his letter of 29 June [1866].

[3] See letter to W. E. Darwin, 29 June [1866] and n. 3.

[4] William had enclosed flowers of the two male forms of *Rhamnus cathartica* with his letter of 29 June [1866].

[5] See letter from W. E. Darwin, 29 June [1866] and n. 2. In *Forms of flowers*, p. 295, CD reported William's belief that the two sub-forms of the same sex did not grade into one another. No correspondence between William and CD in 1867 regarding *Rhamnus* has been found.

[6] William had apparently gone to Paris to meet Henrietta Emma Darwin and accompany her back to England. Henrietta had been in France from 15 March to mid-June with Elinor Mary Bonham-Carter and Elinor's aunt, Julia Smith (see letter to H. E. Darwin, [14–21 April 1866] and n. 4). According to CD's Account book–banking account (Down House MS), Elinor was paid £2 16*s.* 6*d.* on 14 July 1866.

[7] A napoleon was a twenty-franc coin (*OED*).

[8] See letter to W. E. Darwin, [24 June 1866] and n. 5.

To J. D. Hooker 30 June [1866]

Down. | Bromley. | Kent. S.E.
June 30

My dear Hooker

I have heard from Sulivan (who poor fellow gives a very bad account of his own health) about the fossils.[1] His son goes with Capt. Mayne & Capt Richards the hydrographer helped Sulivan as his Lieut. in collecting the bones.[2] Sulivan meant to speak to Capt. Mayne; but if you c^{d} influence the Duke of S. that w^{d} be by far the most important.[3]

The place is Gallegos on the S. coast of Patagonia. Sulivan says that in the course of 2 or 3 days all the boats in the ship could be filled twice over; but to get good specimens out of the hardish rock 2 or 3 weeks w^{d} be requisite. It w^{d} be a grand haul for paleontology.[4]

I have been thinking over your lecture. Will it not be possible to give enlarged drawings of some leading forms of trees?[5] You will of course have a large map; & George tells me that he saw at Sir H. James's at Southampton a map of the world on a new principle, as seen from within, so that almost $\frac{4}{5}$ of the globe was shewn at once on a large scale. W^d it not be worth while to borrow one of these from Sir H. James as a curiosity to hang up?[6]

Remember you are to come here before Nottingham.[7]

I have almost finished the last number of H. Spencer & am astonished at its prodigality of original thought. But the reflection constantly recurred to me that each suggestion, to be of real value to science, w^d require years of work.[8] It is also very unsatisfactory the impossibility of conjecturing where direct action of external circumstances begins & ends, as he candidly owns in discussing the production of woody tissue in the trunks of trees on the one hand, & on the other in spines & the shells of nuts.[9] I shall like to hear what you think of this number when we meet

yours affectly | Ch. Darwin

Thanks about Lupine[10]

Endorsement: '/66'
LS(A)
DAR 115: 292

[1] In his letter of 27 June 1866, Bartholomew James Sulivan discussed the navy's plan to return to the Río Gallegos in Patagonia, where he had discovered bones of fossil mammals in 1845.

[2] CD refers to James Young Falkland Sulivan, Richard Charles Mayne, and George Henry Richards (see letter from B. J. Sulivan, 27 June 1866 and nn. 6 and 8).

[3] CD refers to the twelfth duke of Somerset, Edward Adolphus Seymour Seymour, first lord of the Admiralty. See letter from B. J. Sulivan, 27 June 1866.

[4] On the results of the expedition, see the letter from B. J. Sulivan, 27 June 1866, n. 11.

[5] Hooker was to give a lecture on insular floras at the meeting of the British Association for the Advancement of Science in Nottingham in August (J. D. Hooker 1866a). No illustrations were referred to in the published lecture; however, one report noted that the lecture 'was illustrated by representations of some extraordinary plants arranged on a screen on either side of a geometrical projection of two-thirds of the sphere' (J. D. Hooker 1866b, p. 22; see n. 6, below). CD discussed trees on oceanic islands in *Origin*, pp. 392, 396. Hooker remarked that CD's theory of trans-oceanic migration explained why so many of the island genera tended 'to grotesque or picturesque arborescent forms' (J. D. Hooker 1866a, p. 75).

[6] George Howard Darwin had visited his brother William Erasmus Darwin in Southampton on 21 June (see letter from W. E. Darwin, 20 June [1866]). Henry James was director-general of the Ordnance Survey, based in Southampton. To aid his talk (see n. 5, above), Hooker used a map that had been developed in 1858 by James for the topographical department of the War Office (see James 1860). James described the design of the map as presenting a 'continuous symmetrical projection of the whole surface of the globe, or any part . . . in which the meridians and parallels intersect rectangularly; there being no distortion of form or area along or near the central meridian' (James 1868, p. 5). James published a variety of maps showing two-thirds of the earth using this method (for example, James 1862). Hooker remarked that the map used in his talk represented the islands and continents in the Atlantic and Indian Oceans 'more truly in position than in a Mercator's or other projection' (J. D. Hooker 1867, p. 7).

[7] Hooker visited Down on 18 August (letter from J. D. Hooker, [17 August 1866]).

[8] Herbert Spencer's *Principles of biology* was published in instalments to subscribers between 1863 and 1867; the most recent issue appeared in June 1866, and discussed the formation of inner and outer tissues of plants and animals (see Spencer 1864–7, 1: Preface, 2: Preface and 241–320). CD's annotated instalments of Spencer 1864–7 are in the Darwin Library–CUL bound as a single volume (see

Marginalia 1: 769–73). For more on CD's and Hooker's general reservations regarding Spencer's work, see the letter from J. D. Hooker, 14 December 1866 and n. 4.

9 Spencer argued that various plant tissues were formed by the adjustment or 'equilibration' of an individual organism to external forces, although some tissues evolved through the operation of natural selection on the species. The woody tissue of trees, he claimed, developed in response to the mechanical stresses to which individual plants were exposed (Spencer 1864–7, 2: 258–60); however, thorns and the shells of nuts, he maintained, could not have resulted 'from any inner reactions immediately called forth by outer actions; but must have resulted mediately through the effects of such outer actions on the species'. Spencer suggested that natural selection was a 'mediate' or 'indirect' force, which did not cause alterations in the structure of individual organisms, but operated on the structure of the species as a whole (*ibid.*, p. 274).

10 No letter to Hooker on *Lupinus* has been found; however, CD may have discussed the plant with Hooker during his visit to Down on 23 June. CD later sent Hooker a specimen of *Lupinus* to identify (see letter to J. D. Hooker, 21 [July 1866]).

To George Bentham [July–September 1866][1]

P.S.[2] If you are on Council of Linn. Soc. do consider whether it is necessary to be so much stricter about Books than the other Societies.[3] Now I have six books which I must refer to; & this will take me 3 weeks to do, & will cost me paying carriage *three* times up to London & *3 times* back;—& I wish only to glance over a short paper in each case.—

Royal allows 4 Books.—. Geolog. I think, 6 Books.[4]

AL incomplete
Royal Botanic Gardens, Kew (Bentham letters: 714)

1 The date range is established by Bentham's reply (see letter from George Bentham, 25 September 1866 and n. 1).

2 The main section of the letter has not been found. In his letter to CD of 25 September 1866, Bentham refers to two memoranda from CD, one of which is this postscript.

3 Bentham was president of the Linnean Society. CD was a fellow of the society, and had been given liberal borrowing privileges under the previous secretary, John Joseph Bennett (see *Correspondence* vol. 5, letter from J. D. Hooker, [before 7 March 1855]). The current secretary and librarian was Richard Kippist.

4 CD refers to the Royal Society of London and the Geological Society of London.

From John Lubbock 1 July [1866][1]

High Elms
1 July

My dear Mr. Darwin

I return you Muller with many thanks.[2] I wish I had read it before delivering my lecture on metamorphoses.[3]

On some points he seems to me to contradict himself, & in places his meaning is obscure, but it is certainly a remarkable memoir.

Hoping you continue to improve I remain | Yours affect | John Lubbock

C Darwin Esq

DAR 170: 52

[1] The year is established by the reference to Lubbock 1866 (see n. 3, below).

[2] Lubbock refers to Fritz Müller's paper 'On the metamorphoses of the prawns' (F. Müller 1864a). For CD's interest in the paper, see the letter to Fritz Müller, 11 January 1866 and n. 8.

[3] Lubbock's lecture, 'On the metamorphoses of insects', was given at the Royal Institution of Great Britain on 9 March 1866 (Lubbock 1866a). A lightly annotated copy is in the Darwin Pamphlet Collection–CUL. See also *Correspondence* vol. 11, letter from John Lubbock, 23 [February 1863] and n. 5.

From J. D. Hooker 2 July 1866

Kew
July 2d. /66.

Dear Darwin

Many thanks for your note.[1] I shall write to James for the map & take your advice about some sketches or diagrams of leading forms.[2]

With regard to the Gallegos fossils, could we not have a memorial drawn up by Huxley & other Geologists.[3] The matter not being Botanical I would rather not myself bring it forward, though I would write to the Duke privately backing it, if brought forward by Geologists.[4] Perhaps Murchison would take it up.[5]

I am extremely sorry for your account of poor Sullivan[6]—but do not wonder— I really think, his brain must be affected from what I saw of him last, some 5 months ago.

Spencer last number I hope to read soon[7]

F. & Brian enjoyed their stay at Down amazingly.[8]

I find the Beech twigs I spoke of to be deformed—[9]

Smith[10] knows nothing of origin of cut-leaved.

Alkanna hispidifolia we never had—[11]

I cannot find the name of any *Lamium campanulatum*[12]

The other questions will soon be answered.

Ever yrs affec | J D Hooker

DAR 102: 79–80

[1] Letter to J. D. Hooker, 30 June [1866].

[2] See letter to J. D. Hooker, 30 June [1866] and nn. 5 and 6. CD had suggested that Hooker use a map designed by the director-general of the Ordnance Survey, Henry James, and some enlarged drawings of trees for his lecture on insular floras to be given at the 1866 meeting of the British Association for the Advancement of Science (J. D. Hooker 1866a).

[3] In his letter of 27 June 1866, Bartholomew James Sulivan had discussed the navy's plan to return to the Río Gallegos in Patagonia, where he had discovered bones of fossil mammals in 1845. See also letter to J. D. Hooker, 30 June [1866]. Hooker refers to Thomas Henry Huxley.

[4] In his letter of 30 June [1866], CD had suggested that Hooker contact the twelfth duke of Somerset, Edward Adolphus Seymour Seymour, first lord of the Admiralty.

[5] Roderick Impey Murchison was director-general of the Geological Survey of Great Britain (*DNB*).
[6] CD had informed Hooker of Sulivan's poor health in his letter of 30 June [1866]; see also letter from B. J. Sulivan, 27 June 1866.
[7] Hooker refers to the June 1866 instalment of Herbert Spencer's *Principles of biology* (Spencer 1864–7, 2: 241–320). See letter to J. D. Hooker, 30 June [1866] and n. 8.
[8] Hooker's wife, Frances Harriet Hooker, had visited Down House from 23 to 29 June 1866 (Emma Darwin's diary (DAR 242)). Brian Harvey Hodgson Hooker, the Hookers' fifth child, was 6 years old.
[9] Hooker may have spoken of the twigs during his visit to Down from 23 to 25 June (Emma Darwin's diary (DAR 242)).
[10] Hooker refers to John Smith (1821–88), curator of the Royal Botanic Gardens, Kew.
[11] CD had requested *Alkanna* seed from Hooker in 1862 after having been informed by Alphonse de Candolle that *A. hispidissima* was 'double-formed' (see *Correspondence* vol. 10, letter from Alphonse de Candolle, 13 June 1862, and letter to J. D. Hooker, 3 November [1862]). For CD's interest in the plant in connection with his research on heterostyly, see *Correspondence* vol. 10, letter to Alphonse de Candolle, 17 June [1862]. *A. hispidifolia* is not a recognised species name.
[12] There is no such species.

To the Lords of the Admiralty [2–4 July 1866][1]

[Down]

To the L of the Admiralty

We the undersigned having heard that one of H.MS ships under the comm of Capt. M accompanied by a naturalist will soon proceed to survey parts of the Str of Magellan,[2] beg permission to call the attention of your Lordships to the fact that several years ago A. S. C.B.[3] discovered at Gallegos River in the extreme S. part of Patagonia a great deposit of the bones of extinct species of quadrupeds. Many of these collected with the aid of Hydrographer Capt Richards R.N. & afterwards in the B. Museum.[4] These *[illeg]* remains apparently belong to a more ancient period, than the collection by Mr Darwin on H.MS. Beagle[5] & by other Naturalists, & currently of extreme interest to science—

Some of the fossils have been described by R. O. F.RS in the Transactions of the Philoso Soc for 1853, & their characters have been shown to be highly remarkable[6]

We the undersigned have been informed by Admiral S., that in the course of a few days several boat-loads of these bones could be collected, & thus if a week or two were given to the work, perfect specimens could probably be disinterred.[7]

We therefore earnestly request your L. to take into your favourable consideration the benefit which wd conferred on Natural Science, if orders were given for a Collection to be made of these fossils under the present favourable circumstances, by the aid of the Naturalist who accompanies Capt Mayne.

Adraft
DAR 96: 25–6

[1] The date is established by the relationship between this letter, the letter from J. D. Hooker, 2 July 1866, and the letter to T. H. Huxley, 4 July [1866].

[2] HMS *Nassau*, under the command of Richard Charles Mayne, surveyed the Straits of Magellan from 1866 to 1869; the naturalist on the voyage was Robert Oliver Cunningham (see letter from B. J. Sulivan, 27 June 1866 and nn. 6 and 7).

[3] A. S. C.B.: Admiral Sulivan, CB. Bartholomew James Sulivan, who discovered the Gallegos fossils (see n. 4, below), was a rear admiral and a Commander of the Order of the Bath (*DNB*).

[4] Sulivan had discovered the bones in January 1845, while commanding HMS *Philomel* (see letter from B. J. Sulivan, 27 June 1866 and n. 7). George Henry Richards served with Sulivan as lieutenant on HMS *Philomel* (Sulivan ed. 1896, p. 56); he became hydrographer to the Admiralty in 1863 (*Modern English biography*). Some of Sulivan's fossils are described in the *Catalogue of the fossil Mammalia in the British Museum (Natural History)* 3: 167–8.

[5] CD's fossil mammal specimens from the *Beagle* voyage were described by Richard Owen in *Fossil Mammalia*.

[6] R. O. F.RS: Richard Owen, FRS. Sulivan's fossils were sent to Owen who, in a paper published in the *Philosophical Transactions of the Royal Society of London* (Owen 1853), established a new genus, *Nesodon*, on the basis of the fossils.

[7] See letter from B. J. Sulivan, 27 June 1866.

From A. R. Wallace 2 July 1866

Hurstpierpoint, Sussex
July 2nd. 1866.

My dear Darwin

I have been so repeatedly struck by the utter inability of numbers of intelligent persons to see clearly or at all, the self acting & necessary effects of *Nat Selection*, that I am led to conclude that the term itself & your mode of illustrating it, however clear & beautiful to many of us are yet not the best adapted to impress it on the general *naturalist public*.[1] The two last cases of this misunderstanding are, 1st. The article on "*Darwin & his teachings*" in the last "Quarterly Journal of Science", which, though very well written & on the whole appreciative, yet concludes with a charge of something like blindness, in your not seeing that "*Natural Selection*" requires the constant watching of an intelligent "chooser" like man's selection to which you so often compare it;[2]—and 2nd., in Janet's recent work on the "*Materialism of the present day*", reviewed in last Saturday's "Reader", by an extract from which I see that he considers your weak point to be, that you do not see that "*thought & direction are essential to the action of 'Nat. Selection'*."[3] The same objection has been made a score of times by your chief opponents, & I have heard it as often stated myself in conversation.

Now I think this arises almost entirely from your choice of the term "*Nat. Selection*" & so constantly comparing it in its effects, to *Man's selection*, and also to your so frequently personifying *Nature* as "*selecting*" as "*preferring*" as "*seeking only the good of the species*" &c. &c.[4] To the few, this is as clear as daylight, & beautifully suggestive, but to many it is evidently a stumbling block. I wish therefore to suggest to you the possibility of entirely avoiding this source of misconception in your great work, (if not now too late) & also in any future editions of the "Origin", and I think it may be done without difficulty & very effectually by adopting Spencer's term (which he generally uses in preference to Nat. Selection) viz. "*Survival of the fittest*."[5]

This term is the plain expression of the *facts*,—*Nat. selection* is a metaphorical expression of it—and to a certain degree *indirect* & *incorrect*, since, even personifying Nature, she does not so much *select* special variations, as *exterminate* the most unfavourable ones.

Combined with the enormous multiplying powers of all organisms, & the "struggle for existence" leading to the constant destruction of by far the largest proportion, —facts which no one of your opponents, as far as I am aware, has denied or misunderstood,—"*the survival of the fittest*" rather than of those who were less fit, could not possibly be denied or misunderstood. Neither would it be possible to say, that to ensure the "*survival of the fittest*" any *intelligent chooser* was necessary,—whereas when you say *natural selection* acts so as to choose those that are fittest it *is* misunderstood & apparently always will be. Referring to your book I find such expressions as "Man selects only for his own good; Nature only for that of the being which she tends".[6] This it seems will always be misunderstood; but if you had said "Man selects only for his own good; Nature, by the inevitable "survival of the fittest", only for that of the being she tends",—it would have been less liable to be so.

I find you use the term "Natural Selection" in two senses, 1st for the simple preservation of favourable & rejection of unfavourable variations, in which case it is equivalent to "*survival of the fittest*",—or 2nd. for the *effect* or *change*, produced by this preservation, as when you say, "To sum up the circumstances favourable or unfavourable to *natural selection*",[7] and again "Isolation, also, is an important element in the process of *natural selection*",[8]—here it is not merely "*survival of the fittest*" but, *change produced by survival of the fittest*, that is meant— On looking over your fourth Chap. I find that these alterations of terms can be in most cases easily made, while in some cases the addition of "*or survival of the fittest*", after "*natural selection*" would be best; and in others, less likely to be misunderstood, the original term may stand alone.[9]

I could not venture to propose to any other person so great an alteration of terms, but you I am sure will give it an impartial consideration, and if you really think the change will produce a better understanding of your work, will not hesitate to adopt it.

It is evidently also necessary not to *personify* "nature" too much,—though I am very apt to do it myself,—since people will not understand that all such phrases are metaphors.

Natural selection, is, when understood, so necessary & self evident a principle, that it is a pity it should be in any way obscured; & it therefore occurs to me, that the free use of "*survival of the fittest*",—which is a compact & accurate definition of it,—would tend much to its being more widely accepted and prevent its being so much misrepresented & misunderstood.

There is another objection made by Janet which is also a very common one. It is that the chances are almost infinite again the particular kind of variation required being coincident with each change of external conditions, to enable an animal to become modified by Nat. Selection in harmony with such changed conditions;

especially when we consider, that, to have produced the almost infinite modifications of organic beings this coincidence must have taken place an almost infinite number of times.[10]

Now it seems to me that you have yourself led to this objection being made, by so often stating the case *too strongly* against yourself. For Example, at the Commencement of Chap. IV. you ask, if it is "*improbable that useful variations should sometimes occur in the course of thousands of generations*";[11]—and a little further on you say, "*unless profitable variati⟨ons⟩ do occur natural selection can do nothing.*"[12] Now such expressions h⟨ave⟩ given your opponents the advantage of assuming that *favourable variations* are *rare accidents*, or may even for long periods never occur at all, & thus Janet's argument would appear to many to have great force. I think it would be better to do away with all such qualifying expressions, and constantly maintain (what I certainly believe to be the fact) that *variations* of *every kind* are *always occurring* in *every part* of *every species*,—& therefore that favourable variations are *always ready* when wanted. You have I am sure abundant materials to prove this, and it is, I believe, the grand fact that renders modification & adaptation to conditions almost always possible. I would put the burthen of proof on my opponents, to show, that any one *organ structure* or *faculty* does *not vary*, even during one generation among all the individuals of a species,—and also to show *any mode or way* in which any such *organ* &c. does not vary. I would ask them to give any reason for supposing that *any organ* &c. is ever *absolutely identical* at any *one time* in *all the individuals* of a species,—& if not then it is always varying, and there are always materials which, from the simple fact, that "*the fittest survive*", will tend to the modification of the race into harmony with changed conditions.

I hope these remarks may be intelligible to you, & that you will be as kind as to let me know what you think of them.

I have not heard for some time how you are getting on.

I hope you are still improving in health, & that you will be able now to get on with your great work for which so many thousands are looking with interest.[13]

With best wishes | Believe me My dear Darwin | Yours very faithfully | Alfred R. Wallace—

C. Darwin Esq.

DAR 106: B33–8

CD ANNOTATIONS

5.4 "To sum . . . *selection*" 5.5] *cross in margin, pencil*
6.1 I could . . . adopt it. 6.4] *crossed pencil*

[1] CD had discussed the meaning of 'natural selection' at length in correspondence with Charles Lyell, Asa Gray, and Joseph Dalton Hooker (see *Correspondence* vols. 8–10). He had attempted to clarify his use of the expression in *Origin* 3d ed., pp. 84–5. On CD's use of the term 'natural selection' in *Origin* and the ensuing debate over it, see Young 1985, pp. 92–112.

[2] The anonymous article, 'Darwin and his teachings', appeared in the April 1866 issue of the *Quarterly Journal of Science*; it contained a discussion of CD's use of the expression 'natural selection' in *Origin*,

and criticised CD for having endowed nature with 'the intelligent faculty of designing and planning' (Anon. 1866, pp. 152–3). A lightly annotated presentation copy of the article is in the Darwin Pamphlet Collection–CUL. See also letter from James Samuelson, 8 April 1866.

3 The review of Paul Janet's *The materialism of the present day* (Janet 1866) appeared in the 30 June 1866 issue of the *Reader*, pp. 618–19. The final chapter of Janet 1866 contained a lengthy discussion of CD's theory of descent. The review included two extracts from Janet's book; however, Wallace is paraphrasing the remark of the reviewer: 'In conclusion, M. Janet states that natural selection only becomes a fruitful principle by admitting choice and direction' (*Reader* 6 (1866): 619). Janet had also emphasised the importance of final causes in a previous review of *Origin* (Janet 1863); see *Correspondence* vol. 12, letter from E. A. Darwin, 5 January 1864.

4 In *Origin*, p. 469, CD wrote: 'Why, if man can by patience select variations most useful to himself, should nature fail in selecting variations useful, under changing conditions of life, to her living products?' CD does not write about 'Nature preferring' or 'seeking only the good of the species' in *Origin*; however, he wrote of natural selection 'favouring the good and rejecting the bad' (p. 469), 'preserving and adding up all that is good', and acting 'only through and for the good of each being' (p. 84).

5 Herbert Spencer first used the expression 'survival of the fittest' in the October 1864 instalment of *Principles of biology* (Spencer 1864–7, 1: 444–5): 'This survival of the fittest, which I have here sought to express in mechanical terms, is that which Mr. Darwin has called "natural selection, or the preservation of favoured races in the struggle for life"'.

6 The sentence appears in *Origin*, p. 83, and is unchanged in later editions (Peckham ed. 1959, p. 168).

7 This phrase from *Origin*, p. 107, was changed in the fifth edition as follows: 'To sum up the circumstances favourable and unfavourable for the production of new species through natural selection' (*Origin* 5th ed., p. 123).

8 *Origin*, p. 104; this sentence was substantially altered, and 'natural selection' deleted, in the fifth edition (*Origin* 5th ed., p. 121).

9 Chapter 4 of *Origin* was headed 'Natural selection'. In the fifth edition of *Origin*, CD added the expression 'survival of the fittest' to the heading of chapter 4, and inserted 'survival of the fittest' at seven places in the text of that chapter (*Origin* 5th ed., pp. 92, 95, 103, 105, 125, 145, 160). CD added 'survival of the fittest' at six other places in the fifth edition of *Origin* (*Origin* 5th ed., pp. 72, 168, 226, 239, 421, and 556). For more on CD's adoption of this phrase, and his use of Spencer's work, see Paul 1988 and Haines 1991. In his own copy of *Origin* (Rare books–CUL), Wallace deleted 'natural selection' and inserted 'survival of the fittest' at various points in the text.

10 See n. 3, above. This criticism from Janet 1866, p. 182, is printed in the *Reader*, 30 June 1866, p. 619.

11 In *Origin*, p. 80, CD wrote: 'Can it, then, be thought improbable, seeing that variations useful to man have undoubtedly occurred, that other variations useful in some way to each being in the great and complex battle of life, should sometimes occur in the course of thousands of generations?' The passage was unchanged until the sixth edition, in which 'thousands of generations' was changed to 'many successive generations' (*Origin* 6th ed., p. 63).

12 The passage appears in *Origin*, p. 82; in the fifth edition, 'profitable variations' is replaced by 'such' (*Origin* 5th ed., p. 94).

13 CD had been working on *Variation* since January 1860 (see *Correspondence* vol. 8, Appendix II).

From Asa Gray 3 July 1866

Cambridge.
July 3^{d}. 66.

My Dear Darwin,

I am delighted to hear, in various ways, such good accounts of your health. Esto perpetua![1] But take capital care of yourself.

I should have earlier replied to yours of 25th May.[2] But the Appleton's do not behave well.[3] I wrote them on receiving your letter, June 9. They waited till 18th. to reply, as enclosed.[4] I wrote back to tell them that I had received no sheets yet—which was true (I have since received up to p. 192);[5] but urged the impracticability of altering the plates, and your aversion to that, so that would be unjust to you.— Said we wanted now a neat & permanent library edition.—[6]

No reply to that yet. But yesterday I wrote saying I now had some sheets, and asked if I should send them, Or, if they thought it not worth while to reprint, if they would object to my offering the sheets to some other publisher.

I think it likely they will play *dog in the manger*[7]—for which part they have advantages,—as they might reprint your additions and issue with their old stereotype pages, without regard to appearance or decency, and so spoil the venture of any other publisher. At least the fear of it might deter any other publisher We shall soon see if I do them injustice.

So there is war on the continent;[8]—really a war "for Empire"—as Lord Russell said our war was.[9] Now our war was a simple necessity; this continental one a *crime*, in which all parties participate. I wish, but no not expect, Prussia to be crushed as one result. I wish all her coast could be annexed to Denmark! However, it is no affair of ours,—being on the other side of the Atlantic. And when a nation can get strength and power by robbery, it will be likely to rob.

Ever Yours | A. Gray

[Notes by A.G. on verso of cover][10]

Passiflora acerifolia is active—

Temp. 88°–92°.— tentril $5\frac{1}{2}$ inches long. You can plainly see the motion of revolution through the quicker part of circle readily; in one case the point moved 45° in a minute, (4 inches) but that was in straightening, after the base had been moving faster than the upper part. Full revolutions made 40′ (including 7′ lost by a going backwards) in 45′, in 38 h, in 46′, and now $\frac{1}{2}$ a revolution in 15′.[11]

A.G. July 3.

DAR 165: 151

1 'Esto perpetua': let it be forever (Latin).

2 CD's letter has not been found.

3 Gray was trying to arrange for the publication of a new American edition of *Origin* by the New York firm D. Appleton & Co. (see letter from Asa Gray, 7 May 1866 and nn. 3–4).

4 The enclosure has not been found.

5 Gray refers to sheets from the fourth English edition of *Origin*, the printing of which was nearly complete (see letter from John Murray, 25 May [1866]).

6 On Appleton's use of solid plates, or stereotyping, to produce the first American edition of *Origin*, see the letter to Asa Gray, 16 April [1866] and n. 11. The firm did not publish a revised edition until 1870 (Freeman 1977).

7 Dog in the manger: 'a person who will not let others enjoy what they themselves have no use for' (*Chambers*).

8 Gray refers to the Austro-Prussian war, fought by Prussia against Austria, Bavaria, Saxony, Hanover, and other German states during June and July 1866. On events leading up to the war, see the letter from E. Schweizerbart'sche Verlagsbuchhandlung, 10 May 1866 and n. 5.

9 John Russell, first Earl Russell, was the British foreign secretary from 1859 to 1865. Gray had been critical of Russell (see *Correspondence* vol. 13, letter from Asa Gray, 6 November 1865).

10 The notes are apparently an answer to a question CD asked in the missing letter to Gray of 25 May 1866.

11 Gray's observations of *Passiflora acerifolia* were summarised in *Climbing plants* 2d ed., p. 154 n. CD had discussed the revolution of tendrils in other *Passiflora* species in 'Climbing plants', pp. 89–91.

To Thomas Henry Huxley 4 July [1866][1]

Down. | Bromley. | Kent. S.E.
July 4.

My dear Huxley

Hooker tells me of an expedition going to survey the St of Magellan.[2] Admiral Sulivan several years ago discovered an astonishingly rich accumulation of fossil bones not far from the Straits[3] & he will tell the Captain of the vessel & the Naturalist exactly where they cd be found.[4] During many years it has seemed to me extremely desirable that these shd be collected; & here is an excellent opportunity. Hooker has suggested a memorial to the Lords of the Admiralty to be signed by a few leading Geologists & Paleontologists.[5] Please read the enclosed, & observe that I do not know in the least the proper form of a Memorial & therefore the enclosed may be corrected to any extent & shall be re-copied, or shall go as it stands.[6] Now please consider whether you will sign this, & shew it to Sir Roderick Murchison & ask him whether he will head the list;[7] perhaps he wd shew it to Professor Owen & ask him if he wd like to sign; for I do not want to have any communication with Owen.[8] If in addition, the Pres. of Geolog. Soc. & Ramsay wd sign,[9] that I shd think wd be ample, & the Memorial might be sent in at once, for there is no time to lose. If it will do as it stands & all goes smooth, will you forward it to the Admiralty & let me have a line to hear the result, as I must inform Sulivan. I may just add that some the fossils here referred to are allied to Toxodon.[10]

My dear Huxley | ever yours sincerely | Ch. Darwin

LS(A)
Imperial College of Science, Technology, and Medicine Archives (Huxley 5: 231)

1 The year is established by the relationship between this letter and the letter from T. H. Huxley, 6 July 1866.

2 CD had been told of the expedition to the Straits of Magellan in the letter from J. D. Hooker, 4 February 1866. See also letter from B. J. Sulivan, 27 June 1866, and letter to J. D. Hooker, 30 June [1866].

3 See letter from B. J. Sulivan, 27 June 1866 and n. 7. Sulivan was a rear admiral (*DNB*).

4 Richard Charles Mayne was captain of HMS *Nassau*, and Robert Oliver Cunningham was ship's naturalist (see letter from B. J. Sulivan, 27 June 1866 and nn. 6 and 7).

5 See letter from J. D. Hooker, 2 July 1866 and n. 3.

6 The memorial has not been found: a draft of it, dated [2–4 July 1866], is reproduced in this volume.

[7] Roderick Impey Murchison was director-general of the Geological Survey of Great Britain (*DNB*).

[8] Richard Owen had established a new mammalian order on the basis of some of the fossils found by Sulivan in Patagonia (see Owen 1853). On CD's deteriorating relationship with Owen, especially following Owen's critical review of *Origin* ([Owen] 1860), see, for example, *Correspondence* vol. 8, letter to Asa Gray, 25 April [1860], and *Autobiography*, pp. 104–5.

[9] The president of the Geological Society of London was William John Hamilton; Andrew Crombie Ramsay was a vice-president (*List of the Geological Society of London*, *DNB*).

[10] *Toxodon* is a genus of rhinoceros-like notoungulates; it was described by Owen (Owen 1838 and *Fossil Mammalia*, pp. 16–35), based on specimens collected in Patagonia by CD (see *Correspondence* vols. 1 and 2, and *South America*, pp. 180–1). Owen had also described the affinities between *Toxodon* and the fossils found by Sulivan, which he identified as belonging to a new genus, *Nesodon* (Owen 1853, pp. 298–99, 309).

From W. B. Tegetmeier 4 July 1866

Muswell Hill | London | N
July 4. 1866

My dear Sir.

All the blocks are engraved except that of the Rock dove which is now in the artist's hands—[1] I had a good deal of difficulty in procuring a specimen that I could rely on as not being crossed with dovecot pigeons, but have now two in the flesh, from the Coast of Lewis (Western Islands) and from Stromness (Orkneys)—[2] To show the wing bars etc. as you wished I have had one hung up by the leg, and drawn after a photograph. In this position the bars on the wings & wing coverts, the white rump feathers—tail bars etc are really admirably shewn and if you do not object to a drawing looking like an artistic sketch of "dead game", I think it will suit, as the plumage is much better shewn than in a natural position, at least as regards the characteristic markings[3]

⟨*one third of page excised*⟩

Will you be so good as ⟨to⟩ read the article by M[r] Teeba⟨y⟩ ⟨in⟩ the July Number of the Po⟨ultry Book⟩ chapter on spangled Hamburghs it will interest you ⟨ ⟩ how nearly two varieties ⟨ ⟩ fowls), can approach in Me⟨ ⟩ ⟨ ⟩ yet be incapable of amalgamation[4]

Teebays statements are perfectly reliable— he is a most practised breeder and fair describer

⟨*one third of page excised*⟩

AL incomplete
DAR 178: 72

[1] On Tegetmeier's procurement of engravings of pigeons and poultry for *Variation*, see the letter to W. B. Tegetmeier, 16 January [1866] and n. 2, and the letter from W. B. Tegetmeier, 22 January [1866] and nn. 1–7. The artist was Luke Wells.

[2] The Isle of Lewis is in the Outer Hebrides off the north-west coast of Scotland; Stromness is a town at the south-west end of the island of Mainland in the Orkney Islands, off the north coast of Scotland.

[3] An illustration of a dead specimen of *Columbia livia*, the rock pigeon, appeared in *Variation* 1: 135. The specimen was shown hanging upside down.

[4] Richard Teebay's article in *The poultry book* (Tegetmeier 1867, pp. 154–8) is annotated in CD's copy in the Darwin Library–CUL (see *Marginalia* 1: 800–3). Teebay described various golden-spangled and silver-spangled varieties of Hamburgh fowl, and the effects of crossing on their plumage patterns. *The poultry book* was issued in parts.

From Frederick Currey 5 July 1866

3, New Square, Lincolns Inn. W.C.
July 5th. 1866

My dear Sir,

Herr Müllers paper on climbing plants is about to be printed in our Journal with such illustrations as may be necessary—[1] I understand from the enclosed letter which was written by you to Mr. Kippist[2] that you only consider the 3 figures marked with the blue cross necessary, (viz. No. 7, one half of No. 2, & a third not numbered) & that we may therefore strike out of the M.S. the references to the other figures—

My immediate object in writing however is to ask whether in your opinion there would be any objection to reducing the size of the figures— The Council have authorized three *octavo* plates, but if the three figures only are necessary, & may be reduced in size, it appears to me that one plate, or two at the outside, might be sufficient—[3] In case you should like to refer to the M.S. I send it (with the drawings & your letter) by Bookpost & if you will kindly let me know what you think I shall be very much obliged—

Believe me | my dear Sir | Your's very truly | Fredk Currey

Chas Darwin Esqr.

DAR 161: 307

CD ANNOTATION

End of letter: 'Proportion given on plate | Proofs | I have struck out each [*interl*] reference & given' *pencil*

[1] Fritz Müller's paper, 'Notes on some of the climbing plants near Desterro, in southern Brazil', appeared in the *Journal of the Linnean Society (Botany)* 9 (1866): 344–9 (F. Müller 1865b). The text had been edited by CD from parts of three letters sent by Müller in 1865 (see *Correspondence* vol. 13, letter from Fritz Müller, [12 and 31 August, and 10 October 1865]).

[2] CD's letter to Richard Kippist has not been found.

[3] One plate, containing three figures, accompanied the paper (F. Müller 1865b, tab. 9); it is reproduced in *Correspondence* vol. 13, p. 217.

From J. T. Moggridge 5 and 6 July [1866][1]

3 Marlborough Villas
July 5.

Dear Mr. Darwin

Yesterday I obtained from Mr. J. G. Baker (late of Thirsk)[2] the seed of *Ononis Columnæ* which I enclose—[3]

Packet N°. 1, contains seed from one individual only—

Packet N°. 2 seed from several individuals of this species—

Mr. Baker tells me that in *Mentha hirsuta* many variations in the relative lengths of Pistil, Stamens & Corolla occur in the same head—[4]

July 6th. Yours received this morning— The best reward you can give me for a well executed commission is to entrust me with another.—[5]

With very kind regards to all your circle[6] | Believe me | Yrs. very sincerely | J. Traherne Moggridge.

I fear that Herbarium seed often fails so I shall try to obtain some more, &, if possible, some from living plants.[7]

DAR 171: 209

1 The year is established on the basis of the appointment of John Gilbert Baker to the herbarium at the Royal Botanic Gardens, Kew, in 1866 (see n. 2, below), and by the references to seed of *Ononis columnae* (see n. 7, below).

2 Baker had owned a drapery business in Thirsk, Yorkshire, until 1864, when his home and premises were destroyed by fire; he became an assistant in the herbarium at the Royal Botanic Gardens, Kew, in 1866 (*DSB*).

3 CD was interested in the cleistogamic flowers of *Ononis*, and described those of *O. columnae* in *Origin* 5th ed., p. 153, and *Forms of flowers*, pp. 325–6.

4 *Mentha hirsuta* and other species of mint belong to a category of dimorphic plants that CD later called 'gyno-dioecious'; it is briefly mentioned in the introduction to the section on 'gyno-dioecious' plants in *Forms of flowers*, p. 298. CD's notes on *M. hirsuta*, based on specimens received from William Erasmus Darwin and dated 28 August 1862, are in DAR 109: A3; see *Correspondence* vol. 10, letter to W. E. Darwin, [5 May 1863].

5 CD's letter has not been found; see, however, the letter from J. T. Moggridge, 3 August [1866].

6 Moggridge had met Henrietta Emma Darwin during her trip to France, and had visited the Darwin family in Down from 23 to 25 June 1866 (see letters from J. T. Moggridge, 21 May [1866], nn. 7 and 8, and 14 June [1866], n. 2).

7 Moggridge enclosed seeds of *Ononis columnae* from Mentone with his letter of 3 August [1866]. CD evidently planted these seeds in 1866; in a note dated 8 May 1867, he described the flowers of *O. columnae* raised from seed sent to him from northern Italy by Moggridge (DAR 111: A21).

To A. R. Wallace 5 July [1866][1]

Down. | *Bromley.* | *Kent. S.E.*
July 5th.

My dear Wallace

I have been much interested by your letter which is as clear as daylight.[2] I fully agree with all that you say on the advantages of H. Spencer's excellent expression of "the survival of the fittest.[3] This however had not occurred to me till reading your letter. It is, however, a great objection to this term that it cannot be used as a substantive governing a verb; & that this is a real objection I infer from H. Spencer continually using the words natural selection.[4]

I formerly thought, probably in an exaggerated degree, that it was a great advantage to bring into connection natural & artificial selection; this indeed led me to use a term in common, and I still think it some advantage. I wish I had received your letter two months ago for I would have worked in "the survival etc" often in the new edition of the Origin which is now almost printed off & of which I will of course send you a copy.[5] I will use the term in my next book on Domestic Animals etc[6] from which, by the way, I plainly see, that you expect *much* too much. The term Natural selection has now been so largely used abroad & at home that I doubt whether it could be given up, & with all its faults I should be sorry to see the attempt made. Whether it will be rejected must now depend "on the survival of the fittest". As in time the term must grow intelligible, the objections to its use will grow weaker & weaker. I doubt whether the use of any term would have made the subject intelligible to some minds, clear as it is to others; for do we not see even to the present day Malthus on Population absurdly misunderstood.[7] This reflexion about Malthus has often comforted me when I have been vexed at the misstatement of my views. As for M. Janet he is a metaphyscian & such gentlemen are so acute that I think they often misunderstand common folk.[8] Your criticism on the double sense in which I have used Natural Selection is new to me and unanswerable; but my blunder has done no harm, for I do not believe that anyone excepting you has ever observed it. Again I agree that I have said too much about "favourable variations;" but I am inclined to think that you put the opposite side too strongly: if every part of every being varied, I do not think we should see the same end or object gained by such wonderfully diversified means.

I hope you are enjoying "the country & are in good health", and are working hard at your Malay Arch. book, for I will always put this wish in every note note I write to you, like some good people always put in a text.[9]

My health keeps much the same or rather improves & I am able to work some hours daily.

With many thanks for your interesting letter, believe me, | my dear Wallace, yours sincerely | Ch. Darwin

P.S. I suppose you have read the last number of H. Spencer; I have been struck with astonishment at the prodigality of Original thought in it; but how unfortunate it is that it seems scarcely ever possible to discriminate between the direct effect of external influences & "the survival of the fittest".—[10]

LS
British Library (Add 46434, f. 70)

[1] The year is established by the relationship between this letter and the letter from A. R. Wallace, 2 July 1866.

[2] See letter from A. R. Wallace, 2 July 1866.

[3] Herbert Spencer introduced the expression 'survival of the fittest' in *Principles of biology* (Spencer 1864–7, 1: 444–5). See letter from A. R. Wallace, 2 July 1866 and n. 7.

[4] Spencer used the term 'natural selection' in a lengthy discussion of CD's theory (Spencer 1864–7, 1: 445–57), and at other places in *Principles of biology* (for example, *ibid.*, 1: 234, 237, 2: 273–4).

[5] Although the printing of the fourth edition of *Origin* was completed in July, the publisher, John Murray, delayed publication until November 1866 (see letter from John Murray, 18 July [1866] and n. 3). Wallace's name is on the presentation list for the fourth edition of *Origin* (see Appendix IV). On CD's use of the expression 'survival of the fittest' in the fifth edition of *Origin*, see the letter from A. R. Wallace, 2 July 1866, n. 11.

[6] CD used the expression 'survival of the fittest' six times in *Variation* (see *Variation* 1: 6, 2: 89, 192, 224, 413, 432); however, CD also defended his use of 'natural selection' in *Variation* 1: 6: 'The term "natural selection" is in some respects a bad one, as it seems to imply conscious choice; but this will be disregarded after a little familiarity.'

[7] CD refers to *An essay on the principle of population* by Thomas Robert Malthus; an annotated copy of the sixth edition (Malthus 1826) is in the Darwin Library–CUL (see *Marginalia* 1: 562–3). CD had previously remarked on the general misunderstanding of Malthus in a letter to Charles Lyell, 6 June [1860] (*Correspondence* vol. 8). On the importance of Malthus's work in the evolutionary debates of the Victorian period, see Young 1985, pp. 23–55.

[8] CD refers to Paul Janet; see letter from A. R. Wallace, 2 July 1866 and n. 3.

[9] Wallace was living in the Sussex village of Hurstpierpoint, the home of his father-in-law, William Mitten (Raby 2001, pp. 182–3, 187–8). CD refers to Wallace's book on his travels to the Malay archipelago (A. R. Wallace 1869; see *Correspondence* vol. 13, letter to A. R. Wallace, 22 September [1865] and n. 3).

[10] The most recent instalment of Herbert Spencer's *Principles of biology* appeared in June 1866 (see Spencer 1864–7, 1: preface, 2: preface and 241–320). On Spencer's discussion of external conditions in relation to the operation of natural selection, see the letter to J. D. Hooker, 30 June [1866] and n. 9.

From T. H. Huxley 6 July 1866

The Athenaeum
July 6th. 1866

My dear Darwin

If I had got your Memorial signed & sent to 'My Lords',[1] My Lords would simply have remitted it to the Hydrographer—so as I know Richards & have always found him a pleasant & helpful sort of man—I thought my best course was to go to him at once with your memorial in my pocket.[2]

I have just done so & find that he knows all about the place having been one of the party who dug up the bones which were obtained at Gallegos[3] He thoroughly interests himself in the object of your Memorial (which I have left with him) & promises to give all the requisite instructions to Capt. Mayne.[4]

Dr Cunningham,[5] the Naturalist, is in communication with me & I will see he is properly primed on the same subject

Evil man that you are you say not a word about yourself—so I hope that you are prospering & Mrs. Darwin[6] better than she was

Ever | Yours faithfully | T H Huxley

DAR 166: 311

[1] The memorial to the Lords of the Admiralty, enclosed with the letter to Huxley of 4 July [1866], has not been found; a draft of it, dated [2–4 July 1866], is published in this volume.

[2] George Henry Richards was hydrographer to the Admiralty (*Modern English biography*).

[3] Richards had served as lieutenant on HMS *Philomel*, and had helped to collect fossil bones of mammals along the Río Gallegos in Patagonia in 1845 (see letter from B. J. Sulivan, 27 June 1866 and nn. 7 and 8).
[4] Richard Charles Mayne was captain of HMS *Nassau*, which surveyed the Straits of Magellan from 1866 to 1869 (*DNB*).
[5] Robert Oliver Cunningham.
[6] Emma Darwin.

From George Stacey Gibson 7 July 1866

Saffron Walden
7/7 1866

Sir,

Knowing the interest you take in the investigation of the phenomena of nature, I venture to ask whether you have ever tried an experiment, which when first mentioned to me I put aside as too absurd to deserve attention, although I knew that a similar result had been reported for many years past. What first induced me to try it, was a visit I paid to an intelligent farmer in this neighbourhood two years ago, who asked me to look at some barley which he had grown from the seed of oats. He had several rods of ground, which he had sown the previous year with *oats*, but cut them down to prevent their flowering, and this year the whole of the plants were *barley*, of a luxuriant character. I immediately sowed some oats, cut them down in a similar manner, and all that survived the winter came barley; from one of these plants I cut 107 ears.

Last year I again sowed oats, and being a mild winter, most of it has lived, and all except about 3 or 4 plants, out of probably 50, are barley; the 3 or 4 are oats. My friend Joshua Clarke has also tried it, though with a less decided result; he has several plants of barley, one of wheat, and the rest remains oats. I believe many will try the experiment this year, as it is a very curious one: I cannot see any possible mistake in my experiment, and yet I can hardly conceive that the differences between two plants so widely dissimilar as oats & barley have only been caused by cultivation.[1]

Can you offer any solution of it? or if, as I expect, you will not believe the fact, will you object to try it for yourself?

I tried several other annual grasses last year in a similar way but without any change being apparent.

Hoping you will excuse the liberty I have taken as a stranger in thus addressing you I remain | yours respectfully | G S Gibson

Charles Darwin Esq

DAR 165: 40

[1] For earlier discussions of the relationship between oats, barley, and wheat, see *Correspondence* vol. 10, letter to J. B. Innes, 22 December [1862], and *Correspondence* vol. 12, letter from C. S. Bate, 6 January 1864. CD discussed these cereal plants in *Variation* 1: 312–20.

To W. B. Tegetmeier 9 July [1866][1]

Down. | Bromley. | Kent. S.E.
July 9

My dear Sir

I am much obliged for your note & for all the trouble which you have so kindly taken about the Rock Pigeon.[2] I shall be glad to see the proofs when I can. All the skulls &c are now in the engraver's hands.[3]

I am sorry but not at all surprized to hear the result of your experiment with the Cochin & Spanish fowls; I think Mr Zurhorst must have made a mistake.[4]

I have read with interest Mr. Teebay's article & I should have read it without your pointing it out as I re-read all the numbers & an excellent book it appears to me to be.[5]

My dear Sir | yours very sincerely | Ch. Darwin

LS
Archives of The New York Botanical Garden (Charles Finney Cox collection) (Tegetmeier 94)

[1] The year is established by the relationship between this letter and the letter from W. B. Tegetmeier, 4 July 1866.

[2] See letter from W. B. Tegetmeier, 4 July 1866 and nn. 1 and 3.

[3] Chapter 5 of *Variation* contained six engravings of pigeon skulls (pp. 163–7). The drawings were made by Luke Wells, and the engraving was done by the firm of Butterworth and Heath (see *Correspondence* vol. 13, letter from W. B. Tegetmeier to John Murray and R. F. Cooke, 17 April 1865). Tegetmeier had provided many of the skulls for CD's study of the anatomical characteristics of different breeds (see *ibid.*, letter to W. B. Tegetmeier, 27 February [1865]).

[4] Tegetmeier's information was evidently in a missing portion of his letter of 4 July 1866. CD had suggested an experiment on the eggs from a cross between Cochin and Spanish fowl, in order to test findings of an earlier experiment by Frederick William Zurhorst. See letter from W. B. Tegetmeier, 22 January [1866] and n. 9. See also letter from W. B. Tegetmeier, 10 December [1866].

[5] The article by Richard Teebay appeared in Tegetmeier 1867, pp. 154–8. See letter from W. B. Tegetmeier, 4 July 1866 and n. 4. On Tegetmeier's new edition of *The poultry book*, see the letter from W. B. Tegetmeier, 22 January [1866] and nn. 11 and 12.

From Charles Kingsley 12 July 1866

Eversley Rectory, Winchfield.
July 12/66

My dear M^r. Darwin

I flee to you, as usual in ignorance & wonder.[1]

Have you investigated the migration of the eye in Flatfish? I have been reading a paper on it by Prof^f. Thompson in Nat. Hist. Mag. for May 1865.—[2]

I look to your methods for explaining *how* the miracle takes place; whether the eye passes through the scull, or round the soft parts, is a minor question.[3]

Will you kindly do me the honour to look at 2 lectures of mine on Science & Superstition g^n at the Royal Institution, & reprinted in Frazer's Mag. for June & July?[4]

I think you will find that I am not unmindful of your teaching.

I heard with extreme pleasure that your health is much improved.

Yours ever with deep respect & attachment | C Kingsley

DAR 169: 34

[1] CD and Kingsley began to correspond soon after the publication of *Origin* (see *Correspondence* vol. 7, letter from Charles Kingsley, 18 November 1859).

[2] Kingsley refers to the article by Charles Wyville Thomson, 'Notes on Prof. Steenstrup's views on the obliquity of flounders', in the *Annals and Magazine of Natural History* for May 1865 (C. W. Thomson 1865). Thomson gave an abstract, with commentary, of a paper by Japetus Steenstrup on the migration of the eye of flounders.

[3] CD discussed the migration of the eye in Pleuronectidae, or flatfish (now righteye flounders), in *Origin* 6th ed., pp. 186–8, citing Malm 1867. He argued that, when young and still with their eyes on opposite sides, the fish cannot long retain their vertical position, owing to the excessive depth of their bodies, the small size of their lateral fins, and the absence of a swimbladder; growing tired, they fall to the bottom on one side, and while at rest twist their lower eye upwards. Eventually the fish remain permanently on their side, and the eye on the under side gradually shifts around to the upper side. CD concluded that the repositioning of the eye was a result of the inherited effects of use, possibly strengthened by natural selection. See Vorzimmer 1969–70.

[4] The references are to Kingsley 1866a and 1866b.

To John Murray 15 July [1866][1]

Down. | Bromley. | Kent. S.E.
July 15

My dear Sir

As I have rec^{d} the last clean sheets, the new Edit. of the Origin will now soon be bound.[2] I therefore enclose a list of copies which I shall be much obliged if you will have the kindness to distribute.[3]

I would suggest for your consideration whether or not it w^{d} be worth while to send copies to a few of the scientific periodicals which might notice it. I have sent a copy to M^{r}. Samuelson the Ed. of the Q. Journal of science.[4] The London Rev. w^{d} I think be likely to notice it, but you will be much the best of judge of all this.[5] If you advertise I hope you will specify that the work is corrected & enlarged.

I am making decided progress with my next work—[6]

My dear Sir | yours sincerely | Ch. Darwin

P.S. I wish I c^{d} persuade you to have the pages of the Origin cut. It is such an *immense* advantage in any work which has to be referred to by the aid of the index; it keeps it cleaner looks better & saves trouble at first; in fact nothing but insanity will account for this not being done in England—[7]

LS
John Murray Archive

[1] The year is established by the relationship between this letter and the letter from John Murray, 25 May [1866].

[2] Although Murray printed the fourth edition of *Origin* in May, it was not published until November 1866 (*Publishers' Circular*).

[3] This list has not been found; see also letter from John Murray, 23 July [1866]. CD also prepared a different presentation list for the fourth edition of *Origin* (see Appendix IV).

[4] James Samuelson was co-editor of the *Quarterly Journal of Science*, in which a long article on CD's work had recently appeared (see letter from James Samuelson, 8 April 1866, and letter from A. R. Wallace, 2 July 1866).

[5] The *London Review of Politics, Society, Literature, Art and Science* had reviewed the first volume of Richard Owen's *On the anatomy of vertebrates* (Owen 1866–8) in April 1866, and had printed an exchange of letters between Owen and the editor about CD's theory of transmutation (see letter to J. D. Hooker, 31 May [1866], n. 11).

[6] CD sent his manuscript of *Variation* to Murray in December (see letter to John Murray, 21 and 22 December [1866]).

[7] For more on this point, see the letter to J. D. Hooker, 28 [December 1866] and n. 6.

From Searles Valentine Wood 16 July 1866

Brentwood, Essex,
July 16. *1866*

My dear Sir

Most probably you are aware of what I am going to tell you but if not it may be interesting. A friend of mine has a relation a farmer in Cambridgeshire who I am informed regularly sows Oats which are fed off the first year & the stalks are permitted to remain in the ground during the Winter. these come up Barley in the following Summer & this mode of husbandry is commonly adopted on that farm.[1] If you sho[d] be unacquainted with this method of raising a crop of Barley & wo[d] like me to obtain for you further particulars I shall have great pleasure in doing so so that you might yourself verify the fact

I will also mention another circumstance (curious to me) of which I have been informed by an old resident in New Zealand viz that they get the finest Peaches out of the Bush Country grown there on Trees which have sprung from Peach stones thrown away by the Natives without any culture[2]

Yours very truly | Searles Wood

Cha[s]. Darwin Esq.

DAR 181: 145

[1] See letter from G. S. Gibson, 7 July 1866 and n. 1.

[2] For CD's interest in the characteristics of seedling fruit trees, see *Correspondence* vol. 5, letter to *Gardeners' Chronicle*, [before 29 December 1855] (*Collected papers* 1: 263–4), and *Correspondence* vol. 10, letter to Thomas Rivers, 23 December [1862]) and n. 5. CD discussed the peach in *Variation* 1: 337–45.

From Julius von Haast 17 July 1866

Glückauf near Christchurch
17 July 1866.

My dear Mr Darwin

I have to thank you very much for your letter of the 26th of Decbr last with the capital photograph but was very sorry to hear that you have been ill.[1] Our mutual friend Dr Jos Hooker has since told me, that you are much better which news I was delighted to hear.[2] A notice in the English newspapers announces the fact that we may soon expect a new work from your pen.[3] It will give me infinite pleasure to study it.

Some time ago, when kept near the sources of the Rakaia in my tent by bad weather I have written some notes on the theory of the origin of species.— As soon as I have time I shall send them to you.[4] Many thanks for your assistance on behalf of the Royal Soc; I shall wait patiently, till my turn comes.[5] I am just writing a paper for the Geological S. of London on the glacier period of our West coast, with sections, in which I shall give some interesting details of that instructive region.[6] I just returned from the West coast, where we buried my poor brother in law, George Dobson, a very promising young engineer & explorer, who has been murdered by a gang of robbers.[7] Fortunately the wretches are now in safe custody; they have killed many people in a few months. You see the unfortunate thrust after gold brings along horrid crimes to our hitherto so peaceful New Zealand.

The interesting labours of Agassiz will without doubt interest you highly;[8] glaciers after all as you pointed out long before played a great part in the physical geology of the globe.[9]

My report of the headwaters of the Rakaia, which is just being printed by the Gov^t. with numerous sections & sketches will make you aquainted with a highly glacialized region—[10]

My best wishes for the restoration of your health.

With [my truly] kind regards | believe me my dear Mr Darwin | ever yours very sincerely | Julius Haast.

DAR 166: 9

1 CD had enclosed his photograph with his letter to Haast of 26 December [1865] (*Correspondence* vol. 13). He reported that he had been ill since April 1865.

2 On Joseph Dalton Hooker's correspondence with Haast, see H. F. von Haast 1948.

3 CD's publisher, John Murray, had advertised *Variation* in the *Reader*, 15 April 1865, p. 427, and again in the 1 August 1865 issue of the *Publishers' Circular*, p. 386. *Variation* was not published until 1868.

4 Haast explored the area around the head-waters of the Rakaia river in the Southern Alps of New Zealand in March and April 1866 (see H. F. von Haast 1948, pp. 463–75). The notes on species have not been found. On Haast's earlier support of *Origin*, see *Correspondence* vol. 11, letter to Julius von Haast, 22 January 1863.

5 In his letter of 26 December [1865] (*Correspondence* vol. 13), CD had agreed to support Haast's candidacy for fellowship of the Royal Society, adding that Haast would probably not be elected for a year or two. See also letter to Julius von Haast, 5 May [1866].

6 Haast's paper on the glacial deposits in the Southern Alps of Canterbury Province, New Zealand, was published in the *Quarterly Journal of the Geological Society* (J. F. J. von Haast 1867). On CD's interest in the evidence from New Zealand on the Pleistocene glacial period, see *Correspondence* vol. 11, letter to Julius von Haast, 22 January 1863, and *Correspondence* vol. 12, letters from J. D. Hooker, 15 June 1864 and n. 10, and 2 December 1864 and n. 28. CD incorporated some of Haast's observations in *Origin* 4th ed., pp. 442–3.

7 The circumstances of Dobson's death are described in H. F. von Haast 1948, pp. 476–9.

8 Haast refers to Louis Agassiz's expedition to South America from April 1865 to August 1866, a major objective of which was to find evidence of glaciation. CD discussed Agassiz's theory extensively in 1866; see, for example, letters to Charles Lyell, 7 February [1866] and 15 February [1866].

[9] CD had discussed the effects of glaciers in *Journal of researches*, pp. 279–88.

[10] See n. 4, above. Haast's report on the region was published by the provincial government of Christchurch in June 1866 (J. F. J. von Haast 1866; see H. F. von Haast 1948, p. 1092).

From Alfred Hanson 17 July 1866

Inland Revenue Office, London, W.C. | *Legacy and Succession Duty Department*
17th. July *1866*.

Register KM. 3. *of the year 1866 folio* 618.

Sir

I beg to enclose abstracts of the Acts by which duties are charged upon legacies and other Successions to property, for the guidance of the persons liable to account for and pay any duty in consequence of the death of Emily Catherine Langton[1]

I am Sir | *Your obedient Servant* | Alfred Hanson

LS
DAR 186: 45

[1] The enclosures have not been found. CD's sister Catherine had died in February 1866. See letter from J. D. Hooker, 4 February 1866, n. 1.

From B. D. Walsh 17 July 1866

Rock Island, Ill. U.S.
July 17, 1866

Chas. Darwin Esq.
My dear Sir,

I sent you by mail last week a short paper of mine exposing some misquotations of Prof. Dana's, which I hope you have received.[1]

I received in due course your welcome letter of April 20, & was rejoiced to find that you were preparing a new Edition of the Origin.[2] As you are kind enough to promise me a copy, please forward it to me through Baillière 219 Regent S^{t}. to Baillière Bros. of New York, with whom I deal, to be sent thence to me by Express.[3] The Smithsonian Institution is so awfully slow in their operations, that they quite put me out of patience.[4] Curiously enough, the same mail that brought me your last letter brought me also one from Wilson Armistead, saying that he had only just received my box of galls, though I had sent it to the Smithsonian the preceding autumn.[5] He was delighted with what I sent, & like Oliver Twist calls out for more.[6] I am gathering together another lot for him. I had sent him two bottles of galls packed in common salt brine, by way of experiment, & he says it is a complete success & far superior to alcohol—the chief disadvantage being that it is so vulgarly cheap.

I had a copy sent me the other day of an "Analysis of Darwin Huxley & Lyell, by Henry A. Dubois of New York" being a reprint in pamphlet form from the "American Quarterly Church Review", which by the way I never heard of before.[7] The writer is a beautiful compound of fool & knave & makes some most ludicrous blunders in Natural History; besides accusing you of setting up a new God—yes, a real, personal, omniscient, omnipotent, omnipresent God—called "Natural Selection".[8] Hence, one would infer that you must be a Deist. But when he comes to attack Huxley, he talks of "the atheistical views embraced in Darwin's hypothesis"; so that you must be Deist & Atheist both at the same time.[9] "Throw plenty of mud, & some of it is sure to stick". My correspondent (W^m. Edwards of N.Y.)[10] wanted me to review the review; but I thought it answered itself sufficiently, & that anyhow "the game would not pay for the candle".[11]

I believe I have done some little good, at all events among N.A. entomologists, in the way of converting them to the true philosophical faith on the origin of species.[12] For I find a great many of them now who take much the same ground as Rev. Herbert,[13] but cannot as yet "go the whole hog", as we say out West.

Have you read Clark's book on "Mind in Nature"? He strikes me as having almost as illogical a mind as Prof. Agassiz. From one end to the other of the Book I don't see a single new fact or new argument to carry out his thesis, namely that "Mind" exists in Nature. But, so far as I am a judge, his original investigations seem very valuable.[14] I never knew before the history of Agassiz's treatment of him. It always puzzled me why there was no titlepage to the two first parts of the "Contributions", but now I fully understand the why & the wherefore.[15]

You mentioned some time ago the case of a foreign gall-fly having suddenly spread over England.[16] Was it not a species that made its gall on the leaf, so that leaf & gall together might be blown great distances by the wind? I have often remarked that our "Oak-apples" are carried by the wind hundreds of yards with the living insect in them; but the species that make their galls in the twig, so that they are part & parcel of the twig itself, infest the same tree year after year, without spreading, except very slowly indeed sometimes, to adjoining trees.

I find that my Paper on Dimorphism in *Cynips* was reviewed by D^r. Reinhard in the Berlin Entom. Periodical;[17] & that he proposes two hypotheses to account for my facts, *1*^st. that *spongifica* & *aciculata* are distinct species, making undistinguishable galls on the same oak, 2nd. that *spongifica* is an inquiline.[18] But my this year's experiments confirm the fact that *aciculata* generates *spongifica* & *aciculata* indiscriminately; & by next fall I shall in all human probability have facts to show that *aciculata* (A) generates *aciculata* (B), & that in the following season aciculata (B) generates *aciculata* (C), all of them being ♀ ♀ & agamous. I have little doubt now that this process goes on for a considerable number of years in certain species—commonly called agamous—say for 10 or 15 years, until at last a brood of ♂ ♂ appears. This would be altogether analagous to the case of *Aphis* ♀ producing 8 or 9 broods of ♀ ♀ through the summer by parthenogenesis & finally in the autumn ♂ ♂.[19] I am aware that the Germans maintain that the agamous *Aphis* has no true ovary or "egg-stock" but only a "bud-stock"; but this seems to me a mere verbal distinction.

Is it not essential to gemmative reproduction that it should be on the surface of the plant or animal & not in its interior?[20]

I have the concluding part of my Willow Gall Paper now ready for the press. There are some facts in it respecting Galls that I think will please you, showing that Gall-making insects must have originated according to your theory.[21] In the autumn I shall probably throw together the facts respecting Dimorphism in *Cynips*, which I have been accumulating now for two years.

I discovered this morning that a pale green fleshy gall on the leaf of the Grape-vine, which had been described by Dr. Fitch as Aphidian & referred to the genus *Pemphigus*, though he was unacquainted with the winged insect, is in reality the work of a **Coccus**!!! I believe this is the first recorded instance of any species of that family producing galls; at least my books mention none such.[22] The gall is about like this  & globular, & occurs very abundantly, some leaves being almost covered with them. Inside there is a true wingless *Coccus* with a parcel of eggs—say 100—many of which are already hatched out—& no powdery or cottony matter among the young lice, as is always the case with the young plant-lice in galls. Besides, eggs are never found in Aphidian galls, the mother-louse generating viviparously. I wonder if you have any such galls in England.

Yours very truly | Benj. D. Walsh

Field Museum of Natural History, Chicago

CD ANNOTATIONS
3.1 Analysis of . . . York 3.2] *double scored blue crayon*
5.1 Have . . . Nature"?] *double scored blue crayon*
6.2 Was . . . wind? 6.3] *double scored blue crayon*
7.4 But . . . indiscriminately; 7.5] *double scored blue crayon*

1 Walsh refers to his article on James Dwight Dana (Walsh 1866c) and to Dana's article (Dana 1866). Walsh had previously criticised Dana's theory of classification in Walsh 1864a, pp. 238–49.

2 In his letter to Walsh of [19] April [1866], CD remarked that he was preparing a fourth edition of *Origin*. Walsh's name is on the presentation list for the book (see Appendix IV).

3 The French bookselling and publishing firm of Hippolyte Baillière had offices at 219 Regent Street, London, and 290 Broadway, New York (Baillière 1853, *Post Office London directory* 1866).

4 Walsh refers to the Smithsonian Institution in Washington, DC.

5 See letter from B. D. Walsh, 13 March 1866 and n. 8, and letter to B. D. Walsh, [19] April [1866] and n. 5.

6 The eponymous hero of Charles Dickens's novel *Oliver Twist* (Dickens 1838), asked for more gruel after three months in the workhouse.

7 Walsh refers to 'The origin and antiquity of man: Darwin, Huxley and Lyell' by Henry Augustus Dubois. The three-part article was published anonymously in the 1865 volume of *American Quarterly Church Review and Ecclesiastical Register* ([Dubois] 1865), and evidently issued as an offprint under the author's name.

8 Dubois claimed that in *Origin*, CD had defined natural selection as a 'blind and materialistic' force, but that 'with singular inconsistency' he had invested 'physical agents with the attributes of a provident Deity' ([Dubois] 1865, pp. 174, 190). For a discussion of similar criticisms of *Origin*, see the letter from A. R. Wallace, 2 July 1866 and nn. 2 and 3.

[9] Dubois claimed that in *Man's place in nature* (T. H. Huxley 1863a), Thomas Henry Huxley sought 'to disseminate the atheistical views embraced in Darwin's hypothesis' ([Dubois] 1865, p. 337).

[10] Walsh refers to William Henry Edwards.

[11] A variation of the expression 'The game is not worth the candle'.

[12] On Walsh's enthusiastic support of CD's theory, see Walsh 1864d, *Correspondence* vol. 12, letter from B. D. Walsh, 7 November 1864, and Sorensen 1995.

[13] CD discussed William Herbert's work on plant hybridisation in *Origin*, pp. 246–51, and added a summary of his view on species in the historical sketch in *Origin* 3d ed., p. xiv: 'the Dean believes that single species of each genus were created in an originally highly plastic condition, and that these have produced, chiefly by intercrossing, but likewise by variation, all our existing species'. For other remarks by CD on Herbert, see the letter to George Henslow, 15 [June 1866] and nn. 6–8.

[14] Walsh refers to *Mind in nature: or, the origin of life, and the mode of development of animals* by Henry James Clark, a former student and assistant of Louis Agassiz at the Museum of Comparative Zoology at Harvard. Clark defended spontaneous generation on the grounds that it allowed for the continuous operation of 'the Creator's controlling hand' (H. J. Clark 1865, pp. 28–9), and concluded, 'Thus it appears that there is a plainly visible, intelligent, *controlling power*, which is manifested, with *unvarying regularity of character*, in each of the five groups of animals' (*ibid.*, p. 314). CD's annotated copy is in the Darwin Library–Down (see *Marginalia* 1: 166–7). He cited H. J. Clark 1865 on the close relationship between reproduction by self-division and budding in his chapter on pangenesis in *Variation* 2: 358–9.

[15] Clark had been employed by Agassiz in 1855 to assist him in the preparation of *Contributions to the natural history of the United States of America.* The four-volume work appeared with Agassiz as the sole author (J. L. R. Agassiz 1857–62), although Clark had performed much of the microscopical and embryological research and had written substantial portions of the sections on jellyfish. A dispute arose between the men, partly over Clark's efforts to gain acknowledgment as an independent author. Clark circulated a statement of his case against Agassiz to zoologists and scientific societies in America and Europe, and reiterated his claim in H. J. Clark 1865, pp. 37–8 n. For an account of the dispute, see Winsor 1991, pp. 47–65.

[16] CD had reported that a new gall had recently appeared in England and spread rapidly (see *Correspondence* vol. 13, letter to B. D. Walsh, 19 December [1865] and n. 3).

[17] Walsh's paper, 'On dimorphism in the hymenopterous genus *Cynips*' (Walsh 1864c), was reviewed by Hermann Reinhard in *Berliner Entomologische Zeitschrift* (Reinhard 1865). CD's annotated copy of Walsh's paper is in the Darwin Pamphlet Collection–CUL. Walsh had argued that the gall insect *Cynips quercus aciculata* was a dimorphic female form of *C. q. spongifica* (Walsh 1864c, pp. 447–8). See also *Correspondence* vol. 12. Reinhard has not been further identified.

[18] See Reinhard 1865, p. 9.

[19] Walsh gave a similar account of his research on *Cynips*, noting the analogy with reproduction in *Aphis*, in his letter to CD of 12 November 1865 (*Correspondence* vol. 13).

[20] Walsh and CD had previously discussed reproduction by gemmation in *Aphis* and other species (see *Correspondence* vol. 13, letter to B. D. Walsh, 19 December [1865] and nn. 7 and 8).

[21] The reference is to Walsh 1866b. There is a heavily annotated copy in the Darwin Pamphlet Collection–CUL. Walsh had sent CD the first part of the paper the previous year (Walsh 1864b; see *Correspondence* vol. 13, letter from B. D. Walsh, 1 March 1865 and n. 14). Walsh remarked that the study of gall-making insects had important implications for the origin of species (Walsh 1866b, p. 274). In his concluding remarks, he stated that the distribution of gall insects among different genera was inexplicable according to 'the Creative Theory'; he added: 'if our modern species were genetically derived from pre-existing species, several new species being generated from one old one, and whole groups from time to time becoming extinct, the actual state of facts . . . is precisely that which we should . . . expect to meet with' (Walsh 1866b, pp. 287–8). The paper is cited in *Variation* 2: 282.

[22] Walsh described the gall insect in Walsh 1866b, pp. 283–4, noting that it had been wrongly classified by Asa Fitch within the genus of gall-forming aphids, *Pemphigus*, and claiming that it 'must become the type of a new and very aberrant genus' of the family *Coccidae* (*ibid.*, p. 284 n.).

From Asa Gray 18 July 1866

Cambridge,
July 18, 1866

Dear Darwin

I received the enclosed to-day.[1] The Appleton's have the sheets up to p. 288, (to sign n.)[2] I have just collated the sheets **O**, **Q**, R, (**P**, has not come), and it is perfectly clear that the Appletons *cannot alter their plates* so as really to reproduce your revised work.[3]

I have written to them that the collation I have made shows me that you could not do otherwise than object decidedly, as you did in your letter, to the course they propose to pursue;[4]—that I am bound to respect your expressed wishes and that I must ask them to return to me the sheets I finished. In consequence there will be *no reprint* here at present. For no publisher would venture to spite the Appletons by taking it up, without buying up their worthless stereotype plates.

I wish you would arrange to have your publisher supply the U.S. market at a lowish rate, as, at present, the Engl. ed. could well compete with any American one, should such be attempted.[5]

If the Appleton's were not in the way, Messrs Ticknor & Fields would reprint the book,[6] and pay the author 10 pr cent on retail price of the book.—in the hope of being favored with early sheets of the vol. on *Variation & Domestication* on the same terms.[7]

But Dog-in-the-Manger prevents.[8]

Our July is fearfully hot, so far— I am to be off next week, for a short holiday.

Ever Yours sincerely | A. Gray

[Enclosure]

Statement of Sales of "Darwin's Origin of Species"[9]

to 1st Feby *1866*

by D. APPLETON & CO., for account of Asa Gray

On hand last account,	197	*On hand this date,*	290
Printed since,	250	*Given away,*	
		Sold to date,	157
	447		447

Sold 157 *Copies.* $2 *Rate* 5%	*$* 15.70
Jany 1/65. Copyrights due	69.91
	$85.61

John Murray Archive; DAR 159: 80

CD ANNOTATIONS
1.1 I received . . . finished. 2.4] *crossed ink*
6.1 Our . . . holiday.] *crossed ink*

[1] Gray may have enclosed the statement of sales for the US edition of *Origin* printed here. CD and Gray had recently discussed the sale of the book, with Gray noting that he had received 'nothing from Appleton's for years' (see letter from Asa Gray, 7 May 1866 and n. 3, and n. 8, below).
[2] Gray was forwarding proof-sheets of the fourth edition of *Origin* to the publisher D. Appleton and Company for a proposed new American edition of the work. See letter from Asa Gray, 3 July 1866 and n. 5. 'Sign n.': i.e., signature N. A signature is a letter or number placed at the foot of a page to indicate the sequence of sheets, or the pages formed by each sheet when folded and cut (*Chambers*).
[3] On the use of solid plates, or stereotyping, in the production of the American edition of *Origin*, see the letter to Asa Gray, 16 April [1866] and n. 11.
[4] CD's letter and Appleton's proposal have not been found; see letter from Asa Gray, 3 July 1866.
[5] CD forwarded Gray's letter to his publisher, John Murray (see letter to John Murray, 16 October [1866], and letter from John Murray, 18 October [1866]).
[6] Gray had previously approached the Boston firm of Ticknor & Fields about publishing the first American edition, but they withdrew on learning that D. Appleton & Co. had already stereotyped and printed the book for sale in the United States (see *Correspondence* vol. 8, letter from Asa Gray, 23 January 1860 and n. 2, and Appendix IV).
[7] *Variation* was published in the United States in 1868 by Orange Judd & Company of New York, with a preface by Gray (Freeman 1977, p. 124).
[8] See letter from Asa Gray, 3 July 1866, n. 7.
[9] The statement of sales for the American edition of *Origin* was originally enclosed in a letter to Gray from D. Appleton & Co. Other statements, giving the amounts credited to Gray's or CD's account, for 1867 to 1870, 1872, and 1874 to 1881, are in DAR 159; no statements for the years before 1866 have been found. For more information on the sale of the American edition of *Origin*, see the letter from Asa Gray, 7 May 1866 and n. 3.

From John Murray 18 July [1866][1]

50^{A}, Albemarle S^{t} | W.
July 18

My Dear Sir

The season for literary publication is so far passed & people are so destracted by gaieties travelling & War Bulletins[2] that I am keeping back all my new books until the beginning of November

I intended to do this with regard to the new Edition of your work on Species & unless you have some very special reason for bringing it out *now*, I w^{d} beg your consent to the delay wch so far from an injury will prove advantageous to the book.[3] If you agree to this I will take care that your List of presentation copies shall be sent out before the end of October[4]—my selected time for publication being the season when days grow short & nights cold.

If you desire a copy for yourself meanwhile you shall have it with the greatest pleasure

I believe I told you I have made the Edition 1250[5]

My Dear Sir | Yours very faithfully | John Murray

PS. The insanity of English booksellers in not cutting the edges of books arises from the propensity of Englishmen & women to read books without buying them—stantes pede in suo in the booksellers shops—[6] They have various other devices by wch they try to effect the same illaudable object—eg by borrowing I have one friend who has borrowed the Quarterly Review from me regularly for 40 years—

Chas Darwin Esq

DAR 171: 336

[1] The year is established by the relationship between this letter and the letter to John Murray, 15 July [1866].

[2] Murray refers to the Austro-Prussian war. See letter from Asa Gray, 3 July 1866 and n. 8.

[3] The fourth edition of *Origin* was published between 1 and 15 November 1866 (*Publishers' Circular*).

[4] See letter to John Murray, 15 July [1866] and n. 3.

[5] Murray printed 1500 copies of the fourth edition of *Origin* (Peckham ed. 1959, p. 776). In his letter of 25 May [1866], he had indicated that 1000 copies would be printed; on learning of the substantial additions CD had made to the new edition, he then proposed 1500 copies in his letter of 30 May [1866].

[6] 'Stans pede in uno': 'standing on one foot', effortlessly (Ehrlich 1985). Murray altered the phrase to mean, 'Standing (pl.) on their foot'. In the postscript to his letter of 15 July [1866], CD had tried to persuade Murray to have the pages of the fourth edition of *Origin* cut.

To J. D. Hooker 21 [July 1866]

Down.
21st

My dear H.

If you can name enclosed, I shall be grateful. By gardening books I conclude it is L. hirsutus; according them it can**not** be L. pilosus.—[1] The standard is often reddish purple instead of white. I sent to nursery garden, whence I bought seed,[2] & could only hear that it was "the common blue Lupine" The man saying "he was no scholard & did not know Latin & that parties who *make* experiments ought to find out the names.—"

Yours affect | C. Darwin

He might have added & not trouble their friends.

Endorsement: 'July | 1866'
DAR 115: 293

[1] CD was interested in the species of *Lupinus*, subsequently identified by Hooker as *L. pilosus* (letter from J. D. Hooker, [24 July 1866]), as illustrating the difficulty of crossing papilionaceous flowers (see second letter to *Gardeners' Chronicle*, [before 11 August 1866]).

[2] No record of the purchase of lupin seed has been found. CD often obtained specimens and seed from the nursery firm of James Veitch (see *Correspondence* vol. 13).

To Christian Gottfried Ehrenberg 22 July [1866?][1]

Down. | *Bromley.* | *Kent. S.E.*
July 22

Dear & honoured Sir

I beg leave to return you my sincere thanks for your two papers on the Tuff of Mexico & on the "Organisations-Präparate", with its beautiful illustrations, shewing for what a wonderful length of time your method has preserved the specimens.[2]

I feel sincerely honoured by your kind remembrance of me & for the valuable assistance which many years ago you were so good as to afford me[3]

With the most sincere respect | I remain dear Sir | yours truly obliged | Ch. Darwin

LS
Archiv der Berlin-Brandenburgischen Akademie der Wissenschaften, Nachlaß C. G. Ehrenberg, Nr. 321

[1] The year is conjectured from the reference to Ehrenberg 1866 (see n. 2, below).

[2] CD refers to 'Über einen Phytolitharien-Tuff als Gebirgsart im Toluca-Thale von Mexico' ('On a phytolith-tuff as a kind of rock in the Toluca valley of Mexico'; Ehrenberg 1866), and 'Über seit 27-Jahren noch wohl erhaltenen Organisations-Präparate des mikroskopischen Lebens' ('On a well-preserved 27-year-old specimen of microscopic life'; Ehrenberg 1862).

[3] CD had corresponded with Ehrenberg between 1844 and 1846 (see *Correspondence* vol. 3). CD sent him material collected in South America and in the Subantarctic that he thought was likely to contain infusoria. Ehrenberg's analysis and identifications helped CD to establish that dust falling on ships in the Atlantic Ocean had come from Africa (see 'An account of the fine dust which often falls on vessels in the Atlantic Ocean', *Quarterly Journal of the Geological Society of London* 2 (1846): pt 1, 26–30; *Collected papers* 1: 199–203), and that the pampas formations of Argentina had been deposited under brackish or estuarine conditions, rather than in cataclysmic deluges (see *South America*, p. 117).

To Friedrich Hildebrand 22 July [1866][1]

Down. | *Bromley.* | *Kent. S.E.*
July 22.

My dear Sir

I received the enclosed from Dr Masters this morning & have read it again with *extreme* interest. It will be most useful for me to quote.[2]

In the paragraph marked 4 I think there is a serious mis-print of *two* instead of *ten.*[3] I hope it will not be too late for correction, if you will be so good as immediately to return the enclosed to me. I have also suggested with pencil a few trifling corrections, as more usual expressions not but that you write excellent English.

Will you be so good as to tell me where your paper on Oxalis is published, as I suppose you cannot send me a copy.[4]

Believe me my dear Sir | yours faithfully | Charles Darwin

P.S. I have only recently seen a kind & favourable review on my Lythrum paper in the Bot: Zeitung, & which from the initials I suppose was written by you.[5]

LS(A)
Courtesy of Eilo Hildebrand (photocopy)

[1] The year is established by the reference to Hildebrand 1866d (see n. 2, below).

[2] CD refers to proof-sheets of Hildebrand's paper on *Corydalis cava* (Hildebrand 1866d), which was published in the report of the International Horticultural Exhibition and Botanical Congress. CD had received the manuscript from Hildebrand, and had forwarded it to Maxwell Tylden Masters, honorary secretary of the congress (see letter to Friedrich Hildebrand, 16 May [1866] and nn. 3–5).

[3] The correction was made in the published version of the paper (see Hildebrand 1866d, p. 157).

[4] The reference is to Hildebrand 1866c. For CD's interest in the paper, see the letter from Friedrich Hildebrand, 11 May 1866 and nn. 2 and 3, and the letter to Friedrich Hildebrand, 16 May [1866] and nn. 9 and 10.

[5] Hildebrand's review of 'Three forms of *Lythrum salicaria*' appeared in the January 1865 issue of *Botanische Zeitung*, pp. 50–2 (Hildebrand 1865b).

From John Murray 23 July [1866][1]

50A, Albemarle St. | W.
July 23

My Dear Sir

Your wishes regarding the Six copies for England & America of your new Edition shall be carefully attended to[2] & I hope you will suffer no inconvenience from the delay of publication until November[3]

Yours very faithfully | John Murray

Chas Darwin Esq

DAR 171: 337

[1] The year is established by the relationship between this letter and the letter from John Murray, 18 July [1866].

[2] See letter to John Murray, 15 July [1866] and n. 3.

[3] See letter from John Murray, 18 July [1866].

From Friedrich Hildebrand 24 July 1866

Bonn
July 24th | 1866.

Dear and honoured Sir

I must excuse myself that I have not answered your former letter, but I was waiting for the copies of my paper on Oxalis to send you one of them;[1] Prof. A. Braun intended to read it in the Berlin Academy but was prevented by a severe illness; after being recovered he has read it now, and I hope that I shall be able to send you a copy in the next time.[2] I see from the proof-sheet that my expressions have not been quite clear, I hope that they will be so now. I thank you very much for your kind corrections of the mistakes I have made in your language.[3]

I must answer a passage in your first letter of March, because I see, that you have thought my experiments made only on one plant of Corydalis cava, "that might have been individually peculiar".[4] I see from an English flora that you have not this plant in England,[5] it is quite different from the C. lutea where you have a lot of racemes on every plant, here you never have more than one; therefore the experiments made on different racemes are made on as many different plants.[6]

Further you say in your letter of March that you would be surprised if I did not come at last to the belief in ⟨*2 or 3 words*⟩ of individuals[7]—you ⟨*2 or 3 words*⟩ this short expression.— I ⟨*2 or 3 words*⟩ that from the first time I ⟨*1 or 2 words*⟩ your excellent "Origin of S⟨pecies"⟩ I have believed in it, and ⟨*1 or 2 words*⟩ strongly insist on this point ⟨*1 or 2 words*⟩ writing after some time—perhaps ⟨*1 word*⟩ on the different kinds of plants-⟨fer⟩tilisation.—[8] A new proof of this law I lastly found in Aristolochia Clematitis that is weiblich-männlich dichogamisch.[9] Sprengel has made here a mistake: the Insects find only the stigma developped in the young flower,— soon this stigma is covered and spoiled, then the anthers open themselves, and now the Insects can get out of the flower to bring the pollen to a younger one.[10]

⟨*1 or 2 words*⟩ ⟨revie⟩w of your paper on ⟨Lythrum salicaria w⟩as written by me,[11] I hope ⟨*2 or 3 words*⟩ have been content with ⟨*1 or 2 words*⟩ ⟨pe⟩rhaps I shall get a copy ⟨*1 or 2 words*⟩ remarks on Corydalis—

⟨I⟩ am in a great hurry to ⟨post⟩ your letter, & therefore you ⟨must⟩ excuse me— Take my best ⟨than⟩ks for your two very kind ⟨le⟩tters and believe me dear Sir | yours | faithfully | Hildebrand

DAR 166: 204; DAR 49: 150

CD ANNOTATION
Bottom of second page: '(Dichogamy) Hildebrand' *pencil*

1 CD had requested a copy of Hildebrand's paper on *Oxalis* (Hildebrand 1866c) in his letter of 16 May [1866]; he asked where it had been published in his letter to Hildebrand of 22 July [1866]. For CD's interest in the paper, see also the letter from Friedrich Hildebrand, 11 May 1866, nn. 2 and 3.

2 Alexander Carl Heinrich Braun read Hildebrand 1866c at the 21 June 1866 meeting of the Königlichen Akademie der Wissenschaften zu Berlin (Royal Academy of Sciences in Berlin).

3 CD had corrected the proof-sheets of Hildebrand's paper on *Corydalis cava* (Hildebrand 1866d). See letter to Friedrich Hildebrand, 22 July [1866])

4 For CD's comments on Hildebrand 1866d, see the letter to Friedrich Hildebrand, 16 May [1866] and nn. 5 and 6. Hildebrand evidently wrote 'March' in error.

5 *Corydalis cava*, now treated as a synonym of *C. bulbosa*, is found in central and southern Europe (Tutin *et al.* eds. 1964–80, vol. 1). According to Lindley 1859, *C. bulbosa* was found in parts of Britain; however, Bentham 1865 describes only *C. lutea* and *C. claviculata* as British species.

6 See letter to Friedrich Hildebrand, 16 May [1866] and n. 6.

7 See letter to Friedrich Hildebrand, 16 May [1866] and n. 13.

8 Hildebrand alludes to CD's claim in *Origin*, p. 97, 'that no organic being self-fertilises itself for an eternity of generations'. Hildebrand first supported CD's view on crossing in print in Hildebrand 1867, p. 5.

9 The literal translation is 'female–male dichogamic'. Hildebrand published his observations of dichogamy in *Aristolochia clematitis* in Hildebrand 1866–7a. For more on *Aristolochia clematitis* and CD's interest in Hildebrand's paper, see the letter from Friedrich Hildebrand, 23 October 1866 and nn. 4 and 5.

10 Christian Konrad Sprengel described pollination in *Aristolochia clematitis* in Sprengel 1793, pp. 418–29. For more on Sprengel's observations, see the letter from Friedrich Hildebrand, 23 October 1866 and n. 3.

11 Hildebrand had written a review of 'Three forms of *Lythrum salicaria*.' See letter to Friedrich Hildebrand, 22 July [1866] and n. 5.

From J. D. Hooker [24 July 1866][1]

Kew
Tuesday

Dear old Darwin

Your Lupin is certainly *L. pilosus* admirably figured in Sibthorp's Fl. Græca—[2] (*L. hirsutus* is a little thing—quite different)—[3] It is a Mediterranean species, very many thanks for the specimen.

I am groaning over my Lecture—[4] I have done Madeira, & am at Canaries, I am utterly puzzled by the absence of alpine or even of subalpine plants in Madeira— it reminds me of what I have heard of Sardinia—I think—& indeed of all European mts south of Pyrenees[5] & alps more or less; & of Atlas again.[6] Then again I am more impressed & staggered than ever with the number of rare local things common to Madeira & Canaries, which are not littoral plants, & which I cannot account for without land extension[7]

Take *Dracæna Draco.*, on mts. of Madeira, of Canaries & of Cape de Verds! or *Bencomia*, a **dioeceous tree**—of which one ♂ plant has been found at top of rocks in Madeira, & one female by a peasant & which is found only else in Canaries & then is excessively rare *Myrica Faya*, found only in West Portugal, Madeira Azores & Canaries!—& so on. An Atlantis is the only possible guess that holds water[8]

Most of the alpine Cameroons plants are natives of Cape de Verd Mts, Canary Mts, & of Madeira & Azores.[9]

I have been reading Ed^d. Forbes again & with admiration, despite its faults:— how near he was to being a very great man; dear old fellow as he was— I had not read it for years, & it reminded me of how we had worked together & made me melancholy. I shall allude to it, as a Brit. Ass. affair—[10] Was his the first *scientific* proposition of the Atlantis?[11]

How disappointing are the Introductory Remarks to Wollaston's Catalogue of Mad & Canarian Coleoptera.[12] Has he any where indicated the apterous proportion, or the strength of European elements in the Entomology of these groups.[13] The Madeiran Catalogue remarks are the best of the two.[14] If I remember aright, all the Kerguelens land insects were apterous, including the moth![15]

Is it not odd that there is a direct relation between the numerical rarity & endemic character of Madeiran plants— thus out of 193 *strictly indigenous* species & varieties *identical* with European

134 are common (61. ccc) (very common)
59 are scarce (11 rrr) (very rare)[16]

Of 16 Madeiran plants that are local varieties of European
1 is a common plant
15 are scarce (4 rrr.)

Of 65 non European plants chiefly Madeiran, but a few common also to the Canaries
21 are common (5 of them ccc)
44 are rare (17 rrr.!)

the more endemic (or the ultra endemic as Wollaston calls them) the more rare.[17]

It looks as if later climatic conditions had favored the prevalence of the European elements at the expense of the Endemic.

Of the extra European types the most curious are *Clethra* & Persea species of very large American genera found no where in the Old World. *Apollonias*, a genus of Laurels, having only 2 species, this Madeiran & a Nilgherrie Mt one. The aforesaid *Dracæna Draco* & several tropical African genera, of trees as *Pittosporum*, *Sideroxylon*, *Myrsine* &c.[18] It is also curious that the majority of the Extra European genera are arbroeous![19]

I am now doing Canaries, the Vegetation is more peculiar than I thought—still no alpine or even *cold* temperate European plants except a few of the Cameroons ones.

It is curious that Wollaston finds the Insects *proportionately* fewer than in Madeira,[20] for I think the Flora is *proportionately* richer—a good deal,

How does your health hold?

Ever yrs affec | Jos D Hooker

My wife takes the children to S^t^. Alban's for 6 weeks—[21]

DAR 205.2 (letters): 239

CD ANNOTATIONS

2.2 even . . . Madeira—] *scored pencil*
2.2 subalpine] *underl pencil*
2.3 & indeed . . . less; 2.4] *scored pencil*
2.6 which are . . . extension 2.7] *scored pencil*
3.5 An Atlantis . . . water] *double scored pencil*
4.1 Most . . . Azores. 4.2] *scored pencil*
4.2 Madeira] *underl pencil*
5.4 Was his . . . Atlantis? 5.5] *scored pencil*
6.1 How . . . Catalogue] *scored pencil*
6.2 the apterous . . . elements 6.3] *scored pencil*
7.1 Is it . . . plants— 7.2] *scored pencil*
7.13 the more . . . rare.] *scored pencil*
8.1 It looks . . . Endemic. 8.2] *scored pencil*
9.5 It is . . . arbroeous! 9.6] *scored pencil*
10.1 still . . . alpine 10.2] *scored pencil*

1 The date is established by the relationship between this letter and the letters to J. D. Hooker, 21 [July 1866] and 30 July [1866]. In 1866, 24 July was the only intervening Tuesday.

2 CD had enclosed a specimen of lupin for identification (see letter to J. D. Hooker, 21 [July 1866] and n. 1). Hooker refers to John Sibthorp. *Lupinus pilosus* is illustrated and described in Sibthorp 1806–40, vol. 7, plate 684 and p. 77.

3 CD had tentatively identified the specimen as *Lupinus hirsutus* (see letter to J. D. Hooker, 21 [July 1866]).

4 Hooker was preparing a lecture on insular floras for the meeting of the British Association for the Advancement of Science to be held at Nottingham in August 1866 (see letter from J. D. Hooker, 16 January 1866 and n. 9). For bibliographical details of the lecture, see the letter from J. D. Hooker, [28 August] 1866, n. 3. The full text of the lecture was serialised in the *Gardeners' Chronicle* (J. D. Hooker 1866a) and later published, in a corrected version, as a pamphlet. This pamphlet has been reproduced with a critical introduction in Williamson 1984.

[5] Hooker in fact refers to the mountains of the northern shore of the Mediterranean (see letter from J. D. Hooker, 31 July 1866).

[6] In his lecture on insular floras (see n. 4, above), Hooker noted that many species were identifiable with those of a 'mother continent', and allowed for the possibility of a former connection between islands and their 'mother continent' (J. D. Hooker 1866a, p. 50). The absence of alpines on Madeira and the Canary Islands (*ibid.*, pp. 6, 27) would have puzzled Hooker as an example of difference between island and continental floras. For comment on this topic, see Williamson 1984, pp. 55–8.

[7] In his lecture, Hooker speculated on the causes of rarity among non-littoral endemic species on oceanic islands (J. D. Hooker 1866a, p. 7). Hooker also suggested that the rare endemics common to Madeira and the Canary Islands might be relics of a former distribution that extended over adjacent continents and intervening land that had since been submerged (J. D. Hooker 1866a, p. 50).

[8] In his lecture, Hooker referred to the presence on Madeira of *Dracaena*, derived from Africa, and of a single female and male plant of *Bencomia caudata* from the Canary Islands. Hooker also referred to Edward Forbes's hypothesis of Atlantis (J. D. Hooker 1866a, p. 50). According to Forbes, a continent had once linked the Iberian peninsula with the Azores and with Ireland, thus providing a land-bridge over which plant species dispersed during the Miocene period (Forbes 1845 and 1846). For extensive discussions of Forbes's Atlantis hypothesis, and CD's and Hooker's earlier correspondence on the derivation of the floras of the Atlantic islands, see *Correspondence* vols. 3 and 5–7.

[9] CD and Hooker had earlier corresponded extensively about the relationships of the plants of the Cameroon mountains (see *Correspondence* vols. 10 and 11). In a published account of those plants, Hooker enumerated forty-nine that grew at an altitude of 9000 feet or higher, and noted their geographical origins (J. D. Hooker 1863). In his lecture on insular floras (see n. 4, above), Hooker considered, in turn, the plant species of Madeira, the Canary Islands, the Azores and the Cape Verde Islands. See also letter from J. D. Hooker, 13 May 1866 and n. 13, and letter to J. D. Hooker, 16 May [1866] and n. 5.

[10] Hooker refers to Edward Forbes and to his 'On the distribution of endemic plants' (Forbes 1846); a summary was published in the *Report of the 15th meeting of the British Association for the Advancement of Science* (Forbes 1845; see also n. 8, above). Hooker had worked with Forbes for the Geological Survey of Great Britain between 1845 and 1847 (L. Huxley ed. 1918, 1: 206–22).

[11] Forbes appears to have been the first to invoke an Atlantic land-bridge in the nineteenth century (see n. 8, above); however, Justus Lipsius had speculated in the seventeenth century on a migration of animals from Africa to America by way of Atlantis (Browne 1983, p. 12). Oswald Heer advanced a further Atlantis hypothesis in which Europe, Africa, and North America were connected by a land-bridge (Heer 1855 and 1860). See also *Correspondence* vol. 13, letter from Charles Lyell, 16 January 1865 and n. 19, and letter to Charles Lyell, 21 February [1865] and nn. 3 and 4.

[12] Thomas Vernon Wollaston's works on Coleoptera include *Catalogue of the coleopterous insects of Madeira* (T. V. Wollaston 1857), *Catalogue of the coleopterous insects of the Canaries* (T. V. Wollaston 1864), and *Coleoptera atlantidum* (T. V. Wollaston 1865), in which beetles of both Madeira and the Canaries are described. Hooker probably refers to Wollaston 1865.

[13] In his letter to Hooker of 7 March [1855] (*Correspondence* vol. 5), CD had remarked on the 'astounding proportion' of Coleoptera that were apterous in Wollaston's *Insecta Maderensia* (see T. V. Wollaston 1854, p. xii; see also T. V. Wollaston 1856, pp. 82–7). Wollaston also considered a few examples of similarities between Madeiran Coleoptera and European species in T. V. Wollaston 1856 (pp. 137–44), arguing that they provided evidence in support of Forbes's hypothesis (see n. 8, above). CD referred to Wollaston's work on Madeiran beetles in *Origin*, pp. 135–6, suggesting that insects without wings were less susceptible to being blown out to sea and were therefore favoured by natural selection.

[14] See n. 12, above.

[15] Hooker had visited Kerguelen's Land, a subantarctic island in the south Indian Ocean, in 1840 (R. Desmond 1999, pp. 38–43), but found only three different species of insect there (*Correspondence* vol. 3, letter from J. D. Hooker, [mid-July 1845]). In his letter of [before 17 March 1855] (*Correspondence* vol. 5), Hooker had remarked, 'The fact of Apterous Coleoptera strikes me too as extremely curious &

reminds me of an old remark I made that not only the few beetles of Kerguelens land were apterous but the only Lepidopterous insect on the Island was so too!'

16 The categories r (rare), rr (very rare) and rrr (extremely rare), and the equivalent categories of c for commonness, are to be found in the first volume of *A manual flora of Madeira* (Lowe 1868), on which Hooker probably relied for his analysis of the flora of Madeira. See also letter from J. D. Hooker, 13 May 1866.

17 In his studies of beetles in Madeira, Wollaston had distinguished between endemic species, which he thought had been created in the places where they were found, and those that had migrated from another area; the former he termed 'ultra-indigenous' (T. V. Wollaston 1857, p. viii). In the account of Madeira in his lecture, Hooker noted that the islands contained many indigenous species that were also rare (J. D. Hooker 1866a, p. 7).

18 In his lecture, Hooker reiterated this information on insular species belonging to genera that elsewhere were represented only on distant continents; he referred to all the non-European genera named here, except *Pittosporum* and *Sideroxylon* (J. D. Hooker 1866a, p. 7). The Nilgiri Hills or Nilgiris are in the southern Indian state of Tamil Nadu (*Times atlas*).

19 Hooker intended to write arboreous.

20 See J. D. Hooker 1866a, p. 27. For Wollaston's statistics on the relative abundance of coleopterous insects in Madeira and the Canaries, see, for example, T. V. Wollaston 1864, p. xi.

21 Hooker and his wife, Frances Harriet, had four surviving children, William Henslow (aged 13), Harriet Anne (12), Charles Paget (11), and Brian Harvey Hodgson (6) (Allan 1967). St Albans is a market-town in Hertfordshire, England. The Hookers had friends in St Albans (*Correspondence* vol. 12, letter from J. D. Hooker, 29 March 1864; see also Allan 1967, p. 180).

From Ellen Frances Lubbock to H. E. Darwin [28 July? 1866][1]

Dear Miss Darwin

I am so sorry you were prevented from coming on Friday, & also that we shall not have the pleasure of seeing M^r. Darwin today—[2] Do you think, when he feels pretty well, he would be so kind as to write some thing like this on a piece of paper for me—

Please deliver to the bearer a copy of the new edition of the Origin of Species—, & sign it— The fact is, John has promised a copy to Philip Norman, & as he is going to India, directly, he wishes to take it with him—& he went the other day to Murray's, but was refused a copy, as M^r. Murray did not know him personally, & thought M^r. Darwin would not like them to give him one before the work is published—[3] But I do not think M^r. Darwin would mind, & if he will kindly scratch down the order, I will send it to Phil—

I am so sorry to trouble him—

With Kindest regards to you all, believe me yours affectly | El Lubbock

DAR 170: 11

1 The year is established by the reference to the fourth edition of *Origin* (see n. 3, below). The day and month are conjectured by the entries in Emma Darwin's diary (DAR 242), and by the reference to presentation copies of *Origin* (see nn. 2 and 3, below).

2 Emma Darwin's diary (DAR 242) records that CD had a headache on Friday 27 July 1866; Emma also noted that she attended a 'fete at High Elms' (the Lubbock family home) on 28 July.

[3] The fourth edition of *Origin* was printed by mid-July 1866 (see letter to John Murray, 15 July [1866]), but CD's publisher, John Murray, had recently informed CD that he wished to delay publication until November (letter from John Murray, 18 July [1866]). Norman's father, George Warde Norman, was a good friend of the Darwin family and had received a presentation copy of the first edition of *Origin* (see *Correspondence* vol. 8, Appendix III).

To J. D. Hooker 30 July [1866]

Down
July 30

My dear Hooker

Many thanks about the Lupine. Your letter has interested me *extremely* & reminds me of old times.[1] I suppose by your writing, you would like to hear my notions. I cannot admit the Atlantis connecting Madeira & Canary Islands without the strongest evidence & all on that side: the depth is so great; there is nothing geologically in the islands favouring the belief; there are no endemic mammals or batrachians;[2] did not Bunbury shew that some orders of plants were singularly deficient?[3] But I rely chiefly on the large amount of specific distinction in the insects & land-shells of P. Santo & Madeira; surely Canary & Madeira c^{d} not have been connected if Mad. P. Santo had long been distinct.[4] If you admit Atlantis, I think you are bound to admit or explain the difficulties.

With respect to cold temperate plants in Mad: I of course know not enough to form an opinion; but admitting Atlantis I can see their rarity is a great difficulty; otherwise seeing that the latitude is only a little N. of the Persian Gulph & seeing the long sea transport for seeds, the rarity of N. plants does not seem to me difficult.[5] The immigration may have been from a Southerly direction & it seems that some few African, as well as coldish plants are common to the M^{ts} to the South.[6]

Believing in occasional transport, I cannot feel so much surprize at there being a good deal in common to Mad. & Canary; These being the nearest points of land to each other.[7] It is quite new & very interesting to me what you say about the endemic plants being in so large a proportion rare Species. From the greater size of the workshop (i.e. greater competition & greater number of individuals &c) I sh^{d} expect that continental forms, as they are occasionally introduced, w^{d} always tend to beat the insular forms; & as in every area there will always be many forms more or less rare tending towards extinction, I sh^{d} certainly have expected that in Islands a large proportion of the rarer forms w^{d} have been insular in their origin.[8] The longer the time any form has existed in an island, into which continental forms are occasionally introduced, by so much the chances will be in favour of it's being peculiar or abnormal in nature, & at the same time scanty in numbers. The duration of its existence will also have formerly given it the best chance, when it was not so rare, of being widely distributed to adjoining archipelagos. Here is a wriggle; the older a form is the better the chance will be of its having become developed into a tree![9] An island from being surrounded by the sea will prevent free immigration & competition, hence a greater number of ancient forms will survive on an island than on the nearest continent whence the island was stocked; & I have always looked at Clethra & the other extra-european forms as remnants of the tertiary flora which formerly inhabited Europe.[10] This preservation of ancient forms in islands appears to me like the preservation of ganoid fishes in our present fresh waters.[11]

You speak of no northern plants on mountains south of the Pyrenees; does my memory quite deceive me that Boissier published a long list from the mountains in *southern* Spain?[12]

I have not seen Woollaston's catalogue but must buy it, if it gives the facts about rare plants which you mention.[13]

And now I have given more than enough of my notions which I well know will be in flat contradiction with all yours. Remember that you have to come here if you possibly can before Nottingham.[14]

Wollaston in his Insecta Maderiensis 4to. p. xii & in his Variation of Species p. 82–87 gives case of Apterous insects, but I remember I worked out some additional details. I think he gives in these same works the proportion of European insects.—[15]

I sh^d be most grateful for loan of Book with enclosed Title, if you have it; for I presume I could no how else see it—[16]

Yours affect | C. Darwin

LS(A)
Endorsement: '/66'
DAR 115: 294, 294b

1 See letter from J. D. Hooker, [24 July 1866]. On CD's earlier debates with Hooker about geographical distribution, see the letter to Charles Lyell, 15 February [1866], n. 6.

2 See letter from J. D. Hooker, [24 July 1866] and n. 8. In 1856, CD had objected to the Atlantis hypothesis, citing the same reasons as evidence against a continental connection between Madeira and Africa (*Correspondence* vol. 6, letter to Charles Lyell, 25 June [1856]). On the Atlantis hypothesis, see Forbes 1846, especially pp. 348–9. For CD's views on the means by which oceanic islands were populated, see *Origin*, pp. 388–406.

3 Charles James Fox Bunbury had noted the absence from Madeira of many European plants which would have been expected if Madeira and Europe had formerly been connected (C. J. F. Bunbury 1855, pp. 19–20); CD's lightly annotated unbound copy of C. J. F. Bunbury 1855 is in the Darwin Library–CUL. Among CD's notes on island floras is a record of a conversation dated 25 March 1855 in which Bunbury had said that *Cistus* and *Ophrys* did not grow in Madeira, and that northern genera in Madeira were represented by different species from those of the mainland (DAR 205.4: 68).

4 Porto Santo lies within 50 km of Madeira in the Madeiran archipelago, over 500 km from the Canary Islands. Richard Thomas Lowe had found the land snails of Madeira and Porto Santo to be very different (Lowe 1854; see also *Correspondence* vol. 5). For the geological inferences drawn from Lowe's observation, see, for example, *Correspondence* vol. 8, letter from Charles Lyell, [13–14 February 1860] and n. 10. On the differences between the land shells of Porto Santo and Madeira and those of other islands, see the letters from R. T. Lowe, 19 September 1854 (*Correspondence* vol. 5).

5 In his letter of [24 July 1866], Hooker had noted the absence of alpine and subalpine plants in Madeira. Hooker and CD held differing views of the means by which plants were distributed among continents and islands (see, for example, *Correspondence* vol. 13, letter to J. D. Hooker, 22 and 28 [October 1865] and nn. 11–13). The colonisation of islands, and the differences between island and continental species, are discussed in *Origin*, pp. 388–406. CD considered that continental extension,

as in Edward Forbes's Atlantis hypothesis, would have resulted in more continental species on islands than are actually found; instead, CD suggested that the rarity of continental species on islands was attributable to distance from the mainland and to the subsequent modification by natural selection of any species that had reached an island by occasional transport (see *Origin*, pp. 396–9).

6 In *Origin*, pp. 367–8, CD described the migration of temperate plants at the end of the glacial period. Hooker's observation that native plants of Madeira were also to be found in the Cameroon mountains is in his letter of [24 July 1866]. Bunbury had described species of plants common to the Cape region of South Africa and the mountains around Funchal in the south of Madeira (C. J. F. Bunbury 1855, p. 5).

7 In his letter of [24 July 1866], Hooker had written about certain rare species of plants present in both Madeira and the Canaries, though not in the coastal zones, and Hooker had suggested that this could be explained according to the hypothesis of continental extension. For CD's belief in the importance of occasional, or accidental, means of transport in the colonisation of islands by plants, see *Origin*, pp. 356–65. CD's definition of occasional transport encompassed the transport of seeds by the sea and by animals, especially birds flying across the sea from one land mass to another (*Origin*, pp. 358–65).

8 Hooker discussed the rarity of endemic Madeiran plants in his letter of [24 July 1866]. CD suggested that naturalised plant species on islands and mountains could become dominant over native ones owing to the larger areas or 'workshops' for natural selection in which the naturalised species had originated in *Origin*, pp. 379–80.

9 On CD's and Hooker's joke about 'wriggling', see the letter to Charles Lyell, 15 February [1866], n. 11. In *Origin*, p. 392, CD gave a similar account of the possibility that, on islands that had been treeless, trees might have developed gradually by the action of natural selection on the most vigorous herbaceous plants. For CD's initial observations of vegetation that 'deserved the title of a wood' in the Galápagos Islands, see *'Beagle' diary*, p. 361.

10 *Clethra* is a genus of sixty-four tropical American and Asian species, with one species in North America and one in Madeira (Mabberley 1997). In *Origin*, p. 107, CD noted Oswald Heer's view that the flora of Madeira resembled the extinct tertiary flora of Europe (see Heer 1855, p. 8 *et seq.*).

11 CD argued that the survival of primitive forms was favoured on islands and in fresh water, because competition between organisms was less pronounced in those environments than on continents or in oceans, in *Origin*, pp. 106–7. As an illustration CD referred to the 'remnants of a once preponderant order', the freshwater ganoid fishes, arguing that there was less competition in any freshwater basin than in the sea (*Origin*, p. 107).

12 CD refers to Pierre-Edmond Boissier and to Boissier 1839–45. Boissier 1839–45 includes lists of mountain plants from the province of Granada in southern Spain that also occur in the Pyrenees, and in the French and Swiss Alps, together with a table of the altitudes at which the plants are found in the different regions (Boissier 1839–45, 1: 227–8, 237–8).

13 CD misunderstood the references to Thomas Vernon Wollaston in the letter from J. D. Hooker, [24 July 1866], as implying that he had published a new work on the plants of Madeira. However, Wollaston's publications about the Atlantic islands were confined to their entomology and conchology.

14 Hooker visited CD in Down on 18 August before giving his lecture on insular floras at the meeting of the British Association at the Advancement of Science in Nottingham on 27 August 1866 (see letters from J. D. Hooker, [17 August 1866] and 18 August 1866).

15 CD refers to T. V. Wollaston 1854, p. xii, and T. V. Wollaston 1856, pp. 82–7; there is an annotated copy of the former, and a heavily annotated copy of the latter, in the Darwin Library–CUL (see *Marginalia* 1: 875–9). CD's detailed abstract of T. V. Wollaston 1854, with his additional calculations of the proportions of winged and apterous beetles on Madeira, is in the Darwin Archive–CUL (DAR 197: 1). Inside the back cover of his copy of *Insecta Maderensia* (T. V. Wollaston 1854), CD pasted his own estimate of the number of endemics among the insect species mentioned in the book. Although Wollaston noted that some of the 200 apterous beetles of Madeira were also distributed in Europe (T. V. Wollaston 1856, p. 83; see also T. V. Wollaston 1854, p. xiii), no specific proportion was given in

the works to which CD refers here. CD quoted Wollaston's data on the apterous beetles of Madeira in *Origin*, pp. 135–6.

[16] The enclosure has not been found.

From J. D. Hooker 31 July 1866

Kew
July 31/66

Dear Darwin

Is there an evidence that the South of England & of Ireland, were *not submerged* during the Glacial Epoch, when the W. & N. of England were Islands in a glacial sea? And supposing they were above water, could the present Atlantic & N.W. of France Floras we now find there, have been there during the Glacial Epoch?— yet this is what Forbes demands, p 346. At p 347 he sees this objection & *wriggles* out of his difficulty by putting the date of the Channell "towards the close of the Glacial Epoch"[1]

What does Austin make the date of the Channell—ante or post glacial?[2]

Origin Ed III. top of p. 344, how can the breaking of an isthmus give rise to an **ir**ruption of new inhabitants?[3]

I think you are wrong in Origin in implying that the true character of Insular Flora is altogether (or almost) due to herbaceous forms of nearest continent becoming arboreous: though the latter is a strong element too. N. Zealand is a heavy case to the contrary.[4] Is DeCandolle right in saying Trees have restricted ranges?[5] it is quite the contrary with Pines, Oaks, Beeches, Birches

Thanks for yours just received, which I should like to discuss with you—[6] I had before your main arguments, quite clear, but you now send me some important developements.

You must not suppose me to be a champion of Continental Connection, because I am not agreeable to transoceanic migration.[7] I have no fixed opinion on the subject—& am much in the state regarding this point, that the Vestiges left me in regarding species.[8] What we want is, not new facts, but new ideas analogous to yours of Natural selection in its application to origin— Either hypothesis appears to me well to cover the facts of oceanic Floras, but there are grave objections to both, Botanical to your's, Geological to Forbes.[9]

I intend to discuss the point with as little prejudice as I can at Cambridge[10]—in fact to d—d both hypotheses, or if you like to d—n Ed. Forbes & double d—n yours! for I suppose that is how *you* will take my **fair play**. I own that it is *most disgusting* to have no side, & I cannot tell you how it dispirits me with the whole thing. I shall make up for it by blessing Nat. selection & Variation—& they shall be blest—as necessary to either hypothesis, & therefore proving them to be twice as right as if it only fitted one![11]

By saying mountains south of Pyrenees I spoke foolishly. & should have said of North shore of Mediterranean.[12] Boissier gives a capital list—. of Grenadan alpines common to North.—[13] I forgot all about S. Spain having mountains— I referred to Appenines, M^{ts} of Sardinia & of Atlas, in which I think no alpine plants occur, I think.

The absence of *any* alpine or subalpine plant of Spain in Madeira or Canaries puzzles me greatly, as they must have been Islands in **your** glacial sea (there is a sneer for you) & yet you must expect it from there being no boulders.[14]

?Have you anywhere stated that you regard the *old* elements of Madeira flora as remains of Tertiary epoch?[15]

I quite grant that the oldest forms have best chance of being developed into Trees.

I should like to look for old moraines on Pico. Erica Daboeci, a native of W. Ireland & Asturias, being common in two Islands, & Calluna on 3 are staggering facts.[16]

With regard to the specific differences between Porto Santo & Madeira, it seems pretty much most marked in *shells*,[17] & they do seem to change very fast under some circumstances. Of course I should include them in the same continent: & should have thought its peculiarities quite as good evidence of the sunk continent theory as of the reverse— Two adjacent lands sink, gradually, till all that remains of one is a barren sunburnt rock, of the other a lofty moist wooded mountain. I should expect the organisms common to both, to be most changed by the struggle in the smaller & drier area.

The Azorean Flora is almost identical with the Madeiran, It has about 30 endemic species & varieties, which with 25 Maccronesian species,[18] make 55 sp. out of about 350 difft. from Europe— Though upwards of 500 miles N. of Madeira & with M^{ts}. 7000 ft high, it contains only 3 plants of more boreal character than Madeira, viz. Viola palustris & *Calluna vulgaris*, both which however reached Grenada, & *Littorella lacustris*, a more boreal water plant which may have brought to the Lake by Gulls' feet— Considering how much nearer these Islands are to Newfoundland on one hand & Britain on the other, this absence of more plants of either country seems marvellous.[19] It also appears strange to me that Madeira should have contributed 25 of her otherwise endemic forms to such a distance & that they should have kept their characters.

The Islands want better exploring however.

Of course you know that the sea currents all set from the Atlantic Islands to the Mediterranean,—but that is a trifle to a sound migrationist![20]

We have not Duvernoya.[21]

Acropera will be sent tomorrow to be left at Bromley station.[22]

Ever yr aff | J D Hooker

DAR 102: 81–6

CD ANNOTATIONS[23]

1.1 England] *underl pencil*

1.1 Ireland . . . Epoch, 1.2] *scored pencil*; 'Yes' *added pencil*

1.3 could the . . . Epoch?— 1.4] *scored pencil*; 'No' *added pencil*; 'as soon believe that those of France c^{d} not exist on summit of Mt B' *added pencil*

2.1 What . . . glacial?] *scored pencil*; 'I forget' *added pencil*
3.1 Origin . . . inhabitants? 3.2] *doubled scored pencil*
4.4 Is DeCandolle . . . ranges?] *double scored pencil*
6.1 You . . . Connection,] *scored pencil*; 'Coral Islets' *added pencil*
6.6 but there . . . to Forbes. 6.7] *scored pencil*; 'I shall much like to hear Botanical reasons against occasional migration— Remember *[illeg]*' *added pencil*
6.7 Botanical] *underl pencil*
7.5 thing.] *closing square bracket added after, pencil*
9.1 or Canaries] 'or' *del pencil*
10.1 ?Have you . . . epoch? 10.2] *double scored pencil*
13.1 it seems . . . *shells*, 13.2] *scored pencil*
14.1 It has . . . than Madeira, 14.4] *scored pencil*; 'No doubt great difficulties' *added pencil*
14.7 Considering . . . other, 14.8] *scored blue crayon*
16.1 Of course . . . Mediterranean 16.2] *double scored pencil*
Top of letter: 'Book— Acropera' *pencil*

[1] Hooker refers to Edward Forbes and to Forbes 1846. Forbes argued that the flora of Kent had migrated from north-western France (Forbes 1846, p. 346), and noted that the distinct floras of south-western England and south-eastern Ireland was closely related to that of the Channel Islands and the extreme west of France (*ibid.*, p. 347; see also *ibid.*, p. 338). Although Forbes favoured pre-glacial migrations for these flora, he conceded that their survival might have been endangered later by low temperatures around the glacial sea in the area of the English channel. Forbes went on to suggest their more recent migration, and that the English Channel might be of post-Pliocene origin (*ibid.*, p. 347; see also J. D. Hooker 1866a, p. 50, for Hooker's summary of Forbes's hypothesis).

[2] According to Robert Alfred Cloyne Godwin-Austen, the English Channel was formed during the Pleistocene period, that is in the post-Pliocene, after the coldest phase of the Glacial Period (Austen 1849, pp. 87–9, 95; see also Imbrie and Imbrie 1979, pp. 90–2).

[3] The passage at the top of page 344 in the third edition of *Origin* was altered by CD in the fifth edition, where he specified that the new inhabitants irrupted 'into an adjoining sea' after the breaking of an isthmus (*Origin* 5th ed., p. 390).

[4] The reference is to *Origin*, p. 392 (see letter to J. D. Hooker, 30 July [1866] and n. 9). In his lecture on insular floras, Hooker alluded to the absence of gum (eucalyptus) trees in New Zealand and their presence in Australia as an example of an island's tree population being derived independently of the adjacent continent (J. D. Hooker 1866a, p. 75); however, *Eucalyptus* does not include any herbaceous species (Mabberley 1997).

[5] In *Origin*, p. 392, CD wrote: 'trees, as Alph. De Candolle has shown, generally have, whatever the cause may be, confined ranges'. The reference is to A. de Candolle 1855, 1: 527–32.

[6] Letter to J. D. Hooker, 30 July [1866].

[7] CD and Hooker had long disagreed about the geographical distribution of species, continental extensions, and occasional transport: see letter to Charles Lyell, 15 February [1866], n. 6.

[8] The reference is to *Vestiges of the natural history of creation* ([Chambers] 1844); for Hooker's initial reactions to it, see *Correspondence* vol. 3, letter from J. D. Hooker, 30 December 1844. For an analysis of the arguments concerning the origin of species in [Chambers] 1844, see Secord 2000, pp. 104–8.

[9] In his lecture, Hooker cited CD on the persistence during recent geological periods of islands and continents, and of the general form of the sea bed, as a geological argument against continental extension (J. D. Hooker 1866a, p. 51). As botanical evidence against CD's doctrine of occasional transport as the means by which island floras originated, Hooker referred to a number of rare plants that were unique to some islands. Hooker noted a further botanical objection to CD's doctrine of occasional transport was that certain plants on Kerguelen's Land were also to be found in Tierra del Fuego but not in South Africa or New Zealand, both of which are closer to Kerguelen's Land (J. D. Hooker 1866a, pp. 50–1, 75).

[10] Hooker was to deliver his lecture on insular floras (J. D. Hooker 1866a) at Nottingham rather than Cambridge.

[11] In his lecture, Hooker evaluated CD's and Forbes's hypotheses concerning the derivations of the floras of oceanic islands, and urged that a distinction be made between CD's doctrines of occasional transport and of variation and natural selection; he concluded in his summary that CD's hypothesis of migration across the sea was more satisfactory than Forbes's (J. D. Hooker 1866a, pp. 50–1, 75).

[12] See letter from J. D. Hooker, [24 July 1866], and letter to J. D. Hooker, 30 July [1866].

[13] See letter to J. D. Hooker, 30 July [1866] and n. 12.

[14] The absence of alpine and subalpine plants in Madeira had been discussed in the letter from J. D. Hooker, [24 July 1866], and the letter to J. D. Hooker, 30 July [1866]. Hooker's reference to the absence of erratic boulders apparently implies his belief that plants could not have arrived on the islands by means of icebergs; in *Origin*, p. 363, CD had argued on the basis of reported evidence of erratic boulders that some of the flora of the Azores had derived from progenitors that had been transported there by icebergs.

[15] In *Origin*, CD had cited Oswald Heer on the similarity between the flora of Madeira and the tertiary flora of Europe (see letter to J. D. Hooker, 30 July [1866] and n. 10).

[16] Hooker refers to the island of Pico in the Azores; moraines would provide evidence of former glacial action (see also n. 14, above). *Daboecia azorica* is native to the Azorean islands of Foyal and Pico (Underhill 1971, p. 203). In his lecture, Hooker noted the presence of St Dabeoc's Heath (*Daboecia* sp.) and *Calluna vulgaris* in the Azores and their absence from Madeira and the Canaries; Hooker also stated that *Daboecia* only occurred elsewhere in the west of Ireland, and in the Pyrenean region (J. D. Hooker 1866a, p. 27).

[17] Hooker mentioned differences between the floras of Madeira and Porto Santo in his lecture (J. D. Hooker 1866a, p. 7). On the differences between the land shells of Madeira and Porto Santo, see also *Origin*, pp. 402–3. See letter to J. D. Hooker, 30 July [1866].

[18] Macaronesia is a biogeographical region that includes the archipelagos of the Azores, Madeira, the Salvage Islands, the Canary Islands, and the Cape Verde Islands (Sunding 1979).

[19] In his lecture, Hooker noted that a similar number of species of American plants were represented in the floras of the Azores, Madeira, and the Canary Islands, despite the relative proximity of the Azores to America. He also noted an unexpected paucity of boreal plants. (J. D. Hooker 1866a, p. 27.)

[20] In his lecture, Hooker asserted his belief that the plants of the Atlantic islands had originally migrated from the continent of Europe, but also noted that the sea currents favoured transport in the opposite direction (J. D. Hooker 1866a, pp. 50, 75).

[21] The genus *Duvernoya* (family Acanthaceae) is now subsumed within *Justicia* (Mabberley 1997). However, the reference is probably to the book for which CD had asked Hooker (see letter to J. D. Hooker, 30 July [1866] and n. 16). CD was writing the second volume of *Variation*, in which there is a reference to Duvernoy 1834 (*Variation* 2: 137 n. 67).

[22] For CD's earlier interest in *Acropera*, see *Correspondence* vols. 9–12. *Acropera* is a genus of tropical orchids now subsumed within *Gongora* (Bailey and Bailey 1976).

[23] CD's annotations are notes for his letter to Hooker of 3 and 4 August [1866].

To Casimir de Candolle 1 August [1866][1]

Down. | *Bromley.* | *Kent. S.E.*
Aug 1.

Dear Sir

I am much obliged to you for your kind present of your Mem. on the "Pipéracées".[2] I am sorry to say that I have not sufficient knowledge of botany fully to understand all the points which you discuss, but I can see that some of them are extremely interesting.

I should be much obliged if you w^{d} give my sincere thanks to your father for the extremely kind letter which he wrote me when in London;[3] I should have written to him at once had I known his address. It caused me sincere regret that the state of my health prevented me attending the Congress & having the great pleasure & honour of conversing with your father.[4]

With my best thanks pray believe me my dear Sir | yours very faithfully. | Charles Darwin

LS
Archives de la famille de Candolle

[1] The year is established by the relationship between this letter and the letter from Alphonse de Candolle, 3 June 1866.
[2] The reference is to Casimir de Candolle's paper on the pepper family (A. C. P. de Candolle 1866).
[3] See letter from Alphonse de Candolle, 3 June 1866.
[4] Alphonse de Candolle was president of the International Horticultural Exhibition and Botanical Congress, held in London from 22 to 31 May 1866 (*International Horticultural Exhibition* 1866).

To John Lubbock 2 August [1866][1]

Down. | Bromley. | Kent. S.E.
Aug 2—

My dear Lubbock

I am much obliged for your invitation for the 11th. which I should much like to accept but doubt whether I shall have the spirit, but I may perhaps call before the collation.

What I sh^{d} like very much better would be to call on Lady Lubbock & you some morning between 12 & 1 when I take my ride;[2] but I must find out on what day you generally stay at home. I have read the abstract of your paper in the Athenæum & must tell you how cordially I admired it.[3] I do not think I ever read in my life any thing more clearly, concisely & conclusively put.

Believe me ever yours | very truly | Ch. Darwin

P.S. I fear you will think me a great bore but if ever you come across my Primula paper let me have it again.[4]

LS
DAR 263: 63

[1] The year is established by the relationship between this letter and the letter from John Lubbock, 4 August 1866.
[2] The reference is to Ellen Frances Lubbock. According to Emma Darwin's diary (DAR 242), CD started riding on 4 June 1866. CD was advised by Henry Bence Jones to go riding every day (see letter from H. B. Jones, 10 February [1866] and n. 3).
[3] The *Athenæum* for 21 July 1866, pp. 79–82, carried an abstract of Lubbock's paper 'On the present state of archæological science', delivered at the annual congress of the Archaeological Institute of Great Britain and Ireland, held in London from 17 to 19 July 1866. Lubbock had been invited to serve as president of the primeval antiquities section of the congress (see Hutchinson 1914, 1: 82). The paper discussed the methods of archaeology, considered as a branch of science. See Van Riper 1993, pp. 200–1; for more on Lubbock and archaeology, see *Correspondence* vol. 13.
[4] CD refers to 'Dimorphic condition in *Primula*'.

From Fritz Müller 2 August 1866

Desterro, Brazil
August. 2. 66.

My Dear Sir,

Your kind letter of May 23^d^ arrived here only July 24th.—[1] In the meantime I could observe but a few specimens of one of our species of *Oxalis*; the length of the styli is very variable even in the flowers of the same plant, but whether the species is really trimorphic, I am not yet able to say.[2]

In my last letter I gave you a short account of an Orchid having three fertile stamens.[3] The species is not very rare and I have already seen numerous ears, all the flowers of which showed the same number of fertile stamens. In a closely allied species from Bahia,[4] which I saw in the garden of a Frenchman, I was much surprised at finding but one fertile stamen as in other plants of the tribe. It is curious, that the number of fertile stamens while it furnishes an excellent character for dividing the Orchids into two main groups, in this case is not even of generic value.[5]

Have you ever seen the flowers of *Notylia*?[6] The stigma forms a very narrow slit, to which I found it impossible to cause the pollinia to adhere; at the same time the ovula have a very rudimentary appearance. Thus for some time I supposed the plant to be a male one, but afterwards I met with seed-capsules, the columna of which had evidently borne an anthera, while the stigma seemed to have been of the same form as in the supposed male flowers. Besides I convinced myself that in some other Orchids the ovula are in a very rudimentary estate at the time when the flower is expanded and that only some weeks afterwards they become ready for impregnation. This is, for instance, the case with two self-fertilizing species of the tribe of Epidendreae; (one of them belongs to the genus *Isochilus*).— Of these species I can send you some drawings if you sh^d^ desire it.—[7]

The fine Orchid, of which I send you a drawing, seemed to me to be interesting by the two stigmas being widely separated and situated at the inside of leaf-like processes projecting beyond the anther.—[8]

In your paper on the dimorphism of *Linum* you say that it had occurred to you, that possibly a species might be dimorphic in function, though not in structure.[9] Some observations, which I casually made, seem to confirm this view and to prove that some species are completely barren or nearly so with pollen of the same individual plant. Thus I saw a large plant of an *Octomeria*; it had more than eighty monophyllous stalks,[10] each with about a dozen yellow flowers; on most of the stigmas which I examined I found numerous (6–12) pollinia; but this plant yielded only *two* seed-capsules. Afterwards I have seen other plants, apparently of the same species, with numerous seed-capsules. I must add, that in the neighbourhood of the first plant I could not detect any other plant of the same species.— A very large plant of a *Serjania*, widely spreading over a hedge, and as far as I know, about a mile distant from the next plant of the same species, (the same, from which the fig. 20 of my paper on the wood of climbing plants[11] was taken) was covered for many weeks by thousands of flowers, which were visited all the day long by numberless insects, (—humble-bees, beetles, butterflies, etc.—); but only very few seed-capsules were produced in the last weeks and I suppose, from their appearance, that none of these capsules, (as yet unripe), will give good seed.— Last year I had raised some plants of *Eschscholtzia californica*; one of them began to flower about a month before the others, and in this time it yielded not even a single seed-capsule; but no sooner had a neighbouring plant expanded its first flowers, than germens[12] of the former plant began to swell; the second plant was fertile from the beginning.—

⟨*one or more sheets missing*⟩

Seeds use to fall to the ground, as soon as the seed-capsules open and in this case they are commonly dark-coloured;[13] if on the contrary, they remain attached to the open valvæ,[14] in all the cases, I know, either the seeds themselves, or the arillus, or the interior of the valvæ are brightly coloured so as to attract the attention,[15] which may carry the seeds to distant places. Thus the large valvæ of a *Tabernaemontana* are filled with a bright red pulpa;—the black and shining seeds of a *Paullinia* are half-imbedded into a white arillus and fixed to red valvæ,—and the seeds of a fine small tree related to Acacia or Inga, which also for some time remain attached to the valvæ, are black and white and visible at a great distance.—

⟨*half a page excised*⟩ hundred miles beyond the actual sea-coast was once covered by a huge glacier!—?—[16]

I am very glad to hear that Nägeli and my old friend Oscar Schmidt are with us.—[17] My brother, Dr. Hermann Müller of Lippstadt, (Prussia) who is thoroughly conversant with the natural history of mosses, is collecting the facts bearing on the change of species, which these plants may offer.—[18]

Wishing that this letter may find you in good health, believe me, dear Sir, with sincere respect very truly yours

[Enclosure 1][19]

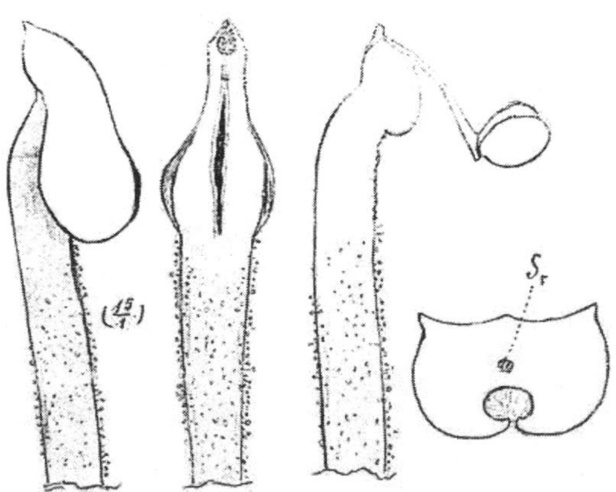

Columna of *Notylia*. *a*. from the side. *b*. front view.
c. from the side after removing anther. *d* transversal section.—

[Enclosure 2][20]

June. 5 66.

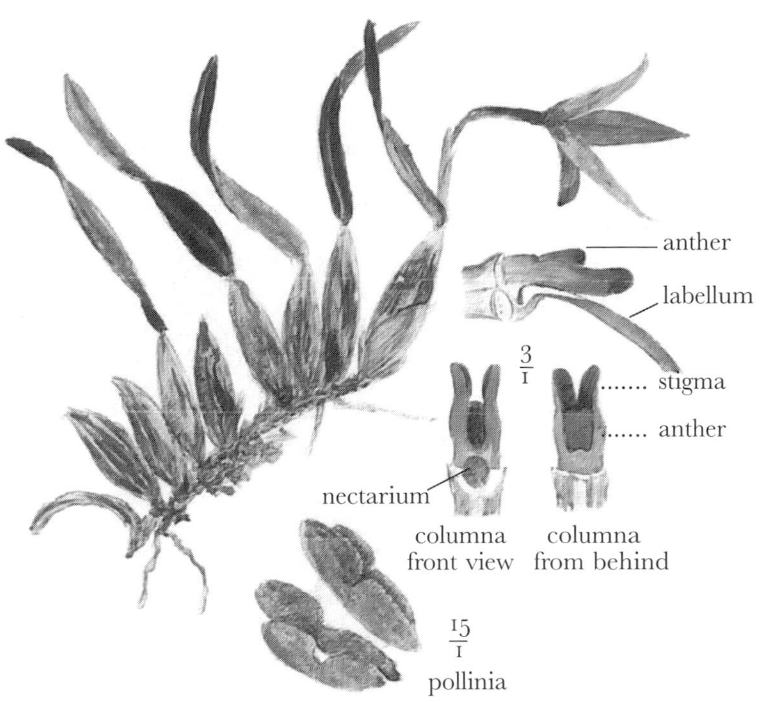

F.M. pinx.[21]

AL incomplete
DAR 76: B33, 33a; DAR 157a: 81, 102; DAR 142: 38

CD ANNOTATIONS

1.1 Your kind . . . desire it.— 3.11] *crossed ink*
4.1 The fine . . . the same species. 5.10] 'Dichogamy *Fr. Muller* Aug 22—1866—' *added in margin blue crayon*
5.1 In your . . . beginning.— 5.21] *scored ink*
5.5 *Octomeria*] 'Malaxideæ?' *added above ink* [22]
5.17 Last year . . . beginning.— 5.21] *scored red crayon*; 'Escholtzia' *added red crayon*; 'Dichogamy Fritz Muller Aug 2. 1866—' *added ink*
6.1 Seeds . . . distance.— 6.9] *enclosed in square brackets, blue crayon*
7.1 hundred . . . yours— 9.2] *crossed ink*
Enclosure 1: 'stigma so narrow a slit that pollinia cannot be inserted (Probably long [*interl*] pedicel in)' *ink*[23]

CD note:
Beauty of seeds or of inside of pods for dissemination: F. Muller. Aug. 1866 | In Portfolio for addition to Dom. Animals, a letter with coloured drawings of other seeds.[24]

1 See letter to Fritz Müller, 23 May 1866.

2 In his letter of 23 May 1866, CD had mentioned Friedrich Hildebrand's recent work on trimorphic species of *Oxalis* and asked Müller to investigate whether there were different forms in species of *Oxalis* in his area. CD put the specimens that Müller enclosed in an envelope labelled 'Oxalis Brazil variable F. Muller Aug 2^{d}/66/'. The specimens are in DAR 142: 97.

3 Müller refers to his letter of 3 April 1866, which has not been found (see letter to Fritz Müller, 23 May 1866). He did, however, give an account of the orchid with three fertile anthers in letters to Max Johann Sigismund Schultze (2 June 1866) and Hermann Müller (1 July 1866; the letters are reproduced in Möller ed. 1915–21, 2: 83–4, 86–9). Müller described the orchid as a species of the orchid tribe Epidendreae with three fertile anthers, two in the outer whorl and one in the inner whorl (see Möller ed. 1915–21, 2: 87–8).

4 Bahia is a state (formerly a province) in north-eastern Brazil. CD described the area in his *Journal of researches*, pp. 589–91.

5 The 'two main groups' that Müller refers to are the Cypripedioideae (lady's slipper orchids), which have two fertile anthers, and most other orchids, which have one. Müller later published his observations on the species of *Epidendrum* with three fertile anthers (see F. Müller 1868a, 1869, and 1870) and CD added a reference to Müller's work in *Orchids* 2d ed., p. 148.

6 See first enclosure. Müller sent CD specimens of *Notylia* attached to the diagram. These are in DAR 142: 38.

7 In botanical nomenclature, a 'tribe' is a subdivision of a family, and contains a number of genera. *Isochilus* is one genus within the tribe Epidendreae. No drawings of *Isochilus* by Müller have been found in the Darwin Archive–CUL, but a diagram found in Müller's papers, dated 24 July 1866, and identified as *Isochilus*, is reproduced in Möller ed. 1915–21, 2: 87.

8 Müller enclosed an unlabelled drawing of an orchid and a specimen of the flower with this letter. These are in DAR 76: B33a. See second enclosure and n. 21. The orchid in the drawing has been identified as *Sophronitella violacea*, a Brazilian member of the subtribe Laeliinae, which also includes *Isochilus* (identification made by Robert L. Dressler from a scan of Müller's drawing; see also Dressler 1981, p. 226, and Dressler 1993, p. 275).

9 Müller refers to 'Two forms in species of *Linum*', p. 82 (*Collected papers* 2: 104).

10 Monophyllous: 'of a plant: having a single leaf or leaflet' (*OED*).

11 The reference is to F. Müller 1866b, and figure 20 of the table that accompanied the article.

12 Germen: 'an ovary' (*OED*).

13 CD pasted this paragraph into his Experimental notebook and added some notes (DAR 157a: 81; the fragment has since been moved to DAR 157a: 102). See CD note transcribed below the letter.

14 Valve: 'one of the halves or sections of a dehiscent pod, pericarp, or capsule' (*OED*).

15 Müller presumably meant 'to attract the attention of birds'. In another letter in which he discussed the function of brightly coloured seeds, Müller wrote that the mechanism was clearly designed to attract birds (see letter from Fritz Müller to Hermann Müller, 29 October 1866, reproduced in Möller ed. 1915–21, 2: 94–8; the reference is on p. 95).

16 The preceding part of this section of the letter has not been found. Müller may be referring to the hypothesis advanced by Louis Agassiz that the Amazon valley was once covered by a huge glacier (see letter from Asa Gray, 27 August 1866 and nn. 3 and 4). Müller had mentioned Agassiz's research on the Amazon river in an earlier letter (see *Correspondence* vol. 13, letter from Fritz Müller, 5 November 1865).

17 Müller refers to Carl Wilhelm von Nägeli and Oskar Schmidt (see letter to Fritz Müller, 23 May 1866 and n. 16). Schmidt had been a friend of Müller's ever since they were students at Greifswald (Möller ed. 1915–21, 3: 25).

18 Hermann Müller later published a group of articles on mosses in *Verhandlungen des botanischen Vereins der Provinz Brandenburg* vol. 8; one of these presented evidence from mosses that supported Darwinian transmutation theory (H. Müller 1866). CD's annotated copy is in the Darwin Pamphlet collection–CUL.

[19] Müller affixed a specimen of *Notylia* to the diagram. CD put the diagram and specimen into an envelope labelled, 'Orchids. F. Muller Aug 2. 1866'. See n. 6, above.
[20] See n. 8, above.
[21] F. M. pinxit: 'F. M. drew [it]' (Latin).
[22] The genus *Octomeria* was included in the orchid tribe Malaxideae (Malaxeae) by John Lindley (see Lindley 1853, p. 181). It is now generally put in the tribe Epidendreae (see Mabberley 1997).
[23] CD described the pedicel of the pollinium in *Orchids*, pp. 6–7. In modern orchid terminology, the pedicel of the pollinium is called the stipe (Dressler 1981, p. 315).
[24] CD refers to a portfolio of notes and material for *Variation*. He kept a number of such portfolios, amassed over a long period of time and since dispersed. The likely contents of some portfolios were reconstructed when some of CD's papers were catalogued in 1932 (see DAR 220: 13). One portfolio is described as follows: 'Scraps and notes on variation'.

From W. B. Tegetmeier 2 August 1866

Muswell Hill | N
Aug 2./66

My dear Sir

I enclose a letter from Mr Hewitt[1] to myself with some feathers of a sebright hen that has assumed Male plumage—*not the plumage of the hen feathered sebright cock* but the more complete male plumage of a full feathered bird, this is rather curious I think—[2] Of course she has diseased or abortive ovaria— Will you send the feathers back when you have done with them— You shall have a photo of the bird when it has moulted again, and some of the other feathers if you wish for them

I forward by this post all the proofs and hope they will meet your approbation— Shall I direct the engravers to forward the blocks to Murrays—and the Artist to send in his account also—[3]

Did you ever see a half bred Gallus Varius? or Eneus? with common fowl.— He was some years since in the Zoological Gardens. He was remarkable as having transverse bright blue bands on his tail coverts like a so called "cuckoo cock" I have some of the feathers if you would like to see them[4]

If you should have occasion to quote any points from the Poultry Book, would you kindly refer to the *current edition* by myself— the other was never completed and except your own numbers and one set in the B. Museum Library I do not know where a copy could be seen— I ask you this favour without wishing to disguise the fact that your mention of the work would be of great service to me.[5]

I am sorry to say that I am not enjoying good health—but I have too many hostages in the hands of Fortune to cease "the struggle for life".

I trust you are enjoying good health and that we may soon be gratified with a sight of the new work.— Should you like me to look over the proofs of the poultry and pigeon chapters I should be much pleased to do so.—

Believe me My dear Sir | Very truly Yours | W B Tegetmeier

C Darwin Esq.

Pray excuse copy slips but I forgot I was writing a letter.[6]

DAR 178: 73

CD ANNOTATION
Verso of last page: 'Name of Artist | Return Proofs' *ink*

[1] Tegetmeier refers to Edward Hewitt; his observations of poultry are cited extensively in *Variation*. The enclosure has not been found.
[2] The Sebright hen with male plumage is described in *Variation* 2: 54, as a case of reversion to the Polish fowl or common bantam, whence it originated as a cross: 'we thus see that . . . masculine characters derived from the first progenitors of the breed, removed by a period of above sixty years, were lying latent in this hen-bird'. CD cited Hewitt's account of the hen (Hewitt 1864), and Tegetmeier's discussion of the lineage of the Sebright fowl (Tegetmeier 1867, pp. 241–2), adding that he had examined the feathers of Hewitt's bird 'through the kindness of Mr. Tegetmeier' (*Variation* 2: 54 n. 61).
[3] Tegetmeier had read the manuscripts, and had overseen the making of illustrations, for CD's chapters on pigeons and fowls for *Variation*. The artist was Luke Wells, and the engravers were Butterworth and Heath. See *Correspondence* vol. 13, letter to W. B. Tegetmeier, 2 June [1865], and this volume, letter from W. B. Tegetmeier, 22 January [1866] and nn. 4 and 7. The publisher of *Variation* was John Murray.
[4] Hybrids between *Gallus varius* (native to Java and the lesser Sunda Islands) and the common hen are described in *Variation* 1: 234–5; CD remarked that the hybrids were once thought specifically distinct, and were named *G. aeneus*. CD reported Tegetmeier's observation that hybrids bred in the Zoological Gardens in Regent's Park, London, had transverse blue bands on their tail feathers similar to those found on some domestic fowls from Borneo, possibly indicating that the latter had been affected by crosses with *G. varius*. CD briefly discussed '"Cuckoo" sub-breeds' of fowl as cases of 'analogous variation'; such birds were characterised by slaty-blue or grey feathers, transversely barred with darker lines, resembling the plumage of the cuckoo (*Variation* 1: 244).
[5] Tegetmeier had edited a revised edition of Wingfield and Johnson 1853; the work had not been completed because the publisher went out of business. A new edition, with Tegetmeier as author, was issued in instalments, beginning in January 1866 (Tegetmeier 1867). See letter from W. B. Tegetmeier, 22 January [1866] and nn. 10–12. Tegetmeier refers to the library of the British Museum.
[6] The letter is written on small sheets of blue-lined paper.

To ? 2 August [1866][1]

Down. | Bromley. | Kent. S.E.
Aug 2^d.

My dear Sir

Although you tell me not to write I must have the pleasure of thanking you for your never failing kindness in remembering what interests me.—[2] I have not seen Bäers paper, but I read long extracts in one of Wagner's papers after publishing my historical sketch.—[3]

The case of the hairy & toothless family (so like the Turkish dog) I knew of from Crawfurds Embassy & Yules Travels;[4] but I had not heard of the case being brought before the B. Association.—[5]

I am now hard at work on the very obscure subject of the causes of Variability in domestic productions & hope to get to press in the winter or spring.—[6]

With my sincere thanks | Yours very faithfully | Charles Darwin

American Philosophical Society (318)

1 The year is established by the reference to CD's work on *Variation* (see n. 6, below).

2 The letter referred to has not been found.

3 CD refers to 'Über Papuas und Alfuren' by Karl Ernst von Baer (Baer 1859). Extracts of the paper appeared in *Zoologisch-Anthropologische Untersuchungen, I* by Rudolph Wagner (Wagner 1861, pp. 50–2). CD's lightly annotated copy of Wagner 1861 is in the Darwin Library–CUL (see *Marginalia* 1: 831). CD first added a 'historical sketch' to *Origin* in the US edition of 1860. He added a short discussion of Baer's paper, as reported in Wagner 1861, to the historical preface of *Origin* 4th ed., pp. xx–xxi, noting that Baer supported the view 'that forms now perfectly distinct' had 'descended from a single parent-form'. In 1860, Thomas Henry Huxley had sent CD a copy of a note from Baer in which Baer remarked that he had 'expressed the same ideas on the transformation of types or origin of species as Mr. Darwin' (see *Correspondence* vol. 8, letter from T. H. Huxley, 6 August 1860; see also Baer 1859, p. 343).

4 CD refers to *Journal of an embassy from the governor general of India to the court of Ava* by John Crawfurd, and to *A narrative of the mission sent by the governor-general of India to the court of Ava in 1855* by Henry Yule; the authors described different members of a family whose entire bodies were covered with hair and who lacked canine and molar teeth (see Crawfurd 1834, 1: 320, and Yule 1858, pp. 93–4). CD mentioned the case in *Variation*, in his discussion of the inheritance of different characters at corresponding periods of life (*Variation* 2: 77), and the laws of correlated variability (*ibid.*, pp. 327–8); see also *Descent* 2: 378. The 'Turkish dog' is mentioned in *Variation* 1: 30 and 2: 227.

5 The reference is to the annual meeting of the British Association for the Advancement of Science. The case has not been found in the British Association reports.

6 CD sent the manuscript of *Variation* to his publisher in December 1866 (letter from John Murray, 24 December [1866]).

To J. D. Hooker 3 and 4 August [1866][1]

Down.
Aug. 3rd.

My dear Hooker

Manny thanks for Acropera & about the book. I will take your letter seriatim.[2] There is good evidence that S.E. England was dry land during glacial period. I forget what Austin says but mammals prove, I think, that England has been united to the Continent since the glacial period.[3] I don't see your difficulty about what I say on the breaking of an isthmus: if Panama was broken thro', wd. not the fauna of the Pacific flow into the W. Indies, or vice versâ, & destroy a multitude of creatures.[4] Of course I'm no judge, but I thought De Candolle had made out his case about small areas of trees—[5] You will find at P. 112 3rd. edit. Origin a too concise allusion to the Madeira flora being a remnant of the tertiary European flora.[6]

I shall feel deeply interested by reading your botanical difficuties against occasional immigration. The facts you give about certain plants such as the Heaths are certainly very curious. I thought the Azores flora was more boreal: but what can you mean by saying that the Azores are nearer to Britain & Newfoundland than to Madeira? on the Globe they are nearly twice as far off.[7] With respect to sea-currents, I formerly made enquiries at Madeira but cannot now give you the results but I remember that the facts were different from what is generally stated; I think that a ship wrecked on the Canary Islands was thrown up on the coast of Madeira.[8] You speak as if only land shells differed in Madeira &

P^{o}. Santo: does my memory deceive me that there is a host of representative insects?[9]

When you exorcise at Nottingham occasional means of transport, be honest, & admit how little is known on the subject.[10] Remember how recently you & others thought that Salt-water would soon kill seeds.[11] Reflect that there is not a coral-islet in the ocean which is not pretty well clothed with plants: & the fewness of the species can hardly with justice be attributed to the arrival of few seeds, for coral-Islets close to other land support only the same limited vegetation.[12] Remember that no one knew that seeds w^{d} remain for many hours in the *crops* of birds & retain their vitality; that fish eat seeds & that when the fish are devoured by birds the seeds can germinate &c &c—[13] Remember that every year many birds are blown to Madeira & to the Bermudas. Remember that dust is blown 1000 miles over the Atlantic.[14] Now bearing all this in mind, w^{d} it not be a prodigy if an *unstocked* Island did not in the course of ages receive colonists from coasts, whence the currents flow, trees are drifted, & birds are driven by gales. The objections to islands being thus stocked are, as far as I understand, that certain species & genera have been more freely introduced & others less freely than might have been expected. But then the sea kills some sorts of seeds, others are killed by the digestion of birds & some w^{d} be more liable than others to adhere to birds feet; but we know so very little on these points that it seems to me that we cannot at all tell what forms w^{d} probably be introduced & what w^{d} not.[15]

I do not for a moment pretend that these means of introduction can be proved to have acted; but they seem to me sufficient, with no valid or heavy objections, whilst there are, as it seems to me, the heaviest objections, on geological & on geographical-Distribution grounds, (p. 387, 388, Origin) to Forbes' enormous continental extensions.[16] But I fear that I shall & have bored you.—

Yours ever affect— | C. Darwin.

P.S. Murray will not bring out, & be hanged to him, the new Edit. of Origin, though all printed off, till November.—[17] I have persuaded him to send Lyell a copy; I do not suppose you w^{d}. care to have your copy at once; if you did, I would ask Murray, but for some reason, he does not seem much to like sending out the copies.—[18]

Dont answer unless you like, for you must be very busy.—

P.S. Here is a bad job, the Acropera has not arrived.— I hope it was not sent off, as soon as you thought. I sent this evening (Friday) but no parcel at Station. If not there tomorrow it must be lost. It is a bad job for me & for you, if the plant is valuable.—[19]

P.S. 2^{d}. As you were asking about Books on "Origin"; a very good Zoologist Claus has just published one, with my name on title-page—the subject being an investigation of the amount of individual variability in the Copepodous Crustaceans & he shows it is wonderfully great in many organs & that some *co existing* vars, are apparently passing into distinct species.—[20]

☞**Acropera** all safe Saturday morning

LS(A)
DAR 115: 295, 295b

[1] The year is established by the relationship between this letter and the letter from J. D. Hooker, 31 July 1866. In 1866, 4 August was a Saturday.
[2] See letter from J. D. Hooker, 31 July 1866 and nn. 21 and 22.
[3] See letter from J. D. Hooker, 31 July 1866 and n. 2. Robert Alfred Cloyne Godwin-Austen considered the presence of mammals in the area of the English Channel and North Sea during the glacial and post-glacial periods, and showed their distribution during the 'new Tertiary' period in a map, in Austen 1851, pp. 131–5.
[4] See letter from J. D. Hooker, 31 July 1866 and n. 3.
[5] CD refers to Alphonse de Candolle. See letter from J. D. Hooker, 31 July 1866 and n. 5.
[6] See letter from J. D. Hooker, 31 July 1866 and n. 15.
[7] See letter from J. D. Hooker, 31 July 1866 and n. 19.
[8] CD's enquiry about sea currents to the Atlantic islands, and the response, have not been found. The only ship wrecked in the Canary Islands between 1836 and 1866 was the British steamship *Niger*. The *Niger* was wrecked at Santa Cruz, Tenerife, on 12 June 1857, but no records of its drifting thereafter have been found, nor any contemporary records of wrecks at Madeira. (Hugh Brown, International Registry of Sunken Ships, personal communication; see also *The Times*, 5 September 1857, p. 8.)
[9] Representative species, in contemporary terminology, were similar but distinct species in different localities (see also *Correspondence* vol. 8, letter to C. J. F. Bunbury, 9 February [1860] and n. 4). The representative species of insects in Porto Santo and Madeira were discussed in Wollaston 1856, pp. 122–4; the representative land shells of the two islands were discussed in Wollaston 1856, pp. 128–35. There is an annotated copy of Wollaston 1856 in the Darwin Library–CUL (see *Marginalia* 1: 876–9). For more on representative species, see Affolter 1980, p. 7.
[10] In his lecture at the British Association for the Advancement of Science meeting at Nottingham in August 1866, Hooker considered the evidence for both Edward Forbes's 'Atlantis' and CD's 'occasional transport' hypotheses about how similar species arrived at different points of the globe, referring to the latter as 'trans-oceanic migration' (J. D. Hooker 1866a, pp. 51, 75–6). For further information on the lecture and its publication, see the letter from J. D. Hooker, [24 July 1866], n. 4. For more on CD's position on geographical distribution, see *Correspondence* vol. 6, and, this volume, letter to J. D. Hooker, 30 July [1866] and n. 7.
[11] The fact that seeds could survive immersion in seawater was included in Hooker's lecture as one of CD's 'many powerful arguments' for trans-oceanic migration (J. D. Hooker 1866a, p. 51). On Hooker's earlier disbelief in the ability of seeds to remain viable after contact with salt water, see *Correspondence* vol. 13, letter to J. D. Hooker, 22 and 28 [October 1865], n. 11. The results of CD's experiments on the resistance of seeds to salt water are given in his paper 'On the action of sea-water on the germination of seeds', read on 6 May 1856 at the Linnean Society (*Collected papers* 1: 264–73), and in *Origin*, pp. 358–61.
[12] In his lecture, Hooker reported CD as pointing out that coral islands, which had not ever been connected with continents, were well stocked with plants, and that oceanic islands were poor in plant species, lacking whole groups of continental plants, which would not have been the case had there been continental extension (J. D. Hooker 1866a, p. 51). See also *Origin*, pp. 360–1, 388–90.
[13] See J. D. Hooker 1866a, p. 51. See also *Origin*, pp. 361–2, 387.
[14] See J. D. Hooker 1866a, p. 51. On birds being blown to Bermuda and Madeira, see *Origin*, p. 90. In 1832, CD noted that dust from Africa fell on vessels in the Atlantic ocean (*Journal of researches*, p. 4). See also *Correspondence* vol. 2, and CD's paper 'An account of the fine dust which often falls on vessels in the Atlantic Ocean', read on 4 June 1845 at the Geological Society of London (*Collected papers* 1: 199–203).
[15] CD noted that islands supported fewer species of plants than equivalent continental areas in *Origin*, pp. 389–90. CD's own experiments on seeds showed that species differed in their capacity to survive

immersion in salt water (see *Correspondence* vol. 5, letters to *Gardeners' Chronicle*, 21 May [1855] and 21 November [1855]). On CD's interest in the distribution of seeds by adhesion to birds' feet, see *Correspondence* vol. 13, letter from Alfred Newton, 27 October 1865, n. 5.

16 CD refers to the third edition of *Origin* and to Edward Forbes's hypothesis of continental extension. See also letter from J. D. Hooker, 31 July 1866 and nn. 1 and 9.

17 CD refers to the fourth edition of *Origin*. See letter from John Murray, 18 July [1866].

18 Charles Lyell was probably named by CD in a now missing list of people who were to receive advance copies of the fourth edition of *Origin* (see letter to John Murray, 15 July [1866] and n. 3). On Murray's inclination to dispatch presentation copies in November 1866, see the letter from John Murray, 23 July [1866].

19 CD had been informed by Hooker that a specimen of *Acropera* would be despatched on Wednesday 1 August, for collection at Bromley railway station (see letter from J. D. Hooker, 31 July 1866 and n. 22).

20 The reference is to Claus 1866, a paper on the copepods of Nice; there is a lightly annotated copy in the Darwin Pamphlet Collection–CUL. In his interpretation of copepod morphology and variations, Carl Friedrich Claus referred to CD's transmutation theory; the subtitle of the paper may be translated, 'An essay on the characteristics of the form and their variation "in the Darwinian sense"'.

From J. T. Moggridge 3 August [1866][1]

3 Marlborough Villas | Richmond
Aug. 3

Dear Mr. Darwin

I received this morning from M. Ardoino—a botanist at Mentone—the small packet of seed of Ononis Columnæ enclosed, which he kindly spared me from his herbarium.—[2]

With a view to finding out what species of Ononis there might be answering to your description I looked through the genus at Kew, & found one bit of Ononis Columnæ labelled in Mr. Bentham's handwriting, "var. vernalis apetala"— —[3]

I then referred to MM. Grenier & Godron's *Flore de France* (I. 377) where mention is made of abortion in the following terms "Corolle plus courte que le calice ou l'égalant, presque avortée dans les fleurs automnales (Vill.)"— —[4] It seems, however, from the quotation of Villars name that MM. G. & G. had not observed the fact themselves—

In Villars' *Histoire des Plantes de Dauphiné* (III, 430) I find the following passage alluding to this plant— "—dans les derniers temps de sa floraison, en automne, ses petales deviennent si petits, qu'ils restent cachés sous le germe, dans le fond du calice, de maniere qu'on ne les apperçoit pas du tout— Le fruit n'avorte cependant pas—" —[5]

I have applied in several other quarters for seed, & if successful I shall send it at once— —

Pray remember me very kindly to Mrs. Darwin[6] & all your circle | & believe me | yrs. very sincerely | J. Traherne Moggridge.

We remain at the above adress till Sept. 4, after which date I shall be in Wales for a month the adress being J. D. Llewelyn Esq Penllergare near Swansea—[7]

I do hope that some of your sons will look me up *here* some day!

DAR 111: A86–7

CD ANNOTATIONS
2.2 & found . . . handwriting, 2.3] *scored red crayon*
5.1 I have . . . Swansea—7.2] *crossed blue crayon*
Top of letter: 'Keep | (/Barents/)' *pencil, del pencil*; 'Ononis Columna' *pencil*

1 The year is established by the relationship between this letter and the letter from J. T. Moggridge, 5 and 6 July [1866].

2 Moggridge refers to Honoré Jean Baptiste Ardoino. CD evidently planted the seeds in 1866 (see *Forms of flowers*, p. 326; see also letters from J. T. Moggridge, 5 and 6 July [1866] and nn. 3 and 7, and 9 November [1866] and n. 3).

3 No letter from CD to Moggridge containing a description of *Ononis* has been found. The reference is to George Bentham, who had donated his plant collections to the Royal Botanic Gardens, Kew.

4 Moggridge refers to the description of *Ononis columnae* in *Flore de France* by Charles Grenier and Dominique Alexandre Godron (Grenier and Godron 1848–56, 1: 377). The passage may be translated as 'Corolla shorter than the calyx or equal, almost aborted in autumn flowers.'

5 The reference is to the description of *Ononis columnae* in *Histoire des plantes de Dauphiné* by Dominique Villars (Villars 1786–9, 3: 430). The passage may be translated as 'in the final phase of flowering, in autumn, its petals become so small that they remain hidden under the ovary in the base of the calyx, in such a way that they cannot be seen at all— The fruit, however, does not abort.'

6 Emma Darwin.

7 Moggridge refers to John Dillwyn Llewelyn.

To Asa Gray 4 August [1866][1]

Down. | Bromley. | Kent. S.E.
Aug 4th.

My dear Gray

I am going to write only a line to thank you most cordially for all the *great* trouble which you have taken about the new edit. of the Origin. From what you say it is evidently hopeless, & I am sorry for it for my own sake & for all your labour in vain.[2]

I will let Murray hear your suggestion of sending copies to the Un. States.[3] Although the book is complete & bound, Murray for trade reasons will not sell it till November; but he promised to send a copy to you.[4]

I hope to begin printing my new book towards the close of the year & I will send sheets as printed in hopes that you will have the great kindness to agree for an American edition.[5] What a misfortune for scientific works is your american plan of stereotyping.[6]

With cordial thanks | believe me my dear Gray | Yours most sincerely | Ch. Darwin

LS
Gray Herbarium of Harvard University (85)

[1] The year is established by the relationship between this letter and the letter from Asa Gray, 27 August 1866.
[2] Gray was in communication with the American publisher D. Appleton & Co. about a revised US edition of *Origin* (see letter from Asa Gray, 18 July 1866).
[3] Gray had suggested that CD's publisher, John Murray, supply copies of the fourth edition of *Origin* for the American market (see letter from Asa Gray, 18 July 1866).
[4] On Murray's reasons for delaying publication of the fourth edition of *Origin*, see the letter from John Murray, 18 July [1866]. See also letter from John Murray, 23 July [1866]. For CD's own presentation list for the book, see Appendix IV.
[5] CD refers to *Variation*. Gray apparently forwarded this letter to the American publisher James Thomas Fields, of the firm Ticknor & Fields, adding the following note to the last page: 'Cambridge 27th Aug. 66 | Dear Mr Fields | Perhaps you will draft me a line, which I can forward to Mr Darwin, to encourage him in his disposition to send on advance sheets of his new book. | Truly Yours | Asa Gray'. In the event, the first American edition of *Variation* was published by Orange Judd & Co. in 1868 (Freeman 1977).
[6] On the process of stereotyping used to produce the American edition of *Origin*, see the letter to Asa Gray, 16 April [1866] and n. 11.

From J. D. Hooker 4 August 1866

Kew
Aug 4/66

Dear Darwin

You mention (Journals) no land birds, except introduced, upon St Helena—[1] Beatson (Introd. XVII) mentions one in "considerable numbers" resembles Sand Lark—is called "Wire bird" has long greenish legs like wires, runs fast, eyes large, bill moderately long, is rather shy, does not possess much powers of flight.—[2] What was it? I have written to ask Sclater also about Birds of Madeira & Azores.[3]

It is a very curious thing, that Azores does not contain the (non European) American genus *Clethra*, that is found in Madeira & Canaries; & that the Azores contain *no trace* of American element, (beyond what is common to Madeira), except a species of *Sanicula*, a genus with hooked bristles to the small seeds— The European *Sanicula* roams from Norway to *Madeira*, *Canaries*, *Cape Verds*, *Cameroons*, *Cape Good Hope*: & from Britain to Japan, & also is *I think* in N. America; *but does not occur in Azores*, where it is replaced by one that is of a decidedly American type.[4]

This tells heavily against the doctrine that joins Atlantis to America, & is much against your transoceanic migration—for considering how near Azores are to America *&* in the influence of the Gulf stream & prevalent winds it certainly appears marvellous. Not only are the Azores in a current that sweeps the coast of U. States, but it is in the S.W. winds, & in the eye of the S.W. hurricanes!.

I suppose you will answer that the European forms are prepotent—but this is riding prepotency to death

R. T. Lowe has written me a capital letter on the Madeiran, Canaries & Cape Verd Floras.[5]

I misled you if I gave you to understand that Wollaston's catalogue said anything about rare **plants**—[6]

I am worked & worried to death with this Lecture: & curse myself as a soft headed & hearted imbecile—to have accepted it.[7]

Ever Yrs | J D Hooker

DAR 102: 87–8

CD ANNOTATION

1.2 Beatson . . . "Wire bird" 1.3] *scored pencil*

[1] See *Journal of researches*, p. 584.

[2] The reference is to Beatson 1816, pp. xvii–xviii, in which the wire bird is described as a land bird; Alexander Beatson noted its occurrence all year round in St Helena and concluded that it was indigenous. The wire bird, or St Helena plover, is now named *Charadrius sanctaehelenae* (*Birds of the world* 3: 428).

[3] Philip Lutley Sclater was a leading authority on birds throughout the world (*DSB*). In his lecture at the British Association for the Advancement of Science meeting at Nottingham in August 1866, Hooker argued that the species of birds in the Azores were derived from Europe, citing Sclater on their close similarity to European species (J. D. Hooker 1866a, p. 75).

[4] The Azores are nearer to America than are the Canary Islands or Madeira; Hooker therefore thought they would be more likely to support an American flora if migration had occurred according to CD's theory of occasional transport. However, CD shared Oswald Heer's belief that *Clethra*, and other non-European genera of plants in the Atlantic islands, were remnants of a European flora that had become extinct in continental Europe (see letter to J. D. Hooker, 30 July [1866] and n. 10). In his lecture, Hooker referred to the probability that hooked bristles on the 'seeds' (fruits) of *Sanicula* had enabled birds to spread the genus eastward from America (J. D. Hooker 1866a, p. 27).

[5] Richard Thomas Lowe was completing his flora of Madeira (Lowe 1868), and had spent two recent winters in the Cape Verde Islands (see letter from J. D. Hooker, 13 May 1866). On Lowe's botanical studies in this area, see Nash 1990, pp. 181–3.

[6] See letter to J. D. Hooker, 30 July [1866] and n. 13.

[7] After the president of the British Association for the Advancement of Science, William Robert Grove, invited him to lecture 'on the Darwinian theory' at its meeting in August 1866, Hooker had commented to CD on the difficulty of the task (see letter from J. D. Hooker, 16 January 1866 and nn. 9 and 10).

From John Lubbock 4 August 1866

4 Aug/66

Dear Mr. Darwin

I am delighted at the prospect of your coming to lunch & fully expect to see you out with our beagles before the season is over.[1]

We will let you know next time I have a holiday.

I am very glad you liked my address.[2]

I send you back your Primula paper, & would have done so before, but I thought you said I might keep it.[3]

Believe me always | Yours most sincerely | John Lubbock

DAR 170: 53

[1] See letter to John Lubbock, 2 August [1866].

[2] See letter to John Lubbock, 2 August [1866] and n. 3.

[3] Lubbock refers to 'Dimorphic condition in *Primula*'. See letter to John Lubbock, 2 August [1866].

To W. B. Tegetmeier 4 August [1866][1]

Down. | Bromley. | Kent. S.E.
Aug 4th.

My dear Sir

I am much obliged for all you have done for me, and it would be a pleasure if I could do anything for you in return.[2]

I am sincerely sorry to hear that your health has failed; with your numerous occupations this must be a severe trial.

I like the woodcuts much; but in the four enclosed, I should be glad of an alteration. Firstly in the fantail the tips of the tailfeathers seem to curl over: surely this is wrong? & if possible, which I fear is not the case, I should like it corrected.[3] I wish the lower part of the neck in the three cocks' heads to be cut away, but not abruptly, so that the lower edge should appear nearly as at present.[4] I am sure the cuts will look better this way. I also want the cloud at the back of the comb of the Polish & Hamburgh to be greatly reduced or wholly removed. The block to be cut close on the top & bottom so that type may go above & below.[5] Also do you not think that the top of the comb in the Hamburgh looks unnatural with so many & sharp little cones.[6] When these corrections are made, I should like to see proofs; & the blocks can then be sent to Mr Murray with the account; & I will write to him.[7] *Please tell me the name of the artist*, for I have forgotten, as I wish to state in text by whom they are done, under *your superintendance*.[8]

I had noticed with interest Mr. Hewitt's account of the bantam hen, & therefore you could not have pleased me more than by letting me see the feathers.[9] I observe they are saffron coloured, which is not stated, I think, in the original account. I should like to see, but not to keep, the photograph when made. I should like to see the barred feathers of Gallus various; for I have quoted you about pencilling in crosses, & I presume this is something of the same kind.[10]

I will correct all the references, though they are very numerous, to the New edit. of the Poultry book.[11] I will remember your kind offer about correcting proofs, but hope to have no occasion to avail myself of it. I expect to go to press towards the close of the year.[12]

My dear Sir | Yours very faithfully | Charles Darwin

LS
Archives of The New York Botanical Garden (Charles Finney Cox Collection) (Tegetmeier 95)

[1] The year is established by the relationship between this letter and the letter from W. B. Tegetmeier, 2 August 1866.
[2] See letter from W. B. Tegetmeier, 2 August 1866 and n. 3.
[3] The enclosure has not been found. The English fantail pigeon is illustrated in *Variation* 1: 147.
[4] Engravings of the heads of male Spanish, Hamburgh, and Polish fowls appear in *Variation* 1: 226, 228, and 229, respectively.

[5] See *Variation* 1: 228–9.

[6] CD described the comb of the Hamburgh fowl as covered with numerous small points (*Variation* 2: 227).

[7] CD's publisher was John Murray.

[8] The drawing for the pigeon and fowl engravings was done by Luke Wells (see *Correspondence* vol. 13, letters to W. B. Tegetmeier, 6 April [1865] and [7 April 1865]). He is acknowledged for some of the drawings, along with Tegetmeier for selecting the birds to be illustrated, in *Variation* 1: 135 n. 6.

[9] Edward Hewitt's account of the Sebright hen (Hewitt 1864) is discussed in *Variation* 2: 54. See letter from W. B. Tegetmeier, 2 August 1866 and n. 2.

[10] See letter from W. B. Tegetmeier, 2 August 1866 and n. 4; CD refers to *Gallus varius*. CD cited Tegetmeier in *Variation* for information on 'the frequent appearance, in mongrel fowls, of pencilled or transversely-barred feathers, like those common to many gallinaceous birds' (*Variation* 2: 40).

[11] See letter from W. B. Tegetmeier, 2 August 1866 and n. 5.

[12] CD sent the manuscript of *Variation* to Murray in December 1866 (see letter to John Murray, 21 and 22 December [1866]).

From W. B. Tegetmeier [after 4 August 1866][1]

⟨*two lines excised*⟩

My dear Sir.

I am glad that you like the cuts generally,—with respect to the alterations; the fantail I am certain can be altered so as to remove the effect to which you object[2]

There will be no difficulty in reducing the blocks of the cocks heads. The Hamburgh was a genuine portrait of a bird that I obtained for Mr Wells to draw, but I will have the extreme regularity a little broken, if possible.[3]

The name of ⟨*two lines excised*⟩[4]

The bantam feathers that you returned were from a golden sebright or laced hen and consequently would have the saffron colour— You allude to the original account of Mr Hewitt respecting this hen, but I do not at the present recollect having seen it, can you tell me if you saw it in print—[5]

If the skulls of the polish in the last number of the poultry book would be of any use to your new volume I could easily supply you with electrotypes to print from[6]

Many thanks for your kindness in correcting the references, irrespective altogether of its being of great benefit to me personally, I think it is desirable, as references to a volume that cannot be seen, are not of any great value[7]

I enclose the feathers of the cross bred wild Gallus— I took them myself from the living bird in the Zoological Gardens some years since—. The neck (hackle) feathers are very curious—[8]

I have no doubt of being able to send you the amended proofs of the blocks in a few days at the farthest.— I have been staying in your drysoiled and sunny county for a few days and am better in consequence

I have just looked for the Gallus varius? cross bred feathers and find also some of a half bred Sonnerat—which I enclose, thinking possibly you may like to see them; they also were taken by myself from the living bird, but I have no doubt you saw Dr Salters paper respecting them in the Natural History Review.—[9]

I am afraid I weary you with my hobby, and will conclude | Yours very truly | W B Tegetmeier

Incomplete
DAR 178: 74

CD ANNOTATIONS
4.4 can you ... print] *double scored blue crayon*
5.1 If ... book] *double scored blue crayon*
7.1 I enclose ... Gallus—] *double scored blue crayon*
9.2 a half bred Sonnerat] *double scored blue crayon*

1 The date is established by the relationship between this letter and the letter to W. B. Tegetmeier, 4 August [1866].
2 See letter to W. B. Tegetmeier, 4 August [1866].
3 The reference is to Luke Wells. See letter to W. B. Tegetmeier, 4 August [1866], n. 8.
4 In his letter of 4 August [1866], CD had asked Tegetmeier for the name of the artist, Luke Wells, who had drawn the pigeon and fowl specimens for *Variation*.
5 Tegetmeier refers to Edward Hewitt and to Hewitt 1864. See letter to W. B. Tegetmeier, 4 August [1866] and n. 9.
6 Illustrations of two skulls, one from a golden-spangled Polish hen, the other from a silver-spangled Polish cock, were published in *The poultry book* (Tegetmeier 1867, p. 174). Tegetmeier had written a short paper on the skulls of Polish fowl (Tegetmeier 1856).
7 Tegetmeier had asked CD to change the references in *Variation* from an earlier and incomplete edition of *The poultry book* to his own edition (Tegetmeier 1867). See letter from W. B. Tegetmeier, 2 August 1866 and n. 5.
8 In his discussion of reversion in *Variation*, CD described the neck-hackles and tail-feathers of a hybrid between the common fowl and *Gallus varius*, received from Tegetmeier, as transversely striped with dark metallic blue and grey, 'a character which could not have been derived from either immediate parent' (*Variation* 2: 40).
9 In *Variation*, CD described the feathers of hybrids raised in the Zoological Gardens in Regent's Park, London, between a male *Gallus sonneratii* and a red game-hen, noting that the feathers exhibited the character of those of *G. sonneratii*, but with much smaller horny laminae (*Variation* 1: 234 n. 13). CD remarked that *G. sonneratii* had once been thought to be the ancestral stock of all domestic varieties, but that numerous crossing experiments made at the Zoological Gardens between *G. sonneratii* and other breeds had resulted in offspring that were almost entirely infertile. On the basis of this and other evidence, CD concluded that the species was not the parent of any domestic breed (*Variation* 1: 233–4). The crossing experiments had been overseen by Samuel James Augustus Salter. CD cited Salter's paper on the subject, published in the *Natural History Review* (S. J. A. Salter 1863; see *Variation* 1: 234 n. 15). For more on CD's interest in the bird, see *Correspondence* vol. 13, letter to W. B. Tegetmeier, 27 February [1865] and n. 3.

To J. D. Hooker 5 August [1866][1]

Down
Aug 5

My dear Hooker

Beatson's bird appears to be one of the Grallatores & such ought not to be called land birds & in my journal I especially exclude them, but state that they are the first immigrants on almost every island.[2] At p. 422 of Origin you will find something about land birds on islands, which with respect to Madeira stands in New. Ed. thus corrected. There are 99 kinds, of which one alone is peculiar tho' very closely related to a European form & 3 or 4 other species are confined to this island & the Canaries.[3] About the birds of the Azores I know nothing except that I saw several European kinds there.[4]

It makes me rather miserable to see how differently we look at every thing: I sh^{d} not have expected many American plants in the Azores, seeing that the *temperate* parts are nearly twice & a half as distant as is Europe; seeing that the sea-currents flow only from the tropical states; & lastly as the American birds which are annually blown to Europe cross the ocean, as lately shewn by Dr Baird U.S., in the lat. of Ireland & Heligoland.[5] Formerly, at least judging from the erratic boulders, currents must have reached the Azores from the North.[6]

I heartily wish all your labours were over yours affectionately | Ch. Darwin

Whilst trying to find whether I had not a note about Birds being blown to the Azores from Europe—I came across these words "Seeds could arrive at Madeira & Azores by *Rennell's current* & then be swept to the south"—[7] What this means I now know not.—

LS(A)
DAR 115: 296

[1] The year is established by the relationship between this letter and the letter from J. D. Hooker, 4 August 1866.

[2] See letter from J. D. Hooker, 4 August 1866 and n. 2. CD refers to Alexander Beatson and to the former order Grallatores of wading birds. In *Journal of researches*, p. 543, CD implied that members of the order of wading birds should not be considered true land birds.

[3] CD refers to *Origin* 3d ed., p. 422; in *Origin* 4th ed., p. 465, CD added that only one of the ninety-nine forms of land birds in Madeira was endemic, and that it was closely related to a European form; he added that three or four species were confined to Madeira and the Canary Islands.

[4] CD had observed starlings, water wagtails, chaffinches, and blackbirds in the Azores during the *Beagle* voyage (*Journal of researches*, p. 595).

[5] Hooker maintained that it was difficult to account for the scarcity of American plants in the Azores, given that a few American species occurred on other Atlantic islands, and the fact that the Azores were closer than the other Atlantic islands to America (see letter from J. D. Hooker, 4 August 1866; see also J. D. Hooker 1866a, p. 27). CD countered that the Azores, which were temperate, were closer to Europe than to the temperate regions of America; that the sea currents from America to the Azores flowed only from the tropical regions, and that migratory birds, which might carry seeds, crossed from America to Europe too far north to touch on the Azores. On the last point, CD refers to Spencer Fullerton Baird's paper 'The distribution and migrations of North American birds' (Baird 1865–6; there is a lightly annotated copy in the Darwin Pamphlet Collection–CUL). Heligoland (now Helgoland) is off the coast of Denmark (*Columbia gazetteer of the world*).

[6] CD used observations of erratic boulders in the Azores as evidence that European plants could have been carried to the Azores as seeds on floating ice (*Correspondence* vol. 7, letter to Charles Lyell, 26 April [1858] and n. 2; *Origin*, p. 363; see also *Origin* 3d ed., pp. 393–4).

[7] Neither note has been found in the Darwin Archive–CUL. Early in the nineteenth century, James Rennell described a current that flowed southward from Cape Finisterre to the Canary Islands (Baker 1963, pp. 146–7). In his copy of Alphonse de Candolle's *Géographie botanique raisonnée* (A. de Candolle 1855, 2: 1022), CD added a note on the possibility that seeds were carried to the Azores or Spain by Rennell's current during the glacial period (*Marginalia* 1: 142).

From J. D. Hooker [6 August 1866][1]

Kew
Monday.

Dear Darwin

Again thanks for your letter.[2]

You need not fear my not doing justice to your objections to the Continental Hypothesis.![3]

Referring to p. 344 again, it never occurred to me that you alluded to extinction of **Marine** life— an isthmus is a piece of land, & you go on in the same sentence about "an island", which quite threw me out: for the destruction of isthmi makes Islands![4]

Bentham is away, but I will put your query on his desk.[5]

I surely did not say Azores nearer to Britain & N.F.L "than to Madeira", but "than Madeira is to said places"[6]

With regard to Madeira Coleoptera I rely very little on local distrib. of Insects— they are so local themselves.[7] A butterfly is a great rarity in Kew, even a white, though we are surrounded by Market Garden— all insects are *most rare* with us, even the kinds that abound on opposite side of Thames.[8]

So with shells, we have literally 0—not a *Helix* even, though they abound in the lanes 200 yards off the Gardens.

of the 89 Dezertas Insects—only 11 are peculiar.
of the 162 Porto Santan, 113 are Madeira, & 51 Dezertan.[9]

Never mind bothering Murray about the new Edn of the Origin for me.[10] You will tell me anything bearing on my subject.

AL
DAR 102: 89–90

[1] The date is established by the relationship between this letter and the letter to J. D. Hooker, 3 and 4 August [1866]. In 1866, the first Monday after 4 August was 6 August.

[2] Letter to J. D. Hooker, 3 and 4 August [1866].

[3] CD commented on the colonisation of oceanic islands by plants, listing various points in favour of occasional transport (or trans-oceanic migration) and against continental extension, in his letter to Hooker of 3 and 4 August [1866].

[4] Hooker refers to *Origin*, p. 344. See letter from J. D. Hooker, 31 July 1866 and n. 3, and letter to J. D. Hooker, 3 and 4 August [1866].

[5] Hooker refers to George Bentham. The enclosure has not been found.

[6] Hooker had written ambiguously about the distance to Britain and Newfoundland from the Azores and Madeira in his letter to CD of 31 July 1866; see letter to J. D. Hooker, 3 and 4 August [1866].

[7] CD had asked Hooker why he had discussed differences between the land shells of Porto Santo and Madeira, but not considered differences between the insect populations of the islands (see letter to J. D. Hooker, 3 and 4 August [1866] and n. 9).

[8] In 1868, the commercial residents of the village of Kew included three market gardeners, two florists and one gardener; the Royal Botanic Gardens, Kew, are in a western suburb of London on the south bank of the river Thames (*Post Office London suburban directory* 1868).

[9] Hooker's information is taken from Wollaston 1857, pp. xiv–xv. The Desertas are a group of islands south-east of Madeira; Porto Santo is a small island north-east of Madeira. Both Porto Santo and the Desertas belong to the Madeiran group of islands (*EB*).

[10] Hooker refers to the fourth edition of *Origin*. See letter to J. D. Hooker, 3 and 4 August [1866] and nn. 17 and 18.

From Asa Gray 7 August 1866

Cambridge
Aug. 7, 1866

My Dear Darwin

When I received yours of July 15,[1] I had just returned from a week of sailing on our New England coast, I have now had a week of pottering at home, and next week I go into the country for 10 days. When I return I must set down to a new ed. of my Manual of Botany, and other stuff.[2]

I will soon send you a brief note on a complete, symmetrical, regular, but 2–merous Orchid flower,—in Cypripedium.[3]

Brace's full name is *Charles Loring Brace*. Curious that Dr. Wells should have first propounded Nat. selection.[4] But a man far-seeing in one line is likely to be so in others.[5]

Appleton has, at my request, returned the sheets I had sent him, as he persisted in the idea of making what he called the essential alterations on his old stereotype plates, I thought for any petty pecuniary advantage, even connive at such doings.[6] I wish your publisher would arrange with some American bookseller to supply the market here at a rate which would make the English edition generally available.[7]

When your Variation-book is ready, we will see what can be done with that, & perhaps at the same time may then get a satisfactory reprint of Origin[8]

I shall take your sheets with me for rail-way reading. I have now got *all* the sheets.— Intending to amuse hours of travel with them, I had not till this moment read the passage, on *Owen* in the *Hist. Sketch*. Owen's proceedings are characteristic. And your note is the *prettiest piece of work of the kind I ever had the pleasure to see*.[9] I never read a more telling page. Owen must be mad enough at being "knocked into a cocked hat"—as we say,— But I see not how he can complain.

I wait with interest the result about *Rhamnus*. I enclose fls of R. lanceolatus.[10]

Clarke was of the greatest use to Agassiz and I cannot but think that A. used him very unfairly as soon as he no longer wanted him or found it difficult to pay for his services.[11] C. is a capital observer; but a man of a lumbering sort of mind. His book was founded on a small course of lectures,—of which I heard only one, and found then—and in conversation with him too—that he was quite incapable of understanding what Natural Selection meant—as much so as Agassiz himself—only the former would like to understand it, and the latter wilfully would not.[12]

You should study Wyman's observations in his own papers. He is always careful to keep his inferences close to his facts, & is as good an experimenter, I judge, as he is an observer. He has a new series of observations to publish. I think, that he has not at all *pronounced* in favor of spontaneous generation—but I will *bet* on his experiments against Pasteur, any day.[13]

I am so glad you are so well: pray keep so,

Ever Yours affectionately | Asa Gray

DAR 165: 153

[1] CD's letter to Gray of 15 July 1866 has not been found.

[2] The fifth edition of Gray's *Manual of the botany of the northern United States* was published in 1867 (A. Gray 1867).

[3] Dimerous: i.e.: with two members in each part or whorl. Flowers of *Cypridedium* normally have three sepals and petals. In *Orchids* 2d ed., p. 235 n., CD referred to the description of a 'monstrous flower of *Cypripedium candidum*' that Gray published in the *American Journal of Science and Arts* (A. Gray 1866). CD and Gray had corresponded extensively on the pollination mechanism of *Cypripedium* (see *Correspondence* vols. 10 and 11).

[4] Brace was a nephew of Gray's wife, Jane Loring Gray. He had informed CD of an article by William Charles Wells, 'An account of a white female, part of whose skin resembles that of a Negro; with some observations on the causes of the differences in colour and form between the white and negro races of men'; the paper was published together with two other essays in W. C. Wells 1818. In the historical sketch of *Origin* 4th ed., p. xv, CD quoted Wells's remark that nature had formed varieties of humans fitted to their environment in a similar way to that in which agriculturalists improved domestic animals by selection, though more slowly. CD also cited Brace for calling his attention to the article. For a discussion of Wells's paper, see K. D. Wells 1973.

[5] Wells had received the Rumford Medal of the Royal Society of London for *An essay on dew, and several appearances connected with it* (W. C. Wells 1814; see *DNB*).

[6] Gray refers to the sheets of the fourth edition of *Origin*. On the process of stereotyping used by the publisher D. Appleton & Co. to produce the American edition of *Origin*, see the letter to Asa Gray, 16 April [1866] and n. 11. Apparently William Henry Appleton, the head of the firm, had proposed making small changes to individual stereotype plates, as any substantial revision would alter the pagination of the volume and entail a recasting of all the stereotypes. Gray had enclosed a letter from Appleton with his letter of 3 July 1866, but this enclosure has not been found.

[7] See letter to Asa Gray, 4 August [1866] and n. 3.

[8] The first American edition of *Variation* was published by Orange Judd & Co. in 1868. A revised American edition of *Origin* was published by D. Appleton & Co. in 1870.

[9] CD had considerably revised his account of Richard Owen's work in the historical sketch to *Origin* 4th ed., pp. xvii–viii (see letter to J. D. Hooker, 31 May [1866] and n. 11; see also letter to B. D. Walsh, [19] April [1866]).

[10] CD and his son William Erasmus Darwin were investigating the different flower forms of *Rhamnus cathartica*. CD had become interested in *Rhamnus* in 1861, when Gray informed him that *R. lanceolatus* was dimorphic. See also letter to W. E. Darwin, 22 June [1866] and n. 10.

[11] On the dispute between Henry James Clark and his former teacher, Louis Agassiz, see the letter from B. D. Walsh, 17 July 1866 and n. 15.

[12] Clark's book, *Mind in nature*, was based on a series of lectures given at the Lowell Institute in Boston in 1864 (see H. J. Clark 1865, iii). For more on Clark's book, see the letter from B. D. Walsh, 17 July 1866 and n. 14.

[13] Gray alludes to experiments performed by his colleague at Harvard University, Jeffries Wyman, in order to test the claims of Louis Pasteur to have disproved the theory of spontaneous generation (see Wyman 1862 and 1867). Gray had previously defended Wyman as an accurate observer in the context of debates over spontaneous generation (see *Correspondence* vol. 11, letter from Asa Gray to

J. D. Hooker, 6 July 1863, and letter from Asa Gray, 21 July 1863). On the role of Wyman's work in these debates, see Strick 2000.

From J. D. Hooker 7 August 1866

Kew
Aug. 7th/66

Dear old Darwin

You must not let me worry you. I am an obstinate pig—but you must not be miserable at my looking at the same thing in a different light from you—[1] I must get to the bottom of this question—& that is all I can do— some clever fellow one day will knock the bottom out of it, & see his way to explain what to a Botanist without a theory to support must be very great difficulties— True enough, all *may* be explained as you reason it will be, I quite grant this: but meanwhile all is not so explained, & I cannot accept a hypothesis that leaves so many facts unaccounted for.—[2]

You say temp. parts of N. Am nearly $2\frac{1}{2}$ times as distant from Azores as Europe is. According to a rough calculation on Col James' chart I make

East. Azores to Portugal 850
West do to N. F. Land 1500[3]

but I am writing to a friend at Admiralty to have the distance calculated (which looks like cracking nuts with Nasmyth's hammer!—[4]

Are European birds blown to America?

Are the Azorean erratics an established fact? I want them very badly, though they are not of much consequence, as a slight sinking would hide all evidence of that sort.[5]

I do want to sum up impartially, leaving verdict to jury, I cannot do this without putting all difficulties most clearly— how do you know how you would fare with me if you were a continentalist!— Then too we must recollect that I have to meet a host who are all on the continental side, in fact pretty nearly *all* the thinkers, Forbes, Hartung, Heer, Unger, Wollaston, Lowe, (Wallace I suppose) & now Andrew Murray.[6] I do not regard all these, & snap my fingers at all but you: in my inmost soul I conscientiously say I incline to your theory—but I cannot accept it as an established truth, or unexceptionable hypothesis.

The "Wire bird" being a grallator is a curious fact favorable to you.[7] Sclater never heard of it.[8] How I do yearn to go out again to St Helena.[9]

Ever yrs affec | J D Hooker

Of course I accept the Ornithological evidence as tremendous strong—though why they should get blown *Westerly*, & not changed specifically as Insects shells & plants have done, is a mystery.[10]

DAR 102: 91–2

CD ANNOTATION
8.1 though ... specifically 8.2] *triple scored pencil*

1 See letter to J. D. Hooker, 5 August [1866].

2 Hooker and CD had been debating since Hooker's letter of [24 July 1866] the means by which oceanic islands had become populated by plants. Hooker was preparing a lecture for the meeting of the British Association for the Advancement of Science at Nottingham in August 1866. Hooker refers to CD's hypothesis of occasional trans-oceanic transport (see letter to J. D. Hooker, 30 July [1866] and n. 7).

3 See letter to J. D. Hooker, 5 August [1866] and n. 5. Hooker used a new map of the earth by Henry James to illustrate his lecture (see n. 2, above). See also letter to J. D. Hooker, 30 June [1866] and n. 6.

4 The industrial steam hammer was commonly known as Nasmyth's hammer, after James Nasmyth, who designed the prototype in 1839 (*DNB*).

5 See letter to J. D. Hooker, 5 August [1866] and n. 6. Hooker refers to the possibility that erratic boulders deposited by icebergs on islands might later be submerged owing to subsidence.

6 According to Edward Forbes, continental Europe formerly included Britain; southern Ireland and Portugal were once connected by land; and the western parts of Europe and north Africa had extended far into the Atlantic encompassing the Canary Islands, Madeira, and the Azores (Forbes 1846). Oswald Heer proposed that Madeira, the Canaries, Porto Santo, and the Azores were the remnants of a sunken land-mass, or 'Atlantis', that in the Tertiary period had been connected to America and Europe by a land-bridge (Heer 1855). Franz Unger, Thomas Vernon Wollaston, and Andrew Murray also promoted the theory of continental extension in their writings (see, for example, Wollaston 1856, Unger 1860, and Murray 1866). Alfred Russel Wallace had considered the possibility that land connections had existed between neighbouring countries now separated by sea (A. R. Wallace 1857). For Wallace's summary of the difference between his and CD's views on geographical distribution, see A. R. Wallace 1905, 2: 20–1. Hooker also refers to Georg Hartung and Richard Thomas Lowe, who had worked on the geology and natural history of the Atlantic Islands (see, for example, Hartung 1864 and Lowe 1868).

7 Hooker accepted CD's claim that the wire bird was not a land bird (see letter to J. D. Hooker, 5 August [1866] and n. 2); in his lecture, he stated that there were no land birds on St Helena (J. D. Hooker 1866a, p. 75).

8 Hooker refers to Philip Lutley Sclater; see also letter from J. D. Hooker, 4 August 1866 and n. 3.

9 Hooker visited St Helena while returning from the Antarctic expedition aboard HMS *Erebus* in 1843 (L. Huxley ed. 1918, 1: 96–9; R. Desmond 1999, pp. 30–4, 84). Between 1843 and 1845, CD and Hooker had corresponded about the flora of St Helena in comparison with that of the Galápagos Islands (*Correspondence* vols. 2 and 3).

10 In his letter of 5 August [1866], CD recollected seeing several European species of birds in the Azores but said that he had not found any 'note about Birds being blown to the Azores from Europe'. In the same letter, CD referred Hooker to *Origin* 3d ed., p. 422, on the land birds of Madeira being derived from Europe and Africa. On the same page, to which Hooker apparently refers, CD contrasted Madeira's lack of indigenous birds with its richness in indigenous species of land shells. For more on the indigenous insects and plants of Madeira, and their variations among the islands of the archipelago, see Wollaston 1857 and Lowe 1868.

To J. D. Hooker 8 August [1866]

Down. | Bromley. | Kent. S.E.
Aug 8

My dear Hooker

It w[d] be a very great pleasure to me if I c[d] think that my letters were of the least use to you. I must have expressed myself badly for you to suppose that I look at islands being stocked by occasional transport as a well established hypothesis:[1] we both give up creation & therefore have to account for the inhabitants of islands either by continental extensions or by occasional transport; now all that I maintain is that of these two alternatives, one of which must be admitted notwithstanding very many difficulties, that occasional transport is by far the most *probable.*[2]

I go thus far further that I maintain, knowing what we do, that it w$^{d.}$ be inexplicable if *unstocked* isl^{ds} were not stocked to certain extent at least, by these occasional means.—[3]

European birds are occasionally driven to America but far more rarely than in the reverse direction: they arrive viâ Greenland (Baird): yet a European lark has been caught in Bermuda.[4] By the way you might like to hear that European birds regularly migrate, viâ the Northern Islands, to Greenland.[5]

About the erratics in the Azores see Origin p. 393: Hartung c^{d} hardly be mistaken about granite blocks on a volcanic island.[6]

You must understand that I do not know, only suppose, that Beatson's bird was a Wader.[7]

I do not think it a mystery that birds have not been modified in Madeira. Pray look at p. 422 of Origin.[8] You w^{d} not think it a mystery if you had seen the long lists which I have (somewhere) of the birds annually blown, even in flocks, to Madeira. The crossed stock would be the more vigorous.—[9]

Remember if you do not come here before Nottingham, if you do not come afterwards I shall think myself diabolically ill-used.[10]

yours affectionately | Ch. Darwin

P.S. Ought you not to measure from the Azores, not to Newfoundland, but to the more Southern & temperate States?[11]

Endorsement: '/66'
LS(A)
DAR 115: 297

[1] See letter from J. D. Hooker, 7 August 1866. See also letters to J. D. Hooker, 30 July [1866] and 3 and 4 August [1866].

[2] On occasional transport, see the letter to J. D. Hooker, 30 July [1866], n. 7. For CD's earlier evaluation of the hypotheses of occasional transport and continental extension, see *Origin*, pp. 357–65. See also CD's arguments in favour of occasional transport in his letter to Hooker of 3 and 4 August [1866]. For CD's earlier rejection of the hypothesis of continental extension, see, for example, *Correspondence* vol. 6, letter to Charles Lyell, 25 June [1856].

[3] See also letter to J. D. Hooker, 3 and 4 August [1866] and n. 12.

[4] Spencer Fullerton Baird thought that prevailing winds accounted for the greater movement of birds from America to Europe, rather than in the reverse direction (Baird 1865–6, pp. 344–5). He also noted that *Alauda arvensis*, the European skylark, had been observed in Bermuda (*ibid.*, p. 342).

[5] European birds that had been seen in Greenland and Iceland are listed in Baird 1865–6, pp. 337–9. In his lecture, among the arguments made by CD in favour of trans-oceanic migration, Hooker mentioned American birds that were transported annually to Europe and European birds that flew to Greenland (J. D. Hooker 1866a, p. 51).

[6] The reference is to the third edition of *Origin*. Georg Hartung had observed erratic boulders in the Azores (see *Correspondence* vol. 7, letter to Charles Lyell, 26 April [1858]). See also letter to J. D. Hooker, 5 August [1866] and n. 6.

[7] The references are to Alexander Beatson and to what he called the wire bird (now the St Helena plover). See letter to J. D. Hooker, 5 August [1866] and n. 2.

[8] CD's discussion of the birds of Madeira and their lack of modification is in *Origin*, p. 391. The reference in this letter is to the third edition of *Origin*, which preserved the sentence added in the second edition on the lack of modification of the bird species of Bermuda: 'Any tendency to modification will also have been checked by intercrossing with the unmodified immigrants from the mother-country.' See also Peckham ed. 1959, p. 621.

[9] CD probably refers to the lists of birds identified in Madeira in Harcourt 1855 and in the letter from E. W. V. Harcourt, 31 May 1856 (*Correspondence* vol. 6). CD's annotated presentation copy of Harcourt 1855 is in DAR 196.4. In the section on oceanic islands in the second and later editions of *Origin*, CD argued that species of Madeiran birds gained increased vigour by occasionally crossing with continental members of the same species (see, for example, *Origin* 3d ed., pp. 421–2).

[10] Hooker was to attend the meeting of the British Association for the Advancement of Science at Nottingham later in August 1866; he visited Down on 18 August (see letters from J. D. Hooker, [17 August 1866] and 18 August 1866).

[11] See letter from J. D. Hooker, 7 August 1866 and n. 3.

From J. D. Hooker 9 August 1866

Kew
Aug 9/66

My dear Darwin

If my letters did not génér you,[1] it is impossible that you should suppose that your's were of no use to me! I would throw up the whole thing were it not for correspondence with you; which is the only bit of silver in the affair. I do feel it disgusting to have to *make a point* of a speciality in which one cannot see one's way—a bit further than I could before I began.—[2] To be sure I have a very much clearer notion of the pros & cons on both sides—(though these were rather forgotten facts than rediscoveries) I see the sides of the well further down & more distinctly but the bottom is as obscure as ever—[3]

I think I know Origin by heart in relation to the subject.—& it was reading it that suggested the queries about Azores boulders & Madeira bird: the former you & I have talked over, & I thought I remembered that you wanted it confirmed.[4] The latter strikes me thus— Why should plants & insects have been so extensively changed & Birds not at all? I perfectly understand & feel the force of your argument—in reference to Birds per se but why do these not apply to insects & plants?[5]

Can you not see, that this suggests the conclusion, that the plants are derived one way & the Birds another!

I certainly did *take it for granted* that you supposed the stocking by occasional transport to be something even *more* than a "well established hypothesis"—but disputants seldom stop to measure the strength of their antagonists opinion.[6]

I shall be with you on Saturday week I hope.[7] I should have come before, but have made so little progress that I could not. I am now at St Helena, & shall then go to & finish with, Kerguelen's Land.[8]

Cape Roch to S^t. Michaels 741
Cape Race to Flores 1035.[9]

Azores to nearest temperate State is nearly double the distance—but to my mind does not mend the matter.—for I do not ask why Azores have even proportionally (to distance) *smaller* number of American plants, but why they have *none*, seeing the winds & currents set that way.[10]

The Bermudas are all American in Flora—but from what Col Munro[11] informs me, I should say they have nothing but common American weeds & the Juniper. (Cedar)[12]—no changed forms—yet they are as far from America as Azores from Europe. I suppose they are modern & out of the pale.[13]

You say ("Coral Reefs" 205) that they "ought to have been colored red"— but you do not say on what map. I do not find them on 3.[14]

There is this, to me, *astounding* difference between certain Oceanic Islands which were stocked by continental extension & those stocked by immigration (following in both definitions your opinion)—that the former do contain many types of the more distant continent, the latter do not any!!!! Take Madagascar with it's many Asiatic Genera unknown in Africa;—Ceylon with many Malayan types not Peninsula Indian.— Japan with many non Asiatic American types—[15]

Baird's fact of Greenland migration I was aware of since I wrote my Arctic paper—[16] I wish I was as satisfied either of continental or of transport means, as I am of my Greenland hypothesis! oh dear me what a comfort it is to have a belief—(sneer away—)[17]

Ever yr affec | J D Hooker

DAR 102: 94–7

CD ANNOTATIONS

2.6 but why . . . & plants?] *scored pencil*; 'because not introduced in body at same time or so finally *[one word illeg]' added pencil*
5.1 I shall . . . hope] *scored pencil*
6.3 yet they . . . the pale. 6.4] *scored pencil*
7.1 You say . . . map. 7.2] *scored pencil*
7.2 3.] *underl pencil*; 'I do not understand' *added pencil*

1 'Gêner': to embarrass or to annoy (French).

2 Hooker refers to the writing of his lecture on insular floras (J. D. Hooker 1866a) and to recent correspondence with CD on the subject of the geographical dispersal of plants to oceanic islands.

3 Hooker refers to the alternative hypotheses of occasional trans-oceanic transport and continental extension. For more on these hypotheses, see *Origin*, pp. 357–65. See also letter from J. D. Hooker, [24 July 1866] and letter to J. D. Hooker, 30 July [1866] and n. 7.

4 Hooker had questioned CD about the veracity of reports of erratic boulders in the Azores (see letter from J. D. Hooker, 7 August 1866). In his letter of 4 August 1866, Hooker had informed CD that he had written to Philip Lutley Sclater for information on the birds of Madeira. In *Origin*, CD considered the erratic boulders of the Azores on page 363 and the birds of Madeira on page 391. On CD's prediction of erratic boulders in the Azores, and their subsequent discovery, see *Correspondence* vol. 7, letter to J. D. Hooker, 26 [April 1858].

5 CD recognised that there were no endemic species of birds on Madeira, whereas there were numerous endemic species of insects and land shells (*Origin*, p. 391). On the plants and insects of oceanic islands, see *Origin*, pp. 389–402.

6 In his letter of 8 August [1866], CD denied that he regarded occasional transport as a 'well established hypothesis' but expressed his belief that it was far more probable than continental extension as the means by which islands had become colonised by plants. On occasional transport, see letter to J. D. Hooker, 30 July [1866], n. 7. See *Correspondence* vol. 6, letter to Charles Lyell, 25 June [1856], for CD's rejection of Edward Forbes's hypothesis of continental extension.

7 In 1866, the second Saturday after 9 August was 18 August. Hooker visited CD at Down on that date (see letters from J. D. Hooker, [17 August 1866] and 18 August 1866).

8 In the first part of his lecture, Hooker described in turn the principal features of the floras of the Madeiran, Canarian, Azorean, and Cape Verde islands, followed by St Helena, Ascension and Kerguelen's Land (J. D. Hooker 1866a).

9 Cape Roche is on the south-western coast of Spain, São Miguel (St Michael's) is an island in the south-eastern Azores, Cape Race is at the south-eastern extremity of Newfoundland, and Flores is the most westerly island in the Azores (*Times atlas*). For Hooker's earlier approximation of the distances in miles between America and the Azores and between the Azores and Europe, see the letter from J. D. Hooker, 7 August 1866 and n. 3.

10 In his letter of 8 August [1866], CD suggested that Hooker measure the distance from the Azores to the more temperate southern states of North America rather than to Newfoundland. See also letter to J. D. Hooker, 5 August [1866] and n. 5.

11 For many years, William Munro had provided Hooker with information on botany from the different continents in which he served as an army officer (see L. Huxley ed. 1918).

12 The common name of the Bermudan native *Juniperus bermudiana* is Bermuda cedar (Bailey and Bailey 1976).

13 CD had noted that the Bermuda islands were fringed by coral reefs (*Coral reefs*, p. 205), and presented evidence that islands with 'fringing reefs' had been formed more recently than other islands (*ibid.*, pp. 131–8). Hooker implies that there had not been time for endemic species to develop on Bermuda by the action of natural selection.

14 Plate 3 in *Coral reefs* distinguishes three different classes of coral islands by colour; however, the West Indies appear at the edge of the plan, which consequently shows no Atlantic islands lying east of Barbados. In *Coral reefs*, p. 205, CD wrote that the Bermuda islands 'ought to have been coloured red' owing to their fringing reefs (see n. 13, above), but that they were left uncoloured because they had some features in common with another class of coral island, the lagoon island or atoll.

15 For CD's general views on the derivation of the flora and fauna of oceanic islands from continents, see *Origin* pp. 388–406. On the affinity between the floras of Madagascar and islands of the Indian Ocean, see *Correspondence* vol. 9, letter to J. D. Hooker, 7 November [1861]). The identity of elephants in Ceylon (now Sri Lanka) and India had been used as evidence that Ceylon and India were once connected by dry land (Falconer 1863, pp. 94–6). CD also believed that Japan was once similarly joined to mainland China (*Correspondence* vol. 7, letter to Asa Gray, 11 August [1858]).

16 Hooker refers to Baird 1865–6 and J. D. Hooker 1860a. See letter to J. D. Hooker, 8 August [1866] and nn. 4 and 5.

17 In his essay 'Outlines of the distribution of Arctic plants' Hooker hypothesised that Greenland represented the western boundary of the European flora, owing to the predominance of European species and lack of Asiatic and American species (J. D. Hooker 1860a, p. 252). Hooker also endorsed CD's theory of plant migrations southward from the Arctic during a former cold period (see *Origin*, pp. 365–82), and argued that Greenland has an anomalous flora, because of its lack of a former southward connection to land on which migration could have proceeded (J. D. Hooker 1860a, p. 254). Hooker and CD subsequently discussed continental extension and occasional transport in relation to the flora of Greenland (*Correspondence* vol. 10). See also *Correspondence* vol. 13, letter to J. D. Hooker, 15 [February 1865] and n. 6.

To W. B. Tegetmeier 10 August [1866][1]

Down. | Bromley. | Kent, S.E.
Aug 10

My dear Sir

I am very much obliged for the sight of the feathers now returned; they are extremely curious & I will add a sentence after your remark about pencilling. I have seen the feathers of the other hybrids which you have sent me.[2]

Many thanks for the offer of the electro types; but nearly similar drawing are now being cut for me on wood.[3]

I enclose a scrap with reference to Mr Hewit's paper: I find I was wrong, for it refers to the Gold laced bantam.[4]

Many thanks about the wood-cuts.[5]

Believe me yours very faithfully | Ch. Darwin

LS
Archives of The New York Botanical Garden (Charles Finney Cox collection) (Tegetmeier 83)

[1] The year is established by the relationship between this letter and the letter to W. B. Tegetmeier, 4 August [1866].

[2] Tegetmeier had remarked on the transverse blue bands on the tail feathers of a hybrid between *Gallus varius* and the common hen (see letter from W. B. Tegetmeier, 2 August 1866 and n. 4). He had enclosed the feathers of the bird, together with those of a hybrid between *G. sonneratii* and the red game-hen with his letter of [after 4 August 1866] (see letter from W. B. Tegetmeier, [after 4 August 1866], and nn. 8 and 9).

[3] See letter from W. B. Tegetmeier, [after 4 August 1866] and n. 6.

[4] CD had remarked that the saffron colour of the feathers of a Sebright hen had not been mentioned in Edward Hewitt's published account of the bird (see letter to W. B. Tegetmeier, 4 August [1866]). Tegetmeier asked for the reference to Hewitt's paper (Hewitt 1864), and noted that as the feathers were from a golden Sebright or laced hen, they would have this colour (letter from W. B. Tegetmeier, [after 4 August 1866]).

[5] Tegetmeier had agreed to have changes made to several of the woodcuts for *Variation*. See letter from W. B. Tegetmeier, [after 4 August 1866].

To *Gardeners' Chronicle* [before 11 August 1866][1]

Oxalis Bowei.—[2] I should be much obliged to any one who will be so kind as to look at his flowers of this Oxalis, and observe where the summits of the branching stigmas stand with respect to the two sets of anthers. In all my plants the stigmas stand close beneath the lower anthers; but I have good reason to believe that two other forms exist—one with the stigmas standing above both sets of anthers, and the other with the stigmas between the two sets. If any one has flowers in either of these latter states, that is long-styled or mid-styled, I should be grateful if he would send me a few rather young flowers wrapped up in tin-foil or oil-silk; for I should thus be enabled to fertilize my own flowers and obtain seed.[3]

Charles Darwin

Down, Bromley, Kent

Gardeners' Chronicle and Agricultural Gazette (1866): 756

1 The letter was published in the *Gardeners' Chronicle and Agricultural Gazette* on 11 August 1866; see also *Collected papers* 2: 132.

2 The species, which CD also referred to as *Oxalis bowii*, is now known as *O. bowiei.*

3 On CD's interest in trimorphism in *Oxalis*, see the letter to Friedrich Hildebrand, 16 May [1866] and n. 10. In *Forms of flowers*, p. 179, CD remarked that he had cultivated the short-styled form of a species purchased under the name of *O. Bowii* but had some doubts whether it was rightly named, noting that it was sterile when self-pollinated. In a note dated July 1866, CD wrote, 'Oxalis bowii I can perceive in short-styled no certain difference in pollen of two sets of anthers' (DAR 109: B101). *Oxalis* has an inner and outer series of stamens; those forming the inner series are longer.

To *Gardeners' Chronicle* [before 11 August 1866][1]

All who have tried have found much difficulty in crossing papilionaceous flowers.[2] Several years ago, Dr. Herbert remarked to me that with the exception of Erythrina no hybrids had been made in this great family.[3] Gärtner crossed 36 flowers of different varieties of the common Pea, and he did not get a single pod perfectly developed and with the full complement of seed; he crossed 10 flowers of Kidney Beans, and did not get a single pod.[4] Some years ago I crossed the varieties of the Sweet Pea, and many more flowers dropped off unimpregnated than were fertilised.[5] The difficulty arises from the anthers opening at so early an age that they must be removed long before the flower expands. After the operation the immature stigma is liable to exposure to the air; and it is difficult to judge when to apply the pollen. Moreover there is some reason to suspect that the stigma requires successive applications of pollen. To show the difficulty of fertilising papilionaceous flowers, I may mention that I lately removed all the pollen that I could with a soft brush from six recently expanded flowers of Lupinus pilosus[6] protected from the visits of insects, and then applied pollen from a distinct individual of the same species. Although in this case there was no operation at an early age, yet five flowers out of the six dropped off unimpregnated. Had these flowers remained untouched, all, judging from the others, probably would have set, and the only difference would have been that their stigmas would have been surrounded by a mass of pollen as long as the flowers continued in bloom. This case is worth mentioning as showing how erroneous the belief is that fertilisation usually takes place in unopened flowers, in which the pollen is shed at an early age. These trials on the Lupines, and others formerly on Sweet Peas, led me to try the following plan. I rolled up thin paper into a cylinder, rather thinner than a knitting needle. I then tied a thread tight round, and cut off the cylinder beneath the thread, so that a little pipe closed at one end or cap, about the fifth of an inch in length, was left. This was easily filled with pollen from the keel-petal of any desired variety, and could then be placed on the pistil and secured below the stigma by being tied with a thread. I then castrated four flower-buds of the Sweet Pea, and placed on the young stigmas caps filled with pollen from another variety, and four fine pods were soon formed. I also fertilised eight castrated flowers of two species of Lupins with pollen from distinct plants of the same species, but from these I have got only four pods. I may add, that as an experiment I filled one of the little caps with pollen of Lathyrus grandiflorus and placed it on the stigma of a Sweet Pea (Lathyrus odoratus), and to my great surprise, considering how distinct these species are, a fine pod has been formed. I am certain no pollen could have been left in the flower of the Sweet Pea, as the anthers were removed whilst quite immature; and if these hybrid seeds grow, a curious hybrid will be produced. I should not have thought this plan of fertilising papilionaceous flowers worth mentioning had it not been applicable in all cases in which early castration is necessary, and likewise in certain cases mentioned by Gärtner, in which the stigma requires, or is benefited by, successive applications of pollen. In all such cases some trouble would be saved and certainty gained by the use of the little caps filled with the desired kind of pollen.

Charles Darwin

Down, Bromley, Kent

Gardeners' Chronicle and Agricultural Gazette (1866): 756

1 The letter was published in the *Gardeners' Chronicle and Agricultural Gazette* on 11 August 1866; see also *Collected papers* 2: 132–4.

2 CD began artificially pollinating leguminous flowers in 1857 as a means of investigating the role of insects in pollination, and of testing his belief that no plant self-fertilises perpetually. See his discussion of Leguminosae in *Natural selection*, pp. 68–71, and *Correspondence* vols. 6 and 7. See also *Correspondence* vol. 13, letter from George Henslow, 1 November 1865, nn. 8 and 9.

3 CD had corresponded with William Herbert on plant hybridisation and reversion (see *Correspondence* vol. 2) and had visited Herbert in 1845 (*Correspondence* vol. 3, Appendix II). *Erythrina* is mentioned in *Natural selection*, p. 70 n. 4, as one of the few cases of hybrids forming in the family Leguminosae.

4 CD refers to Karl Friedrich von Gärtner's crossing experiments with *Pisum* and *Phaseolus* (see Gärtner 1849, p. 720).

5 On CD's experiments with sweetpeas (*Lathyrus odoratus*), see *Natural selection*, pp. 70–1, and *Correspondence* vol. 9, letter to *Journal of Horticulture*, [before 14 May 1861] and n. 7.

6 CD had asked Joseph Dalton Hooker to identify the species in his letter of 21 [July 1866]. For more on CD's experiments with *Lupinus pilosus* and his publication of the results, see *Correspondence* vol. 13, letter from W. A. Leighton, 29 May 1865, n. 2.

To J. D. Hooker 12 August [1866]

Down. | Bromley. | Kent. S.E.
Aug 12th

My dear Hooker

I write one line to say how heartily glad we shall be to see you on Saturday or any other day.[1] Let us know train & we shall probably be able to send tax-cart or pony carriage—

I will not talk over some of the points in your last letter until we meet;[2] but I now plainly see that one chief cause of our difference is that you look much higher than I do and expect to solve the problem far more completely than I have ever thought to be possible. Your letters have interested me quite awfully as the boys say.

yours aff^{dy}. | Ch. Darwin

Endorsement: '/66'
LS
DAR 115: 298

[1] In his letter of 9 August 1866, Hooker wrote that he hoped to visit Down on 'Saturday week', which was 18 August.
[2] Letter from J. D. Hooker, 9 August 1866.

From J. D. Hooker [17 August 1866][1]

Dear Darwin

I hope to arrive at Bromley with my blessed mss[2] tomorrow by the Train that leaves Charing X at 5.15. & arrives at Bromley at 6 PM

Ever | J D Hooker

Kew Friday.

DAR 102: 93

[1] The date is established by the references to Hooker's manuscript (see n. 2, below) and by the relationship between this letter and the letter to J. D. Hooker, 12 August [1866]. In 1866, the Friday following 12 August was 17 August.
[2] Hooker refers to the manuscript of his lecture on insular floras (J. D. Hooker 1866a), delivered at the meeting of the British Association for the Advancement of Science on 27 August 1866.

To Ernst Haeckel 18 August [1866]

Down. | *Bromley.* | *Kent. S.E.*
Aug 18

My dear Sir

I received a few days ago a sheet of your new work, & have read it with great interest.[1] You confer on my book, the "Origin of Species", the most magnificent eulogium which it has ever received, & I am most truly gratified, but I fear if this part of your work is ever criticized, your reviewer will say that you have spoken much too strongly.[2] Your abstract seems to me wonderfully clear & good; & one little fact shews me how clearly you understand my views, namely your bringing prominently forward, which no one else has ever done, the fact & the cause of Divergence of Character.[3] Oddly enough, as it now appears to me, it was many years before I clearly saw the necessity of admitting a tendency to divergence of character, & some more years until I could see the explanation.[4]

I have read with much interest your discussion on Inheritance &c; & all the more so as I give in my next work, which will not be published for half a year, several chapters on this & other allied subjects.[5] So that I shall feel very curious to read your remaining chapters when published; but it is a terrible evil to me that I cannot read more than one or two pages at a time of German, even when written as clearly as is your book.

I suppose you have seen Prof. Claus new work on Copepoda in which he discusses individual variability, & alludes to your work; I have been interested by it.[6] I heartily congratulate you that your great undertaking is so nearly completed & with my cordial thanks for the great honour which you have done me & with a full belief that you will do excellent service in the cause which we have both at heart, I remain my dear sir | yours very sincerely Ch. Darwin

Endorsement: '*1866*'
LS(A)
Ernst-Haeckel-Haus (Bestand A-Abt. 1: 1-52/10)

1 The reference is to a proof-sheet of Haeckel's *Generelle Morphologie* (Haeckel 1866). CD's annotated copy of the book, which he later received, is in the Darwin Library–CUL (see letter from Ernst Haeckel, 19 October 1866 and n. 3; see also *Marginalia* 1: 355–7). For Haeckel's discussions of his work on the book, see *Correspondence* vols. 12 and 13.

2 In a section about the history of the theory of descent, Haeckel wrote that *Origin* was the book through which CD founded a new era in general morphology and physiology and also in anthropology and the whole of science in general (Haeckel 1866, 2: 163).

3 See Haeckel 1866, 2: 249–56, and *Marginalia* 1: 357. For CD's discussion of divergence, see *Origin*, pp. 111–26.

4 CD's notes on divergence and classification are in DAR 205.5. See *Correspondence* vols. 3 and 6 for some early discussions of the principle of divergence.

5 See Haeckel 1866, 2: 170–90. CD refers to *Variation*, which was published in January 1868 (Freeman 1977). In *Variation* 2: 397 n., CD cited Haeckel 1866, 2: 170, on the simplest form of inheritance.

6 Carl Friedrich Claus's monograph on the copepods of Nice (Claus 1866) presented a classification scheme influenced by Darwinian transmutation theory; it focused particularly on the role of environmental factors in determining morphological features in the sub-class Copepoda. CD had earlier recommended it to Joseph Dalton Hooker (see letter to J. D. Hooker, 3 and 4 August [1866] and n. 20). Claus referred to Haeckel's conclusions on variability within the copepod family, Corycaeidae, but did not cite a specific work (Claus 1866, p. 2).

From J. D. Hooker 18 August 1866

Royal Gardens Kew
Aug 18/66.

My dear Darwin

I found to my vexation that I had brought away vol I instead of III of Felix Holt.[1] I return I & II. with the Coddington, which was under my nose on my writing table![2]

I shall find out what it cost & hold your 10/ till then.

Smith will send you our small plant of *Drosera binata.* the leaves of our other are much bigger than I told you.[3] Give yours a nice sphagnum pot as you treat rotundifolia in a pot full of crocks & stand it in a pan of a water in a damp coolish house—[4]

I have told Smith you would keep yourself to Acropera.[5]

I forgot to ask you if your beef diet had improved your Pitcher plant.[6]

Ever yrs affcc | J D Hooker

My Mother is very unwell at Yarmouth with Diarrhœa & I am in dread of being sent for.[7]

The "Nation" says that Agassiz has shown that the Amazon valley was made since the Glacial Epoch & consists of 3 deposits—no particulars.[8]

DAR 102: 104–5

CD ANNOTATIONS
1.1 I found . . . till then. 2.1] *crossed pencil*
3.1 Smith . . . *binata.*] '(*Susan*)' *added pencil*
Top of 2d page: '*[one word illeg]* both 10th' *pencil, circled & del pencil*

1 The reference is to *Felix Holt the radical* by George Eliot (Eliot 1866).

2 The reference is to a microscope made with a lens popularised by Henry Coddington (see Bradbury 1967, pp. 102, 173). CD acquired a microscope of this type in 1831 (see *Correspondence* vol. 1, letter from [J. M. Herbert], [early May 1831] and n. 3).

3 Hooker refers to John Smith (1821–88). *Drosera binata* (syn. *D. dichotoma*) is described in *Insectivorous plants*, pp. 281–4. CD had requested a specimen from Hooker in 1864 (see *Correspondence* vol. 12, letter to J. D. Hooker, [27 January 1864] and n. 9).

4 CD had begun extensive experiments with *Drosera rotundifolia*, the common sundew, in 1860 (see *Correspondence* vol. 8, and *Correspondence* vol. 9, Appendix IV).

5 See letter from J. D. Hooker, 31 July 1866 and n. 22.

6 CD had kept several specimens of *Nepenthes*, a genus of pitcher-plant, for his research on climbing plants (see 'Climbing plants', pp. 46–7).

7 The reference is to Maria Hooker.

8 The notice of Louis Agassiz's view on the formation of the Amazon valley has not been found in the *Nation.* For more on Agassiz's glacial theory, see the letters to Charles Lyell, 7 February [1866] and 15 February [1866].

From William Darwin Fox 20 August [1866][1]

Delamere Rectory | Northwich
August 20

My dear Darwin

Though very unwilling to give you trouble, I cannot quite cease writing to you and hoping for a few lines whenever you are able to write.

Erasmus[2] gave a better account of you when I saw him in the Spring— I hope this may have continued, and that your wretched health, has been less wretched than usual.

Nothing but mental rest will ever give you any comfort and you have got into such a normal state of requiring the stimulus of mental activity, that you must have it, & the poor body go to the wall.

How goes on *the Book*?[3] Requiring so many additions and corrections, that it never approaches its end I suppose.

I am anxiously looking for your work on domestic animals, which will I suppose soon be out.[4] Possibly it may be so already, for I am sadly behind hand with knowledge of what is going on in the literary world. Except Sir P Egerton[5] I have no literary bot Hist[y] friends here—& he is never at home for more than a few weeks.

I was deeply grieved a few days since, to hear of poor Susans suffering state, from Frank Parker.[6] I knew she was very ill, but I hoped not in such pain as he told me she was.

Erasmus I thought looking extremely well. He gets younger, not having a Book to destroy him.

We have all been at Whitby.—a famous place in any point of view.— I just left it before Sir C. Lyell arrived there.[7] I should have much liked to see him again. There were some grand specimens of Ichthyosaurus & Plesiosaurus there for 〈 〉 Inspection.

Possibly you may be interested in the fact of Smerinthus Ocellatus & Populi being now regularly bred between. They are cognate species—The eyed Hawk Moth & the Poplar. I imagine there is little difficulty in procuring the mules. I have a lot of the caterpillars of each & hope next year to try whether the mules will breed again.[8]

Possibly this may be proved by others this year.

When you write, if you ever do, tell me how you all are—and also how Caroline[9] & her belongings are.

My Brood are all well I am thankful to say— it is a good deal to say of *16*.[10]

With our kindest regards to Mrs Darwin[11] Believe me Ever yours affec[ly] | W. D. Fox

DAR 164: 184

[1] The year is established by the relationship between this letter and the letter to W. D. Fox, 24 August [1866].

[2] Erasmus Alvey Darwin, CD's brother.

[3] Fox refers to the fourth edition of *Origin*, which CD had recently finished, but which had not yet been published (see letter from John Murray, 18 July [1866]).

[4] *Variation* was not published until January 1868 (Freeman 1977).

[5] Philip de Malpas Grey-Egerton.

[6] The references are to Susan Elizabeth Darwin, CD's sister, and Francis Parker, CD's nephew.

[7] Fox refers to Whitby, a seaside town in North Yorkshire, and to Charles Lyell.

[8] Fox refers to two species in the family Sphingidae, *Smerinthus ocellatus*, the eyed hawk-moth, and *S. populi* (now *Laothoe populi*), the poplar hawk-moth. The species interbreed in captivity, but only sterile hybrids are produced.

[9] Caroline Sarah Wedgwood.

10 Fox had four surviving children from his first marriage and twelve from his second (*Darwin pedigree*).
11 Emma Darwin.

To B. D. Walsh 20 August [1866]

Down. | Bromley. | Kent. S.E.
Aug 20

My dear Sir

I am sorry to say that before receiving your letter of July 17th the new edit. of the Origin had been despatched by Murray for you.[1] I received safely your paper exposing Dana's mis-quotations; I never cd. persuade myself that there was much or any thing in Dana's paper, but I see it is taking effect in the United States[2]

I have read Prof. Clark's book[3] & was interested by it on psychological principles as shewing how differently two men viz. the writer & the reader can view the same subject. I am heartily glad that you are making progress with your Cynips experiment.[4] The new gall which has spread so wonderfully in England (& about which by the way there was a letter 2 days ago in the Times)[5] is attached not to the leaf but to twigs; so that the bushes are rendered conspicuous in the winter by their numbers. I do not think any one can define an ovule from a bud; the only difference being, as many now view the case, that the former must be fertilized.

Have you seen Balbiani's extraordinary paper on the vivaparous aphides being at a very early age hermaphrodites:[6] he is a capital observer, & Sir J. Lubbock tells me that he has no doubt the appearances are true, for he has seen the same in Coccus, whether the interpretation be correct or not.[7]

Some of the Germans, as Prof. Claus, have been taking up a subject which I am glad of, namely to ascertain the amount, in order to test my views, of the individual variability of some of the commoner lower animals; & they find it very great.[8]

My dear Sir | yours very sincerely | Ch. Darwin

Postmark: AU 21 66
LS
Field Museum of Natural History, Chicago (Walsh 5)

1 In his letter of 17 July 1866, Walsh had asked CD to send a copy of the fourth edition of *Origin* to him via Baillière Bros., London and New York. John Murray was CD's publisher.
2 CD refers to Walsh 1866c, to James Dwight Dana and to Dana 1866. See letter from B. D. Walsh, 17 July 1866 and n. 1.
3 Henry James Clark's book, *Mind in nature* (H. J. Clark 1865), discussed spontaneous generation as proof of the existence of a Creator (see letter from B. D. Walsh, 17 July 1866 and n. 14).
4 See letter from B. D. Walsh, 17 July 1866 and nn. 17–19.
5 See letter from B. D. Walsh, 17 July 1866 and n. 16. A letter, signed 'C.', commenting on the large increase in galls and proposing the employment of children to collect the galls in order to contain any further spread of the insects, appeared in *The Times*, 17 August 1866, p. 10. A second letter, signed A. W. Digby & Co. (*The Times*, 18 August 1866, p. 12), offered to test the commercial value of any galls collected. Some oak galls are used in making inks and dyes.
6 Edouard-Gérard Balbiani's paper 'On the reproduction and embryogeny of the *Aphides*' (Balbiani 1866) appeared in instalments in the July and August issues of *Annals and Magazine of Natural History*.

Balbiani claimed to have detected male reproductive elements in viviparous aphids, and argued that this was positive proof of the hermaphrodite nature of these insects (*ibid.*, p. 62). CD's annotated copy of the article is in his collection of unbound journals in the Darwin Library–CUL.

7 John Lubbock had discussed two species of *Coccus* (soft scale insects) in his paper 'On the ova and pseudova of insects' (Lubbock 1858) and had described in detail the development of the embryo.

8 CD refers to Carl Friedrich Claus and Claus 1866 (see letter to Ernst Haeckel, 18 August [1866] and n. 6).

To Fritz Müller 23 August [1866][1]

Down. | Bromley. | Kent. S.E.
Aug 23

My dear Sir

I have been very neglectful in not having thanked you sooner for your valuable letter of June 1st, but I have rather more work to do than I can manage & so my correspondence suffers.[2]

Many of the facts which you mention are very curious & interesting, & if ever I publish a supplement to my Orchis book I shall make use of some of them.[3] I am much surprized at what you say about those with large flowers seeding so badly.[4] I am especially interested in the case of one of the Epidendreæ which has pollinia for removal by insects & others for self-fertilization.[5]

Your letter with its elegant drawings & dried flowers is quite a pretty object. The case of the Bourlingtonia is entirely new.[6] As for the course of the vessels in the various organs of the flower I dare say your interpretation may be right, & I have little doubt that mine was wrong.[7]

I am glad to say that I received the other day a proof of your paper on climbing plants, & when I receive copies I will send one for the Bot. Zeitung, another for the American Journ. of Science, another to the Soc. Bot. of Paris & retain one for myself, sending the remainder to you.[8]

You will receive at about the same time with this note a copy of the new Ed. of the Origin.[9] I do not know how much you attend to plants but if it wd be of much service to you, I should be happy to send you the two parts as yet published of "Bentham & Hookers Genera Plantarum", for I have often thought of buying a second copy for the sake of adding to the sale,—which has been small.[10]

Have you seen Prof. Claus recent pamphlet on Copepoda in which he treats of their individual variability:[11] he speaks most respectfully of your work, but seems to feel some doubt with respect to the two forms of Orchestia.[12]

With every good wish & sincere respect Pray believe me yours very faithfully | Charles Darwin

P.S. I have forgotten to thank you for the beautiful drawing of the Vanilla-like plant.[13]

LS(A)
British Library (Loan 10: 8)

[1] The year is established by the reference to receiving a proof copy of Müller's paper on climbing plants (see n. 8, below).
[2] Müller's letter of 1 June 1866 has not been found.
[3] CD mentioned several of Müller's observations in 'Fertilization of orchids' and *Orchids* 2d ed.
[4] No other mention has been found of large flowers of orchids seeding badly.
[5] See letter from Fritz Müller, 2 August 1866 and nn. 3 and 5. In F. Müller 1869, p. 226, Müller noted that in this unnamed species of *Epidendrum*, the two anthers located on either side of the middle anther were for self-fertilisation while the middle anther had pollinia that could only be removed by insects. CD mentioned the additional anthers for self-fertilisation in *Orchids* 2d ed., p. 291.
[6] None of the drawings or dried flowers that Müller enclosed with the letter of 1 June 1866 has been found. In a letter to Müller of [9 and] 15 April [1866], CD had suggested that Müller should 'observe any cases of flowers which catch insects by their probosces'. Müller's remarks about *Burlingtonia* may have concerned his observation of two fork-like projections of the pistil reaching over the stigma, which, he explained, served to detach pollen from the proboscis of an insect visiting the flower and deposit it into the stigmatic cavity. Müller later mentioned the phenomenon in a letter to his brother, Hermann, of 30 May 1867 (see Möller ed. 1915–21, 2: 123–7; a diagram made by Müller in May 1866 of the stigmatic projections of *Burlingtonia* is on p. 125). In *Orchids*, pp. 182–94, CD had discussed the movement of the pedicel ('stipe' in modern orchid terminology; see Dressler 1981, pp. 61–2) as an aid to pollination in various genera of the orchid tribe Vandeae, including two species of *Rodriguezia* (*Rodriguezia* is a synonym for *Burlingtonia*). He had not observed the projections that Müller described. Müller had noted the elastic pedicel but observed that in his specimen the stigma was not capable of detaching a pollen-mass owing to its weakly adhesive surface, but that the fork-like projections, by grasping the pollen-masses from an insect's proboscis above the stigmatic cavity, detached them and deposited them on the stigma (Möller ed. 1915–21, p. 125).
[7] CD is probably referring to Müller's description of a *Vanilla*-like flower with two rudimentary stamens in the outer whorl (see letter to Fritz Müller, 23 May 1866 and nn. 2 and 3). CD's interpretation of the labellum as a compound structure made up of a petal and two sterile petaloid stamens (*Orchids*, p. 294) was cast into doubt by this observation, but he maintained his view of the nature of the labellum (see *Orchids* 2d ed., p. 238; for a modern assessment of the structure of the labellum, see Dressler 1981, pp. 43–4).
[8] The reference is to F. Müller 1865b, which appeared in the 29 November 1866 issue of the *Journal of the Linnean Society (Botany)* (see letter from Frederick Currey, 5 July 1866 and n. 1). The other journals to which CD refers are the *Botanische Zeitung*, the *American Journal of Science and Arts*, and the *Bulletin de la Société Botanique de France*, which published a notice of F. Müller 1865b (*Bulletin de la Société Botanique de France* 14 (1867): 70–1).
[9] Although the fourth edition of *Origin* was printed by mid July 1866, the publisher, John Murray, did not release it for sale until November 1866; however, Murray agreed to send presentation copies to selected recipients before publication (see letter to John Murray, 15 July [1866] and n. 3, and letter from John Murray, 18 July [1866]). Müller's name is on CD's presentation list for the fourth edition of *Origin* (Appendix IV).
[10] Bentham and Hooker 1862–83 was published in seven parts. The first two parts appeared in 1862 and 1865. CD's complete set is in the Darwin Library–CUL.
[11] CD refers to Carl Friedrich Claus's monograph on the copepods of Nice (Claus 1866). CD had commented on the book to several correspondents (see second postscript to letter to J. D. Hooker, 3 and 4 August [1866], letter to Ernst Haeckel, 18 August [1866], and letter to B. D. Walsh, 20 August [1866]).
[12] Claus praised Müller's book, *Für Darwin* (F. Müller 1864c), referring to it as excellent, full of noteworthy observations and remarkable facts. While Claus agreed in principle with the possibility of two forms of males having come about as a result of different environmental pressures, in the case of *Orchestia* he questioned whether one might be the sexually mature form of the other, as was the case with another amphipod, *Phronima* (see Claus 1866, pp. 1 and 2; see also F. Müller 1864c, pp. 16–17).

[13] The drawing referred to was probably one sent with the letter from Fritz Müller, 3 April 1866. Neither the letter nor the drawing has been found. It is possible that CD returned the drawing (see letter to Fritz Müller, 23 May 1866 and nn. 2 and 4).

To W. D. Fox 24 August [1866]

Down. | Bromley. | Kent. S.E.
Aug 24th.

My dear Fox

It is always a pleasure to me to hear from you & about you, patriarch as you are with your countless children, & grand children—[1] I feel a mere dwarf by your side. My own children are all well & two of my boys are touring in Norway.[2] Poor Susan is in a terrible suffering state & I fear there is no hope for her except the one & last hope for all.[3]

We expect Caroline here with her three girls on Monday & I will give her your kind enquiries.[4] As for myself my health is very decidedly better though I am not very strong. I attribute my improvement partly to Bence Jones' diet & partly, wonderful to relate, to my riding every day which I enjoy much.[5] I don't believe in your theory of moderate mental work doing me any harm—any how I can't be idle.[6] I am making rapid progress with my book on domesticated animals which I fear will be a big one & has been laborious from the number of references.[7] I hope to begin printing towards the close of this close of this year & when it is completed I will of course send you a copy, as indeed I am bound to do as I owe much information to you.[8] I should have begun printing before this had I not lost nearly three months by the troublesome labour of largely correcting a new edit. of the Origin.[9] I think I have heard of hybrids between the Sphinx-moths which you mention; I shall be surprised if the hybrids are fertile[10]

Believe me, my dear old Friend | yours affectly | Charles Darwin

LS
Postmark: 'AU25 66'
Smithsonian Institution Libraries, Dibner Library of History of Science and Technology

[1] See letter from W. D. Fox, 20 August [1866]. Fox had sixteen children and five grandchildren (see *Correspondence* vol. 13, letter from W. D. Fox, 6 January [1865]).

[2] CD refers to George Howard Darwin and Francis Darwin (letter from G. H. Darwin to H. E. Darwin, [June–July 1866] (DAR 251: 2240)). Emma Darwin's diary (DAR 242) recorded, 'Boys went to Norway' on 16 August 1866.

[3] CD's sister, Susan Elizabeth Darwin, was seriously ill.

[4] The reference is to Caroline Sarah Wedgwood. Her daughters were Katherine Elizabeth Sophy, Margaret Susan, and Lucy Caroline Wedgwood (Freeman 1978, s.v. Josiah Wedgwood III).

[5] CD first consulted Henry Bence Jones in July 1865 and began following the diet he recommended shortly after (see letter to H. B. Jones, 3 January [1866] and nn. 2 and 4). He started riding on 4 June 1866 (Emma Darwin's diary (DAR 242)); see also letter to John Lubbock, 2 August [1866], n. 2.

[6] See letter from W. D. Fox, 20 August [1866].

[7] CD refers to *Variation*.

[8] CD sent the manuscript of all but the last chapter of *Variation* to his publisher in December 1866, but the book was only published in January 1868 (letter to John Murray, 21 and 22 December [1866], and Freeman 1977). In *Variation*, CD made several references to information received from Fox.

[9] The reference is to the fourth edition of *Origin*.

[10] Sphinx-moths or hawk-moths, as Fox had referred to them, belong to the family Sphingidae. Fox had reported crossing two species (see letter from W. D. Fox, 20 August [1866] and n. 8).

From Asa Gray 27 August 1866

Cambride, Mass.
Aug. 27, 1866.

My Dear Darwin.

I have yours of the 4th. inst. which I think has crossed a line from me, telling you that I had got the sheets of Origin back from the Appleton's.

You rightly infer that there is no hope at present for an Amer. reprint, unless you agree to fall in with Appleton's shabby ways—which I think you will not be tempted to do.[1]

But I am encouraged to think that I can make a *good arrangement* with Messrs. Ticknor & Fields, of Boston, to bring out the new book, & allow Author 12 per cent. I shall confer with Mr. Fields.[2]

Agassiz is back (I have not seen him), and he went at once down to meeting of National Academy of Sciences—from which I sedulously keep away—and, I hear *proved* to them that the glacial period covered the *whole continent of America with unbroken ice*, and closed with a significant gesture and the remark "So *here is the end of the Darwin* theory"![3] How do you like that.

I said last winter, that Agassiz was bent upon covering the whole continent with ice,—and that the *motive* of the discovery he was sure to make was, *to make it sure* that there should be no coming down of any terrestial life from tertiary or post tertiary period to ours.[4]

You cannot deny that he has done his work *effectually*, in a truly imperial way!

I am glad your new ed. is not to be issued for 3 months yet. I want to read the sheets at odd moments and give a notice of the new ed. in some periodical—tho' I can give little time to it.[5]

Ever dear Darwin, | Yours cordially | A. Gray

Charles Darwin, Esq | Down | Bromley | Please post

DAR 165: 154

CD ANNOTATIONS

4.1 Agassiz . . . way! 6.1] *enclosed in square brackets, pencil*

Back of letter: 'Lenny thanks | Lyell about Agassiz | Perfect case | copy of Origin | if Appleton | non-seeding Plants | *Domestic animals* woodcuts | Rhamnus'[6] *pencil, crossed pencil*

CD note:[7]

P.S. I have just received a letter from Asa Gray with following passage, so that according to this I am chief cause of Agassiz's absurd views

1 See letter to Asa Gray, 4 August [1866], and letter from Asa Gray, 7 August 1866 and n. 6. D. Appleton & Co. was the American publisher of *Origin.*

2 James Thomas Fields was the head of the publishing firm Ticknor & Fields. See the letter to Asa Gray of 4 August [1866] and n. 5.

3 Louis Agassiz headed an expedition to Brazil that left New York on 1 April 1865 and returned on 6 August 1866 (Lurie 1960, p. 346). On 12 August 1866, he read a paper 'Traces of glaciers under the tropics' to the annual meeting of the National Academy of Sciences in Washington; in this paper he advanced the hypothesis that glaciers had covered great areas in Brazil and concluded that a new creation of plants and animals occurred after the glaciers receded (Lurie 1960, p. 353). For Gray's opinion of the fledgling National Academy of Sciences, see Dupree 1959, pp. 313–24, and Lurie 1960, pp. 334–5.

4 During the winter of 1864 to 1865, Agassiz had delivered a series of lectures at the Lowell Institute in Boston, in which he argued that glaciers in South America destroyed all life, and offered this claim as a proof of the fallacy of transmutation theory. He also suggested that an expedition to gather direct evidence of glacial action should be mounted (Lurie 1960, p. 345). For earlier discussion of Agassiz's glacier theory, see the letters to Charles Lyell, 7 February [1866] and 15 February [1866].

5 Gray refers to the fourth edition of *Origin*, which had been printed in mid July but was only published in November 1866 (see letter from John Murray, 18 July [1866]). No review by Gray has been found.

6 CD's notes are for his reply to Gray's letter (see letter to Asa Gray, 10 September [1866]).

7 CD's note is a rough draft for a part of his letter to Charles Lyell, 8[–9] September [1866].

From J. D. Hooker [28 August][1] 1866

British Association for the Advancement of Science, | *Nottingham*
Tuesday. *1866.*

Dear old Darwin

The whole thing went off last night in very good style— the audience were well fed & conformable, they followed the whole lecture with admirable good nature & were sent into fits by the conclusion.[2] I made myself well & easily heard without unreasonable effort & have all the more reason to bless my stars that I not earlier given way to popular lecturing—for which I am already besought!

I never was so glad to get a thing out of hand & mind. & now I must in the course of the winter cast it into Scientific form for publication.[3]

I am awfully busy as you may suppose, & only just beginning to enjoy the fun—

Huxley is getting on splendidly in §D.[4] He returned thanks for my Lecture in the most skilful graceful & perfect way— I never heard anything so hearty & thoroughly good—no coarse flattery, or fulsome praise—but an earnest, thoughtful & I believe truthful eulogy of what he thought good & happy in the treatment of the subject, with a really affectionate tribute to myself.

Ever your affectionate | Jos D Hooker

DAR 102: 98–9

1 The date is established by the reference to Hooker's lecture to the British Association, which was delivered on Monday 27 August 1866 (J. D. Hooker 1866a, p. 6).

2 The reference is to Hooker's lecture 'Insular floras', which he concluded with a humorous allusion to the acceptance of CD's theory of transmutation since the appearance of *Origin* (see J. D. Hooker 1866a, pp. 75–6; see also letter to J. D. Hooker, 30 August [1866] and n. 3).

[3] The text of Hooker's lecture appeared in *Gardeners' Chronicle* (1867): 6–7, 27, 50–1, 75–6 (J. D. Hooker 1866a). Summarised versions appeared in the edited report of the papers and discussions at the Nottingham meeting (J. D. Hooker 1866b) and the *Journal of Botany* for 1867 (J. D. Hooker 1867), and a French translation in *Annales des Sciences Naturelles*, 1866 (J. D. Hooker 1866c). CD's annotated copy of the edited offprint from the *Gardeners' Chronicle* version is in the Darwin Pamphlet Collection–CUL. This version is also reprinted in Williamson 1984.

[4] Thomas Henry Huxley was the president of section 'D' Biology (*Report of the thirty-sixth meeting of the British Association for the Advancement of Science held at Nottingham*, p. xxxi).

To J. D. Hooker 30 August [1866][1]

Down | Bromley Kent
Aug 30th.

My dear Hooker

I was very glad to get your note & the Notts Newspaper. I have seldom been more pleased in my life than at hearing how successfully your lecture went off.[2] Mrs. H. Wedgwood sent us an account, saying that you read capitally & were listened to with profound attention & great applause. She says when your final allegory began "For a minute or two we were all mystified, & then came such bursts of applause from the audience. It was thoroughly enjoyed amid roars of laughter & noise making a most brilliant conclusion."[3]

I am rejoiced that you will publish yr. lecture, & felt sure that sooner or later it wd come to this; indeed it would have been a sin if you had not done so.[4] I am especially rejoiced, as you give the arguments for occasional transport with such perfect fairness, these will now receive a fair share of attention, as coming from you a professed botanist.[5] Thanks also for Grove's address; as a whole it strikes me as very good & original but I was disappointed in the part about species; it dealt in such generalities, that it would apply to any view or no view in particular.[6]

I have also to thank you much for a lot of things sent by Parslow—[7] I must get Sclater's M.S. copied & then return it, which I will do in a few days.[8] The Codrington has come safe—[9] I shall be delighted to receive the Drosera.[10] As for Acropera I must beg leave to keep it for some time for it is making new flower stalks, & I have already I find had much better success in fertilising it, than I expected when you were here; so that I am sure I shall find out the dodge.[11] And now I have got to beg another favour: I want very much a book which is not in Royal or Linn. libraries— it is "*Séringe* Bullet. bot. 1830 p. 117. on the St Valery apple"—[12]

And now farewell— I do most heartily rejoice at your success, & for Grove's sake at the brilliant success of the whole meeting.

Yours affectly. | Charles Darwin

I have made abstract of Sclater & return it herewith.—

LS(A)
DAR 115: 299

[1] The year is established by the relationship between this letter and the letter from J. D. Hooker, [28 August] 1866.

[2] See letter from J. D. Hooker, [28 August] 1866. Hooker evidently enclosed a local Nottingham newspaper report on his lecture on insular floras at the meeting of the British Association for the Advancement of Science, but no copy has been found in the Darwin archive. The *Nottingham Journal* and the *Nottingham Daily Express* both carried accounts of Hooker's lecture on 28 August 1866. The latter account claimed that Hooker had succeeded in making a not very attractive subject highly interesting.

[3] The reference is to Frances Emma Elizabeth Wedgwood. Her letter has not been found but her account of Hooker's lecture was copied in a letter from Emma Darwin to William Erasmus Darwin, [September 1866] (DAR 219.1: 84). She described the humorous conclusion to the lecture as follows:

> D[r] Hooker took just 1 ½ hour & perhaps it was as well you shortened him & also he read capitally & was listened to with profound attention— There was a crammed theatre the house being quite full for an hour before. When the *Sachem* began, for a minute or two we were all mystified & then there came such bursts of applause from the audience first & going on— It was so thoroughly enjoyed amid roars of laughter & noise making a most brilliant conclusion.
>
> (Now I must explain a little what the Sachem was. D[r] Hooker said that in his travels he had come upon a tribe of Indians who were firmly of opinion that the moon was a fresh creation every month & they thought him very impious for telling them it was the same moon "as if God could not create a fresh moon every month." However seven years afterwards on meeting the same tribe he found that many of the medicine men & Sachems had begun to see the truth & the opinion was gradually making way with them & then he added that he need not tell them that his first visit to the tribe was at Oxford 7 years ago & that his second was at Notts. now)
>
> I thought M[r] Grove's address as good as it c[d] be— how I longed for you to hear the noise they made when Charles' name was mentioned.

For more on the Oxford meeting of the British Association for the Advancement of Science in 1860, see *Correspondence* vol. 8, Appendix VI.

[4] See letter from J. D. Hooker, [28 August] 1866 and n. 3.

[5] Both newspaper accounts of the lecture had noted that Hooker discussed continental extension and occasional transport as explanations for the similarities in island and continental floras (see *Nottingham Journal* and *Nottingham Daily Express*, 28 August 1866). On occasional transport, see the letter from J. D. Hooker, 30 July [1866], n. 7. For Hooker's presentation of the theory of seed dispersal through occasional transport, see J. D. Hooker 1866a, pp. 50–1, 75.

[6] William Robert Grove's address as president of the British Association contained a section on transmutation of species (W. R. Grove 1866, pp. lxxi–lxxix). Grove gave examples of recent research that supported transmutation, but did not distinguish between different theories, focusing instead on the idea that continuity was the 'law of nature' that underlay the gradual process of change (*ibid.*, p. lxxix). Grove had requested more information on CD's theory while preparing his address (see letter from J. D. Hooker, 29 May 1866, and letter to J. D. Hooker, 31 May [1866]).

[7] Joseph Parslow was Darwin's butler.

[8] Philip Lutley Sclater probably sent Hooker a manuscript with information on the birds of Madeira and the Azores (see letter from J. D. Hooker, 4 August 1866 and n. 3).

[9] The reference is to the Coddington lens; see letter from J. D. Hooker, 18 August 1866 and n. 2.

[10] Hooker told CD he would send a specimen of *Drosera binata*, the fork-leafed sundew, an insectivorous plant (see letter from J. D. Hooker, 18 August 1866).

[11] Hooker had sent CD a specimen of *Acropera*, which CD received on 4 August 1866 (see letter from J. D. Hooker, 31 July 1866 and n. 22, and letter to J. D. Hooker, 3 and 4 August [1866]). CD had tried on many previous occasions to artificially pollinate flowers of this genus without much success; he first pollinated *Acropera* in 1863 (see *Correspondence* vol. 11, letter to John Scott, 7 November [1863] and n. 6). CD later described his method for pollinating *Acropera* in *Orchids* 2d ed., pp. 168–9. Hooker had visited Down on 18 August (see letters from J. D. Hooker, [17 August 1866] and 18 August 1866).

[12] The reference is to an article on the monstrous apple tree of St Valery, which appeared in *Bulletin Botanique ou Collection de Notices Originales et d'Extraits des Ouvrages Botaniques* (Seringe 1830).

From W. R. Grove 31 August 1866

Southill House | Shepton Mallet
Aug 31 1866

Dear Darwin

Many thanks for your letter[1] I thought I had expressed the adaptation theory in the passage p 30 beginning "The doctrine of Cuvier"— Possibly you mean that I have not given examples of the special means—[2] as to special facts if I had given only one or two (& more than a few I had no space for), they would have been cavilled at—their value greatly depending on their number I was anxious to put forward such arguments as seemed to me unanswerable & which addressed themselves not merely to specialists—

I said not much about the adaptation view though entirely agreeing with it because the answer would have been that the argument cut both ways as whether an animal by circumstance Natural selection &c became suited to locality in conformation habits &c—or was specially created for p⟨arti⟩cu⟨lar⟩ circumstances the adaptation would equally be a necessity— an animal or plant must within limits be adapted to circumstance or not *be* at all—

I wanted the authorities much to press on you the chair of the British Assn. but all agreed your health would not stand it & *I* now agree, for it is most trying & exciting work even when as at Nottingham most successful[3]

yrs most truly | W R Grove

I have only just returned

DAR 165: 231

[1] CD's letter has not been found.

[2] The page number evidently refers to a manuscript version of Grove's address to the meeting of the British Association for the Advancement of Science, which has not been found. In W. R. Grove 1866, the passage mentioned begins on page lxxv and offers a Lamarckian explanation of adaptation. Grove refers to Georges Cuvier. For CD's reaction to Grove's speech, see the letter to J. D. Hooker, 30 August [1866] and n. 6.

[3] Grove refers to his experience as president of the British Association, which met at Nottingham in 1866.

To Robert Swinhoe [September 1866][1]

Cordial Thanks for so kindly remembering my wish— when I come to subject—*Apis Indica*—,[2] Your kindness will lead you to be glad to hear that my health much improved, though yet far from strong—[3] my eternal book, you a copy, if not returned before this date.[4] I am delighted to hear that you keep on your zealous love & work for Nat History & British Assoc—[5] New discussion—on modification of species

President's address—[6] Hooker capital lecture[7]—but I hear Wallace's paper best—[8]

I wish I could tell you any news, but I have not been in L. since Spring[9] & seen nobody socially except Sir J. Lubbock—who was down chiefly comparing his collection to Archaeologs.[10]

I suppose you see Zoolog Proc—the case of the N American antelopes so intermediate between hollow & solid-horned ruminants, is one of more curious facts I have lately heard with respect to higher animals.—[11]

Adraft
DAR 177: 329r

[1] The date is established by the reference to the meeting of the British Association for the Advancement of Science (see nn. 5–7, below). The draft was written on the back of Swinhoe's letter to CD of 28 March 1866.

[2] See letter from Robert Swinhoe, 28 March 1866 and nn. 3 and 4.

[3] CD had recently told his cousin William Darwin Fox that he attributed his improved health to the diet and exercise recommended by his doctor (see letter to W. D. Fox, 24 August [1866]). He had started riding for exercise on 4 June 1866 (Emma Darwin's diary (DAR 242)).

[4] CD began work on *Variation* in 1860; he had been unable to complete it because of long intervals of poor health and numerous interruptions revising or writing other works (see letter to W. B. Tegetmeier, 16 January [1866] and n. 1). *Variation* was not published until 1868. Presumably CD planned to send a copy of *Variation* to Swinhoe in China if he had not returned to England before the book appeared.

[5] Swinhoe had been a member of the British Association since 1863 and had presented a paper at the 1865 meeting (Swinhoe 1865).

[6] The annual meeting of the British Association took place in Nottingham from 22 to 30 August 1866 (*Athenæum*, 11 August 1866, p. 161). In his presidential address, William Robert Grove had discussed CD's theory of the transmutation of species and recent work in the field (W. R. Grove 1866). For CD's reaction to the address, see the letter to J. D. Hooker, 30 August [1866] and n. 6.

[7] On 27 August 1866, Joseph Dalton Hooker gave an evening lecture on insular flora at the British Association meeting (J. D. Hooker 1866a; see letter from J. D. Hooker, [28 August] 1866 and n. 3).

[8] Alfred Russel Wallace presented a paper, 'On reversed sexual characters in a butterfly, and their interpretation on the theory of modifications and adaptive mimicry (illustrated by specimens)', at the British Association meeting on 27 August 1866 (A. R. Wallace 1866a; see also A. R. Wallace 1866b). An abstract, including a report of related discussion, appeared in the *Athenæum*, 8 September 1866, p. 309, and the paper was also reported in the *Reader*, 6 October 1866, p. 847; see also C. H. Smith ed. 1991, p. 485. Earlier, Hooker told CD that he had recommended Wallace's research on Malayan butterflies to Grove as among the work providing the best evidence for the transmutation theory (see letter from J. D. Hooker, 29 May 1866 and n. 6; see also W. R. Grove 1866, p. lxxiv).

[9] The Darwins were in London from 21 April to 1 May 1866 (Emma Darwin's diary (DAR 242)).

[10] Over the preceding five years, John Lubbock, CD's neighbour, had made several trips to sites of archaeological interest in Denmark, Switzerland, France, and Scotland and had written a book in which he summarised recent archaeological evidence for the antiquity of the human race (Lubbock 1865). Lubbock evidently had a large collection of specimens. While he was on an expedition to France, Ellen Frances Lubbock noted that he said that they 'filled two carriages in one day' with flints (see *Correspondence* vol. 13, letter from E. F. Lubbock, [27 August – 1 September 1865]; see also Hutchinson 1914, 1: 135–6).

[11] CD refers to a paper in *Proceedings of the Zoological Society of London* in which the author claimed that, contrary to the then prevalent view that the prongbuck (*Antilocapra americana*) had permanent horns, the horns were shed annually (Canfield 1866, p. 108; CD's lightly annotated copy is in the collection of unbound journals, Darwin Library–CUL). Hollow-horned ruminants like antelope have horns made of a permanent bony inner layer covered with an outer layer of keratin, which are never shed. Solid-horned ruminants like deer have antlers made entirely of bone and shed their horns annually. The prongbuck,

now more commonly known as the pronghorn, is not a true antelope but is the only member of a separate family, Antilocapridae. Its horns are like those of antelope in that they consist of a keratinous sheath over a bony inner layer, but differ because the sheath is shed periodically. (Nowak 1999.)

From J. D. Hooker [4 September 1866][1]

Kew
Tuesday

Dear old Darwin

I am very proud of your letter—[2] I thought I might have exaggerated the effect I produced on my audience, & did not like to think too much of it— I do now pray to be another "Single speech Robinson"![3] I wish you could have heard Huxley's eloge, it pleased me so immensely, & was so much better than all the applause.[4] I had set my head heart & mind on earning your's, Groves, Huxley's, Tyndalls, & the Lubbocks (especially Lady L'!) good opinion, & I cared little for other peoples.[5] I have not seen Tyndall since, nor heard how he liked it.— He came up to me in the forenoon, evidently most anxious for my success, & questioned me about it. When I told him it was a written discourse, & that I intended to *read* it, his countenance fell & I saw he was cut.— he turned away first, but came back & with great delicacy & loving kindness gave me some hints; to learn passages by heart &c—(I had done this copiously already) & to put myself en rapport with the audience &c &c. I saw in short that he prognosticated a dead failure, & I spared no pains that afternoon in preparing myself to succeed in his eyes. I hope I did.—

Huxley made a capital President of §D.—& was very conciliatory prudent & amusing too—[6] I really heard few papers & none of any consequence. Wallaces was no doubt the best in our line.[7]

As to Grove's address, I can quite understand your disappointment at the Species part of it—[8] I only wonder he did it so well, for when I have talked the subject with him, he has shown so little appreciation of its *difficulties* that I was rather pleased than otherwise that he thought it needful to discuss it— I knew too that he had left it all to me— indeed he, on accepting the Presidentship, *retained* me as champion of the cause.[9] I wished him at the Devil, but felt flattered at the selection—puzzled as I was then, & am now, to make out why he should have thought me worthy of so responsible a post—on so critical an occasion. I had always a notion that he looked on me as a very weak vessell, & my branches of Botany as mild child's play. Then too he had no hints or instructions for me I was to "back him up" & "to carry Darwinism through the ranks of the enemy" after he had sounded the charge: & whether or no his "Continuity" Address[10] was well received. In short I was a stink-pot,[11] which he was to pitch into the Enemies decks, whether sinking or swimming himself.

The only excursion I went on, was to Belvoir castle, a really grand place, & well worth a visit.[12] The pictures & the grounds delighted me.

I am so glad that you are succeeding with Acropera I should not like you to be beat by any orchid.[13]

I sent off Seringe to day, & the Drosera shall go soon.[14]
Ever yr aff | J D Hooker

DAR 102: 100–2

1 The date is established by the relationship between this letter and the letter to J. D. Hooker, 30 August [1866]. In 1866, the first Tuesday after 30 August was 4 September.

2 In his letter to Hooker of 30 August [1866], CD had expressed great satisfaction on hearing how well Hooker's lecture on insular floras, delivered at the meeting of the British Association for the Advancement of Science on 27 August 1866, had gone. He also applauded Hooker's plan to publish the text of the lecture. For the publication details of Hooker's lecture, see the letter from J. D. Hooker, [28 August] 1866, n. 3.

3 Hooker possibly meant 'single-speech Hamilton', a misleading nickname for William Gerard Hamilton, who had been well-known as an orator. His lengthy maiden speech in the House of Commons on 13 November 1755 was much admired (*DNB*).

4 Thomas Henry Huxley had praised Hooker's lecture on insular floras in remarks made after the speech was delivered (see letter from J. D. Hooker, [28 August] 1866).

5 In addition to Huxley, Hooker refers to William Robert Grove, John Tyndall, and John and Ellen Frances Lubbock.

6 The British Association meeting for 1866 was divided into seven sections. As the president of section D, biology, Huxley moderated the discussion of the papers presented in the section.

7 Hooker refers to Alfred Russel Wallace's paper on adaptive mimicry in butterflies (A. R. Wallace 1866a; see letter to Robert Swinhoe, [September 1866] and n. 8).

8 For CD's reaction to the address given by Grove as president of the British Association, see the letter to J. D. Hooker, 30 August [1866] and n. 6.

9 In January 1866, Grove had asked Hooker to deliver a lecture on 'the Darwinian theory' at the British Association meeting (see letter from J. D. Hooker, 16 January 1866). While preparing his own presidential address, Grove had asked Hooker for examples of recent work supporting CD's theory of transmutation (see letter from J. D. Hooker, 29 May 1866).

10 Hooker refers to Grove's speech as his 'Continuity' address because Grove maintained that continuity was a 'law of nature' and the underlying principle on which the argument in favour of transmutation could be made (W. R. Grove 1866, pp. lxxii, lxxix).

11 Stink-pot: 'A hand-missile charged with combustibles emitting a suffocating smoke, used in boarding a ship for effecting a diversion while the assailants gain the deck' (*OED*).

12 The excursion to Belvoir Castle took place on 30 August 1866. A brief description of the excursion is given in Robertson ed. 1866, p. 290. The castle is in Leicestershire, near Grantham.

13 CD reported to Hooker that he was having better success than he had expected with the new specimen of *Acropera* that Hooker had sent (see letter to J. D. Hooker, 30 August [1866] and n. 11).

14 CD had asked Hooker to send him an article (Seringe 1830) that he was unable to find elsewhere (see letter to J. D. Hooker, 30 August [1866] and n. 12). Hooker had also promised to send CD a specimen of *Drosera binata*, the fork-leafed sundew, a carnivorous plant (see letter from J. D. Hooker, 18 August 1866).

From Julius von Haast 8 September 1866

Christchurch
Sept 8. 1866

My dear Mr Darwin

I have to thank you heartily for your kind letter of the 5th of May and the trouble you have taken concerning my election to the R. S.—[1] Prof Ramsay told me already some months ago, that I had very little chance for the first year but I have no doubt, that with your powerful assistance and that of other kind friends my election will take place next year.[2]

I am delighted to hear from other English friends, that your health has so much improved & trust, that it will continue to do so, so that you will be able to take a more active part in scientific life, than you were able to do for the last few years.[3]

I am just occupied to plot my alpine work on a large scale which will take me another 3 months, but I hope then to publish a map of the Southern Alps proper which will not be uninteresting—[4] Our Western goldfields continue to become every day more extensive and another rush from Australia is beginning to set in towards that part of New Zealand[5] It is wonderful to behold how the wandering after that golden vliess[6] brings such busy life into the wilderness; towns spring up as by enchantment & men battle successfully against nature & nature has to give way at the end.

Fearing to miss the mail, I have to be short this time but shall write soon again
Believe me my dear Mr Darwin | ever yours very sincerely | Julius Haast.

DAR 166: 10

[1] See letter to Julius von Haast, 5 May [1866]. CD told Haast that although he had written on Haast's behalf to the Royal Society of London, he had never received Haast's proposal paper for his signature.

[2] Andrew Crombie Ramsay had officially proposed Haast as a candidate for Royal Society fellowship (H. F. von Haast 1948, p. 505). Haast became a fellow of the Royal Society on 6 June 1867 (*Record of the Royal Society of London*).

[3] Haast probably heard about CD's health from, among others, Joseph Dalton Hooker, with whom he had corresponded since 1861 (see H. F. von Haast 1948, pp. 247–50, 513).

[4] As provincial geologist for Canterbury province, New Zealand, Haast had made a number of expeditions to the Southern Alps. Early in 1866, he explored the area around the head-waters of the Rakaia river. In June 1866 he wrote a report on the area, including a map (J. F. J. von Haast 1866; see H. F. von Haast 1948, pp. 472–3, 1092). His map of the whole of the Southern Alps was eventually published by the Royal Geographical Society of London (J. F. J. von Haast 1870; see H. F. von Haast 1948, p. 1095).

[5] After the first discovery of gold in 1864, the provincial government had been interested in finding routes from Canterbury through the Southern Alps to the goldfields of the west coast. Haast explored much of the region looking for passes (see H. F. von Haast 1948, pp. 405–33; see also *Correspondence* vol. 11, letter from Julius von Haast, 5 March 1863 and n. 2). For a history of the 1860s gold rushes on the west coast of New Zealand, see May 1967.

[6] Haast refers to 'das Goldene Vlies', the golden fleece of Greek mythology.

To Charles Lyell 8[–9] September [1866][1]

Down. | Bromley. | Kent. S.E.
Sep 8

My dear Lyell

It has been a great disappointm^t^ to me putting off your visit; as it has proved we might have had you.[2]

My sister's state varies a little but she suffers greatly & there is no hope of recovery.[3]

We are very glad that you think you will be able to come here in Oct.[4]

Many thanks for the pamphlet which was returned this m^{g}.[5] I was very glad to read it, though chiefly as a psychological curiosity. I quite follow you in thinking Agassiz glacier-mad. His evidence reduces itself to supposed moraines which w^{d} be difficult to trace in a forest-clad country; & with respect to boulders, these are not said to be angular & their source cannot be known in a country so imperfectly explored. When I was at Rio I was continually astonished at the depth (sometimes 100 feet) to which the granitic rocks were decomposed in situ;[6] & this soft matter w^{d} easily give rise to great alluvial accumulations: I well remember finding it difficult to draw a line between the alluvial matter & the softened rock in situ.[7] What a splendid imagination Agassiz has! & how energetic he is! What capital work he w^{d} have done if he had sucked in your Principles with his mother's milk.[8] It is wonderful that he sh^{d} have written such wild nonsense about the valley of the Amazon; yet not so wonderful when one remembers that he once maintained before the Brit. Assoc that the chalk was all deposited at once.[9]

With respect to the insects of Chili, I knew only from Bates that the species of Carabus shewed no special affinity to northern species; from the great difference of climate & vegetation, I sh^{d} not have expected that many insects w^{d} have shewn such affinity.[10] It is more remarkable that the birds on the broad & lofty Cordillera of Tropical S. America shew no affinity with European species.[11] The little power of diffusion with birds has often struck me as a most singular fact, even more singular than the great power of diffusion with plants. Remember that we hope to see you in the autumn

yours affectionately | Charles Darwin

Sunday Morning

P.S. I have just received a letter from Asa Gray with the following passage, so that according to this, I am the chief cause of Agassiz' absurd views.[12]

"Agassiz is back (I have not seen him) & he went at once down to Nat. Accad. of Sciences—from which I sedulously keep away—& I hear proved to them that the Glacial period covered the *whole continent of America with* unbroken ice, & closed with a significant gesture & the remark, "So here is the end of the Darwin Theory". How do you like that?

I said last winter, that Agassiz was bent on covering the whole continent with ice & that the *motive* of the discovery he was sure to make was *to make sure* that there shd be no coming down of any terrestrial life from tertiary or post-tertiary period to ours. You cannot deny that he has done his work effectually, in a truly imperial way."

P.S. There is a capital paper in the Sept. no^{r} of Annals & Mag, translated from Pictet & H. on fossil fish of Lebanon; but you will I daresay have received the original.— It is capital in relation to modification of species; I would not wish for more confirmatory facts, though there is no direct allusion to the modification of species.—[13] Hooker, by the way, gave an admirable Lecture at Nottingham; I read it in M.S. or rather heard it.— I am glad it will be published, for it was capital.—[14]

LS(A)
American Philosophical Society (319)

[1] The year is established by the relationship between this letter and the letter from Asa Gray, 27 August 1866. In 1866, 9 September was a Sunday.

[2] No correspondence between CD and Lyell concerning the cancelled visit has been found. CD may have postponed a visit from Lyell owing to the severity of his sister's illness (see n. 3, below).

[3] Susan Elizabeth Darwin died on 3 October 1866 (Emma Darwin's diary (DAR 242)).

[4] Charles and Mary Elizabeth Lyell eventually visited the Darwins from 16 to 19 November 1866 (Emma Darwin's diary (DAR 242)).

[5] CD refers to an article by Louis Agassiz that appeared in two parts in *Atlantic Monthly* (J. L. R. Agassiz 1866a).

[6] Agassiz put forward the theory that the Amazon valley had been covered by a glacier that had descended from the Cordilleras (the Andes mountains) to the west. He conceded that he had not found any of the characteristic traces of glacier movement, but claimed that the tropical climate was responsible for the decomposition of rocks that would have shown such evidence (J. L. R. Agassiz 1866a, pp. 162–3). In a series of lectures given during the winter of 1864 to 1865, Agassiz, arguing against the theory of the transmutation of species, had hypothesised that a continental ice sheet in South America had destroyed all life, so there could be no connection between species of the past and those of the present (see Lurie 1960, p. 345).

[7] In *South America*, pp. 143–4, CD had remarked that the depth of decomposed gneiss and other granitic rocks in the district of Rio de Janeiro was close to 100 feet. Agassiz had admitted that the depth of decomposition of underlying rock made it difficult to distinguish between it and the drift (J. L. R. Agassiz 1866a, p. 50).

[8] CD refers to *Principles of geology* (C. Lyell 1830–3). Lyell's book had made a great impression on CD when he took the first volume of it on the *Beagle* voyage (see *Autobiography*, p. 77).

[9] CD may be referring to the 1840 meeting of the British Association for the Advancement of Science, at which he met Agassiz (Lurie 1960, p. 100). At this meeting, Agassiz gave a paper on glaciers in Switzerland that summarised his book on the topic (J. L. R. Agassiz 1840a, 1840b). Lyell gave a paper, 'On ancient sea cliffs and needles in the chalk of the valley of the Seine in Normandy', in which he hypothesised that the valley was excavated during the slow and intermittent upheaval of land from the sea, resulting in several distinct levels of cliffs (C. Lyell 1840, p. 113). Agassiz may have made a remark about chalk deposition in discussion following Lyell's paper.

[10] In his article, Agassiz had remarked on the scarcity of insects in general and beetles in particular in the Amazon valley, but had not commented on differences of genera in different locations (J. L. R. Agassiz 1866a, p. 59). Henry Walter Bates had earlier informed CD about a Chilean subgenus of the beetle genus *Carabus* that he described as being quite distinct from all other species. See *Correspondence* vol. 10, letter from H. W. Bates, 30 April 1862 and n. 3, and letter to H. W. Bates, 4 May [1862] and n. 5. In *Origin* 4th ed., p. 454, CD speculated that the distinctiveness of the Chilean beetles indicated that their ancestors had been introduced at some very early period.

[11] Agassiz had noted striking differences in gallinaceous birds of the Amazon valley compared with those in the rest of the world (J. L. R. Agassiz 1866a, p. 59).

[12] CD copied the passage, with minor alterations, from the letter from Asa Gray, 27 August 1866.

[13] The article in the *Annals and Magazine of Natural History* on fossil fishes referred to the 'study of organic development throughout the course of geological time' (Pictet de la Rive and Humbert 1866, p. 242), suggesting a tacit acceptance that some fish species had been modified over time, but it made no

specific reference to the theory of the transmutation of species. CD's annotated copy is among his unbound journals in the Darwin Library–CUL.

[14] CD refers to Joseph Dalton Hooker's lecture on insular floras delivered on 27 August 1866 at the meeting of the British Association for the Advancement of Science and later published in *Gardeners' Chronicle* (J. D. Hooker 1866a). For the publication details of Hooker's lecture, see the letter from J. D. Hooker, [28 August] 1866, n. 3.

From W. R. Grove 9 September 1866

Southill House
Sept 9 1866

Dear Darwin

The enclosed evidently from a working man is so remarkable that I think it will interest you as showing that ideas are spread[1]

Yrs vy truly | W R Grove

DAR 165: 232

[1] The enclosure has not been found.

To Asa Gray 10 September [1866][1]

Down. | Bromley. | Kent. S.E.
Sep 10

My dear Gray

Perhaps you will remember when one of my boys was terribly ill you sent him some stamps which he looked at, & then after a long silence there came out the words "He is awfully kind".[2] He never said a truer thing. In the 1st place your note about Agassiz has interested & amused me much;[3] for the day before I had been reading the Atlantic Monthly & the copy of a letter from Mme. Agassiz to Lyell & one from him all about the Amazonian glacier.[4] We were both lost in astonishment at the nonsense which Agassiz writes & I cd not resist sending to Lyell a copy of part of your note, for his pre-determined wish partly explains what he fancies he observed. The evidence advanced by him is so weak that I do not think it wd be admitted for the former existence of glaciers even in a temperate region.[5]

With respect to the Origin, you speak of reading the sheets, but Murray promised me to send you a bound copy.[6] After all as there is no chance of a new edition perhaps it wd be as well to let the Appletons have the sheets if they wd make any use of them; though on the other hand it is hardly worth while taking trouble about giving a few of the additions.[7]

With respect to my next book "on domestic animals" I am in perplexity, though most grateful to you for the capital bargain which you have made with Messrs Ticknor.[8] My perplexity is this that I really have no idea whether it will be in the least degree popular; I am sure some chapters are curious, but then many others enter into far too minute details for the general reader: hence I do not quite like

Mess[rs] Ticknor to agree to publish until they have seen some of the sheets. And here comes the difficulty; there are about 42 wood-cuts & it w[d] save great expence if metal copies were procured of these, & to do this Mess[rs] Ticknor w[d] have to make up their minds soon & enter into some arrangement with Murray, as I think I c[d] not ask Murray, who publishes at his own risk, to give copies; *though as far as I am concerned I w[d] willingly do so*. I feel pretty sure that I shall not even begin to print till the beginning of next year.

Many thanks for the specimens of the Rhamnus; my son & self have both looked at the pollen of both forms but alas! can make out no difference.[9] The difference seems confined to the pistil & to the peduncles. We cannot even conjecture whether this species is reciprocally dimorphic like Primula or is merely tending to become dioecious.[10] This is a great disappointment to us & the nature of the two forms c[d] only be made out by experiment or by observing their seed-production in their natural state.

I suppose this species c[d] not be purchased in your nursery gardens—

In my last letter I asked you whether you knew of any striking cases of endemic or naturalized plants which never flowered or which never seeded; if at no time I get an answer I shall understand that you know of no cases like the Acorus or horse-radish in Europe.[11]

The only point which I have made out this summer which c[d] possibly interest you is that the Common Oxlip found every where more or less commonly in England, is certainly a hybrid between the primrose & cowslip; whilst the P. elatior found only in the Eastern Counties (*Jacq.*) is a perfectly distinct & good species; hardly distinguishable from the common oxlip except by the length of the seed-capsule relatively to the calyx. This seems to me rather a horrid fact for all systematic botanists.[12]

I have just begun a large course of experiments on the germination of the seed & on the growth of the young plants when raised from a pistil fertilized by pollen from the same flower, & from pollen from a distinct plant of the same or of some other variety.[13] I have not made sufficient experiments to judge certainly, but in some cases the difference in the growth of the young plants is highly remarkable.

I have taken every kind of precaution in getting seed from the same plant, in germinating the seed on my own chimney-piece, in planting the seedlings in the same flower pot, & under this similar treatment I have seen the young seedlings from the crossed seed exactly twice as tall as the seedlings from the self-fertilized seed; both seeds having germinated on same day. If I can establish this fact (but perhaps it will all go to the dogs) in some 50 cases, with plants of different orders, I think it will be very important, for then we shall positively know why the structure of every flower permits, or favours, or necessitates an occasional cross with a distinct individual.[14] But all this is rather cooking my hare before I have caught it. But somehow it is a great pleasure to me to tell you what I am about.

Believe me my dear Gray | ever yours most truly | & with cordial thanks | Ch. Darwin

LS(A)
Gray Herbarium of Harvard University (92)

[1] The year is established by the relationship between this letter and the letter from Asa Gray, 27 August 1866.

[2] When Leonard Darwin was recovering from scarlet fever, Gray had sent a selection of American postage stamps for his collection (see *Correspondence* vol. 10, letters to Asa Gray, 10–20 June [1862] and 28 July [1862]).

[3] See letter from Asa Gray, 27 August 1866.

[4] Elizabeth Cabot Cary Agassiz's letter to Charles Lyell has not been found. It is likely that she enclosed a copy of Louis Agassiz's article from the *Atlantic Monthly* (J. L. R. Agassiz 1866a), which Lyell then passed on to CD along with her letter. Lyell's letter to CD has not been found, but see the letter to Charles Lyell, 8 [–9] September [1866] and n. 5.

[5] For the portion of Gray's 27 August 1866 letter that CD copied and sent to Lyell, see the postscript to the letter to Charles Lyell, 8[–9] September [1866]. On the reasoning behind Agassiz's theory, see the letter to Charles Lyell, 8[–9] September [1866] and n. 6.

[6] See letter from Asa Gray, 27 August 1866. CD had asked his publisher, John Murray, to send copies of the fourth edition of *Origin* to a number of people (see letter to John Murray, 15 July [1866] and n. 3). Gray's name appears on CD's presentation list for the fourth edition of *Origin* (see Appendix IV).

[7] CD's American publisher, D. Appleton & Co., printed from stereotypes. Since CD had made major revisions (see *Origin* 4th ed., pp. xi–xii), Appleton's would have had to recast most of the book. See letter from Asa Gray, 18 July 1866 and n. 6.

[8] CD refers to *Variation*; Gray had told CD that he thought he could make an arrangement with the Boston firm Ticknor & Fields to publish it (see letter from Asa Gray, 27 August 1866).

[9] Gray had enclosed specimens of the flowers of *Rhamnus lanceolatus* with his letter of 7 August 1866. In CD's notes on *R. lanceolatus* (DAR 109: A42 and 44), a table of pollen-grain sizes indicates a slight difference between those of long-styled and those of short-styled forms. In *Forms of flowers*, pp. 295–6, CD noted a ratio of 10 to 9 in the diameter of pollen-grains in the two forms. CD's son William Erasmus Darwin had observed a difference in the size of the pollen-grains of the two male forms of a related species, *R. cathartica* (see letter from W. E. Darwin, 20 June [1866] and n. 5, and *Forms of flowers*, p. 295). William's notes on the *R. lanceolatus* specimens received from Gray, dated 28 August 1866, are in DAR 186: 43.

[10] In *Forms of flowers*, pp. 295–6, CD noted that the pistil of the short-styled form of *Rhamnus lanceolatus* was half to two-thirds the length of that of the long-styled form. Moreover, he noted the slightly larger size of pollen-grains in the long-styled form. He suggested that *R. lanceolatus* was a hermaphrodite plant that was becoming dioecious. In earlier work on various dimorphic species of *Primula*, CD had shown that heteromorphic unions resulted in complete fertility whereas homomorphic unions were incompletely fertile ('Dimorphic condition in *Primula*', p. 91). CD later referred to this phenomenon as reciprocal dimorphism (see 'Three forms of *Lythrum salicaria*', p. 191).

[11] The letter to Gray requesting information on plants which never flowered or seeded has not been found. *Acorus calamus* (sweet flag) is a perennial herb propagated by rhizome division; horseradish is propagated by pieces of root. CD's question about *Acorus* and horseradish was related to his work on sterility from the excessive development of the organs of growth or vegetation; he refers to the sterility of the two plants, and others, in *Variation* 2: 170.

[12] In crosses of long-styled primrose (*Primula vulgaris*) with pollen of short-styled *P. elatior*, CD found only minimal fertility, compared with the high rate of fertility he had recorded in earlier experiments using pollen from the common oxlip (now *P. veris* x *vulgaris*) with *P. vulgaris*. CD's interpretation of the results emphasised the necessity of going beyond structural criteria in classifying species (see 'Specific difference in *Primula*', pp. 449–51). CD's notes for his crossing experiments made in 1866 with the common oxlip and *P. elatior* (which he called the Bardfield oxlip), are in DAR 108: 8–10; the bulk of

CD's notes on *Primula* are in DAR 108–11. CD's discussion of the common oxlip and *P. elatior* is in *Forms of flowers*, pp. 55–73.

13 This work marked a departure from many of CD's previous crossing experiments, which were designed to assess the regulation of cross-fertility and self-fertility by variation in flower structure. Earlier experiments had focused on the number of seeds produced in controlled crosses while the new work concerned the relative growth of plants raised from such seeds (see Allan 1977, pp. 250–1). CD later published the results of these and further experiments in *Cross and self fertilisation*; see especially pp. 285–311.

14 In *Cross and self fertilisation*, p. 303, CD concluded that seedlings from a cross between distinct plants were generally superior in height, weight, and constitutional vigour to those that were self-pollinated.

From W. B. Tegetmeier 12 September 1866

Muswell Hill | London | N
Sept. 12./66

My dear Sir

I have had the blocks cut as you desired and forward proofs.[1] One I have returned to the engraver to have a little more shade cut away—

Would you have any objection to sign the enclosed[2] I should feel it a high honour to be recommended by you, in conjunction with my friend M[r] Flowers.[3]

If you would kindly return the paper this week it would be ready for the next meeting of the Council[4]

I send you with this a number of the Field containing a rather graphic account of the habits etc of the Jungle fowl—[5]

The suggestion that certain breeds are derived from the Sonnerattii are obviously incorrect and I consequently wrote a short reply in the paper of the following week.[6]

Trusting you are enjoying good health | Believe me | Very truly Yours | W B Tegetmeier

C Darwin Esq

DAR 178: 75

1 CD had asked Tegetmeier to have alterations made to four of the woodcuts for *Variation* (see letter to W. B. Tegetmeier, 4 August [1866]). The proof copies he sent to CD have not been found, but see *Variation* 1: 147, 226, 228, and 229 for the illustrations to which he refers.

2 Tegetmeier evidently enclosed a letter of application for membership in the Zoological Society of London (see letter to W. B. Tegetmeier, 14 September [1866]).

3 The reference is probably to William Henry Flower, who had been on the Council of the Zoological Society of London since 1862 (*DNB*).

4 No record of the date of the council meeting has been found, but Tegetmeier did become a member in 1866.

5 The article was part of a series on Indian birds by an author writing under the name 'Ornithognomon' (see the *Field*, 1 September 1866, p. 183). The author suggested that the domestic fowl showed affinity to two wild species, the common red junglefowl, *Gallus ferrugineus* (CD used the synonym, *G. bankiva*; see *Variation* 1: 226), and the grey junglefowl, *G. sonneratii*.

6 Tegetmeier, though not mentioning specific works, cited CD and Edward Blyth to support the view that all varieties of domestic poultry derived from the common junglefowl (see *Field*, 8 September 1866, p. 191). In 1865, CD had compared the feathers of *Gallus sonneratii* with those of some domestic breeds as part of his investigation into the ancestry of domestic breeds (see *Correspondence* vol. 13, letter to W. B. Tegetmeier, 27 February [1865] and n. 5). See also letter from W. B. Tegetmeier, [after 4 August 1866] and n. 9.

To W. B. Tegetmeier 14 September [1866][1]

Down. | Bromley. | Kent. S.E.
Sept. 14th

My dear Sir

I have had much pleasure in signing the enclosed. No one has a better right to be a member of the Zoological Soc. than yourself.[2] Many thanks for the blocks, which I think are greatly improved by being cut.[3] When I receive the last I will write to Mr Murray about paying for the lot.[4]

Many thanks for the Field: it is an interesting article, but contains nothing particularly new.— How hydra-headed the error is about the Gallus Sonneratii[5]

My dear Sir | Yours sincerely | Ch. Darwin

Your note is dated 12th. but I only got **this** morning & I am very sorry that I quite forgot it was Friday, but you ought to receive this tomorrow, Saturday)

Archives of The New York Botanical Garden (Charles Finney Cox Collection) (Tegetmeier 96)

1 The year is established by the relationship between this letter and the letter from W. B. Tegetmeier, 12 September 1866.

2 Tegetmeier had asked CD to sign a letter of application for membership in the Zoological Society of London (see letter from W. B. Tegetmeier, 12 September 1866).

3 See letter from W. B. Tegetmeier, 12 September 1866 and n. 1.

4 CD's letter to his publisher, John Murray, regarding payment for the woodcuts for *Variation* has not been found, but see the letter to W. B. Tegetmeier, 16 October [1866].

5 CD refers to the claim made in a recent issue of the *Field* that some domestic breeds of fowl were descended from *Gallus sonneratii* (see letter from W. B. Tegetmeier, 12 September 1866 and nn. 5 and 6).

To Albert Gaudry 17 September [1866][1]

Down. | Bromley. | Kent. S.E.
Sep 17.

Dear Sir

I received some time ago your kind present of your Considerations Génerales . . . de Pikermi; but I have delayed thanking you until I had time to read your work.[2] I have now done so with the greatest possible interest. Your observations on many points, especially on the various intermediate fossil forms, seem to me most valuable;[3] & I formerly read with great interest some of your memoirs in the

Bull. Soc. Geolog. de France, especially that on fossil monkeys.[4] I will venture to make one little criticism, namely that you do not fully understand what I mean by "the struggle for existence, or concurrence vitale;[5] but this is of little importance as you do not at all accept my views on the means by which species have been modified.

With my sincere appreciation of the value of you paleontological discoveries, & with my thanks for your obliging present

I have the honour to remain | Dear Sir | yours faithfully & obliged | Charles Darwin

LS
Museo Civico di Storia Naturale, Milan

[1] The year is established by the reference to Gaudry's paper (see n. 2, below).

[2] The paper that Gaudry had sent CD was an offprint of the second chapter of a larger work on the fossil animals of Greece (Gaudry 1862–7). CD's separately paginated offprint, published in 1866 under the title *Considérations générales sur les animaux fossiles de Pikermi* (Gaudry 1866), is in the Darwin Pamphlet Collection–CUL; it is annotated.

[3] Gaudry noted that many of the Miocene fossils he found at Pikermi in Greece showed characteristics of two or more groups of animals. He wrote that one could see the passage from order to order, family to family, genus to genus, and species to species in these intermediate forms, noting, for example, how the horns of *Tragocerus* showed characteristics of both the antelope and the goat (see Gaudry 1862–7, p. 347). He included several graphs showing the branching from one or two Miocene species to several related species in later epochs (*ibid.*, pp. 348–55).

[4] Gaudry claimed that a Miocene fossil monkey (*Mesopithecus*) he had found in Greece showed characteristics of two modern genera, macaques (*Macaca*) and *Semnopithecus*; he referred to the monkey as a 'type transitionnel' (see Gaudry 1862, p. 1023). Although CD did not cite this article specifically, he referred to Gaudry's finding in *Descent* 1: 197.

[5] In the conclusion of his monograph, Gaudry argued that his research had shown not that Greece had been a scene of conflict and disorder ('un théâtre de luttes et de désordres') in the distant past, but rather that everything existed in harmony. He then suggested that the gradual transformation of species was effected by the creator himself, working like an artist, and that each transformation reflected his infinite beauty (Gaudry 1862–7, p. 370). CD may have been alluding to this statement as a misunderstanding of the notion of struggle for existence.

From J. D. Hooker 19 September 1866

Royal Gardens Kew

Dear old Darwin

Seringe has come all safe.[1]

Mrs Hooker tells me of the distress you are again in—[2] My dear friend we do feel deeply for you—

The *Drosera* shall go in a day or two—[3]

Ever yr affec | J D Hooker

Kew Sept. 19/66.

DAR 102: 103

[1] Hooker refers to Seringe 1830 (see letter from J. D. Hooker, [4 September 1866] and n. 14).
[2] The reference is to Frances Harriet Hooker. Hooker probably alludes to the illness of CD's sister, Susan Elizabeth Darwin, who died two weeks later. Her death was thought to have been imminent at the end of August (see letter to W. D. Fox, 24 August [1866]).
[3] Hooker had promised to send a specimen of *Drosera binata* (see letter from J. D. Hooker, 18 August 1866).

From George Warde Norman 20 September 1866

Bromley | Kent
20 Septr. 1866

My dear Darwin,

You are so much interested in the habits of animals, that I think you may like to peruse the Paper, which accompanies this—[1]

It comes from the wife of our Curate M^r. Holland an intelligent man, who lodges with a Tenant of mine—named Roots—at Bence Well on Bromley Common—[2]

Please to return it at your convenience—

I have known a Cat, bring up Ducks but never Squirrels before—[3]

I earnestly hope that you may be progressing towards perfect recovery & should like to assure myself of this, through the means of an early Visit to Down—[4]

With kind Regards to M^rs. Darwin—[5] | Believe me | Yrs mo. truly | Geo W^de Norman

C. R. Darwin Esqre

DAR 172: 74

[1] The paper referred to has not been identified.
[2] George Roots lived at Bencewell, Bromley Common, Kent (*Post Office directory of the six home counties* 1870). Richard George Holland became curate of Holy Trinity Church, Bromley Common, in 1866 (*Crockford's clerical directory* 1868). His wife has not been further identified.
[3] Evidently, the paper reported the case of a cat adopting a squirrel.
[4] CD's health had generally improved in 1866 (see, for example, letter to Robert Swinhoe, [September 1866] and n. 3). Emma Darwin's diary (DAR 242) makes no mention of a visit by Norman, but as a neighbour of CD's, Norman may have visited informally (see Freeman 1978, pp. 127, 216).
[5] Emma Darwin.

To Lucy Caroline Wedgwood [before 25 September 1866][1]

My dear Lieutenant Lucy.—

If the Book with many vols. with coloured plates be the Botanical Mag. please look at Pl. 356 & see whether it mentions that the flowers of the plant, viz Erica Massoni, are glutinous, or the leaves—& whether the glutinous matter is secreted by glandular hairs.—[2]

How about the Pæony seeds—do the pods open & are they brilliantly coloured—? do Birds eat them? Have the seeds any thin fleshy coat?[3]

Your affectionate Uncle & Commander | Ch. Darwin

CUL (Add 4251: 336)

[1] The date is established by the relationship between this letter and the letter to Fritz Müller, 25 September [1866] (see n. 3, below), and the letter to J. D. Hooker, 25 September [1866] (see n. 2, below). By 25 September CD had received specimens of peony seeds and would not have needed to ask whether they had 'any thin fleshy coat' (see n. 3, below).

[2] The description of *Erica massoni* in *Botanical Magazine* (9 (1801): facing 356) mentions that the flowers 'are so extremely viscous that scarcely a winged insect can settle on them and escape with its life'. The leaves are described as 'hoary', but there is no mention of the hairs secreting any substance. CD was investigating insectivorous plants at this time, and wanted to compare the glandular hairs of *E. massoni* with those of *Drosera* (see letter to J. D. Hooker, 25 September [1866]).

[3] In the letter to Fritz Müller, 25 September [1866], CD mentioned that he received peony seeds from a friend the day after he received Müller's letter of 2 August 1866 (he wrote to Müller that he had 'just' received the August letter). It is likely that Lucy sent the peony seeds. She and her sisters had provided CD with specimens in the past (see *Correspondence* vol. 10, letter to K. E. S., L. S., and M. S. Wedgwood, 4 [August 1862]). In his Experimental notebook (DAR 157a: 81), CD noted: 'Lucy W. case at Leith Hill nothing touches or eats the Pæony seeds.'

From George Bentham 25 September 1866

25, Wilton Place, | S.W.
Sept 25 1866

My dear Darwin

On returning to my labours at Kew this morning after an absence of nearly three months I find on my table two memoranda of yours to which I hasten to reply[1]

I have never spoken of species of thistles in England not producing fertile seed—[2] All I have said was in my address of 1862 p. 19 in which I observed "How is it that when our hedges are annually loaded with the fruit of the bramble or our fields covered with the down of Carduus arvensis we seldom see a seedling of the one or the other?— Nature having concurrently provided for their propagation by the marching and rooting stems of the former and the creeping rhizomes of the latter"[3] which was strongly taken up by Hewett Watson[4] who sent me a box of young seedling Brambles.— I meant and ought to have said a *full-grown* seedling I never intended to deny that seeds are formed and shed and that they germinate in Autumn— but meant (as it appears to me to be clear from what follows) merely to show that we do not know what becomes of them in winter for in spring the infinite majority of the plants in these species in our climate are the result of propagation from buds (marching stems or creeping rhizomes) and not from seeds. So much is this the case that some Norfolk farmers say that Carduus arvensis will not propagate from seed and I heard when there that one farmer had said that he would give $5^{s}/$ to any one who would prove that it could be raised from seed— I may possibly have repeated this story and that may have led some one to suppose that I believe that C. arvensis did not produce fertile seed—whereas I am perfectly aware that it is often introduced into fields by seed— when there it generally spreads by its rhizomes In the above quoted passage I referred to what requires investigation not to undoubted facts.

Secondly about borrowing books from the Linnean Society.[5] Strict regulations were rendered necessary by the abuse of the privilege on the part of non-scientific or careless fellows but there was always an understanding that these regulations admitted of exceptions in the case of working Naturalists—both as to number of volumes and as to time, and also as to the privilege of borrowing valuable works which we cannot lend out to everybody. The great difficulty is that our Librarian[6] who is in many respects invaluable is sometimes too great a stickler to forms and does not like the responsibility of discretionary power, but in any case of doubtful exception to rules he ought to apply to the Secretary[7] instead of refusing peremptorily. I feel confident however that when you want to borrow more than the regulation number at a time if you write to him saying you wish to do so he would let you have them—or if he does not pray let me know that I may speak to him— We of the Council are particularly anxious that the Library should be made as useful as possible to working Naturalists especially to such as yourself—and at the same time that books should not be kept away from the Library and thus out of reach of the great mass of Fellows by those who really make no use of them.

I have been much gratified by the accounts of your improved health and sincerely trust you may go on progressing[8]—and that we may soon see the new work Murray has so long announced[9]

Yours very sincerely | George Bentham

DAR 160: 158

[1] Bentham had spent ten weeks away from Kew, leaving on 7 July and returning on 22 September 1866 (see B. D. Jackson 1906, p. 206). CD's letter to Bentham of [July–September 1866] is incomplete; the memoranda to which Bentham refers were evidently two postscripts to the letter, one of which is now missing.

[2] CD's remark about thistles must have been in the missing portion of his letter to Bentham of [July–September 1866].

[3] Bentham refers to a statement from his address to the Linnean Society meeting of 24 May 1862 (Bentham 1862, p. lxxxii). The page number given by Bentham refers to a separately paginated offprint. *Carduus arvensis*, a thistle, is a common weed on open ground. CD's query was related to his work on plants that did not generally propagate by seed (see letter to Asa Gray, 10 September [1866] and n. 11).

[4] Hewett Cottrell Watson.

[5] In his letter to Bentham of [July–September 1866], CD had asked to borrow more than the usual two books at a time. Bentham was president of the Linnean Society.

[6] Richard Kippist was the librarian of the Linnean Society.

[7] George Busk and Frederick Currey were secretaries of the Linnean Society.

[8] CD's health had generally improved in 1866 (see letter to Robert Swinhoe, [September 1866] and n. 3).

[9] CD's publisher, John Murray, had advertised *Variation* in the *Reader*, 15 April 1865, p. 427, and again in the 1 August 1865 issue of the *Publishers' Circular*, p. 386.

To J. D. Hooker 25 September [1866][1]

Down. | Bromley. | Kent. S.E.
Sept. 25th

My dear Hooker

My poor sister still lives, but is dying.[2] It is a great comfort that she has now ceased suffering & doses nearly all day long. She wishes poor thing earnestly for death, & really death is nothing compared with much suffering. It will soon now all be over.—

Many thanks for two kind notes from you, & for the loan of Sering.[3] It will please me much to receive Drosera; not that I am in the least hurry.[4] Can you give me another plant *Erica Massoni*; for I presume it is not to be bought, being described by Loudon as "grotesque". I see it is said to catch very many insects & even once a Kitty-wren. I want to look at its glands in comparison with those of Drosera.—[5]

Have you read or heard of Agassiz's new doctrine that the whole of the valley of Amazons was filled from Cordillera to beyond mouth of river with gigantic glacier! & that all striæ have disappeared owing to Tropical climate!! There never was so monstrous a notion.[6] Asa Gray says he started with determination to prove the whole globe covered with ice for purpose of destroying all terrestrial productions & thus destroying "Darwinian views". He rushed down immediately on his arrival to the Academy, & announced my destruction.—[7]

Talking of my views, did you see a Review in last Gard. Chronicle on Murray: by Jove if Masters wrote that he is up to snuff, & he will stand much higher than before in my estimation of his powers. It seemed to me *very* good.— It hits the nail on the head so truly & so hard & yet so gently.—[8]

Have you seen Frankland's Lecture on muscular force read before Royal In^n.— he was so kind as to send it me, & I have liked it very much, though here & there there were bits I could not fully understand.—[9]

I suppose you are, as usual, very very busy. I wonder when you will find time to finish off your Lecture, & when you will publish it.[10] All your doings at Nottingham seem to have troubled much the good people at Dundee, who dread such infidel doctrines.[11] I hope Wallace's paper will be published; I have seen not even a moderate abstract of it—[12]

Farewell | my dear old Friend.— | Yours affect^ly | C. Darwin

DAR 115: 300

[1] The year is established by the relationship between this letter and the letter from J. D. Hooker, 19 September 1866.
[2] Susan Elizabeth Darwin died on 3 October 1866 (Emma Darwin's diary (DAR 242)).

[3] CD refers to the letters from J. D. Hooker, [4 September 1866] and 19 September 1866. CD had recently returned Seringe 1830.

[4] Hooker had promised to send a specimen of the insectivorous plant *Drosera binata* (see letters from J. D. Hooker, 18 August 1866 and 19 September 1866).

[5] CD refers to John Claudius Loudon's description of *Erica massoni* in Loudon 1841, p. 306. The source for the report of a kitty-wren (*Troglodytes vulgaris*) being caught by *E. massoni* has not been further identified. For CD's interest in *Erica massoni*, see also the letter to L. C. Wedgwood, [before 25 September 1866] and n. 2.

[6] Louis Agassiz advanced the theory that the Amazon valley had been covered by a huge glacier in J. L. R. Agassiz 1866a. CD also discussed Agassiz's claim in correspondence with Charles Lyell, Asa Gray, and Fritz Müller (see letter to Charles Lyell, 8[–9] September [1866], letter to Asa Gray, 10 September [1866], and letter to Fritz Müller, 25 September [1866]).

[7] Gray told CD that Agassiz had gone to a meeting of the National Academy of Sciences in Washington as soon as he returned from his South American trip (see letter from Asa Gray, 27 August 1866 and n. 3; for a brief description of Agassiz's address to the Academy, given 12 August 1866, see Lurie 1960, p. 353).

[8] The unsigned review of Andrew Murray's study of the geographical distribution of mammals (Murray 1866) appeared in the 22 September 1866 issue of *Gardeners' Chronicle*, p. 902. Maxwell Tylden Masters was the editor of *Gardeners' Chronicle*. The reviewer, later identified as Hooker (see letter from J. D. Hooker, 28 September 1866), was critical of Murray's concept of species change, which, he claimed, was unsupported by any evidence and failed to take into account many of CD's views. When Murray first told CD about his plan to write on geographical distribution, CD had expressed doubts about Murray's ability to do this (see *Correspondence* vol. 12, letter to J. D. Hooker, 3 November [1864]).

[9] Edward Frankland's lecture on the source of muscular power, delivered on 8 June 1866 at the Royal Institution of Great Britain, discussed his calorimetric experiments, which included the first measurements of the calorific value of various foods (Frankland 1866). CD's copy of the paper has not been found in the Darwin Archive–CUL. For more on Frankland's study and its significance, see Russell 1996, pp. 421–5.

[10] CD refers to Hooker's lecture on insular floras, delivered on 27 August 1866 at the British Association for the Advancement of Science meeting in Nottingham (for the publication details of Hooker's lecture, see the letter from J. D. Hooker, [28 August] 1866, n. 3).

[11] Dundee, Scotland, was the venue of the 1867 meeting of the British Association. CD is probably alluding to remarks by members of Brechin Town Council reported in the *Athenæum*. Dundee Town Council, in a meeting on 4 September 1866, had resolved to issue circulars to various regional civic and corporate bodies inviting them to co-operate with Dundee to ensure a successful meeting (Dundee City Archives, ref: IF15/24/9). The Brechin meeting was evidently a response to such an invitation. One member said that the British Association propagated nothing but infidelity and another expressed disapproval of the president, William Robert Grove (*Athenæum*, 22 September 1866, p. 371). Brechin is about 25 miles north-east of Dundee.

[12] CD refers to Alfred Russel Wallace's paper on sexual modifications and adaptive mimicry in butterflies, read at the British Association meeting at Nottingham (A. R. Wallace 1866a).

To Fritz Müller 25 September [1866][1]

Down Bromley Kent
Sep & 25th

My dear Sir

I have just recd your letter of Aug. 2nd & am as usual astonished at the number of interesting points which you observe. It is quite curious how by coincidence you have been observing the same subjects that have lately interested me.[2]

Your case of the Notylia is quite new to me; but it seems analogous with that of Acropera, about the sexes of which I blundered greatly in my book.[3] I have got an Acropera now in flower & have no doubt that some insect with a tuft of hairs on its tail removes by the tuft the pollinia, & inserts the little viscid cap & the long pedicel into the narrow stigmatic cavity, & leaves it there with the pollen-masses in close contact with, but not inserted into, the stigmatic cavity. I find I can thus fertilize the flowers; & so I can with Stanhopea, & I suspect that this is the case with your Notylia.[4] But I have lately had an orchid in flower, viz. Acineta, which I could not any how fertilize.[5] Dr Hildebrand lately wrote a paper shewing that with some orchids the ovules are not mature & are not fertilized until months after the pollen-tubes have penetrated the column; & you have independently observed the same fact, which I never suspected in the case of Acropera.[6] The column of such orchids must act almost like the Spermatheca of insects. Your Orchis with 2 leaf-like stigmas is new to me; but I feel guilty at your wasting your valuable time in making such beautiful drawings for my amusement.[7]

Your observations on those plants being sterile which grow separately or flower earlier than others are very interesting to me. They w^{d} be worth experimenting on with other individuals: I shall give in my next book several cases of *individual* plants being sterile with their own pollen. I have actually got on my list Escholtzia for fertilizing with its own pollen, though I did not suspect it w^{d} prove sterile, & I will try next summer.[8] My object is to compare the rate of growth of plants raised from seed fertilized by pollen from the same flower & by pollen from a distinct plant & I think from what I have seen I shall arrive at interesting results.[9] Dr Hildebrand has lately described a curious case of Corydalis cava, which is quite sterile with its own pollen, but fertile with pollen of *any* other individual plant of the species.[10] What I meant in my paper on Linum about plants being dimorphic in function alone was that they sh^{d} be divided into two equal bodies functionally but not structurally different.[11] I have been much interested by what you say on seeds which adhere to the valves being rendered conspicuous: you will see in the new Edit. of the origin why I have alluded to the *beauty* & bright colours of fruit;[12] after writing this, it troubled me that I remembered to have seen brilliantly coloured seed, & your view occurred to me. There is a species of Peony in which the inside of the pod is crimson & the seeds dark purple. I had asked a friend to send me some of these seeds, to see if they were covered with any thing which c^{d} prove attractive to birds.[13] I rec^{d} some seeds the day after receiving your letter; & I must own that the fleshy covering is so thin that I can hardly believe it w^{d} lead birds to devour them; & so it was in an analogous case with Passiflora gracilis.[14] How is this in the cases mentioned by you? The whole case seems to me rather a striking one.

I wish I had heard of Mikania being a leaf-climber before your paper was printed; for we thus get a good gradation from M. scandens to Mutisia with its little modified leaf-like tendrils.[15] I am glad to hear that you can confirm (but render still more wonderful) Haeckel's most interesting case of Liriope: Huxley told me that he thought that the case w^{d} somehow be explained away.[16]

As for Agassiz & his glaciers in the valley of the Amazons, it seems to me sheer madness, as it does likewise to Lyell; the evidence being wholly insufficient.[17] Prof. Asa Gray tells me that A. started with the determination to prove that the whole world had been covered with ice in order to annihilate all Darwinian views.[18]

I hope I have not troubled you with this long letter & believe me yours very sincerely

Charles Darwin

LS(A)
British Library (Loan 10: 9)

[1] The year is established by the relationship between this letter and the letter from Fritz Müller, 2 August 1866.

[2] In his letter of 2 August 1866, Müller had discussed dimorphism in Brazilian species of *Oxalis*, self-sterility in various plants, and brightly coloured seeds.

[3] In *Orchids*, pp. 203–10, CD described *Acropera* (now placed in synonymy with *Gongora*) as dioecious, concluding that the specimens he examined were male; however, in 1862 John Scott succeeded in pollinating flowers with pollen from the same plant. CD himself eventually pollinated *Acropera* (see *Correspondence* vol. 11, letter to John Scott, 7 November [1863] and n. 6, and the experimental note in DAR 70: 114). In August 1866, CD began experimenting with *Acropera* once more, and had recently been successful in pollinating a specimen (see letter to J. D. Hooker, 30 August [1866] and n. 11). Müller had reported that he initially supposed that a specimen of *Notylia* was male because he could not get pollinia to adhere to the stigma and the ovules seemed rudimentary, but that he later found seed capsules (see letter from Fritz Müller, 2 August 1866).

[4] Müller later confirmed CD's description in experiments with *Cirrhaea*, a genus related to *Acropera*. He described the process by which the pollinium was gradually sucked into the stylar canal after one end was inserted into the narrow entrance of the stigmatic chamber (F. Müller 1868b, pp. 630–1). CD referred to Müller's description in 'Fertilization of orchids', p. 153 (*Collected papers* 2: 150), and in *Orchids* 2d ed., p. 206. CD's annotated copy of F. Müller 1868b is in the Darwin Pamphlet Collection–CUL. For CD's finding on *Stanhopea*, see his notes, dated 11 to 20 August 1866, in DAR 70: 122–8, and *Orchids* 2d ed., p. 171; see also *Correspondence* vol. 12.

[5] In a note written on 3 July 1866 (DAR 70: 117), CD described his inability to pollinate *Acineta*, another orchid genus related to *Acropera*, noting that the stigmatic opening was so small that pollen could hardly enter and would not stick. He concluded that he could not conceive how the flower was fertilised. In 'Fertilization of orchids', p. 153, CD mentioned *Acineta* as one of the genera of orchids with a narrow entrance to the stigmatic chamber for which the means of pollination was not yet known, but added that insect agency of some kind was certain. For more on the pollination mechanisms of *Acineta* and the other orchid genera discussed in nn. 3 and 4, above, see Dressler 1981, pp. 102–3, 258–9.

[6] Friedrich Hildebrand reported his results from pollinating and cross-pollinating several species of orchids in Hildebrand 1863 and 1865c. CD's annotated copies of both papers are in the Darwin Pamphlet Collection–CUL. Hildebrand concluded that pollen caused the ovary to swell and the ovule to develop, after which fertilisation could occur (Hildebrand 1865c, p. 249). CD cited Hildebrand's articles in 'Fertilization of orchids', p. 153, and in *Orchids* 2d ed., p. 172. After observing specimens of *Notylia* as well as other orchids, Müller had suggested that the ovules of some orchids, especially among the tribe Epidendreae, did not develop until the flower had been opened for some time (see letter from Fritz Müller, 2 August 1866).

[7] See letter from Fritz Müller, 2 August 1866 and n. 8.

[8] The list of plants to which CD refers has not been found. Müller had observed some plants, including *Eschscholtzia californica*, all of which appeared to be sterile with their own pollen but fertile with pollen

from another individual plant of the species (see letter from Fritz Müller, 2 August 1866). CD discussed self-sterility in *Variation* 2: 131–40, including many of Müller's findings.

9 See letter to Asa Gray, 10 September [1866] and n. 13.

10 Hildebrand had sent CD a copy of his paper on *Corydalis cava* (Hildebrand 1866d; see letter from Friedrich Hildebrand, 11 May 1866 and n. 5).

11 CD made the comment on functional dimorphism in 'Two forms in species of *Linum*', p. 82 (*Collected papers* 2: 104). See also letter from Fritz Müller, 2 August 1866.

12 In *Origin* 4th ed., p. 240, CD argued that the beauty or bright coloration of fruit served 'merely as a guide' to attract birds or mammals so that their seed might be disseminated. See letter to C. W. Nägeli, 12 June [1866] and n. 4. For more on CD's views on beauty see also the letter to James Shaw, 11 February [1866].

13 CD probably refers to his niece Lucy Caroline Wedgwood (see letter to L. C. Wedgwood, [before 25 September 1866] and n. 3).

14 Müller had discussed the brightly coloured seeds of various plants in his letter of 2 August 1866.

15 CD refers to F. Müller 1865b, which appeared in the 29 November 1866 issue of the *Journal of the Linnean Society* (*Botany*) (see letter from Frederick Currey, 5 July 1866 and n. 1). In *Climbing plants* 2d ed., pp. 116–17, CD added the information from Müller that a Brazilian species of *Mikania* was a leaf-climber; he noted the gradation in *Climbing plants* 2d ed., pp. 195–6.

16 Müller's remarks on *Liriope* were in a now missing section of his letter of 2 August 1866; however, in a letter to Ernst Haeckel of 3 June 1866 (Möller ed. 1915–21, 2: 84–6), Müller informed Haeckel that he had recently confirmed Haeckel's findings concerning reproduction in certain Hydromedusae species (Haeckel 1865d; see *Correspondence* vol. 13, letter to Ernst Haeckel, 6 December [1865] and n. 9). Haeckel claimed to have discovered a new form of alternation of generations, having observed the apparent budding of individuals of *Cunina rhododactyla* (now *Pegantha rubiginosa*) from a parent *Geryonia hastata* (now *G. proboscidalis*). Müller reported that he observed a parent of *Liriope catharinensis* (now *L. tetraphylla*), a species closely related to *G. hastata*, with buds of *C. köllikeri* (now *C. octonaria*). Müller further observed that all the offspring were males of *C. köllikeri* and speculated whether, as in the case of some dimorphic plants, males of one form fertilised females of the other (see Möller ed. 1915–21, 2: 85). It is now generally accepted that larvae of *C. octonaria* develop parasitically in the stomach pouches of other medusae such as *Liriope* (see Kramp 1961, p. 282). Thomas Henry Huxley had worked on the anatomy and classification of the Medusae (see, for example, T. H. Huxley 1849).

17 Müller's comments about Louis Agassiz's theory that the Amazon valley had been covered by a glacier were in a now missing section of his letter of 2 August 1866; CD refers to his own recent correspondence with Charles Lyell discussing Agassiz's claims (see letter to Charles Lyell, 8[–9] September [1866] and n. 6).

18 See letter from Asa Gray, 27 August 1866; see also Lurie 1960, p. 345.

To William Bowman 26 September [1866][1]

Down. | *Bromley.* | *Kent. S.E.*
Sep 26

My dear Mr Bowman

I am very much obliged to you for having so kindly sent me your Address;[2] the whole has greatly interested me, & there is much in it quite new to me. I have been pleased to see your remarks on life having been continuous on this globe, & I admire your boldness tempered with due caution on the origin of Man.[3]

You read an excellent lesson to bigots of all kinds & that is a very striking passage in which you call the well-ascertained results of science "vox Dei".[4]

With my thanks for the pleasure which you have given me believe me | yours very sincerely | Charles Darwin

LS(A)
Roy Davids Ltd (1996)

[1] The year is established by the reference to Bowman 1866 (see n. 2, below).
[2] The reference is to Bowman's address given at the annual meeting of the British Medical Association at Chester, on 9 August 1866 (Bowman 1866). CD's copy is in the Darwin Pamphlet Collection–CUL.
[3] For Bowman's remarks on the continuity of life and the origin of the human species, see Bowman 1866, pp. 191–2. Although he did not mention CD's work, Bowman argued that evidence strongly suggested a continuity of life from the earliest times, 'through successive *generative* links of evolution', to the present. Referring to humans, Bowman suggested that the possibility that the human species belonged to an 'ascending . . . series in the scale of being' need not detract from human dignity.
[4] CD refers to a section of the address in which Bowman makes a plea for Church leaders to embrace science, concluding that the 'true results' of scientific inquiry become '*vox Dei*' (the voice of God; Bowman 1866, p. 192).

To George Bentham 27 September [1866][1]

Down. | *Bromley.* | *Kent. S.E.*
Sep 27

My dear Bentham

I am very much obliged to you for your note & I am sorry that I have troubled you in vain.[2] I was anxious to hear of any cases like that of Acorus calamus.[3] My memory deceived me for I now recollect the passage, & believe that at the time I did not misunderstand it.

With respect to the Linnean Library, not very long ago I applied for more than two books, but was told that it was against rules. I am sure it w^{d} be of no use my asking Mr Kippist for more books unless he receives instructions, for though nobody can be more obliging & kind than he is, he is rigid to what he considers his duty.[4]

With many thanks for your note believe me | yours very sincerely | Ch. Darwin

LS
Royal Botanic Gardens, Kew (Bentham letters: 705)

[1] The year is established by the relationship between this letter and the letter from George Bentham, 25 September 1866.
[2] See letter from George Bentham, 25 September 1866. In a missing portion of his letter to Bentham of [July–September 1866], CD had asked about species of thistle not producing fertile seed .
[3] See letter to Asa Gray, 10 September [1866] and n. 11, and letter from George Bentham, 25 September 1866 and nn. 2 and 3.
[4] CD had asked Bentham, who was president of the Linnean Society, whether it would be possible to borrow more than two books at a time from the society's library (see letter to George Bentham, [July–September 1866], and letter from George Bentham, 25 September 1866). Richard Kippist was the society's librarian.

From Thomas Francis Jamieson 27 September 1866

Ellon. Aberdeen$^{sh.}$
27 Sep. 1866

My Dear Sir,

I have the pleasure of sending you per Book post copy of a paper of mine on the *Glacial phenomena of Caithness*[1]—where, it seems to me, we have a very interesting example of glaciation having taken place under *marine* conditions, & where the means of proving this are unusually good.[2]

In the first place the glacial scoring on the soft shaly flags of that district runs from N.W to S.E. *across the angle* or extreme north-east corner of Scotland—with a N.W. stos-seite.— Secondly—the drift covering these ice worn rocks—very generally contains fragments of Arctic shells— Foraminifera &c—and what is very interesting—the shells are often very well *ice-marked*—being rubbed & scratched like the stones.[3]

—As you may not care about reading all the paper I have marked some of the passages which I have thought might most interest you—

The Table, no. II, at p. 280 contains some facts w$^{h.}$ seem to me very interesting—as for example the remarkably high proportion of N.E. American forms in what seem to be the older glacial marine beds of Scotland.[4]

Caithness is just the place where we might expect traces of marine conditions during the glacial period—being a low outlying region—a jutting-out corner—not likely to be covered by glaciers, but very likely to be in the way of drifting ice.

I am | Yours very truly | Tho$^{s.}$ F. Jamieson

Cha$^{s.}$ Darwin Esq. F.R.S. | &c &c

DAR 168: 46

1 The reference is to Jamieson 1866. CD's copy has not been found in the Darwin Library–CUL or the Darwin Library–Down.

2 Jamieson was a supporter of the theory of glacial submergence that became popular in the mid nineteenth century. The theory tried to reconcile evidence of glacial striation of land surfaces with evidence that some erratic material had been transported from low-lying areas to mountain regions by proposing that the land had been alternately submerged and covered by glaciers and that some deposition had been the result of icebergs melting. For more on the competing glacial theories of the mid to late nineteenth century, see Davies [1969], pp. 294–313.

3 Stoss: 'designating the side of any object that faces a flow of ice or water' (*OED*). The stoss-seite or stoss-side refers to the weathered or smooth side of a hill. Because of the geographical relationship of Caithness to the sea, Jamieson interpreted the north-west to south-east movement of ice as suggesting that marine conditions prevailed during the deposition of the Caithness drift; he also claimed that sea-borne ice could accumulate unstratified mud indistinguishable from that found underneath a glacier moving over land, except for the presence of marine shells (see Jamieson 1866, p. 269 n.)

4 The table referred to contains a comparison of the distribution of fossil molluscs grouped by geographic occurrence found in a number of Scottish glacial beds.

From J. D. Hooker 28 September 1866

Kew
Sept 28/66

Dear Old Darwin.

The *Drosera* has gone I hope, with *Erica Massoni*.[1] The *Drosera* attains twice the size you have it here. It should die down in winter, & be kept cold & moist: but not too close. I do not think your plant will grow bigger this season

I have heard of Agassizs new doctrine, but had not of the manure (your theory) that *raised* it.[2] Had you heard that his brain had been a little disordered?

I did *not* read the article on Murray in the Gardeners' Chronicle—having had no time to look at the number;— I wrote it—however, as I think you suspect, from the most welcome praise you give it, which I find to be *very* sweet.[3]

I tried Franklands lecture, but it was altogether too deep for me— it seemed very learned & good. & I only wished I could understand it.[4]

I shall probably send my Lecture to Gard. Chron., if they will print it in a reasonable-sized type.[5]

What a capital joke is the Dundee Town Councils discussion.[6] it reminds me of the Edinburgh T. C. when I was Candidate for poor Graham's Chair:[7] I long to see Wallaces paper also.[8]

Lady Lyell & Mr & Mrs Pertz were here the other day—[9] he is a very agreeable & able man. S^r^ C could not come. I hope he is not overdoing his "Principles".[10]

I am very busy, out of doors 6-hours a day, & delighting in my occupation. I can make even Kew 50 percent better than it is.[11]

I must get on with Gen. Plant. soon again.[12] Bentham goes to Cranworth's in a fortnight & hopes to see you—[13]

Do let me have one line by Henrietta when your poor sister is gone.[14]

Ever yr affec | J D Hooker

Old Gœppert of Breslau sends Photog. & asks yours in return.[15]

DAR 102: 106–7

CD ANNOTATION

Top of letter: 'Peas | My crossed seed'[16] *pencil*

[1] CD had asked Hooker to send a specimen of *Erica massoni* as well as the previously promised specimen of *Drosera binata* (see letter to J. D. Hooker, 25 September [1866] and nn. 4 and 5).

[2] CD had told Hooker of Asa Gray's view that Louis Agassiz had constructed the theory that the whole of the Amazon valley was once covered by a glacier in order to disprove CD's theory of transmutation (see letter to J. D. Hooker, 25 September [1866] and n. 7; see also letter to Charles Lyell, 8[–9] September [1866] and n. 6).

[3] CD had speculated that the article, a review of Andrew Murray's book on the geographical distribution of mammals, might have been written by Maxwell Tylden Masters (see letter to J. D. Hooker, 25 September [1866] and n. 8).

[4] Hooker refers to Edward Frankland's lecture at the Royal Institution of Great Britain (Frankland 1866). See letter to J. D. Hooker, 25 September [1866] and n. 9.

[5] The reference is to Hooker's lecture on insular floras, delivered on 27 August 1866 at the meeting of the British Association for the Advancement of Science in Nottingham (see letter from J. D. Hooker, [28 August] 1866, n. 3). The *Gardeners' Chronicle* used three sizes of type in the main text, 8pt, 7pt, and 6pt, 8pt generally being reserved for leading articles. Hooker's lecture was set in 7pt type (J. D. Hooker 1866a).

[6] Hooker probably refers to disparaging remarks made by members of Brechin Town Council, not Dundee Town Council, reported in the *Athenæum* (see letter to J. D. Hooker, 25 September [1866] and n. 11).

[7] Hooker refers to political manoeuvring by Edinburgh Town Council in awarding the chair of botany at Edinburgh University following the death of the incumbent, Robert Graham, in 1845. For a detailed explanation of the council's role in the matter, see L. Huxley ed. 1918, 1: 204–5.

[8] CD had expressed a desire to see Alfred Russel Wallace's paper on butterflies, read at the British Association meeting at Nottingham in August 1866 (see letter to J. D. Hooker, 25 September [1866] and n. 12).

[9] Hooker refers to Mary Elizabeth Lyell, Georg Heinrich Pertz, and Leonora Pertz, who was Mary Lyell's sister.

[10] Charles Lyell was working on a new edition of *Principles of geology*. The ninth edition had appeared in 1853; the tenth edition, in two volumes, was published in 1867 and 1868 (C. Lyell 1853, 1867–8).

[11] After the death of his father, William Jackson Hooker, in 1865, Hooker became director of the Royal Botanic Gardens, Kew. For Hooker's view of the difficulties of Kew administration and his efforts to promote scientific botany and horticulture, see *Correspondence* vol. 12, letter from J. D. Hooker, 20 April 1864, and *Correspondence* vol. 13, letter from J. D. Hooker, [7–8 April 1865] and nn. 5 and 6 (see also Allan 1967, pp. 211–13).

[12] *Genera plantarum* (Bentham and Hooker 1862–83) was published in seven parts. The second part appeared in 1865, the third in 1867.

[13] George Bentham was a friend of CD's neighbour, Robert Monsey Rolfe, first Baron Cranworth.

[14] Hooker refers to Henrietta Emma Darwin and to Susan Elizabeth Darwin, who was gravely ill.

[15] No photograph of Heinrich Robert Göppert has been found in the Darwin Archive–CUL.

[16] CD's annotation relates to his discussion of cross-pollination in peas in his letter to Hooker of 2 October [1866].

From Francis Trevelyan Buckland 29 September 1866

37. Albany S^t^ | Regent's Park. | N. W.
Sept 29 | 1866.

My Dear Mr Darwin

Will you allow me to call your attention to "Land & Water" a copy of which I now send you.[1]

The Field behaved so badly to me that I simply withdrew from them[2]—& I now conduct the portions of the paper to which my name is affixed—[3]

The work I assure you is perfect slavery.

Will you kindly patronize me, & make my columns the medium for obtaining any information you require. I have a large staff of zoologists working for me at home, & a large correspondence abroad.

Trusting that you are much better in health

Yours ever | Most obedient & obliged | Frank Buckland

C Darwin Esq

DAR 160: 360

[1] The first issue of *Land and Water*, which Buckland had started in association with friends, appeared on 27 January 1866 (Bompas 1885, p. 155). The copy sent to CD has not been found in the Darwin Archive–CUL.
[2] Buckland had been a contributor to the *Field* since 1856, but had severed his connection in 1865 (for more on Buckland's falling-out with editors of the *Field*, see Burgess 1967, pp. 113–16). CD had sought information on various topics in letters to the *Field* in 1861 (see *Correspondence* vol. 9).
[3] Buckland was editor of Practical Natural History for *Land and Water* (Bompas 1885, p. 155).

To George Bentham 1 October 1866

Down. | *Bromley.* | *Kent. S.E.*
October 1st. 1866

My dear Bentham,

I write one line to thank you for your note, which will be very useful to me,[1] and to say how very glad I shall be to see you when you are at Holwood.—[2] Would it suit Mrs. Bentham[3] and yourself to fix any day and come here to luncheon at half past one? I may just mention that by my doctors orders I ride every day from 12 to luncheon time.[4]

Believe me | Yours very sincerely | Charles Darwin

LS
Royal Botanic Gardens, Kew (Bentham letters: 707)

[1] Bentham's letter has not been found, but see the letter from George Bentham, 25 September 1866 and n. 5, and the letter to George Bentham, 27 September [1866]. CD had asked Bentham, who was president of the Linnean Society, whether he could borrow more than two books at a time from the library. He suggested that the librarian, Richard Kippist, would not allow him to do so without explicit instructions from Bentham. Bentham's note was evidently a confirmation of CD's special borrowing privileges.
[2] Holwood Park, a mile and a half north of Down House, was the home of Robert Monsey Rolfe. Bentham was planning to visit Rolfe later that month (see letter from J. D. Hooker, 28 September 1866 and n. 13).
[3] Sarah Bentham.
[4] CD's doctor, Henry Bence Jones, had recommended a strict diet and exercise (see letter to H. B. Jones, 3 January [1866], nn. 2–4). CD had begun walking regularly in August 1865; he started riding on 4 June 1866 (Emma Darwin's diary (DAR 242)).

From E. F. Lubbock [1 October 1866][1]

Dear Mr. Darwin

Mr. Herbert Spencer, who is staying here, has a very great desire to see you, and I write to ask if you would allow him to call upon you, or if you would, in the course of one of your rides,[2] stop here for a short time—

We should be only too glad if we could persuade you either to lunch or dine with us—but please will you tell us what you feel equal to, or if you would rather not see Mr. Spencer at all.

With our kindest regards to you all, believe me yours most truly | Ellen Lubbock

John goes to Yorkshire either tomorrow or Wednesday, to open some barrows.[3]

DAR 170: 8

[1] The date is established by the relationship between this letter and the letter to J. D. Hooker, 2 October [1866], and by the reference to 'tomorrow or Wednesday'; in 1866, 1 October was a Monday.

[2] CD had started riding daily from 4 June 1866 (Emma Darwin's diary (DAR 242)). He usually went out from 12 noon to 1 P.M. (see letter to John Lubbock, 2 August [1866]).

[3] John Lubbock had visited several sites of archaeological interest in Britain and Europe as part of his research into early humans. He had published a book on the subject a year earlier (Lubbock 1865).

To E. F. Lubbock [1 October 1866][1]

[. . .] Mr. Herbert Spencer. I will call tomorrow about half past 12. [. . .]

With my sincere thanks, yours truly obliged, Charles Darwin

Incomplete
Henry Bristow (Catalogue 265)

[1] The date is established by the relationship between this letter and the letter to J. D. Hooker, 2 October [1866].

From Fritz Müller 1 and 3 October 1866

Desterro, Brazil
Octbr. 1st. 1866.

My dear Sir.

In your last letter (of May 23rd) you wished me to observe whether Oxalis here exhibits different forms.[1] I already wrote you that in one of our species I found the relative lengths of the styli and stamens to be variable; I have now satisfied myself that this species is dimorphic.[2] In both the forms the stigmas reach to, or project a little beyond, the mouth of the calyx and the longer stamens are fully one third longer than the styli. The shorter stamens in one form are about half as long, whereas in the other they are about as long as the styli.— Thus far the species offers no particular interest; but there is one circumstance which renders it highly curious. At least 99 per cent of the plants of the second form have perfectly sterile anthers, not producing a single pollen-grain. Specimens of this form having all the anthers of all their flowers fertile are extremely rare. There are three different estates of the anthers: with good pollen—with small aborted pollen-grains—and without pollen; they blend into one another by insensible steps; (thus you may find anthers with only two or three good pollen-grains); but notwithstanding they are generally to be distinguished even without the aid of the microscope, the fertile anthers being bright yellow, those with aborted pollen-grains pale yellow and the pollen-less anthers white.[3]

Now in nine stalks the flowers showed the following combinations of the different anthers:

	Number of	Long stamens			Short stamens		
	Anthers	A.	B.	C.	A.	B.	C
I	2.	5	.	.	5.	.	.
	1.	4	.	1	4.	.	1.
II.	4.	.	.	5	.	.	5.
	1.	.	2	3	.	2	3
	1.	.	5.	.	.	5	.
	1.	.	2.	3	3	3.	2
	1.	.	4.	1.	1	2	.
III.	2.	.	.	5.	.	.	5.
	1.	.	3.	2.	.	.	5
	1.	5	.	.	.	5	.
	1.	.	3.	2.	.	5	.
IV.	3.	.	.	5	.	.	5.
	1.	5	.	.	.	.	5
V.	1.	1.	2.	2.	.	1	4
	1.	4.	.	1	5	.	.
	1.	5	.	.	.	5	.
VI.	2.	.	.	5	.	.	5.
	2.	5	.	.	5	.	.
	1.	5	.	.	4	.	1.
VII.	2.	5	.	.	.	5	.
VIII	1.	.	1	4	.	5	.
	1.	.	.	5	.	5	.
	1.		1.	4.	.	4.	1.
IX	1.	.	.	5	.	.	5
	1.	5	.	.	.	.	5
	1.	.	.	5	1	.	4
	36	64	23	93	37	52	91
		180			180		

A bright yellow
B pale yellow } anthers.
C white

In the first form the anthers are always fertile; but even here, as in the fertile anthers of the second form there is among the good pollen a large amount of aborted pollen-grains.

In some rather rare specimens of the second form,—but only, as far as I know, among those with sterile anthers,—the length of the stamens is very variable; (such were casually the few plants, which I had examined, when writing my last letter).[4] Sometimes, in a single flower the longer stamens are hardly as long, and the shorter ones half as long as the styli; but even in those specimens the stamens and styli of the majority of flowers use to show the characteristic lengths of the form.

It is not very rare to find one or two of the white pollen-less anthers transformed into small leaflets, and I met with a single plant, (now in my garden), in which all the anthers are transformed into petala-like leaves, sometimes exceeding ten in number; the ovaries form five open leaves with green stigmas on the tip, but without ovula, and in the midst of these ovarial leaves there is a great number of petala-like leaves, among which sometimes some sepala may be distinguished.[5]

Although the plant is extremely common (thousands flourishing in the very streets of our town) I have not yet been able to find a single seed-capsule. This sterility may be owing in part to the circumstance of the two forms but seldom growing mingled.[6] You may find your way bordered, for a mile or more, by one of the two forms exclusively, which then suddenly is substituted by the other.

A second very common species of *Oxalis*, with small yellow flowers, is monomorphic, the styli reaching to the level of the longer stamens; this species produces plenty of seed-capsules.[7]

Of a third species with fine crimson flowers, ressembling in shape, size and colour those of Linum grandiflorum, I have as yet seen only one plant, in which the styli were intermediate in length between the two sets of stamens; although the stigmas of all the flowers were densely covered with pollen, I found no seed-capsules; thus I am inclined to think that it will prove dimorphic or trimorphic.[8]

In short, I hope to have an opportunity of examining a fourth species of Oxalis with woody stem.—

To the list of dimorphic plants I may add a *Cordia*, of which I enclose a short-styled as well as a long-styled specimen; as soon as they are ripe, I shall send you seeds of either form.—[9]

In my last letter (of Aug. 2^d) I alluded to the circumstance of brightly coloured seeds remaining attached to the valves of the capsules after their opening.[10] I have since found two more plants, in which this is the case. One is a twining Leguminosa, perhaps a Rhynchosia, with black and red seeds. The other is a tree, probably belonging to the Mimoseae, which after the opening of the seed-capsules presents a truly magnificent aspect, being covered over and over with large and elegant curls of pale yellowish silk, (the spirally contracted valves) beset with brilliant red pearls.[11]

Octbr. 3. Yesterday I procured to calculate the number of seeds contained in a large capsule of an Orchid (Maxillaria?); the seeds weighed $42\frac{1}{2}$ grains; I extended half a grain of the seeds into a narrow heap and by counting a small portion I found them to be 20661, so that the capsule would contain the prodigious quantity of 1.756.440 seeds![12]

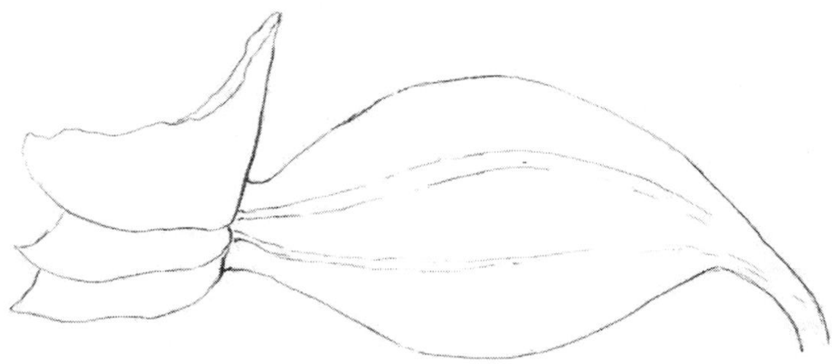

Hoping that this will find you in good health I am dear Sir with the most sincere respect | Yours very truly | Fritz Müller

Do the aërial roots of all the species of Catasetum grow perpendicularly upwards into the air, as they do in our Cat. mentosum?[13]

DAR 142: 99; DAR 157a: 103

CD ANNOTATIONS

1.5 the longer stamens ... the styli.— 1.7] *scored red crayon*
1.10 Specimens of ... anthers white. 1.17] *scored red crayon*
3.1 In the first ... pollen-grains. 3.3] *scored red crayon*
4.2 —the length ... variable;] *scored red crayon*
4.2 very] *underl red crayon*
5.2 small leaflets] *underl red crayon*
6.2 I have not ... seed-capsule.] *scored red crayon*
6.4 You may ... the other. 6.5] *scored red crayon*
7.1 A second] '[' *added before, blue crayon*
7.1 monomorphic 7.2] *underl red & blue crayon*
7.3 seed-capsules.] ']' *added after, blue crayon*
8.1 Of a third ... form.— 10.3] *crossed blue crayon*
10.1 To the list ... form.— 10.3] *scored blue crayon, crossed pencil*
12.1 *Octbr. 3.* ... very truly 13.2] *crossed pencil*

[1] See letter to Fritz Müller, 23 May 1866.

[2] See letter from Fritz Müller, 2 August 1866 and n. 2. After further observations, Müller later came to regard this species of *Oxalis* as trimorphic (see n. 6, below).

[3] In his work on dimorphic and trimorphic flowers, CD noted any differences in the pollen of different forms of flowers (see 'Dimorphic condition in *Primula*', 'Two forms in species of *Linum*', and 'Three forms of *Lythrum salicaria*'). CD had recently been interested in the observations made by his son William Erasmus Darwin on the differences in the size of pollen-grains in *Rhamnus cathartica*, but was unsure of the significance of such differences. William had suggested that *R. cathartica* was an example of a dimorphic species becoming dioecious (see letter to W. E. Darwin, 22 June [1866] and n. 3). CD included Müller's description of this species of *Oxalis* in *Forms of flowers*, pp. 180–1.

[4] Müller initially had noted considerable variation in the length of the styles, even in flowers of the same plant (see letter from Fritz Müller, 2 August 1866).

[5] In *Forms of flowers*, p. 180, CD mentioned that the stamens in some of the flowers were 'partially converted into petals'.

[6] Müller eventually reinterpreted the cause of sterility in this species of *Oxalis*, as well as its dimorphic status, in light of CD's experimental results with the illegitimate offspring of various heterostyled species. He concluded that the plants might be the variable and sterile offspring of a single form of a trimorphic species, accidentally introduced and afterwards propagated asexually (see *Forms of flowers*, pp. 180–1; see also letter from Fritz Müller, 31 October 1868, *Calendar* no. 6439).

[7] CD discussed this monomorphic species of *Oxalis* in *Forms of flowers*, pp. 181–2.

[8] In *Forms of flowers*, p. 180, CD referred to a trimorphic *Oxalis* with red flowers that, according to Müller, had never produced seed.

[9] The specimens have not been found (see letter to Fritz Müller, [before 10 December 1866] and n. 5).

[10] CD cut out the following paragraph and pasted it into his Experimental notebook along with his own notes on brightly coloured seeds (DAR 157a: 80; the fragment has since been moved to DAR 157a: 103). For Müller's earlier comments on the topic, see the letter from Fritz Müller, 2 August 1866 and nn. 14 and 15.

[11] Müller evidently sent specimens of these seeds, but they have not been found (see letter to J. D. Hooker, 5 December [1866] and letter to Fritz Müller, [before 10 December 1866]).

[12] The sketch is reproduced at approximately 80 per cent of its original size.

[13] *Catasetum mentosum* is a synonym of *C. atratum*.

To F. T. Buckland 2 October 1866[1]

I am much obliged for the Paper which is full of interesting matter and for your note. I am sure I should be very glad to be of any assistance to you but my health is too weak for me to offer to be a correspondent; nor do I think it likely that I should have any questions to ask, and so take advantage of your obliging offer.[2] I am endeavouring to complete a book which has been many years on hand.[3] Perhaps you may remember my asking you about the feet of otter hounds.[4] You obtained some information but never sent it me, being I have no doubt so much pressed with other business.[5] I now enclose a query on the same subject, if you will be so kind as to insert it; if you were to back it up with an editorial request my chance of answer would be better, though I am not sanguine.[6] I have ordered from my news vendor "Land and Water" for the next six months.[7]

With every good wish for your success and that your labour may grow lighter. | Believe me | Yours very faithfully | Charles Darwin

LS incomplete[8]
Rendells

[1] The date 2 October 1866 is given in the sale catalogue.

[2] Buckland had sent CD a copy of *Land and Water* and asked him to direct any inquiries through the magazine (see letter from F. T. Buckland, 29 September 1866 and n. 1).

[3] CD refers to *Variation*, which was not published until 1868. For more on CD's work on the manuscript of *Variation*, see the letter to W. B. Tegetmeier, 16 January [1866] and n. 1.

[4] CD requested information about the feet of otter-hounds in his letter to F. T. Buckland, 11 December [1864] (*Correspondence* vol. 12). For a more detailed query regarding the feet of otter-hounds, see *ibid.*, letter to T. C. Eyton, 29 December [1864?].

[5] In December 1864 Buckland informed CD that a friend had promised him a dead otter-hound to examine (see *Correspondence* vol. 12, letter from F. T. Buckland, 13 December 1864 and n. 1).

[6] CD's note appeared in the 6 October 1866 issue of *Land and Water* (see letter to *Land and Water*, [2 October 1866]).

[7] CD's copies of the magazine have not been found.

[8] The original letter is complete and is described in the sale catalogue as being three pages long.

To J. D. Hooker 2 October [1866][1]

Down.
Oct 2d Tuesday | Evening

My dear Hooker

I thank you heartily for the two plants which arrived safe on Saturday.[2] The Drosera is extraordinary & I hope when vigorous will behave in an extraordinary manner.

The Acropera shall be returned tomorrow by Rail; carr: paid to London by Carrier: I have succeeded with it only moderately well.—[3]

I supposed it possible but did *not* believe that you wrote the review of Murray: all my surprise at its being so well done has disappeared.—[4] I cannot help feeling that Gardeners' Chronicle is not good or permanent enough a place for your Lecture: few will ever be able to refer to it: think of this.—[5]

I have sent Photograph to Göppert.—[6]

As you did not read last Gardeners' Chronicle, you will not have read an article by a Mr. T. Laxton (I wonder who he is, he is a gentleman, but not scientific) on direct action of pollen of peas on the seed & pod:[7] I wrote to him & he sent me the specimens & they are wonderful & not to be mistaken.[8] This is a grand physiological fact & delightful for my pangenesis.—[9]

I went this afternoon to the Lubbocks to have an interview with Herbert Spencer, & enjoyed my talk much, though he does use awesomely long words. I plainly made out that Lady L. thinks him, like you do, not a small bore.[10] It is worth going to High Elms to see such lovely children.—[11]

My poor sister has rallied a little & is still alive & does not suffer, or but in a small degree; but her improvement is only temporary & we must soon hear of the end of a most sweet & loving character.[12]

Farewell dear old friend | C. Darwin

DAR 115: 301

[1] The year is established by the relationship between this letter and the letter from J. D. Hooker, 28 September 1866.

[2] CD refers to specimens of *Drosera binata* and *Erica massoni* (see letter from J. D. Hooker, 28 September 1866 and n. 1).

[3] CD had been trying to artificially pollinate an *Acropera* sent to him by Hooker in August (see letter from J. D. Hooker, [4 September 1866] and n. 13).

4 The reference is to an unsigned review of Andrew Murray's study of the geographical distribution of mammals (Murray 1866) in the 22 September 1866 issue of *Gardeners' Chronicle* (see letter to J. D. Hooker, 25 September [1866] and n. 8).

5 Hooker had told CD that he planned to publish his lecture on insular floras in *Gardeners' Chronicle*, provided the magazine used a large enough type-face (see letter from J. D. Hooker, 28 September 1866 and n. 5).

6 Heinrich Robert Göppert had sent Hooker a photograph to be forwarded to CD and had requested CD's photograph in return (see letter from J. D. Hooker, 28 September 1866 and n. 15).

7 In the 22 September 1866 issue of *Gardeners' Chronicle*, pp. 900–1, Thomas Laxton, a nurseryman from Stamford, reported that both pods and seeds of crosses made with sugar peas and purple-pod peas showed characteristics of both parents. His report was a response to CD's second letter to *Gardeners' Chronicle*, [before 11 August 1866]. CD's copy of the article has not been found; it was cut out of his copy of *Gardeners' Chronicle* (Cory Library, Cambridge University Botanic Garden). CD cited Laxton's findings in *Variation* 1: 397–8, in a section headed 'On the direct or immediate action of the Male Element on the Mother Form'. See also *ibid.*, pp. 401–3, and letter to Asa Gray, 16 April [1866] and n. 13.

8 The letters have not been found, but see the letter to Thomas Laxton, 31 October [1866].

9 In *Variation* 2: 387–8, CD suggested that gemmules within the pollen that were derived from parts near the reproductive organs might sometimes affect the same parts in the mother-plant, including the seeds and seed-coats, while they were still developing. For more on CD's theory of pangenesis and the operation of gemmules, see the letter to J. D. Hooker, 4 April [1866] and nn. 5–10.

10 Spencer was a guest of CD's neighbours, John and Ellen Frances Lubbock, at their house, High Elms (see letter from E. F. Lubbock, [1 October 1866]). For CD and Hooker's earlier discussions of Spencer and his publications, see *Correspondence* vols. 12 and 13.

11 The Lubbocks had six children (see Hutchinson 1914, 1: facing p. 1).

12 Susan Elizabeth Darwin had been seriously ill for some time (see letter to Charles Lyell, 8[–9] September [1866] and n. 3).

To *Land and Water* [2 October 1866][1]

Sir,—

I should be very much obliged to any one who keeps otter hounds if he would have the kindness to examine the feet of two or three dogs, and compare them with respect to the membrane between the toes with some other dog of a named breed. It would be best to compare the feet with those of some other sort of hound. With some otter hounds the skin between the toes is certainly more largely developed than in the case of common dogs, and I am anxious to know whether this is the general rule. It should be stated to which part or joint of the toes the skin extends, and whether it is much hollowed out in the middle. I should be very grateful for information sent to me either by letter or through LAND AND WATER.[2]

Charles Darwin

Down, Bromley, Kent

Land and Water, 6 October 1866, p. 244

1 The date is established by the relationship between this letter and the letter to F. T. Buckland, 2 October 1866. CD enclosed the original of this letter with his letter to Francis Trevelyan Buckland. The original letter has not been found.

2 In *Variation* 1: 40, CD referred to a response to his query from Charles Otley Groom-Napier, who reported on the webbing of the hind feet of otter-hounds in *Land and Water*, 13 October 1866, p. 270.

From George Bentham 4 October [1866][1]

25, Wilton Place, | S.W.
Oct 4

My dear Darwin

Thanks for your kind note but as at Holwood[2] we depend on the arrangements of others I fear we cannot *fix* a day for coming over to your luncheon till we are there— I shall at any rate in walking over avoid the time of your riding out[3]

Yours very truly | George Bentham

DAR 160: 159

[1] The year is established by the relationship between this letter and the letter to George Bentham, 1 October 1866.

[2] The reference is to Holwood Park (see letter to George Bentham, 1 October 1866 and n. 2).

[3] CD had told Bentham that he rode daily from noon until lunch-time (see letter to George Bentham, 1 October 1866 and n. 4).

From F. T. Buckland 4 October [1866][1]

37. Albany St. | Regent's Park. | N. W.
Oct 4.

Dear Mr Darwin,

Thanks for patronizing my efforts. I will not rest till I have obtained what you want to know in Re Otter dogs[2]

See "Land & Water" Saturday[3] Pray make use of me—*in any way*

I am so very sorry to hear that you are still unwell I trust you will soon be better.

I cant help smiling at the fightings & disputes between your disciples & your non disciples at the British Association.[4]

Did you ever see a pack of hounds fighting for a bone, when the huntsman's back is turned. Just so our friends attack & defend your theories thrown down into the middle of them.

Please throw us down *another* bone to fight about, the old bone is nearly picked clean now—

Yours ever | Frank Buckland

DAR 160: 361

[1] The year is established by the reference to CD's query in *Land and Water* about otter-hounds (see n. 3, below).

[2] See letter to F. T. Buckland, 2 October 1866 and nn. 4–6.

[3] CD's query on otter-hounds appeared in the 6 October 1866 issue of *Land and Water*, p. 244 (see letter to *Land and Water*, [2 October 1866]).

[4] Buckland is referring to the recent meeting of the British Association for the Advancement of Science held in Nottingham from 22 to 30 August 1866 (*Athenæum*, 11 August 1866, p. 161). In his presidential address, William Robert Grove had mentioned CD's works among others in natural history that were

supportive of transmutation of species rather than successive creations (W. R. Grove 1866). Buckland attended the meeting and presented papers (see *Report of the thirty-sixth meeting of the British Association for the Advancement of Science held at Nottingham*, pp. 70–1). For more on the reception of Grove's address, see the letter from Charles Pritchard, 8 October 1866 and nn. 3 and 4.

From E. A. Darwin 4 October [1866][1]

Oct 4

Dear Charles

Some little time ago Susan said that she wished George to have the Indian Chessmen.[2] I suggested to her that it would probably be an inconvenient gift & that they were scarcely ornamental now in which she agreed but said you can ask Charles whether he likes to have them.

Before I leave Shrewsbury I had better settle something about the house. I have no power to act without the consent of all parties.[3]

Caroline[4] is looking very much worn and it is a great mercy that she did not break down alltogether just at last. It has been a most painful time

with love to Emma | Yours affec. | Eras Darwin

DAR 105: B44–5

[1] The year is established by the reference to arrangements following Susan Elizabeth Darwin's death (see n. 2, below).

[2] Susan had died on 3 October 1866 (see letter to J. D. Hooker, [4 October 1866] and n. 1). The reference is to CD's son George Howard Darwin.

[3] Susan had resided at the Darwin family home, The Mount, in Shrewsbury. Robert Waring Darwin had bequeathed the house to his children with CD and Erasmus each receiving a quarter share while his four daughters (Marianne, Caroline, Susan, and Emily Catherine (Catherine)) each received an eighth share. The will further stipulated that his unmarried daughters could live in the house and collect rents from properties attached to it as long as they remained unmarried (will of Robert Waring Darwin, Department of Manuscripts and Records, National Library of Wales, Aberystwyth). The surviving children, Erasmus, CD, and Caroline Sarah Wedgwood, agreed to sell the house after Susan's death. It was advertised for sale at auction on 30 November 1866 (*Shrewsbury Chronicle*, 16 November 1866), but was not sold. The house was then let and eventually sold the next year (see *Correspondence* vol. 15, letter from Salt & Sons, 17 July 1867).

[4] Caroline Sarah Wedgwood, CD's eldest surviving sister.

To J. D. Hooker [4 October 1866]

Down
Thursday Evening

My dear Hooker

We have just heard that my poor sister is at rest & thank God has had no more suffering, having been tranquil & half unconscious for many days.[1]

Yours affectionately | C. Darwin

Do not write.

Endorsement: 'Oct. 4th/66'
DAR 115: 302

[1] Susan Elizabeth Darwin's date of death is registered in Shrewsbury as 3 October 1866.

From William Bowman 5 October 1866

Dumbleton Hall
Oct 5. 1866

Dear Mr Darwin

I must write one line to say how pleased I am that any little effort of mine should have met your approval—[1] With no wide or accurate acquaintance with the grounds of the great argument to which you have contributed so much and so powerfully, I cannot say I have any remaining doubt as to how the future will regard it. So that I could not honestly have expressed myself otherwise than I did if I touched upon it at all—and I felt that the occasion called for or at least admitted of some allusion to it.[2]

I was very near troubling you with an afternoon call one Sunday last Summer which I was spending with Lord Cranworth—[3] Yesterday I had the pleasure of inscribing my name near yours in Mrs Dent's book at Sudeley.[4]

Yrs very sincerely | W Bowman

C. Darwin Esq

DAR 160: 266

[1] CD had praised Bowman's recent address to the annual meeting of the British Medical Association (see letter to William Bowman, 26 September [1866] and n. 2).
[2] Bowman is referring to his remarks on the continuity of life and the origin of humans (see letter to William Bowman, 26 September [1866] and n. 3).
[3] Robert Monsey Rolfe, Lord Cranworth, was a neighbour of CD's.
[4] Bowman refers to Emma Dent and Sudeley Castle, near Winchcombe, Gloucestershire. Although there is no evidence that CD ever visited Sudeley, he may have contributed his signature for one of Dent's autograph books, as she was an avid collector. The page referred to has not been found in the archives at Sudeley Castle.

From E. A. Darwin 7 October [1866][1]

Oct. 7

Dear Charles

There is some confusion about the Soup Tureen.

Some time ago Caroline inquired of Armstrong & he said that one had been sent to you & the other Susan wished to go to Carolines children—[2] Caroline thinks you must have received it & forgotten about it so you had better ascertain—

The frame of the Fox Glove is in perfectly good order.

I am going to London on Wednesday & perhaps Caroline also but that is not certain—

Frank[3] has fractured the ankle bone most unluckily so cannot come to the Funeral.

yours affec. | E D

I am bringing away a large packet of your letters from abroad.[4]

Frank & Henry are the Exōrs[5]

DAR 105: B46–7

1 The year is established by the reference to Susan Elizabeth Darwin's funeral; see n. 2, below.

2 The references are to Caroline Sarah Wedgwood and Susan Elizabeth Darwin. Susan died on 3 October 1866 (see letter to J. D. Hooker, [4 October 1866] and n. 1). Armstrong has not been identified. Caroline had four daughters, one of whom died in infancy (see Freeman 1978, s.v. Josiah Wedgwood III).

3 Frank Parker was CD's nephew (Freeman 1978).

4 For CD's letters home while on the *Beagle* voyage, see *Correspondence* vol. 1.

5 Henry Parker and his brother Frank were the executors of Susan's will (Susan Elizabeth Darwin's will, Probate Registry, York).

From Charles Pritchard 8 October 1866

Freshwater
1866 Oct 8.

Dear Mr Darwin,

As a matter of dutiful courtesy to you I take the liberty of sending you a copy of a Sermon lately preached before the British Assoc^n^ at Nottingham.[1] In the *Appendix* Note *A*. I have stated certain reasons why I disagree with your (apparent) view of the gradual genesis of the Human Eye by Natural Selection.[2] You will I am sure as gladly accord to the views held as a Math^n^ or Astron^r^—as I respectfully do to you as a great Naturalist & I trust you will for once at all events see that an Orthodox Clergyman can write & speak of a view which he does not accept, as a gentleman ought.

I grieve to say my eloquent colleague D. Moore indulges in railery where he ought either to have been silent or have given *reason* for outspeech.[3]

Should you read my preface you will see what is the spirit in which I think seekers after truth ought to meet each other.[4]

I rejoice greatly to hear of the well being of your boys,[5] & am dear Sir | very Sincerely yrs | C. Pritchard

DAR 174: 78

1 The reference is to the published version of Pritchard's sermon (C. Pritchard 1866) given in response to William Robert Grove's presidential address at the meeting of the British Association for the Advancement of Science in Nottingham (W. R. Grove 1866). Grove's address supported the idea of the transmutation of species. CD's annotated copy of the sermon is in the Darwin Pamphlet Collection–CUL.

2 Pritchard opposed the view that the development of the human eye could be explained by the operation of natural selection over several millions of years (see however, letter to Charles Pritchard,

12 October [1866] and n. 3). His chief objection, based on William Thomson's calculations of the age of the earth, was that there was not enough time for the changes CD described to have occurred (see W. Thomson 1862a and 1862b; for more on the controversy about the age of the earth, see Burchfield 1990).

[3] Pritchard alludes to the disparaging remarks made by Daniel Moore about Grove's presidential address and Darwinian theory in the introduction to his sermon preached at Nottingham on the occasion of the British Association meeting (see D. Moore 1866, pp. v–vi).

[4] In the preface to his sermon, Pritchard argued that there should be no conflict between faith and scientific inquiry, since each new fact would be a new illustration of divine truth. He was critical of 'suspicious timidity regarding science and scientific men' and of ignorant attacks on the supposed tendencies of science made by some in religious circles (C. Pritchard 1866, pp. vii–viii).

[5] Until 1862, Pritchard had been headmaster of Clapham Grammar School, where CD's sons George, Francis, and Leonard were pupils (*DNB*).

From Thomas Rivers 8 October 1866

Bonks Hill, | Sawbridgeworth.
Oct 8/66

My dear Sir/

I have had some scores of purple fruited nut trees searched but not a nut can be found— the boys I suspect have been before us. I have however just heard that a neighbour near Saffron Walden has some I have therefore written to him to send me a few, as soon as they arrive I will despatch them[1]

Pray never hesitate to write me for anything that I am likely to have to help you with yr. interesting enquiries I only wish you were my neighbour I so often see little matters which I should like to submit to you

I am My Dear Sir | Yrs. very truly | Thos. Rivers

DAR 176: 168

[1] No letter from CD requesting specimens of purple nuts has been found, but see the letter to Thomas Rivers, 13 October [1866] and n. 2.

To Charles Lyell 9 October [1866][1]

Down.
Oct 9th

My dear Lyell

One line to say that I have received your note & the Proofs safely, & will read them with greatest pleasure;[2] but I am *certain* I shall not be able to send any criticism on the Astronomical Chapter, as I am as ignorant as a pig on this head.[3]

I shall require some days to read what has been sent. I have just read Chapter IX & like it *extremely*: it all seems to me very clear, cautious & sagacious.[4] You do not allude to one very striking point enough or at all, viz the classes having been formerly less differentiated than they now are; & this specialisation of classes must, we may conclude, fit them for different general habits of life, as well as the specialisation of particular organs.—

p. 162 I rather demur to your argument from Cetacea; as they are such greatly modified mammals, they ought to have come in, rather late in the series.[5]

You will think me impudent, but the discussion at end of Ch IX on man, who thinks so much of his fine self, seems to me too long or rather superfluous & too orthodox, except for the beneficed clergy.—[6]

Ever yours | C. Darwin

American Philosophical Society (320)

[1] The year is established by the reference to receiving proofs of C. Lyell 1867–8 (see n. 2, below).

[2] Lyell's note has not been found. CD refers to proofs of the first volume of the tenth edition of *Principles of geology* (C. Lyell 1867–8). The first volume of C. Lyell 1867–8 was advertised in *Publishers' Circular*, 15 November 1866, p. 722.

[3] The reference is to chapter 13 of C. Lyell 1867–8, 'Vicissitudes of climate, how far influenced by astronomical changes' (1: 268–304).

[4] Chapter 9 of C. Lyell 1867–8 (1: 146–73), which dealt with the progressive development of organic life, had been entirely re-written (see C. Lyell 1867–8, 1: iii).

[5] CD refers to Lyell's argument that, since whale bones could hardly escape the notice of collectors, the fact that no cetacean fossils had ever been found in pre-Eocene strata suggested that it was highly unlikely that many fossil mammals would be found in earlier strata (C. Lyell 1867–8, 1: 163).

[6] CD refers to the section 'Introduction of man, to what extent a change of the system' (C. Lyell 1867–8, 1: 167–73). For CD's differences with Lyell over human origins, and on his disappointment with *Antiquity of man* (C. Lyell 1863), see especially *Correspondence* vol. 11.

From Asa Gray 10 October 1866

Cambridge Mass.
Oct. 10. 66

My Dear Darwin

Thanks for very interesting letter of Sept. 10—[1] I am much pressed now, or would write a long gossiping letter.

The "bound copy' of Origin is just received from Murray—[2] Many thanks. I will send Appleton the sheets—tho' I don't think he will use them to the extent he ought.[3]

Ticknor & Fields, timid souls, after all fear to touch the new book either.[4] Perhaps Appleton will reprint it. But, I would advise you to ask Murray to throw in to the American Market—which he can now do—a stock of Origin, & of the new book too—and let us rely on *that.*

I meant to have written an early review of new ed. of *Origin.* But I doubt now if I can possibly get time to do it.

Had you asked a little earlier I could have sent you a stock of seeds of Rhamnus lanceolatus—from our single bush here.[5] I send the few I could find on the ground. I think *Acorus* really fruits here—where it is *seemingly* native— But I am not sure.

I believe I *have seen* a pod or two of Horseradish—but rare.[6] Your *germinations* show curious resemblance of *dimorphic-crosses* with *hybrid-crosses* as shown by Naudin—[7] Very interesting & capital point for you.

Ever Yours | A. Gray

DAR 165: 155

[1] See letter to Asa Gray, 10 September [1866].

[2] CD had asked his publisher, John Murray, to send a bound copy of the fourth edition of *Origin* to Gray (see letter to Asa Gray, 4 August [1866]). When Gray mentioned in his letter of 27 August 1866 that he was about to read proof-sheets, CD responded that he ought to have been sent a bound copy by Murray (see letter to Asa Gray, 10 September [1866] and n. 6).

[3] CD's American publisher, D. Appleton & Co., was reluctant to bring out a new edition of *Origin* because of the cost of typesetting the substantial number of revisions and additional material (see letter to Asa Gray, 10 September [1866] and n. 7).

[4] Gray had spoken to the Boston publishing firm, Ticknor & Fields, about producing an American edition of *Variation* as well as the new edition of *Origin* and had hoped to get better terms for CD (see letter from Asa Gray, 27 August 1866 and n. 2).

[5] Gray had sent CD specimens of the dimorphic flowers of *Rhamnus lanceolatus* with his letter of 7 August 1866. CD had reported that he was unable to detect differences in the size of the pollen-grains of the different forms and asked whether it would be possible to obtain plants of *Rhamnus* from a nursery (see letter to Asa Gray, 10 September [1866] and n. 9).

[6] CD had asked Gray for information on plants in America that never flowered or seeded, and mentioned *Acorus* and horseradish (*Cochlearia armoracia*) as two European examples (see letter to Asa Gray, 10 September [1866] and n. 11). *Acorus calamus* is native to North America (Mabberley 1997).

[7] CD had reported to Gray the early results of his experiments on the relative growth and vigour of seedlings raised from cross-pollinated and self-pollinated plants; these indicated that the crossed seedlings were significantly larger than the seedlings from self-pollinated plants (see letter to Asa Gray, 10 September [1866] and nn. 13 and 14). In a short article on two studies of hybrid crosses, Gray had referred to Charles Victor Naudin's experimental results from crossing two species of thorn apple, noting that the hybrids were at least twice the size of their parents (A. Gray 1865, p. 108). CD's annotated copy of the two-page article is in DAR 205.7: 5. For more on Naudin's work with hybrids, see *Correspondence* vol. 13.

From E. A. Darwin 11 October [1866][1]

Q A.
Oct 11

Dear Charles

Caroline was going to have an examination of the Plate list as it almost seems as if there were 3 tureens or else Susan forgot all about the matter.[2] She says that of course if it cannot be cleared up the Tureen belongs to you. The other matters I have attended to. £100 is left to each of your children except William & Henry will write to him about the Deeds of Claythorpe being sent to him.[3]

I took possession of all the letters & papers in the Bureau as I considered that they belonged to us as Exōrs & an immense big box they fill— Caroline wishes to have a letter or two of D[r] D—[4] I will keep them for a time for the chance of having energy to look at them & then you can have them— There is a pedigree among them, & there is also a pedigree among Susan's papers which Caroline was going to copy & then send to George.[5] There were in Susan's desk a pair of scissors & smelling Bottle marked with the names of Henrietta & Lizzy which I pointed out to Charles.[6]

I never saw anything so miserably ill as Caroline is looking She is tired of her present doctor & I recommended Paget & she is going to consult him— She seems to suffer most severe pain—[7]

Yours affec.| E D

P.S.

I asked Henry to send you Richmonds pictures of self & Emma.[8]

DAR 105: B48–51

[1] The year is established by the reference to Susan Elizabeth Darwin and her estate (see n. 2, below).

[2] Susan Darwin had died on 3 October 1866 (letter to J. D. Hooker, [4 October 1866], n. 1). In an earlier letter discussing the disposal of Susan's effects, Erasmus mentioned that a soup tureen might already have been sent to CD (see letter from E. A. Darwin, 7 October [1866]). In a codicil to her will, Susan had bequeathed a silver soup tureen to Caroline Sarah Wedgwood. No other tureen is mentioned in the will (will of Susan Elizabeth Darwin, Probate Registry, York).

[3] William Erasmus Darwin, CD's eldest son, inherited the farm at Claythorpe, Lincolnshire. Susan had inherited the property from her father, Robert Waring Darwin, who had purchased another farm, for CD, at Beesby, near Claythorpe, in 1845 (see *Correspondence* vol. 3). Henry Parker was one of the executors of Susan's estate (see letter from E. A. Darwin, 7 October [1866] and n. 5).

[4] 'D[r] D' is probably a reference to Erasmus Darwin, but may refer to Robert Waring Darwin. CD and Erasmus Alvey Darwin were the executors of Robert Waring Darwin's will (will of Robert Waring Darwin, Department of Manuscripts and Records, National Library of Wales, Aberystwyth).

[5] CD's son George Howard Darwin was interested in genealogy and collected information on the family. See letter from E. A. Darwin, [before 20 February 1866] and n. 2.

[6] The references are to Henrietta Emma and Elizabeth Darwin. Erasmus probably meant to write 'Henry' instead of 'Charles'.

[7] Caroline's health had suffered after the death of another sister, Emily Catherine Langton (see letter from E. A. Darwin, 19 February [1866] and n. 6). The reference is to the surgeon James Paget.

[8] George Richmond made portraits of CD in 1839 and 1840, of Emma Darwin in 1840 and 1842, and of Erasmus Alvey Darwin in 1850 (Lister 1981, p. 156; see also frontispieces to *Correspondence* vols 1 and 2).

To Charles Lyell 12 October [1866][1]

Down
Oct 12

My dear Lyell

I have read all the sheets (returned by this post) with nothing less than enthusiastic admiration. I do not think you have ever published any thing better than these amended chapters.[2] I began to mark, thinking that you w[d] like to hear, the passages which struck me most, but I soon desisted for I found I sh[d] have to score so much. I do not suppose that you care for any criticisms on these corrected chapters, & indeed I have none worth sending. Nevertheless I will make 2 or 3 remarks.

p. 188. I am rather sorry you did not limit the remark about the increased severity of the climate destroying the mammoth as acting through the vegetation; for is it not known that they survived in America the coldest period?[3]

Slip p. 14. I cannot but think that the marked passage is too strong. Any one with your knowledge & skill c[d] make out a striking case on the permanence of our continents,—from the continuity of allied terrestrial forms on the same continent,—from the dissimilarity of the marine Fauna during the present & past tertiary ages on the opposite sides of some continents,—& from the present distribution of mammals & indeed of all organic beings.[4]

slip 15. Is not this line bold, not to say rash; seeing that in the islands of the great oceans we have not a fragment of any secondary or even true Plutonic rock?[5]

I wish you joy at having so nearly completed this extremely difficult part of your work; & as far as I can judge it is admirably completed.[6]

yours affectionately | Ch. Darwin

P.S. The passage about the evaporation of the Snow, which is only conjectural, though I have no doubt that the fact was correctly reported, is at p. 245 of my Journal, in a note to passage about the great curvature of the snow-line.—[7]

P.S. Did you know that according to Airy, Adams & others (as stated in Prichards Pres. Astronom. Soc. in his Nottingham sermon) the day is slowly increasing in length; so that a million x million years ago it must have been only the $\frac{1}{200}$th part of a second in length! & in the same period in futurity, each day will be 80 years in length.—[8]

LS(A)
American Philosophical Society (321)

[1] The year is established by the relationship between this letter and the letter to Charles Lyell, 9 October [1866].

[2] Lyell had sent CD proof-sheets of the first volume of the tenth edition of *Principles of geology* (C. Lyell 1867–8). In addition to several minor alterations, he had re-written three chapters and added two new ones (for a list of the revisions, see C. Lyell 1867–8, 1: iii–v). CD had already commented on changes to chapter 9, concerning the development of organic life (see letter to Charles Lyell, 9 October [1866] and nn. 4–6).

[3] Lyell argued that the disappearance of animals like the mammoth could be explained without resorting to speculation about sudden climate change; he proposed that a moderate decrease in temperature would result in a diminution of vegetation, which in turn would cause the extinction (C. Lyell 1867–8, 1: 187–8).

[4] It is not clear to which passage CD is referring, as the proof-sheets he marked have not been found. In the printed version, Lyell argued that even though present continents had existed since long before the Eocene, the fossil record indicated that the distribution of land and sea during the Eocene must have been vastly different (C. Lyell 1867–8, 1: 253–5). For earlier arguments between CD, Lyell, and Joseph Dalton Hooker on the possible changes of land and water surface areas and their potential effect on climate change, see, for example, *Correspondence* vol. 12, letter to J. D. Hooker, 23 October [1864] and n. 10; see also Ospovat 1977.

[5] The passage referred to has not been identified, but see C. Lyell 1867–8, 1: 142–5 for Lyell's discussion of the characteristics and origin of plutonic and metamorphic rocks.

[6] The first volume of C. Lyell 1867–8 was advertised in *Publishers' Circular*, 15 November 1866, p. 722.

CD's lightly annotated copy, signed and dated 29 November 1866 by the author, is in the Darwin Library–CUL (see *Marginalia* 1: 543–4).

7 In the printed version of C. Lyell 1867–8, Lyell included this reference to the second edition of *Journal of researches* to support the view that snow and ice could evaporate in cold, dry regions without first becoming liquid (see C. Lyell 1867–8, 1: 286–7).

8 CD refers to George Biddell Airy, John Couch Adams, and Charles Pritchard, who was president of the Royal Astronomical Society in 1866 (*DNB*). In his sermon at the meeting of the British Association for the Advancement of Science (see letter from Charles Pritchard, 8 October 1866 and nn. 1 and 2), Pritchard had cited recent astronomical calculations indicating that the length of a day was constantly increasing. He suggested that if CD were right about the great age of the earth, then at the earliest times, a day would have been a fraction of a second in length (see C. Pritchard 1866, pp. 35–6).

To Charles Pritchard 12 October [1866][1]

Down,
Oct. 12*th.*

My Dear Mr Pritchard,—

I have read with much interest your sermon, with its appendices, & I thank you sincerely for having sent it me.[2]

I should be a very cross-grained man to object to a single word that you have said. You pay me the most elegant compliments, and attack me with much spirit and force. Even if I could you would not thank me for making a long defence; but I may make two remarks. When I refer to the extremely simple eyes of the *articulata* (*i.e.*, insects, spiders, etc.), you translate this into the human eye.[3] Should there be a second edition, I hope you will correct this, for I have always spoken of the human eye as the pinnacle of difficulty.

You speak of the necessity of various parts of the eye changing simultaneously in order that it may become adapted for even slightly changed work; but many a short-sighted person can see an object distinctly at a distance which renders the image confused to others.[4]

What a very curious case about the increasing length of day![5] I have that profound respect for mathematics which profound ignorance gives, but I cannot help observing that when applied to uncertain subjects, such as geology, it gives as uncertain results as geologists arrive at by other means; for instance, how Thomson and others differ about the thickness of the crust of the earth and the rate of cooling.[6]

My son George has been much interested by your sermon, and begs to be very kindly remembered to you.—[7]

With my best thanks, pray believe me, yours very sincerely, | Ch. Darwin

That is a very foolish episode of mine about the Wealden, and was struck out in later editions.[8]

A. Pritchard comp. 1897, p. 93

1 The year is established by the relationship between this letter and the letter from Charles Pritchard, 8 October 1866.

2 The reference is to C. Pritchard 1866 (see letter from Charles Pritchard, 8 October 1866 and n. 1).

[3] Pritchard had misinterpreted a remark from *Origin*, p. 188, in which CD suggested that the change from a simple optic nerve to an eye of any member of the Articulata could be plausibly explained as the result of natural selection. Pritchard assumed CD meant an eye 'as perfect as the human eye' (C. Pritchard 1866, p. 32). CD had expanded his discussion of the possible development of the eye in *Origin* 4th ed., pp. 216–18.

[4] CD noted Pritchard's argument (C. Pritchard 1866, p. 33) in his discussion of the possible incremental steps in the development of the eye in *Variation* 2: 222–3.

[5] CD refers to another argument Pritchard made against Darwinian theory, based on astronomical evidence that the length of a day was constantly increasing (see letter to Charles Lyell, 12 October [1866] and n. 8).

[6] The physicist William Thomson (later Lord Kelvin) had recently calculated the age of the earth based on its cooling from a molten ball. He concluded that the earth could not possibly have existed with its crust in a similar state as at present for the length of time proposed by geologists (W. Thomson 1865).

[7] George Howard Darwin had been a student at Clapham Grammar School while Pritchard was headmaster there (see letter from Charles Pritchard, 8 October 1866 and n. 5).

[8] In *Origin*, p. 287, CD had written that the denudation of the Wealden district in Kent took longer than 300 million years. In response to criticism, he revised his estimate downwards to 150 or 100 million years in *Origin* 2d ed., p. 287. No reference was made to the Wealden in the third or later editions of *Origin* (see Peckham ed. 1959, pp. 483–4). See also *Correspondence* vol. 12, letter from A. C. Ramsay, 10 July 1864 and n. 3.

To Francis Darwin [after 12 October 1866][1]

If you endorse this cheque you can pay M^{r}. Burns with it, so as not to bother yourself with passing it through your Bank.—[2] But you ought to enter it **in your accounts** as received from me & paid by you.—

AL
DAR 211: 2

[1] The date is established by the reference to Mr Burn (see n. 2, below).

[2] Robert Burn was Francis's tutor at Trinity College, Cambridge, where Francis was an undergraduate from 29 September 1866 until April 1870, when he received his BA (*Admissions to Trinity College, Cambridge* 5: 329, *Cambridge University calendar* 1870, p. xxiv; see also *Correspondence* vol. 13, letter to Robert Burn, 2 December [1865]). CD's Classed account books (Down House MS) record a payment to Francis of £100 on 1 October 1866. Emma Darwin's diary (DAR 242) records that Francis left home on 12 October 1866. CD's instructions probably refer to the first payment Francis received while at university.

To Thomas Rivers 13 October [1866][1]

Down Bromley Kent
Oct 13th

My dear Sir

I thank you most sincerely for all the trouble which you have so kindly taken about the purple nuts. I was greatly interested in the case, but I find after seeing your specimens that I dare not trust my case.[2]

Indeed I wish most truly that I lived near you, or was strong enough to pay you a visit that I might profit by some of your varied knowledge; but such cannot be.

With many thanks, believe me | Yours truly obliged | Ch. Darwin

DAR 185: 86

[1] The year is established by the relationship between this letter and the letter from Thomas Rivers, 8 October 1866.

[2] Rivers had written to CD that he would send specimens of purple nuts from a neighbour's tree (see letter from Thomas Rivers, 8 October 1866). CD's request for the specimens has not been found, but it is likely that he had asked for nuts of a purple-leaved hazel (*Corylus* sp.). In *Variation* 2: 330, CD mentioned the variety in his discussion of correlated variability as an example of a plant in which the leaves, fruit, and seeds vary together in colour.

From Thomas Rivers 14 October 1866

Bonks Hill, | Sawbridgeworth.
Oct 14/66

My Dear Sir/

When looking over some grass a species of Bromus from the North Western coast of America—with a friend & botanist we noticed some oats that were producing ears of barley this led to the assertion made by Elihu Burritt in his "Walk through the Eastern Counties" that a farmer at St. Ives Hunts had for years "transmuted" oats into barley.[1] doubting this I wrote to the writer of the enclosed[2] a farmer of 1600 acres a Member of the Council of the Royal Agricultural Society & above all a good & truthful gentleman. The subject may possibly be an old one with you but to me so curious & well authenticated as to tempt me to trouble you.[3] The writer's name is Mr. Jno. Claydon[4]

I am My Dr. Sir | Yrs. very truly | Thos. Rivers

DAR 176: 169

[1] Burritt's claim that oats 'transmuted' into barley appeared in *A walk from London to John O'Groat's* (Burritt 1864, pp. 170–1). St Ives is near Huntingdon in Cambridgeshire.

[2] The enclosure has not been found.

[3] For earlier discussions on the transmutation of oats into barley, see letter from G. S. Gibson, 7 July 1866, and letter from S. V. Wood, 16 July 1866.

[4] Rivers probably refers to John Clayden of Littlebury, Saffron Walden, Essex, a member of the council of the Royal Agricultural Society (*Journal of the Royal Agricultural Society of England* 2d ser. 2 (1866): ii).

From W. B. Tegetmeier 15 October 1866

Muswell Hill | London | N
Oct 15, 66.

My dear Sir

The Engravers inform me that they have delivered the blocks to Mr Murray, and have been paid—[1] Mr Wells posted me the enclosed—[2] I hardly know whether I should have directed him to call or forward it to Mr Murray, or whether it requires your signature to be paid

I have had some pleasant correspondence with Prof Newton respecting an original dodo picture I discovered—[3] He also seems to have discovered that varieties and variation are not altogether beneath the notice of naturalists.

I hope your work will be out before very long. I am very anxious to read it— I think in my marginal

AL incomplete
DAR 178: 76

[1] Butterworth and Heath, a firm of wood-engravers with premises at 356 Strand, London, engraved the blocks of Luke Wells's illustrations for *Variation* (*Post Office London directory* 1866; see *Correspondence* vol. 13, letter from W. B. Tegetmeier to John Murray and R. F. Cooke, 17 April 1865). John Murray was CD's publisher.

[2] The enclosure from Wells has not been found, but see letter to John Murray, 16 October [1866]. Tegetmeier had overseen the illustrations of pigeons and fowls for *Variation* (see *Correspondence* vol. 13, letter from W. B. Tegetmeier, 27 March 1865).

[3] Alfred Newton, professor of zoology and comparative anatomy at Cambridge University, corresponded with Tegetmeier about a seventeenth-century painting of a white dodo that Tegetmeier had discovered in a private collection. Tegetmeier had exhibited the picture at a meeting of the Zoological Society of London, 10 April 1866 (*Proceedings of the Zoological Society of London* 14 (1866): 201). Tegetmeier supplied Newton with a photograph of the original and Newton published an article including a reproduction of the picture (Newton 1867; several letters written by Tegetmeier to Newton about the painting between October 1866 and February 1867 are in the Alfred Newton Papers–CUL).

To John Murray 16 October [1866][1]

Down Bromley | Kent
Oct 16th.

My dear Sir

I have heard the wood cutter has sent in his account to you & I now enclose Mr. Luke Wells' account for drawing the same & will tell him to call for the amount.[2]

But as you have not agreed to publish my work until seeing the M.S. would you not prefer my sending you a cheque for the amount & likewise for the second set of engravings now being made by Mr. Sowerby.[3] Pray do as you like.

I trust I shall begin printing in the beginning of next year but I cannot say quite positively— Please to read over the second page of the enclosed note from Professor Asa Gray & then tear it up; twice over he has urged the same plan & be so good as to consider it & act as you think fit.[4] I may repeat what I said before that I have not the least idea whether my new book will get many readers; all that I can say in its favour is that I am sure that some of the chapters contain very curious matter.[5]

My dear Sir | yours sincerely | Charles Darwin

LS
John Murray Archive

[1] The year is established by the relationship between this letter and the letter from W. B. Tegetmeier, 15 October 1866.
[2] The reference is to the wood-engraving firm of Butterworth and Heath. See letter from W. B. Tegetmeier, 15 October 1866 and nn. 1 and 2.
[3] George Brettingham Sowerby Jr had made illustrations for some of CD's other works (see *Correspondence* vols. 5 and 9). For CD's interest in having Sowerby contribute illustrations to *Variation*, see the letter to John Murray, 22 February [1866] and n. 14.
[4] CD enclosed the letter from Asa Gray, 18 July 1866. Gray had suggested that John Murray should supply the American market with copies of the fourth edition of *Origin*. See also the letter from Asa Gray, 10 October 1866.
[5] The first printing of the first edition of *Variation* sold out in a week (letter to Alphonse de Candolle, 6 July 1868 (*Calendar* no. 6269); also printed in *LL* 3: 99–100).

To W. B. Tegetmeier 16 October [1866][1]

Down Bromley | Kent
Oct 16th.

My dear Sir

Very many thanks for all your kind assistance now completed.

I have written to Mr. Murray to pay Mr. L. Wells when he calls for payment.[2] I hope to begin printing in the beginning of next year but I can work only slowly. I need not say that one of the first copies shall be sent to you.[3]

My dear Sir, | Yours sincerely | Ch. Darwin

LS
Archives of The New York Botanical Garden (Charles Finney Cox Collection) (Tegetmeier 97)

[1] The year is established by the relationship between this letter and the letter from W. B. Tegetmeier, 15 October 1866.
[2] CD refers to John Murray and Luke Wells (see letter from W. B. Tegetmeier, 15 October 1866 and nn. 1 and 2).
[3] The reference is to *Variation*, which was published in January 1868 (Freeman 1977). Tegetmeier's name appears on CD's presentation list for *Variation* (DAR 210.11: 33).

From John Murray 18 October [1866][1]

50A, Albemarle St. | W.
Oct. 18

My Dear Sir

After publishing for you two such works as the Origin of Species & the Orchids I can have no hesitation in offering at once, even without seeing the MS.S to publish your "Domesticated Animals" on the same terms as I publish the Origin— viz paying you a sum equal to $\frac{2}{3}$d of the profits—for every edition consistent with the number of copies[2]

If this be satisfactory to you I shall of course pay Mr Wells Bill, as I have done that of Mr Sowerby—including them in the expences of the works.[3]

I shall not lose sight of Dr Asa Greys suggestions— I have no objection to let Mess Ticknor & Field know that they can have 250 copies of the new Edition at half price—[4]

I could supply them either with early sheets of your new Book or with stereotype plates if they prefer them

I remain My Dear Sir | Yours very faithfully | John Murray

Chas Darwin Esqr

DAR 171: 338

CD ANNOTATION

End of letter: 'This was [*above del* 'shall be'] changed into half-profits, I think'[5] *pencil*

[1] The year is established by the relationship between this letter and the letter to John Murray, 16 October [1866].

[2] The works referred to are the first four editions of *Origin*, *Orchids*, and *Variation.* For the terms of CD's agreement with John Murray for *Origin*, see the letter from John Murray, 24 February [1866] and n. 4.

[3] Murray refers to Luke Wells and George Brettingham Sowerby Jr, both of whom provided illustrations for *Variation.* See letter to John Murray, 16 October [1866].

[4] Ticknor & Fields was a Boston firm that Asa Gray had approached about publishing *Origin* and *Variation* (see letter to John Murray, 16 October [1866] and n. 4).

[5] Murray later told CD that although he was prepared to publish his new book (*Variation*), he would offer CD only half the profits rather than two-thirds because he felt he was taking a greater risk in publishing a work that would have less popular appeal than *Origin.* See *Correspondence* vol. 15, letter from John Murray, 28 January [1867].

From Ernst Haeckel[1] 19 October 1866

London | 8 Clarges Street | Piccadilly.
19 Oct. 66

Theurer, hochverehrter Herr!

Endlich geht einer meiner sehnlichsten Wünsche seiner Erfüllung entgegen, indem ich die Hoffnung habe, Sie in kurzer Zeit selbst sehen und sprechen zu können. Ich denke, dass Ich Ihnen vielleicht Sonntag (*Sunday* 21. Oct) meinen Besuch machen darf, und bitte Sie, mir mit wenigen Worten zu sagen, ob dieser Tag Ihnen angenehm ist, und *zu welcher Stunde* (at what o'clock) ich nach Down. Bromley kommen darf. Ich bin nur auf kurze Zeit in London, da ich mit dem nächsten Dampfschiffe nach Madeira und Teneriffa gehen werde, um dort den Winter zu bleiben und zoologische Untersuchungen anzustellen.[2]

Meine "*generelle Morphologie der Organismen*, begründet durch die von Charles Darwin reformirte Descendenz-Theorie" ist jetzt vollendet, und Sie werden dieselbe in den nächsten Wochen erhalten.[3] Der *erste Band* umfasst die allgemeine Einleitung und die Grundzüge der generellen Anatomie; der *zweite Band* enthält eine allgemeine Darstellung der Descendenz- und Selections-Theorie, und die Grundzüge der generellen Entwickelungsgeschichte. Weiteres davon darf ich Ihnen vielleicht bald selbst mittheilen.

Hoffentlich treffe ich Sie in bestmöglicher Gesundheit an. Mit der vorzüglichsten Verehrung bleibe ich Ihr von ganzem Herzen ergebener | Ernst Haeckel

DAR 166: 43

[1] For a translation of this letter, see Appendix I.

[2] Haeckel had travelled from Bonn to London at the beginning of October 1866. He travelled on to Lisbon, where he met two students who accompanied him to Madeira and Tenerife in November 1866. In December, they arrived at Lanzarote, where they spent three months studying hydrozoans and siphonophores. (Krauße 1987, pp. 76–7.)

[3] The reference is to Haeckel 1866. CD's annotated copy is in the Darwin Library–CUL (see *Marginalia* 1: 355–7). For Haeckel's earlier discussions of Haeckel 1866, see *Correspondence* vols. 12 and 13.

From J. D. Hooker 19 October 1866

Royal Gardens Kew
October 19/66

My dear Darwin

The shrubs for your lawn are gone to day.—[1] plant them singly in good light loamy soil & *not too near other trees*.

Lyell was here the other day very well, but blinder than ever I fear.[2] He sent me his chapters X, XI, XIII[3] I pointed out a few inadvertencies in X & XI. My great objection to XII is that he ignores vapor,—which plays so important a part in modifying climate— if you push the land to the Poles or to the Equator, you may not necessarily thereby alter the temp. of the globe.—only alter its distribution over the Globe[4]

Ever yr aff | J D Hooker

The Govt. (Lord J. Manners) has arranged that the Treasury will propose to Parliament next session to purchase my fathers collection[5]

Herbarium	£5000
Choice of books	£1000
Portraits, mss, Correspondence &c	£1000
	£7000

This is what I asked. it relieves me of a great strain.

Ever yr aff | J D H

DAR 102: 108–9

[1] On 19 October 1866 Hooker sent CD the following plants: *Abies douglasii* (*Pseudotsuga menziesii*, Douglas fir), *A. canadensis* (*Tsuga canadensis*, hemlock, or *Picea glauca*, white spruce), *Retinospora obtusa* (unidentifiable; *Retinospora* is a name formerly used for 'many scale-leaved conifers in the juvenile needle-leaved stage' (Mabberley 1997)), *Wellingtonia gigantea* (*Sequoiadendron giganteum*, giant sequoia), *Cupressus lawsoniana*

(*Chamaecyparis lawsoniana*, Port Orford cedar), *C. macrocarpa* (Monterey cypress), and *Thujia lobbii* (*Thuja plicata*, western red cedar); (Royal Botanic Gardens, Kew, Outwards book).

2 Charles Lyell's eyesight had always been poor, requiring him to be read aloud to and to dictate much of what he wrote (K. M. Lyell ed. 1881, 2: 381).

3 Hooker refers to proof-sheets of chapters in the first volume of the tenth edition of Lyell's *Principles of geology* (C. Lyell 1867–8). CD had recently sent Lyell comments on the proof-sheets he had been sent (see letters to Charles Lyell, 9 October [1866] and 12 October [1866]). Hooker wrote 'XIII' by mistake for 'XII' (see n. 4, below).

4 In the section referred to in chapter 12 (C. Lyell 1867–8, 1: 233–67), Lyell discussed the relationship between temperature and the relative position of land and sea. He discussed the role of the ocean in equalising and moderating temperature (*ibid.*, pp. 236–9) but did not consider vapour in a similar context. In a letter to Hooker, 20 October 1866, Lyell said he would send chapter 13 and hoped it would clear up difficulties arising from current climate theories that predicted huge temperature differences between the hemispheres because of the greater proportion of land in the northern hemisphere. He suggested that vapour, to which Hooker had alluded, could be a factor in equalising temperature (see K. M. Lyell ed. 1881, 2: 410–11). See also letter from J. D. Hooker, [after 28 April 1866] and nn. 7 and 8.

5 John James Robert Manners was commissioner of works (*DNB*). Before his death in 1865, Hooker's father, William Jackson Hooker, had written a memorandum stating that his herbarium would be left to his son on the understanding that it might be purchased by the government as part of the crown property attached to the Royal Botanic Gardens, Kew (Allan 1967, pp. 216–17).

To Mary Elizabeth Lyell [19? October 1866][1]

Down
Friday

My dear Lady Lyell

I should be delighted & honoured by M[rs] Somerville's using any of the diagrams in my Orchid book.[2] But it is more M[r] Murray's affair than mine.[3] If this note were shewn to him I have no doubt he would give permission & do what is necessary.

Pray believe me yours sincerely | Ch. Darwin

LS
Bodleian Library, Dep. c. 370, folder MSD-1 (on loan from Somerville College, Oxford)

1 The date is conjectured from the relationship between this letter and the letter from Mary Somerville, 30 October 1866, and the estimated time needed for post to go to and from Italy.

2 The letter requesting permission for Mary Somerville to use the illustrations has not been found. Somerville used fourteen illustrations from *Orchids* in her book *On molecular and microscopic science* (Somerville 1869, 1: 389–403). CD's copy of Somerville 1869 is in the Darwin Library–Down House.

3 John Murray, CD's publisher, owned the woodcuts for the illustrations of *Orchids*.

To George Brettingham Sowerby Jr 19 October [1866][1]

Down
Oct 19.

My dear Sir

I like all the drawings very much, but 2 or 3 must be corrected;[2] but it will not I think cause much trouble. I must see the blocks again when corrected, & the specimens in question must be returned at the same time with my MS Instructions for the same. When corrected please to address them to—

C. Darwin Esq
care of Down Postman
Bromley Kent.
per Rail

When the blocks are cut & I have proofs, please to be sure return **all** my M.S instructions.

I think you have got one number of Waterhouse's Mammalia belonging to me.[3]

(Corrections.)[4]

Fig 1. The muzzle looks almost ridiculous from both nostrils being so visible & standing so high. The head is too prominent near the eyes. One hind hoof looks cleft. The front fetlocks rather too thin. Pray improve the head, & I send with the block a rather good engraving. Please observe that all four shoulder-stripes & leg-stripes are decidedly too dark. The lower end of anterior shoulder-stripe ought to be more square see the original drawing. I think the head w[d] look better if it was in profile.

Fig 4. The snout is a little exaggerated & too much upturned like a proboscis.

Fig 5 The projecting bristles on right side of head much too coarse; you had better remove them altogether.

Fig. 10 This does not well show what is wanted; a little shading above the great occipital foramen of both figures w[d] at once tell the story. As the condyles are shewn on each side, it is necessary that a small portion of the skull, shading away indefinitely, should be given above. Please look at the specimens in the "Rabbit box".

Fig 26 Lower jaw C. of Pigeon spec. 129. must be altered; the upper rim of the jaw is considerably too much reflexed; the very object of the wood cut is to shew the contrast in this respect between jaw C. 129 & jaw B. 116. As the jaw is seen from vertically above, the upper edge in the terminal portion of the jaw entirely hides the lower portion or margin. The basal part of the jaw is also made, as seen from vertically above, too broad; & does not contrast enough with Fig B. Please compare these jaws; they are in a labelled pill-box & to save you trouble are put in the "*Rabbit box*".

Fig 33 C. Skull of Fowl There is an important error here, against which I guarded you in my M.S. instructions & in the outline given. The error can however be corrected by erasing a small portion of the pre-maxillary bone. Pray read my instructions & look at my sketch; & compare the entire skull marked "White crested" with the skull of which a section is here given. I wished you to imagine an exactly medial section through the entire "White crested" skull; by holding this skull & the section of skull in the same position, & by looking at my outline I think you will understand the alteration which is necessary. One of the 2 points of bone shewn in your Fig. 32 A[5] will project just behind or beyond the line of section. You will understand why all this is necessary, when I tell you that it is quite an anomaly in the breed of which the section of the skull is given to have the pre-maxillary bone extending up & united to the skull. I have put these 2 skulls which you will require for the correction in whity brown paper in the "Rabbit Box"

Fig 35 Is drawn upside down, but by merely altering the lettering, as I have done, all comes right.—

In the Pea pod (*un numbered*)[6] the dark shading near the extremity ought to terminate more abruptly or be more defined. Look at the original drawing folded up with the block.—

I hope these corrections will not give you great trouble. Please observe that I must see all these corrected blocks again. I am much pleased with the whole lot & thank you sincerely

I am my dear Sir | yours very faithfully | Ch. Darwin

Will it not be adviseable to let the Wood-cutter have the specimens, when he is cutting; but of this you will judge best.

Pray put him to work at once in order, I hope to have proofs to affix to my M.S. & give proper references by middle of December.—

Woodcuts No 1, 10, 26, & 33 are those which I must see again— I forgot to observe whether you have given letter of Reference *in all cases* in which there is more than one figure on same block— Please attend to this—

See that the Blocks are ultimately cut close for the Printed number above & Description below.—[7]

LS(A)
DAR 96: 21–4

[1] The year is established by the relationship between this letter and the letter to John Murray, 16 October [1866].

[2] The reference is to illustrations made by Sowerby for *Variation* (see letter to John Murray, 16 October [1866] and n. 3).

[3] Waterhouse 1846–8 was issued in twenty-two instalments, later appearing in a two-volume edition. CD's unbound copies are in the Darwin Library–CUL (see *Marginalia* 1: 845–9). CD may have lent Sowerby part 12, on the Rodentia (Waterhouse 1846–8, 2: 1–48; it is the only part that has CD's signature on the front cover). CD had annotated the plate showing the skull and lower jaw of *Lepus timidus*, the common hare. In *Variation* 1: 116–20 various features of the skull of the wild rabbit are compared to those of domestic breeds, and figures 6 to 11 illustrate this part of the text.

[4] The figure numbers that CD gives correspond to those in the printed version of *Variation* except for figure 33 C, which is figure 36, the skull of a horned fowl, in the printed version. Figure 1 is of the Devonshire pony; figure 4 is of the old Irish pig; figure 5 is of the half-lop rabbit; figure 10 is of the occipital foramen of rabbits; figure 26 is the skull of a runt (a pigeon); figure 35 is of longitudinal sections of skulls of fowls.

[5] This number evidently corresponds to Sowerby's own list; based on the description, it is figure 36 in the printed version (see *Variation* 1: 265).

[6] 'Pods of the common pea' is figure 41 in the list of illustrations (see *Variation* 1: viii, 328).

[7] In the printed version, the figure number and description usually but not invariably appear below the illustration.

To Ernst Haeckel [20 October 1866][1]

Down Bromley | Kent
Sat.

My dear Sir

It will give me the most sincere & cordial pleasure to see you tomorrow.[2]

On Sundays there are not many trains to choose from. You must go to the "London Chatham & Dover department" of the *Victoria station* for the trains which start either at 10.25 arriving at Bromley 11.3 or leaving Victoria at 2.0 arriving at Bromley 2.40.

My carriage, which you will recognize by a white horse with a chestnut one, will meet both trains at Bromley so that you can take your choice.[3] We live 6 miles from Bromley Station. Take care to get out at *Bromley* station. We hope that you will of course sleep here & we can convey you to the station the next morning.

My health is a good deal improved but I find it impossible to converse with any one for more than a quarter or half an hour at a time. So you must forgive me for often leaving you.[4]

I know that you read English perfectly, & I hope that you speak it, as I am ashamed to say I can neither speak German or French. It will give me the most sincere pleasure to see you.

Believe me | yours very faithfully | Ch. Darwin

You had better direct your cab. to Victoria Station, which is little more than half a mile from Clarges St.[5]

LS
Ernst-Haeckel-Haus (Bestand A-Abt. 1-52/11)

1 The date is established by the relationship between this letter and the letter from Ernst Haeckel, 19 October 1866.

2 Haeckel had asked if he could visit CD on Sunday 21 October 1866 (see letter from Ernst Haeckel, 19 October 1866).

3 According to a letter circulated to his friends, Haeckel took the morning train to Bromley (see Kraußе 1987, pp. 76–7).

4 For more on the improvement in CD's health, see the letter to W. D. Fox, 24 August [1866]. CD often excused himself from social occasions on the grounds that conversation with visitors exhausted him (see *Correspondence* vol. 13, Appendix IV and n. 9).

5 Haeckel had written to CD from 8 Clarges Street, Piccadilly, London (see letter from Ernst Haeckel, 19 October 1866).

To J. D. Hooker [21 October 1866][1]

Down
Sunday

My dear Hooker

The Bearer of this is Prof. Ernst Häckel, a first-rate Zoologist, who wishes much to know you, so I could not refuse a note of introduction, but I hope he will not take up very much of your time.—[2]

Your splendid present of trees & conifers has arrived all safe & Emma is very much obliged to you.—[3]

I am delighted to hear about the Government & your Fathers Herbarium & Books; though £7000 is a good big sum, I suppose it is a mere fraction of what your Father must have spent on them.—[4]

Lyell sent me the same chapters to read: they seemed to me very good indeed, not that I am convinced that change of land & water will do all that he thinks.—[5]

I am tired so good night.

Ever Yours | C. Darwin

DAR 115: 303

[1] The date is established by the reference to Ernst Haeckel, who visited CD on 21 October 1866 (Emma Darwin's diary (DAR 242)).

[2] Haeckel visited CD while on his way to Madeira to conduct research (see letter from Ernst Haeckel, 19 October 1866 and n. 2).

[3] See letter from J. D. Hooker, 19 October 1866 and n. 1.

[4] Hooker had told CD that the government was planning to purchase the herbarium and books of his late father, William Jackson Hooker, for the price Hooker had requested (see letter from J. D. Hooker, 19 October 1866 and n. 5).

[5] Charles Lyell sent proof pages of chapters 10 to 12 of the first volume of the tenth edition of his *Principles of geology* (C. Lyell 1867–8). Lyell had argued that the relative distribution of land and water over the globe was a modifying influence on climate (see letter from J. D. Hooker, 19 October 1866 and n. 4).

From John Lubbock [21 October 1866][1]

High Elms

My dear Mr. Darwin

I cannot very well come up to Down this afternoon.

You will I am sure be tired & must not overdo yourself. I wish you would send Haeckel down here to dinner & I would send him over to the station if he must go to night, or give him a bed & take him up in the morning if he could stay till then.[2]

Believe me | Yours most sincerely | John Lubbock

Pray tell him I am very anxious to make his acquaintance.

JL

DAR 170: 51

[1] The date is established by the reference to Ernst Haeckel's visit to CD, which took place on Sunday 21 October 1866 (Emma Darwin's diary (DAR 242)).

[2] There is no evidence that Haeckel visited Lubbock.

From Friedrich Hildebrand 23 October 1866

Bonn
Oct 23^{d} | 1866.

Dear and honoured Sir

I received your kind letter this morning, but I am very sorry that I cannot satisfy your wishes about the seeds of Oxalis rosea, I spent all of them this spring to see what forms I might get from the seeds produced by the three different manners of fertilisation—all of them were long-styled like the mother-plants.[1] I have not made any other experiments about this matter and I am really sorry that I cannot send you the wanted seeds.— Perhaps it will interest you that I have experimentized last summer, besides other plants, with the flowers of Aristolochia Clematitis.[2] Sprengel has made a mistake when thinking that each flower of this species is fertilised by insects agency with its own pollen.[3] My observation have shown to me quite the contrary, for we have here a very interesting and curious case of "weiblich-männlich Dichogamia.[4] When the flower openes only the stigma is ripe, the anthers are not opened as yet and besides secured by the form of the kettle from the insect's touch. Some time after this first state of the flower the stigmatic surface besides withering is turned upwards and rolled up in a way that it cannot be touched any more, now the anthers open and can be touched by the insect because the under part of the kettle has become larger and is moved away from them. Now the hairs in the corollas mouth wither and the little flies get out, covered with pollen, to bring it now to the open stigma of a younger flower; the fertilisation with the flowers own pollen is quite impossible.

This case of dichogamie is quite different from the others known as yet, because the insect must wait in the flower the stigma of which it has fertilised, till the anthers of this same flower are opened— I hope that I shall be able to publish some thing about this matter, where the figures will make clearer this curious construction—but I fear it shall last again some time before I can sent you something about it;[5] you have seen how long the publication of my paper on Oxalis has been delayed, that was written on the end of the last year.[6]

I was very glad to see by the letter written with your own hand that you are recovered now, sending you my best wishes for your further health[7]

I remain | dear Sir | yours | truly | F Hildebrand

DAR 166: 205

CD ANNOTATIONS
1.1 I received . . . seeds.— 1.6] *crossed blue crayon*
Top of letter: 'Dichogamy Aristolochia' *blue crayon*

[1] CD's letter requesting seeds of *Oxalis rosea* has not been found, but in an earlier letter he had asked for details of Hildebrand's recent paper on *Oxalis* (Hildebrand 1866c; see letter to Friedrich Hildebrand, 22 July [1866]). Hildebrand had already informed CD that he had only been able to experiment with a single form of *O. rosea* (see letter from Friedrich Hildebrand, 11 May 1866 and n. 3). He later sent CD a copy of the paper, which included information on pollination experiments with the

long-styled form of *O. rosea*, including the amounts of seed produced by artificially self-pollinating and cross-pollinating flowers with pollen from 'upper and lower anthers'; that is, longer and shorter stamens (Hildebrand 1866c, pp. 371–4; see letter from Friedrich Hildebrand, 24 July 1866).

2 Hildebrand had given CD a brief description of his observations on *Aristolochia clematitis* in his letter of 24 July 1866.

3 Hildebrand refers to Sprengel 1793, pp. 418–29. CD first recorded reading Sprengel 1793 in 1841 (see *Correspondence* vol. 4, Appendix IV). His annotations on Christian Konrad Sprengel's comments on *Aristolochia clematitis* indicate that he was sceptical about several points in the account. For example, he questioned whether flies were really imprisoned in the flower and queried, 'Why do so few flowers, then, produce seed which he has insisted on as explained?' (annotations to Sprengel 1793, pp. 423, 425; CD's copy is in the Darwin Library–CUL; for all CD's annotations on *A. clematitis* in Sprengel 1793, see *Marginalia* 1: 777, 784–5). See also letter from Friedrich Hildebrand, 24 July, 1866.

4 The literal translation is 'female–male dichogamy'. Sprengel had used this expression to refer to the development of the pistil before the stamens (see Sprengel 1793, p. 19). Hildebrand later coined the word 'protogyny' for this condition; see Hildebrand 1867, pp. 16–17 n. 3.

5 Hildebrand reported his observations of dichogamy in *Aristolochia clematitis* in Hildebrand 1866–7a. CD's annotated copy of the article is in the Darwin Pamphlet Collection–CUL. CD referred to Hildebrand's demonstration of the cross-pollination of *Aristolochia* in *Cross and self fertilisation*, p. 417, but he did not cite the article. See also letter to Fritz Müller, [9 and] 15 April 1866 and n. 8.

6 Hildebrand had explained the delay in publication of Hildebrand 1866c in his letter of 24 July 1866.

7 CD's letter has not been found, but his earlier letter to Hildebrand of 22 July [1866] was written by an amanuensis.

To John Murray 23 October [1866][1]

Down Bromley | Kent
Oct 23rd.

My dear Sir

I asked Dr Gray to tell Messrs. Ticknor & Field that you would let them have 250 copies of New Edit. of Origin at $\frac{1}{2}$ price; but a letter from Gray has crossed mine on the road.[2] He sends the enclosed note from Messrs Ticknor, which I do not understand for I do not see what "Da & Co" means.[3] Anyhow Gray says that they are afraid of the Appletons & will not publish an edit. of my new book. You see they recommend, as does Gray that you shd send copies for the American Market.[4] But there is no hurry about this.

With respect to the Origin I do not suppose that Gray will communicate again with Messrs Ticknor & Field & it is not fair to ask him to take any more trouble. So you must do what you think best about sending copies of the Origin to some House in America.

Gray is going to review the new edit. & evidently thinks there would be some sale for it.[5] It has just occurred to me that if Gray does communicate with Messrs. Ticknor & they accept the 250 copies it would be an awkward predicament if they were sent elsewhere. You must decide what had better be done.

My dear Sir | Yours very faithfully | Ch. Darwin

Please let me hear what you decide.—

LS(A)
John Murray Archive

[1] The year is established by the relationship between this letter and the letter from Asa Gray, 10 October 1866.

[2] See letter from John Murray, 18 October [1866]. Gray had approached the Boston firm of Ticknor & Fields about publishing the fourth edition of *Origin* as well as *Variation*, but had recently informed CD that they had declined both offers (see letters from Asa Gray, 18 July 1866, 27 August 1866, and 10 October 1866).

[3] The enclosure has not been found. The reference is to D. Appleton & Co., which CD usually referred to as 'Appletons'. They were reluctant to bring out a new edition of *Origin* because of typesetting difficulties (see letter to Asa Gray, 10 September [1866] and n. 7).

[4] See letter from Asa Gray, 10 October 1866.

[5] No review by Gray of the fourth edition of *Origin* has been found.

From John Murray 25 October [1866][1]

50^A Albemarle S^t. | W.
Oct 25

My Dear Sir

Under the circumstances considering Mess. T & F's position the best course for me to pursue perhaps is to ask D Appletons Co. agent here if he is willing to take the 250 copies new Ed^n. as proposed— if not agreed to we must trust to a certain demand for single copies from the US[2]

Had I contemplated sending away 250 copies, I w^d have printed more than 1250 for this Edit^n[3]

My Dear Sir | Yours very faithfully | John Murray

I thank you for your kind & considerate letter of Oct 20[4]

Ch Darwin Esq

DAR 171: 339

[1] The year is established by the relationship between this letter and the letter to John Murray, 23 October [1866].

[2] Murray refers to the American publishing firms Ticknor & Fields and D. Appleton & Co. CD had conveyed Asa Gray's advice that Murray send copies of the fourth edition of *Origin* for the American market (see letter to John Murray, 23 October [1866] and n. 2).

[3] According to the publisher's ledger, 1500 copies of the fourth edition of *Origin* were printed (see Peckham ed. 1959, p. 776).

[4] No letter from CD bearing this date has been found.

From E. Schweizerbart'sche Verlagsbuchhandlung[1] 26 October 1866

Stuttgart
den 26 October 1866.

Verehrtester Herr!

Seit ich das letztemal an Sie geschrieben habe, ist eine geraume Zeit vergangen, während welcher Sie so gütig waren mir nach und nach die Bogen der neuen Auflage Ihres Origin zu senden.[2]

Sie wissen dass die traurige Zeit des deutschen Krieges nicht geeignet war zu literarischen Unternehmungen;[3] dem ungeachtet habe ich die neue Auflage nicht ausser Acht gelassen, sondern mich, nachdem Herr Prof. Geinitz und Herr Prof Leonhard der Aufgabe nicht sich zu unterziehen meinten, auf Empfehlung des Ersteren an Herrn Prof. Dr Victor Carus in Leipzig gewendet.[4]

Ich habe die grosse Befriedigung Ihnen anzeigen zu können daß derselbe aufs Bereitwilligste meinen Antrag angenomen hat und sich wegen der Sache sich mit Ihnen in brieflichen Verkehr setzen wird;[5] einstweilen sandte ich ihm das Exemplar Ihres Werkes welches ich von Ihnen erhalten habe, dazu 1 Ex der deutschen Ausgabe.[6] Nach allem was mir Herr Carus schreibt ist er ganz der rechte Mann für das Buch; er behält sich ganze Freiheit vor von den Anmerkungen des Herrn Bronn wegzulassen was er selbst nicht wissenschaftlich vertreten könne;[7] Hr Carus ist ein erklärter Anhänger Ihrer Theorie und will seinerseits solche durch allgemein physikälisch-physiologische Gründe zu stützen und zu bekräftigen versuchen. H^r^ Carus wird sich selbst brieflich an Sie wenden; ich dachte aber Ihnen diese Mittheilung gleich machen zu müssen, damit Sie wissen wie es damit steht.

Indem ich Ihnen nochmals meinen Dank sage für all die Freundlichkeit der ich mich von Ihnen zu erfreuen hatte bin ich mit größter Hochachtung und Verehrung

Ihr ergebenster
E Schweizerbart

DAR 177: 73

CD ANNOTATIONS
2.5 Herrn . . . Leipzig] *double scored pencil*
Top of letter: 'Note on Hybrid Chapter'[8] *pencil*

[1] For a translation of this letter, see Appendix I. It was written by Christian Friedrich Schweizerbart, the head of E. Schweizerbart'sche Verlagsbuchhandlung, who used the signature E. Schweizerbart in business communications.

[2] See letter from E. Schweizerbart'sche Verlagsbuchhandlung, 10 May 1866. Page proofs of the fourth edition of *Origin* were available by mid-July 1866 (see letter to John Murray, 15 July [1866]).

[3] The reference is to the Austro-Prussian War. Stuttgart, where the Schweizerbart firm was located, was the capital of Württemberg, one of the German states that sided with Austria (see letter from E. Schweizerbart'sche Verlagsbuchhandlung, 10 May 1866 and n. 5).

[4] Schweizerbart had originally approached Gustav von Leonhard to supervise the third German edition of *Origin*, but he declined, recommending Hans Bruno Geinitz as his replacement. Geinitz also declined but suggested that Julius Victor Carus would be well qualified for the job (see letter from E. Schweizerbart'sche Verlagsbuchhandlung, 10 May 1866).

[5] See letter from J. V. Carus, 7 November 1866.

[6] Schweizerbart refers to *Origin* 4th ed. and Bronn trans. 1863.

[7] For more on Heinrich Georg Bronn's annotations to the German translation of *Origin*, see the letter from J. V. Carus, 7 November 1866.

[8] CD's annotation refers to a note added to the chapter on hybridism in the second German edition of *Origin* (Bronn trans. 1863, p. 274 n.; see letter to J. V. Carus, 10 November 1866).

From Rudolf Oldenbourg 28 October 1866

Munich | Bavaria
28th. October 1866.

Dear Sir!

I hope you will excuse the liberty I take in writing this letter to you, which, I am afraid, will come too late reach its purpose.

I read in the papers, that your work "domesticated animals and cultivated plants" is just out,[1] and I wish to publish a german translation of it through my house (firm: Cotta & Coy. in Stuttgart, and Munich),[2] if you have not allready disposed of such a translation, what I allmost must guess through a letter, which you wrote in June to my friend Professor Nägeli.[3]

I thought, to have the translation to be done by Dr. Peschel, the author of some works of best repute (Geschichte der Erdkunde),[4] if you would give your consent to such a plan.

Being for many years a personal admirer of your studies, I had reason to regret, that the german translations of your works, untill now, allways fell into hands, which were not quite fit for it, though the translators were respectable men.

I recollect, that when 12 years ago I read your journey in South America, translated by Dieffenbach, I could not help smiling at the remarquable awkwardness of poor Mr. Dieffenbach's translation, who in a life of travel-toil had forgot his german.[5] More serious are the insufficiencies of Mr. Bronn's translation of your "origin" because they have actually caused misunderstandings and doubts, which could be removed only by those, who were able to recur to the English original[6]

Your friend Prof Huxley was much better introduced into the german world, and my sincere wish would be to give your eminent productions a german garment equally worthy of their great merits.[7]

As to the respectability of my house you will easily get information in any of the foreign bookselling-houses in London, Messrs Williams and Norgate or Duleau.[8]

I am, dear Sir, | your most obedt. servant | R. Oldenbourg

Prof Nägeli told me yesterday that he was going to write to you in a few days[9]

Charles Darwin Esqr. | Down | Bromley | Kent S.E.

DAR 173: 12

CD ANNOTATION

On verso: 'Oldenbourg on Translation of Domestic Animals' *ink*

[1] The reference is to *Variation*, which was not published until January 1868. CD's publisher had advertised the book as forthcoming as early as April 1865 (*Reader*, 15 April 1865, p. 427). The book was also advertised in the 1 August 1865 issue of the *Publishers' Circular*, p. 386, under the title: 'Domesticated Animals and Cultivated Plants, or the Principles of Variation, Inheritance, Reversion, Crossing, Interbreeding, and Selection under Domestication'.

[2] Oldenbourg was the business manager for the Munich branch of the firm J. G. Cotta'schen Buchhandlung (Bosl ed. 1983). The German edition of *Variation* (Carus trans. 1868) was published by E. Schweizerbart'sche Verlagsbuchhandlung.

[3] The reference is to Carl Wilhelm von Nägeli, who was professor of botany at Munich. CD had written to Nägeli on 12 June [1866] to praise his paper on the origin and concept of species (Nägeli 1865). He told Nägeli that the fourth edition of *Origin* would be translated into German but did not mention *Variation*.

[4] Oldenbourg refers to Oscar Ferdinand Peschel and Peschel 1865.

[5] The reference is to Ernst Dieffenbach and Dieffenbach trans. 1844.

[6] For more criticisms of Heinrich Georg Bronn's translations of *Origin* (Bronn trans. 1860 and Bronn trans. 1863), see the letters from Rudolf Suchsland, 16 March 1866 and 2 April 1866.

[7] Thomas Henry Huxley's book, *Evidence as to man's place in nature* (T. H. Huxley 1863a) had been translated into German by Julius Victor Carus (Carus trans. 1863). Carl Vogt translated *On our knowledge of the causes of the phenomena of organic nature* (T. H. Huxley 1863b; Vogt trans. 1865).

[8] The booksellers and publishers Williams & Norgate specialised in foreign scientific literature, with premises at Covent Garden, London, and South Frederick Street, Edinburgh. Dulau & Co., who specialised in foreign language books, had premises at 37 Soho Square, London (*Publishers' Circular* 1866).

[9] No letter from Nägeli to CD from this period has been found.

From Mary Somerville 30 October 1866

La Spezia Piemonte
30th Octr 1866

Dear Mr Darwin

I beg of you to accept my very sincere thanks for your kindness in granting me permission to make use of the illustrations in your admirable work on the Orchids,[1] which I have taken the liberty to refer to very extensively in a sketch on the present state of microscopic science which I have just finished[2]

Believe me | very gratefully yours | Mary Somerville

DAR 177: 217

[1] Somerville refers to *Orchids*. In a letter to M. E. Lyell, [19? October 1866], CD had indicated his approval of Somerville's request, but pointed out that permission to use the illustrations had to be obtained from the publisher John Murray, who owned the woodcuts.

[2] The reference is to Somerville 1869 (see letter to M. E. Lyell, [19? October 1866] and n. 2).

To Thomas Laxton 31 October [1866][1]

Down. | Bromley Kent.
Oct 31.

Dear Sir.

The Box arrived safe this evening I have not yet opened it— I will never open 2 parcels at the same time. or if I ever do it shall be on *separate* tables., so you may rely on the seeds not getting mixed.— I am most grateful for the confidence you place in me by allowing me to look at your collection, which fairly astonishes me from the amount of labour which must have been bestowed on so many crosses.—[2] I will consider your generous offer of keeping certain peas;[3] but I certainly shall want very few & possibly none, for it is not at present the character of the full grown offspring, only certain points in germination which interest me.[4] But I shall be able to judge best after examining the Peas—

I am delighted at the opportunity of seeing so many crosses

With cordial thanks— In haste | Yours very faithfully. | Ch. Darwin.

I will keep the Box only for a few days or a week at most & will advise you when despatched.

P.S. | I have not expressed myself half strong enough. It must have cost you much time & trouble to have so kindly selected all these pods & their parents.

All that I can say is, is that as far ⟨as⟩ interest in the subject goes, your trouble & kindness have not been thrown away.

Copy
DAR 146: 35

[1] The year is established by the relationship between this letter and the letter to J. D. Hooker, 2 October [1866].
[2] Laxton evidently sent CD the entire collection of seeds of pea varieties with which he had experimented. He had already sent CD some specimens of pods and seeds of a cross between the sugar pea and the purple-pod pea (see letter to J. D. Hooker, 2 October [1866] and n. 7).
[3] The letter from Laxton in which he made this offer has not been found.
[4] CD had mentioned to Joseph Dalton Hooker that Laxton's results with crosses between the sugar pea and the purple-pod pea showed the direct action of pollen on the mother plant, and thus seemed to support the theory of pangenesis (see letter to J. D. Hooker, 2 October [1866] and n. 9).

From Frances Harriet Hooker 1 November [1866][1]

My dear Mr. Darwin

In case you do not see "Notes & Queries", I cannot help sending you this paragraph from this week's No.[2]

"It is not generally known that the views on the development of life, which have been made popular by Mr. Darwin's work on the Origin of Species, are entirely due to his grandfather, Dr. Darwin. For proof of this see "A sketch of the Life & works of Erasmus Darwin", published by Lewis, 136, Gower St."— —[3]

Honour to whom honour is due!—[4]

Joseph seems to have enjoyed his stay at Lord Lovelace's pretty place in Somerset very much—[5] he is now at Pembroke Dock, with Dr. Lyall—[6]

Your two foreigners made their appearance with your letter of introduction one day this week— of course they were disappointed of seeing Joseph—[7]

With kind love to Mrs. Darwin & your daughters,[8] | believe me | Yours affectly. | F H Hooker

Kew. W.
Novr. 1.

DAR 104: 242–3

[1] The year is established by the reference to the article in *Notes and Queries* (see n. 2, below).
[2] The reference is to an article discussing the date of Erasmus Darwin's death, signed 'D.', that appeared in the 27 October 1866 issue of *Notes and Queries*, pp. 343–4.
[3] The writer refers to Dowson 1861. CD's views on descent are compared with those of Erasmus Darwin on pp. 35–7.
[4] Rom. 13: 1–7.
[5] The references are to Joseph Dalton Hooker, William King-Noel (first Earl Lovelace), and the Lovelace estate of Ashley Combe in Somerset (see Woolley 1999, p. 171).
[6] Pembroke Dock, a town on the Cleddau river in west Wales, had a government dockyard where ships were built for the Royal Navy. David Lyall had served with Hooker on the Antarctic expedition of 1839 to 1843 (R. Desmond 1994).
[7] CD had given Ernst Haeckel a letter of introduction to Hooker (see letter to J. D. Hooker, [21 October 1866]). Haeckel's companion was probably the German zoologist, Richard Greeff, who accompanied Haeckel to Lisbon on his way to Madeira (Krauße 1987, p. 77).
[8] Emma Darwin, Henrietta Emma Darwin, and Elizabeth Darwin.

To J. D. Hooker 1 November [1866]

Down
Nov 1

My dear Hooker

The trees are planted & look very well, but I write now to say that I have despatched carr. p^{d} to London the two empty hampers & 2 mats, which my gardener says are well worth returning.[1] What success have you had with Euryiale or any other water lily?[2] please remember that I sh^{d} like to have the pods to count, weigh, & germinate some of the seeds of the crossed & uncrossed pods. But how to germinate them I sh^{d} much wish to know. The main quantity of seed c^{d} be returned if desired.

Did Hæckel call on you? if so I hope he did not bore much. He is a very nice fellow & a first-rate zoologist but talks atrocious English.[3]

My dear Hooker | ever yours | Ch Darwin

Endorsement: '/66'
LS
DAR 115: 304

[1] Hooker had recently sent trees and shrubs for CD's lawn (see letter from J. D. Hooker, 19 October 1866 and n. 1).
[2] CD became interested in *Euryale ferox*, a large waterlily, when Robert Caspary mentioned it as an example of a plant that was perpetually self-pollinating, but that maintained its vigour over numerous generations (Caspary 1865b, p. 20; see letter from Robert Caspary, 25 February 1866 and nn. 3 and 13). CD asked William Robinson, foreman of the herbaceous department at the Royal Botanic Society, Regent's Park, London, to perform crossing experiments with *Euryale ferox* to see whether crossing had an effect on the fertility of the plant (see letter to William Robinson, [29 April 1866]).
[3] CD had given Ernst Haeckel a letter of introduction to Hooker after Haeckel had visited Down House (see letter to J. D. Hooker, [21 October 1866]). In an entertaining account of that visit, Henrietta Emma Darwin told her brother George Howard Darwin that Haeckel 'could stumble on very decently' in English, adding a few examples of his idiosyncratic usage, such as his comment on

dining in London, 'I like a good bit of flesh at a restoration' (letter from H. E. Darwin to G. H. Darwin, [22 October 1866] (DAR 245: 269)).

From Fritz Müller [2 November 1866][1]

I alluded in one of my letters to the sterility of Eschscholtzia and some other plants, when fertilized with pollen from the same individual plant.[2] I have at present in my garden one old large plant of Eschscholtzia, which for about six weeks is producing a large number of flowers, (just now I had them counted by my children, who tell me, there are to day 103), without yielding a single seed capsule. The stigmas of all the flowers, I examined, were covered with pollen-grains, which emitted their tubes; but never the tubes appeared to enter deeply the tissue of the stigmas.— Yesterday expanded the first flower of the present year"s seedlings; I fertilized with its pollen two of the old plants flowers, and the seedlings flower with the old plants pollen, and now (24 hours after fertilization) I see, that the stigmas of these three crossed flowers behave very differently from those of all others; the stigmas of the latter (A) are diverging in a more or less horizontal direction, those ⟨of the f⟩ormer (B) have become erected, ⟨*4 or 5 words missing*⟩ ⟨ ⟩ered.—

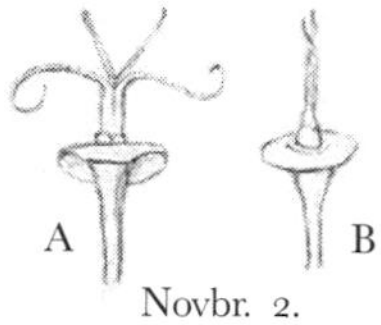

A B
Novbr. 2.

I fertilized also numerous ⟨*4 or 5 words missing*⟩ with pollinia from the same ⟨*4 or 5 words missing*⟩ a single seed-capsule. On the ⟨*3 or 4 words missing*⟩ ⟨fer⟩tilized with the very same flowers pollinia is yielding a seed-capsule.

During the last month I have been very fortunate in enlarging the list of our dimorphic plants,—adding once in half an hour four new species (Cordia, Oxalis, Hedyotis Villarsia).

But before passing to the new species, allow me some more remarks on the dimorphic Oxalis, of which I told you in my last letter.[3] How could this species by natural selection arrive to the extremely miserable estate of its male reproductive system, the anthers of one form being in most cases perfectly steril, while those of the other form also contain much aborted pollen? Perhaps the question might be answered in the following way: The plant producing an uncommonly large number of bulbilli, natural selection might have been less severe regarding the sexual reproduction. The anthers of the one form, one set of which equals in length the pistils, might have been rendered steril by natural selection, to prevent self-fertilization. (Thus, for instance, in some Malpighiaceae those anthers, which would be able to fertilize without the intervention of insects, the own flowers stigmas, have become barren).[4] Lastly the partial barrenness of the anthers of the other form might have been inherited from the form with barren anthers. I feel not quite sure, whether this answer will do.— At all events the plant will offer far more difficulty to those who look at species as *perfect* productions of a supreme intelligence.

Now to the recently found dimorphic plants of our flora. ⟨*diagram excised*⟩

1, a second of *Cordia*.[5]

2, a frutescent *Oxalis* (alread⟨y⟩ alluded to in my last letter).[6] The species is probably trimorphic. I observed but two plants, growing close together, one being long-styled and the other short-styled, both yielding plenty of seed-capsules.

3, a *Plumbago*, from the continent. I saw but two plants, from which I brought home about half a dozen of long-styled and as many short-styled ears. These continued to yield fresh flowers for about a week. The length of the styli of the long-styled form ⟨*4 or 5 words missing*⟩ ⟨v⟩ariable, while in the short-sty⟨led⟩ ⟨*4 or 5 words missing*⟩ ⟨s⟩tigmas & each is rather variable. ⟨*4 or 5 words missing*⟩ ⟨s⟩ame level with the anthers; but ⟨*4 or 5 words missing*⟩ ⟨rea⟩ch even to their bases, while in other cases they project beyond the anthers, but never so far as the stigmas of the long-styled flowers do. There is no difficulty in distinguishing the two forms. I may add, that a Plumbago with pale-blue flowers is frequently to be met with in the gardens of Desterro; this is always pro⟨pag⟩ated by cuttings and never seeds here (as far as ⟨*three quarters of page missing*⟩

6, a small *Hedyotis*. The pollen-grains are larger in the short-styled form.[7] ⟨*diagram excised*⟩

Villarsia is, as you know, an aquatic plant; the *Hedyotis* grows in wet sand near the edge of small fresh-water pools.[8] Both the dimorphic and trimorphic *Oxalis* are preferring humid places, whereas our monomorphic *Oxalis* is to be found even in so dry and barren places as the fissures of a naked rock. All this confirms the view, you suggested, of aquatic and marsh-plants being more liable, than others, to dimorphism.[9]

⟨*three quarters of page missing*⟩

Als ich heute einen Franzosen, Herrn Hippolyte Gautier, besuchte, der Orchideen zum Verkauf sammelt, sah ich in seinem Garten eine schöne blaue Ipomoea.[10] Er erzählte mir, er habe eine einzige Pflanze gezogen aus Samenkörnern, die er aus den nördlichen Provinzen Brasiliens erhalten hätte; diese Pflanze blühte einige Jahre schon sehr reichlich und brachte Blumen in grosser Zahl fast das ganze Jahr hindurch, ohne jedoch Samenkapseln zu liefern. Ich dachte natürlich, die Pflanze möchte dimorph sein, und fand bei Untersuchung der Blumen, dass der Griffel weit über die Ebene der Staubgefässe hinausragte.[11] Wir haben hier, auf dem Festlande, eine nahe verwandte Art, welche ich vielleicht nächsten Monat untersuchen kann.

Bei der Untersuchung der dimorphen Blumen unseres gemeinen Erythroxylon ("Fruta de pomba") war ich überrascht von der Verschiedenheit, welche ein kurzgriffliger Baum in den einzelnen Blüthentheilen darbot.[12]

Unter 253 Blumen dieses Baumes hatten:

5	sepala,	5	petala,	10	stamina,	3	styli,	192	Blumen	
5	"	6	"	10	"	3	"	1	"	1)
6	"	6	"	10	"	3	"	3	"	
6	"	6	"	11	"	3	"	3	"	
6	"	6	"	12	"	3	"	20	"	
6	"	6	"	12	"	3–4	"	1	"	2)
6	"	6	"	12	"	4	"	25	"	
6	"	7	"	12	"	3	"	1	"	
6	"	7	"	13	"	4	"	1	"	
6	"	7	"	14	"	3	"	1	"	
7	"	7	"	12	"	3	"	1	"	
7	"	7	"	12	"	4	"	1	"	
7	"	7	"	14	"	3	"	1	"	
7	"	7	"	14	"	3–4	"	1	"	2)
7	"	7	"	14	"	4	"	2	"	

1) Eines der sepala war an der Spitze gekerbt.

2) Einer der drei styli war doppelt so dick als jeder der beiden andern und mit einem zweilappigen stigma versehen.

Von den Blumen mit vier Griffeln hatten zehn zwei Ovula. Unter zahlreichen Blumen von anderen kurz- und langgriffligen Bäumen fand ich nur eine einzige kurzgrifflige mit sechs Kelch-, sechs Blumenblättern, zehn Staubfäden und drei Griffeln und eine langgrifflige mit 4 Kelch-, 4 Kronenblättern, 8 Staubgefässen, 4 Griffeln und *keinem* Ovulum.

Aber ich fürchte, Ihre Geduld schon erschöpft zu haben und will schliessen und einen Fall von merkwürdiger Veränderlichkeit des Kelches, den ich bei einer Hillia beobachtete, für einen andren Brief versparen.[13]

Erlauben Sie, dass ich Ihnen noch einmal herzlich für Ihren freundlichen Brief und die "Origin" danke,[14] und glauben Sie, dass ich, werther Herr, mit aufrichtiger Hochachtung treulichst der Ihrige bin | Fritz Müller.

P. S. Habe ich Ihnen schon mitgetheilt, dass ich einen unterirdischen Käfer fand, dem die Tarsen an allen Füssen fehlen?

AL incomplete
DAR 111: B59, DAR 142: 100, 101, 105, Möller ed. 1915–21, 2: 93–4

CD ANNOTATIONS
1.1 I alluded . . . Villarsia). 2.3] *crossed blue crayon*
2.1 During . . . Villarsia). 2.3] *crossed pencil*
3.1 But before . . . Oxalis, 3.2] 'Oxalis' *added blue crayon*
3.12 Lastly . . . anthers. 3.13] '*[*Plumbag*]*' *in margin pencil*
3.15 supreme intelligence. 3.16] ']' *added after, blue crayon*
7.1 3, . . . week. 7.3] *crossed pencil*; 'next Famy to Primulaceæ'[15] *added ink*
7.4 ⟨v⟩ariable . . . far as 7.10] *crossed blue crayon*
8.1 6, a small *Hedyotis*.] 'Pontederia aquatica'[16] *added above, ink*

9.1 *Villarsia* ... dimorphism. 9.6] *scored red crayon*; 'Keep' *added blue crayon*
Top of letter: 'Fritz Muller Nov. 2^d^—1866.'
on cover: 'Fritz Muller. Letter of Nov. 2^d^. 1866' *ink, crossed blue crayon*; 'Oxalis with imperfect anthers.' *ink, circled red crayon*; '*Escholtzia* self-sterile' *ink, crossed pencil and blue crayon*: '*Dimorphic, Plumbago Findlaya*[17] [*interl*] *Cordia*— Erythroxylum—(Sethia is sub-genus)[18] Villarsia. allied to Menyanthes Hedyotis, Cinchonaceæ Gesneria??'[19] *ink, crossed blue crayon*; 'Dimorphic Portfolio'[20] *pencil, crossed blue crayon*

[1] The date is established by CD's annotations at the top of the letter and on the envelope in which part of it was found. The letter contained specimens attached to the page at various places. Some of these were cut out by CD, probably to be added to his 'Dimorphic Portfolio', and have not been found (see n. 20, below). The letter text has been reconstructed from more than one source. The text in German is transcribed from Möller ed. 1915–21, 2: 93–4, Alfred Möller having translated the original English fragment, which has not been found. For an account of the reconstruction of Müller's letters to CD, see the letter from Fritz Müller, 13 February 1866, n. 1. Möller dated this fragment of the letter 1 October 1866, but CD's annotations as well as his reply of [late December 1866 and] 1 January 1867 refer to items mentioned only in this part of the letter (see n. 11, below). For a translation of the German portion of the letter, see Appendix I.

[2] See letter from Fritz Müller, 2 August 1866.

[3] See letter from Fritz Müller, 1 and 3 October 1866 and nn. 2–6.

[4] In the family Malpighiaceae the presence of sterile as well as fertile stamens is common (Mabberley 1997).

[5] Müller had sent CD specimens of two forms of another species of *Cordia* (see the letter from Fritz Müller, 1 and 3 October 1866 and n. 9). CD discussed *Cordia* in *Forms of flowers*, pp. 117–18, 253.

[6] Frutescent: 'having the appearance or habit of a shrub' (*OED*). Müller enclosed pressed specimens of both long-styled and short-styled forms of *Oxalis* with this letter (DAR 142: 100 v.). He had mentioned his intention of examining an *Oxalis* with a woody stem in his letter of 1 and 3 October 1866.

[7] CD had recently expressed the view that the pollen-grains from longer stamens in the short-styled forms of a wide variety of dimorphic plants usually were the largest (see letter to W. E. Darwin, 22 June [1866] and nn. 5 and 6). In *Forms of flowers*, pp. 249–54, CD discussed the relative size of pollen-grains in several heterostyled species.

[8] In *Forms of flowers*, pp. 116, 133, CD discussed *Villarsia* and *Hedyotis* specimens that he received from Müller.

[9] See letter to Fritz Müller, 23 May 1866 and n. 13.

[10] This section of the letter, published in Möller ed. 1915–21, 2: 93–4, was dated 1 October 1866 by Möller, but is clearly part of the present letter (see n. 1, above). Hippolyte Gautier has not been further identified.

[11] In his reply to Müller of [late December 1866 and] 1 January 1867, CD referred to Müller's observation of evidence for dimorphism in *Ipomoea*, calling it *Convolvulus* (in *Cross and self fertilisation*, p. 28, CD stated that in England *Ipomoea purpurea* was often called *Convolvulus major*).

[12] 'Fruta de pomba': fruit of the dove (Portuguese). In *Forms of flowers*, pp. 121–2, CD referred to the dried flowers of *Erythroxylum* (*Erythroxylon* was an alternative spelling) and included a sketch of the two forms that Müller had sent him. He also noted Müller's observations on the variation in the number of flower parts.

[13] The observations on *Hillia* are in the letter from Fritz Müller, 1 December 1866.

[14] See letter to Fritz Müller, 23 August [1866]. According to Müller's endorsement, he received the letter on 25 October 1866; in a letter to his brother Hermann Müller of 29 October 1866, he mentioned having just received a copy of the fourth edition of *Origin* (see Möller ed. 1915–21, 2: 95). CD's publisher, John Murray, had agreed to send out some copies before the general release of the new edition in mid-November 1866 (see letter from John Murray, 23 July [1866]).

[15] In John Lindley's classificatory arrangement, the family Primulaceae is adjacent to the family Plumbaginaceae (see Lindley 1853, p. 641).

[16] The section of the letter containing the reference to *Pontederia aquatica* has not been found. Most of the fourth page is missing. Müller's findings on *Pontederia*, collected over the next five years, were mentioned in *Forms of flowers*, pp. 183–6.
[17] The genus *Findlaya* was placed in the family Primulaceae by Lindley (see Lindley 1853, p. 646), but is now placed in the Plumbaginaceae.
[18] *Sethia* is now subsumed within *Erythroxylum*. CD's remarks on heterostyly in *Sethia* are in *Forms of flowers*, p. 122.
[19] Müller's remarks on *Gesneria* were contained in a now missing part of the letter, but see the letter to Fritz Müller, [late December 1866 and] 1 January 1867 and n. 8.
[20] The annotation refers to a portfolio of notes on dimorphism where CD may have kept specimens and sections of the letter that he cut out. CD kept a number of such portfolios, amassed over a long period of time and since dispersed. The likely contents of some portfolios were reconstructed when some of CD's papers were catalogued in 1932 (see DAR 220: 13), but part of that material has since been lost. Some of CD's extant notes on dimorphism are in DAR 108–11, including one fragment of this letter. A list of species, including representatives of many genera mentioned in this letter and containing information on relative pollen-grain sizes of long-styled and short-styled forms is in DAR 111: 34.

From Herbert Spencer 2 November 1866

37 Queen's Gardens | Bayswater W.
2 Nov 66

Dear M^r. Darwin

I was glad to hear from Miss Darwin on Saturday last that your sympathies are with us in the Eyre prosecution matter.[1] We want to have as weighty a list of names as we can. Will you let us add yours to the selected list I send herewith.[2] Your signature will not involve any active part. On this understanding Huxley has given us his— I inclose a capital letter he has just published[3]

very truly yours | Herbert Spencer

DAR 177: 226

[1] Spencer refers to Henrietta Emma Darwin and to the Jamaica Committee, which was formed in December 1865 to lobby for the criminal prosecution of the former colonial governor Edward John Eyre for his actions in suppressing an uprising of the ex-slave population in Jamaica. An opposing Eyre Defence Committee was formed in August 1866, and both sides in the controversy sought the support of prominent individuals (see Semmel 1962, pp. 62–5, 105 ff.).
[2] The list has not been found.
[3] The copy of Thomas Henry Huxley's letter has not been found. The letter appeared in the *Pall Mall Gazette*, 31 October 1866, p. 3 (the text of the letter is reproduced in L. Huxley ed. 1900, 1: 279–81). Huxley had written in response to an editorial comment in the paper that suggested that his 'peculiar views on the development of species' inclined him to treat 'the negro' as well as 'the ape' as a brother (*Pall Mall Gazette*, 29 October 1866, p. 9, and L. Huxley ed. 1900, 1: 279).

From J. D. Hooker 3 November 1866

Pembroke Dock
Nov 3/66.

Dear Darwin

I am here on a short visit to my old Antarctic companion Dr Lyall, who is married & settled here—[1] I return to Kew on Tuesday—

My wife tells me that Mr Haeckel called in my absence, I am sorry for it, as I should have much liked to make his acquaintance.[2]

I left such stringent *written* orders about the Euryale seeds that I cannot but hope they are carried out faithfully & will see when I get back:[3] but the labor & difficulty I experience in getting anything scientifically done by practical men is untold.

I called yesterday on Mr Henry Wedgwood, but found him ill in bed I am sorry to say— I had the pleasure of seeing Mrs Wedgwood & her daus.[4] They have a lovely view from their windows: the only pretty one I have seen in this neighbourhood

How odd Huxley joining the Eyre prosecution fund— I suppose you approve—[5] I have no notion of kicking a poor devil when he is down, & as to *principles* they are fiddle sticks under such circumstances of mismanagement. The nation tacitly submits to have Governors made of heaven born politicians; Geograph. Soc: Lions,[6] & nine days wonders, & when the poor devils make a mess of it (which they are sure to do when difficulty arises) we persecute them *on principle*.—

Euryale germinates promptly in a pan of mud placed in a warm place, inside your *Nepenthes-hutch* should suit it I would say.[7]

Ever yr affec | J D Hooker

I think I told you that the Treasury have agreed to put in a vote next year for purchase of my fathers Herb^{m}. books, mss, portraits &c &c—£7000 in all.[8]

DAR 102: 110–11

CD ANNOTATIONS

5.1 How odd . . . fund—] *scored pencil*

6.1 Euryale . . . would say. 6.2] 'Drosera'[9] *added pencil*

End of letter: 'Pangenesis'[10] *pencil*

[1] The reference is to David Lyall (see letter from Frances Harriet Hooker, 1 November [1866] and n. 6).

[2] Hooker refers to Ernst Haeckel (see letter from Frances Harriet Hooker, 1 November [1866] and n. 7).

[3] CD had asked Hooker for pods of *Euryale* or any waterlily for his experiments on cross and self-pollination (see letter to J. D. Hooker, 1 November [1866] and n. 2).

[4] Jessie and Henry Allen Wedgwood had three daughters, Louisa Frances, Caroline, and Anne Jane (Freeman 1978).

[5] Thomas Henry Huxley was a member of the Jamaica Committee, which sought to have Edward John Eyre prosecuted for his role in the suppression of an uprising of the ex-slave population (see letter from Herbert Spencer, 2 November 1866 and n. 1; for more on Huxley's participation, see A. Desmond 1994–7, 1: 351–4).

[6] Eyre was elected a fellow of the Royal Geographical Society in 1857 (*Journal of the Royal Geographical Society* 27 (1857): xii). On Hooker's dislike of the practice of societies like the Geographical of 'lionising' individuals, see L. Huxley ed. 1918, 1: 405–7.

[7] CD had experimented with *Nepenthes*, a tropical genus of pitcher plant, for 'Climbing plants'. He initially had trouble growing the specimens (see, for example, *Correspondence* vol. 11, letter to J. D. Hooker, 5 March [1863]) and may have set aside a special area in his hothouse, but no other reference to a 'Nepenthes hutch' has been found.

[8] See letter from J. D. Hooker, 19 October 1866 and n. 5.

[9] Hooker had recently sent a specimen of *Drosera binata* to CD (see letter from J. D. Hooker, 28 September 1866, n. 1). The annotation may refer to the location in CD's hothouse where he planned to put the *Euryale*, since the plants required similar conditions.

[10] CD and Hooker had corresponded on the topic of pangenesis earlier in the year (see letter to J. D. Hooker, 4 April [1866], and letter from J. D. Hooker, [6 April 1866] and nn. 4 and 5).

To Thomas Laxton 3 November [1866][1]

Down. | Bromley. | Kent. S.E.
Nov 3.—

Dear Sir

I have spent some hours during the last few days in examining with the greatest possible interest your Peas.[2] After all, I could not resist your very kind offer, & have kept one pea out of the packets marked 7. 10. 11. 12. 13. & the purple pea N°. 14. I never saw anything more curious than the lots 12 & 13. Will you have the kindness to look at the pod of N°. 13, & you will see that the rim close to the suture is red; pray tell me whether you think this has been caused by the pollen of the purple pod.—[3] These two cases & that of the purple pea are truly wonderful; the others are less striking But I observe in lot 1 (except one pea) & in a lesser degree in 2, & in 3. 5. 6. & 8 that the crossed peas are smooth like the paternal stock, & not wrinkled & cubical like the mother pea— Can this loss of wrinkling be due to mere variation, or to the effect of some peculiar culture, or is it the direct result of the pollen of the father? I should be grateful for an answer on this head— I know I am rather unreasonable, but I should be very much obliged if you would write a single word in answer to 3 queries on the enclosed paper.[4]

You ask me to return some peas next season; but I had intended planting them at once as I want now to observe some points in their growth; I should keep them in the greenhouse, but whether they would seed there I do not know. Hence if you are anxious about the product I must delay my observations & I will not sow till I hear again from you, I will take care that no one gets any seed if my plants seed.—[5] I shall send a servant to London on Wed mg. & he shall that day book & pay carriage for the box to Stamford—[6] I will enclose your list in it— Pray accept my *cordial* thanks for your very great kindness—

Dear Sir | Yours faithfully & obliged | Charles Darwin

P.S. Many thanks for your answer about the Gooseberry.[7]

Copy
DAR 146: 36

[1] The year is established by the relationship between this letter and the letter to Thomas Laxton, 31 October [1866].

[2] See letter to Thomas Laxton, 31 October [1866] and n. 2.

[3] CD was looking for evidence of direct action of the male parent on the female parent in crossing experiments to support his hypothesis of pangenesis (see letter to J. D. Hooker, 2 October [1866] and nn. 7 and 9).

[4] The enclosure has not been found.

[5] Laxton's own experiments crossing different varieties of peas were made in order to develop new varieties for sale.
[6] Laxton's home address was St Mary Hill, Stamford, Lincolnshire (*Post Office directory of Lincolnshire* 1868).
[7] CD and Laxton's correspondence on the gooseberry has not been found, but see *Variation* 1: 376.

From James Scott Bowerbank [4 November 1866?][1]

2 East Ascent | St Leonards on S⟨ea⟩

My Dear Sir

I have sent back th⟨e⟩ Proof to the Printer with insertion of your name as you suggested.[2]

I have long wanted some slight stimulus to induce me to write to you, on one or two little facts in natural history that may interest you.

1st. When a Boy of 14 while on a visit at Ightham Court Lodge in Kent I chanced to see a litter of Puppies under a Pointer Bitch & was much surprised to find half had all the characters of Pointers ⟨wh⟩ile the remainder had ⟨eve⟩ry appearance of Setters ⟨A⟩t my expressing my surprise to the old Huntsman that ⟨i⟩t should be the case he ⟨ex⟩plained it by saying that ⟨t⟩he Father was a Setter an ⟨ac⟩cidental mis-alliance Well then said I how is it that they are not mongrels a⟨n⟩d he told me that if they had been low bred dogs such would have been the case but that with pure Breeds mismatched it was often as I saw it. & he moreover assured me that each puppy as it grew up would follow the instincts indicated by ⟨its⟩ appearance.

2nd. Some years since o⟨ur⟩ Housekeeper at Sun ⟨Street⟩ London[3] had a little hairless Barbary B⟨itch⟩ who never had had puppies. When she went to heat I ⟨com⟩menced a negociation with a man in Covent garden who had a Dog of ⟨the⟩ same species but while I was negociating our Young Dog a mongrel Spaniel with long brown hair was operating & so the negociation became useless, and in due course there came a litter of 5 puppies. Who all died before they were ⟨ ⟩ months old. 3 of these ⟨pu⟩ppies were black & hairless ⟨like the⟩ Mother & the other ⟨2 were⟩ covered with *short* ⟨brown⟩ hair like the Father ⟨in⟩ colour. The Bitch had ⟨a⟩ second Litter of puppies but this time we secured ⟨the⟩ right Father a regular black thorough Bred Barbary dog, but alas the mischeif had been implanted in the mother and again about half the litter looked like pure Barbarys & the other half like the short haired progeny of the first Father Again all of the puppies died but one, a short brown haired dog which lived to be 2 years old

AL incomplete
DAR 160: 261

CD ANNOTATIONS
1.1 I have ... years old 4.13] *crossed pencil*
Top of first page: 'J. S. Bowerbank | Ch. on Crossing | Effects of 1st Cross on subsequent *[illeg]* | Nov. 4 186⟨ ⟩' *pencil*; 'Ch IX'[4] *brown crayon*

[1] The year is conjectured from Bowerbank's address and the reference to the insertion of CD's name in a page-proof (see n. 2, below). Bowerbank moved from London to St Leonard's-on-Sea between

January and November 1864 (*Palæontographical Society* 18 (1864), 19 (1865), *List of the Geological Society of London* 1864). The rest of the date is established from the CD annotation.

2 Bowerbank probably refers to proof-sheets of *A monograph of the Foraminifera of the Crag*, part 1 (Jones *et al.* 1866). The volume was published by the Palaeontographical Society in December 1866. CD's *Fossil Cirripedia* (1854) is cited on page iii of the preface. CD's monograph had also been published by the society.

3 Bowerbank refers to the premises of the family business, Edward Bowerbank & Sons, distillers, at 77½ Sun Street, London (*Post Office London directory* 1860).

4 CD's annotation indicates that he included Bowerbank's letter among his notes on hybridism. 'Ch IX' refers to CD's chapter on hybridism in *Natural selection.* Even after the publication of *Origin*, CD continued to make notes that he labelled for this chapter. Some of this material was eventually used in *Variation* (see *Natural selection*, pp. 387–8). The breeding of dogs is not mentioned in *Natural selection.* The reference in CD's annotation to a chapter on crossing is probably to chapter 11 of *Variation* (1: 373–411), which included a section headed 'On the effects in female animals of a first impregnation on the subsequent offspring'. In this section, CD gave examples of such effects in horses and pigs, and mentioned in a note similar effects in dogs, but did not cite Bowerbank's observations (see *Variation* 1: 404).

From Richard Trevor Clarke 6 November [1866][1]

Dear Mr Darwin

As some good matter appeared in our first number of the new issue of the RHS transactions on the subject of hybridism I shall have to say my word in the second;[2] my object in writing to you is to know if you would mind my publishing my observation on the change of colour in Matthiola seed produced by pollen agency before germination. Having sent it to you to add to *your* collection of facts I would not publish it now unless entirely agreeable to you—[3]

Naudin and Vichura's observations are good & interesting, especially the "loves of the Willows", highly confirmatory, but new, *no.*[4] I have not a scrap of novelty for you this season,—any more than the Frenchman.

I have been making some splendid cross bred cottons, but I fear the posterity will not come up to the first crosses always vigorous and good vide also Vichura.[5]

The Oriental Gossypia will not cross with Barbadense.—[6]

Very truly y^rs | R Trevor Clarke

Welton Place
Novr 6th

Sea Island cottons[7] are dimorphous occasionally, style sometimes exserted, beyond anthers, sometimes covered; no concomitant phenomena yet observed.

DAR 161: 163

1 The year is established by the reference to the first number of the new series of the *Journal of the Royal Horticultural Society*; see n. 2, below.

2 The *Journal of the Royal Horticultural Society* n.s. 1 (1866) carried two papers on hybridism, an English translation of Naudin 1864 (pp. 1–9) and an English abstract of Wichura 1865 (pp. 57–82). There was no article by Clarke in volume 2 of the *Journal of the Royal Horticultural Society*.

[3] CD noted Clarke's observations of *Matthiola* in *Variation* 1: 398–9, citing Clarke's paper on *Matthiola* read at the International Horticultural Exhibition, London, in May 1866 (Clarke 1866). No previous correspondence on the subject has been found.

[4] Clarke refers to Charles Victor Naudin and Max Ernst Wichura, and to Naudin 1864 and Wichura 1865. CD's copy of Naudin 1864 is in the Darwin Pamphlet Collection–CUL; his annotated copy of Wichura 1865 is in the Darwin Library–CUL (see *Marginalia* 1: 871–3). CD had finished reading Wichura's paper in early February 1865, noting in a letter to M. E. Wichura, 3 February [1865] (*Correspondence* vol. 13): 'the extreme frequency of Hybrid Willows is quite a new fact to me'. CD commented on Naudin's theory of the reversion of hybrids in the same letter.

[5] Wichura had given instances where hybrid willows were so vigorous that they outnumbered their parent species (Wichura 1865, pp. 64–5; see *Correspondence* vol. 13, letter to M. E. Wichura, 3 February [1865] and n. 3).

[6] In a published account of a lecture given at the Royal Horticultural Society on the cultivation of cotton, Clarke discussed the variability of the genus *Gossypium*, noting that it included two main divisions, which he referred to as Asian and American, and mentioned growing the Asian species *G. arboreum* (see *Gardeners' Chronicle* 1864, p. 1086). The cross that Clarke unsuccessfully attempted was probably between *G. arboreum* and *G. barbadense*. For more on Clarke's observations, see *Correspondence* vol. 12, letter from R. T. Clarke, 25 November [1864].

[7] 'Sea island' was the name given to a cultivar of *Gossypium barbadense* grown in a limited coastal region of the south-eastern United States (see C. W. Smith and Cothren eds. 1999, pp. 154–7, 831; see also *Correspondence* vol. 12, letter from R. T. Clarke, 25 November [1864], n. 3).

From Asa Gray 6 November [1866][1]

C—
Nov. 6.

Dear Darwin

Thanks for yours of 19th Oct.[2]

You can say to Murray that as Ticknor & Fields sell only their own publications, they cannot avail themselves of his offer of copies of Origin for Amer. sales at $\frac{1}{2}$ price.[3]

But I could wish that offer made—say to Messrs. *Scribner & Co.* New York—whose agent in London is *Mr. Welford*[4]—who must be known at Murray's, & in all the *Row*[5]

I want you to know that Mr. Agassiz—having sent to me, thro, a mutual friend—a handsome apology for some very bad conduct to me— —a mere outbreak of spoiled temper, $1\frac{1}{2}$ years ago, we are now on amicable terms—[6] Till then, I was obliged to ignore him.

Ever Yours | A. Gray

DAR 165: 156

[1] The year is established by the relationship between this letter and the letter from John Murray, 18 October [1866] (see n. 3, below).

[2] The letter to Gray of 19 October has not been found.

[3] John Murray, CD's publisher, had offered to supply the Boston firm Ticknor & Fields with 250 copies of the fourth edition of *Origin* at half price (see letter from John Murray, 18 October [1866]).

[4] The reference is to Charles Scribner and Company, Brick Church Chapel, Park Row, New York. Charles Welford, Charles Scribner's partner in the book-importing firm Scribner & Welford, had

moved to London in 1864 to oversee the European side of the business (*New York Times*, 20 May 1885, p. 5).

[5] Gray refers to Paternoster Row, Cheapside, London, where several publishers and booksellers had premises.

[6] Gray's falling out with his Harvard colleague Louis Agassiz was precipitated by a disagreement over the election in 1864 of Spencer Fullerton Baird, assistant secretary and curator at the Smithsonian Institution, as a member of the National Academy of Sciences (see Lurie 1960, pp. 340–4). The 'mutual friend' who conveyed Agassiz's apology was Joseph Henry, secretary of the Smithsonian (see letter from Joseph Henry to Asa Gray, 31 October 1866, Historic Letters file, Gray Herbarium Archives, Harvard University).

From Julius Victor Carus 7 November 1866

39, Elsterstrasse | Leipzig,
Nov. 7 1866.

My dear Sir,

Probably you will know already, that Mr. Schweizerbart, the publisher of Bronn's translation of your work on the origin of species, has asked me to revise this translation, to mend and correct it as far as possible.[1] It is with the greatest pleasure that I will try to do it, partly because I am fully convinced that this work is the most important of our time, partly as it give me the opportunity to thank you not only for the copy of your work you sent me when it came out first,[2] but especially for the immense good you did with it to organic sciences in general. Yet, I should have scarcely ventured to write to you directly, if I had not to ask you to help me out of a puzzle. Surely the late Professor Bronn was one of our ablest naturalists and I have the greatest regard for his truly philosophical and earnest endeavours to bring Zoology on a higher, a more scientifical footing. But for one reason or another, because he was a "natural philosopher" of the old German school[3] or because he was too much of a describing Zoologist, he was too anxious to allow your work to act freely upon the German public. According to the opinion of most of my younger colleagues he did not even deal fairly with it. I should not like to go as far as this, but I must confess, that I dislike strongly that sort of authoritative doubt and that sometimes quite ludicrous display of a so called higher scientific argumentation which he shows in his "Anmerkungen" and especially in his Epilogue.[4] But here comes my difficulty. You will be of course the most interested that your work should be presented to the German reader in a fair and unprejudiced form. Now do you think it fair of me, when I leave off all those remarks of Bronn's which are according to my scientific conscience almost equal to nothing. Do you think it compatible with the due regard to Bronn's memory if I was to separate his "Schlusswort"[5] from the body of your work, with which it had nothing at all to do, and to modify it according to *my* views of the question? I think I may do it. As the first two editions of his translation are existing, the history of the Science will take due notice of his position. But for my part I should not like to propagate his doubts, especially as I pointed already 1853 in my System of animal morphology (p. 5) to the *genealogical* connexion of the present and past forms of animal life.[6] If you would be so good as to write with one word that I may have liberty to do as I like best, I should be very much obliged to you.

Mr. Schweizerbart sent me some corrections Dr. Caspary had pointed out.[7] Most of these I knew before. With regard to the Guinea-fowl which is said to have been wrongly translated by Bronn, I must say, here Bronn was right. It is the Perlhuhn. But in that place you marked (p. 17 of the first English edition) you changed Guinea-fowl into Goose.[8]

Allow me once more to say how much I am delighted to be able to associate my name in a way ever so humble with your work and believe me | My dear Sir | Yours most truly and respectfully. | Prof J. Victor Carus

DAR 161: 53

[1] Christian Friedrich Schweizerbart approached Carus to supervise the production of a translation of the fourth edition of *Origin* after the job had been turned down by Gustav von Leonhard and Hans Bruno Geinitz (see letter from E. Schweizerbart'sche Verlagsbuchhandlung, 26 October 1866 and n. 4). Two earlier German editions of *Origin* (Bronn trans. 1860 and 1863) had been translated by Heinrich Georg Bronn, who died in 1862.

[2] Thomas Henry Huxley had recommended Carus for CD's presentation list for the first edition of *Origin* (see *Correspondence* vol. 8, Appendix III).

[3] Carus refers to *Naturphilosophie*: 'the theory . . . that there is an eternal and unchanging law of nature, proceeding from the Absolute, from which all laws governing natural phenomena and forces derive' (*OED*). For more on *Naturphilosophie* and research in natural history, see Rehbock 1983 and Jardine 1996.

[4] CD had suggested that Bronn append 'notes of *refutation* or confirmation' to the translation of *Origin* (see *Correspondence* vol. 8, letter to H. G. Bronn, 4 February [1860]). The first two German editions of *Origin* (Bronn trans. 1860 and Bronn trans. 1863) contained several notes added by Bronn, elaborating on certain points or engaging in theoretical discussion of CD's views. In addition, a twenty-five page epilogue written by Bronn attempted to guide the reader's assessment of CD's theory in light of Bronn's own critical review of what he considered to be the main issues (see Bronn trans. 1860, pp. 495–520).

[5] 'Schlusswort': epilogue.

[6] The reference is to *System der thierischen Morphologie* (Carus 1853).

[7] Robert Caspary's letter to Schweizerbart has not been found.

[8] In the fourth edition of *Origin*, CD had changed the word 'guinea-fowl' to 'goose' in the sentence that, in the first three editions, read, 'Has the little variability of the ass or guinea-fowl . . . prevented their domestication?' (see *Origin* 4th ed., p. 18, and Peckham ed. 1959, p. 90).

From James Shaw 7 November 1866

Tynron Parish School | Dumfries
7 Nov/66

Dear Sir,

Allow me to return sincere thanks for receipt of a Copy of the 'Origin' by to-days' post—to be henceforth ranked with the *Lares* & *Penates*.[1]

The difference between the tastes of cultivated man & that of savages & birds is not so great when we expand your remark on the modern feeling for scenery &c by tracing how gradually it has arisen[2]

(*Cosmos* vol II.)[3] The Sublime & Beautiful of the heroic ages were accessory to Power & Love. De Quincy somewhere remarks that Shakespeare was the first English poet who has alluded to clouds *per se* & that in terms far removed from Shelley's rapturous poem.[4]

What we call ugliness may sometimes be for an animals' good as is its stench, repulsive to its enemies as perfume is attractive to its mate; witness the manner of frightening birds by horrid painted screens, depriving them almost of sense for a little (practised in Palestine), & then shooting or catching them.

Keats's exquisite description of a venomous serpent:—

"She was a Gordian shape of dazzling hue,
vermilion spotted, golden, green, & blue"[5] &c

shows that the idea of danger being eliminated as regards the describer something remains pleasing to the eye.

In very ancient Chinese sculpture their method of catching tigers with a box-trap & mirror is represented.

Again thanking you for the handsome present, | I am, Dear Sir, | Yours truly | Ja.s Shaw

Ch. Darwin Esq.re

P.S. I can so far verify your remarks on the colour of fruit being a guide to birds as I observed that blackbirds &c preyed quite as much on red geans in my garden as on the ripened black ones, whereas the coloured gooseberries suffered far more from them than even the ripe green ones.[6]

J.S.

DAR 177: 151

1 The reference is to the fourth edition of *Origin*, which CD's publisher, John Murray, had recently released for sale (the book was advertised in the 17 October and 1 November 1866 issues of the *Publishers' Circular*, pp. 617, 666). The book had been printed by the end of July 1866, but Murray did not release it until November for marketing reasons (see letter from John Murray, 18 July [1866]). Shaw's name appears on CD's presentation list for this edition (see Appendix IV). *Lares* and *penates*: 'household gods; valued personal or household objects' (*Chambers*).

2 Shaw refers to CD's comment, 'The idea also of beauty in natural scenery has arisen only within modern times' (*Origin* 4th ed., p. 239).

3 Shaw refers to volume 2 of Humboldt 1846–58 (*Cosmos: sketch of a physical description of the universe*); volume 2 has two sections, 'Incitements to the study of nature' and 'History of the physical contemplation of the universe'. CD read this volume in May 1848 (see CD's reading notebooks, *Correspondence* vol. 4, Appendix IV, 119: 21a; see also *Correspondence* vol. 4, letter to Edward Cresy, [May 1848]). There is a copy of it in the Darwin Library–Down.

4 Thomas De Quincey wrote in his essay 'On Wordsworth's poetry' that cloud architecture had been little noticed by earlier poets, claiming that there was no distinct sketch of the appearance of clouds before William Shakespeare's *Antony and Cleopatra* (see Masson ed. 1889–90, 11: 317–18). Shaw refers to Percy Bysshe Shelley's poem 'The cloud' (Shelley 1834, 2: 469–72).

5 The quotation is from John Keats's poem 'Lamia' (Keats 1820, p. 6).

6 CD had added a new passage to the fourth edition of *Origin* criticising the view that organic beings had been created beautiful for the benefit of human beings (*Origin* 4th ed., pp. 238–41). In it he

claimed (*ibid.*, p. 240) that the beauty of fruits served 'merely as a guide to birds and beasts', so that the fruit might be eaten and the seeds disseminated.

To W. E. Darwin 8 November [1866][1]

Down
Nov. 8th

My dear William.

Taking the valuation of Claythorpe, at 13,500£ I have resolved to charge you in my Will (which I will at once have altered) 8500£; so that you will in fact receive 5000£ more than my other sons, as being eldest & more especially as Susan has bequeathed this estate to you.[2] But I think I mentioned to you that Susan clearly understood and agreed with my intention of deducting the value of the estate. As 4500£ was advanced when you joined the Bank, the total deduction will be 13,000£.[3] As far as I can judge, by including what Aunt Catherine has left all you children, & if Uncle Eras bequeaths us any share,[4] I expect you will receive on our deaths beyond the 13,000£ about 10,000£ in addition.— When you receive your whole rent you ought to save somewhat.— I request that you will *soon* consult your Solicitor about your will, for Land requires special notice in a will, & deliberate carefully what you think will be best to do with all property which you may die possessed of.—

I wish to God I could leave you better off, but I have not been extravagant or wasted our property.

My dear old son | Your affect. Father | C. Darwin

This note is miserably expressed & written, but I am tired.—

DAR 210.6: 120

[1] The year is established by the reference to the Claythorpe farm (see n. 2, below).

[2] Susan Elizabeth Darwin had bequeathed Claythorpe farm to William (see letter from E. A. Darwin, 11 October [1866] and n. 3).

[3] CD's will was altered as described. For the advance given to William when he became a partner in the Southampton and Hampshire Bank, see *Correspondence* vol. 9, letter to W. E. Darwin, 22 October [1861] and n. 3.

[4] The references are to Emily Catherine Langton, who had died in February 1866 (see letter from J. D. Hooker, 4 February 1866, n. 1), and Erasmus Alvey Darwin.

From J. T. Moggridge 9 November [1866][1]

St. Roch | Mentone
Nov. 9

Dear Mr. Darwin

I have gathered you some seeds of Ononis minutissima which I enclose.—[2] They are the product of fully developed flowers, which are the only ones out now & seem to be amply fertile.[3]

About the Peas;—when I was leaving London I went to Butler & M'Culloch's, Seedsmen in Covent Garden, & bought packets of each of the varieties of Sweet Peas & two of the most marked forms of eatable Peas for sowing here.—[4] I then asked the ⟨*third of page excised*⟩

⟨ ⟩ varieties I am selling you are artificial hybrids, as for example this one', & he took up a packet marked 'Clarks hybrid'.[5]

I asked the same question of an intelligent gardener here at Mentone, & he likewise said that these plants are always separated when seed is wanted from different varieties—.

These answers may perhaps only point to a common prejudice in favour of separating all varieties for seed; & I shall try to get evidence of spontaneous crossing if possible—[6] ⟨*third of page excised*⟩

AL incomplete
DAR 171: 201

[1] The year is established by the relationship between this letter and the letter from J. T. Moggridge, 5 and 6 July [1866].

[2] Moggridge had earlier sent CD seeds of *Ononis columnae* that he had obtained in England and later sent seeds obtained from Mentone, a region of the French and Italian Riviera, where Moggridge lived during the winter months (see letters from J. T. Moggridge, 5 and 6 July [1866] and n. 3, and 3 August [1866]).

[3] *Ononis minutissima* bears both opening and non-opening flowers. Moggridge's seeds were from opened flowers. CD reported his observations on the seed produced by both types of flowers of *O. minutissima* in *Forms of flowers*, pp. 326–7, and further observations on the seedlings of both types in *Cross and self fertilisation*, pp. 167–8.

[4] Butler & M'Culloch had premises at South Row, Covent Garden, London (*Post Office London directory* 1866). In the second letter to *Gardeners' Chronicle*, [before 11 August 1866], CD had reported on some of his experiments in crossing peas, noting that he had succeeded in crossing *Lathyrus odoratus* (sweetpea) and *L. grandiflorus* (everlasting pea).

[5] 'Clarks hybrid' has not been further identified.

[6] In *Cross and self fertilisation*, pp. 168–9, CD observed that although varieties of *Lathyrus odoratus* did not intercross in England, they were believed to do so in northern Italy. He suggested that efficient insect pollinators were lacking in England.

To J. V. Carus 10 November 1866

Down. | Bromley. | Kent. S.E.
Nov 10th. 1866

My dear Sir

I thank you for your extremely kind letter.[1] I cannot express too strongly my satisfaction that you have undertaken the revision of the new edition, & I feel the honour which you have conferred on me. I fear that you will find the labour considerable, not only on account of the additions, but I suspect that Bronn's translation is very defective, at least I have heard complaints on this head from quite a large number of persons.[2]

It would be a great gratification to me to know that the translation was a really good one, such as I have no doubt you will produce. According to our English practise you will be fully justified in entirely omitting Bronn's appendix, & I should be very glad of its omission.[3] A new edition may be looked at as a new work. I should however feel very doubtful whether you would be justified in altering this appendix by Bronn.

On the other hand you could add any thing of your own that you liked, and I should be much pleased. Should you make any additions, or append notes, it appears to me that Nägeli "Entstehung und Begriff" etc would be worth noticing, as one of the most able pamphets on the subject.[4] I am however far from agreeing with him that the acquisition of certain characters, which appear to be of no service to plants, offers any great difficulty, or affords a proof of some innate tendancy in plants towards perfection.[5] If you intend to notice this pamphlet, I should like to write hereafter a little more in detail on the subject.

Will you be so good as to observe that in the 2nd German Edition I added a note to the chapter on Hybridism which note I now wish destroyed, as I believe the view to be false.[6]

I wish I had known when writing my Historical sketch that you had in 1853 published your views on the genealogical connection of past & present forms.[7]

I suppose you have the sheets of the last English edition on which I marked with pencil all the chief additions, but many little corrections of style were not marked.

Pray believe that I feel sincerely grateful for the great service & honour which you do me by the present translation.

I remain, my dear Sir | yours very sincerely | Charles Darwin

P.S. I shd. be *very much* pleased to possess your Photograph, & I send mine in case you should like to have a copy.—[8]

LS(A)
Staatsbibliothek zu Berlin, Sammlung Darmstaedter (Carus 1)

[1] See letter from J. V. Carus, 7 November 1866.

[2] For criticisms of Heinrich Georg Bronn's translations of *Origin* (Bronn trans. 1860 and Bronn trans. 1863), see the letter from Rudolf Suchsland, 16 March 1866, the enclosure to the letter from Rudolf Suchsland, 2 April 1866, and the letter from Rudolf Oldenbourg, 28 October 1866.

[3] CD refers to the 'epilogue' added by Bronn as the last chapter in the German editions of *Origin* (Bronn trans. 1860 and Bronn trans. 1863); Carus had suggested separating this epilogue from the main text and altering it to reflect his (Carus's) own views (see letter from J. V. Carus, 7 November 1866 and n. 4). In the new German edition, Carus did not include Bronn's epilogue and he deleted most of Bronn's notes with the exception of those that related to the translation. He did retain two notes in which Bronn had commented on CD's response to some of his objections (see Bronn trans. 1863, pp. 149–50, and Bronn and Carus trans. 1867, pp. 159–61).

[4] CD refers to Carl Wilhelm von Nägeli and Nägeli 1865 (see letter to C. W. von Nägeli, 12 June [1866] and nn. 2, 4, 7–10). In the new German edition, Carus did not make any editorial comments in the text that did not relate to translation.

[5] CD discusses Nägeli's objection in *Origin* 5th ed., pp. 151–7.

[6] CD refers to the note on page 274 of Bronn trans. 1863. The note is appended to the sentence, 'On the theory of natural selection the case [of hybrid sterility] is especially important, inasmuch as the

sterility of hybrids could not possibly be of any advantage to them, and therefore could not have been acquired by the continued preservation of successive profitable degrees of sterility' (*Origin*, p. 245). The original English text of the note has not been found, but in CD's annotated copy of the third edition of *Origin* an asterisk has been added at the end of the sentence to which the note was to be appended and the word 'Footnote' is written in pencil in the margin. The German text of the note reads:

> Obwohl mir dieser Satz nahezu wahr zu seyn scheint, so habe ich doch bis jetzt zu berücksichtigen vergessen, dass daraus noch keineswegs folge, dass nicht Unfruchtbarkeit für zwei im Entstehen begriffene Spezies von grossen Vortheilen soferne seyn könne, als sie dieselben getrennt hält und für verschiedene Lebens-Beziehungen geeignet macht. Die Unfruchtbarkeit der Bastarde mag eine unvermeidliche Folge der erlangter Unfruchtbarkeit [?] ihrer Ältern seyn; aber ich will nicht mehr sagen, weil einige Versuche, die ich in Bezug auf diese wichtige Frage durchzuführen beschäftigt bin, noch nicht zum Abschluss gelangt sind. (Im April 1862.)

English translation:

> Although this sentence seems nearly true, I have forgotten until now to consider that it in no way follows that a lack of sterility for two nascent species could be a great advantage provided they (themselves) remain separated and are adapted to different conditions. The sterility of hybrids may be an unavoidable consequence of the acquired sterility [?] of their parents; but I will not say more as I am occupied carrying out some experiments in connection with this important question, which are not yet complete. (April 1862.)

For CD's changing views on the subject of the sterility of hybrids as a selected quality, see *Correspondence* vol. 13, letter to M. E. Wichura, 3 February [1865] and n. 9. For the changes to this section of *Origin* in all the English editions, see Peckham ed. 1959, pp. 424–5.

7 CD had added a preface to the first German edition and the revised American edition of *Origin* giving a historical background to the idea of transmutation of species (Bronn trans. 1860, pp. 1–6, and *Origin* US ed., pp. i–xi; see *Correspondence* vol. 8, Appendix IV, and Freeman 1977). The 'Historical sketch' published in *Origin* 3d ed., pp. xiii–xix, included new material, and more additions were made to the preface of the second German edition (Bronn trans. 1863, pp. 1–10). CD expanded the sketch again in *Origin* 4th ed., pp. xiii–xxi. For the changes to this section of *Origin* in all the English editions, see Peckham ed. 1959, pp. 59–70.

8 CD may have sent a photograph of himself taken by Ernest Edwards during his visit to London in April 1866 (see *Correspondence* vol. 13, letter from E. A. Darwin to Emma Darwin, 25 [November 1865] and n. 3).

From Armand de Quatrefages[1] 10 November 1866

Paris
10 9bre. 66[2]

Monsieur et cher confrère

MM Williams et Norgate libr. sont chargés de vous faire parvenir un exemplaire de mon Histoire des Annélides (fig. col.)[3] Si mon livre tardait trop a vous arriver, Soyez assez bon pour le faire reclamer. Cet ouvrage m'a couté bien de la peine car je ne sais pas d'animaux plus pénibles à déterminer que les Annélides et j'ai mis tout mon soin a être exact. Accueillez le comme bon souvenir de votre bien dévoué confrere qui desirerait fort faire votre connaissance personnelle

De Quatrefages

DAR 175: 4

[1] For a translation of this letter, see Appendix I.
[2] '9bre': Novembre (from the Latin for 'nine': novem).
[3] The booksellers and publishers Williams & Norgate specialised in foreign scientific literature. CD's copy of Quatrefages 1865 is in the Darwin Library–Down. 'Fig. col.' is probably an abbreviation for 'figures colorés', referring to the coloured plates of the work.

From T. H. Huxley 11 November 1866

26 Abbey Place
Novr. 11th. 1866

My dear Darwin

I thank you for the New Edition of the 'Origin'[1] & congratulate you on having done with it for a while—so as to be able to go on to that book of a portion of which I had a glimpse years ago—[2]

I hear good account of your health—indeed the last was that you were so rampageous you meant to come to London & have a spree among its dissipations[3]

May that be true—

I am in the thick of my work & have only had time to glance at your 'Historical sketch'—

What an unmerciful basting you give "Our Mutual friend"— I did not know he had put forward any claim![4] And even now that I read it black & white, I can hardly believe it—

I am glad to hear from Spencer that you are on the right (that is *my*) side in the Jamaica business— But it is wonderful how people who commonly act together are divided about it—[5]

My wife joins with me in kindest wishes to Mrs Darwin[6] & yourself | Ever yours truly | T H Huxley

Actual Potential

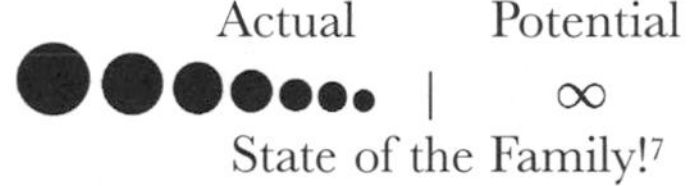

| ∞

State of the Family![7]

You will soon receive an Elementary Physiology book—not for your reading but for Miss Darwin's—[8] Were you not charmed with Haeckel?[9]

DAR 166: 312

[1] The reference is to the fourth edition of *Origin*. Huxley's name appears on CD's presentation list for the fourth edition (Appendix IV).
[2] Huxley refers to *Variation*, which was published in 1868. CD had sent Huxley a draft of the chapter on pangenesis (see *Correspondence* vol. 13, letter to T. H. Huxley, 27 May [1865]).
[3] According to Emma Darwin's diary (DAR 242), CD was in London from 22 to 29 November 1866.
[4] The 'Historical sketch' at the beginning of the fourth edition of *Origin* had been revised to include a reference to Richard Owen's recent claim that he had presented a theory of descent as early as 1850 (see *Origin* 4th ed., pp. xvii–xviii). See letter to J. D. Hooker, 31 May [1866] and n. 11. Charles Dickens's *Our mutual friend* (London: Chapman and Hall) was published in 1865.
[5] Herbert Spencer had solicited CD's support for the Jamaica Committee (see letter from Herbert Spencer, 2 November 1866 and n. 1). While CD, Spencer, and Huxley supported the move to

prosecute the former governor of Jamaica, Edward John Eyre, friends of theirs, notably Joseph Dalton Hooker and John Tyndall, were opposed to prosecution (see letter from J. D. Hooker, 3 November 1866; for Tyndall's role on the Eyre Committee, see Semmel 1962, pp. 123–7).

6 Emma Darwin. Huxley's wife was Henrietta Anne Huxley.

7 Presumably the dots in the diagram represent Huxley's seven children, the last of whom, Ethel, had been born in May 1866 (see letter from J. D. Hooker, 13 May 1866, n. 17). The second column contains the mathematical symbol for infinity.

8 The references are to T. H. Huxley 1866 and Henrietta Emma Darwin.

9 Ernst Haeckel had visited CD on 21 October 1866 (see letter from Ernst Haeckel, 19 October 1866). He also visited Huxley at around the same time (Krauße 1987, pp. 76–7).

From Clair James Grece 12 November 1866

To Cha: Darwin, Esqre. | Bromley, | London, S.E.

Sir,

I enclose a slip from the Morning Star,[1] lest the fact it records should escape your attention; and, I will add my attestation to its substantial correctness. That the animal has no skin is, of course, not strictly true; but it has cast its entire skin from the snout to the tail, together with subcutaneous fat of from one to three inches in thickness, leaving a second skin now exposed to the external air. The animal was in a stye to be fatted, but about three weeks ago was observed to be off its appetite, and portions of the skin of the belly peeled off; but the owner could not foresee that the whole skin was to slough off. However, one morning he found the skin, with fat as aforesaid, lying in the stye, having obviously, come off in a mass during the night, and the pig, like the snake in Virgil,[2] resplendent in a delicate new attire. The former skin was black and bristly, the new one was, at first, entirely flesh coloured but is changing to black by degrees.— The animal, after the crisis was over, recovered its appetite, and, to all appearance, has now naught the matter with it. The skin is preserved. Many persons have visited it, but, I believe, no one as yet of natural historical knowledge.

You may recollect me as having some year or two since pointed out to you a passage from Aristotle, shewing that "Natural Selection" was known to the ancients.[3]

I remain, Sir, | your very ob^t. serv^t, | Clair J. Grece.

Redhill Surrey
12th. Novr. 1866.

P.S. Should you like to see the animal, it is on the premises of one M^r. Jennings,[4] a baker, in Horley Row about one mile north of the Horley Station of the London and Brighton railway.

A fly might not be procurable at that station, so that you might prefer to alight at the Redhill Station, where vehicles are readily obtainable, and whence it is about four miles to the southward.

C.J.G.

[Enclosure]

Freak of Nature.— One of those extraordinary freaks of nature can now be witnessed by any person who will take the train from London Bridge to Horley station, within five minutes' walk of the Chequers' Inn, at Horley. A living pig may be seen at Mr. Jennings's, without a skin on it, the animal having adopted the course of throwing off its entire coat from head to tail, with hair and flesh, the latter nearly three inches thick. It is doing well, and the coat hangs on one of the trees adjoining the stye. It is quite a curiosity, and may become matter for future discussion at the Anthropological Society. The flesh is like good pork, fat and lean, and has no appearance of disease. In fact, he is a specimen grunter, without a coat, and the new one is growing nicely.

Morning Star: Saturday the 10th. November 1866.

DAR 165: 220 and 220a

1 The enclosure is an article from the London newspaper, the *Morning Star*, 10 November 1866.

2 The reference is to a passage from Virgil's *Aeneid*:

> So shines, renew'd in youth, the crested snake,
> Who slept the winter in a thorny brake,
> And, casting off his slough when spring returns,
> Now looks aloft, and with new glory burns.

Bk 2, ll. 471–4, trans. Dryden.

3 The letter from Grece containing the reference to Aristotle has not been found, but CD added Grece's information to the historical sketch in *Origin* 4th ed., p. xiii n.

4 Stephen Jennings was a baker and shopkeeper in Horley, Surrey (*Post Office directory of the six home counties* 1866).

To J. T. Moggridge 13 November [1866][1]

Down Bromley
Nov. 13.

My dear Mr. Moggridge

I am very much obliged for your very interesting letter, for the seeds, and especially for the trouble which you have taken about the peas.[2] I have often received vague information about sw. and common peas crossing; but on the other hand some careful raisers have assured me positively (and in one case I saw the seed-beds) that they get seed from beds of adjoining vars., and each var. comes true. I have the particulars of one case in which one var. of common pea was raised for a number of generations near other peas and yet kept true. From the action of Bees and from analogy the whole case perplexes me much. Perhaps if you come across any nursery gardener you will enquire whether they have actually known adjoining vars. to cross.

Last autumn I saw a peculiar bee visiting and apparently fertilising my sweet peas and I have saved seed to see if they come true.

But I shall be very much more interested by hearing what takes place in a warmer country.[3]

What you tell me about Jordan's subspecies interests me much. I hope M. Thuret or D^r. Bornet will publish their results.— If you see them again, can you find out if they have so large a stock of seed that they could spare me a little. I should like to cross some of these five forms, and likewise grow them separately and in adjoining beds.—[4] I am glad to hear about the orchids: mine are growing well.—[5]

One word more about the peas; it would be of some value, if you could ascertain that it was a *general* practice to grow the vars. of sweet and common peas separate; for this is certainly not commonly done in England.

With *cordial* thanks for all your great kindness, believe me, | Yours very sincerely | Ch. Darwin

Copy
DAR 146: 375

[1] The year is established by the relationship between this letter and the letter from J. T. Moggridge, 9 November [1866].

[2] Moggridge had made enquiries about hybridisation in peas (see letter from J. T. Moggridge, 9 November [1866]). For CD's earlier work on sweetpeas and other leguminous plants, see the second letter to *Gardeners' Chronicle*, [before 11 August 1866] and nn. 2, 5, and 6.

[3] See letter from J. T. Moggridge, 9 November [1866] and n. 6.

[4] The remarks on Alexis Jordan's sub-species were in a now missing portion of the letter from J. T. Moggridge, 9 November [1866], but probably referred to the several new species within the genus *Papaver* described in Jordan 1864; these were being studied by Edouard Bornet in the Antibes garden of Gustave Adolphe Thuret. Bornet later sent CD seeds of some *Papaver* varieties, so he could perform crossing experiments (see letter to Edouard Bornet, 1 December 1866 and n. 1).

[5] The remarks on orchids were in a now missing portion of the letter from J. T. Moggridge, 9 November [1866]; Moggridge frequently sent orchid specimens to CD (see *Correspondence* vol. 13, letter from J. T. Moggridge, 27 December [1865] and, this volume, letter from J. T. Moggridge, 21 May [1866]). Moggridge may also have brought specimens when he visited CD in June (see letter from J. T. Moggridge, 14 June [1866] and n. 2).

From J. V. Carus 15 November 1866

39, Elsterstrasse, | Leipzig
Novbr, 15. 1866.

My dear Sir,

First of all let me thank you for your photograph, by which you made me *happy*. I longed for it and yet I did not venture to ask you directly. As you were so kind to express your wish with regard to mine, I enclose it being proud of the quite undeserved honour conferred upon my figure.[1]

As for the translation I try to make it a really true one; to make it good, that is rather impossible without rewriting it.[2] Yet I do my best to make it at any rate more German and readable. Some mistakes of Bronn's are quite ridiculous[3] For instance he translates "turnspit dog" by "that sort of dogs used in England to turn the spits". You mean the Canis fam. *vertagus*, where already Linnaeus gives the quotation: "Turnspit, Pennant, Brit. Zool."[4] It is our "Dachshund", which word Bronn uses as the translation of "terrier", which is on the contrary our Pinscher, viz. Canis fam. *gryphus*.[5] These places of course you did not mark. I am obliged to read and compare the whole verbatim. Till now I did the first three chapters. There is one thing in these I must ask you. You mention the sweet pea. Bronn translates "Sugar-pea", which is false.[6] I am almost sure of the plant you mean, but cannot get hold of our German name without knowing first the botanical. On p. 23 of the fourth edition (which I have got) you mention the laugher. There Bronn doubts if you had meant Columba risoria.[7] I think there is no occasion for doubting. I should therefore leave off his note, as I do with the others where he did not give an addition of yours[8] For myself I shall not append notes, as I do not think it proper to bring my individuality forward in such a way. All I should do would be to give a short appendix especially on the mechanical or physiological relations of every germ, whether egg or bud or the product of partition, on which variability depends, and, if you allow it, on spontaneous generation with special regard to Haeckel's new book.[9] As to Nägeli's pamphlet I should feel very much obliged if you should write a note on it and tell me the place where I ought to put it.[10] He gives some very striking instances of selection in certain alpine plants and so on; but he is not quite consistent, what I felt just in the opinion of his, which you mentioned.[11]

Before I beg leave, may I ask you another great kindness? The publisher of one of our Cyclopaedias, who knows that I am acquainted with a pretty number of English naturalists thought me the right man to write biographical articles on your dear life and on that of Th Huxley.[12] I shall never forget that meeting of the combined sections of the British Association when at Oxford 1860, where Admiral Fitzroy expressed his sorrows for having given you the opportunities of collecting facts for such a shocking theory as yours. The poor man is gone, and yet we thank him.[13] As I welcome the opportunity of giving to the public in a widely spread work for reference an abstract of your results I should be very much pleased if I could rely for the little biographical sketch on the best authority possible, on yourself Now, if it gives not too much trouble to you, would you be so very kind as to give me some details on your life? Birthday, school, and so on. If you should not like it I trust you will tell me quite openly and will not be angry with me. In the meantime I shall go on with your work, and whenever I find some doubts, will you excuse my writing again and trespassing on your time?

Once more my most hearty thanks for the kind gift. Believe me, | My dear Sir, | Yours very sincerely. | J. Victor Carus

DAR 161: 54

CD ANNOTATIONS

1.1 First of all … *happy.*] *scored pencil*
2.10 You mention … the botanical. 2.12] *scored blue crayon*
2.13 There Bronn … for doubting. 2.15] *scored blue crayon*
2.21 As to Nägeli's … put it. 2.23] *scored blue crayon*

3.11 would you be so very . . . and so on. 3.13] *scored blue crayon*
3.15 will you excuse . . . your time? 3.16] *scored blue crayon*

[1] CD had sent a photograph of himself and requested one of Carus (see letter to J. V. Carus, 10 November 1866). The photograph of Carus has not been found.

[2] Carus was producing a new German edition of *Origin* based on the fourth English edition (Bronn and Carus trans. 1867). He did not simply translate the revisions CD had made, but revised the whole translation.

[3] Heinrich Georg Bronn had prepared the first and second German editions of *Origin* (Bronn trans. 1860 and 1863).

[4] See Bronn trans. 1863, p. 41. *Canis familiaris* var. *vertagus* is described in Linnaeus 1858–9, 1: 50.

[5] Carus replaced Bronn's phrase with the word 'Dachshund' (see Bronn and Carus trans. 1867, p. 45). On the translation of 'terrier', see Bronn trans. 1863, p. 27, and Bronn and Carus trans. 1867, p. 31.

[6] See *Origin* 3d ed., p. 76, and Bronn trans. 1863, p. 88, where Bronn uses 'Zuckererbsen' (sugar pea; *Pisum sativum* var. *saccharatum*) rather than 'wohlriechenden Platterbse' (sweetpea; *Lathyrus odoratus*). Carus used only the botanical name, *Lathyrus odoratus*, in his translation (see Bronn and Carus trans. 1867, p. 98).

[7] Carus refers to the fourth edition of *Origin*, which was published in November 1866. CD had earlier sent page proofs to his German publisher (see letter from E. Schweizerbart'sche Verlagsbuchhandlung, 26 October 1866 and n. 2). In Bronn trans. 1863, p. 32 n., Bronn writes, '*the laugher*, die Lachtaube' (literally 'laughing dove'), but adds that from the context, the breed of pigeon CD meant was probably 'die Trommeltaube' (literally 'drumming dove'). 'Lachtaube' is the German common name for *Columba risoria* (now *Streptopelia roseogrisea*), the African collared dove.

[8] In his translation, Carus called the bird 'die Lachtaube', but appended a note stating that he learned, from correspondence with the author, that the 'laugher' was not *Columba risoria*, but another eastern variety of *C. livia* apparently unknown in Germany (see Bronn and Carus trans. 1867, pp. 36–7).

[9] Carus refers to Ernst Haeckel and his *Generelle Morphologie der Organismen* (Haeckel 1866), in which he had speculated on the possibility of spontaneous generation (see Haeckel 1866, 2: 174; for more on Haeckel's theories of the development of living organisms from inorganic matter, see Rehbock 1975 and Rupke 1976). There is no appendix to Bronn and Carus trans. 1867.

[10] There is no note on Carl Wilhelm von Nägeli's pamphlet in Carus's revised translation (Bronn and Carus trans. 1867; see also letter to J. V. Carus, 10 November 1866 and n. 4). CD added a reference to Nägeli's work on the morphological character of plants in *Origin* 5th ed., p. 151.

[11] See Nägeli 1865, p. 24, for Nägeli's comments on adaptation in alpine plants. For CD's criticism of Nägeli, see the letter to J. V. Carus, 10 November 1866 and n. 5.

[12] Thomas Henry Huxley. The encyclopedia for which Carus wrote biographies of CD and Huxley has not been identified.

[13] Robert FitzRoy had commanded the *Beagle* during the voyage of 1832 to 1836 on which CD served as naturalist. In 1860, he attended the British Association for the Advancement of Science meeting at Oxford, where he presented a paper to the meteorological section (FitzRoy 1860) and also made comments during the discussion of CD's theory (see *Correspondence* vol. 8, Appendix VI, and F. Darwin ed. 1892, p. 239). He committed suicide in 1865 (see *Correspondence* vol. 13).

To John Lubbock 15 November 1866

Down.
15th Nov. 66.

Dear Lubbock

Would you oblige me by looking in indices (for I suppose such there are) to Microscopical Journal, & see if you can find Paper by Mr Hincks or Hickes on the fertilisation or on structure of the Polyzoa or Bryozoa or on the Flustraceæ;[1] & if you can find such paper will you kindly lend me y^{r} part.

If there be no indices it will be hopeless; but if there be it will not, I trust, cause you much trouble—

Yours very sincerely | C. Darwin

DAR 261.7: 1

[1] The reference is to Thomas Hincks and Hincks 1861. For CD's earlier interest in reproduction in Bryozoa, see *Correspondence* vol. 6, letter to T. H. Huxley, 8 June [1856].

From A. R. Wallace 19 November 1866

9, S^{t}. Mark's Crescent, | *Regent's Park,* N.W.
Novr. 19th. *1866*

Dear Darwin

Many thanks for the 4th. Ed. of the "**Origin**",[1] which I am glad to see grows so vigorously at each moult, although it undergoes no metamorphosis. How curious it is that D^{r}. Wells should so clearly have seen the principle of Nat. Select^{n}. 50 years ago and that it should have struck no one that it was a *great principle* of universal application in Nature![2]

We are going to have a discussion on "*Mimicry*, as *producing abnormal sexual characters*" at the Entomological tonight.[3] I have a butterfly (a *Diadema*) of which the female is *metallic blue*, the male *dusky brown* contrary to the rule in all other species of the genus, & in almost all insects;—but the explanation is easy;—it mimics a metallic blue *Euplœa*, and so gets a protection perhaps more efficient than its allies derive from their sombre colours, & which females require much more than males. I read a paper on this at the B. Ass^{n}.[4] Have you the report published at Nottingham in a volume by D^{r}. Robertson, if so you can tell me if my paper is printed at full?[5]

I suppose you have read Agassiz' marvellous theory of the,—*Gt. Amazonian Glacier*! *2000 miles long*!!![6] I presume that will be a *little* too much even for you. I have been writing a little popular paper on "*Glacial Theories*" for the Quarterly Journ. of Science of Jan. next in which I stick up for *Glaciers* in N. America and *Ice bergs* in the Amazon![7]

I was very glad to hear from Lubbock that your health is permanently improved.[8] I hope therefore you will be able to give us a volume per. annum of your "**op. mag.**", with all the facts as you now have them, leaving *additions* to come in new *editions*.[9]

I am working a little at another family of my butterflies & find the usual interesting & puzzling cases of variation, but no such strange phenomena as in the *Papilionidæ*.[10]

With best wishes | Believe me | My dear Darwin | Yours very faithfully | Alfred R. Wallace—

C. Darwin Esq.

DAR 106: B39–40

[1] Wallace's name appears on CD's presentation list for the fourth edition of *Origin* (Appendix IV).

[2] CD had added a reference to William Charles Wells and his essay 'An account of a female of the white race of mankind, part of whose skin resembles that of a negro; with some observations on the causes of the differences in colour and form between the white and negro races of men', published in W. C. Wells 1818, to the historical sketch at the beginning of the fourth edition of *Origin* (pp. xiv–xv). See letter from Asa Gray, 7 August 1866 and n. 4.

[3] An account of the discussion was reported in the *Transactions of the Entomological Society of London* (*Journal of the Proceedings*) 3d ser. 5 (1865–7): xxxvi–xli (19 November 1866).

[4] In his paper 'On reversed sexual characters in a butterfly' (A. R. Wallace 1866a, p. 186), Wallace suggested the name *Diadema anomala* (now *Hypolimnas anomala*) to highlight the fact that it was the female of the species that mimicked the male *Euploea midamus*. An abstract of the paper (A. R. Wallace 1866b) appeared in the *Report of the thirty-sixth meeting of the British Association for the Advancement of Science held at Nottingham*.

[5] Wallace refers to William Tindal Robertson and Robertson ed. 1866, in which the full text of Wallace's paper and some comments were reproduced (A. R. Wallace 1866a).

[6] The reference is to Louis Agassiz's article in *Atlantic Monthly* (J. L. R. Agassiz 1866a), in which he put forward a theory that the Amazon valley had been covered by a glacier (for more on the theory, see, for example, the letter to Charles Lyell, 8[–9] September [1866] and n. 6).

[7] In his paper 'Ice marks in north Wales. With a sketch of glacial theories and controversies' (A. R. Wallace 1867), Wallace discussed the evidence for glaciers in the area around Snowdon and Cader Idris in Wales. He argued that there was no evidence for Agassiz's claim that a glacier once covered the Amazon valley, but suggested that some evidence existed that icebergs once floated over a submerged Amazonian plain (*ibid.*, p. 41).

[8] John Lubbock. On CD's improved health, see the letter to W. D. Fox, 24 August [1866].

[9] The 'opus magnum' or 'great work' to which Wallace refers was the three-part work on variation in domestic and wild species and the principle of natural selection, of which *Variation* was originally intended to be the first part (see *Variation* 1: 3–9 for CD's outline of all three proposed works).

[10] For Wallace's earlier work on Malay Papilionidae, see *Correspondence* vol. 12 and A. R. Wallace 1864b.

To J. D. Hooker 20 November [1866][1]

Down
Nov 20

My dear Hooker

Thanks for your Pembroke note.[2]

We are coming up to 6 Q. Anne St on Wed. ie. tomorrow[3] Now if I am supernatural & the weather decent I sh^{d} like *very much* to drive down soon after breakfast & have an hour's walk with you about the garden, & I think this w^{d} not put you out much as I believe you go to the garden in the morning.

Emma will like to come with me to see Mrs Hooker.[4] I know you will ask us to lunch but it will be more prudent in me to leave you sooner— Let me have a line in answer at Q. A. St

When with you I can hear about the seeds of Euryale.[5]

And now I want to beg for something else viz. for roots of two species of Mirabilis, not M. jalapa which I have as I want to try a curious ex. in crossing them,[6] but I dont know whether you have other species; if you have & can spare roots I can take them away with me.

Your Drosera is unfolding new leaves beautifully.[7] You will shriek at me when you hear that I have just subscribed to the Jamaica committee.[8] For the more I hear about it the more atrocious the case appears—

Ever yours affecttely | Ch. Darwin

Impudence is a noble quality

Saxifraga Fortunei (on account of nectary) w^{d} be gratefully received.[9]

LS(A)
DAR 115: 305

[1] The year is established by the relationship between this letter and the letter from J. D. Hooker, 3 November 1866.

[2] Hooker had written to CD while on a visit to Pembroke Dock in south-west Wales (see letter from J. D. Hooker, 3 November 1866).

[3] Six Queen Anne Street was the address of CD's brother, Erasmus Alvey Darwin, with whom CD usually stayed on visits to London (Freeman 1978). According to Emma Darwin's diary (DAR 242), the Darwins went to London on 22 November 1866 and CD and Henrietta returned on 29 November.

[4] CD refers to Emma Darwin and Frances Harriet Hooker.

[5] Hooker planned to supply CD with seeds of the waterlily *Euryale ferox* and had already advised him on the best place for them to be planted to ensure germination (see letter from J. D. Hooker, 3 November 1866).

[6] In *Variation* 2: 88, during his discussion of the absorption of one species by another after repeated crosses, CD referred to crossing experiments made by Joseph Gottlieb Kölreuter between *Mirabilis vulgaris* (probably *M. jalapa*) and *M. longiflora*. In *Cross and self fertilisation*, pp. 298, 377, CD referred to experiments with *Mirabilis* that concerned the number of pollen-grains needed to fertilise an ovule.

[7] Hooker had sent CD a specimen of *Drosera binata* (see letter from J. D. Hooker, 28 September 1866).

[8] The Jamaica Committee sought to prosecute Edward John Eyre, the former governor of Jamaica, for his role in the suppression of an uprising of the ex-slave population (see letter from Herbert Spencer, 2 November 1866 and n. 1, letter from J. D. Hooker, 3 November 1866, and letter from T. H. Huxley, 11 November 1866 and n. 5). CD recorded a payment of £10 under the heading 'Jamaica' for 19 November 1866 in his Account books–cash account (Down House MS).

[9] CD was investigating insectivorous plants. He had obtained a specimen of *Erica massoni* in order to compare the glandular hairs of the nectary with those of the insectivorous plant *Drosera* (see letter to J. D. Hooker, 25 September [1866], and letter from J. D. Hooker, 28 September 1866). He probably requested a specimen of *Saxifraga fortunei* for similar observations (see *Insectivorous plants*, pp. 345–8, for his discussion of two other species of *Saxifraga*).

To J. V. Carus 21 November 1866

Down. | Bromley. | Kent. S.E.
Nov. 21st. 1866

My dear Sir

I am much obliged for your letter & especially for your photograph.[1] I shall be most happy at all times to answer when able any questions.

The sweet-Pea is *Lathyrus odoratus*[2] The Laugher-pigeon is an Eastern Var. of *Columba livia* & not C. risoria; it appears not to be known in Germany, for a man who knows the German var.s well & gives synonyms for all others excepting this one kind.[3]

I have pleasure in enclosing a copy of a short biographical sketch of myself which I lately had to give for an English biographical dictionary.[4]

With respect to a note on Nägeli I find on consideration it would be too long; for so good a pamphlet ought to be discussed at full length or not at all.[5] He makes a mistake in supposing that I say that useful characters are always constant.[6] His view about distinct species converging & acquiring the same identical structure is by implication answered in the discussion which I have given on the endless diversity of means for gaining the same end.[7]

The most important point as it seems to me in the pamphlet is that on the morphological characters of plants & I find I could not answer this without going into much detail.[8] The answer would be as it seems to me that important morphological characters, such as the position of the ovules & the relative position of the stamens to the ovarium (hypoginous, periginous &c &c)[9] are sometimes variable in the same species, as I incidentally mention when treating of the ray-florets in the Compositæ & Umbelliferæ; & I do not see how Nägeli could maintain that differences in such characters prove an inherent tendancy towards perfection.[10]

I see that I have forgotten to say that you have my fullest consent to append any discussion which you may think fit to the new edition. As for myself I cannot believe in spontaneous generation,[11] & though I expect that at some future time the principle of life will be rendered intelligible, at present it seems to me beyond the confines of science.

With my sincere thanks, Believe me | My dear Sir— Yours very sincerely— | Charles Darwin.

LS(A)
Staatsbibliothek zu Berlin, Sammlung Darmstaedter (Carus 2); DAR 143: 212

[1] See letter from J. V. Carus, 15 November 1866 and n. 1.

[2] See letter from J. V. Carus, 15 November 1866 and n. 6.

[3] Carus had mistakenly thought that the 'laugher' was the same as the German 'Lachtaube' (literally 'laughing dove') and that Heinrich Georg Bronn had erred in his translation (see letter from J. V. Carus, 15 November 1866 and n. 7). The reference is probably to William Bernhard Tegetmeier, who was CD's principal source for information on pigeons.

[4] CD probably sent the biographical sketch written for Reeve and Walford eds. 1863–7 (see letter to Robert Hunt, 3 May [1866] and n. 1).

[5] Carus had asked whether CD would write a note on Carl Wilhelm von Nägeli's paper on the origin of species (Nägeli 1865; see letter from J. V. Carus, 15 November 1866 and n. 10). There is a heavily annotated copy of Nägeli 1865 in the Darwin Pamphlet Collection–CUL.

[6] Nägeli claimed that CD stated that neutral characteristics were variable and useful ones were constant (Nägeli 1865, p. 28). CD marked the passage in his copy and added the comment, 'no–when part becomes variable, then if variation not useful; not made constant.'

[7] Nägeli argued that two species that were subject to the same conditions and eventually became perfectly adapted to them would necessarily converge into a single species (Nägeli 1865, p. 26). For CD's discussion of the diversity of means for gaining the same end, see *Origin* 4th ed., pp. 228–32.

[8] Nägeli wrote that what could be termed 'useful adaptations' in the plant kingdom were exclusively physiological and that no morphological modification could be explained by the theory of usefulness (Nägeli 1865, p. 27; see also letter to C. W. von Nägeli, 12 June [1866] and n. 8). He added that changes in morphological characteristics could be accounted for by his 'perfectibility principle' ('Vervollkommnungsprincip'; *ibid*, p. 30). CD discussed Nägeli's paper in *Origin* 5th ed., pp. 151–7.

[9] Hypogynous, perigynous.

[10] For CD's discussion of correlated variation and the shape of ray florets in the Compositae and Umbelliferae, see *Origin* 4th ed., p. 172.

[11] See letter from J. V. Carus, 15 November 1866 and n. 9. In the first German translation of *Origin*, Bronn had added a final chapter of his own commentary in which he discussed spontaneous generation within the context of CD's theory (see Bronn trans. 1860, pp. 495–520). For more on Bronn's argument that CD's theory was incomplete until it could account for the origin of life, see Bronn's review of *Origin* (Bronn 1860b) and *Correspondence* vol. 8. For more on CD's view of spontaneous generation, see *Correspondence* vol. 11, letter to *Athenæum*, 18 April [1863] and n. 3. On the Victorian debate about spontaneous generation within the context of Darwinism, see Strick 2000.

From J. D. Hooker [22 November 1866][1]

Kew
Thursday.

Dear Darwin

We shall be delighted to see any & all of you & at any hour.[2] I shall be at home all the week— I have such lots of things to show you— I will enquire about *Mirabilis*— we have not *Saxif. Fortunei*, but have a similar one that would I hope suit your purpose.[3]

I do *not* shriek at your subscribing to the Jamaica Committee, though I entirely disapprove of it's persecution of Eyre (for whom I have *no* respect but much pity) individually. I have not a syllable to say for his acts.—[4] Logically you are right; but there are a vast many considerations besides & above mere logic & law and *sentiment*, that, I think, should influence us in such cases: & the balance in my mind is in favor of letting bad alone.— You can do no good, & may make bad worse. You may guess how far I go with & beyond you in sentiment, when I add, that I hold it to be morally unlawful criminal if you will to take the life of animals *for sport*. & I can draw no line logical, between taking the life of a partridge for sport, or a man (white or black) for anger or revenge—

I returned from Shrewsbury yesterday!, where I went, impelled by various motives, to attend the Sale.[5] I was rewarded & very pleased by having seen your birth place &c &c &c—but grievously disappointed to find the Wedgwood bought in— there was one that I had been trying to get ever since I began to collect.—a Medallion Emblematic of the Colonization of N S. Wales,—also a head of B. Franklin.[6] So you may enjoy a counter shriek at my Wedgwood-mania breaking out in such force. Don't you *despise* my folly— I know what you will say.— laugh away.—[7] per contra I have not given up the thought of expanding my Lecture into a Treatise.[8]

Ever yr affec | J D Hooker

Let me know as early as possible if you find you cannot come & I will run in & see you.

DAR 102: 112–13

[1] The date is established by the relationship between this letter and the letter to J. D. Hooker, [23 November 1866].

[2] According to Emma Darwin's diary (DAR 242), CD was in London from 22 to 29 November 1866. CD told Hooker he would like to visit one morning (see letter to J. D. Hooker, 20 November [1866]).

[3] CD had asked whether Hooker could give him the roots of some species of *Mirabilis* other than *M. jalapa*. He also requested a specimen of *Saxifraga fortunei*. See letter to J. D. Hooker, 20 November [1866] and nn. 6 and 9.

[4] CD told Hooker that he had subscribed to the Jamaica Committee. The group sought to have criminal charges brought against Edward John Eyre, the former governor of Jamaica (see letter to J. D. Hooker, 20 November [1866] and n. 8).

[5] The sale of the contents of the Mount, the Darwin family home until the death of Susan Elizabeth Darwin in October 1866, was held from 19 to 24 November 1866 (*Shrewsbury Chronicle*, 16 November 1866). Hooker attended the sale on 20 and 22 November 1866 and bought several Wedgwood items (Fontaines ed. 1968; see item nos. 44, 60, 61, 72, and 175).

[6] Hooker later discovered that CD's sister Caroline Sarah Wedgwood had bought the items mentioned (see letter from J. D. Hooker, [12 December 1866] and n. 7). The medallion representing 'Hope encouraging Art and Labour under the influence of Peace' was made in 1790 and celebrated the founding of the settlement at Sydney Cove in 1788. Erasmus Darwin, CD's grandfather, had been given a medallion and composed verses to go with it (Reilly 1992, pp. 329–30). The portrait medallion of Benjamin Franklin was made in 1777 (*ibid.*, p. 236).

[7] Hooker was an avid collector of Wedgwood ware, particularly medallions. CD, despite his Wedgwood family connections, did not share Hooker's interest and occasionally joked about the subject (see, for example, *Correspondence* vol. 11, letter to J. D. Hooker, 13 January [1863]; see also Allen 1967, pp. 215–16).

[8] After Hooker told CD that he planned to publish his lecture on insular floras given at the recent meeting of the British Association for the Advancement of Science (J. D. Hooker 1866a) in *Gardeners' Chronicle*, CD had expressed reservations about the magazine, arguing that it was not 'good or permanent enough' and that few would be able to refer to it (see letter to J. D. Hooker, 2 October [1866] and n. 5). For the complete publication history of the lecture, see the letter from J. D. Hooker, [28 August] 1866 and n. 3.

To J. D. Hooker [23 November 1866]

6. Queen Anne St | W.
Friday

My dear Hooker

I will start, *weather & stomach permitting*, on Tuesday morning at 9° so shall be at Kew about 10°: Emma thinks she will not be able to come, perhaps Henrietta will.—[1] We will go to Mrs Hooker's house, & if you are not there will go on to Herbarium, after staying a few minutes with Mrs Hooker,[2] then a walk in the garden & home again

Ever yours | C. Darwin
If I fail on Tuesday, I will try on Wednesday.

Endorsement: 'Nov. 23/66'
DAR 115: 306

[1] CD visited Hooker on Tuesday 27 November 1866 (see letter from J. D. Hooker, 4 December 1866). There is no mention of the visit in Emma Darwin's diary (DAR 242) and no record of whether Henrietta Emma Darwin accompanied CD.
[2] Frances Harriet Hooker.

To James Shaw 24 November [1866][1]

24 November

[Saying he has seen the Athenæum & admires his article on beauty.][2]

Sotheby's New York (1986)

[1] The year is established by the reference to Shaw's article (see n. 2, below).
[2] The reference is to an article, 'Feeling of beauty among the animals', that appeared in the 24 November 1866 issue of the *Athenæum* (Shaw 1866b). CD cited the article in *Descent* 2: 71. For CD and Shaw's earlier discussions on the subject of beauty in relation to natural selection, see the letters to James Shaw, 11 February [1866] and [23 or 30 April 1866], and the letters from James Shaw, [6–10 February 1866], 14 February 1866, 19 April 1866, and 7 November 1866; see also *Correspondence* vol. 13.

From Anne Marsh-Caldwell 27 November [1866][1]

Linley Wood | Nr. Lawton | Cheshire
Nor. 27th

My dear Mr. Darwin

I long to say My dear Charles—but cannot venture upon that liberty with so renowned a man—[2]

Rosamond is at present staying with the Corbets—at the nice place they have taken near Oxford[3]—& she has just written to ask me by Mr. Corbets desire to write to you— He is the blind Mr. Corbet—who is I believe an acquaintance of yours[4]—but any how he has sent to ask me to write—&, as one never denies that dear Mr. Corbet anything—I trouble you with this— He has been troubled now, for more than a year—with poor health—nothing very important the matter—I believe—only just the destruction of all his comfort from constant malaise—fits of sleeplessness—depression of spirit—dislike to mental exertion—even a dread of those scientific & intellectual conversations in which he used to take all his delight— in short every one who has been thoroughly out of order knows the whole horrid *dragons* of such a state— Hearing from Rosamond what diet has done for you[5]—in which all to your most distant friends so heartily rejoice—he has desired her—"to ask if you would mind to Mr. Charles Darwin to ask what was the diet he pursued— he is an old friend of Mr. Corbets but they have not corresponded for some years— he would be glad if you would tell him— he has often thought of his old friend & felt for his sufferings— I have told Mrs Corbet[6] how much better Mr Darwin has been for diet—& he is anxious to know the particulars— I am convinced a great part of his miserable feelings arise from his inattention to these matters—. . . . Poor man he suffers very much— if Mr Darwin or Mrs. Darwin[7] would write to him straight—he would be very glad—& would like so much to hear from his old friend" So far Rosamond—& if you or Mrs. Darwin would be so kind as to write direct to him—I am sure that the letter would be a great gratification—as well as far more likely to have its due effect— I must beg of you not to give one moment of your precious strength to acknowledging this letter— I have just heard from Elizabeth W[8] how well you are & heartily heartily rejoice

Kindest love to Emma (Mrs. Darwin) I mean— I did so grieve to lose my own share—in sweetest Susan[9]—but they go away so sadly fast—those I loved in early happy days

Always believe me to be | very truly yours | Anne Marsh Caldwell

DAR 171: 41

[1] The year is established by the reference to the death of Susan Elizabeth Darwin (see n. 9, below).

[2] The Caldwell family of Linley Wood, Talke, Staffordshire had been neighbours and frequent visitors of Josiah Wedgwood II and his wife, Elizabeth (Wedgwood and Wedgwood 1980, p. 175). Anne lived at Linley Wood until she married in 1817 and resumed residence there with her three unmarried daughters in 1860 (*DNB*). Emma Darwin referred to the Caldwells as 'old friends' (letter from Emma Darwin to G. H. Darwin, [28 November 1881] (DAR 210.3: 32)).

[3] Rosamond Jane Marsh-Caldwell, Anne's daughter, was staying with Richard Corbet and his son Rowland William Corbet at Headington Hill house, Oxford (*Post Office directory of Northamptonshire* 1869; *Alum. Cantab.* s.v. Rowland William Corbett).

[4] Richard Corbet had formerly resided at Adderly Hall, Adderly, near Market Drayton in Shropshire (*Post Office directory of Gloucestershire, with Bath, Bristol, Herefordshire, and Shropshire* 1863). It is likely that he first became acquainted with CD when CD was still living at the family home in Shrewsbury.

[5] For more on CD's health and diet, see the letter to H. B. Jones, 3 January [1866], and letter to W. D. Fox, 24 August [1866].

[6] Eleanor Corbet.

[7] Emma Darwin.

[8] The reference is to Sarah Elizabeth Wedgwood.

[9] Susan Elizabeth Darwin died in October 1866.

From Alfred Newton 27 November 1866

Magd: Coll: | Cambridge.
27 Novr. 1866.

My dear Sir,

Pray accept my sincere thanks for the copy of your new edition which you have been so kind as to send me.[1] I should take it as a very great compliment that you have thus honoured me—were it not that I feel I owe the gift much more to your own good nature which prompts you to recognize the insignificant efforts of the humblest followers of natural science, than to any other cause—

I have had great pleasure in making (through my colleague Prof. Humphry) the acquaintance of your son at Trinity—[2] So far as regards the rewards given at present by the University it is perhaps well that his studies should be directed elsewhere—but I hope these will not in future occupy all his attention—[3]

You will I am sure be glad to hear that my lectures have been much better attended than I had any reason to hope, and that the study of Zoology seems to be not merely popularly but scientifically pursued among the Undergraduates—[4]

Trusting that your health will permit you with all speed to finish the great work we have been so long expecting,[5] | I remain, my dear Sir, With very great respect, | Yrs. most truly | Alfred Newton

C. Darwin, Esqre.

DAR 172: 46

[1] Newton refers to the fourth edition of *Origin*.

[2] George Murray Humphry was professor of human anatomy at Cambridge (*DNB*). George Howard Darwin was an undergraduate at Trinity College, Cambridge (*Alum. Cantab.*).

[3] Newton is probably alluding to the fact that George was studying mathematics rather than natural sciences which, at the time, was still a fledgling tripos within the university (see n. 4, below). George was considering a career as an engineer and had discussed the topic with CD's friend, Edward Cresy, a civil engineer (see *Correspondence* vol. 13, letter to Edward Cresy, 7 September [1865] and n. 2, and letter from Edward Cresy, 18 October 1865 and n. 4).

[4] Newton was the first holder of the newly created professorship of zoology and comparative anatomy at Cambridge University (see *Correspondence* vol. 13, letter from Alfred Newton, 27 October 1865 and n. 1, and A. F. R. Wollaston 1921, p. 133).

[5] Newton refers to *Variation*, which was published in 1868.

From B. D. Walsh [28 November 1866][1]

a favorable review of what the author is pleased facetiously to call the Darwinian Theory.[2] Funnily enough, the writer makes the same silly mistake that Agassiz made, & argues throughout on the supposition that Darwinism means the transmutation of species through the "conditions of life", utterly ignoring Natural Selection.[3] Certainly the fools are not all dead yet.

As you may see from the heading of this Paper, I am now Sole Editor of the "Practical Entomologist".[4] I have sent you a number or two of it, which I thought contained matter that might possibly interest you.[5] I wish you would correct any errors into which you may notice that I have fallen there or elsewhere. For example, Osten Sacken tells me that modern research has shown that *Ornithorhynchus parodoxus* is *not* oviparous. Is this so? And how came such a mistake to be made?[6] I have seen the statement in I don't know how many books.

If you happen to know any Ornithologist who wishes to exchange European Birds for North American birds, I have a particular friend here, "Dr. Velie, Rock Island, Illinois", who has a very fine collection & is an excellent manipulator of bird's-skins.[7] He is also an honorable man to exchange with, which is more than can be said of certain naturalists. But don't put yourself to any trouble on account of this matter.

The conclusion of my Paper on Willow Galls is at last about to be printed. It was finished last summer, but the Society being short of funds could not print it until now. When published I shall of course do myself the pleasure to send you a copy.[8]

Yours ever very truly, | Benj. D. Walsh.

Chas. Darwin Esq.

P.S. I suppose you heard long ago of the Human Skull found in California in *Pliocene* rock, covered by two solid strata of lava. Authority Prof. Whitney, one of our best geologists.[9] Casts said to have been sent to Europe.

Incomplete
American Philosophical Society (324a)

CD ANNOTATIONS
1.1 a favorable . . . books. 2.7] *crossed pencil*
4.1 The conclusion . . . Europe. 7.3] *crossed pencil*

1 The date is established by Walsh's endorsement on the envelope of the letter to B. D. Walsh, 20 August [1866], 'answered Nov. 28, 1866'.

2 The review has not been further identified.

3 Walsh refers to arguments in Louis Agassiz's *Methods of study* (J. L. R. Agassiz 1863), which he had criticised at length in an article in the *Proceedings of the Entomological Society of Philadelphia* (Walsh 1864a: see especially pp. 223–5; see also *Correspondence* vols. 12 and 13 for earlier discussions between CD and Walsh on this topic). CD's lightly annotated copy of J. L. R. Agassiz 1863 is in the Darwin Library–Down House (see *Marginalia* 1: 13); his heavily annotated copy of Walsh 1864a is in the Darwin Pamphlet Collection–CUL.

4 The monthly periodical *Practical Entomologist* began publication in October 1865 and ended in September 1867. Walsh's title, on the front page of each issue, was 'associate editor'.

5 CD's copy of the issue for 29 September 1866 is in the Darwin Pamphlet Collection–CUL. An article by Walsh on the gooseberry saw-fly (Walsh 1866a) is heavily annotated.

6 Walsh refers to Carl Robert Romanovich von der Osten Sacken. Evidence that *Ornithorhynchus paradoxus* (now *O. anatinus*, the platypus) laid eggs was provided in 1884 by William Hay Caldwell. Earlier studies based on dissection of the reproductive system of the platypus had suggested that it might be ovoviviparous (Griffiths 1978, p. 5).

7 Walsh refers to Jacob W. Velie. CD forwarded a page from this letter to Philip Lutley Sclater (see letter to P. L. Sclater, 24 December [1866], and letter to B. D. Walsh, 24 December [1866]).

8 The reference is to the second part of a paper on insects inhabiting the galls of certain species of willow (Walsh 1866b), published in the *Proceedings of the Entomological Society of Philadelphia*. CD's

annotated copy is in the Darwin Pamphlet Collection–CUL. Walsh had sent CD the first part of the paper the previous year (Walsh 1864b; see *Correspondence* vol. 13, letter from B. D. Walsh, 1 March 1865 and n. 14).

9 The reference is to the 'Calaveras skull', found in February 1866 in a mine in Calaveras County, California. The skull was 130 feet below the surface, beneath a layer of lava. Josiah Dwight Whitney, state geologist of California, acquired the skull and announced its discovery in July 1866 at a meeting of the California Academy of Sciences (Whitney 1866). He claimed that it was evidence of the existence of Pliocene age humans in North America. For more on the discovery and the ensuing controversy about the authenticity of the skull, see Dexter 1986.

From Herbert George Henry Norman 30 November 1866

Oakley | Bromley | Kent.

Dear Sir—

You asked me many years ago if I ever found a partridges foot with earth attached, you would like to examine it, as affording a means of dispersing the seeds of plants—[1] I shot a woodcock today and enclose the foot with some earth attached— Should it be of any use to you, I should much like to know the results, if it is not giving you too much trouble—[2]

I am yours truly— | Herbert G H Norman

Nov. 30th/66

DAR 172: 75

1 CD had obtained the foot of a red-legged partridge (*Caccabis rufa*) from Alfred Newton in 1863 (see *Correspondence* vol. 11, letter from Alfred Newton, 31 October 1863 and nn. 2 and 4). He may have asked Norman, who was a neighbour, for a similar specimen around this time.

2 There is an entry in CD's Experimental notebook (DAR 157a: 83) that reads:

> Dec. 2d. 1866 Mr Herbert Norman of Oakley near Bromley sent me leg of Woodcok with tarsus coated with mud, which *when dry* weighed 8–9 grains. Planted on burnt sand, Decr 3d. Dec. 8th a monocot: plant, apparently a rush, has [*after del* 'or Luzula'] has germinated!!! turns out *Juncus bufonius* or toad rush—

No record was made of any other plants having germinated. CD added the information to *Origin* 5th ed., p. 440. See also letter to J. D. Hooker, 10 December [1866].

To H. G. H. Norman [after 30 November 1866][1]

[thanking his correspondent for remembering to send him a woodcock's leg and informing him that 'from a ball of earth attached to the leg of a Red Partridge no less than 82 plants germinated'][2]

Incomplete
Christie's (dealers) (20 June 1990)

[1] The recipient and date are established by the relationship between this letter and the letter from H. G. H. Norman, 30 November 1866.

[2] See letter from H. G. H. Norman, 30 November 1866. For the germination of seeds in a ball of earth attached to the foot of a partridge, see *Correspondence* vol. 12, letter to Alfred Newton, 29 March [1864] and nn. 3 and 4.

From J. D. Hooker [December 1866?][1]

Kew
Saturday.

Dear Darwin

Will you send to Grove 115 Harley Street the titles of Walsh's & Fritz Mueller's papers, that he alluded to in his address, & the references to where published.[2]

Ever | J D Hooker

DAR 102: 120

[1] The date is conjectured on the basis of an endorsement in an unknown hand and by the reference to William Robert Grove's presidential address to the British Association (see n. 2, below).

[2] In his presidential address to the British Association for the Advancement of Science in August 1866 (W. R. Grove 1866, p. lxxiv), Grove referred to Benjamin Dann Walsh's research on the effect of food on the formation of insect races (Walsh 1864–5) and to Fritz Müller's observations on organs of different structure acquiring similar functions (F. Müller 1864c; both works are cited on p. lxxxii). While composing the address, Grove had asked for references to recent work supporting CD's theory (see letter from J. D. Hooker, 29 May 1866, and letter to J. D. Hooker, 31 May [1866]).

To Edouard Bornet 1 December 1866

Down. | Bromley. | Kent. S.E.
Dec 1st. 1866

Sir

Absence from home has prevented me from sooner thanking you most sincerely for your very great kindness in sending me the seeds of Papaver with the sketches & for your obliging letter.[1] I have long wished to see some of these closely allied sub-species, & I hope to make some experiments in crossing them.[2]

The subject seems to me extremely curious, & is closely parallel with Brehm's observations on the sub-species of several European birds.[3] I am much obliged for your permission to make use of the abstract of your very interesting experiments on hybrid Cisti:[4] at present I am not writing on hybridism, but incidentally I much wish to allude to one of your observations. I hope that you will soon publish your experiments in full detail.[5] I beg that you will present my most respectful compliments to M. Thuret; I feel that his message to me is a great honour, for during many years I have much admired his admirable observations on Algæ.[6]

Pray accept my thanks & with sincere respect believe me, dear Sir, | yours truly obliged | Charles Darwin

P.S. I do not know whether you feel any interest with respect to Climbing Plants, but I venture to send you by this post a paper on this subject, the last which I have published.[7]

LS
Muséum National d'Histoire Naturelle (Département Systématique & Evolution; Cryptogamie, Ms 501 fol. 387)

[1] Bornet's letter and the sketches have not been found. According to Emma Darwin's diary (DAR 242), CD was in London from 22 to 29 November 1866. CD had asked John Traherne Moggridge to find out whether Bornet or Gustave Adolphe Thuret could spare him some poppy seeds (letter to J. T. Moggridge, 13 November [1866]).

[2] CD was interested in the work of Alexis Jordan, who had argued that there was a group of poppies similar to *Papaver dubium* that ought to be classed as separate species because they bred true even when grown together for several years (Jordan 1860, pp. 467–8; see letter to J. T. Moggridge, 13 November [1866] and n. 4). CD mentioned experimenting with seeds of *P. vagum*, *P. depressum*, *P. lecoqii*, and *P. pinnatifidum* the next year (see *Correspondence* vol. 15, letter to Edouard Bornet, 20 August [1867]). In *Cross and self fertilisation*, pp. 108–9, CD reported the results of his experiments with *P. vagum*, and thanked Bornet for providing the seeds. *Papaver vagum*, *P. depressum*, and *P. lecoqii* are now considered to be varieties of *P. dubium*.

[3] The reference is to Christian Ludwig Brehm's study of German birds (Brehm 1831). In the manuscript of his 'big book' on species (*Natural selection*, p. 114), CD had observed that Brehm's classification created 576 new German bird species and commented that while it might be proper to ignore 'fine differences as specific', such variations certainly existed.

[4] The abstract that Bornet sent to CD has not been found, but in *Variation* 2: 140, CD wrote, 'I have heard from Dr. E. Bornet, of Antibes, who has made numerous experiments in crossing the species of Cistus, but has not yet published the results, that, when any of these hybrids are fertile, they may be said to be, in regard to function, diœcious; "for the flowers are always sterile when the pistil is fertilised by pollen taken from the same flower or from flowers on the same plant. But they are often fertile if pollen be employed from a distinct individual of the same hybrid nature, or from a hybrid made by a reciprocal cross."' CD also referred to information received from Bornet via John Traherne Moggridge (*Variation* 1: 389; see letter from J. T. Moggridge, 21 May [1866] and n. 6).

[5] No publication by Bornet on *Cistus* has been found.

[6] CD had read Thuret's study of the fertilisation of *Fucus* in 1857 (Thuret 1854–5; see *Correspondence* vol. 6, letter to J. D. Hooker, 4 December 1857) and had cited his observations on reciprocal crosses in species of *Fucus* in *Origin*, p. 258.

[7] CD refers to 'Climbing plants'. The paper first appeared in June 1865 in a double issue of the *Journal of the Linnean Society* (*Botany*), and offprints of the paper were produced in August 1865. For more on the publication history of the paper, see *Correspondence* vol. 13.

From Daniel Hanbury 1 December 1866

Plough Court, Lombard Street | E.C.
1 Dec. 1866.

Dear Sir

Some months ago you presented to the Linnean Society a communication (just now printed) from a certain *Fritz Müller* of Desterro in Brazil.[1]

Will you tell me whether this gentleman is still in that locality, and whether being so, I might address him for information on one or two pharmacological matters?[2]

I do not know in which province Desterro is situated.[3] The gazetteer I have at hand does not mention it.

Believe me to remain | Yours faithfully
Danl Hanbury.

C. Darwin Esq.

DAR 166: 93

[1] The reference is to Fritz Müller's 'Notes on some climbing plants near Desterro, in south Brazil' (F. Müller 1865b; see also letter to Fritz Müller, 23 August [1866] and n. 8). The paper is also published in *Correspondence* vol. 13 as the letter from Fritz Müller, [12 and 31 August, and 10 October 1865].

[2] Much of Hanbury's research focused on the botanical origin of drugs (see Ince ed. 1876, p. 496).

[3] Destêrro (now Florianópolis) was located on Santa Catarina Island in the province (now state) of Santa Catarina, Brazil (*Columbia gazetteer of the world*).

To Charles Lyell 1 December [1866][1]

Down.
Dec 1.

My dear Lyell

Emma has brought me your grand book, & I thank you sincerely for it, & still more for the inscription on the first page, which pleases me much.—[2]

Your additions are prodigious. (N.B an error, for p. 136, read 146)[3] & I long to read them & especially the climate chapter,[4] but I must refrain for some weeks, for my present work is actually delayed until I get through 5 or 6 books & long papers, & my strength for reading is not great.—[5] I heartily congratulate on the completion of so much of what is really a gigantic work.[6]

Believe me with cordial thanks | Your sincere friend
Ch. Darwin

American Philosophical Society (322)

[1] The year is established by the reference to the tenth edition of Lyell's *Principles of geology* (see nn. 2 and 3, below).

[2] The first volume of the tenth edition of *Principles of geology* (C. Lyell 1867–8) was published in November 1866 (*Publishers' Circular*, 15 November 1866, p. 722). The inscription in CD's copy (Darwin Library–CUL) reads, 'Charles Darwin from his affectionate friend Charles Lyell Nov[r]. 29. 1866'.

[3] CD refers to an incorrect page number in the list of changes that appeared in the front matter of C. Lyell 1867–8.

[4] Lyell had made significant changes to the material on climate, adding a new chapter on the fossil evidence for climate change during different geological periods (C. Lyell 1867–8, 1: 212–32).

[5] CD was preparing *Variation* for publication (see 'Journal' (Appendix II)).

[6] The second volume of the tenth edition of *Principles of geology* was published in March 1868 (*Publishers' Circular*, 1 April 1868, p. 179).

To Anne Marsh-Caldwell 1 December [1866][1]

Down Bromley Kent
Dec 1st

My dear Mrs Marsh Caldwell

Your very kind note has pleased me much. I shd. have answered it sooner, but there has been some delay, owing to our return yesterday from London, where we have been staying with Erasmus, who is only very moderately well.[2]

I am ashamed to say that I forgot the Christian name of Mr Corbet;[3] nor do I know his address; so will you be so kind as to direct the enclosed note for him.[4]

I have given him all the information which I could, but it is worse than useless to try by mere chance experiments in diet.—[5]

Emma has brought back a cold from London & is in bed, other wise she would have written & sent a note better worth receiving than this.

Pray believe me, my dear Mrs. Marsh Caldwell | Yours very sincerely | Ch. Darwin

American Philosophical Society (323)

1 The year is established by the relationship between this letter and the letter from Anne Marsh-Caldwell, 27 November [1866].

2 See letter from Anne Marsh-Caldwell, 27 November [1866]. According to Emma Darwin's diary (DAR 242), CD returned from London on 29 November 1866 and Emma herself returned the next day. Erasmus Alvey Darwin, CD's brother, lived at 6 Queen Anne Street, London (*Post Office London directory* 1866).

3 The reference is to Richard Corbet (see letter from Anne Marsh-Caldwell, 27 November [1866] and nn. 3 and 4).

4 The enclosure has not been found.

5 On Corbet's interest in CD's diet, see the letter from Anne Marsh-Caldwell, 27 November [1866].

From Fritz Müller[1] 1 December 1866

Desterro, Brazil,
1. December 1866.

Verehrter Herr!

Vor einer Woche erhielt ich Ihren freundlichen Brief vom 25. Septb. und danke Ihnen herzlich;[2] er ist sehr werthvoll und äusserst interessant für mich, da er sich mit Gegenständen beschäftigt, die gerade jetzt meine Aufmerksamkeit lebhaft fesseln.

Schon Dr. Hildebrand hat, wie ich durch Ihren Brief zu meiner Freude erfahre, beobachtet, dass die Ovula mancher Orchideen zur Blüthezeit nicht reif sind.[3] Dies scheint ganz allgemein bei Epidendren und Vandeen vorzukommen; wenigstens habe ich noch keine Art von diesen Familien kennen gelernt, welche ihre Ovula zu dieser Zeit ganz fertig hätte. Bei meinem Epidendrum triandrum, wie es heissen mag,[4] sind selbst jetzt—ungefähr 6 Monate nach der Blüthe—die Ovula noch nicht ganz reif. Das Säulchen solcher Orchideen pflegt nach dem Welken der Blüthe stark zu schwellen; die Pollenschläuche dringen bald in den Griffel ein und bilden sechs Fäden, die an seinen Wänden entlang laufen; diese Fäden kann man mit grosser Leichtigkeit von einander trennen. Bei Leptotes bicolor waren in einer Blume zwei Monate, nachdem sie mit ihren eigenen Pollinien befruchtet war, diese Fäden sehr dick und schneeweiss mit einem seidenartigen Glanze. Der Pollen scheint in vielen Fällen lange Zeit frisch zu bleiben, während er bei anderen Arten trocken und schwärzlich wird, bald nachdem die Schläuche in den Griffel eingedrungen sind. So ist es z. B. der Fall bei einem kleinen sich selbst befruchtenden Epidendrum (verwandt mit E. caespitosum). Die Caudiculi bleiben unverändert und Pollenschläuche werden nicht gebildet, weder bei dieser, noch, soweit ich weiss, bei irgend einer anderen Art von Epidendren. Wenn die Befruchtung durch Insecten-Thätigkeit bewirkt wird, so pflegen die Caudiculi gewöhnlich an dem Insectenkörper festgeheftet zu bleiben, an dem sie durch die klebrige Substanz des Rostellum angeklebt sind.

Was Pflanzen betrifft, die mit ihrem eigenen Pollen unfruchtbar sind, so vermuthe ich stark, dass manche von ihnen in der That wirklich dem Wesen nach dimorph sind.[5] Es stehen z. B. ein paar Büsche einer Ximenia nicht weit von meinem Hause und einige andere Büsche etwa eine Meile entfernt. Diese verschiedenen Büsche haben im Laufe von 10 Jahren nur zwei Früchte hervorgebracht. Unter der Annahme, dass die verschiedenen Pflanzen an jeder der beiden Oertlichkeiten zu derselben, in ihrer Function verschiedenen, obwohl in der Form nicht zu unterscheidenden Gruppe gehören, würde sich diese Unfruchtbarkeit leicht erklären. In anderen Fällen ist sicher kein Dimorphismus vorhanden, wie ich mich jetzt überzeugt habe, sondern (wie bei Dr. Hildebrand's Fall von Corydalis cava)[6] Unfruchtbarkeit mit dem eigenen, Fruchtbarkeit aber mit dem Pollen irgend einer andern Pflanze derselben Art. Dies fand ich z. B. bei vier Pflanzen von Eschscholtzia in meinem Garten, an denen ich einige Versuche machte. Diese vollkommene Unfruchtbarkeit mit eigenem Pollen würde kaum unbemerkt geblieben sein können, wenn sie bei allen Individuen einer so häufigen Gartenpflanze existirte; vielleicht mag sie bei meinen Pflanzen auf die Kultur unter abweichenden klimatischen Verhältnissen zurückzuführen sein.[7] Die Verschiedenheit der beiden Pollen wird an sonnigen Tagen 4–5 Stunden, nachdem der Pollen auf die Narbe gebracht ist, sichtbar, da alsdann der Pollen einer fremden Pflanze bewirkt, dass die Narbe sich aufrichtet, während der eigene Pollen keine Bewegung hervorruft.

Oncidium flexuosum ist auch ganz unfruchtbar mit eigenem Pollen und fruchtbar mit dem Pollen irgend einer andern Pflanze derselben Art.[8] Ich habe mehr als 100 Blumen befruchtet und unveränderlich dasselbe Ergebniss erhalten. Während der ersten drei Tage, nachdem man die Pollinien auf die Narben gebracht hat, ist kein Unterschied zwischen den eigenen und denen von einer anderen Pflanze. Die Narbenkammer hat so zu sagen zwei Thüren, welche in der nicht befruchteten Blüthe weit offen stehen. Im Lauf des ersten Tages wird die innere Thür, im Lauf des zweiten Tages die äussere, welche von den beiden seitlichen unfruchtbaren Staubfäden gebildet ist, geschlossen. Bald beginnen die Pollinien sich aufzulösen oder sich zuerst in Gruppen von vier und dann in einzelne Körner zu sondern, und diese einzelnen Körner senden Schläuche aus, von denen einige am Ende des dritten Tages schon von erheblicher Länge sind; das Säulchen erscheint leicht geschwollen. Im Lauf des vierten Tages erscheint bei den Blüthen, welche mit eigenem Pollen befruchtet sind, eine mattbräunliche Linie, welche die Pollinien von der Narbe trennt, und diese Linie nimmt schnell an Breite zu und wird dunkler, so dass am Ende dieses Tages oder etwas später das ganze Pollinium und die Oberfläche der Narbenkammer dunkelbraun geworden ist. Die Pollenkörner und Schläuche sind verschrumpft. Diese mit eigenem Pollen befruchteten Blumen welken etwas schneller als die mit dem Pollen einer andern Pflanze befruchteten. Die Fruchtknoten der letzteren beginnen bald zu schwellen und die rudimentären Fransen der Placenta wachsen schnell, obwohl 23 Tage nach der Befruchtung die Ovula noch weit von der Reife entfernt sind; die Pollenschläuche haben sich zu dieser Zeit bis über mehr als die Hälfte der Griffelsäule verlängert.

Ich dachte zuerst, dass das Schliessen der Thüren von der Narbenkammer und das Austreiben von Pollenschläuchen als Zeichen der beginnenden Befruchtung der Blumen angesehen werden könnte, fand aber später, dass—auch wenn man die Pollinien einer so weit verschiedenen Art, wie z. B. Epidendrum fragrans auf die Narbe von Oncidium flexuosum bringt—die Narbenkammer sich schliesst, die Pollinien sich auflösen und Pollenschläuche hervortreiben.

Ein altes Pollinium, welches ich 9 oder 10 Monate früher von einer anderen Art von Oncidium genommen hatte, löste sich nicht auf, sondern war, nachdem es 4 Tage lang in der Narbenkammer von Oncidium flexuosum gelegen hatte, schwarz geworden.

Ich bin jetzt in der Lage, Ihnen zwei neue Beispiele von Pflanzen zu geben, welche auffällige Samen haben und an den Klappen der Frucht festsitzen bleiben. Eines ist ein kleiner Baum, der zu den Meliaceen gehört, wahrscheinlich eine Guarea; die Pflanze hat acht ziegelrothe Samen, welche an den Klappen der Frucht befestigt bleiben (sie sind zu gross, um sie in einem Briefe zu senden); das Andere ist ein grosser Baum aus der Gattung Talauma (Magnoliacee).[9] Ich erinnere mich noch meines Erstaunens, als ich vor etwa 12 Jahren seine zahlreichen leuchtend gefärbten Samen an einer grossen Ananas ähnlichen Frucht baumeln sah. In dem Falle von Paullinia mag wohl der fleischige Arillus Vögel veranlassen, die Samen zu verschlucken; bei den Mimoseen und bei Rhynchosia ist keine fleischige Hülle vorhanden, aber die Samen sind ungewöhnlich hart, und da Hühnervögel häufig kleine Steine verschlucken, um die Zerkleinerung ihres Futters zu beförden, so habe ich mir gedacht, dass diese harten auffälligen Samen wohl zu demselben Zwecke von unsern Jacús (Penelope) oder andern Vögeln verschluckt werden möchten. Endlicher sagt von Talauma, dass die Samen eine "testa subossea" hätten.[10] Die Samen von Guarea haben weder eine fleischige Hülle noch sind sie sehr hart.

Unsere strauchartige Oxalis ist wirklich dimorph; ich habe jetzt die mittelgrifflige Form auch gefunden.[11] Diesmal kann ich nur zwei Arten zu der Liste der dimorphen Pflanzen hinzufügen:

1) Ein Lipostoma mit blauen Blüthen;[12] es wächst in kleinen Gräben zusammen mit der merkwürdigen moosähnlichen Mayaca; die Antheren der kurzgriffligen Form sind länger, die Pollenkörner grösser. Ich glaube, dass man unter den Rubiaceen noch manche dimorphen Pflanzen finden wird; denn in Endlicher's Gattungsbeschreibungen lese ich häufig: "stamina inclusa, stigma exsertum" oder "stamina exserta, stigma inclusum".[13]

2) Eine Statice, welche an der Küste wächst, aber auch feuchte Stellen liebt.

Nun zu der Veränderlichkeit des Kelches bei Hillia, auf die ich in meinem letzten Briefe hingewiesen habe.[14] Die Gattung Hillia, welche man auf den ersten Anblick nach der Form der Blumenkrone, der Samenkapsel und der Samen eher für eine Apocynee als für eine Rubiacee halten möchte, soll nach Endlicher einen "limbus calycis biquadripartitus" haben.[15] Nun kann man bei unserer Art an derselben Pflanze Calyces finden mit einem ganz verkümmerten Limbus, andere mit zwei, mit vier oder sogar sechs Laciniae. Die Länge der zwei Paare von Blättern, die unmittelbar unter dem Fruchtknoten stehen, ist ebenso veränderlich wie die Zahl der Laciniae des Kelches. Ich mass sie bei 19 Blumen. Bei 11 von diesen Blumen hatte der Kelch einen verkümmerten Limbus, bei sechs zwei Laciniae; in einer Blüthe waren vier Laciniae vorhanden, von denen zwei 6 mm und zwei kaum 1 mm lang waren, und in einer Blume endlich hatte der Kelch sechs Laciniae von 4 mm Länge. Die Länge des obersten Blätterpaares schwankte von 3 bis zu 50 mm, die der Stipulae von ganz verkümmerter Ausbildung bis 15 mm, das nächste Blätterpaar hatte 5 bis 118 mm, die Stipulae verkümmert und bis zu 32 mm. Die Krone hatte immer 6 Laciniae.

Sie hatten ganz recht mit der Vermuthung, dass in dem Falle des Lancettfischchens der Kampf ums Dasein mit Gliedern der wirbellosen Klassen stattfinden werde.[16] Hier wenigstens ist sein einziger Begleiter und Nebenbuhler in dem unfruchtbaren Sande, in welchem es lebt, eine Ophelia, welche dem Lancettfisch im allgemeinen Aeussern und in der Bewegung so ähnlich ist, dass ich, als ich sie zuerst sah, eine neue rothblütige Art von Amphioxus entdeckt zu haben glaubte.[17] Die Ophelia sieht in der That den meisten andern Anneliden so wenig ähnlich, wie der Lancettfisch anderen Fischen. Unser Lancettfisch scheint von der europäischen Form specifisch nicht verschieden zu sein; wenigstens konnte weder Johannes Müller, der von Kröyer gesammelte Exemplare untersuchte, noch Max Schultze, dem ich einige gesandt hatte, irgend welchen Unterschied von dem Lancettfisch aus Neapel auffinden.[18]

Indem ich Ihnen ein glückliches neues Jahr wünsche, bin ich, werther Herr, mit aufrichtiger Hochachtung treulichst der Ihrige. | Fritz Müller.

Möller ed. 1915–21, 2: 99–102.

[1] For an account of the reconstruction of Fritz Müller's letters to CD, see letter from Fritz Müller, 13 February 1866, n. 1. For a translation of this letter, see Appendix I.

[2] See letter to Fritz Müller, 25 September [1866].

[3] CD had mentioned Friedrich Hildebrand's observations on the development of the ovules in some orchid species (Hildebrand 1865c) in his letter to Müller of 25 September [1866].

[4] *Epidendrum triandrum* is a nomenclatural synonym of *Epidendrum cochleatum* var. *triandra*, a variety that does not occur in Brazil. It seems likely that Müller used the name here simply to refer to a three-anthered, self-pollinating form of *Epidendrum* (Robert Dressler, personal communication). CD added Müller's information on the immature state of the ovules at the time of flowering in orchids of the tribes Epidendreae and Vandeae to *Orchids* 2d ed., p. 173.

[5] Müller refers to the concept of 'functional dimorphism' that CD introduced in 'Two forms in species of *Linum*', p. 82 (*Collected papers* 2: 104; see letter from Fritz Müller, 2 August 1866 and n. 9). CD clarified his use of the phrase 'dimorphic in function' as referring to plants that could be 'divided into two equal bodies functionally but not structurally different' in his letter to Müller of 25 September [1866].

[6] The reference is to Hildebrand 1866d (see also the expanded German version of the paper, Hildebrand 1866–7b). CD had corresponded with Hildebrand on the pollination mechanism of *Corydalis cava*, and had communicated Hildebrand's paper to the International Horticultural Exhibition (see letter to Friedrich Hildebrand, 16 May [1866] and n. 3).

[7] Müller refers to *Eschscholzia californica*, a plant not native to Brazil (see letter from Fritz Müller, 2 August 1866). His suspicion that self-sterility in this plant might be related to the climate in which it was grown was later confirmed by CD. In *Cross and self fertilisation*, pp. 331–3, CD described changes in the degree of self-sterility in plants raised from seeds of *E. californica* sent to him by Müller and also gave the results of reciprocal experiments made by Müller on plants raised from seeds sent by CD.

[8] CD discussed Müller's observations of *Oncidium flexuosum* in *Variation* 2: 134–5.

[9] Müller had described plants with brightly coloured seeds attached to the valve of the fruit in his letters of 2 August 1866 and 1 and 3 October 1866.

[10] Müller refers to Stephan Ladislaus Endlicher's generic diagnosis of *Talauma* (Endlicher 1836–42, 1: 837). 'Testa subossea': somewhat bony seed-coat.

[11] Müller probably meant to write 'trimorphic', or Alfred Möller may have incorrectly transcribed or translated the word. (Like all of Müller's letters to CD, the letter was written in English and later translated into German for Möller ed. 1915–21. The original letter has not been found.) Müller had earlier told CD he thought the species was probably trimorphic, but had only found specimens of the long-styled and short-styled forms (see letter from Fritz Müller, [2 November 1866]).

[12] *Lipostoma* is now placed in synonymy with *Coccocypselum*. In *Forms of flowers*, p. 134, CD described flower specimens of *Lipostoma* sent to him by Müller.

[13] Müller refers to Endlicher 1836–42. 'Stamina inclusa, stigma exsertum': stamens not projecting, stigma exserted. 'Stamina exserta, stigma inclusum': stamens exserted, stigma not projecting.

[14] See letter from Fritz Müller, [2 November 1866].

[15] 'Limbus calycis biquadripartitus': lobe of the calyx biquadripartite (see Endlicher 1836–42, 1: 556). For a recent revision of the genus *Hillia*, see Taylor 1994.

[16] In *Origin* 4th ed., pp. 143–4, CD had remarked that the lancelet (*Branchiostoma lanceolatum*, formerly *Amphioxus lanceolatus*) would not compete with other fish, but more probably with invertebrates. CD added Müller's information to *Origin* 5th ed., p. 146. The lancelet was initially classed as a primitive fish but has now been moved to its own subphylum, Cephalochordata.

[17] *Ophelia* is a genus of the class Polychaeta (marine worms). For more on the similarity between some forms of Opheliidae and *Branchiostoma*, see Rouse and Pleijel 2001, pp. 53–6.

[18] Johannes Peter Müller reported that he received a specimen of *Branchiostoma* collected in Brazil by Henrik Nikolaj Krlyer (see J. P. Müller 1844, p. 8 n. 3). Max Johann Sigismund Schultze had written a paper on young specimens of lancelet (Schultze 1851).

From J. D. Hooker 4 December 1866

Kew
Dec 4/66.

Dear Darwin

How are you after your visit here last Tuesday? & how did you get home. It was a great treat to see you looking so well.[1]

I have no news, having been away in Norfolk to see my Mother, who appears to be comfortably settled at Norwich.[2] I received Lyells volume last night & am very anxious to begin it. What a comfort it is that he has returned to the old typography.[3] We must now keep him straight anent origin & development.[4] I dine with them on Tuesday, to meet Bunbury—to whom I shall give a hint on the subject.[5]

Have you seen the new part of Herbert Spencer,[6] some of it is interesting, but much of it is ponderous verbose & sesquipedalian to the last degree. Good God fancy a luckless school boy of 10 centuries hence having to translate it into the vernacular of his epoch!— Some passages trench on your subject of Pangenesis.[7]

Huxleys little book on Elementary Physiology is very clear & good for those who have a good knowledge of the subject, but what the "boys & girls" for whom it is intended can make of it passes my comprehension.[8]

I have just finished the New Zealand Manual, & am thinking about a discussion on the Geograph. distrib &c of other plants.[9] There is scarce a single *indigenous* annual plant in the group.[10] I wish that I knew more of the past condition of the Islands & whether they have been rising or sinking There is much that suggests the idea, that the Islands were once connected during a warmer epoch, were afterwards seperated & much reduced in area to what they now are, & lastly have assumed their present size. The remarkable *general* uniformity of the flora, even of the arboreous Flora, throughout so many degrees of latitude, is a very remarkable feature, as are the representation in the Southern half of certain species of the north, by very closely allied varieties or species; & lastly there is the immense preponderance of certain genera whose species all run into one another & vary horribly. & which suggest a rising area.—[11] I hear that a whale has been found some miles inland.[12]

Do you care to see Haast's lecture on the West-coast of Canterbury—[13] It is I think quite worth glancing over: as is Doyne's report on the formation of the lower plains of Canterbury, I can lend you both.[14]

At Cambridge I heard that Babington was very ill,[15] with a sudden attack of illness that puzzled the Doctor, Rheumatism Gout & Paralysis were all talked of.

I suppose you never were insane enough to speculate upon the status of life on the globe: but this question of replacement of species, plus a dose of Malthus which I took the other day, has set me to stupifying myself over the question as to whether the total amount of life, i.e. of living organized matter on the globe varies materially within the limits of our knowledge:[16] putting of course temperature on one side, a rise in which would I suppose largely increase the amount of organized matter existing at any one time, Temperature I suppose determines the amount of living matter existing at any time on the globe,—its fluctuations or unequal distribution the variety of life, & so forth. This may be all great nonsense, but I suppose the time may come when the inorganic equivalent of the organized matter on the globe may be measured or weighed.

What a curious discovery this is of Balfour Stewarts at the Kew Observatory, that the spots on the sun are connected with the positions of Venus & other planets, which thus either drag on one side patches of the Sun's photosphere, or otherwise so influence it that it disperses in spots that are exposed to their influence.[17]

This is a precious idle gossip, but it is like holding on to your coat-tails, after you have left Kew, yourself. & calling "Papa come back"—

My wife is much the same; eats well, which I suppose is everything at this time.[18]

Ever Yr affectionate | Jos D Hooker.

DAR 102: 114–17

CD ANNOTATIONS

1.1 How ... Norwich. 2.2] *crossed ink*
2.4 We must ... comprehension. 4.3] *crossed ink*
8.2 but this ... other day, 8.3] *scored blue crayon*
End of letter: 'Red seeds'[19] *pencil*; 'Woodcut Proc 8 or 9'[20] *ink*

1 CD was in London from 22 to 29 November 1866 (Emma Darwin's diary (DAR 242)). The Tuesday was 27 November.

2 Hooker's mother, Maria Hooker, had recently moved to Norwich to be close to her daughter Elizabeth Evans-Lombe (Allan 1967, p. 224).

3 Hooker refers to the first volume of the tenth edition of Charles Lyell's *Principles of geology* (C. Lyell 1867–8). The new edition was printed in the larger type-face of the first edition (C. Lyell 1830–3).

4 Lyell had entirely re-written the ninth chapter of his book, on progressive development of organic life, conceding that the geological record supported the case for transmutation, but maintaining that human beings were distinct from all other species (C. Lyell 1867–8, 1: 146–73; see also Rudwick 1998).

5 Hooker refers to Lyell and his wife, Mary Elizabeth Lyell, and Charles James Fox Bunbury, Lyell's brother-in-law.

6 The most recent instalment of *Principles of biology* (Spencer 1864–7), no. 17 (2: 321–400), appeared in November 1866. CD's annotated bound copy of the work is in the Darwin Library–CUL (see *Marginalia* 1: 769–73).

7 Hooker probably refers to chapter 10 of *Principles of biology* (Spencer 1864–7, 2: 377–88), in which Spencer discussed the heritability of variations occurring during an organism's lifespan. For more on CD's theory of pangenesis, see the letter to J. D. Hooker, 4 April [1866] and nn. 5–10.

8 The reference is to Thomas Henry Huxley's *Lessons in elementary physiology* (T. H. Huxley 1866). The book was 'primarily intended to serve the purpose of a text-book for teachers and learners in boys' and girls' schools' (*ibid.*, p. v).

9 The second volume of Hooker's *Handbook of the New Zealand flora* (J. D. Hooker 1864–7) appeared early in 1867 (Yaldwyn and Hobbs eds. 1998, p. 78 n. 2). Hooker had talked about writing a general book on the geographical distribution of plants on previous occasions (see *Correspondence* vol. 13, letter from J. D. Hooker, 1 January 1865 and n. 13).

10 In his recent lecture on insular floras (J. D. Hooker 1866a, p. 6), Hooker had commented on the rarity of annual plants on oceanic islands.

11 Hooker had speculated about the geological conditions affecting the islands of New Zealand in his introductory essay to the *Flora Novae-Zelandiae*, referring especially to the theories of Lyell and Edward Forbes (J. D. Hooker 1853, pp. xxi–xxvii; see also Turrill 1953, pp. 143–9). He and CD had long discussed various aspects of the geographic distribution of plants in New Zealand (see *Correspondence* vols. 5, 6, 10–12).

12 In the introductory essay to the *Flora Novae-Zelandiae*, Hooker had commented on the equable climate throughout the south temperate zone and speculated about how a change in the relative positions of

sea and land could affect climate (J. D. Hooker 1853–5, 1: xxiii–xxiv). In his study of the geology of New Zealand, Ferdinand von Hochstetter had reported the discovery of whale bones in the Waitaki Beds, which form the boundary between Otago and Canterbury provinces (Hochstetter 1959, p. 24).

13 The reference is to Julius von Haast and to J. F. J. von Haast 1865.

14 Hooker refers to William Thomas Doyne. Doyne made two reports for the New Zealand government on the plains and rivers of Canterbury (Doyne 1864 and 1865).

15 Charles Cardale Babington was professor of botany at Cambridge.

16 The reference is to Thomas Robert Malthus's *An essay on the principle of population* (Malthus 1826). In his essay, Malthus concluded that, although population increase was inevitably limited by the means of subsistence, it was impossible to put a definite limit on the 'power of the earth to produce subsistence' (*ibid.*, 2: 451). On the influence of Malthus on CD, see *Correspondence* vol. 12, letter to Ernst Haeckel, [after 10] August – 8 October [1864] and n. 8.

17 The observation is noted in Stewart 1865, p. 380.

18 Frances Harriet Hooker was expecting her sixth child (Allan 1967 s.v. 'Hooker pedigree').

19 CD's annotation refers to the seeds that he had recently received from Fritz Müller (see letter to J. D. Hooker, 5 December [1866], and letter to Fritz Müller, [before 10 December 1866] and n. 6).

20 CD's annotation probably refers to the woodcut that accompanied Müller's article on climbing plants, published in *Journal of the Linnean Society (Botany)* 9 (1866): 344–9. The journal's title had recently changed from *Journal of the Proceedings of the Linnean Society*. See also *Correspondence* vol. 13, letter from Fritz Müller, [12 and 31 August, and 10 October 1865].

To W. B. Tegetmeier 4 December [1866][1]

Down Bromley | Kent
Dec 4th.

My dear Sir

You will remember the note you sent me about Mr. Zurhorst & the eggs; & it seems so distinct that although your experiments were contradictory, I am tempted to give the case.[2] Pray tell me what you think. If Mr. Z. actually saw the eggs himself I would rely on him. Perhaps you will be so kind as to give me his address & I will write & ask.

I was very sorry not to see you in London but was unable to break my previous engagement.[3] I am now looking through my pigeon & fowl M.S. & am profitting by your remarks.[4] I hope in a fortnight to send the whole to press.[5]

My dear Sir | Yours very faithfully | Ch. Darwin

LS
Archives of The New York Botanical Garden (Charles Finney Cox collection) (Tegetmeier 99)

1 The year is established by the relationship between this letter and the letter to W. B. Tegetmeier, 9 July [1866] (see n. 2, below).

2 CD had asked Tegetmeier whether Frederick William Zurhorst would repeat an experiment that involved crossing a Cochin hen with a Spanish fowl in order to study the eggs produced (see letter to W. B. Tegetmeier, 16 January [1866] and n. 5). No letter reporting Zurhorst's observations has been found, but Tegetmeier evidently made the experiment himself and reported his results to CD (see the letter to W. B. Tegetmeier, 9 July [1866] and n. 4).

3 CD was in London from 22 to 29 November 1866 (Emma Darwin's diary (DAR 242)).

4 CD refers to the three chapters on pigeons and fowls in *Variation* 1: 131–275. He had asked Tegetmeier to comment on the manuscript of these chapters the previous year (see *Correspondence* vol. 13).

[5] CD sent the manuscript of all but the last chapter of *Variation* to his publisher on 22 December 1866 (see letter to John Murray, 21 and 22 December [1866]).

To J. D. Hooker 5 December [1866]

Down
Dec 5th.

My dear Hooker

I will send tonight (if I can find basket; if not next week) both forms of Mitchella repens, Leersia & some plants of Peloric antirrhinum;[1] these you can throw away if you like but they are well worth keeping, & I never saw anybody so pleased with a plant as was Häckel[2] with these monsters. I enclose some seeds of a twining Leguminous plant from Southern Brazil which you can throw away if you like; they adhere to the open pod.[3] As for the splendid crimson seeds I am going to pass them through a fowl & if they are not ground up & grow you shall have the plants; Müller describes the appearance of the tree as magnificent when in fruit.[4] I enjoyed my visit to Kew exceedingly & was only moderately knocked up. I was very glad to see Mrs. Hooker looking so well.[5]

yours affecately. | Ch. Darwin

P.S. I am ungrateful dog & quite forgot at time to thank Mrs. Hooker for telling me of life of my grandfather, of which I had not heard, but have now got it.—[6]

Endorsement: '/66'
LS(A)
DAR 115: 307

[1] CD had obtained specimens of *Mitchella repens*, a plant native to eastern North America, from Asa Gray in 1863 (see *Correspondence* vol. 11, letter to Asa Gray, 2 January [1863] and n. 5). He performed crossing experiments with the heterostyled flowers in 1864 and 1865, and reported his results in *Forms of flowers*, pp. 125–7. William Bennett had supplied CD with specimens of *Leersia oryzoides* in 1864 (see *Correspondence* vol. 12, letter from William Bennett, 25 May 1864 and n. 1). CD had sent Hooker peloric flowers of *Antirrhinum majus* and reported that all the progeny of self-pollinated specimens of peloric flowers were also peloric (see *Correspondence* vol. 13, letter to J. D. Hooker, 1 June [1865] and n. 11).

[2] Ernst Haeckel had recently visited CD at Down (see letter to J. D. Hooker, [21 October 1866], n. 1).

[3] Fritz Müller had reported finding the seeds of a leguminous twining plant with black and red seeds, probably of the genus *Rhynchosia*, in his letter of 1 and 3 October 1866, and evidently sent specimens to CD. At the top of this letter, Hooker wrote 'Abrus precatorius??', a guess as to the identity of the seeds.

[4] For Müller's description of the tree and the appearance of these seeds, see the letter from Fritz Müller, 1 and 3 October 1866.

[5] CD visited Kew on 27 November; Frances Harriet Hooker gave birth to her sixth child, Reginald Hawthorn Hooker, on 12 January 1867 (Allan 1967 s.v. 'Hooker pedigree').

[6] The reference is probably to Dowson 1861 (CD's copy is at CUL). CD already knew about the biography of Erasmus Darwin written by Anna Seward (see *Correspondence* vol. 13, letter from Hermann Kindt, 13 November 1865 and n. 3).

To Miss Behrens 7 December 1866

Down Bromley Kent
Dec. 7 1866

Mr Darwin has much pleasure in sending to Miss Behrens[1] his signature.
Charles Darwin

Michael Silverman (Catalogue 13) 1994

[1] Miss Behrens has not been identified.

To Linnean Society 7 December [1866][1]

Down | Bromley, Kent
Dec 7th

My dear Sir

Will you be so kind as to have author's spare copies of F. Müllers paper on Climbing Plants sent here to me that I may forward them to him[2]

Yours very faithfully | Ch. Darwin

Linnean Society of London, Misc. loose letters, case 1: C. Darwin (5)

[1] The year is established by the relationship between this letter and the letter to Fritz Müller, [before 10 December 1866].

[2] The reference is to Fritz Müller and F. Müller 1865b (the paper is also reproduced in *Correspondence* vol. 13 as the letter from Fritz Müller, [12 and 31 August, and 10 October 1865]).

From Robert Monsey Rolfe 8 December 1866

Dogmersfield Park | Winchfield
8 Decr 1866

My dear Mr Darwin

Your letter was forwarded to me in the Country where we are passing a few days in visiting some friends in Hampshire— But we hope to be back at Holwood[1] on Monday— I am sorry that you sh^d have had the trouble of writing to me, but I lose no time in sending you a cheque for my annual contribution to the Downe Charities—[2] We have met here Mr Charles Kingsley an old friend of ours, & he & Mrs Kingsley[3] have promised next month to pay us a visit— I hope you may then be strong enough to be able to see us if we call on you—[4]

Yours very truly | Cranworth

DAR 161: 234

[1] CD's letter has not been found. Holwood House, Rolfe's family seat, was 1½ miles from Down (Freeman 1978).

[2] Rolfe was a regular subscriber to the Down Friendly Club and the Down Coal and Clothing Club, of which CD was treasurer (Freeman 1978; see letter from Harriet Lubbock, [April? 1866], n. 4). CD

recorded a contribution of £2 2s. from Rolfe in 1866 in his Down Coal and Clothing Club account book (Down House MS).

3 Frances Eliza Kingsley.

4 The Kingsleys visited Rolfe from 15 to 19 January 1867 and evidently saw CD on 16 January (see *Correspondence* vol. 15, letter from R. M. Rolfe, 14 January 1867).

To Fritz Müller [before 10 December 1866][1]

Down Bromley Kent

My dear Sir

I have so much to thank you for that I hardly know how to begin. I have received the bulbillas of Oxalis & your most interesting letter of Oct 1st.[2] I have planted half the bulbs & will plant the other half in the spring. The case seems to me very curious & until trying some experiments in crossing I can form no conjecture what the abortion of the stamens in so irregular a manner can signify.[3] But I fear from what you say the plant will prove sterile like so many others which increase largely by buds of various kinds. Since I asked you about Oxalis Dr. Hildebrand has published a paper showing that a great number of species are trimorphic like Lythrum, but he has tried hardly any experiments.[4]

I am particularly obliged for the information & specimen of *Cordia* & shall be most grateful for seed: I have not heard of of any dimorphic species in this Family.[5] Hardly anything in your letter interested me so much as your account & drawing of the valves of the pod of one of the Mimoseæ with the really beautiful seeds.— I will send some of these seeds to Kew to be planted.[6] But these seeds seem to me to offer a very great difficulty. They do not seem hard enough to resist the triturating power of the gizard of a gallinaceous bird, though they might resist that of some other birds, for the skin is as hard as ivory. I presume that these seeds cannot be covered with any attractive pulp. I soaked one of the seeds for 10 hours, in warm water which became only very slig⟨htly⟩ mucilaginous. I think I will try whether they will pass through a fowl uninjured.[7] I hope you will observe whether any bird devours them, & could you get any young man to shoot some & observe whether the seeds are found low down in the intestines. It would be well worth while to plant such seeds with undigested seeds for comparison. An opponent of ours might make a capital case against us by saying that here beautiful pods & seeds have been formed not for the good of the plant but for the good of birds alone. These seeds would make a beautiful bracelet for one of my daughters if I had enough. I may just mention that ⟨E⟩uonymus Europæus is a case in point; the seeds are coated by a thin orange layer which I find is sufficient to cause them to be devoured by birds.[8] I have received your paper on Martha; it is as wonderful as the most wonderful orchis:[9] Ernst Haeckel brought me the paper & stayed a day with me. I have seldom seen a more pleasant, cordial & frank man. He is now in Madeira where he is going to work chiefly on the Medusæ[10] His great work is now published & I have a copy, but the german is so difficult I can make out but little of it, & I fear it is too large a work to be translated.[11]

Your fact about the number of seeds in the capsule of the Maxillaria came just at the right time as I wished to give one or two such facts.[12] Does this orchid produce many capsules? I can not answer your question about the aerial roots of Catasetum.[13] I hope you have received the new Edition of the "Origin"—[14] Your paper on climbing plants is printed & I expect in a day or two to receive the spare copies, & I will send off three copies as before stated, & will retain some in case you should wish me to send them to anyone in Europe, & will transmit the remainder to yourself[15]

With cordial thanks for all your great kindness, believe me, | My dear Sir, | Yours sincerely | Ch. Darwin

Endorsement: 'Received January 24th. 1867.— Answered February 2^{d}.—'
LS(A)
British Library (Loan 10: 10)

1 The date is established by the relationship between this letter and the letter to J. D. Hooker, 10 December [1866] (see nn. 6 and 7, below).

2 See letter from Fritz Müller, 1 and 3 October 1866. 'Bulbillas': i.e. bulbils.

3 Müller had found that 99 per cent of the plants he had observed of one form of a species of Brazilian *Oxalis* had sterile anthers. The specimens with fertile anthers ranged from those with good pollen to those with aborted pollen-grains and ultimately to those with no pollen (see letter from Fritz Müller, 1 and 3 October 1866 and nn. 2 and 6).

4 CD refers to Hildebrand 1866c. See letter from Friedrich Hildebrand, 23 October 1866 and n. 1.

5 *Cordia* belongs to the family Boraginaceae. In *Forms of flowers*, pp. 117–18, CD described the specimens sent by Müller with his letter of 1 and 3 October 1866, concluding that they were probably heterostyled.

6 See letter from Fritz Müller, 1 and 3 October 1866. Müller had sent these seeds and seeds of a twining leguminous plant (see letter to J. D. Hooker, 5 December [1866]). CD enclosed some of the seeds (later identified by Joseph Dalton Hooker as *Adenanthera pavonina*) with his letter to J. D. Hooker, 10 December [1866].

7 CD recorded the trial feeding of these seeds to a fowl in his Experimental notebook (DAR 157a: 80) and reported the outcome of the experiment in his letter to J. D. Hooker, 10 December [1866].

8 CD had referred to spindle-wood (*Euonymous europaeus*), in arguing that beauty or bright colour in fruits and seeds had developed as a means of attracting birds and other animals who would eat and disseminate the seeds, in *Origin* 4th ed., p. 240.

9 The reference is to F. Müller 1866a, where Müller described the mechanism by which *Martha fragrans* prevented self-pollination. CD discussed the process in *Cross and self fertilisation*, p. 5; he referred to the plant as *Posoqueria fragrans*. *Martha fragrans* and *Posoqueria fragrans* are synonyms of *Posoqueria densiflora*.

10 Haeckel visited CD on 21 October 1866 (Emma Darwin's diary (DAR 242)). For more on Haeckel's research trip, see the letter from Ernst Haeckel, 19 October 1866 and n. 2.

11 CD refers to Haeckel's *Generelle Morphologie* (Haeckel 1866).

12 See letter from Fritz Müller, 1 and 3 October 1866. CD included Müller's estimate of the number of seeds in *Maxillaria* in *Variation* 2: 379, in 'Fertilization of orchids', p. 158 (*Collected papers* 2: 155), and in *Orchids* 2d ed., p. 278. In 1864, CD had received information from John Scott on the number of seeds in an *Acropera* capsule (see *Correspondence* vol. 12, letter from John Scott, 28 March 1864 and n. 9).

13 Müller had asked CD whether all species of *Catasetum* had upward projecting aerial roots (see letter from Fritz Müller, 1 and 3 October 1866; for a description of such roots and their function, see Dressler 1981, pp. 30, 90–2).

14 CD sent a copy of the fourth edition of *Origin* to Müller in August (see letter to Fritz Müller, 23 August [1866]). Müller received it in late October (see letter from Fritz Müller, [2 November 1866] and n. 14).

[15] CD refers to F. Müller 1865b (see letter to Fritz Müller, 23 August [1866]; this paper is also published in *Correspondence* vol. 13 as the letter from Fritz Müller, [12 and 31 August, and 10 October 1865]). See letter to Linnean Society, 7 December [1866].

To Edward Blyth 10 December [1866][1]

Down Bromley Kent
Dec. 10th

My dear Mr Blyth

I hope that you will forgive me troubling you; when I had the very agreeable walk with you at Zoolog. Gardens,[2] you said that you shd. give in "Land & Water" case of tame deer in Isd. of Aral sea.— I have carefully looked in vain for this account.[3]

Will you have the kindness to give the Vol. year & page in Geograph. Journal, where I can find this account & oblige me much?[4]

Believe me | Yours very faithfully | Ch. Darwin

American Philosophical Society (Getz 4950)

[1] The year is established by the reference to Blyth's article in *Land and Water* (see n. 3, below).

[2] CD had been in London from 22 until 29 November 1866 (Emma Darwin's diary (DAR 242)); he refers to the Zoological Gardens in Regent's Park.

[3] Blyth's notice on the 'tame deer' (see n. 4, below) appeared in *Land and Water*, 15 December 1866, p. 495, under the pseudonym 'Zoophilus', which he used for his contributions to the paper. The Aral Sea, which is an inland sea or salt lake, is in central Asia in Kazakhstan and Uzbekistan.

[4] The reference is to the account of tame saigas (*Saiga tatarica*) by Aleksey Ivanovich Butakoff in his 'Survey of the Sea of Aral', published in the *Journal of the Royal Geographical Society* (Butakoff 1852, pp. 94–5).

To J. D. Hooker 10 December [1866]

Down.
Dec 10

My dear Hooker

Your letter which you speak of as containing nothing, interested me much.—[1] I enclose 3 seeds of the Mimoseous tree, of which the pods open & wind spirally outwards & display a lining like yellow silk, studded with these crimson seeds, & looking gorgeous.[2] I gave two seeds to a confounded old cock, but his gizzard ground them up; at least I cd. not find them during 48° in his excrement. Please Mr. Deputy-Wriggler explain to me why these seeds & pods, hang long & look gorgeous, if Birds only grind up the seeds, for I do not suppose they can be covered with any pulp.— Can they be disseminated like acorns merely by birds accidentally dropping them. The case is a sore puzzle to me.—[3]

Speaking of distribution Mr Norman sent me a woodcock's leg with 8–9 gr. of dry clay clinging to its *tarsus*, & by Jove this morning a little monocot., like a microscopical rush, has sprung up: of course this fact does not really make the means any more probable, but it is satisfactory & all the more as the Bird is a migrant & belongs to the order which first visits oceanic islands.[4]

I have now read the last no^{r} of H. Spencer: I do not know whether to think it better than the previous number;[5] but it is wonderfully clever & I daresay mostly true. I feel rather mean when I read him; I could bear & rather enjoy feeling that he was twice as ingenious & clever as myself, but when I feel that he is about a dozen times my superior, even in the master art of wriggling, I feel aggrieved. If he had trained himself to observe more, even if at the expence, by the law of balancement, of some loss of thinking power, he w^{d}. have been a wonderful man.— I have not yet read either Lyell's great work or Huxley's little work,[6] for I have at present much reading for my book;[7] & therefore will not borrow the papers on N. Zealand Glaciers.—[8]

I am *heartily* glad you are taking up the distribution of plants in New Zealand & suppose it will make part of your new book.[9] Your view, as I understand it, that N.Z. subsided & formed two or more small islands & then rose again, seems to me extremely probable. Your fact about the annual plants is extraordinary, & I shall be very curious to hear whether the prevalence of annual plants under different climates & on islands, throws any light on the problem.[10] When I puzzled my brains about N.Z. I remember I came to the conclusion, as indeed I state in the Origin, that its flora as well as that of other Southern lands, had been tinctured by an antarctic Flora which must have existed before the glacial period.[11] I concluded that N.Z never c^{d} have been closely connected with Australia, though I supposed it had received some few Australian forms by occasional means of transport. Is there any reason to suppose that N Z. c^{d} have been more closely connected with S. Australia during the glacial period when the Eucalypti &c might have been driven further north? Apparently there only remains the line, which I think you suggested, of sunken islands from New Caledonia.[12] Please remember that the Edwardsia was certainly drifted there by the sea.[13]

I remember in old days speculating on the amount of life, i.e. of organic chemical change, at different periods. There seems to me one very difficult element in the problem, namely the state of development of the organic beings at each period; for I presume that a Flora & Fauna of cellular cryptogamic plants, of protozoa & radiata w^{d} lead to much less chemical change than is now going on.[14]

But I have scribbled enough.— Yours affectionately | Ch. Darwin

I sent the plants off last Wednesday.[15]

Endorsement: '/66'
DAR 115: 308, 308b

[1] See letter from J. D. Hooker, 4 December 1866.

[2] CD had received the seeds from Fritz Müller (see letter to Fritz Müller, [before 10 December 1866] and n. 6). Müller had described the pods in his letter of 1 and 3 October 1866. Hooker wrote at the top of the letter, 'Adenanthera pavonina', his identification of the tree.

[3] CD had added a section on beauty as acquired through natural selection to *Origin* 4th ed., pp. 238–41. He had argued that the beauty of fruit served merely as a guide to animals to ensure seed dissemination

and that seeds were always disseminated by being first eaten (*Origin* 4th ed., p. 240). Bright seeds with no nutritive value to potential dispersers presented a problem for CD's hypothesis. CD recorded the experiment of feeding the seeds to the fowl in his Experimental notebook (DAR 157a: 80). For more on the dispersal of seeds like those of *Adenanthera pavonina*, see Galetti 2002.

4 CD refers to Herbert George Henry Norman (see letter from H. G. H. Norman, 30 November 1866). In his Experimental notebook (DAR 157a: 83), CD identified the plant as *Juncus bufonius*, toadrush. The woodcock (*Scolopax rusticola*) belonged to the Grallae or Grallatores, an order of birds that included all the waders. It now belongs to the order Charadriiformes, which includes gulls and shorebirds.

5 The reference is to instalment number 17 of Spencer 1864–7 (see letter from J. D. Hooker, 4 December 1866 and n. 6). For CD's comment on the previous instalment, see the letter to J. D. Hooker, 30 June [1866].

6 CD refers to the first volume of C. Lyell 1867–8 and to T. H. Huxley 1866 (see letter from J. D. Hooker, 4 December 1866 and nn. 3 and 8).

7 CD was preparing to send the manuscript of all but the last chapter of *Variation* to his publisher, John Murray (see letter to John Murray, 21 and 22 December [1866]).

8 Hooker had offered to send two papers he recently received from New Zealand (see letter from J. D. Hooker, 4 December 1866 and nn. 13 and 14).

9 Hooker had just finished the second volume of his handbook of New Zealand flora (J. D. Hooker 1864–7). He planned to write a general work on geographical distribution (see letter from J. D. Hooker, 4 December 1866 and n. 9).

10 Hooker had found hardly any annual plants indigenous to New Zealand (see letter from J. D. Hooker, 4 December 1866 and nn. 10 and 11).

11 See *Origin*, p. 399.

12 CD is probably referring to the argument made by William Branwhite Clarke and added to the fourth edition of *Origin*, that New Zealand and New Caledonia should be considered as 'appurtenances' of Australia (see *Correspondence* vol. 10, letter from W. B. Clarke, 16 January 1862 and nn. 13 and 14, and *Origin* 4th ed., p. 466).

13 CD refers to the tree *Edwardsia microphylla*, a species known only in Chile and New Zealand. CD and Hooker had argued for years about whether seeds could be transported by oceanic migration. CD had recently found further support for his view that some seeds could survive exposure to salt water in an article by Henry Hammersley Travers in which Travers had suggested that seeds of *Edwardsia* had been carried by ocean currents from New Zealand to the Chatham Islands (Travers 1864, p. 143; see *Correspondence* vol. 13, letter to J. D. Hooker, 22 and 28 [October 1865] and n. 11).

14 Hooker had suggested that temperature was a factor in predicting the amount of living matter existing on the planet at a given time (see letter from J. D. Hooker, 4 December 1866). In *Origin* 3d ed., p. 142, CD had written that the amount of life (as opposed to the number of species) supported on any area must be limited by physical conditions.

15 See letter to J. D. Hooker, 5 December [1866].

From W. B. Tegetmeier 10 December [1866][1]

Muswell Hill
Monday Decr 10.

My dear Sir

I did not write before as I expected to see Mr Zurhorst at Birmingham,— — From the conversation I have had with him respecting the eggs I do not think his information is sufficiently definite to be of use— It really amounts only to this, that a spanish hen running with his cochins laid dark eggs.— Whether she did so before or not he does not know[2]

My single experiment was that a spanish hen running with cochins laid *perfectly white* eggs, that were fertilized by the cochin and from which I hatched chickens

I regretted much not seeing you[3] I wished to ask you your conclusions respecting the original stock of the Guinea fowl, the Duck—The so called Buenos Ayres duck[4] and the Goose— I know practically very little of the origin of these birds and should like to be in accord with you in the Poultry Book[5]

Trusting you are quite strong | Believe me | Yours very truly | W B Tegetmeier.

C Darwin Esq

Should you like to write to Mr Zurhorst his address is

Belleville
Donny brook
Co Dublin

DAR 178: 77

[1] The year is established by the relationship between this letter and the letter to W. B. Tegetmeier, 4 December [1866].

[2] CD had asked for Frederick William Zurhorst's address in order to ask him about the eggs of a cross between a Cochin hen and a Spanish fowl (see letter to W. B. Tegetmeier, 4 December [1866] and n. 2).

[3] CD had been unable to see Tegetmeier in London during his November visit (see letter to W. B. Tegetmeier, 4 December [1866] and n. 3).

[4] The Buenos Aires duck was also referred to as the Labrador or the East Indian duck (see Tegetmeier 1867, p. 306, and *Variation* 1: 276). CD described the Labrador duck in *Variation* as having entirely black plumage and as a variety of the common domestic duck, descended from the common wild duck, *Anas boschas* (*Variation* 1: 276–7).

[5] The reference is to Tegetmeier 1867 (see letter from W. B. Tegetmeier, 22 January [1866] and nn. 10 and 11).

From J. D. Hooker [12 December 1866][1]

Kew
Wednesday.

Dear Darwin

The plants arrived all safe & are *most* acceptable, many thanks.[2]

I am getting up a good bed of Monsters, amongst which the *Antirrhinum* will come.[3] I am now busy rearranging & replanting our whole Herbaceous Ground, which will take all winter to get into order.[4]

I had a delightful dinner party at Lyells yesterday 2 Bunburys, (& Lady B)—Lecky the rationalist & Miss B. Coutts.[5] I have rarely really enjoyed a dinner party. Lyell looks uncommonly well & in great spirits.

I shall be glad to hear the result of passing the Leguminous seeds through a fowl, the red one you sent me resembles little Crab's eyes (Abrus precatorius)—

What are the splendid crimson seeds you allude to—anything difft from those you sent?—[6]

I hear that the Wedgwoods at Shrewsbury were bought by a Mrs Wedgwood of London—probably, as you supposed, of *Leith* hill—[7]

Lubbock gave a most interesting account at Linn. Soc. of a new sort of Centipede which gave rise to an able discussion by Busk & Huxley as to whether it was a new order or not. I thought Huxley's view the most rational.[8]

Ever yrs affec | J D Hooker

DAR 102: 118–19

[1] The date is established by the relationship between this letter and the letter to J. D. Hooker, 10 December [1866]. In 1866, the first Wednesday after 10 December was 12 December.

[2] CD had sent the plant specimens to Hooker on 5 December 1866 (see letters to J. D. Hooker, 5 December [1866] and 10 December [1866]).

[3] CD had sent a specimen of peloric *Antirrhinum majus*, the common snapdragon (see letter to J. D. Hooker, 5 December [1866] and n. 1).

[4] The arrangement of the herbaceous ground (or order beds) was based on taxonomic classification. From 1856, Hooker had begun to rearrange the beds, including fewer representative species of each genus, while increasing the actual number of plants (see R. Desmond 1995, pp. 183, 248).

[5] Hooker refers to Charles and Mary Elizabeth Lyell, Charles James Fox Bunbury, Edward Herbert Bunbury, Frances Joanna Bunbury, William Edward Hartpole Lecky, and Angela Georgina Burdett-Coutts. Charles Bunbury recorded recollections of the event in his journal (see F. J. Bunbury ed. 1891–3, *Later life* 1: 237–8).

[6] Fritz Müller had sent CD brightly coloured seeds of two plants, one of which he suggested might be a *Rhynchosia*, while the other he described as probably belonging to the Mimoseae, comparing the seeds to 'brilliant red pearls' (see letter from Fritz Müller, 1 and 3 October 1866, and letter to J. D. Hooker 5 December [1866] and n. 3). *Abrus precatorius* and *Rhynchosia precatoria* have very similar-looking black and red seeds. CD sent specimens of the black and red seeds with his letter to Hooker of 5 December [1866]. He sent the crimson seeds to Hooker with his letter of 10 December [1866].

[7] Hooker refers to the Wedgwood medallions that he failed to acquire at the sale in Shrewsbury of Susan Elizabeth Darwin's effects (see letter from J. D. Hooker, [22 November 1866] and nn. 5–7). CD's sister, Caroline Sarah Wedgwood, lived at Leith Hill Place near Dorking, Surrey (Freeman 1978).

[8] John Lubbock read his paper 'On *Pauropus*, a new type of centipede' at the meeting of the Linnean Society on 6 December 1866 (Lubbock 1866b). Lubbock later gave the animal the name *Pauropus huxleyi*. In modern classification, *Pauropus* is a member of the class Pauropoda, not of the class Chilopoda (centipedes). Hooker also refers to George Busk and Thomas Henry Huxley.

To W. B. Tegetmeier 12 December [1866][1]

Down Bromley | Kent
Dec 12

My dear Sir

Many thanks about Mr Zurhorst; I will not write.[2]

With respect to the duck I have considered the case well & am convinced that all the breeds including the Black Labrador & Penguin are the descendants of the common Wild Duck.[3] With respect to the goose there is more difficulty from the existence of 3 or 4 closely allied European wild species, & there is no indirect evidence as in the case of the duck. The evidence as far as it goes supports the belief of many good naturalists that the domestic bird is descended from the wild Grey Lag Goose, anser ferus.[4]

I have not attended to the guinea fowl & did not know that there was any doubt about its origin; I saw plenty of the wild bird in the Cape de Verd islands.[5]

I hope this is the kind of information which you require

My dear Sir | Yours very faithfully | Ch. Darwin

LS

Archives of The New York Botanical Garden (Charles Finney Cox collection) (Tegetmeier 100)

[1] The year is established by the relationship between this letter and the letter from W. B. Tegetmeier, 10 December [1866].

[2] See letter from W. B. Tegetmeier, 10 December [1866] and n. 2.

[3] In *Variation* 1: 279, CD concluded that several distinct breeds of duck, including the Labrador and the penguin (now more generally referred to as the Indian runner) were all descended from *Anas boschas* (see letter from W. B. Tegetmeier, 10 December [1866]; see also Tegetmeier 1867, p. 310).

[4] According to CD, *Anser ferus* (now *A. anser*) was probably the wild species from which the domestic goose was descended (see *Variation* 1: 287–8; see also Tegetmeier 1867, p. 312).

[5] In *Journal of researches*, pp. 3–4, CD recorded having seen a large flock of guinea fowl near the village of Fuentes on the island of St Jago (Santiago) in the Cape de Verd (Cape Verde) Islands.

From Edward Blyth 13 [December] 1866[1]

7 Princess Terrace, | Regent's Pk, N.W.

*[*Dec^{r}.*]* 13/66—

My dear Sir,

I only received your letter yesterday evening.[2] The notice which you refer to of saigas fearless of mankind is in type, but not yet published. I will see to the insertion of it, in the No: of 'Land & Water' for next Saturday.[3] I remember, however, that it occurs in a letter from Commander Alexey Butakoff to Sir R. I. Murchison, published in the 23^{d}. Volume of the Geographical Society's Journal.[4]

The pair of saigas in the Z. G. have greatly improved in appearance, & are likely to do well— they looked rather weakly on their arrival.[5]

A very interesting little beast just arrived is the *Hyomoschus aquaticus* from W. Africa, very like the Indian *memmina*,[6] but peculiar among all existing ruminants for having the metacarpal bones (& I think the metatarsal also) separate, or not united to form a cannon-bone,—approximating to the fossil *Dichobune*,[7] &c.

Bartlett told me that as he was going over the Gardens with a visitor who had been long in New Zealand, as they were looking at the Cassowary the bird voided about half a pint of pebbles, as is occasionally also observed of the Ostrich, Rhea, & Emeu.[8] The New Zealand colonist remarked that he then understood, at once, the origin of the similar heaps of pebbles, amounting to a quart or so, that he had commonly seen in N. Zealand and the meaning of which had hitherto puzzled him. Undoubtedly they had been similarly voided by the species of *Deinornis*![9]

The recent discovery of the complete skeletons of the "Solitaire" of Rodriguez I hear anounced for the next No. of Buckland's paper.[10]

Yrs sincerely, | E. Blyth

DAR 160: 207

[1] The month is confirmed by the reference to articles forthcoming in *Land and Water* (see nn. 3 and 10, below). In 1866, the Saturday following 13 December was on 15 December.

[2] Letter to Edward Blyth, 10 December [1866].

[3] Blyth's notice appeared in *Land and Water*, 15 December 1866, p. 495, under his pseudonym 'Zoophilus'. In it, Blyth referred to a report on saiga antelope found in an isolated island in the Aral Sea (see n. 4, below).

[4] The references are to Aleksey Ivanovich Butakoff and Roderick Impey Murchison, and to Butakoff 1852. Animals that were fearless of humans interested CD, who had observed tame birds in the Falkland Islands and the Galápagos archipelago, and considered that animal species acquired instinctive timidity only after prolonged exposure to humans (*Journal of researches*, pp. 475–8, and *Origin*, p. 212).

[5] In 1864, the Zoological Society of London purchased one saiga, which was received at the Zoological Gardens in Regent's Park on 21 November (*Proceedings of the Zoological Society of London* (1864): 728). Another saiga arrived there on 21 January 1865 (*Proceedings of the Zoological Society of London* (1865): 856). CD may have seen the saigas when he visited the Zoological Gardens in November 1866 (see letter to Edward Blyth, 10 December [1866] and n. 2).

[6] Blyth described *Hyomoschus aquaticus* (now *Hyemoschus aquaticus*), the water chevrotain of West Africa, as resembling *Tragulus meminna*, the spotted mouse-deer from India and Ceylon (Blyth 1864, p. 483; see also Grzimek ed. 1972, 13: 134, 150–1). The animal arrived at the Zoological Gardens on 11 December 1866 (*Proceedings of the Zoological Society of London* (1866): 619). It died in June 1867 and was dissected by William Henry Flower (*Proceedings of the Zoological Society of London* (1867): 954–60).

[7] *Dichobune* is an extinct genus of the order Artiodactyla (even-toed ungulates), found in Europe from the mid Eocene to early Oligocene (Lambert 1985, p. 186). *Hyemoschus* is a genus of the sub-order Ruminantia. In all modern ruminants the bones in the feet (metapodials) are fused to form a cannon bone, although in *Hyemoschus* this does not occur until after maturity (Nowak 1999, 2: 1081). When Flower dissected the specimen he described it as 'not quite full-grown' (*Proceedings of the Zoological Society of London* (1867): 955).

[8] Abraham Dee Bartlett was superintendent of the Zoological Gardens, Regent's Park (*Modern English biography*). Cassowary, ostrich, rhea, and emu are all large flightless birds (ratites), which consume hard substances to aid digestion. The Zoological Society's gardens first received a cassowary in 1857, and acquired a pair of Bennett's cassowaries (*Casuarius bennettii*) in 1858.

[9] *Dinornis* had four known species, including the New Zealand giant moa (*D. giganteus*), all of which became extinct approximately four hundred years ago (Feduccia 1996, p. 281).

[10] The Rodriguez solitaire, *Pezophaps solitarius*, a relative of the dodo, became extinct on Rodriguez Island in the Indian Ocean about 1790 (*EB*). Francis Trevelyan Buckland was the editor of *Land and Water*; the article on the solitaire appeared in the issue for 15 December 1866, pp. 493–4.

From Mary Everest Boole 13 December 1866

Private

Dear Sir

Will you excuse my venturing to ask you a question to which no one's answer but your own would be quite satisfactory to me.

Do you consider the holding of your Theory of Natural Selection, in its fullest & most unreserved sense, to be inconsistent,—I do not say with any particular scheme of Theological doctrine,—but with the following belief, viz:

That knowledge is given to man by the direct Inspiration of the Spirit of God.

That God is a personal and Infinitely good Being.

That the effect of the action of the Spirit of God on the brain of man is *especially* a moral effect.

And that each individual man has, within certain limits, a power of choice as to how far he will yield to his hereditary animal impulses, and how far he will rather follow the guidance of the Spirit Who is educating him into a power of resisting those impulses in obedience to moral motives.

The reason why I ask you is this. My own impression has always been,—not only that your theory was quite *compatible* with the faith to which I have just tried to give expression,—but that your books afforded me a clue which would guide me in applying that faith to the solution of certain complicated psychological problems which it was of practical importance to me, as a mother, to solve.[1] I felt that you had supplied one of the missing links,—not to say *the* missing link,—between the facts of Science & the promises of religion. Every year's experience tends to deepen in me that impression.

But I have lately read remarks, on the probable bearing of your theory on religious & moral questions, which have perplexed & pained me sorely.[2] I know that the persons who make such remarks must be cleverer & wiser than myself. I cannot feel sure that they are mistaken unless you will tell me so. And I think,—I cannot know for certain, but I *think*,—that, if I were an author, I would rather that the humblest student of my works should apply to me directly in a difficulty than that she should puzzle too long over adverse & probably mistaken or thoughtless criticisms.

At the same time I feel that you have a perfect right to refuse to answer such questions as I have asked you. Science must take her path & Theology hers, and they will meet when & where & how God pleases, & you are in no sense responsible for it, if the meeting-point should be still very far off. If I receive no answer to this letter, I shall infer nothing from your silence except that you felt I had no right to make such inquiries of a stranger.

I remain | Dear Sir | Yours truly | Mary Boole

43 Harley Street | London W.
Decr. 13th. 1866

DAR 160: 249

[1] Boole was the mother of five daughters. She was employed as a librarian in Queen's College, Harley Street, London, the first women's college in England. Although she had no formal teaching duties, she gave Sunday evening talks in which she discussed the relationship of different forms of knowledge. She was especially interested in the psychology of learning and her ideas on child psychology and learning were later taken up by educators in America (Cobham 1951).

2 Boole may have come across the remarks on CD's theory and religion while preparing her book, *The message of psychic science to mothers and nurses* (Boole 1883; for Boole's discussion of CD's theory, see *ibid.*, pp. 33–43). In the preface to Boole's *Collected works* (Boole 1931, 1: vii–viii), Ethel Dummer wrote that Boole's book was a 'series of talks to a group of London mothers who, finding their religion threatened by Darwin's new theories, sought Mrs. Boole's philosophic wisdom'. Although only published in 1883, Boole's book was completed in 1868 (see Boole 1931, 1: 81).

From Eleanor Corbet 13 December 1866

Dear M^r^. Darwin

M^r^. Corbet[1] does not like y^r^ kind letter to remain unnoticed, and therefore I promise to write and thank you for it, & at the same time I am to tell you, that tho' something better than he has been, yet he is so far from well that he does not feel equal to dictating a letter—[2]

Irritation of the mucous membrane is thought to be the cause of his distressing sensations, & there is no doubt that a very great deal is done by the strictest care in diet—& we endeavor as far as possible to get him to persevere in exercising every precaution.

He desires to send his best regards & believe me dear M^r^. Darwin | Y^rs^. very truly | Eleanor Corbet

Headington Hill | Oxford
Dec. 13th | 1866

DAR 161: 225

1 Richard Corbet.
2 CD's letter has not been found, but see the letter to Anne Marsh-Caldwell, 1 December [1866]. On hearing of the improvement in CD's health, Richard Corbet wanted to know what diet CD's doctor had recommended (see letter from Anne Marsh-Caldwell, 27 November [1866]).

To M. E. Boole 14 December 1866

Down. Bromley. Kent.
Decr. 14. 1866.

Dear Madam.

It would have gratified me much if I could have sent satisfactory answers to y^r^. questions, or indeed answers of any kind.[1] But I cannot see how the belief that all organic beings including man have been genetically derived from some simple being, instead of having been separately created bears on your difficulties.— These as it seems to me, can be answered only by widely different evidence from Science, or by the so called "inner consciousness". My opinion is not worth more than that of any other man who has thought on such subjects, & it would be folly in me to give it; I may however remark that it has always appeared to me more satisfactory to look at the immense amount of pain & suffering in this world, as the inevitable result of the natural sequence of events, i.e. general laws, rather than from the direct intervention of God though I am aware this is not logical with reference to an omniscient Deity— Your last question seems to resolve itself into the problem of Free Will & Necessity which has been found by most persons insoluble.[2]

I sincerely wish that this note had not been as utterly valueless as it is; I would have sent full answers, though I have little time or strength to spare, had it been in my power.

I have the honor to remain dear Madam. | Yours very faithfully | Charles Darwin.

P.S. I am grieved that my views should incidentally have caused trouble to your mind but I thank you for your Judgment & honour you for it, that theology & science should each run its own course & that in the present case I am not responsible if their meeting point should still be far off.

Copy
DAR 143: 121

[1] See letter from M. E. Boole, 13 December 1866.

[2] CD refers to Boole's question whether natural selection was consistent with the belief that each individual had the power to choose how far to yield to 'hereditary animal impulses' and how far to follow 'moral motives' (see letter from M. E. Boole, 13 December 1866).

From J. D. Hooker 14 December 1866

Royal Gardens Kew
Dec 14/66

Nothing to answer
Dear Darwin

The Scarlet seed is that of *Adenanthera pavonina* a native of India.[1] I am well acquainted with itself & with its habits from the year $-\infty$ (minus infinity)— At that rather (Geologically) early period it was a low bush, & the seeds were all black, (an allied species has seeds half-black & half-red, which *proves* this statement).[2] Gallinaceous birds were, *after its creation*, introduced into the part of the globe where I first saw it, & these sought the seeds with avidity: so that finally only those vars of climbing habit alone survived & thus got out of the way of the gallinaceous birds (which are not perchers)— its' chances of dissemination being thus diminished, the tendency to scarlet next developed itself in excess, being determined by the perchers (whose gizzards would not grind the seeds) & which were attracted by the color, & soon led to the extinction of all but the full scarlet forms.

Nonsense apart, I should suppose that it is to imitate a scarlet insect & thus attract insectivorous birds, or frugiferous perchers, of weak digestions, that the color is acquired. The plant is a very common Indian one, & it would be easy to ascertain how far it is a prey to birds.[3]

It is all very easy for Spencer to wriggle without facts, & if he spent a fraction of his brain & time in observing & experimenting, he would not wriggle so lithely—he is all oil & no bone.[4] Though I must confess that his sap & wood paper in the Linnean is a confoundedly good piece of scientific work—[5] I was disgusted with his wriggles *against* facts in the matter of some Umbelliferous flowers, & utterly so when he declined to bring the specimen to analysis, preferring to argue on the bare possibility of being right, against Bentham's Master's & my assurances that he was wrong & would find himself so if he would be honest & look his observations in the face.[6] I think he is now ashamed of this. He always reminds me of a thinking pump; though I can attach no meaning to the simile. it ought to have one.

I do not see how the M^{ts} of N. Zealand S. Australia & Tasmania could have been peopled to so large an extent by Antarctic forms common to Fuegia, without some intercommunication, & I have always supposed this was *before* the immigration of Asiatic plants into Australia, & of which plants the temperate & tropical plants of that country may be considered as altered forms.[7] The presence of so many of these temperate & cold Australian & New Zealand genera on the top of Kini Balou in Borneo (under the Equator) is an awful staggerer, & demands a very extended northern distribution of Australian temperate forms.[8] It is a frightful assumption, that the plains of Borneo were covered with a temperate cold vegetation that was driven up Kini balou by the returning cold.[9]

Then there is the very distinct distribution of a few Australian types Northwards to the Phillippines China & Japan, that is a fearful & wonderful fact,—though as these plants are New Zealand too for the most part, the migration northward may have been East of Australia.

Bentham was at Zoolog. Soc. last night & heard a very interesting paper by Gunther on fishes of oceans E & W. of Panama being the same; a fact which staggered the conclave.—[10] Considering the seabirds & short distance I should rather have wondered if it were not so. The Fish of the fresh water Lakes there seem very curious

I saw Grove at Athenæum— he had read abstract of my lecture in the publication of the meetings proceedings, & was so disappointed with the wind up, that he swears I have altered it—[11] I had difficulty in assuring him it was not so, & that it was "all in the telling" which is *quite* what I all along expected, & one reason why I have delayed publication— The sooner after delivery it is read, the poorer it will appear to those who heard it read. Now that the abstract is out, I send the entire affair to Gard. Chron—where I *intreat* you to overhaul it—, as I shall immediately reprint it for private circulation.[12] The G. C. will give me 40/ a column for it, which I am very glad of, as I have made a confounded fool of myself buying Wedgwood—[13]

I had not quite overlooked the state of development of life in the matter of bulk or weight of organic matter, but I think it may be wriggled through.[14] true enough the cellulares[15] would give rise to less chemical change if their vital phases were as slow as those of phenogams, but does not a Mucor effect more chemical change than a 10000 times bigger phenog. plant?[16]

I am so glad that you are at your big book.[17]

Huxley was telling me how much he wondered at the sensation of novelty that Grove's paper excited in the *hoi polloi* (I forget the greek letters!)—& was amused when I told him what I believe the real facts of the case to be, viz. that Grove's continuity doctrine was received at Nottingham as a sort of corollary flowing from, & subsequent to, your development theory!!![18] Of this I have no doubt whatever. Do not say that this is a cynical invention of mine, for I am sure it is a fact,—as it is that I am cynic enough to enjoy it—

Fancy my dining the next night after Lyell's at the W. Spottiswoods, where Lecky turned up again!—it was a nice party, Huxley, Sir B & Lady Brodie Greg (Creed of C^{m}.)—H Wedgwood,[19]—their house is a *Gorgeous* one. S. & his wife do a vast deal for their work-people, lecturing & so on, & are very nice & friendly but these London dinners are the ruin of Science, & I must now get on with "Genera Plantarum".[20]

So no more from your affec | Jos D Hooker—

DAR 102: 121–6

CD ANNOTATIONS

1.5 Gallinaceous . . . avidity: 1.6] 'No gizzards— Mr Dep^{ty} wrg[21] I soaked the seed hours' *added pencil*
3.2 he is . . . bone 3.3] *scored blue crayon*
3.9 He always . . . to have one. 3.11] *double scored blue crayon*
4.8 It is . . . vegetation 4.9] *scored blue crayon*
6.1 a very . . . being the same; 6.2] *scored blue crayon*
7.6 Now that . . . circulation. 7.8] *scored blue crayon*
10.6 Do not say . . . enjoy it— 10.7] *scored blue crayon*
11.1 Fancy . . . again!— 11.2] *scored blue crayon*
End of letter: 'Crossing Experiment' *pencil*; 'Australian flora Revue Horticole' *blue crayon*; 'Plumbago' *pencil*[22]

[1] Hooker refers to seeds, described by CD as crimson, which had been collected by Fritz Müller in Brazil. See letter to J. D. Hooker, 10 December [1866] and n. 2.

[2] *Adenanthera abrosperma* and *A. bicolor* are species with red and black seeds.

[3] CD had given some seeds of *Adenanthera pavonina* to a fowl, but reported to Hooker that they had been ground up in the bird's gizzard (see letter to J. D. Hooker, 10 December [1866] and n. 3). 'Frugiferous': i.e. frugivorous.

[4] In his letter to Hooker of 10 December [1866], CD referred to Herbert Spencer, whose *Principles of biology* (Spencer 1864–7) was appearing in instalments. CD and Hooker often discussed the latest number as they received it and commented on the speculative nature of Spencer's writing (see, for example, *Correspondence* vol. 12, letter from J. D. Hooker, 24 January 1864, and letter to J. D. Hooker, 3 November [1864]).

[5] Spencer's paper 'On circulation and the formation of wood in plants' (Spencer 1866) described the results of his experiments on the absorption of dyes by plants.

[6] Hooker refers to George Bentham and Maxwell Tylden Masters. Spencer had argued that the size and shape of individual umbelliferous flowers were related to the density and shape of the inflorescences (Spencer 1864–7, 2: 157; see *Correspondence* vol. 13, letter from Charles and Emma Darwin to J. D. Hooker, [10 July 1865] and nn. 7 and 8, and letter from J. D. Hooker, 13 July 1865 and n. 24).

[7] CD had discussed the possibility of a closer connection between Australia and New Zealand during a glacial period, allowing certain plants to move north, and at the same time, speculated about occasional transport as a means of distribution in his letter to Hooker of 10 December [1866]. Hooker had earlier favoured the explanation of a former land-bridge but had recently conceded that occasional transport was a viable means of distribution (J. D. Hooker 1866a). In *Origin*, p. 399, CD had suggested that New Zealand, South America, and other southern lands shared a common flora that came from the Antarctic islands before the Glacial Period.

[8] Mt Kinabalu (4095 m), in the state of Sabah, in the northern part of the island of Borneo, Malaysia, contains one of the most diverse assemblages of plants in the world (Beaman and Beaman 1998).

[9] Hooker meant to write 'returning warmth'. In *Origin*, pp. 378–80, CD had argued that temperate forms of vegetation had migrated towards the equator from both northern and southern hemispheres during glacial periods, then receded when temperatures became warmer again, leaving isolated remnants on mountains, as in Borneo.

[10] Hooker refers to George Bentham. An account of Albert Charles Lewis Günther's paper, 'Fishes of the states of Central America' was given in *Proceedings of the Zoological Society of London* (1866): 600–4. The complete monograph was later published in *Transactions of the Zoological Society of London* (Günther 1864–6). Günther reported that about a third of fish species were identical on either side of the Isthmus of Panama and suggested that at an earlier time the isthmus had been an island chain. He concluded that the species stayed the same even after the land-barrier separated the Atlantic and Pacific Oceans because the conditions on either side of the isthmus remained constant (see *ibid.*, pp. 397–400).

[11] Hooker refers to William Robert Grove, who was the president of the British Association for the Advancement of Science for 1866, and to the Athenaeum Club, Pall Mall, London. Hooker had given an evening lecture on insular floras at the British Association meeting at Nottingham on 27 August 1866 (see letter from J. D. Hooker, [28 August] 1866 and n. 3). The abstract Hooker refers to appeared in a report of the meeting published in November 1866; the closing part of the lecture was quoted in full (see J. D. Hooker 1866b, p. 227).

[12] The full text of Hooker's lecture was printed in instalments in *Gardeners' Chronicle* from 5 January to 23 February 1867 (J. D. Hooker 1866a). An offprint of the lecture with slight alterations to the text was printed for private circulation; CD's copy is in the Darwin Pamphlet Collection–CUL. The offprint is reproduced in Williamson 1984.

[13] Hooker had bought a number of items of Wedgwood ware at the sale of Susan Elizabeth Darwin's effects (see letter from J. D. Hooker, [22 November 1866] and n. 5).

[14] See letter to J. D. Hooker, 10 December [1866] and n. 14.

[15] Hooker refers to the 'plantae cellulares' or non-vascular plants of some older classificatory systems, among which would generally be included mosses, lichens, and algae.

[16] *Mucor* is a genus of filamentous fungus whose growth rate is several times that of a phaenogam (flowering plant).

[17] Hooker refers to *Variation* (see letter to J. D. Hooker, 10 December [1866] and n. 7).

[18] Thomas Henry Huxley was commenting on popular reaction to Grove's presidential address at the British Association meeting in Nottingham. On Hooker's reference to the speech as the 'Continuity' address, see the letter from J. D. Hooker, [4 September 1866] and n. 10.

[19] Hooker had been a guest of Charles and Mary Elizabeth Lyell on 11 December 1866 (see letter from J. D. Hooker, [12 December 1866] and n. 5). He refers to William Spottiswoode and his wife, William Edward Hartpole Lecky, Thomas Henry Huxley, Benjamin Collins Brodie, Philothea Margaret Brodie, William Rathbone Greg, and Hensleigh Wedgwood. He also refers to Greg's book, *The creed of Christendom* (Greg 1851).

[20] The second part of *Genera plantarum* (Bentham and Hooker 1862–83) was published in 1865, the third in 1867.

[21] CD had referred to Hooker as 'M^r^. Deputy-Wriggler' in his letter of 10 December [1866].

[22] CD's annotations are notes for his reply to this letter (see letter to J. D. Hooker, 24 December [1866] and nn. 5, 12, and 13).

To William Turner 14 December [1866][1]

Down. | Bromley. | Kent. S.E.
Dec. 14th

My dear Sir

Your kindness when I met you at the Royal Socy. makes me think that you would grant me the favour of a little information, if in your power.[2] I am preparing a book on "Domestic Animals," & as there has been so much discussion on the bearing of such views as I hold, on Man, I have some thoughts of adding a chapter on this subject.—[3]

The point on which I want information is in regard to any part which may be fairly called rudimentary in comparison with the same part in the Quadrumana or any other mammal.—[4] Now the os coccyx is rudimentary as a tail, & I am anxious to hear about its muscles. Mr Flower[5] found for me in some work that its one muscle (with striæ) was supposed only to bring this bone back to its proper position after parturition. This seems to me hardly credible. He said he had never particularly examined this part, & when I mentioned your name, he said you were the most likely man to give me information. Are there any traces of other muscles? it seems strange if there are none. Do you know how the muscles are in this part in the Anthropoid Apes? The muscles of the ear in man may, I suppose, in most cases be considered as rudimentary; & so they seem to be in the Anthropoids; at least I am assured in Zoolog. Gardens,[6] they do not erect their ears. I gather that there are a good many muscles in various parts of body which are in this same state; could you specify any of the best cases.— The mammæ in man are rudimentary. Are there any other glands or other organs, which you can think of.— I know I have no right whatever to ask all these questions & can only say that I shd be grateful for *any* information.

If you tell me anything about the os coccyx or other structures, I hope that you will permit me to quote the statement on your authority, as that would add so greatly to its value.—[7] Pray excuse me for troubling you & do not hurry yourself in the least in answering me.

Pray believe me | My dear sir | Yours sincerely | Ch. Darwin

I do not know whether you would care to possess a copy, but I told my Publisher to send you a copy of the new Edit. of the "Origin" last month.—[8]

Edinburgh University Library, DC. 2. 96/5 folio 1

[1] The year is established by the references to the Royal Society of London and to the presentation copy of *Origin* (see nn. 2 and 8, below).

[2] CD had attended a reception at the Royal Society on 28 April 1866 (Emma Darwin's diary (DAR 242)), where he met Turner. Turner then sent CD some of his publications (see letter to William Turner, 5 June [1866] and n. 2).

[3] The reference is to *Variation*, which was published in 1868. Although CD began collecting material for a chapter on humans, he soon decided that the subject needed a separate volume and eventually the material was used in *Descent* (see *Correspondence* vol. 15, letter to J. D. Hooker, 8 February [1867]).

[4] CD discussed rudimentary organs in animals and plants in *Variation* 2: 315–18, 397–8. He extended his discussion, including rudimentary organs in humans, in *Descent* 1: 17–31.
[5] William Henry Flower.
[6] The reference is to the Zoological Gardens of the Zoological Society of London in Regent's Park, London.
[7] Turner's response to CD's queries has not been found. CD included information from Turner on the muscles of the coccyx in *Descent* 1: 29–30.
[8] CD refers to the fourth edition of *Origin*, which was published in November 1866 (*Publishers' Circular*, 1 November 1866, p. 666). Turner's name appears on the presentation list for the book (see Appendix IV).

From W. B. Tegetmeier 15 December [1866][1]

Muswell Hill
Dec[r] 15

Dear Sir

Thanks for your kind note it contained precisely the information I wanted[2]

I hardly know whether you care to read the enclosed—[3]

When writing to me please return it at your convenience but do not trouble to write purposely.

Yours very truly | W B Tegetmeier

D[r] Sclater told me that statement about the Numida ptiloryncha in the last number of the Poultry Book[4]

DAR 178: 78

[1] The year is established by the reference to the most recent instalment of the *Poultry book* (see n. 4, below).
[2] CD had supplied Tegetmeier with information on the origin of the domestic duck and goose (see letter to W. B. Tegetmeier, 12 December [1866] and nn. 3 and 4).
[3] The enclosure has not been found. CD returned it to Tegetmeier with his letter of 18 [December 1866].
[4] The reference is to Philip Lutley Sclater. Tegetmeier's *Poultry book* (Tegetmeier 1867) was issued in fifteen monthly instalments, the most recent (part 12, pp. 266–88) dated December 1866. CD's unbound annotated copy is in the Darwin Library–CUL. Tegetmeier wrote that *Numida ptilorhyncha*, the Abyssinian guinea fowl, was probably the ancestor of the domestic variety (Tegetmeier 1867, p. 288; see also *Variation* 1: 294). The name is no longer valid, having been subsumed within *N. meleagris* (*Birds of the world*).

To Charles Lovegrove? 16 December [1866?][1]

Down Kent
December 16

I beg leave to acknowledge & thank you & Mrs. Love[2] for your very kind subscription of Emma[3] and I. 2/2/[0] to the Down [Coal & Clothing] Club.[4]

Incomplete
North Star Rare Books & Manuscripts

[1] The identity of the recipient is conjectured from CD's Down Coal and Clothing Club account book (Down House MS). The only year in which a contribution is listed from both 'C. Lovegrove' and 'M[rs] Lovegrove' is 1866. The original letter is complete and is one page long.
[2] Henrietta Lovegrove.
[3] Possibly a reference to Emma Darwin, although the transcription in the sale catalogue appears to be flawed.
[4] CD recorded a payment of £2 2*s.* from 'C. Lovegrove' and 'M[rs] Lovegrove' in his Down Coal and Clothing Club account book (Down House MS).

From M. E. Boole 17 December [1866][1]

43 Harley S[t.]
Dec[r.] 17[th.]

Dear Sir,

Thank you sincerely for your kind letter.[2] You have told me all I wanted to know from you. The criticisms to which I referred were such as seemed to take for granted that all such speculations as yours,—in fact, as it seemed to me, *all* independent untheological speculations on Creation as we find it,—must be incompatible with any belief in a moral government of the world. I have always taken the liberty of telling the people who brought such criticisms under my notice, that, in my opinion, the authors of them were simply talking about what they had never examined into. But still, when one is studying alone, & so ignorant too as I am, one gets frightened, & loses faith in one's own principles. And I thought, for my own satisfaction, I should like to have *your* assurance that moral & religious faith are things quite independent of theories about the *process* of Creation. You have given me that assurance and again I thank you.

With sincere wishes for improvement in your health

I remain | dear Sir | Yours truly | Mary Boole

DAR 160: 250

[1] The year is established by the relationship between this letter and the letter to M. E. Boole, 14 December 1866.
[2] See letter to M. E. Boole, 14 December 1866.

To Henry Walter Bates 18 December [1866][1]

Down Bromley | Kent
Dec. 18th

Dear Bates

Will you kindly do me a favour?— M[r] Blyth tells me that in 23[d] vol. of your R. G. Journal, there is a letter from Commander $\frac{\text{R?}}{\text{B}}$utakoft to Sir R. Murchison, in which the tameness of the deer on recently visited Isl[d.] in Lake Aral is mentioned.[2] Now if passage is quite short, will you have it copied for me, with man's name—proper volume, date, of vol. & page.— If passage is long, can you send me Vol. by Post & it shall soon be returned, as I want it soon.—

Forgive me troubling you | & believe me | Dear Bates | Yours very sincerely | Ch. Darwin

Cleveland Health Sciences Library (Robert M. Stecher collection), FF7

[1] The year is established by the relationship between this letter and the letter from H. W. Bates, 19 December 1866.
[2] Bates was assistant secretary of the Royal Geographical Society of London. CD had asked Edward Blyth for the reference to Aleksey Ivanovich Butakoff's article, which was communicated to the society by Roderick Impey Murchison (Butakoff 1852; see letter to Edward Blyth, 10 December [1866] and n. 4, and letter from Edward Blyth, 13 [December] 1866).

To W. B. Tegetmeier 18 [December 1866][1]

Down Bromley Kent
18

My dear Sir

I return the enclosed with thanks.—[2] I fully believe in the statement, but I have facts enough & this statement is anonymous. I had overlooked about Guinea-fowl & am obliged to you for calling my attention to it, for though I give only one paragraph to the Guinea-fowl, I sh^{d} have been vexed to have blundered about its parentage[3]

Yours very sincerely | Ch. Darwin

P.S I shall *very* soon now be able to return your 2 or 3 skulls, which I have kept for so enormous a time.—[4]

Archives of The New York Botanical Garden (Charles Finney Cox collection) (Tegetmeier 98)

[1] The month and year are established by the relationship between this letter and the letter from W. B. Tegetmeier, 15 December [1866].
[2] The enclosure has not been found.
[3] See letter from W. B. Tegetmeier, 15 December [1866] and n. 4.
[4] CD refers to skulls of the white-crested Polish fowl and the horned fowl. He had borrowed Tegetmeier's collection of fowl skulls in 1861 (see *Correspondence* vol. 9, letters to W. B. Tegetmeier, 25 February [1861] and 1 March [1861]). He sent the skulls of the white-crested Polish and the horned fowl to George Brettingham Sowerby Jr in October 1866 to assist Sowerby in making corrections to plates for *Variation* (see letter to G. B. Sowerby, 19 October [1866]). He returned the skulls to Tegetmeier in January 1867 (see *Correspondence* vol. 15, letter to W. B. Tegetmeier, 6 January [1867]). CD included illustrations of these skulls in *Variation* 1: 262, 265.

From H. W. Bates 19 December 1866

Royal Geographical Society | 15, Whitehall Place, S.W.
Decem 19th 1866

My dear Mr Darwin

On the other side is the extract you require.[1] I presume "saigak" means the same as "saiga", therefore the animals were the saiga antelope.[2] The islands were new *discoveries*; the Kirghises of the Aral shores did not know of their existence.[3]

Yours sincerely | H W Bates

I am now reading Lyells 1st vol. New Ed. Principles, with intense pleasure & great profit[4]

DAR 160: 82

[1] See letter to H. W. Bates, 18 December [1866]. Bates evidently affixed a separate piece of paper with a short extract from the *Journal of the Royal Geographical Society* (Butakoff 1852, pp. 94–5) to the verso of the letter, but the extract is now missing.

[2] In Russian, 'saigak' is a slightly older variation of 'saiga' (*Saiga tatarica*; *SSRLI*).

[3] Butakoff found the saigas on a newly discovered island in the Aral Sea that he named Nicolas 1st Island. The Kirghiz are a Mongolian people of west central Asia who inhabit the area around the Aral Sea.

[4] Bates refers to the first volume of the tenth edition of *Principles of geology* (C. Lyell 1867–8), which appeared in November 1866 (*Publishers' Circular*, 15 November 1866, p. 722).

To John Murray 21 and 22 December [1866][1]

Down. | *Bromley.* | *Kent. S.E.*
Dec. 21.

My dear sir

I herewith send all the M.S. excepting the last chapter which I can write before I get the proof sheets, & excepting a chapter on Man,—though it will depend upon circumstances whether I shall write this.—[2] I fear I shall never get the book done by April[3] & certainly not if I give the chapter on Man; but I am most anxious to begin at once printing otherwise I shall go on adding forever.

The wood blocks are ready except revising.[4]

Please to look at the enclosed instructions, about foot-notes & size of page & please be sure to forward the paper of Instructions with the M.S.

I enclose two titles for you to give your opinion which you like best,— that is if it is not too late to make any change.[5]

After going through all my M.S. I have come to the conclusion, which I am very sorry for, that the book probably will not have a large sale. Perhaps Chap. 1 w^{d} give a fair & favorable idea of the interest of the first ten Chapters; but the latter chapters are the most valuable, though now illegible.

I shall wish to hear how large the book will be—

My dear Sir | yours very sincerely | Ch. Darwin

Dec 22^{d}. P.S. I have just seen all my M.S. together & am utterly dismayed at its bulk; it must be two volumes I fear & large volumes.— The end of Chapt X or XI. w^{d} be best division.— I add a mere list of chapters for your use.—[6]

LS(A)
Herb Sewell (private collection)

[1] The year is established by the reference to the manuscript of *Variation* (see n. 2, below).

[2] CD refers to the manuscript of *Variation*. On his proposed chapter on humans, see the letter to William Turner, 14 December [1866] and n. 3.

[3] CD may be alluding to the fact that Murray usually released new works only in spring and autumn (see *Correspondence* vol. 15, letter to W. B. Tegetmeier, 6 January [1867]). *Variation* was published in January 1868 (Freeman 1977).

[4] Luke Wells and George Brettingham Sowerby Jr provided illustrations for *Variation* (see letter from John Murray, 18 October [1866] and n. 3). CD had asked Sowerby to make some revisions to his woodcuts in October (see letter to G. B. Sowerby, 19 October [1866]).

[5] The enclosures have not been found. *Variation* had been advertised the previous year under the title 'Domesticated Animals and Cultivated Plants, or the Principles of Variation, Inheritance, Reversion, Crossing, Interbreeding, and Selection under Domestication' (*Publishers' Circular*, 1 August 1865, p. 386).

[6] The enclosed list has not been found. In the printed version, the first volume ends with chapter 11.

From Lydia Ernestine Becker 22 December 1866

10 Grove st | Ardwick. Manchester
Dec. 22. 1866.

My dear Mr. Darwin

Before proceeding to the object of my letter I must try to recall my name to your recollection. I scarcely dare flatter myself, that I can do this successfully, though the remembrance of your great kindness and courtesy to me will never fade from my mind and is a constant source of pride and pleasure.

In the summer of 1863 I ventured to send you some flowers of *Lychnis diurna* which seemed to present some curious characteristics, and though they proved on examination not to possess the interest you at first thought they might have with respect to your own investigations you were good enough to write me several notes about them.[1] You also did me the honour to send me a copy of a paper you had read to the Linnæan Society on two forms in the genus *Linum* and I had the greatest pleasure in immediately procuring a pot of seedlings of crimson flax—and watching the appearances you had recorded[2]

At first the plants which bloomed had long styled flowers only, and at this point my correspondence with you came to a natural close, leaving you under the impression that there had been a failure in my observations. I have often since wished that I could have expressed to you the admiration and delight with which I perceived how, when the short styled flowers at last made their appearance, the capsules which till then, had withered away with the petals, seemed to start into life—how they grew and they swelled and rapidly became vigorous and healthy fruits— But I had no pretext for troubling you with any further communication and I feared I had already trespassed too much on your attention.

I have not been able to pursue my study of the Lychis flowers nor my endeavours to penetrate the mystery of their alteration in form, for since then we have ceased to reside in the country and now, surrounded by acres of bricks and mortar—and an atmosphere laden with coal smoke, I have no opportunity of watching living plants.[3]

But living in a town has its advantages, among others it makes possible such societies as that indicated in the circular I have taken the liberty to enclose. A few ladies have joined together hoping for much pleasure and instruction from their little society, which is quite in its infancy and needs a helping hand. Am I altogether too presumptuous in seeking this help from you? Our petition is—would you be so very good as to send us a paper to be read at our first meeting[4] Of course we are not so unreasonable as to desire that you should write anything specially for us, but I think it possible you may have by you a copy of some paper such as that on the *Linum* which you have communicated to the learned societies but which is unknown and inaccessible to us unless through your kindness. In your paper on the *Linum* you mention your experiments on *Primula*[5] which greatly excite my interest and curiosity, for last spring as I was gathering primroses I was forcibly struck with the difference between the "pin eyed" flowers, and those in which the stigma was concealed beneath the anthers. I have known of this difference in the Polyanthus[6] from childhood, but not until I read your paper was I aware of its interest or importance and now I have just enough information to excite and tantalise, but not to satisfy, a strong desire for more. If you will pardon the presumption of the request, I would beg that your goodness might prompt you to send something you may have on hand in the form of pamphet or paper which would help us to learn the meaning of these curious differences in the flowers, and as we may all hope during the coming spring for the pleasure of luxuriating on a primrose bank we should indeed be grateful for the kindness that had guided us to look more closely into the beautiful things we were enjoying.

I send this with much misgiving lest you may be displeased at the liberty I have taken if I have a hope of pardon it rests entirely on your goodness.

Believe me always | yours much obliged | Lydia E. Becker.

DAR 160: 113

[1] Becker and CD had corresponded in the spring and summer of 1863, but only one of CD's letters to Becker has been found (see *Correspondence* vol. 11, letter to L. E. Becker, 2 August [1863]). Becker's observations on the flowers of *Lychnis diurna* (she had earlier referred to it as *L. dioica*) suggested that the species might be dimorphic, but the apparent differences were the result of a parasitic fungus (see *Correspondence* vol. 11, letter from L. E. Becker, 28 May [1863]; see also Becker's later paper on the topic, Becker 1869).

[2] CD had sent Becker a copy of 'Two forms in species of *Linum*', inspiring her to make her own observations (see *Correspondence* vol. 11, letter from L. E. Becker, 31 July [1863]). Crimson flax, *Linum grandiflorum*, was one of the species discussed in 'Two forms in species of *Linum*' (see pp. 69–75; *Collected papers* 2: 93–8).

[3] In 1865 Becker had moved from Altham, Lancashire, to Manchester (Blackburn 1902, pp. 28–9).

[4] The enclosure has not been found. Becker was the president of the Manchester Ladies' Literary Society, whose inaugural meeting was held at the Royal Institution, Manchester, on 30 January 1867 (Blackburn 1902, p. 31). Becker presented CD's 'Climbing plants' at the meeting (see *Correspondence* vol 15, letter from L. E. Becker, 6 February 1867).

[5] See 'Two forms in species of *Linum*', p. 70 (*Collected papers* 2: 94). CD was referring to the experiments published in 'Dimorphic condition in *Primula*'.

[6] Polyanthus is the common name of a hybrid group derived from some species of the genus *Primula*.

To T. H. Huxley 22 December [1866][1]

Down. | *Bromley.* | *Kent. S.E.*
Dec. 22^{d}

My dear Huxley

I suppose that you have received Häckels book some time ago, as I have done.[2] Whenever you have had time to read through some of it, enough to judge by, I shall be very curious to hear your judgment.— I have been able to read a page or two here & there, & have been interested & instructed by parts. But my *vague* impression is that too much space is given to methodical details, & I can find hardly any facts or detailed new views. The number of new words, to a man like myself weak in his Greek, is something dreadful. He seems to have a passion for defining, I daresay very well, & for coining new words.[3] From my very vague notions on the book & from its immense size, I sh^{d}. fear a Translation was out of the question. I see he often quotes both of us with praise.—

I am sure I sh^{d}. like the book much, if I could read it straight off instead of groaning & swearing at each sentence.

I have not yet had time to read your Phys. book except one chapter; but I have just reread your book on "Man's Place &c", & I think I admire it more this second time even than the first.[4] I doubt whether you will ever have time, but if ever you have, do read the Chapt. on Hybridism in new Edit. of Origin,[5] for I am very anxious to make you think less seriously on that difficulty.— I have improved the Chapt. a good deal I think, & have come to more definite views— Asa Gray & Fritz Müller (the latter especially) think that the new facts on illegitimate offspring of dimorphic plants throw much indirect light on the subject.—[6] Now that I have worked up Domestic Animals I am convinced of the truth of the Pallasian view of loss of sterility under Domestication & this seems to me to explain much.—[7]

But I had no vile intention, when I began this note, of running on at such length on Hybridism, but you have been Objector-General on this head.—[8]

Ever my dear Huxley | Your sincere friend | Ch. Darwin

Imperial College of Science, Technology, and Medicine Archives (Huxley 5: 196)

[1] The year is established by the reference to Ernst Haeckel's *Generelle Morphologie* (see n. 2, below).

[2] Haeckel had arranged in October 1866 to have a copy of his book, *Generelle Morphologie* (Haeckel 1866), sent to CD (see letter from Ernst Haeckel, 19 October 1866 and n. 3).

[3] Among the neologisms in Haeckel's book are 'ontogeny' (Ontogenie), 'phylogeny' (Phylogenie), and 'ecology' (Œcologie; see Haeckel 1866, 1: 53, 57 and 2: 286). On Haeckel's coining of new words, see S. J. Gould 1977, p. 76.

[4] CD refers to *Lessons in elementary physiology* (T. H. Huxley 1866) and *Evidence as to man's place in nature* (T. H. Huxley 1863a). CD's annotated copy of T. H. Huxley 1863a is in the Darwin Library–CUL (see *Marginalia* 1: 424). For CD's original criticism, see *Correspondence* vol. 11, letter to T. H. Huxley, 26 [February 1863].

[5] See *Origin* 4th ed., pp. 292–338.

[6] Huxley had frequently maintained that natural selection could not be fully accepted as a mechanism of the origin of species until a new species created by means of artificial selection had been produced (see, for example, T. H. Huxley 1863b, pp. 147–9). His position was based on the widely accepted view

that sterility of hybrids was an essential criterion of species. Huxley's critique served as an important impetus to CD's investigations into cross and hybrid sterility. For a summary of CD's and Huxley's earlier discussions on the topic, and some of CD's unpublished notes on hybridity, see *Correspondence* vol. 10, Appendix VI. In *Origin* 4th ed., p. 323, CD remarked that 'the physiological test of lessened fertility, both in first crosses and in hybrids, is no safe criterion of specific distinction'. Asa Gray had recently written that the resemblance of dimorphic crosses to hybrid crosses was a 'Very interesting & capital point' in favour of CD (see letter from Asa Gray, 10 October 1866 and n. 7). Müller had been collecting information on dimorphic and trimorphic plants since CD had asked him to observe whether Brazilian varieties of *Oxalis* exhibited different forms (letter to Fritz Müller, 23 May 1866; see letters from Fritz Müller, 2 August 1866, 1 and 3 October 1866, and [2 November 1866]).

7 The reference is to Pyotr Simon Pallas and his view that under a long period of domestication the tendency to sterility in crosses was eliminated (see Pallas 1780 and *Origin*, pp. 253–4). CD's notes on this work are in DAR 196.5; see also *Correspondence* vol. 8 for more on CD's view of Pallas.

8 See n. 6, above.

From John Murray 22 December [1866][1]

Albemarle St
Decr 22

My Dear Sir

The copy of your new Ed^n^. addressed to Benj. D. Walsh Esq—was despatched from this in parcel—enclosed to Scribner & Co New York—on the 6th. of August last by Mr Sampson Lowe— I cannot doubt that it has reached its destination ere this. However obeying your injunction I have sent off another copy to care of Baillière—[2]

I am— | My Dear Sir | Yours faithfully | John Murray

Ch Darwin Esq

DAR 171: 340

1 The year is established by the reference to the new edition of *Origin* (see n. 2, below).

2 CD had arranged for Murray to send an advance copy of the fourth edition of *Origin* to Benjamin Dann Walsh before receiving instructions from Walsh to send the book to Baillière Bros in New York (see letter from B. D. Walsh, 17 July 1866, and letter to B. D. Walsh, 20 August [1866]). Charles Scribner & Co. was a New York publishing firm. Sampson Low, Son & Marston, American publishers, had premises at Milton House, Ludgate Hill, London (*Post Office London directory* 1866). In his letter of [28 November 1866], Walsh evidently wrote that he had not received the book, but in a part of his letter that is now missing (see letter to B. D. Walsh, 24 December [1866]).

To J. D. Hooker 24 December [1866]

Down
Dec 24

My dear Hooker.

I am going to amuse myself by scribbling a bit to you about your last long letter.[1] But first you must congratulate me in your mind when you hear that I have sent M.S. (such an awful, confounded pile, two volumes I much fear) of "Domestic

Animals & Cult. Plants" to Printers.[2] I am now writing concluding chapter, & shall perhaps insert, but am much perplexed on this head, a Chapt. on Man; just to say how I think my views bear on him.—[3]

We have all the Boys at home & are very jolly, & William has come for 3 days.[4] He has brought back the Introduction to Australian Flora, after having read it over *three* times & liked it *extremely*. I mention this because it shows how interesting & valuable a book you might produce for general readers on Insular Floras.[5] I feel, however, sure that you will grapple with this work now.— I see in Müllers letter that I assumed without any grounds that the Adenanthera was a native Brazilian plant:[6] it is not worth enquiring in India about, though it is a perplexing case, for I can hardly admit your wriggle of the seeds being devoured by birds with weak gizzards: at least soaking for 10 hours in a little warm water got out hardly anything soluble from one of the seeds. Yet I must believe that they hang long on the tree & look so gaudy to attract birds.—[7]

I read aloud your simile of H. Spencer to a thinking pump, & it was unanimously voted first-rate, & not a bit the worse for being unintelligible.[8]

One word more about about the flora derived from supposed pleistocene Antarctic Land, requiring land intercommunication, this will depend much, as it seems to me, upon how far you finally settle whether Azores, Cape de Verdes, Tristan d'Acunha, Galapagos Juan Fernandez &c &c &c have all had land intercommunication. If you do not think this necessary might not New Zealand &c have been stocked during intervening glacial period by occasional means from Antarctic Land?[9] As for lowlands of Borneo being tenanted by a moderate number of temperate forms during Glacial period, so far from appearing a "frightful assumption", that I am arrived at that pitch of bigotry that I look at it as *proved*![10]

I had another letter from Fritz Müller yesterday & in one day's collecting he found six genera of dimorphic plants! One is a Plumbago.—[11] Now have you seed of any species; I see none are on sale in Carter's list.[12] I want a second favour; could you lend me for *short time* a recent number of Revue Horticole, with an account by Carrière of curious effect of grafting an Aria, given in last Gard. Chronicle.—[13]

Yours affect | C. Darwin

Endorsement: '/66'
DAR 115: 309, 309b

[1] See letter from J. D. Hooker, 14 December 1866.

[2] CD refers to the manuscript for *Variation*, which he had recently sent to his publisher, John Murray (see letter to John Murray, 21 and 22 December [1866]).

[3] On the proposed chapter on humans, see the letter to William Turner, 14 December [1866] and n. 3.

[4] According to Emma Darwin's diary (DAR 242), Leonard and Horace Darwin returned from Clapham Grammar School, and George Howard and Francis Darwin returned from Cambridge University, on 14 December 1866. William Erasmus Darwin lived in Southampton (Freeman 1978).

[5] Hooker's essay on the Australian flora (J. D. Hooker 1859) was written as an introduction to his taxonomic work *Flora Tasmaniæ* (J. D. Hooker 1860b), but was published separately. CD's annotated copy of J. D. Hooker 1859 is in the Darwin Library–CUL (see *Marginalia* 1: 394–8). CD had encouraged

Hooker to publish the text of his lecture on insular floras delivered at the British Association for the Advancement of Science meeting in August 1866 (J. D. Hooker 1866a), and had been disappointed when Hooker decided to publish the piece in the *Gardeners' Chronicle* (letter to J. D. Hooker, 2 October [1866]). See also letter from J. D. Hooker, 4 December 1866 and n. 9.

6 The reference is to Fritz Müller and his description of crimson seeds found in Brazil (see letter from Fritz Müller, 1 and 3 October 1866). Hooker identified the seeds as those of *Adenanthera pavonina*, and noted that the species was native to India (see letter from J. D. Hooker, 14 December [1866]).

7 CD had tried giving the seeds to a fowl but reported that the bird's gizzard had ground them up, whereupon Hooker suggested the seeds might be consumed by birds with 'weak digestions' (see letter from J. D. Hooker, 14 December 1866 and n. 3).

8 See letter from J. D. Hooker, 14 December 1866 and n. 4.

9 The Azores are a small group of islands in the Atlantic Ocean, west of Portugal. The Cape Verde islands lie to the west of Senegal. Tristan da Cunha is a remote island in the mid South Atlantic. The Galápagos islands are in the Pacific Ocean, west of Ecuador. The Juan Fernandez islands lie to the west of Chile. In *Origin*, pp. 381–2, CD had suggested that an isolated Antarctic flora was dispersed from a common centre over the southern hemisphere by means of occasional transport.

10 See letter from J. D. Hooker, 14 December 1866 and n. 9.

11 See letter from Fritz Müller, [2 November 1866]; some of the information on dimorphic plants is in a now missing section of the letter.

12 CD wanted *Plumbago* seeds for his crossing experiments with dimorphic plants (see *Correspondence* vol. 15, letter to J. D. Hooker, 29 January [1867]). He refers to a list of seeds from the firm Carter, Dunnett & Beale; the list had been published annually since 1837 (R. Desmond 1994).

13 *Gardeners' Chronicle*, 22 December 1866, p. 1217, reported on Elie Abel Carrière's grafting experiments with *Aria vestita*, which had been described in *Revue Horticole*, 1 December 1866, pp. 457–8 (Carrière 1866). CD reported Carrière's findings in *Variation* 1: 387 n. 84.

From John Murray 24 December [1866][1]

Albemarle St
Decr 24

My Dear Sir

Your two parcels of MS. reached me on Sat^{y} night with your instructions[2] I was very glad to receive them but they arrive just at the beginning of Xmas Holidays & no real work can be got out of the Printers before Thursday next. This will account for a little delay—but proceedings shall be taken in earnest when once begin & we will endeavour to make up for lost time—

Permit me to wish you the Comps of the Season & to remain My Dear Sir | yours very faithfully | John Murray

Ch Darwin Esq

DAR 171: 341

1 The year is established by the relationship between this letter and the letter to John Murray, 21 and 22 December [1866].

2 CD had sent the manuscript of all but the last chapter of *Variation*, along with instructions about footnotes and page size, and two possible titles (see letter to John Murray, 21 and 22 December [1866]).

To P. L. Sclater 24 December [1866][1]

Down Bromley | Kent.
Dec 24

Dear Sclater

I have thought you might like to see the enclosed proposal, & if you thought fit you c[d] communicate directly with the man.[2] Do not trouble yourself to acknowledge this.

yours very sincerely. | Ch. Darwin

LS
American Philosophical Society (324)

[1] The year is established by the relationship between this letter and the letter from B. D. Walsh, [28 November 1866] (see n. 2, below).

[2] CD enclosed a page of a letter from Benjamin Dann Walsh in which Walsh asked whether CD knew of any ornithologist who might want to trade bird skins with the American collector, Jacob W. Velie (see letter from B. D. Walsh, [28 November 1866] and letter to B. D. Walsh, 24 December [1866]).

To William Turner 24 [December 1866][1]

Down, Bromley, Kent.
24th.

My dear Sir,

I have been working so hard to get a certain job done that I have neglected to thank you sooner for your note of Dec 15th., which contained much of the very information which I wanted—[2] If hereafter you can give me any more information about rudimentary parts in man, & allow me to quote you, I shall be truly obliged—

I have received your paper on the gestation of Arius but have not yet read it from same reason that has made me delay thanking you; but I have now got it out & will read it this evening, for I can see that the subject is a very curious one—[3]

With cordial thanks | Believe me | Yours very sincerely | Ch. Darwin

Copy
DAR 148: 152

[1] The month and year are established by the relationship between this letter and the letter to William Turner, 14 December [1866].

[2] The letter from Turner has not been found, but see the letter to William Turner, 14 December [1866] and n. 7. CD had been working on his manuscript of *Variation* (see CD's 'Journal' (Appendix II)).

[3] Turner had sent CD a copy of a paper 'On a remarkable mode of gestation in an undescribed species of Arius (*A. Boakeii*)' (Turner 1866b). CD's annotated copy is in the Darwin Pamphlet Collection–CUL. Turner described how the male *Arius boakeii* (now *A. arius*, the threadfin sea catfish) incubated eggs in its mouth (Turner 1866b, p. 79). CD referred to the phenomenon and cited Turner's paper in *Descent* 1: 210.

To B. D. Walsh 24 December [1866]

Down. | Bromley. | Kent. S.E.
Dec 24.

My dear Sir

A copy of the Origin for you was sent on Aug 6 through Sampson Low to Scribner & Co New York;[1] but as this copy is lost I have now ordered a new one to be sent to Messrs Bailliére New York for you.[2] I am sorry that the first copy failed.

I have rec^{d} 2 numbers of the Practical Entomol.; the first about naturalized insects interested me greatly, & seemed very well done.[3]

I am rather sorry that you are Editor, as I have always heard that an Editor's life is one of ceaseless trouble & anxiety.[4]

I believe the reproduction of the Ornithorhyncus is not yet thoroughly known, & recently one little bit of evidence rather favours its being oviparous.[5]

I will send your proposal from Dr Velie to Dr Sclater Sec. Zoolog. Soc., as he is our greatest ornithologist.[6]

With respect to Aphis you must not trust my recollection, but Balbiani has shewn that the so-called pseudo-ovum contains a peculiar cell, & this so far is certain.[7] Lubbock finds the same in Coccus.[8] Now this cell according to B. contains spermatic matter & fertilises the other part of the pseudo-ovum.— I have asked 2 or 3 good judges & no one knows what to think, but all agree that B. is an excellent observer. According to this view the viviparous Aphides are all hermaphrodites with the 2 sexual elements in close union, & the oviparous Aphides unisexual.[9]

I shall be glad to receive your paper on galls—[10]

I am tired & not well today—so no more—

Yours very sincerely | Ch. Darwin

LS(A)
Postmark: DE 24 66
Field Museum of Natural History, Chicago (Walsh 8)

[1] The reference is to the fourth edition of *Origin*. CD's publisher, John Murray, had sent a copy through the publishers Sampson Low, Son & Marston to Charles Scribner & Co., New York (see letter from John Murray, 22 December [1866] and n. 2).

[2] Walsh had earlier asked CD to send the book to Baillière Bros, New York (see letter from John Murray, 22 December [1866] and n. 2).

[3] The 29 September 1866 issue of the *Practical Entomologist* contained Walsh's article on the naturalised gooseberry saw-fly (Walsh 1866a); CD's heavily annotated copy is in the Darwin Pamphlet Collection–CUL. The other issue has not been found.

[4] Walsh was associate editor of the *Practical Entomologist.* See letter from B. D. Walsh, [28 November 1866] and n. 4.

[5] Walsh had told CD of a report that the platypus (*Ornithorhynchus*) was not oviparous (see letter from B. D. Walsh, [28 November 1866] and n. 6). It is not known to what evidence CD refers.

[6] The references are to Jacob W. Velie and to Philip Lutley Sclater. See letter to P. L. Sclater, 24 December [1866].

[7] The section of Walsh's letter of [28 November 1866] discussing the genus *Aphis* is now missing, but see the letter from B. D. Walsh, 17 July 1866, and the letter to B. D. Walsh, 20 August [1866]. CD refers to Edouard-Gérard Balbiani and his study 'On the reproduction and embryogeny of the

Aphides' (Balbiani 1866). CD's annotated copy of the article is in his collection of unbound journals in the Darwin Library–CUL.

[8] John Lubbock had discussed two species of *Coccus* in a paper 'On the ova and pseudova of insects' and had observed a 'vitelligenous cell' containing green granules, which he did not further identify (Lubbock 1858, pp. 363–4). CD's copy of the article, in his collection of unbound journals, is uncut.

[9] See Balbiani 1866, p. 64.

[10] The reference is to Walsh 1866b (see letter from B. D. Walsh, [28 November 1866] and n. 8).

From J. D. Hooker 25 December 1866

Kew
Dec 25/66

Dear Darwin

I was about to write today, when your jolly letter came this morning[1] to tell you that after carefully going over the N. Z. Flora, I find that there are only about 30 *reputed* indigenous Dicot **annuals**, of which almost half, not being found by Banks & Solander, are probably non-indigenous.[2] This is just $\frac{1}{20}$ of the Dicots. or excluding the doubtful about $\frac{1}{40}$th. whereas the British proportion of annuals is $\frac{1}{4-6}$ amongst Dicots.!!! Of the **Naturalized** New Zealand plants, one-half are annual![3]

I suppose there can be no doubt but that a deciduous leaved vegetation affords more conditions for vegetable life than an evergreen one—& that it is hence that we find countries characterized by uniform climates to be poor in species & these to be evergreen— I can now work this point out for New Zealand & Britain.

Japan may be an exception It is an Extraordinary Evergreen country & has many species *apparently*, but it has so much novelty that it may not be so rich in species really as it hence looks, & I do believe it is *very poor*. It has very few annuals.

Then again I think that the number of plants with irregular flowers, & especially such as require insect agency, diminishes much with *Evergreenity*

Hence in all humid temperate regions we have as a rule Few species,—many evergreens, few annuals,—few Leguminosæ & Orchids,—few Lepidoptera & other flying Insects—many Coniferæ, Amentacea,[4] Gramineæ Cyperaceæ & other wind fertilized trees & plants &c.

Orchids & Leguminosæ are scarce in Islets because the necessary fertilizing insects have not migrated with the plants. Perhaps you have published this[5]

Ever | J. D Hooker.

DAR 102: 127–8

CD ANNOTATIONS[6]

2.1 I suppose ... one— 2.2] *triple scored pencil*; 'is not this one of results?' *added pencil*
2.2 & that ... evergreen— 2.4] 'How in Arctic Region & Tropics, not subject to doubt' *added pencil*
5.1 Hence ... regions] 'does not here imply equability' *added pencil*
6.1 Orchids ... this 6.2] *scored pencil*; 'No' *added pencil*
End of letter: 'Keeling Is' *pencil del pencil*; 'Coral islet any irregular flower' *pencil*

[1] See letter to J. D. Hooker, 24 December [1866].
[2] Hooker refers to his *Flora Novæ-Zelandiæ* (J. D. Hooker 1853–5) and to Joseph Banks and Daniel Carl Solander, botanists on the *Endeavour* voyage of 1768 to 1771 (*DNB*). 'Dicot.': dicotyledonous.
[3] See letter from J. D. Hooker, 4 December 1866 and n. 10.
[4] 'Amentaceae': an old grouping of catkin-bearing plants, since separated into a number of families in modern systems of classification (Lindley 1853, p. xxxiii; Mabberley 1997, s.v. Amentiferae).
[5] In *Origin*, p. 97, CD had argued that the fertility of papilionaceous plants (Leguminosae) was greatly reduced if bees were excluded. He had suggested in a letter to Hooker that the 'remarkable absence' of papilionaceous plants in New Zealand might be explained by the absence of hive bees (see *Correspondence* vol. 7, letter to J. D. Hooker, 12 January [1858]; see also letter to the *Gardeners' Chronicle*, [before 13 November 1858] (*Collected papers* 2: 19–25)). CD had suggested that Hooker compare the number of species that, like members of the Leguminosae, had irregular flowers in New Zealand and England (see *Correspondence* vol. 13, letter to J. D. Hooker, 7 January [1865] and nn. 9 and 10).
[6] CD's annotations mostly refer to points he wanted to bring up in his reply to Hooker (see *Correspondence* vol. 15, letter to J. D. Hooker, 9 January [1867]).

From B. J. Sulivan 25 December 1866

Bournemouth
Decr. 25 | 66.

My dear Darwin

Many happy returns of the season to you and M^{rs}. Darwin[1] as well as all your party. The last account of your health was so much more cheering that I hope to hear it has continued to improve. I have had my Turkish bath at work for six weeks and I think my head gets steadily better, though slowly, and for the first time for some years I have gone so far into winter without the slightest cold or cough.[2] I am thankful to say I can say the same of all our party so I hope Bournemouth will suit us all—[3]

A few days since I went to Bristol to see our Mission schooner ready for sea, and also to see the Fuegian lads before they return.[4] They have been with a farmer who speaks highly of their conduct

I should have known Jimmy's son from the likeness, he is said to be a very nice lad & good disposition—but not so intelligent as one of them from Packsaddle Bay.[5] One can hardly believe that this lad was the same race as those we saw along side in that Bay where we taught them to rub their noses and say "Old Stokes"—[6] There is another lad of that party who has been at the Falkland Station,[7] and lately a Merchant vessel taking refuge there this lad went on board and asked the Capt to tell M^{r}. Stirling (our clergyman there), to come back to them soon[8]—and he was so anxious to go away in the schooner to the Falklands that the Father insisted on his leaving her & did not bring him again. This shows that some good influence is beginning to work & I hope that even now a shipwrecked crew would be safe with those families.[9]

Jimmy's son told me several things his Father used to tell them about the Beagle and "Cappen FitzRoy"—[10] M^{r}. Stirling again gives up the Secretaryship & goes out to the Fuegian work—[11]

We have been lately amusing ourselves with finding fossil leaves in the Eocine beds here. A gentleman came to examine them from the B. Association[12]—and he asked me to look out for portions of the bed when the cliff falls. Though only found in a few places the first little fall brought down some good bits of the bed, & of a second one distinct from the other; and though we destroy twenty leaves to get one we have now numerous specimens; some I hope different from any described in the ⟨Ge⟩ology of the Isle of Wight.[13] If any of them would be of use or interest to you I should be glad to send you any after M^{r}. Mitchell[14]—who comes again soon—has seen them. It would amuse you to see me with a party of five or six young ladies working away till they are in a nice mess with wet clay, making the good folks of Bournemouth stare sometimes when they see us returning— Tho', I fear the workers spoil more specimens every ten minutes than they save in a whole forenoons working. At present we are hoping for some more cliff to fall before fine days in spring come.

What do you think of an old *Turk*, a M^{r}. Packe M.P., a cousin of Hamonds'[15] refusing permission to M^{r}. Michell to go up a ravine on his land where the bed was most easily accessible, though he knew M^{r}. M was employed by the B. Asso^{n}.

When you see Hooker[16] will you say to him that if he wants any specimens of these leaves I shall be glad to get all I can for him. I suppose it is more in his line than yours.

I see in the last Cambridge book a "Darwin" in the First Class of the first year's men. I hope that is your second boy.[17] My youngest[18] has just been trying the senior Local exam^{n}. of Cambridge at Southampton I hope he may do as well as he did in the junior one two years ago, as he got the 9th position in Mathematical honors out of 760—candidates & seven of the eight above him were a year older & had gone up once before. If he does as well now I hope, when he is a year older, he may have a chance of winning a scholarship at Cambridge;[19] I think of his trying at Caius or Pembroke—

The return of Christmass day always recalls strongly that one we passed on an Island of Chiloe, after you left our boat party,[20] when after three weeks wet by night and day and that morning going without breakfast because the rain put the fire out, after the tent was blown down on us—& then when Paddy S.[21] & I returned from egg hunting for the pudding finding the party in the Priest's house, which a kind head Indian had opened for them, and where round a roaring fire they were drying our things and *cooking a sheep*, and we had the luxury of dry clothes & dry blankets for the first time for weeks—

You will perhaps have heard that last year a law was passed in Chile giving free toleration to all religions—[22] we have lately heard from an English gentleman who was at the time in Santiago; that our missionary clergyman at Lota, Allen Gardiner,[23] was referred to by more than one speaker in the House—and the good he was doing there used as an argument for toleration. He has now made friends with the Araucanian chiefs and they are helping him to establish stations in their country.[24]

Old Harris made particular enquiries for us all (at Rio Negro)[25] He & his family were very kind to Stirling and his poor wife during her illness & death,[26]

& now wishing you again many happy christmass & new year's days, & with our kind regards to Mrs Darwin, Believe me | yours very sincerely | B. J. Sulivan

DAR 177: 287

1 Emma Darwin.

2 Sulivan may have acquired a Turkish bath after undergoing treatment in Ireland at the hydrotherapy establishment of the physician Richard Barter (see letter from B. J. Sulivan, 27 June 1866 and nn. 4 and 5).

3 After retiring from the Board of Trade in April 1865, Sulivan moved from London to Bournemouth (see *Correspondence* vol. 13, letter from B. J. Sulivan, 8 May [1865]).

4 The Patagonian Mission Society (the name was changed to South American Mission Society in 1865) owned a ship, the *Allen Gardiner*, which was built in 1854 to serve as an offshore base for the society's missionary work in the islands of Tierra del Fuego (Hazlewood 2000, pp. 161–2). In August 1865, the superintendent missionary, Waite Hockin Stirling, had returned to England from Tierra del Fuego with four Yahgan boys, Uroopa, Mamastugadagenges, Sesoienges, and Wammestriggins, who was called Threeboys (see below, n. 5). They left for Tierra del Fuego on 8 December 1866 (*ibid.*, pp. 313–16). The Yahgan are one of the three indigenous peoples of Tierra del Fuego, found in the most southerly parts of the islands (*OED*).

5 The Yahgan Orundellico, known to the British as Jemmy Button, was brought to England in 1830 and returned to his native land in 1833 on the *Beagle* by Robert FitzRoy (see *Correspondence* vol. 1). One of his sons, Wammestriggins, known as Threeboys, was among the Yahgan boys brought to England in 1865 (see n. 4, above). Packsaddle Bay was located off Hardy Peninsula in the south-eastern part of Tierra del Fuego (*British Admiralty chart no. 1373*, 1841).

6 The reference is to John Lort Stokes, who was mate and assistant surveyor on the *Beagle* voyage with CD (*Correspondence* vol. 1). For CD's account of the mimicry skills of Fuegians, see *Journal of researches*, p. 229.

7 The Falkland missionary station was on Keppel Island (Hazlewood 2000, p. 165).

8 The reference is to Waite Hockin Stirling (see n. 4, above).

9 Sulivan may be alluding to an incident that took place at Wulaia, Tierra del Fuego, in November 1859, when some Englishmen were killed by a group of Yahgans (see Hazlewood 2001, pp. 249–53).

10 FitzRoy was commander of the *Beagle* from 1828 to 1836; see also n. 5, above.

11 Stirling had been secretary of the Patagonian Mission Society from 1857 to 1862, when he became the society's superintendent missionary for Tierra del Fuego (*Crockford's clerical directory*).

12 William Stephen Mitchell had reported to the British Association for the Advancement of Science meeting in August 1866 on the fossil leaf-bed at Alum Bay, Isle of Wight (W. S. Mitchell 1866).

13 The reference is to a list of Eocene plants published in the *Memoirs of the Geological Survey of Great Britain* (Harpe and Salter 1862) that included material collected at Bournemouth. Mitchell noted in his report that many new forms had been discovered since the list was published (W. S. Mitchell 1866, p. 147).

14 See n. 12, above.

15 Robert Nicholas Hamond had served with Sulivan and CD on the *Beagle* voyage (Sulivan ed. 1896, p. 202). Charles William Packe, MP for South Leicestershire, owned the Branksome Tower estate in Poole, Dorset (*Thom's Irish almanac* 1866).

16 Joseph Dalton Hooker.

17 George Howard Darwin achieved a first class in the 'Junior Sophs' examination, Michaelmas term 1865 (*Cambridge University calendar* 1866, p. 388).

18 Henry Norton Sulivan (see *Correspondence* vol. 13, letter from B. J. Sulivan, 8 May [1865] and nn. 20 and 21).

19 No record of Henry Norton Sulivan's attending Cambridge University has been found, but Sulivan later reported that his son left Cambridge after only a few weeks owing to ill health (letter from B. J. Sulivan, 19 March 1868, *Calendar* no. 6026).

20 Sulivan refers to Christmas 1834, which he spent on Chiloé Island, off the south coast of Chile (see Sulivan 1896, p. 44). CD had remained on the *Beagle* while Sulivan and a party of men surveyed Chiloé (see *Journal of researches*, p. 342).

21 The reference is to Peter Benson Stewart (see *Correspondence* vol. 12, letter from B. J. Sulivan, 18 March [1864], where 'Paddy' is incorrectly transcribed as 'Padeby'). For a list of the people on the *Beagle* between 1831 and 1836, see *Correspondence* vol. 1, Appendix III.

22 Article 5 of the Chilean constitution of 1833 prohibited the public practice of any religion other than Roman Catholicism. An amendment of 1865 made it legal to practice other religions and to establish non-Catholic schools on private property. (Bizzarro 1987, s.v. Constitution.)

23 Lota is a coastal city in the Región del Biobío, over 200 miles south of Santiago, Chile. Allen Weare Gardiner took up his missionary post in Chile around 1865 (*Clergy list* 1864, *Crockford's clerical directory* 1865).

24 'Araucana' was the name the Spanish gave to the native people (who called themselves 'Mapuche') occupying the area between the rivers Biobío and Toltén in southern Chile (Blancpain 1990, p. 20). The Araucanians were not under the control of the Chilean government.

25 James Harris, a trader based at Patagones (now known as Carmen de Patagones), near the mouth of the Río Negro, Patagonia, had acted as CD's guide in Argentina (see *Journal of researches*, p. 79).

26 Louisa Jane Stirling died in October 1864, ten weeks after her arrival at Patagones (Macdonald 1929, p. 59).

From L. E. Becker 28 December [1866][1]

10 Grove st | Ardwick | Manchester
Dec. 28.

My dear Sir

Will you please to accept my hearty thanks for the paper on "Climbing Plants, which you have generously bestowed on me, and for the loan of the others which I will take great care of, and return to you before long—[2] You do not name *Primula farinosa* in your paper[3]—but will not be surprised to hear that in looking over my dried specimens of this plant, nine in number—I find 5 long styled, and 4 short styled plants. I have taken the liberty of enclosing one of each in proof of my words and remain | dear Sir | yours sincerely | Lydia E Becker

DAR 160: 114

1 The year is established by the relationship between this letter and the letter from L. E. Becker, 22 December 1866.

2 Becker had asked CD to send one of his papers for presentation to a ladies' group (see letter from L. E. Becker, 22 December 1866 and n. 4). In addition to 'Climbing plants', CD sent 'Dimorphic condition in *Primula*' (see n. 3, below) and probably 'Three forms of *Lythrum salicaria*' (see *Correspondence* vol. 15, letter from L. E. Becker, 6 February 1867).

3 In 'Dimorphic condition in *Primula*', CD discussed the results of experiments with *Primula veris*, *P. sinensis*, and *P. auricula*. CD later included information on *P. farinosa* (bird's eye primrose), based on John Scott's experiments with the species, in *Forms of flowers*, pp. 45, 224, 273.

To J. D. Hooker 28 [December 1866][1]

Down
28th

My dear Hooker

Many thanks for the Revue Horticle,[2] which I return by this Post.—

I had a long & very pleasant letter from Sulivan[3] this morning & he is in somewhat better health.— He has been collecting fossil leaves in Eocene(?) beds at Bournemouth & has got, as he believes new forms.— Mr Mitchell from British Assoc. has first pick & he offers me others & then recollecting that they wd be of no use to me, offers them to you.—[4] Now when you write say whether you wd like to have them for yourself or Heer,[5] & whether he shall send them to Kew. I will not write to Sulivan till I have a line from you.— The Athenæum has been admitting letters urging Publishers to sell their Books cut & I have, like an ass, sent a long letter, which they will perhaps insert.—[6]

Yours affecty | C. Darwin

DAR 115: 310, 310b

1 The month and year are established by the relationship between this letter and the letter from B. J. Sulivan, 25 December 1866.

2 See letter to J. D. Hooker, 24 December [1866] and n. 13.

3 Bartholomew James Sulivan (see letter from B. J. Sulivan, 25 December 1866).

4 CD refers to William Stephen Mitchell (see letter from B. J. Sulivan, 25 December 1866 and n. 12).

5 Oswald Heer was a Swiss palaeobotanist who had published on the flora of the Tertiary period, including the Eocene (Heer 1860).

6 CD had encouraged his publisher, John Murray, to bring out the fourth edition of *Origin* with the pages cut (see letter to John Murray, 15 July [1866]). Two letters had already been printed in the *Athenæum* on the subject (*Athenæum*, 15 December 1866, p. 803, and 22 December 1866, p. 848). CD's letter was published in the *Athenæum*, 5 January 1867, pp. 18–19 (see *Correspondence* vol. 15, letter to *Athenæum*, 1 January 1867).

From J. D. Hooker [29 December 1866][1]

Kew
Saturday

Dear Darwin

By all means let Heer have the Bournemouth leaves, I have no time even to look at them; & Heer works them better than anyone— They are usually so fragile that they should be so packed at once, as not to be disturbed till in the hands of Heer. & Sulivan had better take a little time & patience about that point. How to get them to Heer is another point, I will write & ask him.[2]

I am very glad you have taken up the Book-cutting matter.[3] I had a great mind to— The Yankees are far ahead of us in all such matters.[4] Our Publishers are Penny-wise Pound foolish, Penurious, Pragmatical Prigs— there then— I have spoken to several on the subject, but none would even listen.

Ever yrs | J D Hooker.

I go on Monday to Norwich for 3 days

DAR 102: 129–30

[1] The date is established by the relationship between this letter and the letter to J. D. Hooker, 28 [December 1866]. In 1866, the first Saturday after 28 December was 29 December.

[2] Bartholomew James Sulivan had offered to send Hooker specimens of fossil leaves he had found in Eocene beds near Bournemouth (see letter from B. J. Sulivan, 25 December 1866). CD had suggested that Oswald Heer might be interested in them (see letter to J. D. Hooker, 28 [December 1866]). Heer was a professor of botany and entomology at Zurich, Switzerland (*DSB*).

[3] See letter to J. D. Hooker, 28 [December 1866] and n. 6.

[4] From the 1850s, North American publications had the pages trimmed (see Tebbel 1972, pp. 260–1).

From John William Salter 31 December 1866

8 Bolton Road | St. Johns Wood.
Dec 31/66

Dear Mr Darwin.

I think you know how badly off I have been these last ⟨ ⟩ years—struggling with the most adverse circumstances—as well as frequent nervous prostration which takes more than half the life & sense out of me when I want it most.[1]

This last year I have broken down for 4 months—and have been pressed beyond measure in circumstances, in consequence.

Are you rich enough to aid me at all—and make me your debtor for any help I can give in looking over the paleozoic part of your reasonings in your great book.[2] I do not know how else to help you.

Everything I have tried has failed more or less—but I have work to do of various kinds—which will keep me just afloat if the pressure of anxiety is taken off my mind.[3]

We have retrenched & retrenched, & wife & daughters keep school,[4] & in spite of all they & I can do I cannot get rid of £200 debt.

Of course you will understand how hard it is for me thus to speak but my unfortunate relations with the Survey prevents Murchison from doing anything to aid me.[5]

I have a work, the only property now left me, which I have tried to sell & cannot except at ruinous loss., nor can I since the money crisis, borrow at all.[6]

I am trying to get aid from the Roy. Soc. fund (as Hawkins did)[7] but all this is uncertain & unlikely too I fear. Can I do any literary work for you? I know you will forgive my asking you—for I have tried to be independent & failed— And I do not justify my faults of temper, which now I think have had a large share in pulling me down—

It is hard to establish a new business when one is 46— So few channels are open— the British Museum is closed against all but young men.[8] Lecturing failed with me—& I lost money by it— Engraving I still do, but want of capital of any kind obliges me to do all the mechanical part as well, and even a young unmarried man finds that a badly paying affair.

Thank God, my family are all well now, & one at least is off my hands.[9]

Yours truly | J. W. Salter.

I trust you will burn my letter— I had hoped for so different a career—& even yet I trust to get on—if I can once get over the pressure which keeps £.s.d. in letters of fire before me—

DAR 177: 12

[1] Salter had resigned his post as palaeontologist to the Geological Survey of the United Kingdom in 1863, after which he was unable to find permanent employment (Secord 1985, pp. 68–9).

[2] The reference is to *Origin*. Salter was recognised as the leading expert on Palaeozoic palaeontology in Great Britain and had contributed information on the subject to the works of notable geologists such as Roderick Impey Murchison and Charles Lyell (Secord 1985, pp. 65–6).

[3] Salter supported himself through lecturing and writing, arranging the palaeontological cabinets of museums and individuals, and engraving and woodcutting (Secord 1985, p. 68).

[4] Sarah Salter, Salter's wife, had started a school shortly after Salter left the Geological Survey (Secord 1985, p. 68).

[5] Salter had left the Geological Survey after disputes with other employees at all levels. Thomas Henry Huxley, naturalist to the survey, had even threatened to step down if Salter did not leave (Secord 1985, p. 67). Murchison was director-general of the Geological Survey.

[6] Salter refers to the *Supplement to the English Botany of the late Sir J. E. Smith and Mr. Sowerby* (W. J. Hooker, Sowerby, [*et al.*] 1831–63). This was published in quarterly instalments, the last of which appeared in May 1865. Salter had been the proprietor of the work since 1849, when it had been passed on to him by his father-in-law, James de Carle Sowerby. On the inside cover of the last instalment, Salter warned that publication would cease if new subscribers could not be found.

[7] The Royal Society of London established a Scientific Relief Fund in 1859 (*Record of the Royal Society of London*, p. 111). Payments from the fund were recorded in the Royal Society Council minutes, but the recipients were not named. Salter received a £50 grant from the fund (Secord 1985, p. 68). Salter probably refers to Benjamin Waterhouse Hawkins.

[8] On Salter's attempts to get employment at the British Museum, see Secord 1985, p. 69.

[9] Salter had seven children, none of whom has been identified (Secord 1985, p. 68).

To B. J. Sulivan 31 December [1866][1]

Down Bromley | Kent
Dec 31

My dear Sulivan

I sincerely rejoice that you are able to give a some what improved account of your health, & I hope it may continue improving.[2] Your letter has interested me exceedingly all about S. America & the Fuegians. I never thought the latter c^d have been civilized, but it appears that I shall be proved wrong. I wish poor Fitz-Roy was alive to hear the result of his first attempt for the civilization of the Fuegians.[3]

Do you know Mr Stirling[4] well enough to ask him to grant me a great favour? Namely to observe during a few months the expression of countenance under different emotions of *any* Fuegians but especially of those who have not lived much in contact with Europeans, & to take the trouble to write me a letter on the subject.

It is an old hobby-horse of mine on which I am very curious, & on which I have vainly sought for information. I will write a few questions on a separate piece of paper, & if you can oblige me you might send it to Mr S. with the request that he w^d^ hereafter write to me by address on the paper.—[5]

I have written to Hooker about the fossil leaves; he fully appreciates their value but says he has no time to work at them.[6] He agrees with me that they w^d^ be of *much* more service for science in the hands of Prof. Heer of Switzerland than in those of any other man in Europe. If you are inclined to send a collection to him, Hooker w^d^ find out the best means, but as he remarks, the specimens would require much trouble in packing.[7]

I am glad to hear so capital an account of y^r^ younger son,[8] & I sh^d^ think he w^d^ be sure to get a scholarship at Cambridge. It was my 2nd son George, & he was first in Mathematics at Trinity.[9]

My health is very much improved, & this is wholly due to diet & to riding daily, but I am never quite well for 24 hours[10] Nevertheless I have just sent off to the printers a great bundle of M.S for a book on "domestic animals".[11]

Again I must thank you for your very interesting letter, & with our very kind remembrances to Mrs Sulivan[12] believe me my dear Sulivan | yours very sincerely | Charles Darwin

LS(A)
E. Sulivan (private collection)

[1] The year is established by the relationship between this letter and the letter from B. J. Sulivan, 25 December 1866.

[2] See letter from B. J. Sulivan, 25 December 1866 and n. 2.

[3] See letter from B. J. Sulivan, 25 December 1866 and n. 5. Robert FitzRoy had been dismayed to see the reversion of Jemmy Button to his 'uncivilised' state when the *Beagle* stopped in Tierra del Fuego in 1834 (Browne 1995, pp. 268–9). For CD's reaction to the encounter with Jemmy Button, see *Correspondence* vol. 1, letter to Catherine Darwin, 6 April 1834. FitzRoy died in 1865 (see *Correspondence* vol. 13).

[4] Waite Hockin Stirling.

[5] The enclosure has not been found, but the questions were probably similar to the questions listed in the letter to Thomas Bridges, 6 January 1860, and to later questionnaires (see *Correspondence* vol. 15). CD received answers in 1867 to the questions that he had sent to Thomas Bridges via Stirling (see *Correspondence* vol. 8, CD annotations to the letter from Thomas Bridges, [October 1860 or after], and *Correspondence* vol. 15, letter from B. J. Sulivan, 11 January 1867).

[6] Sulivan had offered to send fossil leaves to Joseph Dalton Hooker (see letter from B. J. Sulivan, 25 December 1866).

[7] CD refers to Oswald Heer. See letter to J. D. Hooker, 28 [December 1866], and letter from J. D. Hooker, [29 December 1866].

[8] Henry Norton Sulivan (see letter from B. J. Sulivan, 25 December 1866 and n. 18).

[9] George Howard Darwin (see letter from B. J. Sulivan, 25 December 1866 and n. 17).

[10] For more on CD's health, see the letter to W. D. Fox, 24 August [1866] and n. 5.

[11] The reference is to the manuscript of *Variation*, all but one chapter of which CD had recently sent to his publisher, John Murray (see letter to John Murray, 21 and 22 December [1866]).

[12] Sophia Sulivan.

To Fritz Müller [late December 1866 and] 1 January 1867[1]

Down. | Bromley. | Kent. S.E.

My dear Sir

Your letter of Nov 2. contains an extraordinary amount of interesting matter.[2] What a number of dimorphic plants S. Brazil produces; you observed in one day as many or more dimorphic genera than all the botanists in Europe have ever observed.[3] When my present book is finished I shall write a final paper upon these plants, so that I am extremely glad to hear of your observations & to see the dried flowers; nevertheless I sh^{d} regret *much* if I prevented you from publishing on the subject. Plumbago is quite new to me, though I had suspected it.[4]

It is curious how dimorphism prevails by groups throughout the world, shewing as I suppose that it is an ancient character: thus Hedyotis is dimorphic in India: the two other genera in the same sub-family with Villarsia are dimorphic in Europe & Ceylon: a sub-genus of Erythroxylum is dimorphic in Ceylon ?& Oxalis with you & at the C. of Good Hope[5] If you can find a *dimorphic* Oxalis it will be a new point, for all known species are trimorphic or monomorphic.[6] The case of Convolvulus will be new if proved.[7] I am doubtful about Gesneria & have been often myself deceived by varying length of pistil.[8] A difference in the size of the pollen-grains w^{d} be conclusive evidence; but in some cases experiments by fertilization can alone decide the point. As yet I know of no case of dimorphism in flowers which are *very* irregular; such flowers being apparently always sufficiently visited & crossed by insects. Your case of the Eschholtzia is extremely curious.[9] With Orchids I know of many facts like that which you give about Oncidium.[10]

Will you be so kind as to remember to tell me, when you next write, whether the Oncidium is an *endemic* species.

I do not know what to think about y^{r} curious speculation on the retarded fertilization of certain Orchids: I believe the pollen-tubes do not reach the ovule in some coniferous trees until many months have elapsed.[11] The little bulbs of the semi-sterile Oxalis have begun to grow & I hope will flower;[12] I sh^{d} suspect that their sterility was nearly of the same nature with that of many cultivated plants.

I have sent off Bentham's & Hooker's Genera by post to you.[13] With respect to the scarlet seeds sent in a former letter I gave 2 to a fowl but they were ground up by its gizzard & disappeared. The remainder I sent to Dr Hooker; he knows the seeds well, & says they belong to an Indian plant the Adenanthera pavonina.[14] Is it a garden-plant with you? The dissemination of its seeds is a puzzling problem.

With *cordial* thanks for all y^{r} great kindness believe me yours very sincerely | Charles Darwin

P.S. Jan 1 1867

By some unaccountable delay I have only this moment received copies of your paper. I will send off 3 copies as before stated;[15] I transmit to you by this post 11 copies; I retain 10 copies any or all of which I will send as you may direct.

British Library (Loan 10: 11)

[1] The date is established by the postscript.

[2] See letter from Fritz Müller, [2 November 1866].

[3] Müller sent a list of dimorphic plants he had recently found (see letter from Fritz Müller, [2 November 1866]).

[4] CD was working on the final chapter of *Variation* (see CD's 'Journal' (Appendix II)). CD wrote a further paper ('Illegitimate offspring of dimorphic and trimorphic plants') and eventually a book (*Forms of flowers*) on this subject. Müller sent CD dried flowers of some of the plants he referred to in his letter (see letter from Fritz Müller, [2 November 1866] and n. 1). A species of *Plumbago* was one of those identified by Müller as dimorphic.

[5] See letter from Fritz Müller, [2 November 1866] and nn. 8 and 12.

[6] Müller had written in an earlier letter about a species of *Oxalis* that he thought was dimorphic (see letter from Fritz Müller, 1 and 3 October 1866 and nn. 2 and 6).

[7] In his German translation of Müller's letter, Alfred Möller refers to the plant as *Ipomoea* (see letter from Fritz Müller, [2 November 1866] and n. 11).

[8] Müller's remarks on *Gesneria* were contained in a now missing part of his letter of [2 November 1866]. He later sent CD seeds of *Gesneria pendulina*; CD reported the results of his experiments with this species in *Cross and self fertilisation*, pp. 92, 322.

[9] Müller had described his observations on *Eschscholzia californica*, noting its infertility with pollen of the same individual plant (see letters from Fritz Müller, 2 August 1866 and [2 November 1866]).

[10] Müller's remarks on *Oncidium* were contained in a now missing part of his letter of [2 November 1866]. For his additional remarks on this orchid genus, see the letter from Fritz Müller, 1 December 1866.

[11] Müller had speculated that in many orchids the ovules were in a rudimentary state when the flower first opened and only developed weeks later to a stage where they were ready for fertilisation (see letter from Fritz Müller, 2 August 1866).

[12] CD had received bulbils of *Oxalis* sent by Müller in October 1866 (see letter to Fritz Müller, [before 10 December 1866] and n. 2).

[13] CD had offered to send the first two parts of *Genera plantarum* by George Bentham and Joseph Dalton Hooker (Bentham and Hooker 1862–83; see letter to Fritz Müller, 23 August [1866]).

[14] Müller had sent the seeds with his letter of 1 and 3 October 1866 (see letter to Fritz Müller, [before 10 December 1866], and letter to J. D. Hooker, 10 December [1866] and n. 3).

[15] The reference is to Müller's paper on climbing plants, which had been sent to the Linnean Society by CD (F. Müller 1865b; see also *Correspondence* vol. 13, letter from Fritz Müller, [12 and 31 August, and 10 October 1865]). CD planned to send copies of the paper to the *Botanische Zeitung*, the *American Journal of Science and Arts*, and the *Bulletin de la Société Botanique de France* (see letter to Fritz Müller, 23 August [1866] and n. 8).

APPENDIX I
Translations of letters

From Ernst Haeckel[1] 11 January 1866

Jena (Saxe-Weimar)
11 January 1866

Most esteemed Sir!

First of all wishing you a very happy New Year and above all that your health may be fully restored, I acknowledge the receipt of your two kind letters (of 6 Dec. and 5 Jan.).[2] They are and will remain, as is the case with all mementos of you, always of the greatest value for me.[3]

I am pleased that you have received my latest works in good order.[4] My publisher (*Engelmann in Leipzig*) had sent ⟨them⟩ to *Williams & Norgate* last September.[5] ⟨I hope⟩ the ⟨*Protogenes*⟩ *primordialis* (in the paper: "⟨Sarcodekörper⟩ der Rhizopoden") will be of particular interest to you.[6] I ⟨believe that⟩ such organisms (quite ⟨homogeneous⟩ masses of gelatinous material or protoplasm ⟨ ⟩ emerged spontaneously in the beginning of organic life ⟨on⟩ earth, and ⟨that⟩ initially various kinds of *cells* developed from them by "natural selection". By differentiation of these cells the few, large *main classes* of the animal and vegetable kingdoms evolved, under which we can subsume all the various organisms.[7] I take it there are roughly 10 or 12 such main classes (types, branches, embranchments) in all, and I will attempt to prove this assumption in my general book, which is about to appear, by drawing up the entire family tree (a genealogical table) for each of them.[8] The printing of this book is advancing vigorously; however, it will probably be several months yet before it appears.[9] A very important chapter (*general principles ⟨and⟩ laws of the embryonic* and its ⟨*parallel*⟩ *palaeontological development*) I ⟨shall⟩ rework completely.[10] This and ⟨a few other⟩ chapters have already been reworked ⟨several⟩ times. But ⟨it is very⟩ difficult to ⟨make⟩ progress in such a ⟨novel⟩ and uncultivated field. It is like a dense, ⟨still⟩-untrodden virgin forest where ⟨the⟩ weeds of prejudice and the ⟨thorns⟩ of dogma impede every step.

You can imagine how much I concern myself with *you*, dear Sir, in this difficult undertaking which absorbs all my energy and which thereby at the same time best distracts me from my unhappy fate.[11] Every time I succeed in making a new discovery in the intellectual field of the philosophical study of nature that you have newly opened up for us, I want to hurry to Down, Bromley, Kent, in order to talk to you about it. I am certain that you would be pleased about it, and I know already that you will enjoy my book very much. For no one has yet recast *the whole of morphology* in accordance with the principles discovered by Darwin and attempted to apply the theory of descent to *all of its branches* with *force* and *persistence.* It is very difficult for me to convey *any details* to you now, however, because the whole consists of a continuous *chain of philosophical investigations.*

In my book I invariably juxtapose *Darwin's* views with those of *Agassiz,* who indeed achieved the maximum of wrongheadedness and unnatural treatment of nature.[12] This is the most didactic proof of the follies to which the dogma of the constancy of species and the teleological–dogmatic treatment of morphology can lead. However, that his views still find the support of many goes to show how far we still have to go.[13]

My public lectures "On Darwin's theory" have, as I think I have already written to you, attracted the largest audiences of any lectures held here this winter,[14] and I hope thereby to be spreading many a fertile seed, which will grow into powerful support for the theory of descent.

Lastly I have a big favour to ask of you, my dear Sir, which I have wanted to bring up for a long time. It is one of my keenest wishes to possess a larger portrait of you. Above my desk hangs the larger photograph (without full beard), the one at the front of the second edition of your work.[15] Underneath it I have the *excellent* smaller photograph which you kindly sent me 2 years ago.[16] However, the first for sure is poor and the second too *small* to satisfy. I have already made inquiries in all bookshops of Berlin and other larger towns whether there are any larger lithographs or photographs of you, but I have not found any. Perhaps such a one exists in England, and you would do me an extraordinary favour if you could send me one. I am often visited by many students and friends who would like to see your picture and it always saddens me that your small photograph (with the full beard) cannot be enlarged four or six times. I have often been begged for the little photograph (in calling card format). If you could send me about $\frac{1}{2}$ or 1 dozen of these, I would in turn send you just as many photographs of German admirers of Darwin and supporters of his teachings. Please excuse my perhaps childish request—but it is of great importance to me.[17]

I enclose a photograph of myself from last October, so that you can see how much I have aged in 2 years.[18]

Wishing with all my heart, dear Sir, that your health may improve very soon so you will remain with us for a long time yet for our benefit and that of science, I remain | with all my heart | Yours truly devoted | Ernst Haeckel.

DAR 166: 41

[1] For a transcription of this letter in its original German, see pp. 6–8.

[2] For the letter to Haeckel of 6 December [1865], see *Correspondence* vol. 13; the letter to Haeckel of 5 January 1866 has not been found.

[3] CD and Haeckel had been corresponding since 1863 or earlier. Their earliest extant correspondence refers to earlier letters (see *Correspondence* vol. 11, letter to Ernst Haeckel, 30 December [1863] – 3 January [1864]).

[4] In his letter of 11 November 1865, Haeckel listed three publications that were to be sent to CD (see *Correspondence* vol. 13). These were Haeckel 1865a, 1865b and 1865c, all papers on marine invertebrates

of the class Coelenterata. A lightly annotated copy of Haeckel 1865a, inscribed by the author, is in the Darwin Pamphlet Collection–CUL. CD's copy of Haeckel 1865b was listed in CD's library catalogue (DAR 240), but was not listed in later catalogues. It has not been found in the Darwin Library–CUL or at Down. In his letter to Haeckel of 6 December [1865], CD acknowledged receipt of two other papers of Haeckel's (Haeckel 1864 and 1865d). For a discussion of the role of Coelenterata in nineteenth-century debates over zoological classification and theories of descent, see Winsor 1976.

[5] Wilhelm Engelmann was a publisher of scientific books (*NDB*; see also *Correspondence* vol. 13, letter from Ernst Haeckel, 11 November 1865). Williams & Norgate, booksellers and publishers of Covent Garden, London, and of Edinburgh, specialised in foreign and scientific literature (*Modern English biography* s.v. Williams, Edmund Sidney).

[6] The reference is to Haeckel 1865a, a paper on rhizopods in which his newly discovered primitive species, *Protogenes primordialis*, was described and illustrated. Haeckel had previously drawn CD's attention to this 'organism', emphasising its significance for his transmutation theory (see *Correspondence* vol. 13, letter from Ernst Haeckel, 11 November 1865 and nn. 11 and 12); a protoplasmic aggregate, without differentiation, organisation, or nucleus, it was able to surround and assimilate foreign bodies, and to reproduce by simple division (Haeckel 1865a, pp. 360–3). It is not recognised in modern taxonomic literature.

[7] In his book *Generelle Morphologie der Organismen*, published later in 1866, Haeckel classified *Protogenes primordialis* in a new phylum, the Monera, comprising the most basic forms of life; he argued that the Rhizopoda might have evolved from a *Protogenes* species (Haeckel 1866, 2: XXII–XXIII). The taxonomic hierarchy proposed by Haeckel reflected CD's transmutation theory, being based on descent from primitive life forms (Haeckel 1866, 2: XVII–XXII; see also n. 8, below). For discussions of Haeckel's theories of protoplasm and the development of living organisms from inorganic matter, see Rehbock 1975 and Rupke 1976. On the Victorian debates over spontaneous generation, see Strick 2000.

[8] The reference is to Haeckel 1866. Haeckel had previously written to CD about his work on this book (see *Correspondence* vol. 12, letter from Ernst Haeckel, 26 October 1864 and n. 8, and *Correspondence* vol. 13, letter from Ernst Haeckel, 11 November 1865 and n. 4). Inside the back cover of the second volume are eight genealogical trees, drawn by Haeckel, displaying the possible relationships among all living organisms. The first tree summarises all subsequent trees and has a central section representing the kingdom of 'Protista' (including unicellular organisms, fungi and sponges) flanked by the animal and plant kingdoms. Haeckel showed eleven main classes (subkingdoms): six within the plant and five within the animal kingdom (for a definition of Haeckel's taxonomic categories, see Haeckel 1866, 2: 374–91). Haeckel's evolutionary trees established a standard iconography for phylogeny (see, for example, S. J. Gould 1990, pp. 263–7). Their epistemological significance is considered in Bouquet 1995, pp. 47–51. CD earlier used a tree-like diagram to illustrate the divergence of offspring from parental types (*Origin*, facing p. 117; see also Winsor 1976, pp. 172–4). For Haeckel's theoretical discussion of his phylogenetic categories, see Haeckel 1866, 2: XVII–XX, XXXI–XXXII, XLVIII–L, and 406–17.

[9] Haeckel 1866 was published on or after 14 September 1866, the date appearing at the foot of the foreword.

[10] Haeckel probably refers to chapter 21, 'Begriff und Aufgabe der Phylogenie' (Concept and function of phylogeny; Haeckel 1866, 2: 303–22), in which he developed arguments in support of the principle that ontogeny recapitulates phylogeny: 'During its own rapid development . . . an individual repeats the most important changes in form evolved by its ancestors during their long and slow palaeontological development' (Haeckel 1866, 2: 300; translated in S. J. Gould 1977, p. 76). For an extensive modern examination of Haeckel's attempted theoretical connection of long-term evolutionary change with short-term growth and development, and a comparison with CD's views, see S. J. Gould 1977.

[11] After Haeckel's wife, Anna Sethe, died on 16 February 1864, Haeckel wrote to CD: 'a stroke of fate has destroyed all prospects of happiness in my life, and . . . I shall pursue the one goal in my life, namely to disseminate, to support and to perfect your theory of descent' (English translation; see

Correspondence vol. 12, letter from Ernst Haeckel, 9 [July 1864]; see also *Correspondence* vol. 13, letter from Ernst Haeckel, 11 November 1865 and n. 13).

12 There are approximately ten references to Louis Agassiz in Haeckel 1866; most make no direct comparison with CD. For more on Agassiz's and Haeckel's interpretations of taxonomic hierarchies, and their differing implications for evolutionary theory, see Bryant 1995, pp. 197–202 and 207 *et seq.*

13 For Agassiz's views on the constancy of species, and his arguments against CD and Haeckel during the 1860s, see Morris 1997. On support for Agassiz's anti-Darwinian rhetoric in the early 1860s, see Lurie 1960, pp. 309–11.

14 According to Haeckel, over 150 people from a wide range of disciplines regularly attended his public lectures on CD's theory in the academic year 1864 to 1865 (see *Correspondence* vol. 13, letter from Ernst Haeckel, 11 November 1865). Records of the university of Jena indicate that 120 people attended the lectures on Darwinian theory given by Haeckel in the main lecture theatre during the winter of 1865 to 1866 (Uschmann 1959, pp. 43–6, 196–8).

15 This photograph, procured from London by the German publisher, E. Schweizerbart'sche Verlagsbuchhandlung, was used as the frontispiece to the second German edition of *Origin* (see *Correspondence* vol. 10, letter from E. Schweizerbart'sche Verlagsbuchhandlung, 7 June 1862 and n. 5); it was taken by Maull & Polyblank, *circa* 1857. The photograph is reproduced as the frontispiece to *Correspondence* vol. 8.

16 Haeckel refers to the first photograph of CD with a beard, taken in 1864 by his son William Erasmus Darwin. The photograph is reproduced as the frontispiece to *Correspondence* vol. 12. See *ibid.*, letter to Ernst Haeckel, 19 July [1864] and n. 7.

17 CD exchanged photographs with many of his correspondents during the 1860s (see *Correspondence* vols. 9–13, and Browne 1998, pp. 253–80).

18 The photograph has not been found. However, there is a portrait of Haeckel dated 1865 at the Ernst Haeckel Haus in Jena. An earlier portrait, presumably taken during 1863, was sent to CD in summer 1864, and included Haeckel's late wife, Anna Sethe (see *Correspondence* vol. 12, letter from Ernst Haeckel, 10 August 1864; see also *ibid.*, plate facing p. 280).

From Ernst Haeckel[1] 28 January 1866

Jena (Saxe-Weimar)
28. Jan. 66.

Dear, most esteemed Sir!

Thank you very much for kindly sending your precious portraits with which you have pleased my friends greatly.[2] With the exception of Schleiden, who is no longer here,[3] I have forwarded your picture to the other five naturalists and they have given me theirs to send to you.[4]

So you will receive the enclosed portraits of the most important and keenest naturalists who disseminate your teachings in Germany. But these are almost the only important naturalists among us who *openly* battle for your teachings, whereas most of the others who are convinced of their truth are too cowardly and fainthearted to say so openly. They will admit to the truth in private but are afraid to say this in public and they fear the consequences of speaking out.[5]

All the six naturalists, whose pictures you receive, have spoken and written openly and freely, as I have, for the truth of the Darwin theory. A. Braun and Virchow, and Leydig too, are my teachers.[6] The youngest, Dohrn, who is now my assistant, has not written much yet. But I have great expectations of him because he is almost as honestly devoted to your teachings as I am, and he sees in it a complete reform of the entire science of morphology and physiology, just as I have taught him.[7] Do not believe that I exaggerate the credit due to you. It *cannot* be exaggerated given the deplorable state into which zoology and botany have fallen due to the species dogma, and to the total reform of which you have been *first* to make a beginning.— I would like to write you in English but I can not write, only read.— I am extraordinarily pleased to hear that you are better. May your recovery always advance thus!

That is the most sincere wish of your, with all his heart devoted, Ernst Haeckel

DAR 166: 42

[1] For a transcription of this letter in its original German, see p. 27.
[2] See letter to Ernst Haeckel, 20 January [1866]. Haeckel requested photographs of CD in his letter of 11 January 1866.
[3] Matthias Jacob Schleiden had resigned from his professorship of botany at Jena in 1862; from 1864, he lived elsewhere as a private scholar (*ADB*, *DBE*).
[4] CD had sent six photographs of himself for Haeckel to forward to German scientists (see letter to Ernst Haeckel, 20 January [1866]). The photographs CD received were evidently of Alexander Carl Heinrich Braun, Rudolf Carl Virchow, Franz von Leydig, and Anton Dohrn, probably together with that of Schleiden, and one other, possibly Carl Gegenbaur, whom Haeckel had mentioned in letters to CD (see nn. 6 and 7, below, and *Correspondence* vol. 12).
[5] On the reception of CD's theory in Germany, see *Correspondence* vol. 11, letter from Friedrich Rolle, 26 January 1863 and nn. 6–14, and *Correspondence* vol. 12, letters from Ernst Haeckel, 9 [July 1864], 10 August 1864, and 26 October 1864. See also Corsi and Weindling 1985, Montgomery 1988, Junker 1989, Engels ed. 1995, and Nyhart 1995.
[6] In the early 1850s, Haeckel attended Braun's lectures at the University of Berlin, and between 1852 and 1856, Virchow's and von Leydig's lectures at the University of Würzburg (*DSB*, Krauße 1987, pp. 18–28, and *DBE*). Haeckel had previously informed CD of Braun's and Virchow's support for his work in his letters of 9 [July 1864] and 26 October 1864 (*Correspondence* vol. 12).
[7] Dohrn was a student of Haeckel's at Jena. By January 1866, he had published more than a dozen scientific papers, including his 1865 article 'Die Darwin'sche Theorie und das Experiment' (Dohrn 1865; see also Kühn 1950, pp. 18, 186–7). For an account of Dohrn's relationship with Haeckel, see Heuss 1991, pp. 35–47.

From Friedrich Rolle[1] 28 January 1866

Homburg von der Hoehe bei Frankfurt am Main
28 January 1866

Dearest Sir,

After you have received Part I of my book "Man" last summer, as I saw from your kind notice, you will now also have received Parts 2–5 from my publisher.[2]

I hope that my work will win your approval; it is designed according to the principles of your theory; on specific points one can certainly differ; the basic principles are, however, so firmly drawn that the true spirit of the view appears to be already quite firmly established.

Where doubts are present, I have taken pains to judge carefully.

So especially in connection with the singularity or multiplicity of origin—and whether the unity of humankind is on this side or beyond the human stage.[3]

To be sure, in the final analysis findings will decide this question.

But rational suppositions are permitted—and throw light on the path one should probably take and the difficulties which one will still have to overcome.

It seems to me that the roots of the human stock may lie

in the Negroes of Africa

in the bushy-frizzy haired men of South Africa and those of New Guinea, Tasmania, etc.

finally third in a not well-known short-headed people (Brachycephali) from South Asia.

Where and how these three roots originate is still not clear to me.

But all straight-haired, civilised people seem to me to be improved, civilised people among whom long-headed, medium-headed, and short- headed are frequently mixed.[4]

This would seem to be similar to the races of domestic animals.

With regard to nomenclature, Bronn has translated "natural selection" with "natürliche Auswahl" into German. I translated it with "natürliche Auslese" this expression comes closer to the concept of passivity.[5] Lately I have begun to translate with "Entfallung" or "Aussterbe-Etat". "Entfallen" means "to fall out of" (dilabi, elabi)[6]

e.g. the aurochs and the wisent have reached the state of extinction and have fallen out.[7]

⟨*6 lines excised*⟩

Proponents fight with the resistance of the old school and are obviously disregarded when positions are filled.

Dr. Jaeger in Vienna is unfortunate, the Vienna zoological garden is bankrupt and Jaeger has little prospect of keeping his position in Vienna.[8]

Dr. Weinland has left his position in Frankfurt.[9] ⟨He was⟩ publishing a journal in Würtemberg "Der Thiergarten", which was supposed to become an organ for the breeding of domestic animals and to support the theory of transmutation. Unfortunately, it lasted for only one year, 1864, and was shut down.[10]

But Prof. Rütimeyer in Basel is very active in developing the descent and transmutation of mammals from mammalian palaeontology.[11]

He sent me ⟨*6 lines excised*⟩

Prof. Goeppert wrote an opposing paper (Ueber die Darwin'sche Transmutations-Theorie in Beziehung auf die fossilen Pflanzen) in the Neues Jahrbuch für Mineralogie. Year 1865. Stuttgart. (pag. 296–306.)[12]

With best wishes for your health and ⟨your⟩ future successful activity, dearest Sir | Your devoted servant | Dr. Friedr. Rolle

DAR 176: 202

[1] For the transcription of this letter in its original German, see pp. 28–9.

[2] In May 1865, CD had thanked Rolle for the first part of Rolle's *Der Mensch* (Rolle 1866), a study of the development of human society in the light of *Origin* and recent discoveries in geology (*Correspondence* vol. 13, letter to Friedrich Rolle, 6 May [1865]). It was published by Friedrich Emil Suchsland of Frankfurt-am-Main in five parts; the first part on 1 May 1865 (*Börsenblatt für den Deutschen Buchhandel und die mit ihm verwandten Geschäftszweige* 32 (1865): 954), the second and third parts on 17 November 1865 (*ibid.* 32 (1865): 2634), and the fourth and fifth parts on 15 January 1866 (*ibid.* 33 (1866): 103). CD's lightly annotated copy of Rolle 1866 is in the Darwin Pamphlet Collection–CUL. CD cited Rolle 1866 in *Descent* 1: 4 and 246 n.

[3] In his complex discussion, Rolle contrasted his scientific treatment of the origin of human beings with theological explanations, allowing that humans might have derived from one or several pairs of parents. He also considered evidence for the genus *Homo* comprising one or more species, and whether human races had arisen relatively recently, as geographical varieties of a single species, or as distinct and immutable species of more distant origin (Rolle 1866, pp. 253–7). For more on Rolle's work, and CD's use of it, see Martin and Uschmann 1969, pp. 28–36, 68–9.

[4] Rolle discussed the primeval races from which he considered humans to have originated in Rolle 1866, pp. 257–64. Rolle believed that certain physical traits, including the straightness of the hair and the shape of the skull, defined a superior type: 'Diese höhere Form der Menschheit trägt mehr oder minder den Charakter einer Aristokratie der Cultur . . .' ('This higher form of mankind bears more or less the character of an aristocracy of civilisation . . .') (Rolle 1866, pp. 260–1). For more on craniometry in relation to racial difference in the period, see S. J. Gould 1997, pp. 62–141, especially pp. 130–2; see also Bowler 1987, pp. 55–6, and Stocking 1987.

[5] In his translation of *Origin* (Bronn trans. 1860), Heinrich Georg Bronn used 'natürliche Züchtung', 'natürliche Zuchtwahl', and 'natürliche Auswahl' to translate CD's 'natural selection'. See also Browne 2002, pp. 141–2. Rolle used both 'natürliche Auslese' and 'natürliche Auswahl' (Rolle 1866, pp. 72, 105), although only the former appeared in the section and chapter titles of Rolle's books (Rolle 1863, p. 155; Rolle 1866, p. 104). While the different translations implied differing degrees of choice, CD wished to dispel notions that natural selection implied conscious choice (*Origin* 3d ed., pp. 84–5).

[6] Rolle used various terms to describe the process of extinction. For his use of the words 'Entfallung' and 'Aussterbe-Etat', see Rolle 1866, pp. 142–4. The former denotes 'falling out' or disappearance, and the latter a state of extinction. 'Dilabi': to fall apart; 'elabi': to fall away (Latin; see Lewis and Short 1969).

[7] Aurochs and wisent are mentioned several times in Rolle 1866 (pp. 317, 324–5, 328). The aurochs, *Bos primigenius*, became extinct in western Europe in 1627 (Grzimek ed. 1972, p. 369), whereas wisent (or European bison), *Bison bonasus bonasus*, were in danger of extinction in the nineteenth century (*ibid.*, pp. 394–5).

[8] The zoologist Gustav Jäger was CD's most active supporter in Vienna, where Rolle had worked before leaving in March 1862 to settle in Homburg (*Correspondence* vol. 11, letter from Friedrich Rolle, 26 January 1863 and n. 4). Jäger was an organiser and director of the zoological garden in Vienna; in March 1866, Jäger was replaced as director. The zoological garden had financial problems from its outset in 1863 and closed in September 1866 (Weinreich 1993, 48–64).

[9] David Friedrich Weinland was a supporter of CD (*Correspondence* vol. 11, letter from Friedrich Rolle, 26 January 1863 and n. 12). In December 1863, Weinland moved from Frankfurt to his parents' estate in Württemberg, having resigned as secretary of the zoological society in Frankfurt and editor of *Der Zoologischer Garten*, the foremost journal for zoological gardens in Germany (Weinland 1863).

[10] Weinland founded *Der Thiergarten* in 1864. Only one volume appeared, comprising twelve parts.

[11] Ludwig Rütimeyer had recently published a history of the genus *Bos* based on palaeontological work (Rütimeyer 1865). For Rütimeyer's earlier correspondence with CD on the origins of domestic cattle, and references to Rütimeyer in CD's publications, see *Correspondence* vol. 13, letter from Ludwig Rütimeyer, 3 January 1865 and nn. 3 and 4.

[12] Rolle refers to Göppert 1865a, in which the author rejected the principle of genealogical connections among extinct and living species of plants (Göppert 1865a, p. 297). The *Neues Jahrbuch für Mineralogie*

(1865): 301–6 contained a different paper in which Heinrich Robert Göppert considered transmutation in relation to geology (Göppert 1865b). In 1864 and 1865, Göppert had published a series of papers criticising CD's theory of common descent from the perspective of botanical palaeontology (see, for example, Göppert 1864, of which there is a lightly annotated copy in the Darwin Pamphlet Collection–CUL). For Göppert's views on transmutation, see Junker 1989, pp. 95–98.

From Fritz Müller[1] 13 February 1866

Desterro,
13 February 1866.

Dear Sir!

I have received your kind letters of 17 October and 9 December and also your "Journal of Researches", for which I convey my sincere thanks.[2] I am currently reading the book with the greatest interest.

You note (p. 30) that the light was clearly green in all the different species of luminous animals that you have observed.[3] I have made the same observation in maritime animals (Renilla, Noctiluca, Beroe etc.), but there are some exceptions among insects. The various species of luminous Elaters that I have seen possess not only the two lights on the thorax but also a luminous spot on the belly of the first abdominal segment. When the insect is still or crawls around, this spot remains invisible, but it becomes visible as soon as the abdomen is bent into the air or the Elater flies. The light from this spot is even brighter than that from the two others and it is yellow in colour, quite different from the greenish light of the thoracic spots.

. . . . . One small Elater species has two more luminous spots on the hind part of the abdomen, just like those of glow-worms. About 12 years ago I found a very strange luminous beetle larva in the jungle by the Itajahy river.[4] It had luminous spots on all its abdominal annuli, of which some (if I remember correctly, those at the front end) were bright red, some were yellow, and most were green. The larva was capable of dimming some or all of its luminous spots; when it was irritated they all radiated a splendid light.[5] The larva seems to be very rare; my brother, who has lived by the Itajahy since 1852,[6] has encountered it only once.

I am highly flattered that you found my comments on climbers worthy of being presented at the Linnean Society.[7]

. . . . . Last month I spent three weeks travelling to the Itajahy river, where I enjoyed the splendour of the jungles anew. I looked for climbers, but I noticed only one single example of a plant that climbed a broad tree trunk (roughly 5 feet in circumference). Judging by the structure of the wood and the bitter flavour I think it was a Menispermum; it was about 3 inches in diameter and climbed in a loose spiral from left to right. Most of the climbers scaling broad-girthed trees were root-climbers (ferns, Aroides, Begonia etc.), but I also found a few hook-climbers (Haplolophium, Bignonia, Cissus etc.).—[8] At the upper Itajahy I saw numerous black strings (ranging from a few lines to an inch in diameter), wound in spirals around a number of huge trees; at first I thought they were climbers scaling the trees, but later I discovered that they were aerial roots of a Philodendron that lived on the branches of those trees, from where it sent roots towards the earth. There are some other species of Philodendron whose aerial roots always hang down freely from the branches, growing vertically towards the ground, often reaching a length exceeding 50 m.[9]

. . . . . Concerning orchids, I have good opportunities to observe species from all the various groups and to see so many of the wonderful adaptations that are described in your orchid book, and thus to convince myself of the correctness of your observations. . . .[10]

Incomplete
Möller 1915–21, 2: 79–80

[1] For a transcription of this letter in the German of its published source, see pp. 55–6. According to Alfred Möller, all Fritz Müller's letters to CD were written in English (see Möller ed. 1915–21, 2: 72 n.); most of them have not been found. Many of the letters were later sent by Francis Darwin to Möller, who translated them into German for his *Fritz Müller: Werke, Briefe und Leben* (Möller ed. 1915–21). Möller also found final drafts of some Müller letters among the Fritz Müller papers and included these in their original English form (*ibid.*, 2: 72 n). Where the original English versions are missing, the published version, usually appearing in German translation, has been used.

[2] See *Correspondence* vol. 13, letters to Fritz Müller, 17 October [1865] and 9 December [1865]; for CD's offer to send a copy of the *Journal of researches*, see *Correspondence* vol. 13, letter to Fritz Müller, 20 September [1865] and n. 14. CD probably sent the second edition, which had been reprinted in 1860 (Freeman 1977, p. 40).

[3] In *Journal of researches* 2d ed., pp. 29–30, CD had written:

> It is remarkable that in all the different kinds of glowworms, shining elaters, and various marine animals (such as the crustacea, medusæ, nereidæ, a coralline of the genus Clytia, and Pyrosoma), which I have observed, the light has been of a well-marked green colour.

[4] The river to which Müller refers is the Itajaí Açu in Santa Catarina province, Brazil.

[5] As evidence against the role of luminosity in the behaviour of mating insects, CD cited Müller's observation that a beetle larva was the most luminous insect that he had seen in Brazil (*Descent* 1: 345).

[6] Fritz Müller and his brother August emigrated together from Germany to Brazil in 1852. For an account of their settlement on the Itajaí Açu river, and Fritz Müller's return visits from Destêrro, where he taught mathematics from 1856, see Möller ed. 1915–21, 3: 45 *et seq.*; see also West 2003, pp. 65–96.

[7] CD had edited comments relating to 'Climbing plants', made by Müller in three letters to CD, and communicated them to the Linnean Society (see *Correspondence* vol. 13, letter from Fritz Müller, [12 and 31 August, and 10 October 1865] and n. 1); the paper was read on 7 December 1865, and published as F. Müller 1865b.

[8] CD added to F. Müller 1865b a short account of the climbing of a trunk roughly five feet in circumference by a probable member of the Menispermaceae (see also *Correspondence* vol. 13, letter from Fritz Müller, [12 and 31 August, and 10 October 1865] and n. 19). The structures of the wood of the climbing plants listed in this letter are described and illustrated in F. Müller 1866b, of which there is an annotated copy in the Darwin Pamphlet Collection–CUL.

[9] CD added Müller's description of the aerial roots to *Climbing plants* 2d ed., p. 188 n., and added:

> These roots therefore seem to be true twiners, though they use their powers to descend, instead of to ascend like twining plants. The aërial roots of some other species of Philodendron hang vertically downwards, sometimes for a length of more than fifty feet.

[10] Müller refers to *Orchids*; CD added new information provided by Müller to the second edition. See, for example, letters from Fritz Müller, 2 August 1866, n. 5, and 1 December 1866, n. 4.

From Fritz Müller[1] 6 March 1866

Desterro, Brazil,
6 March 1866.

Dear Sir,

Since I sent off a letter only a few weeks ago I am writing today only to tell you that I have received your kind letter of 11 January in good order and to thank you for the valuable present which you kindly offered.[2] Since everything coming from you is always very welcome and since everything regarding your theory is always certain to command my greatest interest, I shall receive the second edition of the German translation of "Origin" with great satisfaction and cordial thanks.

Here the last two summers (1863–64 and also 64–65) have been unusually dry, and this drought, while not severe enough to cause much damage to agriculture, has nevertheless brought about a number of changes in the relative frequency of many of our animals and plants.[3] Various species seem to have disappeared from places where they used to occur in profusion.— For instance, the edges of a number of ditches near "Villa do Itajahy"[4] used to be covered by a very dainty Aeschynomene, but when I last passed by I did not find one single specimen; now there is an even more beautiful leguminous plant in its place, a Daubentonia.[5] I never saw this plant prior to the great inundation of 1855, but since then it has become very common on the banks of the Itajahy.—[6] In a little ditch near the coast there used to be myriads of delicate Closterium;[7] this ditch dried out completely and remained so until the current rainy summer refilled it with water. Now the Confervæ, the Cypris, the Cyclops, etc. have reappeared,[8] but I looked in vain for the Closterium of which Max Schultze wanted drawings for his Archive.—[9] A couple of days ago I wanted to show a friend the movement in the root hairs of one of the Hydrocharideæ (Limnobium).[10] For this purpose I went to a ditch that I had to cross daily in previous years and that was then covered almost exclusively by this plant. Now I was barely able to collect a couple of specimens, as the plant had been completely replaced by an extremely common Heteranthera.—[11] Our only orchid from the Ophrys group (Bonatea) also seems to have succumbed to the drought on our island: it now occurs only on the mainland.—[12] Orchestia Darwinii had become exceedingly rare following the drought; now the larger part of the area it used to occupy to the exclusion of every other species of Amphipoda has been seized by Orch. Tucuranna, and while it occurs in great profusion in the small area that it still holds, I did not succeed in finding one single specimen of either male form, both of which used to be equally common, it seemed.—[13] No doubt there will be a great number of other plants and animals that have been influenced by this drought. I was prompted to pay attention to the ones I mentioned for various unrelated reasons and so I noticed the changes by chance.

Even at times when no extraordinary changes in the physical conditions influence the outcome of the "struggle for survival", the relative numbers of various animal and plant inhabitants of a land or an ocean by no means remain unchanged. Rather, in my opinion the numbers fluctuate considerably, and probably much more so where the primeval vegetation covers the whole land than where human culture has left wild animals and plants barely a minimum of surface area on which to struggle for survival. I recall that in the last 10 years many changes have occurred in the fauna of the narrow coastal strip close to my house.[14] In earlier years, I did not anticipate such changes, alas, and it did not occur to me that they might be of any scientific importance. Thus I am not in a position to provide you with a precise report. One of the cases that surprised me the most is the following: there is a small rock near the coast, only a few feet across, that was covered with large bushes of a brown bryozoan during the first years of my stay here. Some 6 or 7 years ago I noticed for the first time some specimens of another very gracious white bryozoan on a neighbouring rock. It remained quite rare for a few years, but some 4 or 5 years later it suddenly became very common and covered all the rocks in the neighbourhood; on our small rock every branch of the brown bryozoan was covered with small bushes of the white one and all specimens of the former died. But the reign of the white species was brief; approximately half a year after its greatest diffusion it began to die off and become rarer and rarer. At the moment I no longer know of any rock on which you could get it. The strangest thing about it seems to me to be that the brown bryozoan did not recover its dominant position on the rock after the intruder had disappeared, despite the fact that for many years it had covered it almost exclusively. But now there is a completely new fauna and amongst the attached species a Clavellina[15] is predominant.

Incomplete
Möller 1915–21, 2: 80–2

1 For a transcription of this letter in the German of its published source, see pp. 93–5. According to Alfred Möller, all Fritz Müller's letters to CD were written in English (see Möller ed. 1915–21, 2: 72 n.); most of them have not been found. Many of the letters were later sent by Francis Darwin to Möller, who translated them into German for his *Fritz Müller: Werke, Briefe und Leben* (Möller ed. 1915– 21). Möller also found final drafts of some Müller letters among the Fritz Müller papers and included these in their original English form (*ibid.*, 2: 72 n). Where the original English versions are missing, the published version, usually appearing in German translation, has been used.

2 Müller refers to his letter to CD of 13 February 1866; in his letter to Fritz Müller of 11 January 1866, CD offered to send him a copy of the second German edition of *Origin* (Bronn trans. 1863).

3 For an account of deforestation, agricultural intensification, and climatic instability in coastal south-eastern Brazil during the nineteenth century, see Dean 1995, pp. 191–6 *et seq.*

4 Müller refers to the town of Itajahy (now Itajaí) at the mouth of the Itajaí Açu river on the Brazilian mainland.

5 *Aeschynomeme* and *Daubentonia* (now *Sesbania*) are both large genera of leguminous plants (Mabberley 1997).

6 Müller refers to the Itajaí Açu river. Müller's homestead was beside the river about twenty-five miles inland from the the town of Itajahy, and was later incorporated within the town of Blumenau. In November 1855, flooding had caused the river to rise nearly ten metres above its normal level (Möller 1915–21, 3: 63–4).

7 *Closterium* is a genus of freshwater green algae.

8 Müller refers to filamentous freshwater algae; to *Cypris*, a genus of ostracods or minute freshwater crustaceans; and to *Cyclops*, a genus of copepods that are also minute freshwater crustaceans. Müller

referred to *Cypris*, *Cyclops*, and other copepods in several parts of *Für Darwin* (F. Müller 1864c; translated as Dallas trans. 1869).

9 Max Johann Sigismund Schultze founded *Archiv für mikroskopische Anatomie* in 1865; the journal did not publish illustrations of *Closterium* during its first ten years, the period of Schultze's editorship (Möller 1915–21, 2: IV *et seq.*). Schultze corresponded with Müller and in 1857 gave him a microscope to assist his biological work (*ibid.*, 1: 75).

10 *Limnobium* is a genus of the family Hydrocharitaceae; protoplasmic streaming, that is, the movement of the contents of the protoplasm within individual cells, may be observed in the root hairs of the floating herb *L. spongia* (Mabberley 1997).

11 *Heteranthera* is a genus of aquatic plants in the family Pontederiaceae.

12 The flora of Santa Catarina state, where Müller lived, includes one species of the orchid genus *Bonatea*, *B. pratensis*, now *Habenaria pratensis*.

13 Müller refers to the small crustaceans *Orchestia darwinii* and *O. tucurauna* (see F. Müller 1864c, p. 54, and Dallas trans. 1869, pp. 79–80).

14 Müller refers to the coast of the island of Santa Catarina, Brazil. As well as his homestead beside the Itajaí Açu river in the mainland part of Santa Catarina state, Müller had a house at Destêrro on the island of Santa Catarina (*DSB*).

15 Müller refers to *Clavelina*, a genus of sea squirts in the class Ascidiacea.

From E. Schweizerbart'sche Verlagsbuchhandlung[1] 23 March 1866

Stuttgart
23 March 1866.

My dear Sir,

Since I last had the pleasure of corresponding with you regarding the 2^{d} edition of the German version of "on the origin etc. and the translation of Orchids $3\frac{1}{2}$ years have already passed.[2]

Your famous work has found many friends also in Germany, but at the same time it has not lacked enemies.[3] This could not be otherwise with a book that has had such a profound effect upon views earlier held. As the unforgettable Bronn said in his prospectus: "that no scientist who had not familiarised himself with the facts and new viewpoints presented in this book was scientifically up-to-date etc."[4] Thus, I see that the sales of the German edition—although small by comparison with those in England—are, nonetheless, vigorous and that younger scientists in particular are very much in favour of the book and keep recommending it.[5] Allow me now, dear Sir, to inform you that I have to consider a new edition and that—should you find it appropriate to make additions to this new German edition, I would be very glad to receive them quite soon so as to be able to begin printing the edition.[6]

I will hand over the revision of the type as well as the translation of possible additions or changes to Professor Geinitz—in Dresden, who has replaced Mr Bronn as editor of the Jahrbuch für Mineralogie und Palaeontologie.[7]

I look forward to your kind reply and remain with the highest esteem and admiration Yours | truly | E. Schweizerbart.[8]

DAR 177: 71

1 For a transcription of this letter in its original German, see pp. 105–6.

[2] See *Correspondence* vol. 10, letter from E. Schweizerbart'sche Verlagsbuchhandlung, 16 October 1862. The firm had published two German editions of *Origin* (Bronn trans. 1860 and 1863), and a German edition of *Orchids* (Bronn trans. 1862).

[3] On the reception of *Origin* in Germany, see the letter from Ernst Haeckel, 28 January 1866 and n. 5.

[4] Heinrich Georg Bronn's prospectus for the first German edition of *Origin* was published in *Neues Jahrbuch für Mineralogie, Geologie und Palaeontologie* (Bronn 1860a); Bronn was co-editor of the journal.

[5] A thousand copies of the second German edition of *Origin* (Bronn trans. 1863) were printed. See *Correspondence* vol. 10, letter from E. Schweizerbart'sche Verlagsbuchhandlung, 7 June 1862.

[6] See also letter from Rudolf Suchsland, 16 March 1866. Suchsland had criticised Bronn's translation of *Origin*, and had asked permission on behalf of his father, Friedrich Emil Suchsland, to publish a new translation.

[7] After Bronn's death in 1862, Hans Bruno Geinitz replaced him as editor of the *Neues Jahrbuch für Mineralogie, Geologie und Palaeontologie* (*Jubiläums-Katalog*, p. xvii). In the event, Geinitz was unable to undertake the revision, and the third German edition of *Origin* (Bronn and Carus trans. 1867) was overseen by Julius Victor Carus (see letter from E. Schweizerbart'sche Verlagsbuchhandlung, 10 May 1866).

[8] In his business communications, C. F. Schweizerbart continued to use the signature of his uncle, Wilhelm Emanuel Schweizerbart, from whom he had purchased the publishing firm in 1841 (*Jubiläums-Katalog*, pp. x–xi).

From Friedrich Rolle 12 April 1866[1]

Homburg vor der Hoehe | bei Frankfurt am Main
12 April 1866

Most esteemed Sir!

Yesterday I learned from my publisher that he has been in touch with with you on the subject of translations, and that Professor *Geinitz* in *Dresden* will take care of the new edition of your work "On the origin".[2] Thus I venture to take this opportunity firstly to say how glad I am that my work "Der Mensch" has reached you and stirred your interest,[3] and secondly to send you a sheet with excerpts from *Leonhardt* and *Geinitz's* "Jahrbuch", from which you can see that the editors *oppose* your teachings and primarily give a platform to the compromises of the opposition.[4] I find nothing *in favour* of your theory in it, but the reviews in the Jahrbuch are unfavourable and malicious!

There has been only one paper in the Jahrbuch dealing with your theory, and this too was written by an *opponent*.

Goeppert. Ueber die Darwinsche Transmutations-Theorie mit Beziehung auf die fossilen Arten

·/· Neues Jahrbuch für Min. 1865. pag. 296. ·/· [5]

Since you found my earlier notes on the literature regarding your theory interesting, I shall take the liberty of continuing this practice.[6]

G. Schwartz von Mohrenstern. Ueber die Familie der Rissoiden. II Rissoa. (Denkschriften der Kaiserlichen Akademie der Wissenschaften 1864. XIX. 4°) Vienna 58 pag. 4 plates.[7] (Has also appeared as an offprint)

This excellent work provides a monograph on and the genealogical tree of the genus Rissoa. It contains a genealogical diagram from which one can glean the geological sequence of fossil and living Rissoa and, based on the *Darwinian* theory, their probable descent.[8] (The author asked for my advice with the composition of text and diagram, and I helped him substantiate his views and bring them into accordance with yours.

In Vienna a work, "Zoologische Briefe", by Dr. *Gustav Jaeger* has come out, in which he discusses the logical elements of the theory of transmutation. He includes several very original tables illustrating the genealogy of species in direct projection and after the onset of branches, extinctions and migrations One part of this work was already written when your Origin of Species became known in Germany![9]

The first issue in a series of lectures by Professor *Virchow* of *Berlin*, the famous physiologist and member of parliament, has appeared; he told me in person that he intends to speak out *in favour* of your theory from the perspective of embryology. The text in question contains a popular dissertation of his on archaeology.[10]

In the hope that my comments are of interest to you | I take my leave with profound respect | Yours most devoted | Dr. Rolle

DAR 176: 203

1 For a transcription of this letter in its original German, see pp. 125–6.

2 Rolle refers to the publisher Friedrich Emil Suchsland. See letters from Rudolf Suchsland, 16 March 1866 and 2 April 1866. Two German editions of *Origin* had been published by E. Schweizerbart'sche Verlagsbuchhandlung; Hans Bruno Geinitz had been asked to undertake the revisions necessary for a third German edition (see letter from E. Schweizerbart'sche Verlagsbuchhandlung, 23 March 1866).

3 The reference is to Rolle 1866. See letter to Friedrich Rolle, 1 February [1866].

4 The list of excerpts has not been found. Rolle refers to the *Neues Jahrbuch für Mineralogie, Geologie und Palaeontologie*, edited by Gustav von Leonhard and Geinitz.

5 The reference is to Göppert 1865a. See letter from Friedrich Rolle, 28 January 1866 and n. 12.

6 In his letter of 28 January 1866, Rolle had discussed recent work by Ludwig Rütimeyer and David Friedrich Weinland.

7 The reference is to Schwartz von Mohrenstern 1864; however, Rolle apparently confused this paper with an earlier article on Rissoidae, a mollusc family, that appeared in volume 19 of *Denkschriften der kaiserlichen Akademie der Wissenschaften. Mathematisch-naturwissenschaftliche Classe* (*Wien*) (Schwartz von Mohrenstern 1861).

8 The genealogical tree is on plate 4 of Schwartz von Mohrenstern 1864.

9 Rolle refers to Jäger 1864. The genealogical trees appear in plates 1 to 5. In the preface, Gustav Jäger suggests that parts of the work were written prior to the publication of *Origin* (Jäger 1864, p. vi). The first German edition of *Origin* was published in 1860 (Bronn trans. 1860).

10 The reference is to *Ueber Hünengräber und Pfahlbauten* (Megalithic graves and lake-dwellings) by Rudolf Carl Virchow (Virchow 1866).

From E. Schweizerbart'sche Verlagsbuchhandlung[1] 10 May 1866

Stuttgart
10 May 1866

Most honoured Sir

I am very grateful to you for your kind and prompt reply and hope you will not interpret my late response as a sign of inattentiveness.[2] The delay has come about for several reasons. Prof. Geinitz was approached on my behalf by Prof. Leonhard to see whether he had the time and inclination to oversee a new edition of your work and also to translate another work from your pen. He was very late in declining, which prompted me to write to him myself, but I met with no greater success.[3] Herr Geinitz then sent me the enclosed letter and once again recommended Prof. Carus in Leipzig.[4]

You will be aware from newspapers of the critical state in which we currently find ourselves in Germany, where the presumption bordering on treason of a single individual is about to plunge us into civil war as he pursues his ambitious plans contrary to all lawfulness and against the will of the entire German nation, and even allies himself with foreign nations![5] Under such circumstances, it is inevitable that business would be totally paralysed. I will therefore also restrict myself to essentials, for at the moment it would be pointless to bring out new books.

As you know Prof. G. Leonhard has been co-editing the "*Jahrbuch*" with Herr Bronn, and he now also has to take care of the administrative side of the editing.[6] Since the translation is Bronn's and checking the new edition is just a question of effort, Herr Leonhard, who has translated into German Murchison's *Geology of Russia* and also Sedgewick and Murchison's publication: "*paleozoic rocks*", should know the English language well enough to revise the 3rd edition of your Origin in accordance with the most recent English edition.[7] I have, therefore, made this proposal to him rather than to Herr Carus, who lives far from here, because I also have commitments to Bronn's widow, and I expect that Herr Leonhard is more likely to come to terms with us as he has long been a friend of the Bronn family.[8]

So, I would respectfully ask you to send the relevant material for the 3rd German edition. We will then have the time to compare it with the 2nd German edition and to make the necessary changes.[9]

With regard to the shortcomings of Herr Bronn's work, which has been criticised by a number of people, I do not think the text contains fundamental errors, as Herr Bronn is master both of the ancient languages and of the most important modern ones. If anyone was qualified through his own work to carry out the translation of your book, then it was he, for he was eminently knowledgeable.[10]

With regard to your other work,* of which you were so kind to offer me page proofs for translation, I am happy to accept; but for the moment we have to wait until the political situation has cleared. For this work I am thinking of approaching Herr Carus, but I would ask you first to send me the printed proofs (sheets).[11]

Be assured that I take a personal interest in having the work carried out properly, as it is most important to me to completely satisfy you who approached us with such kindness.

We have read with much pleasure that you are well again.

I look forward to further kind news from you and remain with the highest esteem your most devoted | E. Schweizerbart[12]

* Domestic animals & cultivated Plants &c

[Enclosure]

Most honoured Herr Schweizerbart!

Although I feel honoured by the trust in me displayed by *Darwin* and you with regard to the revision of the new German edition of his famous work and the translation of a new work[13] by this excellent scientist, I cannot, however, take on this job. In particular, because I just finished my book on bituminous coal last year, a number of other very attractive scientific projects have been left for longer than I can answer for. In addition to these, all the work that I can not delay for our Jahrbuch, for the Royal Museum under my command, and for the lecture courses at the polytechnic will keep me more than busy for many years to come.[14]

Although I do not belong to the *extreme* followers of Darwinism, I still pursue with great interest the important direction shown us by Darwin and do not cease to examine the facts with thorough impartiality in my field of speciality.[15]

I had ventured to point you in the direction of Prof. Victor Carus in Leipzig as my replacement and I still believe that he is the most suitable person for the task in hand, not only because he is a great admirer of Darwinian teaching but also because he has complete mastery of the English language, having spent several years at Oxford. As Professor of physiology he is also closer to these questions than I could be from the geological–paleontological perspective.[16]

I remain with the highest esteem
Your most devoted | H. B. Geinitz

Dresden 29 April 1866
Herrn E. Schweizerbart in Stuttgart.

DAR 177: 72

[1] For a transcription of this letter in its original German, see pp. 166–8.

[2] The letter to E. Schweizerbart'sche Verlagsbuchhandlung has not been found; however, see the letter from E. Schweizerbart'sche Verlagsbuchhandlung, 23 March 1866.

[3] Schweizerbart refers to a third German edition of *Origin* and to *Variation.* Gustav von Leonhard was co-editor with Hans Bruno Geinitz of the *Neues Jahrbuch für Mineralogie, Geologie und Palaeontologie*, published by E. Schweizerbart'sche Verlagsbuchhandlung.

[4] Julius Victor Carus. See enclosure.

[5] Schweizerbart refers to the measures taken by Otto von Bismarck to expand Prussian influence and territory within the German lands. Many of Bismarck's efforts were directed against Austria, the other principal power in the German confederation of states. On 9 April 1866, Prussia had formed an alliance with Italy, effective for ninety days, that committed the two states to assist each other in the event of war with Austria. On Bismarck's diplomacy during the years leading up to the Austro-Prussian war, and the opposition to his policies by liberal political parties and the German press, see Sheehan 1989, Pflanze 1990, vol. 1, and Wawro 1996.

[6] Leonhard assumed editorial responsibilities for the *Neues Jahrbuch für Mineralogie, Geognosie, Geologie und Petrefaktenkunde* in 1861. He edited the journal jointly with Heinrich Georg Bronn until the latter's death in July 1862, when the name of the journal was changed to *Neues Jahrbuch für Mineralogie, Geologie und Palaeontologie.* Bronn was succeeded as co-editor by Geinitz in 1863. See *Jubiläums-Katalog*, p. xvii.

7 The first two German editions of *Origin* had been translated by Bronn (Bronn trans. 1860 and Bronn trans. 1863), who had arranged for its publication by E. Schweizerbart'sche Verlagsbuchhandlung (see *Correspondence* vol. 8). Leonhard had translated Murchison and Sedgwick 1842 and Murchison *et al.* 1845 into German; both translations were also published by E. Schweizerbart'sche Verlagsbuchhandlung (Leonhard trans. 1844 and 1848). In the event, the third German edition was overseen by Carus (Bronn and Carus trans. 1867). The references are to Adam Sedgwick and Roderick Impey Murchison.

8 Bronn's widow has not been further identified.

9 The second German edition of *Origin* (Bronn trans. 1863) was based on the third English edition, but with additional changes (see *Correspondence* vol. 10, Appendix VIII). The third German edition was based on the fourth English edition.

10 For criticisms of Bronn's translation of *Origin*, see the letters from Rudolf Suchsland, 16 March 1866 and 2 April 1866; see also letter from Rufolf Oldenbourg, 28 October 1866, letters from J. V. Carus, 7 November 1866 and 15 November 1866, and letter to J. V. Carus, 10 November 1866.

11 CD's letter to Schweizerbart has not been found. The reference is to proofs of *Variation*. A German edition of *Variation*, translated by Carus, was published by E. Schweizerbart'sche Verlagsbuchhandlung in 1868 (Carus trans. 1868).

12 See letter from E. Schweizerbart'sche Verlagsbuchhandlung, 23 March 1866, n. 8.

13 Geinitz refers to a third German edition of *Origin* and to *Variation*.

14 Geinitz refers to H. B. Geinitz ed. 1865. He was director of the Mineralogisches Museum, and professor of geology and mineralogy at the Technische Bildungsanstalt, Dresden (*ADB*).

15 On the reception of CD's work in Germany, see the letter from Ernst Haeckel, 28 January 1866 and n. 5.

16 Carus had been conservator of the comparative anatomy collection at Oxford from 1849 to 1851; in 1853 he was appointed professor of comparative anatomy at Leipzig University (*DSB*).

From Alphonse de Candolle[1] 3 June 1866

London
3 June 1866

My dear Sir.

I have just spent 15 days in London in a most agreeable manner. One thing, however, distresses me, but since it was the result of an error on my part alone, I am happy enough to explain it to you. The first time that I attended a meeting of the Committee in connection with the Botanical Congress, I asked for news about you and whether we would have the pleasure of seeing you.[2] One of the gentlemen answered me that you were ill, and he added (or I misunderstood what he said in English) that you were absent. I understood that you were going on a trip to the south and with many regrets I gave up the idea of meeting you. Later I learned from Mr Caspary[3] and Sir Charles Lyell that you were in the country, but it was too late for me to be able to present my compliments. Allow me to tell you that I really regretted this, especially since Madame de Candolle[4] and I are going to travel in the vicinity of Oxford and to the north of Great Britain so that it will not be possible to put right my negligence.

Perhaps you and Sir Charles Lyell do not have a very precise idea of what Mr Lecoq said about plants from the Auvergne and about the glacial period.[5] I had the impression that he particularly objected to the idea of lowered temperature as a cause of glacial extension and that he insisted on the possibility of large glaciers when there was a great deal of humidity in the air. I do not recall that he completely denied that there had been a glacial period.[6] He insisted on the possibility of the transportation of seeds over great distances by wind, birds, etc, which I carefully investigated and I persist, personally, in believing that one has often taken possibilities for realities.[7] Observation has shown me that in 2 or 3 centuries, in the countries where most research has been carried out, no phanerogam has been naturalised except through the direct or indirect action of *man*. One will have to read the improvised lecture by Lecoq in the Proceedings to get a better idea of this.[8]

Mr Ruprecht has published in German in the Bulletin de l'Academie de St Petersbourg a curious memoir on the black earth of south Russia.[9] He proved through plant remains and the absence of any marine or other sediment in the soil that it was a substantial island dating back to the tertiary era, in which the grasses formed an enormous accumulation of detritus. Consequently we might have there a source for our European vegetation before and after the glacial period. I had this article translated for the Bibliothèque Universelle de Genève in order to understand it better, because at first reading of a badly edited German text I could not easily understand the author's opinion.[10] I have reason to believe that Mr Ruprecht is a good observer and what he said will merit your attention as well as that of Sir Charles and the other geologists.

Accept, my dear Sir, the assurance of my sincere devotion and all my best wishes for an improvement in your health | Alph. de Candolle.

P.S. Please pay my respects to Madame Charles Darwin.

DAR 161: 12

1 For a transcription of this letter in its original French, see pp. 194–5.

2 Candolle had delivered the presidential address at the opening meeting of the International Horticultural Exhibition and Botanical Congress on 23 May 1866 (A. de Candolle 1866). CD was on the congress committee, but did not attend the meeting for reasons of health (see letter from M. T. Masters, March 1866, and letter to Friedrich Hildebrand, 16 May [1866]). CD had been invited to two dinner parties at which Candolle was to be present (letter from J. E. Gray, 9 April 1866, and letter from C. W. Dilke, 24 April 1866), and had asked Joseph Dalton Hooker to convey his regrets at not seeing Candolle in London (letter to J. D. Hooker, 16 May [1866] and n. 8).

3 Robert Caspary had attended the Botanical Congress, and had visited CD at Down (letter from Robert Caspary, 7 May 1866 and n. 3).

4 Jeanne-Victoire-Laure de Candolle.

5 See letter from M. T. Masters, 20 April 1866. Maxwell Tylden Masters had informed CD of a paper on the migration of plants to be delivered by Henri Lecoq at the International Horticultural Exhibition and Botanical Congress (Lecoq 1866). CD had been corresponding at length with Charles Lyell about plant dispersal during the glacial period (see, for example, letter to Charles Lyell, 7 February [1866]).

6 See letter from M. T. Masters, 20 April 1866 and n. 5.

7 See letter from M. T. Masters, 20 April 1866 and n. 6.

8 Candolle refers to Lecoq 1866.

9 Franz Josef Ruprecht's paper, 'Neuere geo-botanische Untersuchungen über den Tschornosjom' (New geo-botanical studies of the Russian black earth), appeared in the 1866 volume of the *Bulletin de l'Académie Impériale des Sciences de St.-Pétersbourg* (Ruprecht 1865).

[10] Candolle refers to Ruprecht 1866. Ruprecht published mainly in Russian; for a bibliography of his works, see *Bulletin de l'Académie Impériale des Sciences de St.-Pétersbourg* 16 (1871): Supplement.

From Ernst Haeckel[1] 19 October 1866

8 Clarges Street Piccadilly London
19 Oct. 1866

Dear, most honoured Sir!

At last one of my fondest wishes is to be fulfilled. I hope to be able to meet and talk to you shortly. I think that I could perhaps visit you Sunday (*Sunday* 21 Oct), and ask you to tell me briefly if this day suits you and *at what time* (at what o'clock) I may come to Down, Bromley. I am only in London for a short time, as I will be going on the next steamship to Madeira and Tenerife where I will stay the winter and conduct zoological research.[2]

My "*generelle Morphologie der Organismen*, based on Darwin's reformed theory of descent" is now finished and you will receive it in the next couple of weeks.[3] *Volume one* includes a general introduction and the elements of general anatomy. *Volume two* contains a general description of descent and selection theory and the fundamentals of general developmental history. I may soon, perhaps, tell you more about it in person.

Hopefully I will find you in the best possible health. With the most excellent admiration I remain yours with wholehearted devotion | Ernst Haeckel

DAR 166: 43

[1] For a transcription of this letter in its original German, see pp. 353–4.

[2] Haeckel had travelled from Bonn to London at the beginning of October 1866. He travelled on to Lisbon, where he met two students who accompanied him to Madeira and Tenerife in November 1866. In December, they arrived at Lanzarote, where they spent three months studying hydrozoans and siphonophores. (Krauße 1987, pp. 76–7.)

[3] The reference is to Haeckel 1866. CD's annotated copy is in the Darwin Library–CUL (see *Marginalia* 1: 355–7). For Haeckel's earlier discussions of Haeckel 1866, see *Correspondence* vols. 12 and 13.

From E. Schweizerbart'sche Verlagsbuchhandlung[1] 26 October 1866

Stuttgart
26 October 1866

Most respected Sir,

Since I last wrote to you, a long time has passed, during which you kindly sent me the proofs of the new edition of your Origin.[2]

You know that the sad time of the German war was not appropriate for literary undertakings;[3] this notwithstanding, I have not left the new edition unattended, but, after Prof. Geinitz and Prof. Leonhard said they would not undertake the task, on the recommendation of the former I have approached Prof. Victor Carus in Leipzig.[4]

I take great pleasure in reporting to you that he has accepted my proposal most readily, and will be writing to you in this regard;[5] meanwhile I have sent him the copy of your work that I received from you, along with one copy of the German edition.[6] From all Mr Carus has written to me, he is exactly the right man for the book; he requests complete freedom to delete from Mr Bronn's annotations anything that he cannot himself support from a scientific standpoint.[7] Mr Carus is an acknowledged proponent of your theory and will try on his part to support and strengthen it through general physical-physiological grounds. Mr Carus will write to you himself about this; I thought however I had better give you this information at once, so that you would know how things stand.

Thanking you once again for all the kindness I have enjoyed from you, I am with great esteem and admiration | Yours truly | E. Schweizerbart

DAR 177: 73

1 For a transcription of this letter in its original German, see pp. 362–3. It was written by Christian Friedrich Schweizerbart, the head of E. Schweizerbart'sche Verlagsbuchhandlung, who used the signature E. Schweizerbart in business communications.

2 See letter from E. Schweizerbart'sche Verlagsbuchhandlung, 10 May 1866. Page proofs of the fourth edition of *Origin* were available by mid-July 1866 (see letter to John Murray, 15 July [1866]).

3 The reference is to the Austro-Prussian War. Stuttgart, where the Schweizerbart firm was located, was the capital of Württemberg, one of the German states that sided with Austria (see letter from E. Schweizerbart'sche Verlagsbuchhandlung, 10 May 1866 and n. 5).

4 Schweizerbart had originally approached Gustav von Leonhard to supervise the third German edition of *Origin*, but he declined, recommending Hans Bruno Geinitz as his replacement. Geinitz also declined but suggested that Julius Victor Carus would be well qualified for the job (see letter from E. Schweizerbart'sche Verlagsbuchhandlung, 10 May 1866).

5 See letter from J. V. Carus, 7 November 1866.

6 Schweizerbart refers to *Origin* 4th ed. and Bronn trans. 1863.

7 For more on Heinrich Georg Bronn's annotations to the German translation of *Origin*, see the letter from J. V. Carus, 7 November 1866.

From Fritz Müller[1] [2 November 1866][2]

Today, when I visited a Frenchman, Mr Hippolyte Gautier, who collects orchids for sale, I saw a beautiful blue Ipomoea in his garden.[3] He told me he had raised a single plant from seed that he had received from the northern provinces of Brazil; this plant had already flowered for some years, very abundantly, and had large numbers of blooms throughout the year, without, however, producing seed capsules. I naturally thought the plant could be dimorphic, and found, upon investigation of the flowers, that the style projected far above the stamens.[4] We have here on the mainland a closely related species which I can probably examine next month.

While investigating the dimorphic flowers of our common Erythroxylon ("Fruta de pomba") I was amazed by the variation presented in every flower part in a short-styled tree.[5]

Out of 253 flowers on this tree there were:

sepala	petala	stamina	styli	flowers	
5 sepala,	5 petala,	10 stamina,	3 styli,	192 flowers	
5 "	6 "	10 "	3 "	1 "	1)
6 "	6 "	10 "	3 "	3 "	
6 "	6 "	11 "	3 "	3 "	
6 "	6 "	12 "	3 "	20 "	
6 "	6 "	12 "	3–4 "	1 "	2)
6 "	6 "	12 "	4 "	25 "	
6 "	7 "	12 "	3 "	1 "	
6 "	7 "	13 "	4 "	1 "	
6 "	7 "	14 "	3 "	1 "	
7 "	7 "	12 "	3 "	1 "	
7 "	7 "	12 "	4 "	1 "	
7 "	7 "	14 "	3 "	1 "	
7 "	7 "	14 "	3–4 "	1 "	2)
7 "	7 "	14 "	4 "	2 "	

1) A few of the sepala were notched at the tip.

2) One of the three styli was twice as thick as each of the other two and had a bilobed stigma.

Of the flowers with four styles, ten had two ovula. Among numerous flowers of other short- and long-styled trees I found only a single short-styled with six sepals, six petals, ten filaments, and three styles, and one long-styled with 4 sepals, 4 petals, 8 stamens, 4 styles and no ovulum.

But I am afraid I've exhausted your patience and will close, and I will save for another letter a case of remarkable variability of the calyx that I observed in a Hillia.[6]

Allow me to give you my heartfelt thanks once again for your friendly letter and the "Origin",[7] and believe me, I am, dear sir, with sincere respect, very truly yours | Fritz Müller

P. S. Have I already told you that I found an underground beetle whose tarsi lacked any feet?

Möller 1915–21, 2: 93–4

[1] For the transcription of this section of Müller's letter in the German of its printed source, see pp. 369–70. This section of the letter, the original of which has not been found, was translated into German by Alfred Möller and published in Möller ed. 1915–21, 2: 93–4 (see letter from Fritz Müller, 13 February 1866, n. 1). Möller dated the fragment of the letter 1 October 1866, but CD's annotations as well as his reply of [late December 1866 &] 1 January 1867 refer to items mentioned only in this part of the letter (see n. 6, below).

[2] The date is established by CD's annotations at the top of the letter and on the envelope in which part of it was found (see pp. 370–1).

[3] This section of the letter, published in Möller 1915–21, 2: 93–4, was dated 1 October 1866 by Möller, but is clearly part of the present letter (see n. 1, above). Hippolyte Gautier has not been further identified.

[4] In his reply to Müller of [late December 1866 and] 1 January 1867, CD referred to Müller's observation of evidence for dimorphism in *Ipomoea*, calling it *Convolvulus* (in *Cross and self fertilisation*, p. 28, CD stated that in England *Ipomoea purpurea* was often called *Convolvulus major*).

[5] 'Fruta de pomba': fruit of the dove (Portuguese). In *Forms of flowers*, pp. 121–2, CD referred to the dried flowers of *Erythroxylum* (*Erythroxylon* was an alternative spelling) and included a sketch of the two forms that Müller had sent him. He also noted Müller's observations on the variation in the number of flower parts.

[6] The observations on *Hillia* are in the letter from Fritz Müller, 1 December 1866.

[7] See letter to Fritz Müller, 23 August [1866]. According to Müller's endorsement, he received the letter on 25 October 1866; in a letter to his brother Hermann Müller of 29 October 1866, he mentioned having just received a copy of the fourth edition of *Origin* (see Möller ed. 1915–21, 2: 95). CD's publisher, John Murray, had agreed to send out some copies before the general release of the new edition in mid-November 1866 (see letter from John Murray, 23 July [1866]).

From Armand de Quatrefages[1] 10 November 1866

Paris
10 November. 66

Dear Sir and Colleague,

Messrs Williams and Norgate bksellr have been instructed to send you a copy of my History of the Annelids (fig. col.)[2] If my book is too slow in reaching you, be so good as to make a request for it. This work has cost me a great deal of trouble, for I do not know of any animals that are more of a nuisance to classify than the Annelids and I have taken every care to be accurate. Receive it as a memento from your very devoted colleague who would so much like to meet you in person | De Quatrefages

DAR 175: 4

[1] For a transcription of this letter in its original French, see p. 384.

[2] The booksellers and publishers Williams & Norgate specialised in foreign scientific literature. CD's copy of Quatrefages 1865 is in the Darwin Library–Down. 'Fig. col.' is probably an abbreviation for 'figures colorés', referring to the coloured plates of the work.

From Fritz Müller[1] 1 December 1866

Desterro, Brazil,
1. December 1866.

My dear Sir!

A week ago I received your kind letter of 25 Sept for which I thank you very much.[2] It is very valuable and extremely interesting for me since it deals with objects that currently fascinate me.

Dr. Hildebrand has already observed, as I am pleased to learn from your letter, that the ovula of many orchids are not ripe at the time of flowering.[3] This seems to be common among the Epidendreae and the Vandeae; at least I have not yet encountered one species in these families in which the ovula were ready at this time. In my Epidendrum triandrum, as it may be called,[4] the ovula are not even quite ready now, approximately six months after flowering. The little column of such orchids usually swells up a lot after the flower has withered; soon the pollen tubes penetrate the style and form six threads that run along its walls. The threads are very easily separated from one another. In a flower of Leptotes bicolor these threads were very thick and snow white with a silky sheen two months after it had been fertilised with its own pollinia. The pollen seems in many cases to remain fresh for a long time whereas in other species it dries up and turns black soon after the penetration of the tubes into the style. For instance, this is the case with a small self-fertilising Epidendrum (related to E. caespitosum). The caudiculi remain unchanged and pollen tubes are not formed, either in this species or, as far as I know, in any other species of Epidendreae. When the fertilisation is effected by insect activity the caudiculi usually remain on the insect body by means of the sticky substance of the rostellum.

In plants that are infertile with their own pollen, I strongly suspect that many of them are really, in essence, dimorphic.[5] For example, there are a couple of bushes of a Ximenia not far from my house and several more about a mile away. These various bushes have only produced two fruits in the course of 10 years. Assuming that the various plants in each of the two locations, different in their function but indistinguishable in form, belong to the same group, it would be easy to explain this infertility. In other cases, as I have now convinced myself, there is certainly no dimorphism, rather infertility with own pollen but fertility with that of another plant of the same species, as in Dr. Hildebrand's case of Corydalis cava.[6] I found this, for example, in four plants of Eschscholtzia in my garden on which I have made some experiments. This complete infertility with own pollen could hardly have remained unnoticed, had it existed in all individuals of such a common garden plant. Perhaps in the case of my plants it can be attributed to their cultivation in divergent climatic conditions.[7] The difference between the two pollens becomes visible on sunny days 4 to 5 hours after the pollen has been put on the stigma, for the pollen from a foreign plant causes the stigma to stand up erect whereas its own pollen does not give rise to any movement.

Oncidium flexuosum is also completely infertile with its own pollen and fertile with the pollen of any other plant of the same species.[8] I have fertilised more than 100 flowers and without fail always had the same result. There is no difference between own pollen and that from another plant during the first three days after having brought the pollinia on to the stigma. The stigmatic chamber has two doors, so to speak, which are widely open in the unfertilised flower. In the course of the first day the inner door will be closed; in the course of the second, the outer, which is formed from the two lateral, infertile filaments, will be closed. Soon the pollinia begin to disintegrate or at first to separate into groups of four and then into single grains; and these single grains emit tubes, some of which by the end of the third day are of considerable length. The little column appears slightly swollen. During the fourth day, in flowers fertilised with their own pollen, a pale brownish line appears that separates the pollinia from the stigma and this line quickly gets wider and darker so that at the end of this day, or soon after, the entire pollinium and the surface of the stigmatic chamber have become dark brown. The pollen-grains and tubes have shrivelled. These flowers fertilised with their own pollen wither somewhat faster than those fertilised with pollen from another plant. The ovaries of the latter soon begin to swell up and the fringe of the placenta grows quickly, although the ovula are still far from ripeness 23 days after fertilisation. The pollen tubes have by this time lengthened by up to more than half the length of the stylar column.

At first I thought that the closing of the doors to the stigmatic chamber and the emission of the pollen tubes could be seen as a sign of the beginning fertilisation of the flowers, but later I found that—even when the pollinia of such a widely differing species as Epidendrum fragrans are brought onto the stigma of Oncidium flexuosum—the stigmatic chamber closes, the pollinia dissolve and the pollen tubes begin to grow.

An old pollinium that I had taken from a different species of Oncidium 9 or 10 months earlier did not dissolve but turned black after it had lain in the stigmatic chamber of Oncidium flexuosum for 4 days.

I am now in a position to give you two new examples of plants that have conspicuous seeds stuck to the valve of the fruit. One is a small tree of the Meliaceae, probably a Guarea. The plant has eight brick-red seeds stuck to the valve of the fruit (they are too big to be sent in a letter). The other is a big tree of the genus Talauma (Magnoliaceae).[9] I still remember my surprise about 12 years ago when I saw its numerous brightly coloured seeds dangling on a large pineapple-like fruit. In the case of Paullinia the fleshy arillus may prompt birds to swallow the seeds. With Mimosa and Rhynchosia there is no fleshy hull but the seeds are exceptionally hard and since gallinaceous birds often swallow small stones in order to promote the breaking up of their food, I imagined that these hard and conspicuous seeds could well serve the same purpose when swallowed by our Jacús (Penelope) or other birds. Endlicher says of Talauma that the seeds have a "testa subossea".[10] The seeds of Guarea neither have a fleshy hull nor are they very hard.

Our bush-like Oxalis really is dimorphic; I have now also found the mid-styled form.[11] This time I can only add two species to the list of dimorphic plants:

1) A Lipostoma with blue flowers;[12] it grows in small ditches with the strange, moss-like Mayaca. The anthers of the short-styled kind are longer, the pollen-grains bigger. I think that one can still find many dimorphic plants among the Rubiaceae because in his descriptions of genera Endlicher often writes: "stamina inclusa, stigma exsertum" or "stamina exserta, stigma inclusum".[13]

2) A Statice which grows on the coast but also likes humid spots.

Now on to the variability of the length of the calyx in Hillia, which I referred to in my last letter.[14] The genus Hillia, which at first glance might be taken for an Apocynaceae rather than a Rubiaceae on account of the shape of its corolla, seed capsule and seeds, ought to have a "limbus calycis biquadripartitus" according to Endlicher.[15] Now, in our species of this plant one finds calyces with a completely rudimentary limbus, others with two, four, or even six laciniae. The length of the two pairs of leaves that are directly under the ovary is just as variable as the number of laciniae of the calyx. I measured it in 19 flowers. In 11 of these flowers the calyx had a withered limbus, in 6 of them there were 2 laciniae; in one flower four laciniae were found of which two were 6 mm long and two barely 1 mm, and finally in one flower the calyx had six laciniae 4 mm long. The length of the upper pair of leaves ranged from 3 to 50 mm, that of the stipules from completely rudimentary to 15 mm. The next pair of leaves were from 5 to 118 mm, the stipules from rudimentary to 32 mm. The corolla always had 6 laciniae.

Your conjecture that in the case of the lancelet the struggle for survival takes place in competition with members of the invertebrate classes was thoroughly justified.[16] Here at least, its only companion and rival in the infertile sand that it inhabits is an Ophelia which in general appearance and movement resembles the lancelet so closely that at first I thought I had discovered a new red-blooded Amphioxus species.[17] The Ophelia indeed resembles the other Annelida as little as the lancelet resembles other fish. Our lancelet does not seem to differ specifically from the European type; at least neither Johannes Müller, who examined samples collected by Kröyer, nor Max Schultze, whom I had sent some, could find any difference from the Neapolitan lancelet.[18]

In wishing you a happy new year, I remain, honoured Sir, sincerely yours. | Fritz Müller.

Möller ed. 1915–21, 2: 99–102.

[1] For an account of the reconstruction of Fritz' Müller's letters to CD, see the letter from Fritz Müller, 13 February 1866, n. 1. For a transcription of this letter from its published German source, see pp. 405–8.

[2] See letter to Fritz Müller, 25 September [1866].

[3] CD had mentioned Friedrich Hildebrand's observations on the development of the ovules in some orchid species (Hildebrand 1865c) in his letter to Müller of 25 September [1866].

[4] *Epidendrum triandrum* is a nomenclatural synonym of *Epidendrum cochleatum* var. *triandra*, a variety that does not occur in Brazil. It seems likely that Müller used the name here simply to refer to a three-anthered, self-pollinating form of *Epidendrum* (Robert Dressler, personal communication). CD added Müller's information on the immature state of the ovules at the time of flowering in orchids of the tribes Epidendreae and Vandeae to *Orchids* 2d ed., p. 173.

[5] Müller refers to the concept of 'functional dimorphism' that CD introduced in 'Two forms in species of *Linum*', p. 82 (*Collected papers* 2: 104; see letter from Fritz Müller, 2 August 1866 and n. 9). CD clarified his use of the phrase 'dimorphic in function' as referring to plants that could be 'divided into two equal bodies functionally but not structurally different' in his letter to Müller of 25 September [1866].

[6] The reference is to Hildebrand 1866d (see also the expanded German version of the paper, Hildebrand 1866–7b). CD had corresponded with Hildebrand on the pollination mechanism of *Corydalis cava*, and had communicated Hildebrand's paper to the International Horticultural Exhibition (see letter to Friedrich Hildebrand, 16 May [1866] and n. 3).

[7] Müller refers to *Eschscholzia californica*, a plant not native to Brazil (see letter from Fritz Müller, 2 August 1866). His suspicion that self-sterility in this plant might be related to the climate in which it was grown was later confirmed by CD. In *Cross and self fertilisation*, pp. 331–3, CD described changes in the degree of self-sterility in plants raised from seeds of *E. californica* sent to him by Müller and also gave the results of reciprocal experiments made by Müller on plants raised from seeds sent by CD.

[8] CD discussed Müller's observations of *Oncidium flexuosum* in *Variation* 2: 134–5.

[9] Müller had described plants with brightly coloured seeds attached to the valve of the fruit in his letters of 2 August 1866 and 1 and 3 October 1866.

[10] Müller refers to Stephan Ladislaus Endlicher's generic diagnosis of *Talauma* (Endlicher 1836–42, 1: 837). 'Testa subossea': somewhat bony seed-coat.

[11] Müller probably meant to write 'trimorphic', or Alfred Möller may have incorrectly transcribed or translated the word. (Like all of Müller's letters to CD, the letter was written in English and later translated into German for Möller ed. 1915–21. The original letter has not been found.) Müller had earlier told CD he thought the species was probably trimorphic, but had only found specimens of the long-styled and short-styled forms (see letter from Fritz Müller, [2 November 1866]).

[12] *Lipostoma* is now placed in synonymy with *Coccocypselum*. In *Forms of flowers*, p. 134, CD described flower specimens of *Lipostoma* sent to him by Müller.

[13] Müller refers to Endlicher 1836–42. 'Stamina inclusa, stigma exsertum': stamens not projecting, stigma exserted. 'Stamina exserta, stigma inclusum': stamens exserted, stigma not projecting.

[14] See letter from Fritz Müller, [2 November 1866].

[15] 'Limbus calycis biquadripartitus': lobe of the calyx biquadripartite (see Endlicher 1836–42, 1: 556). For a recent revision of the genus *Hillia*, see Taylor 1994.

[16] In *Origin* 4th ed., pp. 143–4, CD had remarked that the lancelet (*Branchiostoma lanceolatum*, formerly *Amphioxus lanceolatus*) would not compete with other fish, but more probably with invertebrates. CD added Müller's information to *Origin* 5th ed., p. 146. The lancelet was initially classed as a primitive fish but has now been moved to its own subphylum, Cephalochordata.

[17] *Ophelia* is a genus of the class Polychaeta (marine worms). For more on the similarity between some forms of Opheliidae and *Branchiostoma*, see Rouse and Pleijel 2001, pp. 53–6.

[18] Johannes Peter Müller reported that he received a specimen of *Branchiostoma* collected in Brazil by Henrik Nikolaj Krlyer (see J. P. Müller 1844, p. 8 n. 3). Max Johann Sigismund Schultze had written a paper on young specimens of lancelet (Schultze 1851).

APPENDIX II
Chronology 1866

This appendix contains a transcription of Darwin's 'Journal' for the year 1866. Darwin commenced his 'Journal' in August 1838 and continued to maintain it until December 1881. In this small notebook, measuring 3 inches by $4\frac{1}{2}$ inches, Darwin recorded the periods he was away from home, the progress and publication of his work, and important events in his family life.

The version published by Sir Gavin de Beer as 'Darwin's Journal' (de Beer ed. 1959b) was edited before the original 'Journal' had been found and relied upon a transcription made by an unknown copyist. The original, now in the Darwin Archive in Cambridge University Library (DAR 158), reveals that the copyist did not clearly distinguish between the various types of entries it contains and that the transcription made was incomplete.

From 1845 onward, Darwin recorded all that pertained to his work (including his illnesses, since these accounted for time lost from work) on the left-hand pages of the 'Journal', while the periods he was away from home, and family events, were noted on the right-hand pages. In order to show clearly Darwin's deliberate separation of the types of entries he made in his 'Journal', the transcription has the left- and right-hand pages labelled.

All alterations, interlineations, additions, and the use of a different ink or pencil have been noted. In addition, the editors have inserted additional information relevant to Darwin's correspondence throughout this transcription of the 'Journal' for 1866. These interpolations are enclosed in square brackets to distinguish them from Darwin's own entries, the source of the information being given in the footnotes.

[**Left**]
1866
Continued correcting Chapts of Domestic Animals.—[1]
March 1st Began on 4th[2] Edit of Origin of 1250 Copies:— (Received for it 238 £[3] making 7500 copies altogether.
May 10th Finished Origin except Revises & began going over[4] Ch. XIII. of Dom. Animals.
Nov[5] 21. Finished Pangenesis.[6]
Dec. 21. Finished regoing[7] over all Chapters, & sent them to Printers[8]
Dec. 22. Began Concluding[9] chapter of Book.[10]

[**Right**]
1866
[24–6 March. Joseph Dalton Hooker visited.][11]
[2 April. George Henslow visited for two days; George Varenne Reed, John Brodie Innes, and Thomas Selwood Stephens to dinner.][12]
April 21st to May 2^{d} to Erasmus.[13] [28 April. CD attended Royal Society of London soirée.][14]
[27 May. Robert Caspary visited.][15]
May 29th to June 2^{d} Leith Hill Place[16]
[23–5 June. John Traherne Moggridge, J. D. Hooker, and Frances Harriet Hooker visited. Frances left on 29 June.][17]
[18 August. J. D. Hooker visited.][18]
[2 October. CD met Herbert Spencer at High Elms.][19]
[21 October. Ernst Haeckel visited.][20]
[16–19 November. Charles and Mary Elizabeth Lyell visited.][21]
Nov. 22 to 29th to Erasmus.
Febr. 2 Catherine died[22]
Oct 3. Susan died.[23]

1 *Variation.*
2 After del 'new'.
3 '(Received . . . £': interl.
4 'going over': interl.
5 Above del 'Dec.'
6 Chapter 27 of *Variation* (2: 357–404).
7 're': interl.
8 See letter to John Murray, 21 and 22 December [1866].
9 'C' over 'c'.
10 Chapter 28 of *Variation* (2: 405–32).
11 Emma Darwin's diary (DAR 242).
12 Emma Darwin's diary (DAR 242); letter to J. D. Hooker, 4 April [1866].
13 CD's brother Erasmus Alvey Darwin lived at 6 Queen Anne Street, London.
14 Emma Darwin's diary (DAR 242).
15 Emma Darwin's diary (DAR 242).
16 Leith Hill Place, near Dorking, Surrey, was the home of CD's elder sister Caroline Wedgwood and her husband, Emma Darwin's brother, Josiah Wedgwood III.
17 Emma Darwin's diary (DAR 242).
18 Letters from J. D. Hooker, [17 August 1866] and 18 August 1866.
19 Letter to J. D. Hooker, 2 October [1866].
20 Emma Darwin's diary (DAR 242).
21 Emma Darwin's diary (DAR 242).
22 Emily Catherine Langton was CD's younger sister; her date of death is registered in Shrewsbury as 1 February 1866.
23 Susan Elizabeth Darwin was CD's elder sister.

APPENDIX III

Diploma presented to Charles Darwin

In 1866, Darwin received the following diploma from the Botanical Society of Edinburgh. Although not a letter in the conventional sense, it represents significant communication between Darwin and a scientific society, and the citations in such diplomas often provide valuable indications of those aspects of Darwin's work that were considered worthy of honour. In view of this, it has been included here, together with a translation. Also in 1866, Darwin was elected an honorary member of the Royal Irish Academy (see letter from William Reeves, 10 April 1866), but the diploma has not been found.

From the Botanical Society of Edinburgh 11 January 1866

VICTORIÆ
BRITANNIARUM REGINÆ
AUSPICIIS.
SOCIETAS BOTANICA,
die XI Januarii *Anni Salutis Humanæ MDCCC*LXVI
apud Edinburgum conventu,

Sodalem Honorarium *sibi cooptavit, atque privilegiorum quibus Sodales* Honorarii *fruuntur participem fecit,*

Carolum Darwin

In cujus rei fidem, hoc Diploma, sigillo suo, Præsidisque ac scribæ chirographis munitum, expediri jussit.

Robert Kaye Greville *Præses.*
Joannes Hutton Balfour MD. *Scriba.*

[Translation]

Under the auspices of Queen Victoria of Great Britain and Ireland. On 11 January *1866, the Botanical Society, in a meeting at Edinburgh, elected* Charles Darwin *an* honorary *fellow, and granted him the privileges enjoyed by* honorary *fellows. In earnest of this fact, it commanded this diploma, furnished with its seal, and the signatures of the president and secretary, to be prepared.*
Robert Kaye Greville *President.*
John Hutton Balfour MD. *Secretary.*

DAR 229: 15

APPENDIX IV
Presentation list for the fourth edition of *Origin*

The fourth edition of *Origin*, published in 1866, was the most extensively revised edition yet published, with two pages added to the historical sketch at the beginning of the book, and fifty-two new pages of text (Peckham ed. 1959, p. 21). John Murray, Darwin's publisher, in a letter dated 21 February [1866], had notified Darwin that the third edition was sold out, and asked whether Darwin agreed to a new edition, and if so, whether he had any changes to make. Darwin may well have made more than Murray expected; he worked intensively on the new edition between 1 March and 10 May 1866, largely abandoning work on *Variation* in order to do so (CD's Journal (Appendix II), letter to Charles Lyell, 22 February [1866]). 'Natural Hist. progresses so quickly that I must make a good many corrections', Darwin warned Murray in his reply, dated 22 February [1866]. In view of the changes, Murray increased the print run from 1250 to 1500 copies (letter from John Murray, 25 May [1866]).

Darwin resented the loss of time from *Variation*, but was heartened to find that his work would be timely for the preparation of a third German edition of *Origin*, correspondence about which began in March 1866 (letter to Asa Gray, 16 April [1866]). A further complication surrounding the new edition was Darwin and Asa Gray's desire to see a new American edition. The first American edition had been based on the second British edition (see *Correspondence* vol. 8, Appendix IV), and was now considerably out of date; however, the stereotype plates that the publishers had had made were difficult to correct. After some frustrating and fruitless negotiations with American publishers, Gray suggested that Darwin ask Murray to supply the US market with 250 copies (letter from Asa Gray, 18 July 1866). Murray was perfectly willing, but (perhaps forgetting that he had already increased the print run to 1500) remarked that if he had known 250 copies were required for the US, he would have ordered more than 1250 (letter from John Murray, 25 October [1866]).

Printing of the new edition was nearly complete on 25 May, and Murray offered Darwin eighteen free copies (letters from John Murray, 25 May [1866] and 30 May [1866]). CD sent a list of copies for Murray to distribute—possibly based on the list published here, which contains twenty-two names of persons or institutions—with his letter of 15 July [1866]. Murray then announced that he was delaying all his new books until the beginning of November, and offered to send out Darwin's presentation copies at the end of October (letter from John Murray, 18 July [1866]). Evidently this was not quite satisfactory to Darwin, for shortly afterwards Murray wrote to him, 'Your wishes regarding the Six copies for England & America of your new edition shall be carefully attended to' (letter from John Murray, 23 July [1866]). From remarks in letters to the persons concerned, it seems likely that the six included Charles Lyell in England, Asa Gray and Benjamin Dann Walsh in the US, and Fritz Müller in Brazil. They did not include Joseph Dalton Hooker, who declined an early copy, confident that Darwin would tell him anything he needed to know (letter from J. D. Hooker, [6 August 1866]), or Thomas Henry Huxley, James Shaw, or Alfred Russel Wallace, all of whom wrote thanking Darwin for their copies in November. William Turner's copy was also probably sent in October or November (letter to William Turner, 14 December [1866]). Alfred Newton, who is not on the list, wrote to thank Darwin for his copy on 27 November 1866.

For biographical details of each recipient (except Darwin himself), see the Biographical register and index to correspondents in this volume.

Origin 4th. Edition

(1) Self
Hackel[1]
F. Muller[2]
Asa Gray
Walsh[3]
J. Shaw[4]
Dr. W. Turner[5]
Lubbock[6]
Lyell[7]
Hooker[8]
Huxley[9]
Wallace[10]
Bates[11]
Royal Soc.
Linnean
Geolog. Soc
Anthropolog Soc
Entomolog. Soc Bedfor[12]
Zoolog[13]
J. Samuelson[14]
2 copies for Foreign Edits
—
22

DAR 210.11: 21

[1] Ernst Haeckel.
[2] Fritz Müller.
[3] Benjamin Dann Walsh.
[4] James Shaw.

[5] William Turner.
[6] John Lubbock.
[7] Charles Lyell.
[8] Joseph Dalton Hooker.
[9] Thomas Henry Huxley.
[10] Alfred Russel Wallace.
[11] Henry Walter Bates.
[12] The Entomological Society of London's apartments were at 12 Bedford Row, London (*Transactions of the Entomological Society of London*, 1866).
[13] Zoological Society of London.
[14] James Samuelson, co-editor of the *Quarterly Journal of Science*; see letter to John Murray, 15 July [1866].

MANUSCRIPT ALTERATIONS AND COMMENTS

The alteration notes and comments are keyed to the letter texts by paragraph and line numbers. The precise section of the letter text to which the note applies precedes the square bracket. The changes recorded are those made to the manuscript by CD; changes of hand in letters written partly by CD and partly by amanuenses are also recorded. Readers should consult the Note on editorial policy in the front matter for details of editorial practice and intent. The following terms are used in the notes as here defined:

del	deleted
illeg	illegible
interl	interlined, i.e., inserted between existing text lines
omitted	omitted by the editors to clarify the transcription
over	written over, i.e., superimposed

To a local landowner [1866]
1.1 now] *interl*
1.3 immediately attend] *interl above del* 'see'
1.3 though . . . the sake 1.5] *above del* 'as a magistrate I must attend to this, and if I send for the'
1.3 I . . . very] *interl*
1.5 A] *over* 'a'
1.5 A conviction] *after del* 'Perhaps you may not be aware that'
1.6 on sufficient . . . produced] *interl*
1.7 compelled] *above del* 'forced'
1.7 vainly] *interl*
1.7 by letter] *interl*
1.8 come down here &] *interl*
1.9 Mr Ainslie] *above del* 'he'
1.9 at the] 'the' *interl*
1.9 Bromley] *before omitted point*
1.10 at once] *above del* 'give'
1.11 not to . . . neck] *interl*
2.1 I remain] *after del* 'with every'

To Henry Bence Jones 3 January [1866]
4.1 with . . . Ch. Darwin] *in CD's hand*

To Philip Lutley Sclater 6 January [1866]
1.5 & . . . opinion?] *interl in CD's hand*

To William Bernhard Tegetmeier 16 January [1866]
1.5 not chequered] *interl after del* 'd[rawn]'
1.6 drawn,] *interl*
2.3 & let me see eggs. 2.4] *interl*
3.1 &] *over illeg*

To Joseph Dalton Hooker 21 [January 1866]
0.2 21] '1' *over* '2'
2.1 or rather nothing] *interl*

To Jeffries Wyman 2 February 1866
3.4 hexagonal combs] 'hexagonal' *in CD's hand above del* 'hexagonal'

To Frederick Ransome [6 February 1866]
1.2 (in hope . . . Co^y^)] *interl*
1.4 finally] *interl*
1.4 Companies] *after del* 'affairs of your'
1.4 is] *above del* 'are now'
1.4 more] *interl*

To Alfred Russel Wallace [6 February 1866]
2.5 I sh^d.^ think] *interl in CD's hand*
2.5 at first] *interl in CD's hand*

To Charles Lyell 7 February [1866]
1.3 after] *interl in CD's hand*

5.4 (which . . . improve)] *interl in CD's hand*
10.1 Remember . . . Equator.— 12.4] *in CD's hand*
11.8 genera of Plants] *above del* 'forms'
12.2 to the sea] 'to' *interl*

To Charles Lyell 15 February [1866]
0.2 Feb 15th] *added in CD's hand*

To Robert Caspary 21 February [1866]
3.2 Ch. Darwin . . . 21st. 4.1] *in CD's hand*

To John Murray 22 February [1866]
12.1 P.S. . . . **Post**.— 12.2] *in CD's hand*

To J. D. Hooker [28 February 1866]
0.1 Down . . . dozen physicists. 1.11] *in the hand of an amanuensis*
0.2 Wednesday] *in CD's hand below del* 'Tuesday'
1.4 on the glacial affair 1.5] *interl in CD's hand*
1.11 ten . . . more] *interl in CD's hand*
2.9 Tropical] *interl*
2.9 cool] *after del* 'gla'

To Charles Lyell [3 March 1866]
2.1 earlier] *interl*
2.2 new facts] *interl*
2.3 they] 'th' *over* '&'
2.7 to . . . seedlings] *interl*
3.3 but . . . folio.—] *interl*

To Charles Lyell 8 March [1866]
2.10 themselves.] *interl in CD's hand*
4.1 Yours . . . Darwin] *in CD's hand*

To Richard Kippist 31 March [1866]
1.3 in . . . members] *interl*

To J. D. Hooker 4 April [1866]
2.1 Bonatea & the] *interl*
2.1 case. Ask 2.2] *altered from* 'case: ask'
2.2 ever] *interl*
4.2 (which] *after* 'of its contents' *interl and del*
4.3 or increases] *interl*
4.3 reproduces] *after del* '& finally'
4.6 tubes] *above del* 'grains'
5.3 are capable] 'are' *interl*
6.2 of the external 6.3] 'of the' *interl*
6.3 similarly] *after del* 'a'
6.3 atoms . . . or 6.4] *interl*
7.4 now] *interl*
7.6 of the view] *interl*
7.9 mutual action &] *interl*
8.1 or sneers] *interl*

To J. D. Hooker [5 April 1866]
1.1 where the] 'the' *interl*
1.2 a var.] 'a' *interl*
1.2 fruit] *interl*

To Fritz Müller [9 and] 15 April [1866]
0.2 15th.] *in CD's hand below del* '9th'
2.5 Apocyneæ] *in CD's hand above del* 'Asclepiadæ'
4.1 I am . . . Ch. Darwin 7.2] *in CD's hand*
5.2 as yet] *interl*
6.5 not] *interl*

To Henrietta Emma Darwin [14–21 April 1866]
1.3 & spontaneously] *interl*
2.4 If . . . Mogg.— 2.5] *added pencil*

To Asa Gray 16 April [1866]
2.5 Germany, is] 'is' *interl*
4.1 makes] *altered from* 'made'
4.5 quite stopped,] 'stopped,' *interl*

To J. D. Hooker [16 April 1866]
2.2 at] *over* 'in'
2.2 (which . . . honour)] *parentheses over commas*

To Benjamin Dann Walsh [19] April [1866]
5.5 in the] 'the' *interl*
5.6 the summer] 'the' *added*
5.9 about] *after del closing quotation marks*

To Friedrich Hildebrand 20 April [1866]
3.3 or fully] *interl*

To J. D. Hooker [22 April 1866]
2.1 we] *over* 'I'

To James Shaw [23 April 1866]
1.2 interesting] *interl*
1.4 (so . . . facts) 1.5] *interl*

To William Robert Grove [26 April 1866]
2.2 for . . . hour] *interl*
3.1 of writing] *after del* 'I'
3.1 to contrary] *interl*

To Thomas Rivers 27 April [1866]
1.2 make] *after del* 'send'
2.3 hence] *interl*

To J. D. Hooker [28 April 1866]

2.3 Can you . . . to Down.] *interl*
3.2 when] *after del* 'at'

To William Robinson [29 April 1866]
2.2 (though . . . aid me)] *parentheses over commas*
2.3 one flower] 'one' *interl*
2.5 the seeds] 'the' *interl*
2.8 advanced] *after del* 'been'
3.3 expanded] *above del* 'open'

To William Robinson 5 May [1866]
1.4 from insects] *interl*

To ? 10 May [1866?]
1.6 the . . . unequal] *interl*

To J. D. Hooker [12 May 1866]
1.2 I doubted] 'I' *over* 'it'
1.3 letter] *after del illeg*

To J. D. Hooker 31 May [1866]
2.1 & . . . Archeopteryx 2.2] *added pencil*
2.1 much] *interl*
3.2 soon] *interl*
3.3 by half-dozens] *interl*
7.1 I . . . *much.*—] *added pencil*

To George Henslow 15 [June 1866]
2.3 Reversion in] *interl*
2.3 appeared] *after del* 'are'
2.3 clear] *above del* 'clear'
2.4 have not] 'have' *above del* 'did'
2.4 thought] *above del* 'think'
3.1 believed] 'd' *added*
3.2 & as] 'as' *interl*
3.2 is] *interl*

To William Erasmus Darwin 19 [June 1866]
1.3 or Hermaphrodite] *interl*
1.4 pistil is] 'is' *interl*
1.4 the male] 'the' *interl*

To W. E. Darwin 22 June [1866]
5.1 (miserable . . . compared.— 6.4] *added in CD's hand*
6.2 The long-styled 6.3] *altered from* 'In the long-styled'
6.3 fruit] *interl*

To W. E. Darwin [24 June 1866]
1.2 pollen of] *interl pencil*
2.3 & damp] *interl*
2.3 ; & then . . . tin-foil. 2.4] *interl*
7.1 Does . . . shade??] *added pencil*

To W. E. Darwin 30 [June 1866]
2.1 this morning] *interl*
3.1 £2"16"8] *above del* '2£ 80 dd'

To J. D. Hooker 30 June [1866]
7.1 Thanks . . . Lupine] *in CD's hand*

To George Bentham [July–September 1866]
1.4 wish] *above del* 'have'

To the Lords of the Admiralty [2–4 July 1866]
1.2 accompanied . . . naturalist] *interl*
1.2 will soon proceed] *after del* 'is going to'; 'soon' *interl*
1.4 at Gallegos] 'at' *pencil above del pencil* 'near the mouth of the'
1.4 in the extreme . . . Patagonia 1.5] *interl*
1.5 deposit of the bones] 'of the' *pencil above del pencil* 'of fossil [*above del* 'Fossil']'
1.5 species of] *interl pencil*
1.5 quadrupeds] *above del* 'forms of Mammalia'
1.5 quadrupeds. Many] '. Many' *pencil above del pencil* ', many'
1.6 these collected] 'these' *pencil below del pencil* 'which he'
1.6 with the aid . . . R.N.] *interl*; 'Hydrographer' *interl*
1.6 & afterwards] *after del* 'the'
1.6 afterwards] *below del* 'deposited'
1.7 These *[illeg]*] '*[illeg]*' *interl pencil*
1.8 collection . . . Beagle & 1.8] *interl pencil above del pencil* 'many Mammalian [*above del* 'other coll'] remains of *allied animals, [*below del* 'extinct quads;' *above del* 'other allied Mammalia'] brought from S. America'
1.8 other] *after del* 'the'
1.8 , & . . . fossils 2.1] *interl pencil above del* 'attached to the last expedition of H.MS. Beagle under the care of Capt'
2.1 have been . . . remarkable 2.2] *added in margin, pencil*
3.1 We the undersigned] *interl pencil del pencil* '& are consequently [*added and del pencil*] of extreme interest to Science.'
3.1 in] *after del* 'I'
3.2 bones] *pencil above del pencil* 'extraordinary fossils [*above del* 'remains']'
3.2 collected] *above del* 'collected'
3.3 perfect] *after del pencil* 'singularly'

3.3 could probably] 'could' *after del* 'could'; 'probably' *interl*
4.1 We . . . Mayne. 4.4] *on a separate sheet, pencil*
4.2 the benefit . . . conferred] *pencil above del pencil* 'advantages to'
4.2 orders . . . for a] *interl pencil*; 'a' *over* 'the'
4.3 Collection] *after* 'extensive' *interl pencil and del pencil*
4.3 to be made] *interl pencil*
4.3 under] *after del pencil* 'to be made *by the Naturalist accompanying Capt Mayne [*interl pencil*]'
4.3 present] *altered from* 'presently'

To Thomas Henry Huxley 4 July [1866]
1.3 not . . . Straits] *interl in CD's hand*
1.17 some] *interl in CD's hand*

To Friedrich Hildebrand 22 July [1866]
2.2 immediately 2.3] *interl in CD's hand*

To J. D. Hooker 30 July [1866]
1.9 had long] 'had' *altered in CD's hand from* 'have'
2.4 the rarity] 'the' *altered in CD's hand from* 'their'
2.4 of N. plants] *interl in CD's hand*
2.6 African, as well as] *interl in CD's hand*
3.2 of land] *interl in CD's hand*
3.11 in favour] *interl in CD's hand*
3.13 duration] *in CD's hand above del* 'length'
3.13 its existence] 'its ex' *in CD's hand above del* 'its ex'
3.13 formerly] *interl in CD's hand*
3.17 survive] *in CD's hand above del* 'exist'
3.18 the island was] *interl in CD's hand*
7.1 Wollaston . . . C. Darwin 9.1] *in CD's hand*
7.1 82] *after del* '28'
8.1 Book with] *interl*

To J. D. Hooker 3 and 4 August [1866]
1.2 evidence] *interl in CD's hand*
3.6 same] *interl in CD's hand*
3.7 of birds] *interl in CD's hand*
3.10 to the Bermudas] 'to' *interl in CD's hand*
4.1 I do not . . . morning 10.1] *in CD's hand*
4.3 objections, on] 'on' *interl*
4.4 (p. . . . Origin)] *interl*
4.4 Forbes'] *after del* 'the'
6.4 sending] *after del* 'to'
7.1 Dont . . . busy.—] *added, blue crayon*
9.4 in many organs] *interl*
9.4 *co existing*] *interl*
10.1 ☞**Acropera** . . . morning] *added, blue crayon*

To J. D. Hooker 5 August [1866]
4.1 Whilst . . . not.— 4.4] *in CD's hand*

To J. D. Hooker 8 August [1866]
2.1 I . . . means.— 2.3] *added in CD's hand; large brace on left-hand side in MS*
6.4 The . . . vigorous.—] *added in CD's hand*

To Ernst Haeckel 18 August [1866]
1.7 , which . . . done,] *interl in CD's hand*
2.1 &c] *interl in CD's hand*

To Fritz Müller 23 August [1866]
2.5 by insects] *interl in CD's hand*

To J. D. Hooker 30 August [1866]
2.3 with . . . fairness, 2.4] *interl in CD's hand*
6.1 I have . . . herewith.—] *in CD's hand*
6.1 return] *altered from* 'returned'

To Robert Swinhoe [September 1866]
1.1 Cordial] *added above* 'Thanks'
1.1 for so . . . wish] *interl*
4.3 animals.—] *after del illeg*

To Charles Lyell 8[–9] September [1866]
11.1 P.S. There is . . . capital.— 11.6] *in CD's hand*
11.1 the Sept.] *after del illeg*
11.4 of species 11.5] *interl*

To Asa Gray 10 September [1866]
1.7 Agassiz] *in CD's hand above del* 'he'
1.8 fancies] *in CD's hand above del* 'thinks'
4.4 like Primula] *interl in CD's hand*
9.3 young] *interl in CD's hand*
9.5 both . . . day.] *interl in CD's hand*
10.1 & with cordial thanks] *added in CD's hand*

To J. D. Hooker 25 September [1866]
3.4 the whole globe 3.5] *interl*
4.2 than before 4.3] *interl*

To Fritz Müller 25 September [1866]
0.2 & 25th] *added in CD's hand after del* '22'
3.2 very] *interl in CD's hand*
4.3 little modified] *interl in CD's hand*

To William Bowman 26 September [1866]
2.2 Dei] 'D' *in CD's hand over* 'd'

To J. D. Hooker 2 October [1866]
2.1 by Rail] *interl*

3.2 surprise] *interl*
5.4 the specimens] 'the' *interl*

To Charles Lyell 9 October [1866]
1.3 as ignorant] 'as' *interl*
3.2 have] *interl*

To Charles Lyell 12 October [1866]
5.1 at] *in CD's hand above del* 'of'
6.1 Ch. Darwin . . . length.— 8.5] *in CD's hand*

To Thomas Rivers 13 October [1866]
2.2 knowledge] *above del* 'fortune'

To George Brettingham Sowerby Jr 19 October [1866]
1.3 with my . . . the same. 1.4] *interl in CD's hand after* 'I have retained for the time my M.S. instructions' *added and del in CD's hand*
1.9 **all**] *interl in CD's hand*
2.1 one] *in CD's hand over* 'a'
3.1 (Corrections.)] *in CD's hand, square brackets in MS*
7.4 above.] *interl in CD's hand*
8.1 of Pigeon] *interl in CD's hand*
9.1 Skull of Fowl] *interl in CD's hand*
9.4 entire] *interl in CD's hand*
9.6 entire] *interl in CD's hand*
9.6 this skull] *altered in CD's hand from* 'the 2 skulls'
9.6 & the section of skull 9.7] *interl in CD's hand*
13.1 Ch. Darwin . . . below.— 17.2] *in CD's hand*

To John Murray 23 October [1866]
1.4 see] *in CD's hand over* 'say'
1.4 what] *interl in CD's hand*
4.1 Ch. Darwin . . . decide.— 5.1] *in CD's hand*

To W. E. Darwin 8 November [1866]
1.1 at 13,500£] *interl*
1.2 in fact] *interl*
1.5 and agreed] 'and' *over* 'that'
1.8 on our deaths 1.9] *interl*
1.10 *soon*] *interl*
1.12 carefully] *interl*
1.12 which you may] 'you' *interl*

To Julius Victor Carus 10 November 1866
9.1 P.S. . . . copy.— 9.2] *in CD's hand*

To J. D. Hooker 20 November [1866]
2.1 ie. tomorrow] *interl in CD's hand*
8.1 Impudence . . . received. 9.1] *in CD's hand*

To J. V. Carus 21 November 1866
5.1 as . . . me] *interl in CD's hand*
5.5 (hypoginous . . . &c)] *added in CD's hand*

To Charles Lyell 1 December [1866]
2.1 for] *after del* 'read'

To J. D. Hooker 5 December [1866]
3.1 P.S. . . . it.— 3.2] *in CD's hand*
3.2 my] *interl*

To Linnean Society 7 December [1866]
1.1 author's] *after del* 'F. Müller'

To Fritz Müller [before 10 December 1866]
2.7 of the gizard . . . sincerely 4.2] *in hand of amanuensis*
2.18 Europæus] *interl in CD's hand*
3.6 some] *in CD's hand above del* 'a few'

To J. D. Hooker 10 December [1866]
1.2 the pods open &] *interl*
1.4 two seeds] 'seeds' *interl*
1.5 during] *above del* 'after'
1.7 Birds] *after del* 'the'
2.1 Mr Norman] 'M[r]' *over* 'a'
3.9 ; &] *altered from* '.—'
4.1 I am . . . going on. 5.5] *in hand of amanuensis*
4.10 N.Z] *in CD's hand above del* 'it'
4.15 Caledonia] 'e' *altered from* 'i'; 'donia' *in CD's hand above del* 'fornia'

To William Turner 14 December [1866]
2.9 it seems . . . none.] *interl*
2.13 of body] *interl*
2.14 of . . . cases.] *interl*

To John Murray 21 and 22 December [1866]
1.5 at once] *interl in CD's hand*
3.2 of Instructions] *interl in CD's hand*
8.1 Dec 22[d] . . . use.— 8.3] *in CD's hand*
8.3 mere] *interl*
8.3 use.—] *below del* 'inspection—'

To T. H. Huxley 22 December [1866]
1.6 detailed] *altered from* 'details'
1.6 new views.] *interl*
1.8 very vague] 'very' *interl*
2.1 am] *over illeg*
2.1 straight] *above del* 'strait'
3.4 do] *above del* 'to'
3.6 have come] 'have' *interl*

3.7 new] *interl*
3.10 Domestication] *after del* 'of'

To J. D. Hooker 24 December [1866]
1.6 bear] *altered from* 'bears'
2.2 Introduction] 'In' *over* 'Au'
2.4 for general readers] *interl*
2.6 without any grounds] *interl*
2.9 a little] 'a' *interl*
2.10 the seeds] 'the' *altered from* 'these'
2.10 the tree] *interl*
3.1 a thinking] *after del* 'to'
4.3 upon] *after del illeg*
4.6 intervening] *interl*
4.8 appearing] *above del* 'being'
5.2 genera of] *interl*
5.4 by Carrière 5.5] *interl*

To B. D. Walsh 24 December [1866]
6.2 this so far] 'this' *interl in CD's hand*
6.3 Now . . . Ch. Darwin 9.1] *in CD's hand*

To J. D. Hooker 28 [December 1866]
2.4 others] *after del* 'remain'

To Bartholomew James Sulivan 31 December [1866]
2.3 but . . . those] *interl in CD's hand*
3.4 by . . . paper.—] *added in CD's hand over point*
4.3 *much*] *interl in CD's hand*
4.5 the specimens] 'the' altered from 'they'; 'specimens' *interl in CD's hand*

To Fritz Müller [late December 1866 and] 1 January 1867
2.4 ?& . . . Hope 2.5] *interl in CD's hand*
2.11 apparently] *interl in CD's hand*
2.12 Eschholtzia] 't' *added in CD's hand*

BIOGRAPHICAL REGISTER

This list includes all correspondents and all persons mentioned in the letters and notes that the editors have been able to identify. Dates of letters to and from correspondents are given in chronological order. Letters to correspondents are listed in roman type; letters from correspondents in italic type; third-party letters are listed in italic type with the name of the recipient given in parentheses.

Adams, John Couch (1819–92). Astronomer and mathematician. Co-discoverer of the planet Neptune. Fellow and tutor, St John's College, Cambridge, 1843–52; Pembroke College from 1853. Lowndean professor of astronomy and geometry, Cambridge University, 1858; director of the Cambridge Observatory, 1861. FRS 1849. (*DNB*, *DSB*.)

Agassiz, Elizabeth Cabot Cary (1822–1907). Educator. A founder of the educational establishment for women that later became Radcliffe College, Cambridge, Massachusetts. President of Radcliffe College, 1894–9; honorary president, 1900–3. Married Louis Agassiz in 1850. (*ANB*.)

Agassiz, Jean Louis Rodolphe (Louis) (1807–73). Swiss-born zoologist and geologist. Professor of natural history, Neuchâtel, 1832–46. Emigrated to the United States in 1846. Professor of zoology and geology, Harvard University, 1847–73. Established the Museum of Comparative Zoology at Harvard in 1859. Foreign member, Royal Society of London, 1838. (*ANB*, *DAB*, *DSB*, *Record of the Royal Society of London*.)

Ainslie, Robert (1802/3–76). Independent unitarian minister and religious writer. Resident at Pond House (later renamed Tromer Lodge), Down, 1845–58. Minister of New Court Chapel, Carey Street, London. Secretary of the London City Mission and of the Congregational Board of Education. Minister of Christ Church, Brighton, 1860–74. (Ainslie 1865; *Calendar* no. 12842, letter from O. A. Ainslie, 23 November 1880; *Correspondence* vol. 3, letter to Susan Darwin, 3[–4] September 1845; *Correspondence* vol. 7, letter to W. E. Darwin, 14 [May 1858]; G. E. Evans 1897; *The Times*, 23 August 1876, p. 16.)

Airy, George Biddell (1801–92). Astronomer. Plumian Professor of astronomy and director of the Cambridge Observatory, 1828–35. Astronomer royal, 1835–81. FRS 1836. (*DNB*, *DSB*.)

Allen, Emma (1780–1866). Daughter of John Bartlett Allen and Elizabeth Allen. Emma Darwin's aunt. (*Darwin pedigree*, *Emma Darwin* (1915).)

Allen, Frances (Fanny) (1781–1875). Daughter of John Bartlett Allen and Elizabeth Allen. Emma Darwin's aunt. (*Darwin pedigree*, *Emma Darwin* (1915).)

Anderson, Thomas (1832–70). Scottish physician and botanist. Entered the Bengal medical service in 1854. Superintendent, Calcutta botanic garden, 1861–8; conservator of forests, Bengal, 1864–9; retired because of ill health. Instituted experiments that led to the successful cultivation of *Cinchona* in India. (R. Desmond 1992, pp. 100–1; R. Desmond 1994; *DSB*; Stebbing 1922–6, 1: 515.)

Anon.
10 May [1866?], 2 August [1866]

Appleton, Thomas Gold (1812–84). American essayist, poet, and artist. Promoted the growth and improvement of Boston; a trustee of the Athenaeum and the Public Library; founder and benefactor of the Museum of Fine Arts. (*ANB.*)
2 March [1866]

Appleton, William Henry (1814–99). American publisher. Partner in the New York firm D. Appleton & Co., 1838–48. Became head of the firm in 1848 on the retirement of his father, Daniel Appleton. D. Appleton & Co. published works by British scientists such as CD and Herbert Spencer. (*ANB.*)

D. Appleton & Co. New York publishing house. Founded by Daniel Appleton (1785–1849) in 1831. His son William Henry Appleton (1814–99) was taken into partnership in 1838. American publishers of works by CD and Herbert Spencer. (*ANB.*)

Ardoino, Honoré Jean Baptiste (1819–74). French–Italian botanist at Menton. (*Taxonomic literature.*)

Argyll, duke of. *See* Campbell, George Douglas.

Armistead, Wilson (1818–68). Entomologist. Specialist in gall insects. (*Entomologist* 4 (1868–9): 49.)

Babington, Charles Cardale (1808–95). Botanist, entomologist, and archaeologist. Involved in natural history activities at Cambridge for more than forty years; an expert on plant taxonomy. A founding member of the Cambridge Entomological Society and the Cambridge Antiquarian Society. Editor of *Annals and Magazine of Natural History* from 1842. Chairman, Cambrian Archaeological Association, 1855–85. Professor of botany, Cambridge University, 1861–95. FRS 1851. (*DNB*, *DSB.*)

Baer, Karl Ernst von (1792–1876). Estonian zoologist and embryologist. Professor of anatomy at Königsberg University, 1819; professor of zoology, 1826–34. Professor of zoology at the Academy of Sciences, St Petersburg, 1834–67. Demonstrated the existence of the mammalian egg, 1826. Propounded the influential view that embryological development proceeds from the general to the specific. Foreign member, Royal Society of London, 1854. (*DSB*, *NDB*, *Record of the Royal Society of London.*)

Baillière, Hippolyte. French publisher. Partner in the French publishing and bookselling firm of Jean Baptiste Baillière, founded in Paris in 1818, specialising in science and medicine; had offices in London and New York. (*Dictionnaire des lettres françaises. XIX siècle*; Baillière 1853.)

Baird, Spencer Fullerton (1823–87). American zoologist and scientific administrator. Professor of natural history, Dickinson College, 1846. Assistant secretary and curator of the Smithsonian Institution, 1850; secretary, 1878–87. Science editor for *Harper's Weekly*, 1871–9. (*ANB.*)

Baker, John Gilbert (1834–1920). Botanist. Draper in Thirsk, Yorkshire, 1847–64. Active in the Thirsk Natural Historical Society. Assistant in the herbarium at the Royal Botanic Gardens, Kew, 1866–99; keeper of the herbarium and library, 1890–99. Lectured on botany at the London Hospital Medical School, 1869–81, and at the Chelsea Physic Garden from 1882. Contributed to a wide range of colonial floras. FRS 1878. (*DSB.*)

Balbiani, Edouard-Gérard (1823–99). French biologist. Licencié in natural science, Paris, 1845; MD, 1854. Director of histological research, Muséum National d'Histoire Naturelle, 1867. Professor of embryogeny, Collège de France, 1874. Co-founder, *Archives d'Anatomie Microscopique*, 1897. (*DBF*, *DSB.*)

Balfour, John Hutton (1808–84). Scottish physician and botanist. Professor of botany, Glasgow University, 1841–5. Professor of botany, University of Edinburgh, and regius keeper of the Royal Botanic Garden, Edinburgh, 1845–79. Founding member of the Botanical Society of Edinburgh, 1836. Founder of the Edinburgh Botanical Club, 1838. Co-editor of the *Edinburgh New Philosophical Journal*. FRS 1856. (*DNB*, *DSB.*)

Banks, Joseph (1743–1820). Botanist. Travelled around the world on HMS *Endeavour*, 1768–71. President of the Royal Society, 1778–1820. Created baronet, 1781; privy councillor, 1791. FRS 1766. (R. Desmond 1994, *DNB.*)

Barter, Richard (1802–70). Physician. Qualified at the London College of Physicians. Founded St Anne's hydrotherapy establishment, Blarney, County Cork, Ireland, 1842; developed treatments using hot-air baths and Turkish baths. (*DNB.*)

Bartlett, Abraham Dee (1812–97). Zoologist. Taxidermist, 1834–52. Superintendent of the natural history department, Crystal Palace, 1852–9; of the Zoological Society's gardens, Regent's Park, 1859–97. (*Modern English biography.*)

Bateman, James (1812–97). Industrialist, banker, landowner, and horticulturalist. Built Biddulph Grange in north Staffordshire and established a well-known garden there. Cultivated tropical plants, especially orchids. Acquired orchids in Central and South America, and published important works on the Orchidaceae. President of the North Staffordshire Field Club, 1865–70. FRS 1838. (R. Desmond 1994, *DNB*, Hadfield *et al.* 1980.)

Bates, Henry Walter (1825–92). Entomologist. Undertook a joint expedition to the Amazon with Alfred Russel Wallace, 1848–50; continued to explore the area, after Wallace returned to England, until 1859. Provided the first comprehensive scientific explanation of the phenomenon subsequently known as Batesian mimicry. Published an account of his travels, *The naturalist on the River Amazons*, in 1863. Assistant secretary, Royal Geographical Society of London, 1864–92. President, Entomological Society of London, 1868, 1869, and 1878. FRS 1881. (*DNB*, *DSB.*)

18 December [1866], *19 December 1866*

Battersby, Charles Henry (1836–1909?). Irish physician. Practised medicine in Cannes and collected plants in the south of France. (R. Desmond 1994.)

Beale, Lionel Smith (1828–1906). Physician and microscopist. Professor of physiology and general and morbid anatomy, King's College, London, 1853–69; professor of pathological anatomy, 1869; professor of medicine, 1876–96. FRS 1857. (R. Desmond 1994, *DNB*.)
9 February 1866

Beatson, Alexander (1759–1833). Army officer and experimental agriculturalist. Governor of St Helena, 1808–13. (*DNB*.)

Becker, Lydia Ernestine (1827–90). Leading member of the women's suffrage movement, botanist, and astronomer. Published *Botany for novices* (1864); awarded a Horticultural Society Gold Medal, 1865. Founder and president of the Manchester Ladies' Literary Society, 1867. Secretary to the Manchester Women's Suffrage Committee from 1867, and later to the Manchester National Society for Women's Suffrage. Member of the Manchester School Board, 1870. Editor of and regular contributor to the *Women's Suffrage Journal* from 1870. Secretary to the London Central Committee for Women's Suffrage from 1880. (Blackburn 1902, R. Desmond 1994, *DNB*, *Macmillan dictionary of women's biography*.)
22 December 1866, *28 December [1866]*

Behrens, Miss.
7 December 1866

Bennett, Edward Turner (1797–1836). Surgeon and zoologist. Secretary, Zoological Society of London, 1833–6. (R. Desmond 1994, *DNB*.)

Bennett, George (1804–93). Physician and naturalist. Collected plants around the Pacific and in Australia. Travelled in Australia, 1832–4; settled in Sydney in 1836. (R. Desmond 1994.)

Bennett, John Joseph (1801–75). Botanist. Assistant keeper of the Banksian herbarium and library at the British Museum, 1827–58; keeper, 1858–70. Secretary of the Linnean Society of London, 1840–60. FRS 1841. (*DNB*.)

Bennett, William (1804–73). Tea-dealer and botanist. Member of the Society of Friends. Retired to Brockham Lodge, Betchworth, Surrey, in 1851. Father of Edward Trusted Bennett (1831–1908) and Alfred William Bennett (1833–1902). (R. Desmond 1994, *DNB* s.v. Bennett, Alfred William.)

Bentham, George (1800–84). Botanist. Donated his botanical library and collections to the Royal Botanic Gardens, Kew, in 1854, and was provided with facilities there for his research from 1861. President of the Linnean Society of London, 1861–74. Published *Genera plantarum* (1862–83) with Joseph Dalton Hooker. FRS 1862. (*DNB*, *DSB*.)
[July–September 1866], *25 September 1866*, 27 September [1866], 1 October 1866, *4 October [1866]*

Bentham, Sarah (d. 1881). Daughter of Harford Jones Brydges. Married George Bentham in 1833. (B. D. Jackson 1906).

Bentley, Robert (1821–93). Botanist. Lecturer in botany, London Hospital medical school, from *circa* 1850. Later, professor of botany, London Institution and King's College, London, and professor of botany and materia medica, Pharmaceutical Society. (R. Desmond 1994, *DNB*.)

Berkeley, Miles Joseph (1803–89). Clergyman and botanist. Perpetual curate of Apethorpe and Wood Newton, Northamptonshire, 1833–68. Vicar of Sibbertoft, Northamptonshire, from 1868. Editor of the *Journal of the Royal Horticultural Society*, 1866–77. An expert on British fungi; described fungi from CD's *Beagle* voyage. Royal Society Royal Medallist, 1863. FRS 1879. (*DNB*, *DSB*.)

Bessemer, Henry (1813–98). Engineer. Inventor of the Bessemer steel-manufacturing process of melting pig iron using air pressure or steam to abstract carbon. (*DNB*.)

Binney, Edward William (1812–81). Solicitor and palaeobotanist. A founder of the Manchester Geological Society, 1838; president, 1857–9, 1865–7. FRS 1856. (R. Desmond 1994, *DNB*.)

Birch, Samuel (1813–85). Egyptologist and archaeologist. Assistant keeper of the department of antiquities in the British Museum, 1844–61; keeper of the oriental, British, and medieval antiquities, 1861–85. Translator of classical Chinese texts. (*DNB*.)

Bismarck, Otto Eduard Leopold (Otto) von (1815–98). German politician. Prime minister of Prussia, 1862–73. Chancellor of Germany, 1871–90. (*EB*.)

Blyth, Edward (1810–73). Zoologist. Pharmacist in Tooting, London. Wrote and edited zoological works under the pseudonym Zoophilus. Curator of the museum of the Asiatic Society of Bengal, Calcutta, India, 1841–62. Provided CD with information on the plants and animals of India in correspondence between 1855 and 1858. Returned to Britain in 1863, and continued to write on zoology and on the question of the origin of species. (*Correspondence* vols. 5–7, *DNB*, *DSB*.)

10 December [1866], *13 [December] 1866*

Blyth, Sarah Clara (1815–91). Sister of Edward Blyth. Cared for Blyth in London, after his return from India in 1863. (Chris Brandon-Jones, personal communication; letters from Clara Blyth to Alfred Newton, 1 December 1865, 31 March 1866, and 18 June 1868 (Alfred Newton papers–CUL).)

Boissier, Pierre-Edmond (1810–85). Swiss botanist, natural historian, and traveller. (*Index biographique de l'Académie des Sciences*, *Taxonomic literature*.)

Bonham-Carter, Elinor Mary (1837–1923). Daughter of Joanna Maria Bonham-Carter, a family friend of the Darwins. The family lived at Keston, Kent, from 1853. Married Albert Venn Dicey (*DNB*) in 1872. (Bonham-Carter 1960, *Burke's landed gentry* 1965.)

Boole, Mary Everest (1832–1916). Writer and educator. Educated privately in France. In 1852, studied calculus with George Boole, whom she married in 1855. Matron, Queen's College, London, 1865–73. Secretary to the doctor and philosopher James Hinton from 1873. Popular writer on mathematics and philosophy. Originator of Boole's Sewing Cards, an aid in teaching geometry. Many of her works focused on the psychology of learning. (*BDWS*.)

13 December 1866, 14 December 1866, *17 December [1866]*

Bornet, Jean-Baptiste-Edouard (Edouard) (1828–1911). French botanist. Collaborated with Gustave Adolphe Thuret at Thuret's garden in Antibes. Worked

Bornet, Jean-Baptiste-Edouard, cont.
especially on algae and lichens. (*DBF.*)
1 December 1866

Bourcier, Jules (d. 1874). French ornithologist. (*Ibis* 3d ser. 14 (1874): 186.)

Bowerbank, James Scott (1797–1877). London distiller and geologist. Had a special interest in London Clay fossils; devoted his later career to the study of sponges. Founder of the Palaeontographical Society, 1847. FRS 1842. (*DNB*, *Record of the Royal Society of London*, Sarjeant 1980–96.)
[4 November 1866?]

Bowman, William (1816–92). Surgeon. Author of works on physiology. Assistant surgeon, King's College Hospital, London, 1840–56; elected professor of physiology and of general and morbid anatomy, King's College, London, 1848; assistant surgeon at the Royal London Ophthalmic Hospital, Moorfields, 1846–51; surgeon, 1851–76. Created baronet, 1884. FRS 1841. (*DNB*, *DSB.*)
26 September [1866], *5 October 1866*

Brace, Charles Loring (1826–90). American philanthropist and social reformer. After studying theology at Yale University and the Union Theological Seminary, New York City, toured Europe, 1850–1. One of the founders of the New York City Children's Aid Society, 1853; secretary, 1853–93. (*ANB.*)

Braun, Alexander Carl Heinrich (1805–77). German botanist. Professor of botany, Freiburg, 1846–50. Professor of botany and director of the botanic garden, University of Berlin, 1851–77. Brother-in-law of Louis Agassiz. Deeply influenced by *Naturphilosophie*; studied plant morphology. Established the doctrine of spiral phyllotaxy. (*DSB*, *NDB.*)

Brehm, Christian Ludwig (1787–1864). German clergyman and ornithologist. His bird collection formed the basis of the Rothschild museum in Tring, Hertfordshire. (*NDB.*)

Bridges, Thomas (1842–98). Missionary on Keppel Island, West Falklands, 1856–69; established a mission at Ushuaia in the Beagle Channel. Author of a Fuegian grammar and dictionary. (Bridges 1948.)

Brodie, Benjamin Collins (1817–80). Chemist. Awarded a doctorate at Giessen, Germany, in 1850 for his analysis of beeswax. Waynflete Professor of chemistry, Oxford, 1865–72. Devised an alternative approach to chemistry from that based on atomic theory, and developed a calculus of chemical operations. Created baronet, 1862. FRS 1849. (*Alum. Oxon.*, *DNB*, *DSB.*)

Brodie, Philothea Margaret. Daughter of John Vincent Thompson. Married Benjamin Collins Brodie in 1848. (*DNB* s.v. Benjamin Collins Brodie.)

Bronn, Heinrich Georg (1800–62). German palaeontologist. Professor of natural science at Heidelberg University, 1833. Translated and superintended the first German editions of *Origin* (1860) and *Orchids* (1862). (*DSB*, *NDB.*)

Brown, Robert (1773–1858). Scottish botanist. Naturalist to the expedition surveying the coast of Australia, 1801–5; published descriptions of the plants he collected. Librarian to the Linnean Society of London, 1806–22; to Sir Joseph Banks, 1810–20. Continued as curator of Banks's collections after his death in

1820 and negotiated their transfer to the British Museum in 1827. Keeper of the botanical collections, British Museum, 1827–58. FRS 1811. (*DNB*, *DSB*.)

Buckland, Francis Trevelyan (1826–80). Naturalist, popular science-writer and surgeon. Son of William Buckland. Trained and practised medicine at St George's hospital, London, 1848–53. Assistant surgeon in the Life Guards, 1854. Staff writer for the *Field*, 1856–65. In 1865, appointed scientific referee to the South Kensington Museum, where he established an exhibit on pisciculture. Launched a weekly journal, *Land and Water*, in 1866. Inspector of salmon fisheries from 1867. (Bompas 1885, *DNB*.)

29 September 1866, 2 October 1866, *4 October [1866]*

Bullock, Charles James (*fl.* 1850s–1880s). Naval officer. Mate in the Royal Navy, 1853; lieutenant, 1855; commander, 1863; captain, 1870; went off the active list in 1873; rear admiral, 1887. (*Navy list*, *The Times*, 8 January 1887, p. 7.)

Bunbury, Charles James Fox, 8th baronet (1809–86). Botanist. Collected plants in South America, 1833–4; in South Africa, 1838–9. Accompanied Charles Lyell to Madeira in 1853. Justice of the peace and deputy lieutenant for Suffolk; high sheriff, 1868. Succeeded to the baronetcy, 1860. FRS 1851. (*County families* 1875, R. Desmond 1994, Sarjeant 1980–96.)

3 February 1866 (Charles Lyell), *20 February 1866* (Charles Lyell)

Bunbury, Edward Herbert, 9th baronet (1811–95). Geographer. Brother of Charles James Fox Bunbury. BA Trinity College, Cambridge, 1833; MA 1836; classical examiner, 1842. MP for Bury St Edmunds, 1847–52. Wrote on the ancient geography of Greece and Rome. Succeeded to the baronetcy, 1886. (*Alum. Cantab.*, *Modern English biography*.)

Bunbury, Frances Joanna (1814–94). Daughter of Leonard Horner. Married Charles James Fox Bunbury in 1844. Published memorials of her husband (1890–3) and his life and letters (1894). (*Burke's peerage* 1863 and 1980, *CDEL*, *County families* 1875.)

Burchell, William John (1781–1863). Explorer and naturalist. Collected plants on St Helena and in South Africa and Brazil. (R. Desmond 1994, *DNB*.)

Burdett-Coutts, Angela Georgina (Baroness Burdett-Coutts) (1814–1906). Heiress and philanthropist. Daughter of Sir Francis Burdett (*DNB*). Assumed the additional surname of Coutts on inheriting a share in the London banking firm Coutts in 1849. Endowed two geological scholarships at Oxford University in 1861. Presented Karl Friedrich Schimper's herbarium of mosses to the Royal Botanic Gardens, Kew. Patroness of a wide range of charities. (*DNB*.)

Burn, Robert (1829–1904). Clergyman, scholar, and archaeologist. Published on the archaeology, literature, and art of ancient Rome. Fellow of Trinity College, Cambridge, 1854–1904; tutor, 1856–72; dean, 1861–3. Ordained priest, 1862. (*Alum. Cantab*, *DNB*.)

Burritt, Elihu (1810–79). American social reformer, writer, and linguist. Published *Christian Citizen*, 1846–51. Founded the League of Universal Brotherhood, a pacifist group, after his arrival in England in 1846; organised a series of peace conventions in Europe, 1848–51. Campaigned in England and America for low overseas

Burritt, Elihu, cont.
postage rates. Appointed US consular agent at Birmingham, 1865. Returned to America in 1869. (*ANB*.)

Busk, Ellen. Daughter of Jacob Hans Busk. Married her cousin, George Busk, in 1843. (*DSB* s.v. Busk, George.)

Busk, George (1807–86). Russian-born naval surgeon and naturalist. Served on the hospital ship at Greenwich, 1832–55. Retired from medical practice in 1855. Member of several scientific societies. President of the Microscopical Society, 1848–9; of the Anthropological Institute, 1873–4. Zoological secretary of the Linnean Society of London, 1857–68. Hunterian Professor of comparative anatomy, Royal College of Surgeons of England, 1856–9; council member, 1863; member of board of examiners, 1868; president, 1871. Specialised in palaeontology and in the study of Bryozoa. FRS 1850. (*DNB*, *DSB*, Plarr 1930.)

Butakoff, Aleksey Ivanovich (b. 1812 or 1816, d. 1869). Russian naval officer, navigator, and hydrographer. Explored and surveyed the Aral Sea, 1848–9; applied Mercator's projection and enabled publication of first map of the sea in 1850. (*GSE*, s.v. Butakov, Alexei Ivanovich, *Russkii biograficheskii slovar'*.)

Butler, Samuel (1774–1839). Educationalist and clergyman. Headmaster of Shrewsbury School, 1798–1836. Bishop of Lichfield and Coventry, 1836; of Lichfield, 1836–9. (*DNB*.)

Butterworth and Heath. Firm of wood-engravers with premises at 356 Strand, London. (*Post Office London directory* 1866.)

Button, Jemmy (d. 1861). A Fuegian of the Yahgan tribe. His birth name was Orundellico. Brought to England in 1830 by Robert FitzRoy; returned to Tierra del Fuego on the *Beagle* in 1833. (Hazlewood 2000.)

Button, Threeboys (b. *c.* 1846 d. 1867). Fuegian of the Yahgan tribe. Son of Jemmy Button. His birth name was Wammestriggins. Brought to England in 1865 by Waite Hockin Stirling; died shortly after returning to Tierra del Fuego. (Hazlewood 2000.)

Caldwell, William Hay (b. 1859). Zoologist and businessman. Demonstrator in comparative anatomy, Cambridge University, 1882. Fellow of Gonville and Caius College, Cambridge, 1883–9. First holder of the Balfour studentship. Confirmed the long-disputed fact that the platypus laid eggs. Went into business as a paper manufacturer. (*Alum. Cantab.*)

Campbell, Archibald (1805–74). Surgeon and administrator. Assistant surgeon, East India Company, 1827. Superintendent of the Darjeeling station, where he implemented social and economic improvements and developed profitable tea plantations, 1840–62; responsible for political relations between the British and the Sikkim government. Wrote many papers on Himalayan geography. Travelled with Joseph Dalton Hooker in Sikkim in 1849, and was imprisoned with Hooker by the Sikkim rajah. (E. Balfour 1885, R. Desmond 1994, J. D. Hooker 1854, L. Huxley ed. 1918, W. B. Jackson 1854.)

Campbell, George Douglas, 8th duke of Argyll (1823–1900). Scottish statesman and author of works on science, religion, and politics. A defender of the concept of design in nature. Chancellor of St Andrews University, 1851. President of the Royal Society of Edinburgh, 1861–4. Privy seal, 1853–5, 1859–60, 1860–6, and 1880–1; postmaster-general, 1855–8 and 1860; secretary of state for India, 1868–74. Succeeded to dukedom in 1847. FRS 1851. (*DNB*, *Proceedings of the Royal Society of London*.)

Campbell, Helen Maria (1842–1922). Eldest daughter of Archibald Campbell. Married James Henry Loch in 1869. (D. Campbell 1925, p. 36; Robin K. Campbell, Newark, Nottinghamshire, personal communication.)

Candolle, Alphonse de (1806–93). Swiss botanist, lawyer, and politician. Active in the administration of the city of Geneva until 1860. Responsible for the introduction of postage stamps to Switzerland. Professor of botany and director of the botanic gardens, Geneva, from 1835. Concentrated on his own research after 1850. Foreign member, Royal Society of London, 1869. (*DSB*, *Record of the Royal Society of London*.)
3 June 1866

Candolle, Anne Casimir Pyramus (Casimir) de (1836–1918). Swiss botanist. Son of Alphonse de Candolle; assistant and colleague of his father. Published monographs of several families of plants. Foreign member, Linnean Society of London, 1893. (*DBS*, *Proceedings of the Linnean Society of London* (1918–19): 51–2.)
1 August [1866]

Candolle, Augustin Pyramus de (1778–1841). Swiss botanist. Resident in Paris, 1796–1808; professor of botany, Ecole de Médecine and Faculté des Sciences, Montpellier, 1808–16; professor of natural history, Academy of Geneva, 1816–35. Foreign member, Royal Society of London, 1822. (*DSB*, *Record of the Royal Society of London*.)

Candolle, Jeanne-Victoire-Laure de. Daughter of Jean-Jacques Kunkler. Married Alphonse de Candolle in 1832. (*Historisches Lexikon der Schweiz* vol. 2.)

Carlyle, Thomas (1795–1881). Essayist and historian. (*DNB*.)

Carpenter, William Benjamin (1813–85). Physician and naturalist. Fullerian Professor of physiology at the Royal Institution of Great Britain, 1844–56; professor of forensic medicine, University College, London; physiology lecturer, London Hospital, 1845–56. Registrar of the University of London, 1856–79. Founding member of the Marine Biological Association. FRS 1844. (*DNB*, *DSB*.)

Carrière, Elie Abel (1818–96). French botanist and horticulturalist. Started work at the Muséum d'Histoire Naturelle at the age of 14 and rose to the rank of head perennial grower. Head of the botanic garden, Zaragossa, Spain, in the early 1860s; head of the nursery, Muséum d'Histoire Naturelle, from 1862; resigned in 1869. Editor of the *Revue Horticole* from 1862; editor-in-chief, 1869–96. Worked on peach trees, dimorphism, and hybridity. (Barnhart comp. 1965, *Revue Horticole* (1896): 389–97, Tort 1996.)

Carruthers, William (1830–1922). Botanist. Assistant, botany department, British Museum, 1859; keeper, 1871–95. Botanist, Royal Agricultural Society, 1871–1909. President, Linnean Society of London, 1886–90. FRS 1871. (R. Desmond 1994.)

Carter, Dunnett & Beale. Seedsmen with premises at 237, 238, and 261 High Holborn, London. Founded by James Carter (*circa* 1797–1885) under the name 'James Carter & Company'. (R. Desmond 1994, *Post Office London directory* 1866.)

Carus, Julius Victor (1823–1903). German comparative anatomist. Conservator of the Museum of Comparative Anatomy, Oxford University, 1849–51. Professor extraordinarius of comparative anatomy and director of the zoological museum, University of Leipzig, 1853. Translated the third German edition of *Origin* (1867) and, subsequently, twelve other works by CD. (*DSB*, *NDB*.)
7 November 1866, 10 November 1866, *15 November 1866*, 21 November 1866

Caspary, Johann Xaver Robert (Robert) (1818–87). German botanist. Director, Bonn herbarium, 1856. Professor of botany and director of the botanic gardens at the University of Königsberg from 1858. Specialised in aquatic plants. (*ADB*.)
21 February [1866], *25 February 1866*, 4 March 1866, *26 April 1866*, *7 May 1866*, *25 May 1866*, *[after 9 June 1866]*

Cattell, John. Florist, nurseryman, and seedsman in Westerham, Kent. (R. Desmond 1994, *Post Office directory of the six home counties* 1859–66.)

Chapman, John (1822–94). Physician, author, and publisher. Studied medicine in Paris and then at St George's Hospital, London, from 1844. Publisher and bookseller at 142 Strand until 1860. Editor and proprietor of the *Westminster Review*, 1851–94. MD, St Andrews, 1857; practised as a physician. Advocated the application of an ice-bag to the spine as a remedy particularly for seasickness and cholera. (*DNB*.)

Charles VII (1403–61). King of France, 1422–61. (*EB*.)

Chatfield, Caroline A. Duncombe (d. 1880). Mother-in-law of Charles Wentworth Dilke. Her daughter, Mary, married Dilke in 1840. (Gwynn and Tuckwell 1917.)

Clark, Henry James (1826–73). Zoologist. Student and assistant of Louis Agassiz. Assistant curator, Museum of Comparative Anatomy, Harvard, from 1859. Assistant professor of zoology, Lawrence Scientific School, Harvard, 1860–5. Professor of botany, zoology, and geology, Pennsylvania State University, 1866–9. Professor of natural history, University of Kentucky, 1869–72. Professor of veterinary science, University of Massachusetts, from 1872. (*ANB*.)

Clarke, Joshua (1805–1890). Botanist. Mayor of Saffron Waldon. Patron of the Saffron Waldon museum. Fellow of the Linnean Society of London, 1853. (*Journal of Botany* 28 (1890): 192.)

Clarke, Richard Trevor (1813–97). Army officer and horticulturalist. Major in the Northampton and Rutland Infantry Militia, 1862. Bred nearly thirty new varieties of begonias and many new strains of cotton. Awarded a gold medal by the Cotton Supply Association of Manchester. Member of the Royal Horticultural Society; served on the council and scientific committee for many years; awarded the society's Veitchian medal, 1894. (*Army list*; R. Desmond 1994; *Gardeners' Chronicle*, 17 April 1897, p. 263.)
6 November [1866]

Clarke, William Branwhite (1798–1878). Clergyman and geologist. Emigrated in

1839 to Australia, where he carried out extensive geological surveys. Discovered gold in New South Wales in 1841. Incumbent of Willoughby parish, Sydney, New South Wales, 1847–70. FRS 1876. (*DNB*, *DSB*.)

Claus, Carl Friedrich (1835–99). German zoologist. Studied medicine, mathematics, and zoology at Marburg and Giessen, 1854–7. Professor of zoology, Marburg, 1863; Göttingen, 1870. Professor of zoology and head of the institute of zoological and comparative anatomy at Vienna, 1873. Founder and first director of the zoological research station at Trieste, 1873. Did major research in environmental influences on variability, especially in Crustacea. A strong supporter of Darwin in both his writing and lecturing. His zoology textbook was a standard work in the last three decades of the nineteenth century. (*DBE*, *NDB*, *OBL*.)

Clayden, John. Farmer at Littlebury, Saffron Walden, Essex. Member of the Council of the Royal Agricultural Society of England. (*Journal of the Royal Agricultural Society of England* 2d ser. 2 (1866): ii.)

Clowes, William & Sons. Printers. William Clowes (1807–83), eldest son of William Clowes (1779–1847), joined his father's printing business in 1823 and the name of the firm was changed to William Clowes & Sons in 1846. Printed the offical catalogue of the Great Exhibition of 1851. Introduced improvements in type-music printing. Printers to John Murray. (*DNB*.)

Coddington, Henry (1798/9–1845). Mathematician. Tutor, Trinity College, Cambridge, 1822–33. Brought into general use the grooved-sphere lens that bears his name. FRS 1829. (*Alum. Cantab.*, *DNB*.)

Collingwood, Cuthbert (1826–1908). Naturalist and writer on religious topics. Lecturer on botany at the Royal Infirmary Medical School, Liverpool, 1858–66. Also lectured on biology at the Liverpool School of Science. Served as surgeon and naturalist on HMS *Rifleman* and HMS *Serpent* on voyages of exploration in the China seas, 1866–7; carried out research in marine zoology. On his return to Liverpool, became senior physician of the Northern Hospital and took a leading part in the intellectual life of the city. (R. Desmond 1994, *DNB*.)

15 February 1866, 16 February [1866], *20 February 1866*

Corbet, Eleanor. Daughter of the Reverend Croxton Johnson, rector of Wilmslow, Cheshire. Wife of Richard Corbet. (A. E. Corbet [1915–19], 2: 363.)

13 December 1866

Corbet, Richard. Acquaintance of CD's. Resided at Adderly Hall, Adderly near Market Drayton, Shropshire, afterwards at Headington Hill, Oxford. (*Post Office directory of Gloucestershire, with Bath, Bristol, Herefordshire, and Shropshire* 1863; *Post Office directory of Northamptonshire, Huntingdonshire, Bedfordshire, Buckinghamshire, Berkshire, and Oxfordshire* 1869.)

Corbet, Rowland William (1839–1919). Clergyman, author. BA, Trinity College, Cambridge, 1861; MA, 1864. Son of Richard Corbet. (*Alum. Cantab.*)

Couch, Jonathan (1789–1870). Zoologist and surgeon. Specialist in British fishes and Cetacea. (*Modern English biography*.)

Crawfurd, John (1783–1868). Scottish-born physician, diplomat, and orientalist.

Crawfurd, John, cont.

Joined the East India Company medical service in 1803. Held several civil and political posts in Java, India, Siam, Cochin China, Singapore, and Burma. Returned to England in 1827; promoted the study of Indo-China and campaigned on behalf of the Singapore trading community against the East India Company. Published papers on ethnological and other subjects in various journals. President of the Ethnological Society of London, 1861–7. FRS 1818. (*DNB*, *Record of the Royal Society of London*, *Transactions of the Ethnological Society of London* n.s. 6 (1867): 6–7, Turnbull 1989, pp. 25–30.)

Cresy, Edward (1824–70). Surveyor and civil engineer. Son of Edward Cresy (1792–1858), the architect and civil engineer who advised CD about the purchase and improvement of Down House. Worked as an architectural draftsman in his father's office as a young man. Assisted his father in preparing his *Cyclopædia of civil engineering* in 1845. Assistant surveyor under the commissioners of sewers, 1849; afterwards engineer. Principal assistant clerk at the Metropolitan Board of Works, 1859. Architect to the fire brigade, 1866. Founder member of the Geologists' Association, 1858; president, 1864–5; vice-president, 1865–70. (*Annual Report of the Geologists' Association* 1859–70; Census returns 1861 (Public Record Office RG9/422: 118a); *DNB* s.v. Cresy, Edward (1792–1858); *Engineer* 30 (1870): 409.)

Crewsden, William Dilwerth. Resided at Helm Lodge, Kendal, Westmorland. (*Post Office directory of Northumberland.*)

Crocker, Emma Harriet Agnes. *See* Robinson, Emma Harriet Agnes.

Croll, James (1821–90). Scottish physical geologist. Worked for the Geological Survey of Scotland, 1867–81. Worked on oceanic circulation patterns, the mechanics of glaciers, and causes of the glacial epoch. FRS 1876. (*DNB*, Sarjeant 1980–96.)

Crüger, Hermann (1818–64). German pharmacist and botanist. Apothecary in Trinidad in the West Indies from 1841; government botanist and director of the botanic garden, Trinidad, from 1857. Collected plants in Jamaica, Trinidad, and Venezuela. (R. Desmond 1994, S[chlechtenda]l 1864.)

Cunningham, Robert Oliver (1841–1918). Naturalist. MD Edinburgh. Collected plants in South America. Naturalist to HMS *Nassau* on an expedition to the Strait of Magellan and the west coast of Patagonia, 1866–9. Professor of natural history, Belfast, 1871–1902. (Cunningham 1871, R. Desmond 1994, Newman 1993.)

Currey, Frederick (1819–81). Mycologist. Called to the bar, 1844. Secretary, Linnean Society of London, 1860–80; vice-president and treasurer, 1880–1. One of the editors of the *Natural History Review.* FRS 1858. (*Alum. Cantab.*, *DNB.*)

5 July 1866

Cuvier, Jean Léopold Nicolas Frédéric (Georges) (1769–1832). French systematist, comparative anatomist, palaeontologist, and administrator. Professor of natural history, Collège de France, 1800–32; professor of comparative anatomy, Muséum d'Histoire Naturelle, 1802–32. Permanent secretary to the Académie des Sciences from 1803. Foreign member, Royal Society of London, 1806. (*DBF*, *DSB.*)

Dallas, William Sweetland (1824–90). Entomologist, author, and translator. Prepared lists of insects for the British Museum, 1847–58. Curator of the Yorkshire Philosophical Society's museum, 1858–68. Assistant secretary to the Geological Society of London, 1868–90. Translated Fritz Müller, *Für Darwin* (1869); prepared the index for *Variation* and the glossary for *Origin* 6th ed. Editor, *Annals and Magazine of Natural History*, 1868–90, *Popular Science Review*, 1877–80. (Freeman 1978, *Geological Magazine* n.s. decade 3, vol. 7 (1890): 333–6, *Modern English biography*, Sarjeant 1980–96.)

Dana, James Dwight (1813–95). American geologist and zoologist. Geologist and mineralogist with Charles Wilkes's expedition to the South Seas, 1838–42; wrote reports on the geology, zoophytes, and Crustacea. An associate editor of the *American Journal of Science and Arts* from 1846. Professor of natural history, Yale University, 1855–64; professor of geology and mineralogy, 1864–90. Foreign member, Royal Society of London, 1884. (*ANB*, *DSB*, *Record of the Royal Society of London*.)

Darwin, Caroline Sarah. *See* Wedgwood, Caroline Sarah.

Darwin, Elizabeth (Bessy) (1847–1926). CD's daughter. (*Darwin pedigree*, Freeman 1978.)

Darwin, Emily Catherine. *See* Langton, Emily Catherine.

Darwin, Emma (1808–96). Youngest daughter of Josiah Wedgwood II. Married CD, her cousin, in 1839. (*Emma Darwin* (1904) and (1915).)

Darwin, Erasmus (1731–1802). CD's grandfather. Physician, botanist, and poet. Advanced a theory of transmutation similar to that subsequently propounded by Jean Baptiste de Lamarck. FRS 1761. (*DNB*, *DSB*, King-Hele 1999.)

Darwin, Erasmus Alvey (1804–81). CD's brother. Attended Shrewsbury School, 1815–22. Matriculated at Christ's College, Cambridge, 1822; Edinburgh University, 1825–6. Qualified in medicine but never practised. Lived in London from 1829. (*Alum. Cantab.*, Freeman 1978.)

17 February [1866], 19 February [1866], [before 20 February 1866?], 10 April [1866], 4 October [1866], 7 October [1866], 11 October [1866]

Darwin, Francis (1848–1925). CD's son. Botanist. BA, Trinity College, Cambridge, 1870. Qualified as a physician but did not practise. Collaborated with CD on several botanical projects, 1875–82. Lecturer in botany, Cambridge University, 1884; reader, 1888–1904. Published *LL* and *ML*. President of the British Association for the Advancement of Science, 1908. Knighted, 1913. FRS 1882. (*DNB*, *DSB*.)

[after 12 October 1866]

Darwin, George Howard (1845–1912). CD's son. Mathematician. BA, Trinity College, Cambridge, 1868; fellow, 1868–78. Called to the bar in 1872 but did not practise. Plumian Professor of astronomy and experimental philosophy, Cambridge University, 1883–1912. President of the British Association for the Advancement of Science, 1905. Knighted, 1905. FRS 1879. (*DNB*, *DSB*.)

[1866]

Darwin, Henrietta Emma (1843–1927). CD's daughter. Married Richard Buckley Litchfield (*Alum. Cantab.*) in 1871. Assisted CD with some of his work. Edited *Emma*

Darwin, Henrietta Emma, cont.
Darwin (1904) and (1915). (*Burke's landed gentry* 1952, *Correspondence* vol. 11, Freeman 1978.)

[14–21 April 1866], *[c. 10 May 1866]*

Darwin, Horace (1851–1928). CD's son. Civil engineer. BA, Trinity College, Cambridge, 1874. Apprenticed to an engineering firm in Kent; returned to Cambridge in 1875 to design and make scientific instruments. Founder and director of the Cambridge Scientific Instrument Company. Mayor of Cambridge, 1896–7. Knighted, 1918. FRS 1903. (*Alum. Cantab.*, *DNB.*)

Darwin, Leonard (1850–1943). CD's son. Military engineer. Attended the Royal Military Academy, Woolwich. Commissioned in the Royal Engineers, 1870; major, 1889. Served on several scientific expeditions, including those for the observation of the transit of Venus in 1874 and 1882. Instructor in chemistry and photography, School of Military Engineering, Chatham, 1877–82. Intelligence service, War Office, 1885–90. Liberal Unionist MP, Lichfield division of Staffordshire, 1892–5. President, Royal Geographical Society of London, 1908–11; Eugenics Education Society, 1911–28. Chairman, Bedford College, London University, 1913–20. (Margaret Keynes 1943, Sarjeant 1980–96, *WWW.*)

Darwin, Marianne. *See* Parker, Marianne.

Darwin, Robert Waring (1766–1848). CD's father. Physician. Had a large practice in Shrewsbury and resided at The Mount. Son of Erasmus Darwin (*DNB*) and his first wife, Mary Howard. Married Susannah, daughter of Josiah Wedgwood I (*DNB*), in 1796. FRS 1788. (Freeman 1978.)

Darwin, Susan Elizabeth (1803–66). CD's sister. Lived at The Mount, Shrewsbury, the family home, until her death. (*Darwin pedigree*, Freeman 1978.)

Darwin, Susannah (1765–1817). CD's mother. Daughter of Josiah Wedgwood I. Married Robert Waring Darwin in 1796. (*Darwin pedigree.*)

Darwin, William Erasmus (1839–1914). CD's eldest son. Banker. BA, Christ's College, Cambridge, 1862. Partner in the Southampton and Hampshire Bank, Southampton, 1861. Chairman of the Southampton Water Company. Amateur photographer. (*Alum. Cantab.*, F. Darwin 1914.)

[7 May – 11 June 1866], *8 May [1866]*, *[18 June 1866]*, 19 [June 1866], *20 June [1866]*, *21 June [1866]*, 22 June [1866], *[23 June 1866]*, [24 June 1866], *29 June [1866]*, 30 [June 1866], 8 November [1866]

Davidson, Thomas William St Clair (1817–85). Artist and palaeontologist. Fellow of the Geological Society of London. Expert on fossil brachiopods. FRS 1857. (*DNB*, Sarjeant 1980–96.)

Dawes, Richard (1793–1867). Clergyman. Mathematical tutor and bursar of Downing College, Cambridge, 1818. Rector of King's Somborne, Hampshire, 1836–50; dean of Hereford, 1850; master of St Catherine's Hospital, Ledbury, 1861. Founded schools for the children of the poor and took an interest in Ledbury's national schools. (*DNB.*)

Dawson, John William (1820–99). Canadian geologist and educationalist. Investigated the geology of the maritime provinces with Charles Lyell in 1842 and

1852. Superintendent of education for common schools in Nova Scotia, 1850. Appointed principal and professor of geology at McGill University, 1855. Knighted, 1884. FRS 1862. (*DNB*, *DSB*.)

Dent, Emma (d. 1900). Née Brocklehurst. Married John Coucher Dent in 1847. With her husband, restored Sudeley Castle, Winchcombe, Gloucestershire. (*Burke's peerage*, *CDEL*.)

De Quincey, Thomas (1785–1859). Author. (*DNB*.)

Dick, William (1793–1866). Veterinary surgeon. Founded Edinburgh Veterinary College, 1818. Veterinary surgeon to the queen for Scotland. (*Modern English biography*.)

Dickens, Charles (1812–70). Novelist. (*DNB*.)

Dickson, John (d. 1872). Physician. Co-founder of the Dumfriesshire and Galloway Natural History and Antiquarian Society, 1862; secretary 1862–7. Medical superintendent, Government Lunatic Asylum, Port Louis, Mauritius, from 1868. (Gladstone 1913, James Williams, personal communication.)

Dieffenbach, Ernst (1811–55). German physician, naturalist, and geologist. Studied medicine at Giessen, 1828–33; received medical degree at Zurich, 1835. Surgeon and naturalist to the New Zealand Company, 1839–40. Professor extraordinarius of geology and director of the mineralogical collection at Giessen, 1851–5. Translated CD's *Journal of researches* into German (1844). (*DBE*, *DNZB*.)

Dilke, Charles Wentworth (1810–69). Magistrate and politician. Son of Charles Wentworth Dilke, 1789–1864 (*DNB*). Served on the executive committee of the Great Exhibition. MP for Wallingford, 1865–8. Magistrate for Westminster and Middlesex. Vice-president of the Royal Horticultural Society. Founder of the *Gardeners' Chronicle*. (*Athenæum*, 15 May 1869; *DNB*; *The Times*, 12 May 1869, p. 5.)

24 April 1866

Dobson, George (b. *c.* 1840 d. 1866). Engineer. Engineer and surveyer for the office of Public Works, Canterbury Province, New Zealand. Brother of Mary Dobson, who married Julius von Haast in 1863. (H. F. von Haast 1948.)

Dohrn, Felix Anton (Anton) (1840–1909). German zoologist. Studied medicine and zoology at various German universities. PhD, Breslau, 1865. Studied with Ernst Haeckel and became Haeckel's first assistant at Jena, where he habilitated in 1868. Founded the Zoological Station at Naples, built between 1872 and 1874. The station was the first marine laboratory, and served as a model for other similar institutions throughout the world. (*DBE*, *DSB*, Heuss 1991.)

Dorrell, Mr. Head of typesetting at William Clowes and Sons, printers to CD's publisher, John Murray. (Letter from ?, 10 May [1866]; letter to Mr Dorrell, 9 August 1870 (*Calendar* no. 7298).)

Doyne, William Thomas (1823–77). Irish-born engineer. Trained as a civil engineer on the London Southwestern Railway, 1840. Worked on a number of railways from 1843 to 1850. Served with the Army Work Corps in the Crimean War in 1851, then worked in India and Ceylon. Went to New Zealand in 1859; employed by the government from 1861 in connection with harbours and rivers,

Doyne, William Thomas, cont.
and served on the Commission on Railways. Established a private practice in Melbourne, Australia, in 1866. (Furkert 1953.)

Dubois, Henry Augustus (1808–84). Physician. Educated at Columbia University and College of Physicians and Surgeons, New York. President, Virginia Cannel Coal Company. Resided in New Haven, Connecticut, from 1854. LLD, Yale University, 1864. (*American medical biography.*)

Dulau & Co. Booksellers with premises at 37 Soho Square, London. Specialised in foreign-language books. (*Post Office London directory* 1866, *Publishers' Circular* 1866, p. 908.)

Duméril, Auguste-Henri-André (1812–70). French herpetologist and ichthyologist. Son of André Marie Constant Duméril, with whom he worked at the Jardin des Plantes, Paris, 1853–7. Professor, 1857–70. Bred axolotls in captivity. Author of works on reptiles, fish, and animal physiology. (*DBF*, *DSB.*)

Dunn, Robert (1839–1902). Clergyman. Attended Rugby School and Christ's College, Cambridge. Curate of Gatcombe, Isle of Wight, 1866–9. Friend of William Erasmus Darwin. (*Alum. Cantab.*, letter from W. E. Darwin to Emma Darwin, [December 1887] (DAR 210.5: 37).)

Edwards, Ernest (1837–1903). Photographer. Ran a photographic studio in London, specialising in portraits, 1864–9. Moved to Boston, and later New York, where he opened commercial firms in landscape photography and colour printing. (Johnson 1990, *Post Office London directory*, M. Pritchard 1994.)

Edwards, William Henry (1822–1909). Entomologist, lawyer, and businessman. Author of *A voyage up the river Amazon* (1847) and *The butterflies of North America* (1874–97). (*ANB.*)

Egerton, Philip de Malpas Grey-, 10th baronet (1806–81). Palaeontologist. Of Oulton Park, Cheshire. Tory MP for South Cheshire, 1835–68; for West Cheshire, 1868–81. Specialised in fossil fish. FRS 1831. (*DNB*, Sarjeant 1980–96.)

Ehrenberg, Christian Gottfried (1795–1876). German zoologist, comparative anatomist, and microscopist. Wrote extensively on infusoria and the development of coral reefs. Professor of medicine at Berlin University, 1839. Foreign member, Royal Society of London, 1837. (*DSB*, *NDB.*)
22 July [1866?]

Eliot, George. *See* Evans, Marian.

Endlicher, Stephan Ladislaus (1804–49). German botanist. (*NDB.*)

Engelmann, Wilhelm. German publishing firm. Founded in 1833, based in Leipzig. Publisher of *Zeitschrift für wissenschaftliche Zoologie* from 1848. (*NDB*, *Zeitschrift für wissenschaftliche Zoologie.*)

Evans, John (1823–1908). Paper manufacturer in Hemel Hempstead, Hertfordshire; archaeologist, geologist, and numismatist. In 1859, his study of chipped flints helped to establish the antiquity of humans in western Europe. Published an important paper on the fossil bird, *Archeopteryx*, in 1865. Developed a theory of evolution with regard to coins, 1849–50, and later applied natural selection to numismatics. Active member of many archaeological, scientific, and industrial societies. Vice-president of the Royal Society of London from 1876; treasurer, 1878–89. Honorary secretary of the Geological Society of London, 1866–74; president, 1874–6. Knighted, 1892. FRS 1864. (*DNB*.)

Evans, Marian (or Mary Anne) (1819–80). Novelist. Published under the name George Eliot. (*DNB* s.v. Cross, Mary Ann.)

Evans-Lombe, Elizabeth (1820–98). Sister of Joseph Dalton Hooker. Married Thomas Robert Evans-Lombe in 1853. (L. Huxley ed. 1918, Allan 1967.)

Eyre, Edward John (1815–1901). Colonial administrator. Emigrated to Australia in 1833. Lieutenant-governor of New Zealand, 1846–53. Governor of St Vincent 1854–60. Captain-general of Jamaica, 1861; governor, 1864–66. Suspended, 1866, then recalled for his role in the suppression of the uprising known as the 'Morant Bay rebellion'. Faced criminal and civil charges but was never convicted and received a government pension. (*DNB*.)

Farrar, Frederic William (1831–1903). Anglican clergyman and headmaster. Master at Harrow school, 1855–70. Canon of Westminster, 1876–95. Dean of Canterbury, 1895–1903. Promoted scientific education. Noted for his school stories, writings on language, and biographies of Christian figures. FRS 1866. (*DNB*.)

1 February [1866], 3 February [1866], *5 February 1866*

Fields, James Thomas (1817–81). American publisher, editor, writer, and lecturer. Partner in the firm Ticknor & Fields, 1854–70. Editor of *Atlantic Monthly*, 1861–70. Known as the literary partner of the firm, for his encouragement of many writers. After his retirement from publishing, he continued to write essays and toured as a lecturer. (*ANB*.)

Fitch, Asa (1809–79). American entomologist. Received his MD from the Vermont Academy of Medicine in 1829. Gave up medicine and took up entomology *circa* 1838. State entomologist for New York, 1854–73. Published extensively on practical entomology. (*ANB*.)

FitzRoy, Maria Isabella (d. 1889). Daughter of John Henry Smyth of Heath Hall, Wakefield, Yorkshire. Second wife of Robert FitzRoy, whom she married in 1854. (*Burke's peerage* 1999, s.v. Grafton, duke of, *County families* 1864, s.v. FitzRoy, Robert.)

FitzRoy, Robert (1805–65). Naval officer, hydrographer, and meteorologist. Commander of HMS *Beagle*, 1828–36. Tory MP for Durham, 1841–3. Governor of New Zealand, 1843–5. Superintendent of the dockyard at Woolwich, 1848–50. Chief of the meteorological department at the Board of Trade, 1854; chief of the Meteorological Office from 1855. Rear-admiral, 1857; vice-admiral, 1863. FRS 1851. (*DNB*, *DSB*.)

FitzRoy, Robert O'Brien (1839–96). Naval officer. Son of Robert FitzRoy. Entered the navy in 1853; captain, 1872. Served in the China war, 1857–8. (*Modern English biography*.)

Flower, William Henry (1831–99). Anatomist and zoologist. Curator of the Hunterian Museum, Royal College of Surgeons of England, 1861–84; Hunterian Professor of comparative anatomy, Royal College of Surgeons, 1870–84.

Flower, William Henry, cont.
Director of the Natural History Museum, London, 1884–98. President of the Zoological Society of London, 1879–99. President of the British Association for the Advancement of Science, 1889. Knighted, 1892. FRS 1864. (*DNB.*)

Forbes, David (1828–76). Geologist and philologist. Brother of Edward Forbes. Supervised mining and metallurgical works in Norway, *circa* 1847–57. Travelled in South America, 1857–60, in search of ores of nickel and cobalt for the firm of Evans & Askins, nickel-smelters of Birmingham. After more years of travelling, he settled in England and became foreign secretary to the Iron and Steel Institute. FRS 1856. (*DNB.*)

Forbes, Edward (1815–54). Zoologist, botanist, and palaeontologist. Naturalist on board HMS *Beacon*, 1841–2. Appointed professor of botany, King's College, London, and curator of the museum of the Geological Society of London, 1842. Palaeontologist with the Geological Survey of Great Britain, 1844–54. Professor of natural history, Edinburgh University, 1854. FRS 1845. (*DNB*, *DSB.*)

Fox, William Darwin (1805–80). Clergyman. CD's second cousin. A friend of CD's at Cambridge; shared his enthusiasm for entomology. Maintained an active interest in natural history throughout his life and provided CD with much information. Rector of Delamere, Cheshire, 1838–73. Spent the last years of his life at Sandown, Isle of Wight. (*Alum. Cantab.*, *Autobiography*, *Correspondence.*)
20 August [1866], 24 August [1866]

Frankland, Edward (1825–99). Chemist. Professor of chemistry, Putney College for Civil Engineering, 1850, and Owens College, Manchester, 1851–7. Lecturer in chemistry, St Bartholomew's Hospital, London, 1857–64. Professor of chemistry, Royal Institution, 1863–8, and Royal College of Chemistry, 1865. President of the Chemical Society, 1871–3; of the Institute of Chemistry, 1877–80. Knighted, 1897. FRS 1853. (*DNB*, *DSB.*)

Galton, Francis (1822–1911). Traveller, statistician, and scientific writer. CD's cousin. Explored in south-western Africa, 1850–2. Carried out various researches on heredity. Founder of the eugenics movement. FRS 1860. (*DNB*, *DSB.*)

Gardeners' Chronicle
[before 10 February 1866], [before 11 August 1866], [before 11 August 1866]

Gardiner, Allen Francis (1794–1851). Naval officer and missionary. Entered the navy in 1810; commander, 1826. Founded a missionary station at Port Natal, South Africa, 1834. Worked in Chile among the Araucana (Mapuchu) people, 1838–43. Attempted to establish a Patagonian mission in 1844, but returned to England in 1845. A second attempt to establish a mission ended in disaster, when he and his party died of starvation after being stranded on Picton Island in 1851. (*DNB*, *Modern English biography.*)

Gardiner, Allen Weare (1831/2–78). Clergyman and missionary. Son of Allen Francis Gardiner. BA, Oxford, 1855; MA 1857. Minister, Nailsworth, Gloucester, 1860–5. Chaplain of Lota, Chile, from 1869 to 1873 or 1874. Chaplain to the bishop of Bathurst, NSW, Australia, 1874–8. (*Alum. Oxon.*, *Clergy list*, *Crockford's clerical directory.*)

Gardner, George (1812–49). Botanist. Collected plants in Brazil, 1836–41. Superintendent of the botanic garden, Peradeniya, Ceylon, 1844. (R. Desmond 1994, *DNB*.)

Gärtner, Karl Friedrich von (1772–1850). German physician and botanist. Practised medicine in Calw, Germany, from 1796, but left medical practice in 1800 to pursue a career in botany. Travelled in England and Holland in 1802. Studied plant hybridisation from *circa* 1824. Elected a member of the Deutsche Akademie der Naturforscher Leopoldina, 1826. Ennobled, 1846. (*ADB*, *DBE*, *DSB*.)

Gaudry, Albert-Jean (Albert) (1827–1908). French palaeontologist. Assistant to his brother-in-law, Alcide d'Orbigny, professor of palaeontology at the Muséum d'Histoire Naturelle. Carried out excavations at Pikermi, Attica, in 1855 and 1860, and published *Animaux fossiles et géologie de l'Attique* (1862–7). Studied the fossils of small reptiles and batrachians, 1866–92. Taught a course in palaeontology at the Sorbonne, 1868–71; appointed professor of palaeontology at the Muséum, 1872. (*DBF*, *DSB*.)

17 September [1866]

Gegenbaur, Carl (or Karl) (1826–1903). German anatomist and zoologist. A supporter of CD; emphasised the importance of comparative anatomy in evolutionary reconstruction. Professor extraordinarius of zoology, Jena, 1855–8; professor of anatomy and zoology, 1858–62; of zoology, 1862–73. Professor of anatomy and comparative anatomy, Heidelberg, 1873–1901. Elected to the Deutsche Akademie der Naturforscher Leopoldina, 1857. (*DBE*, *DSB*, *NDB*.)

Geinitz, Hans Bruno (1814–1900). German geologist and paleontologist. Teacher at the Technische Bildungsanstalt in Dresden from 1837; professor of geology and mineralogy from 1850. Director of the Mineralogischen Museum in Dresden from 1857. (*DBE*.)

Geoffroy Saint-Hilaire, Etienne (1772–1844). French zoologist. Professor of zoology, Muséum d'Histoire Naturelle, 1793. Devoted much attention to embryology and teratology. (*DBF*, *DSB*.)

Gibson, George Stacey (1818–83). Botanist and banker. Regular contributor to the *Phytologist*, 1842–51. Author of *Flora of Essex* (1862). Mayor of Saffron Walden, 1877–8. Fellow of the Linnean Society of London. (*DNB*.)

7 July 1866

Gladstone, William Ewart (1809–98). Statesman and author. Chancellor of the Exchequer, 1852–5 and 1859–66. Prime minister, 1868–74. FRS 1881. (*DNB*.)

14 May 1866

Godman, Frederick DuCane (1834–1919). Ornithologist and entomologist. Educated at Eton, and Trinity College, Cambridge. Travelled in Central America and the Azores. Undertook, with Osbert Salvin, a comprehensive serial publication on the botany and zoology of Central America. FRS 1882. (*Ibis* 9th ser. 2 (1908): 81–92, *Record of the Royal Society of London*.)

Godron, Dominique Alexandre (1807–80). French botanist, zoologist, and ethnologist. In 1854, became head of the science faculty at Nancy, where he established a natural history museum and a botanic garden. (*DBF*.)

Godwin-Austen, Robert Alfred Cloyne (1808–84). Geologist. Noted for his work on the stratigraphy of southern England. Predicted the existence of coal-bearing strata in the south-east. Secretary of the Geological Society of London, 1843–4 and 1853–4. Assumed the additional name Godwin from 1854. FRS 1849. (*DNB*, *DSB*.)

Goethe, Johann Wolfgang von (1749–1832). German poet and naturalist. (*DSB*, *NDB*.)

Göppert, Heinrich Robert (1800–84). German botanist. Lecturer in medicine and botany at the University of Breslau, 1827–31; professor extraordinarius, 1831–9; ordinary professor from 1839. Studied plant physiology and fossil trees. One of the founders of German palaeobotany. (*BHGW*, *NDB*.)

Gould, John (1804–81). Ornithologist and artist. Taxidermist to the Zoological Society of London, 1826–81. Described the birds collected on the *Beagle* and *Sulphur* expeditions. FRS 1843. (*DNB*.)
10 May 1866

Graham, Robert (1786–1845). Physician and botanist. Regius professor of botany, Edinburgh University, 1820–45. Physician to the Edinburgh Infirmary. (*DNB*.)

Gray, Asa (1810–88). American botanist. Fisher Professor of natural history, Harvard University, 1842–88. Wrote numerous botanical textbooks and works on North American flora. President of the American Academy of Arts and Sciences, 1863–73; of the American Association for the Advancement of Science, 1872; a regent of the Smithsonian Institution, 1874–88. Foreign member, Royal Society of London, 1873. (*DAB*, *DSB*, *Record of the Royal Society of London*.)
16 April [1866], *7 May 1866*, *3 July 1866*, *18 July 1866*, 4 August [1866], *7 August 1866*, *27 August 1866*, 10 September [1866], *10 October 1866*, *6 November [1866]*

Gray, Charlotte Frances (1811–85). Younger sister of John Edward Gray. Married Samuel Birch in 1838. (Gunther 1975.)

Gray, George Robert (1808–72). Zoologist; an expert on insects and birds. Assistant in the zoological department of the British Museum, 1831–72. Brother of John Edward Gray. FRS 1865. (*DNB*, Gilbert 1977.)

Gray, Jane Loring (1821–1909). Daughter of Charles Greely Loring, Boston lawyer and politician, and Anna Pierce Brace. Married Asa Gray in 1848. Edited the *Letters of Asa Gray* (1893). (Barnhart comp. 1965; Dupree 1959, pp. 177–84.)

Gray, John Edward (1800–75). Botanist and zoologist. Assistant keeper of the zoological collections at the British Museum, 1824; keeper, 1840–74. President, Botanical Society of London, 1836–56. FRS 1832. (R. Desmond 1994, *DNB*.)
28 February 1866, *9 April 1866*, *13 April 1866*

Grece, Clair James (d. 1905/6?). Solicitor and philologist. Town clerk of Reigate and clerk to the Reigate Local Board. Member of the Philological Society, 1862–1905. Wrote works on various legal topics and translated a German study of English grammar. (*Post Office directory of the six home counties* 1866, *Transactions of the Philological Society*.)
12 November 1866

Greeff, Richard (1829–92). German zoologist. Professor of zoology and comparative anatomy, Marburg, 1871. His research focused on the structure and reproductive system of rhizopods. (*DBE*, *NDB*.)

Greg, William Rathbone (1809–81). Essayist. Pursued a career in business, 1828–50. Commissioner at the Board of Customs, 1856; comptroller of the Stationery Office, 1864–77. Regular contributor to the periodical press. (*DNB*.)

Grenier, Jean Charles Marie (Charles) (1808–75). French botanist. Professor of botany and zoology, Besançon, 1845. (*DBF*.)

Greville, Robert Kaye (1794–1866). Scottish botanist, entomologist, and social reformer. President, Botanical Society of Edinburgh, 1838 and 1866; honorary secretary, from *circa* 1861 until 1866. Edited the *Amethyst, or Christian's Annual*, 1832–4; secretary of the Sabbath Alliance; one of the compilers of the *Church of England hymn-book* (1838). Vice-president of the Anti-slavery Convention, 1840. Earned a living as a landscape painter in his later years. (*DNB*, *Medical directory* 1861–7, *Modern English biography*, *Transactions of the Botanical Society* [*of Edinburgh*] 1 (1844).)

Grierson, Thomas Boyle (1818–89). Physician and promoter of rural education. Founded museum at Thornhill, Dumfriesshire, *circa* 1852; co-founder of the Dumfriesshire and Galloway Natural History and Antiquarian Society; president 1886–8. (Gladstone 1913, Truckell 1966.)

Griffith, William (1810–45). Botanist. Travelled extensively in India, making natural history collections with the aim of compiling a flora of India. Superintendent of the Calcutta botanic garden and professor of botany at the Calcutta Medical College, 1842–4. Died of hepatitis in Malacca. (*DNB*, *DSB*.)

Groom-Napier, Charles Otley (1839 – before 1895). Writer. Wrote books and articles on natural historical topics from a Christian natural theological standpoint. Adopted the additional name Napier in 1865. Strong anti-Darwinian. (*Modern English biography*, Tort 1996.)

Grove, William Robert (1811–96). Lawyer, judge, and natural philosopher. Professor of experimental philosophy, London Institution, 1847. An active member of the Royal Society of London; treasurer and chairman of the executive committee of the Philosophical Club, 1847; Royal Medallist, 1847. Member of the Royal Commission on the Law of Patents, 1864. Appointed to the bench, Court of Common Pleas, 1871. FRS 1840. (*DNB*, *DSB*.)

26 April 1866, [26 April 1866], *31 August 1866*, *9 September 1866*

Günther, Albrecht Carl Ludwig Gotthilf (Albert Charles Lewis) (1830–1914). German-born zoologist. Commissioned to complete the British Museum's catalogues of amphibia, reptiles, and fish, 1857; officially joined the staff in 1862. Assistant keeper of the zoological department, 1872–5; keeper, 1875–95. Edited the *Record of Zoological Literature*, 1865–9. FRS 1867. (*DNB*, *NDB*.)

Gurney, John Henry (1819–90). Financier and ornithologist. MP, King's Lynn, Norfolk, 1854–65. (*Modern English biography*, Stenton 1976.)

Haast, John Francis Julius (Julius) von (1822–87). German-born explorer and geologist. Travelled to New Zealand in 1858 to report on the prospects for

Haast, John Francis Julius von, cont.
German emigration. Explored the western districts of Nelson province at the request of the provincial government in 1859. Appointed provincial geologist, 1861. Conducted the first geological survey of Canterbury province, 1861–8. Became a British national in 1861. Founded the Philosophical Institute of Canterbury in 1862, and the Canterbury Museum in 1863. Professor of geology, Canterbury College, 1876–87. Member of the senate of the University of New Zealand, 1879–87. Knighted, 1886. FRS 1867. (*DNB*, *DNZB*, *DSB*, H. F. von Haast 1948.)
5 May [1966], *17 July 1866*, *8 September 1866*

Haeckel, Anna (1835–64). Cousin of Ernst Haeckel, whom she married in 1862. (*DSB* s.v. Haeckel, Ernst; Uschmann 1984, p. 317.)

Haeckel, Ernst Philipp August (Ernst) (1834–1919). German zoologist. MD, Berlin, 1857. Lecturer in comparative anatomy, University of Jena, 1861–2; professor extraordinarius of zoology, 1862–5; professor of zoology and director of the Zoological Institute, 1865–1909. Specialist in marine invertebrates. Leading populariser of evolutionary theory. His *Generelle Morphologie der Organismen* (1866) linked morphology to the study of the phylogenetic evolution of organisms. (*DSB*, *NDB*.)
11 January 1866, 20 January [1866], *28 January 1866*, 1 February 1866, 18 August [1866], *19 October 1866*, [20 October 1866]

Hallier, Ernst (1831–1904). German botanist. PhD, Jena, 1858; professor extraordinarius, 1864. Worked on isolating micro-organisms responsible for disease. (*NDB*.)

Hamilton, Edward (d. *c.* 1903). Physician and ornithologist. MD, 1842. Based in London. (*List of the Linnean Society of London*, *Medical directory*, *Royal Society catalogue of scientific papers*.)

Hamilton, William Gerard (1729–96). Politician. Chancellor of the Exchequer in Ireland, 1763–84. Called 'single-speech Hamilton' because of his maiden speech in Parliament, which lasted nearly fifteen hours and was admired by Horace Walpole. (*DNB*.)

Hamilton, William John (1805–67). Geologist. MP for Newport, Isle of Wight, 1841–7. Secretary of the Geological Society of London, 1832–54; president, 1854 and 1865. (*DNB*, Sarjeant 1980–96.)

Hamond, Robert Nicholas (1809–83). Naval officer. Lieutenant, 1827. (*Burke's landed gentry* 1952, O'Byrne 1849.)

Hanbury, Daniel (1825–75). Pharmacist. Partner in the London firm Allen & Hanbury of Lombard Street, London. Member of a number of scientific societies in London, including the Royal Society, the Linnean Society, the Chemical Society, and the Microscopical Society. Member of the board of examiners of the Pharmaceutical Society, 1860–72. FRS 1867. (*DNB*.)
1 December 1866

Handel, George Frideric (Georg Friedrich) (1685–1759). German-born composer. Granted English naturalisation, 1727. (*DNB*, G. Grove 1980.)

Hanson, Alfred (1816–86). Barrister. Comptroller of legacy and succession duties at Somerset House, 1865–86. (*Modern English biography.*)
17 July 1866

Hardwicke, Robert (1823–75). Printer and publisher at 192 Piccadilly, London. One of the founders of the Quekett Microscopical Club, 1865. Published *Hardwicke's Science Gossip*, 1865–75. (*Modern English biography.*)

Harris, James. English trader at the Rio Negro, Patagonia, from whom Robert FitzRoy hired two boats for surveying parts of the coast too shallow for the *Beagle.* (*Journal of researches*, p. 79, *Narrative*, vol. 2.)

Hartung, Georg (1822?–91). German geologist. Investigated Madeiran geology with Charles Lyell, 1852–3. Author of numerous travel books. (Freeman 1978, *NUC.*)

Harvey, Elizabeth Lecky. Born Elizabeth Lecky Phelps. Married William Henry Harvey in 1861, having known him since childhood. (Ducker 1988.)

Harvey, William Henry (1811–66). Irish botanist. Colonial treasurer in Cape Town; collected plants in South Africa, 1836–42. Keeper of the herbarium, Trinity College, Dublin, from 1844; professor of botany, Royal Dublin Society, 1848–66; professor of botany, Trinity College, Dublin, 1856–66. Published works on South African plants, including *Flora Capensis* (1859–65) with Otto Wilhelm Sonder. Specialist in marine algae. FRS 1858. (R. Desmond 1994, *DNB*, *DSB.*)

Haughton, Samuel (1821–97). Irish clergyman, mathematician, geologist, and palaeontologist. Professor of geology, Dublin University, 1851–81. Became registrar of the medical school after graduating in medicine in 1862. Co-editor of the *Natural History Review*, 1854–60. President of the Royal Irish Academy, 1887. FRS 1858. (R. Desmond 1994, *DNB*, Sarjeant 1980–96.)

Hawkins, Benjamin Waterhouse (1807–89). Artist, sculptor, geologist, and popular natural history lecturer and author. Assistant superintendent of the Great Exhibition, 1851. Commissioned by the Crystal Palace Company to construct life-size replicas of extinct animals for the park in 1852. Illustrated *Fish* (part 4) and *Reptiles* (part 5) for the *Zoology of the voyage of HMS Beagle.* (Freeman 1978, *Men and women of the time* 1865.)

Hay, Arthur, Viscount Walden, 9th marquess of Tweeddale (1824–78). Ornithologist. Joined the Grenadier Guards in 1841, retiring as colonel in 1863 having served in campaigns in India and the Crimea. President of the Royal Zoological Society, 1868–78. FRS 1871. (*Burke's peerage*, *DNB.*)

Hector, James (1834–1907). Scottish geologist. Surgeon and geologist on the government expedition to the western parts of British North America, 1857–60. Geologist to the provincial government of Otago, New Zealand, 1861–5. Director of the Geological Survey of New Zealand, 1865. Director of the meteorological department of the New Zealand Institute, of the Colonial Museum, and of the botanical garden, Wellington, 1866–1903. Knighted, 1887. FRS 1866. (*DNZB.*)

Heer, Oswald (1809–83). Swiss biogeographer, palaeontologist, and botanist. An expert on Tertiary flora. Lecturer in botany, University of Zürich, 1834–5;

Heer, Oswald, cont.
director of the botanic garden, 1834; associate professor, 1835–52; professor of botany and entomology, 1852–83. (*DSB*, *NDB*.)

Hegel, Georg Wilhelm Friedrich (1770–1831). German philosopher. Professor of philosophy, University of Berlin, from 1818. (*EB*.)

Hennessy, Henry (1826–1901). Irish physicist and mathematician. Initially an engineer, became librarian at Queen's College, Cork, in 1849. Professor of physics at the Roman Catholic University, Dublin, 1855. Professor of applied mathematics, Royal College of Science, Dublin, 1874; dean, 1880 and 1888. Specialised in meteorology, climatology, and terrestrial physics. FRS 1858. (*DNB*.)

Henry, Joseph (1797–1878). American physicist and scientific administrator. Professor of mathematics and natural philosophy, Albany Academy, 1826. Professor of natural philosophy, College of New Jersey, 1832. Secretary of the Smithsonian Institution, 1846–78. President, National Academy of Sciences, 1868–78. (*ANB*.)

Henslow, Frances Harriet. *See* Hooker, Frances Harriet.

Henslow, George (1835–1925). Clergyman, teacher, and botanist. BA, Christ's College, Cambridge, 1858. Headmaster at Hampton Lucy Grammar School, Warwick, 1861–4; at the Grammar School, Store Street, London, 1865–72. Lecturer in botany at St Bartholomew's Hospital, 1866–80. Younger son of John Stevens Henslow. (*Alum. Cantab.*, *Crockford's clerical directory*, R. Desmond 1994.)
8 March 1866, *12 March 1866*, *17 March [1866]*, *[18–30 March 1866]*, *7 April 1866*, 16 April [1866], [before 19 April 1866], *[after 19 April 1866]*, *18 May 1866*, *11 June [1866]*, 12 June [1866], *[13 or 14 June 1866]*, 15 [June 1866], *19 June 1866*

Henslow, John Stevens (1796–1861). Clergyman, botanist, and mineralogist. CD's teacher and friend. Professor of mineralogy, Cambridge University, 1822–7; professor of botany, 1825–61. Extended and remodelled the Cambridge botanic garden. Curate of Little St Mary's Church, Cambridge, 1824–32; vicar of Cholsey-cum-Moulsford, Berkshire, 1832–7; rector of Hitcham, Suffolk, 1837–61. (*DNB*, *DSB*, *Historical register of the University of Cambridge*.)

Herbert, John Maurice (1808–82). Lawyer. BA, St John's College, Cambridge, 1830; fellow, 1832–40. Barrister, 1835. County court judge, South Wales, 1847–82. Friend of CD's. (*Alum. Cantab.*, *Correspondence* vol. 1, *Modern English biography*.)

Herbert, William (1778–1847). Naturalist, classical scholar, linguist, politician, and clergyman. Noted for his work on plant hybridisation. Rector of Spofforth, Yorkshire, 1814–40. Dean of Manchester, 1840–7. (*DNB*, *DSB*.)

Johann Christian Hermann'sche Verlagsbuchhandlung. German publishers and booksellers, based in Frankfurt, headed by Friedrich Emil Suchsland. (*Börsenblatt für den deutschen Buchhandel* 3 (1836): 830, 36 (1869): 434.)

Herschel, John Frederick William, 1st baronet (1792–1871). Astronomer, mathematician, chemist, and philosopher. Member of many learned societies. Carried out astronomical observations at the Cape of Good Hope, 1834–8. Master of the Royal Mint, 1850–5. Created baronet, 1838. FRS 1813. (*DNB*, *DSB*.)

Hewitt, Edward. Judge of poultry exhibitions. Resided in Sparkbrook, Birmingham. (Wingfield and Johnson 1856–7, p. 89.)

Hildebrand, Friedrich Hermann Gustav (Friedrich) (1835–1915). German botanist. After studying mineralogy, geology, and agriculture at Berlin, he took up botany, studying at Bonn, then from 1855 to 1858 at Berlin, where he received his doctorate. Habilitated at Bonn, becoming privatdozent there, in 1859. Professor of botany, Freiburg im Breisgau, 1868–1907. Worked mainly on hybridity, dimorphism, and generation. (Correns 1916, Junker 1989, Tort 1996.)
20 April [1866], *11 May 1866*, 16 May [1866], 22 July [1866], *24 July 1866*, *23 October 1866*

Hincks, Thomas (1818–99). Clergyman and zoologist. Unitarian minister in Leeds, 1855–69. Studied Polyzoa. FRS 1872. (*DNB*.)

Hitchcock, Edward (1793–1864). American geologist and clergyman. Professor of chemistry and natural history, Amherst College, 1825–45; president, 1844–54; professor of geology and natural theology, 1845–64. Served on the Massachusetts, New York, and Vermont geological surveys. (*DAB*, *DSB*.)

Hochstetter, Ferdinand von (1829–84). German geologist. Geologist for the Reichsanstalt in Vienna, 1854–6. Lecturer in geology, University of Vienna, 1856–7. Naturalist on the *Novara* expedition, 1857–9. Professor of geology and mineralogy at the Polytechnic Institute in Vienna, 1860–81. Undertook further travels, acting as geological adviser on the construction of the Turkish (1869) and trans-Siberian (1872) railways. Director of the Hofmuseum, Vienna, from 1876. (*BHGW*, *DBE*, *NDB*.)

Holland, Richard George (*fl.* 1857–70). Clergyman. BA, Kenyon College, Ohio, 1857; MA, 1860. Curate of Holy Trinity Church, Bromley Common, Kent. (*Crockford's clerical directory* 1870.)

Hooker, Brian Harvey Hodgson (1860–1932). Fifth child of Frances Harriet and Joseph Dalton Hooker. (Allan 1967 s.v. 'Hooker pedigree'.)

Hooker, Charles Paget (1855–1933). Physician and surgeon. Third child of Frances Harriet and Joseph Dalton Hooker. Trained at St Bartholomew's Hospital, London; made a licentiate of the Royal College of Physicians of London and the Royal College of Surgeons, Edinburgh, 1879, before being appointed to the staff of the Hertfordshire General Infirmary. Cottishall Cottage Hospital, Norfolk, 1880–5; Cirencester Cottage Hospital, Gloucestershire, 1885–1912. (Allan 1967, *Medical directory* 1881–1933, *Medical who's who* 1914.)

Hooker, Elizabeth. *See* Evans-Lombe, Elizabeth.

Hooker, Frances Harriet (1825–74). Daughter of John Stevens Henslow. Married Joseph Dalton Hooker in 1851. (Allan 1967, *DNB* s.v. Hooker, Joseph Dalton.)
1 November [1866]

Hooker, Harriet Anne (1854–1945). Second child of Frances Harriet and Joseph Dalton Hooker. (Allan 1967 s.v. 'Hooker pedigree'.)

Hooker, Joseph Dalton (1817–1911). Botanist. Worked chiefly on taxonomy and plant geography. Son of William Jackson Hooker. Friend and confidant of CD. Accompanied James Clark Ross on his Antarctic expedition, 1839–43, and

Hooker, Joseph Dalton, cont.
published the botanical results of the voyage. Appointed palaeobotanist to the Geological Survey of Great Britain, 1846. Travelled in the Himalayas, 1847–50. Assistant director, Royal Botanic Gardens, Kew, 1855–65; director, 1865–85. Knighted, 1877. FRS 1847. (*DNB*, *DSB*.)

15 [January 1866], *16 January 1866*, 21 [January 1866], *23 January 1866*, *4 February 1866*, *21 February 1866*, *[26 or 27 February 1866]*, [28 February 1866], *[19 March 1866]*, *[21 March 1866]* (Emma Darwin), 4 April [1866], [5 April 1866], *[6 April 1866]*, [9 April 1866], [16 April 1866], [22 April 1866], [28 April 1866], *[after 28 April 1866]*, [12 May 1866], *13 May 1866*, 16 May [1866], *[17 May 1866]*, *29 May 1866*, 31 May [1866], [31 May 1866], *[2 June 1866]*, [4 June 1866], 30 June [1866], *2 July 1866*, 21 [July 1866], *[24 July 1866]*, 30 July [1866], *31 July 1866*, 3 and 4 August [1866], *4 August 1866*, 5 August [1866], *[6 August 1866]*, *7 August 1866*, 8 August [1866], *9 August 1866*, 12 August [1866], *[17 August 1866]*, *18 August 1866*, *[28 August] 1866*, 30 August [1866], *[4 September 1866]*, *19 September 1866*, 25 September [1866], *28 September 1866*, 2 October [1866], [4 October 1866], *19 October 1866*, [21 October 1866], 1 November [1866], *3 November 1866*, 20 November [1866], *[22 November 1866]*, [23 November 1866], *[December 1866?]*, *4 December 1866*, 5 December [1866], 10 December [1866], *[12 December 1866]*, *14 December 1866*, 24 December [1866], *25 December 1866*, 28 [December 1866], *[29 December 1866]*

Hooker, Maria (1797–1872). Eldest daughter of Dawson Turner. Married William Jackson Hooker in 1815; acted as her husband's secretary. Mother of Joseph Dalton Hooker. (Allan 1967 s.v. 'Turner pedigree', R. Desmond 1994.)

Hooker, Maria Elizabeth (Minnie) (1857–63). Fourth child of Frances Harriet and Joseph Dalton Hooker. (Allan 1967 s.v. 'Hooker pedigree'.)

Hooker, Reginald Hawthorn (1867–1944). Sixth child of Joseph Dalton and Frances Harriet Hooker. Took B-ès-Sc. in Paris, and studied mathematics at Trinity College, Cambridge. Assistant to the director of the Intelligence Department of the Board of Agriculture, and subsequently head of the statistical branch. Secretary, Royal Statistical Society; president, Royal Meteorological Society. Married Olive Marion Rücker in 1911. (Allan 1967.)

Hooker, William Henslow (1853–1942). Eldest child of Frances Harriet and Joseph Dalton Hooker. Civil servant, India Office, 1877–1904. Encouraged imperial ties between metropolitan institutions (particularly the Royal Botanic Gardens, Kew) and British East Africa, *circa* 1896–1906. (Allan 1967; *India list* 1904–5; *Zanzibar Gazette*, 5 February 1896, p. 6, and 28 November 1900, p. 5.)

Hooker, William Jackson (1785–1865). Botanist. Father of Joseph Dalton Hooker. Regius professor of botany, Glasgow University, 1820. Appointed first director of the Royal Botanic Gardens, Kew, 1841. Knighted, 1836. FRS 1812. (*DNB*, *DSB*.)

Hope, James (1808–81). Naval officer. Entered the navy in 1822. Commander-in-chief in North America and the West Indies from 1863. Admiral, 1870. (*DNB*.)

Hopkins, William (1793–1866). Mathematician and geologist. Tutor in mathematics at Cambridge University. President of the Geological Society of London, 1851–3. Specialised in quantitative studies of geological and geophysical questions. FRS 1837. (*DNB*, *DSB*, *Record of the Royal Society of London*.)

Hornby, Geoffrey Thomas Phipps (1825–95). Naval officer. Entered the navy in 1837; commodore on the west coast of Africa, 1865–7; admiral, 1879; admiral of the fleet, 1888. (*DNB*.)

Horner, Anne Susan (1789–1862). Daughter of Gamaliel Lloyd of Yorkshire. Married Leonard Horner in 1806. (Freeman 1978.)

Horner, Ann Susan (Susan) (1815/16–1900). Author and translator. Daughter of Leonard Horner. Author of works on Italian history and other subjects. (*CDEL*, Freeman 1978, *Modern English biography*, *NUC*.)

Horner, Joanna B. (b. 1822?). Author and translator. Daughter of Leonard Horner. Author, with Susan Horner, of *Walks in Florence and its environs* (1873) and translator, with Leonora Pertz, of German works. (Freeman 1978, *NUC*.)

Horner, Katharine Murray. *See* Lyell, Katharine Murray.

Horner, Leonard (1785–1864). Scottish geologist and educationalist. Founded the Edinburgh School of Arts in 1821. Warden of University College, London, 1828–31. Inspector of factories, 1833–56. A promoter of science-based education at all social levels. President of the Geological Society of London, 1846 and 1860–2. Father-in-law of Charles Lyell. FRS 1813. (*DNB*, *DSB*.)

Horner, Leonora. *See* Pertz, Leonora.

Huber, François (1750–1830). Swiss entomologist. (*NBU*.)

Huber, Jean Pierre (1777–1840). Swiss entomologist. Son of François Huber and editor of his father's works. (*NBU*.)

Humboldt, Friedrich Wilhelm Heinrich Alexander (Alexander) von (1769–1859). Prussian naturalist, geographer, and traveller. Official in the Prussian mining service, 1792–6. Explored equatorial South America, Cuba, Mexico, and the United States, 1799–1804. Travelled in Siberia in 1829. Foreign member, Royal Society of London, 1815. (*DBE*, *DSB*, *NDB*.)

Humphry, George Murray (1820–96). Surgeon and anatomist. Admitted to the Royal College of Surgeons, 1841. Lecturer in human anatomy, Cambridge University, 1847; professor, 1866–83; professor of surgery from 1883. FRS 1859. Founder and co-editor of the *Journal of Anatomy and Physiology*, 1867. (*DNB*.)

Hunt, Robert (1807–87). Scientific writer. Professor of experimental physics at the School of Mines, Jermyn Street. Published the first English treatise on photography, 1841. Keeper of mining records, 1845–78. FRS 1854. (*DNB*.)

3 May [1866]

Hutton, Frederick Wollaston (1836–1905). Geologist and army officer. Served with the Royal Welsh Fusiliers in the Crimea and India, 1855–8. Captain, 1862. Left the army in 1865, and emigrated to New Zealand in 1866. Employed by Auckland provincial government to survey coal deposits. Assistant geologist to the geological survey of New Zealand, 1871–3. Provincial geologist of Otago, 1873–6. Professor of natural science, University of Otago, 1877–80. Professor of

Hutton, Frederick Wollaston, cont.
biology, Canterbury College, 1880–93. Curator of Canterbury Museum from 1893. FRS 1892. (*DNZB*, Stenhouse 1990, G. M. Thomson 1884–5.)

Huxley, Ethel Gladys (1866–1941). Daughter and youngest child of Henrietta Anne and Thomas Henry Huxley. Married artist–author John Collier in 1889. (R. W. Clark 1968, p. 110, A. Desmond 1994–7, 1: 348.)

Huxley, Henrietta Anne (1825–1915). Born Henrietta Anne Heathorn. Emigrated to Australia in 1843. Met Thomas Henry Huxley in Sydney, Australia, in 1847, and married him in 1855. (A. Desmond 1994–7, Freeman 1978.)

Huxley, Thomas Henry (1825–95). Zoologist. Assistant-surgeon on HMS *Rattlesnake*, 1846–50, during which time he investigated Hydrozoa and other marine invertebrates. Lecturer in natural history, Royal School of Mines, 1854; professor, 1857. Appointed naturalist to the Geological Survey of Great Britain, 1855. Hunterian Professor, Royal College of Surgeons of England, 1863–9. Fullerian Professor, Royal Institution of Great Britain, 1863–7. President of the Royal Society of London, 1883–5. FRS 1851. (R. W. Clark 1968, A. Desmond 1994–7, *DNB*, *DSB*, *Record of the Royal Society of London.*)
4 July [1866], *6 July 1866*, *11 November 1866*, 22 December [1866]

Innes, John Brodie (1817–94). Clergyman. Perpetual curate of Down, 1846–68; vicar, 1868–9. Left Down in 1862 after inheriting an entailed estate at Milton Brodie, near Forres, Scotland; changed his name to Brodie Innes in 1861 as required by the entail. Priest in charge of Milton Brodie Mission and general licentiate of the diocese of Moray, 1861. Chaplain to the Bishop of Moray, 1861–80 and 1886–94. (*Clergy list*, *County families* 1864, *Crockford's clerical directory*, Freeman 1978, J. R. Moore 1985.)

Jäger, Gustav (1832–1917). German physician and zoologist. Co-founder and director of the Vienna zoological garden, 1858–66. Professor of zoology and anthropology, Hohenheim Academy, from 1867; Stuttgart Polytechnic, from 1870. Taught physiology and histology at the Veterinary School, Stuttgart, from 1874. Co-editor of *Kosmos*, 1877–9. Returned to medical practice in 1884. (*DBE*, Freeman 1978, *NDB*, Weinreich 1993.)

James, Henry (1803–77). Military officer. Lieutenant, Royal Engineers, 1831; captain, 1846; colonel, 1857. Joined the staff of the Ordnance Survey in 1827. Local superintendent, Geological Survey of Ireland, 1843–6. Transferred to admiralty employment in 1846, but returned to the Ordnance Survey in 1850; director-general, 1854–75. Director of the topographical and statistical department of the War Office, 1857–70. (*DNB*.)

Jamieson, Thomas Francis (1829–1913). Scottish agriculturalist and geologist. Factor on the Ellon estate, Aberdeenshire, for many years; later took the farm of Mains, Waterton. Appointed Fordyce Lecturer on agricultural research, University of Aberdeen, 1862. Carried out notable researches on Scottish Quaternary geology and geomorphology. Became a fellow of the Geological Society of London in 1862. (*Geological Magazine* 50 (1913): 332–3, Sarjeant 1980–96.)
27 September 1866

Janet, Paul Alexandre René (Paul) (1823–99). French philosopher with an interest in entomology. Professor of logic, Lycée Louis le Grand, Paris, 1857–64. Professor of history of philosophy, Sorbonne, after 1864. Published *Le matérialisme contemporain en Allemagne: examen du système du docteur L. Büchner* (1864), in which he criticised CD's theory of natural selection. (*Dictionnaire universel des contemporains*; Tort 1996, p. 2382.)

Jardine, William, 7th baronet (1800–74). Naturalist. A founder of the *Annals and Magazine of Natural History*, 1841. Commissioner for the salmon fisheries of England and Wales, 1860. President, Dumfriesshire and Galloway Natural History and Antiquarian Society, 1862–74. FRS 1860. (*DNB*, Gladstone 1913, *Record of the Royal Society of London.*)

Jenner, William, 1st baronet (1815–98). Physician. Professor of pathological anatomy at University College, London, 1849; Holme Professor of clinical medicine, 1860. Assistant, then full, physician to University College Hospital, 1849–76; consulting physician, 1879. Physician extraordinary to Queen Victoria, 1861; physician-in-ordinary, 1862. Established, through clinical studies, definitive evidence that typhus and typhoid were different diseases. FRS 1864. (*DNB.*)

Jennings, Stephen. Baker and shopkeeper. Premises at Horley, Surrey. (*Post Office directory of the six home counties* 1866.)

Joan of Arc (b. *c.* 1412 d. 1431). National heroine of France. Led the French to victory over the English at Orléans, 1429. Captured by the English, 1430; burned as a heretic, 1431. (*EB.*)

Johnson, Andrew (1808–75). American politician. United States senator for Tennessee, 1857–63. Vice-president of the United States, 1864. Became president following the assassination of Abraham Lincoln, 1865. (*ANB.*)

Johnson, George William (1802–86). Barrister and writer on gardening. Barrister, Gray's Inn, 1836. Professor of moral and political economy at the Hindu College, Calcutta, 1839–42. Founded the *Cottage Gardener* (later *Journal of Horticulture*) in 1848. (R. Desmond 1994, *DNB.*)

Jones, Henry Bence (1814–73). Physician and chemist. Physician to St George's Hospital, 1846–62. Secretary of the Royal Institution from 1860. In his chemical studies, devoted himself especially to the application of chemistry to pathology and medicine. FRS 1846. (*DNB.*)

3 January [1866], *10 February [1866]*, 13 April [1866], [23 April 1866?]

Jordan, Claude Thomas Alexis (Alexis) (1814–97). French botanist. Conducted field research, 1836–46, to complete and correct existing French floras. Assembled an important private herbarium. After giving up his botanical expeditions, worked in his own experimental gardens, trying to demonstrate the stability of species. A strong opponent of transmutation theory. (*DSB*, Tort 1996.)

Jurine, Louis (1751–1819). Swiss zoologist. Professor of medicine, l'Académie de Genève, from 1802; professor of zoology from 1808. (Sigrist *et al.* 1999.)

Keats, John (1795–1821). Poet. (*DNB.*)

Kempson, Louisa Frances (1834–1903). Daughter of Henry Allen and Jessie Wedgwood. Married William John Kempson in 1864. (Freeman 1978.)

Kent Church Penitentiary Society
[before 21 February 1866]

Key, Thomas Hewitt (1799–1875). Latin scholar and grammarian. Professor of pure mathematics, University of Virginia, 1825–7. Professor of Latin, London University, 1828–42; professor of comparative grammar, 1842–75. Headmaster of University College school from 1833. President of the Philological Society of London. FRS 1860. (*DNB*.)

King-Noel, William, 1st Earl Lovelace (1805–93). Politician. Served abroad in various diplomatic posts; appointed lord lieutenant of Surrey, 1840. Created Earl Lovelace, 1838. FRS 1841. (*Modern English biography* s.v. Lovelace.)

Kingsley, Charles (1819–75). Author and clergyman. Lecturer on English literature, Queen's College, London, 1848–9. Professor of modern history, Cambridge University, 1860–9. Rector of Eversley, Hampshire, 1844–75. Chaplain to the queen, 1859–75. (*Alum. Cantab.*, *DNB*.)
12 July 1866

Kingsley, Frances Eliza (1814–91). Née Grenfell. Wife of Charles Kingsley. Acted as his amanuensis and edited his memoirs after his death. (*DNB* s.v. Kingsley, Charles; *The Times*, 14 December 1891, p. 7.)

Kippist, Richard (1812–82). Botanist. Librarian of the Linnean Society of London, 1842–80. Specialist in Australian plants. (R. Desmond 1994, *DNB*.)
31 March [1866]

Kirk, John (1832–1922). Colonial official, botanist, and physician. MD, Edinburgh University. Served as physician and naturalist to David Livingstone on his second expedition to the Zambezi, 1858–63; entered the consulate of Zanzibar in 1866, rising to the position of consul general, 1873. Knighted, 1881. FRS 1887. (*DNB*.)

Knight, Charles (1791–1873). Publisher and journalist. Wrote works of popular instruction; edited the *Plain Englishman* and other popular periodicals. Publisher to the Society for the Diffusion of Useful Knowledge, 1829–46. (*DNB*.)

Koenig, Johann Samuel (1712–57). German mathematician and physicist. Studied under Johann Bernoulli I and his son Daniel, but entered legal practice in Bern in 1737 after failing to obtain a professorship in mathematics. Wrote extensively on the shape of the earth, bee cells, and other geometrical subjects. Formulated several physical laws and a controversial critique of Pierre Louis Moreau de Maupertuis's principle of least action. (*DSB*.)

Kölreuter, Joseph Gottlieb (1733–1806). German botanist. Assistant keeper of the natural history collections, Imperial Academy of Sciences, St Petersburg, 1756–61. Professor of natural history and director of the gardens of the margrave of Baden, Karlsruhe, 1763–86. Carried out extensive hybridisation experiments on plants. (*ADB*, *DBE*, *DSB*, *NDB*, *Taxonomic literature*.)

Krlyer, Henrik Nikolaj (1799–1870). Danish zoologist. Specialised in fish. Collected in South America, 1840–1. (*DBL*.)

Lamarck, Jean Baptiste Pierre Antoine de Monet (Jean Baptiste) de (1744–1829). French naturalist. Held various botanical positions at the Jardin du Roi, 1788–93. Appointed professor of zoology, Muséum d'Histoire Naturelle,

1793. Believed in spontaneous generation and the progressive development of animal types; propounded a theory of transmutation. (*DSB.*)

Land and Water

[2 October 1866]

Langton, Charles (1801–86). Rector of Onibury, Shropshire, 1832–41. Left the Church of England in 1841. Resided at Maer, Staffordshire, 1841–7, and at Hartfield Grove, Hartfield, Sussex, 1847–63. Married Emma Darwin's sister, Charlotte Wedgwood, in 1832. After her death, married CD's sister, Emily Catherine Darwin, in 1863. (*Alum. Oxon.*, *Emma Darwin* (1915), Freeman 1978.)

Langton, Edmund (1841–75). Son of Charles and Charlotte Langton. BA, Trinity College, Cambridge, 1864. Admitted at Lincoln's Inn, 1864. (*Alum. Cantab.*, *Emma Darwin* (1915).)

Langton, Emily Catherine (Catherine) (1810–66). CD's sister. Married Charles Langton in 1863. (*Darwin pedigree.*)

[6 and 7? January 1866] (Emma and Charles Darwin)

Laxton, Thomas (1830?–93). Nurseryman. Raised new varieties of peas, beans, and strawberries. Conducted breeding experiments on *Pisum* for CD. (R. Desmond 1994.)

31 October [1866], 3 November [1866]

Leach, William Elford (1790–1836). Naturalist. Assistant keeper of the natural history department, British Museum, 1813–21. FRS 1816. (*DNB*, Gilbert 1977.)

Lecky, William Edward Hartpole (1838–1903). Historian and essayist. Elected to the Athenaeum Club, 1867. Wrote on Irish history and politics. Privy councillor, 1897. (*DNB.*)

Lecoq, Henri (1802–71). French naturalist and vulcanologist. Professor of natural history, University of Clermont-Ferrand, and director of the city's botanic garden, 1826–54. Taught at the Preparatory School of Medicine and Pharmacy, Clermont-Ferrand, from 1840; professor, science faculty, from 1854. Published widely on botany, agriculture, and meteorology. (*Grande encyclopédie*, Sarjeant 1980–96.)

Leonhard, Gustav von (1816–78). German geologist. Professor extraordinarius of mineralogy, Heidelberg University, 1853. Son of Karl Cäsar von Leonhard. (*ADB*, Sarjeant 1980–96.)

Leydig, Franz von (1821–1908). German zoologist. Lecturer in physiology, University of Würzburg, 1849–55; professor extraordinarius, 1855–7. Professor of zoology, Tübingen, 1857–75; of comparative anatomy, Bonn, 1875–87. Foreign member, Royal Society of London, 1901. (*DSB*, *NDB.*)

Lindley, John (1799–1865). Botanist and horticulturalist. Assistant in Joseph Banks's library and herbarium, 1818 or 1819. Garden assistant secretary, Horticultural Society of London, 1822–7; general assistant secretary, 1827–41; vice-secretary, 1841–58; honorary secretary, 1858–62. Lecturer on botany, Apothecaries' Company, 1836–53. Professor of botany, London University (later University College, London), 1829–60. Horticultural editor of the *Gardeners' Chronicle* from 1841. FRS 1828. (R. Desmond 1994, *DNB*, *DSB.*)

Linnean Society of London
7 December [1866]

Lipsius, Justus (Lips, Joest) (1547–1606). Flemish humanist, classicist, moral and political theorist, and historian. (*EB.*)

Llewelyn, John Dillwyn. Resident of Penllergare, Swansea, Wales. (*Pigot & Co.'s royal, national, and commercial directory* 1844.)

Local landowner
[1866?]

Lonsdale, William (1794–1871). Geologist. Served the Geological Society of London, 1829–42, first as curator and librarian, and after 1838 as assistant secretary and librarian. Suggested fossils were a reliable basis for estimating the age of geological strata. (*DNB*, *DSB.*)

Lords of the Admiralty
[2–4 July 1866]

Loudon, John Claudius (1783–1843). Landscape gardener and horticultural writer. Travelled in northern Europe, 1813–15; in France and Italy, 1819–20. Urban and rural landscape designer. A prolific author; founded and edited the *Gardener's Magazine*, 1826–43, and the *Magazine of Natural History*, 1828–36. (R. Desmond 1994, *DNB.*)

Lovegrove, Charles (b. 1827/8). Merchant in the City of London, and churchwarden of St Mary's, Down. (Census returns 1861 (Public Record Office RG9/462: 73), Freeman 1978.)
16 December [1866?]

Lovegrove, Henrietta (b. 1832/3). Wife of Charles Lovegrove. (Census returns 1861 (Public Record Office RG9/462: 73).)

Low, Sampson (1797–1886). Publisher. Senior partner in the publishing firm Sampson Low, Marston & Co., with offices in Ludgate Hill, London. Publisher of the *Publishers' Circular.* (*DNB*, *Modern English biography.*)

Lowe, Richard Thomas (1802–74). Clergyman and botanist. English chaplain in Madeira, 1832–54. Rector of Lea, Lincolnshire, 1854–74. Published a flora of Madeira (1857–72). (R. Desmond 1994, *DNB.*)

Lubbock, Ellen Frances (1834/5–79). Daughter of Peter Hordern, clergyman, of Chorlton-cum-Hardy, Lancashire. Married John Lubbock in 1856. (*Burke's peerage* 1970, Census returns 1861 (Public Record Office RG9/462: 75).)
[28 July? 1866] (H. E. Darwin), *[1 October 1866]*, [1 October 1866]

Lubbock, Harriet (1810–73). Neé Hotham. Married John William Lubbock in 1833. (Freeman 1978.)
[April? 1866]

Lubbock, John, 4th baronet and 1st Baron Avebury (1834–1913). Banker, politician, and naturalist. Son of John William Lubbock and a neighbour of CD's in Down. Studied entomology and anthropology. A partner in the family bank from 1849. Liberal MP for Maidstone, Kent, 1870 and 1874; for London University, 1880–1900. Succeeded to the baronetcy in 1865. Created Baron Avebury, 1900. FRS 1858. (*DNB*, *DSB*, Hutchinson 1914, *Record of the Royal Society of London.*)

1 July [1866], 2 August [1866], *4 August 1866*, *[21 October 1866]*, 15 November 1866

Ludwig, Camilla. German governess. Governess to the Darwin family, 1860–3. Translated German works for CD. Married Reginald Saint Pattrick, vicar of Sellinge, Kent (*Alum. Oxon.*), in 1874. (CD's Classed account books (Down House MS); letter from R. S. Pattrick, 19 October 1881 (*Calendar* no. 13416).)

Lyall, David (1817–95). Botanist. Assistant surgeon on HMS *Terror* in James Clark Ross's Antarctic voyage, 1839–43. Surgeon and naturalist on HMS *Acheron* in New Zealand; on HMS *Assistance* in the Arctic, 1852. On British Columbia Boundary Commission, 1858–61. Collected plants in the Antarctic, Australia, New Zealand, the United States, and Canada. Friend of Joseph Dalton Hooker. (R. Desmond 1994, *Proceedings of the Linnean Society of London* (1894–5): 33–5.)

Lyell, Charles, 1st baronet (1797–1875). Scottish geologist. Uniformitarian geologist whose *Principles of geology* (1830–3), *Elements of geology* (1838), and *Antiquity of man* (1863) appeared in many editions. Professor of geology, King's College, London, 1831. President of the Geological Society of London, 1835–6 and 1849–50; of the British Association for the Advancement of Science, 1864. Travelled widely and published accounts of his trips to the United States. CD's scientific mentor and friend. Knighted, 1848; created baronet, 1864. FRS 1826. (*DNB*, *DSB*.)

3 February 1866 (C. J. F. Bunbury), 7 February [1866], 15 February [1866], 20 February 1866 (C. J. F. Bunbury), 22 February [1866], *1 March 1866*, [3 March 1866], *5 March 1866*, 8 March [1866], *10 March 1866*, 8[–9] September [1866], 9 October [1866], 12 October [1866], 1 December [1866]

Lyell, Henry (1804–75). Army officer in India. Married Katharine Murray Horner in 1848. Brother of Charles Lyell. (*Burke's peerage* 1980.)

Lyell, Katharine Murray (1817–1915). Daughter of Leonard Horner. Married Henry Lyell, brother of Charles Lyell, in 1848. Collected plants in India. Edited *Life, letters and journals of Sir Charles Lyell* (1881), and memoirs of Charles James Fox Bunbury and Leonard Horner. (R. Desmond 1994, Freeman 1978.)

Lyell, Mary Elizabeth (1808–73). Eldest child of Leonard Horner. Married Charles Lyell in 1832. (Freeman 1978.)

[19? October 1866]

Macfarlane, Robert. Resident of Thornhill, Falkirk, Scotland. (*County directory of Scotland* 1868.)

Mackintosh, Robert James (1806–64). Emma Darwin's cousin. Barrister-at-law, Lincoln's Inn, 1833. (*Alum. Oxon.*, O'Leary 1989, Wedgwood and Wedgwood 1980.)

Maguire, Thomas Herbert (1821–95). Irish painter and lithographer. Specialised in lithographed portraits and produced a series of portraits of men of science known as the Ipswich Museum portraits, published in 1851 by George Ransome. Lithographer to the queen, 1854. Exhibited at the Royal Academy and the British Institution. (Bénézit 1976, *DIA*.)

Malthus, Thomas Robert (1766–1834). Clergyman and political economist. First professor of history and political economy at the East India Company College,

Malthus, Thomas Robert, cont.
Haileybury, 1805–34. Quantified the relationship between growth in population and food supplies in *An essay on the principle of population* (1798). FRS 1818. (*DNB*, *DSB*, *Record of the Royal Society of London*.)

Mamastugadagenges (b. 1852/3). Fuegian of the Yahgan tribe. Brought to England in 1865 by Waite Hockin Stirling. Later known as 'Jack'. On his return from England in 1867 he settled at the mission station at Ushuaia, Tierra del Fuego. (Hazlewood 2000.)

Mamiani della Rovere, Terenzio (1799–1888). Italian politician and philosopher. (*EI*.)

Manners, John James Robert (1818–1906). Politician. Entered Parliament, 1841. Became first commissioner of works, 1852; held the post again, 1858, 1866–8. Postmaster-general, 1874–80. Became seventh duke of Rutland in 1888. (*DNB*.)

Maraldi, Giacomo Filippo (1665–1729). Italian astronomer and mathematician. Also interested in entomology and horticulture. Settled in Paris in 1687 and started a catalogue of the fixed stars. (*NBU*.)

Marsh-Caldwell, Anne (1791–1873). Novelist. (*DNB*.)
27 November [1866], 1 December [1866]

Marsh-Caldwell, Rosamond Jane (1823–1911). Daughter of Anne Marsh-Caldwell. (*Burke's landed gentry* 1862; J. J. Heath-Caldwell, personal communication.)

Martius, Karl Friedrich Philipp von (1794–1868). German botanist and ethnologist. Assistant to the conservator of the Munich botanic garden, 1814. Accompanied the Austrian expedition to Brazil, 1817–20, returning with several thousand specimens for the botanic garden. Professor of botany, Munich, 1826; principal conservator of the botanic garden, institute, and collections, 1832. Secretary of the physiomathematical section, Royal Bavarian Academy, Munich, 1840. (*DSB*.)

Masters, Maxwell Tylden (1833–1907). Botanist, surgeon, and general medical practitioner. Sub-curator, Fielding Herbarium, University of Oxford, *circa* 1853–7. Lecturer on botany at St George's Hospital medical school, 1855–68. Editor of the *Gardeners' Chronicle*, 1865–1907. Active in the Royal Horticultural Society, succeeding Joseph Dalton Hooker as the chairman of the scientific committee; secretary of the International Horticultural Congress, 1866. FRS 1870. (Clokie 1964, pp. 106, 208; R. Desmond 1994; *DNB*; *Medical directory* 1857–1908.)
March 1866, *20 April 1866*

Maull & Polyblank. Photographic artists of Piccadilly and Gracechurch Street, London, 1856–65; moved to Fulham Road, 1865. A partnership between Henry Maull and George Henry Polyblank. (*Post Office London directory* 1856–65, M. Pritchard 1986.)

Maw, George (1832–1912). Tile manufacturer, geologist, botanist, and antiquarian. Partner with his younger brother Arthur in the encaustic tile company, Maw & Co., of Brosley, Shropshire. Established a well-known garden at his residence at Benthall Hall, Shropshire; an expert on crocuses. Wrote on the geology of western England and North Wales. Travelled to Morocco and Algeria with Joseph

Dalton Hooker in 1871 and independently in 1873, writing on the geology of these countries. (Benthall 1980; R. Desmond 1994; *Gardeners' Chronicle*, 12 February 1881, pp. 205–6, 208, 209; Sarjeant 1980–96.)
18 June 1866, 21 June [1866]

Maxwell, James Clerk (1831–79). Scottish physicist. Fellow, Trinity College, Cambridge, 1855. Professor of natural philosophy, King's College, London, 1860–5. Member of the newly formed electrical standards committee of the British Association for the Advancement of Science, 1862. Superintended the building of the Cavendish Laboratory at Cambridge; first professor of experimental physics, University of Cambridge, 1871. Wrote papers on colour vision, the kinetic theory of gases, electricity, and magnetism. FRS 1861. (*DNB*, *DSB*.)

Mayne, Richard (1796–68). Commissioner of police. BA, Trinity College, Dublin. Joint commissioner of the London metropolitan police, 1829–50; chief commissioner from 1850. Knighted, 1848. (*DNB*.)

Mayne, Richard Charles (1835–92). Naval officer and explorer. Entered the navy in 1847. Commanded the survey expedition to the Strait of Magellan, 1866–9. Retired as rear admiral in 1879. MP for Pembroke and Haverfordwest, 1886–92. Knighted, 1879. (*DNB*.)

Mendel, Johann Gregor (1822–84). Austrian monk and botanist. Laid the mathematical foundations of the science of genetics. Conducted plant breeding experiments in the monastery garden at Brno from 1856. Published 'Versuche über Pflanzenhybriden', 1866. The Mendelian laws of segregation and independent assortment derive from his work. (*DSB*, Orel 1996.)

Meyer, Jürgen Bona (1829–97). German philosopher. PhD, Berlin, 1854; Privatdozent, 1862. Professor of philosophy, Bonn, 1868; rector, 1887–8. (*ADB*.)

Miers, John (1789–1879). Botanist and engineer. Travelled and worked in South America, 1819–38. Author of many papers describing South American plants. FRS 1843. (R. Desmond 1994, *DNB*.)

Millais, John Everett (1829–96). Painter. An originator of the Pre-Raphaelite movement. Knighted, 1885. (*DNB*.)

Miller, William Hallowes (1801–80). Mineralogist and crystallographer. Professor of mineralogy, Cambridge University, 1832–80. FRS 1838. Foreign secretary, Royal Society of London, 1856–73; Royal Medallist, 1870. (*DNB*, *DSB*.)

Miquel, Friedrich Anton Wilhelm (1811–71). Dutch botanist. Described the flora of the Dutch East Indies. Director, Rotterdam botanic garden, 1835–46. Professor of botany, Amsterdam, 1846–59; Utrecht, 1859–71. (*DSB*.)

Mitchell, Donald (d. 1896). Journalist and editor. Reporter for the *Dumfries Courier* from 1855; editor and proprietor from 1871. Member of the Dumfriesshire and Galloway Natural History and Antiquarian Society. (*Dumfries Courier*, 4 October 1896; *Transactions and Journal of the Proceedings of the Dumfriesshire & Galloway Natural History and Antiquarian Society* (1862–3): 16.)

Mitchell, William Stephen (1840–92). Botanist and businessman. BA, Cambridge, 1866. Did some work on fossil leaves. Went into business as a wine merchant. (*Alum. Cantab.*, R. Desmond 1994.)

Mitten, Annie. *See* Wallace, Annie.

Mitten, William (1819–1906). Pharmaceutical chemist and bryologist. Authority on mosses and liverworts. Corresponded with William Jackson Hooker. Resided at Hurstpierpont, Sussex. Described the liverworts for Joseph Dalton Hooker's *Flora Novae Zelandiae* (1853–5) and *Flora Tasmaniae* (1860). (*Journal of Botany* 44 (1906): 329–32.)

Moggridge, John Traherne (1842–74). Entomologist and botanist. Wintered in Mentone, France, and studied the flora of the area. (R. Desmond 1994, *Gardeners' Chronicle* n.s. 2 (1874): 723, Gilbert 1977.)

15 February [1866], 10 May [1866], 21 May [1866], 25 May [1866], 14 June [1866], 5 and 6 July [1866], 3 August [1866], 9 November [1866], 13 November [1866]

Moggridge, Matthew (1803–82). Botanist. Father of John Traherne Moggridge. Accompanied him to Mentone, France, and helped him collect plants there. Fellow of the Linnean Society of London, 1877. (R. Desmond 1994, *Proceedings of the Linnean Society* 1882–3, 42–3.)

Moggridge, Matthew Weston (1838–91). Clergyman. Brother of John Traherne Moggridge. Curate of St John's Church, Leicester, 1864–6, and Long Ditton, Kingston-on-Thames, 1866–73. Author of works on charitable giving and social improvement. (*Crockford's clerical directory* 1878, H. T. Moggridge, personal communication.)

Montagu, George (1751–1815). Writer on natural history. His collections of birds and other animals were purchased by the British Museum after his death. (*DNB*.)

Moore, Daniel (1809–99). Clergyman and writer. Honorary chaplain in ordinary to the queen, 1866; chaplain in ordinary, 1871. Rural dean of Paddington from 1885. Published numerous sermons and other religious books. (*Modern English biography*.)

Müller, Albert (d. 1922). Swiss entomologist. Director of the zoological garden in Basel, 1874. Published chiefly on gall insects. (Barnhart comp. 1965, *Royal Society catalogue of scientific papers*, Sarasin ed. 1924.)

28 March 1866, 28 March [1866], *31 March 1866*

Müller, August (b. 1825). German settler in Brazil from 1852. Brother of Johann Friedrich Theodor (Fritz) Müller. (Möller ed. 1915–21, 3: 45 *et seq.*)

Müller, Hermann (1829–83). German botanist and entomologist. Brother of Johann Friedrich Theodor (Fritz) Müller. Schoolteacher in Schwerin, 1854–5. Studied blind cave insects in Krain, 1855. Teacher of natural sciences at the Realschule in Lippstadt, 1855–83; became director of the school. After settling in Lippstadt, studied the local flora, in particular the mosses. CD's *Orchids* directed Müller's attention to the pollination and fertilisation of flowers, on which he published several papers and books. (Gilbert 1977, *Science* 2 (1883): 487–8.)

Müller, Johannes Peter (1801–58). German comparative anatomist, physiologist, and zoologist. Became professor of anatomy and physiology at Berlin University in 1833. Foreign member, Royal Society, 1840. (*ADB*, *DSB*.)

Müller, Johann Friedrich Theodor (Fritz) (1822–97). German naturalist. Emigrated to the German colony in Blumenau, Brazil, in 1852. Taught science at the Lyceum in Destêrro (now Florianópolis), 1856–67. Appointed *Naturalista Viajante* of the National Museum, Rio de Janeiro, 1876–92. His anatomical studies on invertebrates and work on mimicry provided important support for CD's theories. (*ADB*, *DBE*, Möller ed. 1915–21, *NDB*.)

11 January 1866, *13 February 1866*, *6 March 1866*, [9 and] 15 April [1866], 23 May 1866, *2 August 1866*, 23 August [1866], 25 September [1866], *1 and 3 October 1866*, *[2 November 1866]*, *1 December 1866*, [before 10 December 1866], [late December 1866 and] 1 January 1867

Munro, Robertson (*fl.* 1868–1900). Scottish nurseryman and florist. Premises at 6 St Andrew Street (South), Edinburgh, and nurseries at Jock's Lodge and Abercorn. Published a paper on fertility in *Passiflora* (Munro 1868). Associate member of the Botanical Society of Edinburgh, 1870–1900. (*Post Office Edinburgh directory* 1870–1, 1890–1, *Transactions of the Botanical Society of Edinburgh* 21 (1900): 372.)

Munro, William (1818–80). English soldier and botanist. Specialised in grasses. Served in India, the Crimea, Canada, and Bermuda. (*DNB*.)

Murchison, Roderick Impey, 1st baronet (1792–1871). Geologist and army officer. Served in the British army, 1807–14. Noted for his work on the Silurian system. President of the Geological Society of London, 1831–3 and 1841–3; of the British Association for the Advancement of Science, 1846–7; of the Royal Geographical Society of London, 1843–4, 1851, 1857–8, 1862–70. Director-general of the Geological Survey of Great Britain, 1855. Knighted, 1846; created baronet, 1866. FRS 1826. (*DNB*, *DSB*, *Journal of the Royal Geographical Society*.)

Murray, Andrew (1812–78). Lawyer, entomologist, and botanist. Practised law in Edinburgh until 1860. Assistant secretary to the Royal Horticultural Society, 1860–5. An expert on insects harmful to crops. In entomology, specialised in the Coleoptera; in botany, in the Coniferae. (*Entomologist's Monthly Magazine* 14 (1878): 215–16, Gilbert 1977, *Proceedings of the Royal Horticultural Society* 5 (1865): 1.)

Murray, John (1808–92). Publisher, and author of guide-books. CD's publisher from 1845. (*DNB*, Freeman 1978.)

21 February [1866], 22 February [1866], *24 February [1866]*, *25 May [1866]*, 28 May [1866], *30 May [1866]*, 15 July [1866], *18 July [1866]*, *23 July [1866]*, 16 October [1866], *18 October [1866]*, 23 October [1866], *25 October [1866]*, 21 and 22 December [1866], *22 December [1866]*, *24 December [1866]*

Nägeli, Carl Wilhelm von (1817–91). Swiss botanist. Maintained a teleological view of evolution. Originally studied medicine, but transferred to botany under Alphonse de Candolle at Geneva. Worked for eighteen months with Matthais Jacob Schleiden at the University of Jena, then worked in Zurich, where he collaborated with Carl Cramer, 1845–52. Professor of botany, University of Freiburg, 1852; professor of botany, University of Munich, 1857. (*DSB* s.v. Naegeli, Carl Wilhelm von.)

12 June [1866]

Nasmyth, James (1808–90). Scottish engineer. Son of the artist Alexander Nasmyth. Designer of an industrial steam hammer, first produced in France in 1841 and commonly known as Nasmyth's hammer. Manufacturer and developer of steam engines and machine tools. Wrote on astronomy. (*DNB.*)

Naudin, Charles Victor (1815–99). French botanist. Joined the herbarium staff at the Muséum d'Histoire Naturelle and became professor of zoology at the Collège Chaptal, Paris, in 1846. Resigned his professorship almost immediately owing to a severe nervous disorder. Appointed aide-naturaliste at the Muséum d'Histoire Naturelle, 1854. Established a private experimental garden at Collioure in 1869, earning his living by selling seeds and specimens. First director of the state-run experimental garden at Antibes, 1878. Experimented widely on plants, particularly on acclimatisation and hybridity. Published a theory of transmutation based on hybridisation. (*DSB*, *Taxonomic literature.*)

Newton, Alfred (1829–1907). Zoologist and ornithologist. Travelled extensively throughout northern Europe and North America on ornithological expeditions, 1854–63. Professor of zoology and comparative anatomy, Cambridge University, 1866–1907. FRS 1870. (*DNB.*)
27 November 1866

Norman, George Warde (1793–1882). Writer on finance. Merchant in the Norway timber trade, 1810–30. A director of the Bank of England, 1821–72. A founder member of the Political Economy Club, 1821. Exchequer bill commissioner, 1831; public works loan commissioner, 1842–76. A director of the Sun Insurance Office, 1830–64. Succeeded to his father's estate at the Rookery, Bromley Common, Kent, in 1830. A family friend of the Darwins. (*Burke's landed gentry* 1965, *DNB*, Freeman 1978, *Post Office directory of the six home counties* 1859.)
20 September 1866

Norman, Herbert George Henry (b. 1838). Barrister. Son of Henry Norman of Oakley, Kent; nephew of George Warde Norman. BA, Christ Church, Oxford, 1859. Entered Lincoln's Inn, London, 1860. Called to the bar, 1863. (*Alum. Oxon.*, Filmer 1977, *Men-at-the-bar*, *Post Office directory of the six home counties* 1862.)
30 November 1866, [after 30 November 1866]

Norman, Philip (1842–1931). Writer, painter, and antiquarian. Son of George Warde Norman. Attended Eton, 1855–9. Studied art at the Slade school in the early 1870s and exhibited at the Royal Academy, 1877–1904. Fellow of the Society of Antiquaries, 1886; vice-president, 1913–17. Best known for his books on and drawings of old London. (*Eton school lists*, Kent 1939, Wood 1995.)

Oldenbourg, Rudolf (1811–1903). German publisher. Founder of the Munich-based firm R. Oldenbourg, 1858. Business manager of the Munich branch of J. G. Cotta'schen Buchhandlung, 1836–69. (Bosl ed. 1983, *NDB.*)
28 October 1866

Oliver, Daniel (1830–1916). Botanist. Assistant in the herbarium of the Royal Botanic Gardens, Kew, 1858; librarian, 1860–90; keeper, 1864–90. Professor of botany, University College, London, 1861–88. FRS 1863. (R. Desmond 1994,

List of the Linnean Society of London, 1859–91.)

[after 13 May 1866], 9 June 1866

Oliver, Francis Wall (1864–1951). Palaeobotanist and ecologist. Lecturer in botany, University College London, 1888; professor, 1890–1929. Professor of botany, Cairo University, 1929–35. Son of Daniel Oliver. FRS 1905. (R. Desmond 1994.)

Oliver, Hannah. Daughter of James Wall of The Hills, Sheffield. Married Daniel Oliver in 1861. (*The Friend: a Religious, Literary, and Miscellaneous Journal* n. s. 5 (1917): 28.)

Orundellico. *See* Button, Jemmy.

Osten Sacken, Carl Robert Romanovich von der (1828–1906). Russian entomologist and diplomat. Joined the Russian diplomatic corps in 1849. Russian consul-general in New York City, 1862–71. Most of his entomological work was on flies and mosquitoes; published major surveys of the Diptera of North America. Returned to Europe in 1877. (*ANB.*)

Owen, Richard (1804–92). Comparative anatomist. Assistant conservator of the Hunterian Museum, Royal College of Surgeons of England, 1827; Hunterian Professor of comparative anatomy and physiology, 1836–56. Superintendent of the natural history departments, British Museum, 1856–84; prime mover in establishing the Natural History Museum, South Kensington, in 1881. President of the British Association for the Advancement of Science, 1858. Described the *Beagle* fossil mammal specimens. Knighted, 1884. FRS 1834. (*DNB*, *DSB.*)

Packard, Alpheus Spring, Jr (1839–1905). American entomologist. Studied under Louis Agassiz. Qualified as a physician but practised for only a few months. In 1867, co-founder, with Edward Sylvester Morse, Alpheus Hyatt, and Frederic Ward Putnam, of the *American Naturalist*, which he edited for approximately twenty years. Professor of zoology and geology at Brown University, 1878–1905. (*ANB*, *DSB.*)

Packe, Charles William (1792–1867). Member of Parliament for South Leicestershire, 1836–67. (*Modern English biography.*)

Paget, James, 1st baronet (1814–99). Surgeon. Assistant surgeon at St Bartholomew's Hospital, London, 1847; surgeon, 1861–71. Arris and Gale Professor of anatomy and surgery at the Royal College of Surgeons of England, 1847–52. Lectured on physiology in the medical school, St Bartholomew's, 1859–61; on surgery, 1865–9. Appointed surgeon-extraordinary to Queen Victoria, 1858; serjeant-surgeon, 1877. Created baronet, 1871. FRS 1851. (*DNB.*)

Palgrave, Reginald Francis Douce (1829–1904). Lawyer and civil servant. Cousin of Joseph Dalton Hooker. Clerk to the House of Commons, 1886–1900. Accomplished amateur painter and sculptor. Knighted, 1892. (Allan 1967, *DNB.*)

Pallas, Pyotr Simon (1741–1811). German naturalist and geographer. Travelled widely in the Russian empire. Foreign member, Royal Society of London, 1764. (*ADB*, *DSB*, *Record of the Royal Society of London.*)

Panizzi, Anthony (1797–1879). Librarian. Italian exile in Britain. Assistant librarian of the British Museum, 1831; principal librarian, 1856–66. (*DNB.*)

Parker, Francis (Frank) (1829–71). Solicitor in Chester. Third son of Henry and Marianne Parker. CD's nephew. (*Darwin pedigree.*)

Parker, Henry (1827/8–92). Fine art specialist. Scholar, Oriel College, Oxford, 1846–51; fellow, 1851–85. Son of CD's sister, Marianne Parker. (*Alum. Oxon.*, *CDEL*, *Darwin pedigree.*)

Parker, Marianne (1798–1858). CD's eldest sister. Married Henry Parker in 1824. (*Darwin pedigree.*)

Parker, William Kitchen (1823–90). Comparative anatomist. Hunterian Professor of comparative anatomy, Royal College of Surgeons, from 1873. Known principally for his research on the skull. FRS 1865. (*DNB*, *Record of the Royal Society of London.*)

Parslow, Joseph (1811/12–98). CD's manservant at 12 Upper Gower Street, London, *circa* 1840–2, and butler at Down House until 1875. (Census returns 1861 (Public Record Office RG9/462: 74), Freeman 1978.)

Passerini, Giovanni (1816–93). Italian botanist. Professor of botany and director of the botanical garden at Parma, 1844–49 and 1853–93. (*Taxonomic literature.*)

Pasteur, Louis (1822–95). French chemist and microbiologist. Professor of chemistry, Strasbourg University, 1849–54. Professor of chemistry and dean of the science faculty, Lille University, 1854–7. Administrator and director of scientific studies, Ecole Normale, Paris, 1857–67; director of the laboratory of physiological chemistry, 1867–88. Professor of chemistry, the Sorbonne, Paris, 1867–74. Director of the Institut Pasteur, Paris, 1888–95. Renowned for his work on fermentation and for experiments providing evidence against the theory of spontaneous generation. Foreign member, Royal Society of London, 1869. (*Dictionnaire universel des contemporains*, *DSB*, *Record of the Royal Society of London.*)

Pedder, William Henry (1826–1900). Consular official. Entered consular service in China in 1848. Worked chiefly in Amoy; consul at Amoy from 1861. Retired in 1878 owing to impaired sight. Brother-in-law of Robert Swinhoe. (Coates 1988, *Foreign Office list* 1901.)

Pertz, Georg Heinrich (1795–1876). German historian. Historian of medieval Germany; published important source material in *Monumenta Germaniae historica.* Archives secretary, royal library, Hanover, 1823; principal keeper, 1827. Called to Berlin as chief librarian, 1842. Married Leonora Horner in 1853. (*ADB*, *EB.*)

Pertz, Leonora (b. 1818). Daughter of Leonard Horner. Translator, with her sister Joanna B. Horner, of German works. Married Georg Heinrich Pertz in 1853. (*ADB* s.v. Pertz, Georg Heinrich, *NUC.*)

Peschel, Oscar Ferdinand (1826–75). German geographer. Studied law and history at Heidelberg and Leipzig, 1845–8. Editor, *Augsburger Allgemeine Zeitung*, 1850. Chief editor at J. G. Cotta'schen Buchhandlung in Augsburg, 1854. Director of the weekly geographical newspaper *Das Ausland*, 1854. First chair of the geography department, University of Leipzig, 1871. Introduced Darwinian concepts of change and distribution as analytical tools in geography. (*NDB.*)

Pott, August Friedrich (1802–87). German linguist and philologist. A founder of Indo-European historical linguistics. Lecturer in linguistics, University of Berlin, 1830–3. Professor of linguistics at the University of Halle from 1833. (*DBE*, *EB*.)

Powys, Thomas Littleton, 4th Baron Lilford (1833–96). Ornithologist. Educated at Harrow, and Christ Church, Oxford. Founding member of the British Ornithologists' Union, 1858. (*DNB*.)

Pritchard, Charles (1808–93). Clergyman and astronomer. Headmaster of Clapham Grammar School, 1834–62, where he established an observatory. Hulsean Lecturer, Cambridge University, 1867. Savilian Professor of astronomy, Oxford University, 1870–93. President of the Royal Astronomical Society, 1866. FRS 1840. (*Alum. Cantab.*, *DNB*, *DSB*.)
8 October 1866, 12 October [1866]

Putnam, Frederic Ward (1839–1915). American archaeologist and anthropologist. Studied under Louis Agassiz. Curator of several museums in Massachusetts, and superintendent of the Museum of the Essex Institute, Salem, during the 1860s; director, Peabody Academy of Science, Salem, 1869–73, and Peabody Museum of Archaeology and Ethnology, Harvard, from 1874. Permanent secretary, American Association for the Advancement of Science, 1873–98; president from 1898. (*DAB*, *DSB*.)
29 January 1866

Quatrefages de Bréau, Jean Louis Armand de (Armand de Quatrefages) (1810–92). French zoologist and anthropologist. Doctorate in the physical sciences, University of Strasbourg, 1830; doctorate in medicine, 1832. Founded *Journal de médicine et de chirurgie de Toulouse*, 1836. Moved to Paris and took a doctorate in the natural sciences, 1840. Professor of natural history at the Lycée Henri IV, Paris, 1850; professor of anthropology, Muséum d'Histoire Naturelle, 1855. Foreign member, Royal Society of London, 1879. (*DSB*, *Record of the Royal Society of London*.)
10 November 1866

Ramsay, Andrew Crombie (1814–91). Geologist. Appointed to the Geological Survey of Great Britain, 1841; senior director for England and Wales, 1862; director-general, 1871–81. Professor of geology, University College, London, 1847–52; lecturer on geology at the Royal School of Mines, 1852–71. President of the Geological Society of London, 1862–4. Knighted, 1881. FRS 1862. (*DNB*, *DSB*.)
15 June [1866]

Ransome, Frederick (1818–93). Inventor of an artificial sandstone. The material was used for building in Britain and in the colonies. (*Modern English biography*.)
[6 February 1866], *7 February 1866*, *10 February 1866*

Rauwenhoff, Nicolas Willem Pieter (1826–1909). Dutch botanist. Lecturer at the medical college of Rotterdam and high school teacher, 1860–71; professor of botany and director of the Utrecht botanical garden, 1871–96. (*Taxonomic literature*.)

Réaumur, René Antoine Ferchault de (1683–1757). French mathematician, physicist, and natural historian. Invented the thermometer scale that bears his name. Foreign member, Royal Society of London, 1738. (*DSB*.)

Reed, George Varenne (1816–86). Clergyman. Curate of Hayes, Kent, 1837–9; of Tingewick, Buckinghamshire, 1839–54. Rector of Hayes, 1854–86. Tutor to George Howard, Francis, Leonard, and Horace Darwin. (*Alum. Cantab.*, Freeman 1978.)

Reed, John Williams (d. 1873). Naval officer. Second master in the Royal Navy, 1851; master, 1857; staff commander, 1868. (*Navy list.*)

Reeves, William (1815–92). Irish bishop and antiquary. Member of the Royal Irish Academy from 1846. Bishop of Down, Connor, and Dromore from 1886. Published on Irish ecclesiastical history. (*DNB*.)
10 April 1866

Reichenbach, Heinrich Gustav (1824–89). German botanist. Appointed professor extraordinarius of botany, Leipzig, in 1855. Director of the botanic gardens in Hamburg, 1863–89. Wrote extensively on orchids. (*ADB*.)

Renan, Joseph-Ernest (1823–92). French philologist. Assistant, department of manuscripts, Bibliothèque Nationale, 1851. Member of the Académie des Inscriptions et Belles Lettres, 1856. Professor of Hebrew and Chaldaic languages, Collège de France, 1862–4. Lost the professorship following publication of his highly controversial *Vie de Jésus* in 1863; reinstated, 1870. Member of the Académie Française, 1878. (*Dictionnaire universel des contemporains*, *EB*.)

Rennell, James (1742–1830). Geographer and oceanographer. Royal Navy, 1756–63; surveyor, East India Company, 1764–77. Published on the geography of Asia, North Africa, and the currents of the North Atlantic. Awarded the Copley Medal of the Royal Society of London, 1791. FRS 1781. (Baker 1963, *DSB*.)

Richards, George Henry (1820–96). Naval officer. Entered the navy in 1832. Hydrographer to the Royal Navy, 1863–74. Knighted, 1877. FRS 1866. (*DNB*.)

Richmond, George (1809–96). Portrait-painter. After two years travelling and painting in Italy, worked exclusively and successfully in England. Until about 1846, worked almost entirely in crayon and watercolour, then began to paint in oils. (*DNB*.)

Rivers, T. Francis (1831–99). Nurseryman. Son of Thomas Rivers. Known for his experimental work on prolonging the growing season of various fruit trees. (R. Desmond 1994, *Gardeners' Chronicle* 3d ser. 26 (1899): 179.)

Rivers, Thomas (1798–1877). Nurseryman. Succeeded to the family business in Sawbridgeworth, Hertfordshire, in 1827. Specialised in the cultivation of roses and fruit. Author of works on rose and fruit culture; contributed extensively to gardening journals. A founder of the British Pomological Society, 1854. (*DNB*.)
27 April [1866], *17 May 1866*, *20 May 1866*, *6 June 1866*, 8 June [1866], *8 October 1866*, 13 October [1866], *14 October 1866*

Robertson, William Tindal (1825–89). Physician. MD, Edinburgh, 1853. Physician to Nottingham General Hospital, 1854. Active as a speaker and organiser;

member of Nottingham Town Council. Local secretary, British Association for the Advancement of Science meeting at Nottingham, 1866. Became blind from glaucoma and retired to Brighton in 1874. Remained active in local politics, becoming an MP in 1886. Knighted, 1888. (*DNB*.)

Robinson, Charles Frederick. Naval officer. Husband of Eleanor Robinson, and father of Charles John Robinson. (*Biograph and Review* 6 (1881): 144–6.)

Robinson, Charles John (1833–98). Clergyman. Incumbent of Harewood, Herefordshire, 1864. Vicar, Norton Canon, Herefordshire, 1865–77; West Hackney, London, 1877–87; Horsham, 1887–94. Founder of Harleian Society, 1869. Professor of theology and principal, Queen's College, London, from 1894. Author of a register of scholars of the Merchant Taylors' school and works on the history of Herefordshire and West Sussex. (*Biograph and Review* 6 (1881): 144–6, *Guardian*, 9 November 1898, pp. 1727–8, *Modern English biography*.)
[1866?]

Robinson, Eleanor. Née Rocke. Wife of Charles Frederick Robinson, and mother of Charles John Robinson. (*Biograph and Review* 6 (1881): 144–6.)

Robinson, Emma Harriet Agnes. Née Crocker. Wife of Charles John Robinson. (*Biograph and Review* 6 (1881): 144–6.)

Robinson, William (1838–1935). Irish-born gardener and writer. Under-gardener at the Royal Botanic Society, Regent's Park, 1861–3; foreman of the herbaceous department, 1863–7. Travelled in France, 1867–8, and North America, 1870. Promoted the use of perennials. Founded the *Garden*, 1871, and *Gardening Illustrated*, 1879. (Allan 1982, R. Desmond 1994, *Gardeners' Chronicle* 3d ser. 97 (1935): 323–4.)
[29 April 1866], 5 May [1866]

Robson, John (d. 1886). Gardener at Linton Park, Kent, until 1876. Contributor to *Journal of Horticulture*. (R. Desmond 1994.)

Rocke, Eleanor. *See* Robinson, Eleanor.

Rolfe, Robert Monsey, 1st Baron Cranworth of Cranworth (1790–1868). Statesman and jurist. Whig MP for Penryn and Falmouth, 1832–9. Solicitor-general, 1834 and 1835–9. Created Baron Cranworth of Cranworth, 1850. Lord justice of appeal, 1851–2. Lord chancellor, 1852–8 and 1865–6. Holwood Park, his country residence, was a mile and a half north of Down House, the Darwins' residence. (*DNB*, *Dod's parliamentary companion*, Freeman 1978.)
8 December 1866

Rolle, Friedrich (1827–87). German geologist, palaeontologist, and natural history dealer. Assistant at the Kaiserlich-königliche Hofmineralien-Cabinett, Vienna, 1857–9; associate, 1859–62. Returned to Bad Homburg in 1862. Author of *Ch. Darwin's Lehre von der Entstehung der Arten und ihre Anwendung auf die Schöpfungsgeschichte* (1863). (*ADB*, *BLKO*, Martin and Uschmann 1969, Sarjeant 1980–96.)
28 January 1866, 1 February [1866], *12 April 1866*, 21 April 1866

Roots, George. Tenant of George Warde Norman. Resided at Bencewell, Bromley Common, Kent. (*Post Office directory of the six home counties* 1870.)

Ruprecht, Franz Josef (1814–70). German-born botanist and physician. Practised medicine in Prague. Curator of the botanical collections of the Academy of Sciences at St Petersburg, 1839; assistant director, St Petersburg botanical gardens, 1851–5; director, botanical museum of the academy, 1855; professor of botany at the Paedagogium, St Petersburg, 1855–9. (*ADB*, *Taxonomic literature*.)

Russell, Arthur (1825–92). Politician. Private secretary to John Russell, 1849–54. Liberal MP for Tavistock, 1857–85. Member of the Metaphysical Society. Fellow, Royal Geographical Society; Linnean Society. (A. W. Brown 1947, Stenton 1976.)

Russell, John, 1st Earl Russell (1792–1878). Statesman. Liberal prime minister, 1846–52 and 1865–6. Home secretary, 1835–9; secretary of state for foreign affairs, 1852–3; for the colonies, 1839 and 1855. Foreign secretary under Lord Palmerston, 1859–65. Created Earl Russell of Kingston Russell, 1861. In later life, occupied with literary work. President of the Royal Historical Society, 1872. FRS 1847. (*DNB*, *Record of the Royal Society of London*.)

Rütimeyer, Karl Ludwig (Ludwig) (1825–95). Swiss palaeozoologist and geographer. Professor of zoology and comparative anatomy, University of Basel, 1855; rector, 1865; professor in the medical and philosophical faculties, 1874–93. Made important contributions to the natural history and evolutionary palaeontology of ungulate mammals. (*DSB*.)

Salisbury, Richard Anthony (1761–1829). Botanist. In 1785, changed his name from Markham to Salisbury as the condition of a gift of £10,000. Secretary of the Horticultural Society of London, 1805–16. FRS 1787. (R. Desmond 1994, *DNB*.)

Salter, John William (1820–69). Geologist and palaeontologist. Apprenticed to James de Carle Sowerby in 1835. Assistant to Adam Sedgwick, 1842–6. Assistant to Edward Forbes on the Geological Survey of Great Britain, 1846; palaeontologist to the survey, for which his duties included the preparation of specimens for exhibition in the Museum of Practical Geology, 1854–63. (*DNB*.)
31 December 1866

Salter, Samuel James Augustus (1825–97). Surgeon. House surgeon and physician, King's College Hospital; dental surgeon, Guy's Hospital, London. FRS 1863. (*Modern English biography*.)

Salter, Sarah (Sally) (1819–92). Daughter of James de Carle Sowerby. Married John William Salter in 1846. (Secord 1985.)

Salvin, Osbert (1835–98). Ornithologist and entomologist. Undertook natural history explorations in North Africa, 1857, and Central America, 1857–60, 1861–3, 1873–4. Strickland Curator of ornithology, University of Cambridge, 1874–82. FRS 1873. (*DNB*.)

Samuelson, James (b. 1829). Writer on scientific and social issues. Called to the bar, 1870. Editor, *Popular Science Review* and *Quarterly Journal of Science*. (*Men-at-the-bar*.)
8 April 1866

Schacht, Hermann (1814–64). German botanist. Practised pharmacy until 1847.

Private lecturer, Berlin, 1853–60. Professor of botany and director of the botanical garden at Bonn, 1860–4. Specialised in plant anatomy and embryology. (*Taxonomic literature.*)

Schleicher, August (1821–68). German linguist and philologist. Professor of philology, University of Prague, 1853–6; University of Jena, 1857–68. (*ADB.*)

Schleiden, Matthias Jacob (1804–81). German botanist, author, and lecturer. Trained and practised as a lawyer but abandoned the profession in 1833 for medical and botanical studies at Göttingen and Berlin. Honorary professor of botany, University of Jena, 1846; professor, 1850–62. Professor of plant chemistry, University of Dorpat, 1863–4. Thereafter a private lecturer, residing in various German cities. (*ADB*, *DBE*, *DSB.*)

Schmidt, Eduard Oskar (Oskar) (1823–86). German zoologist. Professor extraordinarius of zoology, Jena, 1849; director of the zoological museum, 1851. Professor of zoology and comparative anatomy, Graz, 1857; director of the agricultural and zoological museum, 1863. Professor of zoology and zootomy, Strasbourg, 1872. His major research interest was the anatomy of sponges. His inaugural lecture supporting Darwinism, made in 1865 at the University of Graz, led to conflict with the Catholic Church in Austria and sparked a wider debate between Catholic and German nationalist circles at the university. (*ADB*, *OBL.*)

Schomburgk, Moritz Richard (1811–91). German-born botanist. Travelled to British Guiana in 1840. Director of the Adelaide Botanic Garden, South Australia, from 1865. (R. Desmond 1994.)

Schultze, Max Johann Sigismund (1825–74). German anatomist. MD, Greifswald, 1849; Privatdozent, 1850–4. Assistant professor of anatomy, Halle, 1854–9. Professor of anatomy and director of the anatomical institute, Bonn, 1859. Founder and editor of *Archiv für mikroskopische Anatomie*, 1865–74. Noted for his work in microscopy, the reform of cell theory, and descriptive and taxonomic studies of rhizopods and sponges. (*DSB*, *DBE.*)

Schweizerbart, Christian Friedrich (1805–79). German publisher. Director of E. Schweizerbart'sche Verlagsbuchhandlung of Stuttgart, 1841–67. Publisher of the German translations of *Origin* (1860, 1863, 1867) and *Orchids* (1862). (*Jubiläums-Katalog.*)

Per pro. E. Schweizerbart'she Verlagsbuchhandlung: *23 March 1866*, *10 May 1866*, *26 October 1866*

Schweizerbart, Wilhelm Emanuel (1785–1870). German publisher. Founded E. Schweizerbart'sche Verlagsbuchhandlung in Stuttgart in 1830. Publisher of many German scientific works. Retired in 1841. (*Jubiläums-Katalog.*)

E. Schweizerbart'sche Verlagsbuchhandlung. German publishing company in Stuttgart; founded by Wilhelm Emanuel Schweizerbart in 1830; conducted by his nephew Christian Friedrich Schweizbart from 1841. (*Jubiläums-Katalog.*)

23 March 1866, *10 May 1866*, *26 October 1866*

Sclater, Philip Lutley (1829–1913). Lawyer and ornithologist. One of the founders of *Ibis*, 1858; editor, 1858–65 and 1878–1912. Secretary of the Zoological Society

Sclater, Philip Lutley, cont.
of London, 1860–1903. FRS 1861. (*DSB*, Scherren 1905.)
6 January [1866], 24 December [1866]

Sclater-Booth, George (1826–94). Politician. Educated at Winchester, and Balliol College, Oxford. Conservative MP for North Hampshire, 1857–87. Held a variety of financial posts in the government, including financial secretary to the Treasury, 1868. Privy councillor. Created Lord Basing, 1887. FRS 1876. (*DNB*, *Record of the Royal Society of London*, Stenton 1976.)

Scott, John (1836–80). Scottish botanist. Gardener at Chatsworth House, Derbyshire, before becoming foreman of the propagating department at the Royal Botanic Garden, Edinburgh, in 1859. Through CD's patronage emigrated to India in 1864, and worked briefly on a *Cinchona* plantation before taking a position as curator of the Calcutta botanic garden in 1865. Carried out numerous botanical experiments and observations on CD's behalf. Fellow of the Linnean Society of London, 1873. (*Correspondence* vol. 13, letter from John Scott, 21 July 1865, R. Desmond 1994, Freeman 1978, *Transactions of the Botanical Society* [*of Edinburgh*] 14 (1883): 160–1.)

Scribner, Charles (1821–71). American publisher of books and magazines. The firm was continued by his sons. (*ANB*.)

Scudder, Samuel Hubbard (1837–1911). American entomologist. Graduated from the Lawrence Scientific School in 1862; assistant to Louis Agassiz, 1862–4. Librarian and custodian of collections, Boston Society of Natural History, 1864–70; vice-president, 1874–80; president, 1880–7. Palaeontologist, United States Geological Survey, 1886–92. (*ANB*.)

Sedgwick, Adam (1785–1873). Geologist and clergyman. Woodwardian Professor of geology, Cambridge University, 1818–73. Prebendary of Norwich Cathedral, 1834–73. President, Geological Society of London, 1829–31; British Association for the Advancement of Science, 1833. FRS 1821. (*DNB*, *DSB*, *Record of the Royal Society of London*.)

Seemann, Berthold Carl (1825–71). German-born traveller and botanist. Studied botany at the Royal Botanic Gardens, Kew, 1844–6. Naturalist to HMS *Herald*, 1847–51. Commissioned in 1860 to report on the Fiji Islands and published a botanical catalogue of the islands. Editor of *Bonplandia*, 1853–62; of the *Journal of Botany, British and Foreign*, 1863–71. Travelled in Venezuela in 1864; in Nicaragua, 1866–7. (R. Desmond 1994, *DNB*.)

Sesoienges (b. 1853/4). Fuegian of the Yahgan tribe. Brought to England in 1865 by Waite Hockin Stirling. Returned to his family in Tierra del Fuego in 1866–7. (Hazlewood 2000.)

Sethe, Anna. *See* Haeckel, Anna.

Seward, Anna (1747–1809). Poet. Active in Lichfield literary circles. Wrote a biography of CD's grandfather Erasmus Darwin (1804). (*DNB*.)

Seymour, Edward Adolphus Seymour, 12th duke of Somerset (1804–85). Statesman. Liberal MP for Okehampton, 1830; for Totnes, 1834–55. Lord of the

Treasury, 1835; secretary to the Board of Control, 1839; under-secretary, Home Department, 1841; commissioner of works, 1851–2; first lord of the Admiralty, 1859–66. (*DNB.*)

Shakespeare, William (1564–1616). Poet and dramatist. (*DNB.*)

Shaw, James (1826–96). Scottish writer and schoolmaster. Apprenticed as a pattern designer. Worked in the calico printing trade. Began training as a schoolmaster in 1855. After a succession of posts, became schoolmaster in Tynron, Dumfriesshire, 1862–96. Member of the Dumfriesshire and Galloway Natural History and Antiquarian Society. (R. Wallace ed. 1899.)

[6–10 February 1866], 11 February [1866], *14 February 1866*, *19 April 1866*, [23 April 1866], *7 November 1866*, 24 November [1866]

Shelley, Percy Bysshe (1792–1822). Poet. (*DNB.*)

Sibthorp, John (1758–96). Botanist. Professor of botany and director of the Botanical Garden, Oxford, 1784–96. Collected plant specimens in Greece. (*Taxonomic literature.*)

Simpson, Wilfred Huddleston (1828–1909). Geologist and ornithologist. Specialist in Jurassic gastropods. President, Geological Society of London, 1892–4. FRS 1884. (*DNB.*)

Smith, Frederick (1805–79). Entomologist in the zoology department of the British Museum from 1849. Specialised in the Hymenoptera. President of the Entomological Society of London, 1862–3. (*Entomologist* 12 (1879): 89–92, Gilbert 1977.)

March 1866

Smith, John (1798–1888). Scottish gardener and pteridologist. Gardener at the Royal Botanic Garden, Edinburgh, 1818; at the Royal Botanic Gardens, Kew, 1822. Curator of the Royal Botanic Gardens, Kew, 1842–64. (R. Desmond 1994, *Taxonomic literature.*)

Smith, John (1821–88). Scottish gardener. Gardener to the duke of Roxburgh; to the duke of Northumberland at Syon House, Middlesex, 1859–64. Curator, Royal Botanic Gardens, Kew, 1864–86. (R. Desmond 1994.)

Smith, Julia. Aunt of Elinor Mary Bonham-Carter. Lived with her sister, Joanna Maria Bonham-Carter, at Keston House, two miles north-west of Down, Kent, from 1862. (Bonham-Carter 1960, *Post Office directory of the six home counties* 1862.)

Snow, George (1820/1–85). Coal-dealer, Down, Kent. Operated a weekly carrier service between Down and London. (Census returns 1861 (Public Record Office RG9/462: 72); gravestone inscription, Down churchyard; *Post Office directory of the six home counties* 1862.)

Solander, Daniel Carl (1733–82). Swedish botanist. Assistant librarian, British Museum, 1763. Engaged by Joseph Banks to accompany him on Cook's voyage in the *Endeavour*, 1768–71, and to Iceland, 1772. Keeper of the natural history department, British Museum, 1773. FRS 1764. (*DNB*, *DSB.*)

Somerville, Mary (1780–1872). Writer on science and mathematics. Advocate of higher education for women and women's suffrage. (*BDWS*, *DNB*, *DSB.*)

30 October 1866, *13 December 1866*

Sowerby, George Brettingham Jr (1812–84). Conchologist and illustrator. Assisted his father, George Brettingham Sowerby, in a business selling natural history specimens; succeeded to the business in 1854. Illustrated numerous works on shells. Fellow of the Linnean Society of London, 1844. (*DNB*.)
19 October [1866]

Sowerby, James de Carle (1787–1871). Naturalist and scientific illustrator. An expert on fossil conchology. Founding member of the Royal Botanic Society and Gardens, Regent's Park, London, 1838; secretary, 1839–69. (R. Desmond 1994, *DNB*.)

Spencer, Herbert (1820–1903). Philosopher. Civil engineer on the railways, 1837–41 and 1844–6. Became sub-editor of the *Pilot*, a newspaper devoted to the suffrage movement, in 1844. Sub-editor of the *Economist*, 1848–53. From 1852, author of papers on evolution and numerous works on philosophy and the social sciences. (*DNB*, *DSB*.)
2 November 1866

Spottiswoode, William (1825–83). Mathematician and physicist. Succeeded his father as queen's printer in 1846. Throughout his life pursued mathematical studies in which he supplied new proofs of known theorems and also did important original work; produced a series of memoirs on the contact of curves and surfaces. President of the mathematical section of the British Association for the Advancement of Science, 1865; of the Royal Society of London, 1878–83. FRS 1853. (*DNB*.)

Sprengel, Christian Konrad (1750–1816). German botanist. Rector of the Great Lutheran Town School, Spandau, where he taught languages and natural science, 1780–94. Moved to Berlin, where he worked as a private tutor. Published his major work on the pollination of flowers in 1793. (*ADB*, *DSB*.)

Spruce, Richard (1817–93). Botanist and schoolteacher. Schoolteacher at Haxby and at the Collegiate School, York. Collected plant specimens in the Pyrenees, 1845–6; in South America, 1849–64. PhD, Berlin University, 1864. Retired in poor health to Coneysthorpe, Yorkshire, where he worked on his plant collections. (R. Desmond 1994, *DNB*.)

Steenstrup, Johannes Japetus Smith (Japetus) (1813–97). Danish zoologist. Professor of zoology and director of the Zoology Museum, University of Copenhagen, 1846–85. Foreign member, Royal Society of London, 1863. (*DBL*, *DSB*.)

Stephens, Thomas Sellwood (b. 1825). Clergyman. Curate at Wanstead, Essex, 1853–9; at Down, Kent, 1859–67. Rector of St Erme, Cornwall, 1867–1904. (*Alum. Oxon.*, *Crockford's clerical directory*.)

Stewart, Balfour (1828–87). Physicist and meteorologist. Assistant, Kew Observatory, 1856; director, 1859–71. Professor of natural philosophy, Owens College, Manchester, 1870–87. Worked on radiant heat and the phenomena of sunspots and terrestrial magnetism. (*DNB*, *DSB*.)

Stewart, Peter Benson (d. 1864). Naval officer. Mate on HMS *Beagle*, 1831–6. Lieutenant on HMS *Alligator*, serving off the coast of Australia and the East

Indies, 1837–41. His last period of sea duty was as commander in the Coast Guard, 1841–8. Captain, 1857. (*Correspondence* vol. 12, letter from B. J. Sulivan, 18 March [1864], *Narrative* 2: 19–20, *Navy list* 1837–64.)

Stirling, Louisa Jane (d. 1864). Wife of Waite Hockin Stirling, whom she married in 1853. (Macdonald 1929.)

Stirling, Waite Hockin (1829–1923). Clergyman and missionary. Secretary, Patagonian Mission Society, 1857–62. Superintendent missionary of Tierra del Fuego, 1862–9. Bishop of the Falkland Islands, 1869–1900. Assistant bishop of Bath and Wells, 1901–11; canon of Wells, 1901–20; precentor, 1903–20. (*Alum. Oxon.*, *Crockford's clerical directory* 1923, Hazlewood 2000, Macdonald 1929.)

Stokes, John Lort (1812–85). Naval officer. Midshipman on HMS *Beagle*, 1825–30; mate and assistant surveyor, 1831–6; lieutenant, 1837–41; commander, 1841–3. Captain on HMS *Acheron*, surveying off New Zealand, 1847–51; on half pay, 1851–60; employed surveying the Channel coasts, 1860–3; rear admiral, 1864; vice-admiral, 1871; admiral, 1877. (*DNB*, *Navy list* 1847–64, O'Byrne 1849.)

Suchsland, Friedrich Emil (1808–1903). German publisher and bookseller. Head of the publishing firm Johann Christian Hermann'sche Verlagsbuchhandlung, based in Frankfurt-am-Main, 1836–68. Published Friedrich Rolle's *Ch. Darwin's Lehre von der Entstehung der Arten* (1863) and sought to publish a German translation of *Origin* in 1866. (Letter from Rudolf Suchsland, 16 March 1866; *Börsenblatt für den deutschen Buchhandel* 3 (1836): 830, 36 (1869): 434; Martin and Uschmann 1969.)

Suchsland, Georg Rudolf Emil (Rudolf) (1839–1921). Son of the German publisher Friedrich Emil Suchsland. Emigrated to Britain and became a mining director in Swansea in 1854. (Family information.)

16 March 1866, *2 April 1866*, *16 April 1866*

Sulivan, Bartholomew James (1810–90). Naval officer and hydrographer. Lieutenant on HMS *Beagle*, 1831–6. Surveyed the Falkland Islands in HMS *Arrow*, 1838–9. Commander of HMS *Philomel*, 1842–6. Resided in the Falkland Islands, 1848–51. Commanded HMS *Lightning* in the Baltic, 1854–5. Naval officer in the marine department of the Board of Trade, 1856–65. Admiral, 1877. Knighted, 1869. (*DNB*.)

27 June 1866, *25 December 1866*, 31 December [1866]

Sulivan, Henry Norton (b. 1848/9). Son of Sophia and Bartholomew James Sulivan; edited his father's *Life and letters*. (Sulivan ed. 1896.)

Sulivan, James Young Falkland (1838/9–1901). Naval officer. Eldest son of Sophia and Bartholomew James Sulivan. Sub-lieutenant on HMS *Firefly* in the Mediterranean, 1864; lieutenant on HMS *Nassau*, surveying the Straits of Magellan, 1866–7; on HMS *Favorite* in North America and the West Indies, 1868–9; on HMS *Indus* at Devonport, 1870. Stationed in China, 1870–5; studied at the Royal Naval College, Greenwich, 1875–6; lieutenant and commander of HMS *Britomart* at Southampton, 1876–9; served in the Coast Guard, 1882–8. Commander, 1889. (*DNB* s.v. Sulivan, Bartholomew James, *Navy list* 1864–1901.)

Sulivan, Sophia (1809/10–90). Daughter of vice-admiral James Young, of Barton End, near Stroud, Gloucestershire. Married Bartholomew James Sulivan in 1837. (*County families* 1871, s.v. Sulivan, B. J.; *DNB*, s.v. Sulivan, B. J.; Sulivan ed. 1896, pp. xii, 395.)

Sulivan, Sophia Henrietta (b. 1837/8). Daughter of Sophia and Bartholomew James Sulivan. Married the surgeon Henry Bullock in 1882. (Census returns 1881 (Public Record Office RG11/1194: 136); Marriage register, Holy Trinity Church, Bournemouth (1882): 176.)

Sulivan, Thomas Edward (d. 1873). Naval officer. Second son of Sophia and Bartholomew James Sulivan. Sub-lieutenant on HMS *Gannet*, 1865–6, and lieutenant on HMS *Duncan*, stationed in North America and the West Indies, 1866–7; Transport Service, 1867–8; surveyed the Mediterranean in HMS *Newport*, 1868–70; lieutenant on HMS *Pert*, stationed off the Cape of Good Hope, 1870, and the south-east coast of America, 1871–3. (*Navy list* 1865–73, Sulivan ed. 1896.)

Swinhoe, Robert (1836–77). Diplomat and ornithologist. Attached to the British consulate in Hong Kong, 1854; in Amoy, China, 1855. British vice-consul, Taiwan, 1860–5; consul, 1865–73. Acting consul, Amoy, 1865–71; Ning-po, 1871–3. Consul, Ning-po, 1873–5. Collected plants and animals in Eastern Asia. FRS 1876. (*Foreign Office list* 1877, P. B. Hall 1987.)

28 March 1866, [September 1866]

Teebay, Richard (*fl.* 1850s–1880s). Farmer and poultry breeder. Resident at Fulwood, Lancashire. (*Post Office directory of Lancashire, Liverpool and Manchester*; *The Times*, 3 December 1856, p. 12, 13 November 1883, p. 3.)

Tegetmeier, William Bernhard (1816–1912). Editor, journalist, lecturer, and naturalist. Pigeon-fancier and expert on poultry. Pigeon and poultry editor of the *Field*, 1864–1907. Secretary of the Apiarian Society of London. (*Field*, 23 November 1912, p. 1070; E. W. Richardson 1916.)

16 January [1866], *22 January [1866]*, *[after 24 January 1866]*, *4 July 1866*, 9 July [1866], *2 August 1866*, 4 August [1866], *[after 4 August 1866]*, 10 August [1866], *12 September 1866*, 14 September [1866], *15 October 1866*, 16 October [1866], 4 December [1866], *10 December [1866]*, 12 December [1866], *15 December [1866]*, 18 [December 1866]

Tennent, James Emerson (1804–69). Traveller, politician, and author. Assumed the name Tennent on his marriage in 1832. MP for Belfast, 1832–45. Civil secretary to the colonial government of Ceylon, 1845–50. Appointed governor of St Helena in 1850, but never assumed office. FRS 1862. (*DNB*.)

Thayer, Nathaniel (1808–83). American financier and philanthropist. Partner in the Boston investment banking house John E. Thayer & Brother. Benefactor of Harvard College; sponsored the construction of a herbarium, 1863–5. Overseer, Harvard College, 1866; member of the board of fellows, 1868–75. (*DAB*; Dupree 1959, pp. 237–8.)

Thomson, Charles Wyville (1830–82). Naturalist and oceanographer. Professor of mineralogy and geology, Queen's College, Belfast, 1854–60; of natural science from 1860. Professor of botany, Royal College of Science, Dublin, 1868–70. Appointed regius professor of natural history, University of Edinburgh, 1870. Interested in deep-sea researches; appointed chief of the civilian scientific staff of the *Challenger* expedition, 1872–6. Knighted, 1877. FRS 1869. (*DNB*, *DSB*.)

Thomson, Thomas (1817–78). Naturalist. MD, Glasgow, 1839. Travelled to India as assistant surgeon to the East India Company. Curator of the Asiatic Society's museum, Calcutta, 1840. Accompanied Joseph Dalton Hooker to the Himalayas, 1849–51, and collaborated with him on various botanical publications. Superintendent of the Calcutta botanic garden and professor of botany at the Calcutta Medical College from 1854 until his return to England in 1860 or 1861. FRS 1855. (R. Desmond 1994, *DNB*.)

Thomson, William, Baron Kelvin (1824–1907). Scientist and inventor. Professor of natural philosophy, Glasgow, 1846–99. Formulated laws of equivalence and transformation in thermodynamics and a doctrine of available energy. Pioneered telegraphic systems and assisted in the laying of the first transatlantic cable. Wrote on the age and cooling of the earth. Proposed a hydroelectric scheme for Niagara. Created Baron Kelvin of Largs, 1892. FRS 1851. Awarded the Copley Medal, 1883. (*DNB*, *DSB*.)

Thuret, Gustave Adolphe (1817–75). Botanist. French lawyer and attaché in Constantinople, 1840. Gave up his diplomatic career to devote himself to botanical research. Published a number of papers on the seaweed genus *Fucus*. Resided in Cherbourg, 1852–6, and later at Cap d'Antibes on the Mediterranean in order to carry out research on living algae. (*DSB*.)

Thwaites, George Henry Kendrick (1811–82). Botanist and entomologist. Superintendent of the Peradeniya botanic gardens, Ceylon, 1849; director, 1857–80. FRS 1865. (R. Desmond 1994, *DNB*.)

Ticknor & Fields. Boston publishing house, founded in 1854 by William Davis Ticknor (*ANB*) and James Thomas Fields. Published the works of many leading British and American writers, as well as the journal *Atlantic Monthly* from 1861. (*ANB*.)

Todd, Robert Bentley (1809–60). Physician, physiologist, and medical editor. Professor of physiology at King's College, London, 1836–53. FRS 1838. (*DNB*.)

Tollet, Georgina. Daughter of George Tollet. A close friend of the Wedgwoods and Darwins. Edited the manuscript of *Origin*. (Freeman 1978.)

Travers, Henry Hammersley (1844–1928). Plant collector. Studied New Zealand flora with his father, William Thomas Locke Travers. Collected plants in the Chatham Islands for Ferdinand von Mueller, 1864, and for the Botanic Garden, Wellington, 1870–1. (R. Desmond 1994.)

Treviranus, Ludolph Christian (1779–1864). German botanist. Professor of botany, University of Breslau, 1816–30; University of Bonn, 1830–64. (*ADB*, *DSB*.)

Trimen, Roland (1840–1916). Zoologist and entomologist. Emigrated to South Africa in 1858. Arranged the Lepidoptera at the South African Museum. Held

Trimen, Roland, cont.
civil-service positions in the Commission of Land and Public Works, the governor's office, and the colonial secretary's office. Became part-time curator of the South African Museum in 1873; full-time curator, 1876. FRS 1883. (*DSAB.*)

Tristram, Henry Baker (1822–1906). Clergyman and ornithologist. Secretary to the governor of Bermuda, 1847–9. Rector of Castle Eden, Durham, 1849–60. Canon residentiary of Durham, 1874. Formed extensive ornithological collections from travels in Algeria, Palestine, Egypt, and Japan. FRS 1868. (*DNB.*)

Turner, William (1832–1916). Anatomist and administrator. Senior demonstrator to Sir John Goodsir, professor of anatomy, University of Edinburgh, 1854–67; professor of anatomy, 1867–1903; principal, 1903–16. Published papers on anthropology and comparative anatomy from 1854. Knighted, 1886. FRS 1877. (*DNB*, *DSB.*)
[after 28 April 1866?], 5 June [1866], 14 December [1866], 24 [December 1866]

Tylor, Edward Burnett (1832–1917). Anthropologist. Educated at the School of the Society of Friends, Grove House, Tottenham. Keeper of Oxford University Museum, 1883; reader in anthropology, Oxford University, 1883; professor, 1896; professor emeritus, 1909. President of the Anthropological Society, 1879–80, 1891–2. Brother of Alfred Tylor. Knighted, 1912. FRS 1871. (*DNB*, *Men and women of the time* 1899.)

Tyndall, John (1820–93). Irish physicist, lecturer, and populariser of science. Professor of natural philosophy, Royal Institution of Great Britain, 1853; superintendent, 1867–87. Scientific adviser to Trinity House and the Board of Trade, 1866–83. FRS 1852. (*DNB*, *DSB.*)

Unger, Franz (1800–70). Austrian botanist. Practised medicine in Stockerau and Kitzbühel, 1828–35. Professor of botany and zoology and director of the botanic garden, Johanneum, Graz, 1835–49. Professor of plant anatomy and physiology, University of Vienna, 1850–69. Considered one of the founders of palaeobotany; wrote in favour of species transmutation as early as 1852 and suggested hybridisation as a source of new species. (*ADB*, *DBE*, *DSB.*)

Uroopa (d. 1867). Fuegian of the Yahgan tribe. Brought to England in 1865 by Waite Hockin Stirling; became ill on the return journey and died in Stanley, Falkland Islands. (Hazlewood 2000.)

Veitch, James (1815–69). Nurseryman. In partnership with his father, James Veitch (1792–1863), proprietor of a nursery in Chelsea, London, from 1853. (R. Desmond 1994.)

Velie, Jacob W. (b. 1829). Curator. Moved from New York to Rock Island, Illinois, where he had a dental practice, 1856. Assistant, Chicago Academy of Sciences, 1871; secretary and curator, 1872. Made field trips throughout America to replenish the natural historical collection lost in the fire of 1871. (Andreas 1884, p. 536.)

Verlot, Bernard (1836–97). French botanist and horticulturalist. Head of propagation, Muséum d'Histoire Naturelle. (*NUC*, Tort 1996, Verlot 1864.)

Villars, Dominique (1745–1814). French physician and botanist. Professor of botany and director of the Jardin des Plantes in Montpellier, 1778–1803. Professor of botany and medicine, University of Strasbourg, from 1803. (*Taxonomic literature.*)

Virchow, Rudolf Carl (1821–1902). German physician, pathologist, medical reformer, and politician. Professor of pathological anatomy at the University of Würzburg, 1849–56. Professor of pathological anatomy and director of the Pathological Institute, University of Berlin, from 1856. Foreign member, Royal Society of London, 1884; awarded the Copley Medal, 1892. (*BLA*, *DBE*, *DSB*, *Record of the Royal Society of London*, Wrede and Reinfels eds. 1897.)

Vogt, Carl (1817–95). Swiss naturalist. Collaborated with Louis Agassiz on a treatise on central European freshwater fish. Professor of zoology, Giessen, 1847. Forced to leave Giessen for political reasons in 1848; settled in Geneva. Professor of geology, Geneva, 1852; director of the Institute of Zoology, 1872. (*ADB*, *DSB.*)

Wagner, Rudolph (1805–64). German anatomist, physiologist, and anthropologist. Professor of physiology, comparative anatomy, and natural history at Göttingen University, 1840. (*ADB*, *DSB.*)

Wallace, Alfred Russel (1823–1913). Naturalist. Collector in the Amazon, 1848–52; in the Malay Archipelago, 1854–62. Independently formulated a theory of evolution by natural selection in 1858. Lecturer and author of works on protective coloration, mimicry, and zoogeography. President of the Land Nationalisation Society, 1881. Wrote widely on socialism, spiritualism, and vaccination. FRS 1893. (*DNB*, *DSB.*)

22 January 1866, *4 February 1866*, [6 February 1866], *2 July 1866*, 5 July [1866], *19 November 1866*

Wallace, Annie (1848–1914). Eldest daughter of William Mitten. Married Alfred Russel Wallace in 1866. (Marchant ed. 1916, 2: 252–3.)

Walsh, Benjamin Dann (1808–69). Entomologist, farmer, and timber merchant. Student at Trinity College, Cambridge, 1827–31; fellow, 1833. Emigrated to the United States, where he farmed in Henry County, Illinois, 1838–51; lumber merchant, Rock Island, Illinois, 1851–8. Retired from commerce in about 1858 and concentrated on entomology, making contributions to agricultural entomology. Suggested the use of natural enemies to control insect pests. Author of several papers in agricultural journals. Associate editor of the *Practical Entomologist*, 1865. Acting state entomologist, Illinois, 1867. (*Alum. Cantab.*, *DAB.*)

13 March 1866, [19] April [1866], *17 July 1866*, 20 August [1866], *[28 November 1866]*, 24 December [1866]

Walton, John.

[after 4 April 1866]

Wammestriggens. *See* Button, Threeboys.

Waterhouse, Alfred (1830–1905). Architect. Designed public buildings in Cambridge, Oxford, Manchester, and London, including the Museum of Natural History, South Kensington. (*DNB.*)

Waterhouse, George Robert (1810–88). Naturalist. A founder of the Entomological Society of London, 1833. Curator of the Zoological Society of London, 1836–43. Assistant in the mineralogical and geological branch of the natural history department of the British Museum, 1843–50; keeper, 1851–6; keeper, geology department, 1857–80. Described CD's mammalian and entomological specimens from the *Beagle* voyage. (*DNB*, Gilbert 1977.)

Watson, Hewett Cottrell (1804–81). Botanist, phytogeographer, and phrenologist. Edited the *Phrenological Journal*, 1837–40. Collected plants in the Azores in 1842. Wrote extensively on the geographical distribution of plants. (*DNB*, *DSB*.)

Waugh, Andrew Scott (1810–78). Army officer. Employed on the trigonometrical survey of India, 1832–43; surveyor-general of India, 1843–61. Lieutenant-colonel of the Bengal Engineers, 1847; major-general, 1861. FRS 1858. (*DNB*.)

Wedgwood, Anne Jane (1841–77). Daughter of Henry Allen and Jessie Wedgwood. Married Ralph Edward Carr in 1864. (Freeman 1978.)

Wedgwood, Caroline (Carry) (b. 1836). Daughter of Henry Allen and Jessie Wedgwood. (*Emma Darwin* (1915).)

Wedgwood, Caroline Sarah (1800–88). CD's sister. Married Josiah Wedgwood III, her cousin, in 1837. (*Darwin pedigree*.)

Wedgwood, Elizabeth (Bessy) (1764–1846). Eldest daughter of John Bartlett Allen. Married Josiah Wedgwood II in 1792. (*Emma Darwin* (1915).)

Wedgwood, Emma. *See* Darwin, Emma.

Wedgwood, Henry Allen (Harry) (1799–1885). Barrister. BA, Jesus College, Cambridge, 1821. Married Jessie Wedgwood, his cousin, in 1830. (*Alum. Cantab.*)

Wedgwood, Hensleigh (1803–91). Philologist and barrister. Emma Darwin's brother. Fellow, Christ's College, Cambridge, 1829–30. Metropolitan police magistrate at Lambeth, 1832–7; registrar of metropolitan carriages, 1838–49. An original member of the Philological Society, 1842. Published *A dictionary of English etymology* (1859–65). Married Frances Emma Elizabeth Mackintosh in 1832. (*DNB*, Freeman 1978.)

Wedgwood, Jessie (1804–72). CD's and Emma Darwin's cousin. Married Henry Allen Wedgwood in 1830. (*Emma Darwin* (1915).)

Wedgwood, Josiah I (1730–95). Master-potter. Founded the Wedgwood pottery works at Etruria, Staffordshire. Grandfather of CD and Emma Darwin. Greatly interested in experimental chemistry. Contributed several papers on the measurement of high temperatures to the Royal Society of London's *Philosophical Transactions*. Actively associated with scientists and scientific societies. FRS 1783. (*DNB*, *DSB*.)

Wedgwood, Josiah II (1769–1843). Master-potter. Partner in the Wedgwood pottery works at Etruria, Staffordshire, 1795–1841. Resident at Maer Hall, Staffordshire. Whig MP for Stoke-on-Trent, 1832–4. Emma Darwin's father. (*Burke's peerage* 1980, *Emma Darwin* (1915), Freeman 1978.)

Wedgwood, Josiah III (1795–1880). Master-potter. Partner in the Wedgwood pottery works at Etruria, Staffordshire, 1841–4; moved to Leith Hill Place, Surrey, in 1844. Emma Darwin's brother. Married CD's sister Caroline, his cousin, in 1837. (Freeman 1978.)

Wedgwood, Katherine Elizabeth Sophy (Sophy) (1842–1911). Daughter of Caroline Wedgwood and Josiah Wedgwood III. CD's niece. (*Darwin pedigree*, Freeman 1978.)

Wedgwood, Louisa Frances. *See* Kempson, Louisa Frances.

Wedgwood, Lucy Caroline (1846–1919). Daughter of Caroline Wedgwood and Josiah Wedgwood III. CD's niece. Married Matthew James Harrison in 1874. (*Darwin pedigree*, Freeman 1978, Wedgwood and Wedgwood 1980.)
[before 25 September 1866]

Wedgwood, Margaret Susan (1843–1937). Daughter of Caroline Wedgwood and Josiah Wedgwood III. CD's niece. Married Arthur Charles Vaughan Williams in 1869. Mother of Ralph Vaughan Williams (*DNB*). (*Emma Darwin* (1915), Freeman 1978.)

Wedgwood, Sarah Elizabeth (Elizabeth) (1793–1880). Emma Darwin's sister. Resided at Maer Hall, Staffordshire, until 1847, then at The Ridge, Hartfield, Sussex, until 1862. Moved to London before settling in Down in 1868. (*Emma Darwin* (1915), Freeman 1978.)

Wedgwood, Susannah. *See* Darwin, Susannah.

Weinland, David Friedrich (1829–1915). German theologian and zoologist. Travelled extensively in North America and Haiti. Assistant to Louis Agassiz, 1855–8. Lecturer in zoology at the Senckenberg Museum, Frankfurt, and secretary of the Zoological Society, 1858. Founder and editor of *Der Zoologische Garten*, 1859. Director of the Senckenberg naturalist society, 1859–63. (*DBE*, *Zoologischer Beobachter* 57 (1916): 160.)

Welford, Charles (1815–85). Bookseller. Settled in New York after leaving London in 1833 and became a clerk at the publishers D. Appleton & Co. Partner, Bartlett & Welford, 1839–52. With Charles Scribner, founded the firm Scribner & Welford for the importation of foreign books in 1857. Returned to London in 1864 to oversee the European side of the business. (*New York Times*, 20 May 1885.)

Wells, Luke. Artist. Resided at 59 Great Percy Street, Pentonville, London. (*Post Office London directory* 1865.)

Wells, William Charles (1757–1817). Physician. Born in South Carolina, of Scottish parents, and educated in Scotland. Elected assistant physician to St Thomas's Hospital, London, 1795; physician, 1800–17. Awarded the Rumford Medal of the Royal Society for his 'Essay on dew' (1814). FRS 1793. (*DNB*.)

Welwitsch, Friedrich Martin Josef (Friedrich) (1806–72). Austrian-born botanist. Resided in Lisbon, 1839–53, where he became director of the botanic garden at Coimbra. Collected and travelled in Portuguese West Africa (Angola), 1853–61. Resided in London, 1863–72. (*DNB*.)

Westwood, John Obadiah (1805–93). Entomologist and palaeographer. Founding member of the Entomological Society of London, 1833; honorary president,

Westwood, John Obadiah, cont.
1883. Hope Professor of invertebrate zoology, Oxford University, 1861–93. Entomological referee for the *Gardeners' Chronicle.* Royal Society Royal Medallist, 1855. (*DNB*, Gilbert 1977.)

Whewell, William (1794–1866). Mathematician, historian, and philosopher of science. Professor of moral philosophy, Cambridge University, 1838–55. Master of Trinity College, Cambridge, 1841–66. FRS 1820. (*DNB*, *DSB*.)

Whitley, Charles Thomas (1808–95). Attended Shrewsbury School, 1821–6. BA, St John's College, Cambridge, 1830. Reader in natural philosophy and mathematics, Durham University, 1833–55. Vicar of Bedlington, Northumberland, 1854–95. (*Alum. Cantab.*, *Modern English biography*.)

Whitney, Josiah Dwight (1819–96). American geologist. Professor of chemistry, University of Iowa, 1855–8. California state geologist, 1860–74. Professor of geology, Harvard, 1865; dean of the School of Mining and Practical Geology, 1868. (*ANB*.)

Wichura, Max Ernst (1817–66). German lawyer and botanist. Prussian government official in Breslau, 1859–66. Devoted his spare time to botany and made frequent excursions to study European flora. Published a number of papers, including one on dimorphism in *Scabiosa* and *Lythrum* ('Ueber unvollkommene Diklinie', *Jahresberichte der schlesischen Gesellschaft für vaterländische Kultur* 36 (1858): 65–6), and a major work on hybridisation, *Die Bastardbefruchtung im Pflanzenreich erläutert an den Bastarden der Weiden* (1865). (*ADB*.)

Wilberforce, Samuel (1805–73). Clergyman. Rector of Brightstone, Isle of Wight, 1830–40; of Alverstoke, Hampshire, 1840–3. Chaplain to Prince Albert, 1841. Dean of Westminster, 1845. Bishop of Oxford, 1845–69. FRS 1845. (*DNB*, Sarjeant 1980–96.)

Williams & Norgate. Booksellers and publishers. Specialised in foreign scientific literature; premises at Covent Garden, London, and South Frederick Street, Edinburgh. A partnership between Edmund Sydney Williams (1817–91) and Frederick Norgate. Publishers of the *Natural History Review*. (*Modern English biography* s.v. Williams, Edmund Sidney.)
10 February [1866]

Wingfield, William Wriothesley (b. 1815). Clergyman. Vicar of Gulval, Cornwall. Co-author with George William Johnson of a work on poultry breeding and management. (*Alum. Oxon.*, *NUC*.)

Wollaston, Thomas Vernon (1822–78). Entomologist and conchologist. Passed many winters in Madeira, where he collected insects and shells. Wrote a series of works on the Coleoptera. (*DNB*, Gilbert 1977.)

Wood, James Julius (1800–77). Scottish clergyman. Minister of the Free Church, Dumfries, 1847–77. (*Modern English biography*.)

Wood, Searles Valentine (1798–1880). Palaeontologist. Officer in the East India Company's navy, 1811–25. Became a partner in a bank at Hasketon, near Woodbridge. Curator of the Geological Society of London, 1838–9; fellow, 1839.

Studied the fossils of the East Anglian Crag, specialising in Eocene fossil Mollusca. (*DNB*, Woodward 1907.)
16 July 1866

Woodbury, Thomas White (1818–71). Journalist and beekeeper. From 1850 devoted himself exclusively to beekeeping. Introduced Ligurian bees to Britain in 1859 and developed the 'Woodbury hive', marketed by the London apiarian specialists George Neighbour & Sons. As 'A Devonshire Beekeeper', a regular contributor to the *Cottage Gardener*, the *Journal of Horticulture*, the *Gardeners' Chronicle*, and *The Times*. (R. H. Brown 1975, Ron Brown 1994, Dodd 1983, Fraser 1958, Neighbour 1865.)

Woolner, Thomas (1825–92). Sculptor and poet. Established his reputation in the 1850s with medallion portrait sculptures of Robert Browning, Thomas Carlyle, and William Wordsworth. Went on to make acclaimed busts of CD, Charles Dickens, Thomas Henry Huxley, Adam Sedgwick, and Alfred Tennyson, and life-size studies of Francis Bacon, John Stuart Mill, and William Whewell. (*DNB*.)

Wyman, Jeffries (1814–74). American comparative anatomist and ethnologist. Curator of the Lowell Institute, Boston, 1839–42. Travelled in Europe, 1841–2. Professor of anatomy and physiology, Hampden-Sydney College, Virginia, 1843–8. Hersey Professor of anatomy, Harvard College, 1847–74. Curator, Peabody Museum of Archaeology and Ethnology, Harvard, 1866–74. (*ANB*, *DSB*.)
11 January 1866, 2 February 1866

Yule, Henry (1820–89). Scottish engineer and colonial official. Entered the Bengal Engineers in 1840. Based in India until 1862. Author of works on India and south-east Asia. Knighted, 1863. (*DNB*.)

Zurhorst, Frederick William. Irish merchant and poultry breeder. Premises at 17 St Andrew Street, Dublin. Leading breeder of white Cochin poultry. (*Thom's Irish almanac* 1865, *Correspondence* vol. 13, letter from W. B. Tegetmeier, 10 April 1865.)

BIBLIOGRAPHY

The following bibliography contains all the books and papers referred to in this volume by author–date reference or by short title. Short titles are used for some standard reference works (e.g., *DNB, OED*), for CD's books and papers, and for editions of his letters and manuscripts (e.g., *Descent, LL, Notebooks*). Works referred to by short titles are listed in alphabetical order according to the title; those given author–date references occur in alphabetical order according to the author's surname. Notes on manuscript sources are given at the end of the bibliography.

ADB: *Allgemeine deutsche Biographie.* Under the auspices of the Historical Commission of the Royal Academy of Sciences. 56 vols. Leipzig: Duncker & Humblot. 1875–1912.

Admissions to Trinity College, Cambridge. Edited by W. W. Rouse Ball and J. A. Venn. 5 vols. London: Macmillan. 1911–16.

Affolter, James. 1980. The 'antarctic' flora: researches of Charles Darwin and Joseph Hooker. *Contributions from the University of Michigan Herbarium* 14: 1–9.

Agassiz, Jean Louis Rodolphe. 1840a. On glaciers and boulders in Switzerland. *Report of the tenth meeting of the British Association for the Advancement of Science, held at Glasgow*, Transactions of the sections, pp. 113–14.

——. 1840b. *Etudes sur les glaciers.* Neuchâtel: Jent & Gassmann.

——. 1857–62. *Contributions to the natural history of the United States of America.* 4 vols. Boston, Mass.: Little, Brown & Company. London: Trübner.

——. 1863. *Methods of study in natural history.* Boston, Mass.: Ticknor & Fields.

——. 1866a. Physical history of the valley of the Amazons. *Atlantic Monthly* 18: 49–60, 159–69.

——. 1866b. Aperçu du cours de l'Amazone. *Bulletin de la Société de Géographie* 12: 433–57.

Agassiz, Jean Louis Rodolphe and Agassiz, Elizabeth. 1868. *A journey in Brazil.* Boston: Ticknor and Fields.

Agassiz, Jean Louis Rodolphe and Coutinho, João Martinus da Silva. 1868. Sur la géologie de l'Amazone. *Bulletin de la Société Géologique de France* 2d ser. 25 (1867–8): 685–91.

Ainslie, Robert. 1865. *Discourses delivered in Christ Church, New Road, Brighton.* London: Longmans, Green, Reader, and Dyer. Brighton: J. H. and C. Treacher.

Allan, Mea. 1967. *The Hookers of Kew, 1785–1911.* London: Michael Joseph.

——. 1977. *Darwin and his flowers: the key to natural selection.* London: Faber and Faber.

Allan, Mea. 1982. *William Robinson 1838–1935. Father of the English flower garden.* London: Faber and Faber.

Alum. Cantab.: *Alumni Cantabrigienses. A biographical list of all known students, graduates and holders of office at the University of Cambridge, from the earliest times to 1900.* Compiled by John Venn and J. A. Venn. 10 vols. Cambridge: Cambridge University Press. 1922–54.

Alum. Oxon.: *Alumni Oxonienses: the members of the University of Oxford, 1500–1886: . . . with a record of their degrees. Being the matriculation register of the university.* Alphabetically arranged, revised, and annotated by Joseph Foster. 8 vols. London and Oxford: Parker & Co. 1887–91.

American medical biography: *Dictionary of American medical biography. Lives of eminent physicians of the United States and Canada, from the earliest times.* By Howard A. Kelly and Walter L. Burrage. New York and London: D. Appleton and Company. 1928.

ANB: *American national biography.* Edited by John A. Garraty and Mark C. Carnes. 24 vols. and supplement. New York and Oxford: Oxford University Press. 1999–2002.

Andreas, Alfred Theodore. 1884. *History of Cook County Illinois. From the earliest period to the present time.* Chicago: A. T. Andreas.

Anon. 1866. Darwin and his teachings. *Quarterly Journal of Science* 3: 151–76.

Atkins, Hedley. 1974. *Down: the home of the Darwins. The story of a house and the people who lived there.* London: Royal College of Surgeons.

Aust. dict. biog.: *Australian dictionary of biography.* Edited by Douglas Pike *et al.* 14 vols. [Melbourne]: Melbourne University Press. London and New York: Cambridge University Press. 1966–96.

Austen, Robert Alfred Cloyne. 1849. On the valley of the English Channel. *Quarterly Journal of the Geological Society of London* 6 (1850): 69–97.

——. 1851. On the superficial accumulations of the coasts of the English Channel, and the changes they indicate. *Quarterly Journal of the Geological Society of London* 7: 118–36.

Autobiography: *The autobiography of Charles Darwin, 1809–1882. With original omissions restored.* Edited with appendix and notes by Nora Barlow. London: Collins. 1958.

Baer, Karl Ernst von. 1859. Über Papuas und Alfuren. Ein Commentar zu den beiden ersten Abschnitten der Abhandlung 'Crania selecta ex Thesauris Anthropologicus Academiae Imperialis Petropolitanae.' *Mémoires de l'Académie Impériale des Sciences de Saint-Pétersbourg* 6th ser. 8: 269–345.

Bailey, Liberty Hyde and Bailey, Ethel Zoe. 1976. *Hortus third: a concise dictionary of plants cultivated in the United States and Canada.* Revised and expanded by the staff of the Liberty Hyde Bailey Hortorium. New York: Macmillan. London: Collier Macmillan.

Baillière, Hippolyte. 1853. *Catalogue of scientific books.* London: Schulze & Co.

Baird, Spencer Fullerton. 1865–6. The distribution and migrations of North American birds. *American Journal of Science and Arts* 41 (1866): 78–90, 184–92, 337–47.

Baker, John Norman Leonard. 1963. *The history of geography: papers by J. N. L. Baker.*

Oxford: Basil Blackwell.

Balbiani, Edouard-Gérard. 1866. On the reproduction and embryogeny of the *Aphides*. *Annals and Magazine of Natural History* 3d ser. 18: 62–9, 106–9.

Balfour, Edward. 1885. *The cyclopædia of India and of eastern and southern Asia, commercial, industrial, and scientific; products of the mineral, vegetable, and animal kingdoms, useful arts and manufactures*. 3d edition. 3 vols. London: Bernard Quaritch.

Barnhart, John Hendley, comp. 1965. *Biographical notes upon botanists . . . maintained in the New York Botanical Garden Library*. 3 vols. Boston, Mass.: G. K. Hall.

Bateman, James. 1864. *Guide to cool-orchid growing*. London: Reeve & Co.

Bates, Henry Walter. 1860. Contributions to an insect fauna of the Amazon valley. Diurnal Lepidoptera. [Read 5 March and 24 November 1860.] *Transactions of the Entomological Society of London* n.s. 5 (1858–61): 223–8, 335–61.

——. 1861. Contributions to an insect fauna of the Amazon valley. *Lepidoptera*: *Heliconidæ*. [Read 21 November 1861.] *Transactions of the Linnean Society of London* 23 (1860–2): 495–566.

——. 1863. *The naturalist on the River Amazons. A record of adventures, habits of animals, sketches of Brazilian and Indian life, and aspects of nature under the equator, during eleven years of travel*. 2 vols. London: John Murray.

BDWS: *The biographical dictionary of women in science: pioneering lives from ancient times to the mid-20th century*. Edited by Marilyn Ogilvie and Joy Harvey. 2 vols. New York and London: Routledge. 2000.

'Beagle' diary: *Charles Darwin's* Beagle *diary*. Edited by Richard Darwin Keynes. Cambridge: Cambridge University Press. 1988.

Beale, Lionel Smith. 1865. *On the structure and growth of the tissues, and on life*. London: Robert Hardwicke.

Beaman, John H. and Beaman, Reed S. 1998. *The plants of Mount Kinabalu 3. Gymnosperms and non-orchid monocotyledons*. Kota Kinabalu. London: Natural History Publications (Borneo) in association with Royal Botanic Gardens, Kew.

Bean, William Jackson. 1970–88. *Trees and shrubs hardy in the British Isles*. 8th edition, fully revised by D. L. Clarke and George Taylor. 4 vols. and supplement. London: John Murray.

Beasley, Henry. 1865. *The book of prescriptions, containing more than 3000 prescriptions, collected from the practice of the most eminent physicians and surgeons, English and foreign*. 3d edition. London: John Churchill and Sons.

Beatson, Alexander. 1816. *Tracts relative to the island of St. Helena; written during a residence of five years*. London: W. Bulmer and Co.

Becker, Lydia Ernestine. 1869. On alteration in the structure of *Lychnis diurna*, observed in connexion with the development of a parasitic fungus. [Read August 1869.] *Report of the 39th meeting of the British Association for the Advancement of Science, held at Exeter*, Transactions of the sections, p. 106.

Bénézit, Emmanuel. 1976. *Dictionnaire critique et documentaire des peintres, sculpteurs, dessinateurs et graveurs de tous les temps et de tous les pays par un groupe d'écrivains spécialistes français et étrangers*. Revised edition. 10 vols. Paris: Librairie Gründ.

Bennett, George. 1834. *Wanderings in New South Wales, Batavia, Pedir Coast, Singapore, and China; being the journal of a naturalist in those countries, during 1832, 1833, and 1834.* 2 vols. London: Richard Bentley.

Benthall, Paul. 1980. George Maw: a versatile Victorian. *National Trust Studies* (1980): 11–20.

Bentham, George. 1862. [Anniversary address, 24 May 1862.] *Journal of the Proceedings of the Linnean Society of London (Botany)* 6: lxvi–lxxxiii.

——. 1865. *Handbook of the British flora; a description of the flowering plants and ferns indigenous to, or naturalized in, the British Isles. For the use of beginners and amateurs.* 2 vols. London: Lovell Reeve & Co.

Bentham, George and Hooker, Joseph Dalton. 1862–83. *Genera plantarum. Ad exemplaria imprimis in herbariis Kewensibus servata definita.* 3 vols. in 7. London: A. Black [and others].

BHGW: *Biographisch-literarisches Handwörterbuch zur Geschichte der exacten Wissenschaften enthaltend Nachweisung über Lebensverhältnisse und Leistungen von Mathematikern, Astronomen, Physikern, Chemikern, Mineralogen, Geologen usw.* By Johann Christian Poggendorff. 5 vols. Leipzig: Johann Ambrosius Barth; Verlag Chemie. 1863–1926.

Binney, Edward William. 1846. On the origin of coal. [Read 1 December 1846.] *Memoirs of the Literary and Philosophical Society of Manchester* 2d ser. 8 (1848): 148–94.

Birds of the world: *Handbook of the birds of the world.* By Josep del Hoyo *et al.* 8 vols. to date. Barcelona: Lynx editions. 1992–.

Bishop, P. J. 1974. *A short history of the Royal Humane Society: to mark its 200th anniversary.* London: [the Society].

Bishop, Sherman Chauncey. 1994. *Handbook of salamanders: the salamanders of the United States, of Canada, and of lower California.* Ithaca and London: Comstock Publishing Associates.

Bizzarro, Salvatore. 1987. *Historical dictionary of Chile.* 2d edition. Metuchen, N.J. & London: Scarecrow Press.

BLA: *Biographisches Lexikon der hervorragenden Aerzte aller Zeiten und Völker.* Edited by A. Wernich, E. Gurlt, and August Hirsch. 6 vols. Vienna and Leipzig: Urban and Schwarzenberg. 1884–8.

Blackburn, Helen. 1902. *Women's suffrage: a record of the Women's Suffrage Movement in the British Isles with biographical sketches of Miss Becker.* London: Williams & Norgate.

Blancpain, Jean-Pierre. 1990. *Les Araucans et la frontière dans l'histoire du Chili des origines au XIXe siècle. Une épopée américaine.* Frankfurt am Main: Vervuert Verlag.

BLKO: *Biographisches Lexikon des Kaiserthums Oesterreich, enthaltend die Lebensskizzen der denkwürdigen Personen, welche seit 1750 in den österreichischen Kronländern geboren wurden oder darin gelebt und gewirkt haben.* By Constant von Wurzbach. 60 vols. Vienna: L. C. Zamarski. 1856–91.

Blyth, Edward. 1841. An amended list of the species of the genus *Ovis*. *Annals of Natural History* 7: 248–61.

——. 1864. Notes on sundry Mammalia. *Proceedings of the Zoological Society of London* (1864): 482–86.

——. 1866a. The gaour. *Field* 27: 55–6.

——. 1866b. The gaour and the gayál. *Field* 27: 77.

Boissier, Pierre-Edmond. 1839–45. *Voyage botanique dans le midi de l'Espagne pendant l'année 1837*. 2 vols. Paris: Gide et Cie.

Bompas, George C. 1885. *Life of Frank Buckland*. London: Smith, Elder & Co.

Bonham-Carter, Victor. 1960. *In a liberal tradition: a social biography 1700–1950*. London: Constable.

Boole, Mary Everest. 1883. *The message of psychic science to mothers and nurses*. London: Trübner & Co.

——. 1931. *Collected works*. Edited by E. M. Cobham. Preface by Ethel S. Dummer. 4 vols. London: C. W. Daniel.

Bosl, Karl, ed. 1983. *Bosl's Bayerische Biographie*. Regensburg: Friedrich Pustet.

Boulenger, George Albert. 1882. *Catalogue of the Batrachia gradientia s. caudata and Batrachia apoda in the collection of the British Museum*. 2d edition. London: printed by order of the trustees [of the British Museum].

Bouquet, Mary. 1995. Exhibiting knowledge: the trees of Dubois, Haeckel, Jesse and Rivers at the *Pithecanthropus* centennial exhibition. In *Shifting contexts: transformations in anthropological knowledge*, edited by Marilyn Strathern. London and New York: Routledge.

Bourcier, Jules. 1851. Note sur onze espèces nouvelles de Trochilidées. *Comptes rendus hebdomadaires des séances de l'académie des sciences* 32: 186–8.

Bowlby, John. 1990. *Charles Darwin: a biography*. London: Hutchinson.

Bowler, Peter J. 1987. *Theories of human evolution: a century of debate, 1844–1944*. Oxford: Basil Blackwell.

——. 1989. *The Mendelian revolution: the emergence of hereditarian concepts in modern science and society*. London: Athlone Press.

Bowman, William. 1866. The address in surgery. [Read 9 August 1866.] *British Medical Journal* (1866) pt 2: 186–97.

Boylan, Patrick J. 1998. Lyell and the dilemma of Quaternary glaciation. In *Lyell: the past is the key to the present*, edited by Derek J. Blundell and Andrew C. Scott. London: Geological Society.

Bradbury, Savile. 1967. *The evolution of the microscope*. Oxford: Pergamon Press.

Brandon-Jones, Christine. 1995. Long gone and forgotten: reassessing the life and career of Edward Blyth, zoologist. *Archives of Natural History* 22: 91–5.

——. 1997. Edward Blyth, Charles Darwin, and the animal trade in nineteenth-century India and Britain. *Journal of the History of Biology* 30: 145–78.

Braun, Alexander Carl Heinrich. 1853. Considerations on the phenomenon of rejuvenescence in nature, especially in the life and development of plants. Translated by Arthur Henfrey. In *Botanical and physiological memoirs*, edited by Arthur Henfrey. London: Ray Society.

Brehm, Christian Ludwig. 1831. *Handbuch der Naturgeschichte aller Vögel Deutschlands*. Ilmenau: Bernh. Friedr. Voigt.

Brice, William R. and Figueirôa, Silvia F. de M. 2001. Charles Hartt, Louis Agassiz, and the controversy over Pleistocene glaciation in Brazil. *History of Science* 39: 161–84.

Bridges, Esteban Lucas. 1948. *Uttermost part of the earth.* London: Hodder and Stoughton.

Brinkman, Paul. 2003. Bartholomew James Sulivan's discovery of fossil vertebrates in the Tertiary beds of Patagonia. *Archives of Natural History* 30: 56–74.

Brock, W. H. and Knight, D. M. 1967. The atomic debates. In *The atomic debates: Brodie and the rejection of the atomic theory*, edited by W. H. Brock. Leicester: Leicester University Press.

Bromfield, William Arnold. 1856. *Flora Vectensis: being a systematic description of the phænogamous or flowering plants and ferns indigenous to the Isle of Wight.* Edited by William Jackson Hooker and Thomas Bell Salter. London: William Pamplin.

Bronn, Heinrich Georg. 1860a. Prospectus: Charles Darwin, *Über die Entstehung der Arten im Thier- und Pflanzen-Reich durch natürliche Züchtung, oder Erhaltung der vervollkommneten Rassen im Kampfe um's Daseyn.* Nach der zweiten Auflage mit einer geschichtlichen Vorrede und andern Zusätzen des Verfassers für diese deutsche Ausgabe aus dem Englischen Übersetzt und mit Anmerkungen versehen von Dr. H. G. Bronn. Stuttgart: E. Schweizerbart'sche Verlagshandlung und Druckerei. *Neues Jahrbuch für Mineralogie, Geognosie, Geologie und Petrefakten-Kunde.*

———. 1860b. Review of *Origin of species. Neues Jahrbuch für Mineralogie, Geognosie, Geologie und Petrefakten-Kunde* (1860): 112–16. [Translated in Hull 1973, pp. 120–4.]

———, trans. 1860. *Charles Darwin, über die Entstehung der Arten im Thier- und Pflanzen-Reich durch natürliche Züchtung, oder Erhaltung der vervollkommneten Rassen im Kampfe um's Daseyn.* Stuttgart: E. Schweizerbart.

———, trans. 1862. *Charles Darwin, über die Einrichtungen zur Befruchtung Britischer und ausländischer Orchideen durch Insekten und über die günstigen Erfolge der Wechselbefruchtung.* Stuttgart: E. Schweizerbart.

———, trans. 1863. *Über die Entstehung der Arten im Thier- und Pflanzen-Reich durch natürliche Züchtung; oder, Erhaltung der vervollkommneten Rassen im Kampfe um's Daseyn.* By Charles Darwin. 2d edition. Stuttgart: E. Schweizerbart.

Bronn, Heinrich Georg and Carus, Julius Victor, trans. 1867. *Über die Entstehung der Arten durch natürliche Zuchtwahl oder die Erhaltung der begünstigten Rassen im Kampfe um's Dasein.* By Charles Darwin. 3d edition. Stuttgart: E. Schweizerbart'sche Verlagshandlung und Druckerei.

Brown, Alan Willard. 1947. *The Metaphysical Society; Victorian minds in crisis, 1869–1880.* New York: Columbia University Press.

Browne, Janet. 1983. *The secular ark. Studies in the history of biogeography.* New Haven, Conn., and London: Yale University Press.

———. 1995. *Charles Darwin. Voyaging. Volume I of a biography.* New York: Alfred A. Knopf.

———. 1998. I could have retched all night. Darwin and his body. In *Science incarnate. Historical embodiments of natural knowledge*, edited by Christopher Lawrence and Steven Shapin. Chicago and London: University of Chicago Press.

———. 2002. *Charles Darwin. The power of place. Volume II of a biography.* London: Pimlico.

Brush, Stephen G. 1983. *Statistical physics and the atomic theory of matter: from Boyle and Newton to Landau and Onsager.* Princeton: Princeton University Press.

Bryant, Harold N. 1995. The threefold parallelism of Agassiz and Haeckel, and polarity determination in phylogenetic systematics. *Biology and Philosophy* 10: 197–217.

Buchanan, W. J. 1908. Notes on old Darjeeling. *Bengal Past and Present* 2: 439–58.

Bunbury, Charles James Fox. 1855. Remarks on the botany of Madeira and Teneriffe. [Read 6 March and 3 April 1855.] *Journal of the Proceedings of the Linnean Society (Botany)* 1 (1857): 1–35.

Bunbury, Frances Joanna, ed. 1891–3. *Memorials of Sir C. J. F. Bunbury, Bart. Early life* 1 vol.; *Middle life* vols. 1–3; *Later life* vols. 1–5. Mildenhall: S. R. Simpson.

Burchfield, Joe D. 1990. *Lord Kelvin and the age of the earth. With a new afterword.* Chicago and London: University of Chicago Press.

Burgess, G. H. O. 1967. *The curious world of Frank Buckland.* London: John Baker.

Burke's landed gentry: *A genealogical and heraldic history of the commoners of Great Britain and Ireland enjoying territorial possessions or high official rank but unvisited with heritable honours. Burke's genealogical and heraldic history of the landed gentry.* By John Burke *et al.* 1st–18th edition. London: Henry Colburn [and others]. 1833–1969.

Burke's peerage: *A genealogical and heraldic dictionary of the peerage and baronetage of the United Kingdom. Burke's peerage and baronetage.* 1st– edition. London: Henry Colburn [and others]. 1826–.

Burritt, Elihu. 1864. *A walk from London to John O'Groat's, with notes by the way.* 2d edition. London: Sampson, Low, Son, & Marston.

Butakoff, Aleksey Ivanovich. 1852. Survey of the Sea of Aral. By Commander Alexey Butakoff, of the Imperial Russian Navy. Communicated by Sir Roderick I. Murchison. [Read 13 December 1852.] *Journal of the Royal Geographical Society* 23 (1853): 93–101.

Calendar: *A calendar of the correspondence of Charles Darwin, 1821–1882. With supplement.* 2d edition. Edited by Frederick Burkhardt *et al.* Cambridge: Cambridge University Press. 1994.

Cambridge University calendar: *The Cambridge University calendar.* Cambridge: W. Page [and others]. 1796–1950.

Campbell, Duncan, comp. 1925. *Records of Clan Campbell in the military service of the Honourable East India Company 1600–1858.* London: Longmans, Green and Co.

[Campbell, George Douglas.] 1862. [Review of *Orchids* and other works.] *Edinburgh Review* 116: 378–97.

——. 1865. The reign of law. *Good Words* (1865): 52–8, 126–33, 227–32, 269–74.

Candolle, Alphonse de. 1855. *Géographie botanique raisonnée ou exposition des faits principaux et des lois concernant la distribution géographique des plantes de l'époque actuelle.* 2 vols. Paris: Victor Mason. Geneva: J. Kessmann.

——. 1866. [Presidential address.] *International Horticultural Exhibition* 1866, pp. 29–42.

Candolle, Anne Casimir Pyramus de. 1866. Mémoire sur la famille des Pipéracées. *Mémoires de la Société de Physique et d'Histoire Naturelle de Genève* 18: 219–48.

Canestrini, Giovanni and Salimbeni, Leonardo, trans. 1864. *Carlo Darwin. Sull'origine delle specie per elezione naturale, ovvero conservazione delle razze perfezionate nella lotta per l'esistenza.* Modena, Italy: Nicola Zanichelli.

Canfield, Colbert A. 1866. On the habits of the prongbuck (*Antilocapra americana*), and the periodical shedding of its horns. [Read 27 February 1866.] *Proceedings of the Zoological Society of London* (1866): 105–10.

[Carlyle, Thomas.] 1838. *Sartor resartus: the life and opinions of Herr Teufelsdröckh*. London: Saunders and Otley.

Caroe, Gwendolen Mary. 1985. *The Royal Institution: an informal history*. With a final chapter by Alban Caroe. London: John Murray.

Carpenter, William Benjamin. 1864. Additional note on the structure and affinities of Eozoön Canadense. [Read 23 November 1864.] *Quarterly Journal of the Geological Society of London* 21 (1865): 59–66.

——. 1866. Supplemental notes on the structure and affinities of Eozoon Canadense. *Quarterly Journal of the Geological Society of London* 22: 219–28.

Carrière, Elie Abel. 1866. Transformation de l'Aria vestita par la greffe. *Revue Horticole* 37: 457–8.

Carus, Julius Victor. 1853. *System der thierischen Morphologie*. Leipzig: Wilhelm Engelmann.

——, trans. 1863. *Zeugnisse für die Stellung des Menschen in der Natur*. By Thomas Henry Huxley. Braunschweig: Vieweg und Sohn.

——, trans. 1868. *Das Variiren der Thiere und Pflanzen im Zustande der Domestication*. By Charles Darwin. 2 vols. Stuttgart: E. Schweizerbart'sche Verlagshandlung (E. Koch).

Caspary, Johann Xaver Robert. 1865a. Sur les hybrides obtenus par la greffe. *Bulletin du Congrès International de Botanique et d'Horticulture réuni à Amsterdam* (1865): 65–80.

——. 1865b. Über botanische Untersuchungen, welche in Bezug auf Darwin's Hypothese, dass kein Hermaphrodit sich durch eine Ewigkeit von Generationen befruchten könne, gemacht sind. *Schriften der k. Physikalisch-ökonomischen Gesellschaft zu Koenigsberg* 6: 11–21.

——. 1865c. Über Mischlinge, die durch Pfropfen entstanden sind. *Schriften der k. Physikalisch-ökonomischen Gesellschaft zu Koenigsberg* 6: 4–5.

——. 1866a. On the change of the direction of the branches of woody plants. *International Horticultural Exhibition* 1866, pp. 98–117.

——. 1866b. Nymphaeaceae. *Annales Musei Botanici Lugduno-Batavi* 2 (1866): 241–56.

——. [1878.] *Nymphaeaceae*. In vol. 4 of *Flora Brasiliensis*, edited by Karl Friedrich Philipp von Martius. Leipzig: apud Frid. Fleischer in Comm.

Catalogue of the fossil Mammalia in the British Museum (Natural History). By Richard Lydekker. 5 vols. London: Taylor and Francis. 1885–7.

CDEL: *A critical dictionary of English literature, and British and American authors, living and deceased, from the earliest accounts to the middle of the nineteenth century . . . with forty indexes of subjects*. By S. Austin Allibone. 3 vols. London: Trübner. Philadelphia: Childs & Peterson; J. B. Lippincott. 1859–71. *A supplement to Allibone's critical dictionary of English literature and British and American authors. Containing over thirty-seven thousand articles (authors), and enumerating over ninety-three thousand titles*. By John Foster Kirk. 2 vols. Philadelphia and London: J. B. Lippincott. 1891.

Chambers: *The Chambers dictionary*. Edinburgh: Chambers Harrap Publishers. 1998.

[Chambers, Robert.] 1844. *Vestiges of the natural history of creation*. London: John Churchill.

Chapuis, Félicien. 1865. *Le pigeon voyageur belge*. Verviers: Imprimerie de Ch. Vinche.

Choldin, Marianna Tax. 1985. *A fence around the empire: Russian censorship of western ideas under the tsars*. Durham, N.C.: Duke University Press.

Clark, Henry James. 1865. *Mind in nature; or the origin of life, and the mode of development of animals*. New York: D. Appleton and Company.

Clark, Ronald W. 1968. *The Huxleys*. London: Heinemann.

Clarke, Richard Trevor. 1866. On a certain phenomenon of hybridism observed in the genus Matthiola. *International Horticultural Exhibition* 1866, pp. 142–4.

Claus, Carl. 1866. *Die Copepoden-Fauna von Nizza. Ein Beitrag zur Charakteristik der Formen und deren Abänderungen 'im Sinne Darwin's'*. Marburg and Leipzig: N. G. Elwert'sche Universitäts-Buchhandlung. [Reprinted from *Schriften der Gesellschaft zur Befoerderung der gesammten Naturwissenschaften zu Marburg*.]

Clergy list: *The clergy list ... containing an alphabetical list of the clergy*. London: C. Cox [and others]. 1841–89.

'Climbing plants': On the movements and habits of climbing plants. By Charles Darwin. [Read 2 February 1865.] *Journal of the Linnean Society (Botany)* 9 (1867): 1–118.

Climbing plants: *On the movements and habits of climbing plants*. By Charles Darwin. London: Longman, Green, Longman, Roberts & Green; Williams & Norgate. 1865.

Climbing plants 2d ed.: *The movements and habits of climbing plants*. 2d edition. By Charles Darwin. London: John Murray. 1875.

Clokie, Hermia Newman. 1964. *An account of the herbaria of the department of botany in the University of Oxford*. Oxford: Oxford University Press.

Coates, Patrick Devereux. 1988. *The China consuls: British consular officers, 1843–1943*. Hong Kong and Oxford: Oxford University Press.

Coats, Alice Margaret. 1968. *Flowers and their histories*. London: Adam & Charles Black.

Cobham, Eleanor Meredith. 1951. *Mary Everest Boole; a memoir with some letters*. Introduction by Ethel S. Dummer. Ashingdon: C. W. Daniel Co.

Collected papers: *The collected papers of Charles Darwin*. Edited by Paul H. Barrett. 2 vols. Chicago and London: University of Chicago Press. 1977.

Collingwood, Cuthbert. 1868. *Rambles of a naturalist on the shores and waters of the China Sea: being observations in natural history during a voyage to China, Formosa, Borneo, Singapore, etc., made in Her Majesty's vessels in 1866 and 1867*. London: John Murray.

Colp, Ralph, Jr. 1978. Charles Darwin: slavery and the American Civil War. *Harvard Library Bulletin* 26: 471–89.

——. 1998. *To be an invalid*, redux. *Journal of the History of Biology* 31: 211–40.

Columbia gazetteer of the world: *The Columbia gazetteer of the world*. Edited by Saul B. Cohen. 3 vols. New York: Columbia University Press. 1998.

Cook, L. M. 1995. T. Vernon Wollaston and the 'monstrous doctrine'. *Archives of Natural History* 22: 333–48.

Coral reefs: *The structure and distribution of coral reefs. Being the first part of the geology of the voyage of the* Beagle, *under the command of Capt. FitzRoy RN, during the years 1832 to 1836*. By Charles Darwin. London: Smith, Elder & Co. 1842.

Corbet, A. E. [1915–19.] *The family of Corbet: its life and times*. 2 vols. London: St Catherine Press.

Correns, C. 1916. Friedrich Hildebrand. *Berichte der deutschen botanischen Gesellschaft* 34 (pt 2): 28–49.

Correspondence: *The correspondence of Charles Darwin*. Edited by Frederick Burkhardt *et al.* 13 vols to date. Cambridge: Cambridge University Press. 1985–.

Corsi, Pietro and Weindling, Paul J. 1985. Darwinism in Germany, France and Italy. In *The Darwinian heritage*, edited by David Kohn. Princeton, N.J.: Princeton University Press in association with Nova Pacifica.

Couch, Jonathan. 1871. *The history of Polperro, a fishing town on the south coast of Cornwall.* Truro: W. Lake.

County directory of Scotland. Edinburgh: R. Grant & Son, Arthur Giles. 1862–1912.

County families: *The county families of the United Kingdom; or, royal manual of the titled & untitled aristocracy of Great Britain & Ireland.* By Edward Walford. London: Robert Hardwicke; Chatto & Windus. 1860–93. *Walford's county families of the United Kingdom or royal manual of the titled and untitled aristocracy of England, Wales, Scotland, and Ireland.* London: Chatto & Windus; Spottiswoode & Co. 1894–1920.

Crawfurd, John. 1834. *Journal of an embassy from the governor general of India to the court of Ava . . . With an appendix, containing a description of fossil remains, by Professor Buckland and Mr. Clift.* 2d edition. 2 vols. London: Henry Colburn.

——. 1866. On the migration of cultivated plants in reference to ethnology. *Journal of Botany* 4: 317–32.

Crockford's clerical directory: *The clerical directory, a biographical and statistical book of reference for facts relating to the clergy and the Church. Crockford's clerical directory etc.* London: John Crockford [and others]. 1858–1900.

Croll, James. 1864. On the physical cause of the change of climate during geological epochs. *Philosophical Magazine* 4th ser. 28: 121–37.

——. 1865a. On the physical cause of the submergence of the land during the glacial epoch. *Reader* 6: 270–1, 435–6.

——. 1865b. On the glacial submergence. *Reader* 6: 630–1.

——. 1866a. On the excentricity of the earth's orbit. *Philosophical Magazine* 4th ser. 31: 26–8.

——. 1866b. The glacial submergence. *Reader* 7: 44.

Cross and self fertilisation: *The effects of cross and self fertilisation in the vegetable kingdom.* By Charles Darwin. London: John Murray. 1876.

Crüger, Hermann. 1864. A few notes on the fecundation of orchids and their morphology. [Read 3 March 1864.] *Journal of the Linnean Society (Botany)* 8 (1865): 127–35.

Cunningham, Robert Oliver. 1871. *Notes on the natural history of the Strait of Magellan and west coast of Patagonia, made during the voyage of H.M.S. 'Nassau' in the years 1866, 67, 68, & 69*. Edinburgh: Edmonston and Douglas.

DAB: *Dictionary of American biography*. Under the auspices of the American Council of Learned Societies. 20 vols., index, and 10 supplements. New York: Charles Scribner's Sons; Simon & Shuster Macmillan. London: Oxford University Press; Humphrey Milford. 1928–95.

Dallas, William Sweetland, trans. 1869. *Facts and arguments for Darwin*. By Fritz Müller. London: John Murray.

Dana, James Dwight. 1866. On cephalization; no. IV: explanations drawn out by the statements of an objector. *American Journal of Science and Arts* 2d ser. 41: 163–74.

Darwin, Bernard. 1955. *The world that Fred made: an autobiography*. London: Chatto & Windus.

Darwin, Erasmus. 1789–91. *The botanic garden; a poem, in two parts*. Pt 1. *The economy of vegetation*. London: J. Johnson. 1791. Pt 2. *The loves of the plants*. With philosophical notes. Lichfield: J. Jackson. 1789.

——. 1794–6. *Zoonomia; or, the laws of organic life*. 2 vols. London: J. Johnson.

——. 1797. *A plan for the conduct of female education in boarding schools*. London: J. Johnson.

——. 1800. *Phytologia; or the philosophy of agriculture and gardening. With the theory of draining morasses, and with an improved construction of the drill plough*. London: J. Johnson.

——. 1803. *The temple of nature; or, the origin of society: a poem. With philosophical notes*. 2 pts. London: J. Johnson.

Darwin, Francis, ed. 1892. *Charles Darwin; his life told in an autobiographical chapter, and in a selected series of his published letters*. London: John Murray.

——. 1914. William Erasmus Darwin. *Christ's College Magazine* 29: 16–23.

——. 1916. Memoir of Sir George Darwin. In vol. 5 of *Scientific papers*, by George Howard Darwin. Cambridge: Cambridge University Press.

Darwin pedigree: *Pedigree of the family of Darwin*. Compiled by H. Farnham Burke. N.p.: privately printed. 1888. [Reprinted in facsimile in *Darwin pedigrees*, by Richard Broke Freeman. London: printed for the author. 1984.]

Davies, Gordon Leslie. [1969.] *The earth in decay. A history of British geomorphology 1578–1878*. London: Macdonald Technical and Scientific.

Dawkins, Richard. 2003. Introduction to *The descent of man, and selection in relation to sex*, by Charles Darwin. Reprint of the 2d edition. London: Gibson Square Books.

Dawson, John William. 1864. On the structure of certain organic remains in the Laurentian limestones of Canada. [Read 23 November 1864.] *Quarterly Journal of the Geological Society of London* 21 (1865): 51–9.

Day, Archibald. 1967. *The admiralty hydrographic service, 1795–1919*. London: Her Majesty's Stationery Office.

DBE: *Deutsche biographische Enzyklopädie*. Edited by Walter Killy *et al.* 12 vols. in 14. Munich: K. G. Saur. 1995–2000.

DBF: *Dictionnaire de biographie Française*. Under the direction of J. Balteau *et al.* 18 vols. and part of vol. 19 (A–Latreille) to date. Paris: Librairie Letouzey & Ané. 1933–.

DBL: *Dansk biografisk leksikon*. Founded by Carl Frederick Bricka, edited by Povl Engelstoft and Svend Dahl. 26 vols. and supplement. Copenhagen: J. H. Schultz. 1933–44. 3d edition. Edited by Sv. Cedergreen Bech. 16 vols. Copenhagen: Gyldendal. 1979–84.

DBS: *Dictionnaire historique & biographique de la Suisse*. Under the direction of Marcel Godet, Henri Türler, and Victor Attinger. 7 vols. and supplement. Neuchatel: Administration du Dictionnaire Historique et Biographique de la Suisse. 1921–34.

Dean, Warren. 1995. *With broadax and firebrand: the destruction of the Brazilian Atlantic forest.* Berkeley, Calif., and London: University of California Press.

De Beer, Gavin, ed. 1959a. Some unpublished letters of Charles Darwin. *Notes and Records of the Royal Society of London* 14: 12–66.

——, ed. 1959b. Darwin's journal. *Bulletin of the British Museum (Natural History). Historical Series* 2 (1959–63): 3–21.

Descent: *The descent of man, and selection in relation to sex.* By Charles Darwin. 2 vols. London: John Murray. 1870–1.

Desmond, Adrian. 1994–7. *Huxley.* 2 vols. London: Michael Joseph.

Desmond, Ray. 1992. *The European discovery of the Indian flora.* Oxford: Oxford University Press [in association with the] Royal Botanic Gardens.

——. 1994. *Dictionary of British and Irish botanists and horticulturists including plant collectors, flower painters and garden designers.* New edition, revised with the assistance of Christine Ellwood. London: Taylor & Francis and the Natural History Museum. Bristol, Pa.: Taylor & Francis.

——. 1995. *Kew: the history of the Royal Botanic Gardens.* London: Harvill Press with the Royal Botanic Gardens, Kew.

——. 1999. *Sir Joseph Dalton Hooker, traveller and plant collector.* Woodbridge, Suffolk: Antique Collectors' Club with the Royal Botanic Gardens, Kew.

Dexter, Ralph W. 1986. Historical aspects of the Calaveras skull controversy. *American Antiquity* 51: 365–9.

DIA: *A dictionary of Irish artists.* By Walter G. Strickland. 2 vols. Dublin and London: Maunsel & Co. 1913.

Dickens, Charles. 1838. *Oliver Twist; or the parish boy's progress.* 3 vols. London: Richard Bentley.

Dictionnaire des lettres françaises. Le dix-neuvième siècle. 2 vols. Edited by Georges Grente. Paris: Fayard. 1971–2.

Dictionnaire universel des contemporains: *Dictionnaire universel des contemporains contenant toutes les personnes notables de la France et des pays étrangers . . . Ouvrage rédigé et continuellement tenu à jour avec le concours d'écrivains et des savants de tous les pays.* Edited by Louis Gustave Vapereau. Paris: Libraire Hachette. 1858. 3d edition, 1865. 4th edition, 1870. 5th edition, 1880. 6th edition, 1893.

Dieffenbach, Ernst, trans. 1844. *Reisen nach den Inseln der grünen Vorgebirges, Südamerika, die Feuerlande, den Falkland-Inseln, Chiloe-Inseln, Galapagos-Inseln, Othaheiti, Neuholland,*

Neuseeland, Van Diemen's Land, Keeling-Inseln, Mauritius, St. Helena, den Azoren &c by Charles Darwin. 2 vols. Braunschweig: Vieweg und Sohn.

'Dimorphic condition in *Primula*': On the two forms, or dimorphic condition, in the species of *Primula*, and on their remarkable sexual relations. By Charles Darwin. [Read 21 November 1861.] *Journal of the Proceedings of the Linnean Society* (*Botany*) 6 (1862): 77–96. [*Collected papers* 2: 45–63.]

'Distribution of erratic boulders': On the distribution of the erratic boulders and on the contemporaneous unstratified deposits of South America. [Read 14 April 1841.] *Transactions of the Geological Society of London* 2d ser. 6 (1842): 415–31. [*Collected papers* 1: 145–63.]

Dixon, Edmund Saul. 1851. *The dovecote and the aviary: being sketches of the natural history of pigeons and other domestic birds in a captive state, with hints for their management.* London: John Murray.

DNB: *Dictionary of national biography.* Edited by Leslie Stephen and Sidney Lee. 63 vols. and 2 supplements (6 vols.). London: Smith, Elder & Co. 1885–1912. *Dictionary of national biography 1912–90.* Edited by H. W. C. Davis *et al.* 9 vols. London: Oxford University Press. 1927–96.

DNZB: *A dictionary of New Zealand biography.* Edited by G. H. Scholefield. 2 vols. Wellington, New Zealand: Department of Internal Affairs. 1940. *The dictionary of New Zealand biography.* Edited by W. H. Oliver *et al.* 5 vols. Auckland and Wellington, New Zealand: Department of Internal Affairs [and others]. 1990–2000.

Dod's parliamentary companion: *The parliamentary pocket companion . . . compiled from official documents, and from the personal communications of members of both houses. Dod's parliamentary companion.* London: Whittaker, Treacher, & Arnot; Whittaker & Co. 1833–1914.

Dohrn, Felix Anton. 1865. Die Darwin'sche Theorie und das Experiment. *Entomologische Zeitung* 26: 238–41.

Dowson, John. 1861. *Erasmus Darwin: philosopher, poet, and physician. A lecture to the Literary and Philosophical Society of Whitby.* London: H. K. Lewis.

Doyne, William Thomas. 1864. *Report upon the plains and rivers of Canterbury, New Zealand.* [Illustrated by plans and sections.] 20th June 1864. Christchurch: Printed at the Press Office, Cork-Street.

——. 1865. *Second report upon the River Waimakariri and the lower plains of Canterbury, New Zealand.* [Illustrated by plans and sections.] 30th November 1865. Christchurch: Printed at the Press Office, Cashel-Street.

Dressler, Robert L. 1981. *The orchids: natural history and classification.* Cambridge, Mass., and London: Harvard University Press.

——. 1993. *Phylogeny and classification of the orchid family.* Cambridge: Cambridge University Press.

DSAB: *Dictionary of South African biography.* Edited by W. J. de Kock *et al.* 4 vols. Pretoria and Cape Town: Nasionale Boekhandel Beperk [and others]. 1968–81.

DSB: *Dictionary of scientific biography.* Edited by Charles Coulston Gillispie and Frederic L. Holmes. 18 vols. including index and supplements. New York: Charles Scribner's Sons. 1970–90.

[Dubois, Henry A.] 1865. The orgin and antiquity of man: Darwin, Huxley and Lyell. *American Quarterly Church Review and Ecclesiastical Register* 17: 169–98, 337–66, 505–34.

Ducker, Sophie C., ed. 1988. *The contented botanist. Letters of W. H. Harvey about Australia and the Pacific.* Carlton, Victoria: Melbourne University Press.

Duméril, Auguste. 1866. Observations sur la reproduction dans la ménagerie des reptiles du Muséum d'Histoire Naturelle des axolotls, batraciens urodèles a branchies extérieures du Mexique: sur leurs développement et sur leurs métamorphoses. *Nouvelles Archives du Muséum d'Histoire Naturelle* 2: 265–92.

Duncan, David. 1908. *The life and letters of Herbert Spencer.* London: Methuen & Co.

Dupree, Anderson Hunter. 1959. *Asa Gray, 1810–1888.* Cambridge, Mass.: Belknap Press of Harvard University.

Duvernoy, Johann Georg. 1834. *Untersuchungen über Keimung, Bau und Wachsthum der Monokotyledonen.* Stuttgart: Fr. Brodhag'sche Buchh.

EB: *The Encyclopædia Britannica. A dictionary of arts, sciences, literature and general information.* 11th edition. 29 vols. Cambridge: Cambridge University Press. 1910–11.

Ehrenberg, Christian Gottfried. 1862. Über die seit 27 Jahren noch wohl erhaltenen Organisations-Präparate des mikroskopischen Lebens. *Abhandlungen der Königlichen Akademie der Wissenschaften zu Berlin* (1862): 39–74.

——. 1866. Über einen Phytolitharien-Tuff als Gebirgsart im Toluca-Thale von Mexico. *Monatsberichte der Königlich Preussischen Akademie der Wissenschaften zu Berlin* (1866): 158–68.

Ehrlich, Eugene. 1985. *Nil desperandum. A dictionary of Latin tags and useful phrases.* London: Robert Hale.

EI: *Enciclopedia Italiana di scienze, lettere ed arti.* 35 vols. Rome: Istituto della Enciclopedia Italiana. 1929–39.

Eliot, George. 1866. *Felix Holt: the radical.* Edinburgh and London: William Blackwood and sons.

Ellegård, Alvar. 1990. *Darwin and the general reader: the reception of Darwin's theory of evolution in the British periodical press, 1859–1872.* Reprint edition. Chicago and London: University of Chicago Press.

Emma Darwin (1904): *Emma Darwin, wife of Charles Darwin. A century of family letters.* Edited by Henrietta Litchfield. 2 vols. Cambridge: privately printed by Cambridge University Press. 1904.

Emma Darwin (1915): *Emma Darwin: a century of family letters, 1792–1896.* Edited by Henrietta Litchfield. 2 vols. London: John Murray. 1915.

Endersby, Jim. 2003. Darwin on generation, pangenesis and sexual selection. In *The Cambridge companion to Darwin*, edited by Jonathan Hodge and Gregory Radick. Cambridge: Cambridge University Press.

Endlicher, Stephan Ladislaus. 1836–42. *Genera plantarum secundum ordines naturales disposita.* 2 vols. including 4 supplements. Vienna: Friedrich Beck.

Engels, Eve-Marie, ed. 1995. *Die Rezeption von Evolutionstheorien im neunzehnten*

Jahrhundert. Suhrkamp Taschenbuch Wissenschaft, Nr. 1229. Frankfurt am Main: Suhrkamp.

English cyclopædia: *The English cyclopædia. A new dictionary of universal knowledge.* 22 vols. and 4 supplements. Conducted by Charles Knight. London: Bradbury and Evans. 1854–73.

Eton school lists: *The Eton school lists, from 1791 to 1850.* With short notes by H. E. C. Stapylton. 2d edition. London: Williams. 1864.

Evans, George Eyre. 1897. *Vestiges of Protestant dissent: being lists of ministers . . . included in the National Conference of Unitarian, Liberal Christian, Free Christian, Presbyterian, and other . . . congregations.* Liverpool: F. & E. Gibbons.

Expression: *The expression of the emotions in man and animals.* By Charles Darwin. London: John Murray. 1872.

Fagan, Louis. 1880. *The life of Sir Anthony Panizzi, K.C.B.* 2 vols. London: Remington & Co.

Fairholme, Edward G. and Pain, Wellesley. 1924. *A century of work for animals: the history of the R.S.P.C.A., 1824–1924.* London: John Murray.

Falconer, Hugh. 1863. On the American fossil elephant of the regions bordering the Gulf of Mexico (*E. Columbi*, Falc.); with general observations on the living and extinct species. *Natural History Review* n.s. 3: 43–114.

Farrar, Frederic William. 1857. *The people of England. A lecture, delivered before the Harrow Literary Institution, October 13th, 1857.* London: Longman, Brown, Green, Longmans, and Roberts. Harrow: W. Winkley, Jun.

——. 1860. *An essay on the origin of language, based on modern researches, and especially on the works of M. Renan.* London: John Murray.

——. 1864a. Traditions, real and fictitious. [Read 23 February 1864.] *Transactions of the Ethnological Society of London* n.s. 3 (1865): 298–307.

——. 1864b. On the universality of belief in God, and in a future state. [Read 5 April 1864.] *Anthropological Review* 2: ccxvii–ccxix.

——. 1864c. On hybridity. [Read 5 April 1864.] *Anthropological Review* 2: ccxxii–ccxxv.

——. 1864d. Fixity of type. [Read 8 November 1864.] *Transactions of the Ethnological Society of London* 3 (1865): 394–9.

——. 1865. *Chapters on language.* London: Longmans, Green, and Co.

Feduccia, Alan. 1996. *The origin and evolution of birds.* New Haven and London: Yale University Press.

'Fertilization of orchids': Notes on the fertilization of orchids. By Charles Darwin. *Annals and Magazine of Natural History* 4th ser. 4 (1869): 141–59. [*Collected papers* 2: 138–56.]

Filmer, J. L. 1977. The Norman family of Bromley Common. *Bromley Local History* 2: 16–24.

FitzRoy, Robert. 1860. On British storms, illustrated with diagrams and charts. *Report of the 30th meeting of the British Association for the Advancement of Science, held at Oxford*, Transactions of the sections, pp. 39–44.

Fleming, James Rodger. 1998. Charles Lyell and climatic change: speculation and certainty. In *Lyell: the past is the key to the present*, edited by Derek J. Blundell and Andrew C. Scott. London: Geological Society.

Fontaines, Una des, ed. 1968. The Wedgwood collection of Sir Joseph Dalton Hooker, M.D., F.R.S. (1817–1911). *Proceedings of the Wedgwood Society* 7: 163–85.

Forbes, Edward. 1845. On the distribution of endemic plants, more especially those of the British Islands, considered with regard to geological changes. *Report of the 15th meeting of the British Association for the Advancement of Science held at Cambridge*, Transactions of the sections, pp. 67–8.

——. 1846. On the connexion between the distribution of the existing fauna and flora of the British Isles, and the geological changes which have affected their area, especially during the epoch of the Northern Drift. *Memoirs of the Geological Survey of Great Britain, and of the Museum of Economic Geology in London* 1: 336–432.

Foreign Office list: *The Foreign Office list.* London: Harrison & Sons. 1852–1965.

Forgan, Sophie and Gooday, Graeme. 1994. 'A fungoid assemblage of buildings': diversity and adversity in the development of college architecture and scientific education in nineteenth-century South Kensington. *History of Universities* 13: 153–92.

'Formation of mould': On the formation of mould. [Read 1 November 1837.] *Transactions of the Geological Society of London* 2d ser. 5 (1840): 505–9. [*Collected papers* 1: 49–53.]

Forms of flowers: *The different forms of flowers on plants of the same species.* By Charles Darwin. London: John Murray. 1877.

Fossil Cirripedia (1851): *A monograph on the fossil Lepadidæ, or, pedunculated cirripedes of Great Britain.* By Charles Darwin. London: Palaeontographical Society. 1851.

Fossil Cirripedia (1854): *A monograph of the fossil Balanidæ and Verrucidæ of Great Britain.* By Charles Darwin. London: Palaeontographical Society. 1854.

Fossil Mammalia: Pt 1 of *The zoology of the voyage of H.M.S. Beagle . . . during the years 1831 to 1836.* By Richard Owen. Edited and superintended by Charles Darwin. London: Smith, Elder and Co. 1839–43.

Foster, Michael and Lankester, Edwin Ray, eds. 1898–1903. *The scientific memoirs of Thomas Henry Huxley.* 4 vols. and supplement. London: Macmillan. New York: D. Appleton.

Frankland, Edward. 1864a. On the glacial epoch. [Read January 29 1864.] *Proceedings of the Royal Institution of Great Britain* 4 (1862–6): 166–176.

——. 1864b. On the physical cause of the glacial epoch. *Philosophical Magazine* 4th ser. 27: 321–41.

——. 1866. On the source of muscular power. [Read 8 June 1866.] *Proceedings of the Royal Institution of Great Britain* 4 (1862–6): 661–85.

Freeman, Richard Broke. 1977. *The works of Charles Darwin: an annotated bibliographical handlist.* 2d edition. Folkestone, Kent: William Dawson & Sons. Hamden, Conn.: Archon Books, Shoe String Press.

——. 1978. *Charles Darwin: a companion.* Folkestone, Kent: William Dawson & Sons.

Hamden, Conn.: Archon Books, Shoe String Press.

——. 1984. *Darwin pedigrees*. London: printed for the author.

Furkert, Frederick William. 1953. *Early New Zealand engineers*. Revised and edited by William Langston Newnham. Wellington, NZ: A. H. & A. W. Reed.

Galetti, M. 2002. Seed dispersal of mimetic seeds: parasitism, mutualism, aposematism or exaptation? In *Seed dispersal and frugivory: ecology, evolution and conservation*, edited by D. Levey, *et al*. New York: CABI Publishing.

Gardner, George. 1843. Contributions towards a flora of Brazil. II. Plants from the Organ Mountains. *London Journal of Botany* 2: 329–55.

——. 1845. Contributions towards a flora of Brazil, being the distinctive characters of a century of new species of plants from the Organ Mountains. *London Journal of Botany* 4: 97–136.

——. 1846a. *Travels in the interior of Brazil, principally through the northern provinces and the gold and diamond districts, during the years 1836–1841*. London: Reeve, Brothers.

——. 1846b. The vegetation of the Organ mountains of Brazil. *Journal of the Horticultural Society of London* 1: 273–86.

Gärtner, Karl Friedrich von. 1849. *Versuche und Beobachtungen über die Bastarderzeugung im Pflanzenreich. Mit Hinweisung auf die ähnlichen Erscheinungen im Thierreiche, ganz umgearbeitete und sehr vermehrte Ausgabe der von der Königlich holländischen Akademie der Wissenschaften*. Stuttgart: E. Schweizerbart.

Gaudry, Albert. 1862. Sur le singe fossile de Grèce. *Bulletin de la Société Géologique de France* 2d ser. 19: 1022–5.

——. 1862–7. *Animaux fossiles et géologie de l'Attique, d'après les recherches faites en 1855–56 et en 1860 sous les auspices de l'Académie des Sciences*. 1 vol. and atlas. Paris: Libraire de la Société Géologique de France.

——. 1866. *Considérations générales sur les animaux fossiles de Pikermi*. Extract from *Animaux fossiles et géologie de l'Attique*. Paris: F. Savy.

Geinitz, Hans Bruno, ed. 1865. *Geologie der Steinkohlen Deutschland's und anderer Länder Europa's, mit Hinblick auf ihre technische Verwendung*. München: R. Oldenbourg.

Geison, Gerald L. 1969. Darwin and heredity: the evolution of his hypothesis of pangenesis. *Journal of the History of Medicine* 24: 375–411.

'Geology of the Falkland Islands': On the geology of the Falkland Islands. By Charles Darwin. [Read 25 March 1846.] *Quarterly Journal of the Geological Society of London* 2 (1846): 267–74. [*Collected papers* 1: 203–12.]

George, J. David and George, Jennifer J. 1979. *Marine life: an illustrated encyclopedia of invertebrates in the sea*. London: Harrap.

Gilbert, Pamela. 1977. *A compendium of the biographical literature on deceased entomologists*. London: British Museum (Natural History).

Gladstone, Hugh S. 1913. *The history of the Dumfriesshire and Galloway Natural History and Antiquarian Society*. Dumfries: Dumfriesshire and Galloway Natural History and Antiquarian Society.

Glick, Thomas F., ed. 1988. *The comparative reception of Darwinism*. With a new preface. Chicago and London: University of Chicago Press.

Göppert, Heinrich Robert. 1864. Ueber Aphyllostachys, eine neue fossile Pflanzengattung aus der Gruppe der Calamarien, so wie über das Verhältniss der fossilen Flora zu Darwin's Transmutation-Theorie. *Verhandlungen der Kaiserlichen Leopoldino-Carolinischen deutschen Akademie der Naturforscher* 32 (1865): (III) 1–16.

———. 1865a. Über die Darwin'sche Transmutations-Theorie mit Beziehung auf die fossilen Pflanzen. *Neues Jahrbuch für Mineralogie, Geologie und Palaeontologie* (1865): 296–300.

———. 1865b. Über die Flora der Permischen Formation. *Neues Jahrbuch für Mineralogie, Geologie und Palaeontologie* (1865): 301–6.

Gould, John. 1861a. *An introduction to the Trochilidæ, or family of humming-birds*. London: privately printed.

———. 1861b. *A monograph of the Trochilidæ, or family of humming-birds*. 5 vols. London: John Gould.

Gould, Stephen Jay. 1977. *Ontogeny and phylogeny*. Cambridge, Mass.; London: Belknap Press of Harvard University Press.

———. 1990. *Wonderful life. The Burgess Shale and the nature of history*. London: Hutchinson Radius.

———. 1997. *The mismeasure of man*. Revised and expanded edition. London: Penguin Books.

Grande encyclopédie: *La grande encyclopédie inventaire raisonné des sciences, des lettres et des arts*. Edited by F. Camille Dreyfus *et al.* 31 vols. Paris: H. Lamirault; Société Anonyme de la Grande Encyclopédie. [1886–1902.]

Graves, Algernon. 1905–6. *The Royal Academy of Arts. A complete dictionary of contributors and their work from its foundation in 1769 to 1904*. 8 vols. London: Henry Graves and Co.; George Bell and Sons.

Gray, Asa. 1858. *Introduction to structural and systematic botany, and vegetable physiology, being a fifth and revised edition of the botanical text-book*. New York: Ivison & Phinney.

[———.] 1860. Darwin on the origin of species. *Atlantic Monthly* 6: 109–16, 229–39; Darwin and his reviewers. *Atlantic Monthly* 6: 406–25.

———. 1865. Spontaneous return of hybrid plants to their parental forms. *American Journal of Science and Arts* 2d ser. 39: 107–8.

———. 1865–6. On the movements and habits of climbing plants; by Charles Darwin. *American Journal of Science and Arts* 2d ser. 40: 273–82, 41: 125–30.

———. 1866. Note on a regular dimerous flower of Cypripedium candidum. *American Journal of Science and Arts* 2d ser. 42: 195.

———. 1867. *Manual of the botany of the northern United States*. 5th edition. New York: Ivison, Phinney, Blakeman & Co.

Gray, John Edward. 1860. Revision of the family Pennatulidæ, with descriptions of some new species in the British Museum. *Annals and Magazine of Natural History* 3d ser. 5: 20–5.

———. 1866. *Catalogue of seals and whales in the British Museum*. 2d edition. London: Trustees of the British Museum.

———. 1869. *Catalogue of carnivorous, pachydermatous, and edentate mammalia in the British*

Museum. London: printed by order of the trustees [of the British Museum].

——. 1870. *Catalogue of monkeys, lemurs, and fruit-eating bats in the collection of the British Museum*. London: printed by order of the trustees [of the British Museum].

Greenaway, Frank, ed. 1976. *The archives of the Royal Institution of Great Britain in facsimile: minutes of managers' meeting 1799–1900*. Vols. 11 and 12. Ilkley and London: Scolar Press.

Greg, William Rathbone. 1851. *The creed of Christendom; its foundations and superstructure*. London: J. Chapman.

Grenier, Jean Charles Marie and Godron, Dominique Alexandre. 1848–56. *Flore de France, ou description des plantes qui croissent naturellement en France et en Corse*. 3 vols. Paris: J. B. Baillière.

Griffith, William. 1847–8. *Journals of travels in Assam, Burma, Bootan, Affghanistan and the neighbouring countries*. 2 vols. Arranged by John M'Clelland. Calcutta: Bishop's College Press.

Griffiths, Mervyn. 1978. *The biology of the monotremes*. New York: Academic Press.

Grove, George. 1980. *The new Grove dictionary of music and musicians*. Edited by Stanley Sadie. 20 vols. London: Macmillan.

Grove, William Robert. 1866. Address of the president. *Report of the thirty-sixth meeting of the British Association for the Advancement of Science, held at Nottingham*, pp. liii–lxxxii.

Grzimek, Bernhard, ed. 1972. *Mammals*. Vol. 13 of *Grzimek's animal life encyclopedia*. New York: Van Nostrand Reinhold Company.

——, ed. 1974. *Fishes II and Amphibia*. Vol. 5 of *Grzimek's animal life encyclopedia*. New York: Van Nostrand Reinhold Company.

GSE: *Great Soviet encyclopedia*. Edited by Jean Paradise *et al.* 31 vols. to date, and index to vols. 1–20. New York: Macmillan. London: Collier Macmillan. 1973–. [Translation of the 3d edition of *Bol'shaia Sovetskaia entsiklopediia*, edited by A. M. Prokhorov.]

Günther, Albert Charles Lewis Gotthilf. 1864–6. An account of the fishes of the states of Central America, based on collections made by Capt. J. M. Dow, F. Godman, Esq., and O. Salvin, Esq. [Read 22 March 1864 and 13 December 1866.] *Transactions of the Zoological Society of London* 6 (1869): 377–494.

Gunther, Albert E. 1975. *A century of zoology at the British Museum through the lives of two keepers, 1815–1914*. London: Dawsons of Pall Mall.

Gwynn, Stephen and Tuckwell, Gertrude M. 1917. *The life of the Rt. Hon. Sir Charles W. Dilke*. 2 vols. London: John Murray.

Haast, Heinrich Ferdinand von. 1948. *The life and times of Sir Julius von Haast, explorer, geologist, museum builder*. Wellington, New Zealand: privately published.

Haast, John Francis Julius von. 1864. Glacial deposits in New Zealand. *Natural History Review* n.s. 4: 474–6.

——. 1865. Lecture on the West Coast of Canterbury. [Read 25 September 1865.] *Lyttelton Times*, 28 and 29 September 1865.

——. 1866. *Report on the head-waters of the Rakaia*. Christchurch: government of Canterbury province.

Haast, John Francis Julius von. 1867. Notes on the geology of the province of Canterbury, N.Z., principally in reference to the deposits of the glacial epoch at the western base of the Southern Alps. *Quarterly Journal of the Geological Society* 23: 342–52.

——. 1870. Notes to accompany the topographical map of the Southern Alps, in the province of Canterbury, New Zealand. *Journal of the Royal Geographical Society* 40: 433.

Hadfield, Miles, *et al.* 1980. *British gardeners. A biographical dictionary.* London: A. Zwemmer in association with The Condé Nast Publications.

Haeckel, Ernst. 1864. Beschreibung neuer craspedoter Medusen aus dem Golfe von Nizza. *Jenaische Zeitschrift für Medicin und Naturwissenschaft* 1: 325–42.

——. 1865a. Über den Sarcodekörper der Rhizopoden. *Zeitschrift für wissenschaftliche Zoologie* 15: 342–70.

——. 1865b. *Die Familie der Rüsselquallen (Geryonida.)* Vol. I of *Beiträge zur Naturgeschichte der Hydromedusen.* Leipzig: Wilhelm Engelmann.

——. 1865c. Über fossile Medusen. *Zeitschrift für wissenschaftliche Zoologie* 15: 504–14

——. 1865d. Über eine neue Form des Generationswechsels bei den Medusen und über die Verwandtschaft der Geryoniden und Aeginiden. *Monatsberichte der Königlichen Preußs. Akademie der Wissenschaften zu Berlin* (1865): 85–94.

——. 1866. *Generelle Morphologie der Organismen. Allgemeine Grundzüge der organischen Formen-Wissenschaft, mechanisch begründet durch die von Charles Darwin reformirte Descendenz-Theorie.* 2 vols. Berlin: Georg Reimer.

Haines, Valerie A. 1991. Spencer, Darwin, and the question of reciprocal influence. *Journal of the History of Biology* 24: 409–31.

Hall, Marie Boas. 1984. *All scientists now: the Royal Society in the nineteenth century.* Cambridge: Cambridge University Press.

Hall, Philip B. 1987. Robert Swinhoe (1836–1877), FRS, FZS, FRGS: a Victorian naturalist in Treaty Port China. *Geographical Journal* 153: 37–47.

Hallier, Ernst. 1865. *Darwin's Lehre und die Specification.* Hamburg: Otto Meissner.

Harcourt, Edward William Vernon. 1855. Notes on the ornithology of Madeira. *Annals and Magazine of Natural History* 2d ser. 15: 430–8.

Harpe, Philippe de and Salter, John William. 1862. Notes on the Eocene flora of Alum Bay, &c. In *Memoirs of the Geological Survey of Great Britain and of the Museum of Practical Geology. The geology of the Isle of Wight*, by Henry William Bristow. London: Longman, Green, Longman, & Roberts.

Hart's army list: *The new annual army list . . . with an index.* Compiled by H. G. Hart. London: John Murray. 1840–1900.

Hartt, Charles Frederick. 1870. *Thayer Expedition: scientific results of a journey in Brazil by Louis Agassiz and his travelling companions: geology and physical geography of Brazil.* Boston, Mass.: Fields, Osgood, & Co.

Hartung, Georg. 1864. *Geologische Beschreibung der Inseln Madeira und Porto Santo.* Leipzig: W. Engelmann.

Harvey, William Henry. 1846–51. *Phycologia Britannica: or a history of British sea-weeds.*

4 vols. London: Reeve and Benham.

——. 1859–63. *Thesaurus Capensis: or, illustrations of the South African flora, being figures and brief descriptions of South African plants selected from the Dublin University Herbarium.* 2 vols. in 1. Dublin: Hodges, Smith & Co. London: John van Voorst.

Haught, John F. 2000. *God after Darwin: a theology of evolution.* Oxford and Boulder, Colo.: Westview Press.

Haughton, Samuel. 1865. *Manual of geology.* London: Longman, Green, Longman, Roberts, and Green.

Hazlewood, Nick. 2000. *Savage. The life and times of Jemmy Button.* London: Hodder and Stoughton.

Heer, Oswald. 1855. Ueber die fossilen Pflanzen von St. Jorge in Madeira. [Read 5 November 1855.] *Neue Denkschriften der allgemeinen Schweizerischen Gesellschaft für die gesammten Naturwissenschaften* n.s. 5 (1857): paper 2.

——. 1860. *Untersuchungen über das Klima und die Vegetationsverhältnisse des Tertiärlandes.* Winterthur, Switzerland: Anstalt von Wurster.

——. 1865. *Die Urwelt der Schweiz.* Zurich: Friedrich Schulthess.

Hennessy, Henry. 1864. On the possible conditions of geological climate. *Report of the thirty-fourth meeting of the British Association for the Advancement of Science, held at Bath*, Transactions of the sections, pp. 55–7.

[Henslow, George]. 1863. Phosphate nodules. *Leisure Hour* 12: 436–8.

——. 1864. The wild flowers of Shakespeare. *Leisure Hour* 13: 229–31.

——. 1865. Note on the structure of *Medicago sativa*, as apparently affording facilities for the intercrossing of distinct flowers. [Read 16 November 1865.] *Journal of the Linnean Society (Botany)* 9 (1867): 327–9.

——. 1866a. Note on the structure of *Indigofera*, as apparently offering facilities for the intercrossing of distinct flowers. [Read 19 April 1866.] *Journal of the Linnean Society (Botany)* 9 (1867): 355–8.

——. 1866b. On hybridization among plants. *Popular Science Review* 5: 304–13.

——. 1866c. On the phenomena of motion and sensitiveness in climbing plants. *Popular Science Review* 5: 55–65.

Herbert, William. 1837. *Amaryllidaceæ; preceded by an attempt to arrange the monocotyledonous orders, and followed by a treatise on cross-bred vegetables, and supplement.* London: James Ridgway & Sons.

——. 1846. On hybridization amongst vegetables. [Read 14 October 1846.] *Journal of the Horticultural Society of London* 2: 1–28, 81–107.

Herschel, John Frederick William. 1830. On the astronomical causes which may influence geological phænomena. [Read 15 December 1830.] *Transactions of the Geological Society of London* 2d ser. 3 (1835): 293–9.

——, ed. 1849. *A manual of scientific enquiry; prepared for the use of Her Majesty's Navy: and adapted for travellers in general.* London: John Murray.

Heuss, Theodor. 1991. *Anton Dohrn: a life for science.* Translated from the German by Liselotte Dieckmann. Berlin: Springer Verlag.

Hevly, Bruce. 1996. The heroic science of glacier motion. *Osiris* 11: 66–86.

Hewitt, Edward. 1864. Hen pheasant assuming the plumage of the male bird. *Journal of Horticulture and Cottage Gardener* n.s. 6 (1864): 37–8.

Hildebrand, Friedrich Hermann Gustav. 1863. Die Fruchtbildung der Orchideen, ein Beweis für die doppelte Wirkung des Pollen. *Botanische Zeitung* 21: 329–33, 337–45.

——. 1865a. Experimente zur Dichogamie und zum Dimorphismus. *Botanische Zeitung* 23: 1–6, 13–15.

——. 1865b. Darwin, über die geschlechtlichen Beziehungen der 3 Formen von *Lythrum Salicaria. Botanische Zeitung* 23: 50–2.

——. 1865c. Bastardirungsversuche an Orchideen. *Botanische Zeitung* 23: 245–9.

——. 1866a. Ueber die Vorrichtungen an einigen Blüthen zur Befruchtung durch Insektenhülfe. *Botanische Zeitung* 24: 73–8.

——. 1866b. Ueber die Befruchtung der Salviaarten mit Hülfe von Insekten. *Jahrbücher für wissenschaftliche Botanik* 4 (1865–6): 451–78.

——. 1866c. Über den *Trimorphismus* der Blüthen in der Gattung *Oxalis*. *Monatsberichte der Königlich Preussischen Akademie der Wissenschaften zu Berlin* (1866): 352–74.

——. 1866d. On the necessity for insect agency in the fertilisation of *Corydalis cava. International Horticultural Exhibition* 1866, pp. 157–8.

——. 1866–7a. Ueber die Befruchtung von Aristolochia Clematitis und einiger anderer Aristolochia-Arten. *Jahrbücher für wissenschaftliche Botanik* 5: 343–58.

——. 1866–7b. Ueber die Nothwendigkeit der Insektenhülfe bei der Befruchtung von Corydalis cava. *Jarhbücher für wissenschaftliche Botanik* 5 (1866–7): 359–63.

——. 1867. *Die Geschlechter-Vertheilung bei den Pflanzen und das Gesetz der vermiedenen und unvortheilhaften stetigen Selbstbefruchtung.* Leipzig: Wilhelm Engelmann.

Hincks, Thomas. 1861. Note on the ovicells of the cheilostomatous Polyzoa. [Read at the British Association, September 1861.] *Quarterly Journal of Microscopical Science* n.s. 1: 278–81.

Historical register of the University of Cambridge: *The historical register of the University of Cambridge, being a supplement to the* Calendar *with a record of university offices, honours, and distinctions to the year 1910*. Edited by J. R. Tanner. Cambridge: Cambridge University Press. 1917.

Historisches Lexikon der Schweiz. 2 vols. to date. Basel: Schwabe. 2002–.

Hitchcock, Edward. 1858. *Ichnology of New England. A report on the sandstone of the Connecticut valley, especially its fossil footmarks, made to the government of the Commonwealth of Massachusetts*. Boston: William White.

Hochstetter, Ferdinand von. 1959. *Geology of New Zealand. Contributions to the geology of the Provinces of Auckland and Nelson.* Translated from the German and edited by C. A. Fleming. Wellington: R. E. Owen.

Hodge, M. J. S. 1985. Darwin as a lifelong generation theorist. In *The Darwinian heritage*, edited by David Kohn. Princeton, N.J.: Princeton University Press in association with Nova Pacifica.

Hooker, Joseph Dalton. 1852. On the climate and vegetation of the temperate and cold regions of East Nepal and the Sikkim Himalaya Mountains. *Journal of the*

Horticultural Society of London 7: 69–131.

——. 1853–5. *Flora Novæ-Zelandiæ*. 2 vols. Pt 2 of *The botany of the Antarctic voyage of HM discovery ships* Erebus *and* Terror, *in the years 1839–1843, under the command of Captain Sir James Clark Ross*. London: Lovell Reeve.

——. 1854. *Himalayan journals; or, notes of a naturalist in Bengal, the Sikkim and Nepal Himalayas, the Khasia Mountains, &c.* 2 vols. London: John Murray.

——. 1859. *On the flora of Australia, its origin, affinities, and distribution; being an introductory essay to the flora of Tasmania*. London: Lovell Reeve.

——. 1860a. Outlines of the distribution of Arctic plants. [Read 21 June 1860.] *Transactions of the Linnean Society of London* 23 (1862): 251–348.

——. 1860b. *Flora Tasmaniæ*. 2 vols. Pt 3 of *The botany of the Antarctic voyage of HM discovery ships* Erebus *and* Terror, *in the years 1839–1843, under the command of Captain Sir James Clark Ross*. London: Reeve Brothers; Lovell Reeve.

——. 1861. On the vegetation of Clarence Peak, Fernando Po; with descriptions of the plants collected by Mr Gustav Mann on the higher parts of that mountain. [Read 7 March 1861.] *Journal of the Proceedings of the Linnean Society* (*Botany*) 6 (1862): 1–23.

——. 1862. On the cedars of Lebanon, Taurus, Algeria, and India. *Natural History Review* n.s. 2: 11–18.

——. 1863. On the plants of the temperate regions of the Cameroons Mountains and islands in the Bight of Benin; collected by Mr Gustav Mann, government botanist. [Read 5 November 1863.] *Journal of the Proceedings of the Linnean Society* (*Botany*) 7 (1864): 171–240.

——. 1864–7. *Handbook of the New Zealand flora: a systematic description of the native plants of New Zealand and the Chatham, Kermadec's, Lord Auckland's, Campbell's, and MacQuarrie's Islands*. 2 vols. London: Lovell Reeve & Co.

——. 1866a. Insular floras. [Read 27 August 1866.] *Gardeners' Chronicle* (1867): 6–7, 27, 50–1, 75–6.

——. 1866b. Abstract of Dr. Hooker's lecture on insular floras. In *The British Association for the Advancement of Science. Nottingham meeting, August, 1866. Report of the papers, discussions, and general proceedings*, edited by William Tindal Robertson. Nottingham: Thomas Forman. London: Robert Hardwicke.

——. 1866c. Considérations sur les flores insulaires. *Annales des Sciences Naturelles* (*Botanique*) 5th ser. 6: 267–99.

——. 1867. On insular floras: a lecture. *Journal of Botany* 5 (1867): 23–31.

Hooker, William Jackson, Sowerby, James de Carle [*et al.*]. 1831–63. *Supplement to the English Botany of the late Sir J. E. Smith and Mr. Sowerby*. 5 vols. London: n.p.

Huber, François. 1814. *Nouvelles observations sur les abeilles*. 2d edition. 2 vols. Paris and Geneva: J. J. Paschoud.

Huber, Jean Pierre. 1810. *Recherches sur les mœurs des fourmis indigènes*. Paris and Geneva: J. J. Paschoud.

Hull, David L. 1973. *Darwin and his critics: the reception of Darwin's theory of evolution by the scientific community*. Cambridge, Mass.: Harvard University Press.

Humboldt, Alexander von. 1846–58. *Cosmos: sketch of a physical description of the universe.* Translated [by Elizabeth Juliana Sabine] under the superintendence of Edward Sabine. 4 vols. London: Longman, Brown, Green, and Longmans; John Murray.

Humboldt, Alexander von and Bonpland, Aimé Jacques Alexandre. 1808–9. *Plantes equinoxiales, recueillies au Mexique, dans l'îsle de Cuba, dans les provinces de Caracas, de Cumana et de Barcelone, aux Andes de la Nouvelle- Grenade, de Quito et du Pérou, et sur les bords du Rio-Negro, de l'Orénoque et de la rivière des Amazones.* 2 vols. Paris: F. Schoell. Tübingen: J. G. Cotta.

——. 1822. *Personal narrative of travels to the equinoctial regions of the new continent, during the years 1799–1804. Volume 3.* Translated by Helen Maria Williams. 2d edition. London: Longman, Hurst, Rees, Orme, & Brown.

Humboldt, Alexander von, *et al.* 1815–25. *Nova genera et species plantarum quas in peregrinatione orbis novi collegerunt, descripserunt, partim adumbraverunt Amat. Bonpland et Alex. de Humboldt.* 7 vols. Pt 6 of *Voyage de Humboldt et Bonpland.* Paris: Libraire Grecque-Latine-Allemande [and others].

Hutchinson, Horace Gordon. 1914. *Life of Sir John Lubbock, Lord Avebury.* 2 vols. London: Macmillan.

Hutton, Frederick Wollaston. 1865. Notes on some of the birds inhabiting the southern ocean. [Read 3 March 1865.] *Ibis* n.s. 1: 276–98.

Huxley, Leonard, ed. 1900. *Life and letters of Thomas Henry Huxley.* 2 vols. London: Macmillan.

——, ed. 1918. *Life and letters of Sir Joseph Dalton Hooker, OM, GCSI.* Based on materials collected and arranged by Lady Hooker. 2 vols. London: John Murray.

Huxley, Thomas Henry. 1849. On the anatomy and the affinities of the family of the Medusæ. *Philosophical Transactions of the Royal Society of London* pt 2: 413–34. Reprinted in Foster and Lankester eds. 1898–1903, 1: 9–32.

——. 1863a. *Evidence as to man's place in nature.* London: Williams & Norgate.

——. 1863b. *On our knowledge of the causes of the phenomena of organic nature. Being six lectures to working men, delivered at the Museum of Practical Geology.* London: Robert Hardwicke.

——. 1866. *Lessons in elementary physiology.* London: Macmillan.

'Illegitimate offspring of dimorphic and trimorphic plants': On the character and hybrid-like nature of the offspring from the illegitimate unions of dimorphic and trimorphic plants. By Charles Darwin. [Read 20 February 1868.] *Journal of the Linnean Society of London* (*Botany*) 10 (1869): 393–437.

Imbrie, John and Imbrie, Katherine Palmer. 1979. *Ice Ages: solving the mystery.* London and Basingstoke: Macmillan Press.

Ince, Joseph, ed. 1876. *Science papers, chiefly pharmacological and botanical. By Daniel Hanbury.* London: Macmillan and Co.

Index biographique de l'Académie des Sciences: *Index biographique de l'Académie des Sciences du 22 décembre 1666 au 1er octobre 1978.* Paris: Gauthier-Villars. 1979.

India list: *The East-India register . . . from the official returns received at the East-India House. The India Office list . . . Compiled from official records by direction of the secretary of state for India in council.* London: Wm. H. Allen [and others]. 1806–1937.

Insectivorous plants. By Charles Darwin. London: John Murray. 1875.

International Horticultural Exhibition 1866: *International Horticultural Exhibition and Botanical Congress, held in London, from May 22nd to May 31st, 1866. Report of Proceedings.* London: Truscott, Son, & Simmons.

Jackson, Benjamin Daydon. 1906. *George Bentham.* London: J. M. Dent. New York: E. P. Dutton.

Jackson, Welby B. 1854. *Selections from the records of the Bengal Government. No. XVII. Report on Darjeeling.* Calcutta: Thos. Jones.

Jäger, Gustav. 1864. *Zoologische Briefe.* 1st issue. Vienna: Wilhelm Braumüller.

James, Henry. 1860. Description of the projection used in the Topographical Department of the War Office for maps embracing large portions of the earth's surface. *Journal of the Royal Geographical Society* 30: 106–11.

——. 1862. *Geometrical projection of two-thirds of the sphere.* Sir Henry James: Southampton.

——. 1868. *On the rectangular tangential projection of the sphere and spheroid.* Ordnance Survey Office: Southampton.

Jamieson, Thomas Francis. 1866. On the glacial phenomena of Caithness. *Quarterly Journal of the Geological Society of London* 22: 261–81.

Janet, Paul Alexandre René. 1863. Le matérialisme contemporain. Une théorie anglaise sur les causes finales. *Revue des deux mondes* 48: 556–86.

——. 1866. *The materialism of the present day. A critique of Dr. Büchner's system.* Translated from the French by Gustave Masson. London: H. Baillière.

Jardine, Nicholas. 1996. *Naturphilosophie* and the kingdoms of nature. In *Cultures of natural history*, edited by Nicholas Jardine *et al.* Cambridge: Cambridge University Press.

Jenkins, Brian. 1974–80. *Britain & the war for the Union.* 2 vols. Montreal, Quebec, and London: McGill-Queen's University Press.

Jenkins, Roy. 1995. *Gladstone.* London: Macmillan.

Johnson, William S. 1990. *Nineteenth-century photography: an annotated bibliography, 1839–1879.* Boston: G. K. Hall & Co.

Jones, Thomas Rupert, *et al.* 1866. *A monograph of the Foraminifera of the Crag*, part 1. London: Palaeontographical Society.

Jordan, Alexis. 1860. Diagnoses d'espèces nouvelles ou méconnues pour servir de matériaux à une flore de France réformée. *Annales de la Société Linnéenne de Lyon* 7: 373–518

——. 1864. *Diagnoses d'espèces nouvelles ou méconnues, pour servir de matériaux à une flore réformée de la France, et des contrées voisines.* Paris: F. Savy.

Journal and remarks: *Journal and remarks. 1832–1836.* By Charles Darwin. Vol. 3 of *Narrative of the surveying voyages of His Majesty's ships Adventure and Beagle between the years 1826 and 1836, describing their examination of the southern shores of South America, and the Beagle's circumnavigation of the globe.* London: Henry Colburn. 1839. [Separately published as *Journal of researches.*]

Journal of researches: *Journal of researches into the geology and natural history of the various countries visited by HMS Beagle, under the command of Captain FitzRoy, RN, from 1832 to 1836*. By Charles Darwin. London: Henry Colburn. 1839.

Journal of researches (1840): *Journal of researches into the geology and natural history of the various countries visited by HMS Beagle, under the command of Captain FitzRoy, RN, from 1832 to 1836*. By Charles Darwin. London: Henry Colburn. 1840.

Journal of researches 2d ed.: *Journal of researches into the natural history and geology of the countries visited during the voyage of HMS Beagle round the world, under the command of Capt. FitzRoy RN*. 2d edition, corrected, with additions. By Charles Darwin. London: John Murray. 1845.

Journal of researches (1852): *Journal of researches into the natural history and geology of the countries visited during the voyage of HMS Beagle round the world, under the command of Capt. FitzRoy RN*. New edition [2d edition]. By Charles Darwin. London: John Murray. 1852.

Journal of researches (1860): *Journal of researches into the natural history and geology of the countries visited during the voyage of HMS Beagle around the world, under the command of Capt. FitzRoy RN*. By Charles Darwin. Reprint edition. London: John Murray. 1860.

Jubiläums-Katalog: *Jubiläums-Katalog der E. Schweizerbart'schen Verlagsbuchhandlung (Erwin Nägele) G.m.b.H., Stuttgart, 1826–1926*. Stuttgart: E. Schweizerbart. 1926.

Junker, Thomas. 1989. *Darwinismus und Botanik. Rezeption, Kritik und theoretische Alternativen im Deutschland des 19. Jahrhunderts*. Stuttgart: Deutscher Apotheker Verlag.

Jurine, Louis. 1807. *Nouvelle méthode de classer les hyménoptères et les diptères*. Geneva: J. J. Paschoud.

Keats, John. 1820. *Lamia, Isabella, The eve of St. Agnes, and other poems*. London: Taylor and Hessey.

Kent, William. 1939. *London worthies*. London: Phoenix House.

Keynes, Margaret. 1943. *Leonard Darwin, 1850–1943*. Cambridge: privately printed at Cambridge University Press.

King, William and Rowney, T. H. 1866. On the so-called 'Eozoonal Rock'. *Quarterly Journal of the Geological Society of London* 22: 185–218.

King-Hele, Desmond. 1999. *Erasmus Darwin. A life of unequalled achievement*. London: Giles de la Mare Publishers.

Kingsley, Charles. 1866a. Superstition. A lecture delivered at the Royal Institution, April 24, 1866. *Fraser's Magazine* 73: 705–16.

——. 1866b. Science. A lecture delivered at the Royal Institution. *Fraser's Magazine* 74: 15–28.

Koenig, Johann Samuel. 1739. Lettre de Monsieur Koenig à Monsieur A. B., écrite de Paris à Berne le 29 novembre 1739 sur la construction des alvéoles des abeilles, avec quelques particularités littéraires. *Journal helvétique*, April 1740.

Kohn, David. 1980. Theories to work by: rejected theories, reproduction, and Darwin's path to natural selection. *Studies in History of Biology* 4: 67–170.

Kramp, Paul Lassenius. 1961. *Synopsis of the medusae of the world*. Special volume of

Journal of the Marine Biological Association 40.

Krauße, Erika. 1987. *Ernst Haeckel.* 2d edition. Leipzig: B. G. Teubner.

Kühn, Alfred. 1950. Anton Dohrn und die Zoologie seiner Zeit. *Pubblicazioni della stazione zoologica di Napoli* 22 (Supplement).

Lambert, David. 1985. *The Cambridge field guide to prehistoric life.* Cambridge: Cambridge University Press.

Leach, William Elford. 1852. *Molluscorum Britanniæ synopsis. A synopsis of the Mollusca of Great Britain, arranged according to their natural affinities and anatomical structure.* London: John Van Voorst.

Lecoq, Henri. 1847. *Des glaciers et des climats, ou des causes atmosphériques en géologie.* Paris: P. Bertrand.

——. 1854–8. *Etudes sur la géographie botanique de l'Europe et en particulier sur la végétation du plateau central de la France.* 9 vols. Paris: J. B. Baillière.

——. 1866. De la migration des plantes des montagnes. *International Horticultural Exhibition* 1866, pp. 158–65.

Leeder, M. R. 1998. Lyell's *Principles of geology*: foundations of sedimentology. In *Lyell: the past is the key to the present*, edited by Derek J. Blundell and Andrew C. Scott. London: Geological Society, special publications, 143.

Leonhard, Gustav, trans. 1844. *Ueber die älteren oder paläozoischen Gebilde im Norden von Deutschland und Belgien, verglichen mit Formationen desselben Alters in Grossbritannien, nebst einer Uebersicht der Fauna der paläozoischen Gebilde in den Rheinlanden.* By Adam Sedgwick and Roderick Impey Murchison. Stuttgart: E. Schweizerbart'sche Verlagshandlung und Druckerei.

——, trans. 1848. *Geologie des europäischen Rußlands und des Urals.* By Roderick Impey Murchison *et al.* Stuttgart: E. Schweizerbart'sche Verlagshandlung und Druckerei.

Lewis, Charlton T. and Short, Charles. 1969. *A Latin dictionary, founded on Andrews' edition of Freund's Latin dictionary.* Revised, enlarged, and in great part rewritten. Oxford: Clarendon Press.

Lindley, John. 1853. *The vegetable kingdom; or, the structure, classification, and uses of plants, illustrated upon the natural system.* 3d edition with corrections and additional genera. London: Bradbury & Evans.

——. 1859. *A synopsis of the British flora arranged according to the natural orders. Containing vasculares or flowering plants.* 3d edition. London: Longman, Brown, Green, Longmans, & Roberts.

Linnaeus (Carl von Linné). 1758–9. *Systema naturæ per regna tria naturæ, secundum classes, ordines, genera, species, cum characteribus, differentiis, synonymis, locis.* 10th edition. 2 vols. Stockholm: Laurentius Salvius.

List of the Geological Society of London. London: [Geological Society of London]. 1864–1934.

List of the Linnean Society of London. London: [Linnean Society of London]. 1805–1939.

List of the Royal Society. London: Royal Society. 1775–1924.

Lister, Raymond. 1981. *George Richmond: a critical biography.* London: Robin Garton.

Living Cirripedia (1851): *A monograph of the sub-class Cirripedia, with figures of all the species. The Lepadidæ; or, pedunculated cirripedes.* By Charles Darwin. London: Ray Society. 1851.

Living Cirripedia (1854): *A monograph of the sub-class Cirripedia, with figures of all the species. The Balanidæ (or sessile cirripedes); the Verrucidæ, etc.* By Charles Darwin. London: Ray Society. 1854.

LL: *The life and letters of Charles Darwin, including an autobiographical chapter.* Edited by Francis Darwin. 3 vols. London: John Murray. 1887–8.

Loudon, John Claudius. 1841. *An encyclopædia of plants.* London: Longman, Orme, Brown, Green, and Longmans.

Lowe, Richard Thomas. 1854. Catalogus Molluscorum pneumonatorum Insularum Maderensium: or a list of all the land and fresh-water shells, recent and fossil, of the Madeiran Islands. *Proceedings of the Zoological Society of London* pt 22: 161–218.

——. 1868. *A manual flora of Madeira and the adjacent islands of Porto Santo and the Desertas.* Vol. 1, *Dichlamydeæ.* London: John van Voorst.

Lubbock, John. 1858. On the ova and pseudova of insects. [Read 9 December 1858.] *Philosophical Transactions of the Royal Society of London* 149 (1859): 341–69.

——. 1865. *Pre-historic times, as illustrated by ancient remains, and the manners and customs of modern savages.* London and Edinburgh: Williams & Norgate.

——. 1866a. On the metamorphoses of insects. [Read before the Royal Institution of Great Britain, 9 March 1866.] *Annals and Magazine of Natural History* 3d ser. 17: 375–81.

——. 1866b. On *Pauropus*, a new type of centipede. [Read 6 December 1866.] *Journal of the Linnean Society (Zoology)* 9 (1867): 179–80.

Lucas, Peter. 2002a. 'A most glorious country': Charles Darwin and North Wales, especially his 1831 geological tour. *Archives of Natural History* 29: 1–26.

——. 2002b. Jigsaw with pieces missing: Charles Darwin with John Price at Bodnant, the walking tour of 1826 and the expeditions of 1827. *Archives of Natural History* 29: 359–70.

Lurie, Edward. 1960. *Louis Agassiz: a life in science.* Chicago: University of Chicago Press.

Luteyn, James L. 2002. Key to the species of Ericaceae of Bolivia, including two new species. *Sida, Contributions to Botany* 20: 1–20.

Lyell, Charles. 1830–3. *Principles of geology, being an attempt to explain the former changes of the earth's surface, by reference to causes now in operation.* 3 vols. London: John Murray.

——. 1840. On ancient sea cliffs and needles in the chalk of the valley of the Seine in Normandy. *Report of the tenth meeting of the British Association for the Advancement of Science held at Southampton*, Transaction of the sections, pp. 111–13.

——. 1853. *Principles of geology; or, the modern changes of the earth and its inhabitants considered as illustrative of geology.* 9th edition, entirely revised. London: John Murray.

——. 1863. *The geological evidences of the antiquity of man with remarks on theories of the origin of species by variation.* London: John Murray.

——. 1867–8. *Principles of geology or the modern changes of the earth and its inhabitants considered as illustrative of geology.* 10th edition. 2 vols. London: John Murray.

Lyell, Katherine Murray, ed. 1881. *Life, letters and journals of Sir Charles Lyell, Bart.* 2 vols. London: John Murray.

Lyons, Henry. 1944. *The Royal Society 1660–1940: a history of its administration under its charters.* Cambridge: Cambridge University Press.

Mabberley, David J. 1997. *The plant-book. A portable dictionary of the vascular plants.* 2d edition. Cambridge: Cambridge University Press.

Macdonald, Frederick C. 1929. *Bishop Stirling of the Falklands. The adventurous life of a soldier of the cross whose humility hid the daring spirit of a hero & an inflexible will to face great risks.* London: Seely, Service & Co.

McGreevy, Thomas. 1995. *The basis of measurement.* 2 vols. Edited by Peter Cunningham. Chippenham: Picton Publishing.

McKitrick, Eric. 1988. *Andrew Johnson and reconstruction.* New York: Oxford University Press.

Macmillan dictionary of women's biography: *The Macmillan dictionary of women's biography.* 2d edition. Compiled and edited by Jennifer Uglow, assisted (1st edition) by Frances Hinton. London and Basingstoke, Hampshire: Macmillan Press. 1989.

Malm, August Wilhelm. 1867. Bidrag till kännedom af Pleuronektoidernas utveckling och byggnad. *Kongliga Svenska Vetenskaps-Akademiens Handlingar* 7 (1867–8): (4th paper) 1–28.

Malthus, Thomas Robert. 1826. *An essay on the principle of population; or, a view of its past and present effects on human happiness; with an inquiry into our prospects respecting the future removal or mitigation of the evils which it occasions.* 6th edition. 2 vols. London: John Murray.

Mamiani della Rovere, Terenzio, Count. 1865. *Confessioni di un metafisico.* 2 vols. Florence: G. Barbèra.

Maraldi, Giacomo Filippo. 1712. Observations sur les abeilles. *Mémoires de l'Académie Royale des Sciences* (1712): 297–331.

Marchant, James, ed. 1916. *Alfred Russel Wallace. Letters and reminiscences.* 2 vols. London: Cassell and Company.

Marcou, Jules. 1896. *Life, letters, and works of Louis Agassiz.* 2 vols. London and New York: Macmillan and Co.

Marginalia: *Charles Darwin's marginalia.* Edited by Mario A. Di Gregorio with the assistance of Nicholas W. Gill. Vol. 1. New York and London: Garland Publishing. 1990.

Martin, Gerald P. R. and Uschmann, Georg. 1969. *Friedrich Rolle 1827–1887, ein Vorkämpfer neuen biologischen Denkens in Deutschland.* Leipzig: Johann Ambrosius Barth.

Martius, Karl Friedrich Philipp von, ed. 1840–1906. *Flora Brasiliensis.* 15 vols. Leipzig: R. Oldenbourg.

Masson, David, ed. 1889–90. *The collected writings of Thomas De Quincey.* New and enlarged edition. 14 vols. Edinburgh: Adam and Charles Black.

May, Philip Ross. 1967. *The west coast gold rushes.* 2d edition. Christchurch, New Zealand: Pegasus Press.

Mayne, Richard Charles. 1862. *Four years in British Columbia and Vancouver Island.* London: John Murray.

Medical directory: *The London medical directory . . . every physician, surgeon, and general practitioner resident in London.* London: C. Mitchell. 1845. *The London and provincial medical directory.* London: John Churchill. 1848–60. *The London & provincial medical directory, inclusive of the medical directory for Scotland, and the medical directory for Ireland, and general medical register.* London: John Churchill. 1861–9. *The medical directory . . . including the London and provincial medical directory, the medical directory for Scotland, the medical directory for Ireland.* London: J. & A. Churchill. 1870–1905.

Medical who's who: *The medical who's who.* London: London & Counties Press Association [and others]. 1913–27.

Medvei, Victor Cornelius and Thornton, John Leonard, eds. 1974. *The Royal Hospital of Saint Bartholomew, 1123–1973.* London: St. Bartholomew's Hospital.

Melvill, James Cosmo. 1864. *The flora of Harrow. With notices of the birds of the neighbourhood, by the Hon. F. C. Bridgeman, and the Hon. G. O. M. Bridgeman, and of the butterflies and moths, by C. C. Parr and E. Heathfield.* London: Longman, Green, Longman, Roberts, and Green. Harrow: Crossley and Clarke.

Men and women of the time: *The men of the time in 1852 or sketches of living notables.* 2d edition, 1853. 3d edition, 1856. 4th edition, 1857. New edition, 1865. 7th edition, 1868. 8th edition, 1872. 9th edition, 1875. 10th edition, 1879. 11th edition, 1884. 12th edition, 1887. 13th edition, 1891. 14th edition, 1895. *Men and women of the time: a dictionary.* 15th edition. By Victor G. Plarr. 1899. London: David Bogue [and others]. 1852–99.

Men-at-the-bar: *Men-at-the-bar: a biographical hand-list of the members of the various inns of court, including Her Majesty's judges, etc.* By Joseph Foster. London: Reeves & Turner. 1885.

Meyer, Jürgen Bona. 1866. Der Darwinismus. [Review of Bronn trans. 1863.] *Preussische Jahrbücher* 17: 272–302, 404–53.

Milner, Richard. 1994. *Charles Darwin: evolution of a naturalist.* New York: Facts on file.

Mitchell, Alan. 1996. *Alan Mitchell's trees of Britain.* London: HarperCollins.

Mitchell, William Stephen. 1866. Report of the committee appointed to investigate the Alum Bay leaf-bed. *Report of the thirty-sixth meeting of the British Association for the Advancement of Science, held at Nottingham*, pp. 146–8.

ML: *More letters of Charles Darwin: a record of his work in a series of hitherto unpublished letters.* Edited by Francis Darwin and Albert Charles Seward. 2 vols. London: John Murray. 1903.

Modern English biography: *Modern English biography, containing many thousand concise memoirs of persons who have died since the year 1850.* By Frederick Boase. 3 vols. and supplement (3 vols.). Truro, Cornwall: printed for the author. 1892–1921.

Moggridge, John Traherne. 1864. Observations on some orchids of the south of France. [Read 3 November 1864.] *Journal of the Linnean Society* (*Botany*) 8 (1865): 256–8.

——. 1865–8. *Contributions to the flora of Mentone.* 4 pts. London: Lovell Reeve and Co.

——. 1869. *Ueber Ophrys insectifera L. (part.)* Dresden: E. Blochmann & Sohn. [*Verhandlungen der Kaiserlichen Leopoldino-Carolinischen deutschen Akademie der Naturforscher* 35 (1870): (3d paper) 1–16.]

Möller, Alfred, ed. 1915–21. *Fritz Müller. Werke, Briefe und Leben.* 3 vols in 5. Jena: Gustav Fischer.

Monkswell, Lord. 1911. *French railways.* London: Smith, Elder & Co.

Montagu, George. 1831. *Ornithological dictionary of British birds by Colonel G. Montagu, F.L.S.* 2d edition by James Rennie. London: Hurst, Chance, and Co.

Montgomery, William M. 1988. Germany. In *The comparative reception of Darwinism*, with a new preface, edited by Thomas F. Glick. Chicago and London: University of Chicago Press.

Moore, Daniel. 1866. *The unsearchableness of God: a sermon, preached at St. Matthew's church, Nottingham, on Sunday, 26th August, 1866, on the occasion of the meeting of the British Association for the Advancement of Science.* London, Oxford, and Cambridge: Rivingtons.

Moore, James Richard. 1985. Darwin of Down: the evolutionist as squarson-naturalist. In *The Darwinian heritage*, edited by David Kohn. Princeton, N.J.: Princeton University Press in association with Nova Pacifica.

Morris, Paul J. 1997. Louis Agassiz's arguments against Darwinism in his additions to the French translation of the *Essay on classification*. *Journal of the History of Biology* 30: 121–34.

Müller, Fritz. 1863. Die Verwandlung der Garneelen. *Archiv für Naturgeschichte* 29: 8–23.

——. 1864a. On the metamorphoses of the prawns. *Annals and Magazine of Natural History* 3d ser. 14: 104–15.

——. 1864b. Ein Wort über die Gattung Herklotsia J. E. Gray. *Archiv für Naturgeschichte* 30: 352–8.

——. 1864c. *Für Darwin.* Leipzig: Wilhelm Engelmann.

——. 1865a. Ueber Darwinella aurea, einen Schwamm mit sternförmigen Hornnadeln. *Archiv für mikroskopische Anatomie* 1: 344–53.

——. 1865b. Notes on some of the climbing-plants near Desterro, in south Brazil. By Herr Fritz Müller, in a letter to C. Darwin. [Read 7 December 1865.] *Journal of the Linnean Society* (*Botany*) 9 (1867): 344–9.

——. 1866a. Ueber die Befruchtung der *Martha (Posoqueria?) fragrans. Botanische Zeitung* 24: 129–33.

——. 1866b. Ueber das Holz einiger um Desterro wachsenden Kletterpflanzen. *Botanische Zeitung* 24: 57–60, 65–9.

——. 1868a. Notizen über die Geschlechtsverhältnisse brasilianischer Pflanzen. *Botanische Zeitung* 26: 113–16.

Müller, Fritz. 1868b. Ueber Befruchtungserscheinungen bei Orchideen. Aus einem Briefe an Friedrich Hildebrand. *Botanische Zeitung* 26: 629–31.

——. 1869. Ueber einige Befruchtungserscheinungen. Aus einem Briefe an F. Hildebrand. *Botanische Zeitung* 27: 224–6.

——. 1870. Umwandlung von Staubgefässen in Stempel bei *Begonia*. Uebergang von Zwitterblüthigkeit in Getrenntblüthigkeit bei *Chamissoa*. Triandrische Varietät eines monandrischen Epidendrum. Aus einem Briefe an H. Müller. *Botanische Zeitung* 28: 149–53.

Müller, Hermann. 1866. Thatsachen der Laubmooskunde für Darwin. *Verhandlungen des botanischen Vereins der Provinz Brandenburg* 8: 41–65.

Müller, Johannes Peter. 1844. *Über den Bau und die Lebenserscheinungen des* Branchiostoma lubricum *Costa,* Amphioxus lanceolatus *Yarrell.* Berlin: Drückerei der Königlichen Akademie der Wissenschaften.

Munz, Philip A. 1943. A revision of the genus *Fuchsia* (Onagraceae). *Proceedings of the California Academy of Sciences* 4th ser. 25: 1–138.

Murchison, Roderick Impey, *et al.* 1845. *The geology of Russia in Europe and the Ural Mountains*. 2 vols. London: John Murray.

Murchison, Roderick Impey and Sedgwick, Adam. 1842. *On the distribution and classification of the older or palaeozoic deposits of the north of Germany and Belgium, and on their comparison with formations of the same age in the British Isles.* London: R. and J. E. Taylor.

Murray, Andrew. 1866. *The geographical distribution of mammals.* London: Day and Son.

Nägeli, Carl Wilhelm von. 1865. *Entstehung und Begriff der naturhistorischen Art.* Munich: Verlag der königl. Akademie.

Narrative: *Narrative of the surveying voyages of His Majesty's ships Adventure and Beagle, between the years 1826 and 1836.* [Edited by Robert FitzRoy.] 3 vols. and appendix. London: Henry Colburn. 1839.

Nash, Roy. 1990. *Scandal in Madeira: the story of Richard Thomas Lowe.* Lewes: Book Guild.

Natural selection: *Charles Darwin's Natural selection: being the second part of his big species book written from 1856 to 1858.* Edited by R. C. Stauffer. Cambridge: Cambridge University Press. 1975.

Naudin, Charles Victor. 1858. Observations concernant quelques plantes hybrides qui ont été cultivées au Muséum. *Annales des Sciences Naturelles* (*Botanique*) 4th ser. 9: 257–78.

——. 1863. Nouvelles recherches sur l'hybridité dans les végétaux. *Annales des Sciences Naturelles* (*Botanique*) 4th ser. 19: 180–203.

——. 1864. De l'hybridité considérée comme cause de variabilité dans les végétaux. *Comptes rendus hebdomadaires des séances de l'Académie des Sciences* 59: 837–45.

Navy list: *The navy list.* London: John Murray; Her Majesty's Stationery Office. 1815–1900.

NBU: *Nouvelle biographie universelle depuis les temps les plus reculés jusqu'à nos jours, avec les renseignements bibliographiques et l'indication des sources a consulter.* Edited by Jean

Chrétien Ferdinand Hoefer. 46 vols. in 23. Paris: Firmin Didot Frères. 1852–66.

NDB: *Neue deutsche Biographie.* Under the auspices of the Historical Commission of the Bavarian Academy of Sciences. 21 vols. (A–Rohlfs) to date. Berlin: Duncker & Humblot. 1953–.

Newman, Kate. 1993. *Dictionary of Ulster biography.* Belfast: Institute of Irish Studies, Queen's University of Belfast.

Newton, Alfred. 1867. On a picture supposed to represent the Didine bird of the island of Bourbon (Réunion). [Read 14 February 1867.] *Transactions of the Zoological Society of London* 6 (1869): 373–6.

Nokes, Harriet. 1895. *Thirty-two years in a house of mercy.* London: Society for Promoting Christian Knowledge.

North, John S. 1997. *The Waterloo directory of English newspapers and periodicals, 1800–1900.* 10 vols. Waterloo, Ontario: North Waterloo Academic Press.

Notebooks: *Charles Darwin's notebooks, 1836–1844. Geology, transmutation of species, metaphysical enquiries.* Transcribed and edited by Paul H. Barrett *et al.* Cambridge: Cambridge University Press for the British Museum (Natural History). 1987.

Nowak, Ronald M. 1999. *Walker's mammals of the world.* 6th edition. 2 vols. Baltimore and London: The Johns Hopkins University Press.

NUC: *The national union catalog. Pre-1956 imprints.* 685 vols. and supplement (69 vols.). London and Chicago: Mansell. 1968–81.

Nyhart, Lynn K. 1995. *Biology takes form. Animal morphology and the German universities, 1800–1900.* Chicago and London: University of Chicago Press.

OBL: *Österreichisches biographisches Lexikon 1815–1950.* Edited by Leo Santifaller *et al.* 11 vols. and 2 fascicles of vol. 12 (A–Siegl Emil) to date. Vienna: Osterreichischen Akademie der Wissenschaften. 1957–.

O'Byrne, William R. 1849. *A naval biographical dictionary: comprising the life and services of every living officer in Her Majesty's Navy, from the rank of admiral of the fleet to that of lieutenant, inclusive.* London: John Murray.

OED: *The Oxford English dictionary. Being a corrected re-issue with an introduction, supplement and bibliography of a new English dictionary.* Edited by James A. H. Murray, *et al.* 12 vols. and supplement. Oxford: Clarendon Press. 1970. *A supplement to the Oxford English dictionary.* 4 vols. Edited by R. W. Burchfield. Oxford: Clarendon Press. 1972–86. *The Oxford English dictionary.* 2d edition. 20 vols. Prepared by J. A. Simpson and E. S. C. Weiner. Oxford: Clarendon Press. 1989. *Oxford English dictionary additional series.* 3 vols. Edited by John Simpson *et al.* Oxford: Clarendon Press. 1993–7.

Olby, Robert. 1985. *Origins of Mendelism.* 2d edition. Chicago and London: University of Chicago Press.

O'Leary, Patrick. 1989. *Sir James Mackintosh: the Whig Cicero.* Aberdeen: Aberdeen University Press.

Orchids: *On the various contrivances by which British and foreign orchids are fertilised by insects, and on the good effects of intercrossing.* By Charles Darwin. London: John Murray. 1862.

Orchids 2d ed.: *The various contrivances by which British and foreign orchids are fertilised by insects, and the good effects of intercrossing.* By Charles Darwin. Revised. London: John Murray. 1877.

Orel, Vítězslav. 1996. *Gregor Mendel: the first geneticist.* Translated by Stephen Finn. Oxford: Oxford University Press.

Origin: *On the origin of species by means of natural selection, or the preservation of favoured races in the struggle for life.* By Charles Darwin. London: John Murray. 1859.

Origin 2d ed.: *On the origin of species by means of natural selection, or the preservation of favoured races in the struggle for life.* By Charles Darwin. London: John Murray. 1860.

Origin 3d ed.: *On the origin of species by means of natural selection, or the preservation of favoured races in the struggle for life.* With additions and corrections. By Charles Darwin. London: John Murray. 1861.

Origin 4th ed.: *On the origin of species by means of natural selection, or the preservation of favoured races in the struggle for life.* With additions and corrections. By Charles Darwin. London: John Murray. 1866.

Origin 5th ed.: *On the origin of species by means of natural selection, or the preservation of favoured races in the struggle for life.* With additions and corrections. By Charles Darwin. London: John Murray. 1869.

Origin 6th ed.: *The origin of species by means of natural selection, or the preservation of favoured races in the struggle for life.* With additions and corrections. By Charles Darwin. London: John Murray. 1872.

Origin US ed.: *On the origin of species by means of natural selection, or the preservation of favoured races in the struggle for life.* A new edition, revised and augmented by the author. By Charles Darwin. New York: D. Appleton. 1860.

Origin 2d US ed.: *On the origin of species by means of natural selection, or the preservation of favoured races in the struggle for life.* By Charles Darwin. From the fifth London edition, with additions and corrections. New York: D. Appleton. 1870.

Ospovat, Dov. 1977. Lyell's theory of climate. *Journal of the History of Biology* 10: 317–39.

Owen, Richard. 1838. A description of the cranium of the *Toxodon platensis*, a gigantic extinct mammiferous species, referrible by its dentition to the *Rodentia*, but with affinities to the *Pachydermata* and the herbivorous Cetacea. *Proceedings of the Geological Society of London* 2 (1833–8): 541–2.

———. 1850. On *Dinornis* (Part IV): containing the restoration of the feet of that genus and of *Palapteryx*, with a description of the sternum in *Palapteryx* and *Aptornis*. [Read 26 February 1850.] *Transactions of the Zoological Society of London* 4 (1862): 1–20.

———. 1853. Description of some species of the extinct genus *Nesodon*, with remarks on the primary group (Toxodontia) of hoofed quadrupeds, to which that genus is referable. *Philosophical Transactions of the Royal Society of London* 143: 291–310.

[———.] 1860. [Review of *Origin* and other works.] *Edinburgh Review* 111: 487–532.

———. 1862. On the *Archaeopteryx* of von Meyer, with a description of the fossil remains of a long-tailed species, from the lithographic stone of Solenhofen. [Read

20 November 1862.] *Philosophical Transactions of the Royal Society of London* 153 (1863): 33–47.

——. 1866–8. *On the anatomy of vertebrates.* London: Longmans, Green & Co.

Packard, Alpheus Spring, Jr. 1864. The humble bees of New England and their parasites; with notices of a new species of *Anthophorabia*, and a new genus of *Proctotrupidæ*. *Proceedings of the Essex Institute* 4 (1864–5): 107–40.

Pallas, Pyotr Simon. 1780. Mémoire sur la variation des animaux; première partie. *Acta Academiæ Scientiarum Imperialis Petropolitanæ* 4, pt 2: 69–102.

Paul, Diane B. 1988. The selection of the 'Survival of the Fittest'. *Journal of the History of Biology* 24: 411–22.

Peckham, Morse, ed. 1959. *The Origin of Species by Charles Darwin: a variorum text.* Philadelphia: University of Pennsylvania Press.

Peschel, Oscar Ferdinand. 1865. *Geschichte der Erdkunde bis auf A. v. Humboldt und Carl Ritter.* Vol. 4 of *Geschichte der Wissenschaften in Deutschland. Neuere Zeit.* Munich: J. G. Cotta'schen Buchhandlung.

Pflanze, Otto. 1990. *Bismarck and the development of Germany.* [2d edition.] 3 vols. Princeton: Princeton University Press.

Physicians: *The roll of the Royal College of Physicians of London.* By William Munk. 2d edition, revised and enlarged. 3 vols. London: Royal College of Physicians. 1878. *Lives of the fellows of the Royal College of Physicians of London.* Compiled by G. H. Brown *et al.* 5 vols. London: Royal College of Physicians. Oxford and Washington, D.C.: IRL Press. 1955–89.

Pictet de la Rive, François Jules and Humbert, Aloïs. 1866. Recent researches on the fossil fishes of Mount Lebanon. *Annals and Magazine of Natural History* 3d ser. 18: 237–47.

Pigot & Co.'s royal, national, and commercial directory 1844: *Pigot and Co.'s royal, national and commercial directory and topography of the counties of Berkshire, Buckinghamshire, Cornwall, Devonshire, Dorsetshire, Gloucestershire, Hampshire, Herefordshire, Monmouthshire, Oxfordshire, Somersetshire, Wiltshire, and North and South Wales.* London: I. Slater. 1844.

Plarr, Victor Gustave. 1930. *Plarr's lives of the fellows of the Royal College of Surgeons of England.* Revised by Sir D'Arcy Power. 2 vols. London: Simpkin Marshall.

Post Office directory of Gloucestershire, with Bath, Bristol, Herefordshire, and Shropshire: *Post Office directory of Gloucestershire, with Bath, Bristol, Herefordshire, and Shropshire. Post Office directory of Gloucestershire, Herefordshire, Shropshire, and the City of Bristol. Post Office directory of Shropshire, Herefordshire, and Gloucestershire, with the City of Bristol.* London: Kelly & Co. 1856–79.

Post Office directory of Lancashire, Liverpool and Manchester: *Post Office directory of Lancashire. Post Office directory of Lancashire, Liverpool and Manchester.* London: Kelly & Co. 1858–92.

Post Office directory of Lincolnshire. London: Kelly and Co. [1849]–76.

Post Office directory of Northamptonshire: *Post Office directory of Berkshire, Northamptonshire, Oxfordshire, with Bedfordshire, Buckinghamshire, and Huntingdonshire. The Post Office directory of Northamptonshire, Huntingdonshire, Bedfordshire, Buckinghamshire, Berkshire, and*

Oxfordshire. The Post Office directory of the counties of Bedford, Huntingdon, Northampton, Berks, Buckingham and Oxford. London: Kelly and Co. [1847]–77.

Post Office directory of Northumberland: *Post Office directory of Westmoreland, Cumberland, Northumberland, and Durham.* London: Kelly and Co. 1858.

Post Office directory of the six home counties: *Post Office directory of the six home counties, viz., Essex, Herts, Kent, Middlesex, Surrey and Sussex.* London: W. Kelly & Co. 1845–78.

Post Office London directory: *Post-Office annual directory. . . . A list of the principal merchants, traders of eminence, &c. in the cities of London and Westminster, the borough of Southwark, and parts adjacent . . . general and special information relating to the Post Office. Post Office London directory.* London: His Majesty's Postmaster-General [and others]. 1802–1967.

Post Office London suburban directory: *The Post Office London suburban directory. Kelly's London suburban directory.* London: Kelly & Co. 1860–1903.

Prete, Frederick R. 1990. The conundrum of the honey bees: one impediment to the publication of Darwin's theory. *Journal of the History of Biology* 23: 271–90.

Prévost. 1830. Note sur un Cytise nouveau. *Annales de la Société d'Horticulture de Paris, et Journal Spécial de l'Etat et des Progrès du Jardinage* 7: 93–6.

Pritchard, Ada, comp. 1897. *Charles Pritchard . . . late Savilian Professor of astronomy in the University of Oxford: memoirs of his life.* London: Seeley and Co.

Pritchard, Charles. 1866. *The continuity of the schemes of nature and of revelation. A sermon preached, by request, on the occasion of the meeting of the British Association at Nottingham. With remarks on some relations of modern knowledge to theology.* London: Bell and Daldy.

Pritchard, Michael. 1994. *A directory of London photographers 1841–1908.* Revised and expanded edition. Watford, Hertfordshire: PhotoResearch.

Putnam, Frederic Ward. 1863a. Notes on the habits of some species of humble bees. [Communicated 22 October 1863.] *Proceedings of the Essex Institute* 4 (1864–5): 98–104.

——. 1863b. Notes on the leaf-cutting bee. [Communicated 22 October 1863.] *Proceedings of the Essex Institute* 4 (1864–5): 105–7.

Quatrefages, Armand de. 1865. *Histoire naturelle des annelés marins et d'eau douce. Annélides et Géphyriens.* 2 vols. Paris: Librairie encyclopédique de Roret.

Raby, Peter. 2001. *Alfred Russel Wallace: a life.* London: Chatto & Windus.

Rachinskii, Sergei A., trans. 1864. *Proiskhozhdenie vidov putem estestvennogo podbora.* [*Origin.*] By Charles Darwin. St Petersburg: A. I. Glazunov.

——, trans. 1865. *Proiskhozhdenie vidov putem estestvennogo podbora.* [*Origin.*] By Charles Darwin. St Petersburg: A. I. Glazunov.

Rafferty, Oliver P. 1999. *The church, the state and the Fenian threat, 1861–75.* Basingstoke: Macmillan.

Ramsay, Andrew Crombie. 1866. *The geology of North Wales.* London: Longmans, Green, Reader, and Dyer. [Vol. 3 of *Memoirs of the Geological Survey of Great Britain and of the Museum of Practical Geology.*]

Réaumur, René Antoine Ferchault de. 1734–42. *Mémoires pour servir à l'histoire des insectes.* 6 vols. Paris: De l'imprimerie royale.

Record of the Royal Society of London: *The record of the Royal Society of London for the promotion of natural knowledge*. 4th edition. London: Royal Society. 1940.

Reeve, Lovell Augustus and Walford, Edward, eds. 1863–7. *Portraits of men of eminence in literature, science, and art, with biographical memoirs*. 6 vols. London: Lovell Reeve and Alfred Wm. Bennett.

Rehbock, Philip F. 1975. Huxley, Haeckel, and the oceanographers: the case of *Bathybius haeckelii*. *Isis* 66: 504–33.

——. 1983. *The philosophical naturalists. Themes in early nineteenth-century British biology*. Madison, Wis., and London: University of Wisconsin Press.

Reichenbach, Heinrich Gustav. 1865. *Neotinea intacta, Rchb. fil.*, the new Irish orchid. *Journal of Botany* 3: 1–5.

Reilly, Robin. 1992. *Josiah Wedgwood 1730–1795*. London: Macmillan London.

Reinhard, Hermann. 1865. Die Hypothesen über die Fortpflanzungsweise bei den eingeschlechtigen Gallwespen. *Berliner Entomologische Zeitschrift* 9: 1–13.

Richardson, Edmund William. 1916. *A veteran naturalist; being the life and work of W. B. Tegetmeier*. London: Witherby & Co.

Ringer, Sydney. 1869. *A handbook of therapeutics*. London: H. K. Lewis.

Rivers, Thomas. 1866a. Something more about fruit tree stocks. *Journal of Horticulture* n.s. 10: 237–8.

——. 1866b. Fruit culture. *Journal of Horticulture* n.s. 10: 306–9.

Robertson, William Tindal, ed. 1866. *The British Association for the Advancement of Science. Nottingham meeting, August, 1866. Report of the papers, discussions, and general proceedings*. Nottingham: Thomas Forman. London: Robert Hardwicke.

Robson, J. 1866a. Stocks for grafting on, and the results. *Journal of Horticulture* n.s. 10: 214–16.

——. 1866b. The relative merits of the stocks used for the apple and pear. *Journal of Horticulture* n.s. 10: 269–70.

Rocke, Alan J. 1984. *Chemical atomism in the nineteenth century: Dalton to Cannizzaro*. Columbus: Ohio State University Press.

Rodgers, Andrew Denny III. 1968. *'Noble fellow': William Starling Sullivant*. London and New York: Hafner Publishing.

Rogers, James Allen. 1988. Russia: social sciences. In *The comparative reception of Darwinism*, with a new preface, edited by Thomas F. Glick. Chicago and London: University of Chicago Press.

Rolle, Friedrich. 1863. *Ch. Darwin's Lehre von der Entstehung der Arten im Pflanzen- und Thierreich in ihrer Anwendung auf die Schöpfungsgeschichte*. Frankfurt: J. C. Hermann.

——. 1866. *Der Mensch, seine Abstammung und Gesittung, im Lichte der Darwin'schen Lehre von der Art-Entstehung und auf Grundlage der neuern geologischen Entdeckungen dargestellt*. Frankfurt: J. C. Hermann.

Rouse, Greg W. and Pleijel, Fredrik. 2001. *Polychaetes*. Oxford: Oxford University Press.

Rowlinson, J. S. 1971. The theory of glaciers. *Notes and records of the Royal Society of London* 26: 189–204.

Royal Society catalogue of scientific papers: *Catalogue of scientific papers (1800–1900). Compiled and published by the Royal Society of London.* 19 vols. and index (3 vols.). London: Royal Society of London. Cambridge: Cambridge University Press. 1867–1925.

Royer, Clémence Auguste, trans. 1862. *De l'origine des espèces ou des lois du progrès chez les êtres organisés.* By Charles Darwin. With preface and notes by the translator. Translated from the 3d English edition. Paris: Guillaumin & Cie; Victor Masson.

——, trans. 1866. *De l'origine des espèces par sélection naturelle ou des lois de transformation des êtres organisés.* By Charles Darwin. Augmented in accordance with notes by the author. 2d edition. [Translated from the 3d English edition.] Paris: Guillaumin & Cie; Victor Masson.

Royle, J. Forbes and Headland, Frederick W. 1865. *A manual of materia medica and therapeutics; including the preparations of the British Pharmacopœia, and many other approved medicines.* 4th edition. London: John Churchill & Sons.

Rudwick, Martin John Spencer. 1969. The glacial theory. *History of Science* 8: 136–57.

——. 1998. Lyell and the *Principles of geology.* In *Lyell: the past is the key to the present*, edited by Derek J. Blundell and Andrew C. Scott. London: Geological Society.

Rupke, Nicolaas A. 1976. *Bathybius Haeckelii* and the psychology of scientific discovery: theory instead of observed data controlled the late 19th century 'discovery' of a primitive form of life. *Studies in History and Philosophy of Science* 7: 53–62.

——. 1994. *Richard Owen, Victorian naturalist.* New Haven, Conn., and London: Yale University Press.

Ruprecht, Franz Josef. 1865. Neuere geo-botanische Untersuchungen über den Tschornosjom. [Read 30 November 1865.] *Bulletin de l'Académie Impériale des Sciences de St.-Pétersbourg* 9 (1866): 482–569.

——. 1866. De l'importance scientifique du tschornozome ou terre noire. *Bibliothèque Universelle et Revue Suisse. Archives des Sciences Physiques et Naturelles* n.s. 26: 17–34.

Russell, Colin Archibald. 1996. *Edward Frankland. Chemistry, controversy and conspiracy in Victorian England.* Cambridge: Cambridge University Press.

Russkii biograficheskii slovar'. Edited by A. A. Polovtsov. St Petersburg: Izdanie Imperatorskogo Russkogo istoricheskogo obshchestva. 1896–1918.

Rütimeyer, Ludwig. 1863. *Beiträge zur Kenntniss der fossilen Pferde und zu einer vergleichenden Odontographie der Hufthiere im Allgemeinen.* Basel, Switzerland: Schweighauserische Buchdruckerei.

——. 1865. Beiträge zu einer palæontologischen Geschichte der Wiederkauer, zunächst an Linné's Genus Bos. *Verhandlungen der Naturforschenden Gesellschaft in Basel* 4 (1867): 299–354.

Salisbury, Richard Anthony. 1866. *The genera of plants.* London: Van Voorst.

Salter, Samuel James Augustus. 1863. Note on the fertility, inter se, of hybrids of different species of the genus *Gallus*. *Natural History Review* 3: 276–9.

Sarasin, Fritz, ed. 1924. *Geschichte des zoologischen Gartens in Basel 1874–1924, zur Feier des 50 jährigen Bestehens.* Basel: Kunstanstalt Frobenius A.G.

Sarjeant, William A. S. 1980–96. *Geologists and the history of geology: an international bibliography.* 10 vols. including supplements. London: Macmillan. Malabar, Fla.:

Robert E. Krieger Publishing.

Sarton, George. 1942. Lesquereux (1806–89). *Isis* 34: 97–108.

Schacht, Hermann. 1856–9. *Lehrbuch der Anatomie und Physiologie der Gewächse.* 2 vols. Berlin: G. W. F. Müller.

Scherren, Henry. 1905. *The Zoological Society of London: a sketch of its foundation and development and the story of its farm, museum, gardens, menagerie and library.* London: Cassell.

S[chlechtenda]l, [D. F. L.]. 1864. Personal-Nachrichten [Hermann Crüger]. *Botanische Zeitung* 22: 119–20.

Schmidt, Oskar and Unger, Franz. 1866. *Das Alter der Menschheit und das Paradies.* Vienna: Wilhelm Braumüller.

Schopf, J. William. 2000. Solution to Darwin's dilemma: discovery of the missing Precambrian record of life. *Proceedings of the National Academy of Sciences of the United States of America* 97: 6947–53.

Schultze, Max. 1851. Beobachtung junger Exemplare von Amphioxus. *Zeitschrift für wissenschaftliche Zoologie* 3: 416–19.

Schwartz von Mohrenstern, Gustav. 1861. Über die Familie der Rissoiden und insbesondere die Gattung Rissoina. *Denkschriften der kaiserlichen Akademie der Wissenschaften. Mathematisch-naturwissenschaftliche Classe* 19 (2): 71–188.

——. 1864. Über die Familie der Rissoiden. II. Rissoa. *Denkschriften der kaiserlichen Akademie der Wissenschaften. Mathematisch-naturwissenschaftliche Classe* 23 (2): 1–56.

Scott, John. 1863. Remarks on the sexual changes in the inflorescence of *Zea Mays.* [Read before the Botanical Society of Edinburgh, 10 December 1863.] *Edinburgh New Philosophical Journal* n.s. 19 (1864): 213–20.

——. 1864. On the individual sterility and cross-impregnation of certain species of *Oncidium.* [Read 2 June 1864.] *Journal of the Linnean Society (Botany)* 8 (1865): 162–7.

Scudder, Samuel Hubbard. 1866. Revision of the hitherto known species of the genus Chinobas in North America. *Proceedings of the Entomological Society of Philadelphia* 5: 1–28.

Secord, James A. 1985. John W. Salter: the rise and fall of a Victorian palaeontological career. In *From Linnaeus to Darwin: commentaries on the history of biology and geology. Papers from the fifth Easter meeting of the Society for the History of Natural History, 28–31 March, 1983.* London: Society for the History of Natural History.

——. 1997. Introduction to *Principles of geology*, by Charles Lyell. London: Penguin Books.

——. 2000. *Victorian sensation: the extraordinary publication, reception, and secret authorship of* Vestiges of the natural history of creation. Chicago: University of Chicago Press.

Sedgwick, William. 1861. On sexual limitation in hereditary disease. *British and Foreign Medico-Chirurgical Review* n.s. 27: 477–89; 28: 198–214.

Seeley, Thomas D. 1995. *The wisdom of the hive: the social physiology of honey bee colonies.* Cambridge, Massachusetts and London: Harvard University Press.

Semmel, Bernard. 1962. *The Governor Eyre controversy.* London: Macgibbon & Kee.

Senior, Hereward. 1991. *The last invasion of Canada: the Fenian raids, 1866–1870*. Toronto and Oxford: Dundurn Press.

Seringe, Nicolas Charles. 1830. Pommier monstrueux de St.-Vallery, avec une notice sur la disposition des carpelles de plusieurs fruits. *Bulletin Botanique ou Collection de Notices Originales et d'Extraits des Ouvrages Botaniques* no. 5, May 1830, pp. 117–25.

Shaw, James. 1866a. The appreciation of beauty by animals. *Transactions and Journal of the Proceedings of the Dumfriesshire and Galloway Natural History and Antiquarian Society* (1864–5): 65–70. [Read 6 February 1866: see R. Wallace ed. 1899, p. lvi.]

——. 1866b. Feeling of beauty among the animals. *Athenæum* 24 November 1866, p. 681.

Sheehan, James J. 1989. *German history, 1770–1866*. Oxford: Clarendon Press.

Shelley, Percy Bysshe. 1834. *The works of Percy Bysshe Shelley, with his life*. 2 vols. London: John Ascham.

Sibthorp, John. 1806–40. *Flora græca: characteres omnium, descriptiones et synonyma*. 10 vols. London: Richard Taylor & Co.

Sigrist, René, *et al.* 1999. *Louis Jurine: chirurgien et naturaliste (1751–1819)*. Chêne-Bourg, Switzerland: Georg.

Sloan, Phillip R. 2001. 'The sense of sublimity': Darwin on nature and divinity. *Osiris* 2d ser. 16: 251–69.

Smith, Charles H., ed. 1991. *Alfred Russel Wallace: an anthology of his shorter writings*. Oxford: Oxford University Press.

Smith, C. Wayne and Cothren, J. Tom, eds. 1999. *Cotton: origin, history, technology, and production*. New York: John Wiley & Sons.

Smith, Frederick. 1864. On the construction of hexagonal cells by bees and wasps. [Read 4 April 1864.] *Transactions of the Entomological Society of London* 3d ser. 2 (1864–6): 131–42.

Smith, Hobart M. 1989. Discovery of the axolotl and its early history in biological research. In *Developmental biology of the axolotl*, edited by John B. Armstrong and George M. Malacinski. New York and Oxford: Oxford University Press.

Smyth, Warington W. 1867. *A treatise on coal and coal-mining*. London: Virtue Brothers & Co.

Somerville, Mary. 1869. *On molecular and microscopic science*. 2 vols. London: John Murray.

Sorensen, W. Conner. 1995. *Brethren of the net. American entomology, 1840–1880*. Tuscaloosa and London: University of Alabama Press.

South America: *Geological observations on South America. Being the third part of the geology of the voyage of the Beagle, under the command of Capt. FitzRoy RN, during the years 1832 to 1836*. By Charles Darwin. London: Smith, Elder & Co. 1846.

'Specific difference in *Primula*': On the specific difference between *Primula veris*, Brit. Fl. (var. *officinalis* of Linn.), *P. vulgaris*, Brit. Fl. (var. *acaulis*, Linn.), and *P. elatior*, Jacq.; and on the hybrid nature of the common oxlip. With supplementary remarks on naturally produced hybrids in the genus *Verbascum*. By Charles

Darwin. [Read 19 March 1868.] *Journal of the Linnean Society (Botany)* 10 (1869): 437–54.

Spencer, Herbert. 1864–7. *The principles of biology.* 2 vols. London: Williams & Norgate.

——. 1866. On circulation and the formation of wood in plants. [Read 1 March 1866.] *Transactions of the Linnean Society of London* 25: 405–30.

Sprengel, Christian Konrad. 1793. *Das entdeckte Geheimniss der Natur im Bau und in der Befruchtung der Blumen.* Berlin: Friedrich Vieweg.

Spruce, Richard. 1908. *Notes of a botanist on the Amazon & Andes, being records of travel . . . during the years 1849–1864.* Edited by Alfred Russel Wallace. 2 vols. London: Macmillan and Co.

Stace, Clive Anthony. 1997. *New flora of the British Isles.* 2d edition. London and Cambridge: Cambridge University Press.

Stanek, V. J. 1969. *The pictorial encyclopedia of insects.* London, New York, Sydney, Toronto: Paul Hamlyn.

Stearn, William T. 1981. *The Natural History Museum at South Kensington: A history of the British Museum (Natural History), 1753–1980.* London: Heinemann in association with the British Museum (Natural History).

Stebbing, E. P. 1922–6. *The forests of India.* 3 vols. London: John Lane, The Bodley Head.

Steiner, André L. 1986. Stinging behaviour of solitary wasps. In *Venoms of the Hymenoptera: biochemical, pharmacological and behavioural aspects*, edited by Tom Piek. London and Orlando, Fla.: Academic Press.

Stenhouse, John. 1990. Darwin's captain: F. W. Hutton and the nineteenth-century Darwinian debates. *Journal of the History of Biology* 23: 411–42.

Stenton, Michael. 1976. *Who's who of British members of Parliament.* Vol. 1, *1832–1885.* Sussex: Harvester Press. New Jersey: Humanities Press.

Stewart, Balfour. 1865. On the latest discoveries concerning the sun's surface. [Read 17 March 1865.] *Proceedings of the Royal Institution of Great Britain* 4 (1862–6): 378–80.

Stocking, George W., Jr. 1987. *Victorian anthropology.* New York: The Free Press. London: Collier Macmillan.

Streatfield, J. F. 1857–9. Seven cases of strabismus in one family. *Ophthalmic Hospital Reports and Journal of the Royal London Ophthalmic Hospital* 1: 260–2.

Stresemann, Erwin. 1975. *Ornithology: from Aristotle to the present.* Translated by Hans J. and Cathleen Epstein. Edited by G. William Cottrell. With foreword and epilogue by Ernst Mayr. Cambridge, Mass., and London: Harvard University Press.

Strick, James. 2000. *Sparks of life: Darwinism and the Victorian debates over spontaneous generation.* Cambridge, Mass.: Harvard University Press.

Strickland, Hugh Edwin, *et al.* 1842. Report of a committee appointed 'to consider of the rules by which the nomenclature of zoology may be established on a uniform and permanent basis'. *Report of the 12th meeting of the British Association for the Advancement of Science, held at Manchester*, pp. 105–121.

Sulivan, Henry Norton, ed. 1896. *Life and letters of the late Admiral Sir Bartholomew James Sulivan, KCB, 1810–1890*. London: John Murray.

Sunding, Per. 1979. Origins of the Macaronesian flora. In *Plants and islands*, edited by David Bramwell. London and New York: Academic Press.

Swinhoe, Robert. 1865. Notes on the aborigines of Formosa. *Report of the thirty-fifth meeting of the British Association for the Advancement of Science held at Birmingham*, Transactions of the sections, pp. 129–30.

Taxonomic literature: *Taxonomic literature. A selective guide to botanical publications and collections with dates, commentaries and types*. By Frans A. Stafleu and Richard S. Cowan. 2d edition. 7 vols. Utrecht, Netherlands: Bohn, Scheltema & Holkema. The Hague, Netherlands: W. Junk. 1976–88.

Taylor, C. M. 1994. Revision of *Hillia* (Rubiaceae). *Annals of the Missouri Botanical Garden* 81: 571–609.

Tebbel, John. 1972. *A history of book publishing in the United States*. Vol. 1, *The creation of an industry, 1630–1865*. New York and London: R. R. Bowker.

Tegetmeier, William Bernhard. 1856. On the remarkable peculiarities existing in the skulls of the feather-crested variety of the domestic fowl, now known as the Polish. *Proceedings of the Zoological Society of London* 24: 366–8.

——. 1867. *The poultry book: comprising the breeding and management of profitable and ornamental poultry, their qualities and characteristics; to which is added 'The standard of excellence in exhibition birds', authorized by the Poultry Club*. London and New York: George Routledge & Sons.

Tesch, Friedrich-Wilhelm. 1977. *The eel: biology and management of anguillid eels*. Translated by Jennifer Greenwood, edited by P. H. Greenwood, revised and extended by I. W. Henderson. London: Chapman and Hall. New York: John Wiley & Sons.

Thom's Irish almanac: *Thom's Irish almanac and official directory of the United Kingdom of Great Britain and Ireland*. Dublin: Alexander Thom. 1846–80.

Thomson, Charles Wyville. 1865. Notes on Prof. Steenstrup's views on the obliquity of flounders. *Annals and Magazine of Natural History* 3d ser. 15: 361–71.

Thomson, George Malcolm. 1884–5. Frederick Wollaston Hutton. *The New Zealand Journal of Science* 2: 301–6.

Thomson, William. 1862a. On the age of the sun's heat. *Macmillan's Magazine* 5: 388–93.

——. 1862b. On the secular cooling of the earth. [Read 28 April 1862.] *Transactions of the Royal Society of Edinburgh* 23 (1864): 157–70.

——. 1865. The 'Doctrine of uniformity' in geology briefly refuted. [Read 18 December 1865.] *Proceedings of the Royal Society of Edinburgh* 5 (1866): 512–13.

'Three forms of *Lythrum salicaria*': On the sexual relations of the three forms of *Lythrum salicaria*. By Charles Darwin. [Read 16 June 1864.] *Journal of the Linnean Society (Botany)* 8 (1865): 169–96. [*Collected papers* 2: 106–31.]

Thuret, Gustave Adolphe. 1854–5. Recherches sur la fécondation des Fucacées, suivies d'observations sur les anthéridies des Algues. *Annales des Sciences Naturelles*.

Botanique. 4th ser. 2: 197–214; 3: 5–28.

Times atlas: *'The Times' atlas of the world. Comprehensive edition.* 9th edition. London: Times Books. 1992.

Tinbergen, Niko. 1969. *The study of instinct.* With a new introduction. Oxford: Clarendon Press.

Todd, Robert Bentley, *et al.* 1866. *The physiological anatomy and physiology of man.* New edition by Lionel Smith Beale. London: Longmans, Green, Reader, and Dyer.

Tort, Patrick. 1996. *Dictionnaire du Darwinisme et de l'evolution.* 3 vols. Paris: Presses Universitaires de France.

Travers, Henry Hammersley. 1864. Notes on the Chatham Islands (lat. 44°30′ S., long. 175° W.). [Read 3 November 1864.] *Journal of the Linnean Society* (*Botany*) 9 (1867): 135–44.

Truckell, A. E. 1966. The Grierson collection, Thornhill, and its dispersal. *Transactions of the Dumfriesshire and Galloway Natural History and Antiquarian Society* 3d ser. 43: 65–72.

Turnbull, Constance Mary. 1989. *A history of Singapore 1819–1988.* 2d edition. Oxford: Oxford University Press.

Turner, William. 1863. The present aspect of the doctrine of cellular pathology: a lecture delivered at an evening meeting of the Royal College of Surgeons of Edinburgh. [Read 27 February 1863.] *Edinburgh Medical Journal* 8: 873–97.

——. 1864a. On the textural changes which occur in inflammation of serous membranes. *Edinburgh Medical Journal* 9: 908–14.

——. 1864b. On variability in human structure, with illustrations from the flexor muscles of the fingers and toes. [Read 19 December 1864.] *Transactions of the Royal Society of Edinburgh* 24 (1864–7): 175–89.

——. 1864c. On some malformations of the organs of generation. [Read 7 December 1864.] *Edinburgh Medical Journal* 10: 575–81, 689–95.

——. 1866a. Notes more especially on the bridging convolutions in the brain of the chimpanzee. [Read 18 February 1866.] *Proceedings of the Royal Society of Edinburgh* 5 (1862–6): 578–87.

——. 1866b. On a remarkable mode of gestation in an undescribed species of Arius (*A. Boakeii*). [Read 23 August 1866.] *Journal of Anatomy and Physiology* 1 (1867): 78–82.

Turrill, William Bertram. 1953. *Pioneer plant geography: the phytogeographical researches of Sir Joseph Dalton Hooker.* The Hague: Martinus Nijhoff.

Tutin, Thomas Gaskell, *et al.*, eds. 1964–80. *Flora Europeae.* 5 vols. Cambridge: Cambridge University Press.

'Two forms in species of *Linum*': On the existence of two forms, and on their reciprocal sexual relation, in several species of the genus *Linum.* By Charles Darwin. [Read 5 February 1863.] *Journal of the Proceedings of the Linnean Society* (*Botany*) 7 (1864): 69–83. [*Collected papers* 2: 93–105.]

Tylor, Edward Burnett. 1865. *Researches into the early history of mankind and the development of civilization.* London: John Murray.

Tyndall, John. 1860. *The glaciers of the Alps. Being a narrative of excursions and ascents, an account of the origin and phenomena of glaciers, and an exposition of the physical principles to which they are related.* London: J. Murray.

Tyndall, John and Huxley, Thomas Henry. 1857. On the structure and motion of glaciers. *Philosophical Transactions of the Royal Society of London* 147: 327–46. [Reprinted in Foster and Lankester eds. 1898–1903, 2: 1–25.]

Underhill, Terry L. 1971. *Heaths and heathers:* Calluna, Daboecia and Erica. Newton Abbot, Devon: David & Charles.

Unger, Franz. 1860. *I. Die versunkene Insel Atlantis. II. Die physiologische Bedeutung der Pflanzencultur. Zwei Vorträge gehalten im Ständehause im Winter des Jahres 1860.* Vienna: Wilhelm Braumüller.

Uschmann, Georg. 1959. *Geschichte der Zoologie und der zoologischen Anstalten in Jena 1779–1919.* Jena: VEB Gustav Fischer.

Usov, Sergei A. trans. 1865. *Uchenie Darvina* O proiskhozhdenii vidov *obsheponiatno izlozhennoe Fridrikhom Rolle.* [Rolle 1863.] Moscow: A. I. Glazunov.

Van Riper, A. Bowdoin. 1993. *Men among the mammoths: Victorian science and the discovery of human prehistory.* Chicago and London: University of Chicago Press.

Variation: *The variation of animals and plants under domestication.* By Charles Darwin. 2 vols. London: John Murray. 1868.

Variation 2d ed.: *The variation of animals and plants under domestication.* By Charles Darwin. 2 vols. London: John Murray. 1875.

Variation US ed.: *The variation of animals and plants under domestication.* By Charles Darwin. 2 vols. New York: Orange Judd & Co. [1868.]

Verlot, Bernard. 1864. Mémoire sur la production et la fixation des variétés dans les plantes d'ornement. *Journal de la Société Impériale et Centrale d'Horticulture* 10: 243–56, 305–20, 375–84, 420–32, 468–80, 518–28, 571–6, 624–40.

Verlot, Bernard. 1865. *Sur la production et la fixation des variétés dans les plantes d'ornement.* Paris: J. B. Baillière.

Villars, Dominique. 1786–9. *Histoire des plantes de Dauphiné.* 3 vols. in 4. Grenoble: Chez l'Auteur & Chez les Libraires.

Virchow, Rudolf. 1866. *Ueber Hünengräber und Pfahlbauten.* Berlin: C. G. Lüderitz'sche Verlagsbuchhandlung.

Vladimirskii, M. trans. 1864. *Karla Darvina uchenie o proiskhozhdenie vidov v karstve rastenii i zhivotnykh, primenennoe k istorii mirotvoreniya izlozheno i obyasneno Fridrikhom Rolle.* [Rolle 1863.] With a supplementary biography of Darwin compiled by S. Seneman. St Petersburg: M. O. Vol'fa.

Vogt, Carl, trans. 1865. *Über unsere Kenntniss von den Ursachen der Erscheinungen in der organischen Natur. Sechs Vorlesungen für Laien, gehalten in dem Museum für praktische Geologie.* By Thomas Henry Huxley. Braunschweig: Vieweg und Sohn.

Volcanic islands: *Geological observations on the volcanic islands, visited during the voyage of HMS Beagle, together with some brief notices on the geology of Australia and the Cape of Good Hope. Being the second part of the geology of the voyage of the Beagle, under the command of Capt. FitzRoy RN, during the years 1832 to 1836.* By Charles Darwin. London: Smith,

Elder & Co. 1844.

'Volcanic phenomena and the formation of mountain chains': On the connexion of certain volcanic phenomena in South America; and on the formation of mountain chains and volcanos, as the effect of the same power by which continents are elevated. By Charles Darwin. [Read 7 March 1838.] *Transactions of the Geological Society of London* 2d ser. 5 (1840): 601–31. [*Collected papers* 1: 53–86.]

Vorzimmer, Peter J. 1969–70. Darwin's 'Lamarckism' and the 'flat-fish controversy' (1863–71). *Lychnos* 12: 121–70.

Wagner, Rudolph. 1861. *Zoologisch-anthropologische Untersuchungen, I.* Göttingen: Dieterichschen Buchhandlung.

Wallace, Alfred Russel. 1853. *A narrative of travels on the Amazon and Rio Negro, with an account of the native tribes, and observations on the climate, geology, and natural history of the Amazon valley.* London: Reeve.

——. 1857. On the natural history of the Aru Islands. *Annals and Magazine of Natural History* 2d ser. 20, suppl.: 473–85.

——. 1864a. The origin of human races and the antiquity of man deduced from the theory of 'natural selection'. [Read 1 March 1864.] *Anthropological Review* 2: clviii–clxx.

——. 1864b. On the phenomena of variation and geographical distribution as illustrated by the *Papilionidæ* of the Malayan region. [Read 17 March 1864.] *Transactions of the Linnean Society of London* 25 (1865–6): 1–71.

——. 1865. On the pigeons of the Malay Archipelago. *Ibis* n.s. 1: 365–400.

——. 1866a. On reversed sexual characters in a butterfly. In *The British Association for the Advancement of Science. Nottingham meeting, August, 1866. Report of the papers, discussions, and general proceedings*, edited by William Tindal Robertson. Nottingham: Thomas Forman. London: Robert Hardwicke.

——. 1866b. On reversed sexual characters in a butterfly, and their interpretation on the theory of modifications and adaptive mimicry (illustrated by specimens). *Report of the thirty-sixth meeting of the British Association for the Advancement of Science, held at Nottingham*, Transactions of the sections, p. 79.

——. 1867. Ice marks in North Wales. (With a sketch of glacial theories and controversies.) *Quarterly Journal of Science* 4: 33–51.

——. 1869. *The Malay Archipelago: the land of the orang-utan, and the bird of paradise. A narrative of travel, with studies of man and nature.* 2 vols. London: Macmillan and Co.

——. 1905. *My life: a record of events and opinions.* 2 vols. London: Chapman & Hall.

Wallace, Robert, ed. 1899. *A country schoolmaster: James Shaw, Tynron, Dumfriesshire.* Edinburgh: Oliver and Boyd. London: Simpkin Marshall, Hamilton, Kent & Co.

Walsh, Benjamin Dann. 1863. Observations on certain N.A. Neuroptera, by H. Hagen, M.D., of Kœnigsberg, Prussia; translated from the original French MS., and published by permission of the author, with notes and descriptions of about twenty new N.A. Pseudoneuroptera species. *Proceedings of the Entomological Society of Philadelphia* 2: 167–272.

Walsh, Benjamin Dann. 1864a. On certain entomological speculations of the New England school of naturalists. *Proceedings of the Entomological Society of Philadelphia* 3: 207–49.

——. 1864b. On the insects, coleopterous, hymenopterous and dipterous, inhabiting the galls of certain species of willow. Part 1st.— Diptera. *Proceedings of the Entomological Society of Philadelphia* 3: 543–644.

——. 1864c. On dimorphism in the hymenopterous genus *Cynips*, with an appendix, containing hints for a new classification of Cynipidæ and a list of Cynipidæ, including descriptions of several new species, inhabiting the oak-galls of Illinois. *Proceedings of the Entomological Society of Philadelphia* 3: 443–500.

——. 1864d. On certain entomological speculations of the New England school of naturalists. *Proceedings of the Entomological Society of Philadelphia* 3: 207–49.

——. 1864–5. On phytophagic varieties and phytophagic species. *Proceedings of the Entomological Society of Philadelphia* 3: 403–30, 5: 194–216.

——. 1866a. Imported insects;—the gooseberry sawfly. *Practical Entomologist* 1: 117–25.

——. 1866b. On the insects, coleopterous, hymenopterous and dipterous, inhabiting the galls of certain species of willow.— Part 2d and last. *Proceedings of the Entomological Society of Philadelphia* 6: 223–88.

——. 1866c. Prof. Dana and his entomological speculations. *Proceedings of the Entomological Society of Philadelphia* 6: 116–21.

Walters, Stuart Max and Stow, E. Anne 2001. *Darwin's mentor. John Stevens Henslow 1796–1861.* Cambridge: Cambridge University Press.

[Waterhouse, George Robert.] 1835. Bee. In *The penny cyclopædia of the Society for the Diffusion of Useful Knowledge*, edited by Charles Knight, vol. 4, pp. 149–56. London: Charles Knight.

Waterhouse, George Robert. 1846–8. *A natural history of the Mammalia.* 2 vols. London: H. Baillière.

Wawro, Geoffrey. 1996. *The Austro-Prussian war: Austria's war with Prussia and Italy in 1866.* Cambridge: Cambridge University Press.

Wedgwood, Barbara and Wedgwood, Hensleigh. 1980. *The Wedgwood circle, 1730–1897: four generations of a family and their friends.* London: Studio Vista.

Weinland, David Friedrich. 1863. Was wir gewollt haben. *Der zoologische Garten* 4: 241–3.

Weinreich, Heinrich. 1993. *Duftstofftheorie: Gustav Jaeger (1832–1917); vom Biologen zum 'Seelenriecher'.* Stuttgart: Wissenschaftliche Verlagsgesellschaft.

Wells, Kentwood D. 1973. William Charles Wells and the races of man. *Isis* 64: 215–25.

Wells, William Charles. 1814. *An essay on dew, and several appearances connected with it.* London: Taylor and Hessey.

——. 1818. *Two essays: one upon single vision with two eyes; the other on dew. A letter to the Right Hon. Lloyd, Lord Kenyon and an account of a female of the white race of mankind, part of whose skin resembles that of a negro; with some observations on the causes of the differences in colour and form between the white and negro races of men.* London: Archibald Constable and Co. [and others].

West, David A. 2003. *Fritz Müller. A naturalist in Brazil.* Blacksburg, Va.: Pocahontas Press.

Westwood, John Obadiah. 1831. Hermaphrodite insects. *Annals and Magazine of Natural History* 4: 434–5.

Whitney, Josiah Dwight. 1866. Notice of a human skull recently taken from a shaft near Angels, Calaveras County. [Read 16 July 1866.] *Proceedings of the California Academy of Natural Sciences* 3 (1867): 277–8. [Reprinted in *American Journal of Science and Arts* 43 (1867): 265–7.]

Wichura, Max Ernst. 1865. *Die Bastardbefruchtung im Pflazenreich erläutert an den Bastarden der Weiden.* Breslau: E. Morgenstern.

Williams, Gary. C. 1995. Living genera of sea pens (Coelenterata: Octocorallia: Pennatulacea): illustrated key and synopses. *Zoological Journal of the Linnean Society* 113: 93–140.

Williamson, M. 1984. Sir Joseph Hooker's lecture on insular floras. *Biological Journal of the Linnean Society* 22: 55–77.

Wingfield, William and Johnson, George William. 1853. *The poultry book; comprising the characteristics, management, breeding, and medical treatment of poultry; being the results of personal observation and the practice of the best breeders, including Captain W. W. Hornby, R N.; Edward Bond, Esq.; Thomas Sturgeon, Esq.; Charles Punchard, Esq.; Edward Hewitt, Esq.; and others.* London: Wm. S. Orr and Co.

——. 1856–7. *The poultry book; comprising the characteristics, management, breeding, and medical treatment of poultry; being the results of personal observation and the practice of the best breeders, including Captain W. W. Hornby, R N.; Edward Bond, Esq.; Thomas Sturgeon, Esq.; Charles Punchard, Esq.; Edward Hewitt, Esq.; and others.* Another edition. Re-arranged and edited by W. B. Tegetmeier. London: Wm. S. Orr and Co.

Winkler, Tiberius Cornelis, trans. 1860. *Het ontstaan der soorten door middel van de natuurkeus, of het bewaard blijven van bevoorregte rassen in den strijd des levens.* [*Origin*], by Charles Darwin. Haarlem, Netherlands: A. C. Kruseman.

Winks, Robin. 1960. *Canada and the United States: the Civil War years.* Baltimore: The Johns Hopkins Press.

Winsor, Mary Pickard. 1976. *Starfish, jellyfish and the order of life: issues in nineteenth-century science.* New Haven and London: Yale University Press.

——. 1991. *Reading the shape of nature. Comparative zoology at the Agassiz museum.* Chicago and London: University of Chicago Press.

Wollaston, Alexander Frederick Richmond. 1921. *Life of Alfred Newton, professor of comparative anatomy, Cambridge University, 1866–1907.* With a preface by Sir Archibald Geikie. London: John Murray.

Wollaston, Thomas Vernon. 1854. *Insecta Maderensia; being an account of the insects of the islands of the Madeiran group.* London: John van Voorst.

——. 1856. *On the variation of species with especial reference to the Insecta; followed by an inquiry into the nature of genera.* London: John van Voorst.

Wollaston, Thomas Vernon. 1857. *Catalogue of the coleopterous insects of Madeira in the collection of the British Museum.* London: By order of the Trustees.

——. 1864. *Catalogue of the coleopterous insects of the Canaries in the collection of the British Museum.* London: By order of the Trustees.

——. 1865. *Coleoptera Atlantidum; being an enumeration of the coleopterous insects of the Madeiras, Salvages, and Canaries in the collection of the British Museum.* London: J. van Voorst.

Wood, Christopher. 1995. *Dictionary of British art.* Vol. 4, *Victorian painters.* 2 vols. Research by Christopher Newall and Margaret Richardson. Woodbridge, Suffolk: Antique Collectors' Club.

Woodward, Horace B. 1907. *The history of the Geological Society of London.* London: Geological Society.

Woolley, Benjamin. 1999. *The bride of science: romance, reason and Byron's daughter.* Basingstoke: Macmillan.

Worthen, A. H. 1866. *Geological survey of Illinois.* Vol. 1, *Geology.* [Illinois]: by authority of the legislature of Illinois.

Wrede, Richard and Reinfels, Hans von, eds. 1897. *Das geistige Berlin. Eine Encyklopädie das geistigens Lebens Berlin.* Vols. 1 and 3. Berlin: H. Storm.

Wyman, Jeffries. 1862. Experiments on the formation of Infusoria in boiled solutions of organic matter, enclosed in hermetically sealed vessels, and supplied with pure air. *American Journal of Science and Arts* 2d ser. 34: 79–87.

——. 1863. Description of a 'White Fish,' or 'White Whale,' (*Beluga borealis* Lesson). *Boston Journal of Natural History* 7: 603–12.

——. 1866. Notes on the cells of the bee. [Read 9 January 1866.] *Proceedings of the American Academy of Arts and Sciences* 7 (1865–68): 68–83.

——. 1867. Observations and experiments on living organisms in heated water. *American Journal of Science and Arts* 2d ser. 44: 152–69.

Yaldwyn, John and Hobbs, Juliet, eds. 1998. *My dear Hector. Letters from Joseph Dalton Hooker to James Hector, 1862–1893.* Museum of New Zealand Te Papa Tongarewa Technical Report 31.

Young, Robert M. 1985. *Darwin's metaphor: nature's place in Victorian culture.* Cambridge: Cambridge University Press.

Yule, Henry. 1858. *A narrative of the mission sent by the governor-general of India to the court of Ava in 1855, with notices of the country, government, and people.* London: Smith, Elder and Co.

Zoology: *The zoology of the voyage of HMS Beagle, under the command of Captain FitzRoy RN, during the years 1832 to 1836.* Edited and superintended by Charles Darwin. 5 pts. London: Smith, Elder & Co. 1838–43.

NOTES ON MANUSCRIPT SOURCES

The majority of the manuscript sources cited in the footnotes to the letters are located either in the Darwin Archive, Cambridge University Library, or at Down House, Downe, Kent. Further details about the Darwin Archive are available in the *Handlist of Darwin papers at the University Library Cambridge* (Cambridge: Cambridge University Press, 1960) and the unpublished supplementary handlist available at the library; a new catalogue of the papers is currently being prepared. Further details about the manuscripts at Down House are available in Philip Titheradge, ed. *The Charles Darwin Memorial at Down House, Downe, Kent*, revised ed. ([Downe: Down House Museum], 1981) and from the curator (The Curator, Down House, Downe, Kent, BR6 7JT). In addition, there are a number of named sources that are commonly used in the footnotes: for each of these, the editors have provided brief descriptive notes.

CD's Account books (Down House MS). This series of seventeen account books begins on 12 February 1839, a fortnight after CD and Emma's marriage, and ends with CD's death. The books contain two sets of accounts. From the start, CD recorded his *cash account* according to a system of double-entry book-keeping. On each left-hand page he recorded credits (i.e., withdrawals from the bank, either in the form of cash paid to himself or cheques drawn for others), and on each right-hand page, he recorded debits (i.e., cash or cheques paid to others). CD also recorded details of his *banking account* from the start, but only noted them down in a single column at the bottom of the left-hand page of his cash account. In August 1848, however, he began a system of detailing his banking account according to double-entry book-keeping, in a separate chronological section at the back of each account book. On the left, he recorded credits to the account in the form of income (i.e., investments, rent, book sales, etc.). On the right, he recorded debits to the account (i.e., cash or cheque withdrawals).

CD's Classed account books (Down House MS). This series of four account books, covering the years 1839–81, runs parallel to CD's Account books. For each year, September – August (after 1867, January – December), CD divided his expenditure into different classified headings; in addition, he made a tally for the year of his income, expenditure, cash in hand, and money in the bank. From 1843, CD also compiled at the back of each book a separate account of the total expenditure under the various headings in each year, and from 1844 he added a full account of his income in each year, and of capital invested and 'paid' up. The classification of expenditure varied over time, but for 1864–5 the classes were: 'Miscellaneous', 'Personal', 'Governess & Girls School & Teachers',

'House', 'Boys & William', 'Coals & Firewood', 'Beer', 'Wine', 'Man-servants', 'Repairs, Furniture', 'Medical attendance', 'Stationery, newspapers postage', 'Books', 'Science', 'Gardens', 'Cow, Pigs, Field', 'Stable', 'Travelling Expences', 'Taxes Rates', 'Charities', and 'Gifts, Annual Subscriptions'.

CD's Experimental notebook (DAR 157a). This notebook contains notes on some, though by no means all of the experiments carried out between 13 November 1855 (with some back references) and 20 May 1868, although the majority of the notes date from before 1863. In many cases only the details of the experiment attempted are given, often with cross-references to results recorded in CD's portfolios of notes. The notebook also contains a number of letters to CD.

CD's Investment book (Down House MS). This book records under each of CD's investments the income received during the period 1846–81.

CD's 'Journal'. *See* Appendix II.

CD's Library catalogue (DAR 240). This manuscript catalogue of CD's scientific library was compiled by Thomas W. Newton, assistant librarian of the Museum of Practical Geology, London, in August 1875. Additions to the catalogue were subsequently made by Francis Darwin (who inherited most of his father's scientific library) and by H. W. Rutherford, who apparently used this catalogue as a basis for compiling his *Catalogue of the library of Charles Darwin now in the Botany School, Cambridge* (Cambridge: Cambridge University Press, 1908). However, there are items listed in this manuscript catalogue that do not appear in Rutherford's published catalogue, and which must have been dispersed subsequently to being listed.

Darwin's copy of the *Gardeners' Chronicle* : account of numbers and index to marks & memoranda (DAR 222). This is a bound manuscript index to CD's collection of the *Gardeners' Chronicle and Agricultural Gazette*, 1841–71 (which is at the Cory Library, Cambridge Botanic Garden). It comprises a list showing which numbers of the journal are missing from CD's copy, together with a 'List of the numbers of special interest to Darwin and kept by him in separate parcels'. The latter details the page-numbers and subjects of the articles that were of particular interest to (and annotated by) CD in the numbers that he kept separately. The handwriting of the list is unknown, but probably dates from the late nineteenth century.

Down Coal and Clothing Club account book (Down House MS). CD was for some years treasurer of this charitable organisation. The account book records subscriptions made by honorary subscribers between 1841–76; between 1848 and 1869 the entries are in CD's handwriting. For the years 1841–8 and 1868–76, there is also a statement of expenditures, though not in CD's handwriting.

Emma Darwin's diary (DAR 242). This comprises a series of small pocket diaries, in which Emma recorded details of the health of family members, trips made by herself, CD, and the children, school holidays, and visits to Down by others. The collection at CUL comprises diaries for the years 1824, 1833–4, 1839–45, and 1848–96.

H. E. Litchfield's autobiography (DAR 246). This unfinished autobiography, written in 1926 on forty-two loose leaves, and chiefly concerning Henrietta Emma Darwin's childhood, has never been published.

List of pamphlets (DAR 252.4). This is a catalogue of CD's pamphlet collection prepared by CD and Francis Darwin in 1878 (see the letter from Emma Darwin to Henrietta Emma Litchfield, [June 1878] (DAR 219.9: 175)). From about 1878 CD began to arrange the articles, papers, and reprints he received into a numbered collection. CD maintained this reprint collection until his death, when it was taken over by Francis Darwin. Francis continued the collection, adding new items, the numbers running consecutively from those of his father. Evidently, until this catalogue was prepared, CD used a working index similar to that of his 'List of reviews'. The catalogue is in two sections, a list of the quarto collection and one of the general collection. Both sections are alphabetically arranged with the entries pasted on sheets in a loose-leaf folder.

List of reviews (DAR 262.8: 9–18 (English Heritage MS: 88206151–60)). This manuscript, headed 'List Reviews of Origin of Sp & of C. Darwins Books', was CD's working index to his collection of the reviews of his own books. It corresponds approximately to the review collection in the Darwin Pamphlet Collection–CUL, but includes some items that were dispersed subsequently to being listed.

Reading notebooks. *See Correspondence* vol. 4, Appendix IV. These notebooks comprise sections entitled 'Books Read' and 'Books to be Read'. CD's entries in 'Books Read' often include a brief opinion of the work.

Scrapbook of reviews (DAR 226.1 and 226.2). Many of the reviews contained in these two volumes bear CD's annotations and thus were evidently collected by CD. However, the scrapbook seems to have been assembled by Francis Darwin: the tables of contents are in the handwriting of H. W. Rutherford, an assistant at Cambridge University Library who acted as a copyist for Francis on several occasions (see *ML*, 1: x, and Francis Darwin, ed. *The foundations of the Origin of Species. Two essays written in 1842 and 1844 by Charles Darwin* (Cambridge: Cambridge University Press, 1909)). In addition, the scrapbook is identified as Francis's in a note (DAR 226.1:132a) made in 1935 by Arthur Keith, whose appeal led to the purchase of Down House as a Darwin memorial (see Arthur Keith, *An autobiography* (London: Watts & Co., 1950)). DAR 226.1 bears the inscription 'Reviews of C. Darwin's works' on the spine, and contains, among others, reviews of *Origin* and *Orchids*; DAR 226.2 is inscribed: 'Reviews. Descent. Expression. Insect. Pl. Eras. D.'

W. E. Darwin's botanical notebook (DAR 117). This notebook contains observational and experimental notes on plants made by William, often in consultation with CD. The first observation bears the date 13 July 1862, and, although the date of the last observation is 26 June 1870, most of the notes were made between 1862 and 1864. The notebook originally contained letters from CD, but these were subsequently removed. William entered notes made from botanical textbooks in a separate notebook (DAR 234).

W. E. Darwin's botanical sketchbook (DAR 186: 43). This sketchbook, which contains entries dated 1862–72, was evidently begun in parallel to William's botanical notebook. It contains ink drawings of various parts of plants, and of sections, together with descriptions, which in some cases are very extensive.

INDEX

The dates of letters to and from Darwin's correspondents are listed in the Biographical register and index to correspondents and are not repeated here. Darwin's works are indexed under the short titles used throughout this volume and listed in the bibliography.

Abies canadensis: sent from Kew for Down House garden, 354 n.1

Abies douglasii (Douglas fir): sent from Kew for Down House garden, 354 n.1

Abrus precatorius: brightly coloured seeds, 413 n.3, 420 & 421 n.6

Abyssinia: temperate flora, 46 & 48 nn.13 & 14, 84 & 86 n.8

Academia Caesarea Leopoldino-Carolina Naturae Curiosorum of Dresden: CD a member, 109 & n.7

Academy of Natural Sciences of Philadelphia: CD a corresponding member, 109 & n.9

acclimatisation of plants, 90 & 91 n.5

Acer negundo 'Variegatum': effect of scion wood on colour of stock tissue, 182 & n.4, 197 & 198 n.3, 198 & n.3

Acineta: CD unable to pollinate, 324 & 325 n.5

Acorus calamus (sweet flag): A. Gray believes it fruits, 344 & 345 n.6; sterility, 314 & 315 n.11, 327 & n.2

Acropera: J.D. Hooker sends specimen to CD, 261 & 263 n.21, 271 & 272 & 274 n.19, 296 & n.5, 304 & 305 n.11, 337 & n.3; numbers of seeds produced by, 416 n.12; pollination, 304 & 305 n.11, 308 & 309 n.13, 324 & 325 n.3

Adams, John Couch: day length steadily increasing, 347 & 348 n.8

adaptation of organisms: alpine plants, C.W. von Nägeli's view, 390 n.11; W.R. Grove's view, xxii, 306 & n.2

Adelaide Botanic Garden: M.R. Schomburgk, director, 149 & n.2

Adenanthera pavonina, 416 n.6, 418 nn.2 & 3, 426 & 428 nn.1–3, 439 & 440 n.6, 452 & 453 n.14

Aeschynomeme, 93 & 95 n.5, 464 & 465 n.5

Agassiz, Elizabeth Cabot Cary: correspondence with M.E. Lyell, xvi, 35 & 36 nn.2 & 7, 45–6 & nn.4 & 5, 68 & 69 n.9, 75 & 76 n.6, 313 & 315 n.4

Agassiz, Louis: apologises to A. Gray, 377 & 378 n.6; birds of Amazon valley, 311 & 312 n.11; book on American natural history, dispute with collaborator, 244 & 246 n.15, 283 & 284 n.11; expedition to Brazil, xvi, 10 & 12 n.10, 35 & 36 nn.3, 4 & 7 & 37 nn.8 & 12, 242 & n.8, 303 nn.3 & 4; E. Haeckel's opposition to theories, 7 & 9 n.12 & 10 n.13, 456 & 458 nn.12 & 13; insects scarce in Amazon valley, 312 n.10; *Methods of study*, 400 n.3; theories of glaciation in Brazil, xvi–xvii, 35–6 & n.7 & 37 nn.8 & 12, 45–6 & n.3, 59 & 60 n.3, 72 & 74 nn.2 & 3, 76 & n.8, 98 & 99 n.3, 266 & 268 n.16, 296 & n.8, 302 & 303 nn.3 & 4, 311 & 312 nn.5–7, 9 & 12, 313 & 315 nn.3–5, 322 & 323 nn.6 & 7, 325 & 326 nn.16 & 17, 329 n.2, 391 & 392 nn.6 & 7

Ainslie, Robert, 2 & n.5

Airy, George Biddell: day length steadily increasing, 347 & 348 n.8

Alauda arvensis (skylark): observed in Bermuda, 287 & n.4

Albert Edward, Prince of Wales, xvii

Alfuran people: K.E. von Baer's book, 270 & 271 n.3

Alkanna 'hispidifolia', 225 & 226 n.11

Allen, Emma, 66 & n.10

Allen, Frances, 66 & n.10

Allen Gardiner (missionary ship), 446 n.4

alpine floras: migration of species, 141–2 & nn.4–6, 178 & 179 n.4; natural selection in, 389 & 390 n.11

Amazon river: distinctive character of gallinaceous birds, 311 & 312 n.11; fishes of, 12 n.10, 35 & 36 n.3; whether basin formed by glacial action, 36 n.7, 46 & 47 nn.4, 6 & 7 & 48 nn.9–11, 266 &

Amazon river, cont.
268 n.16, 296 & n.8, 311 & 312 nn.6, 7 & 9, 313 & 315 n.4, 329 n.2, 392 n.6
Ambystoma mexicanum. See axolotl
Amentaceae: few species in humid temperate regions, 443 & 444 n.4
American Academy of Arts and Sciences: J. Wyman's paper on geometry of bees' cells, 34 & n.6
American Journal of Science and Arts: A. Gray, paper on dimerous *Cypripedium*, 284 n.3; F. Müller's paper on climbing plants, 299 & 300 n.8, 453 n.15
American Quarterly Church Review and Ecclesiastical Register: H.A. Dubois, paper on origin and antiquity of man, 243–4 & 245 nn.7–9
Amphioxus lanceolatus. See Branchiostoma lanceolatum
Anas boschas, 6 & nn.3 & 4
Anas poecilorhyncha (spot-billed duck), 6 & n.4
Anchusa azurea: identified by D. Oliver for CD, 198 n.1
Anchusa italica. See Anchusa azurea
Anderson, Thomas: Calcutta botanic garden, superintendent, 81 & 83 n.9; illness, 81
Andromeda: found in Organ Mountains, 46 & 47 n.8
Anguilla bostoniensis (rostrata): malformed specimen found in well, 31 & nn.4–6
Annales de la Société d'orticulture de Paris: Prévost's paper on *Cytisus adami*, CD wishes to read, 148 & n.3
Annales des Sciences Naturelles: insular floras, translation of J.D. Hooker's lecture, 304 n.3
Annales Musei Botanici Lugduno-Batavi: R. Caspary's paper on Nymphaeaceae, 80 n.11; F.A.W. Miquel, editor, 80 n.11
Annals and Magazine of Natural History: article on 'domesticated' white whale, 127 n.4; article on fossil fishes of Lebanon, 311–12 & n.13; E.G. Balbiani's paper on reproduction in aphids, 298 & n.6; CD renews subscription, 53 & 54 n.5; F. Müller's papers on crustaceans, 11 nn.7 & 8; J. Steenstrup, paper on migration of eye in flatfish (abstract), 230 & 240 n.2
annelids: A. de Quatrefages' book on, 384 & 385 n.3, 476 & n.2
Anser (geese): W.B. Tegetmeier seeks information from CD on varieties, 420 & n.4, 421–2 & n.4, 431 & n.2
Antarctica: flora dispersed over southern hemisphere, 439 & 440 n.9
Anthropological Society of London: presentation copy of *Origin*, 485
Antilocapra americana (prongbuck, pronghorn): horns, 307 & n.11
Antirrhinum majus: CD sends specimens of peloric flowers to J.D. Hooker, 413 & n.1, 420 & 421 n.3
ants. *See Formica sanguinea*
Apathus (*Psithyrus*, cuckoo bumble-bee): sting, 87 & 88 n.2
apes: anthropoid, do not erect ears, 430
Aphis: reproduction, 244–5 & 246 nn.19 & 20; reproduction, E.-G. Balbiani's paper, 298 & n.6, 442 & n.7 & 443 n.9
Apis. See under bees
Apocyneae: insects trapped by flowers, 122 & 123 n.9
Apoica pallida. See under wasps
Apollonias, 254 & 256 n.18
apples: monstrous tree at St Valery, 304 & 305 n.12, 309 & n.14, 318 & 319 n.1, 322 & 323 n.3
D. Appleton and Co., publishers of *Origin*, xix, 131 nn.11 & 12, 156 & 157 nn.3 & 4, 231 & nn.3, 6 & 7, 276 n.2, 283 & 284 nn.6 & 8, 302 & 303 n.1, 313 & 315 n.7, 344 & 345 n.3, 361 & 362 nn. 3 & 4, 362 & n.2; 'dog-in-the-manger' attitude, 231 & n.7, 247 & 248 n.8; statement of sales, 246 & 247 nn.1–6 & 9
Appleton, Thomas Gold, 83 n.1, 90 & nn.2–4
Aral Sea: tame saigas in island in, 417 & nn.3 & 4, 422 & 423 nn.3 & 4, 432 & 433 n.2, 433 & 434 nn.2 & 3
Archaeological Institute of Great Britain and Ireland: J. Lubbock's paper read at congress, 264 & n.3, 277 & n.2
Archaeopteryx, 192 & 193 n.5
Archiv für mikroskopische Anatomie, 93 & 95 n.9, 464 & 466 n.9
Archives of Medicine, 51 n.3
Arctic floras: colonisation of Auvergne mountains, 141–2 & n.6; J.D. Hooker's essay, 190 & 191 nn.8 & 9, 192 & 193 nn.9 & 10, 289 & 290 n.17
Arctogale: taxonomic difficulties in classification, 83 & 84 n.6
Ardoino, Honoré Jean Baptiste: gift of seeds to J.T. Moggridge, 274 & 275 n.2
Argentina: conditions of deposition of pampas formations, 250 n.2
Argyll, 8th duke of. *See* Campbell, George Douglas, 8th duke of Argyll
Aria vestita: E.A. Carrière's grafting experiments, 439 & 440 n.13

aristocracy: outcome of natural selection, 181 & 182 n.11; parrot's response to, 136
Aristolochia: pollination mechanisms, 122 & 123 n.8
Aristolochia clematitis: female–male dichogamy in, 252 & n.9, 360 & 361 nn.2–5; pollination, 252 n.10
Aristotle: cited by C.J. Grece, 386 & 387 n.3
Arius boakeii (*A. arius*, threadfin sea catfish): incubation of eggs in mouth, 441 & n.3
Armistead, Wilson: proposed book on gall insects, 101 & 102 n.8, 137 & 138 n.5; B.D. Walsh sends gall insects to, 243 & 245 nn.5 & 6
Armstrong, Mr, 341 & 342 n.2
Arum maculatum: pollination mechanisms, 122 & 123 n.8
Ascension Island: flora, 289 & 290 n.8
Ashley Combe, Somerset: J.D. Hooker's visit to, 366 & 367 n.5
asses: stripes as instance of reversion, 206 & 207 n.8
Athenæum: CD, letter urging publishers to sell books with pages cut, 448 & n.6; J. Lubbock's paper on archaeology, 264 & n.3, 277 & n.2; report of Brechin Town Council's disapproval of British Association for the Advancement of Science, 323 n.11; report of Royal Society soirée, 172 n.3; J. Shaw's article on feeling of beauty among animals, 397 n.2; A.R. Wallace, paper on adaptive mimicry in butterfly, abstract, 307 n.8
Athenaeum Club: J.D. Hooker meets W.R. Grove at, 427 & 429 n.11
Atlantic Monthly: L. Agassiz's article on Amazon valley, 311 & 312 n.5, 313 & 315 n.4, 392 n.6
Atlantis hypotheses, 253 & 255 nn.8, 11 & 13, 257 & 258 nn.2 & 5, 276, 285 & 286 n.6
atomic theory of matter, 116 & 117 n.5
auroch. *See Bos primigenius*
Australia: glacial action in south-east, 48 n.20; J.D. Hooker's essay on flora, 190 & 191 nn.8 & 9, 439 & n.5
Austro-Prussian War, xxiii, 166 & 168 n.5, 231 & 232 n.6, 248 & 249 n.2, 363 & n.3, 469 & 470 n.5, 473 & 474 n.3
axolotl (*Ambystoma mexicanum*), 83 & 84 n.4
Azores: birds of, 276 & 277 n.3, 281 & n.4, 285 & 286 n.10; distance from America, 263 n.19, 276 & 277 n.4, 281 & n.5, 285 & 286 n.2, 287 & 288 n.11; distance from America and Europe, 289 & 290 nn.9 & 10; distance from Madeira, 271 & 273 n.7; erratic boulders, 281 & n.6, 285 & 286 n.5, 287 & 288 n.6, 288 & 289 n.4; flora, 261 & 263 nn.14, 16 & 19, 271 & 273 n.7, 276 & 277 n.4, 281 & nn.5 & 7, 289 & 290 nn.8 & 10, 439 & 440 n.9

Babington, Charles Cardale: Cambridge University, professor of botany, 410 & 412 n.15; illness, 410 & 412 n.15; International Horticultural Exhibition and Botanical Congress, member of committee, 86 & 87 n.2
Baer, Karl Ernst von: paper, 'Über Papuas und Alfuren', 270 & 271 n.3
Bahia: orchid growing in, 265 & 268 n.4
Hippolyte Baillière, publishers and booksellers, 243 & 245 n.3, 298 n.1, 438 n.2, 441 & n.2
Baird, Spencer Fullerton: bird migration from America to Europe, 287 n.4, 289 & 290 n.16; election to National Academy of Sciences, 378 n.6; paper on North American birds, 281 & n.5
Baker, John Gilbert: seeds of *Ononis columnae*, 234 & 235 nn.2 & 4
Baker Channel, Patagonia: survey, 217 & 218 n.12
Balbiani, Edouard-Gérard: paper on reproduction of aphids, 298 & n.6, 442 & n.7 & 443 n.9
Balfour, John Hutton: Botanical Society of Edinburgh, secretary, 483
banking crisis, 172 & 173 n.15
Banks, Joseph, 443 & 444 n.2
bantams. *See under* fowls
Bardfield oxlip (*Primula elatior*): identified as distinct species, 314 & 315 n.12
Barter, Richard: hydrotherapy establishment, 216 & 217 nn.4 & 6
Bartlett, Abraham Dee: observation of cassowary, 423 n.8; Zoological Gardens, Regent's Park, superintendent, 423 n.8
Bateman, James: cool-grown orchids, 61 n.8
Bates, Henry Walter: CD asks for copy of paper on tame saigas, 432 & 433 n.2, 433 & 434 nn.2 & 3; colouring in butterflies, 55 n.6; paper on mimetic butterflies, 190 & 191 nn.7 & 9; papers on variability in butterflies, 192 & 193 nn.9 & 10; presentation copy of *Origin*, 485 & 486 n.11; Royal Geographical Society of London, assistant secretary, 433 n.2; *The naturalist on the river Amazons*, 190 & 191 n.7; travels in Brazil, 35 & 36 n.6
batrachians: larva, 83 & 84 nn.1, 3 & 4, 90 & nn.3–5
bats: difficulties in taxonomical studies, 83 & 84 n.5

Battersby, Charles Henry: physician, 128 & 129 n.5
HMS *Beagle*, 444 & 446 n.10; Christmas festivities at Chiloé, 445 & 447 n.20; fossils collected in Patagonia, 226 & 227 n.5; R.N. Hamond, member of expedition, 445 & 446 n.15; J. Harris, guide in Patagonia, 446 & 447 n.25; P.B. Stewart, member of expedition, 445 & 447 n.21; J.L. Stokes, mate and assistant surveyor, 444 & 446 n.6; voyage, 12 n.13, 151 & 152 nn.6 & 7, 218 n.13
Beale, Lionel Smith: papers on cell biology, 50 & 51 nn.1–3, 54 n.7
beans: climbing French, 183 & 184 & nn.2 & 3; crossing experiments using *Phaseolus* spp., 292 & 293 n.4
Beatson, Alexander: birds of St Helena, 276 & 277 n.2, 280 & 281 n.2, 287 & 288 n.7
beauty: appreciation by animals, 42–3 & 44 nn.1–12, 54 & 55 nn.2–7, 135–6 & 137 nn.1–9, 144 & n.3, 379–80 & nn.2–5, 397 n.2; in humming-birds, 165 n.3; in relation to natural selection, 203 & 204 n.4, 397 n.2, 418 n.2; of seeds or fruit, 267 & 269 n.24, 324 & 326 n.12
Becker, Lydia Ernestine: CD sends copies of 'Climbing plants', 'Dimorphic condition in *Primula*' and 'Three forms of *Lythrum salicaria*', 447 & n.2; CD sends copy of *Linum* paper, 435 & nn.2 & 5; Manchester Ladies' Literary Society, president, 436 & n.4; move to Manchester, 435 & 436 n.3; observations of *Lychnis diurna*, 435 & 436 n.1; sends *Primula farinosa* specimens to CD, 447 & n.2
bee ophrys. *See Ophrys apifera*
beech: fern-leaved. *See Fagus sylvatica* 'Asplenifolia'
bees: *Apis indica*, 306 & 307 n.2; *Apis indica*, honeycomb, 108 & nn.3 & 4; and fertility of papilionaceous plants, 444 & n.5; geometry of hive-bee cells, 12–14 & 15 nn.1–7 & 16 nn.8–10, 33–4 & nn.2–8 & 35 nn.11 & 12; geometry of humble-bee (*Bombus*) cells, 30–31 & nn.1 & 2; lousewort pollination by *Bombus lapidarius*, 140 & 141 n.4; stings, 87–8 & n.1; and their parasites, 31 & n.3
beetles. *See* Coleoptera
Befaria. *See* Bejaria
Begonia phyllomaniaca, 116 & 117 nn.2 & 3, 121 & n.4
Behrens, Miss: CD sends signature to, 414
Bejaria (*Befaria*), 67 & 69 n.6
Beluga orealis. *See under* whales
Belvoir Castle, Leicestershire: excursion from Nottingham, 308 & 309 n.12
Bencomia caudata, 253 & 255 n.8
Bengal: orchids from, 81 & 83 n.11
Bennett, George, 58 n.3
Bennett, John Joseph: International Horticultural Exhibition and Botanical Congress, member of committee, 86 & 87 n.2; Linnean Society of London, librarian, 224 & n.3
Bennett, William: sends *Leersia* specimens to CD, 413 n.1
Bentham, George, 282 & n.5, 427 & 429 n.10; absence from Kew, 320 & 321 n.1; administration and locality of natural history collections, 175 & n.1 & 176 nn.2 & 3; gratified to hear of CD's improved health, 321 & n.8; and J.D. Hooker, *Genera plantarum*, 329 & 330 n.12, 428 & 429 n.20; and J.D. Hooker, *Genera plantarum*, CD offers copies to F. Müller, 299 & 300 n.10, 452 & 453 n.13; hopes to call on CD, 339; Linnean Society of London, anniversary address, 320 & 321 n.3; Linnean Society of London library, borrowing regulations, 321 & nn.5–7, 327 & n.4, 331 & n.1; Linnean Society of London, president, 224 & n.3, 321 n.5; *Ononis columnae* specimen, 274 & 275 n.3; Umbelliferae, controversy with H. Spencer, 427 & 428 n.6; visit to R.M. Rolfe, 329 & 330 n.13, 331 & n.2, 339 & nn.2 & 3
Bentham, Sarah, 331 & n.3
Bentley, Robert: International Horticultural Exhibition and Botanical Congress, member of committee, 86 & 87 n.2
Berkeley, Miles Joseph: International Horticultural Exhibition and Botanical Congress, member of committee, 86 & 87 n.2; translator of C.V. Naudin's paper on hybridism, 205 & 206 n.5
Berliner Entomologische Zeitschrift: review of B.D. Walsh's paper on dimorphism in *Cynips*, 244 & 246 nn.17–20
Bermuda: birds blown to, 272 & 273 n.14, 287 & n.4; flora, 289 & 290 nn.12 & 13
Bermuda cedar. *See Juniperus bermudiana*
Beroe, 55, 462
Bessemer, Henry, 50 & n.4
Bignonia, 56, 462; clefts in wood, 124 n.14
Bignonia capreolata, 157 & n.7
Binney, Edward William: theory of origin of coal, 18 n.8
Bioko. *See* Fernando Po
Birch, Charlotte Frances (née Gray), 127 n.3
Birch, Samuel: British Museum, keeper of oriental antiquities, 127 n.3

birds: appreciation of beauty by, 42–3 & 44 n.6, 54 & 55 nn.4 & 6; blown to Bermuda and Madeira, 272 & 273 n.14, 281, 287 & n.4 & 288 n.9; C.L. Brehm's study of German, 402 & 403 n.3; colour of fruit a guide to ripeness, 380 & n.6; distribution and migration of North American, 281 & n.5; of Madeira and Azores, 276 & 277 n.3, 281 & n.4, 286 n.10, 287 & 288 n.8; opportunity to exchange European and North American specimens, 400 & n.7, 441 & n.2; petrels of north and south hemispheres, 91 & n.7; reaction to portrait and mirror-image, 54 & 55 n.4, 57 & n.3, 144 & n.2; song, 42–3 & 44 n.6. *See also names of individual species and genera*

bird's eye primrose. *See Primula farinosa*

Bismarck, Otto von, 469 & 470 n.5

Bison bonasus bonasus (wisent, European bison), 29 & 30 n.7, 460 & 461 n.7

bizzarria orange: graft hybrid, 79 & 80 n.9

Blarney, Co. Cork: R. Barter's hydrotherapy establishment, 216 & 217 n.4

Blyth, Edward: article on solitaire, 423 & n.10; articles on Indian cattle, 26 & n.5; health and mental problems, 26 & 27 n.5; *Hyomoschus aquaticus*, 422 & 423 nn.6 & 7; meets CD in Zoological Gardens, 417 & n.2; Molina's Pudu and *Antilope mariquensis*, 76 n.5; stones voided by cassowaries, 422 & 423 nn.8 & 9; tame saigas in island of Aral Sea, 417 & n.3, 422 & 423 nn.3 & 4, 432 & 433 n.2

Boissier, Pierre-Edmond: mountain plants, 259 n.12, 260–1 & 263 n.13

Bombus. *See under* bees

Bonatea pratensis. *See Habenaria pratensis*

Bonatea speciosa. *See Habenaria bonatea*

Bonham-Carter, Elinor Mary: holiday in France, 128 & 129 n.4, 222 & n.6

Bonn University: R. Caspary, director of herbarium, 79 & 80 n.8

books: preferably sold with pages cut, 240 & 241 n.7, 249 & n.6, 448 & n.6, 448 & 449 nn.3 & 4

Boole, Mary Everest: whether CD's theories are compatible with religious faith, xxiv–xxv, 423–4 & n.1 & 425 n.2, 432 & n.2

Borneo: lowland flora, 439 & 440 n.10

Bornet, Edouard: sends CD *Papaver* seeds, 388 n.4, 402 & 403 n.3; studies of *Cistus* hybrids, 185 & n.6, 402 & 403 nn.4 & 5

Bos: palaeontological history of genus, 30 n.11, 461 n.11

Bos primigenius (auroch), 29 & 30 n.7, 460 & 461 n.7

Boston Journal of Natural History: article on 'domesticated' white whale, 127 n.4

Botanical Magazine: CD asks L.C. Wedgwood to check description of *Erica massoni*, 319 & 320 n.2

Botanical Society of Edinburgh: CD elected honorary fellow, 483

Botanische Zeitung: F. Hildebrand, paper on dichogamy and dimorphism, 174 & n.2; F. Hildebrand, paper on hybridisation of orchids, 174 & n.4; F. Hildebrand, paper on mechanisms of insect pollination, 132 & nn.2–4, 139 & 140 n.3; F. Hildebrand, review of CD's *Lythrum* paper, 174 & n.3, 250 & 251 n.5, 252 & n.11; F. Müller, paper on wood of climbing plants, 122 & 124 nn.13–15, 453 n.15

bottle-nosed dolphins. *See Tursio* (*Tursiops*)

Bourcier, Jules, 164 & n.1

Bournemouth: Eocene fossils collected at, 445 & 446 nn.12–14, 448 & nn.4 & 5, 448 & 449 n.2; home of B.J. Sulivan, 444 & 446 n.3

Bowerbank, James Scott: monograph on Foraminifera, CD cited, 375 & 376 n.2; observations on breeding dogs, 375 & 376 n.3

Bowman, William, 1 n.2; address to British Medical Association, 326 & 327 n.2, 341 & n.2; and R.B. Todd, book on physiology, 51 n.3; visit to R.M. Rolfe, 341 & n.3

Brace, Charles Loring, 283 & 284 n.4

brambles: full-grown seedlings rare, 320–1 & nn.2 & 4

Branchiostoma lanceolatum (*Amphioxus lanceolatus*, lancelet): competition with invertebrates, xxiii, 408 & 409 nn.16–18, 479 & 480 nn.16–18

Braun, Alexander Carl Heinrich: *Cytisus* hybrid, 198 n.4; exchanges photographs with CD, 27 & 28 n.4, 458 & 459 n.4; E. Haeckel attends lectures, 27 & 28 n.6, 458 & 459 n.6; in poor health, 155; reads F. Hildebrand's *Oxalis* paper, 252 & 252 n.2; on rejuvenescence, 155 n.5

Brazil: L. Agassiz's expedition, 10 & 12 n.10, 35 & 36 nn.3 & 7, 242 & n.8, 303 nn.3 & 4; changes in flora and fauna, 93–4 & 95 nn.3–5, 7, 8, 10–13 & 15, 464–5 & nn.3–5, 7 & 8 & 466 nn.10–13 & 15; dimorphic plants in, 439 & 440 n.12, 452 & 453 n.3; impact of steam-driven transport, 35 & 36 nn.4 & 5; lakes and streams, 36 & 37 n.13; retirement home of F. Müller, 12 n.9, 403 & 404 nn.1 & 3; whether ever glaciated, 35–6 & n.7 & 37 nn.8 & 12, 242 n.8, 302 & 303 nn.3 & 4, 311 & 312 nn.5–7 & 9, 313 & 315 nn.3–5,

Brazil, cont.
322 & 323 nn.6 & 7, 325 & 326 nn.16 & 17, 391 & 392 nn.6 & 7. *See also* Amazon river; Santa Catarina island
Brechin: hostility of town council towards British Association for the Advancement of Science, 323 n.11, 329 & 330 n.6
Brehm, Christian Ludwig: study of German birds, 402 & 403 n.3
Bristol: B.J. Sulivan's visit, 444
HMS *Bristol*: R.O'B. FitzRoy's service, 218 n.17
British Association for the Advancement of Science, 270 & 271 n.5; 1840 meeting (Glasgow), L. Agassiz, paper on glaciers in Switzerland, 312 n.9; 1840 meeting (Glasgow), C. Lyell, paper on Seine valley in Normandy, 311 & 312 n.9; 1842 meeting (Manchester), committee on zoological nomenclature, 164 n.2; 1860 meeting (Oxford), xxi, 21 & 22 n.8, 389 & 390 n.13; 1866 meeting (Nottingham), F.T. Buckland attended, 339 & n.3; 1866 meeting (Nottingham), excursion to Belvoir Castle, 308 & 309 n.12; 1866 meeting (Nottingham), W.R. Grove, presidential address, xx, xxi–xxii, 190 & 191 nn.3–9, 192 n.3, 304 & 305 n.6, 306 & n.2, 306 & 307 n.6, 308 & 309 nn.8–10, 339 & n.4, 402 & n.2; 1866 meeting (Nottingham), J.D. Hooker, lecture on insular floras, xx–xxi, 17 & 18 nn.9 & 10, 21 & 22 n.7, 222–3 & nn.5 & 6, 225 n.2, 253–4 & n.4 & 255 nn.5–9 & 256 nn.16 & 18, 259 n.14, 260 & 263 nn.10, 11 & 20, 272 & 273 nn.10–15, 277 & n.7, 286 nn.2, 3 & 7, 287 n.5 & 288 n.10, 288–9 & nn.2–4 & 290 nn.5, 6 & 8–10, 294 n.2, 303 & n.2 & 304 nn.3 & 4, 304 & 305 nn.2–5, 306 & 307 n.7, 308 & 309 nn.2–5, 322 & 323 n.10, 329 & 330 n.5, 337 & 338 n.5, 396 & n.8, 410 & 411 n.10, 427 & 429 nn.11 & 12, 439 & n.5; 1866 meeting (Nottingham), T.H. Huxley, president of 'D' section, 303 & 304 n.4, 308 & 309 n.6; 1866 meeting (Nottingham), W.S. Mitchell, report on fossil leaf-bed, 445 & 446 n.12, 448 & n.4; 1866 meeting (Nottingham), president's post too arduous for CD to consider, 306 & n.3; 1866 meeting (Nottingham), C. Pritchard, sermon preached at, 342 & n.2 & 343 nn.3 & 4; 1866 meeting (Nottingham), A.R. Wallace, lecture on reversed sexual characters in butterfly, 312 & 313 n.14, 329 & 330 n.8, 391 & 392 nn.4 & 5; 1867 meeting (Dundee), local expressions of disapproval, 322 & 323 n.11, 329 & 330 n.6; R. Swinhoe, member, 307 n.5
British Medical Association: W. Bowman's address to annual meeting, 326 & 327 n.2, 341 & n.2
British Museum: S. Birch, keeper of oriental antiquities, 127 n.3; R. Caspary intends to visit, 145 & 146 n.6; *Catalogue of seals and whales*, 127 & n.6; CD's visit, 148 & n.2; collection of Patagonian fossils, 226 & 227 n.4; G.R. Gray, assistant keeper, 127 n.3; J.E. Gray, keeper of zoological collections, 186 & 187 n.10; memorial to chancellor of the Exchequer on natural history collections, 174–5 & n.1 & 176 nn.2–5; R. Owen, superintendent of natural history departments, 176 n.2; A. Panizzi, principal librarian, 176 n.2; report on batrachian larva, 83 & nn.1, 3 & 4, 90 & n.4; J.W. Salter seeks employment at, 449 & 450 n.8
Brodie, Benjamin Collins: dines at W. Spottiswoode's, 428 & 429 n.19
Brodie, Philothea Margaret: dines at W. Spottiswoode's, 428 & 429 n.19
Bromfield, William Arnold: flora of Isle of Wight, 212 & n.4
Bromley Common: R.G. Holland, curate of Holy Trinity Church, 319 & nn.2 & 3
Bronn, Heinrich Georg: defends theory of spontaneous generation, 395 n.11; translator of *Origin*, xix, 11 nn. 3 & 4, 29 & 30 nn.5 & 6, 102 & 103 n.2, 105 & 106 nn.4 & 7, 111 & 112 nn.3 & 5, 134 n.5, 143 & n.5, 363 & n.7, 364 & 365 n.6, 378 & 379 nn.3–5, 382 & 383 & n.2, 388 & 390 nn.3–11, 460 & 461 nn.5 & 6, 466 & 467 nn.4 & 7, 469 & 471 n.10, 474 & n.7
brooms. *See Cytisus*
Brown, Robert: prediction, 113 & 114 n.11
Bryozoa: changes in populations, 94–5, 465
Buckland, Francis Trevelyan: attends British Association for the Advancement of Science, 339 & n.4; CD seeks information on feet of otter-hounds, 336 & 337 nn.4–6, 339 & n.3; *Field*, severs connection, 330 & 331 n.2; *Land and Water*, editor of Practical Natural History, 330 & 331 nn.1 & 3, 423 n.10; offers services of staff to CD, 330
buckthorn. *See Rhamnus cathartica*; *Rhamnus lanceolata*
bud variations, 208–9 & nn.1 & 2, 212–13 & n.1
buds: CD asks for information on structure and appearance of young, 148
Bulletin Botanique: N.C. Seringe's paper on St Valery apple, 304 & 305 n.12, 309 & n.14, 322 & 323 n.3

Bulletin de la Société Botanique de France: F. Müller's paper on climbing plants, notice, 299 & 300 n.8, 453 n.15
Bulletin de l'Académie Impériale des Sciences de St.-Petersburg: F.J. Ruprecht, paper on Russian black earth, 195 & 196 n.9, 472 & n.9
Bulletin du Congrès International de Botanique et d'Horticulture: R. Caspary's paper on graft hybrids, 71 & nn.2 & 3, 141 & 142 n.1
Bullock, Charles J., 59 n.1
Bunbury, Charles James Fox: comments to C. Lyell on theory of glaciation of Brazil, 35–6 & nn.3 & 7 & 37 nn.8–12, 46–7 & 49 nn.21–2, 67–8 & nn.1–5 & 69 nn.6–13, 75 & 76 n.6; dines with C. and M.E. Lyell, 410 & 411 n.5, 420 & 421 n.5; flora of Madeira, 257 & 258 n.3 & 259 n.6; welcomes news of CD's improved health, 68 & 69 n.12
Bunbury, Edward Herbert: dines at C. Lyell's, 420 & 421 n.5
Bunbury, Frances Joanna, 37 n.14; dines at C. Lyell's, 420 & 421 n.5
Burchell, William John: plant collections from St Helena, 129 & 131 n.6
Burdett-Coutts, Angela Georgina: dines at C. Lyell's, 420 & 421 n.5
Burlingtonia, 299 & 300 n.6
Burn, Robert, 349 & n.2
Burritt, Elihu: oats 'transmuted' into barley, 350 & n.1
Busk, Ellen, 81 & 82 n.5, 84 & 85 n.2; visit to J.D. and F.H. Hooker, 72 & 74 n.1
Busk, George, 81 & 82 n.5; discussion at Linnean Society meeting, 421 n.8; Linnean Society of London, secretary, 321 & n.7; visit to J.D. and F.H. Hooker, 72 & 74 n.1
Butakoff, Aleksey Ivanovich: survey of Aral Sea, 417 n.4, 422 & 423 n.4, 432 & 433 n.2
Butler, Samuel, 151 & 152 n.5
Butler & M'Culloch, seedsmen, 382 & n.4
butterflies: awareness of beauty, 136; H.W. Bates's paper on mimetic, 190 & 191 nn.7 & 9; H.W. Bates's papers on variability in, 192 & 193 nn.9 & 10; beauty displayed in conspicuous parts, 54 & 55 n.5; coexistence of different female forms, 24 nn.4 & 5, 39–40 & n.2, 44 & 45 n.2; males more brilliant than females, 54 & 55 n.6, 57 & 58 n.2; rare at Kew, 282 & n.8; A.R. Wallace's paper on adaptive mimicry, 306 & 307 n.8, 308 & 309 n.7, 322 & 323 n.12, 329 & 330 n.8, 391 & 392 nn.4 & 5; A.R. Wallace's paper on Malayan, xxii, 24 & n.3 & 25 nn.4 & 5, 190 & 191 nn.6 & 9
Butterworth & Heath, engravers, 239 n.3, 270 n.3, 350 & 351 n.1, 351 & 352 n.2
Button, Jemmy, 444 & 446 n.5

Caccabis rufa (red-legged partridge): seeds carried in earth ball on foot of, 401 n.1, 401 & 402 n.2
Caithness, Scotland: T.F. Jamieson's paper on glaciation in, 328 & nn.2–4
Calamus angustifolius, 82 & 83 n.12
Calamus jenkinsianus, 81 & 83 n.12
Calamus lewisianus, 81 & 83 n.12
'Calaveras skull', 401 n.9
Calcutta botanic garden: T. Anderson, superintendent, 81 & 83 n.9; J. Scott, curator, 82 & 83 nn.9 & 14
Caldwell, William Hay: *Ornithorhynchus parodoxus* (*O. anatinus*), proved oviparous, 399–400 & n.6
Calluna vulgaris, 261 & 263 n.16
Cambridge University: C.C. Babington, professor of botany, 410 & 412 n.15; CD a student, 151; F. Darwin a student, 349 & n.2; G.H. Darwin a student, 1 n.1, 66 & n.9, 133 & n.3, 445 & 446 n.17, 451 & n.9; G.M. Humphry, professor of human anatomy, 399 & n.2; A. Newton, professor of zoology and comparative anatomy, 351 n.3
camera lucida, 162 n.2, 213 & 214 n.4
Campbell, George Douglas, 8th duke of Argyll: beauty in birds, 55 n.6, 165 n.3; paper on the reign of law, 42 & 44 n.3
Campbell, Helen Maria: illness, 38 & 39 nn.2 & 3
Canada: invasion threat from Fenian troops, 130 & 131 n.15, 157 & 158 n.9
canary: preening before mirror, 136 & 137 n.3
Canary Islands: birds of, 281 & n.3; flora, 253 & 254 & 255 nn.6–8, 257 & 259 n.7, 261 & 263 n.14, 276, 289 & 290 n.8; *Niger* shipwreck at Tenerife, 273 n.8; sea-currents, 271 & 273 n.8; T.V. Wollaston's catalogues of Coleoptera, 253 & 255 nn.12–14
Candolle, Alphonse de: *Alkanna hispidissima* dimorphic, 226 n.11; dines with C.W. Dilke, 145 & n.1, 180 n.8; dines with J.E. Gray, 120 & nn.1 & 2, 180 n.8; International Horticultural Exhibition and Botanical Congress, president, 86 & 87 n.2, 142 n.9, 194–5 & n.2, 264 n.4, 471 & 472 n.2; missed meeting with CD regretted by both, 179 & 180 n.8, 195 & n.2, 264 & n.4,

Candolle, Alphonse de, cont.
471 & 472 n.2; trees having restricted ranges, 262 n.5, 271 & 273 n.5
Candolle, Augustin Pyramus de: paper on pollination of *Indigofera*, 132 & n.3
Candolle, Casimir de: paper on Piperaceae, 263 & 264 n.2
Candolle, Jeanne-Victoire-Laure de, 196 n.4, 471 & 472 n.4; dines with C.W. Dilke, 145 & n.1
Cape Verde Islands: flora, 172 & 173 nn.13 & 14, 276, 289 & 290 n.8, 439 & 440 n.9; guinea fowl, 422 & n.5; R.T. Lowe and T.V. Wollaston's visit, 172 & 173 n.12
Carabus: distinctive character of Chilean, 311 & 312 n.10
Carboniferous plants: collected on Melville Island, 149 & n.6
Carduus arvensis (thistle): rarity of full-grown seedlings, 320–1 & nn.2 & 3, 327 & n.2
Carlyle, Thomas: origin of clothes, 42 & 44 n.4
Carpenter, William Benjamin: administration and locality of natural history collections, 175 & n.1 & 176 nn.2 & 3; pre-Silurian fossils, 192 n.4
Carrière, Elie Abel: grafting experiments with *Aria vestita*, 439 & 440 n.13
Carruthers, William: International Horticultural Exhibition and Botanical Congress, member of committee, 86 & 87 n.2
Carter, Dunnett & Beale, seedsmen, 439 & 440 n.12
Carus, Julius Victor: exchanges photographs with CD, 383 & 384 n.8, 388 & 390 n.1, 393 & 394 n.1; T.H. Huxley, *Evidence as to man's place in nature*, translator, 364 & 365 n.7; Leipzig University, professor of comparative anatomy, 169 n.16, 471 n.16; Oxford University, conservator of comparative anatomy collection, 169 n.16, 471 n.16; possible translator of *Variation*, 469 & 470 & n.3 & 471 n.11; presentation copy of *Origin*, 378 & 379 n.2; proposed new German edition of *Origin*, xix, 106 n.7, 362–3 & nn.4–6, 378–9 & nn.1–8, 382–3 & nn.2–6 & 384 n.7, 388–9 & 390 nn.2–11, 467 n.7, 469 & 471 n.8, 473–4 & nn.4–6; support for CD's theories, 363, 474; *System der thierischen Morphologie*, 378 & 379 n.6
Caspary, Robert, 195 & 196 n.3, 471 & 472 n.3; CD likes him very much, 192 & 193 n.13; concern for CD's health, 154–5 & n.2; corrections to *Origin*, 379 & n.7; exchanges photographs with CD, 80 & 81 n.14, 91 & 92 nn.1 & 2, 145 & 146 n.5, 163 n.10; giant waterlilies, whether perpetually self-fertile, 148 & n.6, 150–1 & n.5, 367 n.2; graft hybrids, xv, 71 & nn.2 & 3, 79 & 80 nn.4, 5 & 9, 131 n.14, 141 & 142 n.1, 147 & nn.2 & 4; hopes to meet CD in London, 145–6 & nn.4 & 6; interest in *Cytisus adami*, 147 & nn.2 & 4, 198 & n.2; Königsberg University, professor of botany and director of botanic garden, 146 n.7; paper on movements of tree branches as result of cold, 141–2 & n.3, 145 & 146 n.8; *Rhamnus cathartica*, search for female flowers, 199 & 200 & 201 nn.6–13; viability of *Cytisus* pollen, 199 & 200 & 201 nn.2–4; visit to Down House, xviii, 146 n.4, 154–5 & n.3, 170–1 & nn.1–4, 179 & 180 n.7, 181 & n.7, 188 & nn.1 & 2, 190 & 191 n.2, 193 n.13, 196 n.3, 201 n.4, 472 n.3, 482 & n.15
cassowaries: stones consumed to aid digestion, 422 & 423 n.8
cat: adopting squirrel, 319 & n.3
Catasetum: aerial roots, 335 & 336 n.13, 416 & n.13
catfish. *See Arius boakeii*
Cattell, John: florist, nurseryman, and seedsman, 147 & n.3
cattle: E. Blyth's articles, 26 & n.5
Celebes: diversity and distribution of species in, 24 & 25 n.6
cell theory, 197 & n.3
centipedes: *Pauropus*, described by J. Lubbock, 421 & n.8
Cerceris: stings, 87 & 88 n.4
cereals: oats 'transmuted' into barley, 238 & n.1, 241 & nn.1 & 2, 350 & nn.1 & 3
Cetacea, 127 & nn.4–6; fossils not found in pre-Eocene strata, 344 & n.5
chalk: L. Agassiz's hypothesis of deposition, 311 & 312 n.9
Chambers, Robert. *See under Vestiges of the natural history of creation*
Chapman, John, physician to CD, 4 nn.3 & 6; treatment of vomiting, 38 & 39 n.3
Chapuis, Félicien: book on pigeons, 18 & 19 n.4, 22 & 23 n.8, 165 n.4
Charadriiformes, 419 n.4
Charadrius sanctahelenae (wire bird, St Helena plover), 276 & 277 n.2, 285 & 286 n.7, 287 & 288 n.7
Chatfield, Caroline A. Duncombe, 145 & n.2
Chile: Araucanian people, 445 & 447 n.24; Christmas celebrations at Chiloé, 445 & 447 n.20; climate of Chiloé and Valdivia, 68 & 69

Chile, cont.
n.11; distinctive character of beetles, 311 & 312 n.10; religious toleration law passed in, 445 & 447 n.22
China: ducks of, 6 & nn.2–4; honeycomb, 108 & nn.3 & 4
Cirrhaea: pollination, 325 n.4
Cissus, 56, 462
Cistus: believed absent from Madeira, 258 n.3; hybrids, 185 & n.6, 402 & 403 nn.4 & 5
Cistus monspeliensis, 185 & n.6
Clapham Grammar School: G.H., F. and L. Darwin, pupils, 343 n.5; C. Pritchard, headmaster, 343 n.5
Clark, Henry James: dispute with L. Agassiz, 244 & 246 n.14, 283 & 284 n.11; *Mind in nature*, 244 & 246 n.14, 283 & 284 n.12, 298 & n.3
Clarke, Joshua, 238
Clarke, Richard Trevor: crossing experiments with cotton, 376 & 377 n.6; lecture on cultivation of cotton, 376 & 377 nn.5 & 6; paper on *Matthiola*, 376 & 377 n.3
Clarke, William Branwhite, 48 n.20, 419 n.12
Claus, Carl Friedrich: book on variability in copepods, 272 & 274 n.20, 295 & n.6, 298 & 299 n.8, 299 & 300 n.11
Clavelina, 95 & n.15, 465 & 466 n.15
Clayden, John, 350 & n.4
Claythorpe: farm at, 345 & 346 n.3, 381 & n.2
cleistogamic flowers, 80 nn.3 & 13, 235 n.3
Clematis, 67
Clethra, 254 & 256 n.18, 258 & 259 n.10, 276 & 277 n.4
click-beetles. *See* elaters
climate change: acclimatisation of plants, 90 & 91 n.5; changes in Brazilian flora and fauna with, 93–4 & 95 nn.3–5, 7, 8, 10–13 & 15, 464–5 & nn.3–5, 7 & 8 & 466 nn.10–13 & 15; J. Croll's theories, xvii, 74 n.10, 85 n.7, 89 nn.4 & 5, 92 & 93 n.2, 99 nn.8 & 11; H. James's 'wild speculations', 85 n.7; C. Lyell's views, xvi–xvii, 354 & 355 n.4, 404 & n.4; and temperature of space, 84 & 85 n.6; whether cause of extinctions, 347 & n.2
climbing plants: *Adenanthera pavonina*, 416 n.6, 418 nn.2 & 3, 426 & 428 nn.1–3, 439 & 440 n.6, 452 & 453 n.14; CD's observations, 157 n.7, 296 n.6; F. Müller's observations on, 56 & 57 nn.7–10, 122 & 124 nn.13–15, 234 & nn.1–3, 265 & 268 n.11, 299 & 300 n.8, 324 & 326 n.15, 403 & 404 n.1, 411 & 412 n.20, 414 & n.2, 416 & 417 n.15, 452 & 453 n.15, 462–3 & nn.7–10; *Nepenthes*, 296 & n.6, 373 n.7; *Passiflora acerifolia*, A. Gray describes climbing action, 231 & 232 nn.10 & 11. *See also under* Darwin, Charles Robert: publications
Closterium, 93 & 95 n.7, 464 & 465 n.7
clouds: architecture little noticed before Shakespeare, 380 & n.4
William Clowes & Sons, printers, 76–7 & n.5, 169 & n.3
coal: H.B. Geinitz's book on bituminous, 470 & 471 n.14; origin, 17 & 18 n.8, 21 n.6
Coccocypselum. *See Lipostoma*
Coccus: J. Lubbock's paper on embryogeny in, 298 & 299 n.7, 442 & 443 n.8
Cochlearia armoracia (horseradish): thought sterile, 199 & 200 n.5, 314 & 315 n.11, 345 & n.6
Coddington, Henry: microscope, 295 & 296 n.2, 304 & 305 n.9
coelenterates: E. Haeckel's papers, 7 & 9 nn.4, 6 & 7, 20 n.7, 455 & 456 n.4 & 457 nn.6 & 7
Coelogyne hookeriana: specimens sent from Calcutta to Kew, 81 & 83 n.10
Coleoptera: distinctive character of Chilean, 311 & 312 n.10; specimen found without feet, 370, 475; T.V. Wollaston's catalogues, 253 & 255 nn.12–14 & 256 nn.17 & 20, 259 n.15
Collingwood, Cuthbert, 39 n.4; CD's suggestions for researches on *Rifleman* expedition, 64 & nn.1–3 & 65 nn.4–7, 69 & 70 nn.1 & 2; Liverpool Royal Infirmary Medical School, lecturer in botany, 59 n.4; naturalist on *Rifleman* expedition, 58 & 59 nn.1 & 2; sends report of expedition to CD, 65 n.7
Columba livia (rock pigeon): ancestor of all domestic varieties, xiv; illustration for *Variation*, 233 n.3, 239 & n.2; laugher-pigeon, 389 & 390 nn.7 & 8, 394 & n.2
Compositae: shapes of ray-florets, 394 & 395 n.10
compositors: whether arms are of unequal length, 169 & nn.3 & 4
Confervae, 93 & 95 n.8, 464 & 465 n.8
conifers: few species in humid temperate regions, 443; retarded fertilisation in, 452 & 453 n.11
continental extension hypothesis, xxi, 258 n.5, 260 & 262 nn.7 & 9, 272 & 274 n.16, 282 n.3, 285 & 286 n.6, 287 & n.2, 289 n.3 & 290 n.17, 305 n.5
convergence of species, 394 & 395 n.7
Convolvulus (*Ipomoea*): whether dimorphic, 369 & 371 n.11, 452 & 453 n.7, 474 & 476 n.4

copepods: C.F. Claus's book on variability in, 272 & 274 n.20, 295 & n.6, 298 & 299 n.8, 299 & 300 n.11
Corbet, Eleanor, 398 & n.6, 425
Corbet, Richard: seeks advice on diet from CD, 397–8 & nn.3 & 4, 405 & nn.3 & 5, 425 & n.2
Corbet, Rowland William, 397 & 398 n.3
Cordia, 334 & 336 n.9, 368 & 371 n.5, 415 & 416 n.5
Coryanthes: gift from CD to G. Henslow, 117 & 118 n.3
Corydalis bulbosa. *See Corydalis cava*
Corydalis cava, 170 n.5, 176 & 177 nn.3 & 6, 179 & 180 n.15, 250 & 251 nn.2 & 3, 251 & 252 nn.4–6, 324 & 325 n.10, 406 & 409 n.6, 477 & 479 n.6
Corydalis claviculata, 252 n.5
Corydalis lutea, 251 & 252 n.5; self-sterility, 177 n.5
Corydalis solida: self-sterility, 177 n.5
Corylus (hazels): CD seeks nuts from purple-leaved tree, 343 & n.1, 349 & 350 n.2; graft of purple-leaved bud to green-leaved rootstock, 198 n.3
J.G. Cotta'schen Buchhandlung: proposed German edition of *Variation*, 364
cotton. *See Gossypium*
Couch, Jonathan: planned book on British Cetacea, 127 & n.5
cowslip. *See Primula veris*
Crabronidae: stings, 87 & 88 n.3
Cranworth, Baron. *See* Rolfe, Robert Monsey, 1st Baron Cranworth
Crawfurd, John: *Journal of an embassy to the court of Ava*, 270 & 271 n.4; paper on migration of cultivated plants, 171 & 173 n.7, 179 & 180 nn.11 & 12, 181 n.9; supports F.W. Farrar's candidature for Royal Society, 41 & n.3
Cresy, Edward, 399 n.3
Crewsden, William Dilwerth, 209 & n.3
Crocker, Emma Harriet Agnes, 3 n.5
Croll, James: theories of climate change, xvii, 74 n.10, 85 n.7, 89 nn.4 & 5, 93 n.2, 99 nn.8 & 11
Crüger, Hermann: death, 122 & 123 n.12; spiral vessels of orchids, 186 & 187 n.3
Cryptobranchus alleganiensis. *See Protonopsis horrida*
Crystal Palace, Sydenham: performance of *Acis and Galatea*, 104 & n.3
cuckoo humble-bee. *See Apathus*
cucumbers, 112 & 113 n.3, 115 & 116 n.2, 121 & n.5
Cucumis hybrids: sterility in, 202 & n.4
Cunina octonaria (*Cunina köllikeri*): reproduction, 326 n.16
Cunina rhododactyla. *See Pegantha rubiginosa*
Cunningham, Robert Oliver, 39 n.4, 173 n.8, 217 n.7 & 218 n.11, 227 n.2, 237 & 238 n.5
Cupressus lawsoniana (Port Orford cedar): sent from Kew for Down House garden, 354 n.1
Cupressus macrocarpa (Monterey cypress): sent from Kew for Down House garden, 354 n.1
Currey, Frederick, Linnean Society of London, secretary, 321 & n.7; and F. Müller's paper on climbing plants, 234 & nn.1–3
Cuvier, Georges, 306 & n.2
Cyclops, 93 & 95 n.8, 464 & 465 n.8
Cynips: B.D. Walsh's experiment, 298 & n.4; B.D. Walsh's paper on dimorphism in, review, 244 & 246 nn.17–20
Cyperaceae: few species in humid temperate regions, 443
Cypripedium candidum: dimerous flower, 283 & 284 n.3
Cypris, 93 & 95 n.8, 464 & 465 n.8
Cytisus: hybrids, 197 n.2, 198 n.4
Cytisus adami (+ *Laburnocytisus adamii*), xv, 79, 198 & nn.2 & 4, 206 & 207 n.5; CD asks T. Rivers for specimen, 147 & n.2, 182 & n.1; CD requests copy of R. Caspary's paper, 71 & nn.2 & 3; description cited in *Variation*, 149 n.4; viability of pollen, 199 & 200 & 201 n.4
Cytisus alpinus (*Laburnum alpinum*): viability of pollen, 199 & 201 nn.3 & 4
Cytisus multiflorus (white broom), 209 & 210 n.7, 219 & 221 n.7
Cytisus purpureus: viability of pollen, 199
Cytisus purpureus elongatus: CD asks T. Rivers for specimen, 147 & nn.2 & 4, 182 & n.1, 197 & n.3; viability of pollen, 199 & 201 n.4; whether pods are formed, 198 & n.4
Cytisus scoparius (common broom): W.E. Darwin's observations, xx, 135 n.2, 158 & 159–62 & nn.2–5 & 163 nn.11 & 12, 209 & 210 n.7, 219 & 221 n.8; mechanisms of insect pollination, 132 & n.4, 134–5 & n.2, 163 n.6
Cytisus watereri: viability of pollen, 199 & 201 n.4

Daboecia azorica, 263 n.16
Dallas, William Sweetland: administration and locality of natural history collections, 175 & n.1 & 176 nn.2 & 3
Dana, James Dwight: paper on cephalisation, 298 & n.2; presentation copy of *Origin*, 243 & 245 n.3; B.D. Walsh's article on, 243 & 245 n.1, 298 & n.2

Darwin, Charles Robert
—AWARDS AND POSITIONS, 108–9 & nn.2–10; Botanical Society of Edinburgh, honorary fellow, 483; British Association for the Advancement of Science, member of committee on zoological nomenclature, 164 n.2; British Association for the Advancement of Science, proposed for president, 306 & n.2; Geological Society of London, Wollaston Medal, 152 & 153 n.19; International Horticultural Exhibition and Botanical Congress, vice-president, 86–7 & nn.1 & 2; Royal Irish Academy, honorary member 125 & n.1, 483; Royal Society of London, Royal Medal and Copley Medal, 152 & 153 n.19
—FINANCES: E.M. Bonham-Carter, payment of W.E. Darwin's expenses, 222 & nn.6 & 7; F. Darwin, payment to R. Burn, 349 & n.2; R. FitzRoy testimonial fund, subscription, 217 & 218 n.15; Jamaica Committee, donation, 393 & n.8; H.B. Jones, payment, 144 & n.3; Kent Church Penitentiary Society, donations, 70 & n.2 & 71 n.5; C. Ludwig, payment, 203 n.2; *Origin*, 4th edition, payments for presentation copies, 77 & 78 n.10; *Origin*, 4th edition, payments to CD, 75 & n.3, 77 & n.7, 78 & 79 n.4, 481 & 482 n.3; *Origin*, US edition, statement of sales, 247 & nn.1 & 9; F. Ransome, settlement of debt, 41–2 & n.2, 49–50 & nn.3 & 4, 53 & nn.1 & 2; sales of shares in London & North West Railway, 209 & 210 n.8; J. Scott, financial assistance, 81 & 82 n.2 & 83 n.15; *Variation*, payment for illustrations, 78 & 79 nn.5 & 6; *Variation*, payments to CD, 352 & 353 n.5
—HEALTH, xiv, 2 & 3 n.1, 3–4 & nn.3–8 & 5 nn.9–11, 22 & 23 n.3, 58, 68 & 69 n.12, 72, 75 n.4, 85, 96 & n.2, 144 & n.3, 155 & n.2, 182, 189, 216, 230 & 231 n.1, 236, 240, 241, 296–7, 309 & 310 n.3, 319 & n.4, 321 & n.8, 358 & n.4, 361 & n.7, 391 & 392 n.8, 398, 444, 451 & n.10; ability to read, xiv, 17 & n.4; able to work, xiv, 3 & 4 n.5, 6 & n.5, 18 & 19 n.1, 20 & n.8, 21 & n.5, 24, 40 n.1, 46 & 48 n.16, 130, 138, 156 & 157 n.1, 236; better though not very strong, 301 & n.5, 306 & 307 n.3; cannot be idle, xiv, 301 & n.6; coffee effective, xiv, 3 & 4 & n.7 & 5 n.9; diet, xiv, 3–4 & n.2, 52 & n.5, 301 & n.5, 307 n.3, 331 & n.4, 451; diet, details requested on behalf of R. Corbet, 397–8, 405 & nn.3 & 5; digestive disturbances, xiv, 3 & 4 & nn.6 & 8 & 5 n.11, 21 & n.5, 52 & nn.1 & 4, 85, 194, 194 & n.2, 196 & n.2; disinclined to write letters, 129 & 130 n.3; exercise, xiv, 3 & 4 n.3, 130, 264 & n.2, 307 n.3, 331 & n.4; exhausted by visitors, 171 & n.4, 358 & n.4; headaches and 'singing head', 3 & 4 n.6, 85, 256 n.2; T.H. Huxley hears 'rampageous', 385 & n.3; ill with cold and influenza, 116 n.3, 121 & n.3, 124 & n.3, 129 n.8, 129 & 131 n.4; looking well in London, 410; never quite well for 24 hours, 451 & n.10; not quite so brilliant lately, 171; not well enough to travel, 37, 128 & n.2, 148 & n.1, 176 & 177 n.2, 179 & 180 n.6, 264 & n.4; riding, xiv, 52 & n.3, 301 & n.5, 307 n.3, 331 & n.4, 331 & 332 n.2, 339 & n.3, 451; 'so well most days', xvii, 148 & n.5; strength for reading not great, 404; takes muriatic acid, xiv, 4 & 5 n.11, 52 & n.4; takes oxide of iron, 4 & 5 n.10; takes 'potass-ammonia', 52 & n.4; tired and not well, 442; weight, 3 & 4 n.4
—OPPOSITION TO THEORIES: L. Agassiz, xvi, 10–11 & 12 nn.10 & 11, 37 n.8, 302 & 303 nn.3 & 4, 311; H.G. Bronn, 102 & 103 n.2; G.D. Campbell, 44 n.3, 165 n.3; H.A. Dubois, 243–4 & 245 nn.7–9; R. FitzRoy, 389 & 390 n.13; H.B. Geinitz, 133 & 134 n.2; H.R. Göppert, 29 & 30 n.12, 460 & 461 n.12; P. Janet, 227 & 230 nn.3 & 10, 236 & 237 n.8; C. Pritchard, 342 & n.2 & 343 n.3; S. Wilberforce, 22 n.8
—PERSONAL ACTIVITIES AND OPINIONS: administration and locality of natural history collections, 175 & n.1 & 176 nn.2 & 3; attends Royal Society of London soirée, xvii, 171 & 172 n.3, 179 & 180 n.9, 189 & n.3, 430 & n.2, 482 & n.14; Miss Behrens, sends signature to, 414; biographical sketch, xvii–xviii, 151–2 & nn.2–9 & 153 nn.10–21, 389 & 390 n.12, 394 & n.4; A. de Candolle, thanks for kind letter, 264; C. de Candolle, thanks for paper on Piperaceae, 263 & 264 n.2; R. Caspary, likes him very much, 192 & 193 n.13; Down charities, treasurer, 110 & n.4, 414 & n.2, 431 & 432 nn.2–4; C.G. Ehrenberg, correspondence, 250 & nn.2 & 3; executor of R.W. Darwin's will, 65 n.3, 346 n.4; F.W. Farrar's candidature for Royal Society, 31–2 & nn.4 & 5, 37–8 & nn.2 & 3, 41 & n.2; forwards business letters to E.A. Darwin, 213 & 214 n.2; A. Gaudry, thanks for paper on fossils of Greece, 317–18 & nn.2–5; gift of Indian chessmen, 340; W.R. Grove, hopes to visit, 146 & 147 n.3; J. von Haast, supports his candidacy for Royal Society, 153 & n.2 & 154 n.3, 309 & 310 n.1; G. Henslow, assists with paper on C.V. Naudin's work on hybridism, 183

& nn.1–3; G. Henslow, comments on article on C.V. Naudin's researches, 201, 202 & nn.2–4, 204–5 & n.4 & 206 n.5; F. Hildebrand, *Corydalis* paper, corrects proofs, 250 & 251 n.3, 251 & 252 n.3; J.D. Hooker, asks for loan of paper on cultivated plants, 179 & 180 nn.11 & 12; J.D. Hooker, asks for loan of paper on St Valery apple, 304 & 305 n.12, 309 & n.14, 318 & 319 n.1, 322 & 323 n.3; J.D. Hooker, returns borrowed journal to, 448 & n.2; J.D. Hooker, sends *Mitchella*, *Leersia* and *Antirrhinum* specimens to, 413 n.1, 420 & 421 n.2; J.D. and F.H. Hooker, invites to visit him in London, 143 & 144 n.3; humane treatment of animals, 1–2 & nn.4 & 5; ignorant of astronomy, 343 & 344 n.3; intends to read G. Schwarz von Mohrenstern and Virchow papers, 143 & n.3; 'Journal', 481–2 & nn.1–23; C. and F.E. Kingsley, meeting with, 414 & 415 n.4; *Land and Water*, subscribes to, 336 & 337 n.7; letters sent while on *Beagle* voyage, 342 & n.4; Linnean Society, complains borrowing regulations too restrictive, 224 & nn.2–4, 321 & nn.5–7, 327 & n.4; Lubbock family 'such lovely children', 337 & 338 n.11; J. Lubbock, lends him F. Müller's paper on prawns, 224 & 225 nn.2 & 3; J. and E.F. Lubbock, visit to, 264 & n.2, 277 & n.1, 332, 337 & 338 n.10; C. Lyell, *Antiquity of man*, disappointment, 344 n.6; C. Lyell, *Principles of geology*, 343–4 & nn.2–6, 346–7 & nn.2–5 & 348 n.7; C. Lyell, sends material on geographical distribution of plants to, 90–1 & nn.4–6, 97 nn.7 & 8 & 98 nn.9 & 10; T.H. Maguire, portrait drawn by, 124 & n.2; F. Müller, thanks for *Oxalis* specimens, 415 & 416 nn.2–4; D. Oliver, asks to identify plant, 196 n.5, 198 n.1; opposition to slavery, xxiii, 130 & 132 n.17; proposed portrait bust, 172 & 173 n.16; A.C. Ramsay, thanks for book on Welsh geology, 207 & 208 n.2; G. Richmond, portraits painted by, 346 n.8; T. Rivers, *Cytisus* specimens, 198 & nn.2 & 4; T. Rivers, wishes he could visit, 350; sale of The Mount, 340 & n.3; serves as magistrate, 2 nn.4 & 5, 152 & 153 n.21; G.B. Sowerby Jr, lends him book on mammals, 355 & 357 n.3; H. Spencer, meeting at High Elms, 331–2, 332, 337 & 338 n.10, 482 & n.19; squabbles with J.D. Hooker do him good, 60 & 61 n.11; W.H. Stirling, wishes to send questionnaire to, 450–1 & n.5; supports Jamaica Committee, xxiii–xxiv, 385 & n.5, 393 & n.8, 395 & 396 n.4; W.B. Tegetmeier, application for membership of Zoological Society of London, 316 & nn.2–4, 317 & n.2; W.B. Tegetmeier, regrets not meeting, 412 & n.3; W. Turner, thanks for information on rudimentary organs, 441 & n.2; W. Turner, thanks for sending papers on cell theory, 197 & nn.2 & 3; E.B. Tylor, meeting with, 179 & 180 n.10; unable to speak German or French, 358; unrecognisable after growing beard, 171 & 172 n.3; B. Verlot's book lost and found, 16, 17 & n.3, 21 & n.1; weak in Greek, xix, 437; L.C. Wedgwood, description of *Erica massoni*, 319 & 320 n.2; whether natural selection theory is compatible with religious faith, xxiv–xxv, 425–6 & n.2; will, 381 & n.3; would prefer pages of books to be cut, 240 & 241 n.7, 448 & n.6; a 'wretched' German scholar, 20, 92, 203 & n.2, 295; 'wriggling' out of difficulties, 60 & 61 n.11, 213 & & 214 n.6, 257 & 258 n.9

—PERSONAL ACTIVITIES AND OPINIONS: PHOTOGRAPHS: CD sends to J. von Haast, 241 & 242 n.2; CD sends to C.W. von Nägeli, 203 & 204 n.11; exchanged with J.V. Carus, 383 & 384 n.8, 388 & 390 n.1, 393 & 394 n.1; exchanged with R. Caspary, 80 & 81 n.14, 91 & 92 nn.1 & 2, 145 & 146 n.5, 163 n.10; exchanged with German scientists, 8 & 10 n.16, 27 & 28 n.4, 27 & n.2 & 28 nn.3 & 4, 456 & 457 n.17, 458 & 459 nn.2–4; exchanged with H.R. Göppert, 329 & 330 n.15, 337 & 338 n.6; exchanged with E. Haeckel, 8 & 10 nn.15–18, 19 & 20 & nn.2, 3 & 9, 163 n.10, 456 & 458 nn.15–18; exchanged with F. Müller, 10 & 11 n.5, 19 & 20 n.3; frontispiece to *Origin*, 2d edition, 19 & 20 n.2; taken by W.E. Darwin, 19 & 20 n.2, 91 & 92 n.2, 146 n.5, 158 & 163 n.10, 204 n.11; taken by E. Edwards, 137 & n.10, 384 n.8

—PUBLICATIONS:

—'Climbing plants', 152 & 153 n.18; *Bignonia capreolata*, 157 & n.7; cited by F. Müller, 122 & 124 n.14; copy sent to L.E. Becker, 436 n.4, 447 & n.2; copy sent to E. Bornet, 403 & n.7; G. Henslow, duplicate copy, 96 & n.4, 100 & n.4; *Mikania* and *Mutisia*, 324 & 326 n.15; *Nepenthes*, 296 & n.6, 373 n.7; *Passiflora*, revolution of tendrils, 232 n.11; *Phaseolus*, 183 & 184 nn.2 & 3; review by A. Gray, 129 & 130 n.2; *Wisteria*, 182 & n.2

—*Climbing plants*, 2d edition: *Philodendron*, aerial roots, 56 & 57 n.9, 462–3 & n.9

—*Coral reefs*, 136 & 137 n.7, 152 & 153 n.11; Bermuda islands, 289 & 290 nn.13 & 14

—*Cross and self fertilisation*: bees visiting *Pedicularis sylvatica*, 141 n.4; cleistogamic flowers, 80 n.13; *Convolvulus*, nomenclature, 371 n.11, 476 n.4; cross-pollination of *Aristolochia*, 361 n.5; crossing of *Papaver*, 403 n.2; crossing of non-blending varieties, 45 n.4; *Cytisus scoparius*, 162 n.5; *Eschscholtzia californica*, 409 n.7, 479 n.7; F. Hildebrand cited, 178 n.11; *Lathyrus odoratus*, 382 n.6; *Mirabilis*, number of pollen-grains needed to fertilise ovule, 393 n.6; *Ononis minutissima*, 382 n.3; pollination of *Arum* and *Aristolochia*, 122 & 123 n.8; pollination in Fumariaceae, 177 nn.4 & 5; pollination of *Medicago lupulina*, 141 n.4; pollination of *Posoqueria*, 123 n.3; pollination in *Salvia*, 178 nn.11 & 12; pollination and setting of seed in *Euryale*, 148 n.6, 154 n.2; products of crosses of distinct species, 314 & 316 nn.13 & 14; self-sterility in occasional plants or species, 178 n.8

—*Descent*, 44 n.12, 271 n.4, 430 n.3; beauty displayed in conspicuous parts, 55 n.5; birds observing mirror-images, 58 n.3, 144 n.3; catfish incubating eggs in mouth, 441 & n.3; F. Chapuis cited, 165 n.5; effect of use or disuse on body parts, 169 n.4; luminous insects, 57 n.5, 463 n.5; printing and typesetting of, 169 n.3; rudimentary organs, 431 nn.4 & 7, 441 & n.2; J. Shaw cited, 397 n.2; transitional types, 318 n.4; W. Turner cited, 441 & n.3; E.B. Tylor cited, 172 n.5; *Urosticte benjamini*, 165 n.3

—'Dimorphic condition in *Primula*', 152 & 153 n.18, 190 & 191 n.4; CD asks for return of loaned copy, 264 & n.4, 277 & 278 n.3; copy sent to L.E. Becker, 447 nn.2 & 3; differences in pollen grains, 211 n.5, 335 n.3; fertility of heteromorphic crosses, 315 n.10; heterostyly, 210 n.6; homomorphic and heteromorphic crosses of *P. veris*, 117–18 & nn.4 & 5, 139 & 140 nn.5 & 6; intercrossing of hermaphrodites, 80 n.3

—'Distribution of erratic boulders', 152 & 153 n.17

—*Expression*: CD requests information from C. Collingwood, 64 & 65 n.7

—'Fertilization of orchids': *Acineta*, 325 n.6; *Cirrhaea*, pollination, 325 n.4; F. Hildebrand cited, 325 n.6; mechanisms of cross-pollination, 123 n.11; F. Müller cited, 300 n.3, 325 n.4; seeds produced by *Maxillaria*, 416 n.12

—'Formation of mould by earthworms', 152 & 153 n.17

—*Forms of flowers*, 453 n.4; aquatic plants, 186 & 187 n.13; *Cordia*, 371 n.5, 416 n.5; crossing of *Mitchella*, 413 n.1; *Cytisus scoparius*, xx, 162 n.5; *Erythroxylum*, 371 n.12, 476 n.5; gynodioecious plants, 210 n.5, 235 n.4; heterostyly, 210 n.6; *Ilex aquifolium*, 209 n.3; *Lipostoma*, 409 n.12, 480 n.12; *Mentha hirsuta*, 235 n.4; *Ononis columnae*, 235 n.3, 275 n.2; *Ononis minutissima*, 382 n.3; *Oxalis*, 170 n.3, 178 n.10, 292 n.3, 336 nn.5, 7 & 8; *Pontederia*, 372 n.16; *Posoqueria*, pollination, 123 n.3; *Primula*, 210 n.6, 315 n.12, 447 n.3; *Rhamnus cathartica*, xx, 201 nn.8 & 14, 211 nn.5 & 6, 214 n.7, 221 nn.5 & 12, 315 n.9; *Rhamnus lanceolata*, 315 n.10; *Sethia*, 372 n.18; size of pollen-grains in different heteromorphs, 371 n.7; transitional states between hermaphroditism and unisexuality, 51 n.2

—*Fossil Cirripedia*, 152 & 153 n.13; cited by J.S. Bowerbank, 376 n.2; G.B. Sowerby Jr, illustrator, 78 n.14

—in *Gardeners' Chronicle*: letter on crossing of papilionaceous plants, 96 & n.3, 292 & 293 nn.2, 4 & 5; letter on *Leschenaultia* pollination, 123 n.5; letter on partial sex change in unisexual flowers, 51 & nn.1–3

—'Illegitimate offspring of dimorphic and trimorphic plants', 140 n.7, 453 n.4

—*Insectivorous plants*: *Drosera binata*, 296 n.3; *Saxifraga*, 393 & n.9

—*Journal and remarks*. *See Journal of researches*

—*Journal of researches*, 58, 111 & 112 nn.8 & 10, 151 & 152 nn.8 & 9; animals' fear of humans, 422 & 423 n.4; birds of Azores, 281 & n.4; birds of St Helena, 276 & 277 nn.1 & 2; copy sent to F. Müller, 10 & 11 n.2; dust falling on Atlantic vessels, 272 & 273 n.14; effects of glaciers, 242 & 243 n.9; evaporation of snow and ice, 347 & 348 n.7; flocks of guinea fowl, 422 & n.5; flora of Tierra del Fuego, 69 nn.7 & 8; *Fucus*, geographical range, 187 n.7; gift to F. Müller, xxiii, 55 & 56 n.3, 462 & 463 n.3; glaciers descending to the sea, 49 n.25; mimicry skills of Fuegians, 446 n.6; peaches grown in Chile, 69 n.11; wading birds not true land birds, 280–1 & n.2

—*Journal of researches*, 2d edition, 56 n.2, 111 & 112 n.9, 463 n.2; luminous animals, 55–6 & n.3 & 57 n.5, 462 & 463 nn.3 & 5; opposition to slavery, 132 n.17; repeated stinging by wasp, 88 & n.1
—*Living Cirripedia*, 152 & 153 n.13, 187 n.11; G.B. Sowerby Jr, illustrator, 78 n.14
—*Natural selection* ('big book' on species): C.L. Brehm, classification of birds, 403 n.3; chapter on hybridism, 376 n.4; chapter read by C. Lyell, 90–1 & nn.4–6, 97 & n.8, 98 & n.1 & 99 nn.3–5; *Fucus*, geographical range, 187 n.7; geographical distribution of species, 91 & n.6, 97 n.8 & 98 n.9; A. von Humboldt cited, 49 n.24; Leguminosae, 293 nn.2 & 3; migration of plants across Africa, 46 & 48 n.14 & 49 n.23; reversion, 207 n.8
—'On the action of sea-water on the germination of seeds', 84 & 86 n.11
—'On the geology of the Falkland Islands', 152 & 153 n.17
—*South America*, 111 & 112 n.7, 152 & 153 n.12; conditions of deposition of pampas formations, 250 n.2; decomposition of igneous rocks, 311 & 312 n.7; fossil discoveries, 233 n.10; German translation, 364 & 365 n.5; uplift along coast, 12 n.13
—'Specific difference in *Primula*', 315 n.12
—'Three forms of *Lythrum salicaria*', 152 & 153 n.18, 191 n.4; adaptations of flowers facilitating insect pollination, 203 & 204 n.6; copy sent to L.E. Becker, 447 n.2; crossing of non-blending varieties, 45 & n.5; differences in pollen grains, 335 n.3; intercrossing of hermaphrodites, 80 n.3; reciprocal dimorphism, 315 n.11; review by F. Hildebrand, 173 & n.3, 250 & 251 n.3, 252 & n.11
—'Two forms in species of *Linum*', 152 & 153 n.18, 191 n.4; copy sent to L.E. Becker, 435 & nn.2 & 5; differences in pollen grains, 335 n.3; experiments on *Primula*, 436 & n.5; intercrossing of hermaphrodites, 80 n.3; plants dimorphic in function but not in structure (functional dimorphism), 265 & 268 n.9, 324 & 325 n.11, 406 & 409 n.5, 477 & 479 & n.5; whether flowers fertilised in unopened bud, 84 & 86 n.10
—*Variation*, xiv–xv, xxv, 1 n.2, 4 n.5, 20 & n.8, 46 & 48 n.16, 76 & 77 n.3 & 78 n.16, 85 & 86 n.15, 109 & 110 n.2, 157 & 158 n.13, 190 & n.7, 229 & 230 n.13, 240 & 241 n.6, 242 & n.3, 270 & 271 n.6, 301 & n.7 & 302 n.8, 306 & 307 n.4, 336 & n.3, 385 & n.2, 391 & 392 n.9, 399 n.5, 404 n.5, 412 & 413 n.5, 418 & 419 n.7, 428 & 429 n.17, 438–9 & n.2, 440 & n.2, 441 & n.2, 451 & n.11, 481 & 482 nn.1 & 4–10; absorption of one species by another, 393 n.6; advantages of crossing, 92 n.6; adventitious buds, 199 n.2; Arctic floras, 192 & 193 nn.9 & 10; *Aria vestita*, grafting experiments, 439 & 440 n.13; L.S. Beale cited, 51 nn.1 & 2; E. Blyth cited, 26 n.5; E. Bornet cited, 185 n.6; A.C.H. Braun cited, 155 n.5; bud variation, 92 n.5; CD sends ms. to J. Murray, 434 & n.1 & 435 nn.3–6; CD unsure of readership, 351 & 352 n.5; cell theory, 197 n.3; cereals, 238 n.1; F. Chapuis cited, 165 n.5; *Cistus* hybrids, 185 & n.6; R.T. Clarke cited, 377 n.3; classification of cell-like bodies, 20 n.6; correlated variability, 114 n.12, 350 n.2; *Corydalis cava*, 177 n.5; crossing experiments with peas, 337 & 338 n.7; crossing of non-blending varieties, 45 & nn.4 & 5; cultivated plants, 179 & 180 n.12, 181 & 182 n.10; *Cytisus adami*, 71 n.3, 148 n.3; *Cytisus* hybrids, 197 n.2; domestic animals, 64 & 65 n.6; duck varieties, 420 n.4; J.G. Duvernoy cited, 263 n.21; effect of one plant's pollen on another's fruit, 130 & 131 n.13; effect of use or disuse on body parts, 115 n.4, 169 n.4; eye, development by natural selection, 348 & 349 n.4; feral cattle, 26 n.5; fowls, 18 & 19 n.5, 22 & 23 n.7, 77 & 78 n.12, 270 nn.2–4, 278 & n.4 & 279 n.6, 316 & n.5, 357 n.4, 412 & n.4, 433 n.4; W.D. Fox cited, 302 n.8; gall insects, 138 n.5; geese, descent, 421–2 & n.4; gemmules, dormancy and reversion, 113 & 114 n.9; gemmules, operation of, 337 & 338 n.9; gemmules, variability due to modified, 113 & 114 n.10; German translation, 364 & n.2, 469 & 470 & nn.3 & 4 & 471 n.11; graft hybrids, 71 n.3, 80 n.9, 155 n.5; hereditary transmission of characters, 1 n.2, 120 n.4, 271 n.4, 295 & n.5; E. Hewitt cited, 270 n.3, 279 n.9; horses, 357 n.4; hybrids, xvi, 376 n.10; illustrations, xiv, 18–19 & nn.2, 3 & 6, 22 & 23 nn.4–7, 77 & 78 nn.11–14, 233 & nn.1–3, 239 nn.2 & 3, 269 & 270 n.2, 278 & nn.2–4 & 279 nn.5–8, 279 & 280 nn.3 & 6, 291 & nn.3 & 5, 314, 316 & n.1, 317

& nn.3 & 4, 350–1 & nn.1 & 2, 351 & 352 nn.2 & 3, 355–7 & nn.2–7, 433 n.4, 434 & 435 n.4; inheritance, 1 & nn.2 & 3, 295 & n.5; *Laburnum watereri*, 147 n.6; T. Laxton cited, 338 n.7; *Matthiola*, 377 n.3; *Mirabilis*, crossing experiments, 393 n.6; F. Müller's observations, xxiii; *Oncidium flexuosum*, 409 n.8, 480 n.8; pangenesis hypothesis, xv, 11 n.8, 24 n.3, 45 n.5, 71 n.3, 113 & 114 nn.5–10, 115 n.3, 120 n.4, 131 n.13, 180 n.14, 197 n.3, 199 n.2, 385 n.2, 481 & 482 n.6; peaches, 241 n.2; pigeons, xiv, 18–19 & nn.2–4 & 6, 22 & 23 nn.4–7, 77 & 78 n.12, 165 n.5, 270 n.3, 278 & n.3, 357 n.4, 412 & n.4; pigs, 357 n.4; portfolios of notes and materials, 267 & 269 n.24, 371 & 372 n.20; presentation copies, 301 & 302 n.8, 306 & 307 n.4, 352 & n.3, 438 & n.2; projected extent, 434 & 435 n.6; proposed chapter on humans, 430 & n.3, 439 & n.3; publication, 242 n.3, 278 & 279 n.12, 297 & n.4, 302 n.8, 307 n.4, 321 & 322 n.9, 352 & n.3, 364 & n.1; rabbits, 357 n.4; reversion, xv, 179 & 180 n.14, 206 & 207 nn.3, 4, 8 & 10, 270 n.2, 280 n.8; rudimentary organs in animals and plants, 430 & 431 n.4; sales, 351 & 352 n.5, 434; S.J.A. Salter cited, 280 n.9; H. Schacht cited, 198 & 199 n.2; seeds produced by *Maxillaria*, 416 n.12; selection, 115 n.5; self-sterility, 325 n.8; sterile plants, 315 n.11; W.B. Tegetmeier cited, 22 & 23 n.12, 270 n.2, 278 & 279 n.10; title, 434 & 435 n.5; W. Turner cited, 197 n.3; US edition, 247 & 248 n.7, 275 & 276 n.5, 283 & 284 n.8, 313–14 & 315 n.8, 345 n.4, 353 & n.4, 362 n.2; use of term 'survival of the fittest', xxii, 236 & 237 n.6; variability in plants, 16 n.2; variable development in unisexual flowers, 1 n.2, 4 n.5, 20 & n.8, 46 & 48 n.16; A.R. Wallace cited, 24 n.3; webbed feet of otter-hounds, 338 n.2

—*Volcanic islands*, 111 & 112 n.9, 152 & 153 n.12

—'Volcanic phenomena and the formation of mountain chains', 152 & 153 n.17

—*Zoology*, 111 & 112 n.11, 151 & 153 n.10

—READING: K.E. von Baer, 'Über Papuas und Alfuren', 270 & 271 n.3; R. Brown's works, 114 n.11; R. Caspary, paper on graft hybrids, 92 & n.3, 130 & 131 n.14; H.J. Clark, *Mind in nature*, 298 & n.3; C.F. Claus, monograph on copepods, 272 & 274 n.20, 295 & n.6; E. Frankland, lecture on source of muscular power, 322 & 323 n.9; W. Griffith, *Journals of travels*, 114 n.11; on gynandromorphy in insects, 51 n.3; E. Haeckel, *Generelle Morphologie*, xix, 294 & 295 n.1, 437 & nn.2 & 3; E. Haeckel, paper on rhizopods, 9 n.6, 20 & n.4, 457 n.6; F. Hildebrand, paper on *Salvia*, 177 & 178 nn.11 & 12; F. Hildebrand, papers on mechanisms of insect pollinaton, 132 & nn.2 & 3, 140 & 141 nn.1–6; A. von Humboldt, *Cosmos*, 380 & n.3; T.H. Huxley, *Lessons in elementary physiology* and *Evidence as to man's place in nature*, 437 & n.4; J. Lubbock, paper on archaeological methods, 264 & n.3; C. Lyell, *Principles of geology*, 10th edition, 346–7 & nn.2–5 & 348 n.7, 404 & nn.2–4 & 6; F. Müller, critique of J.E. Gray's taxonomic errors, 186 & 187 n.9; F. Müller, papers on sponges and crustaceans, 10 & 11 nn.6–8; A. Murray, paper on geographical distribution of mammals, review, 322 & 323 n.8; C.W. von Nägeli, *Entstehung und Begriff der naturhistorischen Art*, 203 & n.2 & 204 nn.4, 7, 8 & 10; *Pall Mall Gazette*, 21 & 22 n.9; *Practical Entomologist*, 399 & 400 nn.4 & 5; N.C. Seringe, paper on St Valery apple, 322 & 323 n.3; H. Spencer, *Principles of biology*, xxii, 223 & n.8 & 224 n.9, 236 & 237 n.10, 418 & 419 n.5; strength for reading not great, 404; W.B. Tegetmeier, *The poultry book*, 239 & n.5; G.A. Thuret, observations on *Fucus*, 402 & 403 n.6; E.B. Tylor, *The early history of mankind*, 172 n.5; B. Verlot, book on variation in plants, 16 & n.2; A.R. Wallace, paper on distribution of pigeons, 24 & nn.1 & 2; A.R. Wallace, paper on Malayan butterflies, 24 & n.3 & 25 nn.4 & 5, 307 n.8

—SCIENTIFIC OPINIONS: amount of living matter on earth, 418 & 419 n.14; ancestry of domestic fowls, 317 n.6; animals' fear of humans, 423 n.4; aristocracy the outcome of natural selection, 181 & 182 n.11; beauty in flowers, 203 & 204 n.6; belief in reversion, 206 & 207 nn. 2–10; birds and flora of Azores, 281 & n.5; brightly coloured seeds, 324 & 325 n.2 & 326 nn.12 & 14, 415 & 416 nn.6 & 8, 417 & nn.2 & 3, 439 & 440 n.7; changes in global temperature, xvii, 59–60 & n.4, 84–5 & nn.5–7, 88 & 89 n.3; colonisation of oceanic islands, 272, 282 & n.3, 286 n.2, 287 & nn.1–3; denudation of Wealden district, 348 & 349 n.8; development of separate sexes in holly, 209 & n.3; dimorphic forms and varieties, 24 & 25 nn.4 & 5, 452 & 453 nn.3–9; divergence of character, 190 n.5, 294–5 & nn.3 & 4; flowers as decoys attracting pollinators, 43 & 44 n.7; geographical distribution of species, xvii, 37 nn.8 & 9, 59 & 60 n.6, 67 & 68 & nn.2, 4 & 5 & 69 nn.7, 8, 10, 11 & 13, 97 & nn.7 & 8, 257 & 258 n.5; graft hybrids, 92 & nn.4 & 5; hypothesis of continental extensions, xxi, 258 n.5, 260 & 262 nn.7 & 9, 282 n.3, 285 & 286 n.6, 287 & n.2, 289 n.3 & 290 n.17, 305 n.5; insular flora, of New Zealand, 418 & 419 nn.10–13; insular flora, preservation of ancient forms, 257–8 & 259 nn.9–11, 261 & 263 n.15; insular flora, rarity of continental organisms, 258 n.5; insular flora, rarity of endemic island organisms, 257 & 259 nn.8 & 9; limited powers of diffusion shown by birds, 311; *Lupinus*, discussion with J.D. Hooker, 223 & 224 n.10, 257 & 258 n.1; mistrust of generalised statements, 84–5 & 86 nn.10 & 11; morphological characters of plants, 394 & nn. 5 & 6 & 395 nn.7 & 8; non-blending varieties, xxii, 44–5 & nn.3–5; occasional transport hypothesis, xxi, 64 & 65 n.5, 74 n.5, 257 & 259 n.7, 262 nn.7 & 9, 271 & 272 & 273 nn.10 & 11, 282 n.3, 286 n.2, 287 & nn.2 & 3, 288 & 289 n.3 & 290 nn.6 & 17, 305 n.5, 418 & 419 n.13, 429 n.7, 439 & 440 n.9; on *Ophrys*, 128 & n.2 & 129 nn.3 & 7; origin of coal, 17 & 18 n.8, 21 n.6; pangenesis, xv, 11 n.8, 45 n.5, 71 n.3, 113 & 114 nn.4–10, 115 n.3, 116 & 117 n.4, 120 n.5, 121 & n.6, 131 n.13, 373 & 374 n.10, 374 & n.3; rejects Atlantis hypothesis, 257 & 258 nn.2 & 5; relevance of 'law of necessary development', 203 & 204 n.10; reproduction in *Aphis*, 244–5 & n.20; survival of tropical species in world cool period, 59–60 & nn.5–7 & 61 nn.8 & 9; theory of descent, xvi, 7 & 9 n.11, 230 n.3, 455–6 & 457 n.11; transmutation of species, xv, xxii, 12 n.11, 37 n.8, 90 & n.2, 303 n.2; views on development of life, 366 & 367 n.3. *See also* dispersal of species

—SCIENTIFIC WORK: evolution of geometry of bee and wasp cells, 15 n.3, 33–4 & nn.2–9 & 35 nn.10–12; hazel varieties, 343 & n.1, 349 & 350 n.2; J.D. Hooker, suggests study of plants with irregular flowers, 444 n.5; microscope, 295 & 296 n.2, 304 & 305 n.9; *Ononis columnae*, 235 n.7; portfolios of notes and materials, 267 & 269 n.24, 371 & 372 n.20; reproduction in Bryozoa, 390–1 & n.1; sends batrachian larva to J.E. Gray, 83 & 84 nn.1, 3 & 4; whether *Primula* ovules anatropal or amphitropal, 204 n.9

—SCIENTIFIC WORK: BARNACLES, ASSISTANCE FROM J.E. GRAY, 187 nn.10 & 11

—SCIENTIFIC WORK: BUD VARIATIONS, 208–9 & nn.1–3, 212–13 & n.1, 225 & 226 nn.9 & 10

—SCIENTIFIC WORK: CLIMBING PLANTS, 157 n.7, 296 n.6

—SCIENTIFIC WORK: CROSSING EXPERIMENTS: cucumbers, 121 & n.5; *Mirabilis*, 393 & n.6, 395 & 396 n.3; *Papaver*, 388 & n.4, 402 & 403 n.2; papilionaceous flowers, 96 & n.3, 249 & n.1, 253 & 254 nn.2 & 3, 292–3 & nn.2, 4 & 5; peas, 338 n.8, 382 n.4; *Primula*, 139 & 140 n.7, 315 n.12; seedlings from self- and cross-pollinated plants, 314 & 315 nn.13 & 14, 324 & 326 n.9, 345 n.7; sweetpeas, xxii, 44–5 & n.4, 292–3 & n.5, 382 n.4, 387 & 388 n.3; waterlilies, 150 & 151 n.4, 154 & n.2, 367 & n.2, 373 & n.3

—SCIENTIFIC WORK: DIMORPHIC AND TRIMORPHIC PLANTS: *Alkanna 'hispidifolia'*, CD seeks seeds from J.D. Hooker, 225 & 226 n.11; crossing experiments, xv, 439 & 440 n.12; heteromorphy in *Rhamnus cathartica*, xx, 156 n.3, 201 n.8, 208 & nn.2–4, 209 & n.2 & 210 n.4, 211 nn.3, 5 & 6, 213 & 214 nn.3–7, 214 & 215 n.2, 215 & nn.2 & 3 & 216 nn.5 & 6, 221–2 & nn.2–5, 283 & 284 n.10; *Oxalis* trimorphism, 176–7 & 178 n.10, 291 & 292 nn.2 & 3; portfolio of notes and materials, 371 & 372 n.20

—SCIENTIFIC WORK: DISPERSAL OF SPECIES: experimental feeding of seeds to fowl, 415 & 416 n.7, 417 & 418 n.3, 420, 439 & 440 n.7, 452; numbers of indigenous plants on oceanic islands, 133 & n.3; plants that form neither flowers nor seeds, 314 & 315 n.11, 321 n.3, 327 & nn.2 & 3; seeks information on feet of otter-hounds, 336 & 337 nn.4–6, 338 & n.2, 339 & n.3; self-sterile plants, 324 & 325 n.8

—SCIENTIFIC WORK: GRAFT HYBRIDS, 147 & n.4, 201 n.4, 209 n.2

—SCIENTIFIC WORK: INSECTIVOROUS PLANTS, 296 & nn.3 & 4, 304 & 305 n.10, 308 & 309 n.14, 318 & 319 n.3, 319 & 320 n.2, 322 & 323 nn.4 & 5, 393 & nn.7 & 9, 395 & 396 n.3

—SCIENTIFIC WORK: ORCHIDS, 30, 284 n.3, 296 & n.5, 304 & 305 n.11, 308 & 309 n.13, 324 & 325 n.5, 337 & 338 n.3, 388 & n.5; nature of labellum, 299 & 300 n.7; variability in *Ophrys* flowers, 63 nn.3–9

—SCIENTIFIC WORK: POLLINATION STUDIES: Fumariaceae, 176 & 177 n.4; *Leschenaultia*, 121–2

& nn.4 & 5; orchids, 324 & 325 nn.3–5; pollen of different forms of flowers, 335 n.3

—SUPPORT FOR THEORIES, xxi; T.G. Appleton, 90 & n.2; J.V. Carus, 363, 474; C. Gegenbaur, 134 n.4; German scientists, 27 & nn.7–9, 458–9 & nn.7–9; W.R. Grove asks for confirmatory evidences, 190 & 191 nn.3–9, 192 & nn.3 & 4 & 193 nn.5 & 6; J. von Haast, 242 n.4; E. Haeckel, 7–8, 294–5 & nn.1–3, 455–6; F. Hildebrand, 178 n.12, 252 & n.8; J.D. Hooker, 21 & 22 n.7, 190 & 191 n.8, 194 & n.4, 196 & n.4, 285 & 286 n.6; G. Jäger, 30 n.8, 461 n.8; F. Müller, 134 n.4, 193 n.6; H. Müller, 266 & 268 n.18; C.W. von Nägeli, 186 & 187 n.16, 266 & 268 n.17; F. Rolle, 102 & 103 nn.3–5; L. Rütimeyer, 186 & 188 n.17; O. Schmidt, 133–4 & n.4, 186 & 187 n.16, 266 & 268 n.17; F. Unger, 133–4 & n.4; B.D. Walsh, 244 & 246 nn.12 & 13; D.F. Weinland, 30 n.9, 461 n.9

—TRIPS AND VISITS : C.W. Dilke invites to dinner, 145 & nn.1–3; Royal Society of London soirée, xvii, 150 n.1, 171 & 172 n.3, 179 & 180 n.9, 189 & n.3, 197 & n.4, 430 & n.2, 482 & n.14; visit to J.D. Hooker, 392, 395 & 396 n.2, 396–7 & n.2, 413 & n.5; visits to E.A. Darwin, xvii, 52 & n.2, 115 & 116 n.3, 124 & n.3, 128 & nn.1 & 2, 143 & 144 n.2, 144, 146 & n.1, 146 & 147 nn.2 & 3, 148 & n.5, 150 & 151 n.2, 158 & 163 n.8, 171 & n.5, 179 & 180 n.9, 307 & n.9, 385 & n.9, 392 & 393 n.3, 396 & 397 n.1, 405 & n.2, 410 & 411 n.1, 412 & n.3, 482 & n.14; visits to C. and J. Wedgwood III, 52 & n.2, 192 n.2, 482 & n.16; visits Zoological Gardens, xvii, 148 & n.5, 417 & n.2, 423 n.5

Darwin, Elizabeth, 346 & n.6, 366 & 367 n.8; CD's amanuensis, 1 n.5

Darwin, Emma (née Wedgwood), 2 & 3 n.6, 46, 127 & n.7, 152 & 153 n.20, 195, 237 & 238 n.6, 274 & 275 n.6, 297 & 298 n.11, 319 & n.5, 359 & n.3, 366 & 367 n.8, 385 & 386 n.6, 396 & 397 n.1, 398 n.7, 444 & 446 & n.1, 472; in bed with a cold, 405; feverish attack, 214 & 215 n.5, 219 & 221 n.10; ill with influenza, 110 n.5, 116 n.3, 129 n.8, 129 & 131 n.4; portrait, 346 & n.8; visit to E.A. Darwin, xvii, 392 & nn.3 & 4, 405 & n.2

Darwin, Erasmus, 151 & 152 n.3; biography by J. Dowson, 366 & 367 n.2, 413 & n.6; Wedgwood medallion, 396 n.6

Darwin, Erasmus Alvey, 296 & 297 & n.2; CD's visits to, xvii, 52 & n.2, 66, 115 & 116 n.3, 124 & n.3, 128 & nn.1 & 2, 143 & 144 n.2, 144, 146 & n.1, 146 & 147 nn.2 & 3, 148 & n.5, 150 & 151 n.2, 158 & 163 n.8, 171 & n.5, 179 & 180 n.9, 307 & n.9, 385 & n.9, 392 & 393 nn.3 & 4, 396 & 397 n.1, 405 & n.2, 410 & 411 n.1, 412 & n.3, 482 & n.13, 482 & n.14; changes will, 66 n.7, 210 & n.3; G.H. Darwin's interest in family history, 66 & 67 n.2; executor of R.W. Darwin's will, 65 n.3, 340 & n.3, 345 & 346 n.4; health, 405; legacies to CD's children, 381 & n.4; portrait, 346 n.8; return to London, 341; sale of The Mount, 340 & n.3; sends information on wasps' nests to CD, 34 n.9; settlement of E.C. Langton's estate, 65 & n.3, 66 & nn.3 & 4

Darwin, Francis: Clapham Grammar School, pupil, 343 n.5; home for Christmas holidays, 439 & n.4; payment from CD, 349 & n.2; undergraduate at Trinity College, Cambridge, 349 & n.2; visit to Norway, 301 & n.2; visit to Wales, 219 & 221 n.9

Darwin, George Howard: career plans, 399 & n.3; CD consults on mathematics of probability, 1 & n.3; Clapham Grammar School, pupil, 343 n.5, 349 n.7; examination successes at Cambridge, xxv, 133 & n.3, 138 & 139 n.15, 445 & 446 n.17, 451 & n.9; executor of E.A. Darwin's will, 66 & n.7; gift of Indian chessmen, 340; home for Christmas holidays, 439 & n.4; interest in family history, 66–7 & nn.1 & 2, 346 & n.5; interest in C. Pritchard's sermon, 348 & 349 n.7; undergraduate scholar of Trinity College, Cambridge, xxv, 66 & n.9, 399 & n.2; visit to W.E. Darwin, 211 & n.4, 215 & n.4, 222 & 223 n.5; visit to Norway, 301 & n.2

Darwin, Henrietta Emma, 2 & 3 n.6, 346 & n.6, 366 & 367 n.8, 372, 396 & 397 n.1; CD's amanuensis, 214 n.8, 329 & 330 n.14; describes E. Haeckel's visit to Down House, xviii, 367 n.3; T.H. Huxley, gift of physiology textbook, 385 & 386 n.8; meeting with J.T. Moggridge, xviii, 163 & nn.2 & 3, 185 & n.9; painting of Joan of Arc, 172 & 173 n.20; sends *Ophrys* specimen to CD, 128 & n.2; travels to France, 128 & 129 nn.4 & 9, 172 & 173 n.24, 222 & n.6; visit to London, xvii, 393 n.4

Darwin, Horace: home for Christmas holidays, 439 & n.4; visit to Wales, 219 & 221 n.9

Darwin, Leonard: Clapham Grammar School, pupil, 343 n.5; A. Gray's kindness in convalescence, 302 & 303 n.6, 313 & 315 n.2; home for Christmas holidays, 439 & n.4

Darwin, Marianne: share of R.W. Darwin's estate, 340 n.3

Darwin, Robert Waring, 151 & 152 n.4; will, 65 n.3, 340 n.3

Darwin, Susan Elizabeth, 5 & n.3, 46 & 48 n.18, 341 & 342 n.2, 421 n.7; contents of bureau, 345–6 & nn.3–6; death, xxiv, 65 n.4, 322 n.2, 340 n.2, 340 & 341 n.1, 398 & n.9, 482 & n.23; executors of will, 342 & n.5; illness, 297 & n.6, 301 & n.3, 311 & 312 n.3, 318 & 319 n.2, 322, 329 & 330 n.14, 337 & 338 n.12; legacies to CD's children, 345 & 346 n.3, 381 & n.2; legacy of soup tureen to C.S. Wedgwood, 345 & 346 n.2; settlement of E.C. Langton's estate, 65 & n.2; share of R.W. Darwin's estate, 340 n.3

Darwin, William Erasmus: asks CD to forward orders for signature to E.A. Darwin, 211 & n.2, 213 & 214 n.2; botanical interests, brooms, xx, 135 n.2, 158 & 159–62 & nn.2–5 & 163 nn.7, 11 & 12, 209 & 210 n.7, 219 & 221 n.8; botanical interests, *Rhamnus*, xx, 156 & n.3, 201 n.8, 208 & nn.2–4, 209 & n.2 & 210 n.4, 211 & nn.3–6, 211–12 & nn.2–5, 214 & 215 nn.2–4, 218–20 & 221 nn.2–8, 11 & 12, 221–2 & nn.2–5, 283 & 284 n.10, 314 & 315 n.9, 335 n.3; CD's observations of expression in infant, 65 n.7; G.H. Darwin and E. Langton's visit to, 211 & n.4; executor of E.A. Darwin's will, 66 & nn.7 & 8; home for Christmas holidays, 439 & n.4; inherits farm at Claythorpe, 345 & 346 n.3, 381 & n.2; journey to France, 222 & n.6; photographs of CD, xviii, 19 & 20 n.2, 91 & 92 n.2, 146 n.5, 158 & 163 n.10, 204 n.11; sends *Mentha hirsuta* specimens to CD, 235 n.4; Southampton and Hampshire Bank, partner, 156 n.2; will, xxiv, 381

Daubentonia (*Sesbania*), 93 & 95 n.5, 464 & 465 n.5

Dawes, Richard, dean of Hereford, 3 n.1

Dawson, John William: identifies fossil Foraminifera, 192 n.4

day length: whether steadily increasing, 347 & 348 n.8, 348 & 349 n.8

De Quincey, Thomas: essay on Wordsworth's poetry, 380 & n.4

Deinornis. *See Dinornis*

Dent, Emma: autograph book at Sudeley Castle, 341 & n.4

Desertas (island group): insects, 282 & 283 n.9

Destêrro, Santa Catarina island, Brazil, 94 & 95 n.14, 369, 466 n.14; retirement home of F. Müller, 12 n.9, 403 & 404 nn.1 & 3

dew: W.C. Wells's essay on, 284 n.5

Dezertas. *See* Desertas (island group)

Diadema anomala. *See Hypolimnus anomala*

Dichobune, 422 & 423 n.7

dichogamy, 135 n.2, 267; in *Aristolochia clematitis*, 252 & n.9, 360 & 361 nn.2–5; in broom, 135 n.2, 162 n.2; F. Hildebrand's paper, 174 & n.2

Dick, William, 114 & 115 n.2

Dickson, John, 43 & 44 n.9, 54 & 55 n.3

Dieffenbach, Ernst: translator of *South America*, 364 & 365 n.5

A.W. Digby & Co.: offer to test commercial value of galls, 298 n.5

Dilke, Charles Wentworth: invites CD and E. Darwin to dinner, 145 & nn.1–3

dimorphism, xv, 24 & 25 nn.4 & 5, 368 & 371 n.3, 439 & 440 n.11, 452 & 453 nn.3–8; in Brazilian plants, 439 & 440 n.12, 452 & 453 n.3; CD's portfolio of notes on, 371 & 372 n.20; in *Convolvulus*, 369 & 371 n.11, 452 & 453 n.7, 474 & 476 n.4; in *Cordia*, 334 & 336 n.9, 368; in *Cynips*, B.D. Walsh's paper, review, 244 & 246 nn.17–20; W.E. Darwin's observations, 162 n.2; in *Erythroxylum*, 369 & 371 n.12, 474 & 476 n.4; in function but not in structure, 265–6 & 268 n.9, 324 & 325 n.11, 406 & 409 n.5, 477 & 479 n.5; in *Gossypium*, 376 & 377 n.7; in *Hedyotis*, 368 & 369 & 371 n.8, 452 & 453 n.5; F. Hildebrand's paper, 174 & n.2; in *Lipostoma*, 408 & 409 nn.12 & 13, 478 & 480 nn.12 & 13; in *Oxalis*, 323 n.2, 332 & 335 n.2, 368–9 & 371 n.3; reciprocal, 315 n.10; in *Rhamnus*, xx, 156 & n.3, 211 & nn.3, 5 & 6, 211–12 & nn.2–5, 213–14 & nn.3–7, 9 & 10, 218–20 & 221 nn.2–5, 222 & n.8, 283 & 284 n.10, 314 & 315 nn.9 & 10; in *Villarsia*, 368 & 369; whether more prevalent in aquatic and marsh plants, 186 & 187 n.13, 369. *See also* gynodioecious plants

Dinornis, 422 & 423 n.9

dispersal of species, 195 & 196 n.5, 272 & 273 nn.10–15, 472 & n.5; occasional transport hypothesis, xxi, 64 & 65 n.5, 74 n.5, 257 & 259 n.7, 262 nn.7 & 9, 271 & 272 & 273 nn.10 & 11, 282 n.3, 286 n.2, 287 & nn.2 & 3, 288 & 289 n.3 & 290 nn.6 & 17, 305 n.5, 418 & 419 n.13, 429 n.7, 439 & 440 n.9; seeds carried in mud on woodcock's foot, 401 n.2, 401 & 402 n.2

divergence of character, 190 n.5, 294–5 & nn.3 & 4

Dixon, Edmund Saul: book on pigeons, 19 & n.6

Dobson, George: murdered in New Zealand, 242 & n.7

dodo: picture discovered by W.B. Tegetmeier, 351 & n.3

dogs: J.S. Bowerbank's observations on breeding, 375 & 376 n.3; breeding of greyhounds, 114–15 & n.4; CD seeks information on feet of otter-hounds, 336 & 337 nn.4–6, 338 & n.2, 339 n.3; translation of breed names into German, 388–9 & nn.4 & 5

Dohrn, Anton: exchanges photographs with CD, 27 & 28 n.4, 458 & 459 n.4; student of E. Haeckel's, 27 & 28 n.7, 458–9 & n.7

Edmund Robson Dorrell & Son, booksellers, 169 n.3

Dorrell, Mr, typesetter, 169 n.3

Doryphora: thoracic spot patterns, 137 & 138 n.4

Douglas fir. *See Abies douglasii*

Down, Kent: railway service, 294, 358; G. Snow, carrier, 53 & n.3, 77 & n.6, 99–100 & n.3

Down Coal and Clothing Club: CD, treasurer, 110 n.4, 414 & n.2, 431 & 432 n.1; donations from C. and H. Lovegrove, 431 & 432 nn.2–4; donations from Lubbock family, 110 & nn.3 & 4

Down House, Down, 152 & 153 n.21; T.G. Appleton's visit, 90 & n.5; R. Caspary's visit, xviii, 146 n.4, 154–5 & n.3, 170–1 & nn.1–4, 179 & 180 n.7, 181 & n.7, 188 & nn.1 & 2, 193 n.13, 196 n.3, 201 n.4, 472 n.3, 482 & n.15; CD's sons come for holidays, 439 & n.4; E. Haeckel's visit, xviii–xix, 353, 358 & nn.2–5, 359 n.1, 367 n.3, 386 n.9, 413 & n.2, 415, 473, 482 & n.20; G. Henslow's visit, xviii, 95 & 96 & n.1, 99–100 & n.3, 103 & 104 n.4, 104 & nn.1–4, 112 & 113 n.2, 118 nn.3 & 6, 132 n.2, 140 & 141 n.3, 482 & n.12; F.H. and B.H.H. Hooker's visit, 225 & 226 n.8; J.D. Hooker's visits, 17 & 18 n.7, 21 & n.3, 73 & 74 n.12, 85 & 86 n.14, 104 & n.2, 105 & nn.3 & 4, 129 & 131 n.5, 172 & 173 n.23, 179 & 180 n.18, 181 & 182 n.12, 215 & 216 n.7, 223 & n.7, 258 & 259 n.14, 287 & 288 n.10, 288 & 290 n.7, 293–4 & nn.1 & 2, 294, 305 n.11, 482 & nn.11, 17 & 18; C. and M.E. Lyell's visit, 310 & 312 n.4, 482 & n.21; J.T. Moggridge's visit, xviii, 163 & n.4, 185 & n.8, 188 & n.2 & 189 n.3, 206 & n.2, 482 & n.17; G.W. Norman's proposed visit, 319 & n.4; J. Parslow, butler, 304 & 305 n.7; G.V. Reed, J.B. Innes & T.S. Stephens' visit, 482 & n.12; 'Tommy' (horse), 52 n.3; trees and shrubs for garden, 354 & n.1, 359 & n.3, 367 & n.1

Dowson, John: biography of E. Darwin, 366 & 367 n.3, 413 & n.6

Doyne, William Thomas: paper on formation of Canterbury plains, 410 & 412 n.14, 418 & 419 n.8

Dracaena draco, 253 & 254 & 255 n.8 & 256 n.18

dredging: in China Sea, 64 & n.3

Drimys: widespread occurrence, 67–8 & 69 nn.7 & 13, 75 & 76 nn.3 & 4

Drosera: found in Organ Mountains, 46 & 47 n.8; widespread occurrence, 67 & 68 n.4

Drosera binata (fork-leaved sundew): J.D. Hooker sends specimen to CD, 296 & n.3, 304 & 305 n.10, 309 & n.14, 318 & 319 n.3, 322 & 323 n.4, 329 & n.1, 337 & n.2, 373 & 374 n.9, 393 & n.7

Drosera rotundifolia, 296 & n.4

Dubois, Henry Augustus: paper on origin and antiquity of man, 243–4 & 245 nn.7–9

ducks: Chinese, 6 & nn.2–4; W.B. Tegetmeier seeks information from CD on varieties, 420 & n.4, 421 & 422 n.3, 431 & n.2

Dulau & Co., booksellers and publishers, 364 & 365 n.8

Duméril, Auguste-Henri-André: observations of axolotl, 84 n.4

Dumfriesshire and Galloway Natural History and Antiquarian Society: J. Shaw's paper on appreciation of beauty by animals, 42–3 & 44 nn.1–12

Dummer, Ethel, 425 n.2

HMS *Duncan*: T.E. Sulivan, lieutenant, 218 n.18

Dundee: venue for meeting of British Association for the Advancement of Science (1867), 323 n.11

Dunn, Robert, curate of Gatecombe, 219 & 221 n.7

Duvernoy, Johann Georg: cited by CD, 263 n.21

Duvernoya, 261 & 263 n.21

earth: age, 60 n.4, 84 & 85 n.5, 342 n.2, 348 n.8, 348 & 349 n.6; amount of living matter on, 410–11 & n.16, 419 n.14, 427–8 & 429 nn.14–16; rate of cooling of crust, 84 & 85 n.5; temperature of, 88–9; variations in axis tilt, 74 n.4, 84 & 85 n.7, 92 & 93 n.2, 96 & 97 n.4

Edinburgh University: CD a student, 151; J.D. Hooker, candidate for chair of botany, 329 & 330 n.7

Edwards, Ernest: photographs of CD, xvii–xviii, 137 n.10, 384 n.8

Edwards, William Henry, 244 & 246 n.11

Edwardsia microphylla: marine transport of seeds, 418 & 419 n.13

eel. *See Anguilla bostoniensis* (*rostrata*)
Egerton, Philip de Malpas Grey-: acquaintance of W.D. Fox, 297 & n.5
Ehrenberg, Christian Gottfried: CD thanks for sending two papers, 250 & nn.2 & 3
elaters: luminosity, 55 & 56 n.3, 462 & 463 n.3
Eliot, George. *See* Evans, Marian
Endlicher, Stephan Ladislaus: flora, 407 & 408 & 409 nn.10, 13 & 15, 478 & 480 nn.10, 13 & 15
Engelmann, Wilhelm: sends E. Haeckel's papers to CD, 7 & 9 n.5, 20 n.7, 455 & 457 n.5
English Channel: date of formation, 260 & 262 nn.1 & 2, 271 & 273 n.3
Entomological Society of London: meeting on mimicry, 391 & 392 n.3; presentation copy of *Origin*, 485
Eocene fossils: leaf-bed in Isle of Wight, 445 & 446 n.12, 448 & nn.4 & 5, 451 & nn.6 & 7
Eozoon canadense, 192 & n.4
Epidendreae, 265 & 268 nn.3 & 7, 325 n.6; delayed fertilisation in, 405 & 409 n.4, 476–7 & 479 n.4
Epidendrum sp.: having three fertile anthers, 268 n.5, 299 & 300 n.5, 409 n.4, 479 n.4
HMS *Erebus*, 286 n.9
Erica daboeci. *See Daboecia azorica*
Erica massoni: J.D. Hooker sends specimen to CD, 322 & 323 n.5, 329 & n.1, 337 & n.2; whether flowers or leaves glutinous, 319 & 320 n.2
erratic boulders: distribution, 152 & 153 n.17. *See also under* glacial phenomena
Erythrina: hybrid, 292 & 293 n.3
Erythroxylum, 371 & 372 n.18, 452 & 453 n.5; variability of flowers, 369–70 & 371 n.12, 474–5 & 476 n.5
Escallonia, 67, 76 n.3
Eschscholtzia californica: self-sterility, 266 & 267 & 268 n.13, 324 & 325 n.8, 368 & 371 n.2, 406 & 409 n.7, 452 & 453 n.9, 477 & 479 n.7
Ethiopia. *See* Abyssinia
Etruria: J.D. Hooker and R.F.D. Palgrave's visit, 25 & 26 n.3
Eucalyptus: absent from New Zealand, 262 n.4; migration during glacial period, 418 & 419 n.12
Euonymus europaeus (spindle-wood): brightly coloured seeds, 415 & 416 n.8
Euphorbiaceae: variable development of flowers, 51 n.2
European bison. *See Bison bonasus bonasus*
Euryale amazonica (*Victoria regia*, *Victoria amazonica*): self-fertility, 148 & n.6
Euryale ferox: J.D. Hooker plans to send seeds to CD, 392 & 393 n.5; J.D. Hooker's advice on germinating, 373 & n.7; whether perpetually self-pollinating, 80 & n.13, 148 n.6, 150 & 151 nn.4 & 5, 154 & n.2, 367 & n.2
Evans, John: supports F.W. Farrar's candidature for Royal Society, 41 & n.3
Evans, Marian (George Eliot): *Felix Holt the radical*, 295 & 296 n.1
Evans-Lombe, Elizabeth, 180 & 181 n.3, 411 n.2
evolutionary trees, 7 & 9 n.8, 126 & nn.8 & 9, 455 & 457 n.8, 467–8 & nn.8 & 9
extinction: German translation of term, 29 & 30 n.6, 460 & 461 n.6
eye: development by natural selection, 44 n.8, 342 & n.2, 348 & 349 nn.3 & 4
eyed hawk-moth. *See Smerinthus ocellatus*
Eyre, Edward John: J.D. Hooker's views, xxiv, 385 n.5, 395 & 396 n.4; lobby for prosecution of. *See* Jamaica Committee; Royal Geographical Society, elected fellow, 373 & n.6

facial expressions, 64 & 65 n.7, 450–1 & n.3
Fagus sylvatica 'Asplenifolia' (fern-leaved beech): bud variations, 208–9 & nn.1–3; J.D. Hooker's observations, 225 & 226 nn.9 & 10; specimen sent to CD, 212–13 & n.1
Falkland Islands: survey, 216 & 218 n.10
Farrar, Frederic William: master at Harrow School, 41 & n.5; seeks election to Royal Society, 31–2 & nn.2–5, 37–8 & nn.2 & 3, 41 & nn.2–4
Fenian movement, 130 & 131 n.15, 157 & 158 nn.8 & 9
Fernando Po: temperate flora, 46 & 48 n.13, 84 & 86 n.8, 178 & 179 n.5
fertilisers: phosphate, for root crops, 117 & 118 n.2
Field: articles on descent of domestic poultry from junglefowl, 316 & n.5 & 317 n.6, 317 & n.5; E. Blyth's articles on Indian cattle, 26 & n.5; F.T. Buckland withdraws from, 330 & 331 n.2
Fields, James Thomas, 276 n.5, 302 & 303 n.2
Findlaya, 371 & 372 n.17
fireflies, 43
fishes: L. Agassiz's views on geographical distribution of species, 12 n.10; of Amazon river, 12 n.10, 35 & 36 n.3; fossil, of Lebanon, 311–12 & n.13; ganoid, 258 & 259 n.11; A.C.L. Gunther's paper on Central American, 427 & 429 n.10
Fitch, Asa: gall wrongly classified by, 245 & 246 n.22

FitzRoy, Maria Isabella, 217 & 218 n.16
FitzRoy, Robert, 151 & 152 n.6, 218 n.14, 444 & 446 nn.5 & 10; and Fuegian people, 450 & 451 n.3; testimonial fund, 217 & 218 nn.14 & 15; views on CD's theories, 389 & 390 n.13
FitzRoy, Robert O'Brien: promotion to commander, 217 & 218 n.17
Flower, William Henry: dissection of *Hyomoschus*, 423 nn.6 & 7; muscles associated with os coccyx, 430; Zoological Society of London, member of Council, 316 & n.3
Foraminifera: CD cited in J.S. Bowerbank's monograph, 375 & 376 n.2; fossilised, 192 n.4
Forbes, David: glaciation in Cordillera, 46 & 48 n.10
Forbes, Edward: Atlantis hypothesis, 253 & 255 nn.8, 10, 11 & 13; hypothesis of continental extension, xxi, 272 & 274 n.16, 285 & 286 n.6; migrations of western European floras, 260 & 262 n.1 & 263 n.13
fork-leaved sundew. *See Drosera binata*
Formica sanguinea: behavioural differences between British and Swiss colonies, 106 & 107 nn.2 & 3, 107 & nn.3 & 4
fossils: bones in Patagonia, 216 & 217 n.7 & 218 n.11, 222 & 223 n.1, 225 & nn.3 & 4 & 226 n.5, 226 & 227 nn.2–7, 232 & nn.2–6 & 233 nn.7–10, 237 & 238 n.3; cetacean not found in pre-Eocene strata, 344 & n.5; Eocene leaf-bed in Isle of Wight, 445 & 446 n.12, 448 & nn.4 & 5; fishes of Lebanon, 311–12 & n.13; found in caves, 64 & n.2; A. Gaudry's paper on Greek, 318 & nn.2–5; horses, L. Rütimeyer's book on, 109 & n.11; leaf-bed found near Bournemouth, 445 & 446 n.13, 448 & nn.4 & 5, 448 & 449 n.2, 451 & nn.6 & 7; mammals, found in Brazilian caves, 75 & 76 n.5; molluscs found in Scottish glacial beds, 328 n.4; pre-Silurian, 192 & n.4; reptiles in Whitby, 297 & n.7; 'tadpole nests', 14 & 15 n.7, 34 & n.7
fowls: bantams' behaviour before mirror, 135; bantams pecking at snowdrops, 135; descent of domestic poultry from junglefowl, 316 & n.5 & 317 n.6, 317 & n.5; E. Hewitt's observations, 269 & 270 nn.1 & 2, 278 & 279 n.9, 279 & 280 n.5; hybrids, 269 & 270 n.4, 278 & 279 n.10, 279 & 280 nn.8 & 9, 291 & n.2; illustrations for *Variation*, 18 & 19 n.5, 22 & 23 n.7, 26 & n.4, 269 & 270 n.3, 278 & nn.3–5 & 279 nn.6–8, 279 & 280 n.6, 291 & nn.3 & 5, 316 & n.1, 317 & nn.3 & 4; Sebright hen with male plumage, 269 & 270 n.2, 278 & 279 n.9, 279 & 280 n.5, 291 & n.4; skulls, 356–7 & n.4, 433 & n.4; spangled Hamburghs, 278 & 279 n.5; spangled Hamburghs, effect of crossing on plumage variations, 233 & 234 n.4, 239 & n.5; W.B. Tegetmeier, *The poultry book*, 22 & 23 nn. 11 & 12, 53 & 54 n.6, 233 & 234 n.4, 239 & n.5, 269 & 270 n.5, 278 & 279 n.11, 279 & 280 n.6, 420 n.5, 431 & n.4; F.W. Zurhorst's crossing experiment, 18 & 19 n.5, 22 & 23 n.9, 26 & n.3, 239 & n.4, 412 & n.2, 419–20 & n.2, 421 & 422 n.2
Fox, William Darwin: concern for CD's health, 296–7 & n.2; family, 297 & 298 n.10, 301 & n.1; family visit to Whitby, 297 & n.7; plans breeding experiment with hawk-moths, 297 & n.8, 301 & 302 n.10
Frankland, Edward: lecture on source of muscular power, 322 & 323 n.9, 329 & n.4; theories of glacial formation, 141 & 142 n.5
Franklin, Benjamin: Wedgwood portrait medallion, 395 & 396 n.6
Fraser's Magazine: C. Kingsley's lectures on science and superstition, 239 & 240 n.4
fruit: influence of pollen on, 130 & 131 n.13, 157 & n.6
Fuchsia, 69 n.13, 75 & 76 n.4; widespread occurrence, 68 & 69 n.8
Fucus: changes in populations, 186 & 187 n.7; reciprocal crosses, 403 n.6; G.A. Thuret's observations, 402 & 403 n.6
Fuegians. *See* Tierra del Fuego, indigenous people
Fuller, Charles C.: sends batrachian larva to T.G. Appleton, 90 & n.3
Fumariaceae: pollination, 176 & 177 nn.4 & 5, 179 & 180 n.15
functional dimorphism. *See* dimorphism, in function but not in structure

Galápagos Islands: flora, 439 & 440 n.9; woodland vegetation, 259 n.9
gall insects: W. Armistead's proposed book on, 101 & 102 n.8, 137 & 138 n.5; colour variants of *Halesidota tessellaris*, 137 & 138 n.3; gall on grapevine leaf, 245 & 246 n.22; galls growing on twigs, 298 & n.5; making galls on leaves, 244 & 246 n.16; offer to test commercial value of galls, 298 n.5; B.D. Walsh's paper on willow galls, 245 & 246 n.21, 400 & n.8, 442 & 443 n.10
HMS *Gannet*: T.E. Sulivan, sub-lieutenant, 218 n.18

Gardeners' Chronicle: article on *Begonia phyllomaniaca* sports, 121 & n.4; R. Caspary's paper on movement of tree branches as result of cold, 141–2 & n.4; CD, letter on *Oxalis bowiei*, 291 & 292 nn.2 & 3; CD, letter on crossing of papilionaceous flowers, 96 & n.3, 292–3 & nn.2–5; CD's observations of *Leschenaultia* pollination, 123 n.5; greenhouse temperatures for tropical orchids, 60 & 61 n.8; F. Hildebrand's paper on *Corydalis cava*, 170 n.5; J.D. Hooker, lecture on insular floras, xx, 17 & 18 n.9, 254 n.4, 304 n.3, 329 & 330 n.5, 337 & 338 n.5, 427 & 429 n.12; T. Laxton, results of crossing of peas, 337 & 338 n.7; M.T. Masters, editor, 141 & 142 n.2, 322 & 323 n.8; A. Murray, book on geographical distribution of mammals, review, 329 & n.3, 337 & 338 n.4; report of E.A. Carrière's grafting experiments, 439 & 440 n.13

Gardiner, Allen Weare: missionary in Chile, 445 & 447 n.23

Gardner, George: flora of Brazil, 35–6 & 37 nn.10 & 11, 46 & 48 n.12 & 24, 60 n.5

Gärtner, Karl Friedrich von, 96 n.5; difficulty in crossing papilionaceous plants, 292 & 293 & n.4; occasional self-sterility in, 176 & 177 n.7; reversion in hybrids, 206 & 207 nn.3 & 9

Gaudry, Albert: paper on fossils of Greece, 318 & nn.2–5

Gaultheria, 67 & 69 n.13, 76 n.3; found in Organ Mountains, 46 & 47 n.8

gaurs. *See under* cattle

Gautier, Hippolyte, 369 & 371 n.10, 474 & 475 n.3

gayals. *See under* cattle

Gaylussacia, 67 & 68 n.5, 67 & 69 n.13, 76 n.3

geese. *See Anser*

Gegenbaur, Carl, xviii; exchanges photographs with CD, 27 & 28 n.4, 458 & 459 n.4; support for CD's theories, 134 n.4

Geinitz, Hans Bruno: book on bituminous coal, 167 & 169 n.14, 470 & 471 n.14; *Neues Jahrbuch für Mineralogie, Geologie und Palaeontologie*, co-editor, 105–6 & n.7, 167 & 168 n.6, 466 & 467 n.7, 470 & n.6; pressure of work, 167 & 169 n.14, 470 & 471 n.14; proposed translator of *Origin*, 105–6 & n.7, 133 & 134 nn.2 & 3, 143 & n.5, 166 & 167–8, 363 & n.4, 466 & 467 n.7, 469 & 470, 473 & 474 n.4

Geoffroy Saint-Hilaire, Etienne, 142 n.7

geographical distribution of species, xvii, 272 & 274 n.16; L. Agassiz's views, 12 n.10, 37 n.8; Australian and Arctic floras, 190 & 191 n.8; flora of Brazil, 67–8 & nn.2–5 & 69 nn.6–13, 75 & 76 n.3, 93–4 & 95 nn.3–5, 7, 8, 10–13 & 15, 464–5 & nn.3–5, 7 & 8 & 466 nn.10–13 & 15; fossil mammals of Brazil, 75 & 76 n.5; J.D. Hooker and CD disagree, xxi, 59 & 60 n.6, 72–3 & 74 nn.3–8, 81 & 82 n.6, 84 & 85 n.4, 88–9 & nn.3–5, 257 & 258 nn.1 & 5, 262 n.7; J.D. Hooker's lecture on insular floras, xx–xxi, 17 & 18 n.9, 21 & 22 n.7, 222–3 & nn.5 & 6, 225 & n.2, 253–4 & n.4 & 255 nn.5–9 & 256 nn. 16 & 18, 259 n.14, 260 & 263 nn.10, 11 & 20, 272 & 273 nn.10–15, 277 & n.7, 286 nn.2, 3 & 7, 287 n.5 & 288 n.10, 288–9 & nn.2–4 & 290 nn.5, 6 & 8–10, 294 & n.2, 303 & n.2 & 304 nn.3 & 4, 304 & 305 nn.2–5, 306 & 307 n.7, 308 & 309 nn.2–5, 322 & 323 n.10, 329 & 330 n.5, 410 & 411 n.10, 427 & 428 n.11, 439 & n.5; H. Lecoq's views, 141 & 142 nn.4–6; Malayan butterflies, 24 & n.3 & 25 n.6; mammals, A. Murray's paper, review, 322 & 323 n.8, 329 & n.3, 337 & 338 n.4; in New Zealand, J.D. Hooker's views, 410 & 411 nn.9–11, 418 & 419 n.9; organisms of Celebes, 24 & 25 n.6; pigeons and parrots, A.R. Wallace's paper, 24 & nn.1 & 2; plants of Southern hemisphere, 427 & 429 nn.7–9, 439 & 440 nn.9 & 10; temperate flora of Africa, 46 & 48 nn.13–15, 84 & 86 n.8, 178 & 179 n.5. *See also* continental extension hypothesis; dispersal of species

Geological Society of London: W.J. Hamilton, president, 232 & 233 n.9; J.F.W. Herschel's paper on temperature of space and earth's climate, 84 & 85 n.6; presentation copy of *Origin*, 485; regulations for borrowing from library, 224 & n.4; Wollaston Medal awarded to CD, 152 & 153 n.19. *See also Quarterly Journal of the Geological Society*

Geological Survey of United Kingdom: J.W. Salter resigns from, 450 nn.1 & 5

Geranium pratense, 174 & n.2

Geryonia proboscidalis (*Geryonia hastata*): reproduction, 326 n.16

Geryoniidae: E. Haeckel's paper on, 20 n.7

Gesneria, 371 & 372 n.19; whether dimorphic, 452 & 453 n.8

Gesneria pendulina: F. Müller sends seeds to CD, 453 n.8

Gibson, George Stacey: relationship between cereals, 238 & n.1

glacial phenomena: in Brazil, 35–6 & n.7 & 37 nn.8 & 12, 46 & 47 nn.4, 6 & 7 & 48 nn.9–11, 59 & 60 n.3, 68 & 69 nn.9 & 13, 98 & 99 n.3,

glacial phenomena, cont.
242 & n.8 & 243 n.9, 302 & 303 nn.3 & 4, 311 & 312 nn.5–7, 9 & 12, 322 & 323 nn.6 & 7, 325 & 326 nn.16 & 17, 329 n.2, 391 & 392 nn. 6 & 7; in Caithness, T.F. Jamieson's paper, 328 & nn.2–4; in Himalayas and Australia, 48 n.20; in Lebanon, 46 & 48 n.20; in mountains of Malay Archipelago, 64 & 65 n.4; in north Wales, 392 n.7; tropical/subtropical vegetation growing near glaciers, 47 & 49 n.25; worldwide glacial period, xvi–xvii, 37 nn.8 & 9, 47 nn.8, 11 & 15, 72–3 & 74 nn.3–10, 82 n.6, 88–9 & nn.3–5, 90 & 91 nn.3–5 & 92 n.6, 92 & 93 n.2, 97 & nn.5 & 6, 141 & 142 n.5, 149 & n.10, 195 & 196 n.5, 471–2 & n.5

Gladstone, William Ewart: Kent Church Penitentiary Society, founder, 70 n.1; memorials submitted to, 88 & 89 n.1, 90 & 91 n.2, 174–5 & n.1 & 176 nn.2–5

Glycine frutescens. *See Wisteria frutescens*

Godman, Frederick DuCane: administration and locality of natural history collections, 175 & n.1 & 176 nn.2 & 3

Godron, Dominique Alexandre: with C. Grenier, *Flore de France*, 274 & 275 n.4

Godwin-Austen, Robert Alfred Cloyne: formation of English Channel, 260 & 262 n.2, 271 & 273 n.3

Goethe, Johann Wolfgang von, xviii–xix, 142 n.7

Gongora. *See Acropera*

gooseberries, 374 & 375 n.7

gooseberry saw-fly: article by B.D. Walsh, 400 n.5, 442 n.3

Göppert, Heinrich Robert: exchanges photographs with CD, 329 & 330 n.15, 337 & 338 n.6; paper on transmutation in relation to geology, 29 & 30 n.12, 460 & 461 n.12; rejects theory of genealogical connections between plants, 29 & 30 n.12, 125 & 126 n.5, 460 & 461 n.12, 467 & 468 n.5

Gossypium (cotton): R.T. Clarke's lecture on cultivation, 376 & 377 nn.5 & 6; dimorphism in, 376 & 377 n.7

Gould, John: humming-bird nomenclature, 164 & nn.1 & 2 & 165 nn.3 & 4

graft hybrids, xv, 79 nn.4–6 & 8–10, 201 n.4, 209 n.2; R. Caspary's papers, 71 & nn.2 & 3, 79–80 & nn.3–5 & 9, 91–2 & nn.3–5, 130 & 131 n.14, 141 & 142 n.1, 147 & n.4

grafts: E.A. Carrière's experiments using *Aria*, 439 & 440 n.13; effect of stock on scion tissue, 112 & 114 n.4, 130 & 131 n.14, 157 n.6, 182 & n.4, 197 & 198 n.3, 198 & n.3; purple *Cytisus* on *Laburnum*, claim of bark and foliage staining, 148 n.5, 197 & 198 n.3

Graham, Robert, 329 & 330 n.7

Grallatores (wading birds), 280 & 281 n.2, 285 & 286 n.7, 419 n.4

Gramineae (grasses): few species in humid temperate regions, 443

Gray, Asa, xv; *Acorus*, believes it sets fruit, 344 & 345 n.6; on L. Agassiz's dispute with H.J. Clark, 283 & 284 nn.11 & 12; on L. Agassiz's theories of glaciation in Brazil, 302 & 303 nn.3 & 4, 322 & 323 n.7, 325 & 326 n.16; article on hybrid crosses, 345 n.7; on Austro-Prussian war, 231 & 232 n.8; botanical textbooks, 158 & 163 n.7, 283 & 284 n.2; correspondence with J.D. Hooker, 171 & 172 n.1, 178 & 179 nn.2 & 3; dimorphism in *Rhamnus lanceolata*, 214 & n.10; holiday, 283; illegitimate offspring of dimorphic plants, 437 & n.6; *Origin*, presentation copy, 157 & n.5, 313 & 315 n.6, 485; *Origin*, proposed new US edition, xix, 156–7 & nn.2–4, 231 & nn.3–7, 302 & 303 n.1, 313 & 315 n.7, 344 & 345 nn.2–4, 361 & 362 n.2; *Origin*, proposed review, 344; *Origin*, proposed sales of 4th edition in US, 231 & n.4, 275 & 276 n.2, 344, 351 & 352 n.4, 353 & n.4, 361 & 362 n.2, 484; *Origin*, receives bound copy, 344 & 345 n.2; *Origin*, statement of sales, 247 & 248 nn.1–6 & 8 & 9; *Origin*, wishes to read at odd moments, 302 & 303 n.5; R. Owen's views on transmutation of species, 192 & 193 n.12; *Passiflora acerifolia*, climbing action, 231 & 232 nn.10 & 11; reconciliation with L. Agassiz, 377 & 378 n.6; reviews of 'Climbing plants', 129 & 130 n.2; sends *Cypripedium* specimen to CD, 283 & 284 n.3; sends postage stamps to L. Darwin, 313 & 315 n.2; sends *Rhamnus* seeds to CD, 344 & 345 n.5; *Variation*, proposed US edition, 313–14 & 315 n.8, 353 & n.4; J. Wyman an accurate observer, 283–4 & n.13

Gray, Charlotte Frances. *See* Birch, Charlotte Frances

Gray, George Robert: British Museum, assistant keeper, 127 n.3

Gray, John, 172 & 173 n.12

Gray, John Edward: arranges publication of W.E. Leach's book on molluscs, 127 & n.2; assists CD with work on barnacles, 186 & 187 n.11; British Museum, keeper of zoological collections, 186 & 187 n.10; CD sends batrachian larva to, 83 &

Gray, John Edward, cont.
84 nn.1, 3 & 4, 90 n.4; family circumstances, 127 n.3; International Horticultural Exhibition and Botanical Congress, member of committee, 86 & 87 n.2; invites CD and E. Darwin to dinner, 120 & nn.1 & 2, 180 n.8, 182 & n.3; paper on taxonomy of sea-pens, 186 & 187 n.9; rheumatic iritis, 83 & 84 n.2; sends copy of R.A. Salisbury's *The genera of plants* to CD, 127 & nn.1 & 2; studies of bat taxonomy, 83 & 84 n.5

Grece, Clair James: pig's sloughing of skin, 386–7 & nn.2–4

Greece: A. Gaudry's paper on fossils of, 318 & nn.2–5

Greeff, Richard: visit to Royal Botanic Gardens, Kew, with E. Haeckel, 366 & 367 n.7

Greenland: birds migrating via, 287 & n.5, 289 & 290 n.16

Greg, William Rathbone: dines at W. Spottiswoode's, 428 & 429 n.19; *The creed of Christendom*, 428 & 429 n.19

Grenier, Charles: with D.A. Godron, *Flore de France*, 274 & 275 n.4

Greville, Robert Kaye: Botanical Society of Edinburgh, president, 483

Grey-Egerton, Philip de Malpas. *See* Egerton, Philip de Malpas Grey-

Grierson, Thomas Boyle, 43 & 44 n.10; monkey recognising pictures, 136 & 137 n.2

Griffith, William: prediction, 113 & 114 n.11

Groom-Napier, Charles Otley: webbed feet of otter-hounds, 338 n.2

Grove, William Robert: British Association for the Advancement of Science, J.D. Hooker's lecture, 277 n.7, 308 & 309 n.5; British Association for the Advancement of Science, president (1866), 18 n.10, 306 & n.3; British Association for the Advancement of Science, presidential address, xxi–xxii, 190 & 191 nn.3 & 9, 192 & n.3, 192 n.3, 304 & 305 n.6, 306 & n.2, 308 & 309 nn.8–10, 339 n.4, 342 n.1, 402 & n.2, 428 & 429 n.18; disapproval of Brechin Town Council, 323 n.11; forwards letter from working man to CD, 313; meeting with CD in London, 146 & n.1, 146 & 147 n.3, 192 & 193 n.8

Guarea: fruit with brightly coloured seeds, 407 & 409 n.9, 478 & 480 n.9

guinea fowls: ancestor of domestic, 431 & n.4, 433 & n.3; W.B. Tegetmeier seeks information from CD on varieties, 420 & n.4, 422 & n.5

Gunther, Albert Charles Lewis: paper on fishes of Central America, 427 & 429 n.10

Gurney, John Henry: administration and locality of natural history collections, 175 & n.1 & 176 nn.2 & 3

gynandromorphy, 51 n.3

gyno-dioecious plants, 210 n.5, 235 & n.4

Haast, Julius von: correspondence with J.D. Hooker, 310 n.3; explorations of New Zealand, 242 & n.4 & 243 n.10, 310 & nn.4 & 5; lecture on west coast of Canterbury, 410 & 412 n.13, 418 & 419 n.8; map of Southern Alps of New Zealand, 310 & n.4; seeks election to fellowship of Royal Society of London, 153 & n.2 & 154 n.3, 242 & n.5, 309–10 & nn.1 & 2; thanks CD for photograph, 241 & 242 n.2; theory of origin of species, 242 & n.4; vegetation growing beside New Zealand glacier, 49 n.25

Habenaria: found in Organ Mountains, 46 & 47 n.8; widespread occurrence, 67 & 68 n.4

Habenaria bonatea, 112 & 113 n.3

Haeckel, Ernst: alternation of generations in *Liriope*, 324 & 326 n.16; CD gives introduction to J.D. Hooker, 358 & 359 n.2, 367 n.3; coiner of new words, 437 & n.3; delighted with peloric *Antirrhinum*, 413 & n.2; difficulties with spoken English, 27, 367 & n.3, 459; evolutionary trees, 7 & 9 n.8, 455 & 457 n.8; exchange of photographs with CD, 8 & 10 nn.15–18, 19 & 20 n.3, 163 n.10, 456 & 458 nn.15–18; *Generelle Morphologie*, xviii–xix, 7 & 9 nn.8–10 & 12, 20 & nn.4 & 5, 294 & 295 nn.1–3, 353–4 & n.3, 389 & 390 n.9, 415 & 416 n.11, 437 & nn.2 & 3, 455–6 & 457 nn.8–10 & 12, 473 & n.3; high opinion of *Origin*, 19, 294 & 295 nn.1–3; lectures on Darwinian theory, 8 & 10 n.14, 456 & 458 n.14; J. Lubbock wishes to meet, 359 & nn.1 & 2; ontogeny recapitulating phylogeny, 9 n.10, 457 n.10; opposition to L. Agassiz's theories, 8 & 10 nn.12 & 13, 456 & 458 nn.12 & 13; papers on coelenterates, 7 & 9 nn.4, 6 & 7, 20 n.7, 455 & 456 n.4 & 457 nn.6 & 7; a pleasant personality, 367, 385 & 386 n.9, 415; portrait, 10 n.18, 458 n.18; presentation copy of Origin, 485 & n.1; speculations on spontaneous generation, 9 n.7, 389 & 390 n.9, 457 n.7; visit to Down House, xviii–xix, 353, 358 & nn.2–5, 359 n.1, 367 n.3, 386 n.9, 413 & n.2, 415, 473, 482 & n.20; visit to T.H. Huxley, 386 n.9; visit to Madeira and Tenerife, 353 & 354 n.2, 415 & 416 n.10, 473 &

Haeckel, Ernst, cont.
n.2; visit to Royal Botanic Gardens, Kew, with R. Greeff, 366 & 367 n.7, 373 & n.2
Halesidota harrissii, 138 n.3
Halesidota tessellaris: colour variants, 137 & 138 n.3
Hallier, Ernst: criticisms of German translation of *Origin*, 134 & n.5
Hamilton, Edward: administration and locality of natural history collections, 175 & n.1 & 176 nn.2 & 3
Hamilton, William Gerard ('Single-speech Hamilton'), 308 & 309 n.3
Hamilton, William John: and expedition to Patagonia, 232 & 233 n.9
Hamond, Robert Nicholas: served on HMS *Beagle*, 445 & 446 n.15
Hanbury, Daniel: seeks information from F. Müller, 403–4 & nn.1–3
Handel, George Frideric: *Acis and Galatea*, performance at Crystal Palace, 104 & n.3
Hanson, Alfred, 243 & n.1
Haplophium, 56, 462
Hardwicke, Robert: *Popular Science Review*, publisher, 201–2 & n.2
Hardwicke's Science-Gossip: G. Henslow sends copies to CD, 117 & 118 n.1
hares: fleetest in countries where greyhounds are kept, 114–15 & n.4
Harris, James: trader in Patagonia, 446 & 447 n.25
Harrow School, Middlesex, 41 & n.5
Hartung, Georg: erratic boulders in Azores, 287 & 288 n.6; hypothesis of continental extension, 285 & 286 n.6
Harvey, Elizabeth Lecky, 180 & 181 n.3
Harvey, William Henry: authority on algae and South African flora, 181 n.6; illness and death, 81 & 83 n.7, 180–1 & nn.2 & 3; Trinity College, Dublin, professor of botany and keeper of herbarium, 181 & n.5
Haughton, Samuel: rate of cooling of earth's crust, 84 & 85 n.5
Hawkins, Benjamin Waterhouse: grant from Royal Society relief fund, 449 & 450 n.7
Hay, Arthur, Viscount Walden: administration and locality of natural history collections, 175 & n.1 & 176 nn.2, 3 & 5
hazels. *See Corylus*
Hector, James, 153 n.2
Hedyotis, dimorphism, 368 & 369 & 371 n.8, 452 & 453 n.5
Heer, Oswald: Atlantis hypothesis, 255 n.11, 285 & 286 n.6; comments on ant behaviour, 106–7 & nn.2 & 3; Eocene fossil leaves offered to, 448 & n.5, 448 & 449 n.2, 451 & nn.6 & 7; on flora of Madeira, 259 n.10, 263 n.15; Zurich University, professor of botany and entomology, 449 n.2
Hegel, Georg Wilhelm Friedrich, 134 & n.6
Hennessy, Henry: rate of cooling of earth's crust, 84 & 85 n.5
Henry, Joseph: Smithsonian Institution, secretary, 378 n.6
Henslow, George: an engaging personality, 112 & 113 n.2; article on C.V. Naudin's studies on hybridity, 96 & n.5, 100 & n.1, 183 & nn.1–3, 201–2 & nn.2–4, 204–5 & nn.2 & 4 & 206 n.7, 210 & nn.1–3; CD's gift of orchid to, 117 & 118 n.3; commitment at St Stephen's Church, Westminster, 104 n.3; duplicate copy of 'Climbing plants', 96 & n.4, 100 & n.4, 103 & n.2; Grammar School, Store Street, headmaster, 104 n.3; lectures at Royal Institution, 100 & n.2, 103 & 104 n.3, 104 & n.3; loan of books by CD, 99 & 100 n.1, 183 & n.2, 201 & 202 n.2, 202 & 203 n.5, 210 & nn.2 & 3; paper on *Cytisus*, xviii; paper on *Indigofera* pollination, xviii, 132 n.2, 135 n.2, 139 & 140 n.3, 179 & 180 n.16; paper on *Medicago sativa* pollination, xviii, 132 n.4, 141 n.5, 179 & 180 n.16; St Bartholomew's Hospital, botanical lecturer, 139 & 140 n.4; visit to Down House, xviii, 95 & 96 & n.1, 99–100 & n.3, 103 & 104 n.4, 104 & nn.1–4, 112 & 113 n.2, 118 nn.3 & 6, 132 n.2, 140 & 141 n.3
Henslow, John Stevens, 180 & 181 n.4; death, 26 n.2; introduction of phosphate manures, 117 & 118 n.2
Herbert, John Maurice, 2 & 3 n.1
Herbert, William, 96 n.5; belief in reversion, 206 & 207 nn.6–8; difficulty in obtaining papilionaceous hybrids, 292 & 293 n.3; views on origin of species, 244 & 245 n.13
'Herklotsia', 187 n.9
Herschel, John Frederick William: temperature of space and climate change, 84 & 85 n.6
Heteranthera, 94 & 95 n.11, 464 & 466 n.11
heterostyly, 226 n.11; in *Cordia*, 416 n.5; and pollen-grain sizes, 162 n.5, 211 & nn.5 & 6, 213–14 & nn.3–7, 9 & 10, 215 & 216 n.6; in *Primula*, 210 n.6, 436, 447 & n.2

Hewitt, Edward: observations of poultry, 269 & 270 nn.1 & 2, 278 & 279 n.9, 279 & 280 n.5, 291 & n.4

High Elms, Down, home of J. Lubbock: fête, 256 n.2; visit by H. Spencer, 337 & 338 n.10, 482 & n.19

Hildebrand, Friedrich: *Aristolochia*, dichogamy in, 252 & n.9, 360 & 361 nn.2–5; delayed fertilisation in orchids, 324 & 325 n.6, 405–6 & 409 n.3, 476 & 479 n.3; *Oxalis rosea*, unable to send seeds to CD, 360 & n.1; *Oxalis* trimorphism, 169–70 & nn.2 & 3, 176 & 178 nn.9 & 10, 179 & 180 n.17, 186 & 187 n.12, 251 & 252 n.1; paper on *Corydalis cava*, 170 & n.5, 176 & 177 nn.3 & 6, 179 & 180 n.15, 250 & 251 n.2, 324 & 325 n.10, 409 n.6, 479 n.6; paper on dichogamy and dimorphism, 174 & n.2; paper on hybridisation of orchids, 174 & n.4; paper on *Salvia*, 132 & n.5, 140 & 141 n.6, 177 & 178 nn.11 & 12; paper on trimorphic species, 415 & 416 n.4; papers on mechanisms of insect pollination, 132 & nn.2–5, 139 & 140 n.3; protogyny, 361 n.4; review of CD's *Lythrum* paper, 174 & n.3, 250 & 251 n.3; support for CD's theories, 252 & nn.8 & 9

Hillia: variability of flowers, 370 & 371 n.13, 408 & 409 nn.14 & 15, 474–5 & 476 n.6, 478–9 & 480 nn.14 & 15

Himalayas: glacial action in, 48 n.20

Hincks, Thomas: paper on reproduction in Polyzoa, 390–1 & n.1

Hitchcock, Edward: fossil tadpole 'nests', 14 & 15 n.7

Holland, Richard George: curate of Holy Trinity Church, Bromley Common, 319 & n.2; wife's account of cat adopting squirrel, 319 & n.3

holly. *See Ilex aquifolium*

Holwood Park, Kent: home of R.M. Rolfe, 331 & n.2, 414 & n.1

Hooker, Brian Harvey Hodgson: visit to Down House, 225 & 226 n.8; visit to St Albans, 256 n.21

Hooker, Charles Paget: visit to St Albans, 256 n.21

Hooker, Frances Harriet, 25 & 26 n.4, 318 & 319 n.2, 392 & 393 n.4, 396 & 397 n.2; CD hopes will visit in London, 143 & 144 n.3; expecting confinement, 411 & 412 n.18, 413 & n.5; sends CD article on death of E. Darwin, 366 & 367 n.2; tells CD of E. Darwin's biography, 413 & n.6; visit to Down House, 105 n.3, 172 & 173 n.23, 179 & 180 n.18, 181 & 182 n.12, 225 & 226 n.8, 482 & n.16; visit to St Albans, 254 & 256 n.21; visit to Sydenham, 104 & n.3

Hooker, Harriet Anne: visit to St Albans, 256 n.21

Hooker, Joseph Dalton, 75 & 76 n.6, 155 & n.3; *Acropera* specimen loaned to CD, 261 & 263 n.22, 271 & 274 n.19, 296 & n.5, 305 n.11, 337 & n.3; administration and locality of natural history collections, 175 & n.1 & 176 nn.2 & 3; on American Civil War, 171 & 172 n.2; aristocracy the outcome of natural selection, 181 & 182 n.11; assistance with expedition to China Sea, 39 n.4, 58 & 59 n.3; assistance with J. Scott's appointment to Calcutta, 82 & 83 n.14; attends sale at The Mount, 395–6 & nn.5–7; and G. Bentham, *Genera plantarum*, 329 & 330 n.12, 428 & 429 n.20; and G. Bentham, *Genera plantarum*, CD offers copies to F. Müller, 299 & 300 n.10, 452 & 453 n.13; cannot understand E. Frankland's lecture, 329 & n.4; and R. Caspary's visit to Down House, 179 & 180 n.7, 181 & n.7, 188 & n.1, 190 & 191 n.2; CD, asks for bibliographical references, 402 & n.2; CD, asks to see text on cultivated plants, 181 & 182 n.10; CD, better news of health, 241 & 242 n.2; CD, discussion of *Lupinus*, 223 & 224 n.10; CD, meets at Royal Society soirée, 171 & 172 n.3; CD, sends him information on *Begonia phyllomaniaca*, 116 & 117 n.2; CD's visit to, 392, 395 & 396 n.1; CD asks for information on appearance and structure of buds, 148; CD hopes will visit in London, 143 & 144 n.3; CD introduces E. Haeckel, 358 & 359 n.2; CD sends *Lupinus pilosus* specimen for identification, 249 & n.1; CD sends plants to, 296 & n.3, 304 & 305 n.10, 318 & 319 n.3, 329 & n.1, 373 & 374 n.9, 393 & n.7, 413 & n.1, 418 & 419 n.15, 420 & 421 nn.2 & 3; changes in global temperature, 59–60 & n.4, 81 & 82 n.6; collector of Wedgwood ware, 172 & 173 n.22, 395 & 396 nn.5 & 7, 427 & 429 n.13; comments on ms. of *Natural selection*, 47 & 49 n.23, 98 n.10; confirmatory evidence of CD's theories, 190 & 191 nn.3–9, 402 n.2; correspondence with A. Gray, 171 & 172 n.1, 178 & 179 nn.2 & 3, 196 & n.1; J. Crawfurd's paper on migration of cultivated plants 'shocking twaddle', 171 & 173 n.7, 181 & n.9; and cut-leaved beech, 225 & 226 nn.9 & 10; delightful dinner party at C. Lyell's, 420 & 421 n.5; delights in his occupation, 329 & 330 n.11; denies seeing B. Verlot's book, 17 n.3; dines with C. and M.E. Lyell and C.J.F. Bunbury,

Hooker, Joseph Dalton, cont.
410 & 411 n.5; dines with W. Spottiswoode, 428 & 429 n.19; G. Eliot, *Felix Holt the radical*, borrowed from CD, 295 & 296 n.1; endemic organisms largely rare species, 257 & 259 nn.7 & 8; enjoys excursion to Belvoir Castle, 308 & 309 n.12; E.J. Eyre, opposes prosecution, xxiv, 385 n.5, 395 & 396 n.4; flora of Atlantic islands, 281 & n.5; flora of Cameroon Mountains, 172 & 173 nn.13 & 14; *Flora Novæ-Zelandiæ*, 443 & 444 n.2; *Flora Novæ-Zelandiæ*, introductory essay, 410 & 411 nn.9, 418 & 419 n.9; geographical distribution of species, xxi, 59 & 60 n.6, 86 n.8, 191 n.8, 258 n.5, 418 & 419 n.9, 427 & 429 nn.7–9; glaciation in Sikkim, 98 & 99 n.4; W.R. Grove, address at British Association for the Advancement of Science, xxii, 428 & 429 n.18; W.R. Grove, dislike of, 17; W.R. Grove, meets at Athenaeum Club, 427 & 429 n.11; J. von Haast's candidacy for fellowship of Royal Society, 153 n.2; W.H. Harvey, grief at death, 180–1 & nn.2–6; haunted by death, xxiv, 25 & 26 nn.1 & 2; honorary degree from Oxford University, 171 & n.6; T.H. Huxley, role at British Association (1866 meeting), 303 & 304 n.4; identifies *Adenanthera pavonina*, 416 n.6, 418 nn.2 & 3, 426 & 428 nn.1–3, 452 & 453 n.14; International Horticultural Exhibition, 'a tremendous worry', 190 & 191 n.10; International Horticultural Exhibition, urges CD to visit, 172 & 174 n.26; lecture on insular floras, xx–xxi, 17 & 18 n.9, 21 & 22 n.7, 222–3 & nn.5 & 6, 225 & n.2, 253–4 & n.4 & 255 nn.5–9 & 256 nn. 16 & 18, 259 n.14, 260 & 263 nn.10, 11 & 20, 272 & 273 nn.10–15, 277 & n.7, 286 nn.2, 3 & 7, 287 n.5 & 288 n.10, 288–9 & nn.2–4 & 290 nn.5, 6 & 8–10, 294 & n.2, 303 & n.2 & 304 nn.3 & 4, 304 & 305 nn.2–5, 306 & 307 n.7, 308 & 309 nn.2–5, 322 & 323 n.10, 329 & 330 n.5, 410 & 411 n.10, 427 & 428 n.11, 439 & n.5; lecture on insular floras, publication, 304 & 305 n.3, 322 & 323 n.10, 337 & 338 n.5, 396 & n.8, 427 & 428 n.12; London dinners the ruin of science, 428; longs to revisit St Helena, 285 & 286 n.9; C. Lyell's visit, 354 & 355 nn.2–4; A. Murray's book on geographical distribution of mammals, review, 323 n.8, 329 & n.3, 337 & 338 n.4; *Natural History Review*, article on new colonial floras, 60 & n.7; orchids, 149; and pangenesis hypothesis, xv, 116 & 117 n.4; paper on Australian flora, 190 & 191 nn.8 & 9, 439 & n.5; paper on distribution of Arctic plants, 190 & 191 nn.8 & 9, 192 & 193 nn.9 & 10, 196 n.4, 289 & 290 n.17; paper on flora of St Helena, 129 & 131 n.6; plans to send *Euryale ferox* seeds to CD, 392 & 393 n.5; presentation copy of *Origin*, 485 & 486 n.8; pressure of work, 16 & 17 n.2, 72, 81 & 83 n.8, 96 & 97 n.4, 329 & 330 n.11, 448; a probable sceptic on Brazilian glaciation, 36 & 37 n.14; publishers 'penurious pragmatical prigs', 448; rearrangements at Kew, 420 & 421 nn.3 & 4; receives C. Lyell's *Principles of geology*, 10th edition, 410 & 411 n.3; recommends *Pall Mall Gazette*, 17 & 18 n.11; recommends papers on New Zealand geology, 410 & 412 nn.13 & 14, 418 & 419 n.8; Royal Botanic Gardens, Kew, director, 17 n.2, 83 n.8; *Saxifraga fortunei*, CD requests specimen, 393 n.9; seeks remedy for persistent vomiting, 38 & 39 nn.2 & 3; sends trees and shrubs to Down House, 354 & n.1, 359 & n.3, 367 & n.1; 'shaky as to species', 98 & 99 n.5; H. Spencer, *Principles of biology*, finds ponderous and verbose, 410 & 411 nn.6 & 7; H. Spencer, *Principles of biology*, hopes to read soon, 225 & 226 n.7; B.J. Sulivan offers fossil leaf specimens, 445, 448, 448 & 449 n.2, 451 & nn.6 & 7; temperate flora in Africa, 46 & 48 n.13, 74 n.5; theories of climate change, 92 & 93 n.2; Umbelliferae, controversy with H. Spencer, 427 & 428 n.6; visit from E. Haeckel and R. Greeff, 366 & 367 n.7; visit from M.E. Lyell and G.H. and L. Pertz, 329 & 330 n.9; visit to Etruria, 25 & 26 n.3; visit to M. Hooker, 410 & 411 n.2; visit to Kerguelen's Land, 255 n.15; visit to Lord Lovelace, 366 & 367 n.5; visit to Norwich, 448; visit to Pembroke Dock, 366 & 367 n.6, 372 & 373 n.1; visit to Torquay with J. Lubbock, 149 & n.5; visits to Down House, 17 & 18 n.7, 21 & n.3, 73 & 74 n.12, 85 & 86 n.14, 104 & n.2, 105 & nn.3 & 4, 129 & 131 n.5, 172 & 173 n.23, 179 & 180 n.18, 181 & 182 n.12, 215 & 216 n.7, 223 & n.7, 258 & 259 n.14, 287 & 288 n.10, 288 & 290 n.7, 293–4 & nn.1 & 2, 294, 305 n.11, 482 & nn.11, 17 & 18; visits to Down House, brings book and microscope away with him, 295–6 & n.1; and voyage to Magellan Straits, 217 & 218 n.20, 225 & n.4 & 226 n.5, 232 & n.5; welcomes news of CD's improved health, 72; whether limit exists on amount of living matter on earth, 410–11 & n.16, 419 n.14, 427–8 & 429 nn.14–16; on worldwide glacial epoch and distribution of species, 72–3 &

Hooker, Joseph Dalton, cont.
nn.3–10; 'wriggling' out of difficulties, 417, 428 & 429 n.21
Hooker, Maria, 180 & 181 n.3; ill at Yarmouth, 296 & n.7; visit by J.D. Hooker, 410 & 411 n.2
Hooker, Maria Elizabeth: death, 26 n.2, 117 n.7
Hooker, Reginald Hawthorn, 413 n.5
Hooker, William Henslow: visit to St Albans, 256 n.21
Hooker, William Jackson: death, 26 n.2, 83 n.8; government to purchase his collections, 354 & 355 n.5, 359 & n.4, 373 & n.8; *London Journal of Botany*, editor, 35 & 37 n.10; memorial at Kew, 17 & n.6, 25 & 26 n.3
Hope, James, navy commander-in-chief, 217 & 218 n.18
Hopkins, William: rate of cooling of earth's crust, 84 & 85 n.5
Hornby, Geoffrey Thomas Phipps: HMS *Bristol*, commodore, 218 n.18
Horner, Ann Susan, 172 & 173 nn.18 & 19
Horner, Joanna, 172 & 173 n.17
Horner, Katharine Murray. *See* Lyell, Katharine Murray
horseradish. *See Cochlearia armoracia*
horses: inhumane treatment, 1–2 & nn.4 & 5; L. Rütimeyer's book on fossil, 109 & n.11; skull of pony, 357 n.4; stripes as instance of reversion, 206 & 207 n.8
Hottonia: pollen-grain sizes in heterostyled flowers, 213 & 214 n.5
Huber, François: geometry of bees' cells, 13 & 15 nn.5 & 6
humans: antiquity of race, J. Lubbock's book, 307 n.10; descent, F. Rolle's views, 29 & nn.3 & 4, 460 & 461 nn.3 & 4; descent from single stock, 171 & 173 n.6; C. Lyell's view, distinct from all other species, 411 n.4; natural selection in, W.C. Wells's view, 283 & 284 n.4, 391 & 392 n.2; origin and antiquity, H.A. Dubois's paper, 243–4 & 245 nn.7–9; origins, W. Bowman's address, 326 & 327 n.3, 341 & n.2; origins, CD differs from C. Lyell, 344 n.6; origins of races, A.R. Wallace's paper, 190 & 191 n.5; Pliocene skull found in California, 400 & 401 n.9; similarities between races, 171 & 172 n.5
Humbert, Aloïs: with F. Pictet de la Rive, article on fossil fishes of Lebanon, 311–12 & n.13
humble-bee. *See under* bees
Humboldt, Alexander von: *Cosmos*, 380 & n.3; description of *Befaria*, 67 & 69 n.6
humming-birds: nomenclature, 164 & nn.1 & 2 & 165 nn.3 & 4
Humphry, George Murray: Cambridge University, professor of human anatomy, 399 & n.2
Hunt, Robert: biographical sketch of CD, xvii–xviii, 151–2 & nn.1 & 2
Hunter, Mrs: canary and peacock preening before mirror, 136 & 137 n.3; parrot of aristocratic tastes, 136
Hurstpierpoint, Sussex: home of A.R. Wallace, 237 n.9
Hutton, Frederick Wollaston: analogous petrel species, 91 & n.7
Huxley, Ethel Gladys: birth, 172 & 173 n.17, 386 n.7
Huxley, Henrietta Anne, 385 & 386 n.6
Huxley, Thomas Henry: administration and locality of natural history collections, 175 & n.1 & 176 nn.2 & 3; alternation of generations in *Liriope*, 324 & 326 n.16; attacked by H.A. Dubois, 243–4 & 246 n.9; biographical sketch by J.V. Carus, 389 & 390 n.12; British Association for the Advancement of Science, president of section 'D' Biology, 303 & 304 n.4, 308 & 309 n.6; CD consults on pangenesis, xv; concept of 'physiological' species, xv–xvi, 40 n.5; dines at W. Spottiswoode's, 428 & 429 n.19; discussion at Linnean Society meeting, 421 n.8; *Evidence as to man's place in nature*, 364 & 365 n.7, 437 & n.4; and expedition to Patagonia, 232 & nn.2–6 & 233 nn.7–10, 237 & n.2 & 238 nn.3–5; and W.R. Grove's address at British Association for the Advancement of Science, 428 & 429 n.18; identifies Patagonian fossil, 218 n.11; *Lessons in elementary physiology*, 385 & 386 n.8, 410 & 411 n.8, 418 & 419 n.6, 437 & n.4; natural selection, criterion for acceptance of theory, 437 n.6; *On our knowledge of the causes of the phenomena of organic nature*, German edition, 364 & 365 n.7; praise for J.D. Hooker's lecture, 303, 308 & 309 nn.4 & 5; presentation copy of *Origin*, 385 & n.1, 485 & 486 n.9; refuses to work with J.W. Salter, 450 n.5; studies of medusae, 324 & 326 n.16; support for Jamaica Committee, xxiv, 372 & n.3, 373 & n.5, 385 & n.5
hybrids: chapter in *Natural selection*, 376 n.4; chapter in *Origin*, 437 & n.5; *Cistus*, 185 & n.6, 402 & 403 nn.4 & 5; crosses, 345 & n.7; fowls, 269 & 270 n.4, 278 & 279 n.10, 279 & 280 nn.8 & 9, 291 & n.2; of hawk-moths, 297 & n.8, 301 & 302 n.10; F. Hildebrand's paper on hybridisation of

hybrids, cont.
orchids, 174 & n.4; *Lathyrus*, 293; C.V. Naudin's researches, 96 & n.5, 100 & n.1, 183 & nn.1–3, 201–2 & nn.2–4, 204–5 & nn.2 & 4 & 206 n.7, 376 & n.2 & 377 n.4; rare in Leguminosae, 292 & 293 n.3; reversion, xv, 179 & 180 n.14, 205 & nn.3 & 4, 206 & 207 nn. 2–10, 210 & n.1, 270 n.2; sterility in, xv, 45 n.3, 202 & n.4, 383 n.6, 437 & n.6 & 438 n.8; willows, M.E. Wichura's paper, 16 & n.1, 207 n.10, 376 & n.2 & 377 nn.4 & 5. *See also* graft hybrids
hydrotherapy, 216 & 217 nn.4 & 5
Hymenoptera: 'bullae' on wings, 100–1 & nn.3–6 & 102 n.7; J. Lubbock's observations of diving, 191 n.9
Hyomoschus aquaticus (water chevrotain): arrives at Zoological Gardens, 422 & 423 nn.6 & 7
Hypericum: found in Organ Mountains, 46 & 47 n.8; widespread occurrence, 67 & 68 n.4
Hypolimnus anomala: reversed sexual characters, 391 & 392 nn.4 & 5

Ichneumonidae: 'bullae' on wings, 100–1 & nn.3–6 & 102 n.7
Ichthyosaurus, 297
Ilex aquifolium (holly): development of separate sexes, 209 n.3
India: laurels of Nilgiri Hills, 254 & 256 n.18; P. Norman's visit, 256 & 257 n.3. *See also* Calcutta botanic garden
Indigofera: G. Henslow's observations of mechanisms of insect pollination, 132 & nn.2 & 3, 135 & n.2, 140 & 141 n.3, 179 & 180 n.15
inflammation: papers by L.S. Beale, 51 nn.1 & 2, 54 n.7
influenza, 110 n.5, 116 n.3, 121 n.3, 129 n.8, 129 & 131 n.4
inheritance of characteristics, 1 & nn.2 & 3, 63 n.8, 295 & n.5
Innes, John Brodie: visit to Down House, 482 & n.12
insectivorous plants. *See Drosera*; *Erica massoni*; *Saxifraga*
insects: diving Hymenoptera, J. Lubbock's observations, 191 n.9; effect of food on formation of races, 402 n.2; effects of light on, 43; J. Lubbock's lecture on metamorphoses in, 224 & 225 n.3; phytophagic, B.D. Walsh's paper, 191 n.9; pollinators of *Ophrys*, 62 & 64 n.10; rare at Kew, 282 & n.8. *See also individual species and genera*
International Congress of Botany and Horticulture (Amsterdam, 1865): R. Caspary, paper on graft hybrids, 71 & nn.2 & 3, 79 & 80 nn.3–5, 7 & 12, 91–2 & nn.3–5, 141 & 142 n.1
International Horticultural Exhibition and Botanical Congress (London, 1866), 171 & 173 n.10; A. de Candolle, presidential address, 142 & n.9, 195 & n.2, 472 & n.2; R. Caspary, paper on movements of tree branches as result of cold, 141 & 142 n.3, 145 & 146 n.8; R. Caspary plans to attend, 145 & 146 nn.2–4, 155 & n.4, 195 & 196 n.3, 471 & 472 n.3; CD invited to join committee, 86–7 & n.2, 145 & 146 n.3, 155 n.4; CD unable to attend, 155 nn.2 & 4, 170 n.4, 174 n.25, 176 & 177 n.2, 179 & 180 n.6, 184 n.5, 195 & n.2, 471 & 472 n.2; R.T. Clarke, paper on *Matthiola*, 376 & 377 n.3; F. Hildebrand, paper on *Corydalis cava*, 170 & n.5, 176 & 177 n.3, 179 & 180 n.15, 250 & 251 n.2, 409 n.6, 479 n.6; J.D. Hooker finds a 'tremendous worry', 190 & 191 n.10; J.D. Hooker urges CD to visit, 172 & 174 n.25; H. Lecoq, paper on migration of alpine plants, 141–2 & nn.4–6; M.T. Masters, honorary secretary, 86–7 & nn.1–4, 176 & 177 n.3, 250 & 251 n.2; papers presented at, 142 n.8; T. Rivers, paper on seedling peaches and nectarines, 183 & 184 n.6
Ipomoea. *See Convolvulus*
Ipswich Museum: commissions portrait of CD, 124 & n.2
island organisms: endemic organisms largely rare species, 257 & 259 nn.7 & 8; J.D. Hooker, lecture on insular floras, xx–xxi, 17 & 18 n.9, 21 & 22 n.7, 222–3 & nn.5 & 6, 225 & n.2, 253–4 & n.4 & 255 nn.5–9 & 256 nn. 16 & 18, 259 n.14, 260 & 263 nn.10, 11 & 20, 272 & 273 nn.10–15, 277 & n.7, 286 nn.2, 3 & 7, 287 n.5 & 288 n.10, 288–9 & nn.2–4 & 290 nn.5, 6 & 8–10, 294 & n.2, 303 & n.2 & 304 nn.3 & 4, 304 & 305 nn.2–5, 306 & 307 n.7, 308 & 309 nn.2–5, 322 & 323 n.10, 329 & 330 n.5, 337 & 338 n.5, 396 & n.8, 410 & 411 n.10, 427 & 429 nn.11 & 12, 439 & n.5; land birds, 280–1 & n.3; numbers of species dependent on mode of colonisation, 289 & 290 n.15; rarity of orchids and Leguminosae, 443 & 444 n.5
Isle of Wight: Eocene leaf-bed at Alum Bay, 445 & 446 n.12
Isleworth: Society of Friends' Meeting House, 116 & 117 n.9
Isochilus, 265 & 268 nn.7 & 8

isthmus: effect of breaking, 260 & 262 n.3, 271 & 273 n.4, 282 & n.4
Itajaí Açu river, Santa Catarina state, Brazil, 10 & 12 n.9, 55 & 56 & n.4 & 57 n.6, 93 & 95 n.6, 462 & 463 nn.4 & 6, 464 & 465 n.6

Jäger, Gustav: paper on theory of transmutation, 126 & n.9, 468 & n.9; Vienna zoological gardens, director, 29 & 30 n.8, 460 & 461 n.8
Jamaica Committee, xxiii–xxiv, 372 n.1, 373 & n.5, 385 & n.5, 393 & n.8, 395 & 396 n.4
James, Sir Henry: map of world used by J.D. Hooker, 222–3 & nn.5 & 6, 225 & n.2, 286 n.3; speculations on climate change, 85 n.7
Jamieson, Thomas Francis: paper on glacial phenomena in Caithness, 328 & nn.2–4
Janet, Paul: objections to CD's theories, 227 & 230 n.3; *The materialism of the present day*, review, 227 & 230 n.3 & 10
Japan: whether rich in plant species, 443
Jardine, Sir William, 42, 43
Jena University: E. Haeckel's lectures on Darwinian theory, 8 & 10 n.14, 456 & 458 n.14; M.J. Schleiden resigns professorship, 27 & 28 n.3, 458 & 459 n.3
Jenner, William: physician to CD, 4 n.8 & 5 n.10
Jennings, Stephen: owner of pig that sloughed skin, 386 & 387 n.4
Joan of Arc, 173 n.21; paintings, 172 & 173 n.20
Johnson, Andrew: and post-Civil War reconstruction, 130 & 131 n.16, 157 & 158 n.12
Johnson, George William: *The poultry book*, 22 & 23 nn.10–12, 270 n.5
Jones, Henry Bence: advises CD to take holiday, 52 & n.2; advises riding exercise, 52 & n.3, 264 & n.2, 331 & n.4; CD asks to call on him in London, 144 & n.3; CD plans to visit, 128 & nn.1 & 2; physician to CD, xiv, xvii, 3 n.1, 4 nn.2 & 4, 52 & nn.1–6, 96 & n.2, 171 & 172 n.4, 301 & n.5, 307 n.3, 331 & n.4
Jordan, Alexis: subspecies of *Papaver*, 388 & n.4, 403 n.3
Journal of Botany: insular floras, summary of J.D. Hooker's lecture, 304 n.3; B.C. Seemann, editor, 163 & n.5
Journal of Horticulture: correspondence on grafting of trees and shrubs, 148 n.5; T. Rivers's article on fruit culture, 147 & n.2
Journal of the Linnean Society: 'Climbing plants' published in, 96 n.4; F. Müller's paper on climbing plants, 299 & 300 n.8, 412 n.20, 453 n.15
Journal of the Royal Geographical Society: account of tame saigas in island of Aral Sea, 417 n.4, 422 & 423 n.4
Journal of the Royal Horticultural Society: papers on hybridism, 376 & n.2
Juan Fernandez islands: flora, 439 & 440 n.9
Juncus bufonius (toadrush): seed carried on woodcock foot, 401 & n.2, 419 n.4
Juniperus bermudiana (Bermuda cedar), 289 & 290 n.12
Jurine, Louis: book on Hymenoptera and Diptera, 100–1 & nn.3–6 & 102 n.7

Keats, John: 'Lamia', quoted by J. Shaw, 380 & n.5
Kempson, Louisa Frances (née Wedgwood), 373 & n.4
Kent: denudation of Wealden district, 348 & 349 n.8
Kent Church Penitentiary Society: removal of St Mary's Home to Stone, 70 & nn.1 & 2 & 71 nn.3–5
Kerguelen's Land: flora, 262 n.9, 289 & 290 n.8; insects of, 253 & 255 n.15
Kew: St Anne's Church, memorial to W.J. Hooker, 17 n.6
Kew Gardens. *See* Royal Botanic Gardens, Kew
Kew Observatory: B. Stewart, director, 411 & 412 n.17
Key, Thomas Hewitt: supports F.W. Farrar's candidature for Royal Society, 41 & n.3
King-Noel, William, 1st Earl Lovelace: J.D. Hooker's visit to, 366 & 367 n.5
Kingsley, Charles, 239 & 240 n.1; lectures on science and superstition, 239 & 240 n.4; migration of eye in flatfish, 239 & 240 nn.2 & 3; visit to Holwood Park, 414 & 415 n.4; welcomes news of CD's improved health, 240
Kingsley, Frances Eliza: visit to Holwood Park, 414 & 415 n.4
Kippist, Richard: Linnean Society of London, librarian, 108–9 & nn.1–11, 224 & n.3, 234 & n.2, 321 & n.6, 327 & n.4, 331 n.1
Kirk, John: administration and locality of natural history collections, 175 & n.1 & 176 nn.2 & 3
kitty-wren. *See Troglodytes vulgaris*
Knight, Charles: *English cyclopedia*, bird observing portrait and mirror-image, 58 n.3

Koenig, Johann Samuel: measurements of honey-bee cells, 13 & 15 n.1
Kölreuter, Joseph Gottlieb: crossing experiments with *Mirabilis*, 373 n.6; reversion in hybrids, 206 & 207 n.3
Königliche-Preussische Akademie der Wissenschaften: CD an honorary member, 108 & 109 n.4
Königlichen Akademie der Wissenschaften zu Berlin: F. Hildebrand's *Oxalis* paper read, 251 & 252 n.2
Königsberg University, botanic garden, 199 & 201 n.10; R. Caspary, professor of botany and director, 146 n.7
Krlyer, Henrik Nikolaj: study of lancelet, 408 & 409 n.18, 479 & 480 n.18

+ *Laburnocytisus adamii*. *See Cytisus adami*
Laburnum alpinum. *See Cytisus alpinus*
Laburnum x *watereri*, 148 & n.4
Lamarck, Jean-Baptiste de, xix
'*Lamium campanulatum*': a non-existent species, 225 & 226 n.12
lancelet. *See Branchiostoma lanceolatum*
Land and Water, 330 & 331 nn.1 & 3; article on solitaire, 423 n.10; article on tame saigas in island of Aral Sea, 417 n.3, 422 & 423 n.3; F.T. Buckland, editor of Practical Natural History, 330 & 331 n.3, 423 n.10; CD seeks information on feet of otter-hounds, 336 & 337 n.6, 338 n.2, 339 n.3; CD subscribes to, 336 & 337 n.7
land-bridges, 257, 290 n.15, 439 & 440 n.9
Langton, Charles, 5 & 6 n.4
Langton, Edmund: visit to W.E. Darwin, 211 & n.4
Langton, Emily Catherine: death duties, 243 & n.1; last illness and death, xxiv, 5 & nn.1 & 2, 21 & n.4, 25 & 26 nn.1 & 4, 38 & 39 n.1, 46 & 48 n.17, 346 n.7, 482 & n.22; legacies to CD's children, 381 & n.4; settlement of estate, 65 & nn.1 & 3, 66 & nn.3–5; share of R.W. Darwin's estate, 340 n.3
Laothoe populi (poplar hawk-moth): interbreeding with *Smerinthus ocellatus*, 297 & n.8
late spider ophrys. *See Ophrys arachnites*
latent heat theory, 116 & 117 n.5
Lathyrus grandiflorus: hybrid formed with *L. odoratus*, 293, 382 n.4
Lathyrus odoratus (sweetpeas): believed to intercross in Italy, 382 n.6; CD's crossing experiments, xxii, 44–5 & n.4, 292–3 & n.5, 382 n.4, 387 & 388 n.3; crossing of varieties unknown, 387 & 388 n.2; German translation of name, 389 & 390 n.6, 394 & n.2
laughing dove, laugher-pigeon. *See under Columba livia*
Laxton, Thomas: home at Stamford, Lincolnshire, 374 & 375 n.6; results of crossing of peas, 337 & 338 nn.7 & 8, 374 & 375 n.5; sends *Pisum* specimens to CD, 337 & 338 nn.7 & 8, 365–6 & nn.2–4, 374 & nn.2–4 & 375 nn.5 & 6
Leach, William Elford: book on British molluscs, 127 & n.2
Lebanon: fossil fishes, 311–12 & n.13; glacial action in, 46 & 48 n.20
Lecky, William Edward Hartpole: dines at C. Lyell's, 420 & 421 n.5; dines at W. Spottiswoode's, 428 & 429 n.19
Lecoq, Henri: paper on migration of alpine plants, 141 & 142 nn.4–6, 195 & 196 nn.5 & 8, 471–2 & nn.5 & 8; views on glacial period, 195 & 196 nn.6–8, 471–2 & nn.6–8; views on modification and descent of species, 142 n.7
Leersia oryzoides: CD sends specimens to J.D. Hooker, 413 & n.1
Leguminosae: feeding of seeds to fowl, 415 & 416 n.7, 417 & 418 n.3, 420; few species in humid temperate regions, 443; plant with coloured seeds, 334 & 336 n.11, 413 & n.3, 415 & 416 n.6, 439 & 440 nn.6 & 7; rarity of hybrids, 292 & 293 n.3; scarce in islets, 443 & 444 n.5. *See also individual species*
Leicester: St John's Church, M.W. Moggridge, curate, 63 n.3
Leipzig University: J.V. Carus, professor of comparative anatomy, 169 n.16, 471 n.16
Leisure Hour: G. Henslow sends copies to CD, 117 & 118 n.2; G. Henslow's articles in, 117 & 118 n.2
Leith Hill Place, Surrey: home of C. and J. Wedgwood III, 192 n.2, 482 & n.16
Leonhard, Gustav von: *Neues Jahrbuch für Mineralogie, Geologie und Palaeontologie*, co-editor, 166 & 168 n.6, 469 & 470 n.6; opposition to CD's theories, 125 & 126 n.4, 467 & 468 n.4; proposed translator of *Origin*, 186 & 187 n.15, 363 & n.4, 469 & 470 n.6 & 471 nn.7 & 8, 473 & 474 n.4; translator of R.I. Murchison and A. Sedgwick's works, 469 & 471 n.7
Lepidoptera: few species in humid temperate regions, 443
Leschenaultia: pollination mechanisms, 121–2 & 123 nn.4 & 5

Leydig, Franz von: exchanges photographs with CD, 27 & 28 n.4, 458 & 459 n.4; E. Haeckel attends lectures, 27 & 28 n.6, 458 & 459 n.6
Lilford, Baron. *See* Powys, Thomas Littleton, 4th Baron Lilford
Limnobium, 94 & 95 n.10, 464 & 466 n.10
Limonium (*Statice*), 408, 478
Lindley, John: classification of plants, 269 n.21, 371 n.15 & 372 n.16
Linnaeus (Carl von Linné), 388 & 390 n.4
Linnean Society of London: J.J. Bennett, librarian, 224 n.3; G. Bentham, anniversary address (1862), 320 & 321 n.3; G. Bentham, president, 224 n.3, 321 n.5, 327 n.4; G. Busk, secretary, 321 & n.7; CD a fellow, 224 n.3; CD's paper on action of sea-water on germination of seeds, 273 n.11; CD's papers, 152 & 153 n.18; F. Currey, secretary, 234, 321 & n.7; G. Henslow, paper on pollination mechanisms in *Indigofera*, xviii, 139 & 140 n.3; J.D. Hooker, paper on temperate floras of Africa, 86 n.8; R. Kippist, librarian, 108–9 & nn.1–11, 224 & n.3, 321 & n.6, 327 & n.4; list of members, 108 & 109 nn.1 & 2; J. Lubbock, paper on *Pauropus*, 421 & n.8; F. Müller's paper on climbing plants, 56 & 57 n.7, 462 & 463 n.7; presentation copy of *Origin*, 485; regulations for borrowing from library, 224 & nn.2–4, 321 & nn.5–7, 327 & n.4, 331 & n.1; W. Robinson elected a member, 154 & n.3. *See also* *Transactions of the Linnean Society of London*
Linum: pollen of equal size in different flower forms, 213 & 214 n.6
Lipostoma: dimorphism, 408 & 409 nn.12 & 13, 478 & 480 nn.12 & 13
Lipsius, Justus: Atlantis hypothesis, 255 n.11
Liriope (medusa): alternation of generations, 324 & 326 n.16
Littorella lacustris, 261
Liverpool, Royal Infirmary Medical School: C. Collingwood lecturer in botany, 59 n.4
Llewelyn, John Dillwyn, 274 & 275 n.7
Lobelia fulgens: occasional self-sterility, 176 & 177 n.7
London & North West Railway: CD sells shares, 209 & 210 n.8
London Journal of Botany: description of *Begonia phyllomaniaca*, 116 & 117 n.2; G. Gardner's papers on Brazilian flora, 35 & 37 n.10; W.J. Hooker, editor, 35 & 37 n.10, 117 n.2
London Review of Politics, Society, Literature, Art, and Science: R. Owen's book on vertebrate anatomy, review, 241 n.5; R. Owen's claim to have originated natural selection theory, 192 & 193 n.11
Longmans, Green and Co.: R. Owen's book on vertebrate anatomy, publishers, 53 n.4
Longmans, Green, Reader, and Dyer: *Annals and Magazine of Natural History*, publishers, 54 n.5
Lopezia coronata, 140 & 141 n.2
Loudon, John Claudius: description of *Erica massoni*, 322 & 323 n.5
lousewort. *See Pedicularis sylvatica*
Lovegrove, Charles: subscription to Down Coal and Clothing Club, 431 & 432 nn.2–4
Lovegrove, Henrietta: subscription to Down Coal and Clothing Club, 431 & 432 nn.2–4
Lovelace, Earl. *See* King-Noel, William
Lowe, Richard Thomas: flora of Atlantic islands, 276 & 277 n.5; hypothesis of continental extension, 285 & 286 n.6; snails of Madeira and Porto Santo, 258 n.3; stay in Cape Verde Islands, 172 & 173 nn.12–14, 179 n.5, 276
Lubbock, Ellen Frances, 307 n.10; arranges for H. Spencer to meet CD, 331–2 & n.2, 337 & 338 n.10; asks for copy of *Origin* for P. Norman, 256 & 257 n.3; donation to Down Coal and Clothing Club, 110 & n.4; family 'such lovely children', 337 & 338 n.11; J.D. Hooker's lecture at British Association for the Advancement of Science, 308 & 309 n.5
Lubbock, Harriet: donations to Down Coal and Clothing Club, 110 & nn.3–5
Lubbock, John: archaeological interests and specimens, 264 n.3, 277 & n.2, 307 & n.10, 332 & n.3; borrows F. Müller's paper on prawns from CD, 224 & 225 nn.2 & 3; CD asks for loan of T. Hincks's paper on Bryozoa, 390–1 & n.1; donation to Down Coal and Clothing Club, 110 & n.4; J.D. Hooker's lecture at British Association for the Advancement of Science, 308 & 309 n.5; lecture on metamorphoses of insects, 224 & 225 n.3; observations of diving Hymenoptera, 191 n.9; paper on embryogeny in *Coccus*, 287 & 299 n.7, 442 & 443 n.8; paper on *Pauropus*, 421 & n.8; presentation copy of *Origin*, 485 & 486 n.6; reports on CD's improved health, 391 & 392 n.8; returns CD's *Primula* paper, 277 & 278 n.3; visit to Torquay with J.D. Hooker, 149; wishes to meet E. Haeckel, 359 & nn.1 & 2
Ludwig, Camilla: translator of C.W. von Nägeli's *Entstehung und Begriff der naturhistorischen Art*, 203 n.2

Luffa hybrids: sterility in, 202 & n.4
luminous animals, 55–6 & n.3 & 57 n.5, 462 & 463 nn.3 & 5
Lupinus, 223 & 224 n.10, 249 & n.1, 253 & 254 nn.2 & 3, 257 & 258 n.1; CD's crossing experiment, 292–3 & nn.5 & 6
Lychnis diurna, 435 & 436 n.1
Lyall, David: visit by J.D. Hooker, 366 & 367 n.6, 372 & 373 n.1
Lyell, Charles, 85 n.7, 195, 450 n.2, 471; admires amount of work CD can do, 67; *Antiquity of man*, CD's disappointment, 344 n.6; asks to see J.D. Hooker's letter to CD, 81 & 82 nn.4 & 5, 84 & 85 nn.3 & 4, 88 & 89 n.2; attacked by H.A. Dubois, 243–4 & 245 n.7; best to avoid controversy, 138 & 139 n.8; CD sends material on geographical distribution of species, 90–1 & nn.4–6, 97 nn.7 & 8 & 98 nn.9 & 10; correspondence with C.J.F. Bunbury, 35–6 & nn.2–7 & 37 nn.8–15; delightful dinner party, 420 & 421 n.5; dines with J.D. and F.H. Hooker, 72 & 74 n.1; failing eyesight, 354 & 355 n.2; J.D. Hooker and C.J.F. Bunbury dine with, 410 & 411 n.5; humans, distinct from all other species, 411 n.4; humans, origins, 344 & n.4; plant migration in glacial period, 195 & 196 n.5, 471 & 472 n.5; plutonic and metamorphic rocks, characteristics and origin, 347 & n.5; presentation copies of *Origin*, 272 & 274 n.18, 485 & 486 n.7; *Principles of geology*, 1st edition, earth's temperature determined by relative positions of land and sea, 149 & n.7; *Principles of geology*, 10th edition, xvi–xvii, 91 n.5, 149 & nn.6 & 8, 329 & 330 n.10, 347 n.6, 404 & nn.2–4 & 6, 410 & 411 nn.3 & 4, 418 & 419 n.6; *Principles of geology*, 10th edition, asks CD to read proofs, 343–4 & nn.2–6, 346–7 & nn.2–5 & 348 n.7, 359 & n.5; *Principles of geology*, 10th edition, asks J.D. Hooker to read proofs, 354 & 355 nn.3 & 4, 359 & n.5; on progressive development of organic life, 411 n.4; theories of climate, xvi–xvii, 88–9 & n.5, 90–1 & nn.3–5, 92 & 93 n.2, 96–7 & n.6, 98 & 99 nn. 7–10, 347 n.4, 354 & 355 n.4, 359 & n.5, 404 & n.4; views on L. Agassiz's glacial theory, xvi–xvii, 37 nn.8 & 12, 311, 313 & 315 n.5, 325 & 326 n.16; visit to Down House, 310 & 311 & 312 n.4, 482 & n.21; visit to J.D. Hooker, 354 & 355 nn.2–4; visit to Whitby, 297 & n.7
Lyell, Henry, 173 n.18
Lyell, Katharine Murray (née Horner), 172 & 173 n.18
Lyell, Mary Elizabeth, 421 n.5; correspondence with E.C.C. Agassiz, 35 & 36 nn.2 & 7 & 37 n.14; dines with J.D. and F.H. Hooker, 72 & 74 n.1; does not invite G. and E. Busk to social gatherings, 74 n.1; visit to Down House, 311 & 312 n.4, 482 & n.21; visit to J.D. Hooker, 329 & 330 n.9
Lythrum: pollen-grain sizes in heterostyled flowers, 213 & 214 n.5

Macaronesia, 261 & 263 n.18
Macfarlane, Robert: pigeon behaviour, 136 & 137 n.5
Mackintosh, Robert James, 90 n.5
Madeira: birds blown to, 272 & 273 n.14, 285 & 286 n.10; birds of, 276 & 277 n.3, 281 & n.3, 285 & 286 n.10, 287 & 288 n.8, 288 & 289 n.4; Coleoptera, 282; Coleoptera, T.V. Wollaston's catalogues, 253 & 255 nn.12–14 & 256 n.17, 259 n.15; flora, 253 & 254 & 255 nn.6–8 & 256 n.16, 257 & 258 nn.3 & 5 & 259 nn.6–8 & 10, 261 & 263 nn.14, 15 & 17, 271 & 273 n.6, 276 & 277 n.5, 289 & 290 n.8; E. Haeckel's visit to, 353 & 354 n.2, 415 & 416 n.10, 473 & n.2; insects and land-shells distinct from those of Porto Santo, 257 & 258 n.4, 271–2 & 273 n.9, 282 & n.7 & 283 n.9; sea-currents, 271 & 273 n.8
Magellan Straits: expedition to survey, 39 n.4, 171 & 173 n.4, 216 & 217 nn.6 & 7 & 218 nn.11–13, 226 & 227 n.2, 232 & nn.2–6 & 233 nn.6–10
Maguire, Thomas Herbert: portrait of CD, 124 & n.2
maize: variable development of flowers, 51 n.2
Malay Archipelago: butterflies. *See under* Wallace, Alfred Russel; search for fossils and bones in caves, 64 & n.2
mallard. *See Anas boschas*
Malpighiaceae: development of sterile and fertile anthers, 368–9 & 371 n.4
Malthus, Thomas Robert, 410 & 412 n.16; general misunderstanding of views, 236 & 237 n.7
Mamastugadagenges, 446 n.4
Mamiani della Rovere, Terenzio: *Confessioni di un metafisico*, 134 n.6
mammals: Brazilian fossils, 75 & 76 n.5; geographical distribution, review of A. Murray's paper, 322 & 323 n.8, 329 & n.3, 337 & 338 n.4; L. Rütimeyer's book on descent

mammals, cont.
and transmutation, 460 & 461 n.11; G.R. Waterhouse's book on, 356 & 357 n.3
mammoth: causes of extinction, 347 & n.3
Manchester: home of L.E. Becker, 435 & 436 n.3
Manchester Ladies' Literary Society: L.E. Becker, president, 436 & n.4; CD's paper read at inaugural meeting, 436 & n.4, 447 & n.2
Manners, John James Robert, 354 & 355 n.5
Maraldi, Giacomo Filippo: measurements of honey-bee cells, 13 & 15 n.1
Marsh-Caldwell, Anne: diet, details requested on behalf of R. Corbet, 397–8, 405 & nn.3–5; grief at S.E. Darwin's death, 398 & n.8
Marsh-Caldwell, Rosamond Jane: asks for CD's advice on diet on behalf of R. Corbet, 397–8 & nn.3 & 4
Martha fragrans. *See Posoqueria fragrans*
Martius, Karl Friedrich Philipp von: *Flora Brasiliensis*, description of *Begonia phyllomaniaca*, 116 & 117 n.3; *Flora Brasiliensis*, article on Nymphaeaceae, 80 n.11
Masters, Maxwell Tylden: R. Caspary's paper on movements of tree branches as result of cold, 141 & 142 n.3, 145 & 146 n.8; *Gardeners' Chronicle*, editor, 141 & 142 n.2; International Horticultural Exhibition and Botanical Congress (London, 1866), honorary secretary, 86–7 & nn.1–4, 177 n.3, 250 & 251 n.2; Umbelliferae, controversy with H. Spencer, 427 & 428 n.6
Maw, George: bud variations in *Fagus*, 208–9 & nn.1–3, 212–13 & n.1
Maxillaria: numbers of seeds produced by, 334–5 & 336 n.12, 416 & n.12
Maxwell, James Clerk: supports F.W. Farrar's candidature for Royal Society, 41 & n.3
Mayne, Richard: commissioner of London police, 171 & 172 n.9
Mayne, Richard Charles, 39 n.4; HMS *Nassau*, commander, 171 & 173 n.9, 216 & 217 n.6, 222 & 223 n.2, 232 & n.4, 237 & 238 n.4
Medicago: mechanisms of insect pollination, 132 & nn.2 & 3, 179 & 180 n.15
Medicago lupulina: pollination by insects, 140 & 141 n.5
Medicago sativa: pollination mechanisms, 132 n.4, 141 n.5
Medical Times and Gazette: CD subscribes to, 53 & 54 n.7
medusae: alternation of generations, 324 & 326 n.16; E. Haeckel's work on, 20 & n.7, 415 & 416 n.10
Melville Island: Carboniferous plants collected on, 149 & n.6
Menispermum, 56 & 57 n.8, 462 & 463 n.8
Mentha hirsuta: dimorphism, 235 & n.4
Mentone: orchids growing at, 61–2 & 63 nn.3–9
Menyanthes: pollen-grain sizes in heterostyled flowers, 213 & 214 n.5
Mesopithecus: fossil found in Greece, 318 & n.4
Metopius: 'bullae' on wings, 101
Mexico: C.G. Ehrenberg's paper on tuffs of, 250 & n.2
Meyer, Jügen Bona: review of *Origin*, 111 & 112 n.5
microscopy: H. Coddington's instrument, 295 & 296 n.2, 304 & 305 n.9; C.G. Ehrenberg's paper on sample-preservation technique, 250 & n.2; M. Somerville's book, 355 & n.2, 365 & nn.1 & 2. *See also Quarterly Journal of Microscopical Science*
Miers, John: International Horticultural Exhibition and Botanical Congress, member of committee, 86 & 87 n.2
migration of species: alpine plants, 141 & 142 nn.4–6, 178 & 179 n.4; of animals from Africa to America, 255 n.11; Brazilian flora, 68 & 69 nn.8 & 13; carried by icebergs, 263 n.14; J. Crawfurd's paper on cultivated plants, 171 & 173 n.7, 179 & 180 nn.11 & 12, 181 & n.9; of European birds to America, 287 & nn.4 & 5; H. Lecoq's paper on migration of alpine plants, 141–2 & nn.4–6; of petrels of north and south hemispheres, 91 & n.7; of plants crossing Africa, 46 & 48 n.14, 73 & 74 n.5, 88–9 & n.4; of plants during glacial period, 195 & 196 n.5, 471 & 472 n.5; of plants into Azores, 276, 281 & n.5; of plants into Madeira, 257 & 259 nn.6 & 7, 261 & 263 n.20; of temperate plants into tropical regions in glacial period, 173 n.13, 290 n.17, 418 & 419 n.12, 427 & 429 nn.7–9, 439 & 440 n.10. *See also* dispersal of species, occasional transport hypothesis
Mikania scandens: leaf-climber, 324 & 326 n.15
Millais, John Everett: painting of Joan of Arc, 172 & 173 n.20
Miller, William Hallowes: sends information on geometry of bees' cells to CD, 35 n.12
mimicry: H.W. Bates's paper on mimetic butterflies, xvi, 190 & 191 nn.7 & 9; discussion at meeting of Entomological Society of London,

mimicry, cont.
391 & 392 n.3; in Malayan butterflies, A.R. Wallace's views, 39
Mimoseae: plant with brightly coloured seeds, 334 & 336 n.11, 415 & 416 n.8, 417 & nn.2 & 3, 439 & 440 nn.6 & 7
Minas Gerais, mountains, 67 & 69 n.6; former glaciation, 68 & 69 n.9
Miocene fossils: found at Pikermi, 317–18 & nn.2–5
Mirabilis: CD asks J.D. Hooker for specimens, 393 & n.6, 395 & 396 n.3; crossing experiments, 393 & n.6, 395 & 396 n.3; number of pollen-grains needed to fertilise ovule, 393 n.6
Mitchell, Donald: canary preening before mirror, 136 & 137 n.4
Mitchell, William Stephen: report on fossil leaf-bed on Isle of Wight, 445 & 446 nn.12–14, 448 & n.4
Mitchella repens: CD sends specimens to J.D. Hooker, 413 & n.1; pollen-grain sizes in heterostyled flowers, 213 & 214 n.5
Mitten, Annie. *See* Wallace, Annie
Mitten, William, 172 & 174 n.26, 237 n.9
Moggridge, John Traherne: health, 188 & 189 n.3; *Lathyrus* hybrids, 382 & n.5; meeting with H.E. Darwin, xviii, 163 & nn.2 & 3, 235 n.6; observations of *Ophrys*, 61–2 & 63 nn. 2–9, 128 & 129 nn.6 & 7, 163 & 164 n.7, 184–5 & nn.3 & 4; *Ononis columnae*, apetalous flowers, 274 & 275 nn.3–5; *Ononis columnae*, sends seeds to CD, 234–5 & nn.2–5 & 7, 274 & 275 n.2, 382 n.2; *Ononis minutissima*, sends seeds to CD, 381 & 382 n.3; sends orchids to CD, 165 & n.2, 184 & 185 nn.2 & 3; visit to Down House, xviii, 163 & n.4, 185 n.8, 188 & 189 nn.2 & 3, 206 & n.2, 235 n.6, 482 & n.17; wishes to meet CD, 185 & n.8
Moggridge, Matthew, 63 n.2
Moggridge, Matthew Weston, 63 n.2
Möller, Alfred, 56 n.1, 95 n.1, 409 n.11, 463 n.1, 465 n.1, 480 n.11
molluscs: fossils found in Scottish glacial beds, 328 n.4; W.E. Leach's book on, 127 & n.2. *See also* *Vermetus*
Monera: E. Haeckel introduces new term, 9 n.7, 457 n.7
monkeys: fossil, found in Greece, 318 & n.4
Montagu, George: male birds' attraction of females by song, 42–3 & 44 n.6
Monterey cypress. *See* *Cupressus macrocarpa*
Moore, Daniel: response to Darwinian theory, 342 & 343 n.3
Morning Star: report of pig's sloughing of skin, 386–7 & nn.2–4
mosses: H. Müller's studies, 266 & 268 n.18
The Mount, Shrewsbury, 5 n.3, 340 & n.3; furniture, 65 & n.3; sale, xxiv, 395 & 396 nn.5–7, 421 n.7, 429 n.13
mountain floras, 258 & 259 n.12, 260–1 & 263 n.13. *See also* alpine floras
Mucor, 428 & 429 n.16
Müller, Albert: call for more studies of animal behaviour, 109 & 110 n.2; questions CD on ant behaviour, 106–7 & nn.2 & 3, 107 & nn.3 & 4
Müller, August, 56 & 57 n.6, 462 & 463 n.6
Müller, Fritz: beetle without feet, 370, 475; CD's gift of books, xxiii, 10 & 11 nn.2–4, 55 & 56 nn.2 & 3, 462 & 463 nn.2 & 3; changes in Brazilian flora and fauna with climate, 93–4 & 95 nn.3–5, 7, 8, 10–13 & 15, 464–5 & nn.3–5, 7 & 8 & 466 nn.10–13 & 15; *Convolvulus*, whether dimorphic, 369 & 371 n.11, 474 & 476 n.4; *Cordia*, dimorphism, 334 & 336 n.9, 368 & 371 n.5; description of rubiaceous plant, 121 & 123 n.3, 129–30 & 131 nn.7 & 8; dimorphic plants, collection, 439 & 440 n.12, 452 & 453 nn.3 & 4; dimorphic plants, illegitimate offspring, 437 & n.6; dimorphic and trimorphic plants, xxiii; emigration from Germany to Brazil, 57 n.6, 463 n.6; *Erythroxylum*, variability of flowers, 369 & 371 n.12, 474–5 & 476 n.5; exchange of photographs with CD, 10 & 11 n.5, 19 & 20 n.3; *Für Darwin*, 192 & 193 n.6, 299 & 300 n.12; T. Hanbury seeks information from, 403–4 & nn.1–3; *Hedyotis*, dimorphism, 368 & 369 & 371 n.8; *Hillia*, variable flowers, 370 & 371 n.13, 408 & 409 nn.14 & 15, 474–5 & 476 n.6, 478–9 & 480 nn.14 & 15; lancelet, 408 & 409 nn.16–18, 479 & nn.16–18; land uplift at Santa Catarina island, 11 & 12 n.12; letters to CD, preparation for publication, 56 n.1, 462 n.1; *Notylia*, sends drawing and specimen to CD, 265 & 266 & 268 n.6; orchids, xxiii, 57 & n.10, 186 & 188 n.18, 265 & 266 & 268 nn.3 & 5–8, 299 & 300 nn.3–5, 324 & 325 nn.6 & 7, 416 & n.12, 463 & n.10; orchids, delayed fertilisation, 405–6 & 409 n.4, 476–7 & 479 nn.3 & 4; orchids, numbers of seeds produced, 334–5 & 336 n.12, 416 & n.12; orchids, self-sterility, 406–7 & 409 n.8, 477–9 & 480 n.8; organs of different structure acquiring similar functions, 402 n.2; *Origin*, 4th edition, presentation copies, xxiii, 93 & 95 n.2, 122 & 124 n.16, 299 & 300 n.9, 370 & 371 n.14, 416

Müller, Fritz, cont.
n.14, 464 & 465 n.2, 475 & 476 n.7, 485 & n.2; *Oxalis*, whether heteromorphic, xxiii, 186 & 187 n.12, 265 & 268 n.2, 332–4 & 335 nn.2 & 3 & 336 nn.4–8, 368 & 369 & 371 n.6; paper on climbing plants, 56 & 57 n.7, 122 & 124 nn.13–15, 234 & nn.1–3, 265 & 268 n.11, 299 & 300 n.8, 403 & 404 n.1, 411 & 412 n.20, 414 & n.2, 416 & 417 n.15, 452 & 453 n.15, 462 & 463 n.7; paper on *Martha fragrans*, 415 & 416 n.9; paper on prawns, 186 & 188 n.17, 224 & 225 nn.2 & 3; paper on taxonomy of sea-pens, 186 & 187 nn.9 & 11; plants with brightly coloured seeds, 266 & 267 & 268 nn.13–15, 324 & 326 n.14, 334 & 336 nn.10 & 11, 407 & 409 n.9, 413 & nn.3 & 4, 418 n.2, 421 n.6, 439 & 440 nn.6 & 7, 452 & 453 n.14, 478 & 480 n.9; plants dimorphic in function but not in structure, 265–6 & 268 n.9, 406 & 409 n.5, 477 & 479 n.5; retirement home in Brazil, 10 & 12 n.9, 403 & 404 nn.1 & 3; support for CD's theories, 134 n.4; *Vanilla*-like flower, 185 & 186 n.2, 299 & 300 n.7

Müller, Hermann, 186 n.2, 268 n.2; studies of mosses, 266 & 268 n.18

Müller, Johannes Peter: study of lancelet, 408 & 409 n.18, 479 & 480 n.18

Munro, Robertson: self-sterility in *Passiflora*, 176 & 178 n.8

Munro, William, 289 & 290 n.11

Murchison, Roderick Impey, 422 & 423 n.4, 432 & 433 n.2, 449; and expedition to Patagonia, 225 & 226 n.6, 232 & 233 n.7; Geological Survey of the United Kingdom, director-general, 450 n.5; *Geology of Russia*, G. von Leonhard, translator, 469 & 471 n.7

Murray, Andrew: hypothesis of continental extension, 285 & 286 n.6; paper on geographical distribution of mammals, review, 322 & 323 n.8, 329 & n.3, 337 & 338 n.4

Murray, John, publisher: *Orchids*, owner of woodcuts, 355 & n.3; *Origin*, 11 n.3, 298 & n.2; *Origin*, fourth edition planned, xxiii, 75 & nn.2 & 3, 75–6 & n.7, 78 & 79 nn.2–4, 189 & n.2, 191 & 192 nn.2 & 3, 248–9 & nn.2–6, 251 & nn.2 & 3, 257 n.3, 272 & 274 n.17, 275 & 276 n.4, 377 & n.3; *Origin*, presentation copies, 370 & 371 n.14, 438 & n.2, 442 & nn.1 & 2, 475 & 476 n.7; *Origin*, refuses request for pre-publication presentation copy, 256 & 257 n.3; regrets missing CD at Royal Society soirée, 189 & n.3; *Variation*, 314, 350 & 351 nn.1 & 2, 351 & 352 nn.2–5, 352 & 353 nn.2–5; *Variation*, CD submits ms., 434 & n.1 & 435 nn.3–6, 438–9 & n.2, 440 & n.2, 451 & n.11; *Variation*, illustrations, 78 & 79 nn.5 & 6, 278 & 279 n.7, 352 & 353 n.3; welcomes news of CD's improved health, 189, 190

Mutilla: sting, 87 & 88 n.3

Mutisia, 324 & 326 n.15

Myrica faya, 253

Myrsine, 254 & 256 n.18

Nägeli, Carl Wilhelm von, xix, 112 n.5, 364 & 365 nn.3 & 9; criticisms of CD's theories, 203 & 204 nn.7 & 8; *Entstehung und Begriff der naturhistorischen Art*, 203 & n.2 & 204 nn.4, 7, 8 & 10, 383 n.4, 389 & 390 nn.10 & 11, 394 & nn.5 & 6 & 395 nn.7 & 8; natural selection one means of species development, 203 & 204 n.8; support for CD's theories, 186 & 187 n.16, 266 & 268 n.17

Nandinia: taxonomic diffculties in classification, 83 & 84 n.6

Nasmyth, James, 286 n.4

HMS *Nassau*: expedition to Straits of Magellan, 39 n.4, 171 & 173 n.4, 216 & 217 nn.6 & 7 & 218 nn.11–13, 226 & 227 n.2, 232 & nn.2–6 & 233 nn.6–10; R.C. Mayne, commander, 171 & 173 n.9, 216 & 217 nn.6 & 7, 222 & 223 n.2, 232 & n.4; survey of Patagonian anchorages, 217 & 218 nn.12 & 13

National Academy of Sciences (Washington): L. Agassiz's paper on traces of glaciers in the tropics, 302 & 303 n.3, 323 n.7; election of S.F. Baird, 378 n.6

Natural History Review: article on new colonial floras, 60 & n.7; CD regrets cessation of publication, 53 & 54 n.8; S.J.A. Salter's paper on hybrid fowl, 280 n.9

natural selection: in alpine plants, described by C.W. von Nägeli, 389 & 390 n.11; and aristocracy, 181 & 182 n.11; beauty in relation to, 203 & 204 n.4, 397 n.2, 418 n.2; better described as 'survival of the fittest', xxii, 227–9 & nn.1 & 2 & 230 nn.3–12, 235 & 236 n.3; CD's use of term, xxii, 228 & 230 nn.7 & 8, 236; and dimorphic *Oxalis*, 368–9 & 371 n.3; eye development by, 44 n.8, 342 & n.2, 348 & 349 nn.3 & 4; German translation of term, 29 & 30 nn.5 & 6, 460 & 461 nn.5 & 6; in humans, W.C. Wells's view, 283 & 284 n.4, 391 & 392 n.2; T.H. Huxley's criterion for acceptance of theory, 437 n.6; ignored by reviewer, 399 & 400 n.3; misunderstood by L. Agassiz and H.J. Clark, 283 & 284 nn.12;

natural selection, cont.
one means of species development, 204 n.7; R. Owen claims to be originator of theory, xvi, 192 & 193 n.12; J. Samuelson's criticisms of theory, 119 & 120 nn.2–5; speed in predatory animals, 114–15 & nn.4 & 5; H. Spencer sees as 'mediate' force, 224 n.9; H. Spencer's use of term, 235 & 236 n.4; term cannot be abandoned, 236 & 237 n.6; theory necessary to both hypotheses of origin of species, 260 & 263 n.11; whether known to the ancients, 386 & 387 n.3; whether theory compatible with religious faith, xxiv–xxv, 423–4 & n.1 & 425 n.2, 425–6 & n.2, 432 & n.1

Nature: CD's paper on pollination in Fumariaceae, 177 n.4

Naudin, Charles Victor: crossing of thorn apple, 345 n.7; researches on hybrids, M.J. Berkeley, translator, 205 & 206 n.5; researches on hybrids, G. Henslow's article, 96 & n.5, 100 & n.1, 183 & nn.1–3, 201–2 & nn.1–4, 202 & nn.2–4, 204–5 & nn.2 & 4 & 206 nn.5 & 7; reversion in hybrids, 206 & 207 nn.3 & 10

nectarines: T. Rivers, paper on seedlings, 183 & 184 n.6

Negundo fraxinifolia. *See Acer negundo* 'Variegatum'

Neotinea intacta: J.T. Moggridge sends specimens to CD, 165 & 166 n.6; self-fertilisation in, 163 & n.5 & 164 n.6

Nepenthes (pitcher plants), 296 & n.6, 373 n.7

Nesodon, 227 n.6, 233 n.10

Neues Jahrbuch für Mineralogie, Geologie und Palaeontologie: H.G. Bronn, co-editor, 105 & 106 n.4, 166 & 167 & nn.6 & 7; H.B. Geinitz, co-editor, 105–6 & n.7, 167–8 & nn.3 & 6, 466 & 467 n.7, 470 & nn.3 & 6; H.R. Göppert, paper on CD's theory of common descent, 29 & 30 n.12, 125 & 126 n.5, 460 & 461 n.12, 467 & 468 n.5; G. von Leonhard, co-editor, 166 & 168 nn.3 & 6, 470 & nn.3 & 6; opposition to CD's theories, 125 & 126 nn.4 & 5, 467 & 468 nn.4 & 5

New South Wales: Wedgwood medallion commemorating colonisation, 395 & 396 n.6

New Zealand: W.T. Doyne's paper on formation of Canterbury plains, 410 & 412 n.14, 418 & 419 n.8; flora, *Eucalyptus* absent from, 262 n.4; flora, J.D. Hooker's *Flora Novæ-Zelandiæ*, 410 & 411 n.9, 418 & 419 n.9, 444 n.2; flora, indigenous plants, 133 & n.3, 143 & 144 n.2; flora, papilionaceous plants absent, 444 n.5; flora, rarity of indigenous annual plants, 410 & 411 n.10, 418 & 419 n.10, 443 & 444 n.2; flora, whether really tropical, 68 & 69 n.10; glaciers descending to the sea, 47 & 49 n.25; gold rush, 242, 310 & nn.5 & 6; J. von Haast's explorations, 242 & n.4 & 243 n.10, 310 & nn.4 & 5; J. von Haast's lecture on west coast of Canterbury, 410 & 412 n.13, 418 & 419 n.8; J. von Haast's paper on glacial deposits, 242 & n.6; stones voided by *Dinornis*, 422 & 423 n.9; whale bones found in, 410 & 411 n.12

Newton, Alfred: administration and locality of natural history collections, 175 & n.1 & 176 nn.2 & 3; Cambridge University, professor of zoology and comparative anatomy, 351 n.3, 399 & n.4; correspondence and article on white dodo, 351 n.3; presentation copy of *Origin*, 398–9 & n.1, 485; sends bird's foot carrying seeds to CD, 401 n.1

Niger: wrecked in Canary Islands, 273 n.8

Nipa: specimens sent from Calcutta to Kew, 82

Noctiluca, 55, 462

Norman, George Warde: hopes to visit Down House, 319 & n.4; presentation copy of *Origin*, 257 n.3; sends CD description of cat adopting squirrel, 319 & nn.2 & 3

Norman, Herbert George Henry: sends bird's foot carrying seeds to CD, 401 nn.1 & 2, 401 & 402 n.2, 417–18 & 419 n.4

Norman, Philip: presentation copy of *Origin*, 256 & 257 n.3

Norton Canon, Herefordshire: C.J. Robinson, vicar, 3 & n.7

Norway: G.H. and F. Darwin's visit, 301 & n.2

Norwich: J.D. Hooker's visit to, 448; new home of M. Hooker, 410 & 411 n.2

Notes and Queries: article on death of E. Darwin, 366 & 367 n.2

Nottingham Daily Express: report of J.D. Hooker's lecture on insular floras, 305 n.5

Nottingham Journal: report of J.D. Hooker's lecture on insular floras, 305 n.5

Notylia, 265 & 266 & 268 n.6 & 269 nn.19 & 23, 324 & 325 nn.3 & 6

Numida ptilorhyncha (*N. meleagris*), 431 & n.4

Nymphaeaceae: R. Caspary's paper, 80 n.11; crossing experiments, 151, 154 & n.2

oceanic islands: absence of plutonic and metamorphic rocks, 347 & n.5; floras, 273 n.12; numbers of species dependent on mode of colonisation, 289 & 290 n.15. *See also* island organisms

Octomeria sp., 265 & 267 & 268 n.10 & 269 n.21

Oliver, Daniel: CD asks for information on appearance and structure of buds, 148, 149 & n.3; death of daughter, xxiv, 116 & 117 n.7, 121 & n.2, 148 n.4, 174 & n.6; identifies *Anchusa italica* for CD, 198 & n.1; move to Kew, 117 n.7; sends CD details of *Botanische Zeitung* papers, 174 & nn.2–4
Oliver, Francis Wall, 116 & 117 n.8
Oliver, Hannah, 116 & 117 n.8; ill after birth of daughter, 171 & 173 n.11, 174 & n.5
Oncidium divaricatum: self-sterility in, 176 & 178 n.8; whether endemic species, 452 & 453 n.10
Oncidium flexuosum: self-sterility, 406–7 & 409 n.8, 477–8 & 480 n.8
Ononis columnae: apetalous flowers, 274 & 275 nn.3–5; J.T. Moggridge sends seeds to CD, 234–5 & nn.2–5 & 7, 274 & 275 n.2, 382 n.2
Ononis minutissima: J.T. Moggridge sends seeds to CD, 381 & 382 n.3
Ophelia, 408 & 409 n.17, 479 & 480 n.17
Ophius: ovipositor left in wound, 88 & n.5
Ophrys: believed absent from Madeira, 258 n.3; method for marking plants, 62; J.T. Moggridge sends plants to CD, 61 & 63 n.2, 165 & n.2; J.T. Moggridge's observations, 163 & 164 n.7, 184–5 & nn.3 & 4; pollinating insects, 62 & 64 n.10; variability of flowers, 61–2 & 63 nn.3, 5 & 7–9; whether specimen is self-fertile, 128 & n.2
Ophrys apifera (bee ophrys), 63 nn.5 & 7, 128 & 129 n.3; J.T. Moggridge sends specimen to CD, 165 & 166 n.4; possible hybrid, 185 & n.4; self-pollination, xviii, 122 & 123 n.11, 128 & n.2, 164 n.6; whether flower acts as decoy for pollinators, 44 n.7
Ophrys arachnites (late spider ophrys), 63 nn.3, 5 & 9, 129 n.3
Ophrys aranifera (spider ophrys), 61 & 63 nn. 3, 5–7 & 9, 128 & 129 n.6
Ophrys bertolonii: J.T. Moggridge sends specimen to CD, 165
Ophrys fusca, 128 & n.2 & 129 n.7, 163 & n.3
Ophrys insectifera, 63 n.5; whether indeed a single species, 128 & 129 n.6
Ophrys lutea, 128 & n.2 & 129 n.7, 163 & n.2
Ophrys scolopax, 63 n.5, 128 & 129 n.6, 184–5 & n.3; possible hybrid, 185 & n.4; two forms observed by J.T. Moggridge, 165 & n.3
orange: graft hybrid (bizzarria orange), 79 & 80 n.9
Orange Judd & Co.: publishers, 276 n.5, 284 n.8
Orchestia: two forms of, 94 & 95 n.13, 186 & 187 n.8, 299 & 300 n.12, 464 & 466 n.13
Orchestia darwinii, 94 & 95 n.13, 464 & 466 n.13
Orchestia tucurauna, 94 & 95 n.2, 464 & 466 n.13
orchids: delayed fertilisation in, 405–6 & 409 nn.3 & 4, 452 & 453 n.11, 476–7 & 479 n.3 & 4; described by F. Müller, 57 & n.10, 185–6 & n.2 & 188 n.18, 265 & 268 n.3 & 5–8 & 269 n.19, 299 & 300 nn.3–5, 452 & 453 n.10, 463 & n.10; few species in humid temperate regions, 443; A. Gray sends specimen to CD, 283 & 284 n.3; greenhouse temperatures for tropical, 60 & 61 n.8, 73 & 74 n.11; F. Hildebrand's paper on hybridisation, 174 & n.4; J.T. Moggridge sends specimens to CD, 165 & n.2, 388 & n.5; numbers of fertile stamens, 265 & 268 nn.3 & 5; numbers of seeds produced, 334–5 & 336 n.12; parasitic orchids unknown, 149; scarce in islets, 443 & 444 n.5; J. Scott sends Indian specimens to J.D. Hooker, 81–2 & 83 nn.10–13; self-fertilisation in, xviii, 122 & 123 nn.10 & 11, 163 & n.4 & 164 n.5, 265 & 268 n.7, 299 & 300 n.5; spiral vessels, 186 & 187 n.3. *See also individual orchid species*
Orchids, 111 & 112 n.7, 152 & 153 n.16, 190 & 191 n.4; *Acropera*, 325 n.3; *Coryanthes*, 118 n.3; functional origins of beauty, 44 n.3; illustrations, permission for M. Somerville's use in new book, 355 & n.2, 365 & nn.1 & 2; intercrossing between hermaphrodites, 80 n.3; nature of labellum, 300 n.7; *Notylia*, pedical of pollinium, 269 n.23; pedicel movement in Vandeae, 300 n.6; perpetual self-fertilisation unknown, 177 & 178 n.13; sales, 77 & 78 n.9, 78 & 79 n.7; self-pollination, 122 & 123 n.11; G.B. Sowerby Jr, illustrator, 78 n.14
Orchids: 2d edition: C.H. Battersby's supply of specimens acknowledged, 129 n.5; *Cirrhaea*, pollination, 325 n.4; *Coryanthes*, 118 n.3; H. Crüger cited, 187 n.3; *Cypripedium candidum*, dimerous flower, 283 & n.3; F. Hildebrand cited, 325 n.6; information provided by F. Müller, 57 n.10, 300 nn.3 & 5, 463 n.10; mechanisms of cross-pollination, 123 n.11; nature of labellum, 300 n.7; *Ophrys scolopax*, 165 n.3; order of flowering of *Ophrys* spp., 63 n.7; pollination of *Acropera*, 305 n.11; seeds produced by *Maxillaria*, 416 n.12; self-pollination, 164 n.6; *Serapias cordigera*, 166 n.5; *Stanhopea*, 325 n.4
Orchids: German edition, 105 & 106 n.2, 466 & 467 n.2
Orchis coriophora: J.T. Moggridge sends specimen to CD, 184

Orchis papilionacea: J.T. Moggridge sends specimen to CD, 165

Orchis secundiflora. *See Neotinea intacta*

Organ Mountains. *See* Serra dos Organos

Origin, 58, 111 & 112 n.9, 152 & 153 n.14; action of natural selection, 115 n.5; animals' fear of humans, 423 n.4; apterous beetles of Madeira, 259 nn.13 & 15; artificial and natural selection contrasted, 228 & 230 n.6; birds blown to Bermuda and Madeira, 272 & 273 n.14; A. de Candolle cited, 262 n.5; cited by W.R. Grove, 191 n.9; correlation of growth, 113 & 114 n.12; deep-sea conditions in Malay Archipelago, 64 n.3; denudation of Wealden district, 349 n.8; development of eye by natural selection, 44 n.8; development of organs by transitional gradations, 177 & 178 n.12; divergence of character, 190 n.5, 295 nn.3 & 4; domestic animals, 65 n.6; effects of use or disuse on body parts, 169 n.4; erratic boulders in Azores, 288 & 289 n.4; *Fucus*, reciprocal crosses, 403 n.6; G. Gardner cited, 60 n.5; geographical distribution of species, 37 n.8, 46 & 48 n.15, 89 & n.4, 98 n.9; geometry of bee and wasp cells, 34 nn.2, 5, 9 & 12; glaciation in Himalayas and south-east Australia, 48 n.20; hybrid sterility and origin of new species, 45 n.3; intercrossing between hermaphrodites, 80 n.3; island organisms, 133 & n.3, 258 nn.2 & 5, 260 & 262 n.4, 263 n.17, 272 & 273 nn.12 & 15, 288 & 290 nn.5 & 15, 418 & 419 n.11; Leguminosae, fertility dependent on presence of bees, 444 n.5; migration of temperate species in glacial period, 173 n.13, 259 n.6, 290 n.17, 429 n.9; misquoted by S.H. Scudder, 138 n.7; modification of temperate plants during glacial epoch, 47 & 49 n.23; New Zealand flora, 418 & 419 n.11; occasional transport of plant species, 259 n.7; perpetual self-fertilisation unknown, 177 & 178 n.13, 252 & n.8; presentation copies, 77 n.8, 257 n.3, 378 & 378 n.2; publication precipitated by A.R. Wallace's writings, 98 & 99 n.6; reversion, 205 & n.3, 207 n.8; role of environment in selection, 43 & 44 n.11; role of variation in natural selection, 229 & 230 nn.11 & 12; J.W. Salter offers to help with, 449 & 450 n.2; sexual selection, 55 n.3; slave-making behaviour of ants, 106–7 & nn.2 & 3, 107 & nn.3 & 4; stings of bees and wasps, 88 n.1; survival of older or primitive forms, 259 n.11, 261; survival of tropical species in world cool period, 61 n.9; transport of seeds on floating ice, 281 & n.6; trees, whether ranges restricted, 260 & 262 n.5; wolves, 44 n.11, 115 n.4

Origin: 2d edition: denudation of Wealden district, 349 n.8; presentation copies, 77 n.8

Origin: 3d edition, xv, 11 nn.3 & 4, 75 & n.2, 190 n.4; effect of breaking of isthmus, 260 & 262 n.3, 282 n.4; erratic boulders in Azores, 287 & 288 n.6; geographical distribution of species, 272 & 274 n.16; geometry of bees' cells, 35 n.12; glaciation in Cordillera, 46 & 48 nn.10 & 11; historical sketch, 383 & 384 n.7; land birds on islands, 280–1 & n.3, 286 n.10, 287 & 288 n.8; Madeira flora a remnant of tertiary European flora, 271 & 273 n.6; natural selection, 120 n.2; presentation copies, 77 n.8; transport of seeds on floating ice, 281 & n.6; world climate during glacial period, 46 & 47 n.11

Origin: 4th edition, xv–xvi, 11 n.6, 75 & n.4, 75–6 & n.7, 85 & 86 n.15, 111 & 112 n.6, 122–3 & 124 n.18, 130 & 131 n.9, 138 & 139 n.10, 142 n.7, 189 & n.2, 189 & 190 nn.2–4, 203 & 204 n.2, 231 n.5, 236 & 237 n.5, 240 & n.2, 297 & n.3; accidental omissions, 192 & 193 nn.10 & 11, 194 & n.3, 196 & nn.3 & 4; acclimatisation of plants, 91 n.5; alpine floras, xvi; *Archaeopteryx*, 193 n.5; beauty, appreciation of, 144 & n.3; beauty, a guide to birds and beasts, 380 n.6; beauty, in relation to natural selection, 203 & 204 n.4, 418 n.3; C.L. Brace cited, 284 n.4; brightly coloured fruit, 324 & 326 n.12; R. Caspary's corrections, 379 & n.7; CD urges sale with pages cut, 240 & 241 n.7, 249 & n.6, 448 n.6; CD's corrections and additions, xv, 76 & 77 & n.4 & 78 n.17, 78 & 79 nn.2 & 3, 97 n.8, 179 & 180 n.13, 186 & 187 n.14, 189 & 190 nn.3 & 4, 191 & 192 n.3, 192 & 193 n.7, 278 & nn.3 & 4 & 279 n.6, 301 & 302 n.9, 379 n.8, 481 & 482 nn.2 & 3, 484; Compositae and Umbelliferae, shapes of ray florets, 394 & 395 n.10; correlated variation, 394 & 395 n.10; crustacean embryology, xvi; delay in publication, xxiii, 240 n.2, 248–9 & nn.2–6, 251 & n.3, 257 n.3, 272 & 274 n.17, 275 & 276 n.4, 380 n.4, 484; descent with modification, xvi; distinction between variations, races, and true species, 24 n.3 & 25 n. 5; diving Hymenoptera, xvi; fertile and sterile forms of plants, 16 n.2; fertilisation of orchids, 118 n.3; flowers, attraction to insects, 54 & 55 n.7; G. Gardner cited, 60 n.5; geographical distribution of species, 89 n.4, 91 n.4, 97 nn.5, 7 & 8; geometry

Origin: 4th edition, cont.
of bees' cells, xvi, 15 n.2; glacial action, 65 n.4, 91 n.4; glacial deposits of New Zealand, 242 n.6; glaciation in Australia, 48 n.20; historical sketch, xvi, 138 & 139 n.13, 142 n.7, 193 n.11, 270 & 271 n.3, 284 nn.4 & 9, 383 & 384 n.7, 385 & n.4, 387 n.3, 392 n.2; J.D. Hooker cited, 179 n.5; hybridism, 437 & n.6; illustrations, 189 & 190 n.5; insect metamorphosis, xvi; island floras, 133 & n.3; lancelet, competition with invertebrates, 408 & 409 nn.16–18, 479 & 480 nn.16–18; land birds on islands, 280–1 & n.3; Lebanese glaciation, 48 n.20; Malayan Lepidoptera, xvi; migration of temperate species in glacial period, 173 n.13, 178–9 & n.5; mimetic butterflies, xvi; F. Müller cited, 122 & 124 n.18; C.W. Nägeli's views discussed, 394 & 395 n.8; Organ Mountains, 76 & n.7; R. Owen's claim to have originated natural selection theory, xvi, 193 n.11; phytophagic insects, xvi; pig that sloughed skin, 386 & 387 n.3; presentation copies, xxiii, 77 & n.8 & 78 n.10, 93 & 95 n.2, 122 & 124 n.16, 138 & 139 n.12, 144 & n.4, 157 & n.5, 190 & n.6, 191 & 192 n.3, 203 & 204 n.5, 236 & 237 n.5, 240 & n.3, 243 & 245 n.2, 248 & 249 n.4, 251 & n.2, 256 & 257 n.3, 272 & 274 n.18, 275 & 276 n.4, 282 & 283 n.10, 299 & 300 n.9, 313 & 315 n.6, 370 & 371 n.14, 379 & 380 n.1, 385 & n.1, 391 & 392 nn.1 & 2, 416 n.14, 430 & 431 n.8, 438 n.2, 442 & nn.1 & 2, 464 & 465 n.2, 475 & 476 n.7, 484–5 & nn.1–4 & 486 nn.5–14; presentation copies, for review, 240 & 241 nn.4 & 5; print run, 189 & n.2, 191 & 192 n.2, 248 & 249 n.5, 362 & n.3, 484; proposed review, 344; proposed sales in US market, 247 & 248 n.5, 275 & 276 n.3, 344, 377 & n.3; stings of bees and wasps, 88 n.1; A.R. Wallace cited, 24 n.3; B.D. Walsh cited, 138 & 139 n.11

Origin: 5th edition: astronomical explanations of climate change, 85 n.7, 99 n.8; CD's corrections and alterations, 228 & 230 nn.7–9 & 12; *Corydalis cava*, pollination, 177 n.5; J. Croll cited, 85 n.7, 99 n.8; effect of breaking of isthmus, 260 & 262 n.3; ice ages alternating between hemispheres, 89 n.4; F. Müller's observations, xxiii; *Ononis columnae*, 235 n.3; R. Owen's claim to have originated natural selection theory, 193 n.11; pollination mechanisms, 178 n.12; seeds carried on woodcock's foot, 401 n.2; use of term 'survival of the fittest', xxii; views of C.W. von Nägeli, 204 n.10, 383 n.5

Origin: 6th edition: causes of glaciation, 99 n.8; migration of eye in flatfish, 240 n.3

Origin: Dutch edition, 152 & 153 n.14

Origin: French editions, 97 n.8, 152 & 153 n.14

Origin: German editions, xix, 10 & 11 nn.3 & 4, 29 & 30 nn.5–7, 97 n.8, 102 & 103 n.2, 105–6 & nn.2, 4, 5 & 7, 110–12 & nn.2–5, 125 & 126 n.2, 130 & 131 n.10, 143 n.3, 152 & 153 n.13, 186 & 187 n.15, 203 & 204 n.3, 362–3 & nn.4–6 & 8, 364 & 365 n.6, 378–9 & nn.1–8, 382–3 & nn.2–6 & 384 n.7, 460 & 461 nn.5–7, 466 & 467 nn.2, 4, 5 & 7, 467 & 468 n.2, 468–9 & 470 nn.2 & 3 & 471 nn.7, 9, 10 & 13, 473–4 & nn.2 & 4–8, 484; H.G. Bronn's epilogue, xix, 378 & 379 nn.4 & 5; CD's photograph used in, 8 & 10 n.14, 456 & 458 n.15; criticisms, 133–4 & nn.4 & 5, 378 & 379 nn.3 & 4, 382 & 383 n.2, 388–9 & 390 nn.2–11, 469 & 471 n.10; presentation copy offered to C.W. von Nägeli, 203 & 204 n.5; worldwide glacial period, 90 & 91 nn.3–5

Origin: Italian edition, 152 & 153 n.14

Origin: opinions of: German scientists, 103 nn.2 & 4, 105 & 106 n.3, 169 n.15, 466 & 467 n.3, 471 n.15; E. Haeckel, xix, 19, 294 & 295 nn.2 & 3; J.B. Meyer, 111 & 112 n.5

Origin: reviews, xxii, 152 & 153 n.15; J. Crawfurd, 173 n.7; A. Gray, 193 n.12, 361 & 362 n.5; J.B. Meyer, 111 & 112 n.5; *Quarterly Journal of Science*, xviii, 118–19 & 120 nn.1 & 3, 124 & n.5, 136–7 & nn.9 & 10, 227 & 229 n.2, 241 n.4

Origin: Russian edition, 152 & 153 n.14

Origin: US editions, xix, 130 & 131 nn.11 & 12, 138 & 139 n.12, 152 & 153 n.14, 156 & 157 nn.2–4, 230 & 231 nn.3–7, 275 & 276 n.2, 283 & 284 nn.6 & 8, 302 & 303 nn.1 & 2, 313 & 315 n.7, 484; historical sketch, 270 & 271 n.3; H. Lecoq cited, 142 n.7; proposed sales of English edition in US, 247 & 248 n.5, 275 & 276 n.3, 283 & 284 n.7, 344 & 345 nn.2 & 3, 351 & 352 n.4, 352 & 353 n.4, 361 & 362 n.4, 484; statement of sales, 247 & 248 nn.1–6, 8 & 9

Ornithorhynchus parodoxus (*O. anatinus*, platypus): whether oviparous, 399–400 & n.6, 442 & n.5

Orr, William S., publishers, 23 n.10

Orundellico. *See* Button, Jemmy

Osten Sacken, Carl Robert Romanovich von der: *Ornithorhynchus parodoxus* (*O. anatinus*), whether oviparous, 399–400 & n.6

Overend, Gurney & Co., 173 n.15

Owen, Richard, 138 & 139 n.13; book on vertebrate anatomy, 53 & n.4; book on vertebrate

Owen, Richard, cont.
anatomy, review, 193 n.11, 241 n.5; British Museum, superintendent of natural history departments, 176 n.2; CD does not wish to communicate with, 232 & 233 n.8; CD's description of work, 283 & 284 n.9; claims to have originated natural selection theory, xvi, 192 & 193 n.11, 385 & n.4; describes fossil bones from Patagonia, 217 n.7, 226 & 227 n.6, 233 nn.8 & 10
Oxalis: bulbils sent to CD by F. Müller, 452 & 453 n.12; dimorphic form, 325 n.2, 368 & 369, 452 & 453 n.6; frutescent species, 334, 369 & 371 n.6; F. Hildebrand's paper on trimorphism, 187 n.12, 251 & 252 n.1; pollen-grain sizes in heterostyled flowers, 213 & 214 n.5; trimorphism in, 169–70 & nn.2 & 3, 176–7 & 178 nn.9 & 10, 179 & 180 n.17, 186 & 187 n.12, 291 & 292 nn.2 & 3, 408 & 409 n.11, 478 & 480 n.11; variability of flowers, 265 & 268 n.2, 332–4 & 335 nn.2 & 3 & 336 nn.4–8, 415 & 416 nn.2–4
Oxalis bowiei (*bowei*, *bowii*): whether trimorphic, 291 & 292 nn.1–3
Oxalis rosea, 170 & n.3, 360 & n.1
Oxford University: J.V. Carus, conservator of comparative anatomy collection, 169 n.16, 471 n.16; J.D. Hooker awarded honorary degree, 171 & n.6
oxlip: Bardfield, *see* Bardfield oxlip; common, *see Primula veris x vulgaris*

Packard, Alpheus Spring, Jr: paper on bees and their parasites, 31 n.3
Packe, Charles William: refuses access to fossil hunters, 445 & 446 n.13
Packsaddle Bay, Tierra del Fuego, 444 & 446 n.5
Paget, James, 346 & n.7
Paguma: taxonomic diffculties in classification, 83 & 84 n.6
Palaeontographical Society: *Fossil Cirripedia*, publishers, 152 & 153 n.13, 376 n.2
Palgrave, Reginald Francis Douce: memorial to W.J. Hooker, 17 & n.6; travels to Etruria, 25 & 26 n.3
Pall Mall Gazette, 17 & 18 n.11, 21 & 22 n.9; T.H. Huxley's letter supporting Jamaica Committee, xxiv, 372 n.3
Pallas, Pyotr Simon: effect of domestication on sterility in crosses, 438 n.7
Panama: fishes of oceans east and west of, 427 & 429 n.10
pangenesis hypothesis, xv, 11 n.8, 24 n.3, 45 n.5, 51 n.2, 71 n.3, 112–13 & 114 nn.4–10, 115 n.3, 116 & 117 n.4, 120 n.4, 121 & n.6, 131 n.13, 180 n.14, 337 & 338 n.9, 366 n.4, 373 & 374 n.10, 374 & n.3, 385 n.2, 410 & 411 n.7
Panizzi, Anthony: British Museum, principal librarian, 176 n.2
Papaver: E. Bornet sends seeds to CD, 388 & n.4, 402 & 403 n.3; subspecies, 388 n.4, 402 & 403 n.2
Papilio: polymorphism in females, 25 n.4, 39–40 & nn.2–5
Papilio coon, 25 n.4
Papilio memnon, 25 n.4
Papilionaceae: crossing experiment, 249 & n.1, 292–3 & nn.2, 4 & 5; fertility dependent on presence of bees, 444 n.5
Papuan people: K.E. von Baer's book, 270 & 271 n.3
Paradisea apoda: reaction to portrait and mirror-image, 58 n.3
Paradoxurina: taxonomic diffculties in classification, 83 & 84 n.6
Paradoxurus: taxonomic diffculties in classification, 83 & 84 n.6
parasites: of bees, paper by A.S. Packard Jr, 31 & n.3; orchids, unknown, 149
Paris: Muséum d'Histoire Naturelle, A.-H.-A. Duméril's studies of axolotl, 84 n.4
Parker, Francis, 297 & n.6; broken ankle, 342 & n.3; executor of S.E. Darwin's will, 342 & n.5
Parker, Henry: executor of S.E. Darwin's will, 342 & n.5, 345 & 346 & n.3
Parker, William Kitchen: administration and locality of natural history collections, 175 & n.1 & 176 nn.2 & 3
parrots: aristocratic in tastes, 136; A.R. Wallace's paper on distribution, 24 & nn.1 & 2
Parslow, Joseph, 304 & 305 n.7
partridge: red-legged. *See Caccabis rufa*
Passerini, Giovanni, 79 & 80 n.10
Passiflora: occasional self-sterility in, 176 & 178 n.8
Passiflora acerifolia: A. Gray describes climbing action, 231 & 232 nn.10 & 11
Passiflora gracilis, 324 & 326 n.14
Pasteur, Louis: claims to have disproved spontaneous generation theory, 283–4 & n.13
Patagonia: fossil bones found in, xxv, 216 & 217 n.7 & 218 n.11, 222 & 223 nn.1 & 4, 225 & nn.3 & 4 & 226 n.5, 226 & 227 nn.2–7, 232 & nn.2–6 & 233 nn.7–10, 237 & 238 n.3

Patagonian Mission Society, 444 & 446 n.4
Patent Concrete Stone Company, 41–2 & n.2, 50 n.3
Patent Siliceous Stone Company, 41–2 & n.2
Paullinia sp.: seeds, 266
Pauropus huxleyi: described by J. Lubbock, 421 & n.8
peaches: best fruit borne by seedling trees, 241 & n.2; T. Rivers, paper on seedlings, 183 & 184 n.6
peas. *See Pisum*
Pedder, William Henry: takes Chinese honeycomb to CD, 108 & n.1
Pedicularis sylvatica (lousewort): bee pollination, 140 & 141 n.4
Pegantha rubiginosa (*Cunina rhododactyla*): reproduction, 326 n.16
peloric flowers, 413 & n.1, 421 n.3
Pembroke Dock: visit by J.D. Hooker, 366 & 367 n.8, 372 & 373 n.2
Peneus: metamorphosis, F. Müller's paper, 10 & 11 n.8
peony: seeds, 320 & n.3, 324 & 326 n.13
pepper family. *See* Piperaceae
Pepsis: repeated stinging by, 88 n.1
Peradiniya botanic gardens, Ceylon: G.H.K. Thwaites, director, 138 n.5
Persea, 254 & 256 n.18
Pertz, Georg Heinrich: visit to J.D. Hooker, 329 & 330 n.9
Pertz, Leonora: visit to J.D. Hooker, 329 & 330 n.9
Peschel, Oscar Ferdinand: proposed translator of *Variation*, 364 & 365 n.4
petrels: analogous species, 91 & n.7
Pezophaps solitarius (solitaire): skeletons found in Rodriguez Island, 423 & n.10
Phaseolus. *See under* beans
Philanthus: sting, 87 & 88 n.3
Philodendron: aerial roots, 56 & 57 n.9, 462–3 & n.9
HMS *Philomel*: voyage to Patagonia, 217 n.7 & 218 n.8, 227 n.4
Philosophical Transactions of the Royal Society of London: R. Owen's description of Patagonian fossils, 226 & 227 n.6
photographs: CD, exchange with J.V. Carus, 383 & 384 n.8, 388 & 390 n.1, 393 & 394 n.1; CD, exchange with R. Caspary, 80 & 81 n.14, 91 & 92 nn.1 & 2, 145 & 146 n.5, 163 n.10; CD, exchange with German scientists, 8 & 10 n.16, 27 & n.2 & 28 nn.3 & 4, 456 & 457 n.17, 458 & 459 nn.2–4; CD, exchange with E. Haeckel, 8 & 10 nn.15–18, 20 & nn.2, 3 & 9, 163 n.10, 456 & 458 nn.15–18; CD, exchange with F. Müller, 10 & 11 n.5, 19 & 20 n.3; CD, frontispiece to *Origin*, 2d German edition, 8 & 10 n.15, 19 & 20 n.2, 456 & 457 n.15; CD, taken by W.E. Darwin, 8 & 10 n.16, 19 & 20 n.2, 91 & 92 n.2, 146 n.5, 158 & 163 n.10, 204 n.11, 456 & 458 n.16; CD, taken by E. Edwards, xvii–xviii, 137 n.10, 384 n.8; H.R. Göppert seeks exchange with CD, 329 & 330 n.15, 337 & 338 n.6; Sebright hen with male plumage, 269, 278
Phronima, 300 n.12
Pico, Azores: J.D. Hooker wishes to search for moraines, 261 & 263 n.16
Pictet de la Rive, François Jules: with A. Humbert, article on fossil fishes of Lebanon, 311–12 & n.13
pigeons: attracted to mirrors, 136; illustrations for *Variation*, 18–19 & nn.2, 3, 4 & 6, 22 & 23 nn.4–7, 26 & n.4, 233 nn.1–3, 239 n.3, 278 & n.3 & 279 n.8, 279 & 280 n.2; laugher-pigeon, 394 & n.3; males having distinctive plumage, 165 n.5; reversion in domestic breeds, 205 n.3; skulls, 356 & 357 n.4; A.R. Wallace's paper on distribution, 24 & nn.1 & 2. *See also Columba livia*
pigs: skull of Irish, 357 n.4; sloughing of skin, 386–7 & nn.2–4
Piperaceae: C. de Candolle's paper on, 263 & 264 n.2
Pisum (peas): crossing experiments, 292 & 293 n.4, 329 & 330 n.16, 337 & 338 nn.7 & 8, 366 n.4, 375 n.5, 382 & n.4; illustration for *Variation*, 357 & n.6; T. Laxton sends specimens to CD, 337 & 338 nn.7 & 8, 365–6 & nn.2–4, 374 & nn.2–4 & 375 nn.5 & 6
pitcher-plants. *See Nepenthes*
plants: B. Verlot's book on variation in, 16 & n.2, 21 & n.1
platypus. *See Ornithorhynchus parodoxus* (*O. anatinus*)
Plesiosaurus, 297
Pleuronectidae: migration of eye, 240 n.3
Pliocene fossils: human skull found in California, 400 & 401 n.9
Plumbago, 428 & 429 n.22, 439 & 440 n.11, 452 & 453 n.4; variability of flowers, 369
pollen: in *Cytisus* spp., 158 & 160–2, 199 & 201 nn.2–4; effect on another plant's fruit, 130 & 131 n.13; number of grains needed to fertilise ovule, 393 n.6; sizes of grains in different heteromorphs, 162 n.5, 211 & n.5, 213 & 214 n.5, 315 n.9, 335 n.3, 371 n.7

polyanthus: heterostyly in, 436 & n.6
polymorphism: in female butterflies, 39–40 & nn.2–5. *See also* dimorphism
Pompilus: stings, 87 & 88 n.3
Pontaderia aquatica, 370 & 372 n.16
poplar hawk-moth. *See Laothoe populi*
Popular Science Review: G. Henslow's article on C.V. Naudin's studies of hybrids, 96 & n.5, 100 & n.1, 183 & nn.1–3, 201–2 & nn.2–4; G. Henslow's summary of 'Climbing plants', 96 n.4, 100 & n.1, 183 & nn.1–3
porpoise: kept in pond, 127 n.5
Port Orford cedar. *See Cupressus lawsoniana*
Porto Santo: insects, 282 & 283 n.9; insects and land-shells distinct from those of Madeira, 257 & 258 n.4, 261 & 263 n.17, 271–2 & 273 n.9, 282 & n.7 & 283 n.9
Posoqueria fragrans (*Martha fragrans*, *Posoqueria densiflora*): mechanism for preventing self-pollination, 415 & 416 n.9
Possession Bay, Patagonia: survey, 217 & 218 n.12
postage rates, 20 & n.9
postage stamps: gift from A. Gray to L. Darwin, 313 & 315 n.2
Pott, August Friedrich: cited by F.W. Farrar, 32 & n.3
Powys, Thomas Littleton, 4th Baron Lilford: administration and locality of natural history collections, 175 & n.1 & 176 nn.2–4
Practical Entomologist: article on naturalised insects, 442 & n.3; B.D. Walsh, editor, 399 & 400 n.4, 442 & n.4
prawns: F. Müller's paper on, 186 & 188 n.17, 224 & 225 nn.2 & 3
Preussische Jahrbücher: review of *Origin* by J.B. Meyer, 111 & 112 n.5
Prévost, M.: paper on *Cytisus adami*, 148 n.3
primrose. *See Primula vulgaris*
Primula: heterostyly in, 210 n.6, 436; pollen-grain sizes in heterostyled flowers, 213 & 214 n.5; whether ovules anatropal or amphitropal, 204 n.9
Primula auricula, 447 n.3
Primula elatior. *See* Bardfield oxlip
Primula farinosa (bird's eye primrose): heterostyly in, 447 & n.3
Primula sinensis, 447 n.3; 'equal-styled' forms, 139 & 140 n.7
Primula veris (cowslip), 447 n.3; 'equal-styled' forms, 139 & 140 n.7; fertility of different forms compared, 117–18 & nn.4 & 5, 139 & 140 nn.5 & 6
Primula veris x *vulgaris* (common oxlip): identified as hybrid, 314 & 315 n.12
Primula vulgaris (primrose): heterostyly in, 436
Primulaceae, 370 & 371 n.15
printers. *See* compositors
Pritchard, Charles: Clapham Grammar School, headmaster, 343 n.5; day length steadily increasing, 347 & 348 n.8, 348 & 349 n.8; sermon responding to W.R. Grove, 342 & n.2 & 343 nn.3 & 4, 347 & 348 n.8, 348 & 349 nn.3–6 & 8
Proceedings of the Entomological Society of Philadelphia: B.D. Walsh's paper on willow galls, 400 n.8
Proceedings of the Zoological Society of London: A.C.L. Gunther's paper on fishes of Central America, 427 & 429 n.10; paper on prongbuck horns, 307 & n.11
prongbuck (pronghorn). *See Antilocapra americana*
Protogenes primordialis, 7 & 9 nn.6 & 7, 20 & n.4, 455 & 457 nn.6 & 7
Protonopsis horrida, 83 & 84 n.3
protoplasmic streaming, 94 & 95 n.10, 464 & 466 n.10
Pseudotsuga menziesii. *See Abies douglasii*
Psithyrus. *See Apathus*
publishers: 'penurious pragmatical prigs', 448
Publishers' Circular: C. Lyell, *Principles of geology* advertised in, 344 n.2, 347 n.6; *Variation* advertised in, 242 n.3, 322 n.9, 364 n.1, 435 n.5
Pulmonaria: pollen-grain sizes in heterostyled flowers, 213 & 214 n.5
Pulmonaria officinalis, 174 & n.2
Putnam, Frederic Ward: construction of bees' cells, 14 & 16 nn.9 & 10, 30–1 & nn.1 & 2, 34 & n.8; paper on leaf-cutting bees, 31 n.3

Quarterly Journal of the Geological Society: C.G. Ehrenberg's paper on dust falling on ships, 250 n.2; J. von Haast's paper on glacial deposits of New Zealand, 242 n.6
Quarterly Journal of Microscopical Science: T. Hincks's paper on reproduction in Polyzoa, 390–1 & n.1
Quarterly Journal of Science: review of *Origin*, xviii, xxii, 118–19 & 120 nn.1 & 3, 124 & n.5, 136–7 & nn.9 & 10, 227 & 229 n.2, 240 & 241 n.4; J. Samuelson, co-editor, 486 n.14; A.R. Wallace's paper on glacial theories, 391 & 392 n.7
Quatrefages, Armand de: book on annelids, 384 & 385 n.3, 476 & n.2

rabbits: skulls, 357 n.4

railway shares, 209 & 210 n.8

Ramsay, Andrew Crombie, 153 n.2; administration and locality of natural history collections, 175 & n.1 & 176 nn.2 & 3; and expedition to Patagonia, 232 & 233 n.9; gift of book on geology of North Wales to CD, 207 & 208 n.2; J. von Haast's candidacy for Royal Society, 309 & 310 n.1

Ransome, Frederick: loans made by CD, 41–2 & n.2, 49–50 & nn.2–4, 53 & nn.1 & 2

Rauwenhoff, Nicolas Willem Pieter, 79 & 80 n.6

Ray Society: *Living Cirripedia*, publishers, 152 & 153 n.13

Reader: astronomical explanation of climate change, 85 n.7; dimorphism, A.R. Wallace's work compared with CD's, 45 n.5; P. Janet, *The materialism of the present day*, review, 227 & 230 nn.3 & 10; *Variation* advertised in, 242 n.3, 322 n.9, 364 n.1; A.R. Wallace, paper on reversed sexual characters in butterfly, 307 n.8

Réaumur, René Antoine Ferchault de: geometry of bees' cells, 13 & 15 nn.1 & 4, 33 & 34 n.3

red-legged partridge. *See Caccabis rufa*

Reed, George Varenne: visit to Down House, 482 & n.12

Reed, John William, 58 & 59 n.1

Reeve, Lovell Augustus: and E. Walford, *Portraits of men of eminence*, editor, xvii–xviii, 151–2 & nn.1 & 2, 394 n.4

Reeves, William: Royal Irish Academy, secretary, 125

Regia Scientiarum Academia Svecica: CD a foreign member, 108 & 109 n.5

Regia Scientiarum Societas Upsaliensis: CD a fellow, 109 & n.6

Reichenbach, Heinrich Gustav: pollination of orchids within bud, 163 n.5

Reinhard, Hermann: review of B.D. Walsh's paper on dimorphism in *Cynips*, 244 & 246 nn.17–20

rejuvenescence, 155 n.5

religion: W. Bowman, results of science the voice of God, 326 & 327 n.4; C. Pritchard, should be no conflict with scientific inquiry, 342 & 343 n.4; tensions with science, 44 n.3; toleration law passed in Chile, 445 & 447 n.22; whether compatible with natural selection theory, xxiv–xxv, 423–4 & n.1 & 425 n.2, 425–6 & n.2, 432 & n.1

Renan, Joseph-Ernest: cited by F.W. Farrar, 32 & n.3

Renilla, 55, 462

Renilla edwardsii, 187 n.9

Rennell, James, 281 n.7

Rennell's current, 281 & n.7

Retinospora obtusa: sent from Kew for Down House garden, 354 n.1

reversion, xv, 179 & 180 n.14, 205 & nn.3 & 4, 206 & 207 nn. 2–10, 210 & n.1, 270 n.2

Revue Horticole: CD returns journal to J.D. Hooker, 448 & n.2; report of E.A. Carrière's grafting experiments, 439 & 440 n.13

Rhamnus cathartica: R. Caspary's observations, 199 & 200 & 201 nn.6–13; CD asks for flowers and twigs, 215 & nn.2 & 3 & 216 nn.5 & 6; W.E. Darwin's observations, xx, 208 & nn.2–4, 209 & n.2 & 210 n.4, 214 & 215 n.2, 218–20 & 221 nn.2–8, 11 & 12, 221–2 & nn.2–5; pollen, 335 n.3; preferred habitat, 215 & 216 n.8; whether heteromorphic, xx, 156 & n.3, 211 & nn.2–5, 211 & nn.3, 5 & 6, 211–12 & nn.2–5, 213–14 & nn.3–7, 9 & 10, 218–20 & 221 nn.2–5, 222 & n.8, 284 n.10, 314 & 315 n.9

Rhamnus lanceolata: A. Gray, sends seeds to CD, 344 & 345 n.5; whether dimorphic, 156 n.3, 214 & n.10, 283 & 284 n.10, 314 & 315 n.10

Rhizopoda, 7 & 9 nn.6 & 7, 20 & n.4, 455 & 457 nn.6 & 7

Rhynchosia, 413 n.3

Rhynchosia precatoria, 334, 421 n.6

Richards, George Henry: hydrographer to Admiralty, 237 & n.2; lieutenant on HMS *Philomel*, 216 & 217 & 218 n.8, 222 & 223 n.2, 226 & 227 n.4

Richmond, George, 346 & n.8

HMS *Rifleman*: expedition to China Sea, 58 & 59 nn.1 & 2

Rio de Janeiro: decomposition of igneous rocks, 311 & 312 n.6

Rissoa: G. Schwartz von Mohrenstern's paper, 125–6 & nn.7 & 8, 143 & n.3, 467–8 & nn.7 & 8

Rivers, T. Francis, 183 & 184 n.1

Rivers, Thomas, xv; CD asks for nuts from purple-leaved tree, 343 & n.1, 349 & 350 n.2; effect of scion wood on coloration of stock tissue, 182 & n.4, 198 n.3; *Journal of Horticulture*, article on fruit culture, 147 & n.1; long shoot on dwarf French bean, 183 & 184 & nn.2 & 3; oats producing ears of barley, 350 & nn.1 & 4; promises to send specimens to CD, xv, 182 & n.1, 182 & n.2, 197 & n.2; welcomes news of CD's improved health, 182 & n.3

Robertson, William Tindal: British Association for the Advancement of Science, report of proceedings, 391 & 392 n.5
Robinson, Charles Frederick, 3 n.5
Robinson, Charles John: bereavements, 2 & 3 n.4; re-marriage, 3 n.5; vicar of Norton Canon, 3 & n.7
Robinson, Eleanor Rocke, 3 n.5
Robinson, Emma Harriet Agnes (née Crocker), 3 n.5
Robinson, William: CD asks to carry out crossing experiments with *Euryale ferox*, 367 n.2; CD regrets not having met, 150 & 151 n.2; elected a fellow of Linnean Society, 154 n.3; offers help to CD, 150 & 151 n.3; Royal Botanic Society, Regent's Park, foreman of herbaceous department, 367 n.2
Robson, John: correspondence on grafting of trees and shrubs, 147 & 148 n.5
rock pigeon. *See Columba livia*
Rodriguez Island: solitaire skeletons found in, 423 & n.10
Rodriguezia. See Burlingtonia
Rolfe, Robert Monsey, 1st Baron Cranworth: G. Bentham's visit to, 329 & 330 n.13, 331 & n.2, 339 & n.2, 339 & nn.2 & 3; W. Bowman's visit to, 341 & n.3; contribution to Down charities, 414 & n.2; visit to Winchfield, 414 & nn.1 & 2 & 415 nn.3 & 4
Rolle, Friedrich, 133 & 134 n.3; *Ch. Darwin's Lehre*, 102 & 103 nn.3–5; *Der Mensch*, 28–9 & n.2, 102 & 103 nn.3 & 5, 125 & 126 n.3, 459–60 & 461 n.2, 467 & 468 n.3
Roots, George: account of cat adopting squirrel, 319 & nn.2 & 3
rose: graft hybrid, 80 n.4, 92 & nn.3 & 4
Routledge, George, and Sons, publishers, 23 n.12
Royal Botanic Gardens, Kew: J.G. Baker, assistant in herbarium, 235 n.2; G. Bentham's absence, 320 & 321 n.1; G. Bentham's gift of plant collections, 275 n.3; R. Caspary intends to visit, 145 & 146 n.6; CD hopes to visit, 146 & 147 n.2, 148 & n.1; CD requests books from library, 198 & 199 n.3; CD's visit to, 392, 396 & 397 n.1, 413 & n.5; *Euryale ferox* plant dead, 150 & 151 n.4; E. Haeckel and R. Greeff's visit, 366 & 367 n.7; J.D. Hooker, director, 17 n.2, 83 n.8, 329 & 330 n.11; insects very rare, 282 & n.8; rearrangement of herbaceous beds, 420 & 421 nn.3 & 4; J. Smith (1821–88), curator, 17 n.5; trees and shrubs sent to Down House, 354 & n.1
Royal Geographical Society of London: H.W. Bates, assistant secretary, 433 n.2; A.I. Butakoff, article on tame saigas, 432 & 433 n.2; E.J. Eyre elected fellow, 373 & n.6; J. von Haast's map of New Zealand Alps, 310 & n.5
Royal Horticultural Society: R.T. Clarke's lecture on cultivation of cotton, 376 & 377 nn.5 & 6. *See also Journal of the Royal Horticultural Society*
Royal Institution of Great Britain: E. Frankland's lecture on source of muscular power, 322 & 323 n.9, 329 & n.4; G. Henslow's lectures on botany, 100 & n.2, 103 & 104 n.3; C. Kingsley's lectures on science and superstition, 239 & 240 n.4; J. Lubbock's lecture on metamorphoses in insects, 224 & 225 n.3
Royal Irish Academy: CD elected honorary member, 125 & n.1, 483
Royal Prussian Academy of Sciences. *See* Königliche-Preussische Akademie der Wissenschaften
Royal Society of Edinburgh: CD an honorary member, 109 & n.10
Royal Society of London: F.W. Farrar seeks election to fellowship, 31–2 & nn.2–5, 37–8 & nn.2 & 3, 41 & nn.2–4; J. von Haast seeks election to fellowship, 153 & n.2 & 154 n.3, 242 & n.5, 309–10 & nn.1 & 2; list of members, 108 & 109 n.3; medals awarded to CD, 152 & 153 n.19; members of council, 154 n.6; regulations for borrowing from library, 224 & n.4; Rumford Medal awarded to W.C. Wells, 284 n.5; J. Samuelson's paper refuting spontaneous generation theory, 119 & 120 n.5; Scientific Relief Fund, grant sought by J.W. Salter, 449 & 450 n.7; soirée, xvii, 150 n.1, 171 & 172 n.3, 179 & 180 n.9, 189 & n.3, 197 & n.4, 430 & n.2, 482 & n.14. *See also Philosophical Transactions of the Royal Society of London*
Royal Society for the Prevention of Cruelty to Animals, 2 n.5
Royal Society of Sciences of Upsala. *See* Regia Scientiarum Societas Upsaliensis
Royal Swedish Academy of Sciences. *See* Regia Scientiarum Academia Svecica
Rubiaceae, 121 & 123 n.3, 129 & 131 nn.7 & 8
rudimentary organs, 430 & 431 n.4, 441 & n.2
Rumford Medal. *See under* Royal Society of London

Ruprecht, Franz Josef: paper on Russian black earth, 195 & 196 n.9, 472 & n.9
Russell, Arthur John Edward: administration and locality of natural history collections, 175 & n.1 & 176 nn.2 & 3
Russell, John, 1st Earl Russell, 231 & 232 n.9
Russia: F.J. Ruprecht's paper on black earth, 195 & 196 n.9, 472 & n.9
Rütimeyer, Ludwig: book on descent and transmutation of mammals, 460 & 461 n.11; book on fossil horses, 109 & n.11; photograph, 19 & 20 n.3; support for CD's theories, 29 & 30 n.11, 126 n.6, 186 & 188 n.17, 460 & 461 n.11, 468 n.6

Sabine, Edward, xvii
Saiga tatarica: tame, in island of Aral Sea, 417 & nn.3 & 4, 422 & 423 nn.3 & 4, 432 & 433 n.2, 433 & 434 nn.2 & 3; in Zoological Gardens, 422 & 423 n.5
St Bartholomew's Hospital: G. Henslow, botanical lecturer, 139 & 140 n.4
St Dabeoc's heath. *See Daboecia azorica*
St Helena: flora, 286 n.9, 289 & 290 n.8; flora, J.D. Hooker's planned paper, 129 & 131 n.6; J.D. Hooker longs to revisit, 286 n.9; 'wire bird', 276 & 277 n.2, 280 & 281 n.2, 285 & 286 n.7
St Helena plover. *See Charadrius sanctahelenae*
salamanders, 83 & 84 nn.1, 3 & 4
Salisbury, Richard Anthony: *The genera of plants*, 127 n.1
Salter, John William: business failures and financial hardship, 449–50 & nn.6 & 8; grant from Royal Society relief fund, 449 & 450 n.7; resignation from Geological Survey of United Kingdom, 450 nn.1 & 5; seeks employment at British Museum, 449 & 450 n.8; seeks to help CD with *Origin*, 449 & 450 n.2
Salter, Samuel James Augustus: administration and locality of natural history collections, 175 & n.1 & 176 nn.2 & 3; crossing of fowls, 279 & 280 n.9
Salter, Sarah: school, 449 & 450 n.4
Salvia: F. Hildebrand's paper on pollination in, 132 & n.5, 140 & 141 n.6, 177 & 178 nn.11 & 12
Salvia coccinea, 178 n.12
Salvia grahami, 178 n.12
Salvia tenori, 178 n.12
Salvin, Osbert: administration and locality of natural history collections, 175 & n.1 & 176 nn.2 & 3
Sampson Low, Son & Marston, 438 n.2, 441 & n.1
Samuelson, James: paper rejecting spontaneous generation theory, 119 & 120 n.5; presentation copy of *Origin*, 240 & 241 n.4, 485 & 486 n.14; *Quarterly Journal of Science*, co-editor, 486 n.14; use of term 'natural selection', xxii
Sanicula, 276 & 277 n.4
Santa Catarina island, Brazil: flora, 67 & 68 n.5; retirement home of F. Müller, 12 n.9, 403 n.3; whether level has risen, 12 nn.12 & 14
Sarothamnus scoparius. *See Cytisus scoparius*
saw-flies. *See* gooseberry saw-fly
Saxifraga: CD requests specimen from J.D. Hooker, 393 & n.9, 395 & 396 n.3
Scaevola: pollination mechanisms, 121 & 122 & 123 nn.4, 6 & 7
Scalpellum: classification, 186 & 187 n.11
Schacht, Hermann: textbook on anatomy and physiology of perennials, 198 & 199 n.2
Schizanthus pinnata, 140 & 141 n.2
Schleicher, August: sends photograph to CD, 19 & 20 n.3
Schleiden, Matthias Jacob: resigns professorship, 27 & 28 n.3, 458 & 459 n.3
Schmidt, Oskar: support for CD's theories, 133–4 & n.4, 186 & 187 n.16, 266 & 268 n.17
Schomburgk, Moritz Richard: Adelaide Botanic Garden, director, 149 & n.2
Schultze, Max Johann Sigismund, 11 n.6, 93 & 95 n.9, 124 n.13, 186 n.2, 268 n.3, 464 & 466 n.9; paper on lancelet, 408 & 409 n.18, 479 & 480 n.18
Schwarz von Mohrenstern, Gustav: paper on *Rissoa*, 125–6 & nn.7 & 8, 143 & n.3, 467–8 & nn.7 & 8
Schweizerbart, Christian Friedrich: publisher of German edition of *Origin*, xix, xxiii, 10 n.15, 11 n.3, 106 & n.8, 110, 111–12 & nn.2 & 3, 143 n.5, 362–3 & nn.2 & 4–7, 378 & 379 & nn.1 & 7, 458 n.15, 466 & 467 n.8, 468–9 & 470 n.3 & 471 nn.7–9, 473–4 & nn.2 & 4–7; publisher of German edition of *Variation*, 364 n.2, 469 & 471 n.11
Science Gossip. *See Hardwicke's Science-Gossip*
Sclater, Philip Lutley: administration and locality of natural history collections, 175 & n.1 & 176 nn.2 & 3; ancestor of domestic guinea fowl, 431 & n.4; CD seeks information on ducks from, 6 & nn.2–4; J.D. Hooker seeks information on birds of Atlantic islands, 276 & 277 n.3, 285 & 286 n.7, 289 n.4, 304 & 305 n.8; opportunity

Sclater, Philip Lutley, cont.
to exchange bird skins, 400 n.7, 441 & n.2, 442 & n.6; Zoological Society of London, secretary, 442
Sclater-Booth, George: administration and locality of natural history collections, 175 & n.1 & 176 nn.2 & 3
Scolopax rusticola (woodcock): seeds carried in mud on foot of, 401 n.2, 401 & 402 n.2
Scott, John, 96 n.5; Calcutta botanic gardens, curator, 82 & 83 n.14; financial help from CD, 81 & 82 n.2; pollination of *Acropera*, 325 n.3; seeds produced by *Acropera*, 416 n.12; self-sterility in *Passiflora*, 176 & 178 n.8; sends good wishes to CD, 82 & n.6; sends plants and seeds to J.D. Hooker, 81–2 & 83 nn.10–13; thanks J.D. Hooker for previous assistance, 82 & 83 n.14; variable development of unisexual flowers, 51 n.2
Charles Scribner & Co., 377 & n.4, 437 n.2, 441 & n.1
Scudder, Samuel Hubbard: misquotes *Origin*, 138 & n.7
sea-pens: J.E. Gray's taxonomic errors, 186 & 187 nn.9 & 11
Sebright hen. *See under* fowls
Sedgwick, Adam: *Palaeozoic rocks*, G. von Leonhard, translator, 469 & 471 n.7
seeds: brightly coloured, 266 & 267 & 268 nn.13–15, 324 & 325 n.2 & 326 nn.12 & 14, 334 & 336 nn.10 & 11, 408 & 409 n.9, 411 & 412 n.19, 413 & n.3, 415 & 416 n.6, 417 & 418 nn.2 & 3, 420–1 & n.6, 426 & 428 nn.1–3, 439 & 440 nn.6 & 7, 478 & 480 n.9; carried by Rennell's current during glacial period, 281 n.7; occasional transport, xxi, 64 & 65 n.5, 257 & 259 n.7, 272 & 273 nn.11–15, 305 n.5, 401 n.2, 401 & 402 n.2, 418 & 419 n.13, 429 n.7, 439 & 440 n.9; whether killed by sea-water, 84 & 86 n.11, 272 nn.11 & 15
Seemann, Berthold Carl: *Journal of Botany*, editor, 163 n.5; Nicaraguan expedition, 86–7 & n.4
self-sterility, 177 nn.4, 5 & 7 & 178 n.8, 265 & 268 nn.10 & 12, 324 & 325 nn.2 & 8, 368 & 371 n.1, 409 n.7, 477–8 & 479 n.7 & 480 n.8
Sequoiadendron giganteum. *See Wellingtonia gigantea*
Serapias cordigera: J.T. Moggridge sends specimens to CD, 165 & 166 n.5, 184 & 185 n.2
Seringe, Nicolas Charles: paper on St Valery apple, 318 & 319 n.1, 322 & 323 n.3
Serjania sp., 265–6 & 268 nn.11 & 12
Serra dos Organõs, Brazil: flora, 35 & 37 nn.9–11, 46 & 47 n.8 & 49 n.22, 59 & 60 n.5, 67–8 & nn.2–5 & 69 nn.6–8 & 10–13, 76 & n.7; former glaciation, 68 & 69 nn.9 & 13, 76 & n.8, 98 & 99 n.3
Sesbania. *See Daubentonia*
Sesoienges, 446 n.4
Sethe, Anna, 9 n.11 & 10 n.18, 457 nn.11 & 18
Sethia, 371 & 372 n.18; pollen-grain sizes in heterostyled flowers, 213 & 214 n.5
sexual selection, 43, 54 & 55 nn.3 & 6, 58 n.5; in butterflies, 55 n.6; in humming-birds, 165 n.3
Seymour, Edward Adolphus Seymour, 12th duke of Somerset, 39 n.4; first lord of the Admiralty, 216 & 218 n.9, 222 & 223 n.3, 225 n.4 & 226 n.5
Shakespeare, William: *Antony and Cleopatra*, 380 n.4
Shaw, James: appreciation of beauty, 42–3 & 44 nn.1–12, 54 & 55 nn.2–7, 135–6 & 137 nn.1–9, 379–80 & nn.2–5, 397 & n.2; colour of fruit a guide to birds, 380 & n.6; presentation copy of *Origin*, 144 & n.4, 379 & n.1, 485 & n.4
Shelley, Percy Bysshe: 'The cloud', 380 & n.4
shells: distinct in Madeira and Porto Santo, 257 & 258 n.4, 271–2 & 273 n.9, 282 & n.7; rare at Kew, 282 & n.8
Shrewsbury School: CD a pupil, 151
Sibthorp, John: *Flora Græca*, 253 & 254 n.2
Sikkim: moraines in, 98 & 99 n.3; orchids from, 81 & 83 n.10
Silla de Caracas, Venezuela, 47 & 49 n.24
Simpson, Wilfred Huddleston: administration and locality of natural history collections, 175 & n.1 & 176 nn.2 & 3
skylark. *See Alauda arvensis*
slavery: outlawed in US, xxiii, 130 & 132 n.17, 157 & 158 n.11
Smerinthus ocellatus (eyed hawk-moth): interbreeding with *Laothe populi*, 297 & n.8
Smerinthus populi. *See Laothoe populi*
Smith, Frederick: geometry of wasp cells, 34 & n.9 & 35 n.10; observations on ants, 107 & n.3; stings of bees and wasps, 87–8 & nn.2–5
Smith, John: whether effect of stock on scion tissue observed, 112 & 114 n.4
Smith, John (1821–88): crossing of cucumbers, 115 & 116 n.2; cut-leaved beech, 225 & 226 n.10; Royal Botanic Gardens, Kew, curator, 17 n.5, 296 & nn.3 & 5; sends *Drosera* specimen to CD, 296 & nn.3 & 5
Smith, Julia: holiday in France, 128 & 129 n.4, 222 n.6

Smithsonian Institution, Washington DC: J. Henry, secretary, 378 n.6; B.D. Walsh impatient at slowness, 243 & 245 nn.4 & 5
Smyth Channel, Patagonia: survey, 217 & 218 n.12
snails: bird eating, 150 & n.1; of Madeira and Porto Santo, 258 n.3
Snow, George: carrier, 53 & n.3, 77 & n.6
Société des Sciences Naturelles de Neuchâtel: CD a corresponding member, 109 & n.8
Solander, Daniel Carl, 443 & 444 n.2
solitaire. *See Pezophaps solitarius*
Somerset, 12th duke of. *See* Seymour, Edward Adolphus Seymour, 12th duke of Somerset
Somerville, Mary: use of illustrations from *Orchids*, 355 & n.2, 365 & nn.1 & 2
Sophronitella violacea, 265 & 267 & 268 n.20
South Africa: flora, 259 n.6
South American Mission Society, 446 n.4
Southampton and Hampshire Bank: W.E. Darwin a partner, 156 n.2
Sowerby, George Brettingham, Jr: illustrations for *Variation*, 77 & 78 n.14, 78 & 79 nn.5 & 6, 351 & 352 n.3, 352 & 353 n.3, 355–7 & nn.2–7, 433 n.4
Sowerby, James de Carle, 450 n.6
space: temperature, 84 & 85 n.6, 89 & n.6
species: 'analogous', 91 n.7; convergence, 394 & 395 n.7; criteria for, xv–xvi, 437 n.6; modification of, xvi, 142 n.7, 306, 318 n.5; origin, 260 & 262 n.8 & 263 n.11; 'physiological' test, xv–xvi, 40 & n.5; theory of transmutation. *See* transmutation of species
Spencer, Herbert: coiner of term 'survival of the fittest', xxii, 227 & 230 n.5, 235 & 236 n.3; controversy on umbelliferous plants, 427 & 428 n.6; meeting with CD, 331–2, 332, 337 & 338 n.10, 482 & n.19; natural selection a 'mediate' force, 224 n.9; paper on absorption of dyes by plants, 427 & 428 n.5; *Principles of biology*, xxii, 223 & n.8 & 224 n.9, 225 & 226 n.7, 236 nn.3 & 4 & 237 n.10; *Principles of biology*, J.D. Hooker's criticisms, 410 & 411 nn.6 & 7; requests CD's support for Jamaica Committee, xxiv, 372 & nn.1–3, 385 n.5; speculative nature of work, 121 & n.6, 427 & 428 n.4; a 'thinking pump', xxii, 427, 439 & 440 n.8; visit to J. and E.F. Lubbock, 331 & 332 n.2; 'wriggling' out of difficulties, 418, 428
Sphingidae (sphinx-moths, hawk-moths): hybrids, 297 & n.8, 302 n.10
spider ophrys. *See Ophrys aranifera*
spindle-wood. *See Euonymus europaeus*
sponges: F. Müller's paper, 10 & 11 n.6
spontaneous generation: CD unable to believe in, 394 & 395 n.11; E. Haeckel's view, 7 & 9 n.7, 389 & n.9, 455 & 457 n.7; L. Pasteur's claims to have disproved theory, 283–4 & n.13; J. Samuelson's paper rejecting, 119 & 120 n.5; theory defended by H.G. Bronn, 395 n.11; theory defended by H.J. Clark, 246 n.14, 298 & n.3
Spottiswoode, Mrs, 428 & 429 n.19
Spottiswoode, William: dinner party, 428 & 429 n.19
Sprengel, Christian Konrad: pollination in *Aristolochia clematitis*, 252 & n.10, 360 & 361 n.3
Spruce, Richard: travels in Brazil, 35 & 36 nn.5 & 6
squinting: in siblings, 1 & nn.2 & 3
squirrel: adopted by cat, 319 & n.3
Stamford, Lincolnshire: home of T. Laxton, 374 & 375 n.6
Stanhopea, 324 & 325 n.4
Statice. *See Limonium*
Steenstrup, Japetus: migration of eye in flatfish, 239 & 240 n.2
Stephens, Thomas Selwood: visit to Down House, 482 & n.12
stereotype production, xix, 130 & 131 n.11, 139 n.12, 231 & n.6, 248 n.3, 275 & 276 n.6, 283 & 284 n.6, 315 n.7
sterile flowers: *Oxalis*, 332–4 & 336 n.6, 415 & 416 n.3. *See also* hybrids, sterility in; self-sterility
Stewart, Balfour: planetary influences on sunspots, 411 & 412 n.17
Stewart, Peter Benson ('Paddy'): served on HMS *Beagle*, 445 & 447 n.21
Stirling, Louisa Jane: death, 446 & 447 n.26
Stirling, Waite Hockin, 444 & 446 & nn.4, 8 & 11
Stokes, John Lort: mate and assistant surveyor on HMS *Beagle*, 444 & 446 n.6
Streatfield, J.F., 1 n.2
Suchsland, Friedrich Emil: proposed new German edition of *Origin*, 102 & 103 nn.1 & 6, 110–11 & 112 nn.2–5, 125 & 126 n.2, 133 & 134 n.1, 467 & 468 n.2; publisher of F. Rolle's book *Der Mensch*, 29 n.2, 461 n.2
Suchsland, Rudolf: proposed new German edition of *Origin*, xix, 102 & 103 n.2, 133 & 134 n.1
Sudeley Castle, Gloucestershire: visit by W. Bowman, 341 & n.4
Sulivan, Bartholomew James, 448 & n.3; CD asks him to send questionnaire to W.H. Stirling,

Sulivan, Bartholomew James, cont.
450–1 & nn.4 & 5; delays in work on house, 216; discovery of fossil bones in Patagonia, xxv, 216 & 217 n.7 & 218 n.11, 222 & 223 n.1, 225 & nn.3 & 4 & 226 n.5, 226 & 227 nn.3 & 7, 232 & nn.2 & 3; fossil leaf-bed in Isle of Wight, 445 & 446 nn.12 & 13, 448 & n.4, 451 & nn.6 & 7; health, 216 & 217 n.2, 222, 225 & 226 n.6, 444 & 446 n.2, 450 & 451 n.2; hydrotherapy treatment, 216 & 217 n.5, 446 n.2; moves to Bournemouth, 444 & 446 n.3; survey of Falkland Islands, 216 & 218 n.10; Turkish bath, 444 & 446 n.2

Sulivan, Henry Norton: Cambridge University examinations, 445 & 446 n.18 & 447 n.19, 451 & n.8

Sulivan, James Young Falkland: health improved by hydrotherapy, 216; promotion to lieutenant, xxv, 216 & 217 n.3; voyage to Magellan Straits, 216 & 217 n.6, 222 & 223 n.2

Sulivan, Sophia, 216 & 217 n.5, 451 & n.12

Sulivan, Sophia Henrietta, 216 & 217 n.5

Sulivan, Thomas Edward: promotion to lieutenant, 217 & 218 n.18

sunspots: planetary influences on, 411 & 412 n.17

'survival of the fittest': term coined by H. Spencer, xxii, 227 & 230 n.5, 235 & 236 n.3; term favoured by A.R. Wallace, xxii, 227–9 & nn.1 & 2 & 230 nn.3–12

sweet flag. *See Acorus calamus*

sweetpea. *See Lathyrus odoratus*

Swinhoe, Robert: British Association for the Advancement of Science, member, 307 n.5; sends CD information on ducks, 6 & n.2; sends CD pieces of Chinese honeycomb, 108 & nn.3 & 4; transferred from Formosa to Amoy, 108 & n.1

Tabernaemontana sp.: seeds, 266

Talauma: fruit with brightly coloured seeds, 408 & 409 n.9, 478 & 480 n.9

Teebay, Richard: article on spangled Hamburgh fowls in *The poultry book*, 233 & 234 n.4, 239 & n.5

teeth: growing in unusual parts of body, 114 & 115 n.3

Tegetmeier, William Bernhard: book on poultry, 22 & 23 nn. 11 & 12, 53 & 54 n.6, 233 & 234 n.4, 269 & 270 n.5, 278 & 279 n.11, 279 & 280 n.6, 420 n.5, 431 & n.4; CD unable to meet in London, 412 & n.3, 420 & n.3; experiment on fowl cross, 18 & 19 n.5, 26 & n.3, 239 & n.4, 412 & n.2, 419–20 & n.2; feathers from hybrids, 279 & nn.8 & 9, 291 & n.2; health poor, 269; letter paper, 269 & 270 n.6; offers use of electrotypes from *The poultry book*, 291 & n.3; painting of white dodo, 351 & n.3; pigeons, 394 n.3; Sebright hen with male plumage, 269 & 270 n.2, 278 & 279 n.9, 291 & n.4; seeks information from CD on guinea fowl, ducks, and geese, 420 & n.4, 431 & n.2; sends information to CD, xiv, 433 & n.4; *Variation*, illustrations, 18–19 & nn.2–4 & 6, 22 & 23 nn.4–7, 26 & nn.2 & 4, 78 n.12, 233 nn.1–3, 239 & nn.2 & 3, 269 & 270 n.2, 278 & nn.2–4 & 279 nn.5–8, 279 & 280 n.6, 291 & nn.3 & 5, 316 & n.1, 317 & nn.3 & 4, 350–1 & nn.1 & 2; *Variation*, illustrations, CD thanks for help, 352; *Variation*, presentation copy, 352 & n.3; Zoological Society of London, application for membership, 316 & nn.2–4, 317 & n.2

Tenerife: E. Haeckel's visit to, 353 & 354 n.2, 473 & n.2

Tennent, James Emerson: administration and locality of natural history collections, 175 & n.1 & 176 nn.2 & 3

Terai: *Calamus* spp. from, 81 & 83 n.13

Thayer, Nathaniel, 12 n.10

Der Thiergarten: D.F. Weinland, editor, 30 n.10, 461 n.10

thistles. *See Carduus arvensis*

Thomson, Charles Wyville: migration of eye in flatfish, 239 & 240 n.2

Thomson, Thomas: administration and locality of natural history collections, 175 & n.1 & 176 nn.2 & 3

Thomson, William: calculation of age of earth, 60 n.4, 342 n.2, 348 & 349 n.6; rate of cooling of earth's crust, 84 & 85 n.5

threadfin sea catfish. *See Arius boakeii*

Threeboys (Wammestriggins), 444 & 446 nn.4 & 5

Thujia lobbii (*Thuja plicata*, western red cedar): sent from Kew for Down House garden, 354 n.1

Thuret, Gustave Adolphe, 185 & n.5, 402 & 403 n.6

Thwaites, George Henry Kendrick: Peradiniya botanic gardens, Ceylon, director, 138 n.5

thyme: gyno-dioecious character, 209 & 210 n.5

Ticknor & Fields, publishers, xix, 156 & 157 n.4, 247 & 248 n.6, 276 n.5, 302 & 303 n.2, 313–14 & 315 n.8, 353 & n.4, 361 & 362 n.2, 362 & n.2, 377 & n.3

Tierra del Fuego: expression of emotions in, 450–1 & n.3; indigenous people, 444 & 446 nn.5–10

The Times: letter on galls, 298 & n.5
toadrush. *See Juncus bufonius*
Todd, Robert Bentley: and W. Bowman, book on physiology, 51 n.3
Tollet, Georgina, 124 & n.4
'Tommy' (horse), 52 & n.3
Torquay; J.D. Hooker and J. Lubbock's visit, 149
Toxodon: fossils found in Patagonia, 232 & 233 n.10
Tragocerus: horns, 318 n.3
Transactions of the Entomological Society of London: discussion of mimicry, 392 n.3; F. Smith's paper on bees' and wasps' cells, 34 & 35 n.10
Transactions of the Geological Society of London: CD's papers, 152 & 153 n.17
Transactions of the Linnean Society of London: A.R. Wallace's paper on Malayan butterflies, 24 & n.3 & 25 nn.4 & 5, 307 n.8
Transactions of the Zoological Society of London: A.C.L. Gunther's paper on fishes of Central America, 427 & 429 n.10
transmutation of species, xv, xxii, 90 & n.2, 303 n.2; G. Jäger's paper, 126 & n.9, 468 & n.9; mammals, L. Rütimeyer's book, 460 & 461 n.11; R. Owen's views, 192 & 193 n.12; in relation to geology, H.R. Göppert's views, 29 & 30 n.12, 460 & 461 n.12; theory opposed by L. Agassiz, 12 n.11, 37 n.8
Travers, Henry Hammersley: transport of *Edwardsia* seeds, 419 n.13
trees: branch movements in frosty weather, 145 & 146 n.2; whether ranges restricted, 260 & 262 n.5, 271 & 273 n.5
Treviranus, Ludolph Christian: paper on pollination of *Indigofera*, 132 & n.3
Trimen, Roland: sends CD *Oxalis* bulbs, 178 n.10
trimorphism, xv; F. Hildebrand's paper, 415 & 416 n.4; *Oxalis* spp., 165–7 & n.10, 169–70 & nn.2 & 3, 179 & 180 n.17, 186 & 187 n.12, 251 & 252 n.1, 268 n.2, 291 & 292 nn.2 & 3, 336 n.8, 369, 408 & 409 n.11, 478 & 480 n.11
Trinity College, Dublin: W.H. Harvey, professor of botany and keeper of herbarium, 181 & n.5
Tristan da Cunha: flora, 439 & 440 n.9
Tristram, Henry Baker: administration and locality of natural history collections, 175 & n.1 & 176 nn.2 & 3
Trochilus benjamini. *See Urosticte benjamini*
Troglodytes vulgaris (kitty-wren): caught by *Erica massoni*, 322 & 323 n.5
tuffs: C.G. Ehrenberg's paper on Mexican, 250 & n.2
Turner, William: information on rudimentary organs, 430 & 431 nn.4 & 7, 441 & n.2; meets CD at Royal Society soirée, 197 & n.4, 430 & n.2; observation of bird eating snail, 150 & n.1; presentation copy of *Origin*, 430 & 431 n.8, 485 & 486 n.5; sends papers to CD, 197 nn.2 & 3, 441 & n.3
Tursiops (*Tursio*) spp. (bottle-nosed dolphins), 127 n.4
Tylor, Edward Burnett: human customs, evidence favouring theory of common descent, 171; meets CD at Royal Society soirée, 179 & 180 n.10; visit to J.D. Hooker at Kew, 171 & 172 n.5
Tyndall, John: delighted by CD's improved health, xvii, 171 & 172 n.4; J.D. Hooker's lecture at British Association for the Advancement of Science, 308 & 309 n.5; opposes prosecution of E.J. Eyre, 385 n.5; theories of glacial formation, 141 & 142 n.5
Tynron, Dumfriesshire: J. Shaw, schoolmaster, 57–8 & n.6

Umbelliferae: shapes of ray-florets, 394 & 395 n.10; H. Spencer in controversy concerning, 427 & 428 n.6
Unger, Franz: hypothesis of continental extension, 285 & 286 n.6; support for CD's theories, 133–4 & n.4
United States of America: American Civil War, J.D. Hooker's views, 171 & 172 n.2; American Civil War, Union losses, 157 & 158 n.10; batrachian larva from California, 83 & 84 nn.1, 3 & 4, 90 & nn.3–5; books sold with pages trimmed, 448 & 449 n.4; Pliocene skull found in California, 400 & 401 n.9; post-Civil War reconstruction, 130 & 131 n.16; slavery outlawed, xxiii, 130 & 132 n.17, 157 & 158 n.11; will develop an aristocracy, 181 & 182 n.11
Uroopa, 446 n.4
Urosticte benjamini, 164 & n.1 & 165 n.3 & 4

Vaccinium, 67 & 68 n.5; found in Organ Mountains, 46 & 47 n.8
Vandeae: delayed fertilisation in, 405 & 409 n.4, 476–7 & 479 n.4; pedicel movement in, 300 n.6. *See also Burlingtonia*
variation: bud variation, 92 n.5; in butterflies, H.W. Bates's papers, 192 & 193 nn.9 & 10; in butterflies, A.R. Wallace's work, 391 & 392 n.10; in copepods, C.F. Claus's book, 272 & 274 n.20, 295 & n.6, 298 & 299 n.8, 299 & 300 n.11;

variation, cont.
correlated, 114 n.12, 350 n.2, 394 & 395 n.10; difficulty in ascertaining causes, 119 & 120 n.4; in *Erythroxylum*, 370 & 371 n.13, 474–5 & 476 n.5; in geometry of bees' cells, 33 & 34 n.4; in *Gossypium*, 376 & n.6; in *Hillia*, 370 & 371 n.13, 408 & 409 nn.14 & 15, 475 & 476 n.6, 478–9 & 480 nn.14 & 15; in morphological characters of plants, 394 & 395 n.8; in *Ophrys* flowers, 61–2 & 63 nn.3, 5 & 7–9; in palm civets and related genera, 83 & 84 n.6; in pigeons, 19 nn.3 & 6; in plants, B. Verlot's book, 16 & n.2, 17 & n.3, 21 & n.1; theory necessary to both hypotheses of origin of species, 260 & 263 n.11
James Veitch, nurseryman, 249 n.2
Velie, Jacob W., ornithologist, 400 n.7, 441 n.2, 442 & n.6
Verlot, Bernard: book on variation in plants, 16 & n.2, 17 & n.3, 21 & n.1
Vermetus, 12 nn.12 & 14
Vestiges of the natural history of creation, 260 & 262 n.8
Victoria regia (*Victoria amazonica*). *See Euryale amazonica*
Vienna: zoological gardens, 29 & 30 n.8, 460 & 461 n.8
Villars, Dominique: *Histoire des plantes de Dauphiné*, *Ononis columnae*, 274 & 275 n.5
Villarsia, 368 & 369 & 371 & n.8, 452
Viola palustris, 261
Virchow, Rudolf Carl, 143 & n.3; exchanges photographs with CD, 27 & 28 n.4, 458 & 459 n.4; E. Haeckel attends lectures, 27 & 28 n.6, 458 & 459 n.6; lectures on archaeology, 126 & n.10, 468 & n.10
Virgil: quoted by C.J. Grece, 386 & 387 n.2
Vogt, Carl: translator, 364 & 365 n.7

Wagner, Rudolph: book on zoological anthropology, 270 & 271 n.3
Wales: CD's geological field work in, 207 & 208 n.3; Geological Survey, 207 & 208 n.2; A.R. Wallace's discussion of evidence for glaciation, 392 n.7
Wales, Prince of. *See* Albert Edward, Prince of Wales
Walford, Edward: and L.A. Reeve, *Portraits of men of eminence*, editor, xvii–xviii, 151–2 & nn.1 & 2, 394 n.4
Wallace, Alfred Russel, 22 & 23 n.3, 98 & 99 n.6, 137 & 138 n.2; administration and locality of natural history collections, 175 & n.1 & 176 nn.2 & 3; book on Malayan travels, 24 & 25 n.7, 40 & n.6 & 41 n.7, 45 & n.6, 236 & 237 n.9; house in London, 100 & 101 n.1 & 102 n.10; hypothesis of continental extension, 285 & 286 n.6; marriage, 172 & 174 n.26; natural selection better described as 'survival of the fittest', xxii, 227–9 & nn.1 & 2 & 230 nn.3–12; paper on adaptive mimicry in butterflies, 306 & 307 n.8, 322 & 323 n.12, 329 & 330 n.8; paper on distribution of pigeons, 24 & nn.1 & 2; paper on Malayan butterflies, 24 & n.3 & 25 nn.4 & 5, 45 n.5, 100 & 101 n.2, 190 & 191 n.6, 307 n.8; paper on origin of human races, 190 & 191 n.5; presentation copy of new edition of *Origin*, 236 & 237 n.5, 391 & nn.1 & 2, 485 & 486 n.10; sends paper on phytophagic varieties and species to CD, 100 & 101 n.1; travels in Brazil, 35 & 36 n.6
Wallace, Annie, 172 & 174 n.26
Walsh, Benjamin Dann: article on gooseberry saw-fly, 400 n.5, 442 n.3; article on J.D. Dana, 243 & 245 n.1, 298 & n.2; *Cynips*, experiment on, 298 & n.4; *Cynips*, review of paper on dimorphism in, 244 & 246 nn.17–20; effect of food on formation of races, 402 n.2; gall on grapevine leaf, 245 & 246 n.22; opportunity to exchange bird skins, 400 & n.7, 441 & n.2, 442 & n.6; *Origin*, presentation copy, 243 & 245 n.2, 298 & n.1, 438 & n.2, 442 & nn.1 & 2, 485 & n.3; paper on Hymenoptera and Diptera, 100–1 & nn.1 & 4–6 & 102 n.7, 137 & 138 n.2; paper on phytophagic insects, 191 n.9; paper on willow galls, 245 & 246 n.21, 400 & n.8, 442 & 443 n.10, *Practical Entomologist*, editor, 399 & 400 n.4, 442 & n.4; reproduction by gemmation in *Aphis*, 244–5 & 246 nn.19 & 20; reproduction in *Ornithorhynchus*, 399–400 & n.6; sends galls to W. Armistead, 101 & 102 n.8, 243 & 245 nn.5 & 6
Walton, John, 114–15
Wammestriggins. *See* Threeboys
wasps: geometry of cells, 14, 34 & n.9 & 35 n.10; stings, 87–8 & nn.1 & 3–5
water chevrotain. *See Hyomoschus aquaticus*
Waterhouse, Alfred, architect, 176 n.3
Waterhouse, George Robert: book on Mammalia, 356 & 357 n.3; geometry of bees' cells, 14 & 15 n.6; sends information on wasps' nests to CD, 34 n.9
waterlilies, 112 & 113 n.3, 367 & n.2. *See also Euryale*; Nymphaeaceae
Watson, Hewett Cottrell: G. Bentham's view on seedling brambles, 320 & 321 n.4

Waugh, Andrew Scott: supports F.W. Farrar's candidature for Royal Society, 41 & n.3
Wedgwood, Anne Jane, 373 & n.4
Wedgwood, Caroline, 373 & n.4
Wedgwood, Caroline Sarah, 297 & n.9; buys Wedgwood ware from The Mount, 396 n.6, 421 & n.6; CD's visit to, 192 n.2; health, 340 & n.4, 346 & n.7; plans to visit E.A. Darwin, 66 & n.6; possible visit to London, 341; share of R.W. Darwin's estate, 340 & n.3; visit to Down, 301 & n.4; whereabouts of soup tureen, 341 & 342 n.2, 345 & 346 n.2
Wedgwood, Emma. *See* Darwin, Emma (née Wedgwood)
Wedgwood, Frances Emma Elizabeth: J.D. Hooker's lecture on insular floras, 304 & 305 n.3
Wedgwood, Henry Allen, 373 & n.4; illness, 373
Wedgwood, Hensleigh: dines at W. Spottiswoode's, 428 & 429 n.19
Wedgwood, Jessie, 373 & n.4
Wedgwood, Josiah, I, 151 & 152 n.4
Wedgwood, Josiah, III: CD's visit to, 52 & n.2, 192 n.2; plans visit to S.E. Wedgwood's house, 66 & n.10
Wedgwood, Katherine Elizabeth Sophy: visit to Down, 301 & n.4
Wedgwood, Louisa Frances. *See* Kempson, Louisa Frances (née Wedgwood)
Wedgwood, Lucy Caroline: CD asks her to check description of *Erica massoni*, 319 & 320 n.2; sends specimens to CD, 320 n.3, 326 n.13; visit to Down, 301 & n.4
Wedgwood, Margaret Susan: visit to Down, 301 & n.4
Wedgwood, Sarah Elizabeth, 5 & n.2; plans visit to Tenby, 66 & n.10; reports on CD's improved health, 398 & n.8
Wedgwood ware: bought by C.S. Wedgwood, 421 & n.6; J.D. Hooker a collector, 172 & 173 n.22, 395–6 & nn.5 & 7, 427 & 429 n.13; memorial to W.J. Hooker, 17 & n.6, 26 n.3
Weinland, David Friedrich, 126 n.6, 468 n.6; *Der Thiergarten*, editor, 460 & 461 n.10; resigns positions in Frankfurt, 29 & 30 n.9, 460 & 461 n.9
Welford, Charles, 377 & n.4
Wellingtonia gigantea (giant sequoia): sent from Kew for Down House garden, 354 n.1
Wells, Luke: illustrator for *Variation*, 19 n.2, 23 n.7, 78 n.12, 239 n.3, 270 n.3, 278 & 279 n.8, 350 & 351 n.2, 351, 352 & n.2, 352 & 353 n.3
Wells, William Charles: article on human races, 283 & 284 n.4, 391 & 392 n.2; awarded Rumford Medal, 284 n.5
Welwitsch, Friedrich: International Horticultural Exhibition and Botanical Congress, member of committee, 86 & 87 n.2
western red cedar. *See Thujia lobbii*
Westwood, John Obadiah, 101 & 102 n.9
whales: bones found in New Zealand, 410 & 411 n.12; 'domesticated', 127 n.4
Whewell, William: death, 138 & 139 n.14
Whitby, North Yorkshire: fossil reptiles, 297; W.D. Fox's visit, 297 & n.7
Whitley, Charles Thomas, 2 & 3 n.3
Whitney, Josiah Dwight: and 'Calaveras skull', 401 n.9
Wichura, Max Ernst, 96 n.5; paper on hybrid willows, 16 & n.1, 207 n.10; reversion in hybrids, 206 & 207 n.10
Wilberforce, Samuel, bishop of Oxford: opposition to CD's theories, xxi, 22 n.8
Williams & Norgate, publishers and booksellers, 7 & 9 n.5, 364 & 365 n.8, 385 & n.3, 455 & 457 n.5, 476 & n.2; books and journals ordered by CD, 53 & nn.1, 3 & 4 & 54 nn.5–8
willows: hybrids, M.E. Wichura's paper, 16 & n.1, 207 n.10, 376 & n.2 & 377 nn.4 & 5; variable development of flowers, 51 n.2
Winchfield: R.M. Rolfe's visit to Dogmersfield Park, 414 & nn.1 & 2 & 415 nn.3 & 4
Wingfield, William Wriothesley: *The poultry book*, 22 & 23 nn.10–12, 270 n.5
wire bird. *See Charadrius sanctahelenae*
wisent (European bison). *See Bison bonasus bonasus*
Wisteria frutescens: shoots twining back on themselves, 182 & n.2, 183 & 184 n.4
Wollaston Medal. *See under* Geological Society of London
Wollaston, Thomas Vernon: catalogues of Coleoptera, 253 & 255 nn.12–14 & 20, 259 nn.13 & 15, 276 & 277 n.6, 282 & 283 n.9; hypothesis of continental extension, 285 & 286 n.6; stay in Cape Verde Islands, 172 & 173 n.12
wolves, 44 n.11, 115 n.4
Wood, James Julius, 136 & 137 n.8
Wood, Searles Valentine: on cereals and seedling fruit trees, 241 & n.2
Woodbury, Thomas White: comparison of honeycombs, 108 n.4
woodcock. *See Scolopax rusticola*

Woolner, Thomas: memorial to W.J. Hooker, 17 n.6; proposed bust of CD, 172 & 173 n.16
Wordsworth, William: T. De Quincey's essay, 380 & n.4
Wyman, Jeffries, 30 & 31 nn.1 & 4; geometry of bees' cells, 12–14 & 15 nn.1–7 & 16 nn.9 & 10, 33–4 & nn.4–8; A. Gray believes an accurate observer, 283–4 & n.13

Ximenia: functional dimorphism, 406 & 409 n.5, 477 & 479 n.5
Xylonomus: 'bullae' on wings, 101

Yahgan people, 446 nn.4, 5 & 9
Yule, Henry: *A narrative of the mission to the court of Ava*, 270 & 271 n.4

zoological nomenclature, 164 & n.2
Zoological Society of London: W.H. Flower, member of Council, 316 & n.3; paper on fishes of Central America, 427 & 429 n.10; presentation copy of *Origin*, 485 & 486 n.13; Regent's Park gardens, anthropoid apes do not erect ears, 430; Regent's Park gardens, A.D. Bartlett, superintendent, 423 n.8; Regent's Park gardens, cassowaries, 423 n.8; Regent's Park gardens, CD's visits, xvii, 148 & n.5, 417 & n.2, 423 n.5; Regent's Park gardens, hybrid fowls, 279 & 280 n.5; Regent's Park gardens, *Hyomoschus aquaticus*, 422 & 423 nn.6 & 7; Regent's Park gardens, saigas, 422 & 423 n.5; P.L. Sclater, secretary, 442; W.B. Tegetmeier, application for membership, 316 & nn.2–4, 317 & n.2; W.B. Tegetmeier, exhibits painting of white dodo at meeting, 351 n.3. *See also Proceedings of the Zoological Society of London*
Der Zoologischer Garten: D.F. Weinland, editor, 30 n.9, 461 n.9
Zurhorst, Frederick William: experiment on fowl cross, 18 & 19 n.5, 22 & 23 n.9, 26 & n.3, 239 & n.4, 412 & n.2, 419–20 & n.2, 421 & 422 n.2
Zurich University: O. Heer, professor of botany and entomology, 449 n.2